AN ENCYCLOPEDIA OF
HUMAN RIGHTS
IN THE
UNITED STATES

AN ENCYCLOPEDIA OF HUMAN RIGHTS IN THE UNITED STATES

SECOND EDITION
VOLUME 1

H. VICTOR CONDÉ

GREY HOUSE PUBLISHING

PUBLISHER:	Leslie Mackenzie
EDITORIAL DIRECTOR:	Laura Mars
EDITORIAL ASSISTANT:	Diana Delgado
PRODUCTION MANAGER:	Kristen Thatcher
MARKETING DIRECTOR:	Jessica Moody

AUTHOR: H. Victor Condé

AUTHOR, TIMELINE
PEER REVIEW EDITOR, TERMS
CONTRIBUTING AUTHOR, DOCUMENT INTRODUCTIONS: Tina M. Ramirez

Grey House Publishing, Inc.
4919 Route 22
Amenia, NY 12501
518.789.8700 FAX 845.373.6390
www.greyhouse.com
e-mail: books@greyhouse.com

While every effort has been made to ensure the reliability of the information presented in this publication, Grey House Publishing neither guarantees the accuracy of the data contained herein nor assumes any responsibility for errors, omissions or discrepancies. Grey House accepts no payment for listing; inclusion in the publication of any organization, agency, institution, publication, service or individual does not imply endorsement of the editors or publisher.

Errors brought to the attention of the publisher and verified to the satisfaction of the publisher will be corrected in future editions.

Publisher's Cataloging-In-Publication Data
(Prepared by The Donohue Group, Inc.)

Condé, H. Victor, 1947-

Human rights in the United States: a dictionary and documents / H. Victor Condé.—2nd ed.

2 v. : ill., forms ; cm.

Includes bibliographical references and index.
ISBN: 978-1-59237-290-4

1. Human rights—United States—Dictionaries. 2. Human rights—United States—History—Sources. I. Title.
KF4747.5.C37 2011
342.73/085/03

This book is dedicated to
Jean Grech Condé and Simone Thérèse Condé,
and in memory of Salvina Mifsud Grech,
Charles Grech, Captain Harry Victor Condé
and Marie Thérèse Condé

ACKNOWLEDGMENTS

Special acknowledgment goes to my dear colleagues Rita Cantos Cartwright and Tina M. Ramirez for their valuable help and human rights expertise without which this book would not have happened.

I would also like to thank the following persons for their competent and heartfelt help in making this book possible—Robert Cartwright, Jean Condé, Simone Condé, Heather Dickey, Catherine Ancel, Dr. Bernard Bastian and Communauté Puits de Jacob, Msgr. Silvano Tomasi, and also Diana Delgado at Grey House Publishing. Thanks to Robert Savage JD and William Luke Gilbert, law student, for developing the case law appendix. Thanks to Trezlen Drake JD, MSIL, law librarian, for updating the bibliography. Special thanks to Sir Nigel Rodley for his input and correction.

In recognition of the International Institute of Human Rights in Strasbourg, France for the knowledge of human rights and humanitarian law I have received over the past 26 years. I also gratefully honor the memory of Professor Jean-Francois Flauss, its late Secretary-General.

In recognition of the University of California at Davis Law School, Martin Luther King Hall, for my legal education in international law.

In recognition of the University of Essex, Human Rights Center in England, for my graduate human rights legal education under the best human rights professors in the world.

Your work will make the United States of America a better country.

TABLE OF CONTENTS

VOLUME 1

TERMS

PRIMARY DOCUMENTS

VOLUME 2

APPENDICES

America did not invent human rights. In a very real sense it is the other way around. Human rights invented America. Ours was the first nation in the history of the world to be founded explicitly on such an idea.

President Jimmy Carter
Farewell Address, January 1981

The desire to live freely under a government that would respect and protect human rights was the fundamental motivation of our country's Founders—human rights have not only been part of the United States since the beginning, they were the reason our nation was created.

U.S. Universal Periodic Report, August 2010

Legislation and court orders can only declare rights. They can never thoroughly deliver them. Only when people themselves begin to act are rights on paper given life blood.

Martin Luther King, 1929-1969

FOREWORD

Integer uitae scelerisque purus
non eget Mauris iaculis neque arcu
nec uenenatis grauida sagittis,
Fusce, pharetra, siue per Syrtis iter aestuosas
siue facturus per inhospitalem Caucasum
uel quae loca fabulosus lambit Hydaspes.

*Quintus Horatius Flaccus, Horace's Ode 1.22 (translation below)

Two thousand years ago the famous Roman lyric poet, Horace, penned the above verse which speaks universally to our time in this age of terrorism and threats to human security and our weaponized response. He states that those who are morally upright, law abiding and do no moral or criminal wrong need not fear misfortune. He infers that something metaphysical happens to a person who does justice and avoids evil, and they are protected by an invisible force. Horace was satirizing the Roman society which wielded power primarily with the time's latest and most terrifying weapons—poisoned arrows—the weaponized drones of his day.

This quote raises the issue of whether weapons and intelligence are really what keeps us safe, or whether being just and righteous and respecting human rights is more powerful. We have been in the process of constructing a world that combats the evil in terrorism and extremism with massive and expensive military operations, and intelligence hardware systems thus putting justice and human rights on the back burner until that "war" is over.

Based on my years of involvement in international human rights, and seeing how different states treat human beings, my opinion is that the nation with a rule-of-law system that respects human rights regardless of domestic or external threats is more just, safe and secure than the nation without such a system. History is replete with nations fallen or defeated in battle, though armed to the hilt and militarily superior to their enemy. As idealistic as it sounds, I believe that might does not make right. Call me an idealist, but having seen what the other side offers, bristling with destruction, I feel Horace has the more universally correct view. History has proven him right.

Further, the more a nation respects and complies with international human rights law the stronger and safer that nation is. It is my deep desire that the U.S. continue to improve respect for, and compliance with, its international human rights obligations. But in order to do so, its government and people need to know and understand human rights and the international legal obligations voluntarily assumed by their state in the area of international human rights law. This book will educate individuals about human rights law, a field in which I have worked and taught for many years.

Over those years I have worked and taught with other American and foreign experts in the field of international human rights. My impression is that the general American public is largely ignorant about international human rights law and what the U.S. government is doing regarding human rights on behalf of the American people in international institutions such as the U.N. There is a great need for the American people to learn about international human rights. This book will teach international human rights as they relate to the U.S. and as they are understood within the body of law known as international human rights law, the fastest developing area of international law.

Every country commits human rights violations, including the U.S., who practices and respects human rights relatively well, but not completely. The U.S. is not as good as it thinks and says it is, and not as bad as some people say it is, regarding its human rights practice at home and abroad. Even the U.S. can improve its human rights performance. If I were asked what can be done to increase respect for human rights in the whole world, my answer would be to not focus international action against states such as North Korea or Iran or Cuba, but to increase education, awareness, and respect for human rights by the American people. Why? Because the U.S. is not just any nation when it comes to human rights. It is the one single nation most capable of setting the tone and being a good model for other countries in respecting human rights, especially as it struggles against terrorism. To date, no country has done more than the U.S. to establish the system of international human rights laws and institutions concerning human rights. But it has not lived up to its calling. America can create a momentum for positive change internationally by improving its human rights record. It can become better. That is why I wrote this book.

Why should this matter to the U.S.? It is my opinion that when states do not respect human rights this gives ammunition and motivation to their enemies and creates the very terrorism (and more terrorists) they are fighting to overcome. Moral and legal righteousness bring with them a strength of spirit that can not be conquered by human weapons.

From my many years of dealing with governments concerning human rights violations I found that human rights violators are not always evil, heartless, godless fanatics. They are often the "good people" in a society, people of otherwise good character, high office, importance, deep faith and unquestioned patriotism. They do what they think is right for their government, their state, their country, and the world, and what they feel is absolutely necessary. They believe they are good and their opponent is evil, godless and deserving of every evil they think they can get away with. They believe beyond a doubt that their cause is just, often god-ordained. They commit atrocious acts because they believe they are protecting the most cherished values and beliefs, and the very existence, of society. This includes the U.S. Without the tools to know the permissible limits of government power, the American people cannot assure themselves that their government will not commit human rights violations in their name, or how that affects them and our national values.

This work is a tool for Americans to learn about their country's laws, policies, procedures, opinions and record in the international human rights arena. This is done by defining certain human rights terms and setting forth some human rights related documents to instruct Americans in this field. This book is for readers who are interested in being informed about human rights and who may want to take a more active position in influencing their leadership to improve its human rights record. America is a great country. One way to become a greater country is to set the gold standard when it comes to protecting human rights.

Many will disagree with one thing or another in this book. This is typical of any work about human rights, especially if it involves the U.S. in the post 9/11 world. It will engender debates, but the debate must continue. This is about the principles on which America operates and acts as the world's great superpower and the model it gives to all other states. But it is more up to the average American citizen than to the government to make this happen. Education in and for human rights is the key to Americans being enlightened and empowered to do so. I would probably not be exaggerating to say that the world is calling us, the American people, to do this. The world is waiting for the actions of the U.S. to correspond with what the U.S. is saying about its human rights law, policy and practice. If we as a nation can still accord a "decent respect for the opinions of mankind," as the signers of the Declaration of Independence stated, we will take this call, this challenge seriously and shape our government accordingly. First we must learn human rights, the protection of inherent human dignity.

Because of the tremendous impact of 9/11 on the U.S. psyche and on its laws and policies in the so-called war on terrorism, this second edition contains a large amount of material related to human rights and counter terrorism measures and the protection of human security, and to the question of the balance between human rights and national security. It is my opinion that this is what Americans most need to know with regard to the U.S. and human rights.

The person who leads a wholesome and law-abiding life,
and is free from wickedness, O Fuscus, has no need of Moorish bow,
or javelins, or a quiver full of poison arrows, whether he is journeying
through the glowing hot sands of the Syrtes
or he is passing through the inhospitiballe Caucasus, or through
those places celebrated in story and washed by the Hydaspes.

Translation by H. Victor Condé, BA *cum laude* in Classical Philology

Introduction and User's Guide

This Second Edition of *An Encyclopedia of Human Rights in the United States*, the post 9/11 edition, contains a broad range of information about international human rights in the United States context, from the Declaration of Independence to the present. It is a sourcebook of information for the average American who wants to know more about human rights in general, and international human rights law in particular. It is a reference book and a textbook in content and scope. It is a box full of tools to help someone who is unfamiliar with human rights to understand and be able to use those rights as they are found in U.S. legal and political policy and practice. It is not a complete resource, and many readers will find something missing, but it would be impossible to cover all areas of human rights and all documents. There are currently too many human rights documents for a single work such as this.

The average American's understanding of human rights is narrow, inaccurate, and often fully erroneous. Human rights is a term very much misunderstood by many Americans, causing them to fail to support human rights causes. The most important service this text could provide is the imparting of the basic concepts, definitions, and theory of international human rights as they are presently understood in the national and international context.

Arrangement

1. Introductory Essay
This work begins with an in-depth Introductory Essay, providing conceptual background on human rights from an academic perspective. The reader is encouraged to read this Introductory Essay before moving on to the definitions of terms or the primary documents. This step is essential for two reasons. First, the background information will lay a foundation for the philosophical issues that arise as terms are defined. Second, and perhaps most important, is that there are basic human rights terms in italics throughout the Essay that are defined in brief—the tools for fully understanding the individual terms that are more fully defined in the terms section. The Introductory Essay also includes a short narrative explaining the historical background of human rights in the United States, and the role of the three branches of the government in their articulation and application of human rights.

More complete works on the history of human rights are referenced in the bibliography. In fairness to the reader it must be said that there are, no doubt, differing views on the history and application of human rights in the United States. These views can differ as to how human rights are both understood and practiced (or not practiced) by the United States domestically and internationally. It is my intention that this work give a full understanding of the idea of human rights. Reading the Introductory Essay as a whole will increase the learning experience as the other sections of the book are studied.

2. Abbreviations
Following the Introductory Essay is a list of Abbreviations of certain terms and names of human rights documents that are used throughout the rest of the text. The reader would be well served to not only review these Abbreviations, but also the list of terms in the Table of Contents, before continuing onto the actual Terms and Documents sections of the book.

3. Human Rights Terms

Following the Abbreviations is the first major section of *An Encyclopedia of Human Rights in the United States*—the alphabetical dictionary of 324 Human Rights Terms. Each term is defined and its significance explained in the context of the United States and international human rights law. This dictionary focuses on words and phrases that are encountered in the politics, laws, and case law of the new and growing field of studies known as international human rights, as they are found in the U.S. historical, political, and legal experience. As a matter of legal systems, the field of human rights exists at both national and international levels. Human rights are most commonly studied in international context as part of the activity of the international community. This book will look primarily at human rights in the U.S. legal context, although documents and court decisions related to U.S. human rights activity in the international context are also included.

In that spirit, the dictionary attempts to give a simple definition of human rights terms in the U.S. context. To increase the usability of this work to more advanced readers, I have included some official definitions taken from the laws of the United States. Each term is defined in the *Definition* section, which is followed by commentary on the term, under the heading *Significance*. For example:

Basic Human Rights

Definition: This term refers to those human rights that are generally considered necessary or essential to the well-being and human dignity of the individual person. In concept, when basic human rights are guaranteed, those rights help to assure the primary material and nonmaterial needs of human beings so that people can lead a dignified life.

Significance: Basic human rights are the most fundamental requirements for human beings to live a life consistent with their human dignity. Therefore, these rights are given absolute precedence, or priority, in both national and international law and policy. There is no universally accepted list of these rights because they vary somewhat in different cultural contexts. They would include, however, the right to life, food, shelter and medical treatment, and freedom from torture, cruel, degrading and inhuman treatment and punishment, and freedom of religion, freedom of expression, and freedom from slavery.

All human rights are considered equal, interdependent, interrelated and indivisible in theory. However, the term "basic human rights" is used to designate certain human rights that are simply too basic *not* to be respected. Basic human rights mentioned generally in the American Declaration of Independence include life, liberty and the pursuit of happiness. It states that the first and foremost duty of government is to protect the basic human rights of people within its jurisdiction. The United States was created by people who sought to create a place where basic human rights were protected for all. Protecting basic human rights has always been a goal of U.S. law and policy.

Basic human rights are set forth in the following international human rights instruments: UDHR, ICCPR, and ICESCR, though the term basic human rights is narrower than all of the substantive rights set forth in them. It is an abstract concept and not easy to define clearly, but it is often used in human rights discourse. See Documents 6, 8, 16.

See Also Terms: 11, 12, 24, 33, 34, 35, 56, 70, 75, 90, 92, 100, 116, 120, 122, 124, 136, 144, 145, 160, 167, 177, 179, 180, 184, 195, 213, 242, 252, 283, 309, 316.

The *Significance* portion of the definition attempts to further explain how the term fits into U.S. human rights law, history, and discourse and, where possible, refer the reader to the actual human rights legal texts where the term is applied. These texts are found in the primary documents section of the book. Some texts are also treated in the extensive appendices.

The principal documents referred to in the *Significance* commentaries are the legal instruments in which specific human rights standards are defined and spelled out. These documents are principally international human rights treaties. The most important references in the

Significance text are to the specific article of the legal instrument (treaty, convention, covenant, or protocol) in which the term is found. I cannot over-emphasize the importance of referring to the documents noted in the *Significance* and reading the appropriate article itself. In a few instances, I have included the treaty text (article) itself in the *Definition* or *Significance* portion of the term.

Significance may also refer the reader to information contained in the appendices. Such information may be a chart of a certain human rights system, a U.S. statute, or excerpts of a judicial case decision pertinent to the term defined. The reader is encouraged to read the pertinent text of the appendix referred to for the fullest possible understanding of the term in context as it plays out in the U.S. human rights experience.

For additional help in grasping the full significance and meaning of a term, you will find *See also* references—a list of numbers that correspond to the 324 numbered terms defined. For example, *See also*: 1, 3..., refers the reader to Term 1 (Accessibility) and Term 3 (Accountability).

Learning the *Definition* and *Significance* of these terms will help the reader grasp the actual material of human rights—largely legal material—in the primary documents. I have arranged and explained the materials with the goal that they are understandable to the average person. This is a challenging task due to the complexity of international law.

Note: The definitions of the Terms claim to be neither official definitions, nor from any official authoritative source other than those cited. They are not binding on any government, forum, organization, or person, and do not claim to be the officially accepted U.S. definitions. They are solely my opinion and understanding of the meaning of those terms in the U.S. at the time of this writing. My perspective is based on the body of law known as International Human Rights Law and Humanitarian Law.

4. Primary Documents

The second major section of this book is Primary Documents. This section begins with an Introduction to the Documents. This general overview defines the types and functions of the documents, or document excerpts, that follow.

The primary documents contain a representative sample of the many human rights related documents that relate to the United States. These documents are intended to show the reader how a particular term or topic of human rights is dealt with in some of the many arenas of human rights. The representative sample of 106 documents comprise several types—Historical, International, United Nations, Humanitarian, Criminal, etc.—to give the reader a taste of the various types of documents that one encounters in this field of law and politics. These documents are not intended to include all the documents that have been written on human rights, either in general, or in the United States.

Each document is numbered, 1–106. Several include sub-documents. These sub-documents are all part of a process, such as the periodic state reporting process, and, as such, are grouped together and are best read together. Documents are cross-referenced throughout this book by that number. For example, see Documents 6, 8 ... refers the reader to the Universal Declaration of Human Rights (Document 6) and to the International Covenant on Civil and Political Rights (Document 8).

Historically, the documents begin on July 4, 1776, with the Declaration of Independence (Document 1). Extremely important to the entire field of human rights, this document is the greatest gift of the United States to the world of human rights. It sets the philosophical tone of all subsequent human rights instruments, including the famous Universal Declaration of Human Rights.

The main activity of the United States in the field of human rights deals with its obligations under international human rights treaties. These obligations are based on the treaties by which the United States is bound. The United States can violate a treaty obligation only if it has, in fact, ratified that specific treaty. It is crucial, therefore, to know the legal status of a treaty in U.S. law before determining U.S. compliance.

For this reason, and to include relevant background information, each document includes its own introduction that discloses the date on which a treaty (or other instrument) was adopted, how many states have become party to it, its full official name, when and if it became legally binding on the United States, and other important pieces of data. For example:

Document 16
Full Official Title: International Covenant on Economic, Social and Cultural Rights
Short Title/Acronym/Abbreviation: The Economic, Social and Cultural Covenant/ICESCR
Subject: Establish recognition of international legal obligations regarding economic, social and cultural human rights in a multilateral treaty.
Official Citation: G.A. res. 2200A (XXI), 21 U.N. GAOR Supp. (No. 16) at 49, U.N. Doc. A/6316 (1966), 993 U.N.T.S. 3
Date of Document: December 16, 1966
Date of Adoption: December 16, 1966
Date of General Entry into Force (EIF): January 3, 1976.
Number of States Parties to this Treaty as of this printing: 160
Date of Signature by United States: October 5, 1977
Date of Ratification/Accession/Adhesion: United States has not ratified this treaty.
Date of Entry into Force as to United States (effective date): Has not entered into force as to United States.
Type of Document: An international legal instrument, a treaty, with the title of "covenant."
Legal Status/Character of the Instrument/Document as to the United States: This instrument was signed by the United States in 1977 but has never been ratified by the U.S. Senate. The Senate has historically been unreceptive to economic, social and cultural rights, especially as to economic rights. There has been a general reluctance in the United States to fully accept these rights as human rights capable of legal implementation. The reluctance stems in part from questions as to how far the United States, which has a free market economy, would be expected to go in providing jobs, guaranteed income, health services, and other items in these categories that are regularly provided in countries with a more socialistic economy. Thus, it has never ratified this Covenant. However, under certain principles of international law contained in the 1968 Vienna Convention on the Law of Treaties, the United States should act consistently with legal instruments it has signed, as an indication of its good faith intent to act accordingly. Some scholars suggest that the ICESCR could be analyzed and possibly applied, as much as possible, using a free market economy as the standard. In that way, the process of ratification might be expedited.
Caution: The status and applicability of this instrument as to the United States may have changed since date of publication. The above information may be updated by referring to the following site:
Web address: http://www1.umn.edu/humanrts/instree/b2esc.htm

This information was valid and up-to-date as of press time. This information does change over time, however, and the reader should check for updates using the websites included at the bottom of document introduction. Again, most human rights legal standards are spelled out in international legal documents called treaties. They could also be titled Covenant, Convention, Charter, or Protocol. The documents section contains a collection of the most important international human rights treaties that the United States has ratified and, therefore, bound to obey. It also contains certain treaties that the United States has signed but not ratified, and a few the United States has not yet even signed. These latter two categories of treaties are included because of their relative importance in the field of human rights, because the United States may eventually become a state party to these treaties, or because the United States uses them to judge other states.

Most important controversies involving human rights in the United States concern treaties that the United States has already signed and that the U.S. Senate is currently deciding whether or not to ratify. During this stage, the Senate discusses the treaty before it votes for its constitutionally required "advice and consent" to the prior signature by the executive branch. Examples of treaties at this state are the Convention on the Rights of the Child and the Convention on the Elimination of All Forms of Discrimination Against Women. Because the public needs to know something about the text of these treaties before it can give input on public policy structures for or against U.S. ratification, this edition also includes the most important human rights treaties that the United States has signed but not yet ratified. Resources are cited in the bibliography that tells which countries have ratified, and therefore are bounded by, these treaties.

In addition to treaties, documents also include Declarations that are, by definition, not originally legal instruments. They include rules and principles applicable to such things as the treatment of prisoners and death penalty imposition. They are for informative purposes; they can be used as a point of discussion on a particular issue and have sometimes served as guidelines used by courts to correct a human rights problem, such as jail overcrowding.

Also included in the documents are those relating to different human rights systems of which the United States is a member, or those arising from procedures required by a particular treaty. For example, under some U.S. human rights treaties the United States is bound to submit periodic written reports to a treaty body for its review and comment. This is called the "reporting requirements." Several of the rather lengthy documents included herein are reports done by the U.S. government and submitted to international human rights bodies (to the U.N. Human Rights Committee under the International Covenant on Civil and Political Rights [ICCPR]; to the U.N. Committee against Torture under the Convention against Torture, to the U.N. Committee on the Elimination of Racial Discrimination). These are reports by the United States to the international community about what the United States does in its law and practice regarding the subject of human rights. It is a self-examination using human rights standards. Also included in this edition are some of the written responses of those treaty bodies to the U.S. reports with conclusions and recommendations. This shows the interplay between the U.S. and the international human rights body, where the international body may see the U.S. laws or practices are not in sync with the international standards.

Another type of document included is the General Comments of the U.N. Human Rights Committee on different articles of the ICCPR. These state the official interpretation of a norm of the ICCPR along with the treaty text and the U.S. report to the Human Rights Committee, and give an idea of how a particular norm plays out in the procedure and discourse of human rights systems. One General Comment, No 22, is provided as a sample of this type of document. It relates to Article 18 of the ICCPR. Many other General Comments are included in Appendix E and should be consulted any time the reader is using the ICCPR. The ICCPR is, in my opinion, the most important general human rights treaty to which the United States is legally bound.

Still another type of document included is the Special Rapporteur Thematic or Country Report. Those selected for this edition are, in fact, the observations of a non-American expert examining the law and practice of the United States on a particular topic by mandate of the U.N. Human Rights Council, of which the U.S. is a member. The observations are based largely on fact-finding missions to this country and on information and input received from many sources, private and governmental. Similar documents are also included in Appendix L.

Despite the fact that certain documents seem to point out what some believe to be failures of the United States to comply with human rights standards, these documents were not chosen based on the favorable or unfavorable light they may shed onto the United States. They are simply representative of the many documents that are being used in the governmental and non governmental world of human rights as applied to the United States.

5. Appendices

Following the Primary Documents are 18 Appendices, each summarized below. They are cross-referenced throughout the other sections of the book, and are designed to supplement the terms and amplify understanding of the documents. Every term is a springboard to the term's significance, which, in turn, should be a springboard to referenced documents and appendices.

Appendix A—Human rights timeline, the Chronology of Human Rights in Relation to the United States. It highlights the major, historical human rights milestones for the U.S. through 2010.

Appendix B—Breaks down the Universal Declaration of Human Rights into a language understandable for the average reader, and includes two alternatives—Children's Version and Simplified Version.

Appendix C—Chart showing the structure of the United Nations, with information on its human rights bodies and procedures. This information is important because most of the U.S. human rights activity in the international context happens in the institutional context of the United Nations, especially U.N. Human Rights Council.

Appendix D—Schematic on International Human Rights and Humanitarian Law. This set of charts gives the reader a more visual depiction of certain human rights systems and bodies, from the global/universal/regional systems, to inter-governmental, governmental, and non-governmental systems (see term Civil Society). The United States participates as a member of some of these international bodies, and many Americans are members or supporters of the human rights organizations mentioned. The non-governmental organizations named are representative of the several thousand that exist.

Appendix E—Documents to help the reader interpret and understand the meaning of treaties. The Vienna Convention on the Law of Treaties is the major treaty about treaties. Also included are several General Comments from the U.N. Human Rights Committee, and the Siracusa Principles on limitation and derogation clauses, with more advanced treaty concepts, followed by an essay on the application of limitation clauses.

Appendix F—Flowchart of the process in the U.S. legal system whereby an international human rights norm is established in international law and gets transformed into or recognized by the legal system for application by our courts. The reader will see how specific norms in the articles of treaties in the Documents section become either U.S. law, or binding legal obligations. This flowchart gives a general description of the various steps from human rights ideal to binding law. There are many variations and exceptions to the general process not identified here.

Appendix G—Chart of the large spectrum of laws that regulate our society, from local municipal ordinances to international laws to international human rights norms applicable to the United States. It shows how human rights norms, which constitute a body of law applicable in U.S., fit into and influence the U.S. legal system.

Appendix H—List of important human rights treaties signed or ratified by the United States. It includes dates of signature, ratification, and entry into force, if applicable, as well as a few treaties that the United States has not yet signed.

Appendix I—Actual summaries and excerpts of U.S. legislation, both enacted and proposed, aimed at the promotion and protection of human rights here and abroad. Not a complete list, it sets forth some general human rights laws and country-specific laws that are seen as the will of the American people which, so far as it is constitutional, must be carried out by the executive branch and enforced by the judicial branch, of the government. Also included are several Congressional resolutions regarding human rights, showing how Congress sometimes expresses its understanding of a human rights issue or country's human rights record, short of legislation. In some cases, only the reference citation and name of the legislation is included.

Caution: Legislation is subject to change by amendment, or can even be repealed. The current status and content of a law can be found in the appropriate U.S. legal texts, or on websites of congressional representatives listed in the Bibliography.

At the end of Appendix I, excerpts from the authoritative Restatement of the Foreign Relations Law of the United States shows how international human rights law fits into the U.S. legal landscape.

Appendix J—Excerpts of selected case decisions involving the U.S. and human rights. It includes not only cases decided solely within the U.S. Constitution and Bill of Rights framework, but case decisions that have a specific connection to the international law of human rights. Included are decisions from U.S. courts, Supreme Court, and federal courts that provide examples of how human rights have been interpreted and applied in U.S. jurisprudence by U.S. courts. They show the struggle of the courts to deal with the area of human rights law, a field not studied by most judges in law school. Also included are decisions arising from international judicial and quasi-judicial bodies in which either, the United States is a party to the case, or the case involves action by the United States in an area affecting human rights.

These case decisions are only representative samples to show how human rights are interpreted and applied. They were not chosen for being for or against the United States. The reference citation given for each case includes the full case decision for further study.

Appendix K—Universal Periodic Review Process Documents, which represent an important factor in the U.S. experience of human rights. In late 2010 the U.S. appeared before the U.N. Human Rights Council and had its human rights record examined before the international community for the purpose of evaluation and recommendation for improvement. The key document in Appendix K is A Practical Guide to the United Nation's Universal Periodic Review. Primary Documents 86 and 87 relate directly to the UPR documents in this Appendix.

Appendix L—Selected human rights reports from various sources on issues that are very important, at the present time, to human rights in the United States.

Appendix M—Documents relative to Human Rights and Security/War on Terrorism, including international organization investigation and findings about the legality of U.S. counter terrorism measures under international human rights and humanitarian law, i.e. drone assassinations and secret detention sites.

Appendix N—Documents regarding the human rights of immigrants and other non citizens.

Appendix O—Documents relating to human rights and law enforcement from an international legal perspective.

Appendix P—Opinion pieces on the United States and the International Community contains various articles about opposing views of certain human rights issues. These articles present the many different opinions in America about human rights, and the many different ways they are interpreted and applied, particularly in the war on terrorism.

Appendix Q—Human Rights Education as dealt with at the international level. Here you will find the U.N. Draft Declaration on Human Rights Education, a work in progress, the U.N. resolution on the World Programme for Human Rights Education, second phase, and the World Programme for Human Rights Education, evaluation of the frst phase.

Appendix R—Your Human Rights Under the International Bill of Rights, which is a complete list of your human rights found in three of the main historical international human rights instruments, transposed into second person declaratory statements, e.g. "You have the right to life."

6. Bibliography

Organized into 14 categories, including Terminology, U.S. Related Publications, Law Review Articles, and Status of Treaties, this Bibliography not only makes it easy to find complete text of documents that are excerpted in the document section of this book, but also offers valuable guidance for further research from a variety of sources.

7. Index

A detailed subject index offers the reader a quick and easy way to access the enormous amount and variety of material in *An Encyclopedia of Human Rights in the United States*.

The Introductory Essay, Definition of Terms, Primary Documents, Appendices, Bibliography, and detailed Index thoughtfully combine to give the reader an informative overview of human rights, specific examples, practical tools for understanding this complex field, and carefully chosen resources for further research.

As the new millennium unfolds and the world stage becomes more volatile, it becomes crucial that the average American realizes the importance of understanding human rights worldwide and participating in recognizing these rights. Despite the inevitable disagreements on the issue of human rights, it is necessary that the basics are presented in an objective manner for all to understand. We are able to debate more effectively, fairly, and peacefully when we "earn the right to criticize," a right earned by understanding the facts and the law. In the understanding of human rights, as in many other disciplines, education is the first step toward wisdom, and wisdom is always a worthwhile goal.

INTRODUCTORY ESSAY

*Recognition of the inherent dignity and of the equal and inalienable rights of all members of the human family is **the foundation** of freedom, justice and peace in the world.*

Universal Declaration of Human Rights (emphasis added)

THE CONCEPT OF HUMAN RIGHTS

If any sentence would sum up what human rights are, it would be that "they are the legal protection of inherent human dignity." Human rights are claims or entitlements held by individual human beings as inherent attributes of the human personality. They are rights held by every human being in relation to the government, the state, and the public power. They are, in theory, legally enforceable claims that an individual can assert to get the government to do something or refrain from doing something. In concept, they are limitations on the power of government in relation to the individual. They limit the exercise of power by the government to only that which is granted to it by the people. In addition, they limit authorized power to be exercised only in a way that protects and advances, and in any case do not harm human dignity and the development of the human personality. The rights are expressed in rules and principles that are found written into laws at the national and international levels.

The idea of human rights became necessary to keep governments from becoming tyrannical or despotic and limiting human freedom. Living in the United States, it is easy to forget that until recent history, there has been little acceptance by governments of an individual's basic human rights derived from inherent human dignity. Rather, the history of the world has been characterized by sovereigns, whether kings, emperors, or ruling elites, deciding the fate of those over whom they ruled on the basis of their own whims. If a group of people were ruled by a kind and benevolent sovereign, they might be treated with respect. If not, they might see oppression and hardship. However, as more often seemed the case, if they were under the thumb of a cruel tyrant, they had no recourse but to suffer through his reign and eventually hope for some relief. Aside from the early experimentation with democracy in Greece, this scenario was typical.

Therefore, with the relatively modern concept of inalienable human rights based on inherent human dignity evolved the concept of government "recognizing," rather than "creating," these rights. "Recognizing" reflects the acceptance of the fact that human rights exist in every human being without the need of any legislative action. Human beings were born with them. All human beings were to have their rights protected from the "encroaching power of the state." This is expressly what the American colonists declared to England and to the world in the Declaration of Independence. That revered text which we celebrate every 4th of July, states that government is created to protect human rights: "to secure these rights, governments are instituted among men, deriving their just powers from the consent of the governed; that whenever any form of government becomes destructive of these ends, it is the right of the people to alter or to abolish it, and to institute new government, laying its foundation on such principles, and organizing its powers in such form, as to them shall seem most likely to effect their safety and happiness." See Document 1. Principles of human rights and fundamental freedoms under a republican form of government were our foundation and form of governance.

Human rights in their modern sense were first articulated in such documents as the American 1776 Declaration of Independence, along with the 1789 French Declaration of the Rights of Man and of Citizen. These documents present the philosophy that human beings are born with rights that they possess all their lives and that the sovereign, whatever or whoever that might be, cannot violate those rights. In the 1776 Declaration of Independence, it was expressed as "all men are created equal and endowed … with certain unalienable rights, among them life, liberty, and the pursuit of happiness." These rights were not granted by the state or the king or the legislature. Human rights as a discipline has taken up this idea of rights as being what human beings possess as part of their nature and which pre exist law.

This brings up the critical difference between human rights and so-called civil or constitutional rights. Human rights are different from what in the U.S. are called "civil rights," "civil liberties," or "constitutional rights." These three types of rights are all rights granted by the sovereign, who gives them to individuals based on the belief that these rights are necessary for the proper ordering, harmonious functioning, and preservation of the society. By contrast, in modern theory, human rights are not granted by any sovereign, whether king, president, prime minister, legislature or parliament, dictator, or other. The rights exist abstractly in each individual human being. The international human rights instruments in the "Documents" section of this work, makes it clear that neither the nations of the world, nor the United Nations, nor the Organization of American States is creating or granting any rights by those instruments. Instead, they are merely providing for the respect and protection of the rights that they thereby recognize in that treaty as already existing in, and held by, the individual.

Constitutional liberties can be abrogated, or abolished, if the procedure in our Constitution is followed. Our U.S. Bill of Rights could theoretically be thrown out if the correct constitutional process were followed. Human rights, however, cannot be voted or legislated out, because they inhere in Americans; that is, they belong to them by nature. If the government abolished the Constitution or the Bill of Rights, human rights would still exist in all Americans. The Declaration of Independence and other legal documents (treaties) in this work say so. We celebrate that great truth every July 4.

As one reads those treaties, one sees that the ultimate, "rock-bottom" basis for all human rights is human dignity, which is the inherent worth of the human being, merely for being human. Every country in the world now accepts the proposition that human rights exist and that human dignity is the basis of those rights. Countries may differ in many ways on where such dignity comes from and how human rights laws are to be interpreted and applied. But the existence of human rights, its basis in human dignity, and its related principle of equality are accepted as normative in all societies of the globe, even though the actual practice of states leaves much to be desired, and religious and ideological perspectives may warp implementation.

Conceptually, human rights as articulated in international instruments represent a balance of interests. They seek to articulate a fair balance between individual and government. On the one hand is the need of human beings for the freedom to do what they desire and become what they choose. On the other hand, reason dictates that a society must have some limitations on the conduct of individuals or there will be lawlessness, disorder, and the possible disintegration of society. Human rights seek to strike that balance between the needs of individuals to protect their freedom and human dignity and the legitimate needs of government to regulate the actions of some for the common good. This is particularly important in the war on terrorism. The standards themselves, set forth in the documents of this book, did not "fall from the sky" and are not the broadest and most liberal limitations on government conduct. They are, in fact, more of a minimum, common-denominator standard that all the countries of the world would agree to as limitations to be imposed upon their sovereignty. Human rights standards are limitations upon governments that are legally articulated and recognized by international organizations made up of governments, including our own. It is against the nature of any government institution to voluntarily limit itself and its power. But as the preamble to the U.N. Charter manifests, it was the voice of "We the peoples of the United Nations," not governments, who demanded this in light of the horrors of World War II, especially the Holocaust.

Today, in light of the actions of the U.S. government exerting its power in the war on terrorism, these limitations on the power of government are all the more necessary and need to be broadly known. It was Lord Acton who said in 1887 that "Power corrupts and absolute power corrupts absolutely." Given that the U.S. has come as close as any in history to being the most absolute power in the world it behooves the U.S., and implicates all mankind, to have an agreed system of values and norms for judging the rightness and justness of our government's action. The international law of human rights and humanitarian law reflects those universal values.

Governments, republican or democrat, will always be able to justify their action, or to achieve "plausible deniability" when accused of wrongdoing. Each is capable and disposed to abusing power, usually in the name of good. A standard of conduct external to government is the necessary weapon of the free citizen to protect against the abuse of power by state. Our great systemic checks and balances did not prevent human rights violations at Abu Gharib prison in Iraq, and is only slowly and lately resolving human rights issues at Guantánamo Bay detainment facility in Cuba. America needs to set up a better bulwark against abuse of power by all branches of government, and law consistent with our international human rights legal obligations is suggested as the answer. We Americans may, from time to time, need to protect ourselves from our own government. The more we put into place the concept of human rights to limit power the less we will have to resort to deadly and divisive rebellion, the seeds of which are often present in our society. This idea is reflected in the preamble of the Universal Declaration of Human Rights:

> *Whereas disregard and contempt for human rights have resulted in barbarous acts which have outraged the conscience of mankind, and the advent of a world in which human beings shall enjoy freedom of speech and belief and freedom from fear and want has been proclaimed as the highest aspiration of the common people,*
>
> *Whereas it is essential, if man is not to be compelled to have recourse, as a last resort, to rebellion against tyranny and oppression, that human rights should be protected by the rule of law...*

The theory of human rights is still in the process of being articulated both in the U.S. and around the globe. One can, however, expound on some of the most generally accepted doctrines and principles of human rights which constitute the theoretical basis of those rights, which, in my opinion, are listed below.

It must be stated that rights exist outside of the concept of human law. There exist moral rights and some say divine rights as well. This work only addresses human law and the concept of human rights within that field of human law, particularly the law of nations, international law, as it relates to the United States.

A DEFINITION OF HUMAN RIGHTS

A definition of human rights is included in the definition of terms section, but with the caveat that there is no one universally accepted definition of human rights. Simply stated, human rights are legal tools for the protection of inherent human dignity. A more complex definition is given in the definitions section.

ESSENTIAL CHARACTERISTICS OF HUMAN RIGHTS

Human rights have several distinctive characteristics that distinguish them from any other type of legal rights:

Inherent: Human rights are inherent attributes of the human personality. As stated, they inhere in, or are part of, the essential nature of human beings and are not created or bestowed by any earthly authority or constitution. In the Declaration of Independence this idea is expressed as human beings being "endowed" with such rights.

Universal: Human rights are universally held; they are held by all human beings, in that everyone has them. They are not an American right or a democratic right but are universally accepted philosophical and legal principles articulated by all the countries of the world. This is stated in our Declaration of Independence as "All men are created equal and endowed … with certain unalienable rights… ."

Unalienable/Inalienable: Since these rights are not granted or legislated by any public or private authority, they cannot be taken away, that is, alienated, from the holder. The state has, in theory, no right to alienate them from a person. Indeed, as will be seen, the exercise of human rights can be limited by government for certain reasons, but the state may not extinguish one's human rights nor may the state force a person to give them up. They inhere permanently in humans from birth, some say from conception, to death.

PREREQUISITE PRINCIPLES

From these characteristics, there arise three necessary and related human rights principles that are prerequisites for the full respect for human rights by states:

Nondiscrimination: Not only does everyone possess all human rights, but society must ensure that all people can exercise their rights without any discrimination based on their race, religion, color, sex, nationality, or other status. See Document 8, Article 2.1.

Rule of law: Human rights can only be respected in a society characterized by "rule of law," meaning that law is the ultimate authority in society and no one is above the law. As Americans would say, it is "a society of laws and not of men." Human rights instruments, such as the ICCPR, Article 2.2, require states parties to legislate these rights into their national legal system to be legally enforceable against government, federal, state or local. No one in a society, even the President of the United States, can be above the law, even if Congress passed a law to that effect. All this is, of course, consistent with the United States Constitution. In America nothing and no one can violate the Constitution, as it is now.

Effective domestic remedies: There must be effective domestic remedies for violation. Without an effective and accessible legal remedy there can be no legal human right. Human rights would be noble but illusory rights. In theory, human rights can only be protected if the holders of those rights or their representatives have accessible and effective legal remedies in the national "domestic" legal system to enforce their rights. Human rights instruments such as the ICCPR, Article 2.3, require states parties to establish legal procedures in national law to prevent or redress violations. These must be both accessible and effective. The remedies may be judicial, or administrative, so long as the latter has recourse to judicial scrutiny of administrative decision.

COLLECTIVE OR GROUP RIGHTS

In its classic theory, human rights are individual. Each individual is said to be a "bearer" or "holder" of such rights individually, without regard to membership in any given society. It is up to each society (*state*) to set up its legal system so as to protect these individual rights for all.

In modern human rights theory, some hold that human rights can also be *collective*, or *group rights*. This theory is asserted especially, for example, to protect the rights of certain minority groups (racial, religious, linguistic, ethnic) and indigenous groups as a whole. In this theory some argue that the group holds the human right for each of its members, *collectively*, whereas the other (and I think better) theory claims that each individual in the group/collective hold and exercises his or her individual human rights together with the other members of the group, and that human rights can theoretically only be individual. The theory of group or collective rights is not universally accepted but is becoming more and more so, particularly for such groups as indigenous peoples.

PRINCIPAL SOURCES OF HUMAN RIGHTS NORMS:
TREATIES AND CUSTOMARY INTERNATIONAL LAW

Human rights have been articulated as legal rights primarily at the international level in and as part of the field of law known as public international law, also known as the *law of nations*. Human rights as a discipline is first and foremost articulated in legal principles and rules. Principles are broad general statements of desired goals of human rights. Rules are specific, legal, normative standards of conduct that, if followed, will result in the conformity of state conduct with those principles.

There are two "material sources" where one finds human rights legal norms—treaties and customary international law.

Treaties

The international process by which human rights treaties are made usually starts with adoption of a *declaration* of human rights principles in a chosen area, for example children's' rights. The international community first articulates basic human rights principles, which are accepted by states, if they so choose, through the adoption of nonbinding declarations. These declarations state what the consensus principles of the international community are regarding a certain area of human rights. These principles are later followed by elaboration of a formal legal instrument known as a *treaty*, which transforms those principles into specific rules, called *norms*. Norms are standards of conduct for states. They create legal obligations for states which expressly accept to be legally bound by them. These treaties are also called by other names, such as *conventions*, *covenants*, and *charters*, and also may be referred to as human rights *instruments*. These legal instruments are produced by the countries of the world coming together as governments in international organizations, such as the United Nations or the Organization of American States. The United States has been a founding member of these organizations.

These bodies, which were founded in order to seek the mutual benefit, peace, and security of all their members, issue resolutions and declarations about human rights. They then get together to create the legally binding treaties, as part of a process called *standard setting*. These instruments set the norms, which the states who negotiated and adopted the instruments accept as the minimum internationally accepted standard of conduct for governments. Treaties, again, are usually preceded by declarations, which are not intended to create legal obligations for states. It is normally intended by the states that these declarations will later serve as the basis for a legally binding instrument, a treaty.

Treaties are only *binding* upon states which expressly *ratify* (approve or accept) them to comply with their rules. Ratification is a formal act of acceptance by a state of the legal obligation to obey the treaty. This ratification is usually expressed in a formal, written legal instrument deposited with the organization in which the treaty was created, such as the United Nations.

Usually human rights treaties are only effective when they have *entered into force (EIF)* which usually means that they go into effect when a certain specified number of states have ratified the treaty. This is all spelled out in the text of the treaty. Once the treaty enters into force it is binding upon all states that have ratified it, specified in the doctrine of *Pacta Sunt Servanda*, which means Agreements Must be Kept. Only at that time can the provisions of the treaty be violated.

Why do countries like the U.S. enter into treaties, taking on legal obligations towards other states, which is really a limitation of their sovereignty? There are several reasons. One is that it makes a state look good in the eyes of the international community by being concerned with human rights both within the state and outside it. A more important reason is that states believe that by entering into a treaty system they can increase their ability to address an issue, such as torture, or exploitation of children, together with other states. This is particularly so now, in light of globalization and so much transnational movement of people. The U.S. enters into treaties because it gives it a forum to work together with other states to address an issue of mutual concern and common national self interest, such as human trafficking. When a state chooses to stay out of a treaty system it has less ability to make an impact on the direction of the international law and policy in a given area, for example the International Criminal Court. States sometimes stay out of a treaty system because of a strong domestic opposition to the treaty, such as the U.S. and the Convention on the Rights of the Child, or because it perceives that the treaty obligations will limit its power, activity, or strategy or economic interests in a certain sector, such as the U.S. regarding the ICC or the ICESCR. Remember, human rights are limitations on the power of states in relation to individuals. States do not, by their nature, like to limit their power and authority unless they perceive they will achieve something greater in their national interest. Sometimes it is purely for internal political reasons that states chose to ratify or not ratify a treaty, allowing the ruling government party to get elected or stay in power. State choices are not always principled and are too often principled on staying in power or getting elected. This dynamic exists in the U.S. as well.

Customary International Law

Another material source in international law where binding legal norms are formed is known as *customary international law*. A legally binding norm is said to exist if almost all countries of the world consistently act a certain way in the international and domestic spheres, based on a belief that this practice is a matter of international law (called *opinio juris*), and not based on convenience or courtesy. When both of these elements of consistent practice and the *opinio juris* are established we can say that a binding legal norm has "crystallized" or "ripened" in international law. An example is the human right against torture. (See Appendix J, *Sosa vs. Alvarez-Machain and Kiobel vs. Royal Dutch Petroleum.*)

From these two sources of legal norms have come most of the human rights we now know as part of international human rights law. This doctrine of customary international law is based on the theory that states agreed to and consented to a rule of international law by the way they act and perceive that act as obligatory. They consent if they consistently and uniformly act a certain way and do so out of a sense of international legal obligation. This obligation is often expressed in their official pronouncements in international legal and political circles. Such objective action and subjective intention by states can be crystallized into a legal norm as long as there is no substantial persistent objection of the states to such a legal norm.

In theory, it is the intention of the international community that every country sign, ratify, and implement all these human rights norms by treaty and custom into national law at all levels, and create effective legal procedures and remedies in the national administrative and judicial system for violations of these norms. This goal is in process. It takes a long time. The United States, for example, signed the Genocide Convention in 1948 but did not ratify it until 1988. See Document 17. The process for each state (country) to make international human rights law become part of national (domestic) law varies from country to country. The procedure in the United States is set forth in a flowchart in Appendix F. See also Appendix G, Spectrum of Law, which shows the place of these norms in U.S. law.

With respect to treaties, it should be remembered that when a state ratifies a treaty, whatever it is called (convention, covenant, etc.), it sometimes qualifies its acceptance with certain provisions called *reservations, declarations, and understandings* (abbreviated RDUs or RUDs). Roughly speaking, *reservations* seek to modify the state's obligations under the treaty as it stands, for example by stating that it does not accept being bound by one of the human rights rules set out in a certain article of the treaty. *Declarations* set forth the state's position on the jurisdiction of a treaty *organ* (i.e., supervising body) to handle cases against it, or they declare the scope of applicability of the treaty's norms within its territory. *Understandings*, sometimes referred to as an *interpretation*, set forth the state's more precise understanding of the meaning of certain terms in the treaty, as the state intends to apply it, for example, the term "inhuman treatment."

These reservations, declarations, and understandings affect the nature and extent of any U.S. ratification of human rights treaties, such as those found in the "Documents" section. Anyone wishing to comment on whether the United States has violated a human rights treaty norm must know not only whether the United States has ratified a specific treaty but also whether it has done so with any accompanying Reservations, Declarations, or Understandings. See Document 9, the U.S. ratification of the ICCPR, as an example of RDUs.

In addition to treaties and customary law there is another source of related norms called General Principles of Law. These are mainly procedural and ancillary in nature, such as the doctrine of exhaustion of domestic remedies, which plays an important role in human rights complaint systems. One can also look to a subsidiary source of law in international case decisions, such as from the International Court of Justice and even national high courts as well, and the writings of the most eminent legal scholars to help in interpreting norms.

POSITIVE AND NEGATIVE RIGHTS AND OBLIGATIONS

Conceptually most human rights have both a negative and a positive aspect to the exercise of the right, and positive and negative aspects of the states obligation as to each right. All human rights norms have this duality. An example of a human right which can be both positive and negative is freedom of expression. The positive aspect of this right says, "I have a right to say x." That is a positive right to say something. The negative aspect of that right is the right **not** to have to express something: "I have a right not to reply to that question." So the right to freedom of expression is both a positive and a negative right. Positive rights give a person freedom to do something. For each positive right there is a negative obligation of the state to refrain from interfering with that person's freedom. An example of violating that positive right would be not allowing that person to speak his opinions. Some rights are considered negative, either in allowing a person not to have to do something, or in prohibiting the state from doing something to someone, such as torturing someone. Everyone has the negative right not to be tortured and the negative right not to be forced to believe something in which one does not believe. Some negative rights require positive obligations by the state, such as to provide police to protect people's lives and property or schools to provide education.

Positive obligations, again, oblige the state to do something and negative obligations oblige a state to refrain from dong something. Human rights obligations can be violated by states for doing nothing when there is a positive obligation to act. For example, the U.S. government has a negative obligation to avoid interfering with our human rights in the war on terrorism and it has a positive obligation to protect our human right to life by taking positive measures to protect us from terrorist attacks. If the government did nothing to protect us it would violate its positive obligation to take steps to protect us from the harmful acts of others.

For all of the individual rights we have and for all the obligations of state government, there are also duties, responsibilities on every member of society without which human rights cannot be realized. See "Duties" below. There are no human rights without human duties. Every human right has a correlative duty.

FOUR LEGAL OBLIGATIONS EVERY STATE MUST FULFILL UNDER INTERNATIONAL HUMAN RIGHTS LAW

International law is based on the free consent of sovereign and equal states and expressed in the international community in legal agreements or custom. This consent gives rise to freely chosen legal obligations in relation to each other state party to the treaty or to all states under customary international law. There are four separate legal obligations which states, such as the United States, undertakes to fulfill and must fulfill to make human rights real and practical and not illusory and abstract only. These four obligations are:

1. **Obligation to Respect** Human Rights

State (national) government has the legal obligation to refrain, in any way, from interfering with individuals in the full enjoyment of their human rights. This obligation is the conscious recognition of the human rights of individuals and groups, and the conduct and treatment by the states consistent with such recognition.

2. **Obligation to Protect** Human Rights from the actions of others

State (national) government has the legal obligation to prevent or punish acts which result in violations committed by third parties, such as private individuals, or groups or other non state entities or actor or commercial interests.

3. **Obligation to Ensure** Human Rights by other states

States parties to a treaty and states bound by a customary international human rights norm have the legal obligation to act to ensure that all other states parties or other states bound by the customary norm respect and protect such human rights within their territory and all those outside their territory for whom the norms apply. Every state must actively and affirmatively cause other states and non state actors to conduct themselves consistently with those norms, consistent with international law.

4. **Obligation to Fulfill** by all things necessary and proper for full enjoyment

The state (national) government has the affirmative obligation to take administrative, budgetary, legislative, judicial and other measures toward the full exercise and realization of all human rights. The state must take all necessary steps to ensure that all persons within its jurisdiction fully enjoy all substantive and procedural human rights all of the time.

States must fulfill all four of these obligations. Some of these obligations are negative and some are positive. A state can violate its obligation by partially fulfilling an obligation that it has the capacity to fulfill completely.

Obligations Erge Omnes

In international law there are certain obligations deemed so important for the continued existence and development of the international community, and so necessary for the protection of human dignity, that they are known as obligations "*Erge Omnes.*" This Latin term means essentially "towards everyone." They are obligations of every state toward each other. The implication of this is that every state has the right to complain and call for action of other states when any other state is violating *Erge Omnes* norms.

Refraining from torture, genocide, or slavery, for example, are considered obligations *Erge Omnes.* They are also referred to as "Peremptory Norms" of conduct which means that states cannot pass legislation inconsistent with such norms. Caveat: This is not the same, however, as "preemption" in the U.S. constitutional sense. Every state must comply with such obligations all the time and they allow no abrogation, derogation or exception for any reason.

Which obligations are *Erge Omnes* is beyond the scope of this book. Generally speaking, the norms which give rise to *Erge Omnes* obligations are called *Jus Cogens*. This term means a compelling or cogent right from which no limitation or derogation is possible.

Former Characterization of "Generations" of Human Rights

Most human rights have for many years been characterized as belonging to one of three so-called "generations" of human rights. This term was coined by a French jurist, Karel Vasak, for purposes of categorizing human rights as they had developed. This also had something to do with the Cold War and its influence on the development of the concept of human rights. It became common for people to speak of three "generations" of human rights. The "first generation" human rights consisted of the internationally accepted civil and political human rights.

The ICCPR (see Document 8) contains civil and political rights. The "second generation" human rights consisted of the internationally accepted economic, social, and cultural rights (see Document 16, the International Covenant on Economic, Social, and Cultural Rights). The West Bloc (non communist) nations favored civil and political human rights, such as freedom of speech and religion, while the East Bloc states favored economic, social and cultural rights. The "third generation" human rights, also called "solidarity rights," were a mixture of new rights and ideas that were proclaimed as human rights but not universally accepted in the international community as such. These rights include the claimed right to peace, the right to a clean environment, the right to development, the right to humanitarian assistance, and the right to solidarity among nations. These rights find their way into very few legal treaties and are promoted primarily by developing countries.

The use of the term "generation" was never meant to imply any distinct historical difference or hierarchy of one generation over another. Over the years, however, the use of this term caused conceptual problems resulting in political controversy. In recent years scholars and international organizations have discouraged the use of the term "generation" as a means of categorizing human rights. This shift is largely due to the development and articulation of the principles of interdependence, interrelatedness, and indivisibility of all human rights. One does, however, still see this term used in the older human rights literature and even in some new literature. For all intents and purposes, the body of international human rights law consists principally and primarily of first and second generation human rights.

The terms first, second, or third "generation" should not be used in human rights discourse. They are outmoded and inaccurate concepts which lead to confusion and misunderstanding.

BASIC INTERNATIONAL HUMAN RIGHTS LAW PRINCIPLES

The field of human rights is full of principles and rules. This comes with being part of international law. There are certain basic principles which apply to treaties. Most human rights norms are found in treaties, which are contractual agreements between two or more states (countries) governed by international law. The most important for this book are principles concerning the application and implementation of human rights treaties, whether they are global or regional or other international instruments. The following international law principles apply to human rights treaties, whatever they are called (convention, charter, covenant, agreement, protocol):

Pacta Sunt Servanda: Latin expression meaning that agreements (*pacta*) must be kept (*sunt servanda*). Treaties are international legal agreements between two or more states. They are promises voluntarily made by one state to one or more other states. This principle says that states must keep their promises to each other and fulfill their obligations under the treaty. It is like saying treaties have to be obeyed by states conducting themselves according to the treaty.

Bona Fides: Latin expression meaning in good faith. All parties to a treaty must accept and implement and interpret the treaty in good faith with the intent to achieve the object and purpose of the treaty. It is about the state's attitude towards its obligations.

Effectiveness: Principle that states that you have to interpret and apply a treaty in a way that makes the treaty most effective in reaching the object and purpose of the treaty. An interpretation of the treaty that makes it ineffective in protecting human rights would violate the principle of effectiveness.

Proper interpretation: Principle that states how to interpret the meaning of terms in a human rights treaty. When you try to interpret a treaty that is not clear, you must interpret it according to the plain meaning of words in their ordinary context consistent with the object and the purpose of the treaty. See the Vienna Convention on the Law of Treaties, Appendix E, which now states this as a legal rule.

Subsidiarity: Principle that states the protection of individual human rights must be done primarily at the national level, in domestic courts under national law and that the international norms and mechanism are a back up system to be used only when the national level has not properly implemented them. The international system of protection of human rights is secondary or subsidiary to the national system.

This usually means that a person who believes his or her human rights have been violated must first seek and exhaust all accessible and effective recourse in his or her national administrative and judicial system before taking the case to the international human rights mechanisms.

Pro Homine: Most fundamental and important principle applicable to all human rights and all government action, and indeed all action of every member of society. This Latin expression means *for* or *in favor of [hu]mankind*. This is a principle of the application and interpretation of human rights law. Human rights, again, are protections of human beings from the abuse of power by government. They are meant to preserve human dignity. This principle means that human rights laws must be interpreted and applied in every situation and at all times in a way that is the most protective of human beings. In other words, all other things being equal, the protection of human beings takes precedence over the needs and desires of government. Because power corrupts and absolute power corrupts absolutely, and because governments have a tendency to usurp or abuse legal power, and oppress individuals and groups, this principle must always be kept in mind when examining the claims of a state versus the claims of human beings. States were created to protect the rights of humans, not vice versa. This principle applies to the whole process of human rights from their initial recognition to determining violation in a human rights committee, commission or court. According to a Latin maxim: All law (including international law) is ultimately made for the sake of human beings [therefore] all international human rights law and all national laws which implement them should be implemented, applied, and their violation adjudicated, with a view to best protecting human beings.

While this principle is classically expressed as *Pro Homine*, which means "for mankind," it is now sometimes seen as *Pro Persona*, to reflect non-sexist language.

Proportionality: Where a state takes a measure that interferes with the exercise of human rights, the state's agents (such as police, legislators, judges, government bureaucrats) are only permitted to take measures, for example enacting a criminal penalty for certain forms of expression, which constitute a reasonably and proportionally measured action in relation to the particular problem or social need. For example, a state enacting a measure imposing a life sentence for joy riding would be a human rights violation because the punishment is not proportional to the offense. Another example would be a general ordering an air attack to destroy a city of 200,000 because five enemy soldiers were somewhere in the city. This would be a disproportionate (as well as indiscriminate) attack because there is no proportionate relationship between the measure (killing 200,000 innocent civilians) and the objective (killing five enemy soldiers).

Proportionality limits the power of government to take any measures it wants and forces it to take only measures that cause minimal negative consequences against the dignity and freedom of human beings. In the United States we do this when judging whether a government action violates the 8th amendment—constitutional prohibition against cruel or unusual punishment. See U.S. Supreme Court decision in *Graham vs. Florida*, in case law Appendix J.

Proportionality runs throughout all international law, and especially international human rights and humanitarian law. Whenever a state takes a measure, for example surveillance of suspected terrorists, one has to ask whether the measure is proportional to the end sought to be achieved, even if the end aim is legitimate and constitutional. A disproportionate measure is an invalid measure. However laudable or important the government's aim, it may only interfere with freedom to the extent minimally necessary.

Freedom is the rule, limitation of freedom the exception, which must be justified by the government in a context of accountability and transparency.

FUNCTIONAL PRINCIPLES

During the history of human rights, debates have arisen as to which rights were most important, whether there was a hierarchy of rights, whether a state could chose which rights it wished to recognize and implement, and how rights were related to each other. These theoretical principles arose because of certain political disagreements and problems in the way human rights were being used politically; in the way states were accusing their enemies of committing violations; and in the way states were claiming that they could only allow their citizens the enjoyment of certain types of human rights and not others. Certain principles have developed and been accepted in the field of human rights to ensure that human rights are recognized and *implemented* (one does not use the term "enforce") and discussed in a nonpolitical and functional way within the international community. The international community has developed human rights principles to help depoliticize them. These functional principles are *interdependence, interrelatedness, and indivisibility*:

Interdependence of human rights: Each human right is dependent on the enjoyment of each other right for its own enjoyment. Each right depends on each other right for any and all human rights to be enjoyed in reality. Thus, a state cannot deny a person any rights or that person's other rights will also fall. For example, freedom of movement is dependent on the right to adequate medical care. The right to fair trial is dependent on the right to equality before the law.

Interrelatedness of all human rights: All human rights are related to each other, for example, the right to adequate nourishment and freedom of speech, or freedom of religion and the right to vote. There is an intrinsic relationship between every human right and every other human right. They all have as their goal the protection of human dignity. One cannot try to separate them but must deal with all of them when addressing problems or alleged violations.

Indivisibility of human rights: All human rights form one indivisible body of norms that cannot be separated into different sets from which states may pick and choose what they will agree to follow. For example, one cannot say that his or her country's people are so poor that they can only have economic rights but not civil and political rights until all economic rights are fulfilled. Governments cannot divide rights in this way. Civil human rights are indivisible from political human rights, which are indivisible from economic rights, which are indivisible from social rights, which are indivisible from cultural rights, and so on. For most experts the so-called "solidarity rights" (peace, development, solidarity, etc.) would not fit within the scope of this principle.

OTHER HUMAN RIGHTS PRINCIPLES

Margin of Appreciation, sometimes referred to as **Margin of Discretion,** is largely a judicially created doctrine used in evaluating a specific factual situation in a court case to determine if a state has interfered with someone's human rights norm. This principle was judicially created within the European Convention on Human Rights system to allow the European Court to strike a fair balance between individual exercise of human rights in that Convention and the needs of states to deal with sometimes urgent and critical and complex problems on a basis where the state is given a benefit of the doubt, some leeway, some wiggle room, so to speak. It is not a term that has been used in relation to the U.S. In dealing with a human rights issue involving a European country one would be wise to remember this doctrine. It has not been adopted in the Inter American human rights system of which the U.S. is a member.

Human rights norms, again, constitute a balance between the needs of government to take care of matters of state and the freedom of human beings. International human rights law gives the government a little leeway by applying a doctrine known as the Margin of Appreciation, sometimes referred to as a Margin of Discretion. This principle recognizes that the government is sometimes better placed than a human rights court, after the fact, to determine the most appropriate government response or measure to take. In adjudicating the correctness of the state action which interferes with someone's exercise of their rights the adjudicator gives the state a certain judicial deference.

In essence this means that where there is an alleged human rights violation, the government will be given the benefit of the doubt in the assessment of whether its actions were a legitimate restriction of human rights or whether they crossed the line and constituted human rights violations.

For example, police are told that a murderer is hiding somewhere in a large apartment building and they evacuate every apartment and search the apartments without knocking. If a claim of violation of human rights is made, the forum that judges the legitimacy of the state action accords the government a margin of appreciation. If it finds that the search was not within the margin of appreciation, and is a human rights violation. If it finds that the search was within the margin of appreciation, it is not a violation. There are some cases in the European Court of Human Rights system which relate to the U.S. and where one will encounter reference to this doctrine. Some argue for a general margin of appreciation doctrine in international law, but this has not been accepted. This would not be applied in the context of a U.S. human rights case in a U.S. forum nor should it be applied in discussion of U.S. compliance with an international norm.

ABSOLUTE VS "PRIMA FACIE" HUMAN RIGHTS

Some human rights are *absolute*, meaning that they apply in all situations at all times, regardless of the circumstances. Some human rights are not absolute; they can be limited, restricted by the state, depending on the circumstances existing in a particular situation. These are called *prima facie* or *conditional* human rights. An example of an absolute human right is the freedom from torture. This type of right is seen in Article 7 of the ICCPR (Document 8) which reads: "No one shall be subjected to torture or to cruel, inhuman or degrading treatment or punishment." When you read this article there are no qualifiers, no limitations possible.

An example of a prima facie human right is the freedom of movement, as seen in Article 12 of the ICCPR, which reads:

> 12.1 *Everyone lawfully within the territory of a State shall, within that territory, have the right to liberty of movement and freedom to choose his residence.*
> 12.2 *Everyone shall be free to leave any country, including his own.*
> 12.3 *The above-mentioned rights shall not be subject to any restrictions except those which are provided by law, are necessary to protect national security, public order (ordre public), public health or morals or the rights and freedoms of others, and are consistent with the other rights recognized in the present Covenant.*

Articles 12.1 and 12.2 state the norm as an absolute, but Article 12.3 renders it not absolute, that is, prima facie. Article 12.3 is a limitations clause. Any human rights norm which has a limitations clause (see below) in an international treaty is a conditional human right. The right is absolute, except for those express, specific situations spelled out in paragraph 3. States can limit the exercise of the freedom if the measure strictly complies with the limitations clause.

LIMITATIONS OR RESTRICTIONS

The circumstances in which human rights that are prima facie can be limited are called permissible *limitations* or *restrictions*. Each prima facie right is defined within the article that sets forth the right, and then the criteria for the limitation or restriction to be legally valid. In Article 12 of the ICCPR, excerpterd above, the freedom of movement can be limited for such legitimate aims as public safety, public order, public health, or public morals. States can establish limitation measures on the exercise of such human rights so long as they are reasonably based on one of these specified aims, **and no others**, and the measure have been established by proper legal authority and procedure, and they are accessible, clear, and understandable to the public. This principle of limitations/restrictions, again, represents the balance between individual freedoms and the just demands of society for the efficient and effective operation of government.

The battles over human rights violations take place primarily in the limitations clauses. The mechanics of limitations/restrictions clauses is more fully explained in the definition section of Limitation/Restriction (measure/clause) in the terms section of this book. A short explanation of the process for applying a limitation/restriction clause to a particular situation can be found in Appendix E.

DEROGATION IN TIME OF PUBLIC EMERGENCY

Some human rights can be completely suspended in times of a serious and widespread public emergency affecting the very life and existence of the whole country, such as when the state is being invaded militarily by an enemy attack. Such suspension of human rights in times of public emergency is called *derogation*. Some Human Rights treaties contain derogations clauses. (See ICCPR art. 4) International human rights law recognizes the sometimes absolute need of the state government to suspend certain human rights for a certain period of time so as to allow it to deal with the public emergency. For example, if a country were being attacked militarily, a state could restrict freedom of movement or freedom of speech, for so long as it was necessary to protect the state. Only certain rights can be suspended like this. These are called "derogable rights." On the other hand some human rights, such as freedom from slavery, cannot be suspended. These are called "non derogable rights." The derogation clause of the treaty specifies which specific rights cannot be derogated, even in public emergency. See ICCPR art. 12.2.

DUTIES

Many people mistakenly think that human rights are about what we can do with no one being able to stop us from doing it. These people see human rights as a license for everyone to do what they want with no responsibility towards society. This is false. Society itself cannot continue to exist if everyone did what they wanted to do in the name of human rights. The truth is that in human rights law, for every human right there is a correlative duty. Everyone has human rights and everyone has human duties towards others and society, without which society cannot function safely and develop. In theory, every human being has duties to society and the state, such as paying taxes and obeying the motor vehicle rules, without which the state could not ensure respect for human rights. (See Article 29.1 of the Universal Declaration of Human Rights (Document 6).

The continued viability of a state that is supposed to protect human rights depends upon the fulfillment of citizen's duties to the state, unless unable or exempted. Human rights and human duties are interdependent. Rights and duties are two sides of the same coin. The coin is freedom. The connection of duties to human rights helps encourage the members of society to respect others' rights, as well as claim their own.

CULTURAL RELATIVISM VS. UNIVERSALITY OF HUMAN RIGHTS

For many years there was a great debate between different nations and groups regarding the issue of whether human rights were universal and had to be applied the same way to everyone everywhere (the doctrine of universality), or whether they were culturally varied and that each culture could interpret and apply them according to their cultural differences ("particularities" or "specificities"), known as the doctrine of cultural relativism. The interpretation and application of human rights internationally had been inconsistent and varied from culture to culture. This inconsistency has given rise to the claim by Western and developed states that human rights are universal and shall be applied in the same way to everyone in every society without regard to differences in religion, culture, language, customs, income level or extent of poverty, or other differences. Those states, usually developing and Third World, accused of violations usually assert the defense of *cultural relativism*, which claims that human rights should be interpreted in different places in different ways depending on the particular culture, custom, religion, and so on, and not on a universal, one-size-fits-all basis. This debate is called "universality versus cultural relativism." In 1993 the international community announced at the United Nations Vienna Conference on Human Rights that the principle of *universality* of human rights was the internationally accepted one. See Document 51. This debate continues nonetheless. The United States accepts and supports the principle of universality. All human rights must be interpreted and applied to all people everywhere the same way, regardless of cultural particularities. See Document 86.

IMPORTANCE OF LEGAL PROTECTION OF HUMAN RIGHTS

According to the preambles to the UDHR, ICCPR, and ICESCR, respect for human rights is "the foundation of freedom, justice, and peace in the world." This is a statement of vast significance. It says that respect for human rights is *the* foundation of freedom, justice, and peace in every country, including the United States. World War II taught the human race that it cannot let each state be the unaccountable god of all that happens within its territory, that the international community has an interest in and is affected by what happens in other states, and that there are international limits necessary for human civilization to continue. There are indeed various limitations, exceptions, and qualifications to the rather sweeping statement in the preambles of the UDHR, ICCPR, and ICESCR. However, the statement noted above is a fair statement of the general theory of the discipline known as human rights. Protection of human rights is necessary in order to preserve freedom, justice, and peace in the world. If one looks at almost every violent conflict scourging the earth today the issue causing the conflict is always a perception of some that the human rights of others are being violated and no one is doing anything about it. Thus, there must be legal measures to prevent, stop, or remedy violations so that conflicts will not occur or will not be enflamed by a sense of irremediable injustice.

HISTORY OF HUMAN RIGHTS IN THE U.S. EXPERIENCE

> *The concept of universal [human] rights developed by the 18th century political theorists nourished international law, as it also set the stage for American Constitutionalism. Indeed, international human rights law and the constitutional law of the United States are at bottom profoundly related: both seek to limit the authority of states to interfere with the inalienable rights of all individuals without discrimination.*
>
> Assistant Secretary of State John Shattuck, Initial Report of the United States of America to the U.N. Human Rights Committee under the International Covenant on Civil and Political Rights, July 1994

Given the long history of our country it is indeed pretentious to give a short history of human rights in relation to the United States. It is particularly challenging in view of the incredible dynamic in the life of the United States since 9/11. So much has happened. So much has changed. But, as Jimmy Carter stated in his Farewell Address, the United States is a country which was created by human rights out of crisis and revolution. This nation was founded by people who fled oppression and persecution and came here for freedom. They believed they had rights and demanded that their rights be respected. When this did not happen they separated themselves from their oppressor and formed their own society and government and went their own way to create America, the land of the free. This was expressed to the "Powers of the earth" in 1776, in the famous Declaration of Independence:

> *When in the course of human events it becomes necessary for one people to dissolve the political bands that have connected them with another, and to assume among the Powers of the earth, the separate and equal station to which the Laws of Nature and of Nature's God entitle them, a decent respect to the opinions of mankind requires that they should declare the causes that impel them to separation.*
>
> *We hold these truths to be self-evident, that all men are created equal, that they are endowed by their Creator with certain unalienable rights, among these are Life, Liberty and the pursuit of Happiness. That to secure these rights, Governments are instituted among Men, deriving their just powers from the consent of the governed....*
>
> *The history of the present King of Great Britain is a history of repeated injuries and usurpations, all having in direct object the establishment of an absolute Tyranny over these States. To prove this, let Facts be submitted to a candid world.*

Here they set forth a specific list of "injuries and usurpations" by the King. An example of two of these is as follows:

> *For depriving us in many cases, of the benefits of Trial by Jury.*
>
> *He has plundered our seas, ravaged our Coasts, burnt our towns, and destroyed the lives of our people .... We, therefore, ... appealing to the Supreme Judge of the world for the rectitude of our intentions, do ... solemnly publish and declare, That these United Colonies are, and of Right ought to be Free and Independent States ....*
>
> Declaration of Independence, in Congress July 4,
1776 (The unanimous Declaration of the thirteen
United States of America)

It has been said that the history of liberty is a history of limitations of governmental power, not the increase of it. Human rights, "unalienable rights," gave the U.S. the Declaration of Independence and the U.S. Constitution and Bill of Rights. History cannot argue against the fact that human rights abuses led to the drafting of the Declaration of Independence, which led to the founding of the United States. It gave proof that the United States of America was the first country to be created *by* human rights and *for* human rights. By this we mean that it was the awareness and consensus of the leaders of the thirteen colonies that all human beings had individual human rights just by being human, and that the human rights of all of the colonists were being violated by England. That led them to join together in united strength and to express the causes that would justify declaring their independence from England. In the Declaration of Independence, the Founding Fathers together stated to England and the world that they would no longer tolerate the abuse of power resulting in human rights violations against colonists. They no doubt were mindful of the Magna Carta of 1212, which held budding ideas of the rights of the governed against the governor. The great experiment that was to be the United States of America was not only caused by (in reaction against) human rights violations. It also came into being for the protection of human rights in the colonies (and later the states) against any abuse of power by even their own respective governments. They held this view in common. The usurpation or abuse of power by government of any kind would no longer be tolerated in America. Government by the people and for the people was set on making government limited in ways that protected their unalienable right to life, liberty, and the pursuit of happiness. Our history has been a continuous battle and debate over how to balance the freedom of the individual and the needs of the state to protect those freedoms.

The Declaration of Independence did not create the United States. It only resulted in the thirteen colonies becoming separate and equal sovereign international states (e.g., the sovereign state of Massachusetts, the sovereign state of Virginia, etc.). They saw a need to join together with each other to form a union that could accomplish together what they could not do individually. That united entity would be granted authority to handle matters that would otherwise have been within their separate sovereignty, such as immigration, foreign affairs, and national defense from external threat. In their sovereignty as states, they chose to give up some of their sovereignty to a greater entity to become known as the "United States" of America. The Articles of Confederation of 1781 formed them into a confederation with limited central government.

The Constitution in 1789 gave them the legal political institution known as the United States of America, a separate and equal, sovereign, international federal state. This Constitution of the United States was legally a treaty, an international legal instrument, governed by international law, entered into freely by the thirteen colonies, which saw themselves as separate sovereign states. It had to be "ratified" by nine of the thirteen colonies before it entered into force, creating the greatest country in history. This country was known for its freedom and for being governed by law, not human power. This Constitution had its legal basis in international law, the source of the doctrine of sovereignty. This was consciously done by the Founding Fathers who knew international law, then called the law of nations or *lex gentium*. The Constitution is not only the organic instrument through which the U.S. was created, it is an international treaty which is governed by international law and must be interpreted and applied consistent with it, so long as not unconstitutionally. This fact is never discussed but it is legally and historically true. One need only read the Federalist Papers to confirm this.

The U.S. is a federal state, meaning that it is composed of separate subunits called "states." Thus, the colonies first became individual international states and then became a federal republic of equal states, whereupon the individual states retained all the powers of international states, except those granted by the Constitution to the federal government. Most important of these was authority to engage in foreign affairs and national defense. In concept, this arrangement was a precursor of sorts to those individual sovereign states of the world who join together and limit their sovereignty for a common purpose, such as the protection of international human rights norms.

The Constitution contained only a few provisions to provide protection for the unalienable rights of the Declaration of Independence. It set forth a few civil liberties, such as establishing the right to habeas corpus (the right to challenge the lawfulness of one's arrest in a court of law); prohibiting bills of attainder (laws passed with the purpose of punishing one particular person); and prohibiting ex post facto legislation (making a law retroactive, therefore punishing people for breaking a law when it was not yet a law). In the Declaration of Independence, the signers clearly were cognizant of, and made reference to, international law as the basis of their right to secede. They believed that international law was based on the same natural law and Enlightenment philosophies that justified their claim to "unalienable rights." Although it was not yet called "human rights," the Founding Fathers clearly understood and meant this concept, even though the institution of slavery, the mistreatment of Indians, and the limited legal status of women were then still legal and social realities. The United States was nonetheless set upon a path toward achieving still greater rights of human beings, as the subsequent Civil War and civil rights and suffrage movements would attest. These movements helped catalyze national action for greater freedoms.

The Declaration of Independence is one of the two important historical documents that have provided the idea of human rights and its essential philosophy for the whole world. The other key document is the 1789 French Declaration of the Rights of Man and of Citizen. Even though it is not a legal document, the declaration has also established that all human beings are born equal and are created with their rights; that fundamental individual rights are not granted by state governments but are only recognized, respected, and protected by them; and that such protection is the first duty of government.

The United States was founded not only <u>by</u> human rights but also <u>for</u> the protection of the human rights of the colonists, as the subsequent Declaration of Rights (an early document that sought to insert the protection of certain individual freedoms into the Constitution), the Constitution and Bill of Rights would thereafter establish. In the 1791 amendments to the Constitution, Americans enjoyed a Bill of Rights to protect the citizenry from government. Along with the separation of powers, and checks and balances created by legal and institutional structure, Americans have enjoyed a system able to overcome major assaults on human rights, such as slavery and segregation, and to survive a civil war that would have ended most political enterprises.

The Constitution and the Bill of Rights would begin the U.S. legal experience of the protection of individuals from the power of the state. They reflected the belief in a government of limited powers, because human rights norms are limitations on how governments exercise power. Having learned about the abuse of power from its ties with England, the United States knew such legal restraints were necessary. The few individual rights provisions of the Constitution and the first ten amendments of the Bill of Rights, along with the Civil War amendments, would serve the United States as its protection of individual human freedom and as the precursors of modern human rights norms. Another important U.S. instrument in this equation was the Lieber Code, created at the time of the Civil War. This document, drafted by Professor Francis Lieber of Columbia University, established a code of conduct for the Union armed forces. This code set forth limitations on the military conduct of U.S. soldiers during the Civil War. It served as one of the founding documents of the field of international humanitarian law, which is the law of armed conflict. It established the principal of "military necessity," which set limits on the use of military power or force by a government so as to minimize the suffering, death, and destruction of war. This type of code is now embodied in the four Geneva Conventions and their various protocols. It is cited even in cases in other countries and legal systems.

The U.S. experience with human rights would take two tracks, one national and one international. On the national level, there are laws, such as the 1964 Civil Rights Act, and case decisions interpreting constitutionally based human rights, such as *Brown v. Board of Education*. On the international level, there is the U.S. participation in the Second World War; its participation in the Nuremberg trials of Nazi war crimes and the Tokyo trials of Japanese war crimes; and its involvement in the establishment of the United Nations and regional international human rights systems.

The United States has, perhaps more than any other state, given the world the foundations of human rights and many of the specific human rights norms, such as fair trial rights. It has given the field of human rights many of its greatest statespersons, scholars, and activists; created many nongovernmental organizations; and mobilized civil society in human rights issues both nationally and internationally. Of course, none of this means that the United States has been free from committing its own human rights violations. Anyone who would deny this would be ill informed and wrong. However, the United States has, by and large, acted consistently with internationally recognized human rights norms, at least since the end of legal segregation until that ignominious day of 9/11 and the start of what has been called the war on terrorism. Since that date, human rights issues have come to the forefront, with claims and denials of human rights violations by the military, the CIA, the Immigration Service, the prison system, the President, and on and on. Much international criticism has been made against the U.S. for what others see as a double standard and attitude of being above the law, known as exceptionalism.

Since the shocking events of 9/11, a shift of political attitudes has changed U.S. participation in the world of human rights both domestically (i.e abortion, capital punishment, and terrorism) and internationally (i.e Israeli treatment of Palestinians or international terrorism, with arrest and detention of suspected terrorists outside the territory of the U.S. and certain interrogation techniques).

Although domestically, U.S. society is more often and more extensively oriented to the Constitution than to international human rights standards, it is slowly increasing its knowledge of these international norms. In addition, international bodies are increasing their activities regarding U.S. human rights practice and problems. Even in the U.S. Supreme Court one sees the increasing influence of international human rights norms. Institutionally however, one has seen the gradual increase in the importance of the United Nations as it continued to develop international human rights standards and set up special mechanisms to monitor and resolve human rights issues, including those involving the U.S.

THE UNITED NATIONS (U.N.)

The United Nations is increasingly becoming the global focus of human rights for the United States. In recent years it has been perceived as almost a political enemy and a tool of those who hate the U.S. and its allies. In looking at the role of the U.S. in relation to the United Nations one must look to the U.N. Charter, a document strongly influenced by U.S. The United Nations was founded in the United States of America and has its main headquarters in New York. As an international inter-governmental institution it is like a club of governments, though it was created, as the Charter preamble states, by "We the peoples of the United Nations." It is the world's institutional focus for compliance with human rights globally. About this institution and it Charter, Eleanor Roosevelt states:

> The Charter of the United Nations is a guiding beacon along the way to the achievement of human rights and fundamental freedoms throughout the world. The immediate test is not only the extent to which human rights and freedoms have already been achieved, but the direction in which the world is moving. Is there a faithful compliance with the objectives of the Charter if some countries continue to curtail human rights and freedoms instead of to promote the universal respect for an observance of human rights and freedoms for all as called for by the Charter? The place to discuss the issue of human rights is in the forum of the United Nations. The United Nations has been set up as the common meeting ground for nations, where we can consider together our mutual problems and take advantage of our differences in experience. It is inherent in our firm attachment to democracy and freedom that we stand always ready to use the fundamental democratic procedures of honest discussion and negotiation. It is now as always our hope that despite the wide differences in approach we face in the world today, we can, with mutual good faith in the principles of the United Nations Charter, arrive at a common basis of understanding. We are here to join the meetings of this great international Assembly which meets in your beautiful capital of Paris. Freedom for the individual is an inseparable part of the cherished traditions of France. As one of the Delegates from the United States I pray Almighty God that we may win another victory here for the rights and freedoms of all men.
>
> Eleanor Roosevelt, *The Struggle for Human Rights*,
> from Halford Ross Ryan Ed.

> The history of human rights as we know them today began in World War II. The world's reaction to the Holocaust and other horrors of the two major wars led all nations, including the United States, to come to grips with human rights. The main focus of the international human rights activity of the United States would be within the United Nations, which was established in San Francisco in 1945 upon the entry into force of the U.N. Charter. With its participation in the United Nations, a community of sovereign and equal states, the United States joined a larger political group because it saw from the lessons of World War II a need to impose some internationally accepted rules upon states so that holocausts would not happen again. It also saw the need for international cooperation to combat various violent evils that still threatened the world. It saw the increasing interconnectedness and interrelationship of nations.
>
> American Rhetoric from Roosevelt to Reagan,
> Waveland Press: Prospect Heights, IL. 1987.

The United States became a prime mover of the United Nations in all fields, especially human rights. Thus, the United States was instrumental in drafting and promoting the U.N. Charter as well as the Universal Declaration of Human Rights; Eleanor Roosevelt served as a key drafter of that declaration as well as a member of the U.N. Commission on Human Rights. The United States began the work of multilateral dealing with human rights problems in all states, U.N. member or not, and in a broad range of areas.

By ratifying the U.N. Charter, the United States became legally obligated to act to fulfill the purposes of the United Nations. In Article 1.3 it states that one purpose is "to achieve international co-operation in solving international problems of an economic, social, cultural, or humanitarian character and in promoting and encouraging respect for human rights and for fundamental freedoms for all without distinction as to race, sex, language or religion." Under Article 55c, the United Nations is obligated to promote universal respect for, and observance of, human rights and fundamental freedoms for all without distinction as to race, sex, language, or religion. The international legal obligation of the United States as a member state as to human rights is set forth in the U.N. Charter, Article 56, which states that "all Members pledge themselves to take joint and separate action in cooperation with the [United Nations] Organization for the achievement of the purposes set forth in Article 55." The United States is thus legally obligated under the U.N. Charter to work toward these U.N. purposes both at home and globally.

The United States continues to act as a very proactive member of various international organizations dealing with human rights. The United Nations is a key one. It is an international intergovernmental institution, a sort of club of governments of the world. It is not an international government or a "one-world government." As a matter of law, it has no power over any member state other than that which the states give it when they voluntarily ratify the United Nations Charter. Most of the human rights norms that now exist in treaties, such as the ICCPR and CERD (the Convention on the Elimination of All Forms of Racial Discrimination), were produced by the member states of the United Nations acting together as an international organization. The United States has been a prime mover and promoter of the human rights standard-setting, treaty-making activity of the international community.

U.S. representatives sit on the U.N. General Assembly and the U.N. Security Council, where they deal with human rights issues in the political context. Americans have sat as judges on the International Court of Justice (ICJ), which as the legal arm of the United Nations has decided several cases relating to human rights. Up until recently, Professor Thomas Buergenthal, one of the most prominent and well-respected American human rights authorities in the world, sat as a judge on the ICJ. He has been succeeded by American Judge Joan E. Donaghue, who also has a human rights background, among others. The U.S. government has members sitting on, or is involved in, issues before many United Nations human rights bodies, such as the on Human Rights Council, which replaced the Commission on Human Rights in 2006.

As a state party that has chosen to become legally bound to follow the ICCPR and the Convention on Racial Discrimination, the United States submits periodic reports to U.N. bodies created by those treaties concerning the status of, and obstacles to, protection in the United States of the rights provided in those treaties.

In its 1994 Report to the U.N. Human Rights Committee under the ICCPR, the U.S. State Department reported:

> *The International Covenant on Civil and Political Rights was concluded in 1966 and entered into force ten years later, and was ratified by the United States in 1992....*
>
> *Together with the Universal Declaration of Human Rights and the International Covenant on Economic, Social and Cultural Rights, it represents the most complete and authoritative articulation of International Human Rights Law that has emerged in the years following World War II....*
>
> *Human Rights have become recognized as the universal birthright of every man, woman and child on this planet. The faith in inalienable human dignity rests at the core of the international law of human rights. It has many different sources and has been articulated over time in different ways. Indeed, its commanding power rests in no small measure on the very nature of its sources....*

The [ICCPR] contributes to the promotion of international human rights by codifying many of the principles we in the United States hold dear—political freedom, self determination, freedom of speech, opinion, expression, association and religion, and protection of the family against government intrusion. The unfortunate fact that these principles are disregarded in many countries in no way diminishes their commanding authority. The U.S. as a nation was founded on the principle of inalienable individual right. The history of this country is in many ways the history of an ongoing struggle to overcome old and new injustices in our own democracy that continues today. As a part of that struggle, the U.S. is also firmly committed to promoting respect for human rights and fundamental freedoms around the globe.

John Shattuck, supra, pp. ii-iii

In 1993, the United States was a very active major state in advancing the promotion and protection of human rights in the U.N. context at the Vienna Conference on Human Rights. At the U.N. conference the 180 plus countries of the world sought to update and rationalize international efforts and organizational systems to better protect human rights globally. It promoted the acceptance of the doctrine of "universality" of human rights, meaning that human rights apply to all peoples at all times in all countries, regardless of different customs, cultures, religions, and philosophies.

As previously mentioned, however, the United States has chosen to become legally bound by (*ratify*) a few international human rights treaties. It has often not ratified treaties even when it was very active in the very creation of the treaty. And when it has ratified it has usually taken a very long time to do so. As stated previously, it took over forty years for it to ratify the Genocide Convention after it signed that treaty, and fifteen years to ratify the ICCPR. That slow ratification process continues into the new millennium.

Since 9/11 and the U.S. "war on terrorism" the U.S. seems to have alienated much of the world community, including some of its historic friends, and this played out in the U.N. General Assembly. In its addresses to the General Assembly the U.S. continued to defend its actions against claims of violating international law, defending them as necessary to protect the U.S. and indeed the civilized world, from damage and domination by religious extremists. The General Assembly pushed to get the U.S. to respect human rights in its measures taken to protect the U.S. and others. It reminded the U.S. that the international human rights standards were legal obligations and that no state could just pick and choose which norms it wanted to respect, and when. The cry from much of the political world in the U.S. supporting the Government was that human rights treaties were "not a suicide pact". This seems to have meant that the U.S. cannot and must not respect human rights norms if the U.S., particularly the executive branch, perceives that it will lose the war against terrorism if it follows the standards, such as against torture, or fair trial, or discrimination.

The U.N. General Assembly did succeed in passing resolutions each year entitled "Protection of Human Rights and Fundamental Freedoms While Countering Terrorism." See Document 5. In its call to all member states, the United Nations is:

Reaffirming the fundamental importance, including in response to terrorism and the fear of terrorism, of respecting all human rights and fundamental freedoms and the rule of law,
Reaffirming also that States are under the obligation to protect all human rights and fundamental freedoms of all persons,
Reiterating the important contribution of measures taken at all levels against terrorism, consistent with international law, in particular international human rights, refugee and humanitarian law, to the functioning of democratic institutions and the maintenance of peace and security and thereby to the full enjoyment of human rights, as well as the need to continue this fight, including through international cooperation and the strengthening of the role of the United Nations in this respect....

The attitude of many Americans in years leading up to 9/11 and continuing after it has been influenced by events such as the U.N.Oil for Food scandal and the bureaucratic ineptitude and financial wastefulness of that international bureaucracy. The U.N. was also perceived by many Americans as anti American and used as a platform for the Khadafi's and Castros of the world. The U.N. was perceived by many as an organization which not only did not advance the national self interest of the U.S. but actually impeded it. The U.S. was trying to protect itself and the U.N. was seen as standing in its way and criticizing it for the measures it was taking in counter terrorism.

With the election of President Obama the mood both in the U.S. and globally changed to one more optimistic and positive, particularly with regards to hope for changes in human rights and humanitarian law policy. Barack Obama won the Nobel Peace prize and then decided to send more troops to war in Afghanistan, all in continuation of the war of terrorism. He announced to the General Assembly that the U.S. was changing its course as regards detentions and was going to close Guantánamo and make other serious policy changes.

The U.N. Human Rights Council
In 2006, the U.N. General Assembly decided to scrap the politically compromised Commission on Human Rights, which was a charter-based organ under ECOSOC. The General Assembly in 2006 created by resolution 60/251 the Human Rights Council. This would be the primary global forum for discussion of and dealing with international human rights issues. It is a subsidiary organ of the General Assembly. The Council is made up of 47 members elected by the General Assembly from different regions, in an attempt to represent all regions and cultures and legal systems. The Council sits in Geneva, Switzerland.

While the purpose of this Council was to create a more objective and impartial and non political forum to deal with human rights it has turned out to be anything but. The U.S. began to participate in the dealings of the Council though it was not elected a member of the Council. Early in the life of the Council there was a bad relationship between the Bush Administration and the Council, the Administration seeing the Council as a place for states to criticize the U.S. and its ally Israel. There developed in the Council a bloc of 56 Muslim states known as the Organization of Islamic Conferences (OIC), which sought to get the Council to condemn Israel and support the Palestinians. The OIC moved the Council to spend what the U.S. and some other states felt was an inordinate amount of time on the Israel-Palestine issue, condemning Israel. The U.S. criticized the Council for the poor record of some of its 47 members, inferring that with such a composition of human rights violators the Council could not be objective, impartial and effective. In 2007 the U.S. pulled out from attending and participating in the Council sessions. It did, however, occasionally send one of its Mission staff to sit in on a session of particular interest. In the U.S. view the Council was beyond repair.

With the election of Obama the mood in the Council became upbeat. The U.S. issued a Pledge (See Document 81) to the U.N. to the world and to Americans about its new view towards human rights and the international community, particularly with a view towards the U.N. It would rejoin participation with and attend the Council sessions. In 2009 the U.S. was elected by the General Assembly to become a member of the Council, which it accepted. It took its seat in 2010. The U.S. also co-drafted and proposed with Egypt a resolution on freedom of expression that was broadly received. This resolution was directed at one of the critical issues being dealt with by the Council besides Israel and the U.S. and its war on terrorism: so-called "defamation of religion." This was an attempt by the OIC and other states to pass a resolution condemning expressions which were deemed to be offensive to a religion, which was initially exclusively Islam, but later applied to all religions, though everyone knew it was primarily about Islam. It was an attempt by the OIC to counter what it felt were a rising negative stereotyping of Islam as a religion of violence and terror-ism leading to discrimination and violence against Muslims in various parts of the world.

The U.S. took a position in opposition to the OIC on this issue seeing it as a threat to freedom of expression and religion, and that it was not consistent with existing international human rights law. It voted against the resolution each time it came up. Between 2007 and 2010 the resolution continued to be voted on and passed, as it also did in the General Assembly, but with diminishing support each vote. What had been presented as a resolution aimed at tolerance was not seen as a two edged sword which could actually undermine and curtail human rights, particularly in the areas of blasphemy and anti proselytism laws. The U.S. resolution co sponsored with Egypt was an attempt to make the U.S. appear on the side of tolerance and against such negative stereotyping, while still asserting that one must adhere to the international human rights standards such as article 19 of the ICCPR. The U.S. continues to oppose this OIC move on defamation of religion. Just as it seemed that support for the defamation resolution was waning in the HRC, in mid 2010 the Human Rights Council passed an OIC sponsored resolution aimed at creating a position of special investigator to work closely with and monitor mass media organizations "to ensure that they create and promote an atmosphere of respect and tolerance for religious and cultural diversity."

The Obama Administration was not unaware of the weaknesses and defects of the Council, but believed it could make change from within the Council, if it could regain friends lost in the previous administration, and gain new ones. It presented the U.S. as just one state like and equal to all other which had to follow the same legal standards and be subject to the same scrutiny and same procedures of any other state. It tried to overcome the aura of exceptionalism which characterized the previous administration in the eyes of many.

Since 2009, the U.S. has again attempted to become a team player in the Council, pleasing some Americans but not others. The U.S. continues to walk a delicate line as regards Israel, and the frequent condemnations and investigations of its conduct such as the Gaza Invasion in "Operation Cast Lead." In that matter the Council called for an in-depth investigation of whether Israel had committed international crimes, and appointed Judge Richard Goldstone, himself a Jew, to lead the investigation which would bear his name. Israel denounced the investigation as biased since it did not also cover Palestinian violence against Israel. The U.S. position was to call the investigating panel flawed and the results suspect. Whether the administration is democratic or Republican the U.S. holds itself as a staunch ally of Israel, all the while trying to appear not so pro-Israel as to be un-objective or principled or unable to be a positive force in dealing with the Middle East crisis, particularly as regards the Israel-Palestine question.

The U.S. participation in the Human Rights Council would come to a peak in late 2010 to early 2011, when the U.S. was scheduled to have its general human rights record examined for the first time in history by an international inter-governmental human rights forum: the Universal Periodic Review ("UPR") process. It had appeared before "treaty based bodies" such as CERD, regarding its periodic reports, but the UPR was to be a highly visible general examination of how the U.S. does or does not comply with international human rights norms.

When the Council was established the UPR process was to be one its main features: every four years every country in the world would take turns having its human rights record examined by the Council, with the participation of non council states. This way no state could complain that the Council was picking on it or singling it out for political reasons. A random drawing took place and a list and schedule of all 192 states of the U.N. was established, setting the time when each state must go through the process. The time for the U.S. UPR was November 5, 2010. The U.S. accepted this and has been going along with the UPR procedure. The process is explained in Documents 84-85 and in Appendix K "A Practical Guide to the United Nations Universal Periodic Review (UPR)."

This process involves the state under review ("SuR") preparing a report and submitting it to the Council via the U.N. Office of the High Commissioner for Human Rights (OHCHR), which will also prepare its own report to the Council. The review is based on these reports. There will be a set of stages that the U.S. will have passed through, ultimately to a list of recommendations and a vote by the Council on whether to accept the "outcome report" concerning the U.S. as a SuR.

In order to prepare its national report the U.S. State Department has solicited participation from Americans in this UPR process. It has invited Americans to attend and held consultations across the United States and solicited input from NGOs and actually anyone in civil society. That period closed and the State Department prepared to the U.N. the U.S. national report, which is included as Document 86.

This U.S. national report should be read along with the Compilation report prepared by the U.N. Office of the High Commissioner for Human Rights and also that Office's Summary Report of stakeholder contributions found in Appendix K.

The United States appeared before the Council on November 5, 2010 (see Appendix K, 3). The draft UPR outcome report/document by the Troika was adopted November 9, 2010. The final report/document appeared January 4, 2011. See Document 87. It contains the most recommendations of any country to have undergone the UPR process. On March 10, 2011, the U.S. submitted its formal responses to the recommendations of the Outcome Report. See Appendix K, #4. After vigorous debate the Human Rights Council voted to adopt this Outcome Report on March 18, 2011. The U.S. accepted many recommendations and rejected many others. For the next four years the U.S. will be expected to implement those accepted recommendations, as it waits to begin the UPR process again, where, inter alia, its progress in implementation will be evaluated, just as for every other state undergoing the UPR every four years.

There is no enforcement power to force the U.S. to do anything. It is believed that since states know they will be examined every four years, the Council will want to know what they have done to implement the UPR recommendations when they appear at the next review, and that will be incentive to make changes.

Many Americans do not want the U.S. to be subject to a Council, composed of so many states known as gross human rights violators. This is so even though evidence suggests the U.S. itself has committed its share of human rights offenses, as well. Every state violates human rights, some more than others. The question is how far the U.S. will go in participating in this Council body. The U.S. is too important on many levels for the Council to survive and be effective for long without it? It has not yet succeeded. But it is possible that this Council will succumb to the geopolitical wrangling that characterizes international organizations. This, after all, is a body of governments judging other governments, some friend, and some foe, on their human rights records.

If the Council fails for too long to accomplish what it was created to do, promote human rights and fundamental freedoms, it will likely go the way of its predecessor. The Council is still in its infancy and with the U.S. input it is anyone's guess how things will go for human rights at the United Nations. Promotion of respect for human rights is one of the stated purposes of the United Nations, set forth in its Charter.

The Introduction to the U.S. national UPR report submitted to the OHCHR in August 2010, begins:

A more perfect union, a more perfect world

1. *The story of the United States of America is one guided by universal values shared the world over— that all are created equal and endowed with inalienable rights. In the United States, these values have grounded our institutions and motivated the determination of our citizens to come ever closer to realizing these ideals. Our Founders, who proclaimed their ambition "to form a more perfect Union," bequeathed to us not a static condition but a perpetual aspiration and mission.*

2. *We present our first Universal Periodic Review (UPR) report in the context of our commitment to help to build a world in which universal rights give strength and direction to the nations, partnerships, and institutions that can usher us toward a more perfect world, a world characterized by, as President Obama has said, "a just peace based on the inherent rights and dignity of every individual."*

3. *The U.S. has long been a cornerstone of the global economy and the global order. However, the most enduring contribution of the United States has been as a political experiment. The principles that all are created equal and endowed with inalienable rights were translated into promises and, with time, encoded into law. These simple but powerful principles have been the foundation upon which we have built the institutions of a modern state that is accountable to its citizens and whose laws are both legitimated by and limited by an enduring commitment to respect the rights of individuals. It is our political system that enables our economy and undergirds our global influence. As President Obama wrote in the preface to the recently published National Security Strategy, "democracy does*

not merely represent our better angels, it stands in opposition to aggression and injustice, and our support for universal rights is both fundamental to American leadership and a source of our strength in the world." Part of that strength derives from our democracy's capacity to adopt improvements based upon the firm foundation of our principled commitments. Our democracy is what allows us to acknowledge the realities of the world we live in, to recognize the opportunities to progress toward the fulfillment of an ideal, and to look to the future with pride and hope.

4. *The ideas that informed and inform the American experiment can be found all over the world and the people who have built it over centuries have come from every continent. The American experiment is a human experiment; the values, on which it is based, including a commitment to human rights, are clearly engrained in our own national conscience, but they are also universal.*

In the Conclusion to this national UPR report of August 2010, the U.S. expresses its attitude regarding the whole UPR process as follows:

The United States views participation in this UPR process as an opportunity to discuss with our citizenry and with fellow members of the Human Rights Council our accomplishments, challenges, and vision for the future on human rights. We welcome observations and recommendations that can help us on that road to a more perfect union. Delivering on human rights has never been easy, but it is work we will continue to undertake with determination, for human rights will always undergird our national identity and define our national aspirations.

This UPR process is an opportunity for American and international NGOs to input the international human rights processes to seek to influence the human rights direction of the U.S. Much depends on the attitude of the U.S. government as to how U.S. participation will go. If there is little domestic awareness of this process and the U.S. government position, or the response of the international community, one cannot expect much change in U.S. policy and practice.

The main problem is the Human Rights Council itself, which at this time is composed of some of the world's worst human rights violators. Libya was voted off the Council in March 2011 for recent human rights abuses. Other UPR related documents are found in Appendix K.

INTERNATIONAL FINANCIAL INSTITUTIONS (IFIS)

The United States has always been a participant, a major money donor, and a policy making participant in international financial institutions, such as the World Bank, the International Finance Corporation, the International Monetary Fund, and the International Development Association. In most of these institutions it does not have veto power over which countries receive international aid loans. However, because it is a major donor state and has substantial political power, it can exercise its political influence upon these institutions in a way favorable or unfavorable to respect for human rights, even by just voting for or against a particular loan. Federal law, the International Financial Institutions Act, now requires that the United States its "voice and vote" in certain international financial institutions (IFIs) In such as way as to advance human rights by seeking to channel assistance toward countries other than those whose governments engage in a consistent pattern of gross violations of internationally recognized human rights. In addition, the Unites States has been instrumental in getting some IFIs to factor human rights considerations into their policy and deliberations. This U.S. participation reflects on the countries belief that the power of international purse strings can be an effective agent to get some human rights-violating states to change their ways.

THE WORLD TRADE ORGANISATION

The end of the second millennium saw the world shrinking swiftly, thanks to the Internet and the globalization of trade, travel, and finances. The world trade situation, which was greatly affected by the major commercial powers of Asia, brought the major economic powers of the world to establish the World Trade Organization. Its purpose was to create a legal structure that would be most protective of international trade. It would be a specialized agency of the United Nations.

The United States became a member of the WTO because it believed this would help improve its international trade situation. The biggest issue of the United States was the relationship of China, a major exporter to the United States and a major human rights violator, with the WTO. Because of the economic importance and issues such as copyright infringement, counterfeit merchandise, and video/software piracy, the United States was interested in using the WTO to its advantage in relation to China.

In the 1990s and in 2000, the United States encountered major criticism, opposition, and even violence in its efforts to promote the WTO. Violent demonstrations in Seattle in 2000 made it clear that the environmental movement, the human rights movement, and the economic development movement had grave reservations about the impact of the WTO activity. In the area of human rights, the concern was that the WTO would cause economic considerations to be placed in priority over human rights protection, that profit would outweigh human dignity, and that all the legal standards that the world had long fought to establish would be undone.

THE INTERNATIONAL CRIMINAL LAW AND TRIBUNALS

In the years 1900 to 2000 it is estimated that 250,000,000 human beings were killed by governments in many different ways, from regional wars to genocides and civil wars and capital punishment. The holocaust was just a small but important part of that. In addition to that many, many other gross human and systematic human rights violations were committed by government.

Since 1944 the United States has been increasingly active in the development of the field of law known as international criminal law. The aim of this body of international law is to end this killing and other atrocities committed by agents of governments, mostly with complete impunity and no deterrence. The way it was to do this was by imposing criminal punishment upon those who committed acts deemed to be against the whole of humanity.

In the years since 2000 the field known as international criminal law has expanded and developed greatly as the great bloodbaths of the 20th century took place, such as Bosnia and Rwanda, the international community realized that the lessons of World War II had not been sufficiently learned. "Never again" seemed as if it were never ever going to become reality. The world came to the painful awareness that it was not only necessary to have human rights protected at a national level, but that it was necessary for the international community to set criminal legal norms at the international level to deter or punish the worst human rights offenses. This led to the development of the field of international criminal law. International criminal law has existed for hundreds of years and is mentioned in the Constitution. Piracy, which continues today off Somalia, was declared a crime against the whole human race, an international crime allowing every country to catch and prosecute the perpetrators wherever found. The next international crime was slavery.

It was particularly after the Second World War with the Nuremberg Trials and the Tokyo War Crimes trials that the field of international criminal law saw a huge leap forward. This was especially so around 1945-50 with the advent of the U.N. and the acceptance of the so called Nuremberg Principles on individual criminal responsibility and the London Charter defining crimes known as War Crimes, Crimes against Humanity (which then included genocide) and crimes against Peace, also known as the Crime of Aggression, under which the Nazi leadership was prosecuted at Nuremberg and other German cities. International Criminal Law continued to grow but was seldom prosecuted in an objective and impartial manner where applicable. The killing fields of Cambodia attest to that. The slow merging of the fields of International Human Rights Law and International Humanitarian Law, and the call for a culture of accountability to replace a culture of impunity, pushed for greater individual criminal responsibility.

Ever since the Genocide Convention was adopted in 1948 the International community, with the strong input of the United States, called for creation of an international criminal court and a code of international criminal offenses. This was, though, a very delicate geopolitical matter especially as the Cold War was waging. The Cold War put the idea of advancing the international criminal court establishment on the back burner. It was only in the 1990s as the ethnic conflict raged in Bosnia and the "Velvet Revolution" was taking place freeing up Eastern Europe, that the members of the U.N. realized that arresting and punishing those who caused and expanded such conflict was the only solution to restoring peace and stability to those regions.

It essentially took the horrors of Bosnia and of Rwanda to move the world forward towards international criminal law and tribunals.

The International Criminal Tribunal for the Former Yugoslavia (ICTY)

In the aftermath of the Bosnia-Serbia-Croatia conflict and the Dayton Agreement the United National Security Council established the International Criminal Tribunal for the Former Yugoslavia in 1993 under a Chapter VII resolution (Res. 827) binding on all states. This was an "ad hoc" tribunal, meaning it was set up only for a limited and temporary purpose. The purpose of this international criminal tribunal was to prosecute those who committed grave breaches of the Geneva Conventions, against the Laws and Customs of War, crimes against humanity, and genocide, in the bloody Balkans conflict. The reason why this tribunal became necessary was, again, because it was believed that the commission of war crimes and crimes against humanity and genocide were fanning the flame of the conflict and that the violence had descended too deep into the realm of barbarity, in Europe's back yard. It was perceived that establishing individual criminal responsibility for commission of these acts, all of which are also human rights violations, would counteract the ethnic demonization by one group of the others which intensified their mutual hatred and perception that everything was permitted because each group was fighting for its very survival.

The international criminal courts, such as the ICTY were an attempt by the international community to combat what was called a "culture of impunity" where high level government people, mostly military, believed they could do whatever they wanted either because the enemy was evil and a being not worthy of living, or simply that their ethnic group's survival depended on them and would not hold them accountable for whatever they did. Powerful people in high positions often believe that they can hide behind the veil of authority and position of their government who will protect them in relation to external or internal criticism and call for account.

Since 1994 an international criminal court with jurisdiction limited to the Bosnia conflict and for acts happening from 1991, has been prosecuting and punishing perpetrators of such crimes from all three ethnic parties to that conflict. The Court is nearing the end of its existence, but is still hoping to catch the biggest fish of all from this conflict, Radko Mladic, the Serbian general believed responsible for the infamous Srebrenica massacre. Even Slobodan Milosevic, former president of Yugoslavia, was prosecuted in the ICTY under the doctrine of command responsibility. He died while proceedings were still pending.

The U.S. contributed greatly in material ways to this tribunal, including money, computers and IT support, and providing judges, prosecuting attorneys and investigators. The product of the ICTY has been many criminal convictions and international criminals serving time in prison (the death penalty not being a punishment allowed). More importantly is the body of legal precedent handed down by the tribunal, particularly by the appellate branch of the ICTY. This has greatly expanded the scope and interpretation of statutory and customary international criminal law, in particular, and public international law in general.

The International Criminal Tribunal for Rwanda (ICTR)

Likewise, after the horrendous genocide in Rwanda in 1994, the U.N. Security Council by Res. 955 established another ad hoc criminal tribunal to prosecute those who participated in the war crimes, crimes against humanity, and genocide. In this massacre from 800,000 to a million Rwandans were slaughtered by fellow Rwandans of a different ethnic group. The world did very little to stop it.

This Tribunal has also presided over the prosecution, conviction and imprisonment of some of the major perpetrators of the Rwandan genocide. It has also greatly expanded the case law applying and interpreting international criminal law, both treaty and customary. This Tribunal established rape as a possible war crime, and gave the world the first international criminal conviction for the international crime of genocide.

As it had done for the ICTY the United States contributed materially and with personnel to the creation and upkeep of this criminal tribunal. This court was scheduled to end its work in 2010 but the Security Council (S/Res1932[2010]) extended the terms of office of certain trial judges until December 31, 2011, and until December 31, 2012 for certain appeals judges, hoping to have all trials and appeals done by the end of 2012.

The International Criminal Court (ICC)

As previously stated the creation of an international criminal court has been a desired goal of the United States and foreseen by the UN at least even prior to the Genocide Convention. The idea was that in order for the international community to deter and prevent international crimes from happening there needed to be a permanent international criminal court sitting to provide criminal prosecution for commission of the most serious international crimes, particularly genocide. There needed to be an international forum always ready to meet out justice for international crimes that created instability and conflict in the world and violate humankind's minimum standards of human conduct towards fellow human beings. In the article 6 of the 1948 Genocide Convention, properly titled the Convention on the Prevention and Punishment of the Crime of Genocide, states:

> *Persons charged with genocide or any of the other acts enumerated in Article 3 shall be tried by a competent tribunal of the State in the territory of which the act was committed,* **or by such international penal tribunal** *as may have jurisdiction with respect to those Contracting Parties which shall have accepted its jurisdiction. (emphasis added).*

It would take almost 50 years for this tribunal to be formulated and become a reality. The U.S. was a key player on this Tribunal becoming reality. Even more key was the work of civil society, many NGOs who pushed the U.S. to do its best to see this happen.

The U.S. government, particularly the Clinton administration, has also been very active in the promotion and process of establishing a permanent International Criminal Court (ICC). This court has jurisdiction to prosecute the international crimes that are known as war crimes, genocide, crimes against humanity, and eventually, the crime of aggression (waging an aggressive war) once that crime is defined. All such international crimes are considered to be crimes against all of the human race and are, or lead to, serious human rights violations. These criminal offenses apply to every person in every country as a matter of customary law. They are subject to the international legal principle of universal jurisdiction, meaning that those persons who commit such acts anywhere in the world can be prosecuted by the national courts of any state in the world, regardless of their nationality.

In June and July 1998, the United States, along with most other states in the international community, finalized a draft statute (international treaty) for the establishment of a permanent International Criminal Court. It was known as the Rome Statute or the ICC Statute. This process had begun in the early 1950s, but had been put aside because of the Cold War. It took place under the auspices of the United Nations, even though the court is not a U.N. organ and is independent from the U.N. (It is to be related to the United Nations by a special international agreement.)

This court would have jurisdiction secondary to national criminal jurisdictions under the principle of *complementarity* and would have jurisdiction only if a state party were unwilling or unable to prosecute who committed such crimes. The international community completed this process, and on July 17, 1998, voted 120 to 7 with 20 abstentions to adopt this statute and establish the court. The United States voted against adoption of the final proposed statute for legal and political reasons, which largely reflected the position of the Pentagon that no U.S. military personnel should ever be subject to the court's jurisdiction and that the U.S. wanted a veto over prosecutions. The United States did, however, sign the Final Act of the Rome Conference and continues to be a part of the ICC establishment process, even though it has not ratified the statute.

The Rome Statute entered into force in July 2002. The Court was thus created in 2002 and sits in The Hague, in Holland, and has started to handle cases under the Rome Statute for crimes within the jurisdiction of the Court. This is a court of complementary jurisdiction with state courts under the principle of "complementarity." This means that the ICC can take jurisdiction over an act if the court in the state court system where the act occurred, or the state where the perpetrator is a national, is "unwilling or unable genuinely" to carry out the investigation or prosecution.

And jurisdiction lies only in regards to the "most serious crimes of international concern", and then only as regards: (a) The State on the territory of which the conduct in question occurred or, if the crime was committed on board a vessel or aircraft, the State of registration of that vessel or aircraft; (b) The State of which the person accused of the crime is a national.

Cases may be brought before the Court by a state party to the Rome Statute, the UN Security Council acting under Chapter VII, or the Prosecutor. Read the ICC Statute (Document 76) for the precise statement of jurisdiction.

At the time of the first edition of this book President Clinton had signed the ICC statute on the last day of his presidency. As soon as President George W. Bush took office he stated the position of his administration that the U.S. would have nothing to do with the Court, unless the Court granted complete immunity for U.S. soldiers and government agents as the price for its becoming a party to this treaty. This was not given. The Bush Administration announced that it was "unsigning" the ICC Statute, an act that has no precedent in international law. It looked at the ICC as a potential threat to U.S. political, military and intelligence community power. From that moment on The Bush Administration did all it could to neutralize what it saw as a threat to U.S. activity outside the US, particularly military. It got Congress to pass the American Service-member's Protection Act (ASPA) in 2002.(See Appendix I) That act authorizes the President to use "all means necessary and appropriate to bring about the release of any U.S. or allied personnel being detained or imprisoned by, on behalf of, or at the request of the International Criminal Court."

In addition to the ASPA the Bush Administration also entered into many Bilateral Immunity Agreements, also called BIAs or "Article 98 Agreements", after a certain article in the Rome Statute. The purpose of these BIAs was to get the legal agreement of states parties to the Rome Statute not to hand over Americans and certain others to the ICC. A state entering a BIA was promising never to hand over Americans even if they committed crimes under the Rome Statute. It was alleged that the U.S. leaned heavily on states to enter these agreements, even to the point of threatening to withhold certain aid if an agreement was not made. Many ICC states and legal scholars criticized these BIAs because they had the legal effect of rendering the ICC treaty less effective, and interfered with states parties fulfilling their obligations under the statute.

At the time of this second edition there are 113 states in the world who have ratified the Rome Statute and 37 who have signed but not ratified. The U.S. and Russia have both signed but not ratified. There has been no clear word on the position of the Obama Administration with regards to U.S. ratification but the administration has hinted that it would like to cooperate with the ICC to promote its effectiveness.

The U.S. has started to attend the sessions of the Assembly of States parties to the ICC and is somewhat participating in the development of the ICC from the outside. It sent a delegation to the meeting in Kampala, Uganda, where the Assembly of States parties came to an agreement about the trickiest problem of the whole ICC process, the definition of the Crime of Aggression. The ICC Statute will now have the crime of aggression within its jurisdiction though this will not go into effect until 2017. See Document 77. The U.S. team was an active player in the lobby-negotiation process for this definition, as it very much affects the U.S. action in the international community, particularly in terms of peace-keeping missions. The Obama Administration has now become consistently engaged in the ICC process. But because it is still not a state party to the Rome Statute it is not fully able to participate as a voting member in the ongoing process of developing the Court and influencing its direction. This continues to be a sore spot with many nations, friend and foe alike, especially after our history of Abu Gharib and Guantánamo, and extraordinary rendition in the war on terrorism. However, the U.S. is trying from the outside to do what it can, so that if it ever eventually joins the ICC the law and practice of the Court will not be too much to its dislike.

Another positive move by the U.S. in relation to the ICC that bears mentioning was that on one occasion the U.S. did not assert its veto in the Security Council to a certain resolution for referral of a case to the ICC for investigation and prosecution. This allowed the case to move forward and not be impeded by politics.

Regarding the future of the ICC, the Assembly of States Parties is moving forward without the U.S., all the while recognizing the real importance of the U.S. to the effectiveness of the court whether or not it is a party. The ICC is seeking to woo the U.S. into joining it and the U.S. is wooing the Court to not take any action that the U.S. would find problematic and an impediment to joining. It is clear that the U.S. considers this forum very important. The reasons for it not wanting to become a party are several. They include fear of "politically motivated prosecutions" against U.S. service personnel and government officials, and the lack of a veto mechanism, which would allow the U.S. to control what cases do get handled, and particularly against the U.S. and its allies. It is especially here that many voices in the world expressed claims of "exceptionalism" in the U.S. attitude against the ICC. To many people the U.S. attitude says that the U.S. considers itself to be in need of an extra amount of latitude in being the world's only superpower and policeman of the world and wants immunity from international prosecution for international crimes. The international community member states of the ICC do not want to give the United States any special treatment or privilege or immunity, and want the U.S. to takes its place at the ICC table as an equal member of the world community, and subject to the same criminal standards.

With the 2010 passage of the crime of aggression the ICC now has its entire criminal arsenal to attack the culture of impunity. However, the absence of the U.S. will indeed affect its effectiveness. It is hoped by the international community that in any event the U.S. under Obama and beyond will not do anything to adversely affect the Court. The first cases are winding their way through the ICC now and it remains to be seen what effect it will have. In 2011, the Court is still facing a refusal of the African Union states to support the arrest and transfer of Ali al Bashir, the head of Sudan, for international crimes in the Darfur and other areas of Sudan. He is the first sitting head of state to be indicted and issued an international arrest warrant by the ICC for crimes including genocide. There is a claim by certain African states that the ICC is culturally biased and influenced by the strong nations and that the indictment of Bashir reflects that bias.

With regard to the adoption of the definition of aggression, a major step forward for the ICC and for International Criminal Law, Professor David Sheffer, a leader-member of the U.S. delegation at the Rome Conference, said:

> The historical significance of these developments cannot be understated. We have reached yet another plateau in the development of international criminal law and there will be many more to scale in the years ahead, including on the crime of aggression. But this is truly one giant leap. Perhaps, just perhaps, the action in Kampala will finally lock in a credible means to holding powerful individuals, those who intentionally launch massive acts of aggression, accountable for their actions and to instilling, over the years, greater deterrence to the aggressive instincts of insecure leaders. There are those who will be impatient with the wait until at least 2017, but I think in the long view of the future, and of history itself, that is a very tolerable and pragmatic wait.

Despite this non state party status of the U.S., in 2010 Professor Francis Boyle, an American International Lawyer and Professor, filed a complaint with the ICC Prosecutor against George W. Bush and other members of his government requesting that the prosecutor start an investigation into alleged international crimes for their actions in the war on terrorism and the Iraq conflict.

THE OSCE (FORMERLY CSCE)

At the end of the Second World War in Europe, many of the nations of eastern and Western Europe (thirty-five) and the United States and Canada established a political organization that was known as the Conference on Security and Cooperation in Europe (CSCE). It sought to establish the boundaries of post-war Europe, to draft political instruments regarding human rights obligations, and to create mechanisms for dealing with threats to security on both sides to minimize the risk of military action. The human rights component of this organization was based on the 1975 Helsinki Final Act. This document contains four chapters called "baskets." Each basket contains a number of principles. See Document 67.

References to the member obligations on human rights are found primarily in the guiding principles contained in Baskets I and III. Principles VII and VIII refer to the member states' obligation to fulfill their obligations to respect human rights under existing international law. This document was not a legal instrument, and the CSCE succeeded largely because everything was a matter of political and not legal obligation. However, the signing of the act was important historically and legally in the postwar struggle for human rights. It was the first international acknowledgement and acceptance by the USSR and its communist allies that they had an obligation to conform their conduct to international human rights standards. Initially this forum served as the meeting place of the two sides of the Iron Curtain and the principal place for discussions on human rights between the two sides, especially the United States and the Soviet Union during the Cold War era.

Since its founding, numerous follow-up meetings and many documents concerning human rights have been issued from these meetings. These meetings consisted of the exchange of views concerning compliance of members with their human rights obligations and the expansion of the catalogue of human rights. These follow-up meetings gave rise to what is called the Helsinki Process. The 1989 Vienna follow-up document gave rise to the "Human Dimension Mechanism" of the CSCE, which consists of a multistage negotiation, fact-finding, and mediation process between states, as well as bilateral and multilateral negotiations and the use of missions of experts and rapporteurs to deal with specific issues and crises. This process is done in conjunction with the Office of the High Commissioner on National Minorities. This office was to provide early warning and take early action to prevent or end minority-based crises before they degenerate into serious conflicts.

In 1994 the name was changed to Organization for Security and Cooperation in Europe, the OSCE. It is a very important human rights forum for the United States, which has always been a very active political player in this organization. The OSCE has served as the main political vehicle to become involved in, and engaged with, former communist countries in central and Eastern Europe. For example, it was the intense political pressure of the United States and its western European allies upon the former Soviet Union through the CSCE that caused the Soviets to permit the mass emigration of Soviet Jews to Israel, the United States, and elsewhere in the late 1980s and early 1990s. There are now about fifty-three countries in the OSCE. The U.S. Congress has established in Washington a Congressional Commission on Security and Cooperation in Europe, which is deeply engaged in human rights issues concerning Europe.

The OSCE has an Office for Democratic Institutions and Human Rights in Warsaw, Poland and the U.S. State Department engages in human rights activity in the OSCE context via that Office.

ORGANIZATION OF AMERICAN STATES

Because the United Nations was very much limited in its human rights activity in the Cold War, there arose what are known as "regional" human rights systems. Regional systems are open only to member states within a particular geographical area. In theory, these regional systems can create and operate a human rights system more finely attuned to the differing issues and problems (particularities) of the states in a particular region. The Council of Europe was formed in 1950 of western European states, which adopted the European Convention for the Protection of Human Rights and Fundamental Freedoms and set up a human rights system that is the most advanced in the world today. The Organization of African Unity set up a regional system in the early 1980s. The U.S. was to join the western hemisphere regional human rights regime under the Organization of American States, which is headquartered in Washington, D.C.

The United States became a founding member of the Organization of American States (OAS), whose 1948 Charter set up an international inter-governmental organization for all countries in the Americas: North, South, and Central. See Document 61. On May 2nd 1948, the OAS proclaimed the American Declaration of the Rights and Duties of Man (ADHR), the first regional human rights instrument applicable to the United States. See Document 62. The OAS established the Inter-American Commission on Human Rights in 1959. This body has its headquarters in Washington D.C. The OAS among other goals seeks to promote respect for human rights in the Americas and uses the ADHR as its basis of what those rights are. In 1965 the Commission was empowered to receive individual complaints ("petitions") against member states for violations. In 1970 the OAS Charter was amended so as to bootstrap the ADHR into being the legal basis in the Commissions for adjudicating petitions claiming violations. The Inter-American Commission was to become a formal charter organ of the OAS thereafter. The Commission still uses the ADHR as the legal basis for deciding cases against those states which are not party to the American Convention on Human Rights, as explained below.

In 1969 the OAS had adopted the American Convention on Human Rights (ACHR, see Document 63), which entered into force in 1978. The United States signed the treaty in 1977, but it has never been ratified by the U.S. Senate. There have been two protocols to the ACHR, the first on adding economic and social rights, and the second on abolishing the death penalty. See Documents 64, 65. The ACHR sets forth a set of regional human rights substantive norms binding upon states that ratify it (twenty-five as of 2010).

Under the ACHR, individuals and certain groups can file petitions alleging violations against a state party that is bound by the treaty automatically upon the state's ratification of the ACHR. The ACHR also provides for petitions by one state party against another state ("inter-state petitions") if a state so expressly declared, upon ratification. Petitions by and against a state party are handled first by the Inter-American commission, which is a quasi-judicial body. A state party and the state Commission can refer the case to the Inter-American Court of Human Rights. The court has both contentious jurisdiction and advisory jurisdiction. Contentious jurisdiction involves cases of an individual versus a state or a state versus a state, alleging actual violation of one or more rights in the Convention. With advisory jurisdiction, the court interprets the ACHR or other treaty concerning the protection of human rights in the American states or, in response to a member states request, advises that state about the compatibility of its domestic laws with such treaties.

Cases filed either before the Inter-American Commission or the Inter- American Court of Human Rights must first be determined to be *admissible*, that is, they must satisfy all the statutory ('legal') criteria for the Court or Commission to exercise its jurisdiction. These criteria include that the petitioner has exhausted all reasonably accessible and effective domestic remedies prior to filing. In contentious cases, the Commission or Court can request the state to take "provisional" or "interim" measures, such as stopping an execution or a deportation until the case is resolved. This happened in a recent 2008 case called *Ameziane vs. USA* involving a Guantánamo prisoner. See Appendix J, case law.

If the Court finds a violation of the Convention it can enter judgment for the complainants that they be assured of the enjoyment of their human rights by the subject state, and it may award fair compensation to the injured party as reparations These can include so called "project of life" or "life project" (span.: *Provecto de Vida*) damages for the loss of a victim's hopes and aspirations and life plans and potential.

The Obama Administration seemed to have taken a more serious and respectful posture towards the Inter-American system. However, in August 2010, the Inter-American Commission issued a press statement wherein it stated: "The Inter-American Commission on Human Rights (IACHR) deplores the forced transfer of Abdul Aziz Naji to Algeria from the United States Naval Base in Guantánamo, in breach of Precautionary Measures [259/02, granted on March 12, 2002]. The IACHR criticised the Obama Administration for sending this Guantánamo detainee back to where it determined he would likely suffer torture or other mistreatment. Naji had a case pending before the IACHR against the U.S.

The U.S. has never had any cases filed against it in the Court because it has not ratified the Convention. A few cases have been filed against the U.S. in the Commission, under the ADHR. These have involved issues such as abortion, capital punishment, damage from the Granada and Panama invasions, interdictions (stop, arrest, return) of Haitian refugees on the high seas, and Guantánamo prisoners, and even the rights of Native Americans. These cases have been largely unsuccessful.

Little is told to the American public about this human rights forum. As the existence of this human rights forum becomes better known, it may be increasingly resorted to by unsuccessful litigants in U.S. courts, who believe their grievances violate the ADHR's human rights norms. In U.S. case law both the ACHR and the ADHR have been referred to, though not as a rule of decision. They are usually referred to as evidence of customary international law.

One thing that can be said about the U.S. and the "American Convention" is that since the U.S. has signed this Convention it has an obligation under article 18 of the Vienna Conventions on the Law of Treaties to "refrain from acts which would defeat the object and purpose of the treaty." Thus, it cannot be said that the American Convention on Human Rights has no legal bearing on the U.S. government.

THE THREE BRANCHES OF U.S. GOVERNMENT

Many accept that the greatness of the American political experience was largely due to the result of the Founding Fathers' establishment in the Constitution of three distinct branches of the government. The purpose of this was that each branch was to be separate from the other and the three were to act as checks and balances against each other so that none would be able to usurp or misuse power. This was no doubt the result of the many human rights violations experienced by the colonists at the hand of the English king.

The United States government is made up of an executive branch, a legislative branch, and a judicial branch.

EXECUTIVE BRANCH

The executive branch of the United States government is led by the president of the United States. Its function is established by the Constitution. The executive branch has as its role the carrying out of the laws established by Congress and international law binding on the United States. The president is not only the head of the executive branch, but is also the "Head of State" known in the international community as the United States of America. As head of state, the president is the chief of U.S. foreign policy and the principal agent of the United States in international law and relations.

The head of state signs international human rights treaties on behalf of the United States and directs and carries out foreign policy in a way that he or she deems best to promote human rights. This includes not only signing various treaties and thus starting them on the process of ratification but also supporting the ratification of those signed by the previous presidents. In addition, the chief executive may issue executive orders on the subject of human rights to indicate an overall policy regarding the actions of his or her administration. Furthermore, foreign policy decisions through the methods mentioned above will determine whether or not international human rights are actively promoted in that particular administration.

All U.S. presidents since World War II have been substantially in favor of U.S. activity in advancing human rights standard setting, even though the United States has actually ratified few human rights treaties, or has done so only after a long time. Both Democratic and Republican presidents have held this position, though in policy and practice Democratic presidents have been more positive and activist internationally regarding human rights. Actually, it was not until it ratified the Genocide Convention in 1988, during the Reagan administration, that the United States ratified any major human rights treaty. (President Truman had signed the Genocide Convention in 1949.) President Jimmy Carter was particularly involved in advancing the cause of international human rights and himself signed many treaties. During his administration others were ratified as well.

An example of the official attitude of a Republican president toward domestic human rights implementation can be heard in the words of President George H.W. Bush, during whose presidency the ICCPR was ratified by the Senate. In his 1992 letter to the Senate Foreign Relations Committee accompanying his recommendation for ratification, which his administration strongly supported, he stated:

> *The end of the Cold War offers great opportunity for the forces of Democracy and rule of law throughout the world. I believe the United States has a special responsibility to assist those in other countries who are now working to make the transition to pluralistic democracies. ....*
>
> *United States ratification of the Covenant on Civil and Political Rights at this moment in history would underscore our natural commitment to fostering democratic values through international law. The Covenant codifies the essential freedoms people must enjoy in a democratic society, such as the right to liberty and security, and freedom of opinion and expression. Subject to a few essential reservations and understandings, it is entirely consonant with the fundamental principles incorporated in our Bill of Rights. U.S. ratification would also strengthen our ability to influence the development of appropriate human rights principles in the international- al community and provide an additional tool in our efforts to improve respect for fundamental freedoms in many problem countries around the world.*
>
> Letter from President George H.W. Bush to Senate Foreign
> Relations Committee, Rep. of S. Committee on Foreign Relations to
> accompany Exec. E, 95-2 [1992] at 25. August 8, 1991

President Clinton issued an executive order regarding international human rights in December 1998 that laid out an aggressive program for the advancement of international human rights in U.S. policy. His official U.S. policy with respect to human rights was contained in nine objectives:

1. Build new institutions of accountability that will hold violators to account;
2. Link trade and economic relations to human rights;
3. Recognize economic development, political development, human rights protection, and democracy protection as an integrated whole;
4. Build new multilateral institutions to address racial, ethnic, and religious conflict so as to diffuse conflicts before they lead to gross human rights violations;
5. Integrate women's rights into all aspects of our human rights policy;
6. Press for enactment of implementing legislation on the Convention against Torture;
7. Strengthen the United Nations' human rights machinery;
8. Strengthen our relationship with the non-governmental organizations working in many countries to promote democracy and human rights;
9. Tighten the focus and coordination of our programs to promote democracy and human rights abroad.

George W. Bush became President. And then there was 9/11. President Bush began to wage what was to be called the "war on terrorism." He sent captured suspected terrorists to Guantánamo and created a large detention facility there to hold and interrogate these prisoners and designated them "enemy combatants" a legal description taken from a 1951 U.S. Supreme Court case (*Eisentrager*), which found such persons to be without rights to access to the American justice system, particularly habeas corpus. It was the government's belief that since Guantánamo was not under the ultimate sovereignty of the U.S. (it was leased from Cuba) that U.S. law and the Constitution did not apply, and so posed almost no legal limits on the Executive power.

The Bush Administration looked for legal authority to maximize its power to use all possible means to interrogate the suspected terrorists or persons suspected of having intelligence information, such as where Osama Bin Laden may be hiding. Starting in 2002 the U.S. Department of Justice started issuing the so called "Torture Memos" in response to questions presented by the Administration on how far it could go in the robustness of its interrogation methods. Among the methods at issue were waterboarding and placing a certain suspect in a box with insects, knowing he was afraid of insects. See Document 91.

Eventually President George W. Bush set up a military commission to try some of the detainees, but that Commission was ruled unconstitutional. The U.S. Supreme Court ruled against the President on several issues related to Guantánamo, finding that the President had overstepped his power. The President got Congress to pass the Detainee Treatment Act to deprive detainees of access to U.S. courts. He had another Military Commission set up by act of Congress, but that process was interrupted by litigation also. Of utmost importance to the detainees was access to U.S. federal courts to seek habeas corpus review of the legality of their detention. The President sought to keep the Court out of this issue based on a claim of separation of powers cum national security but was rejected by the Supreme Court. The detainees were allowed access to lawyers, federal courts and to file for habeas relief. The GITMO plan of creating a human-rights-free zone in Guantánamo was thwarted by the Court which President Bush had filled with his choices, and which was supposed to be friendly to him.

There were allegations of torture and other mistreatment by the U.S. guards and interrogators particularly incident to interrogations, using what were referred to as "enhanced interrogation techniques". No charges were filed, no one had access to lawyers for a while, and everything was shrouded in utmost secrecy under a claim of national security.

President George W. Bush invaded Iraq and removed from power Sadaam Hussein. He began a process of trying to set up a democracy in Iraq with a system of human rights. Many criticized the Executive on legal grounds for invading Iraq, the pretext for which was the existence of weapons of mass destruction and Sadaam's failure to cooperate in monitoring his nuclear capacity. The threat of a large scale inter-religious conflict between Sunni and Shiite loomed large. The President instituted a military "surge", which seemed to push things in a positive direction and Iraq held elections, the U.S. turned sovereignty back to the Iraqi government, and the military took a lower profile, assisting Iraq to rebuild itself and create a rule of law, human rights respecting system.

Then Barack Obama was elected. He came into office and immediately issued an executive order to start the process of closing Guantánamo, arranging for prosecuting those detainess subject to prosecution. He issued an order stopping official torture and had his Attorney General issue a withdrawal of the so called Torture Memos of his predecessor. See Documents 90, 92. His Attorney General, Eric Holder, openly stated to Americans that the administration considered water boarding to be torture and prohibited by the Torture Convention.

President Obama gave his famous Cairo speech, trying to establish positive relations between America and the Muslim world, and to set the tone for the Middle East peace process. See Document 79. He re-engaged the U.S. in the United Nations Human Rights Council issuing his "Pledge" to the U.N. and the world. See Document 81. He started the process of closing

Guantánamo but was hung up on how and where to prosecute certain detainees, no state wanting them in its back yard or its courts, particularly New York.

On behalf of the President, Secretary of State Hilary Clinton announced the four part Obama plan for human rights in his administration. See Document 80:

1. A commitment to human rights starts with universal standards and with holding everyone accountable to those standards, including ourselves.
2. We must be pragmatic and agile in pursuit of our human rights agenda – not compromising on our principles, but doing what is most likely to make them real.
3. We support change driven by citizens and their communities.
4. We will widen our focus. We will not forget that positive change must be reinforced and strengthened where hope is on the rise, and we will not ignore or overlook places of seemingly intractable tragedy and despair.

President Obama began to tackle the illusive goal of universal health care coverage in view of a scandalous number of uninsured people in the U.S. Noticeable in the debate from a human rights perspective was that no one addressed the issue or raised the claim of whether medical health care was a human right. It remained a market commodity which some people could not afford. No one was discussing the health care issue in the context of human rights law.

He would eventually prevail in getting a compromised bill, but one that fully pleased no one. Having gone as far as he could in healthcare he is now, at the time of this book, turning to the huge financial crisis and intractable problem of illegal immigration and the treatment of aliens, a problem that still divides the nation.

LEGISLATIVE BRANCH

The Congress of the United States is the branch of government whose role is to serve as the legislature, making law and setting foreign policy for the executive branch to carry out. Its purpose is to express the will of the American people as to what U.S. law and policy should be in our democratic society, both as to domestic and international matters. The legislature is made up of the Senate, composed of two members from every state (a total of 100), and the House of Representatives, with a number of representatives based on population.

Perhaps its most important function as to international human rights is the process of ratification of treaties by the Senate. The Constitution gives the president the right to enter into international treaties, but these only become binding when he has received the "advice and consent" of two-thirds of the senators present for voting. This ratification makes international human rights norms part of U.S. law. After the president has signed a human rights treaty, the process of ratification then shifts to the U.S. Senate, where hearings are first held to determine if the Senate will give its advice and consent to the instrument. In the U.S. Senate, the hearings occur in the Senate Committee on Foreign Relations. In this committee, the ramifications of ratifying a particular treaty are discussed in detail. If there is general agreement on the purpose of the treaty, but some perceived problems of its conflicting with the Constitution or current laws of the nation, then the committee discusses possible reservations, declarations, and understandings that may be attached to the treaty and/or various specific articles. In this way, the treaty may be ratified, with "qualifications" the committee deems appropriate considering the overview of U.S. laws. This is the place that the ratification process usually takes a particularly long time, due to political differences on the committee, which represent the usually widely varying opinions of the electorate toward international human rights documents. If the Senate Committee on Foreign Relations agrees to send the treaty on to the full Senate, it is then discussed further and presented for a vote.

Ratification by the Senate is the expression by the representatives of the people that the people agree to ratify the president's signing of a treaty, allowing the United States to become legally bound under international law to fulfill the treaty obligations. Only when the Senate thus ratifies a treaty does the United States become legally bound by that treaty.

The involvement of the Congress in the treaty process then proceeds with the various legislation that is proposed and passed to implement the treaty's norms into domestic law. Furthermore, the Congress is very involved in the promotion of international human rights norms in the area of foreign policy, as it decides whether or not to deal with other nations, depending on their records in the area of upholding human rights norms. This process is particularly familiar in, for example, the decisions regarding "normal trading status," formerly known as "most favored nation status." In U.S. foreign policy decisions regarding China (People's Republic of China), for example, China's poor human rights performance has been the center of controversy in deciding whether or not to trade with them. Trading status has been an area of much debate for the U.S. Congress.

Almost from the beginning, the ratification of international human rights treaties has been a controversial subject, usually involving considerations of U.S. sovereignty. In the early 1950s, Senator John Bricker, a conservative senator from Ohio, headed a group of like-minded legislators who felt there were dangers inherent in U.S. involvement in signing international human rights treaties. Because of cases in the U.S. courts, such as *Sei Fuji v. California* and *Oyama v. California*, they feared that treaty law would subvert the purposes of domestic law. The result of their concerns was the proposed Bricker Amendment to the Constitution (see term in dictionary section), designed to limit treaty-making power and ensure that all international human rights treaties would be non-self-executing. The amendment, in various forms, was debated over the next few years and was eventually defeated. However, a compromise between the Eisenhower administration and the proponents of the amendment established a conservative attitude toward the treaty-making process over the next several years.

In recent years the Congress has been active in legislating both general human rights legislation and country-specific legislation. It also serves as a forum for fact finding and investigation into what is going on in human rights both in the United States and elsewhere. Especially important is congressional processing and deliberating of the Country Reports on Human Rights prepared annually by the State Department. See Documents 82, 83. The very important joint congressional body known as the Commission on Security and Cooperation in Europe is very active in investigating and reporting on human rights issues in Europe, especially former communist states.

In terms of Congress's influence on the human rights practices of other countries it is particularly in the area of appropriation of foreign aid and military and technical assistance that Congress tries to effect change internationally. Occasionally, Congress members engage separately or collectively in human rights diplomacy.

There seems to be an almost constant tension between the President and the Congress over U.S. human rights policy and practice, with domestic partisan politics often being the key factor. The attempt to give China permanent normal trading status in 2000 is a classic example of this phenomenon.

Then came 9/11. This catastrophe turned the U.S. upside down, created a national solidarity and patriotism bordering on nationalism. No sooner had 9/11 occurred then the stalled legislation known as the Patriot Act, the purpose of which was to increase the power of the President and executive branch, passed in a heartbeat, with only one congress member admitting to having read the whole act. The Patriot Act was controversial from the very start and was criticized broadly by human rights and civil liberties groups.

Broadly speaking the Patriot Act was a laundry list of items which the President wanted Congress to legislate, and which had been found by various federal courts to not have been statutorily or constitutionally permitted to the Executive. Where courts had curtailed or limited executive power the President wanted the Congress to expressly restore those judicially deprived powers. It was a legislative attempt to give the President the power he felt he needed to wage the war on terrorism and protect America. Many saw it differently, as a power grab by a conservative president who wanted the power to walk over human rights with impunity, calling him the "Imperial President." The debate continued over where to draw the line between freedom and security, and how much of their freedoms the Executive could ask Americans to give up in return for security.

The government arrested hundreds of aliens, mostly Middle Eastern or Muslim, usually via the immigration system, and detained them in remote areas for reasons claimed to be anti-terrorist. Claims of racial and religious profiling were raised against this action.

Congress has continued to legislate in areas of human rights, for example in passing the Torture Victims Protection Act, and dealing with human trafficking and hate crimes. It is also dealing with other issues such as same sex marriage, abortion related matters, and with violence against women in tribal law and order systems on Native American lands.

The Government had a major restructuring in order to enhance national security post 9/11. The Department of Homeland Security was established, and a national security Czar chosen; airport screening was put under tighter federal control, and the immigration system revamped and tightened. Americans were in a war they did not understand, against a concept which had no definition in international law. The Congress was trying to do its part to keep America safe. Gradually Americans started to feel safer though the country was heading for an economic crisis of epic proportions.

The elections of 2008 brought a feeling of hope and sea change to America. Congress went Democratic. Then in 2010 the House went Republican, vowing to undo some of President Obama's accomplishments, such as the recently enacted health care law. From November 2010 to March 2011 his administration fully participated in the U.N. Human Rights Council Universal Periodic Review in Geneva, the first time the U.S has appeared before an international human rights organ regarding its general human rights record. The government received criticism and recommendations for change from many states and NGOs, to which it responded. That process was completed March 18, 2011, when the Human Rights Council adopted the final Outcome Document of the USUPR Process. See Documents 86, 87, and Appendix K.

President Obama tried to close down Guantánamo but has been unable to find a place to transfer and prosecute the detainees who were suspected of criminal offenses. In early 2011 he had military commission trials started again in Guantánamo. Many Arab states started revolting from oppression and the U.S. President backed the changes, such as in Egypt and Libya. At the Human Rights Council the U.S. gave a strong and successful push to expelling Libya from the Council for its human rights violations in trying to crush the anti-Ghadaffi revolt. The U.S. vetoed a U.N. Security Council resolution against Israel for its continued construction in certain contested areas, and leaving the Israel-Palestine issue in a stalemate. It successfully promoted a Security Council resolution creating a no fly zone in Libya to protect civilians and intervened militarily to enforce the no fly zone, all done under this resolution which referenced the controversial Responsibility to Protect doctrine for the first time. The war against Al Qaeda and the Taliban in Afghanistan continues, and the situation in Iraq seems to continue to wind down, despite occasional violence. Much of the excitement and hope from the 2008 elections has turned into disappointment for many Americans. This is the era, along with severe economic uncertainty, joblessness and a bad housing sector, we find ourselves in at the time of this writing.

JUDICIAL BRANCH

The role of the judicial branch of government (courts) is to determine, interpret, and apply national and international law in a way protective of human rights and fundamental freedoms. They are to ensure that our governments (federal and state) act consistently with international obligations; they prevent and remedy violations, including providing for lawsuits by foreigners against foreigners for certain violations of human rights elsewhere. They must apply the law in a way consistent with our obligations under international law, so long as they do not violate the U.S. Constitution.

Article III of the U.S. Constitution, again, makes international human rights law part of U.S. law. Article VI, 2, makes such law the supreme law of the land:

> This Constitution, and the Laws of the United States which shall be made in Pursuance thereof; and all Treaties made, or which shall be made, under the Authority of the United States, shall be the supreme Law o f the Land; and the Judges in every State shall be bound thereby, any Thing in the Constitution or Laws of any State to the Contrary notwithstanding.

Human rights treaties, if self-executing, are of equal status with federal statutes. The latest in time prevails. Customary international law on human rights has the status of federal common law. If implemented by implementing legislation by Congress, such legislation must be applied and interpreted consistently with the international instrument which they implement. Courts must ascertain and administer international law on human rights. Where no treaty or other legal authority is controlling, the court must look to see if any customary international law norms exist, and, if so, apply them as U.S. law. According to early decisions of the U.S. Supreme Court, U.S. courts are never to interpret any law passed by Congress in any way that violates international law, so long as any other interpretation is possible. This follows from the legal principle that international law is part of U.S. law. Different parts of U.S. law should not be in conflict or inconsistent with each other.

Many of the cases in which U.S. courts are dealing with international human rights law involve lawsuits by foreigners against other foreigners who committed human rights violations against them in other countries. These cases are brought under the Alien Tort Claims Act (see Appendix I, J). Other cases involve human rights abuses alleged to have been committed by the United States or other countries against Americans. Some recent cases involve lawsuits against transnational corporations for physical and environmental harm, alleged to have been committed in connection with some government in violation of international human rights norms.

The record of the American courts, both federal and state, in being open to and applying international human rights law has not, on the whole, been positive. But it is progressing. Courts have been very reluctant to apply international human rights law. Much of this reluctance stems from the relative lack of knowledge of judges (and lawyers in general) of this field of law. Much of this ignorance results from so little being taught about human rights in law schools, though this is improving. There is also political skepticism and fear that international law is something foreign that a foreign body, such as the United Nations, might be trying to force upon the U.S. legal system, in violation of American sovereignty and social values. An interesting case decision showing a U.S. court grappling with international human rights law can be seen in the *Kiobel vs. Royal Dutch Petroleum Co.*, Opinion of 2010 found in Appendix J.

In 1793 the U.S. Supreme Court stated in a case called *Chisholm v. Georgia* that the United States "had, by taking its place among the nations of the earth, become amenable to the law of nations." Regarding the U.S. judicial experience concerning international human rights law, the late Justice Harry A. Blackmun wrote in 1994, after reviewing recent important U.S. cases involving human rights issues, "I would say that, at best, the Supreme Court enforces some principles of international law and some of its obligations some of the time" (Article in the *ASIL Newsletter*, American Society of International Law, March-May 1994). This is an apt description of the track record of U.S. courts in general.

Over the course of time, U.S. jurists are becoming more familiar with international human rights law and are beginning to see that it is neither foreign law nor the dictates of a supranational body to be imposed upon the U.S. in violation of its sovereignty. It is, as has been shown, U.S. law, as understood by the Founding Fathers, who told Americans that the first duty of government is the protection of the unalienable rights of its people.

More and more, U.S. courts are open to looking at the jurisprudence of other legal systems in the area of human rights. The increasing globalization and international intercourse of people and ideas make this inevitable. Though reviewing the case law of other legal systems, the Court did not accept the prevailing international human rights jurisprudence in that case. But, as U.S. Supreme Court Justice Sandra Day O'Connor stated in 1995:

> As our domestic courts are increasingly asked to resolve questions of foreign and international law about which we have no special competence, I think there is a great potential for our [Supreme] Court to learn from the experience and logic of foreign courts and international tribunals...

In 2005, the U.S. Supreme Court ruled in *Roper vs. Simmons* that a sentence of capital punishment on a person who committed a crime while a minor was unconstitutional. See Appendix J. The opinion considered international human rights law.

In a more recent case *Graham vs. Florida*, 2010, involving life sentences imposed on minors the Supreme Court, after looking for a national (U.S.) consensus on such punishment turned to the international law and practice. In concluding that such punishment constituted cruel and unusual punishment in violation of the U.S. Constitution, the Court, through Justice Kennedy stated:

> Society changes. Knowledge accumulates. We learn, sometimes, from our mistakes. Punishments that did not seem cruel and unusual at one time may, in the light of reason and experience, be found cruel and unusual at a later time....
>
> The Court has treated the laws and practices of other nations and international agreements as relevant to the Eighth Amendment not because those norms are binding or controlling but because the judgment of the world's nations that a particular sentencing practice is inconsistent with basic principles of decency demonstrate that the Court's rationale has respected reasoning behind it.

American courts are becoming more sensitive to international human rights law as lawyers learn this law and put it into legal briefs, including amicus curiae briefs, bring international law and jurisprudence into the American judicial mix. After all, international law is part of our American law because the Constitution says so.

In another recent Supreme Court case, *Samantur vs. Yousuf,* the Supreme Court ruled that the Foreign Sovereign Immunities Act (FSIA) did not grant legal immunity to an individual who persecuted the plaintiff while he was a member of a government. (See Appendix J) It allowed the suit by one alien against another alien in U.S. District Court under the Alien Tort Claims Act, saying that Congress did not intend to grant such immunity to former government agents who committed human rights violations.

Of all the cases decided by the Supreme Court since 9/11, the most courageous and beneficial to the limitation of government power, to checks and balances, were the opinions in *Rasul vs. Bush, Hamdan vs. Rumsfeld* and *Hamdi vs. Rumsfeld*, and *Boumediene vs. Bush*. These were especially important as they were checks on the head of state and commander in chief in the war on terrorism. These cases reinforced the principles of rule of law and accountability, and due process of law. They were cases about the limitation of the power of government towards human beings and access to justice. They reasserted that the U.S. is a "nation of laws and not of men," where law rules supreme, even in time of armed conflict, even in a war against terrorists.

See Appendix J, Selected Case Decisions, for other U.S. court decisions involving international human rights issues.

INTERNATIONAL COURT OF JUSTICE CASES AND FEDERALISM

One very important factor affecting international human rights in America is the issue of federalism. The United States of America is a federal state, a country made up of fifty sub states. Under the tenth amendment to the U.S. Constitution all power not granted to the federal government, such as immigration and national defense, was reserved to the individual states:

> The Powers not delegated to the United States by the Constitution, nor prohibited by it to the States, are reserved to the States respectively or to the People.

And that same Constitution states, as cited above, that treaties and other international law are the supreme law of the land, "any thing in the Constitution or Laws of any State to the contrary notwithstanding". The issues of states rights, federalism, and supremacy have a complex and historic effect on the respect for international law in general and international human rights law in particular. This has played itself out not only in the courts of America, but also in the International Court of Justice, the judicial organ of the United Nations.

Over the course of history of the International Court of Justice (ICJ) the U.S. has been involved in several cases directly or indirectly involving human rights. The Nicaragua vs. U.S. case and the Iran Hostage cases are examples. More recently two cases, which went largely unnoticed by America, came to the ICJ: *Germany vs. USA (Legrand)* 2001 and *Mexico vs. USA (Avena)* 2004. Both of these cases involved the issue of whether the U.S. had violated its obligation under the Vienna Convention on Consular Relations. That Convention, which the U.S. had ratified, said that if the nationals of any state party were subject to criminal proceedings for capital crimes in another state party, that the prosecuting country had to inform the defendant that he or she had a right to contact his or her consulate in the prosecuting country for whatever help that the foreigner's state could give, such as assisting in finding competent legal counsel or monitoring the fairness of the proceedings. Thus, this was a legal obligation of the United States under international law.

In two state court capital criminal proceedings the state had not given the defendants that consular advisement. One case involved citizens of Germany, the other 51 Mexican nationals. Given the large number of Mexican nationals in the United States this was a very substantial problem.

Germany and Mexico brought petitions against the U.S. in the ICJ. The U.S. tried to say that such criminal matters were a matter of state (e.g. Texas) laws and it was a matter for their authorities. The U.S. lost in both cases. Regardless of what the federal-state criminal law jurisdictional setup was, the federal government had the obligation to see that states complied with the treaty The ICJ in *Avena* ruled "that the United States had breached Article 36 of the Vienna Convention on Consular Relations in the cases of 51 Mexican nationals [who had been arrested, tried and sentenced to death in the United States] by failing to inform them … of their rights to consular access and assistance." See Appendix J.

In the *LeGrand Case* (*Germany v. United States of America*), the International Court found by fourteen votes to one that, by not informing Karl and Walter LaGrand without delay following their arrest of their rights under Article 36, paragraph 1 (b), of the Vienna Convention on Consular Relations, and by thereby depriving Germany of the possibility, in a timely fashion, to render the assistance provided for by the Convention to the individuals concerned, the United States breached its obligations to Germany and to the LeGrand brothers under the Convention.

In the aftermath of those two ICJ cases a difficult process ensued between the U.S. governments and the state governments involved to try to remedy the problem and make right cases which could still be made right. At issue was due process of law for criminal defendants who could lose their life going through the foreign legal system and the consular help which is the other side of the coin of citizenship and allegiance to a state. The federal- state criminal jurisdictional split wound up costing the U.S. internationally embarrassing judicial losses in the World Court though few Americans even heard about it.

Not unexpectedly, states in America do not like the idea of some international law, international body, or a foreign country meddling in or cluttering their criminal justice system, particularly with death penalty cases. But it must be remembered that the supremacy clause ends with: "any Thing in the Constitution or Laws of any State to the Contrary notwithstanding." The language of the Constitution seems to say the several states must comply with this international norm as a matter of U.S. Constitutional law. Indeed, it is the case that all judges in all courts of the States take an oath or affirmation to support and defend the Constitution of the United States, as well as state law. When any legal proceeding arises out of the constitution of his State or out of any of its laws it is by this clause made his or her duty to be " bound" by the U.S. Constitution and laws, and in the appropriate case to hold that the state constitution or law is void because it is in conflict with "the supreme law of the land."

Much of the problem has to do with communication between the federal government and state governments. Since states are not in the business of treaty making or compliance they are not as up to speed in the international human rights law domain. They must be taught by the federal government what the ramifications of treaties are as well as just learning what the treaties are and the procedures and implications to federal states. This is particularly important as it relates to areas such as criminal law and family law, for example issues such as the death penalty.

A process started to deepen the federal- state interaction regarding human rights and consular law after the *Avena* and *LeGrand* decisions. In early 2010, Harold Koh, the Legal Advisor at the U.S. State Department wrote to the Governors of all 50 states and brought to their attention the main human right treaties binding on the U.S. He made them aware of issues such as preparation of U.S. periodic reports. In that memo he tells the Governors:

MEMORANDUM FOR STATE GOVERNORS
FROM: *Harold Hongju Koh, Legal Adviser*
SUBJECT: *U.S. Human Rights Treaty Reports*

This electronic communication contains information on several human rights treaties to which the United States is party, and which are implemented *through existing laws at all levels of government (federal, state, insular and local). To promote knowledge of these treaties in the United States, we would appreciate your forwarding this communication to your Attorney General's office, and to the departments and offices that deal with human rights, civil rights, housing, employment and related issues in your administration. Specifically, this memorandum provides background information on five human rights treaties to which the United States is a party and on which the United States has filed reports with the United Nations from 2005-2008: the Convention Against Torture and other Cruel, Inhuman or Degrading Treatment or Punishment (CAT); the International Covenant on Civil and Political Rights (ICCPR); the International Convention on the Elimination of All Forms of Racial Discrimination (CERD); and two optional protocols to the Convention on the Rights of the Child —the Optional Protocol on the Involvement of Children in Armed Conflict and the Optional Protocol on the Sale of Children, Child Prostitution, and Child Pornography (CRC Optional Protocols). The United States is party to each of these treaties and, pursuant to obligations under each of these treaties, is obliged to submit reports to treaty monitoring bodies on the implementation of U.S. obligations thereunder.* **Because U.S. treaty obligations may apply to all levels of government throughout the territory of the United States and because of the important issues of U.S. law and practice addressed in our reports, we wish to make you and the appropriate members of your staff aware of these reports.**

United States obligations under the ICCPR, CERD and the CRC Optional Protocols are implemented under existing law; in other words, prior to becoming a party to each of these treaties, the U.S. State Department, coordinating with other relevant agencies, reviewed the treaties and relevant provisions of U.S. law and determined that existing laws in the United States were sufficient to implement the treaty obligations, as understood or modified by reservations, understandings or declarations made by the United States at the time of ratification in order to ensure congruence between treaty obligations and existing U.S. laws. With regard to the CAT, Congress passed specific implementing legislation.

Although these treaties do not give rise directly to individually enforceable rights in U.S. courts, the United States is bound under international law to implement all of its obligations under these treaties and takes these obligations very seriously.

*As noted above, among these obligations are requirements to submit to the United Nations periodic reports of the actions the United States has taken in implementation of these treaties. Subsequent to submission of the reports, representatives of the United States (and in some cases representatives of the states) met with the relevant United Nations committees involved to present these reports, answer questions, and provide further information. In the context of these reports and meetings, the United Nations committees have expressed interest in confirming that the existence and substance of these treaties is made known throughout the territory of the United States. For example, one of these committees expressly urged the United States to "make government officials, the judiciary, federal and state law enforcement officials, teachers, social workers and the public in general aware about the responsibilities of the State party under the Convention." **Because implementation of these treaties may be carried out by officials at all levels of government (federal, state, insular, and local) under existing laws applicable in their jurisdictions, we want to make sure that the substance of these treaties and their relevance to the United States is known to appropriate governmental officials and to members of the public.***

I have attached to this memorandum links to the State Department and other websites containing the relevant treaties, the reports submitted by the United States, committee responses ("Concluding Observations"), and other relevant documents. We ask that you transmit these links to the appropriate offices in your organization or department.

(emphasis added)

Time will tell whether and to what extent the states will cooperate with the Feds to see that the treaties are fully implemented. What can be said is that without state awareness of, and cooperation with the Federal government in complying with international law, binding under the U.S. Constitution, a significant protection gap will exist at the state level. This is not acceptable under international human rights law. The Constitution makes international law the supreme law of the land, including federal and state.

EXTRA-TERRITORIALITY: ARE HUMAN RIGHTS LEGAL OBLIGATIONS LEGALLY BINDING ON THE U.S. OUTSIDE OF ITS BORDERS?

Since even before the war on terrorism began the issue of the extra-territorial effect of international human rights treaty norms has been debated. The issue is as follows: Is the U.S. government legally bound to observe human rights treaty and customary human rights norms outside of the boundaries of the U.S.? Put conversely, can the U.S. be accused of human rights violations for its actions, such as in a peacekeeping or its Iraq or Afghanistan conflict situations? Of course, humanitarian law applies beyond the U.S. boundaries, but here the issue is the territorial scope of human rights obligations, such as the ICCPR and Convention against Torture. The issue became clear when the events of Abu Gharib and Guantánamo detainees and extraordinary renditions became known. In those situations one can ask whether treaties such as the ICCPR and Torture Convention apply to the acts of the U.S. committed in other countries, in addition to any humanitarian law norms.

The position of the Bush government was substantially that international human rights law did not apply outside our borders. It was for internal use only. Therefore only international law applicable outside the U.S. such as the Geneva Conventions would apply. The attitude was particularly that human rights are about what we do at home, even though most Americans had no clue about the existence of international human rights norms. In fact, the attitude of most Americans was that any so called human rights norms were standards with which we judged other countries as to how they treated their own people. Human rights were concepts we used to judge China and Cuba and Iran. Americans have been largely unaware that the U.S. has taken on international legal obligations regarding human rights concerning its own actions. So much less would we wonder whether these legal obligations would bind our government in how it acts in other countries where our troops and other agents are found.

At the level of the international community this issue is being debated and claims of U.S. violations of human rights by us in other countries are being alleged. The position of the U.S. has been either that such standards do not apply to us because we are in the exceptional situation of the war on terrorism and cannot be hindered by human rights norms, and even humanitarian law norms, for that matter; or that as a matter of law these human rights norms do not apply outside the U.S. The two defenses presented against the claim that human rights norms do not apply to the U.S. actions outside the U.S. border are either exceptionalism, that we are above the law because of the need to fight the war on terror unimpeded, or that these norms do not apply to us extraterritorially as a matter of law. U.S. criminal law how ever, has been expanded to apply extra territorially to criminalize and give U.S. courts jurisdiction over acts of torture committed outside our borders. See Primary Document 21. Since the beginning of the war on terrorism the application of U.S. criminal law has been expanded extraterritorially, such as regarding torture or acts of terrorism, but the government has resisted claims that human rights norms apply to the U.S. abroad.

As a matter of international law binding on the U.S. via the U.S. Constitution, most international human rights law norms do apply to the U.S. extra-territorially, at the very least where the U.S. exercises "effective control" of the places and people where we find ourselves acting outside our borders. Human rights norms apply to the U.S. both inside the boundaries of the U.S. and outside the U.S. where we exercise effective control.

To see this issue in the international human rights documents such as the ICCPR, see Primary Document 15, the Annex to the U.S. Second and Third Periodic reports to the U.N. Human Rights Committee, wherein the Dept. of State sets forth its legal position. Its position is primarily that the ICCPR when it was drafted was never meant to apply extra-territorially outside the territory of the states. Thus, it does not apply in such places as Guantánamo or Abu Gharib, and the U.N. human rights treaty bodies could not even bring it up before the U.S. Contrast this with General Comment 31 of the Human Rights Committee, Appendix E, paragraphs 10. The position of the Obama government was somewhat revealed in the U.S. national UPR report, Document 86. There the new government in 2010 stated, as regarding interrogation techniques:

> Individuals detained in any armed conflict shall in all circumstances be treated humanely and shall not be subjected to violence to life and person, nor to outrages upon personal dignity, whenever such individuals are in the custody or under the effective control of the United States Government or detained within a facility owned, operated, or controlled by the United States.

This obviously means wherever such persons are detained and are in the custody and effective control of the U.S. government. The U.S. must accept that under international human rights law it is bound to respect the human dignity and human rights of all human beings, wherever situated, who are in the custody and effective control of the U.S. government. This is the object and purpose and spirit of international human rights norms in such treaties as ICCPR, CAT, and CERD.

Closely related to this issue in the war on terror has been the question of whether, in situation of armed conflict, both international humanitarian law and also human rights norms apply at the same time. This is not a question of extra territoriality but a complex legal question of whether in time of armed conflict regular human rights norms cease to apply and only humanitarian law applies. Otherwise stated, do human rights obligations continue to apply in situations where an armed conflict exists and international humanitarian law applies?

The U.S. position is that only humanitarian law applies and human rights norms, even if they applied extra-territorially, cease to apply during the armed conflict. This is the so called "lex *specialis*" argument, which will not be explained here. See Document 26, para. 24. In the war on terrorism context this has largely meant that where the U.S. is engaged in armed conflict it contends that only humanitarian law applies and human rights norms fall silent. This is incorrect as a matter of international law. Both sets of norms apply during armed conflict, except for those derogable norms which have been officially derogated during the conflict. Thus, for example, the treaty norm (ICCPR, CAT) and customary norm against torture would both apply as well as humanitarian law norms, in a situation of armed conflict and would both apply wherever the U.S. has effective control or custody of a person. For another discussion of this issue of the concurrent applicability of human rights and humanitarian law see Appendix E, General Comment #31, and Appendix M, Document M #1, Summary, and Paras 6-8, and Document M #5, para. 282.

It is my opinion that international human right norms binding upon the U.S. apply both within the territory of the U.S., and outside of it where the U.S. Government, including the military, exercises effective control over persons, and human rights norms, at least non derogable norms apply alongside and concurrently with any applicable humanitarian law norms.

THE SCHOOL OF THE AMERICAS/WHINSEC

One issue that continues to hold the attention of the Executive and Legislative branches is the activities of the School of the Americas, which, in 2001, was replaced by Congress with the Western Hemisphere Institute for Security and Cooperation or WHINSEC. It is headquartered at Fort Benning, Georgia. This Institute is a training facility for training members of the military from Central and South American countries in courses that are given to U.S. military. Courses are in Spanish.

The reason that SOA/WHINSEC has been of concern is that many graduates of this school were alleged to have been taught by the U.S. Dept. of Defense how to commit human rights violations such as torture. It is claimed that many graduates returned to their country and committed serious human rights violations and a few became oppressive dictators. This charge led to a lot of opposition from the human rights NGO community. It led to the establishment of an NGO called School of the Americas Watch, whose goal was the abolition of the SOA and its successor, WHINSEC by Congress. In 2007 Congress fell a few votes short of cutting off funding. The allegations continue that some of its graduates are committing human rights violations. The DOD claims that WHINSEC now offers its students a course in human rights and democracy, and in any case, the U.S. cannot be held responsible for the acts of its graduates when they are back in their country. The human rights community continues to try to mobilize Congress to pass legislation to abolish WHINSEC. School of the Americas Watch has an annual demonstration at Fort Benning every November, calling for its permanent abolition.

DILEMMAS AND CRITICISM OF HUMAN RIGHTS POLICY AND PRACTICE

Most Americans believe in human rights and believe they have them. Most place the source of these rights in the U.S. Constitution, though some have now learned of human rights under international law. Politically speaking in the United States, one sees those who really know and believe in human rights in both U.S. and international law, but more often one sees those who think that international human rights standards are a threat to Americans, being imposed upon them by a non-U.S. source (the United Nations or Organization of American States), which threatens to take away their sovereignty and compromise their fundamental values, such as parental rights.

Many Americans are politically against resorting to international human rights standards, at least when they are directed against the United States as a criticism of its practice. They see them as only a political tool used to make the United States look bad. Many Americans see human rights norms as something we apply to the actions of those in other countries but which are not to be directed against us.

Many believe that U.S. law is fully consistent with international human rights standards and thus they need not become bound by any international human rights treaties. They do not wish to be judged by anyone or by any standard other than U.S. law. Still others believe that what is needed to end the major human rights crises is a one-world government, or world federalism, which they believe would protect the human rights of all humans equally. They see a problem with countries always doing only that which they believe is in their national self-interest and not following international law as to how they treat people within their territory. There are indeed a great variety of American views, from the extreme nationalist, to the extreme world federalist, to the nihilist. Human rights are considered by most people to be as American as apple pie, but how and when they are applied as a matter of law in U.S. law, politics, and policies are often a very controversial matter, especially in delicate issues such as reproductive rights, capital punishment, religious liberty, racial discrimination, and illegal aliens. The greatest factor in this situation is ignorance of the accepted international human rights standards in the various treaties and other instruments, and ignorance of the authority and practice of international bodies dealing with human rights issues. The present work is an attempt to shed some light on how that international dimension of human rights has affected U.S. law and policy, by unveiling some of the language and legal instruments in the field of human rights.

By and large, the focus of U.S. law and human rights has been outward, that is, focused on human rights violations in other countries, especially countries that it views unfavorably. Little official policy and practice specifically regarding international human rights norms has been focused internally, such as at prison conditions, police brutality, or the death penalty system. These have largely remained within the discourse of constitutional law and civil rights. Some criticize that, to a degree, U.S. law sees human rights violations as something other countries "out there" do to their people, and so it does not apply the same standards to judging practices in the United States.

Many countries have criticized the United States for its own human rights record on racial minorities and Native Americans and for acting in its military and commercial interests in other countries. It is accused of applying a double standard: one human rights standard to countries it does not like, but no such standard applies to the United States itself, or its allies. It is accused of hypocrisy in its human rights practice for telling other countries what not to do but doing the same things itself. It is also sometimes accused of tolerating or even aiding other countries with bad human rights records with such things as foreign aid or military or police assets.

Another criticism is that the United States most often will only ratify a human rights treaty in the Senate with a proviso that the treaty is not self-executing, meaning that it cannot thereupon be used in a court of law and applied by a judge as the rule of decision for a case. It must be implemented by subsequent legislation, which may take even more years to make the rights part of U.S. law. Moreover, when the U.S. does ratify human rights treaties it does so with so many reservations, declarations and understandings that it in reality means that nothing has changed legally in the U.S. as a result of its ratification. The legal obligations are all but illusory.

U.S. case law has established that no international human-rights can be interpreted or applied here inconsistently with the U.S. Constitution. No international law may violate the Constitution. The United States may violate an international human rights legal norm but not be in violation of U.S. law. It may violate U.S. law and not be in violation of international human rights law. Otherwise stated, the United States could engage in a certain act because it is required by U.S. law, and such an act could violate an international legal obligation. Again, one is dealing with two levels of law, national and international, and human rights are treated in both spheres, which are not mutually exclusive.

This history aside, it is clear that human rights are now firmly a part of the American legal landscape. It is now time for the average American to learn about them. The United

States is now in the stage of internalizing what it has been creating at the international level, especially at the United Nations. This is called "domestic implementation" and consists of legislating international human norms into U.S. law and teaching human rights to all Americans including government institutions, and causing them to make human rights part of their daily reality including in our courts. This was cogently stated by Eleanor Roosevelt fifty years ago:

> *Where, after all, do universal rights begin? In small places, close to home-so close and so small that they cannot be seen on any maps of the world. Yet they are the world of the individual person; the neighborhood he lives in; the school or college he attends; the factory, farm or office where he works. Such are the places where every man, woman and child seeks equal justice, equal opportunity, equal dignity without discrimination. Unless these rights have meaning there, they have little meaning elsewhere. Without concerned citizen action to uphold them close to home, we shall look in vain for progress in the larger world.*
>
> The Great Question, 1958, cited from *Human Rights Here and Now*, Human Rights Educators Network, 1998, Amnesty International USA

At this time when Americans are beset by terrorism and searching for human security, and debating the proper limits of government authority and curtailment of civil liberties, it behooves them to learn the source of these subjects, human rights. Knowledge is power, human rights knowledge is empowerment. Empowerment of every human being is necessary for the development and protection of human dignity in every person in our generation, and in those to come. An America which knows its human rights will be best able to give its people human security.

In its August 2010, national UPR report, the U.S. Administration stated to the international community:

> *The United States understands its role as a cornerstone in an international system of cooperation to preserve global security, support the growth of global prosperity, and progress toward world peace based on respect for the human rights and dignity of every person.*
>
> *The fundamental truth which grounds the principles of government enshrined in our Constitution—that each person is created with equal value from which flows inalienable rights—is not an exclusively American truth; it is a universal one. It is the truth that anchors the Universal Declaration of Human Rights. It is the truth that underpins the legitimate purposes and obligations not just of our government, but of all governments.*
>
> *We are committed to that universal truth, and so we are committed to principled engagement across borders and with foreign governments and their citizens. This commitment includes, in the words of our Declaration of Independence, according 'decent respect to the opinions of mankind,' and seeking always to preserve and protect the dignity of all persons, because the values that we cherish apply everywhere and to everyone.*

These statements were made in full national conscience of the dangers to this nation and the moral and legal standards which should guide its path. The UPR report continues by stating:

Values and National Security

> *The United States is currently at war with Al Qaeda and its associated forces. President Obama has made clear that the United States is fully committed to complying with the Constitution and with all applicable domestic and international law, including the laws of war, in all aspects of this or any armed conflict. We start from the premise that there are no law-free zones, and that everyone is entitled to protection under law. In his Nobel Lecture, the President made clear that '[w]here force is necessary, we have a moral and strategic interest in binding ourselves to certain rules of conduct ... [E]ven as we confront a vicious adversary that abides by no rules ... the United States of America must remain a standard bearer in the conduct of war.'*

THE FUTURE OF HUMAN RIGHTS IN THE UNITED STATES

The United States of America is the greatest nation on earth and one of the most free. But this freedom cannot be presumed or taken for granted. There must be mechanisms to protect this freedom and standards by which to judge our nation's acts. This country has been a prime mover of the advancement of international human rights law and has told the world that we accept most of its standards as our own values in law and policy. We have not always lived up to these standards. We can do better. In our search for human security we must have not only costly hard power assets to protect us. We need the soft power of a system of rule of law in a democratic state which respects, protects, ensures and fulfils all human rights.

The author respectfully recommends three things to help the U.S. become a better nation as to both internal and international human rights policy and practice.

1. Create a national human rights institution (NHRI) to monitor and promote the U.S. government's compliance with its international human rights legal obligations. Many countries have such NHRIs. Such institution needs to be independent from the government and not subject to manipulation or influence by the government or any special interest. It should be bi-partisan and include non-governmental individuals. It must be able to interface and receive input from the people. It must be able to monitor and promote education of the American people on what is going on in relation to human rights. It must be perceived as a neutral and objective body which examines the government's actions in light of the international instruments to which the U.S. is legally bound and which the U.S. Constitution makes the supreme law of the land. Such NHRI needs to be established and operated in conformity with the Paris Principle on NHRIs.

Such a body will enhance the checks and balances of the tri partite U.S. government, which has been shown to sometimes be unable to prevent human rights violations by the U.S. This will increase a sense of transparency and accountability which this country greatly deserves and needs, both for itself, and as an example to the world. It will enhance a sense of human security.

There must be some central place and office in our public institutions where specifically international human rights law becomes a conscious and generally known part of the fabric of American society. Neither the State Department, which looks outward from the U.S., nor the Attorney General, the nation's chief law enforcement officer, is fulfilling nor can they fulfil this task. The U.S. needs a national human rights institution of the people, by the people and for the people. This was one of the main recommendations to the U.S. in the UPR Outcome Report, Document 87.

2. What is equally needed and practically non existent in the U.S. is human rights education. By this I mean education which includes learning about the international human rights laws and institutions, such as the American Commission on Human Rights. Many countries of the world are incorporating human rights education into their formal education systems. Human rights education is not, generally speaking, part of the American school curriculum, but it should be.

I am convinced from many years of teaching human rights in the U.S. and abroad, that the way to improve human rights in a country is not trying to change the minds of political leaders at the top. With few exceptions, they are too bound up by political interests and considerations. The solution is to educate the whole populace about their human rights, thus empowering them in a way that they can then demand and assure by their vote that the government respects those rights both at home and abroad.

Human rights education must be promoted by the Federal government as much as constitutionally possible, even though education is primarily a state and local matter. See Document 40 and Appendix Q on the obligation of the state to teach human rights.

The United States of America needs human rights education. This book is an attempt to contribute to that need and that process.

3. To restore rule of law and the belief that government and individual members of government are never above the law, America must examine the events that have happened since 9/11 and call them what they really are, not what the political debate or partisan spin says they are. They must create accountability. There must be individual criminal responsibility where members of government, military or civilian, have broken the law, including international law. Partisan politics and political debate cannot be used as shield to the breaking of laws meant to protect human beings from abuse of U.S. power anywhere in the U.S. or elsewhere. This will involve, investigation with a view to prosecution of those who, as perpetrators or those in command responsibility roles, civilian or military, are responsible for violating U.S. law and international human rights and humanitarian law binding on the U.S. as it wages the so called war on terrorism. Political considerations must never be an excuse for anybody not being held accountable for wrongdoing whatever their present nor former place in the government, and whatever the impact on politics. Prosecution of those responsible for acts such as torture or prolonged arbitrary detention is absolutely essential to establishing what these acts are in U.S. law, whether they in fact occurred, and whether the alleged perpetrator or responsible supervisor committed them or ordered them committed, or failed to stop them when in a position to do so. When persons who commit such acts get away with them it sews the seeds for the next group of persons who will act likewise, based on such model of impunity. America needs to counter the culture of impunity of those in high offices, both Democratic and Republican. It is not a partisan matter: it is a justice matter. Moreover, the higher the level of office of a perpetrator, the greater the need to assure accountability.

Justice is truth in action. Until truth comes out justice has not been done, regarding what has happened since 9/11. Such investigation and, where warranted, prosecution of those who violated U.S. and international norms, will show Americans that they are indeed a nation of laws. This could do more to reduce human insecurity than all the gimmicks and gadgets to catch the bad guys. When human rights violations are swept under the rug in the name of moving forward they fester and rot and come back to haunt the society later. They must be dealt with. No justice: No peace. If you want peace, work for justice.

At the time of this printing the Arab world is exploding, country after country. Freedom is the cry and the U.S. is seeking to define its response. Challenges such as these lie ahead. Our own national security is at stake. Human Rights must be part of that response. Americans want peace and Americans want security. They need human security in relation to their own government as well as in relation to those on the outside who seek to do them wrong. Compliance with law at home is necessary to create a country, which is whole and united in itself and can face any threats to it because its government is just and rule of law is secure. America must practice what it preaches. America needs accountability and transparency in government and must not be afraid to tackle the difficult challenge of examining what it has done to itself and what it has done to others. This will make the best country on earth a better country, and a better model of freedom and justice for the rest of the world. God bless America.

ABBREVIATIONS

ACHR	American Convention on Human Rights
ADHR	American Declaration of the Rights and Duties of Man
ATCA	Alien Tort Claims Act
CAT	Convention against Torture, Cruel, Inhuman, or Degrading Treatment or Punishment
CEDAW	Convention on the Elimination of All Forms of Discrimination Against Women
CERD	Convention on the Elimination of All Forms of Racial Discrimination
ECOSOC	United Nations Economic and Social Council
EIF	Entry into Force
EA	Executive Agreement
EO	Executive Order
FSIA	Foreign Sovereign Immunities Act
GA (UNGA)	General Assembly (of the United Nations)
GAOR	General Assembly Official Records
GC	Geneva Conventions of 1949
HFA	Helsinki Final Act
HRCee	Human Rights Committee (U.N.)
HRC	Human Rights Council (U.N.)
I-AComHR	Inter-American Commission on Human Rights
I-ACourtHR	Inter-American Court of Human Rights
ICC	International Criminal Court
ICCPR	International Covenant on Civil and Political Rights
ICESCR	International Covenant on Economic, Social and Cultural Rights
ICRC	International Committee of the Red Cross
ICJ	International Court of Justice
ICTR	International Criminal Tribunal for Rwanda
ICTY	International Criminal Tribunal for the Former Yugoslavia
IDP	Internally Displaced Person
IFI	International Financial Institution
IGO	Inter-Governmental Organization
ILO	International Labour Organization
IRFA	International Religious Freedom Act of 1998
NGO	Non-Governmental Organization
OAS	Organization of American States
OHCHR	Office of the High Commissioner for Human Rights
OP	Optional Protocol
OP 1	First Optional Protocol
OP 2	Second Optional Protocol
OSCE	Organization for Security and Cooperation in Europe
POC	Prisoner of Conscience

ABBREVIATIONS

POW	Prisoner of War
R2P	Responsibility to Protect
RDUs/RUDs	Reservations, Declarations, and Understandings
SuR	State Under Review
TVPA	Torture Victim Protection Act
UDHR	Universal Declaration of Human Rights
U.N.	United Nations
UNCH	United Nations Charter
UNESCO	United Nations Educational, Scientific, and Cultural Organization
UNHCHR	United Nations High Commissioner for Human Rights
UNHCR	United Nations High Commissioner for Refugees
UPR	Universal Periodic Review

HUMAN RIGHTS TERMS
A–Z

A

1. ACCESSIBILITY (PRINCIPLE)
See entry for **Legality**

2. ACCESSION (TO TREATY)
See entry for **Ratification**

3. ACCOUNTABILITY/ACCOUNTABLE
Definition: The obligation or willingness to accept legal, political or moral responsibility to society for one's actions. It means having one's actions subject to public examination and possibly suffering legal or political consequences for wrongdoing. For persons in government it means having to be answerable to the people for how they fulfill their public duties.

Significance: Human rights violations are violations of the inherent human dignity of members of a society. Such violations are committed by those who represent or act on behalf of government and are violations of the law. No one in government has the right to commit human rights violations. Therefore, if someone in government commits such violations they must be held accountable, that is, personally responsible to society for abusing their power and position. This applies to all branches of government. It means, for example, that legislators, policemen, judges, soldiers, generals, prison guards, defense ministers, interior ministers and even presidents, kings and prime ministers all have some type of accountability for human rights violations. This accountability is to the society that they serve, such as a city, county, state or country. It can even involve accountability to all of humanity, such as for war crimes or genocide, as was seen in the Nuremberg trials after World War II.

Accountability is an essential, basic principle in human rights law. It is meant to preserve the rule of law, which means that no one is above the law or exempt from it as it pertains to respect for human rights. In theory, persons in government will not commit violations if they know that they will have to answer for such acts. Civilians are also accountable to society for their actions, usually under criminal laws.

Accountability also occurs at the international inter-governmental level within human rights treaty systems and international organs such as the U.N. Human Rights Council (UNHRC). States parties to a treaty seek to hold other states parties accountable for how they comply with the treaty. In organs such as the UNHRC the Council seeks to implement institutional processes such as special mechanisms/procedures which seek to hold states accountable for their human rights practices. One important procedure in the HRC is the Universal Periodic Review procedure (UPR). In this procedure all member states of the United Nations will have their human rights records examined by the HRC, with input from non-Council member states and civil society. This is an accountability mechanism based on the idea that states will change what they are doing wrong if they know it will be exposed to international public examination.

The United States went through the initial UPR procedure in November 2010. This process was completed in March 2011, with 228 recommendations made to the U.S. See Document 87. The U.S. is in a sense being accountable before the world even though it seriously questions the integrity, objectivity and effectiveness of this process in light of the bad human rights record of some of the HRC members. There is no enforcement mechanism in this process, only political and public opinion pressure.

Accountability needs some ultimate effective recourse, preferably judicial, to succeed. In the international community this works on the basis of the principle of *Pacta Sunt Servanda*, good faith observance of treaties, and comity, a sort of good conduct among nations. And then there are commissions, committees, working groups, general assemblies and ultimately courts, such as the International Court of Justice or the International Criminal Court.

The *Chuckie Taylor, Kadic, In Re Cincinnati,* and *Rasul* decisions in Appendix J are examples of U.S. judicial proceedings to establish the accountability of alleged human rights violators or to hold the U.S. government accountable for its policies and procedures which may violate human rights norms.

With respect to legal responsibility for human rights violations, the opposite of accountability is *impunity*.

See Also Terms: 8, 13, 17, 19, 23, 25, 30, 42, 60, 45, 63, 47, 48, 70, 71, 93, 95, 81, 103, 109, 118, 145, 147, 150, 151, 132, 157, 159, 182, 184, 202, 224, 227, 206, 215, 234, 238, 266, 248, 272, 273, 271, 303, 305, 310, 317, 318.

4. ACTIVIST
(See entry for **Human Rights Defender**)

5. ADMISSIBILITY (OF COMPLAINTS, PETITIONS, COMMUNICATIONS)
Definition: The legal criteria which must be met before a written complaint (sometimes called a communication or petition or application) alleging human rights violations by a state is accepted for consideration or adjudication by a human rights forum, such as a court or commission or committee. Admissibility includes initial prerequisites that an individual, group or state must fulfill before it is permitted to present its written complaint to a particular treaty-monitoring body, other human rights fact-finding or judging organization or court.

Significance: In the international legal system there are certain institutional organs which can receive written complaints against a state claiming that a state has violated human rights. These organs can receive written complaints against a state only if certain prerequisites are fulfilled and the necessary information is contained in the complaint. These are called the admissibility criteria or grounds of admissibility. Each human rights system has its own admissibility criteria but they are all substantially similar.

There are two kinds of complaint systems: 1. individual complaint systems where an individual or a group files a complaint against a state, alleging violation of the rights of the petitioner; and 2. an inter-states complaint system where one state party files a complaint alleging that another state party has violated human rights in a certain treaty.

Usually these complaints are filed in treaty based bodies such as the U.N. Human Rights Committee (HRCee). That organ was created in the ICCPR, Article 28. Under it individual victims and states can file written complaints against states which have ratified the ICCPR. States can file inter-state complaints (called "communications") under Article 41 if they fulfill the admissibility criteria of Article 41. The criteria would include having submitted a declaration recognizing the power of the Committee to receive such complaints and, for example documenting the exhaustion of domestic remedies (41.1(c)). The United States has submitted a declaration accepting the power ("competence") of the HRC allowing other states parties to the ICCPR to file communications against it if they believe the U.S. has violated its obligations under the ICCPR. No state has ever filed a communication against any other state in this system. If any state did so against the U.S. it would first have to meet admissibility criteria in Article 41.

Individual victims can file communications under the Optional Protocol against states which have ratified the first Optional Protocol (OP) to the ICCPR (See Doc. 10) if they fulfill the admissibility criteria in articles 2, 3 and 5 of the OP. The United States has not ratified the First Optional Protocol and therefore individual victims of violations by the U.S. cannot be filed in the Human Rights Committee against the U.S. This would change only if the U.S. ratified the OP.

The first thing a human rights body does when it receives a complaint is to determine whether the complaint as it is written meets all the admissibility criteria. If it does, then it is deemed "admissible" and the body is then considered to be "seised" of the case. The body can then proceed to determine the merits of the case, that is whether a violation has occurred. In some human rights complaint systems the body can make a determination of admissibility at any time in the case and sometimes determines admissibility and the merits at the same time. Each system is different and the Statute and rules of procedure must be read before filing a case so that one can know if a complaint is admissible or not.

Admissibility concerns getting a complaint in the door of the human rights body to be heard as to whether a human rights violation happened and whether the state was the one which committed it. If not, it is deemed "inadmissible" or "non-admissible." A human rights body, such as the HRCee, only has the legal authority to decide certain cases. They cannot accept any other cases. Their terms of reference, that is their operating rules, specify what they can do as a supervising body or judicial organ.

Complaints can also be filed again the U.S. in the Inter-American Commission of Human Rights. (See Appendix J) These complaints use the ADHR as its basis of human rights norms. There have been cases filed against the U.S. in this system, including some regarding the Guantanamo detainees. Who can file, and the grounds of admissibility, are spelled out in the rules of that OAS based body.

One admissibility criteria common to all human rights complaint systems at the international level is that a complainant must first exhaust all reasonable and available national level legal recourse to try to solve the issue. This is because of the principle of subsidiarity which says that the international system is a backup to the national legal systems, which should be the first line of protection of human rights. So if someone wanted to file a complaint against the U.S. in an international human rights forum they would have to have gone through every legal procedure available in the U.S. before filing in an international body, such as the Inter-American Commission. There are, however, some very important exceptions to this rule. One exception is where the victim has been prevented from access to domestic remedies by force or threat.

See Also Terms: 11, 26, 46, 48, 93, 145, 146, 151, 162, 165, 184, 185, 187, 222, 246, 252, 262, 269, 306.

6. ADVICE AND CONSENT OF THE U.S. SENATE

Definition: The approval of a treaty (whether it's called a covenant, convention, charter, etc.), accepted by a two-thirds majority vote of the U.S. Senate. This act constitutes the ratification of the treaty, already signed by the chief executive (President), as head of state on behalf of the United States. The U.S. Constitution, Article II, section 2, establishes the power of the president to enter into treaties but requires that the representative of the people, the Senate, gives its official approval, its "advice and consent," to confirm that such an act is the will of the people. Through this process, the treaty becomes binding as U.S. law and also makes the treaty binding on the United States under international law.

Significance: Human rights norms are found in treaties, which are international contracts entered into between two or more states and governed by international law. In U.S. law, the Constitution gives the president the right to enter into a treaty and legally obligate the United States to act or refrain from acting in a certain way. This includes entering into treaties establishing human rights law, humanitarian law and international criminal law.

The Constitution makes it a requirement for the president to send any treaty he or she signs to the Senate with recommendations for advice and consent, and any suggested reservations, declarations and understandings. The Senate must then deliberate on whether to give its advice and consent. For the treaty to be ratified and create legal obligations on the United States, approval must be voted for by a two-thirds majority of the Senators present. This process is called the ratification of the treaty.

The Senate has often taken a long time to ratify human rights treaties. The process takes a long time because it requires deliberation in committee meetings and a vote of approval by the Senate, but more so because many senators do not like the idea of creating any international legal obligations and having an international body, such as the United Nations, monitoring its compliance with the treaty. For example, the ICCPR was signed in 1977, but the Senate took until 1992 to vote its advice and consent and thus ratify it and bind the United States. The United States signed the Genocide Convention in 1948 but took until 1988 to ratify it. Most of the time when the Senate votes to ratify a treaty, it adds a provision that the ratified treaty is considered "non-self-executing," meaning that the treaty norms do not become U.S. law until they are implemented by congressional legislation.

Human rights norms are also created by customary international law. These norms arise (or "ripen") when most states of the world practice them consistently over time and do so because they believe it is legally required. In such cases no Senate ratification is required. International law, which is based on the concept of the consent of sovereign states, implies a consent to be bound. Such customary law norms become part of federal common law.

See Also Terms: 2, 31, 52, 53, 54, 55, 56, 57, 62, 98, 145, 158, 211, 220, 222, 226, 243, 258, 259, 262, 269, 279, 280, 287, 293, 306.

7. AFFIRMATIVE ACTION

Definition: Action taken by a government as a matter of law or policy to correct or make up for past discrimination, whether it was intentional or not. Such past discrimination is usually against women or members of certain racial, religious or ethnic groups, or persons with disabilities. Affirmative action normally means the granting of certain preferential treatment or giving special consideration to the person possessing such characteristics. The aim or goal is to undo the effects of past discrimination and make things the way they would have been had there been no such discrimination.

Significance: Within the history of any nation, including the United States, there are often groups of people sharing common characteristics who have been the victims of discrimination. Examples of such group characteristics are age, gender, race, ethnicity, religion and disability.

Discrimination is commonly considered to occur when certain human beings are treated differently than others, with a negative impact. In some human rights instruments discrimination is defined as any acts of distinction, exclusion, restriction or preference based on a specific characteristic (e.g., Convention on the Elimination of All Forms of Racial Discrimination (CERD), Article 1, and the Convention on the Elimination of All Forms of Discrimination Against Women (CEDAW), Article 1). See Documents 23, 27. In the field of human rights most forms of discrimination are violations of human rights law, namely the rule of nondiscrimination (ICCPR, Article 2.1). It is argued that as a result of many historical acts of discrimination there have been unequal opportunities for certain jobs or job promotion, academic programs, and athletic and cultural activities. This discrimination results in little or no participation of victim groups in these areas of society. Such discrimination causes the victims to feel they are not full and equal members of society.

Affirmative action programs and policies aim to remedy the negative effects of past discrimination by granting certain preferences or giving special consideration to members of victim groups. In theory, affirmative action makes things the way they would have been if there had not been any discrimination in the past. Affirmative action measures can be enacted through policies, principles, laws and administrative rules and regulations. These can affect the operation and management practices of government or business.

In recent years, affirmative action has been a controversial issue, with some suggesting that special help given to a previously victimized group is done at the expense of another group of people. It is argued that affirmative action discriminates against all those who, through no fault of their own, are not members of the assisted group, an effect called "reverse discrimination." Some states have passed laws banning the use of affirmative action measures.

Under Article 1.4 of CERD and Article 4.1 of CEDAW, measures taken to correct past discrimination are not considered to be acts of discrimination if done only to correct past inequalities and only so long as necessary to correct the problem.

See Also Terms: 86, 100, 126, 145, 194, 205, 216, 237, 244, 260, 270, 277, 283.

8. AGGRESSION

See entry for **Crimes Against Peace**

9. AID CONDITIONALITY

Definition: The process of making U.S. foreign aid of any kind (military, financial, security, technological, etc.) conditioned upon the receiving states' human rights performance. It is a linking of such aid in return for certain conduct or certain results in specific or general areas of human rights.

Significance: This conditionality linkage is meant as an enticement to the receiving state to improve its human rights conditions or else be deprived of such U.S. assistance. For example, Congress or the executive branch could *condition* a group of economic foreign aid funds to a state upon that state granting religious freedom to a religious minority or improving the rights of women by improving their access to health care. If the recipient state refused to change such situations, it would not be granted the aid. If it did not, in fact, put such changes in effect or if it stopped doing so after receiving the money, then such funding could be terminated or a subsequent grant refused. Sometimes this process is also referred to as "linkage."

In the field of international human rights, aid conditionality is the kind of leverage that states exercise to encourage other states to be accountable for their human rights promises. It is hoped that when a state ratifies an agreement it is doing so with the intention of quickly and fully implementing it; sometimes, however, this is not the case. Therefore, the international community may need, through various means, to encourage another state to such action. In this way, all states make a commitment to the improvement of human rights worldwide.

In some of the U.S. legislation, one sees an example of linkage between foreign aid and human rights violations. An example is the linkage between religious persecution and foreign aid, such as in the International Religious Freedom Act of 1998. See Document 89.

See Also Terms: 48, 61, 83, 190, 194, 199, 243, 272, 316.

10. ALIEN TORT CLAIMS ACT (ATCA)

(Also known as the Alien Tort Statute, ATS, or ATCA, or a "1350" action/case)

Definition: A U.S. federal statute enacted in 1789 and found in section 1350 of Title 28 of the *United States Code*. It gives power (subject matter jurisdiction) to federal district courts to hear judicial cases filed by a foreigner (plaintiff) against another foreigner (defendant) for acts committed by the defendant, which constitute "torts in violation of international law," such as torture, disappearances, slavery and summary executions. The text itself reads: "The District Courts shall have original jurisdiction of any civil action by an alien for a tort only, committed in violation of the law of nations or a treaty of the United States."

Significance: Violations of internationally recognized human rights are meant to be remedied in national courts and other bodies before resorting to international systems. International human rights are properly the concern of all states. Many states, including the United States, allow their courts to be used for lawsuits filed for human rights violations that occur in other states and where neither the victim nor the violator are U.S. citizens. The intent of the U.S. Congress in 1789 was to provide our courts as a judicial forum for those injured by certain violations of international law, thus helping to enforce international law.

Many lawsuits have been filed in U.S. federal courts using this act as the basis for court jurisdiction. The decisions in *Kadic v. Karadzic* and *Sosa vs. Alvarez Machain* are examples of these cases. See Appendix J. They are sometimes referred to as 1350 cases or abbreviated ATCA, or ATS which stands for Alien Tort Statute.

See Also Terms: 3, 71, 73, 88, 93, 110, 118, 128, 124, 136, 144, 145, 151, 159, 194, 222, 234, 254, 267, 302, 303.

11. AMERICAN CONVENTION ON HUMAN RIGHTS (ACHR)

Definition: An international general human rights treaty instrument adopted in 1978 by members of the Organization of American States to provide a regional (western hemisphere) system for the protection of human rights.

Significance: See Document Overview and Information Sheet, American Convention on Human Rights, Document 63.

See Also Terms: 12, 33, 52, 70, 84, 92, 99, 110, 113, 114, 116, 123, 124, 136, 144, 145, 151, 160, 165, 167, 169, 170, 184, 185, 196.

12. AMERICAN DECLARATION ON THE RIGHTS AND DUTIES OF MAN (ADHR)

(Also known as the American Declaration of Human Rights [ADHR])

Definition: A human rights document adopted in 1948 by the Organization of American States, an international political organization of North, Central, and South American countries, setting forth the human rights accepted by its member states, including the United States, in a non legally binding instrument.

Significance: See Document Overview and Information Sheet, American Declaration on the Rights and Duties of Man, Document 62. (The *Cherokee Nation and Haitian Centre and Ameziane* cases are examples of two cases filed against the United States in the Inter-American Commission on Human Rights and based on the human rights in the ADHR).

See Also Terms: 11, 20, 21, 33, 70, 74, 100, 110, 113, 116, 122, 123, 124, 144, 145, 160, 167, 169, 170, 184, 185, 189, 195, 196, 216, 222, 226, 231, 242, 245, 252, 259, 264, 272, 282, 283, 291, 297, 302, 309, 312, 322.

13. AMNESTY

Definition: Amnesty, in the human rights context, is an official, blanket legal pardon given by the state, usually to everyone on both sides of a conflict who has broken the law or committed human rights violations during such turmoil. It refers to an act of a government authority to officially forget and waive the legal consequences of crimes and other harmful acts that occurred during a period of violent turmoil or transition. Also used in the U.S. immigration context to refer to a program to normalize the legal status of illegal aliens by disregarding their illegal entry or overstay or violation of their right to stay in the U.S.

Significance: The word amnesty means a *forgetting*. The result of a grant of amnesty is that those who receive this amnesty are thereafter free from any legal responsibility, receiving impunity from the legal consequences of their wrongful acts. Examples of turmoil are revolutions, rebellions or periods of anarchy or oppression, where human rights violations happened, usually on a widespread basis. Amnesty can be granted to specific individuals or to everyone who may have violated human rights in a given conflict.

Amnesty is usually carried out by executive grant or decree by a country's leader, or by parliamentary or congressional legislation. When a society goes through a period of violent turmoil, such as a revolution that overthrows the government, there are often many criminal acts committed by all sides of the conflict. Some of these acts constitute violations of human rights law, such as those found in Articles 6 to 12 of the ICCPR. Examples of such turmoil include Haiti in the early 1990s and the civil war in El Salvador. The United States was politically involved in the resolution of these conflicts, which included grants of amnesty.

Amnesty is usually called for at the end of such turmoil to help the society forget the past and move forward to heal the wounds and repair the damage. Historically, however, where blanket amnesties are given and no one is brought to justice for human rights violations, the turmoil will often arise again. Unless justice is done, or at least the truth of what occurred is revealed, those who were victims will carry around the feeling that their human dignity has been violated and nothing has been done about it. They will seek their own vengeance, leading to more violence. Therefore, an alternative is needed to allow the people to feel that such abuses have been revealed and acknowledged, even if no one is punished. Various methods, such as truth commissions, can be established to get to the truth of what happened. The post apartheid South African Truth Commission is an example of such a process.

In the United States, amnesty also refers to an immigration law and program enacted in 1986. The "Amnesty Law," or the Immigration Control and Reform Act, forgave the illegal entry or overstay of all illegal aliens who had lived in the United States since 1981 or were agricultural workers who had worked for a certain period. The amnesty program allowed such aliens to become legal residents of the United States. Other amnesties have occurred in U.S. history, for example, the amnesty of draft dodgers in the Vietnam War.

See Also Terms: 3, 151, 155, 156, 272, 283.

14. ANTI-SEMITISM

Definition: A hostile, intolerant, or discriminatory attitude against Jews as a racial or religious group. Also used to characterize the acts or statements manifesting such an attitude, usually in a hateful and injurious manner. Actually, the true and full meaning of the word refers to such an attitude against *anyone* of Semitic origin, which includes Arabs as well as Jews, since both groups are Semites. In the United States, however, most people associate this attitude specifically with Jewish people.

Significance: Anti-Semitic attitudes by themselves may not be human rights violations, because they are part of personal beliefs. However, certain actions manifesting anti-Semitic attitudes can be characterized as hate crimes, and if committed by a government or its agents, can be violations of human rights. Such anti-Semitic actions might include defacing synagogues, desecrating cemeteries or physically beating a Semitic person.

The following articles of the ICCPR would come into play in such cases: Article 2.1, non-discrimination on the basis of race, religion, national origin; Article 6, the right to life; Article 7, prohibition of torture, cruel, inhuman, or degrading punishment; Article 9, liberty and security of person; Article 14, equality before courts and tribunals; Article 17, prohibition of unlawful interference with privacy, family, honor and reputation; Article 18, freedom of religion; Article 19, freedom of expression; Article 20.2, prohibition of advocacy of racial or religious hatred that constitutes incitement to discrimination, hostility or violence; Article 24, prohibition of discrimination against children based on race or religion; Article 25, voting and participating in public affairs; Article 26, equal protection of the law; Article 27, the rights of ethnic and religious minorities to enjoy their culture and profess and practice their own religion. See Document 8.

Many anti-Semitic acts would also be prohibited under CERD, Articles 2–4, as a violation of human rights in the context of racial discrimination. See Document 23. Anti-Semitism is a violation of human rights because it treats certain people differently from other people solely on the basis of their race, religion or ethnic group. As history has shown, in its ultimate manifestation, anti-Semitism could lead to genocide and the destruction of those who are Semitic, such as was attempted during the Holocaust.

The international community and human rights organizations have expressed their belief that the key to eliminating anti-Semitism is to teach human rights to everyone. This education will result in increasing tolerance of "the other," regardless of race, religion, ethnic origin or any other such characteristic.

In 2004, the U.S. Congress passed the Global Anti Semitism Review Act. See Document 101. This obligated the State Department to monitor and report on acts of anti-Semitism. It resulted in a specific office being established in the State Department to do this work. Since that time there has been a step up in anti-Semitism awareness and activity by the U.S. government. The U.S. government now has a Special Envoy to Monitor and Combat Anti-Semitism.

See Also Terms: 22, 28, 33, 35, 55, 77, 78, 86, 87, 100, 130, 139, 140, 143, 144, 145, 151, 179, 188, 190, 216, 228, 235, 237, 255, 260, 261, 324.

15. APARTHEID

Definition: A legally enforced social and political system of nearly complete racial separation between a dominant race and dominated race or races.

Significance: This term was used to describe the system in South Africa prior to 1993, wherein the whites created a forced separation between whites and blacks and other nonwhites. This systematic, enforced racial segregation was condemned by nearly every country and in the 1970s was considered by the international community to be an international crime, as an offense against all persons. Though South Africa no longer has apartheid, the term has come to be used in human rights circles for the systematic forced segregation of races, ethnic groups or even religious groups. The idea is that the dominant group wishes to exist separately from the dominated group while still controlling the latter group.

Apartheid is characterized by treating certain races as unequal and as lesser than the dominant group. It is forced racial discrimination, typically resulting in persons of the dominated race being forced to live in separate parts of the state or city. It usually results in the dominated race receiving very few government benefits, having to use separate public facilities, and not mixing with the dominant race. It may include a lack of political power, even a lack of the right to vote or hold office. It usually allows for very limited exercise of civil and political rights. The U.S. now condemns apartheid. In its own history, however, it sanctioned the same kind of discrimination at one time. This situation was rectified through the abolition of slavery and subsequently through the Civil Rights Acts. One does still hear claims that the U.S. policy of putting Native Americans on reservations is a form of apartheid.

See Also Terms: 22, 33, 34, 40, 45, 55, 63, 86, 100, 102, 122, 124, 144, 145, 151, 152, 167, 169, 181, 182, 184, 188, 195, 205, 216, 228, 235, 237, 260, 261, 277, 283, 316.

16. ARBITRARY ARREST/DETENTION

Definition: Arbitrary arrest occurs when a person is taken into custody by the government authorities (federal, state or local) without a proper, well-founded, lawful basis for doing so. Arbitrary detention means keeping a person in detention or custody without taking steps to prosecute or release. Thus, the victim of arbitrary detention appears to be in the position of being held indefinitely, without charges and criminal prosecution.

Significance: In general, arbitrary arrest or detention denies the person his or her rights to "liberty and security of person" and "due process of law." Government may only deprive a person of physical liberty if it is done pursuant to law. In the U.S. context, this usually requires probable cause under the Fourth Amendment and due process of law under the Fifth Amendment to the U.S. Constitution. Because there is no legal justification for a detention that is characterized as arbitrary, it is a violation of one's constitutional rights. Under international human rights law, it is also a violation of international human rights norms because, therein, everyone has a right to liberty and security of person. That means everyone has a right to move around freely, believing that government will not interfere with his or her freedom without having a legal ground to do so, such as evidence that the person committed a crime. Arbitrary detentions are often made simply to harass people that authorities do not like; sometimes they are made merely because authorities suspect that the people are engaged in unlawful activity, though they do not have sufficient evidence to prosecute them.

Under Article 9 of the ICCPR, "Everyone has the right to liberty and security of person. No one shall be subjected to arbitrary arrest or detention." This article sets forth the procedural human rights of arrested and detained persons. Thus, because of the U.S. ratification of the ICCPR, arbitrary arrests and detentions committed in the United States are a violation of international human rights norms.

Arbitrary arrests and detentions are not done solely where the victim is suspected of having committed a crime. It may possibly apply, for example, in the case of a mentally ill street person being institutionalized against his will for too long, or in a so-called administrative detention, wherein police round up and detain people, more for fear of possible future criminal activity without any legitimate factual basis, rather than for having committed a crime. Any type of depriving a person of physical liberty can bring into play this human rights norm.

Arbitrary detentions have occurred in U.S. history. One example is the Japanese internment after Pearl Harbor. Even though at that time those internments were done pursuant to law, it was later determined that such legal basis was not valid. Another example is the detention of Cuban Marielitos, who were criminals sent out of Cuba by the Cuban government to come into the United States. Because they could not be sent back to Cuba, they were housed in prisons around the United States with no criminal charges filed against them and no criminal prosecutions having been commenced. Where such detentions last an unjustifiably long time, as determined by a court, they are referred to as "prolonged arbitrary detentions."

Post 9/11 this issue surfaced repeatedly in the war on terrorism measures taken by the U.S. government, specifically the detention of many terrorism suspects, primarily those detained in Guantanamo. Almost all were detained without any charges and some were held just because it was believed that they possessed information which would help U.S. counter terrorism measures.

Even though done in pursuance of this goal the detentions were arbitrary so long as the U.S. detained them without charge and without access to lawyers and court. The proof of the arbitrariness of the detention was that even until the new President ordered the closure of Guantanamo hardly any of the over 600 detainees had been charged with any criminal wrongdoing and only a few were convicted of any crime. Because of the amount of time spent in such detention this qualified as a prolonged arbitrary detention as to most detainees. This violated the ICCPR, Article 9, which was at all times applicable to Guantanamo, though the U.S. government denies its extraterritorial application.

See Also Terms: 11, 12, 17, 20, 24, 48, 59, 81, 82, 85, 90, 93, 120, 122, 124, 134, 136, 144, 145, 151, 152, 167, 169, 177, 179, 184, 193, 195, 196, 239, 248, 252, 254, 255, 272, 275, 283, 309, 316.

17. ARREST

Definition: Any physical denial of freedom of movement by the government for purposes of detaining a person suspected of having committed a crime. An arrest begins the process of a person being brought physically before law enforcement authorities and courts so as to read and face charges of criminal conduct and, if found guilty, to be punished for such crimes.

Significance: Under international human rights law, freedom is the rule and any limitation on liberty and freedom of movement is the exception and must be legally justified by the state. The first duty of the state is respect for and protection of the human rights of all persons within its jurisdiction. Under the U.S. Constitution, freedom from physical restraint is a substantive due process right guaranteed by the Fifth and Fourteenth Amendments. The state may not arrest or otherwise exercise physical restraint on anyone unless it has a valid legal basis for doing so.

Article 3 of the UDHR states that "Everyone has the right to life, liberty and security of person." Security of person corresponds to freedom from unreasonable search and seizure under the Fourth Amendment to the U.S. Constitution. Article 9 states that "No one shall be subjected to arbitrary arrest, detention or exile." Under Article 11 everyone charged with a criminal offense is presumed innocent. See document 6.

Article 9 of the ICCPR, binding on the United States, states that "everyone has the right to liberty and security of person. No one shall be subject to arbitrary arrest or detention." That article goes on to state the particular human rights held by someone arrested. Article 10 sets forth the right of all persons deprived of their liberty to be "treated with humanity and with respect for the inherent dignity of the human person." Article 14 sets forth human rights required for a fair and just criminal process, known as procedural due process, or criminal defendant's rights, in the U.S. Constitution. See Document 8.

The criminal arrest and prosecution-related provisions of both the UDHR and ICCPR were modeled on the U.S. Constitution's Bill of Rights.

See Also Terms: 3, 11, 12, 16, 24, 33, 34, 49, 59, 81, 82, 90, 93, 117, 122, 124, 134, 145, 153, 155, 156, 161, 167, 175, 177, 179, 184, 193, 195, 196, 234, 238, 248, 252, 283, 309, 316.

18. ASYLUM

Definition: Asylum is legal protection from human rights violations constituting persecution, committed by the government of a person's own country. It is provided by another country to a person who is not its citizen but who flees to that country to escape the persecution. The asylum seeker requests such protection because of past persecution or a well-founded fear of future persecution based on the person's race, nationality, religion, political opinion or membership in a particular social group.

Significance: Under Article 14 of the UDHR, everyone has the right to seek and enjoy asylum. This does not mean that everyone has the right to be granted asylum but only the right to apply for it. See Document 6.

Everyone has the right to be free from persecution in their own country or in the country where they permanently reside. If individuals have their human rights violated by their own country, they have the right to flee to another country and there ask that government to protect them from their own country. Other states have the right to protect the rights of a person when that person's own state will not. Asylum will only be granted to someone who qualifies as a "refugee." The definition of a "refugee" under international law is set forth in Article 1 of the 1951 Refugee Convention. See Document 36.

The United States has not ratified the Refugee Convention but has ratified the 1967 Protocol to that treaty that incorporates and expands the convention definition. In the United States, asylum is granted under the Refugee Act of 1980, federal legislation that implements that 1967 Protocol. See Document 37. A refugee under U.S. law (see 8 U.S.C.A., sec. 1101(a) (42)) is a person who is outside of his own country, or of the last country in which he resided, and is unable or unwilling to avail himself of the protection of that country because of past persecution (which is a violation of human rights), or a well-founded fear of future persecution on account of race, nationality, religion, membership in a particular social group, or political opinion.

Those who flee a country because of generalized violence or to find a better economic situation are not considered eligible for asylum, because they do not qualify officially as "refugees." A person can also become a refugee while in another country when the situation changes in her own country and those changes cause her to be afraid to return to that country for fear of human rights violations against her.

A grant of asylum is discretionary with the host state. There is no automatic right to be granted asylum, only the right to apply for asylum. A state can choose, in its discretion, not to grant asylum. However, if a state denies asylum it nonetheless may not, under the principal of *non-refoulement*, expel or return an alien in any manner to a border ("frontier") of a territory where her life or freedom would be threatened on account of her race, religion, nationality, membership in a particular social group, or political opinion.

Americans often speak about asylum using the term "political asylum." They use this term almost interchangeably with asylum. Actually, asylum can be of five different types, depending on the basis for receiving asylum. These are race, religion, political opinion, nationality, or membership in a particular social group. So it is incorrect to speak merely of "political asylum" or to use that term to refer to all forms of asylum. Of course, political asylum is the most commonly found basis for a person seeking asylum, because most often persons flee their country after being involved in political activity that their government sought to stop by violating the person's human rights.

Prominent examples of persons seeking asylum in the United States include the Vietnamese of the late 1970s–1980s, Haitian refugees of the early 1990s, the Chinese who fled China for fear of forced abortion or sterilization in the mid-1990s, the Eastern European dissidents who fled here during the Cold War, and Iraqi Christians, who came to this country in the aftermath of the Iraqi invasion in 2004.

Many immigrants have come to the United States fleeing persecution in other countries. As a matter of fact, the United States was founded by peoples fleeing countries in Europe where religious and ethnic rights were being violated. This is made clear in the Declaration of Independence. See Document 1.

See *Haitian Centre for Human Rights v. United States* for an interesting case filed against the United States regarding the United States stopping Haitian refugees on the high seas in the early 1990s.

See Also Terms: 11, 12, 13, 20, 33, 37, 51, 70, 73, 79, 109, 122, 124, 125, 144, 145, 146, 151, 152, 155, 156, 167, 169, 177, 179, 184, 185, 195, 219, 235, 238, 239, 240, 249, 253, 254, 259, 263, 265, 272, 283, 287, 293, 294, 302, 309, 316.

19. ATROCITY

Definition: An act or a series of acts usually committed by human beings against other human beings that is particularly and completely brutal, wicked, barbaric and revolting in a civilized world. Sometimes these acts are committed by governments against their own people; sometimes they are committed by private, nongovernmental groups and persons.

Significance: An atrocity is a situation where many different human rights are violated such as: the right to life, freedom from torture, cruel, degrading and inhuman treatment and even genocide. Because atrocities so greatly harm human beings and so greatly shock the human conscience, they are to be condemned as violations of human rights. They may constitute international crimes if they were committed during an armed conflict, or crimes against humanity if committed at other times against the civilian population. Examples in an American context would include the My Lai massacre and the Oklahoma Federal Building bombing.

Such acts are usually characterized by excessive and indiscriminate physical violence, such as a mass murder, and are often acts of hate targeting members of an ethnic group, such as the Holocaust genocide. Atrocities are often referred to in the more extreme instances as "man's inhumanity to man," and in spite of great technological advances in the world today they still continue to occur. International atrocities of recent times include the Rwanda genocide of 1994, the Srebrenica (Bosnia) Massacre of 1995, and Kosovo in the late 1990s. These instances all violated international human rights norms and involved the United States in either peacekeeping, peace brokering, or international humanitarian relief assistance, as well as in dealing with them in the U.N. Security Council.

When those guilty of committing atrocities go unpunished, a "culture of impunity" is created and sows the seeds for future atrocities by way of revenge. The response to atrocities must include restoring the rule of law through justice according to human rights law, and it must include adequate investigation, prosecution, and reparations for and rehabilitation of surviving victims or their families.

See Also Terms: 11, 12, 20, 26, 33, 34, 35, 48, 53, 56, 63, 64, 70, 71, 72, 85, 101, 110, 111, 117, 124, 130, 132, 143, 144, 145, 151, 152, 153, 177, 181, 182, 200, 201, 228, 235, 238, 271, 272, 281, 289, 298, 300, 302, 394, 309, 317, 318, 319, 320.

20. BASIC HUMAN RIGHTS

Definition: This term refers to those human rights that are generally considered necessary or essential to the well-being and human dignity of the individual person. In concept, when basic human rights are guaranteed, those rights help to assure the primary material and nonmaterial needs of human beings so that people can lead a dignified life.

Significance: Basic human rights are the most fundamental requirements for human beings to live a life consistent with their human dignity. Therefore, these rights are given absolute precedence, or priority, in both national and international law and policy. There is no universally accepted list of these rights because they vary somewhat in different cultural contexts. They would include, however, the right to life, food, shelter and medical treatment, and freedom from torture, cruel, degrading and inhuman treatment and punishment, and freedom of religion, freedom of expression, and freedom from slavery.

All human rights are considered equal, interdependent, interrelated and indivisible in theory. However, the term "basic human rights" is used to designate certain human rights that are simply too basic *not* to be respected. Basic human rights mentioned generally in the American Declaration of Independence include life, liberty and the pursuit of happiness. It states that the first and foremost duty of government is to protect the basic human rights of people within its jurisdiction. The United States was created by people who sought to create a place where basic human rights were protected for all. Protecting basic human rights has always been a goal of U.S. law and policy.

Basic human rights are set forth in the following international human rights instruments: UDHR, ICCPR, and ICESCR, though the term basic human rights is narrower than all of the substantive rights set forth in them. It is an abstract concept and not easy to define clearly, but it is often used in human rights discourse. See Documents 6, 8, 16.

See Also Terms: 11, 12, 24, 33, 34, 35, 56, 70, 75, 90, 92, 100, 116, 120, 122, 124, 136, 144, 145, 160, 167, 177, 179, 180, 184, 195, 213, 242, 252, 283, 309, 316.

21. BEARER

Definition: The person who possesses, or who holds, a legal (human) right and has the right and power to take steps to protect or vindicate such a right. In international human rights law it is the individual human being and not the state who is the bearer (also called "holder") of the human right for protection of his or her human dignity.

Significance: The key to understanding the international human rights movement is to understand that it is built on the individual person as the bearer of human rights, based on each person's inherent human dignity. Historically, state sovereigns (rulers or governments) have most often believed that human rights were bestowed by them on the individuals under their rule. This concept only worked well for the individual if the sovereign happened to be benevolent. Often, however, rights were given and taken away from people on the whim of the sovereign. A classic example of the kinds of horrors that can occur with this approach to rights is the Holocaust of World War II. Under the Third Reich, the laws were changed so that the rights of Jews and other designated "enemies of the state" were no longer upheld. Beyond that, it became legal to perpetrate any actions against them and their property that was deemed necessary. At the Nuremberg trials, when the Nazis defended their actions by claiming they were legal according to their country's laws, the response was that the individual's rights cannot be taken away at the whim of the state, no matter what the legal system says. The Jews and other Holocaust victims were *bearers* of inherent human dignity and could not be treated the way they were, because there existed a law higher than the national laws which had permitted such barbarity. This was international criminal law to some, and divine law to others. Throughout history, there have been various attempts to codify laws so that inequities did not occur, as they were bound to under a system in which the government "bestowed" rights on individuals.

The modern human rights movement established from the outset that the individual human being is the bearer or holder of human rights based on human dignity and/or divine law. From this perspective, the state then merely "recognizes" those rights and is bound by duty to protect them. The United States has espoused this approach from the beginnings of the nation in its founding documents. The "inalienable rights" language of the Declaration of Independence and the very existence of the Bill of Rights establish that the United States approaches human rights from the "individual as bearer of the right" basis.

Over the last several years, there has been a controversy in the international human rights movement over individual human rights versus collective or "group" rights. The latter concept suggests that human rights can be held by a group or collection of people, calling the group rights the collection of all the individual human rights being held together by the individual bearers or members of the group. In this approach, a right can be held by the group as a whole and not belong to any individual member. The difficulty with this approach arises when there is a conflict between the group and an individual as to the granting or taking away of a particular right. For example, if a woman who is a member of such a group claims her right to self-determination in certain matters, but the group as a whole does not want to grant her autonomy to make a decision, the concepts of individual and group bearers of rights come into conflict. The woman, in a classic approach to human rights, would be the *bearer* of the right to self-determination in the decisions of her own life (freedom of conscience, expression, etc.) and should have the right to depart from what the group believes.

See Also Terms: 11, 12, 26, 33, 53, 54, 55, 56, 57, 75, 100, 116, 122, 124, 144, 145, 160, 165, 169, 177, 179, 180, 184, 195, 213, 236, 259, 291, 297, 323.

22. BIGOT(ED)/BIGOTRY

Definition: Being strongly and openly biased and prejudiced against another person or group on the basis of a certain distinguishing characteristic or set of beliefs that the bigot does not like.

Significance: Bigotry is an intolerance of characteristic differences between persons and groups. Such an attitude is seen as a danger to respect for human rights and fundamental freedoms, because it looks at another as being unacceptable, less than equal, or rightly to be discriminated against. An example would be a white person who hates blacks and thinks that all blacks are lazy or of lower intelligence, or an American who thinks that all Muslims are terrorists or anti-American. Bigotry is an attitude inconsistent with respect for human dignity and an attitude that human rights education seeks to root out and replace with an attitude of tolerance.

Article 1 of the UDHR states that "All human beings are born free and equal in dignity and rights." See Document 6. They are endowed with reason and conscience and should act towards one another in a spirit of brotherhood." Being bigoted is having an obstinate, irrational and blindly unreasoning attachment to one's own beliefs and opinions and intolerance for any opposite beliefs.

It is important to note that some people use the word "bigot" too loosely, specifically to describe someone who disagrees with them, thus not using the word in its proper spirit. Individuals have the right to freedom of thought, conscience, and religion, and therefore have the right to hold their own personal opinions consistent with their own worldview. Those who vilify such people themselves become intolerant and in the same way create a dilemma. The balance is a difficult one to achieve but must be worked at to establish human rights norms consistent with the inherent human dignity of *each* individual.

Although it is permissible to hold opinions reflecting bigotry, bigotry can lead to harmful acts of intolerance, and those acts can be prevented or punished by society. According to the international community, the best remedy for bigotry is education in human rights.

See Also Terms: 14, 28, 33, 34, 35, 54, 55, 72, 77, 78, 86, 87, 101, 125, 126, 139, 140, 145, 188, 212, 216, 235, 237, 238, 255, 260, 261, 265, 277, 283, 324.

23. BILATERAL IMMUNITY AGREEMENT
See entry for **International Criminal Court**

24. BILL OF RIGHTS
Definition: A term coined to describe the first ten amendments to the U.S. Constitution, which establish, in an indirect way, legal protection of certain basic rights of individuals somewhat similar to human rights.

Significance: When Americans think about legal protection from the abuse of power by government, they naturally think about the Constitution and the Bill of Rights. See Document 2. There are certain human rights–like legal protections in the Bill of Rights, for example the guarantee of freedom of speech in the First Amendment. These are our historical, fundamental freedoms. These freedoms could, though, be taken away if, for example, the Constitution were amended to delete them. For example, the First Amendment could theoretically and legally be amended out of the Constitution.

Human rights, however, are not like the civil rights set forth in the Bill of Rights. They were not created or granted by any body of human beings or by any government. They inhere in human beings by their very nature. They cannot be amended away. Thus, in theory, constitutional rights could possibly be taken away with an overthrow of government and change of constitution; human rights could not.

The United States has recognized that the International Bill of Rights is also a source of rights for all Americans because the United States accepts and makes human rights legal norms a part of U.S. national law by virtue of the Constitution. The Constitution declares human rights treaties and customary norms to be part and parcel of U.S. law.

The American Bill of Rights was indeed the model most used in drafting the International Bill of Rights. In effect, the International Bill of Rights is substantially the U.S. Constitution and Bill of Rights internationalized, rendered part of international law to grant its benefits of liberty to all human beings. They are not the same in scope and substance, but Americans can and should consider their rights from the international human rights perspective as well as from the traditional Constitution and Bill of Rights model. The lack of exposure of Americans as to the existence and scope of international human rights can cause a limitation of legal vision and perspective on human rights worldwide.

It would be advisable at this time for the reader to compare and contrast the U.S. Bill of Rights with the list of rights contained in the International Bill of Rights. The reader will then know his or her freedom rights from all major human rights sources.

See Also Terms: 20, 21, 33, 34, 35, 49, 65, 66, 70, 84, 86, 88, 90, 100, 113, 122, 123, 124, 144, 145, 152, 160, 167, 169, 177, 189, 195, 196, 213, 216, 222, 242, 252, 260, 272, 291, 297, 283, 309, 312.

25. BINDING
Definition: A legal term that describes the legal status or nature of a treaty or customary norm as one with which a state must legally comply. It is a mandatory, obligatory requirement because the state has, in theory, consented to be legally bound by it.

Significance: In the field of human rights law, human rights norms fall into two basic categories: binding and nonbinding. A binding treaty or customary law norm refers to a standard of government conduct that must be obeyed as a matter of legal obligation. It must act internally in compliance with the international norm. If a state has ratified a treaty and the instrument has entered into force, then the instrument is *binding* upon the state and it must comply with that treaty. Only if a treaty is *binding* is a state *bound* to comply with it. Customary international law also establishes norms that are binding on all states.

Before one can accuse the United States or any other state of violating an international human rights standard, one must ascertain whether a particular norm (treaty or custom) is binding or nonbinding. Only noncompliance with a binding norm would lead to a breach or violation of the norm. Such a breach would engage legal remedies because human rights standards are legal standards.

Under the U.S. Constitution, treaties entered into by the president are only binding if they have been ratified by two-thirds of the Senate (see Advice and Consent). A good example of a treaty binding on the United States would be the ICCPR, (see Document 8), which the United States has ratified. A good example of a nonbinding treaty would be the International Covenant on Economic, Social, and Cultural Rights (ICESCR), (see Document 16), which the United States has signed but not yet ratified. A chart on how an international human rights norm becomes binding as a matter of U.S. law is found in Appendix F.

Human rights are often referred to at international organizations in instruments called resolutions and declarations. These instruments are by definition nonbinding and are not meant to create legal obligations. There are some exceptions, such as the Universal Declaration of Human Rights, which is considered by the weight of authority to be binding as a matter of customary international law, at least as to so called "hard core human rights" such as slavery and torture and the right to life. See the *Restatement of the Law of Foreign Relations, Third* in Appendix I.

When determining what human rights norms are binding on the U.S., one must always remember that one must check on customary international norms also, as they are binding upon the U.S. The only possible exception to that rule is the "Persistent Objector Rule," which says that a state which has persistently and expressly refused to accept a customary international norm will not be held bound by such norm. This is so because international law is based on the theory of the consent of states and when a state expresses its objection to a norm it is not consenting to accept it.

See Also Terms: 2, 3, 5, 6, 26, 48, 52, 62, 73, 80, 94, 98, 145, 151, 211, 214, 215, 222, 226, 244, 259, 262, 269, 272, 280, 285, 287, 292, 293, 306.

26. BREACH

Definition: The failure of a state to comply with an international norm is a "breach" of its legal obligation. A state is said to breach its normative obligation under treaty or customary law when its conduct is not up to the standard set by the legal norm.

Significance: International human rights law creates legal obligations on states to act or not act in a certain way, according to the terms of an international treaty or customary law norm. A breach entails international responsibility of the offending state and its agents, depending on the source of the norms violated (treaty or custom). The breach can be of a specific treaty norm, or a norm of customary international law. The breach can be by a state's action or inaction. It can occur when nongovernmental actors commit the acts with state collusion or complicity, or when the state fails to prevent or stop such acts. If a breach is considered a "material breach" it means that the state has either completely rejected and refused to comply with the whole treaty, or has violated a provision essential for accomplishing the object and purpose of the norm.

Because the United States has ratified the Convention against Torture, if U.S. agents were to commit acts of torture on prisoners, then that would constitute a breach of its international legal obligation under that treaty. It would then bring into play certain processes to remedy the breach, so that the injury and damage would be repaired and the act would not occur again. The word "violation" is also used somewhat interchangeably with the word "breach."

"Breach" is a term used for all of international law, but most often it is heard in the context of the law of armed conflict, especially under the Geneva Conventions of 1949. See Document 72. In those conventions and protocols, violations of the four treaties are either considered as regular "breaches" or, for certain enumerated more serious violations, as "grave breaches," with the latter constituting international crimes.

See Also Terms: 3, 25, 41, 42, 48, 60, 70, 71, 73, 88, 93, 98, 104, 119, 129, 132, 259, 267, 272, 273, 276, 291, 293, 297, 306, 307, 311, 317, 318.

27. BRICKER AMENDMENT

Definition: The Bricker Amendment was a series of proposed amendments to the U.S. Constitution in the 1950s that would have amended the treaty power in the Constitution to prevent the president from entering into any self-executing human rights treaties. The amendment also proposed preventing the use of executive agreements on human rights and requiring larger Senate action on international human rights treaty making by the executive.

Significance: From 1952–57, this series of amendments proposed by Senator Bricker was part of a strenuous debate over whether and how the new human rights treaties under the United Nations would apply in U.S. law. This debate was sparked by the political conservatives in reaction to several court decisions, such as the cases of *Sei Fuji v. California* and *Oyama v. California*. In these cases the courts dealt with the applicability of human rights provisions of international treaties, such as the U.N. Charter, which would have invalidated some state laws allowing state racial discrimination against aliens.

The amendments would have prohibited the executive from entering into any self-executing human rights treaties by declaring all such treaties to be non-self-executing, would have required congressional legislation to implement them, and would have limited the use of executive agreements. The proposals were the result of the concerns of Congress that the United States would be criticized for human rights violations before international bodies and sued for violations in U.S. Courts. They were also meant to reverse the effect of the 1920 U.S. Supreme Court case of *Missouri v. Holland*. In that decision the Supreme Court held that the Tenth Amendment did not limit the treaty-making power of the federal government.

The term Bricker Amendment has come to be associated with any strong political contention for limiting the entry of the United States into any human rights treaties that would become part of U.S. law, be binding on both federal and state government, and therefore serve as a basis for claims of international human rights violations. It also has to do with the fear that treaty power is being used in a way that violates state's rights (as in the fifty individual states of the United States) to residual powers under the Tenth Amendment to the Constitution. It was defeated because of the promise of the Eisenhower Administration not to ratify any human rights treaties. To this day, however, these same issues are strongly debated when the United States becomes involved in international human rights agreements.

See Also Terms: 6, 48, 52, 62, 70, 71, 89, 98, 103, 158, 194, 211, 212, 218, 220, 226, 243, 262, 272, 279, 280, 287, 292, 292, 306.

28. BROAD-MINDEDNESS

Definition: An attitude of being open to a society composed of all different types of people with all different kinds of ideas and of having tolerance toward them all. It is the opposite of narrow-mindedness.

Significance: Broad-mindedness is considered a necessary element of the public mind-set in a society that wants to be characterized by respect for human rights. This concept is an important part of the discourse on human rights in today's society. As communications throughout the world have increased in the twentieth century, people have been made aware of cultures they could never have imagined when they were isolated in their own smaller, homogenous spheres of influence. In addition, the development of international finance, not to mention more technologically destructive instruments of war, has created a need to deal with the mind-sets of other worldviews, customs and political and economic systems.

At the very least, to be broad-minded is to not react in fear or anger to opposing ideas without giving a hearing to those ideas. Even if one violently disagrees with his opponent, it is still assumed, in a polite society, that those disagreements can be presented in a orderly and respectful manner. The international human rights movement attempts to bring together those of widely differing views in everything from religion to politics to economics, in order to find common ground regarding the protection of human dignity worldwide. The international human rights instruments are the results of that attempt to find consensus.

The concept of broad-mindedness is especially important in the U.S. context, since the United States is the classic example of a "melting pot" society, largely populated by individuals of different worldviews and national origins who are seeking a free society in which to live and grow. To that end, it would be detrimental to the health of the nation as a whole to have an atmosphere of intolerance or narrow-mindedness toward another person's right to form his or her own opinions. In a democratic society such as the United States, each individual should, at the very least, have the right to this most basic freedom of conscience. The founding documents of this nation have made it clear that this kind of broad-mindedness is essential to the "United States experiment." The Statue of Liberty, with its invitation to the "tired, poor and huddled masses," represents a situation in which broad-mindedness and a basic concept of tolerance is upheld by the government.

For many, the difficulty with the concept of broad-mindedness occurs when they are forced to go beyond *respecting* an individual's right to his or her beliefs, and instead are coerced into accepting as true those beliefs. This concern is appropriate, because if such coercion occurs, then that individual's right to believe what he or she wishes has been compromised. It must be the first duty of government to protect this most basic right of the individual, even if those in office personally disagree with the belief. In this way, the government can demonstrate and encourage an appropriate concept of broad-mindedness for the population at large.

See Also Terms: 22, 69, 70, 72, 78, 87, 123, 139, 140, 144, 145, 188, 237, 241, 255, 260, 261, 323.

29. BUREAU OF HUMAN RIGHTS, DEMOCRACY AND LABOR

Definition: The branch of the U.S. State Department that is primarily charged with monitoring and engaging foreign governments on human rights issues for the U.S. government.

Significance: The Bureau of Democracy, Human Rights, and Labor (DRL) studies the human rights situation in every country of the world and acts as a source of information to the U.S. government about human rights problems outside the United States. DRL is distinct from the Bureau of International Organization Affairs which serves as the primary vehicle at the State Department for engaging with international organizations, including human rights issues. The Department of Democracy, Human Rights, and Labor (DRL) has as its primary role reporting on human rights conditions throughout the world and engaging in U.S. foreign policy, including through multilateral fora, to promote greater respect and protection for these human rights. DRL collaborates with other branches of the State Department, such as the Bureau of International Organization Affairs, when addressing human rights issues within multi-lateral fora.

Its most important function is probably the writing of the yearly "country reports" on the human rights situation of almost all states in the world. It presents this report to Congress each year and Congress uses the report in making its foreign aid or military assistance legislation or appropriations. This tool is essential for them to make an informed decision in these matters. This report also helps U.S. government bodies in the area of human rights by providing country-specific responses for immigration courts in cases where an alien is seeking asylum in the United States. The reports submitted by the United States to the Committee against Torture, contained in Document 21A, is a sample of a document produced by this Bureau.

See Also Terms: 14, 20, 22, 32, 48, 53, 54, 55, 56, 57, 60, 61, 70, 77, 82, 84, 85, 86, 90, 100, 113, 115, 117, 119, 122, 124, 125, 126, 133, 144, 144, 145, 150, 151, 152, 159, 160, 163, 167, 169, 170, 171, 177, 179, 184, 185, 196, 199, 206, 211, 215, 221, 222, 233, 235, 252, 256, 260, 268, 297, 304, 322 .

C

30. CAPITAL PUNISHMENT

Definition: A criminal sentence imposed by a court of law upon conviction, after a trial, ordering the convicted defendant to be put to death as punishment for the commission of a capital offense.

Significance: Capital punishment is imposed by a court of law only upon conviction of the most serious ("capital") crimes, such as murder. It is more commonly known as the death penalty.

It is a very controversial topic in international human rights, with some states favoring it and some opposed. There is clearly an international trend toward abolition of the death penalty. This move toward abolition is based on the belief that this practice violates the human right to life, constitutes cruel and inhuman punishment, constitutes an alienation of all of the person's other "inalienable" human rights, is barbaric, and is subject to too frequent abuse, misuse, and discriminatory application. All of these objections are without regard to how heinous was the crime of the accused. Those who support it, including families of the victims, say it deters serious crime and is an appropriate retributive punishment.

Under existing international human rights law, capital punishment is not prohibited (see ICCPR, Article 6). Nevertheless, a decreasing number of countries have this penalty on their books, and still fewer actually use it. The subject of the Second Optional Protocol to the ICCPR is the abolition of the death penalty (see Document 11). Under generally accepted contemporary human rights standards, it can be imposed only (1) for the most serious crimes; (2) upon conviction by an impartial and independent court with jurisdiction; (3) after a public and fair trial that meets all procedural due process standards accorded to the defendant and that allows a right to appeal for judicial review of the conviction; (4) with the right to petition for clemency, pardon, or commutation of sentence; and (5) in accordance with certain safeguards. The United Nations has established certain human rights safeguards for those facing the death penalty (see "Safeguards Guaranteeing Protection of the Rights of those Facing the Death Penalty," Document 49).

The United States believes that the majority of Americans want the death penalty imposed for certain crimes and does not care what the rest of the world thinks about the human rights implications. Some federal and state laws have recently expanded the number of crimes punishable by capital punishment as a result of their goal to get tough on crime. This is particularly true in the wake of 9/11 and what was called the war on terrorism. Some states in the United States have abolished the death penalty, and, as previously mentioned, there is currently a movement in international human rights worldwide to prohibit it universally.

There are various means of administering this punishment, including lethal injection, the gas chamber, the electric chair, hanging, and firing squad. Some of these have been subjected to scrutiny by U.S. courts. The U.S. Supreme Court has upheld capital punishment under certain conditions and by certain means.

In international human rights law applicable to the United States, capital punishment principally involves the scope and interpretation of the human right to life in Article 6 of the ICCPR, which does not expressly prohibit such punishment. It also involves the scope and interpretation of the human right against cruel, degrading, and inhuman punishment, especially regarding how the death penalty is administered, that is, to avoid unnecessary suffering (see ICCPR Article 7). Capital punishment can also involve Article 2.1 if administered in a discriminatory manner. Article 14 of the ICCPR addresses the rights of the defendant to a fair trial and appeal. In the eyes of international human rights law, a condemned convict is still a human being entitled to treatment as such, regardless of his or her crimes.

In its ratification of the ICCPR in 1992, the United States made a reservation to Article 6.5 to allow it to execute persons younger than 18 who committed crimes. Otherwise, commission of such acts would have constituted a violation of that article. See Document 9.

Several important U.S. Supreme Court cases have discussed the international legal implications of capital punishment and the so-called death row phenomenon relating to the long agonizing wait and numerous legal motions. The U.S. death penalty system has been an issue in several international cases outside the United States. In the famous *Soering v. United Kingdom*, the European Court of Human Rights found that if the United Kingdom were to extradite a young murder suspect from the United Kingdom to Virginia, he would face the famous "death row syndrome," referring again to the long death row wait many face. They said it would violate his human right against cruel, inhuman, and degrading treatment under the European Convention on Human Rights. This case gave rise to many cases regarding extradition or forced return to the United States to face the death row syndrome.

One of the major issues in the U.S. regarding the death penalty is the statistical evidence of it being imposed in a racially discriminatory manner. This has been the subject of much litigation. This brings into play two human rights: equality before the law and non discrimination. In a 2003 Amnesty International study it was found that while African-Americans make up only about 12% of the U.S. population they represented about 40% of convicted criminals on death row, and one in three of those who were actually executed, since 1977.

There have been other issues as well. The Supreme Court ruled in 2005 in *Roper vs. Simmons* that it is cruel and unusual punishment, and thus unconstitutional, to sentence to capital punishment persons who committed crimes as a juvenile. See Appendix J. The High Court also ruled in 2002 in *Atkins v. Virginia*, that capital punishment of the mentally ill is also unconstitutional as a violation of the 8th amendment.

A searching inquiry is being made in many states in the U.S. concerning capital punishment because of the scientific evidence of the number of persons executed who were in fact and law innocent of the capital charges. This has been largely due to forensic science use of DNA evidence which was not available or employed at the time of the criminal proceedings. It calls into question the justice system's ability to correctly determine capital guilt and provide adequate legal representation to assure that the innocent do not die at the hands of the state. A death penalty execution resulting from an incorrect judgment of guilt constitutes a violation of the human right to life, however well intentioned or comprehensive the prosecution.

In its 2010 national report to the OHCHR for the UPR process, the Administration reports about the death penalty in the U.S. Among other things it reports at paragraph 61, 62 and 63:

> The United States may impose the death penalty for the most serious crimes and subject to exacting procedural safeguards. Federal laws providing for the death penalty most often involve serious crimes in which death results. Several non-homicide crimes may also result in the imposition of a death sentence, e.g., espionage, treason, and several carefully circumscribed capital offenses intended to target the threat of terrorist attacks resulting in widespread loss of life.
> 62. The federal government utilizes a system for carefully examining each potential federal death penalty case. This system operates to help ensure that the death penalty is not applied in an arbitrary, capricious, or discriminatory manner, and to promote indigent defendants receiving competent representation by qualified attorneys. Many of our states have adopted procedures of their own to provide experienced counsel for indigent defendants. In addition, existing federal law permits DNA testing in relevant federal and state cases.

63. In 2009, the death penalty was applied in 52 cases in the United States, about half the number of a decade earlier. The death penalty is authorized by 35 states, the federal government, and the U.S. military. There are currently 16 jurisdictions without the death penalty. While state governments retain primary responsibility for establishing procedures and policies that govern state capital prosecutions, the Supreme Court has excluded from application of the death penalty those offenders who, at the time of the offense, were under age 18 or had intellectual disabilities.

See Also Terms: 3, 11, 12, 33, 48, 49, 53, 57, 65, 66, 70, 90, 110, 113, 124, 144, 145, 152, 160, 167, 170, 177, 179, 185, 202, 213, 246, 252, 283, 298, 309, 314, 316, 323.

31. CHARTER

Definition: A type of treaty by which states establish an international inter-governmental organization or sometimes a human rights treaty system. It is usually a formal and solemn international legal instrument, and as a treaty it is legally binding on all states that have ratified it.

Significance: An example is the Charter of the United Nations. See Document 5. Such an instrument is used to establish global or regional inter-governmental organizations, to define and limit their authority, and to designate their principal organs. It sets forth certain basic purposes and principles and serves as their constitutional instrument. Some charters, such as the African Charter on Human and Peoples' Rights (1981), are actually specifically general human rights treaties, binding upon states that are parties to them. They create a human rights system by setting forth substantive human rights norms and establishing a supervisory mechanism to assure implementation.

The United States has ratified the U.N. Charter, and by its ratification it became a member state of the United Nations and voluntarily assumed legal obligations to the United Nations and other members states. These obligations include respecting and promoting human rights, and cooperating with the United Nations in its attempt to get other member states to do so.

See Also Terms: 25, 98, 124, 145, 177, 185, 208, 222, 225, 226, 247, 254, 259, 262, 272, 276, 280, 289, 291, 293, 297, 306, 308.

32. CHILDREN'S RIGHTS

Definition: The totality of those human rights principles conventional norms from treaties, and customary norms, and declarations which seek to protect children through the establishment of specific child-related normative standards. Those standards that are recognized and accepted in international law and within the systems that seek to implement them. The primary source of children's human rights in International Law is the 1989 United Nations Convention on the Rights of the Child.

Significance: Children's human rights have as their purpose the protection, respect, assurance and fulfillment of all human rights of that sector of society which has not reached the age of majority. They are known as sectorial rights. They do not apply to everyone of every age, but only to a specific sector of society which needs particular human rights legal protections given their age and degree of maturity and considering the history of abuse and exploitation of children.

Properly speaking, only those norms found in human rights treaties, such as the Convention on the Rights of the Child and several articles of the ICCPR and certain ILO conventions such as No. 182, can be called hard human rights law. Some principles such as the Declaration on the Rights of the Child, the Minimum Rules for the Administration of Juvenile Justice (U.N. 1985) (so called "Beijing Rules"), the Guidelines for the Prevention of Juvenile Delinquency (U.N. 1990) (so called "Riyadh Guidelines), which are sets of international principles consistent with international human rights law, and could be considered some of the instruments of soft law in the field of children's rights.

The U.S., particularly U.S. based NGOs and other civil society stakeholders, have played a big part in the articulation, promotion and standard setting process in the field of children's human rights. As of 2010, the U.S. has not ratified the CRC, which has become the most ratified treaty in the world. The U.S. has signed the CRC, expressing its intent to eventually ratify.

However, under the Vienna Convention on the Law of Treaties there is an "interim" obligation to refrain from acts which would defeat the object and purpose of [the] treaty. The object and purpose of the CRC is to recognize certain human rights in children and to protect children from harm. The opposition to the CRC is largely concerning perceived interference with U.S. sovereignty as relates to how American law, primarily state law, deals with children, and interference with the rights of parents to decide how to raise their children.

The U.S. has, interestingly, signed and ratified two optional protocols to the CRC, The First Optional Protocol concerns children in armed conflict. It is an attempt to prohibit child soldiers. This OP and the U.S. ratification are found in Documents 29 and 30.

The U.S. has also signed and ratified the Second Optional Protocol which concerns the sale of children, child prostitution and child pornography. This OP and U.S. ratification are in Documents 31 and 32. The periodic state reports of the U.S. to the Committee on the Rights of the Child under these two protocols are found at http://www.state.gov/g/drl/rls/83929.htm and http://www.state.gov/g/drl/rls/84467.htm.

See Also Terms: 11, 12, 20, 21, 41, 49, 57, 58, 60, 65, 66, 68, 84, 92, 100, 104, 115, 124, 144, 145, 147, 149, 150, 151, 152, 167, 169, 177, 179, 180, 184, 191, 192, 204, 236, 282, 283, 287, 289, 304, 311.

33. CIVIL HUMAN RIGHTS

Definition: This is a type of human right held by the individual members of the general society and sometimes by nonmembers who are present within the society. It is a right of individuals to treatment by government as free and equal in their activities, actions, and needs in the general public sphere or in their public affairs. The following are the principal human rights forming this category: the right to life; the right to liberty and security of person; the prohibition of slavery; the prohibition of torture and of cruel, degrading, or inhuman treatment or punishment; the right not to be subject to arbitrary arrest, detention, or exile; the right to a fair trial in both civil and criminal matters; the presumption of innocence; the right to be treated with humanity when deprived of liberty; freedom of movement; freedom of thought, conscience, and religion; freedom of expression and opinion; freedom of assembly; the right to privacy; equal protection of law; the right to legal personality; nondiscrimination on any basis in the exercise of human rights; and access to adequate and effective legal remedies to enforce human rights.

Significance: There are five main categories of human rights: civil; political; economic; social; and cultural. Civil human rights are those that regulate the conduct of government toward individuals in a state to assure that they enjoy a maximum amount of freedom consistent with the common well-being. Civil human rights are distinguished from rights relating solely to religious or military affairs. They are part of what used to be known as the "first generation" human rights, a term we no longer use.

Although the concept sounds similar, these are not the same as "civil rights" as the term is used in the United States. The term civil rights in the United States usually refers to the civil rights acts or rights under the constitutional Bill of Rights, and most often refers to racial and other types of discrimination in the exercise of rights. Some civil rights are also civil human rights; examples would include racial equality and nondiscrimination.

Police brutality and racial discrimination are examples of violations of civil human rights. In the United States, civil rights are granted by the legislature through statutes, whereas human rights belong to a person simply by being human and are merely recognized, respected, and enforced by government. Civil human rights can be found in Articles 6–24, 26, and 27 of the ICCPR. The U.S. became bound to respect these internationally recognized human rights when the U.S. Senate ratified the ICCPR in 1992.

See Also Terms: 7, 11, 12, 16, 17, 20, 24, 30, 34, 35, 39, 49, 51, 52, 53, 54, 55, 56, 57, 58, 59, 60, 62, 65, 66, 75, 81, 82, 84, 86, 90, 100, 101, 110, 111, 113, 115, 116, 117, 120, 122, 123, 124, 126, 136, 139, 140, 141, 142, 144, 145, 146, 147, 148, 150, 152, 155, 156, 160, 162, 167, 169, 170, 171, 177, 179, 184, 189, 195, 196, 198, 205, 216, 222, 233, 235, 238, 248, 249, 250, 252, 253, 254, 255, 256, 259, 260, 265, 270, 272, 275, 277, 281, 283, 289, 291, 297, 298, 299, 302, 303, 304, 306, 307, 309, 311, 312, 316, 320, 322, 324.

34. Civil Liberties

Definition: Civil liberties are legal guarantees established by the governed of a democratic society and are assurances that the basic freedom of the individual will not be curtailed or reduced by the government. Examples of civil liberties include freedom of expression, freedom of peaceable assembly, and the right to a fair criminal trial.

Significance: Civil liberties is a general political term referring to the basic legal protection of an individual from the acts of a state interfering with freedom and equality. This term is not the same as civil rights or civil human rights, although some civil liberties are the same as civil human rights. Civil rights usually refers to the various laws of the Civil Rights Acts; they seek to put into effect the rights contained in the Bill of Rights. Civil human rights are a conceptual category of *specific* human rights that are akin to the general rights of members of society to enjoy freedom and equality in the public sphere. These rights come from the human dignity of each member of society, regardless of any status or characteristic. Civil human rights protect civil liberties. Civil liberties are included within the concept of civil human rights; human rights protect human beings in relation to government. Civil liberties are usually found in a state constitution or bill of rights. In U.S. law they are found in the Constitution and first ten amendments. In a broad sense, the Universal Declaration of Human Rights is an international consensus adopted at the United Nations in 1948, with the United States voting in favor, as to the basic civil liberties of all human beings. This was not originally a legally binding document, but it is now considered by most scholars to be legally binding, at least in terms of the "hard core," basic individual liberties. In the international sphere, it is considered binding as a matter of customary international law.

See Also Terms: 20, 22, 28, 33, 55, 59, 70, 72, 74, 77, 86, 100, 116, 120, 122, 123, 124, 139, 144, 145, 148, 152, 160, 167, 169, 177, 179, 188, 194, 195, 196, 216, 232, 238, 239, 249, 255 256, 260, 261, 265, 266, 270, 272, 275, 277, 283, 298, 299, 302, 305.

35. Civil Rights

Definition: As commonly used in the United States, this term refers to the nonpolitical rights of citizens and certain others to liberty and equality of treatment. These rights are found in the Constitution's Bill of Rights and the so-called Federal Civil Rights Acts.

Significance: The purpose of civil rights is to insure the respect of persons in a civil society. They are granted by the sovereign (person or state) through legislation, such as the U.S. Congress passing the Civil Rights Acts. The object of civil rights is to create a harmonious, peaceful, and stable society that is built on the liberty and equality of all its citizens. Historically, in many countries, the sovereign who grants civil rights can also repeal or amend such civil rights legislation. Civil rights are established by legislation in the United States, for example, so that they can be changed by whoever is in power at the time. In contrast, however, human rights inhere in all human beings by nature. Human rights are not granted by state sovereigns but are only recognized by them in human rights instruments (e.g., treaties such as ICCPR, see Document 8). They are not subject to alienation, termination, annulment, or modification by a sovereign, although some of them can be limited or suspended for a time in public emergency situations.

The term civil rights is also sometimes used in a general sense to refer to "civil human rights," usually by those who do not understand the difference. They are different.

See Also Terms: 7, 11, 12, 16, 17, 20, 22, 24, 33, 55, 59, 70, 75, 78, 86, 87, 97, 100, 116, 120, 122, 123, 124, 126, 139, 144, 145, 151, 160, 167, 169, 177, 179, 188, 195, 205, 216, 228, 235, 237, 238, 242, 249, 252, 255, 260, 261, 265, 270, 275, 277, 283, 309, 312, 320, 324.

36. Civil Society

Definition: All the people and organizations who are not part of government who are actively working to change or improve the public society of the United States or to influence or affect public law and policy.

Significance: Government seems, sooner or later and in small or large ways, to act in ways that are not beneficial to the public or even to the entire international community. Civil society members act as private, but often organized and collectively working, forces to make change. An example of a civil society organization is Amnesty International USA or the League of Women Voters, but civil society can also refer to individuals.

Civil society is becoming an increasingly powerful force affecting government; its ability to affect public policy and practice, and even law, is increasing. The Brady Bill that passed regarding hand gun control was a result of an effort of civil society. The International Criminal Court was not possible without many NGOs working together at the Rome diplomatic conference to lobby, pressure, and provide legal expertise to the governments of the world, to finally establish an international criminal court to stop the culture of impunity. Civil society made the Court happen. Christian Solidarity International revealed to the world at large the genocidal activities of the government of Northern Sudan against Christian and animist groups.

The human rights movement is also made up of this type of grassroots civil society activist. Through letter-writing campaigns and other means, they can help to keep governments accountable to human rights norms, because governments do not want an unfavorable public image.

Civil society had an important role to play in the preparation of the U.S. national report to the OHCHR for the Universal Periodic Review process at the U.N. in 2010. This is recognized in the report itself, at paragraph 8:

> This report is the product of collaboration between the U.S. Government and representatives of civil society from across the United States. Over the last year, senior representatives from more than a dozen federal departments and agencies traveled the country to attend a series of UPR consultations hosted by a wide range of civil society organizations. At these gatherings, individuals presented their concerns and recommendations and often shared stories or reports as they interacted with government representatives. Those conversations shaped the substance and structure of this report. Nearly a thousand people, representing a diversity of communities and viewpoints, and voicing a wide range of concerns, attended these gatherings in New Orleans, Louisiana; New York, New York; El Paso, Texas; Albuquerque, New Mexico; Window Rock, Arizona; the San Francisco Bay Area; Detroit, Michigan; Chicago, Illinois; Birmingham, Alabama; and Washington, D.C. Information about the process was also posted on the website of the U.S. Department of State (www.state). Members of the public were encouraged to contribute questions, comments, and recommendations via that site, and many did so. The consultation process followed a familiar tradition of collaboration and discussion between government and civil society that is vital to the strength of our democracy. The U.S. Government is grateful to all those who hosted meetings and shared their views both in those consultations and online. We also welcome constructive comments and recommendations from other governments and non-governmental organizations through the UPR process.

See Also Terms: 4, 48, 70, 76, 93, 94, 112, 113, 119, 121, 123, 145, 148, 149, 194, 206, 215, 217, 221, 227, 249, 268, 283, 305, 311, 323.

37. CIVIL WAR

Definition: An armed conflict between the government and an opposing force of its own citizens, sometimes for control of the state government and sometimes over some other issue, such as becoming an independent state, self-rule, religious liberty, or social justice. It is more than just isolated incidents of violence; it is a concerted and sustained military conflict. Also called a non-international armed conflict, civil wars often result in many human rights violations. They are covered within the scope of international human rights law, in such treaties as the ICCPR, CERD, the Genocide Convention, the Convention against Torture, and under humanitarian law, the law of armed conflict, particularly common Article 3 of the four GCs, which the U.S. Supreme Court has said is binding customary international law in the U.S. courts.

Significance: The devastating results of civil wars are well known in today's world. Places in the world whose names were previously little known, for example Rwanda or the Congo, are often catapulted onto the world stage because of the tragedies that occur during this kind of conflict. Ethnic cleansings and genocide are sometimes associated with civil war. It is essential that society, although it cannot seem to eliminate war altogether, at least make rules to minimize the effects of this kind of conflict. This field of humanitarian law developed mainly to do just that.

The United States knows the devastation of civil war because of the War between the North and the South fought in the mid-1800s. This conflict centered on the social justice issue of slavery. Even in that conflict, however, an attempt to deal with the problem of human rights violations was made through the Lieber Code, a formal military manual that set forth rules for that armed conflict. The Lieber Code is still cited today in court cases as part of customary international law.

Internationally, as states attempt to find common ground in the area of respect for human rights, the rules for armed conflicts such as civil wars, are essential to minimize the devastation, especially on civilians. All citizens should know of the existence of the rules so that they can hold their governments accountable.

See Also Terms: 13, 41, 42, 45, 48, 70, 72, 129, 132, 137, 144, 145, 152, 176, 177, 178, 179, 180, 181, 182, 184, 185, 192, 197, 201, 206, 218, 221, 243, 257, 259, 271, 272, 276, 278, 283, 287, 292, 309, 314, 323.

38. COLLATERAL DAMAGE

Definition: Incidental damage caused to civilian (nonmilitary) persons and objects by an armed attack, such as a naval or air bombardment or missile attack, during an armed conflict. Strictly speaking, collateral damage is unintended and the unfortunate result of an attack whose damage cannot be limited only to military targets. It is a euphemism for the loss of civilian life and injuries to civilians during an armed attack, as if it were an acceptable amount.

Significance: The Law of Armed Conflict does not permit combatants to attack civilians or civilian property. (See Geneva Convention, Protocol 1, Article 51, Document 73). It does, however, recognize that sometimes when a military force attacks an enemy it cannot avoid all damage to civilian persons and objects, even where, for example, smart bombs are used. The military has coined the term collateral damage to refer to the damage caused incidentally to nonmilitary persons and things (churches, schools, houses) during an armed attack. It did so to lessen the negative public image of armed conflict caused by the knowledge or images of innocent civilians being killed or wounded. It is an attempt to ameliorate public sentiment against a particular conflict or armed conflict in general during that conflict.

Collateral damage can constitute a human rights violation if the amount of collateral damage is disproportionate to the military benefit to be achieved. For example, dropping a large bomb on a machine gun nest manned by two soldiers situated right next to a civilian hospital, thus killing 2,000 civilians to neutralize two enemy soldiers, would most likely be a violation of humanitarian law, that is, a violation of the human rights of those 2,000 dead civilians. Calling a loss to civilians "collateral damage" does not mean that such damage is legally permissible as a matter of human rights law. Each attack must be examined in light of the facts of that attack, especially when judging what information was known by those who planned the attack regarding the possible extent of civilian damage.

See Also Terms: 37, 41, 42, 48, 59, 63, 73, 86, 104, 110, 116, 129, 132, 135, 137, 144, 145, 151, 152, 154, 164, 166, 177, 178, 179, 181, 182, 184, 192, 197, 201, 226, 257, 259, 283, 317, 318, 321.

39. COLLECTIVE HUMAN RIGHTS

Definition: The concept that human rights can be held by a group or collective of people, such as an ethnic minority group or a religious or linguistic group. It is sometimes defined as being the collection of all the individual human rights being held together by the members of the group as a whole, and also defined as a right held by the group as a whole and not belonging to any individual member.

Significance: These rights are generally contrasted with individual rights, which are held by each individual person regardless of his or her belonging to a particular group. Some rights, such as minority or indigenous rights, are said to be collective or group rights. The conception of collective or group rights is controversial and is not universally accepted.

This concept is used in the area of the rights of indigenous peoples. The claim is that an indigenous group, such as a tribe of Indians, holds a right for all its members. There is often a real tension between individual rights and collective or group human rights. For example, a tribe claiming it had the right to determine the sole religion for members of the group, when some members wanted to change to another religion or no religion.

Collective human rights are also known as group human rights. They mean the same thing. Some scholars say that Article 27 of the ICCPR is an example of a collective human right. In the final analysis individual rights must take primacy of place.

See Also Terms: 21, 40, 46, 56, 67, 68, 69, 83, 97, 100, 101, 102, 130, 139, 140, 143, 144, 145, 153, 163, 179, 184, 190, 205, 216, 222, 237, 243, 260, 265, 277, 283, 316.

40. COLLECTIVE PUNISHMENT

Definition: The punishment of persons who have not committed any wrongdoing, as a payback or threat in response to the wrongful act of someone else. It means punishing a group of innocent people for the past wrongdoing of those who are guilty.

Significance: Collective punishment is a violation of the human rights and criminal law principles that people cannot be punished for acts they have not committed. Usually, collective punishment is a response in armed conflict to the harmful acts someone, usually a civilian or guerrilla, has committed against the military force of an occupying army, and it is unknown who committed the act. It happens when certain persons, chosen at random and with no evidence of their individual guilt, are punished instead of those who *are* guilty. The goal of collective punishment is usually to create fear among the people so that they will not commit such acts in the future; to persuade those guilty to not do it again because innocent people will suffer; or to get the innocent to reveal who committed the past acts.

An example of collective punishment would be the following: In a town occupied by enemy soldiers, someone commits sabotage against the military occupiers, who then line up citizens at random and shoot some or all of them as punishment.

Although this term is most commonly found in relation to armed conflict, it can apply to any type of situation. It occurs wherever individuals are punished in a group without any proof of guilt of any member of the group. Collective punishment can be committed by a government against its own citizens.

Collective punishment is a violation of human rights because human beings cannot be punished unless they do something wrong. Individual punishment can only occur where the person is found guilty under the law by a court of law or other lawfully authorized body, and after fair trial with all procedural due process rights. Guilt cannot be collective or by mere association.

References to these prohibitions are in the ICCPR Articles 9, 14, and 15; it is also specifically prohibited in armed conflicts by the Geneva Conventions of 1949 and its Protocols of 1977. See Documents 8, 72, 73.

See Also Terms: 3, 11, 12, 19, 20, 21, 24, 26, 42, 45, 48, 59, 63, 70, 71, 72, 90, 100, 101, 102, 113, 116, 122, 124, 129, 130, 132, 133, 135, 137, 143, 144, 145, 151, 152, 154, 166, 177, 179, 181, 182, 184, 192, 197, 215, 223, 228, 235, 252, 257, 259, 271, 272, 283, 316, 317, 321.

41. COMBATANT

Definition: A person who is legally entitled to engage in armed conflict (has a *jus ad bellum*) and who, if captured, is entitled to the legal status of prisoner of war and treatment pursuant to international humanitarian law as a POW. A person who has the legal right to participate in hostilities.

Significance: The designation of combatant in international law gives a person a license to kill or wound enemy combatants and destroy other enemy military objectives. As a consequence combatants cannot be prosecuted for lawful acts of war in the course of military operations, even though in peacetime this would constitute serious crimes. They can only be prosecuted for violations of international humanitarian law, such as war crimes. Once captured, combatants are entitled to prisoner of war status and come under the protection of the Third Geneva Convention.

This distinction is important not only for what the combatant can do and what protections he or she has but it also provides the basis of an essential principle of humanitarian law. A combatant can only attack military persons and objects and must at all times distinguish between military and civilian object and persons. A combatant can only attack other combatants, not civilians. So, the status of a combatant is very important for several reasons. In the war on terrorism in the U.S. and abroad the issue has been defining the status of persons detained either for engaging in armed conflict against the U.S. and its allies, or how the enemy is to be treated once captured, and more importantly what legal rights they have. Having legal rights to a certain treatment is different from just being given certain treatment as a matter of generosity.

In an armed conflict one is either a combatant or a non-combatant. If you do not meet the criteria of combatant you are a non-combatant, also called a civilian. Thus, non-combatant is a residual description. Within the category of combatant there are lawful combatants and unlawful or unprivileged or illegal combatants. Unlawful and unprivileged are the more appropriate legal terms.

If one is a combatant one has certain legal rights. If one is an unlawful, unprivileged combatant one has different rights, under humanitarian law, but the same rights under international human rights law. If one is a non-combatant one has different rights both under the Geneva Conventions and human rights law. In the category of combatant there has been a lot of debate and criticism of U.S. policy in the war on terrorism, especially with the naming of some detainees as "enemy combatants." Enemy combatants is a term which does not exist in the International Law of Armed Conflict. It comes from the 1950 U.S. Supreme Court Case of *Johnson vs. Eisentrager*. That term is obsolete because it does not reflect the development of international humanitarian law and human rights law since 1950. But this term was still being used by the U.S. government post 9/11 to describe war on terror detainees. As the U.S. government understood it, an enemy combatant was someone who did not meet the criteria for being a combatant under international humanitarian law and thus could not claim status as a POW, and basically had no rights at all in detention.

But under international law the question is whether the detainees are combatants or unprivileged/unlawful combatants, also called unprivileged/unlawful belligerents. In short, U.S. law as applied to detention in the war on terrorism has not been in harmony with international law as to who is a combatant and what are the rights of unlawful combatants.

The International Law of Armed Conflict provides the definition, and legal status and protections, of combatants in armed conflicts. It is a complicated set of criteria which has given rise to many disputes about who is what. It is particularly the body of law known as international humanitarian law where the definition of combatant is found. It has developed over the course of history but in 1907 was defined in the Hague Convention. In order to be a combatant one had to fulfill the following criteria:

1. To be commanded by a person responsible for his subordinates;
2. To have a fixed distinctive emblem recognizable at a distance;
3. To carry arms openly; and
4. To conduct their operations in accordance with the laws and customs of war.

After the Second World War combatants were redefined in The Geneva Convention relative to the Treatment of Prisoners of War, 12 August (GCIII) of 1949 defines the requirements for a captive to be eligible for treatment as a Prisoner of war. A **lawful combatant** is a person who commits belligerent acts but if captured, would be a considered POW. An **unlawful combatant** is someone who commits belligerent acts, but does not qualify under GCIII. A civilian who engages in hostilities remains a civilian under humanitarian law, though he may be attacked, arrested and prosecuted for ordinary crimes. See Articles 4 and 5. Article 4 of the GC on Prisoners of War reads:

A. Prisoners of war, in the sense of the present Convention, are persons belonging to one of the following categories, who have fallen into the power of the enemy:

1. Members of the armed forces of a Party to the conflict as well as members of militias or volunteer corps forming part of such armed forces.

2. Members of other militias and members of other volunteer corps, including those of organized resistance movements, belonging to a Party to the conflict and operating in or outside their own territory, even if this territory is occupied, provided that such militias or volunteer corps, including such organized resistance movements, fulfil the following conditions:

(a) That of being commanded by a person responsible for his subordinates;
(b) That of having a fixed distinctive sign recognizable at a distance;
(c) That of carrying arms openly;
(d) That of conducting their operations in accordance with the laws and customs of war.

3. Members of regular armed forces who profess allegiance to a government or an authority not recognized by the Detaining Power.

4. Persons who accompany the armed forces without actually being members thereof, such as civilian members of military aircraft crews, war correspondents, supply contractors, members of labour units or of services responsible for the welfare of the armed forces, provided that they have received authorization from the armed forces which they accompany, who shall provide them for that purpose with an identity card similar to the annexed model.

5. Members of crews [of civil ships and aircraft], who do not benefit by more favourable treatment under any other provisions of international law.

6. Inhabitants of a non-occupied territory, who on the approach of the enemy spontaneously take up arms to resist the invading forces, without having had time to form themselves into regular armed units, provided they carry arms openly and respect the laws and customs of war.

In 1977 the first Protocol to the Geneva Conventions was adopted and entered into force, reflecting the lessons learned from Korea and Vietnam and elsewhere, particularly regarding guerilla warfare. Protocol I defines combatants residually. However the U.S. has not ratified that Protocol and so the definition of combatant does not apply to the U.S. in applicable conflicts. The U.S. has, though, acknowledged that to some degree Protocol I is declaratory of customary international law.

The problem in the U.S. war on terrorism is the use of the designation of enemy combatant on suspected terrorists, most of whom ended up in Guantanamo. At first there was no access to courts or lawyers to challenge the detention or its conditions and no internal tribunal for determining whether one was a combatant or not. In the post 9/11 era it was enough that the president denominated someone an "enemy combatant" for that person to be arrested, detained indefinitely without charges, not accorded POW status, and not given access to justice, so one could not challenge being called an enemy combatant.

Under international humanitarian law an unlawful or unprivileged combatant when captured is entitled to the coverage of the fourth Geneva Convention on civilians. There is no humanitarian law no man's land where persons have no rights under humanitarian law during armed conflict. The only question is whether one is a combatant or not.

In the U.S. Army Field Manual, sec. 2.22-3 on intelligence gathering it is stated:

Lawful Enemy Combatant: Lawful enemy combatants, who are entitled to protections under the Geneva Conventions, include members of the regular armed forces of a State Party to the conflict; militia, volunteer corps, and organized resistance movements belonging to a State Party to the conflict, which are under responsible command, wear a fixed distinctive sign recognizable at a distance, carry their arms openly, and abide by the laws of war; and members of regular armed forces who profess allegiance to a government or an authority not recognized by the detaining power.

Unlawful Enemy Combatant: Unlawful enemy combatants are persons not entitled to combatant immunity, who engage in acts against the United States or its coalition partners in violation of the laws and customs of war during an armed conflict. For the purposes of the war on terrorism, the term "unlawful enemy combatant" is defined to include, but is not limited to, an individual who is or was part of or supporting Taliban or al Qaeda forces, or associated forces that are engaged in hostilities against the United States or its coalition partners.

In the Military Commissions Act of 2006 this definition was expanded to include those who have "purposefully and materially supported hostilities against the United States," even if they had not taken part in the hostilities themselves.

One of the problems with this process has been that under international humanitarian law, specifically the Geneva Convention, if there is any doubt about the status of a person as a combatant or non-combatant, a state party to the Geneva Conventions is obligated to hold a hearing to look at the facts and determine a person's status. Article 5 of the Third GC reads:

Art 5. The present Convention shall apply to the persons referred to in Article 4 from the time they fall into the power of the enemy and until their final release and repatriation.
Should any doubt arise as to whether persons, having committed a belligerent act and having fallen into the hands of the enemy, belong to any of the categories enumerated in Article 4, such persons shall enjoy the protection of the present Convention until such time as their status has been determined by a competent tribunal.

Eventually the U.S. government set up a Combatant Status Review Tribunal to do just this. The CSRTs were established July 7, 2004 by order of U.S. Deputy Secretary of Defense after U.S. Supreme Court rulings in *Hamdi v. Rumsfeld* and *Rasul v. Bush*. Eventually, litigation and a change of administration changed all this process and even the terminology employed in this area began to change.

In 2009, the U.S. Department of Justice formally changed the designation of the Guantanamo detainees from "enemy combatant." The President announced in 2009 that his authority to detain hostile parties, like war on terrorism suspects, was based on the "Authorization for the Use of Military Force (AUMF) that Congress passed in 2001, which is "informed by principles of the laws of war." He was saying that henceforth those detained will be detained via his Congressionally mandated power and under the International Law of Armed Conflict, and designated and treated consistently under that body of law. That meant that they should no longer be referred to as "enemy combatants." They should be referred to as unlawful or unprivileged combatants. This is the implication of the phrase "informed by principles of the laws of war." This refers to making U.S. policy and practice consistent with the Law of Armed Conflict.

It must always be remembered that when discussing combatants we are discussing human beings who have inherent human dignity and whose human rights are inalienable. In any evaluation of the capture, status and treatment of combatants, whether lawful or unlawful, international human rights law applies, even during time of armed conflict and even extraterritorially wherever the U.S. exercises effective control.

This issue was raised in the U.S. national report to the OHCHR for the UPR process in 2010. See Document 86. In that report at paragraphs 82-88 the Administration explains what has changed in the U.S. law and policy on detentions and the issue of access to justice and the applicability of international law outside of the territory of the U.S. In paragraphs 82-88 the U.S. says:

The United States is currently at war with Al Qaeda and its associated forces. President Obama has made clear that the United States is fully committed to complying with the Constitution and with all applicable domestic and international law, including the laws of war, in all aspects of this or any armed conflict. We start from the premise that there are no law-free zones, and that everyone is entitled to protection under law....[E]ven as we confront a vicious adversary that abides by no rules...the United States of America must remain a standard bearer in the conduct of war."

The report does not even use the term combatants or enemy combatants. It continues, saying:

Executive Order 13491, *Ensuring Lawful Interrogations*, directed that individuals detained in any armed conflict shall in all circumstances be treated humanely and shall not be subjected to violence to life and person, nor to outrages upon personal dignity, whenever such individuals are in the custody or under the effective control of the United States Government or detained within a facility owned, operated, or controlled by the United States....

Individuals detained in armed conflict must be treated in conformity with all applicable laws, including Common Article 3 of the 1949 Geneva Conventions, which the President and the Supreme Court have recognized as providing "minimum" standards of protection in all non-international armed conflicts, including in the conflict with Al Qaeda....

As a matter of domestic law, the Obama Administration has not based its claim of authority to detain individuals at Guantánamo and in Afghanistan on the President's inherent constitutional powers, but rather on legislative authority expressly granted to the President by Congress in 2001. The Administration has expressly acknowledged that international law informs the scope of our detention authority..... Working with our Congress, we have revised our military commissions to enhance their procedural protections, including prohibiting introduction of any statements taken as a result of cruel, inhuman, or degrading treatment.

It appears at the time of writing this book that the U.S. law and policy regarding combatants and enemy combatants is changing to one involving combatants and unlawful or unprivileged combatants, which is consistent with the Law of Armed Conflict.

See Also Terms: 38, 42, 45, 48, 59, 63, 64, 70, 71, 72, 73, 86, 95, 96, 104, 110, 129, 132, 135, 137, 145, 152, 154, 164, 166, 178, 179, 181, 182, 184, 185, 192, 197, 201, 202, 203, 215, 223, 224, 251, 257, 259, 300, 313, 315, 317, 318, 319.

42. COMMAND RESPONSIBILITY

Definition: The legal principle of international humanitarian law that establishes the individual criminal responsibility of commanding officers for the war crimes and crimes against humanity committed by those under their command, where the commander had the required mental awareness of the acts of his or her subordinates. It also creates criminal liability of civilian government officials for acts committed by those in the military subordinated to them.

Significance: The international law applicable in armed conflicts, known as international humanitarian law, establishes the individual criminal responsibility of military commanders for the acts of soldiers under their command in certain situations. Normally the rule is that a commander will be responsible for the crimes of his soldiers where he "knew or should have known under the circumstances" that the wrongful acts were occurring. If he did not take steps to stop and punish such acts when he had the power and authority to do so, then the commander failed or refused to suppress or repress violations of humanitarian law. Command responsibility is a vicarious liability of commanding officers for the acts of soldiers under their command. This places a burden on commanders to know what their troops are doing and to prevent all war crimes and crimes against humanity the troops may try to commit.

If a commanding officer *orders* troops to commit acts that are war crimes or crimes against humanity, then that commander will be directly criminally responsible as a perpetrator of such international crimes. But *command* responsibility applies when the commander fails to control acts of those subordinates where the commander did not plan or order the acts, but failed to stop them when able to do so.

Command responsibility is not to be mistaken with the criminal defense of "superior orders." This defense is raised against war crimes charges by soldiers who claim they were "just following orders." Following the orders of a military superior is not a valid defense for committing a war crime; it may, however, lessen the punishment.

This principle came out of the Second World War as a result of the Nuremberg Trials and establishment of the Nuremberg Principles. See Documents 68, 70, 72 and 76. They have been articulated in certain instruments of international criminal law, such as the ICC statute and Code of Crimes against the Peace and Security of Mankind.

Under this principle the head of state, such as the president of the U.S., can be found guilty of committing international criminal offenses for the acts of those under him. It results in criminal responsibility of civilian authorities for acts of the military and other government agencies, such as the intelligence community.

In the context of the ICTY former president Milosevic was prosecuted for crimes he personally ordered, but also under the command responsibility principle for crimes committed by his military subordinates in the Bosnia conflict.

See Also Terms: 3, 8, 23, 26, 37, 38, 41, 45, 48, 63, 64, 70, 71, 73, 91, 96, 104, 110, 111, 129, 130, 132, 135, 154, 157, 159, 166, 181, 182, 185, 192, 197, 202, 222, 224, 244, 251, 259, 272, 317, 318, 319.

43. Commission on Human Rights

Definition: A former United Nations commission, no longer in existence, comprising a group of representatives of different countries that sits under ECOSOC (*Economic and Social Council*) to deal with situations involving human rights and fundamental freedoms anywhere in the world.

Significance: The Commission on Human Rights was originally established in 1946 by ECOSOC as a subsidiary or auxiliary body. It was replaced in 2006 by the Human Rights Council.

See Also Terms: 147, 173, 208, 289, 290, 308, 316, 322.

44. Commission on Security and Cooperation in Europe

Definition: A commission set up by the U.S. Congress on June 3, 1976 to monitor the activity of the Organization on Security and Cooperation in Europe (OSCE) and which is commonly referred to as the "U.S. Helsinki Commission" pursuant to Public Law No. 94-304, 90 Stat. 661 (codified as amended at 22 U.S.C. 3001-3009).

Significance: The OSCE (formerly known as the Conference on Security and Cooperation in Europe, [CSCE]) is an organization set up after World War II to deal with settling borders, repatriating refugees, and avoiding an outbreak of military hostilities between East and West. The OSCE has always had a human rights component dealing with human rights problems, especially in Central and Eastern Europe, and formerly serving as a forum for Eastern bloc–Western bloc discussions of issues, including human rights. This organization based its human rights activities on the Helsinki Accords, or Final Act, of 1975. See Document 67. It has had an increasingly important human rights and humanitarian component, developing in the 1980s and 1990s, known as the Helsinki "human dimension" mechanisms. Some of the institutions within the OSCE include an Office for Democratic Institutions and Human Rights and a High Commissioner for National Minorities; it also has several Missions in member states to mitigate conflict. This system relies on existing international human rights standards, such as the UDHR, ICCPR, and ICESCR. Moreover, the OSCE is unique in that it operates on the basis of consensus from all members states.

The U.S. Commission on Security and Cooperation in Europe is an independent federal agency that sits in the U.S. Congress. There are nine members of the U.S. Senate and nine members of the

House of Representatives, as well as a representative from the Department of Defense, Department of State, and Department of Commerce that form the commission with the chair and co-chair rotating from the Senate and House every two years. The party in power holds the chairmanship of the commission. The commission actively engages in formulation and execution of U.S. policy with respect to the OSCE by monitoring the activity of the OSCE, holding public hearings to discuss relevant issues related to the implementation of the Helsinki Act, and producing reports to Congress on their findings related to these issues and the OSCE processes. The Secretary of State is required to submit an annual report to the Commission on activities of the OSCE and U.S. policy objectives with respect to the OSCE. The commission staff and members also form part of the U.S. delegation to annual meetings of the OSCE.

See Also Terms: 3, 20, 48, 50, 70, 72, 121, 123, 124, 136, 141, 144, 145, 151, 152, 159, 160, 169, 192, 208, 211, 222, 230, 235, 236, 240, 242, 252, 259, 263, 265, 273, 278, 287, 292, 296, 297.

45. COMMON ARTICLE 3 (GENEVA CONVENTIONS)
See entry for **Geneva Conventions of 1949**

46. COMMUNICATION/COMPLAINT PROCEDURES
Definition: A set of formal legal procedures through which an individual, group, or state (or states) may submit for consideration and decision by some international human rights organ, a formal written document alleging a breach or violation by the named state of some treaty or other legal norm binding on that state for the protection of human rights. A formal written human rights complaint.

Significance: One of the ways human rights are implemented (a word used in place of "enforced") in a human rights system is a procedure or mechanism for filing formal written complaints against a state believed to have violated the legal norms of that system. Such complaints, also referred to as communications, applications, or petitions, can be filed in international human rights systems such as the U.N. Human Rights Committee and the Inter-American Commission on Human Rights. Usually this requires that the state has accepted the jurisdiction ("competence") of the particular organ to which the complaint is submitted.

The organ handling the complaint will go through a process of considering and making a decision about whether it thinks the state has committed a human rights violation as the complaining party alleges. Most often these complaint systems are established in a human rights treaty, which will establish the treaty monitoring/supervising body and set forth the procedures and conditions for filing and processing such complaints. Each human rights system has its own different complaint procedures. For example, Article 28 of the International Covenant on Civil and Political Rights (ICCPR) establishes the U.N. Human Rights Committee (HRCee) and provides for state versus state complaints in Articles 41–42. The First Optional Protocol to the ICCPR sets up procedures for individual victims to file individual complaints against a state if the state has ratified that Optional Protocol. The United States has accepted the jurisdiction of the HRCee to handle state versus state ("interstate") complaints, but has not ratified the Optional Protocol. See Documents 8, 9, 10.

These complaint procedures usually require that the complaining party has exhausted all accessible and effective legal procedures in the complainant's own national legal system before filing a complaint with the international human rights body. This is because the international human rights system is secondary, or a backup, to the human rights protection procedures every state is supposed to provide in its own national laws and procedures. Each human rights system has its own particular rules of procedure.

Some complaint systems have procedures called a request for precautionary measures. These are also sometimes called interim or preventative measures. This is a procedure whereby a petitioner requests that the forum hearing the complaint make a formal request to the respondent state to refrain from certain action which would cause irreparable injury, such as a capital punishment execution or a deportation, which would make the case ineffective or moot. It is somewhat like a request for a temporary restraining order in a case for a preliminary injunction. It is meant to preserve the status quo until the forum can decide if the State's action will violate applicable human rights norms. In some systems the request by the forum (committee, commission, court) has to be obeyed, in others it is voluntary.

In the case of *Ameziane vs. the U.S.A.* which can be found in Appendix J, one can see a petition and request for precautionary measures for a Guantanamo detainee addressed by the Inter-American Commission on Human Rights to the U.S.

The *Cherokee Nation v. United States, Soering v. United Kingdom, Haitian Centre for Human Rights v. United States,* and *Ng v. Canada* case decisions in Appendix J were rendered under international human rights communication/complaint procedures.

See Also Terms: 5, 25, 26, 47, 48, 53, 54, 55, 62, 70, 74, 76, 88, 90, 93, 94, 99, 100, 107, 112, 113, 133, 134, 145, 146, 148, 151, 162, 165, 167, 173, 175, 177, 179, 180, 187, 208, 215, 246, 252, 253, 254, 259, 267, 273, 289, 296, 297, 307.

47. COMPLEMENTARITY OF JUDICIAL SYSTEMS

Definition: A legal principle establishing the relationship between two separate judicial systems, whereby one system is meant to complement, that is, to fill in and make up for the judicial shortcomings, of the other. This is done by giving one of the judicial systems the power (jurisdiction) to decide a case the other system could not or would not handle, but should have handled.

Significance: This principle establishes the one judicial system as a backup to assure that no cases within the jurisdiction of the system would not be fully and justly handled. To "complement" means to fill out or complete something together or along with something else. As used here, complementarity refers to the relationship between an international judicial system and a national judicial system.

Complementarity between national and international judicial systems is a recognition that national court systems sometimes fail to do their job for various reasons, such as political influence, anarchy, racial or religious bias, or corruption. This term is most often seen used in the context of the permanent U.N. International Criminal Court (ICC). This Court would prosecute international crimes that are the worst human rights violations in the world and of concern to all states, such as genocide, war crimes, and crimes against humanity. The treaty (Statute) that established the Court was adopted in Rome in 1998. See Document 76. The United States was a prime supporter of the ICC and accepted the principle of complementarity. However, the United States did not vote in favor of adoption of that statute and has signed but not ratified the statute as of publication of this book. In the context of the ICC Statute, complementarity refers to the relationship between this new international criminal tribunal and domestic (national) criminal courts of states parties to the ICC Statute. This principle is set forth in Articles 1 and 17 of the ICC Statute.

Application of this principle to the ICC would mean that the ICC would be competent to prosecute cases only where states parties are genuinely unable or unwilling to prosecute. Under this principle national courts have primary jurisdiction to prosecute such international crimes and should prosecute those who commit them. The ICC is secondary. It is primarily up to the national courts to assure achievement of the goal of punishment of international crimes. When, and only when, national courts fail in this obligation does the international community bring into play the backup ICC court system. This dynamic is comparable to the principle of "primacy" of jurisdiction, where the international system takes precedence over the national one. (See, for example, the ICTY Statute, Article 9.)

If there were no such backup system, many people who commit international crimes, especially in an official capacity, would escape punishment and others would be encouraged to so the same, believing that they could escape punishment also. The international community established the

ICC primarily to end this "culture of impunity" by doing justice at the international level when national justice fails.

If the United States were to ratify the ICC Statute now that the Court is in existence, then U.S. citizens could be prosecuted by the ICC if, and only if, the United States refused to prosecute, was unable to prosecute, or the prosecution was a sham.

See Also Terms: 5, 48, 88, 93, 94, 107, 159, 181, 182, 184, 185, 253, 254, 259, 296, 306.

48. COMPLIANCE WITH HUMAN RIGHTS NORMS

Definition: Compliance refers to a state acting in a manner consistent with and according to the terms of a human rights legal standard, as contained in a treaty or in customary international law.

Significance: The goal of the international human rights movement is to establish worldwide norms based on the inherent dignity of each human being that will be recognized and upheld by all the governments of the world. If a state party signs a document and thereby agrees to uphold those norms, it is therefore expected to stay in compliance with the guidelines to which it has become bound. The state, in this way, is agreeing to become accountable to the international community for the respect of the norms. Part of that accountability involves agreeing to submit periodic reports and to be monitored regarding how well it is in compliance, or is in non compliance. Each human rights instrument has a method of monitoring compliance with human rights norms.

In reality, however, states often sign international agreements agreeing that they will comply with the norms and in fact do not carry out their promises. This often happens because of situations that make it more difficult to comply and therefore expedient to ignore the norms for a time; sometimes, states have even signed the agreements only for "public relations" purposes and their intent is not fixed on compliance at all costs. When this occurs, the government is said to "breach" the agreement.

The United States is not bound by many international human rights treaties per se, but it is bound by customary international law. Therefore, other states in the world expect the United States to be compliant with human rights norms. In the case of the ICCPR, to which the United States is fully bound, the United States follows procedures, such as yearly reports to the U.N. Human Rights Committee, to show its compliance with those norms. These reporting procedures are essential to monitoring compliance worldwide, not just in the United States. There are also special rapporteurs' reports that follow up any concerns about the compliance with the norms. Special rapporteur reports are included in this work in and in Appendices L and M.

See Also Terms: 70, 72, 144, 145, 146, 147, 151, 152, 211, 215, 222, 241, 243, 244, 259, 268, 272, 283, 286, 297, 305, 306, 307, 311, 316.

49. CONDITIONS OF DETENTION

See entry for **Detention**

50. CONFERENCE ON SECURITY AND COOPERATION IN EUROPE (CSCE)

See entry for **Organization for Security and Cooperation in Europe (OSCE)**. In 1994, the former Conference on Security and Cooperation in Europe changed its name to Organization for Security and Cooperation in Europe, now abbreviated OSCE.

51. CONSCIENTIOUS OBJECTION

Definition: This term refers to the objection of an individual to being forced to do any act, for or on behalf of the state, when the act is against the person's firmly held religious, moral, or ethical beliefs. Although it is commonly used to refer to objection to doing military service or fighting in a particular armed conflict, this term applies to a person's objection to any public act mandated by law on the basis that it is against a person's personal conscience and to the person's refusal to do it.

Significance: Within certain limits, a government cannot force a person to act against his or her deep-seated beliefs, especially religious-based beliefs. The right to conscientious objection as to military service is the most common form of conscientious objection, though this term can apply to any situation in which one refuses to do something the government asks because of a belief in its wrongfulness based on a moral or religious belief. Article 18 of the ICCPR has been interpreted by the Human Rights Committee as allowing for conscientious objection. This interpretation is found in General Comment 22 on Freedom of Thought, Conscience and Religion under Article 18 of the ICCPR (Document 12, and ICCPR Article 18, Document 8).

See Also Terms: 11, 12, 18, 20, 24, 33, 34, 72, 122, 123, 124, 144, 145, 152, 177, 179, 184, 195, 249, 259, 283, 287, 323.

52. CONVENTION

Definition: A convention is an international treaty instrument. It is an international contract between more than two states that is governed by international law. Most international human rights norms are set forth in international legal instruments entitled "Convention on...."

Significance: Examples of conventions include the Convention on the Elimination of All Forms of Racial Discrimination (Document 23), the Convention on the Elimination of All Forms of Discrimination against Women (Document 27), Genocide Convention (Document 17), Convention against Torture (Document 19), Convention on the Rights of the Child (Document 28), Geneva Conventions (Documents 72), Refugee Convention (Document 36), and the Hague Convention IV (Document 69).

See Also Terms: 2, 11, 20, 21, 25, 26, 33, 45, 46, 48, 53, 54, 55, 56, 62, 70, 80, 88, 92, 93, 94, 98, 114, 122, 124, 129, 130, 136, 144, 145, 147, 150, 151, 152, 154, 158, 165, 167, 168, 172, 173, 174, 175, 177, 184, 185, 186, 187, 192, 198, 206, 208, 215, 220, 222, 225, 226, 229, 233, 242, 244, 245, 247, 258, 259, 262, 264, 268, 269, 272, 279, 280, 282, 291, 293, 297, 306, 307, 311, 316.

53. CONVENTION AGAINST TORTURE, CRUEL, INHUMAN OR DEGRADING TREATMENT OR PUNISHMENT

(Also known as the Torture Convention or CAT)

Definition: An international human rights treaty adopted in the United Nations in 1984 and open for ratification by all countries in the world, whose object is to recognize the human right held by everyone to protection of his or her mental and physical integrity and well-being. Its purpose is to provide legal protection for the individual against acts of torture and cruel, inhuman, and degrading treatment or punishment.

Significance: The United States signed this treaty in April 1988, but it took until November 1994 for the Senate to ratify it. The U.S. ratification was subject to reservations, declarations, and understandings.

See Also Terms: 3, 6, 10, 20, 24, 33, 34, 48, 49, 58, 59, 60, 63, 67, 70, 71, 73, 81, 96, 104, 111, 117, 124, 129, 132, 133, 136, 144, 145, 151, 152, 159, 160, 161, 167, 177, 179, 182, 184, 185, 222, 226, 234, 238, 244, 248, 256, 259, 266, 272, 275, 279, 280, 283, 289, 290, 293, 294, 297, 302, 303, 306, 308, 309, 310, 316, 317, 318, 319, 320.

54. CONVENTION ON THE ELIMINATION OF ALL FORMS OF DISCRIMINATION AGAINST WOMEN (CEDAW)

Definition: An international human rights treaty adopted in the United Nations in 1979 and open for ratification by all countries in the world, whose object is to establish legal protection under international law for women, so that they can achieve full enjoyment of all human rights without discrimination based on being female. It is usually called the Women's Convention or CEDAW. See Document 27.

Significance: The United States signed this treaty in July 17, 1980. As of the publication of this work, the United States had not yet ratified it.

See Also Terms: 3, 6, 20, 25, 33, 35, 48, 69, 70, 86, 98, 93, 100, 115, 124, 125, 126, 144, 147, 150, 151, 160, 167, 169, 177, 179, 184, 185, 193, 216, 222, 226, 238, 244, 249, 262, 268, 269, 270, 272, 279, 280, 283, 291, 293, 297, 306, 307, 316, 322, 323.

55. CONVENTION ON THE ELIMINATION OF ALL FORMS OF RACIAL DISCRIMINATION (ICERD)

Definition: An international human rights treaty adopted in the United Nations in 1954 and open for ratification by all states in the world, whose objective is to recognize human rights under international law to protect persons of all racial groups and whose purpose is to eliminate discrimination against anyone, individually or as a group, on the basis of that person's or group's race. In this treaty the term "race" is defined expansively to include "color, descent, or national or ethnic origin." This instrument is sometimes abbreviated ICERD. See Document 23.

Significance: The United States signed this treaty in September 1966, but it took until November 1994 for the Senate to ratify it. See Document 24. The ratification was subject to reservations, declarations, and understandings.

See Also Terms: 3, 6, 7, 14, 15, 20, 22, 24, 28, 33, 34, 35, 46, 48, 59, 60, 70, 72, 75, 78, 86, 87, 93, 97, 98, 100, 107, 122, 124, 126, 139, 140, 144, 147, 150, 151, 160, 165, 167, 169, 177, 179, 182, 184, 185, 188, 205, 216, 220, 222, 226, 233, 235, 237, 238, 252, 255, 259, 260, 261, 262, 268, 269, 270, 272, 277, 280, 283, 291, 293, 297, 306, 307, 316, 324.

56. CONVENTION ON THE PREVENTION AND PUNISHMENT OF THE CRIME OF GENOCIDE

See entry for **Genocide/Genocide Convention**

57. CONVENTION ON THE RIGHTS OF THE CHILD (CRC)

(Also known as the Children's Convention or CRC)

Definition: An international human rights treaty adopted in the United Nations in 1989 and open for ratification by all states of the world, whose object is to recognize certain human rights held by children under international law. The purpose of this treaty is to protect the children of this world, primarily from abuse and exploitation, and to allow development of their maximum potential as human beings. It does this by an attempt to balance the rights of the children, of their parents, and of the state.

Significance: This convention is the most broadly ratified human rights treaty ever, having been ratified by 191 states as of September 1999. See Document 28. The United States signed it in 1995 but the Senate has not ratified it as of November 4, 2010. There are two amendments (Protocols) to the CRC; the first one being non-involvement of children in armed conflict ("OP-CRC-AC"). The U.S. has signed (2000) and ratified (2002) this Protocol. It is aimed at preventing "child soldiers;" the second Protocol covers the sale of children, child prostitution and child pornography (OP-CRC-SC). The U.S. has signed and ratified this Protocol. See Documents 29, 30, 31 and 32. Thus, the U.S. is bound by the two protocols to the CRC, even though not bound by the CRC itself. The U.S. does have to submit periodic reports to the Committee on the Rights of the Child under these Protocols.

See Also Terms: 6, 20, 21, 32, 33, 34, 36, 38, 41, 48, 58, 69, 70, 81, 86, 93, 98, 115, 124, 125, 126, 144, 145, 149, 150, 151, 152, 160, 167, 169, 177, 184, 185, 192, 204, 220, 222, 225, 226, 229, 233, 236, 244, 252, 259, 262, 265, 268, 269, 272, 280, 282, 283, 287, 291, 293, 297, 304, 306, 307, 309, 316.

58. CORPORAL PUNISHMENT

Definition: The intentional infliction of physical harm upon the body of a person, usually as punishment for acts committed.

Significance: Human rights law requires that everyone be treated as a human being, possessing inherent human dignity. This dignity requires respect for the physical and psychological well-being of persons. Under international human rights law generally, corporal punishment is not permissible. More specifically, only when corporal punishment crosses a not-well-defined line of severity and cruelty can it be considered a human rights violation when done by someone in government or with the consent or collusion of government. Human rights law certainly argues for a minimum use of such punishment. This is a delicate and controversial issue.

Whether corporal punishment is a human rights violation depends on who is committing the act, the reason it was committed, the kind and extent of the act, and the injury, if any, suffered by the victim. For example, it is not unlawful for parents to inflict corporal punishment upon their children as a tool of discipline, so long as it is not harmful to the child and does not constitute child abuse under the law. Even though there may be extenuating circumstances for corporal punishment, some argue that all corporal punishment, whether inflicted against children or adults, is cruel and inhuman treatment and thus a human rights violation. Corporal punishment of prisoners is prohibited under human rights law. States have a positive obligation to see that corporal punishment beyond reasonable limits is prescribed, prevented and prosecuted, particularly relating to children.

Police brutality most often consists of acts of corporal punishment. Corporal punishment is usually done as a means of punishing a wrongdoer for unacceptable behavior or for teaching discipline against further wrongdoing, often as an example to others. It is meant to inflict pain and suffering upon the person punished. Whipping, caning, spanking, or beatings are examples of acts of corporal punishment.

When such acts are found to constitute torture or cruel or inhuman punishment they cross the line and become human rights violations. Article 5 of the UDHR and Article 7 of the ICCPR state that no one shall be subjected to torture or cruel, inhuman, or degrading treatment or punishment. See Documents 6, 8. Historically, these human rights provisions got their source from the Eighth Amendment to the U.S. Constitution, the prohibition against cruel and unusual punishment.

The Conventions against Torture would require the state to prohibit and prosecute acts of corporal punishment which would rise to the level of harm referred in the definition of torture or cruel, inhuman or degrading treatment. See Documents 19 and 21, para 124.

See Also Terms: 11, 12, 20, 24, 32, 33, 48, 65, 66, 70, 96, 104, 124, 144, 145, 151, 152, 165, 167, 169, 170, 171, 177, 179, 184, 185, 192, 221, 222, 224, 272, 302, 309.

59. COUNTERTERRORISM MEASURES

Definition: All measures taken by a state to detect, surveil, interdict, terminate and deter any threat or act or conspiracy to commit acts or threats of terrorism. (See entry for Terrorism). These include administrative, political, military, intelligence, police and civilian measures.

Significance: Since 9/11 and the start of the war on terrorism the U.S. and many other countries of the world have been ramping up measures to protect people from terrorism. Examples of counter terrorism measures are airport baggage and body checks, phone tapping, data mining, individual surveillance, unmanned drone reconnaissance and attack missions.

Any measures taken by the U.S. to counter terrorism must be tailored to address and counter only acts that are within the definition of terrorism. The U.S. has established a definition of terrorism for American law. However, it must be remembered that there is no internationally accepted definition of the term terrorism. There is a definition found in U.S. criminal law which would apply to acts and threats of terrorism coming within the scope of U.S. law. That law does not cover all terrorist acts anywhere just because they have something to do with the U.S. Strictly speaking, in the international arena the U.S. cannot act against "terrorism" because the U.S. cannot define terrorism in the international arena. However, the U.S. and most of the rest of the international community have been acting in concert against terrorism outside of U.S. national interests even without an accepted international definition because of the perceived need of all nations for security and stability.

The U.S. cannot take any measures it chooses in its fight to counter terrorism. Any and all measures taken by the U.S. in the international arena must be consistent with international human rights law, humanitarian law, refugee law, and international criminal law. Outside of the jurisdiction of the United States, the U.S. government cannot unilaterally define what is or is not terrorism and determine the lawfulness of its actions. International standards apply because the U.S. has consented to these standards for just such situation as these. If and when the international community can agree on a definition of terrorism then the U.S. may act consistent with such definition in the international arena.

Much of the criticism of the U.S. in the years shortly following 9/11 was that the U.S. was itself deciding what was and was not terrorism, who was or was not a terrorist or unlawful combatant and whether measures it was taking, such as waterboarding, were consistent with its international human rights and humanitarian law obligations. The U.S. took an extremely narrow view of its international legal obligations which gave it the most power and leeway to act, considering the fight against terror as one involving survival of the nation.

Much of the foreign criticism of U.S. counter-terrorism measures came in the context of the United Nations. The U.N. has sought to call the U.S. to comply with its international legal obligations included in the U.N. Charter. In 2010 the U.N. General Assembly passed a resolution (A/RES/64/168) about compliance of counter measures with international law. See Document 55. The General Assembly, of which the U.S. is a member, stated:

Stressing that all measures used in the fight against terrorism, including the profiling of individuals and the use of diplomatic assurances, memorandums of understanding and other transfer agreements or arrangements, must be in compliance with the obligations of States under international law, including international human rights, refugee and humanitarian law,

Recalling Article 30 of the Universal Declaration of Human Rights, and reaffirming that acts, methods and practices of terrorism in all its forms and manifestations are activities aimed at the destruction of human rights, fundamental freedoms and democracy, threatening the territorial integrity and security of States and destabilizing legitimately constituted Governments, and that the international community should take the necessary steps to enhance cooperation to prevent and combat terrorism,

Reaffirming its unequivocal condemnation of all acts, methods and practices of terrorism in all its forms and manifestations, wherever and by whomsoever committed, regardless of their motivation, as criminal and unjustifiable, and renewing its commitment to strengthen international cooperation to prevent and combat terrorism,

Recognizing that respect for all human rights, respect for democracy and respect for the rule of law are interrelated and mutually reinforcing,

Reaffirming that terrorism cannot and should not be associated with any religion, nationality, civilization or ethnic group,

Emphasizing the importance of properly interpreting and implementing the obligations of States with respect to torture and other cruel, inhuman or degrading treatment or punishment, and of abiding strictly by the definition of torture contained in Article 1 of the Convention against Torture and Other Cruel, Inhuman or Degrading Treatment or Punishment, in the fight against terrorism,

Recalling its resolutions 57/219 of 18 December 2002, ...and other relevant resolutions and decisions of the General Assembly, the Commission on Human Rights and the Strategy, adopted on 8 September 2006, 11 reaffirming that the promotion and protection of human rights for all and the rule of law are essential to the fight against terrorism, recognizing that effective counter-terrorism measures and the protection of human rights are not conflicting goals but complementary and mutually reinforcing, and stressing the need to promote and protect the rights of victims of terrorism,

Reaffirms that States must ensure that any measure taken to combat terrorism complies with their obligations under international law, in particular international human rights, refugee and humanitarian law....

(Full text at Document 55.)

For several years the U.N. Security Council, of which the U.S. is a permanent member, has spoken out generally on such measures, as they relate to international peace and security. In a Security Council President's Statement issued in 2010, (S/PRST/2010/11) in connection with the Council's consideration of the item entitled "The promotion and strengthening of the rule of law in the maintenance of international peace and security," the Council President made the following statement on behalf of the Council:

"The Security Council reaffirms its commitment to the Charter of the United Nations and international law, and to an international order based on the rule of law and international law, which is essential for peaceful coexistence and cooperation among States in addressing common challenges, thus contributing to the maintenance of international peace and security.

"The Security Council recognizes that respect for international humanitarian law is an essential component of the rule of law in conflict situations and reaffirms its conviction that the protection of the civilian population in armed conflict should be an important aspect of any comprehensive strategy to resolve conflict and recalls in this regard resolution 1894 (2009).

"The Security Council reaffirms its strong opposition to impunity for serious violations of international humanitarian law and human rights law. The Security Council further emphasizes the responsibility of States to comply with their relevant obligations to end impunity and to thoroughly investigate and prosecute persons responsible for war crimes, genocide, crimes against humanity or other serious violations of international humanitarian law in order to prevent violations, avoid their recurrence and seek sustainable peace, justice, truth and reconciliation.

"The Security Council expresses its commitment to ensure that all U.N. efforts to restore peace and security themselves respect and promote the rule of law. The Council recognizes that sustainable peace building requires an integrated approach, which strengthens coherence between political, security, development, human rights and rule of law activities." (Full text at Document 56.)

All human rights norms in the treaties and customary norms to which the U.S. is obligated to comply were initially drafted or established taking into account the needs of governments to deal with issues including national emergencies. In theory, at least, they constituted a fair balance of protection of maximum freedom for individuals, with provisions in the limitations clauses and derogation clause (see ICCR Article 4) to allow the state to meet any pressing social need, up to and including terrorism. The United States has not declared a period of derogation during the war on terrorism and so it must meet all obligations under every human rights norm under the ICCPR, and all other treaty norms not subject to derogation. And even if it declares a derogation it still has to respect the many non-derogable rights in the ICCPR, and apply those rights legitimately derogated in a nondiscriminatory manner. This includes all counter-terrorism measures.

In its 2010 national UPR report to the OHCHR, the Administration addresses the issue of U.S. compliance with domestic and international law in its counter terrorism measures. See Document 86, paras. 82 to 91. With regards to those persons detained in the war on terrorism and the U.S. treatment of those detainees see Enhanced Interrogation Techniques, below.

See Also Terms: 1, 3, 16, 17, 24, 33, 34, 35, 40, 41, 45, 48, 49, 3, 55, 65, 66, 70, 71, 78, 81, 82, 84, 85, 96, 88, 90, 93, 95, 96, 100, 103, 104, 106, 109, 110, 111, 113, 117, 122, 124, 129, 132, 134, 135, 136, 137, 142, 144, 145, 147, 151, 152, 154, 157, 159, 160, 161, 162, 164, 166, 167, 170, 171, 177, 178, 179, 181, 182, 184, 185, 192, 193, 194, 195, 196, 201, 202, 203, 210, 211, 215, 216, 219, 221, 222, 223, 224, 226, 230, 232, 243, 251, 252, 254, 255, 256, 257, 259, 260, 261, 265, 266, 272, 273, 275, 276, 283, 289, 290, 292, 294, 295, 298, 299, 300, 302, 305, 308, 309, 311, 313, 314, 315, 316, 317, 318, 320, 321, 323.

60. COUNTRY REPORTS

Definition: The Department of State's annual work entitled "Country Reports on Human Rights Practices," is a detailed report prepared by the U.S. Department of State, Bureau of Human Rights, Democracy and Labor, and presented to the Senate Foreign Relations Committee and the House Committee on Foreign Affairs to assist those law-making bodies in U.S. foreign policy and foreign aid. It is updated and presented each year. It is a report of the human rights record of almost every country in the world. See Documents 82, 83.

Significance: A country report is prepared from information supplied to the Department of State by U.S. consulates and embassies, which have human rights officers compiling such information from various sources, such as newspapers, churches, NGOs, and labor unions.

Country reports serve as a primary source of information for many federal departmental bodies, such as immigration courts. The level of U.S. military and foreign economic development aid is based largely upon each state's human rights record. It is important that these reports be made and kept up-to-date because they directly affect the ongoing relationship of the United States with other countries in the world whose human rights conditions may be changing for better or worse.

See Also Terms: 20, 29, 48, 61, 70, 112, 119, 124, 144, 145, 150, 151, 177, 184, 185, 206, 215, 222, 227, 268, 286, 292, 306.

61. COUNTRY-SPECIFIC LEGISLATION

Definition: A law passed by Congress aimed at one particular country in response to its human rights violations and aimed at causing some harm or denying some benefit to that state to encourage it to improve its human rights record.

Significance: The U.S. seeks to improve human rights worldwide by passing both general human rights legislation and country-specific legislation. Country-specific legislation is usually made in response to a specific call by public groups for country-specific measures because of certain specific human rights violations. The measure is usually based on what is deemed appropriate for that country (e.g., Cuba, North Korea), such as instituting a trade embargo, freezing assets in bank accounts, or prohibiting U.S. investment or travel there. The Cuban Democracy Act referred to in Appendix I, Selected U.S. Human Rights Legislation, is an example of country-specific legislation.

See Also Terms: 3, 9, 29, 48, 70, 119, 121, 128, 138, 151, 184, 185, 190, 194, 199, 206, 211, 214, 215, 218, 259, 272, 273, 283, 286, 292.

62. COVENANT

Definition: A covenant is an international legal instrument, a treaty, which sets forth specific, enumerated human rights norms and usually also establishes a supervisory organ (court, commission, committee) to implement the norms by assuring compliance by state parties. See entry for Treaty/International Instrument.

Significance: The two main international human rights documents are called the International Covenant on Civil and Political Rights (ICCPR) and the International Covenant on Economic,

Social, and Cultural Rights (ICESCR). See Documents 8, 16. The ICCPR sets forth most of the generally accepted civil and political human rights. The ICESCR sets forth economic, social, and cultural rights. These two documents are the offspring of the UDHR, which was the initial international statement identifying human rights. See Document 6. Covenant means a promise. A covenant is a treaty, or a contract between more than two different countries, wherein each country promises ("covenants") that it will respect and ensure that everyone respects the human rights of those who are in its territory and therefore are subject to its legal authority or its laws.

The U.S. signed the ICCPR in 1977, and the Senate ratified it in 1992, making it U.S. law. Although the ICESCR was signed in 1977, it has not yet been ratified by the Senate. Until approximately 1993, the United States did not accept all the economic rights described in that covenant as legitimate human rights, at least in the manner in which the covenant wished the state to institute them.

See Also Terms: 3, 6, 20, 25, 26, 48, 52, 80, 88, 93, 98, 114, 124, 144, 145, 151, 167, 175, 279, 280, 291, 293, 297, 306, 307.

63. CRIMES AGAINST HUMANITY

Definition: A group of crimes that the international community of nations has declared to be criminal offenses against the whole human race because they shock the conscience of all mankind and are an affront to humanity. They are such acts as murder, extermination, genocide, enslavement, deportation, and other serious inhuman acts against civilians or the civilian population.

Significance: The international criminal norms known as "crimes against humanity" create international criminal responsibility on individuals under international law for certain horrendous acts of violence against human beings. The philosophical basis in common for this type of crime is a violation of the inherent dignity of individual human beings on a massive or widespread scale in a manner so abhorrent to a civilized world that they threaten the peace and stability of the whole human race. This class of international crime was first established as such in the Nuremberg Charter (London Charter) of 1945, which established the crimes punishable against defeated Nazis in the famous Nuremberg trials. The charter also set forth those acts that constituted war crimes and crimes against peace. The United States helped establish the Nuremberg Tribunal, and U.S. prosecutors and judges participated in the prosecution and judgment of crimes against humanity in those trials. In the charter these crimes were connected to war crimes or crimes against peace before or during an armed conflict.

At the time of these trials genocide was not a separate international crime. It was, however, covered under the heading of crimes against humanity. After the Nuremberg trials the United Nations declared crimes against humanity to be customary international law, binding on all states.

Because the Holocaust of World War II was one of the major catalysts for the modern international human rights movement, the concept of crimes against humanity is essential to comprehend. This is so even though genocide developed into a separate crime and was made into a treaty called the Genocide Convention. Crimes against humanity are actually a certain level of human rights violations that, when committed, engage international criminal responsibility for those who commit or cause these acts.

Currently these same international criminal norms serve as a legal basis for the crimes under the jurisdiction of the recent International Criminal Tribunals for the Former Yugoslavia and for Rwanda. They are also included in the jurisdiction of the International Criminal Court established under the United Nations in 1998, where no connection to armed conflict is necessary. They are now considered to be binding as customary international law. This crime is found in Article 18 of the Draft Code of Crimes against the Peace and Security of Mankind, 1996, which is considered a codification of customary international law. See Document 68.

See Also Terms: 3, 15, 19, 40, 48, 53, 56, 70, 71, 72, 73, 101, 110, 111, 117, 124, 130, 133, 143, 144, 145, 151, 152, 153, 157, 159, 164, 166, 170, 177, 179, 181, 182, 184, 185, 192, 200, 213, 215, 221, 222, 223, 224, 235, 256, 259, 260, 265, 271, 272, 275, 281, 283, 291, 292, 294, 298, 302, 308, 309, 310, 316.

64. CRIMES AGAINST PEACE

Definition: An international crime, crimes against peace is the planning, ordering, preparing, conspiring, initiating, and waging of an unjustified armed conflict against another state, also referred to as aggression.

Significance: Crimes against peace is usually known as the crime of aggression. It was articulated as an international crime at the 1945 Nuremberg trials and was based on international customary law set forth in Article 6 of the London Charter, which served as the basis of the Nuremberg trials. Under it, certain Nazi military and civilian leaders were prosecuted and punished under international law for the Nazi military action against other countries. It is considered binding as a matter of customary international law. The international community has not been able to more fully define this crime.

Until the 2010, new compromise definition by the Assembly of States Parties of the ICC, the international community used U.N. General Assembly Resolution 3314, which was an unsatisfactory and unsuccessful definition. That resolution described acts of aggression as "the most serious and dangerous form of the illegal use of force, being fraught, in the conditions created by the existence of all types of weapons of mass destruction, with the possible threat of a world conflict and all its catastrophic consequences," and defined the international crime of aggression as "the use of armed force by a State against the sovereignty, territorial integrity or political independence of another State, or in any other manner inconsistent with the Charter of the United Nations, as set out in this Definition."

This international crime along with the Nuremberg Principles establishes individual criminal responsibility under international law and gives rise to universal jurisdiction, meaning that any state in the world has jurisdiction to prosecute the perpetrators of crimes against peace.

It was alleged that NATO countries in their bombing of Yugoslavia in early 1999, regarding Kosovo, were committing acts of aggression constituting international crimes. The U.N. charter, Article 2.4, prohibits the use, or threat to use, force against the political independence or territorial integrity of other states and is seen as the prohibition against aggression (crimes against peace) in the U.N. Charter. See Document 5.

The international crime of aggression was included, but not defined, in the 1998 Rome Statute because the states could not agree on a definition. It was too politically charged. The 1998 Statute made reference to such crime to be later defined by the states parties. See document 76. However, as of 2010, it has finally been defined. The Assembly of State Parties finally defined this crime for ICC purposes in 2010 in Kampala, Uganda. This crime is scheduled to be one of the crimes within the jurisdiction of the International Criminal Court starting in 2017. The major issue in the definition of this crime has been the role of the U.N. Security Council, which, under the U.N. Charter, has the sole authority to determine when an "act of aggression" has occurred. The new definition is set forth in the document section. See Document 77.

With this newly defined crime soon within the jurisdiction of the ICC, the international community hopes to deter and prevent acts of aggression, and all the international crimes they spawn, by creating fear of prosecution and punishment for an international crime. This crime is of great importance to the U.S. because of its extensive military activity all over the world.

See Also Terms: 3, 8, 42, 48, 70, 72, 73, 133, 135, 137, 143, 144, 145, 151, 152, 154, 159, 166, 177, 181, 182, 185, 192, 197, 201, 202, 210, 215, 222, 223, 224, 230, 59, 271, 272, 273, 276, 287, 295, 306, 308, 309, 323.

65. CRUEL AND UNUSUAL PUNISHMENT

See entry for **Cruel or Unusual Treatment or Punishment**

66. CRUEL OR UNUSUAL TREATMENT OR PUNISHMENT

Definition: The infliction of pain or suffering by the state in a manner devoid of human feeling, causing injury, fear, or grief, in violation of the human dignity of the victim.

Significance: This term is usually seen in human rights treaty norms, along with acts of torture and inhuman or degrading treatment or punishment. The first major human rights norm was found in Article 5 of the UDHR.

These all represent different levels of severity of treatment or punishment. Cruel treatment and cruel punishment are different. If the cruel acts are not being done for purposes of the punishment of the victim for a prior act, such as for some kind of a violation (criminal or otherwise), then the term "cruel treatment" is used. If the cruel acts were done for purposes of punishing the victim for his prior conduct, such as for a criminal conviction, then the term "cruel punishment" is used.

Both cruel treatment and cruel punishment are inconsistent with a victim's inherent human dignity and are human rights violations. Article 7 of the ICCPR states: "No one shall be subjected to torture or to cruel, inhuman or degrading treatment or punishment." See Document 8.

The United States submitted a reservation to its ratification of the ICCPR to the effect that the terms "torture, cruel, inhuman and degrading treatment or punishment" would be interpreted consistent with the 5th, 8th, and 14th amendments to the U.S. Constitution, which offer somewhat less protection than Article 7 of the ICCPR, as interpreted by the Human Rights Committee. The United States has stated its law and practice as to cruel treatment or punishment under ICCPR, Article 7, in its first, second and third reports to the Human Rights Committee. See Document 15A, Second and Third reports.

The United States has also ratified the U.N. Convention against Torture, Cruel and Degrading Treatment and Punishment, which deals with "cruel treatment or punishment." This instrument is the more expansive definition of the term cruel treatment or punishment. A recent extensive report by the U.S. State Department to the U.N. Committee against Torture sets forth U.S. law and practice on this topic. See Documents 19, 21A, B, and C.

This concept originally came from the eighth amendment of the U.S. Constitution, which speaks of "cruel and unusual punishment." See Document 2. From the perspective of the U.S., the concept of "cruel punishment" is important internationally as it relates to the practice of capital punishment. Since a majority of countries internationally are no longer practicing capital punishment, the U.S. is under more scrutiny and criticism from the international community, especially if the extradition of criminals to the United States to face the death penalty is involved.

As mentioned above in the definition of "capital punishment," the U.S. death penalty system has been an issue in several international cases outside the United States. In the famous *Soering Case (Soering v. UK)* (see Selected Case Decisions, Appendix J), the European Court of Human Rights found that if the UK were to extradite a young murder suspect from the UK to Virginia where he would face the famous "death row syndrome," it would violate his rights against cruel and inhuman punishment under the European Convention on Human Rights. This case gave rise thereafter to many cases regarding extradition or forced return to the United States to face the so called "death row syndrome."

Domestically, many advocates of the abolition of the death penalty claim such punishment should be abolished because it is cruel and inhuman punishment. The U.S. Supreme Court ruled in the cases of *Knight vs. Florida* and *Moore vs. Nebraska* that the death row phenomenon was not cruel and unusual punishment in violation of the U.S. Constitution where the delay was caused by the defendant's appeals. However in 2005 (*Roper vs. Simmons*) the Supreme Court found that capital punishment of those who committed crimes as a minor constituted cruel and unusual punishment, as in 2010 (*Graham vs. Florida*) where life sentences were imposed on minors who committed no capital offenses. See Appendix J.

In determining whether a practice is cruel and unusual punishment in American constitutional law the courts look to see if there is a national consensus of jurisdictions on the practice. If so they will rule accordingly. They may also look at international law and practice to see if there is an international consensus and factor that in as relevant evidence but not legally binding. (See *Graham vs. Florida*, Appendix J).

67. CULTURAL GENOCIDE

See entry for **Genocide/Genocide Convention**

68. CULTURAL HUMAN RIGHTS

Definition: A category of human rights that in general protects a human being's right to personal development and participation in the cultural life of one's own group and the larger society.

Significance: There is no widely accepted definition of cultural human rights. They are part of the what used to be called "second generation" human rights, along with economic and social human rights. Even the term "culture" has no generally accepted meaning in human rights though there is movement towards a definition. It has been defined as the integrated pattern of human knowledge, belief, and behavior that depends upon humanity's capacity for learning and transmitting knowledge to succeeding generations.

Another definition is a set of shared attitudes, values, goals and practices that characterize a society. Still another: the customary beliefs, social forms, language, art, and material traits of a racial, religious or social group.

Various aspects of cultural life relevant to human rights can be seen in the following goals of cultural rights:

1. Preserving and nurturing one's own cultural identity, language and customs, that is, the customary beliefs, social forms and material traits of a racial, religious or social group.

2. Obtaining education necessary to develop intellectual and moral faculties and acquiring the knowledge necessary for earning a living.

3. Sharing in scientific advancement.

4. Protection of one's own moral and material interests in scientific literacy or artistic productions, such as with patents and copyrights.

5. Obtaining of information, training and knowledge for the enjoyment of cultural values and cultural property. This goal refers to acquainting oneself with, and developing a taste in, fine arts, humanities and the broad aspects of science, as distinguished from gaining vocational and technical skills.

The ICESCR, Articles 13–15, lists the major cultural human rights. The ICCPR, Article 27, includes the rights of racial, religious and linguistic minority groups to enjoy their culture. See Documents 8, 16.

69. CULTURAL RELATIVISM

Definition: A philosophy of human rights that says that human rights can be interpreted and practiced by different societies in different ways depending on culture and religion, etc. It means that there are no absolute and universally applicable rights.

Significance: The great debate in the world of human rights is between states that say that all human rights are universal and applied in the same way to everyone, everywhere, and those who say they are relative to the culture in which they are used. Cultural relativism means that one would have to look at a state's human rights practices in light of its distinguishing characteristics, such as religion, customs, mores and political ideology. Under this philosophy, human rights mean whatever a particular society says they mean. This attitude is considered a danger to the consistent compliance with international standards for human rights. Mainly, states like China, the Muslim states, and the Developing World states claim this philosophy. It is used as a defense against a claim of human rights violations, but it is not a valid defense.

The predominant philosophy today is universality: that human rights are universal, applying everywhere, to everyone, in the same way. This philosophy was affirmed in the 1993 Vienna Declaration and Programme of Action.

See Also Terms: 94, 115, 124, 125, 126, 184, 186, 236, 237, 259, 312, 316, 322, 323.

70. CULTURE OF HUMAN RIGHTS

Definition: A generally held social attitude that sees all members of society, indeed all human beings, as possessing inherent human dignity and, as a result, as holding inalienable human rights which the government must respect and protect.

Significance: The international human rights movement of the second half of the 20th century has been seeking to replace intolerance, discrimination, hate crimes, hate speech and attitudes of human superiority or nationalism with attitudes that see human beings primarily as individuals inhabiting this world and not so much as members of a certain society, state, ethnic, religious or linguistic group. It seeks to establish legal standards for the limitation of government power toward human beings. It seeks to prevent abuses of power by the state. This culture of human rights was a term coined in the late 1990s to describe the goal of human rights education, particularly in the context of the United Nations, which declared 1995–2004 to be the "Decade of Human Rights Education."

See Also Terms: 3, 4, 11, 12, 28, 48, 67, 71, 72, 78, 87, 89, 91, 100, 119, 120, 122, 124, 139, 140, 142, 144, 145, 147, 148, 149, 152, 166, 167, 168, 169, 172, 174, 177, 179, 180, 181, 184, 185, 195, 216, 230, 237, 252, 253, 271, 272, 291, 305, 308, 309, 311, 316, 317, 318, 323.

71. CULTURE OF IMPUNITY

Definition: An attitude or perception held by most persons that someone can commit human rights violations, even on a massive and systematic scale, and suffer no legal or other negative consequences for their acts. It also refers to the attitude of those persons committing such violations, who believe that they will never be caught and held accountable, either in their own country or in an international forum, for committing such acts.

Significance: Human rights violations very often happen because those who commit them believe that they will never be caught, held accountable and punished for committing them. They may believe that the government will shield them from personal responsibility since they acted on behalf of the government. Or, they may believe that there is no political will or ability of the state or the legal system, or of the international community, to come after them to hold them accountable. Over the last half of the 20th century this attitude flourished because people saw horrible atrocities take place and nothing seemed to be done about them, even by the international community with all its human rights rhetoric. Gross violators such as Idi Amin, Pol Pot, Papa Doc Duvalier, Sadaam Hussein, and Radovan Karadzic all seemed to have violated the international norms for human rights but never really seemed to be promptly caught and punished for the horrible things they did. This led to the common perception that impunity for human rights violations was just "the way it is" in this world, so why try to stop human rights violations? Now we know that Hussein got his due and Karadzic is in proceedings before the ICTY, meeting accountability head-on in court.

The human rights movement, both governmental and nongovernmental, has been seeking to establish legal standards and institutions for eliminating the culture of impunity so that no one will think they can commit violations with impunity. Even in the United States, the government continues to discover war criminals from WW II living in this country, and is trying to deport them. It is trying to show that even 60 plus years after they committed human rights violations they can, should, and must be held accountable. This is doing justice. The international community has determined that the greatest way to combat the culture of impunity is to educate people about human rights. This is aimed at replacing the culture of impunity with the so-called "culture of human rights," where there is a rule of law society with accountability of everybody and punishment and reparation for violations.

Much U.S. activity and legislation is seeking to combat this culture of impunity. See, for example, the Torture Victim Protection Act and War Crimes Act of 1996 in Documents 97 and 104, and the case of *Kadic v. Karadzic* in Appendix J. At the same time the United States is criticized by many for failing to take certain actions which would go far toward making the threat of punishment more effective against present and future violators. For example, in Bosnia the United States was accused of not doing enough to capture and bring to justice certain indicted war criminals, such as Karadzic and Radko Mladic.

Sometimes the United States is accused not so much of inaction, but of inconsistency or of having a double standard. They are accused of going effectively after certain violators, but not after certain other equally guilty violators, usually because of political or military considerations.

The U.N. international criminal tribunals on the former Yugoslavia and on Rwanda are examples of international organs which the United States has helped establish and fund with a view toward combating impunity. The new International Criminal Court, whose Statute was adopted in the United Nations by a 120 to 7 vote, is the most serious effort of the international community to combat the culture of impunity as regards the most serious human rights violations such as genocide, war crimes and crimes against humanity. The United States wants to see this process succeed, but voted against the Statute because it did not like parts of the Statute. It has been participating as much as it can from the sidelines and the ICC is allowing its input because of its importance to the success of such an international organ. The court is up and running and processing cases.

Slowly, the culture of impunity is giving way to a growing culture of human rights, which breeds a culture of accountability of everyone for their actions affecting human rights. Much of this has been fostered and promoted by NGOs from the United States, such as Amnesty International USA, Human Rights Watch, Lawyers Committee for Human Rights, The Open Society Institute and various other actors in civil society.

The *Chuckie Taylor* U.S. criminal case in Appendix J, is an example of how one country, the U.S., can help fight the culture of impunity against someone who committed international crimes in another country with no U.S. connection.

See Also Terms: 3, 10, 13, 23, 26, 42, 48, 56, 59, 63, 64, 70, 72, 103, 118, 151, 152, 157, 159, 166, 181, 182, 184, 185, 192, 202, 210, 211, 222, 223, 224, 243, 271, 272, 273, 316.

72. CULTURE OF PEACE

Definition: A generally held social attitude that accepts that all disputes at any level should be resolved peacefully, without resort to violence or causing harm, according to prevailing law that is consistent with international human rights standards.

Significance: The 20th century has been characterized by extensive destructive violence between and within many countries. The goal of the human rights system is to provide limitations on the conduct of government in all countries so that armed conflicts and violent rebellions do not occur and so that peace will reign. Respect for human rights is said to be "the foundation for freedom, justice and peace in the world" (UDHR preamble). See Document 6. The international legal community is seeking to educate the world about human rights to help eliminate the causes of violence and promote peace. This effort involves reprogramming societies from more militaristic or belligerent attitudes, which seek to resolve disputes by force, to societies where rule of law prevails and disputes are resolved by judicial organs applying law.

A culture of peace is deemed to be the most conducive to respect for human rights, and vice versa. The Middle East, with its Israeli-Palestinian dispute, is a classic example of a place where the United States is seeking, by its public policy and foreign policy and relations, to get the parties to replace a culture of hate with a culture of peace.

See Also Terms: 8, 11, 12, 20, 48, 51, 59, 63, 64, 70, 76, 120, 124, 129, 141, 144, 145, 148, 152, 160, 177, 181, 182, 184, 188, 192, 210, 218, 230, 272, 276, 283, 286, 308, 309, 311, 316, 317, 318, 323.

73. CUSTOMARY INTERNATIONAL LAW

Definition: A source of human rights standards from international law. This source declares certain human rights standards to be legally binding norms if they are reflected by consistent practices of most countries over a course of time, and if these practices are done by states with an attitude that the practices are a matter of legal obligation.

Significance: Human rights norms which are binding upon the United States come primarily from international human rights treaties, such as the ICCPR and the Convention against Torture. Such norms can also be found in what is known as customary international law, which is based on the actual practice of states, coupled with the belief that international law requires them to act so. Torture is a human rights violation under the Convention against Torture for all states that have ratified it. Torture is now also prohibited by customary international law. Customary international law is legally binding upon all states, even if they have not signed any treaties on the subject.

The United States, for example, has not signed the 1977 First Protocol to the Geneva Conventions of 1949, and has not yet ratified it (see Document 73). The United States considers, though, that some of the norms (rules) in that protocol are declaratory of customary international law. Therefore, those rules are legally binding on the United States even without ratifying the protocol, which is a legal instrument that modifies a treaty.

For a U.S. court decision concerning customary international law see the decision *In Re: Cincinnati Radiation Litigation and Kiobel vs Royal Dutch Petroleum.* See Appendix J. In that first case the federal district judge found that the Nuremberg Code on Medical Treatment has become binding as U.S. law as a matter of customary international law. As such, it can be applied in both civil and criminal proceedings in the United States. In the *Kiobel* case the court found that there was no cause of action for an oil company aiding and abetting a state to commit human rights violations, based on customary international law.

See Also Terms: 8, 15, 16, 25, 26, 42, 45, 48, 53, 56, 63, 64, 65, 66, 90, 110, 111, 113, 117, 130, 135, 136, 154, 161, 164, 166, 177, 179, 182, 184, 185, 192, 197, 223, 224, 252, 254, 256, 259, 260, 265, 272, 275, 281, 291, 292, 297, 298, 300, 302, 308, 309, 316, 317, 318.

D

74. DECLARATION/DECLARATIONS

Definitions: 1. Political instrument: A statement of principles officially adopted and issued by a group of people or members of an institution, such as the United Nations, not meant to be legally binding. It sets forth what they believe should be human rights principles that are applicable in general or to a certain group of people or in certain situations usually characterized by human rights violations.

2. Treaty Legal Instrument: A formal legal instrument submitted by an individual state at the time of its ratification, accession or adhesion to a human rights treaty, wherein the state ratifying, etc., declares the extent to which, or how it accepts the treaty obligations. This type of declaration is a legal formality and part of a legal instrument, which is filed with the instrument of ratification, etc., usually along with reservations and understandings.

Significance: The main example of a human rights declaration is the Universal Declaration of Human Rights. See Document 6. The Declaration of Independence is the main document in the U.S. human rights history. See Document 1. Other examples of the many human rights declarations in which the U.S. government and civil society played a part in creating and promoting are the Declaration on the Right and Responsibility of Individuals, Groups, and Organs of Society to Promote and Protect Universally Recognized Human Rights and Fundamental Freedoms (Document 40) and the Declaration on the Elimination of Violence against Women (Document 43). These are primarily political instruments coming from an international inter-governmental organization, such as the United Nations, to express their common understanding of what human rights are regarding a given subject.

Sometimes this term is seen in the second sense as part of a legal instrument of ratification, etc. In this sense the state declares the extent to which it will be bound to apply a certain provision of the treaty as to, for example, geographical or temporal scope. Or it may relate to acceptance of the jurisdiction ("competence") of a treaty supervisory organ to handle complaints against that state.

Often it is seen as plural ("declarations") to refer to a formal statement submitted along with a state's ratification of a human rights treaty. This is often seen along with the terms, reservations and understandings, that is, "**r**eservations, **d**eclarations, and **u**nderstandings," or "**r**eservations, **u**nderstandings and **d**eclarations" and abbreviated RDUs or RUDs. When used in this context, the word declaration sometimes means a formal written statement by a ratifying state that it accepts the jurisdiction of a treaty-monitoring body to handle written complaints against it for violations of the treaty. For example, when the United States ratified the ICCPR, the U.S. Senate made a declaration that the United States accepted the jurisdiction of the Human Rights Committee to handle complaints against the United States made by other states parties to the ICCPR who had made similar declarations.

It can also declare how, where, and to what extent the state will accept to be bound by a particular obligation. In the U.S. ratification of the First Optional Protocol to the CRC in 2002, Document 30, the U.S. submitted a declaration saying the following:

> "The Government of the United States of America declares, pursuant to Article 3 (2) of the Optional Protocol to the Convention on the Rights of the Child on the Involvement of Children in Armed Conflict that (A) the minimum age at which the United States permits voluntary recruitment into the Armed Forces of the United States is 17 years of age;..."

This type of declaration serves to clarify a state's position, and not to exclude or modify an obligation, as does a reservation. These are often made because if the state were to ratify the treaty with its domestic laws as they are at the time of ratification it would immediately be in violation of its treaty obligations as soon as the treaty entered into force.

See Also Terms: 12, 20, 48, 75, 76, 222, 245, 259, 262, 269, 285, 291, 309, 316.

75. DECLARATION OF INDEPENDENCE

Definition: The Declaration of Independence was the founding document of the establishment of the United States. See Document 1. In it, the 13 colonies, who looked at themselves individually as sovereign nation-states, declared that they were cutting off their relationship with Britain so as to govern themselves. It explained collectively to Britain and the whole world their reasons for secession and proclaimed the unalienable human rights of all human beings.

Significance: While this Document was the basis of the American political and historical human rights experience, celebrated each 4th of July, and still reminds Americans that their rights are inherent and inalienable, it also has served as one of the sources of the philosophical bases of all human rights. This basis was the concept of natural law. It was particularly so with regard to the ideas of human dignity, equality and inherent ("endowed") and inalienable rights. These concepts were so important that it was held that the government's first duty, above all others, was to protect them. This instrument articulated the right to life, liberty and the "pursuit of happiness." This last concept did not mean pursuit of hedonistic pleasure. In its historical context "happiness" referred to having a right relationship to God.

See Also Terms: 20, 21, 26, 33, 34, 35, 37, 39, 40, 48, 65, 66, 70, 71, 98, 100, 104, 108, 109, 110, 113, 122, 124, 136, 144, 145, 151, 152, 157, 159, 160, 167, 169, 170, 175, 177, 195, 196, 211, 213, 222, 228, 242, 252, 253, 259, 272, 278, 292, 323 .

76. DEFAMATION OF RELIGION
See entry for **Freedom of Expression**

77. DEFENDER
See entry for **Human Rights Defender**

78. DEGRADING TREATMENT OR PUNISHMENT

Definition: The term describes ill-treatment or punishment that is designed to arouse feelings of fear, anguish, and inferiority in victims; the purpose of such treatment is to humiliate and debase them and possibly break their physical or moral resistance.

Significance: Degrading treatment or punishment is usually condemned as a violation of human rights treaty norms in an article including torture, cruel and inhuman treatment or punishment. The first such norm was found in Article 5 of the UDHR, which includes the terms torture, cruel treatment or punishment, degrading treatment or punishment, and inhuman treatment or punishment. See Document 6. These all represent different levels of severity of treatment or punishment.

Degrading treatment and degrading punishment are different. If the degrading acts are not being done for purposes of punishment of the victim for a prior act, such as for a criminal or other violation, then the term "degrading treatment" is used. If the degrading acts are done for the purposes of punishing the victim for his prior conduct, such as for a criminal conviction, then the term "degrading punishment" is used.

Both degrading treatment and punishment are inconsistent with the victim's inherent human dignity and constitute human rights violations. Article 7 of the ICCPR states: "No one shall be subjected to torture or to cruel, inhuman or degrading treatment or punishment." See Document 8.

The United States submitted a reservation to its ratification of the ICCPR to the effect that the terms "torture, cruel, inhuman and degrading treatment or punishment would be interpreted consistent with the 5th, 8th, and 14th amendments to the U.S. Constitution, which offer somewhat less protection than Article 7 of the ICCPR, as interpreted by the U.N. Human Rights Committee." See Document 9.

Degrading treatment is part of the criminal jurisdiction of the ICC. In Article 8. 2(b)(xxi) of the Rome Statute, degrading treatment within the context of an armed conflict is one of the predicate acts for a war crime. See Document 76.

See Document 15A, the Second and Third Report of United States of America to the U.N. Human Rights Committee, Article 7, for a statement by the United States as to its law and practice in this area of human rights. The United States has also ratified the U.N. Convention against Torture, Cruel, Inhuman or Degrading Treatment or Punishment, which treats this topic of human rights with greater detail. See Document 19. The Second Periodic report of CAT gives a very recent expansive treatment of this topic from the U.S. legal experience. See Document 21A.

The war of terrorism has engendered some acts of degrading treatment regarding detainees who were suspected terrorists. A very clear example of degrading treatment or punishment was the conduct of the U.S. Army prison guards at Abu Ghraib prison in Iraq in 2006. Photos of treatment of Iraqi prisoners at Abu Ghraib appeared all over the media. They showed the prisoners in degrading situations, such as nakedness, under the watch of U.S. Army military personnel. This has subjected the U.S. to accusations of violating both human rights and humanitarian law. Degrading treatment violates human dignity just as terrorism does.

See Also Terms: 3, 11, 12, 20, 24, 33, 34, 35, 48, 49, 53, 65, 66, 70, 81, 82, 88, 93, 96, 115, 124, 144, 145, 146, 147, 151, 152, 167, 170, 171, 177, 178, 181, 182, 184, 185, 192, 215, 259, 283, 293, 297, 302, 307, 309, 316.

79. DEPORTATION

Definition: Deportation occurs when a country removes and sends an alien back across the border to the country from which he or she came. The reasons for deportation include that the alien's presence is found to be unlawful or that it is detrimental to the public welfare or national security. The term now used in the U.S. is removal.

Significance: There are various reasons that deportation from a country may occur. For example, legal aliens have certain criteria they must adhere to in order to remain in a country. If they ignore any of these criteria, such as by committing illegal acts, they run the risk of deportation.

Deportation can also occur when a person seeks asylum in the United States but is not granted that status after his or her case is reviewed. The deportation would result from the denial of asylum.

In the United States, deportation occurs on a regular basis when illegal aliens cross over the border from Mexico into the United States and when a legal alien's visa expires. Those who are not legal aliens possessing a visa to enter and remain in the United States or who are not citizens of the United States can be deported if they are apprehended.

In the U.S., immigration law and legal system the term "deportation" is no longer used. The term "removal" is now used. The U.S. now legally "removes" those who do not have or who have lost the right to be present here. This covers persons who are in the U.S. illegally and those who are subject to exclusion while trying to enter the U.S. The term deportation is still commonly used in the U.S. and internationally to refer to this act or removal or aliens.

This issue of illegal aliens has become a controversial one, resulting in several ballot measures in California dealing specifically with the rights, if any, of those who are in the United States illegally and how to improve the system of apprehension and deportation. At time of publication, the U.S. President is starting to push for a new comprehensive immigration law to deal with the estimated 12,000,000 illegal aliens in the U.S.

Before the Department of Homeland Security was created, deportation was handled by the Immigration and Naturalization Service (INS). Since the beginning of the war on terrorism this deportation process has come under the U.S. Department of Homeland Security, which has ramped up deportations particularly of suspected terrorists and criminal aliens, and has been accused of having secret detention centers to keep certain detainees incommunicado.

The international community has reminded the U.S. that in all measures taken in the fight against terrorism, including deportations, the state must respect its human rights obligations.

Under the international human rights principle of non-refoulement, the United States cannot deport (remove) an alien in any manner to a border ("frontier") of a territory where his or her life or freedom would be threatened on account of race, religion, nationality, membership in a particular social group, or political opinion. (See the Convention Relating to the Status of Refugees, Article 33, Document 36.)

It is important for nations to be able to work together in this area of deportation/removal to establish proper procedures. International agreements can standardize the process and also encourage the proper treatment of the deported individuals so that their human rights are not violated in the process.

Article 13 of the ICCPR recognizes the right of all aliens lawfully in the territory of a state party, such as the United States, to be expelled from the state only in pursuance to a decision reached in accordance with law and, except where national security reasons compel otherwise, to be allowed the right to submit reasons to the government against their expulsion and have their cases heard by a competent government authority, with legal representation. See Document 8.

The case of *Haitian Centre for Human Rights v. United States* addresses U.S. practice regarding asylum seekers, refugee processing, admission of aliens to the United States, and their deportation.

See Also Terms: 11, 12, 17, 18, 20, 48, 59, 81, 82, 90, 93, 100, 113, 124, 144, 145, 152, 155, 156, 167, 169, 177, 179, 184, 185, 210, 211, 219, 222, 252, 253, 259, 263, 272, 283, 287, 292, 294, 316.

80. DEROGATION/DEROGABLE HUMAN RIGHTS

Definition: Derogation is the act of a state suspending the application and enjoyment of certain human rights upon its declaration of a state of public emergency affecting the life of a whole nation. Derogable human rights are those that can legally be suspended in such a situation of derogation.

Significance: Sometimes major public emergencies occur in a state and need to be dealt with by the government to preserve the state. International human rights doctrine permits a state to derogate from its usual legal human rights obligations to handle a public emergency. The word derogate means to "take away" or "lessen." For example, under martial law during a military invasion, freedom of movement, a human right, may be curtailed so that public safety and order can be maintained.

A "derogation clause" is a treaty clause that sets forth the right and criteria for a state to derogate from its obligations under a treaty. Article 4 of the ICCPR is a "derogation clause." The derogation clause also specifies which rights may be derogated, the so-called derogable rights. It also specifies which rights may never be suspended or "taken away." Such human rights are known as "nonderogable rights;" that is, they may *never* be suspended, no matter what the public emergency circumstances. A good example of such a right would be the right to life or freedom from torture.

Human rights principles make it clear that even when rights are derogable, a state cannot apply this derogation in a discriminatory way on the basis of race, color, sex, and other similar attributes.

To ensure that the derogable rights are only taken away or lessened for so long as absolutely necessary, derogations are subject to supervision by the international organ or supervising body charged with implementation of the treaty. The derogation must be officially declared to the supervising organization pursuant to a human rights instrument and must last only until the emergency no longer exists.

Sometimes certain periods of derogation of human rights are called a "state of exception," "state of emergency," "state of siege," or "martial law."

An example of the derogation clause is Article 4 of the ICCPR:

> 1. In time of public emergency which threatens the life of the nation and the existence of which is officially proclaimed, the States Parties to the present Covenant may take measures derogating from their obligations under the present Covenant to the extent strictly required by the exigencies of the situation, provided that such measures are not inconsistent with their other obligations under international law and do not involve discrimination solely on the ground of race, colour, sex, language, religion or social origin.
>
> 2. No derogation from Articles 6 (*right to life*), 7 (*freedom from torture*), 8 (*slavery*) . . . may be made under this provision.
>
> 3. Any State Party to the present Covenant availing itself of the right of derogation shall immediately inform the other States Parties to the present Covenant, through the intermediary of the Secretary-General of the United Nations, of the provisions from which it has derogated and of the reasons by which it was actuated. A further communication shall be made, through the same intermediary, on the date which it terminates such derogation.

Because the United States is a state party to the ICCPR, any such period of derogation declared by it would be subject to compliance with this article. In the wake of 9/11, and the resulting war on terrorism, the U.S. government has not declared a period of derogation and suspended certain human rights. It expects, though, that everyone will remember the 9/11 factor in evaluating the measures taken in this war. Absent such formal declaration of a state of derogation, all human rights in the ICCPR are fully legally binding as they would be at any other time. Thus, no rights can be suspended by the U.S., nor can they be limited for reasons beyond those listed in the limitations clause nor can any limitation measure have the effect of negatively interfering with the exercise of other human rights. It must be remembered that every human rights norm is written in a way to reflect a balance between the maximum freedom of the individual versus the needs of state to protect rights and human beings under its jurisdiction or effective control.

See Also Terms: 11, 25, 179, 184, 185, 210, 211, 259, 272, 306, 307.

81. DETAINEE/DETENTION FACILITIES

See entry for **Detention**

82. DETENTION

Definition: The exercise of physical restraint upon an individual depriving them of liberty and holding them in government custody for reasons other than to face criminal charges. The term detained usually has the sense of being put in a physical government facility where one is kept from leaving so that one can be processed for legal procedures, held for questioning or as a witness, or held for deportation/removal. Where this is accompanied by concealment by the perpetrators of the whereabouts of the victim, this is called Secret Detention and sometimes Ghost Detention. Those who are the victims of secret or ghost detention are often referred to as Ghost Detainees.

Significance: Detention brings into play the human rights to liberty and security of person. Under international human rights law, freedom is the rule and any limitation on liberty and freedom of movement is the exception and must be legally justified by the state. The first duty of the state is respect for and protection of the human rights of all persons within its jurisdiction. Under the U.S. Constitution, freedom from physical restraint is a substantive due process right guaranteed by the 5th and 14th Amendments. See Document 2. The state may not arrest, detain, or otherwise exercise physical restraint on anyone unless it has a valid legal basis for doing so. Its right to do so is limited by international human rights law binding on the U.S. via the Constitution.

Article 3 of the UDHR states, "Everyone has the right to life, liberty and security of person." Security of person is similar to freedom from unreasonable search and seizure under the 4th Amendment to the U.S. Constitution. Article 9 states, "No one shall be subjected to arbitrary arrest, detention or exile." Under Article 11, everyone charged with a criminal offense is presumed innocent. See Document 6.

Article 9 of the ICCPR, binding on the United States, asserts, "Everyone has the right to liberty and security of person. No one shall be subject to arbitrary arrest or detention." See document 8. That article goes on to state the particular human rights held by someone deprived of their liberty, which include the right to be promptly brought before a judge and to have proceedings taken before a court (habeas corpus) so that the court may rule without delay on the lawfulness of the detention and order release if detention is not proven lawful. The burden of proof of lawfulness is on the government.

Aside from the issue of when a state can detain, another key issue in detention is the conditions of detention, the facilities in which one is detained. They must be such as comport with inherent human dignity, regardless of what the detainee may have done or be feared to do in the future. Conditions of detention brings into play international legal norms both in the Geneva Conventions, where applicable, and International Human Rights Law.

Article 10 of the ICCPR sets forth the right of all persons deprived of their liberty to be "treated with humanity and with respect for the inherent dignity of the human person." Article 7 states categorically that: "No one shall be subjected to torture or to cruel, inhuman or degrading treatment or punishment." Bad detention conditions can violate the norms against cruel, inhuman or degrading treatment or punishment. Conditions of detention can be so bad as to constitute a violation of human rights of the detainee.

At the international level there exists some soft law which applies to the conditions of detention. The United Nations has adopted a "Body of Principles for the Protection of all Persons

Subject to any Form of Detention," which, though not legally binding, should serve as a yard-stick of compliance with treaty norms (see Document 47). It has also adopted a set of "Standard Minimum Rules for the Treatment of Prisoners," which should also be used for those convicted and in prison (see Document 48). There are other soft law principles and guidelines that apply to U.S. detention both domestically and where it detains outside its borders.

Detention has become a major human rights issue in the U.S. since 9/11, in terms of who is detained, why and under what conditions. In the war on terrorism the U.S. has been accused of having placed certain so called "high value" or particularly dangerous detainees into secret detention in various places around the world. The U.S. is said to be placing other suspects in remote detention centers, sometimes incommunicado. The secrecy of both the whereabouts or even the identity of these detainees was claimed to be a matter of national security. Secret detention is dangerous to human rights. Secret detention creates so called "ghost detainees:" no one knows who they are or where they are. Where and how persons are detained can in and of itself constitute a violation of human rights. Anywhere the U.S. exercises effective control over people in detention, the international norms will probably be applicable to the U.S.

Sometimes the U.S. has done this through third country proxies in foreign countries. Regarding U.S. responsibility for such proxy detention of secret or ghost detainees in non U.S. territory it has been asserted by one U.N. Special Rapporteur that:

> Secret detention, involving the denial or concealment of a person's detention, whereabouts or fate has the inherent consequence of placing the person outside the protection of the law. The practice of "proxy detention," where persons are transferred from one State to another outside the realm of any international or national legal procedure ("rendition" or "extraordinary rendition") for the specific purpose of secretly detaining them, or to exclude the possibility of review by the domestic courts of the State having custody of the detainee, or otherwise in violation of the well-entrenched principle of non-refoulement, entails exactly the same consequence. The practice of "proxy detention" involves the responsibility of both the State that is detaining the victim and the State on whose behalf or at whose behest the detention takes place.
>
> 37. According to Article 2, clause 1, of the International Covenant on Civil and Political Rights, each State party undertakes to respect and to ensure to all individuals within its territory and subject to its jurisdiction the rights recognized in the Covenant, without distinction of any kind, such as race, colour, sex, language, religion, political or other opinion, national or social origin, property, birth or other status. The Human Rights Committee clarified, in its general comment No. 31, that a State party must respect and ensure the rights laid down in the Covenant to anyone within the power or effective control of that State party, even if not situated within the territory of the State party. Similarly, the International Court of Justice, in its advisory opinion on the *Legal Consequences of the Construction of a Wall in the Occupied Palestinian Territories*, recognized that the jurisdiction of States is primarily territorial, but concluded that the Covenant extends to "acts done by a State in the exercise of its jurisdiction outside of its own territory." An excessively literal reading of Article 2, paragraph 1 of the Covenant would defeat the very purpose of the Covenant. As far as the Convention against Torture is concerned, Article 2, paragraph 1, and Article 16, paragraph 1, refer to each State party's obligation to prevent acts of torture "in any territory under its jurisdiction."

See also the U.N. Human Rights Council Joint Report of Special Rapporteurs on Secret Detention Centers, Appendix M. The U.N. Special Rapporteur on Protection of Human Rights while Countering Terrorism has said regarding the legal implications of secret detention that, "On a global scale, secret detention in connection with counter-terrorist policies remains a serious problem," and, "If resorted to in a widespread and systematic manner, secret detention might reach the threshold of a crime against humanity." Under international criminal law widespread or systematic secret detention can constitute an international crime against humanity. The well-meaning or patriotism of the perpetrator will not excuse such a crime.

No detention issue has been more acute for the U.S. than the Guantanamo (GITMO) issue. There were over 600 human beings all who were either suspected of waging war or engaging in terrorism against the U.S., or having information claimed to be relevant to fighting the war on terrorism. Many detainees were never charged with any criminal activity nor found to have any useful information. Some were found to have been brought there mistakenly, but they were detained in GITMO for years. Allegations of abuse were made. Some of these detentions would be considered to constitute prolonged arbitrary detention. Though President Obama has ordered GITMO closed the detention issue, especially for future such detentions, goes on in the halls of government and in the military and intelligence offices of America.

This is also an area where one sees the applicability of International Humanitarian law. Where the detainees are considered "enemy combatants," a U.S. term which does not exist in international humanitarian law, they have a right under Article 5 of the Geneva Conventions to a hearing to determine their status as a combatant prisoner of war or not. One is either a combatant covered under the Geneva Convention III or one is a civilian, protected by the GC IV. There is no other classification, though combatants includes persons known as unprivileged or unlawful combatants. Either way, detained combatants have rights under the GCs, either GC IV on protection of civilians or GC III on prisoners of war. Detention includes access to a legal system to determine both the status and legality of the detention. Even where the armed conflict is deemed a noninternational armed conflict, or civil war, common Article 3 of the Geneva Conventions applies as a matter of treaty law and customary international law and provides for access to legal recourse.

The main issue from the side of the detainees was access to legal representation and U.S. federal court to file habeas corpus actions to determine the legality of the detention, and the use of military commissions to determine their status or prosecute them. This was dealt with in several Supreme Court cases such as *Rasul vs. Bush*, *Hamdi vs. Rumsfeld* and *Hamdan vs. Rumsfeld* and *Boumedienne vs. Bush*

The United Nations has adopted a new Convention for Protection of all Persons from Enforced Disappearance, which deals with the issue of detention and forced disappearance. The U.S. has not signed or ratified it. See Document 45.

See Also Terms: 11, 12, 16, 20, 24, 48, 82, 84, 88, 90, 93, 96, 111, 124, 134, 144, 145, 152, 155, 161, 167, 170, 171, 177, 178, 179, 184, 185, 195, 210, 215, 222, 248, 251, 252, 253, 254, 256, 259, 266, 272, 275, 297, 302, 309, 316.

83. DEVELOPMENT (ECONOMIC/SUSTAINABLE)

Definition: Development is a complex, controversial, and difficult concept to define, both generally as a process and as a specific substantive human right. As a process, development has been defined in the 1986 U.N. Declaration on the Right to Development as meaning a "comprehensive economic, social, cultural, and political process, which aims at the constant improvement of all individuals in a society on the basis of their active, free, and meaningful participation in development, and in the fair distribution of the benefits resulting therefrom." As a human right, the "Right to Development" is a subjective human right of groups of individuals to have the freedom, cooperation, methods, and means to develop themselves economically, socially, culturally, and politically as a civil society, and to achieve the goals of human rights: the fullest possible development of the human personality of every individual in society.

Significance: The human right to development is one of the newer human rights to be articulated and defined. It is not universally accepted as a human right. It was originally a right articulated by the developing and non aligned states as one of the so called "Solidarity Rights" which formed part of what used to be known as the "Third Generation Human Rights." The U.S. has long been skeptical and cautious about the development of this right and has seen it as a claim by poor nations for a bigger share of money and material from developed states. It is accepted by the greater part of the international community as a human right and its contours are being defined.

According to the 1986 Declaration above, "the right to development is an inalienable human right by virtue of which every human person and all peoples are entitled to participate in, contribute to, and enjoy economic, social, cultural, and political development, ..."

One of the most important moments in the right to development occurred in 2000 at the United Nations: The U.N. General Assembly adopted the Declaration on the Millenium Development Goals. See Document 50. These goals were goals for all states to try to meet and which were to be scrutinized by scientific evidence of progress. Little has been heard from the U.S. government on these "MDGs" as they are called. The states are to strive to meet these goals by 2015. In adopting the Declaration the U.N. stated:

> We believe that the central challenge we face today is to ensure that globalization becomes a positive force for all the world's people. For while globalization offers great opportunities, at present its benefits are very unevenly shared, while its costs are unevenly distributed. We recognize that developing countries and countries with economies in transition face special difficulties in responding to this central challenge. Thus, only through broad and sustained efforts to create a shared future, based upon our common humanity in all its diversity, can globalization be made fully inclusive and equitable. These efforts must include policies and measures, at the global level, which correspond to the needs of developing countries and economies in transition and are formulated and implemented with their effective participation.

> The eight specific Millenium Development Goals (MDGs) are as follows:

> Goal 1: Eradicate extreme poverty and hunger

> Goal 2: Achieve universal primary education

> Goal 3: Promote gender equality and empower women

> Goal 4: Reduce the child mortality rate

> Goal 5: Improve maternal health

> Goal 6: Combat HIV/AIDS, malaria, and other diseases

> Goal 7: Ensure environmental sustainability

> Goal 8: Develop a global partnership for development

Most people associate development with foreign aid money to help developing states become developed states. It is much more than that. It is a recognition of a need of everyone to develop oneself and strive for one's goals. It would be wrong to assume that the right to development relates only to poor developing countries wanting to have the resources and rights to improve themselves for the well being of their people, or even just for groups and individuals in those countries to develop. It is a right for every human being to develop him or herself in personal autonomy as he or she sees fit, within the bounds of the law.

The right to development is a human right belonging to all Americans and, in fact, to all persons living in America. It does not imply a right to enter or to stay in the U.S., but once here, everyone has the right to development.

In its 2010, national UPR report the U.S. made known its contribution to international development with the example of its donation to Haiti and Pakistan. (See Document 86.) The report stated at paragraph 78:

> Our own efforts to build such a world include our role as the world's largest donor of development aid—including our commitment to disaster relief as seen recently in Haiti and Pakistan. And they include a commitment to using "smart power" in our foreign policy, including a

focus on honest, determined diplomacy and on harnessing the full potential of international institutions to facilitate cooperation.

See Also Terms: 9, 20, 39, 74, 92, 97, 144, 145, 152, 180, 183, 184, 190, 199, 204, 259, 286, 316.

84. DISABILITY

Definition: Genetic and/or acquired physical, mental and psychological conditions that may require accommodation in order for a person to participate fully and equally in society. People who have a disability are called disabled or handicapped but there are certain differences in the meanings of these terms. Definitionally, in the context of health experience, between disability and handicap the terms involved in this area have been defined by the World Health Organization as follows:

Disability: Any restriction or lack (resulting from an impairment) of ability to perform an activity in the manner or within the range considered normal for a human being.
Handicap: A disadvantage for a given individual, resulting from an impairment or disability, that, limits or prevents the fulfillment of a role that is normal, depending on age, sex, social and cultural factors, for that individual.

Handicap is therefore a function of the relationship between disabled persons and their environment. It occurs when they encounter cultural, physical or social barriers which prevent their access to the various systems of society that are available to other citizens. Thus, handicap is the loss or limitation of opportunities to take part in the life of the community on an equal level with others."(International Classification of Impairments, Disabilities and Handicaps (ICIDH), World Health Organization, Geneva, 1980).

Significance: It is estimated that there are about 500,000,000 persons in the world who are disabled as a consequence of mental, physical or sensory impairment. Many of them suffer discrimination, marginalization, lack of physical access, and a denial of the possibility to develop themselves as they so choose, within the limits of their disabilities. At this time the international community is going beyond principles and starting to develop legally binding norms of obligation of states to regiment society in the way that respects all human rights of the disabled. This has started with the adoption in 2006 of the Convention on the Rights of Persons with Disabilities. See Document 44. That Convention entered into force in 2008 and was signed by the U.S. in 2009. The preamble of that Convention reads:

(*a*) *Recalling* the principles proclaimed in the Charter of the United Nations which recognize the inherent dignity and worth and the equal and inalienable rights of all members of the human family as the foundation of freedom, justice and peace in the world,
(*b*) *Recognizing* that the United Nations, in the Universal Declaration of Human Rights and in the International Covenants on Human Rights, has proclaimed and agreed that everyone is entitled to all the rights and freedoms set forth therein, without distinction of any kind,
(*c*) *Reaffirming* the universality, indivisibility, interdependence and interrelatedness of all human rights and fundamental freedoms and the need for persons with disabilities to be guaranteed their full enjoyment without discrimination,
(*e*) *Recognizing* that disability is an evolving concept and that disability results from the interaction between persons with impairments and attitudinal and environmental barriers that hinders their full and effective participation in society on an equal basis with others,...

Human rights treaties have always applied to disabled persons and the nondiscrimination clauses in each treaty prohibited discrimination in the exercise of all human rights in that treaty as an "other status." Certainly ICCPR Articles 2, 12, 14 and 26 would apply in particular ways.

See Document 8. But it was deemed necessary by the international community to have a sectoral treaty specifically on disability to give more concrete and specific expression of the rights of the disabled in binding legal norms.

The U.S. has passed the Americans with Disabilities Act which seeks to meet the concerns of the disabled set forth in the Convention.

Most human rights for disabled or handicapped persons are for purposes of eliminating any unfair exclusion, restriction, limitation or exemption of human beings based on having such characteristics. The goals of such rights are to equalize as much as possible the opportunities of such persons so that they can have a maximum of autonomy, respect and ability to development themselves as equal and productive members of society. In recent years increasing attention has been given to the rights of the disabled in general. The international community is also developing soft law rules aimed at giving states a road map on how to best change society to allow the disabled to fully exercise their human rights. See the Standard Rules On The Equalization Of Opportunities For Persons With Disabilities, and the World Programme Of Action Concerning Disabled Persons.

In its August 2010, national UPR report, (see Document 86) the U.S. reports about the strides it has made in legal protection of the disabled from discrimination, particularly through the Americans with Disabilities Act. The report states at paragraph 33: "The intent of these laws is to prohibit discrimination on the basis of disability and remove barriers to the full and equal inclusion of people with disabilities in U.S. society."

See Also Terms: 11, 12, 20, 24, 33, 34, 35, 49, 70, 86, 87, 99, 100, 122, 144, 146, 147, 152, 160, 167, 169, 177, 179, 180, 184, 195, 216, 237, 242, 254, 278, 282, 283, 309, 316.

85. DISAPPEARANCE

Definition: This term refers to the government taking someone into physical custody for arrest or detention and then denying to their family and the world that they are being held by the government. In the human rights context it is most often called "enforced" or "involuntary" disappearance, to distinguish it from a situation where a person runs away and decides to hide, or is missing for reasons not caused by the government, such as a private kidnapping.

In the 2006 International Convention For The Protection Of All Persons From Enforced Disappearance the term enforced disappearance is defined as follows:

> For purposes of this Convention, "enforced disappearance" is considered to be the arrest, detention, abduction or any other form of deprivation of liberty by agents of the State or by persons or groups of persons acting with the authorization, support or acquiescence of the State, followed by a refusal to acknowledge the deprivation of liberty or by concealment of the fate or whereabouts of the disappeared person, which place such a person outside the protection of the law.

Significance: In many countries the government has at times arrested political opponents and taken them somewhere where no one can find them; they are held secretly to neutralize them politically. This act constitutes a forced disappearance, which is a very serious human rights violation. Often the disappearance is accompanied by torture. Even without torture, it is a cruel and inhuman act to cut someone off from their society, family, job, and friends. It would, for example, violate at least Articles 6, 7, 9, 10, 12, 14, and 16 of the ICCPR for a state like the United States, which is bound by that covenant, to commit disappearances.

A number of times, the United States has been accused of helping other governments commit such acts, such as Argentina, El Salvador, the Philippines, and Guatemala. A government helping another government cause someone to disappear is itself a human rights violation.

Since 9/11, the U.S. has experienced many allegations of disappearances of persons, most of whom were suspected of having ties to terrorism or terrorist cells. There were allegations of secret detention centers all over the world where the U.S. and some of its allies were holding so called "ghost" detainees in these so called "black" sites. There was alleged to have been a network for extraordinary rendition of terrorism suspects whom the governments involved were keeping secret for their families and the world. These were persons who just disappeared from the radar somewhere and are put into incommunicado detention somewhere. Reports on war on terrorism disappearances prepared by U.N special rapporteurs on such disappearances are included in Appendix M. In 2006 an International Convention For The Protection Of All Persons From Enforced Disappearance was adopted at the U.N. to define and prohibit disappearances. See Document 45. It has entered into force. At the time of publication the U.S. had not signed it.

See Also Terms: 11, 12, 17, 20, 24, 48, 53, 59, 63, 70, 73, 81, 82, 88, 90, 93, 100, 111, 117, 124, 134, 136, 144, 145, 151, 152, 161, 167, 177, 179, 182, 184, 185, 195, 196, 215, 222, 227, 244, 248, 252, 253, 254, 256, 259, 272, 275, 297, 302, 306, 309, 316.

86. DISCRIMINATION

Definition: A principle of human rights that is used in two different senses; that is, it has two very different meanings within the context of human rights:

1. Most often this term is used concerning the government or the private sector treatment of persons in different ways based on some characteristic of the victim. It is treating people differently because of their race, religion, ethnic group, color, creed, political opinion, or other status or characteristic, where there is no legal justification for doing so.

2. A second context involves a principle of humanitarian law that states that combatants (soldiers) must at all times distinguish, that is "discriminate," between enemy combatants and enemy civilians when engaging in an armed attack and must only attack combatants.

Significance: A definition found in the U.N. Convention on Elimination of Racial Discrimination defines racial discrimination as: "any distinction, exclusion, restriction or preference based on race, etc.... which has the purpose or effect of nullifying or impairing the recognition, enjoyment or exercise, on an equal footing of human rights and fundamental freedom" (CERD, Article 1). See Document 23.

The United States has ratified CERD and so should use this definition of racial discrimination. See Document 24. There are many different types of discrimination and many laws that seek to prohibit the kind of discrimination that is unacceptable as a matter of law. It is also true that not all types of discrimination are a violation of human rights. Examples are distinctions between adults and children, citizens and noncitizens, men and women. Some distinctions may be made by society but only so long as there exists, in human rights law terms, a "reasonable and objective justification" for such discrimination; there must be no alternative measure that could be taken that would not be inconsistent with human dignity and human rights. All discrimination must comply with basic human rights.

With respect to the humanitarian law principle of discrimination, soldiers may only attack enemy combatants. Failure to discriminate between civilians and combatants makes an armed attack an "indiscriminate attack" and a violation of humanitarian law. This is called the "principle of discrimination" or "principle of distinction" in the Law of Armed Conflict. If, for example, the United States were to bomb a town that had mostly civilians and only a few soldiers, and no measures were taken to only destroy the soldiers, then this attack would most likely be considered an indiscriminate attack and a violation of humanitarian law. It would constitute a failure to comply with the principle of discrimination. See Documents 69, 71, 73. This is also an international crime within the jurisdiction of the ICC. See Document 76.

See Also Terms: 7, 11, 12, 14, 15, 20, 22, 24, 28, 33, 34, 35, 41, 48, 54, 55, 70, 87, 120, 122, 124, 126, 129, 136, 139, 144, 145, 146, 147, 151, 152, 154, 155, 160, 164, 167, 169, 177, 179, 182, 184, 185, 188, 191, 192, 205, 212, 216, 236, 237, 255, 260, 261, 265, 270, 277, 283, 306, 307, 308, 309, 312, 316, 321, 322, 324.

87. DIVERSITY

Definition: The literal definition of the word is "the condition of being different." In the context of human rights, it has come to mean having persons of differing races, colors, gender, languages, religions, ethnic backgrounds, or cultures all coexisting in the same place or society in mutual acceptance, tolerance, and harmony.

Significance: Human beings differ from one another in many ways. Historically, many societies have tried to create a homogeneous society in which everyone is the same. Experience and reality have proven that this does not work, because one group of people will end up trying to make all others like them, as though they themselves were the ultimate criteria of how human society should be. No person or group can claim to be that model. Modern societies tend to be democratic and egalitarian. There is, however, very often a tension between persons who want all others to be more like the main population group, calling for unity and a common shared identity, and others who want to allow everyone to be as different as they like, regardless of the impact on social harmony and cohesiveness. This tension can lead to one, usually dominant, group becoming intolerant and restricting the rights of "the other," that is, those who are not like them. Under human rights principles, everyone has the right to be different and to express that difference as long as it is done within the law and consistent with human rights norms.

The key concept in diversity is that a variety of peoples maintain and develop their own unique and publicly accepted identity and characteristics. They also maintain an autonomous participation in the development of the common civilization. Diversity is the result of a society characterized by equality of all members and nondiscrimination in the enjoyment of all human rights. By its very nature, the concept of diversity presents challenges in creating a legal and social environment in which people with different worldviews, religions, and lifestyles can *all* exercise their basic human rights.

Diversity is often the claimed goal of affirmative action programs that seek to remedy certain areas of society in which discrimination has led to the exclusion of certain groups. Such remedies to past discrimination can result in claims of reverse discrimination.

Where diversity leads to the fractionalization of society into too many opposing groups, it creates a situation where demagogues can rush in, demonize opposing groups, and create a social crisis that can lead to violence and result in human rights violations.

The human rights principles of nondiscrimination, freedom of expression, and equality before the law, articulated in Articles 2, 19, and 26 of the ICCPR and such treaties as the Convention on Elimination of All Forms of Racial Discrimination, are examples of how human rights aim at protecting diversity among members of a society, such that everyone's human dignity is respected. See Documents 8 and 23.

See Also Terms: 7, 11, 12, 15, 20, 28, 33, 34, 35, 54, 55, 56, 67, 68, 70, 101, 102, 123, 144, 145, 156, 177, 179, 184, 205, 216, 237, 241, 260, 261, 265, 270, 277, 283, 292, 309, 316, 323, 324.

88. DOMESTIC REMEDY

Definition: A legal remedy available within the national legal system for remedying violations of internationally recognized human rights, particularly those set forth in human rights treaties like the ICCPR. See Document 8.

Significance: International human rights legal norms are meant to be secondary or subsidiary to national legal protections of human rights. The international system is a backup system to national (domestic) legal systems. To allow states to stand as the first line of defense for human rights and to allow individuals the quickest and most "near-to-home" legal protection of human rights, the international treaties specifically call for ratifying states to ensure that there is an effective and accessible legal remedy within the domestic legal system, where everyone within the jurisdiction can vindicate their rights. If people can protect their rights within their state, they do not need to avail themselves of international legal remedies.

As a matter of law, everyone wishing to commence almost any of the procedures at the international level must first exhaust all domestic legal remedies that are accessible and potentially effective. This is the principle of "exhaustion of domestic remedies."

Article 8 of the UDHR states, "Everyone has the right to an effective remedy by the competent national tribunals for acts violating the fundamental rights granted him by the constitution or by law." See Document 6.

Article 2, paragraph 3, of the ICCPR sets forth the legal obligation of all state parties, including the United States, to create effective domestic remedies for any violations of the substantive rights. This applies only if no such remedy already exists within the legal system procedures existing at the time of ratification. Article 2.3 states, "Each State Party to the present Covenant undertakes: To ensure that any person claiming such a remedy shall have his right thereto determined by competent judicial, administrative or legislative authorities, or by any other competent authority provided for by the legal system of the State, and to develop the possibilities of judicial remedy.

See Also Terms: 1, 3, 5, 12, 46, 48, 70, 90, 93, 107, 113, 134, 144, 145, 152, 162, 163, 167, 177, 179, 184, 194, 220, 222, 226, 244, 252, 253, 254, 259, 267, 272, 279, 292, 296, 316.

89. DOUBLE STANDARD/DUAL STANDARD

Definition: The application by a state of a certain standard of conduct pertaining to human rights by one state but not applying the same standard to other states for committing the very same acts constituting human rights violations. The term can also mean applying a human rights standard to other states but not to your own state for committing the very same acts constituting human rights violations. There is one standard for other countries but not for one's own.

Significance: The double standard approach to honoring human rights norms defeats the purpose of the entire movement worldwide. When the world was compelled to deal with the atrocities of World War II, it was agreed that there were human rights that were *basic* to the dignity of all human beings and that governments must be made to recognize those rights in spite of whatever political or economic reasons might compel them to do otherwise.

If a state practices a double standard in, for example, its trade negotiations with other countries, allowing trade with more lucrative markets with bad human rights records but condemning smaller countries for the same kinds of abuses, it is hypocritical. Understandably, the government of a state tries to balance its decisions in many arenas, such as economically, politically, and socially. The bottom line of human rights law, however, is fairness and equity to all people; the other considerations must take a back seat to this principle if the establishment of human rights in the world is to work. In the scenario just described, that state may decide to trade with *all* countries, contingent on human rights records; that would be a fair and equitable approach. The United States must deal with this kind of dilemma all the time, for example, in decisions about normal trading status, that is, most-favored nation status.

More difficult for states than even that scenario is the temptation to apply a double standard where one's *own* human rights record is concerned. If a state condemns the violations of another state yet commits the same kind of violation, the temptation is to excuse its own behavior because of "extenuating circumstances." Again, however, such an approach is hypocritical. If the state puts every other state up to scrutiny, it must allow itself to be scrutinized also. The provision for "extenuating circumstances" in general is handled in international human rights with the reservations, declarations and understandings (RDUs) that the state adds to its ratification of a certain human rights treaty. At that time, the state can make provisions for its particular situation. Even then, there is a danger of negating the purpose of ratifying the treaty if the RDUs disclaim the basic purposes of it.

The United States has been accused of a double standard in its handling of human rights norms because it is active in trying to bring other states into compliance and yet has ratified relatively few documents itself. The U.N. Human Rights Committee in General Comment 24 (see Appendix E) has also expressed a concern about how the United States used RDUs in the ratification process of the ICCPR. The ratification of treaties and use of RDUs pose a difficult dilemma for the United States, because its human rights record overall is one of the best in the world, and it is largely the model for human rights based on the Declaration of Independence and the U.S. Constitution. However, there is also an ongoing debate on the sovereignty of the United States in these matters of international human rights law; it is essential to resolve this issue so that consistency can be established. Because the people of the United States have excellent access to the political process, their knowledge of these issues should help the politicians make the appropriate decisions.

See Also Terms: 3, 59, 61, 70, 71, 103, 151, 159, 177, 186, 192, 202, 211, 272, 291, 323.

90. DUE PROCESS OF LAW

Definition: Fundamental legal fairness and justice in both substance and procedure. Most often used in the human rights context meaning fairness in legal procedures ("procedural due process"), particularly in criminal proceedings.

Significance: The United States gave the world of international human rights its model for what is known as due process of law, that fundamental fairness that human beings deserve from state governments that they establish to serve them. The world saw in the U.S. Constitutional experiment a system that appeared to do justice to all and that treated all human beings as equal. It was a well-defined system, both in human experience and in vast judicial definition and protection.

There are several different individual human rights with due process functions found in the major international human rights instruments, both global and regional. Among the global instruments the UDHR and ICCPR are the most frequently used. See Documents 6 and 8.

Article 14 of the ICCPR reads:

1. All persons shall be equal before the courts and tribunals. In the determination of any criminal charge against him, or of his rights and obligations in a suit at law, everyone shall be entitled to a fair and public hearing by a competent, independent and impartial tribunal established by law. The press and the public may be excluded from all or part of a trial for reasons of morals, public order (ordre public) or national security in a democratic society, or when the interest of the private lives of the parties so requires, or to the extent strictly necessary in the opinion of the court in special circumstances where publicity would prejudice the interests of justice; but any judgment rendered in a criminal case or in a suit at law shall be made public except where the interest of juvenile persons otherwise requires or the proceedings concern matrimonial disputes or the guardianship of children.

2. Everyone charged with a criminal offense shall have the right to be presumed innocent until proved guilty according to law.

3. In the determination of any criminal charge against him, everyone shall be entitled to the following minimum guarantees, in full equality:

(a) To be informed promptly and in detail in a language which he understands of the nature and cause of the charge against him;

(b) To have adequate time and facilities for the preparation of his defense and to communicate with counsel of his own choosing;

(c) To be tried without undue delay;

(d) To be tried in his presence, and to defend himself in person or through legal assistance of his own choosing; to be informed, if he does not have legal assistance, of this right; and to have legal assistance assigned to him, in any case where the interests of justice so require, and without payment by him in any such case if he does not have sufficient means to pay for it;

(e) To examine, or have examined, the witnesses against him and to obtain the attendance and examination of witnesses on his behalf under the same conditions as witnesses against him;

(f) To have the free assistance of an interpreter if he cannot understand or speak the language used in court;

(g) Not to be compelled to testify against himself or to confess guilt.

4. In the case of juvenile persons, the procedure shall be such as will take account of their age and the desirability of promoting their rehabilitation.

5. Everyone convicted of a crime shall have the right to his conviction and sentence being reviewed by a higher tribunal according to law.

6. When a person has by a final decision been convicted of a criminal offense and when subsequently his conviction has been reversed or he has been pardoned on the ground that a new or newly discovered fact shows conclusively that there has been a miscarriage of justice, the person who has suffered punishment as a result of such conviction shall be compensated according to law, unless it is proved that the nondisclosure of the unknown fact in time is wholly or partly attributable to him.

7. No one shall be liable to be tried or punished again for an offense for which he has already been finally convicted or acquitted in accordance with the law and penal procedure of each country.

U.S. law and practice in this area under the ICCPR was treated in the Initial and Second and Third Reports of the United States to the U.N. Human Rights Committee, under Article 14. Those reports show what the United States discloses about its law and practice with regard to due process of law, as viewed in light of the ICCPR. See Document 15A, Second and Third Periodic Reports.

Due process is referred to in the 2010 national report of the U.S. to the OHCHR for the UPR process. See Document 86. Paragraphs 14 and 56 read:

> People should enjoy fair treatment reflected in due process and equality before the law. Governments have an obligation not to discriminate or persecute and should establish mechanisms for protection and redress.
>
> The U.S. Constitution, as well as federal and state statutes, provides a number of substantive and procedural protections for individuals accused of committing crimes, those being held for trial, and those who are held in prisons or jails. (See Document 2) These include the right to be protected from unreasonable search and seizures, the right to due process under the law, the right to equal protection under the law, the right to an attorney, the right to remain silent during a criminal proceeding, the right to be protected from excessive bail in federal prosecutions, the right to be informed of the nature of the charges filed and of potential punishments, the right to a speedy and public trial, the right to cross-examine witnesses at trial, the right to an impartial jury of peers before someone can be sentenced to a year or more in prison, the right to be protected against being tried for the same crime twice, and the right to be free from cruel and unusual punishment in all prosecutions. (These constitutional rights are generally reflected, at times with different terminology, in international human rights law instruments to which the U.S. is party. In some respects, our constitutional rights go beyond those guaranteed in international law.)

See Also Terms: 1, 11, 12, 20, 24, 33, 34, 35, 48, 59, 70, 73, 93, 95, 99, 100, 109, 111, 113, 124, 136, 146, 147, 151, 154, 162, 167, 177, 179, 184, 185, 193, 202, 222, 252, 253, 254, 259, 272, 283, 297, 309, 316.

91. DUTY

Definition: Duties are the specific obligations owed by every human being to self, family, community, society, state and the world to act in a way that promotes the common interest, or at least does not threaten its existence and harmony and the rights of others. For every human right there is a corresponding duty that goes with it. Paying taxes, supporting one's minor children, not breaking the criminal laws and not committing harmful acts on others, are all examples of acts that fulfill one's duty, without which human rights cannot be fully exercised.

Significance: Article 29.1 of the UDHR (see Document 6) states:

Everyone has duties to the community in which alone the free and full development of his personality is possible.

In the preamble to the ICCPR (see Document 8) it states:

Realizing that the individual, having duties to other individuals and to the community to which he belongs, is under a responsibility to strive for the promotion and observance of the rights recognized in the present Covenant.

Every member of society must fulfill her or his duty to the U.S. and to each other, in order for the state to be able to ensure the full realization of all human rights for everyone in the U.S.

See Also Terms: 11, 12, 51, 70, 107, 145, 179, 184, 221, 222, 259, 272, 309, 316.

92. ECONOMIC HUMAN RIGHTS

Definition: A category of human rights that is concerned with assuring that human beings have the means to obtain and maintain a minimum decent standard of living that is consistent with human dignity. Economic human rights have come to refer to the right to food, health care, social security and work, and to form and participate in trade unions and are set out in the UDHR and the ICESCR.

Significance: Economic rights seek to ensure the everyday needs of humans. Without these basic needs, such as food, their very life and enjoyment of any human rights is in danger. Human beings can only realize their full dignity and worth if they have the means to live a decent life. However, the interpretation and application of this category of rights as it relates to the obligations of the state is a matter of debate without universal consensus.

Conceptually, economic human rights are considered programmatic and progressive rights. "Programmatic" means that government "programs" such as health, housing, or financial assistance are required to fulfill the state's obligation. "Progressive" refers to requiring "progressive" government measures, such as building schools or creating jobs over the course of time, to fulfill the state's obligations. These rights are to be contrasted with "immediate" human rights obligations, such as civil and political rights. These can be enjoyed immediately upon a state's treaty ratification and usually require no implementing measures.

Economic rights are one of five categories of human rights described in the UDHR, which also includes civil, political, social, and cultural rights. In his Four Freedoms speech, President Franklin D. Roosevelt referred to this area of rights as "freedom from want." (See Document 4).

Economic rights seek to ensure the right of each individual to seek provision of their everyday basic needs, such as food, without which their very life and enjoyment of any human rights would be endangered. As such, these rights are intended to provide human beings the ability to realize their full dignity and worth. The principle human rights instruments setting forth economic rights are the UDHR (Articles 22, 23, 25) and ICESCR (especially Articles 6–12). Economic rights are also treated in the Vienna Declaration and Programme of Action of 1993, particularly under the principles of indivisibility, interrelatedness, and interdependence of all human rights. (See Documents 6, 16, 51) The U.S. has signed but not ratified the ICESCR, principally out of continued opposition to the manner of the implementation of the economic rights in the ICESCR.

Historically, economic human rights used to be known as one of the "second generation human rights," along with social and cultural human rights. The term "second generation" is no longer used to describe human rights.

Economic rights have also been referred to as aspirations of social policy by some who believed the economic rights contained in the UDHR were established to ensure that governments provided and protected the fair and equitable conditions by which individuals could realize basic social needs.

This category of human rights was originally promoted internationally by communist countries and, for resulting philosophical and political reasons, they were not accepted by the U.S. as human rights. The U.S. feared that recognition of economic human rights would give rise to claims to receive monetary and material benefits from society and government which was inconsistent with the nature of America's democratic political system and free market economic system. As such, some Americans feared that economic human rights would require a massive expenditure of public funds and a redistribution of wealth.

In advocating for adoption of the Universal Declaration of Human Rights (see Document 7), Roosevelt's wife Eleanor Roosevelt, who had a major role in the formation of the document as the U.S. representative to the U.N. Commission on Human Rights, explained the U.S. position on economic rights as such:

> We in the United States have come to realize it means freedom to choose one's job, to work or not to work as one desires. We, in the United States, have come to realize, however, that people have a right to demand that their government will not allow them to starve because as individuals they cannot find work of the kind they are accustomed to doing and this is a decision brought about by public opinion which came as a result of the great depression in which many people were out of work, but we would not consider in the United States that we had gained any freedom if we were compelled to follow a dictatorial assignment to work where and when we were told. The right of choice would seem to us an important, fundamental freedom.

> In the United States we have a capitalistic economy. That is because public opinion favors that type of economy under the conditions in which we live. But we have imposed certain restraints; for instance, we have antitrust laws. These are the legal evidence of the determination of the American people to maintain an economy of free competition and not to allow monopolies to take away the people's freedom.

> Our trade-unions grow stronger because the people come to believe that this is the proper way to guarantee the rights of the workers and that the right to organize and to bargain collectively keeps the balance between the actual producer and the investor of money and the manager in industry who watches over the man who works with this hands and who produces the materials which are our tangible wealth.

In theory, economic human rights do not require the state to provide basic necessities for free to all who need them. Economic rights do not mean free money from the public trough. It does require that the state take measures to see that the structures exist within society, both through the public and private sectors, through which individuals can obtain their basic needs. This may be done while still requiring recipients to fulfill their duties to society by working or seeking employment and by paying taxes. In theory, a capitalistic economy as well as a socialist one can create a system in which economic human rights can be realized. Up until the mid-1990s, the U.S. government continued to be cold toward economic rights.

Beginning with the administration's position at the 1993 Vienna Conference on human rights, the U.S. position began to change. It unofficially recognized economic, social, and cultural rights. In the aftermath of the cold war and the demise of communism, formal opposition to economic human rights, properly understood, is diminishing. There is still, however, significant opposition to the acceptance of economic human rights, mainly among conservatives.

In 2010, the Administration interestingly referred to economic human rights in its UPR report to the OHCHR even though it is not bound by the Covenant on Economic, Social and Cultural Rights. In paragraph 67, the Report states as follows:

The paradigm elucidated in Franklin Roosevelt's 1941 "Four Freedoms" speech became a reference point for many in the international human rights movement. On subjects such as "freedom from want," the United States has focused on democratic solutions and civil society initiatives while the U.S. courts have defined our federal constitutional obligations narrowly and primarily by focusing on procedural rights to due process and equal protection of the law. But as a matter of public policy, our citizens have taken action through their elected representatives to help create a society in which prosperity is shared, including social benefits provided by law, so that all citizens can live what Roosevelt called "a healthy peacetime life." Often this has included safeguards for the most vulnerable in our society—including the young, the old, the poor, and the infirm. In the wake of the Civil War, legislation was passed to support the well-being of widows and veterans, and to provide land to former slaves. By the early 20th century, all of our states had recognized that children needed schooling in order to become free and engaged citizens and had instituted free education for all. During the Great Depression, new programs were introduced to ensure the security of those who could no longer work. In the 1960s, several administrations announced a "war on poverty," and programs were established to provide health care for seniors and the very poor. And this year saw the passage of major legislation that will greatly expand the number of Americans who have health insurance. In every case, the creation of these programs has reflected a popular sense that the society in which we want to live is one in which each person has the opportunity to live a full and fulfilling life. That begins, but does not end, with the exercise of their human rights.

See Also Terms: 11, 20, 70, 83, 138, 144, 145, 152, 167, 168, 169, 172, 174, 180, 184, 199, 204, 244, 259, 283, 284, 309, 316, 322, 323.

93. Effective Domestic Remedy

Definition: A legal remedy exercisable within the national legal system, which can in fact result in the protection of one's exercise of human rights by force of national law.

Significance: This is an obligation contained in most human rights treaties, so that individuals within the states parties can obtain effective legal recourse within the state's legal system and not have to resort to an international forum to protect human rights. This is in fulfillment of the principle of subsidiarity, which says that the international system for protection is secondary or subordinate to the national system. If they do not already exist, states must create effective legal remedies that individuals can use within the national legal systems when their human rights are violated. Article 8 of the UDHR states, "Everyone has the right to an effective remedy by the competent national tribunals for acts violating the fundamental rights granted him by the constitution or by law." See Document 6. Article 2.3 of the ICCPR (see Document 8) states:

Each State Party to the present Covenant undertakes:
(a)To ensure that any person whose rights or freedoms as herein recognized are violated shall have an effective remedy, notwithstanding that the violation has been committed by persons acting in an official capacity;
(b)To ensure that any person claiming such a remedy shall have his right thereto determined by competent judicial, administrative or legislative authorities, or by any other competent authority provided for by the legal system of the State, and to develop the possibilities of judicial remedy;
(c)To ensure that the competent authorities shall enforce such remedies when granted.

Every state is bound to create effective and accessible domestic remedies that all human rights issues can be resolved in the U.S. under the principle of subsidiarity. Without effective remedies human rights are illusory and the state has failed to fulfill its obligations to its people.

See Also Terms: 11, 25, 26, 48, 70, 71, 76, 88, 90, 107, 113, 118, 134, 151, 158, 162, 165, 177, 179, 184, 194, 222, 244, 252, 253, 254, 259, 272, 283, 296, 297, 316.

94. EFFECTIVENESS (PRINCIPLE OF)

Definition: A general principle of international law that is usually invoked in the interpretation and application of an international legal norm. This principle states that a treaty norm should be interpreted and applied in such a way as to give maximum effect to the treaty in which it is found and which best achieves the treaty's "object and purpose." Also defined more specifically as a general principle of international human rights and humanitarian law which holds that human rights treaty obligations undertaken by states must be interpreted and implemented, that is, put into real practice, in the manner and by such means which best protect all persons, and are interpreted in light of social developments. This principle is expressed in Latin as *ut res magis valeat quam pereat,* which means "so that the thing may be more effective, rather than be wasted/lost."

Significance: Very often in applying the terms of a treaty there is an issue of an individual or a group claiming a human rights violation of specific substantive human rights found in particular articles of a treaty. Often there is a dispute between the parties as to the correct interpretation and application of the treaty.

As an example, suppose an individual lost his home and one of his children to the unlawful action of the government and the case was taken to a local court which applied the international human rights norms to the situation. The court found a violation of the human rights norms and as a remedy ruled that a judicial finding of a violation by the state was sufficient and just satisfaction for the violation, with no monetary reparations (money damages) ordered. This would constitute a violation of the principle of effectiveness because it is the intent of the treaty to cause the state to refrain from violating human rights. If there are no reparations ordered, such as monetary reparation, then the treaty will be ineffective to deter violation by the state. This is because the state will think that it can continue to act as it did in violation of human rights and that it will not suffer any concrete loss for doing so. This failure of the court to impose full and just satisfaction for the losses suffered by the petitioner works against the maximum effectiveness of the treaty's object and purpose to prevent such violations.

As an example in the U.S. situation under the ICCPR, Article 9.5, regarding liberty and security of persons, states that "Anyone who has been a victim of unlawful arrest or detention shall have an enforceable right to compensation." See Document 8. This means nothing less than if one is wrongfully arrested or detained one does have the right to compensation for the loss of freedom and to deter the state from wrongfully arresting or detaining others. However, in the U.S. ratification of the ICCPR, the U.S. submitted an Understanding (See Reservations, Declarations, Understandings, infra) which reads: "that the United States understands the right to compensation referred to in Article 9(5) and 14(6) to require the provision of effective and enforceable mechanisms by which a victim of an unlawful arrest or detention or a miscarriage of justice may seek, and where justified, obtain compensation from either the responsible individual or the appropriate government entity. Entitlement to compensation may be subject to the reasonable requirements of domestic law."

This last sentence, which is extremely vague, and includes legal defense such as sovereign immunity, works against the effectiveness of Article 9(5) on compensation and thus violates the principle of effectiveness.

See Also Terms: 11, 23, 46, 69, 70, 103, 158, 186, 225, 259, 272.

95. ENEMY COMBATANT
See entry for **Combatant**

96. ENHANCED/ROBUST INTERROGATION TECHNIQUES

Definition: A term used by the U.S. government to described methods or means, including physical and psychological, of enticing or coercing a detainee to reveal information, and which methods are more robust and coercive than normal.

Significance: The war on terrorism has had a large part of its battles waged in interrogation rooms where captured terrorist suspects or persons believed to have sensitive information helpful in fighting that war have been interrogated by the U.S. Sometimes these people have been sent to other countries with perhaps more robust techniques. In the U.S. interrogation program since 9/11, much criticism from within and without the U.S. has come regarding how military and intelligence agents extract information from those detainees. The question is whether the government is following U.S. law, and sometimes specifically international law, such as the Torture Convention and the ICCPR. See Documents 6 and 19. Many domestic NGOs and international NGOs and international organizations such as the U.N. have written reports on this subject.

The issue is whether interrogation measures which the U.S. calls "enhanced interrogation techniques" are legal under U.S. law or international human rights and humanitarian law. The issue is whether these practices constitute either torture or cruel or inhuman, or degrading treatment or punishment. Use of a title such as "Enhanced Interrogation Techniques" is not sufficient to make them in compliance with international norms. The actual practice needs to be examined and judged objectively in light of the legal standards, particularly ICCPR Article 7, as interpreted in light of the appropriate U.N. HRCee General Comments (see Appendix E), and the definition of torture in the Torture Convention, as well as the case law, both national and international, on whether these practices are consistent with human right in legal reality. It is also a question as whether they were consistent with the Geneva Conventions, whether the victims were lawful or unlawful combatants or civilians. (See entry for Combatants).

In the period from 2002 to 2005 the Administration operated on certain legal memos from the Office of the Chief Counsel of the Justice in response to certain questions raised by the Administration regarding the lawfulness of certain intelligence practise. These were given the name the "Torture Memos." (See Document 91, and Appendix M). These legal opinions went far in allowing the Administration to engage in a wide variety of actions to wage war on terrorism in the interrogation rooms of Guantanamo and Abu Ghraib and other detention centers, both known and secret. As these techniques were discovered and as eventually the memos became public, there were allegations that these enhanced interrogation techniques were, in fact and law, actually torture or cruel or inhuman or degrading treatment.

It must be remembered that international legal norms from ratified human rights and humanitarian law treaties, and from customary international law are part and parcel of U.S. law by virtue of the U.S. Constitution, Article VI, which makes them the supreme law of the land. In fact, the provision of international human rights law can be used in relation to the 8th amendment prohibition on cruel and unusual punishment, to inform its content. See Document 2.

According to a New York Times report updated August 2009, CIA sources described a list of six "Enhanced Interrogation Techniques" instituted in mid-March 2002. These techniques were said to have been used on a dozen top al Qaeda targets who were detained and held incommunicado at secret locations on military bases which spread from Asia to East Europe. These suspects were known as "high value detainees." It seems a special set of interrogation techniques was used on them as it was deemed most important to get them to talk. The NYT news sources revealed that only a handful of CIA interrogators are trained and authorized to use the following so called enhanced interrogation techniques:

1. **The Attention Grab**: The interrogator forcefully grabs the shirt front of the prisoner and shakes him.

2. **Attention Slap**: An open-handed slap aimed at causing pain and triggering fear.

3. **The Belly Slap**: A hard open-handed slap to the stomach. The aim is to cause pain, but not internal injury. Doctors consulted advised against using a punch, which could cause lasting internal damage.

4. **Long Time Standing**: This technique is described as among the most effective. Prisoners are forced to stand, handcuffed and with their feet shackled to an eye bolt in the floor for more than 40 hours. Exhaustion and sleep deprivation are effective in yielding confessions.

5. **The Cold Cell**: The prisoner is left to stand naked in a cell kept near 50 degrees. Throughout the time in the cell the prisoner is doused with cold water.

6. **Waterboarding**: The prisoner is bound to an inclined board, feet raised and head slightly below the feet. Cellophane is wrapped over the prisoner's face and water is poured over him. Unavoidably, the gag reflex kicks in and a terrifying fear of drowning leads to almost instant pleas to bring the treatment to a halt.

According to the NYT sources, CIA officers who subjected themselves to the water boarding technique lasted an average of 14 seconds before caving in. They said al Qaeda's toughest prisoner, Khalid Sheik Mohammed, won the admiration of interrogators when he was able to last between two and two-and-a-half minutes before begging to confess. Much has been debated about the enhanced interrogation technique known as waterboarding. See entry for Waterboarding, below.

The George W. Bush Administration denied that it was torture. The Obama administration came in and the new President issued an order concerning torture prohibiting such acts, and ordered the Torture Memos rescinded. The Attorney General expressly stated that he considered waterboarding to constitute torture and issued a withdrawal of the Torture Memos. See Document 92.

The issue of appropriate interrogation techniques continued into the Obama administration. This issue has been the subject of certain reports by special rapporteurs on torture and on protection of human rights while countering terrorism, from the U.N. Human Rights Council. These are set forth in Appendix M. These reports include, inter alia, the underlying international law interpretations of the relevant international norms showing how these techniques are regarded in international law.

In November 2010, the U.S. was reviewed before the U.N. Human Rights Council. These enhanced interrogation techniques were an issue. The U.S. national UPR report to the OHCHR addresses this issue. See U.S. report to OHCHR for UPR, Document 86 and the Human Rights Council final Outcome Report Document 87. In paras. 82–84 of Document 86 the U.S. government reports under the title "Values and National Security":

> The United States is currently at war with Al Qaeda and its associated forces. President Obama has made clear that the United States is fully committed to complying with the Constitution and with all applicable domestic and international law, including the laws of war, in all aspects of this or any armed conflict. We start from the premise that there are no law-free zones, and that everyone is entitled to protection under law. In his Nobel Lecture, the President made clear that '[w]here force is necessary, we have a moral and strategic interest in binding ourselves to certain rules of conduct...[E]ven as we confront a vicious adversary that abides by no rules...the United States of America must remain a standard bearer in the conduct of war.'

On his second full day in office, President Obama acted to implement this vision by issuing three Executive Orders relating to U.S. detention, interrogation, and transfer policies and the Guantánamo Bay detention facility. See Documents 90, 92.

Executive Order 13491, *Ensuring Lawful Interrogations*, directed that individuals detained in any armed conflict shall in all circumstances be treated humanely and shall not be subjected to violence to life and person, nor to outrages upon personal dignity, whenever such individuals are in the custody or under the effective control of the United States Government or detained within a facility owned, operated, or controlled by the United States. Such individuals shall not be subjected to any interrogation technique or approach that is not authorized by and listed in Army Field Manual 2-22.3, which explicitly prohibits threats, coercion, physical abuse, and water boarding. See Document 87 and entry for Waterboarding, infra. Individuals detained in armed conflict must be treated in conformity with all applicable laws, including Common Article 3 of the 1949 Geneva Conventions, which the President and the Supreme Court have recognized as providing "minimum" standards of protection in all non-international armed conflicts, including in the conflict with Al Qaeda.

The Executive Order also directed a review of all U.S. transfer policies to ensure that they do not result in the transfer of individuals to other nations to face torture or otherwise for the purpose, or with the effect, of undermining or circumventing the commitments or obligations of the United States to ensure the humane treatment of individuals in its custody or control.

Thus, the United States prohibits torture and cruel, inhuman, or degrading treatment or punishment of persons in the custody or control of the U.S. Government, regardless of their nationality or physical location. It takes vigilant action to prevent such conduct and to hold those who commit acts of official cruelty accountable for their wrongful acts. The United States is a party to the Convention Against Torture, and U.S. law prohibits torture at both the federal and state levels. See Documents 19, 20. On June 26, 2010, on the anniversary of adoption of the Convention Against Torture, President Obama issued a statement unequivocally reaffirming U.S. support for its principles, and committing the United States to continue to cooperate in international efforts to eradicate torture.

See Also Terms: 11, 12, 20, 24, 33, 34, 35, 41, 45, 48, 53, 58, 59, 65, 66, 70, 71, 73, 81, 82, 84, 88, 93, 95, 103, 104, 111, 117, 124, 129, 132, 134, 144, 145, 151, 152, 154, 159, 160, 161, 167, 170, 171, 177, 178, 179, 182, 184, 192, 211, 215, 219, 248, 252, 253, 256, 259, 266, 272, 275, 302, 309, 316, 317, 318, 320.

97. Entry into Force (EIF)

Definition: The stage of the treaty-making process at which a treaty actually becomes legally binding upon any state that has signed and ratified it. It is sometimes abbreviated E.I.F.

Significance: Treaties are a source of most human rights that form part of the U.S. legal landscape. These treaties are contracts entered into by the United States as a sovereign state and governed by international law as opposed to national law. Appendix F, *How an International Human Rights Norm Becomes U.S. Law,* contains a flow chart of the process.

A treaty is first proposed, then a diplomatic conference is convened; the text of the treaty is negotiated until finished, and then it is voted upon and adopted, which establishes the exact official text. Then the treaty is open for signature and signed by whichever states choose to sign, indicating their intent to become legally bound by the treaty after it is ratified by the state. At a certain point in the ratification process, as set forth in the text of the treaty instrument, the treaty actually becomes a binding law between the states who ratified it. That point is called "entry into force." Usually, entry into force happens upon the deposit of a certain numbered ratification, such as seen in Article 49 of the ICCPR, which entered into force ninety days after the 35th state deposited its instrument of ratification with the United Nations. See Document 8.

The United States is not legally bound to comply with a human rights treaty unless the treaty has entered into force and the United States has both signed and ratified it. The United States has signed and ratified the Genocide Convention, which entered into force in 1948. It is thus bound by that convention. The United States has signed but not ratified the American Convention on Human Rights, which entered into force in 1978. The United States signed it in 1974. Because the U.S. Senate has never ratified it, the United States is not legally bound by it.

See Also Terms: 2, 25, 26, 48, 151, 215, 220, 222, 226, 259, 262, 269, 272, 279, 280, 291, 293, 297, 306, 307.

98. ENVIRONMENTAL RACISM

Definition: A hybrid environmental and human rights term which express the disproportionate state of environmental conditions and economic, social and health problems that people of a certain race endure as one aspect of racial discrimination in society.

Significance: Everything which affects the human person and his or her human dignity engages human rights. This includes the effects of the environmental surroundings in which people live, work and play. Everyone knows that there are substantial problems in the U.S. with environmental pollution. This pollution takes many forms, including auto emissions, water pollution, chemical discharges from factories, lead paint, and noise pollution. This could also include the placement of a dam, levee or seawall and its effects on adjacent land. The claim of environmental racism was made in relation to the effects of Hurricane Katrina. This was as much for the state of the Louisiana and adjacent states environmental preparedness, such as the condition of the levees, and the speed and amount of relief response from the government. Under international human rights law every part of the country and every racial group should have the same quality and proportional quantity of environmental preparedness and response to disaster, natural, such as Katrina and man made, such as the BP oil spill of 2010.

Environmental racism occurs where the noxious effects of environmental conditions either intentionally or negligently fall disproportionately upon the poorer classes of Americans and non American residents, and have a deleterious effect upon a certain race of persons, such as Latinos, African-Americans or other politically less powerful racial or ethnic groups. The implication is that the predominant racial group, in the U.S. case, Caucasians, have the power and money and political influence to cause the negative effects of environmental harm to fall away from them and onto those who are politically less powerful, which is usually a minority racial or ethnic group.

Usually the effect of this negative environmental harm is higher disease, higher birth defects, higher incidences of cancer, lower life expectancy. Where this happens a human rights violation would arguably occur if the government, federal, state, or local becomes aware of this disproportionate effect and fails to exercise its affirmative obligation to protect the weaker or more exposed racial group.

The main human rights norms involved in environmental racism are equality and nondiscrimination. Because environmental racism can have a strong impact on economical, social and cultural rights it is hard to say that in America everyone has ESC rights against environmental racism. This is because the U.S. has not ratified the ICESCR. Many of the impacts of environmental racism fall within the scope of economic, social and cultural rights. In this regards U.S. human rights law coverage is weak. It can be argued, though, that because the U.S. has signed the ICESCR, it has a soft or "interim" legal obligation to refrain from acts which would defeat the object and purpose of the ICESCR treaty. (See Appendix E, Vienna Convention.)

Over the past few years there has been a convergence of the international and national legal fields of international human rights law and environmental law. This is logical as any environmental problem which affects humankind brings into play human rights norms. An example is the *Doe vs. UNOCAL* case in the U.S. District Court, over environmental degradation occurring in a foreign country with the alleged participation of a U.S.-based transnational corporation. A few cases involving alleged environmental racism have been litigated in U.S. Courts.

An important case with adverse consequences for the environment and human rights law movement occurred in June 2010 when the Second Circuit Court of Appeals ruled in the case of *Kiobel v. Royal Dutch Petroleum* that the plaintiffs could not assert customary international human rights law in an ATCA cause of action against the corporate oil company defendants for aiding and abetting offenses against the law of nations. See Appendix J. That case could limit the use of human rights law in fighting corporate environmental damage in other countries where corporations are aiding and abetting governments to cause environmental damage that harms a certain sector of the population seriously.

See Also Terms: 20, 39, 40, 55, 70, 72, 83, 92, 144, 145, 151, 152, 167, 177, 179, 221, 260, 261, 283.

99. EQUALITY/EQUALITY BEFORE THE LAW

Definition: Equality is a principle of justice that says that all human beings are equal in value, that they all have the same intrinsic worth and human rights, and thus they should be treated equally because of their inherent human dignity. When used in the term "equality before the law," it means the right of an individual to equal treatment in the administration or application of the law by law enforcement authorities and by the ordinary courts of the land.

Significance: Human equality is a general principle of elementary justice that applies to all human rights. It means that whatever level may be reached in the realization of those rights in a particular country, human rights should be applied in the same way to every individual residing there, without discrimination of any kind. The principle of the equal dignity and worth of every individual in society must be reflected and applied in law and public policy. Even though theoretically every human being is equal, certain differential treatments can be permitted where there is a reasonable and objective justification for doing so, such as for the handicapped, children, pregnant women.

Historically, the United States, more than any other country, gave meaning to the concept of equality in the field of international human rights. Within the United States itself, the equality principle is essential to its democratic system. It is outlined in depth throughout the country's founding documents, including the Declaration of Independence ("all men are created equal") and the Bill of Rights, the first 10 amendments to the Constitution. See Document 2.

Protection of human rights requires a society characterized by equality and rule of law, where no one is "above the law," and where there is a society "of laws and not of man." All public institutions must treat everyone equally, regardless of race, color, wealth, or any other status or characteristic.

There are specific norms establishing this principle in international human rights instruments. The first main example was Article 7 of the UDHR. See Document 6. The major legal instrument to which the United States is a party that contains this principle is the ICCPR preamble and Article 3 (equality between men and women), Article 14.1 (equality before courts), and Article 26 (equality before the law). See Document 8.

In human rights language, "equality before the law" is roughly the same as "equal protection of law" under the U.S. Constitution.

In 2007 the U.N. Human Rights Committee issued General Comment No. 32 entitled: "Article 14: Right to equality before courts and tribunals and to a fair trial." This was largely motivated by the treatment of persons apprehended and prosecuted in the so called war on terrorism, some of whom were prosecuted in military tribunals having little semblance of due process. See the text of this General Comment in Appendix M.

See Also Terms: 7, 11, 12, 14, 15, 20, 24, 28, 29, 33, 34, 35, 48, 54, 55, 69, 76, 73, 75, 86, 90, 99, 113, 124, 144, 145, 146, 151, 160, 162, 167, 169, 177, 179, 184, 202, 205, 216, 222, 252, 253, 254, 259, 260, 265, 272, 309, 316.

100. EQUALITY OF ARMS

See entries for **Due Process of Law** and **Procedural Rights**

101. ETHNIC CLEANSING

Definition: The forcible removal by fear or threat, or the actual physical removal or destruction of an ethnic group or groups from a specified territory, so as to eliminate all but one ethnic group from that territory.

Significance: This term was first coined in the context of the Bosnian conflict in the early 1990s between three different ethnic groups: the Bosnian Serbs, Bosnian Croats, and Bosniaks or Bosnian Muslims. Each of these three groups tried to forcibly and otherwise remove members of the other ethnic groups from a certain territory, which it hoped to control and govern free from the presence of the other, thus creating ethnically pure territories.

Generally speaking, ethnic cleansing is done to render the territory ethnically free from the presence of the other group and to create an ethnically homogeneous (or "pure") territory. It is the removal of the members of all other ethnic groups, except the one doing the cleansing. Ethnic cleansing is a problem that may occur in reaction to diverse, multicultural social situations. It is based on social attitudes that are characterized as nationalistic or ethnocentric, and possibly even racist, in the broadest sense.

At its core, the concept of ethnic cleansing violates the idea of basic human rights and the inherent dignity and equality of every person, regardless of ethnic origin. The acts of ethnic cleansing usually involve violations of the right to life, freedom from torture, cruel, inhuman and degrading treatment and punishment, liberty and security of person, nondiscrimination, freedom of movement, right to protection of family life and right to property, just to name a few. These would constitute violations of the ICCPR, Articles 2.1, 7, 9, 12, 14, and 27, to name a few. See Document 8.

When ethnic cleansing is done in the context of an armed conflict, it violates international law norms found in the body of humanitarian law. Humanitarian law is the law of armed conflict, such as found in the fourth Geneva Convention and Protocol, and in the Laws and Customs of War, under customary international law. (See Article 49, Document 72.)

There is no one specific international legal norm against "ethnic cleansing." Ethnic cleansing is unlawful because it violates many different human rights and humanitarian law norms. See the Statute of the International Criminal Tribunal for the Former Yugoslavia, on the various legal norms relating to acts of ethnic cleansing in the Bosnia conflict.

The United States was very involved as part of its activities under NATO (IFOR/SFOR) and the United Nations in stopping ethnic cleansing in Bosnia and overseeing the return of persons to their home in areas from which they had been removed. Ethnic cleansing not only violates human rights but also creates international crises, usually engaging U.S. political and military activity.

The classic historical example of ethnic cleansing was the attempt by Nazi Germany to get rid of all Jews from Germany, thus making it "Judenrein," meaning "free of Jews." The 1994 Rwanda massacre of Tutsis by Hutus is also an example of such a phenomenon. There ethnic cleansing led to genocide of over 800,000 people.

Under international law there is no legal right for any ethnic, racial or religious group to forcibly remove members of any other group from its territory. The United Nations created an International Criminal Tribunal for the former Yugoslavia in 1994 to prosecute human rights violations for acts constituting ethnic cleansing that were also international crimes. The United States helped establish and supported this court. Convictions rendered by this court proved that ethnic cleansing can constitute an international crime.

Acts constituting ethnic cleansing on a widespread or systematic basis against the civilian population, or in the context of an armed conflict, can be an international crime recognizable under the Rome Statute for an International Criminal Court. See Articles 7.2(d) and 8.2(a). See Document 76.

The decision in the case of *Kadic v. Karadzic*, (see Appendix J) shows how U.S. courts can deal with the international human rights and humanitarian law issues arising from ethnic cleansing in the conflict in the former Yugoslavia.

See Also Terms: 8, 11, 12, 15, 19, 20, 22, 26, 33, 34, 35, 36, 39, 48, 71, 72, 78, 85, 100, 102, 108, 117, 124, 129, 130, 133, 137, 144, 145, 151, 152, 153, 160, 163, 167, 170, 176, 177, 179, 181, 182, 184, 188, 192, 201, 205, 212, 216, 228, 235, 237, 260, 261, 263, 271, 272, 277, 283, 297, 309, 316, 317, 318, 319, 324.

102. ETHNIC MINORITY

Definition: A group of people who identify with each other as being from the same particular stock of human beings and who are different based on their particular characteristics such as physical features, history, customs and homeland. They are a minority because, as a group, they are fewer in number than the majority group in the state.

Significance: Article 27 of the ICCPR reads, "In those States in which ethnic, religious or linguistic minorities exist, persons belonging to such minorities shall not be denied the right, in community with the other members of their group, to enjoy their own culture, to profess and practice their own religion, or to use their own language." See Document 8.

There have been many international instruments dealing in some way with the rights of ethnic minorities. It is an important area of human rights, since many atrocities have occurred worldwide that are based on prejudice against people with common ethnic characteristics. Ethnic cleansing is one of those atrocities, as well as genocide. Aside from the atrocities, however, there are other valid concerns of ethnic minorities, notably their right to a group cultural identity, and these rights are dealt with as well.

Oftentimes, when ethnic minority rights are discussed, there are also philosophical dilemmas involved, such as individual versus group rights and cultural relativism versus universality of rights.

See the Second and Third Reports of the United States to the U.N. Human Rights Committee, Document 15A, regarding U.S. law and practice on minority rights under Article 27.

See Also Terms: 11, 12, 14, 15, 20, 24, 39, 55, 56, 63, 67, 70, 72, 78, 86, 87, 100, 124, 130, 144, 145, 152, 156, 160, 163, 167, 169, 176, 177, 179, 180, 184, 188, 205, 216, 237, 242, 255, 259, 260, 261, 263, 277, 278, 283, 309, 316.

103. EXCEPTIONALISM

Definition: The attitude of a state that certain international human rights standards do not apply to that country or a certain actions of the state, such as the international military peacekeeping. It is the attitude of a state that it *should* be recognized as enjoying a *special* exception or exemption from the applicability of certain human rights/humanitarian law norms because of a unique set of circumstances.

Significance: This term is seen particularly in the area of armed conflicts or peacekeeping and is usually used to describe the attitude and actions of the United States of America in the context of the International Community as regards the applicability of international human rights and humanitarian law, as to war crimes, genocide, crimes against humanity, and aggression. The attitude of the U.S. came into *play* most conspicuously and controversially as to whether the U.S. would ratify the Statute of the International Criminal Court. That statute was adopted in 1998, with the U.S. voting against its adoption. Since its adoption the U.S. has stated the U.S. would ratify the ICC statute if official U.S. government acts and actions of U.S. government and military personnel would be immune from prosecution by the ICC. The U.S. felt that it should enjoy such immunity because of the extensive military presence of the U.S. all over the world, it being the world's policeman and involved in peace keeping activities.

There has been a general perception of many people in foreign countries and many in the U.S. that the U.S. believes is should be above the law as for as international law is concerned, and that it should be above to do whatever it wants if it feels it meets the strategic goals of the war on terrorism.

Much of the attitude of exceptionalism comes from a perception of many in government that international law can pose too great a limitation on the sovereignty of a nation and prevent it from meeting certain perceived critical national security challenges, especially those perceived to be new and different, such as asymmetrical warfare or bio terrorism.

This can lead to a situation where government demonizes a certain group of those causing the threat, such as Al Quaeda, and seeks to portray them as not deserving any human rights because the demonized persons are perceived to be acting in a manner that deprives others of human rights. The perception is that those who deprive others of human rights do not deserve to have any protection from human rights themselves. This is not the law. Nothing the perpetrators do causes them to lose their inalienable human rights. However, they can be captured, arrested, prosecuted and punished for any criminally wrongful acts.

By making these perpetrators out to be undeserving of human rights protection they feel justified in treating them in any way they wish, regardless of the international standards. They tend to either disregard international legal standards or to interpret the international standards in a way that allows the state to act any way it feels necessary to meet the perceived threat. The saying that has usually accompanied such an attitude in the U.S. since the war on terrorism started has been something like: "we cannot let international treaties be a suicide pact." The implication is that if the state complies with its international legal obligations it will not be able to meet its national security threat." This is reinforced when the enemy is perceived as not "playing by the rules."

The problem with the attitude of exceptionalism is that it works against respect for the rule of law among states at the international level and fosters other states following that example and disregarding or too narrowly interpreting the international standards. This has happened in the war on terrorism with a number of states following the U.S. lead passing so called anti terrorism laws which are inconsistent with international standards. Exceptionalism breeds resentment by smaller states which try to follow the standards but see the big nations like the U.S. acting like might makes right.

The attitude of exceptionalism is inconsistent with a culture of human rights and accountability, and a culture of peace. Where the domestic population of a state does not know what the international human rights and humanitarian law standards are they cannot hold the government to compliance with those standards. The remedy is human rights education.

Much of the U.N. human rights activity presented under the theme "protection of human rights while countering terrorism" is actually aimed at addressing this perceived attitude by the U.S. and certain other states. See Documents 54-56 and 58.

In its August 2010, national UPR report the U.S. government very carefully tried to assert that it feels that the U.S., despite its power and importance in the world, must abide by the same standards as every other state in the world. See Document 86, paras. 5 and 82. This is aimed at suggesting that the U.S. no longer sees itself as exceptionalist.

See Also Terms: 3, 13, 23, 48, 59, 70, 71, 72, 89, 96, 104, 110, 111, 117, 145, 147, 151, 154, 157, 159, 177, 179, 181, 182, 184, 185, 193, 201, 210, 211, 212, 215, 222, 225, 226, 239, 243, 244, 252, 259, 272, 275, 283, 292, 299, 306, 308, 309, 312, 316, 317, 318, 320, 323.

104. EXCESSIVE FORCE

Definition: The use of more physical force than is permitted by law, or more than is reasonable under the circumstances, by government agents.

Significance: It is the use of force to a level that violates human rights. It is force that cannot be justified by law, giving the victim a right to make a claim against the government for damages or injuries suffered. It is force that crosses the line from reasonable and lawful use to unreasonable and unlawful use.

It could theoretically also be used in reference to government acts against the property of a person. It is usually committed by law enforcement agents, especially the police, but could be applied to other government agencies. It most often occurs in the attempt to apprehend and search for a person sought by law enforcement.

Human rights violations are the use of power by government in a manner exceeding their lawful powers. When excessive force is used against a human being, it violates their dignity and hence their human rights, engaging the responsibility of the state under both national and, likely, international law.

The use of excessive force could, depending upon the circumstances, motives and degree of force used, violate ICCPR, Article 7, regarding torture or cruel and inhuman treatment or punishment; or if the person dies, Article 6, the right to life. See Document 8. It may, if torture occurs, constitute a violation of the Convention against Torture (see Document 19, Articles 1, 2, and 4).

The beating of Rodney King in the mid-1990s in Los Angeles was considered a classic example of the use of excessive force. Another example is the force used by the United States in the NATO bombing of Yugoslavia in 1999, which many claimed was excessive force. This claim was based on the belief that the force used by the U.S. military (within NATO attacks) was more than was necessary to get the Yugoslav government to cease its alleged atrocities and ethnic cleansing in Kosovo. This claim says that the U.S. use of force was excessive, beyond that lawfully permitted under international law regarding the use of armed force. If this claim were true, the U.S. actions would constitute a violation of the law of armed conflict, especially where an extensive number of civilian persons and property were damaged by the attack.

Humanitarian law norms prohibiting excessive force in armed conflicts can be found in Documents 69, 71, 73 (Articles 35, 57), and 76 (Articles 8.2 (b)(iv) and 8.2(b)(xx).

See Also Terms: 11, 12, 26, 33, 34, 35, 38, 40, 42, 48, 53, 58, 59, 63, 70, 72, 96, 124, 125, 129, 132, 135, 136, 137, 151, 152, 154, 164, 166, 177, 179, 181, 182, 184, 192, 201, 215, 222, 238, 239, 259, 272, 283, 294, 302, 314, 316, 317, 318, 321.

105. EXECUTIVE AGREEMENTS (EA)

Definition: Formal agreements entered into by the President of the United States with another country's leader, looking much like a treaty but not subject to the treaty requirement of the Constitution, Article II, section 2 (two-thirds majority Senate vote). Such agreements normally cover matters not deemed to be the normal subject of treaties.

Significance: The President can enter into executive agreements with other countries that affect the human rights of Americans in foreign countries or of aliens in the United States. Access to the courts, ownership of property, criminal jurisdiction and due process rights are all examples. A Status of Forces agreement would be an example of an executive agreement that could affect not only people in the military but also people harmed by them.

Executive agreements are considered the rough equivalent of treaties. They are often undertaken by the President when he thinks the Senate would not approve a treaty under Article II, Section II of the U.S. Constitution. See Document 2. Although such instruments are not part of the Constitution and thus not the "supreme law of the land" under Article VI, they are still subject to all U.S. Constitutional limitations in the Bill of Rights.

The President is the head of state of the United States, in charge of foreign policy in international relations and law, and he has the power to act internationally with any country. He must act consistent with U.S. international human rights obligations to the extent that those obligations are consistent with the Constitution. Executive agreements cannot violate human rights norms. They cannot change existing U.S. domestic law but must operate within the bounds of that law.

See Also Terms: 70, 177, 184, 193, 194, 210, 211, 222, 243, 259, 272, 286, 287, 292.

106. EXECUTIVE ORDERS

Definition: Formal legal statements issued by the President of the United States concerning an area of international law or policy and applying to the actions of the pertinent U.S. government departments and agencies.

Significance: In U.S. law, treaties are the main source of U.S. national law involving international human rights obligations. Congressional legislation is another source, whether it is part of legislation implementing a treaty or standing on its own. Executive orders (EOs) are another type of legal device used by the President as chief executive of the U.S. government to set the policy and practice of government in certain fields. Such orders have been made by Presidents since the early days of this country. They sound like laws. Human rights can be one of the fields affected by such orders. Such orders can be issued to state the administration's policy on how the U.S. government will fulfill its obligations regarding human rights. They can serve as a policy directive with the force of law when used by the administration to govern the executive branch of government.

In December 1998, President Clinton, on the occasion of Human Rights Day (December 10), issued an executive order wherein he ordered the executive branch of the government to become aware of and to act in compliance with U.S. international human rights obligations. This EO also called for a process of inquiries and complaints regarding human rights violations and established an interagency Working Group on Human Rights Treaties to coordinate all government activities in order to bring the U.S. in compliance with all its human rights treaty obligations. In 2009 President Obama issued an EO ordering the closing of the Guantanamo detention center and an EO stopping what his administration believed was unlawful authorization by the previous administration for commission of acts of torture. See Documents 90, 92.

Although EOs have been used for a long time, they are very problematic politically because they make it appear that the President has law-making power. Under the Constitution it is Congress who has such power. Sometimes when the president issues an EO the Congress reacts as though the president is interfering with Congress's power over government, which happened with the December 1998 EO. EOs are subject to the Constitution and cannot be in violation of it.

See Also Terms: 25, 48, 59, 70, 177, 210, 211, 222, 243, 259, 272, 286, 287, 292, 302.

107. EXHAUSTION OF DOMESTIC REMEDIES

Definition: A principle of human rights law that requires that a person, group, organization or state wishing to file a formal complaint against an alleged violator state go through all legal procedures that are available, accessible and potentially effective within the national legal system before they can file the complaint with an international human rights forum for a formal decision.

Significance: The system of international human rights law created by the international community is a backup system to the laws and procedures each state should have to protect human rights. It is called a secondary or subsidiary system. The international law principle of subsidiarity makes it necessary to exhaust national remedies before going to the international human rights system. The international human rights community hopes that everyone who has been the victim of a violation seeks and finds legal resolution of the issue before the courts and administrative bodies of the state. States have established this principle as a way to avoid the embarrassment of having the case brought to world attention, the so-called "forum of shame." It requires that the matter be handled internally before being handled internationally. Only when the national system does not work or when it has not decided a case according to its international human rights legal obligations can a victim take the case to the international human rights bodies that are set up to handle complaints under a particular treaty.

Most human rights systems such as the U.N. treaty regimes or the OAS have commissions, committees or courts that can handle formal complaints of human rights violations of a state party to a treaty. These are called complaint procedures or mechanisms. See, for example, the International Covenant on Civil and Political Rights (ICCPR), Article 28, and 41–42, and its First Optional Protocol. See Document 8.

A victim or state wishing to bring a formal complaint against a state under international law must first seek domestic remedies through all available and effective domestic procedures. Only then can they resort to international bodies such as human rights commissions or courts. This means that normally one has to take one's case alleging a state violation all the way to the highest court in a state. If not possible, one has to go to the highest possible level in the legal system in a particular matter. Failure to exhaust domestic remedies in the violating state can be a ground for the court, commission or committee to deem the complaint "inadmissible" and to decide not to proceed any further with it.

There are some exceptions under international law principles to the exhaustion requirements. One is when the recourse would be fruitless, or when the victim or their representative is prevented by threat or force from using the procedure. Because of the need to fulfill the exhaustion of domestic remedies principle, many cases are filed years after the alleged violations. Very often the case is never adjudicated, either because the complainant dies, disappears, gives up or the problem gets resolved internally.

See Also Terms: 3, 5, 11, 26, 46, 88, 90, 93, 151, 158, 165, 179, 184, 185, 187, 208, 252, 253, 254, 259, 264, 272, 296, 306, 307.

108. EXPROPRIATION

Definition: Expropriation is a government's confiscation of the property of persons and companies who are from other countries against their will, and sometimes without paying any money or even allowing the victims to go to court to contest the taking or the fairness of any compensation paid.

Significance: U.S. companies operating in foreign countries may sometimes have their assets taken over by the government of the country and converted to use by that state. Such expropriation happens especially where the government dislikes the United States or is a socialist or communist state. An expropriation can constitute a human rights violation but is more a matter of private international law than classical human rights law that protects human beings, not companies. It is often treated in the field of human rights.

The main sources of human rights norms applicable to expropriation are the UDHR (Article 17) as it relates to the right to own property and the ICCPR (Article 14) on procedural due process of law. See Documents 6, 8.

See Also Terms: 11, 12, 20, 24, 33, 34, 35, 48, 70, 73, 83, 88, 90, 92, 93, 113, 124, 144, 145, 151, 152, 161, 167, 169, 177, 179, 184, 185, 193, 195, 252, 253, 257, 259, 267, 272, 283, 284, 287, 294.

109. EXTRADITION

Definition: The legal and political process whereby one state (the requested state) hands over to another state (the requesting state), usually after legal proceedings, a person who is alleged to have committed a crime in the requesting state, or someone who has escaped and fled to the requested state and whose return is requested for purposes of prosecution or punishment.

Significance: Extradition is the process by which the justice system of any country seeks to apprehend an alleged criminal who has fled their particular state and therefore jurisdiction.

It is essential for states to have this kind of arrangement with each other. In a world that values human rights, however, it is essential that the individual is protected, because he or she may be innocent or there may be extenuating circumstances regarding the accusations. Even if the accused turns out to be guilty, however, his basic human rights in the process must be respected in a "due process of law" manner. This process is a characteristic of a society that values the "rule of law."

There may be various circumstances that impede immediate extradition once someone has been apprehended. For example, the person may be seeking political asylum in the country to which she fled and proper asylum procedures would have to be followed. The person, as a refugee, may claim that she was a victim of human rights violations in her own country and had no effective remedy in her own state.

Sometimes, as in the famous *Soering* case, there is a conflict between human rights norms in one state and those in another. The *Soering* case involved a controversy over extraditing a citizen of a country without the death penalty to stand trial in a country that does allow the death penalty. See the *Soering* decision in Appendix J, Selected Case Decisions, for extradition issues involving human rights.

Closely related to extradition is the phenomenon of rendition and extraordinary rendition. These both are acts of one government handing a person over to another government to do something to that person. Sometimes it is a rendition to justice, such as where someone escaped from prison and is returned to the state of escape to serve a sentence, or to be prosecuted where there is no extradition treaty. Where it is not a case of fulfillment of a request under an extradition treaty, this is a rendition. This became a big issue during the so called war on terrorism because it was alleged that the U.S. and some other states purposefully sent terrorism suspects to other countries where they knew they would be persecuted or tortured to extract intelligence information or simply for punishment. This was known as extraordinary rendition. See the U.N. Human Rights Council Joint report of Special Rapporteurs on Secret Detention Centers, Appendix M.

See Also Terms: 3, 11, 12, 17, 18, 20, 24, 30, 33, 34, 48, 49, 53, 59, 65, 66, 70, 79, 81, 82, 88, 90, 93, 113, 122, 124, 134, 144, 145, 152, 160, 167, 169, 177, 179, 184, 195, 196, 211, 219, 238, 240, 248, 252, 253, 254, 256, 259, 263, 266, 272, 275, 283, 287, 292, 297, 306, 309, 316.

110. EXTRAJUDICIAL KILLING

Definition: In the Torture Victim Protection Act of 1992, extra judicial killing is defined as follows: "a deliberate killing not authorized by a previous judgment pronounced by a regularly constituted court affording all judicial guarantees which are recognized as indispensable by civilized peoples. Such term, however, does not include any such killing that, under international law, is lawfully carried out under the authority of a foreign nation." The U.N. Special Rapporteur on Extrajudicial, Summary or Arbitrary Executions stated that the terms "extrajudicial executions" and "unlawful killings" in his reports are used to refer to killings that violate international human rights or humanitarian law.

Significance: See Summary Execution entry, because the terms are synonymous.

The so called war on terrorism has seen an increase in deaths caused, not in battle on the battlefield, but in the targeted killings of suspected terrorists and of enemy leaders whom the government seeks to kill or neutralize in other places, such as by drone airplanes hovering overhead. These are called extrajudicial or summary or extra-legal executions. These attacks cannot ascertain whether they have targeted the right person or whether the person actually committed the acts for which he is getting attacked. In short they are killed without justice being done and are relying only on the presumption of guilt and the absolute justice of their cause, the justice of the killers. Summary executions without prior justice are violations of human rights law. This is not the same thing as a killing on the battlefield. It is a violation of the right to life, even if the victim caused the death of other persons.

See the Report of the Special Rapporteur on Extrajudicial, Summary or Arbitrary Executions, Paul Alston, on Targeted Killings and Drone attacks, Appendix M.

See Also Terms: 11, 12, 19, 20, 24, 25, 30, 33, 34, 35, 48, 59, 63, 70, 71, 73, 85, 88, 90, 93, 104, 124, 129, 132, 133, 135, 136, 137, 144, 145, 146, 151, 152, 154, 159, 160, 166, 167, 169, 175, 177, 179, 181, 182, 184, 185, 200, 201, 223, 224, 234, 235, 238, 259, 272, 294, 295, 298, 300, 309, 316, 317, 318.

111. EXTRAORDINARY RENDITION

See entry for **Rendition**

112. FACT-FINDING

Definition: A human rights process, mission or trip to some other place to gather factual information for purposes of investigating an alleged human rights violation, or to prepare a report on a particular country or theme.

Significance:

1. *Process:* Generally, a fact-finding process is any activity designed to obtain detailed knowledge of the relevant facts of any dispute or situation, conditions in a country or about a particular theme, such as prison conditions.

2. *Mission or Trip:* The human rights investigation mechanism of a fact-finding mission or trip involves an individual or team of persons going in person to a place, usually in another state, to investigate, gather firsthand information and seek the most accurate information. The fact finders then make a report about the true facts concerning a human rights situation, condition or issue, and submit the report back to the organization sponsoring the mission, such as an IGO. The facts are gathered by talking to victims, witnesses, government officials and any others (e.g., NGOs, union leaders, church officials) who can provide factual information about a general or specific human rights matter. In the human rights context, fact-finding most often refers to a process whereby members of an IGO organ, such as a human rights commission or a special rapporteur, go to places where an event, such as a massacre or disappearances, happened to gather evidence to help determine the true facts. The fact-finding often takes place at government offices, hospitals, prisons, police stations, mass grave sites or military bases. It can be fact-finding about a certain theme, general country conditions or a specific case based on a formal complaint.

Included in the document section are several reports by special rapporteurs with the results of their fact-finding trips to the United States. These reports represent an attempt to find out the factual reality of a situation or issue, and are not just the statements of the government or of a victim, individual or organization. They are also called country visits. They are also sometimes referred to as *in situ* or *in loco* investigations when they involve a specific alleged incident.

These may also be for forensic purposes such as when American forensic experts went to Bosnia to gather evidence from mass graves in the early 2000s to support criminal cases in the ICTY.

See Also Terms: 3, 4, 48, 60, 70, 71, 76, 94, 148, 150, 151, 178, 206, 227, 253, 264, 268, 289, 290, 317, 318.

113. FAIR TRIAL

Definition: A judicial or quasi-judicial legal proceeding, whether civil or criminal, which meets all international human rights standards of fairness though due process of law.

Significance: International human rights law imposes an obligation on states to provide a society based on rule of law. This obligation requires that states have a legal system with judicial remedies to enforce human rights and that judicial issues be resolved through resort to legal proceedings that are both fair to all parties and that appear in reality to be fair.

The primary international human rights standards on fair trial are set forth in Article 14 of the ICCPR. See Document 8. This article sets forth many of the specific rights included in the international legal norm. Because the United States has ratified the ICCPR, it has an obligation to provide fair trials to everyone within the United States. The Human Rights Committee can thus monitor fair trial issues to assure that the United States fulfills its obligations under Article 14. Other state parties can also address issues to the United States for denials of fair trial. Having ratified the ICCPR, the matter of fair trials is no longer simply a U.S. national or local issue. The U.S. government often comments on issues of denial of fair trial in other countries, especially in political trials, citing this article and Article 10 of the UDHR, which also deals with fair trial. The UDHR Article 10 is probably binding as a matter of customary international law. See Document 6.

See the Second and Third Reports of the United States to the U.N. Human Rights Committee (Document 15A) for the U.S. position on its law and practice in light of its obligations under the ICCPR, Article 14.

In 2007, the U.N. Human Rights Committee issued its General Comment No. 32(14) on equality before courts and tribunals and right to a fair trial. See Appendix M. It is likely that this General Comment was motivated in part by the Guantanamo detainee dilemma concerning access to courts and a fair trial. In Guantanamo the U.S. government was denying detainees access to civilian courts and even denying access to lawyers to challenge the legality of their detention until ordered to do so. The government tried to set up a military commission to deal with the detainees. The U.S. Supreme Court ruled this unlawful and stated that the detainees, even if they were so called "enemy combatants," had a right to access to U.S. federal courts to determine the legality of detention by habeas corpus. The Supreme Court also found that the initial military commission was not a properly constituted court and did not provide sufficient due process guarantees. (See Case Law section Appendix J, on *Rasul, Hamdan, Hamdi, Boumedienne*).

In its General Comment No 32(14) the Human Rights Committee addresses the issue of the reason for a fair trial and the type of court involved:

> The right to equality before the courts and tribunals and to a fair trial is a key element of human rights protection and serves as a procedural means to safeguard the rule of law. Article 14 of the Covenant aims at ensuring the proper administration of justice, and to this end guarantees a series of specific rights.
>
> The provisions of Article 14 apply to all courts and tribunals within the scope of that article whether ordinary or specialized, civilian or military. The Committee notes the existence, in many countries, of military or special courts which try civilians. While the Covenant does not prohibit the trial of civilians in military or special courts, it requires that such trials are in full conformity with the requirements of Article 14 and that its guarantees cannot be limited or modified because of the military or special character of the court concerned. The Committee also notes that the trial of civilians in military or special courts may raise serious problems as far as the equitable, impartial and independent administration of justice is concerned. Therefore, it is important to take all necessary measures to ensure that such trials take place under conditions which genuinely afford the full guarantees stipulated in Article 14. Trials of civilians by military or special courts should be exceptional, i.e. limited to cases where the State party can show that resorting to such trials is necessary and justified by objective and serious reasons, and where with regard to the specific class of individuals and offences at issue the regular civilian courts are unable to undertake the trials.

Article 14 due process fair trial rights apply legally to Guantanamo and anywhere the U.S. government exercises effective control over persons. The U.S. has argued that they apply only on U.S. territory but this is legally incorrect. They apply extraterritorially to places like Guantanamo where the U.S. government, via the military, exercises effective control.

Article 14 of ICCPR applies even where Common Article 3 of the Geneva Conventions relating to noninternational armed conflict applies. Common Article 3 prohibits "the passing of sentences and carrying out of executions without previous judgment pronounced by a regularly constituted court affording all the judicial guarantees which are recognized as indispensible by civilized people." The fair trial provisions of ICCPR Article 14 actually serve as the "judicial guarantees … recognized as indispensible by civilized people." This is an example of how human rights law supplements and complements international humanitarian law. Violation of this Common Article 3 is a war crime.

Thus, in the war on terrorism there is no one who is not entitled to a fair trial with procedural due process rights under Article 14, unless a derogation is in effect specifically suspending this right. Such suspension could not be applied discriminatorily. As of this time no derogation by the United States has been proclaimed in relation to the so called war on terrorism. The provisions of ICCPR Article 14 apply in wartime as well as in peacetime, subject to derogation in ICCPR Article 4.

See Also Terms: 11, 12, 20, 24, 33, 34, 35, 70, 72, 73, 75, 76, 88, 90, 93, 99, 100, 124, 136, 144, 145, 146, 148, 151, 152, 167, 169, 177, 179, 184, 185, 194, 202, 217, 222, 244, 252, 253, 254, 259, 264, 272, 283, 286, 297, 306, 397, 309, 316.

114. FEDERAL CLAUSE

Definition: A clause in a human rights treaty which states how the treaty applies legally to the political subdivision units of a state party to the treaty.

Significance: The question often arises as to how much the ratification of a treaty by the federal government of a state binds the political sub-units of that state to comply with the treaty. This is usually governed in each country by its constitution. Such political subdivisions can refer to states in a federal system, such as in Canada or the U.S. When the United States ratifies a human rights treaty, it is the federal government that is doing so on behalf of the international federal state known as the United States of America, which is comprised of 50 sub states, such as California, Hawaii, etc.

Each treaty, which is negotiated, drafted and adopted by states of the international community, usually within the context of an IGO like the United Nations, expressly sets down how far it applies to a state party's political subdivisions. This tells the impact or applicability of the treaty norms on the federal sub-units of a state party. See, for example, the federal clause of the ICCPR, Article 50, which, for example, would tell whether or to what extent the Covenant applies legally to the state of California, and not just to the U.S. federal government. See Document 8. This is extremely important, because if the treaty only applies human rights norms to the jurisdiction of the federal government, but not to the states, then the extent of coverage of the norms to the whole country is very limited.

It is the purpose and object of every international human rights treaty to have as broad and effective applicability in the subdivision states as is possible under the constitution of the federal state.

Federalism can create problems for the U.S. in its compliance with its international obligations. This was seen in the cases before the International Court of Justice in the *Legrand* and *Avena* cases against the U.S. There it was alleged that the U.S. did not fulfill its obligations under the Vienna Convention on Consular Relations to inform the defendants from Mexico and Germany, prosecuted for murder, that they could call their consulates and ask for help. They were being prosecuted in state courts in the U.S. The ICJ found the U.S. in breach of its obligations even though the prosecutions were solely under state law in the U.S. constitutional system. It must be remembered though that the U.S. Constitution states that treaties and other international law are the supreme law of the land, "any Thing in the Constitution or Laws of any State to the Contrary notwithstanding." See Document 2. This would seem to imply a Constitutional duty of states to comply with international law where the subject matter is within their jurisdiction.

In international human rights treaties the U.S. has started to employ language in its instrument of ratification, in the RDUs, to expressly deal with the federalism issue: The following language is from the U.S. ratification of the Second Optional Protocol to the CRC:

> (6) IMPLEMENTATION OF THE PROTOCOL ON THE FEDERAL SYSTEM OF THE UNITED STATES. The United States understands that the Protocol shall be implemented by the Federal Government to the extent that it exercises jurisdiction over the matters covered therein, and otherwise by the State and local governments. To the extent that State and local governments exercise jurisdiction over such matters, the Federal Government shall as necessary, take appropriate measures to ensure the fulfillment of the Protocol.
> (See Document 32.)

See Also Terms: 3, 6, 11, 25, 27, 29, 48, 52, 53, 55, 56, 57, 70, 98, 103, 151, 157, 159, 177, 179, 180, 184, 194, 211, 215, 222, 226, 243, 259, 262, 269, 272, 287, 288, 292, 293, 297, 306.

115. FEMALE GENITAL MUTILATION
See entry for **Gender-Based Violence**

116. FIRST GENERATION HUMAN RIGHTS
Definition: A formerly-used term for a classification of human rights that comprised all civil and political human rights.

Significance: It is no longer advisable to use this term because it creates confusion in the discourse of human rights. The term "generation" is still seen in some human rights literature and in the older literature.

See Also Terms: 20, 25, 33, 48, 70, 124, 127, 136, 144, 145, 146, 168, 172, 174, 179, 184, 259, 264, 272, 274, 283, 291, 293, 297, 301, 306, 309, 316.

117. FORCED DISAPPEARANCE
See entry for **Disappearance**

118. FOREIGN SOVEREIGNTY IMMUNITY ACT (FSIA)
Definition: A U.S. statute found in Articles 1601–1611 of Title 28 of the U.S. Code, which limits when a foreign state government can be sued in U.S. federal district courts for certain unlawful acts.

Significance: Many cases have been filed in U.S. federal district courts against foreign governments for committing human rights violations against the plaintiffs or their family members. It is a principle of law that states enjoy sovereign immunity for acts they commit within their jurisdiction. The filing of a suit against a foreign government in U.S. courts can interfere with international diplomatic relations between the defendant state and the United States. For this reason, the U.S. Congress has enacted this statute to spell out just when a foreign state can be sued in U.S. courts. Section 1604 spells out the general rule and section 1605 spells out the exceptions. The text of the FSIA is set forth in Document 105.

If the FSIA applies in a case, the court will dismiss the case unless it falls within one of the exceptions.

The U.S. Supreme Court handed down an important decision in 2010, in the case of *Samantar vs. Yousuf* . See Appendix J. Interpreting the FSIA statute, the Court held that a former Somali government official could not raise the FSIA immunity defense in a case against him for committing human rights violations which he committed while working for the Somali government. The statue was construed to allow this defense only to states. The court allowed the ATCA action by a Somalian against a fellow Somalian for acts that occurred in Somalia to continue. The defendant could not shield himself with state immunity. This is a major victory for human rights in the U.S. and internationally, as many lawsuits against human rights violators happen in the U.S. under the Alien Tort Claims Act. *Samantar* removes one big obstacle to some of this litigation.

See Also Terms: 3, 10, 46, 48, 70, 71, 73, 88, 90, 93, 94, 100, 145, 151, 157, 159, 165, 167, 169, 177, 185, 194, 211, 222, 252, 253, 254, 259, 272, 283, 287, 292, 297.

119. FORUM OF SHAME
Definition: The forum of shame is the public humiliation to which a state or regime is subjected and exposed by having its injustices and human rights violations brought up (paraded) before the world, usually in the media. The forum of shame is most often used by those trying to show how hypocritical a state is being, contrasting what it tells the world it does and what it really does, such as committing torture, disappearances, or sex discrimination.

Significance: Along with establishing human rights norms worldwide, it is important for states to have methods of encouraging other states to comply with those norms to which they have agreed and therefore protect the human rights of their citizens. The forum of shame is such a method. When it is proven that a state has a record of human rights violations, especially gross violations of human rights, this method brings the issue into the public arena. It is hoped that the embarrassment of this exposure will give the state the impetus to abide by its agreements and no longer be hypocritical in its application of the human rights norms.

This forum of shame is carried out largely through the media, because most states are very sensitive to their public image. Oftentimes, states will respond to letter-writing campaigns by the citizens of another state. Again, the knowledge of the average person in the United States about human rights internationally could help others to realize their inherent human dignity. In the United States, citizens have the great advantage of personal freedom to become involved in that kind of process.

While this concept is normally associated with the activities of civil society, it does apply even in international inter-governmental organizations such as the United Nations. The Universal Periodic Review Process in the U.N. Human Rights Council has a mild forum of shame element to it, especially as civil society stakeholders use that forum for some criticisms of states under review. In fact, the Human Rights Council itself has been criticized in Council sessions in attempts to get it to become more effective and less politically influenced.

See Also Terms: 3, 26, 29, 36, 48, 60, 61, 69, 70, 71, 72, 76, 112, 142, 144, 145, 148, 150, 151, 184, 185, 206, 208, 215, 218, 227, 243, 259, 268, 272, 283.

120. "FOUR FREEDOMS"

Definition: Refers to a historical speech given by Franklin Delano Roosevelt on January 6, 1941, for his state of the union address, wherein he stated that the existence of world peace was linked to four essential human freedoms. These freedoms are freedom of expression, freedom of worship, freedom from want (i.e., economic security), and freedom from fear (i.e., reduction of arms).

Significance: This speech later became a key document in the underpinnings of the efforts to establish the United Nations and provided for the promotion of human rights after World War II. The speech was given before the United States entered World War II, but the world wars proved Roosevelt's assertion and vision to be true. This speech gave momentum to those seeking to create an international human rights protection system, one that would have to wait until after the war. The speech reads:

> In future days which we seek to make secure, we look forward to a world founded upon four essential freedoms. The first is freedom of speech and expression—everywhere in the world.
>
> The second is freedom of every person to worship God in his own way—everywhere in the world.
>
> The third is freedom from want, which translated into world terms, means economic understanding which will secure to every nation a healthy peace time life for its inhabitants—everywhere in the world.
>
> The fourth is freedom from fear, which, translated into world terms, means a worldwide reduction of armaments to such a point and in such a thorough fashion that no nation will be in a position to commit an act of physical aggression against any neighbor—anywhere in the world. It is a definite bias for a kind of world attainable in our own time and generation.
>
> (See Document 4.)

See Also Terms: 11, 12, 20, 24, 33, 48, 53, 54, 55, 56, 70, 71, 72, 92, 116, 122, 123, 124, 125, 126, 136, 144, 145, 152, 157, 160, 167, 169, 177, 179, 180, 185, 195, 210, 211, 243, 265, 272, 274, 283, 292, 297, 312, 323.

121. FREE AND FAIR ELECTIONS

Definition: Elections that are conducted in a way that accurately reflects the will of the voting population of a state; they meet international standards for fairness and freedom from any unfair influences or pressure to vote a certain way.

Significance: Elections must be the expression of the will of the people of a state expressed by their votes by secret ballot. To be recognized as legitimate and accepted by other states, a state's national elections must be free and fair. For elections to be free and fair there must be an absence of voter fraud, intimidation and coercion, proven by compliance with international election standards, with adequate monitoring by international observers ("election monitors"). Whether or not a government or its leaders are recognized by other states depends on whether the elections reflected that they were a true expression of the will of the people.

Human rights instruments recognize that the will of the people, as expressed in free and fair elections, is the basis for all government authority in a rule-of-law society. It is also an implication and prerequisite of the emerging international norm of "democratic governance."

See Also Terms: 11, 12, 20, 24, 29, 70, 122, 123, 124, 144, 145, 152, 160, 167, 169, 177, 179, 184, 185, 242, 243, 259, 278, 283, 287, 292, 305, 309, 311, 316, 323.

122. FREEDOM

Definition: Freedom is the power or capacity of acting without any external compulsion; absence of restraint; the power to choose one's actions and develop one's own personality, especially in relation to the state; the state of a person having his or her human rights fully respected.

Significance: Human rights protect human freedom. Often seen in the term "fundamental freedoms," it is a term that denotes a freedom that is deemed absolutely necessary for the maintenance and protection of the dignity of a human being in an organized society. It is a sort of minimum acceptable protection. Its purpose is also the protection of the very existence of society, for when human rights are violated society is harmed and civil unrest and even rebellion and revolution can occur. The lack of freedom for African American slaves and the resulting Civil War are evidence of this. The effects of this lack of freedom and horrible treatment of a class of human beings was addressed in Abraham Lincoln's Emancipation Proclamation.

Under modern human rights theory the purpose of human rights is to protect the fundamental freedoms of all human beings in relation to the government of the state. These fundamental freedoms are those without which human beings are not free to fully develop their personalities and exist in a manner consistent with their inherent human dignity.

The international human rights instruments, such as the UDHR and ICCPR, expressly state in their preambles that respect for human dignity is the basis of all freedom. See Documents 6 and 8. The Declaration of Independence declared that, because Britain had violated the unalienable rights of the colonists, they had a right to break off from the United Kingdom to be able to enjoy their freedoms. It stated that the very purpose of government is the protection of freedom of the members of the society. See Document 1.

International human rights instruments and procedures seek to protect individual freedoms under international law, as a backup to national laws, when national laws or legal systems fail to protect freedom by respecting human rights.

"Freedom" is stronger and broader than "liberty," and is all-encompassing in scope.

See Also Terms: 11, 12, 13, 20, 24, 28, 33, 34, 35, 48, 70, 72, 75, 120, 121, 123, 124, 144, 145, 148, 149, 152, 154, 167, 169, 177, 179, 180, 184, 185, 189, 190, 195, 196, 213, 239, 240, 242, 243, 263, 272, 283, 291, 297, 309, 316, 323.

123. FREEDOM OF EXPRESSION

Definition: A specific substantive human rights norm that allows an individual to externalize information, ideas, opinions and beliefs through any manner of speech, writing or symbol, including artistic expression, without limitation from the state and subject only to certain specified limitations.

Significance: Freedom of expression is a civil human right that is a basic requirement of any free society. It allows for free, unimpeded transmission and exchange of ideas, opinions and beliefs, creating the so-called marketplace of ideas. It has both positive and negative aspects. This right includes the positive right to express something and the negative right not to be compelled to express something. The U.S. equivalent is "freedom of speech." The right to freedom of expression does not, however, have the same scope as the First Amendment free speech clause.

Freedom of expression as found in international human rights instruments includes the freedom to seek, receive and impart information and ideas of all kinds. It can be done either orally, in writing or in the form of art, or through any other media of one's choice. Freedom of expression is one of the "fundamental freedoms," a term that denotes a freedom that is considered absolutely necessary for the maintenance and protection of the dignity of a human being. This freedom is primarily found in Article 19 of the UDHR and Article 19 of the ICCPR. See Document 8.

The exercise of freedom of expression carries with it certain special duties and responsibilities for all members of society. It can be restricted by the state for certain narrowly defined reasons, such as public order, public safety, public morals, national security and the reputation of others. An example of a clause containing such a limitation is found in the ICCPR, Article19.3.

The U.S. position regarding the international human rights standard of free expression is that the scope of the U.S. Constitution's First Amendment is broader than the international standard. See Document 2. For this reason, in its ratification of the ICCPR in 1992, the United States submitted a reservation to Article 20 of the ICCPR regarding that instrument's prohibition of "propaganda for war" or "advocacy of national, racial or religious hatred that constitutes incitement to discrimination, hostility or violence" (see Documents 8 and 9). The United States felt that some of such acts would be permissible under the U.S. Constitution.

The international protection of free expression was largely influenced by the U.S. experience of its free speech clause in the U.S. Constitution, which served as a model for many other states. The international human rights norms of free expression represent a balance between individual freedom on the one hand and the needs of a society to sometimes regulate expression in the broader interest of society on the other hand.

Starting in 1999, a very important issue of freedom of expression arose for the U.S. and the entire international community. The issue of what was called by its proponents "defamation of religion" arose in the context of the United Nations Commission on Human Rights in discussions of racism. The concept raised concerns from many in the Commission with respect to how it potentially interfered with the freedom of expression and freedom of religion. In brief, the countries within the Organization of Islamic Conference wanted to get the United Nations, first the Commission on Human Rights, then primarily the Human Rights Council and General Assembly, to pass a resolution prohibiting what they termed "defamation of religion." As originally introduced, the resolutions focused on the "defamation of Islam," a term that was later broadened. Roughly speaking, the concept of "defamation of religion," as presented by its proponents, was the act of making public statements which negatively ridiculed and stereotyped people belonging to a certain religion, namely Islam, thereby offending the religious sensitivities of the followers of the religion. As presented in the OIC resolutions, "defamation of religion" is a sociological concept and does not exist as a legal concept or principle in the field of human rights or international law. In reality, the concept has often been used to justify national anti-blasphemy legislation, such as the Anti-Ahmadiya blasphemy laws in Pakistan. In addition, defamation is, by definition, a false statement of fact expressed against someone. Who is going to determine the truth or falsehood of a statement concerning a religion?

Proponents of the concept and resolution sought to establish an international mechanism that would criminalize such negative speech. While the resolutions had been passed in each session of the Human Rights Commission since 1999, it was not until certain Danish newspaper cartoons depicted the Islamic Prophet Mohammed in a way deemed offensive to Muslims that the issue was more aggressively pursued by the OIC in the Council and General Assembly. The resolutions presented did not distinguish between statements intended to incite violence and statements intended to provoke public debate that might be used to justify violence, but were not intended to do so. Much of the violence that occurred in response to the Danish cartoons was instigated by those who were offended, rather than individuals responding in hate to the Muslim communities depicted in the cartoons.

This debate over the concept of "defamation of religion" and how the international community should address this issue occurred mainly in the Human Rights Council but also in the

General Assembly, with resolutions on the subject passed annually. States and NGOs countering the resolution in both arenas argued that the concept of "defamation of religion" is objectionable for a variety of reasons including the following: (1) human rights law, as well as the legal concept of defamation, protect individuals and not religions, and establishing a new legal concept to protect against the "defamation of religion" would restrict an individual's established human rights (2) the concept seeks to criminalize speech and expression outside the scope of permissible limitations provided in the ICCPR and in so doing undermines the theoretical basis of all human rights, in addition to being simply an excessive infringement of free speech, (3) the concept seeks to stifle open discussion of issues and criticism of religious beliefs which could potentially restrict the freedom to choose or change one's beliefs within the freedom of religion, thus having particularly damaging effects for minority religious communities or those who object to the state's interpretation of religion, (4) and the attempt to criminalize "defamation of religion" suppresses ideas on the basis of the effect they have on others rather than addressing permissible limitations on speech used to specifically justify violence, and (5) religious intolerance would be better addressed within the context of human rights education as a social issue rather than a legal imperative, insofar as the concept of "defamation of religion" falls outside the scope of permissible limitations on existing human rights norms.

One of the primary issues discussed within the debate at the Council was whether "defamation of religion" and other acts of religious intolerance, including injury to religious feelings and sensitivities, constitute or rise to the level of incitement of religious hatred prohibited in Article 20(2) of the ICCPR, questioning if they should be addressed within that context. If they do fall under Article 20(2), then it would be important to consider the extent to which the rights protected under Article 19 on freedom of expression and Article 18 on freedom of religion or belief suggest the state's responsibilities under Article 20(2) to prohibit them. In considering this issue, the Human Rights Council has addressed the permissible limitations on Articles 18 and 19, as well as the balance necessary in a democratic society between protections for: the freedom of expression – for those wishing to impart views that may be considered offensive to a particular religious group; with the freedom of religion or belief – of those who feel that their ability to have or manifest their religious beliefs is threatened by the expression. There were sharp differences of opinion on this question among the various special rapporteurs tasked with responding to this question.

The U.S. has been opposed to this resolution because it is generally inconsistent with the freedom of expression and religion as established in international law and would curtail these rights if recognized as a matter of criminal law. It has also been opposed to related attempts by the OIC to draft a protocol to the Racism Convention criminalizing "defamation of religion" in meetings of the Ad Hoc Working Group designated for this purpose. If such a protocol were to be adopted, it would be the first time the concept of "defamation of religion" was given validity by an enforceable U.N. treaty. It has become clear to most U.N. observers that this push is intended to create a new international legal principle whereby "religions" are elevated to the status of "rights bearers" under international law, and any "incitement," i.e. critique or truth seeking considered a threat to that religion, might be punishable by law.

When the U.S. rejoined the HRC in 2009 it co-authored a resolution focusing on freedom of expression with Egypt, one of the main sponsors of an international document prohibiting the "defamation of religion," in order to address concerns in the defamation concept without endorsing it as a legal concept. In this resolution, the U.S. reaffirmed the importance of freedom of expression but also spoke against the negative stereotyping, and denigrating, of religions. The proponents have continued the promotion of their resolution and the U.S. still opposes it, but the resolution appears to be losing support in the U.N. for a number of reasons, namely that countries voting on the resolution are more aware of the negative implications the concept has for other established human rights norms.

In March 2008, the Council renewed the mandate of the special rapporteur on freedom of expression, but amended the original mandate to now "report on instances in which the abuse of the right of freedom of expression constitutes an act of racial or religious discrimination" rather than reporting solely on restrictions imposed by governments. At the end of the June 2010 session the HRC passed a resolution calling for a media watchdog to be appointed to monitor the depiction of religions in the media, particularly those involving expressions concerning Islam in relation to terrorism and violence. The U.S. delegation to the HRC voted against the resolution.

In 2010, legislation was passed by Congress on so called "libel tourism" which was designed to protect free speech from libel tourists who sue American authors in English or Welsh Courts and seek to enforce foreign defamation judgments on the authors in the U.S. courts.

In its 2010, national UPR report to the OHCHR (see Document 86) the Administration spoke of freedom of expression thusly:

> The United States maintains robust protections for freedom of expression. As a general matter, the government does not punish or penalize those who peacefully express their views in the public sphere, even when those views are critical of the government. Indeed, dissent is a valuable and valued part of our politics: democracy provides a marketplace for ideas, and in order to function as such, new ideas must be permitted, even if they are unpopular or potentially offensive. The United States has a free, thriving, and diverse independent press—a feature that existed before the advent of electronic and digital media and that continues today.

> We also recognize that privacy is linked to free expression, in that individuals need to feel that they can control the boundaries of their self-disclosure and self-expression in order to be able to express themselves freely: surveillance, especially when practiced by a government, can lead to self-censorship. Although protecting the security of all citizens means that no individual can have an absolute right to privacy or expression, any limitations on these rights are determined in a public process, by representatives of the people in the legislature and by the courts.

See Also Terms: 11, 12, 14, 20, 22, 24, 25, 28, 29, 33, 34, 35, 51, 55, 69, 70, 72, 75, 77, 78, 87, 120, 124, 16, 139, 140, 144, 145, 146, 147, 152, 169, 167, 169, 175, 177, 179, 184, 185, 188, 210, 222, 237, 259, 264, 272, 283, 297, 306, 307, 309, 316, 322, 323.

124. FUNDAMENTAL RIGHTS/FREEDOMS

Definition: Rights and freedoms which are basic and necessary for the government to respect in order to protect and promote individual liberty, as well as preserve the viability of a human society.

Significance: There are many types of freedoms and rights. Those rights and freedoms are fundamental because a society cannot continue to exist in a state of freedom and peace without them. Human rights that are deemed fundamental are those that the international community of most countries in the world have officially and legally recognized as legally binding on all states and that must be protected in national law.

Examples of fundamental rights are the right to life (see ICCPR, Article 6.1); freedom from torture (Article 7); freedom from slavery (Article 8); equality of men and women and equality before the law for everyone (Articles 2.1, 14, 26); freedom of expression (Article 19); and freedom of religion (Article 18). These are only a few of the many fundamental rights. See Document 8.

Human rights have been considered to reflect the fundamental rights and freedoms articulated by the Founding Fathers of the United States in the Declaration of Independence of 1776. That declaration was a source of the philosophy about fundamental rights held by individuals which served as a basis for present international human rights treaties binding upon the United States (See Documents 1 and 2, Bill of Rights).

One of the difficulties with the popular perception of fundamental freedoms is that many Americans think that "bad people should not have any or at least not as many." This is particularly true as to suspected terrorists. Much of the American feeling towards terrorists is this way. They feel that if terrorists do not respect human rights then they should not be able to enjoy them either. Human rights are not about what "bad guys" can or cannot do but is primarily about what government and the state should or should not do to human beings, all of whom have inherent and inalienable human dignity. All are responsible for their actions before society, American or international, and all should be caught and punished for any wrongful conduct; but human rights belong to the good and the bad alike under the principle of universality. We seek to win the so called war on terrorism and eradiate terrorism from this world, which is not only a right but a duty of the state. The state, though, is legally obligated, because of its international obligations, to respect the human rights of all, even the weakest, the most marginalized and the despised, all while it takes measures to counter terrorism.

The U.N. General Assembly has articulated this balance in resolution 64/168 and succeeding resolutions each year entitled "Protection of human rights and fundamental freedoms while countering terrorism" and reminding states such as the U.S. of this balance and the legal obligations involved. See Document 55. States are not free to take whatever measures they want in the war on terrorism. International rule of law requires that states obey international law and implement it in good faith consistent with human rights norms.

See Also Terms: 11, 12, 20, 24, 29, 30, 32, 33, 34, 35, 48, 62, 70, 72, 75, 81, 82, 83, 84, 85, 86, 90, 92, 93, 97, 100, 113, 116, 120, 121, 122, 123, 124, 136, 144, 145, 146, 147, 152, 153, 160, 167, 169, 177, 179, 180, 184, 185, 192, 195, 196, 213, 216, 222, 252, 253, 259, 264, 272, 283, 292, 297, 296, 308, 309, 312, 316, 322, 323.

G

125. GENDER-BASED VIOLENCE

Definition: Violence committed against women as women; violence particular to women, such as rape, sexual assault, female circumcision, or dowry burning; violence against women for failing to conform to restrictive social norms.

Significance: the 1993 Vienna Declaration and Programme of Action specifically recognized gender-based violence as a human rights concern. See Document 51. Any act of gender-based violence that results in, or is likely to result in, physical, sexual or psychological harm or suffering to women, including threats of such acts, coercion or arbitrary deprivation of liberty, whether occurring in public or private life. Violence against women includes, but is not be limited to, the following: a) Physical, sexual and psychological violence occurring in the family, including battering, sexual abuse of female children in the household, dowry-related violence, marital rape, female genital mutilation and other traditional practices harmful to women, non-spousal violence related to exploitation; b) Physical, sexual and psychological violence occurring within the general community, including rape, sexual abuse, sexual harassment and intimidation at work, in educational institutions and elsewhere, trafficking in women and forced prostitution; c) Physical, sexual and psychological violence perpetrated or condoned by the State, wherever it occurs.

The Convention on the Elimination of All Forms of Discrimination against Women and its Committee on the Elimination of Discrimination against Women deal with this very serious issue. One important product of CEDAW is CEDAW General Recommendation No.19, on Violence against Women (eleventh session 1992). This is an influential recommendation of the treaty-monitoring body charged with enforcing the Convention on the Elimination of All Forms of Discrimination against Women. See Document 27. It defines gender violence as a form of discrimination against women.

Gender violence is a serious problem in just about every country in the world, including the U.S. While it is dealt with primarily at the state and local level in the U.S. the international community has become involved in it, particularly in light of the increase in interest in women's human rights internationally.

The U.N. Human Rights Council has a special rapporteur on violence against women as one of its special mechanisms.

One form of gender violence which has manifested itself in the U.S. but occurs mostly in Africa, is female genital mutilation. It is referred to as FGM. This is a process by which females have their sexual organs altered, usually by cutting off the clitoris. It is considered a human rights violation for the state not to take affirmative steps to make illegal and prosecute such conduct.

In its U.S. national UPR report to the OHCHR (see Document 86), the U.S. reported about gender-based violence as follows:

> Moreover, the Administration established the first White House Advisor on 11 Violence Against Women, appointed two women to the U.S. Supreme Court, and created an unprecedented position of Ambassador-at-Large for Global Women's Issues to mobilize support for women around the world. The Obama Administration strongly supports U.S. ratification of the Convention on the Elimination of all forms of Discrimination Against Women and is working with our Senate toward this end.
>
> ....
>
> Addressing crimes involving violence against women and children on tribal lands is a priority. After extensive consultations with tribal leaders, Attorney General Eric Holder announced significant reform to increase prosecution of crimes committed on tribal lands. He hired more Assistant U.S. Attorneys and more victim-witness specialists. He created a new position, the National Indian Country Training Coordinator, who will work with prosecutors and law enforcement officers in tribal communities. The Attorney General is establishing a Tribal Nations Leadership Council to provide ongoing advice on issues critical to tribal communities.
>
> On July 29, 2010, President Obama signed the Tribal Law and Order Act, requiring the Justice Department to disclose data on cases in Indian Country that it declines to prosecute and granting tribes greater authority to prosecute and punish criminals. The Act also expands support for Bureau of Indian Affairs and Tribal officers. It includes new provisions to prevent counterfeiting of Indian-produced crafts and new guidelines and training for domestic violence and sex crimes, and it strengthens tribal courts and police departments ....

See Also Terms: 11, 12, 20, 22, 24, 26, 28, 29, 33, 48, 49, 53, 54, 58, 63, 65, 66, 69, 70, 84, 85, 93, 100, 104, 115, 120, 122, 124, 126, 132, 136, 139, 140, 144, 145, 151, 152, 160, 167, 169, 170, 171, 177, 179, 181, 182, 184, 185, 192, 201, 216, 222, 223, 228, 235, 236, 238, 259, 264, 272, 283, 297, 302, 304, 309, 316, 317, 318, 319, 322, 323.

126. GENDER DISCRIMINATION

Definition: Discrimination based on socially constructed ideas and perceptions of men and women. Any distinction, exclusion, restriction, or preference based on the gender or perceived gender of a person.

Significance: This term is made up of two difficult and complex terms: gender and discrimination.

Gender is a complex and controversial term that does not have a generally accepted definition in international human rights law. Some have defined it as identical to the biological-anatomical description *sex*, as in the male and female of the human species. Sex refers to biological differences between men and women, not the way humans act. Some have defined it as the way women and men are perceived and expected to think and act in a particular social, economic, political, and cultural context. However defined, gender can be affected by other factors such as age, race, class, or ethnicity. It is also regarded as a socially defined or constructed expectation regarding roles, attitudes, and values, which communities and societies ascribe as appropriate for one sex or the other in the public or private domain. To some, gender differences exist because of the way society is organized, not because of biological differences. In the field of human rights this term comes into play mostly in relation to the human rights of nondiscrimination and equality before the law.

Discrimination is a sociological and legal term referring to the treatment taken toward or against a person of a certain group in consideration based solely on class or category. Discrimination is the actual behavior towards another group. It involves excluding or restricting members of one group from opportunities that are available to other groups.

Though gender discrimination and sexism refers to beliefs and attitudes in relation to the gender of a person, such beliefs and attitudes are of a social nature and do not, normally, carry any legal consequences. Sex discrimination, on the other hand, may have legal consequences.

Though what constitutes sex discrimination varies between countries, the essence is that it is an adverse action taken by one person against another person that would not have occurred had the person been of another sex. Discrimination of that nature in certain enumerated circumstances is illegal in many countries.

Currently, discrimination based on sex is defined as adverse action against another person, that would not have occurred had the person been of another sex. This is considered a form of prejudice and is illegal in certain enumerated circumstances in most countries. Sexual discrimination can arise in different contexts. For instance, an employee may be discriminated against by being asked discriminatory questions during a job interview, or because an employer did not hire or promote, or wrongfully terminated an employee based on his or her gender, or employers pay unequally based on gender.

In an educational setting there could be claims that a student was excluded from an educational institution, program, opportunity, loan, student group, or scholarship due to his or her gender. In the housing setting there could be claims that a person was refused negotiations on seeking a house, contracting/leasing a house or getting a loan based on his or her gender. Another setting where there have been claims of gender discrimination is banking; for example if one is refused credit or is offered unequal loan terms based on one's gender.

Gender discrimination, sometimes known as sexual discrimination, is the practice of letting a person's sex unfairly become a factor when deciding who receives a job, promotion, or other employment benefit. It most often affects women who feel they have been unfairly discriminated against in favor of a man. But there have also been cases where males have claimed that reverse discrimination has occurred, that is, the woman received unfairly favorable treatment at the expense of the man.

Gender discrimination can take place in many different settings, but typically occurs most often in the following situations: Employment; Education; Housing; Borrowing or Credit.

United States Federal Laws Prohibits Gender Discrimination.

Gender discrimination in the exercise of substantive human rights in the ICCPR is in violation of ICCPR Article 2.1 and 3. It is also inconsistent with Article 26. It is a violation of UDHR Articles 1, 2, 7, 10, 16. The state has the affirmative (positive) obligation to prohibit and eliminate gender discrimination. See Documents 6, 8.

See the Second and Third U.S. periodic reports to the Human Rights Committee under the ICCPR, Document 15A for the U.S. report about its law and case law and practice regarding the norms of the ICCPR regarding gender discrimination.

See Also Terms: 7, 11, 12, 20, 22, 24, 28, 29, 33, 34, 35, 48, 54, 69, 70, 86, 87, 100, 115, 116, 122, 124, 144, 145, 146, 147, 151, 160, 167, 169, 177, 179, 180, 184, 185, 188, 194, 216, 222, 228, 235, 236, 242, 243, 259, 264, 270, 272, 282, 290, 306, 307, 308, 309, 316, 322, 323.

127. GENERAL COMMENTS (U.N. HR COMMITTEE)

Definition: A statement by a U.N. treaty-based supervisory body such as the U.N. Human Rights Committee under the ICCPR, or Committee on Economic, Social and Cultural Rights under ICESCR, which serve as the official collective statement of the experts on that treaty supervising body to all states parties as to how to interpret, understand and to best fulfill their legal obligations under that treaty instrument.

Significance: General comments will usually be issued concerning one or more specific articles or issues such as state reporting requirement or about the interpretation of an article of the treaty. General comments sometimes contain analysis of the meaning, content and scope of application of a particular substantive norms, such as torture, or to point out deficiencies in and make suggestions on how to improve reports submitted by states or how to clarify the requirements of the treaty in any respect. General comments can suggest ways to overcome obstacles to compliance, or to generally strengthen co-operation among the member states parties in the implementation of the treaty.

Much of the general comments are based on the body's review of the written periodic reports of states and may also reflect the jurisprudence (case law) of the body which engages in quasi-judicial determination of written communications claiming violation of the treaty. While general comments are not, strictly speaking, binding on the states parties they do have a strong moral and political force because of the legal expertise of the committee members and states should follow them in order to fully implement their legal obligations under the treaty. (See ICCPR Article 40.4-5)

A sample General Comment is found at Document 12, General Comment 22(18). Many other General Comments are included in Appendix E.

See Also Terms: 5, 20, 24, 25, 26, 33, 46, 48, 49, 52, 53, 54, 55, 57, 62, 65, 66, 67, 70, 77, 81, 82, 84, 85, 86, 88, 90, 93, 95, 99, 100, 102, 104, 109, 111, 113, 114, 116, 136, 144, 145, 151, 157, 158, 159, 167, 169, 170, 171, 173, 175, 177, 179, 180, 184, 186, 193, 198, 205, 206, 208, 210, 215, 216, 219, 221, 222, 225, 226, 233, 243, 244, 247, 252, 259, 268, 272, 291, 292, 306, 307.

128. GENERAL HUMAN RIGHTS LEGISLATION

Definition: With general human rights legislation, Congress establishes a U.S. law directing how the U.S. will deal with another country's fulfillment of its international human rights obligations. It does this in relation to another state's beneficial relations with the United States, such as in trade, military assistance, foreign aid, finance, and even cultural and other types of activities.

Significance: The U.S. Congress seeks to influence the way other countries respect human rights by passing laws that condition our relations on the fulfillment of their human rights obligations in a certain area or in a certain way. Congress does this by either country-specific legislation or general human rights legislation. The former only applies to one particular country. The latter applies equally to all countries.

An example of general human rights legislation would be the International Religious Freedom Act of 1998 (IRFA). See Document 89. This Act conditions U.S. relations with all other countries upon the fulfillment of their obligation under international law to respect religious freedom, such as under the ICCPR, Article 18. This Act also establishes a committee to monitor countries in this field and to report to Congress so that the information can affect U.S. policy and action. The text of the IRFA and other general human rights legislation is included in the U.S. Human Rights Legislation section of this work.

See Also Terms: 3, 9, 13, 29, 48, 52, 60, 61, 70, 118, 119, 124, 133, 136, 138, 144, 145, 150, 151, 152, 154, 159, 160, 167, 169, 175, 177, 179, 184, 185, 190, 192, 194, 199, 206, 207, 211, 215, 218, 220, 226, 243, 259, 268, 271, 272, 273, 283, 286, 292, 294, 297, 306, 308, 309.

129. GENEVA CONVENTIONS OF 1949 (GC)

Definition: Four international treaties adopted in 1949, which had as their object and purpose the protection of victims of armed conflict, both in international armed conflict between states parties, and in non-international armed conflict within a member state. The Geneva Conventions of 1949 are the principle legal instruments of international humanitarian law. See Document 72.

Significance: International humanitarian law is the body of international law which seeks to render armed conflict as humane and humanitarian as possible to minimize human suffering and loss. The four Geneva Conventions of 1949 offered the protection of humanitarian law to four target groups: GC I, soldiers on land; GC II, sailors and shipwrecked persons at sea; GC III, prisoners of war; and GC IV, civilians. The Geneva Conventions sought to limit death, injury, and pain and suffering in armed conflict to only that which was justified by military necessity and reasonably proportional to that need.

The Geneva Convention of 1929 was in force during the second World War. In light of the experiences of WW II the 1929 Geneva Convention was replaced by the above four separate treaties, no longer to cover only combatants. The 1949 Geneva Convention IV was the first general convention to cover civilians. This reflected the growing awareness that it is primarily civilians who are harmed in armed conflict, not combatants. This fact has become increasingly true since WWII.

The 1949 GCs were amended in 1977 by Protocols I and II, which reflected lessons learned from the Vietnam and Korean Wars. See Documents 73, 74. Protocol I covered international armed conflicts and noninternational conflicts of national liberation, foreign occupation, or against colonialism, or racism. Protocol II covers only noninternational armed conflict such as civil wars, and was the first international instrument to deal with matters which were entirely within a single state and a matter of state sovereignty. The U.S. has signed, but not ratified either Protocol I or II. It has, however, recognized Protocol I, to some degree, reflective of customary international law and, as such, binding on the U.S.

The Geneva Conventions have applied to the armed conflicts engaged in by the U.S. in the Iraq and the Afghanistan theaters. The Geneva Conventions do not apply to the war on terrorism as such because the war against terrorism is a political figure of speech. War, properly understood, is a legal relationship between two or more states characterized by a breaking off of diplomatic relations. War is the legal state of broken diplomatic relationship between states. At this time Israel and Syria are legally at war with each other though no bullets are flying. War is a legal state, not the act of military violence. This is why humanitarian law, and the GCs, are part of what is called the "Law of Armed Conflict." The term "armed conflict" is the humanitarian law term employed in describing what most people call "war." Given this meaning of war, the so called war on terrorism is not really a war. The international Law of Armed Conflict as such does not apply to the so called war on terrorism because it is a war against a concept (terrorism), not even against a specific group of people, much less against a state. However, where the U.S. military is engaged in hostilities or in belligerent occupation, the Geneva Conventions of 1949 are applicable.

In the Iraq war of 2004 the four GCs were applicable. Of greatest importance was the Fourth Geneva Convention (GC IV) on Protection of Civilians. That Convention has a section called the Law of Occupation. It was that law that regulated the actions of the U.S. as an occupying force in relation to the civilian population and Iraqi institutions.

The supervision of GCs and Humanitarian Law in general is by the International Committee of the Red Cross. This was historically why the Red Cross was founded, not to provide humanitarian relief in earthquakes and floods. Its principal task is making sure that the parties to the GCs are obeying the humanitarian law. The ICRC in particular visits and monitors prisoners of war and has a proven tracking system to help reunite persons lost and separated by the conflict.

The U.S. Supreme Court in 2006 in *Hamdan vs. Rumsfeld* dealt with the issue as to the applicability of the Geneva Conventions to an Afghan conflict detainee in Guantanamo, a so called enemy combatant. The U.S. Supreme Court concluded that it did apply, at least Common Article 3, and that that article of the GC required the detainee have access to judicial procedures with judicial guarantees of due process. The Supreme Court stated:

Common Article 3, then, is applicable here and, as indicated above, requires that *Hamdan* be tried by a "regularly constituted court affording all the judicial guarantees which are recognized as indispensable by civilized peoples." 6 U. S. T., at 3320 (Article 3, ¶1(d)). While the term "regularly constituted court" is not specifically defined in either Common Article 3 or its accompanying commentary, other sources disclose its core meaning. The commentary accompanying a provision of the Fourth Geneva Convention, for example, defines "regularly constituted" tribunals to include "ordinary military courts" and "definitely excludes all special tribunals." GCIV Commentary 340.

Certain more serious violations of the Geneva Conventions are known as grave breaches. They constitute war crimes, international crimes with universal jurisdiction of every country to arrest and prosecute violators. The GCs also serve as the basis for war crimes found in the Rome Statute for an International Criminal Court. Violation of Common Article 3 is an international crime, which has been confirmed by the U.S. Supreme Court. (See ICC Statute, Document 76, Article 8.2(4)(iv).)

Common Article 3 gets its name from the fact that it appears just the same as Article 3 of all four GCs. It is referred to as a "mini convention" and it was the first international legal norm regulating purely internal state matters. It is playing a key role in the legality of the war on terrorism concerning detention and access to justice and judicial guarantees. The text of Common Article 3 reads as follows:

In the case of armed conflict not of an international character occurring in the territory of one of the High Contracting Parties, each Party to the conflict shall be bound to apply, as a minimum, the following provisions:

(1) Persons taking no active part in the hostilities, including members of armed forces who have laid down their arms and those placed ' hors de combat' by sickness, wounds, detention, or any other cause, shall in all circumstances be treated humanely, without any adverse distinction founded on race, colour, religion or faith, sex, birth or wealth, or any other similar criteria.
To this end, the following acts are and shall remain prohibited at any time and in any place whatsoever with respect to the above-mentioned persons:
(a) violence to life and person, in particular murder of all kinds, mutilation, cruel treatment and torture;
(b) taking of hostages;
(c) outrages upon personal dignity, in particular humiliating and degrading treatment;
(d) the passing of sentences and the carrying out of executions without previous judgment pronounced by a regularly constituted court, affording all the judicial guarantees which are recognized as indispensable by civilized peoples.
(2) The wounded and sick shall be collected and cared for.
An impartial humanitarian body, such as the International Committee of the Red Cross, may offer its services to the Parties to the conflict.
The Parties to the conflict should further endeavour to bring into force, by means of special agreements, all or part of the other provisions of the present Convention.
The application of the preceding provisions shall not affect the legal status of the Parties to the conflict.

See Also Terms: 3, 8, 11, 13, 16, 19, 20, 21, 25, 26, 33, 37, 38, 40, 41, 42, 45, 48, 49, 56, 59, 63, 65, 70, 71, 72, 73, 79, 81, 86, 90, 93, 95, 96, 100, 101, 103, 104, 110, 113, 120, 124, 132, 133, 135, 136, 137, 143, 144, 145, 151, 153, 154, 157, 159, 164, 166, 170, 171, 177, 178, 181, 182, 185, 191, 192, 197, 200, 201, 202, 203, 210, 211, 215, 221, 222, 223, 224, 243, 251, 252, 253, 254, 257, 259, 267, 272, 283, 297, 306, 313, 314, 315, 316, 317, 318, 319, 320, 321, 323.

130. GENOCIDE/GENOCIDE CONVENTION

Definition: Genocide is an international crime that consists of the commission of harmful acts committed in wartime or in peacetime with the intent to destroy, in whole or in part, a national, ethnic, racial, or religious group of human beings. It is the systematic elimination of a people based on these characteristics. The Genocide Convention of 1948 is an international treaty that prohibits genocide and provides for its prosecution as an international crime. Its full title is the Convention on the Prevention and Punishment of the Crime of Genocide. See Document 17.

The internationally accepted definition of genocide is taken from that convention, which states:

Genocide means any of the following acts committed with intent to destroy, in whole or part, a national, ethnical, racial, or religious group:
(a) Killing members of the group;
(b) Causing serious bodily or mental harm to members of the group;
(c) Deliberately inflicting on the group conditions of life calculated to bring about its physical destruction in whole or in part;
(d) Imposing measures intended to prevent births within the group;
(e) Forcibly transferring children of the group to another group.

Significance: Acts that constitute genocide include acts that kill or seriously injure a group or subject that group to conditions that are calculated to partially or completely destroy them. Genocide is a human rights violation and constitutes an international crime. It is prohibited under both treaty law and as a matter of customary international law; thus, it is binding on all countries, even those that have not ratified the Genocide Convention.

The Genocide Convention was adopted by the members of the United Nations in 1948. Its purpose was to establish a conventional, legal norm that defines and establishes punishment for the act of genocide. In addition to defining genocide, it established international criminal responsibility for acts that violate the convention and it authorized universal jurisdiction for all state parties to prosecute violators in national courts. It does not matter if the person accused acted in an official capacity for a government.

The 1948 convention also makes reference in Article 6 to "such international penal tribunal as may have jurisdiction" to prosecute genocide under the convention. In July 1998, the Rome Statute (treaty) was adopted establishing such a permanent International Criminal Court. The statute (Articles 5 and 6) includes genocide as one of the core international crimes within the court's inherent subject matter jurisdiction. It uses the definition of genocide set forth in the 1948 Genocide Convention. The United States was in favor of including genocide within the ICC's jurisdiction, but for political reasons it voted against adoption of the statute. The International Criminal Court is now in existence and can prosecute crimes of genocide.

The United States was a prime mover in getting the Genocide Convention adopted, and it signed this treaty in December 1948. Nonetheless, the U.S. Senate, because of domestic political considerations, took until 1988 to finally ratify (give its "advice and consent to") this treaty. This convention should be read by everyone, along with the U.S. reservations, declarations and understandings submitted with the U.S. ratification. See Document 18.

Genocide was not a crime prosecuted at the Nuremberg trials in 1945. It was defined as a crime after Nuremberg. The acts that constituted genocide were, however, prosecuted under the classification of "crimes against humanity." A person can also be guilty of committing genocide if he enters into a conspiracy with others to commit genocide, directly and publicly incites others to commit genocide (as happened in Rwanda), or in some way aids and abets genocide before or after the act. Classic historic examples of genocide are the Holocaust of World War II, the Rwanda Genocide of 1994, and the Armenian Genocide of 1915. Genocide is a violation of the collective human rights of members of a particular group. It is not the same thing as ethnic cleansing.

Ethnic cleansing means in some way causing all unwanted groups to leave a particular place so that only one group remains. It does not necessarily imply the destruction of the victim group. If the cleansing state intends to kill or exterminate the victim group as a way to cleanse the area, that could become a genocide if the victims were targeted as members of a group, i.e., national, ethnic, racial, or religious.

In the 1999 U.S.-NATO intervention in Yugoslavia, the NATO countries, led by the United States, claimed that it was justified in bombing to stop certain atrocities, including genocide, allegedly being committed by the Yugoslavian government against the Kosovar Albanians. In response to the NATO bombing, Yugoslavia sued the United States and other NATO countries in the World Court, claiming that the bombing was an act of genocide under element (c) in the Genocide Convention definition. The court ruled that it did not have jurisdiction to decide the case against the United States.

In the ad hoc international criminal tribunals for former Yugoslavia and Rwanda, both, with substantial material and personnel support of the U.S., have been prosecuting the crime of genocide. In fact, the first conviction in an international tribunal for commission of the crime of genocide came out of the Rwanda Tribunal. Genocide is an international crime having universal jurisdiction, meaning that every state in the world has jurisdiction to prosecute those who commit genocide.

The *Kadic v. Karadzic* decision which arose out of alleged underlying genocide issues in Bosnia.

See Also Terms: 3, 8, 11, 12, 14, 19, 22, 28, 23, 29, 40, 42, 48, 53, 56, 63, 67, 70, 71, 72, 73, 78, 85, 86, 97, 101, 102, 110, 117, 124, 132, 133, 135, 136, 139, 143, 144, 145, 151, 152, 154, 157, 159, 160, 166, 167, 169, 177, 181, 182, 184, 185, 192, 200, 201, 202, 203, 205, 216, 222, 223, 224, 233, 243, 246, 259, 260, 261, 265, 271, 272, 283, 295, 306, 308, 309, 316, 317, 318, 321.

131. GOOD GOVERNANCE

Definition: An evolving principle that roughly means that the inherent dignity of individuals and their collective holding of human rights entitle them to "good governance," within state societies, meaning they deserve a government characterized by rule of law, having a democratic political basis (elected by plebiscite), and responsive to the people. Good governance also includes adequately structured state institutions with efficiency and transparency of institutions and procedures and respect by all governmental authorities for the human rights of all persons within the territory of the state. It includes respect by government for rule of law with access by individuals to means for redressing violations of law; accountability of public officials for misconduct, malfeasance, and human rights violations; and a public sector with an active and free civil society, with fairness and equity for all.

Significance: Good governance is a rather uncertain term used generally in human rights discourse and seen a lot in development literature to describe how public institutions conduct public affairs and manage public resources in order to guarantee the realization of human rights. Governance describes the process of decision-making and the process by which decisions are, or are not, implemented. The term *governance* can apply to corporate, international, national, local governance or to the interactions between other sectors of society.

The concept of "good governance" is often used as a model to compare underperforming economies or political bodies with well working economies and political bodies. Because the most "successful" governments in the contemporary world are liberal democratic states concentrated in Europe and the Americas, those countries' institutions often set the standards by which to compare other states' institutions. Very often development aid organizations and the authorities of developed countries will focus the meaning of good governance to a set of requirements that conform to the organization's agenda, making "good governance" imply many different things in many different contexts. It is a government operated in a manner that is essentially free of abuse and corruption, and with due regard for the rule of law.

See Also Terms: 3, 7, 11, 12, 18, 20, 24, 28, 29, 32, 33, 34, 35, 42, 48, 59, 60, 61, 70, 72, 75, 88, 90, 93, 94, 99, 100, 105, 106, 113, 118, 121, 122, 124, 128, 135, 138, 144, 146, 148, 149, 150, 152, 160, 162, 166, 169, 177, 178, 180, 183, 184, 185, 190, 193, 195, 196, 197, 204, 206, 210, 211, 216, 219, 226, 227, 230, 231, 233, 240, 242, 243, 244, 252, 253, 267, 268, 272, 273, 283, 286, 287, 292, 305, 309, 311, 316.

132. GRAVE BREACHES

Definition: Grave breaches are the most serious violations of the most fundamental humanitarian legal standards of the Geneva Conventions of 1949 and Protocol I of 1977, which occur in armed conflicts. Grave breaches are war crimes, violations of international criminal law. See Documents 72, 73.

Significance: Humanitarian law is that branch of international law, which seeks to minimize human and material loss in times of armed conflict. The main international instruments of Humanitarian Law are the Four Geneva Conventions of 1949. In order to deter violations of the most serious humanitarian law norms, states defined what are called grave breaches of the Conventions, which are war crimes and international crimes.

In the Fourth GC grave breaches are found in Article 147:

Article 147. Grave breaches to which the preceding Article relates shall be those involving any of the following acts, if committed against persons or property protected by the present Convention: willful killing, torture or inhuman treatment, including biological experiments, willfully causing great suffering or serious injury to body or health, unlawful deportation or transfer or unlawful confinement of a protected person, compelling a protected person to serve in the forces of a hostile Power, or willfully depriving a protected person of the rights of fair and regular trial prescribed in the present Convention, taking of hostages and extensive destruction and appropriation of property, not justified by military necessity and carried out unlawfully and wantonly.

Each of the four GCs has its own grave breaches article.

Grave breaches are criminalized also in the Code of Crimes against the Peace and Security of Mankind, Document 68, under the title of crimes against the peace and security of mankind.

As war crimes, grave breaches are considered crimes against all humankind because they cause death and suffering beyond that which is militarily necessary to accomplish military objectives. Commission of grave breaches gives rise to universal jurisdiction of all countries of the world to prosecute perpetrators of such war crimes. The particular acts that constitute grave breaches are specified in the Geneva Conventions and Protocol I.

Kadic v. Karadzic is a case decision dealing with such issues. See Appendix J.

See Also Terms: 3, 19, 25, 30, 33, 37, 40, 41, 42, 45, 48, 59, 66, 70, 71, 72, 73, 81, 82, 84, 90, 95, 96, 104, 110, 133, 135, 136, 137, 144, 145, 151, 152, 154, 157, 159, 164, 166, 170, 171, 178, 181, 182, 185, 192, 200, 201, 202, 203, 210, 215, 222, 223, 224, 251, 252, 253, 254, 259, 267, 271, 272, 275, 291, 293, 298, 302, 310, 314, 316, 318, 319, 320, 321.

133. GROSS HUMAN RIGHTS VIOLATION

Definition: Gross human rights violations are the most serious of human rights violations and include murder, extermination, mass deportations, slavery, systematic religious persecution, torture, prolonged arbitrary detention and enforced disappearances. There is no clear, concise definition of this term, either in the international legal system or in U.S. law. Usually this concept includes the idea of serious, systematic and very physically injurious acts intentionally committed by government.

Significance: This term is used in international and U.S. human rights law, but it has never been clearly defined. The Harkin Amendment to the Foreign Assistance Act of 1961 (Section 116) conditions and links U.S. foreign aid to a state not engaging in a consistent pattern of gross violations such as those included in the definition in the previous paragraph.

Section 502 of the Foreign Assistance Act of 1961, as amended, states that "for purposes of this section (1) the term 'gross violations of internationally recognized human rights' includes torture or cruel, inhuman, or degrading treatment or punishment, prolonged detention without charges and trial causing the disappearance of persons and other flagrant denial of the right to life, liberty or the security of persons."

Most general human rights legislation in the United States makes reference to gross violations as the basis for government action under that particular law.

See Also Terms: 8, 15, 19, 48, 53, 56, 63, 64, 65, 66, 71, 84, 85, 96, 101, 111, 130, 132, 143, 144, 145, 151, 152, 153, 179, 181, 182, 185, 200, 281, 298, 302, 303, 306, 307, 316, 317, 318, 319, 320, 321.

134. HABEAS CORPUS PROCEEDINGS

Definition: A civil legal procedure to force the government to prove to the court that it has the legal right and power to keep someone in its custody who has been deprived of liberty by the state.

Significance: Habeas corpus is the prime legal procedure for determining the legality of a government's deprivation of a person's liberty. The state must present that person before the court with evidence of the lawfulness of the arrest and detention. If the state cannot prove the existence of a valid legal basis to hold someone, they will be ordered by the court to free the detained person.

It is a violation of human rights for the state to deprive anyone of their physical freedom without a valid basis in law or in a manner inconsistent with the state's constitution. This principle is spelled out in UDHR Articles 3, 8, 9, and 11. See Document 6. There is no specific human right to a habeas corpus procedure in international human rights instruments to which the United States is a party. The right to this type of relief can be implied from ICCPR Articles 9, 14, and 15. See Document 8.

Habeas corpus arose historically from the Magna Carta as a legal, procedural basis to challenge the exercise of power by the king. It is a procedure used today to protect individuals from the abuse of power by the state.

No legal procedure tests the mettle of a state's rule of law like habeas corpus, for it is most often the most hated, defiled and odious persons who find themselves locked up under the power of state with little hope of freedom. Some may be innocent and some may be guilty. But history, particularly the circumstance of the founding of the U.S., has long taught Americans to mistrust the power of government and have adequate institutions and procedures to test its legality. Such is the legal procedure habeas corpus, which comes from the Latin expression for "may you have (or produce) the body." It is a procedure wherein a judge issues an order to the government to come to court with the person involved and for the government to prove the legality and constitutionality of the deprivation of personal freedom. Freedom is the rule, deprivation of freedom the exception, and the state's heavy burden to prove. If the government cannot justify the legality of the deprivation of liberty it must release the individual. This is to keep the power of the king (state) in check.

Habeas corpus does not test the criminal guilt or innocence of the detainee. It challenges the legal basis of the arrest and detention.

In the war on terrorism, particularly regarding the Guantanamo detainees, habeas corpus has taken on a particularly important role. The U.S. government placed the detainees in Guantanamo in the belief that U.S. law, including the Habeas Corpus Act, would not apply to the detainees and they would not be able to challenge the legality of their arrest and detention, some for almost six years, without any criminal charges being filed against most of them. The government attempted to set a military commission in the 2004 Military Commissions Act, which was ruled unlawful. It then passed the 2006 Military Commissions Act to deal with the detainees.

Habeas corpus petitions were filed in federal district courts and eventually came before the U.S. Supreme Court. See Appendix J, Case Law, *Rasul, Hamdan, Hamdi and Boumedienne*. The government got Congress to pass the Detainee Treatment Act (DTA) of 2005). The DTA is an Act of the United States Congress which, among other things, strips federal courts of jurisdiction to consider habeas corpus petitions filed by prisoners in Guantanamo, or other claims asserted by Guantanamo detainees against the U.S. government. On June 12, 2008, the Supreme Court, in the case of *Boumediene v. Bush*, ruled 5-4 that the Military Commissions Act of 2006 unconstitutionally limited detainee's access to judicial review and that detainees have the right to challenge their detention in conventional civilian courts. It confirmed the line of cases from *Rasul* to *Boumedienne* which said that the White House and Department of Defense did not have the power to prohibit the detainees access to habeas corpus in the American legal system.

Here the government was trying to wage what it called the war on terrorism by, among other things, preventing the detainees access to the procedure of habeas corpus. The Supreme Court decided these cases decisively in a manner showing the vitality of the system of checks and balances. The Supreme Court found it necessary to provide the broadest possible access to this holy writ won with the Magna Carta. Justice Kennedy stated in *Boumedienne*:

> The laws and Constitution are designed to survive, and remain in force, in extraordinary times. Liberty and security can be reconciled; and in our system they are reconciled within the framework of law.
>
> Officials charged with daily operational responsibility for our security may consider a judicial discourse on the history of the Habeas Corpus Act of 1679 and like matters far removed from the nation's present urgent concerns. Establishing legal doctrine, however, must be consulted for its teaching. Remote in time it may be; irrelevant to the present it is not. Security depends on a sophisticated intelligence apparatus and the ability of our armed forces to act and to interdict. There are further considerations, however. Security subsists, too, in fidelity to freedom's first principles. Chief among these are freedom from arbitrary and unlawful restraint and the personal liberty secured by the adherence to the separation of powers.

The habeas corpus proceedings continued in light of these decisions and, with the change of Administration, the battle over what kind of justice and where detainees may seek it, continues. Habeas corpus was preserved as an attempt to preserve the separation of powers established in the Constitution. Habeas corpus is the effective domestic remedy in the U.S. for protecting physical and moral integrity and freedom from deprivation of liberty and security of person. It is a unitary concept meant to preserve human security in the American legal system, even during the most difficult of times.

See Also Terms: 1, 11, 12, 16, 17, 20, 33, 34, 35, 46, 48, 49, 70, 76, 81, 82, 85, 88, 93, 99, 100, 113, 117, 124, 144, 145, 151, 152, 161, 165, 167, 169, 177, 179, 183, 196, 215, 222, 239, 248, 252, 255, 254, 256, 259, 264, 272, 275, 283, 292, 316.

135. HAGUE REGULATIONS

See entry for **Law of Armed Conflict**

136. HARD CORE HUMAN RIGHTS

Definition: A description of certain substantive human rights that are always applicable in all countries at all times in all situations. These rights can never be derogated in time of a public emergency, and they can never be subject to limitations for any public or private reason. Although there is no official list of which human rights are considered "hard core," it would include prohibition of slavery, torture, summary (without trial) execution, and prolonged arbitrary detention.

Significance: These rights are those that cannot be derogated, or suspended, for a time. They are the kind of rights that uphold the dignity of each individual and therefore may never be taken away for any reason. It is the purpose of the international human rights community to establish a common denominator of these rights worldwide and also to establish which human rights can, under certain circumstances, be suspended for a time. The suspension of any human rights by a government should be the exception, not the rule.

In the war on terror and the many changes in the American legal and political system, the concept of hard core human rights is very important because it defines what our rock-bottom legal values are in the relation between the individual and government. With all the discussion about limiting our freedom to allow the government to protect us from terrorism, the hard core human rights are rights that no American should give up or be asked to give up. Otherwise America is no longer America, and is the land of the formerly free.

As previously stated, all human rights, as written in international human rights law, are a compromise between the needs of state to protect society as a whole and the maximum freedom of individual. They are supposed to be a fair balance between these two. The concept of hard core human rights says that there is a certain point beyond which government cannot go in its interference with liberty. For this reason international human rights law makes these norms not subject to any exception whatsoever. They apply fully during the war of terrorism.

See Also Terms: 11, 12, 15, 19, 30, 33, 49, 53, 56, 63, 64, 65, 66, 70, 84, 85, 86, 90, 96, 99, 100, 104, 110, 111, 113, 115, 117, 124, 125, 126, 130, 133, 139, 140, 143, 144, 145, 146, 147, 152, 153, 160, 170, 171, 177, 179, 181, 182, 184, 189, 196, 200, 222, 228, 235, 238, 256, 259.

137. HARD POWER

See entry for **Soft Power**

138. HARKIN AMENDMENT

Definition: An amendment to the Foreign Assistance Act of 1961, Section 116, sponsored by Senator Harkin, which would prohibit U.S. foreign assistance to gross violators of human rights.

Significance: This amendment is found in U.S. law at Title 22, United States Code Annotated Section 215/n of 1994. It establishes general human rights legislation that would prohibit U.S. foreign aid to countries found to "engage in a consistent pattern of gross violations of internationally recognized human rights, including torture or cruel, inhuman or degrading treatment or punishment, prolonged detention without charges, causing the disappearance of persons by abduction and clandestine detention... or other flagrant denial of the right to life, liberty, and the security of person, unless such assistance will directly benefit the needy people in such country."

This amendment creates legal and policy linkage between U.S. aid and the human rights practices of all other countries; it is an effort to use U.S. resources as an incentive to states to not commit gross violations.

The text is set forth in Appendix I, Selected U.S. Human Rights Legislation.

See Also Terms: 9, 29, 48, 60, 70, 83, 124, 128, 133, 144, 145, 151, 152, 177, 184, 194, 199, 207, 211, 215, 218, 222, 259, 272, 283, 286, 292, 297, 309, 322.

139. HATE CRIME

Definition: A hate crime is a criminal offense committed by someone whose actions are motivated by the perpetrator's dislike or hatred for certain types of persons. It is characterized by the willful use of force or threat of force to cause injury, intimidation, oppression or damage to persons or their property.

A hate crime is based on antagonism toward some characteristic of the victim, such as his actual or perceived race, color, religion, ancestry, national origin, disability, gender or sexual orientation.

Significance: Hate crime is a term used both in the general and particular sense. In the general sense it is used to characterize any type of criminal act motivated by such antagonism against race, religion and so on. In the particular sense it can refer to a specific type of criminal statute aimed at eradicating harmful conduct against someone because of their distinguishing characteristics or lifestyle choices, which prevents victims from exercising their constitutional and statutory rights.

Hate crimes are acts of discrimination and abuse of the victim's human equality and dignity. They are intolerable if committed at any time against anyone, whether an individual or a group. If not prevented, they can lead to social strife, conflicts and even war. Hate crimes can be committed by agents of the government or by private individuals or groups.

Hate crime legislation is an attempt by society to assure the equal enjoyment of all human rights by all persons by eliminating the manifestations of intolerance. It is an attempt to get people to treat the "other" humanely and respectfully, without discrimination. It is a human rights obligation of government to investigate, prosecute, educate against and eliminate hate crimes.

In different jurisdictions, states will define hate crimes differently, some including more differing characteristics than others and some creating stiffer penalties than others.

Examples of hate crimes would include defacing of synagogues, Ku Klux Klan cross burning in front of an African-American's house; gay bashing; shooting worshippers in a church; threatening, racist e-mail messages; and beating up an illegal alien. It is constitutionally permitted for everyone to have any opinions they want, but manifesting or expressing that opinion can risk the violation of human rights.

In the aftermath of 9/11, and even since the Oklahoma Bombing, America saw an increase in hate crimes, largely directed at persons from the Middle East, or who appeared to be from there. Such hate crimes continue and the U.S. is trying to educate and prosecute to eradicate hate crimes. Hate crime legislation continues to develop as new forms of hate develop, e.g. internet racism.

In its 2010 national report to the OHCHR for the UPR process, Document 86, the U.S. mentions what it is doing regarding hate crimes. It mentions legislation regarding sexual orientation hate crimes in paragraph 34:

> With the recent passage of the Matthew Shepard and James Byrd, Jr. Hate Crimes Prevention Act of 2009, the United States has bolstered its authority to prosecute hate crimes, including those motivated by animus based on sexual orientation, gender identity, or disability.

In paragraph 36 the report states:

> At our UPR consultations, including the meeting in Detroit, Michigan, Muslim, Arab-American, and South Asian citizens shared their experiences of intolerance and pressed for additional efforts to challenge misperceptions and discriminatory stereotypes, to prevent acts of vandalism, and to combat hate crimes. The federal government is committed to ongoing efforts to combat discrimination: the Attorney General's review of the 2003 Guidance Regarding the Use of Race by Federal Law Enforcement Agencies (discussed below), as well as efforts to limit country-specific travel bans, are examples.

See Also Terms: 14, 15, 22, 28, 29, 33, 34, 35, 55, 70, 72, 77, 101, 120, 125, 126, 130, 136, 140, 143, 144, 145, 151, 152, 177, 179, 181, 182, 184, 188, 235, 259, 260, 261, 265, 272, 283, 306, 307, 309, 316, 322, 323, 324.

140. HATE SPEECH

Definition: Oral and written statements expressing hate, anger, vilification and disdain, demeaning to a certain group of people in a way meant to be offensive or to cast a bad light on the group.

Significance: Article 1 of the UDHR states that all human beings are born free and equal in dignity and rights. They are endowed with reason and conscience and should act toward one another in a spirit of brotherhood. See Document 6.

Hate speech treats other persons as less equal and as having less dignity. It causes others to dislike the victim group and makes violence and damage to them more possible. It can create civil strife in a whole country.

Even though, under international human rights law, everyone has freedom of expression, including speech, this right is not absolute. Article 19 of the ICCPR allows limitations of speech for (1) respect for the rights and freedoms of others; and (2) protection of national security, public order, or public health or morals.

Article 20 of the ICCPR states, "Any advocacy of national, racial or religious hatred that constitutes incitement to discrimination, hostility or violence shall be prohibited by law." See Document 8.

The United States is bound by Article 20 but does not accept this limitation on speech because it believes that the First Amendment to the U.S. Constitution provides greater protection of some levels of such advocacy speech.

The United States is also bound by Article 4 of the Convention on Elimination of All Forms of Racial Discrimination (see Document 23). That Article advocates that "States Parties condemn all propaganda and all organizations which are based on ideas or theories of superiority of one race or group of persons of one colour or ethnic origin, or which attempt to justify or promote racial hatred and discrimination in any form...."

In its reservations, declarations and understandings submitted with its ratification of CERD, (see Document 24) the United States stated a reservation to the effect that:

"Accordingly, the United States does not accept any obligation under this Convention, in particular under Articles 4 and 7, to restrict those rights, through the adoption of legislation or any other measures, to the extent that they are protected by the Constitution and laws of the United States."

This reservation means that the United States will keep its First Amendment free speech standard as defined by the U.S. Supreme Court, instead of the Article 4 of CERD. This is because the U.S. standard is broader.

See Also Terms: 11, 12, 14, 22, 28, 29, 33, 34, 35, 48, 55, 70, 72, 77, 78, 86, 120, 123, 124, 125, 126, 136, 139, 143, 144, 145, 146, 147, 151, 152, 160, 167, 169, 177, 179, 184, 185, 188, 205, 216, 222, 228, 235, 237, 260, 261, 265, 272, 283, 309, 316, 323, 324.

141. HELSINKI FINAL ACT OF 1975/HELSINKI ACCORDS

Definition: A political document adopted in 1975 at the end of the 1972 Conference on Security and Cooperation in Europe, the Helsinki Final Act made reference to human rights and fundamental freedoms for Europeans.

Significance: The act set forth certain human rights principles of government behavior referred to as "Baskets" of ten principles each. Basket III called for cooperation in certain humanitarian and other fields relating to human rights and called all member states (including the United States, which was a member) to fulfill all their international human rights legal obligations set forth in such international documents as the UDHR and ICCPR. The Helsinki Final Act was not a legally binding instrument. Excerpts from the act are found in Document 67.

See Also Terms: 14, 18, 20, 26, 33, 34, 35, 36, 44, 48, 50, 68, 70, 72, 86, 94, 102, 113, 116, 121, 122, 123, 128, 136, 141, 144, 145, 152, 153, 154, 156, 160, 176, 177, 179, 184, 205, 206, 208, 210, 190, 195, 211, 215, 218, 230, 235, 239, 240, 242, 243, 252, 253, 259, 260, 261, 265, 272, 282, 283, 286, 287, 292, 297, 308, 309, 316, 323, 324.

142. HIGH COMMISSIONER FOR HUMAN RIGHTS

Definition: The title of the highest U.N. official (an under-secretary general) charged with coordinating and heading human rights activity at the United Nations.

Significance: As a member of the United Nations, the United States is involved in many different human rights activities, both as a party to certain U.N. treaties, such as the ICCPR and as a participant in special procedures and mechanisms.

The High Commissioner for Human Rights is an office established in 1995 to coordinate and make more efficient all U.N. human rights activities. In addition, the high commissioner travels around the world to check on human rights conditions and makes helpful suggestions to governments for implementing human rights.

The High Commissioner works on the basis of the U.N. human rights instruments such as the UDHR, ICCPR, ICESCR, and other U.N. related treaties. The high commissioner cannot force any country, such as the United States, to do anything.

The person selected as the high commissioner is usually a very high-level political figure who has particular expertise in human rights. See the chart of the United Nations Human Rights Organizational Structure in Appendix C.

The Office of the High Commissioner (OHCHR) is involved in the process of Universal Periodic Review in the U.N. Human Rights Council in Geneva. See Appendix K. In this process the OHCHR prepares a report from the state and various sources on the state under review, SuR, to submit to the Council. This report forms a part of the process.

The OHCHR has offices in many parts of the world, providing a "field presence." It also prepares and submits reports to the Council on different topics, such as defamation of religion.

See Also Terms: 11, 12, 13, 14, 20, 25, 26, 30, 31, 32, 33, 36, 39, 48, 49, 52, 59, 62, 66, 67, 68, 69, 70, 71, 72, 74, 77, 81, 82, 83, 84, 85, 86, 90, 92, 93, 96, 97, 99, 100, 101, 104, 110, 111, 112, 113, 115, 117, 121, 122, 123, 124, 125, 126, 127, 130, 133, 136, 139, 140, 144, 145, 146, 147, 149, 150, 151, 152, 156, 160, 161, 162, 163, 165, 167, 169, 170, 171, 173, 175, 176, 177, 179, 180, 184, 185, 189, 192, 193, 196, 198, 202, 203, 204, 205, 206, 208, 215, 216, 221, 222, 225, 226, 227, 233, 235, 236, 237, 238, 242, 244, 248, 250, 252, 253, 254, 255, 256, 259, 260, 261, 263, 265, 268, 271, 272, 274, 275, 277, 278, 281, 282, 283, 289, 290, 291, 298, 299, 300, 302, 304, 306, 308, 309, 310, 316, 322, 324.

143. HOLOCAUST

Definition: The systematic annihilation of 12 million people by Nazi Germany during World War II.

Significance: The word "holocaust" literally means to burn up the whole of something. Arguably the most horrible event of the 20th century, and certainly of World War II, was the Holocaust of Europe in the early 1940s. This mass annihilation of human beings was based on the victims' race, religion, or other characteristics, all of which Nazi Germany hated and considered subhuman. It was a gross and systematic violation of human rights. The incredible evil of the Holocaust can be seen by the fact that the world is still dealing with the human and material problems created by it. Examples include the continuing prosecution and deportation of newly discovered Nazi war criminals, efforts to seek the return of plundered bank accounts and art treasures, and the rebuilding of destroyed buildings, even now, over fifty years after the end of the war. The United States is still caught up in this aftermath, especially because of the large number of Holocaust survivors and the surprising number of war crime suspects living here in the United States.

The Holocaust is most often used to refer to the killing of those of Jewish background as part of the Nazi "Final Solution." Although most Jews consider this term as applying only to what happened to Jews as a group, it has come to signify something broader, and not solely a Jewish victim phenomenon. Jews were indeed the largest victim group. Estimates are that the Holocaust caused 6 million Jewish victims and 6 million non-Jewish victims. Many others, such as Catholic priests, Gypsies, and homosexuals were also victims of the Holocaust. Despite its biblical significance, the Holocaust has come to signify more than the horror that happened to the Jews.

The importance of the Holocaust for human rights is that its horrors were a major factor in galvanizing the postwar international community to establish human rights and humanitarian law standards in international law to prevent future holocausts. The Holocaust itself had given rise to the prosecution of Nazi war criminals in the Nuremberg trials. The Nuremberg Trials gave rise to the recognition and acceptance of the Nuremberg Rules (the Nuremberg [London] Charter of 1945) and Principles that definitively established crimes against peace (aggression), crimes against humanity, and war crimes to be international crimes against all humankind. Such crimes could result in the individual criminal responsibility of those who commit them.

The Nuremberg Rules and Principles were historical precursors to modern human rights law applicable both in times of peace and of armed conflict. The Genocide Convention of 1948, which was a direct response to the Holocaust and aimed at preventing another like it, was also an important bridge and catalyst to modern human rights (see Document 17). The Holocaust is also the greatest historical factor in the international community's attempt to create a permanent international criminal court, a process that was begun in the early 1950s and rekindled in 1998 with the adoption of the Rome Statute for an International Criminal Court (see Document 76).

The Holocaust taught the world that the national sovereignty of states can never be a shield against responsibility for the commission of human rights violations and that such violations are the legitimate concern of all nations.

See the decision in the case of "*Cincinnati Radiation Litigation*" in Selected Case Decisions, Appendix J, for an example of how legal norms arising from the Holocaust are currently being applied in U.S. Courts.

See Also Terms: 3, 11, 12, 14, 19, 21, 22, 24, 26, 33, 39, 55, 56, 63, 70, 71, 72, 78, 86, 87, 11, 120, 124, 130, 132, 133, 139, 144, 151, 153, 154, 159, 167, 169, 175, 177, 179, 181, 182, 184, 185, 188, 192, 200, 201, 205, 215, 223, 224, 235, 259, 260, 261, 271, 276, 283, 295, 298, 300, 303, 306, 308, 309, 317, 319, 321, 323, 324.

144. HUMAN DIGNITY

Definition: The innate value and worth or worthiness of a human being. Human dignity is an attribute of the human personality, part of the very nature of man and woman.

Significance: Human dignity serves as the juridical basis of all human rights. Because of this intrinsic worth, all human beings are equal and entitled to human rights. Human rights are legal protections of human dignity. This basis of human rights is often referred to as "inherent human dignity." Every state in the world officially accepts the proposition that every individual human being possesses human dignity and that this dignity is the basis of human rights. Of course, states often do not act consistently with this belief.

No one has to do anything to obtain this dignity; one is born with it. It exists by virtue of one being a human being; it is inherent and inalienable. This dignity is preserved and enhanced by the setting of international human rights standards that limit the state from committing acts, or failing to act, in such a way as to violate human dignity. Human rights protect human dignity from the encroaching power of the state. They also direct states to implement laws and programs that enhance the basic value of each person.

The preamble to almost every major human rights instrument makes specific reference to human dignity. The ICCPR, which is binding upon the United States since 1992, states in its preamble that all contracting states are "recognizing that these [human] rights derive from the inherent dignity of the human person." See Document 8. The United States has accepted to be bound by international human rights legal standards that place the existence of human rights in the nature and worth of all human beings and not in the grant of such rights by the state. This is entirely consistent with the Declaration of Independence wherein it states, "all men are created equal and are endowed ... with certain inalienable rights." Human rights for Americans come not from the state but from human nature, or from the God of human nature ("endowed by their Creator") in the eyes of the Founding Fathers. See Document 1.

In its 2010, national report to the OHCHR for the UPR process in late 2010 (see Document 86) the Administration makes reference to human dignity several times showing its importance in human rights discourse. In its introduction to this report the Administration begins:

> We present our first Universal Periodic Review (UPR) report in the context of our commitment to help to build a world in which universal rights give strength and direction to the nations,

partnerships, and institutions that can usher us toward a more perfect world, a world characterized by, as President Obama has said, "a just peace based on the inherent rights and dignity of every individual."

The reports states at paragraphs 12-16:

As we look to the future, the United States stands committed to the enduring promises of protecting individual freedoms, fairness and equality before the law, and human dignity—promises that reflect the inalienable rights of each person....
III. A commitment to freedom, equality, and dignity
12. Article 1 of the Universal Declaration of Human Rights declares that "all human beings are born free and equal in dignity and rights" and that they are "endowed with reason and conscience."

People should be treated with dignity. Governments have an obligation to protect the security of the person and to respect human dignity. In fact, Section III.3 is all about human dignity in different spheres of life such as criminal justice and imprisonment.

See Also Terms: 11, 12, 15, 20, 21, 22, 24, 30, 32, 33, 34, 35, 48, 49, 53, 54, 55, 56, 57, 58, 59, 65, 66, 70, 72, 73, 75, 78, 81, 82, 84, 85, 86, 92, 96, 99, 100, 110, 111, 113, 115, 120, 122, 123, 124, 125, 126, 145, 146, 147, 148, 149, 151, 152, 155, 160, 167, 169, 170, 171, 177, 179, 180, 184, 185, 189, 196, 201, 205, 213, 219, 222, 238, 242, 250, 251, 252, 259, 260, 264, 265, 272, 275, 281, 282, 283, 294, 302, 303, 308, 309, 316, 320, 321, 322, 323, 324.

145. HUMAN RIGHT(S)

Definition: There is no universally accepted and authoritative definition of a human right. Many, however, define a human right as a legally enforceable claim or entitlement that is held by an individual human being in relation to the government of a state, existing and to be asserted for the protection of the inherent dignity of the human being.

Human rights are defined officially in U.S. law in the *Restatement of the Law*, at section 701 as follows:

"Human rights" refers to freedoms, immunities and benefits which, according to widely accepted contemporary values, every human being should enjoy in the society in which he or she lives. By international law and agreement states have recognized many specific human rights and assumed the obligation to respect them (*Restatement of Law Third, Foreign Relations*, Part VII (Protection of Persons), Chapter One (International Law of Human Rights)—section 701, comment a). (See Appendix I, for excerpted text of the *Restatement*.)

Significance: Human rights are legally enforceable limitations on the power of the state in relation to the individual and, some say, to groups. They are minimum common denominator standards of conduct of government established by the international community in treaties (conventions, covenants, agreements, protocols) and declarations and by customary international law. All human rights are held by individual human beings as attributes of their human personality and not as rights granted by any human authority, be it state, monarch or other authority, secular or religious. Individuals are said to be the "bearers" or "holders" of human rights. They are rights that allow human beings to protect their inherent human dignity from the abuse of power.

International human rights norms arising from international treaty or custom are binding as a matter of U.S. law by virtue of Article 6 of the Constitution, which makes them the supreme law of the land. No international human rights norms may, however, violate the provisions of the U.S. Constitution. See Document 2.

They are also called "fundamental freedoms" and are often seen in the phrase "human rights and fundamental freedoms." They are not the same as "civil rights," as used in the sense of the civil rights found in U.S. law. This is because civil rights in the United States are granted by legislative enactment (the "Civil Rights Acts"), whereas human rights are inherent attributes of the human personality. Everyone is born with human rights. The most commonly accepted philosophical foundation for human rights is natural law.

International human rights as a body of law have been most influenced in their genesis by U.S. history, law and jurisprudence, dating all the way back to the Declaration of Independence, the Constitution and the Bill of Rights. Human rights in the United States today are the "certain unalienable rights" mentioned in the Declaration of Independence. But it was especially the Bill of Rights, the first 10 amendments to the U.S. Constitution, that provided the world with the model for contemporary human rights standards.

The U.S. history of involvement with human rights has been described as a "bundle of contra-dictions" by some scholars. The United States has been very active in the standard-setting process of elaborating human rights in international instruments, but it has been very slow to sign and ratify human rights treaties and to implement them into domestic (national) U.S. law. The United States has been accused of applying dual standards of human rights compliance by friend and by foe.

As a matter of practice, the United States substantially respects and complies with interna-tional human rights standards, but it is highly resistant to any international human rights-based criticisms of its practice. Very few Americans, even lawyers, know or have even read the interna-tional human rights instruments, such as the UDHR. See Document 6. Largely for this reason, one hears little reference to them in discourse on human rights issues in the United States.

In the war on terrorism, human rights stand for the legal line between what the state can do to human beings, American citizens and noncitizens, and what it cannot do. The power of govern-ment is not unlimited, even in an age of terrorism even in time of war. Human rights are legal tools to counter the abuse of power by the state.

See Also Terms: All other terms.

146. HUMAN RIGHTS COMMITTEE (U.N.)

Definition: A U.N. organ set up in the International Covenant on Civil and Political Rights (ICCPR) to supervise and monitor implementation of that treaty and its amending protocols by states that have ratified and are thus bound to comply with them.

Significance: Most international human rights treaties (covenants, conventions, etc.) set up a mechanism or organ, such as a commission, committee or court, to monitor and supervise imple-mentation of the substantive norms of the treaty. Article 28 of the ICCPR established the Human Rights Committee (HRCee) as its "treaty-based" implementation organ to monitor compliance with the ICCPR and its two optional protocols. See Document 8. The First Optional Protocol pro-vides a mechanism for the HRCee to handle complaints by individuals claiming to be victims of a violation of the treaty. The Second Optional Protocol calls for the abolition of the death penalty. See Documents 10, 11.

The United States has not signed either of the two optional protocols. Thus, individuals in the United States who are victims of violations by the United States cannot file complaints in the HRC against the United States. Moreover, in its ratification, the United States also submit-ted a declaration stating that the ICCPR was deemed a "non-self-executing" treaty, meaning that it could not be used in U.S. courts as a rule of decision making. Implementing legislation by Congress was thus required to transform the ICCPR into U.S. national law. Therefore, individu-als could not even claim violations of the ICCPR in U.S. federal and state courts, much less the HRCee.

The United States is a state party to the ICCPR as of 1992, when the U.S. Senate ratified this covenant. Its ratification was, however, qualified with certain reservations, declarations and understandings. These affect the extent of the U.S. legal obligations under the ICCPR, creating, in a manner of speaking, legal loopholes for the United States. One of the declarations was an express U.S. acceptance (Article 41) of the power of the HRCee to handle complaints against the

United States filed by other states parties who had also accepted the HRCee's jurisdiction. (It must be said that no state party has ever filed an interstate complaint, or a complaint against another state party).

The HRCee is known as a quasi-judicial organ. Its eighteen members are not judges but legal experts in human rights. They examine complaints and apply the law of the ICCPR to the facts. If the complaint is admissible, the HRCee can handle it, and if the complaint is not resolved to the parties' satisfaction, the HRCee can set up a "Conciliation Commission" to try to resolve it. If this step is unsuccessful, the HRC can submit a report on its findings and its "views" about whether a violation was found (the "merits") and give its recommendations. The HRC can make an urgent request to a respondent state for a halt to imminent state action if immediate protection is needed, such as in a case about deportation or execution. "Views" are not legally binding decisions, but they are usually followed by states. The HRCee has no power to invalidate a respondent state's laws or to order the state to do anything.

In addition, the HRCee will periodically issue General Comments on what it thinks is the scope and content of any particular right in the covenant. This helps states parties understand how the committee views the ICCPR legal obligations. Anyone using or wanting to understand the ICCPR should look to the General Comments, some of which are set forth in Appendix E.

See the decision in the case of *Ng v. Canada* in Appendix J, which is a decision ("views") of the Human Rights Committee involving the U.S. death penalty.

In addition to handling individual and interstate complaints, the HRCee receives and reviews reports submitted by states parties under ICCPR, Article 41, regarding "measures they have adopted that give effect to the rights in the ICCPR and progress made in the enjoyment of those rights." The United States submitted its second and third reports to the HRCee in 2005, and the HRCee issued its comments and observations to it (see Documents 15A and C.)

See Also Terms: 3, 20, 25, 26, 30, 33, 34, 35, 46, 48, 49, 58, 59, 62, 66, 70, 77, 79, 80, 81, 82, 84, 85, 86, 88, 90, 93, 94, 96, 100, 101, 107, 110, 111, 113, 114, 116, 122, 123, 124, 125, 126, 127, 136, 144, 145, 150, 151, 152, 155, 156, 160, 165, 167, 169, 170, 171, 175, 177, 179, 184, 185, 186, 187, 189, 193, 196, 198, 205, 206, 208, 215, 216, 222, 225, 226, 229, 233, 234, 235, 238, 242, 244, 246, 248, 250, 252, 253, 254, 255, 256, 257, 258, 259, 260, 261, 265, 267, 268, 269, 270, 272, 275, 278, 279, 283, 291, 293, 296, 297, 298, 302, 306, 307, 316, 320, 321, 323, 324.

147. HUMAN RIGHTS COUNCIL (U.N.)

Definition: The primary organ of the United Nations which deals with human rights issues issues and replaces the U.N. Commission on Human Rights. (See Appendix C, U.N. Organogram)

Significance: The U.N. Human Rights Council was created by the U.N. General Assembly in 2006 to replace the discredited U.N. Commission on Human Rights. Members of the Council are elected by states in their region. It is a body of governments made up of 47 member states representing every geographical region and different types of political systems in the world. It was established by U.N. General Assembly resolution A Res. 60.251 (see Document 57). According to the resolution the General Assembly stated:

> *Reaffirming* the commitment to strengthen the United Nations human rights machinery, with the aim of ensuring effective enjoyment by all of all human rights, civil, political, economic, social and cultural rights, including the right to development, and to that end, the resolve to create a Human Rights Council,
> 1. Decides to establish the Human Rights Council, based in Geneva, in replacement of the Commission on Human Rights, as a subsidiary organ of the General Assembly; the Assembly shall review the status of the Council within five years;
> 2. Decides that the Council shall be responsible for promoting universal respect for the protection of all human rights and fundamental freedoms for all, without distinction of any kind and in a fair and equal manner;

3. Decides also that the Council should address situations of violations of human rights, including gross and systematic violations, and make recommendations thereon. It should also promote the effective coordination and the mainstreaming of human rights within the United Nations system;

4. Decides further that the work of the Council shall be guided by the principles of universality, impartiality, objectivity and non-selectivity, constructive international dialogue and cooperation, with a view to enhancing the promotion and protection of all human rights, civil, political, economic, social and cultural rights, including the right to development;

5. Decides that the Council shall, inter alia:

(a) Promote human rights education and learning as well as advisory services, technical assistance and capacity-building, to be provided in consultation with and with the consent of Member States concerned;

(b) Serve as a forum for dialogue on thematic issues on all human rights;

(c) Make recommendations to the General Assembly for the further development of international law in the field of human rights;

(d) Promote the full implementation of human rights obligations undertaken by States and follow-up to the goals and commitments related to the promotion and protection of human rights emanating from United Nations conferences and summits;

(e) Undertake a universal periodic review, based on objective and reliable information, of the fulfilment by each State of its human rights obligations and commitments in a manner which ensures universality of coverage and equal treatment with respect to all States; the review shall be a cooperative mechanism, based on an interactive dialogue, with the full involvement of the country concerned and with consideration given to its capacity-building needs; such a mechanism shall complement and not duplicate the work of treaty bodies; the Council shall develop the modalities and necessary time allocation for the universal periodic review mechanism within one year after the holding of its first session;

(f) Contribute, through dialogue and cooperation, towards the prevention of human rights violations and respond promptly to human rights emergencies;

(g) Assume the role and responsibilities of the Commission on Human Rights relating to the work of the Office of the United Nations High Commissioner for Human Rights, as decided by the General Assembly in its resolution 48/141 of 20 December 1993;

(h) Work in close cooperation in the field of human rights with Governments, regional organizations, national human rights institutions and civil society;

(i) Make recommendations with regard to the promotion and protection of human rights;

(j) Submit an annual report to the General Assembly;

6. Decides also that the Council shall assume, review and, where necessary, improve and rationalize all mandates, mechanisms, functions and responsibilities of the Commission on Human Rights in order to maintain a system of special procedures, expert advice and a complaint procedure; the Council shall complete this review within one year after the holding of its first session;

7. Decides further that the Council shall consist of forty-seven Member States, which shall be elected directly and individually by secret ballot by the majority of the members of the General Assembly; the membership shall be based on equitable geographical distribution, and seats shall be distributed as follows among regional groups: Group of African States, thirteen; Group of Asian States, thirteen; Group of Eastern European States, six; Group of Latin American and Caribbean States, eight; and Group of Western European and other States, seven; the members of the Council shall serve for a period of three years and shall not be eligible for immediate re-election after two consecutive terms;

8. Decides that the membership in the Council shall be open to all States Members of the United Nations; when electing members of the Council, Member States shall take into account the contribution of candidates to the promotion and protection of human rights and their voluntary pledges and commitments made thereto; the General Assembly, by a two-thirds majority of the members present and voting, may suspend the rights of membership in the Council of a member of the Council that commits gross and systematic violations of human rights;

9. Decides also that members elected to the Council shall uphold the highest standards in the promotion and protection of human rights, shall fully cooperate with the Council and be reviewed under the universal periodic review mechanism during their term of membership;

In March 2005 U.N. Secretary General Kofi Annan issued a report entitled "In Larger Freedom" in which he called for the replacement of the Commission with a smaller Council that would limit its membership to states with solid human rights records in order to restore credibility in the U.N. system to protect human rights. At the time there was much criticism of the Commission for repeatedly electing egregious human rights violators to serve as Members and for the disproportionate and continued criticism of Israel to the neglect of serious issues in other countries. In June 2005, the Task Force on the United Nations, a body mandated in the FY2005 omnibus appropriations bill at the direction of U.S. Congressman Frank R. Wolf, called for the replacement of the Commission with a Human Rights Council. The Task Force called for a number of other reforms to the Council as well. When the General Assembly voted on the adoption of the resolution to establish the Council, the U.S. was one of four countries that voted against it. U.S. Ambassador to the U.N. John Bolton did not believe that the resolution went far enough in reforming the former Commission. Many questioned how much the Council had been reformed when during the first election cycle countries such as China, Cuba, Saudi Arabia, Russia and Pakistan, were elected to serve as Members despite what many NGOs considered their questionable commitments to human rights.

Council Membership is organized by regions with each regional group electing states in their region to serve on the Council for a three-year term, with 47 total member states which may not be immediately re-elected after serving two consecutive terms. Observer states and even certain NGOs can participate in the Council sessions, such as by written or oral speeches called "interventions."

One of the more controversial elements of the new Council was the requirements of membership since the former Commission was significantly discredited by the membership of egregious human rights violators, such as Sudan. Membership is open to all U.N. member states and each would be expected to "uphold the highest standards in the promotion and protection of human rights". Moreover, when elections were held, "the contribution of candidates to the promotion and protection of human rights and their voluntary pledges and commitments made thereto" would be taken into consideration. Members of the Council that commit gross and systematic violations of human rights may be removed by a two-thirds vote of the General Assembly.

According to the resolution establishing the Council, its work would be "guided by the principles of universality, impartiality, objectivity and non-selectivity, constructive international dialogue and cooperation, with a view to enhancing the promotion and protection of all human rights." Its primary tasks would be to hold regular sessions, undertake a Universal Periodic Review of the human rights fulfillment of the human rights obligations and commitments in all U.N. Member states, establish special mechanisms and procedures to address country-specific or thematic violations of human rights, and submit an annual report directly to the General Assembly.

For the first few years of the Council's existence the U.S. government, as an observer state, was absent from the Council, though working behind the scenes. This was largely due to the Council being perceived as an anti-American bully pulpit, and for what the U.S. deemed its excessive and too frequent criticism of Israel. In 2009, with the Obama administration arriving, the United States was elected as a member of the Human Rights Council. While recognizing the serious defects of this organ, primarily the poor human rights records of many fellow Council members, the U.S. decided to try to improve the HRC from working within it in a collegial and cooperative manner.

Another problem with the Human Rights Council was a political bloc known as the OIC, or the Organization of Islamic Conferences, which used its political influence to push for certain changes in human rights consistent with its Islamic world view and the political issues which it supported, such condemnation of Israel regarding the rights of the Palestinians, and the "defamation of religion" resolutions. The administration was trying to create friendlier relations with the Islamic world. In the wake of his historic speech in Cairo the President's Department of State started to again attend the Council meetings. When it first became a member of the Council in 2009, which coincided with its return to active participation in the Council, it co-drafted with Egypt a proposed resolution on freedom of expression. This resolution was an attempt to do something cooperative with an OIC state, and to address the issue of defamation of religion, and the U.S. fears that the OIC defamation resolution would infringe too far the classical notion of freedom of expression as known in U.S. Constitutional law.

The issue of defamation of religion became one of the major human rights issues of the Council. Defamation of religion has the sense of saying something negative about a religion or its followers that causes offense to the religious sensitivities of the followers of the religion. Defamation of religion is a sociological concept and does not exist as a legal concept or principle in the field of human rights or international law. In the context of the HRC it has primarily been a movement of the OIC to get the U.N. to condemn any expressions which cause offense to a religion, which primarily meant Islam. It was largely a movement in reaction to the negative post 9/11 stereotyping of Muslims as all terrorists. The underlying problem with this OIC push against defamation of religion was that it would result in the undermining of the theoretical basis of all human rights, in addition to being simply an excessive infringement of free speech. In addition, defamation is, by definition, a _false_ statements of fact expressed against someone. Who is going to determine the truth or falsehood of a statement concerning a religion? For these and other reasons the U.S. has continued to opposed these defamation resolutions and the whole anti-defamation movement, while trying at the same time to call for education in tolerance which would diminish anti-religious expressions and increase religious tolerance. This issue seems not to want to go away and the Human Rights Council and the General Assembly are where this issue plays out in the international arena.

It is the U.S. State Department which represents the U.S. at the United Nations. There is a U.S. Ambassador to the U.N. and various State Department staff whose work includes the U.N. Human Rights Council. As of publication, the U.S. sits as a Council member on the 47 member Council which meets four times a year in Geneva. While the Council consists of 47 states, every other state in the world can attend the HRC sessions as "observer states." Observer states, and even certain NGOs, can participate in the sessions, such as by written or oral speeches called " interventions."

One of the key components of the HRC resolution A Res. 60.251 was decision 5(e) which created the process known as Universal Periodic Review. Under this process every country in the U.N. would have its general human rights record examined every four years. It is a sort of national self disclosure on how the country sees itself in compliance with its international human rights norms. There will also be a report drawn up by the OHCHR from various sources and eventually there will be an "outcome document" outlining the views and recommendations of the Council.

The relation of the U.S. and the HRC had its most critical moment on November 5, 2010, when the U.S. government appeared before the HRC in Geneva to have its human rights record reviewed in the (UPR) Process. The procedure and background on the UPR process is set forth in Documents 84 and 85 and Appendix K. Document 86 is the U.S. national report to the Office of the High Commissioner for Human Rights to be used by the HRC. Document 87 is the HRC final Outcome Report summarizing the U.S. UPR procedure and setting forth the recommendations to the U.S. The U.S. UPR process came to a close on March 18, 2011, when the HRC voted to adopt the Outcome Report. Every four years the U.S. will have to undergo the UPR process.

The participation of the U.S. in the Human Rights Council is very much subject to the attitudes of the U.S. Administration and can change depending on the political climate in the U.S. It can change with each Administration and depending on the geopolitical situation.

Aside from the UPR process the HRC has what are called special mechanisms or special procedures. According to the U.N. High Commissioner for Human Rights website, "Special procedures" is the general name given to the mechanisms established by the U.N. Commission on Human Rights to address either specific country situations or thematic issues in all parts of the world. These procedures, which consist mainly of working groups or special rapporteurs or special representatives, are explained in the entry for Special Mechanisms/Procedures, below.

Currently, the HRC remains the primary global forum for the discussion of and dealing with human rights issues in the world. The Human Rights Council has no real enforcement mechanism, except political pressure. It reports to the General Assembly.

See Also Terms: 3, 14, 15, 16, 19, 20, 25, 26, 30, 31, 32, 33, 34, 35, 43, 48, 53, 54, 55, 56, 57, 59, 60, 62, 66, 68, 70, 74, 77, 79, 81, 82, 83, 92, 96, 110, 111, 112, 113, 115, 117, 121, 122, 123, 124, 130, 131, 133, 136, 137, 139, 140, 142, 144, 145, 148, 149, 150, 151, 152, 156, 159, 163, 167, 169, 170, 171, 173, 175, 176, 177, 179, 180, 184, 185, 189, 193, 196, 202, 203, 204, 205, 206, 208, 211, 214, 215, 216, 221, 222, 226, 227, 235, 236, 237, 238, 239, 242, 243, 250, 252, 253, 254, 255, 256, 259, 260, 261, 263, 265, 268, 271, 272, 275, 278, 281, 282, 283, 289, 290, 291, 297, 298, 299, 300, 302, 304, 308, 309, 311, 316, 320, 322, 323, 324.

148. HUMAN RIGHTS DEFENDERS

Definition: Human rights defenders are persons who, based on the principles of universality and indivisibility of human rights, defend the civil, political, economy, social, and cultural human rights of ether persons, including their own. Human rights defenders, whether working for women's rights, land rights, the protection of the environment, or the defense of civil liberties, play a vital role in the promotion and protection of human rights. They are the individuals and organizations involved in the multi-dimensional work of human rights; in civic education, advocacy, investigation, reporting of violations, and the legal defence of victims. (Definition from International Service for Human Rights, Geneva).

Significance: The work of human rights defenders aims to achieve full domestic implementation of international human rights law norms, holding government authorities accountable for the full promotion and protection of all human rights. Human Rights Defenders intentionally act to bring about civic, cultural, economic, political, or social change. These persons' actions support or oppose one side of a controversial argument. Defender activism may refer to a variety of multidimensional actions, including protest, lobbying, writing letters to newspapers or politicians, participating in rallies and street marches, training, human rights education, and many other tactics to bring about change that promotes and protects human rights.

Historically governments have often mistreated, even persecuted human rights defenders because they exposed the human rights violations of the state, which tried to silence them. In response to this need to protect human rights defenders, the international community, through the U.N., adopted in 1998 the "Declaration on the Right and Responsibility of Individuals, Groups and Organs of Society to Promote and Protect Universally Recognized Human Rights and Fundamental Freedoms" (see Document 40.)

In the U.N. Human Rights Council there exists among the "special mechanisms" of the Council a U.N. Special Rapporteur on Human Rights Defenders who is chosen and mandated to report on compliance with the 1998 Declaration. That person, a human rights expert usually with a law background, has no power to force any state to do anything but works through political and moral pressure upon states to respect and protect human rights defenders. It is ultimately the Council which must handle the matters raised. The Special Rapporteur writes reports to the Council about how states are implementing this non-binding Declaration, and he or she can make country visits and meet with governments and human rights defenders, and can also receive and handle "Urgent Action" requests regarding specific instances of violation by a state. Upon receipt of a credible urgent action request the SR can write to the state in question inquiring about the incident and ask the state to investigate and account for itself and remedy the problem where possible. It is hoped that the exposure to the international level scrutiny will persuade the state to act correctly and consistent with the Declaration.

Sometimes human rights defenders are called human rights activists.

See Also Terms: 3, 4, 20, 36, 46, 48, 60, 70, 71, 72, 74, 76, 81, 82, 90, 112, 113, 119, 121, 122, 124, 140, 145, 146, 147, 149, 150, 151, 152, 165, 167, 173, 177, 184, 185, 192, 206, 208, 215, 217, 221, 227, 232, 233, 243, 259, 264, 268, 272, 283, 286, 291, 305, 306, 307, 311, 316.

149. HUMAN RIGHTS EDUCATION

Definition: There are several current definitions for Human Rights Education (HRE).

One states that HRE is education at all levels, status and occupation appropriate levels, both formal and informal, academic and non-academic, aimed at communicating to all society the knowledge of human rights and calling for individual and collective action aimed at respect for and protection of human rights.

Another definition: All learning that develops the knowledge, skills and values of human rights;

Another: the entire process of social life by means of which individuals and social groups learn to develop consciously within, and for the benefit of the national and international community, the whole of their personal capacities, attitudes, aptitudes, and knowledge.

A more official definition is found in the context of the U.N. Human Rights Council. The definition used in the U.N. World Programme for Human Rights Education, 2010-2014, states that "as agreed upon by the international community, human rights education can be defined as any learning, education, training and information efforts aimed at building a universal culture of human rights, including:

(a) The strengthening of respect for human rights and fundamental freedoms;

(b) The full development of the human personality and the sense of its dignity;

(c) The promotion of understanding, tolerance, gender equality and friendship among all nations, indigenous peoples and minorities;

(d) The enabling of all persons to participate effectively in a free and democratic society governed by the rule of law;

(e) The building and maintenance of peace;

(f) The promotion of people-centered sustainable development and social justice."

NB: Human rights education is not to be confused with the human right to obtain an education. The right to an education is found in Article 13 of the International Covenant on Economic, Social and Cultural Rights. Human rights education is necessary so that people can learn about all human rights, including the right to get an education. See Document 16.

Significance: According to the U.N. Office of the High Commissioner for Human Rights the international community has increasingly expressed consensus on the fundamental contribution of human rights education to the realization of human rights. Human rights education aims at developing an understanding of our common responsibility to make human rights a reality in every community and in society at large. In this sense, it contributes to the long-term prevention of human rights abuses and violent conflicts, the promotion of equality and sustainable development and the enhancement of participation in decision-making processes within a democratic system.

There are conceptually two types of human rights education: education *in* human rights and education *for* human rights. Education *in* human rights is the imparting of cognitive knowledge of human rights so that one knows what his rights are and how to defend their full exercise. Education *for* human rights refers to understanding and embracing the principles of human dignity and equality and the commitment to respect and protect the rights of all people, and to have the organs and institutions of society that are engaged in formal or informal education for human rights to reflect in reality and practice those very same human rights. Education for human rights is more about how we act rather than what we know. In the broadest sense HRE is much broader than the classroom. It is about the whole human process whereby one can come to fulfill the commands of the slogan of the recent Vienna World Conference on Human Rights, 1993: "Human Rights: Know them; demand them; defend them."

Promotion of HRE is taking place at the U.N., particularly through the Human Rights Council which is establishing a World Program for Human Rights Education 2010 – 2014. That HRE process at the U.N. is giving rise to a draft Declaration on Human Rights Education. (See Appendix Q). It is intended that eventually human rights education will be a binding human rights obligation. In the Human Rights Council there is also a Special Rapporteur on Human Rights Education who reports on HRE to the Council.

In the mid 1990s the U.N. declared the years 1995 to 2004 to be the "U.N. Decade for Human Rights Education." It included a programme to get all countries to conduct HRE. Little was heard or known about U.N. Decade and nothing was done in the U.S. to increase HRE, even though the U.S. had voted for the Decade and its program.

In 1998, the U.N. adopted the Declaration on Human Rights Defenders. See Document 40. This Declaration, which is not legally binding, sets forth the rights of individuals and groups regarding human rights education, and the state's obligation with regards to providing HRE to the population.

That Declaration provides:

Article 6
Everyone has the right, individually and in association with others:
(a) To know, seek, obtain, receive and hold information about all human rights and fundamental freedoms, including having access to information as to how those rights and freedoms are given effect in domestic legislative, judicial or administrative systems;
(b) As provided for in human rights and other applicable international instruments, freely to publish, impart or disseminate to others views, information and knowledge on all human rights and fundamental freedoms;
(c) To study, discuss, form and hold opinions on the observance, both in law and in practice, of all human rights and fundamental freedoms and, through these and other appropriate means, to draw public attention to those matters.

Article 14
1. The State has the responsibility to take legislative, judicial, administrative or other appropriate measures to promote the understanding by all persons under its jurisdiction of their civil, political, economic, social and cultural rights.
2. Such measures shall include, *inter alia*:
(a) The publication and widespread availability of national laws and regulations and of applicable basic international human rights instruments;

Article 15
The State has the responsibility to promote and facilitate the teaching of human rights and fundamental freedoms at all levels of education and to ensure that all those responsible for training lawyers, law enforcement officers, the personnel of the armed forces and public officials include appropriate elements of human rights teaching in their training programme.

Because humanitarian law is also referred to in this text under the umbrella of human rights, it is appropriate to point out that in humanitarian law, particularly the Four Geneva Conventions of 1949 and their two protocols, there is a call in each of those instruments for basic education by disseminating the basic principles of the GCs. See document 72. For example, Article 144 of the Fourth Geneva Convention, Document 72, reads:

The High Contracting Parties undertake, in time of peace as in time of war, to disseminate the text of the present Convention as widely as possible in their respective countries, and, in particular, to include the study thereof in their programmes of military <u>and, if possible, civil instruction,</u> so that the principles thereof may become <u>known to the **entire** population</u>. (underscoring added)

Despite this state legal obligation to teach the civilian population about the basic principles of the Geneva Conventions there appears to be no dissemination of these basic principles to the civilian population in this country. The reason for teaching the civilian population is that they will ensure that their own government complies with its international legal obligation regarding armed conflict.

See Also Terms: 1, 4, 20, 28, 29, 36, 48, 70, 72, 76, 124, 127, 142, 144, 145, 146, 147, 152, 184, 244, 259, 272, 283, 286, 316.

150. HUMAN RIGHTS REPORTS

Definition: This term usually refers to the Department of State's annual work entitled "Country Reports on Human Rights Practices." This detailed report is prepared by the U.S. Department of State, Bureau of Human Rights, Democracy and Labor, and is presented to the Senate Foreign Relations Committee and the House Committee on Foreign Affairs to assist those law-making bodies in U.S. foreign policy and foreign aid. It is updated and presented each year. It is a report of the human rights record of almost every country in the world. This term can also sometimes be referred to as the periodic reports made by states to treaty monitoring bodies, such as the Human Rights Committee. Generally speaking they also can refer to reports on human rights themes, such as trafficking in humans or about a specific country, whether done by an NGO, such as Freedom House, or an international inter-governmental organization, such as the Organization of American States.

Significance: In the U.S. governmental context, the term "human rights reports" is often used to refer to the annual U.S. State Department "country reports" made pursuant to Sections 116 and 502B of the Foreign Assistance Act of 1961. Country Reports are the most official and most comprehensive reports on the human rights records of all countries to whom the United States gives assistance. The term human rights reports is even found in legislation, such as the 1998 International Religious Freedom Act, which uses the reports as a basis of factual information on religious persecution. See Document 89.

See Also Terms: 3, 4, 11, 29, 48, 60, 70, 76, 112, 119, 124, 133, 142, 144, 145, 146, 147, 148, 159, 167, 169, 173, 179, 184, 185, 206, 208, 215, 217, 227, 233, 243, 259, 268, 272, 289, 290, 292, 293, 297, 306, 307, 311.

151. HUMAN RIGHTS VIOLATION

Definition: The failure of a state to act in a manner consistent with its legally binding international human rights obligations or national laws which implement those international standards.

Significance: Human rights are legal rights found primarily in international treaties and in customary international law. These rights create legal norms, or standards of conduct of government, which a state must meet in order to respect human rights and fulfill its legal obligations. When a state acts in a way that is inconsistent with the standard of conduct in human rights norms, it is said to be violating human rights.

Violations can and should result in certain legal measures being taken, usually as set forth in a human rights treaty, to stop and to redress the violations. These measures are normally taken through courts, commissions, committees and other permanent or ad hoc bodies set up for that purpose.

Human rights violations are acts of a state that violate the human dignity of individuals subject to its jurisdiction. They are the legitimate concern of all people of all states.

Serious violations of human rights can violate international criminal law. The Draft Code of Crimes against the Peace and Security of Mankind (see Document 68) sets forth some of those violations. Some serious violations can bring the perpetrators within the criminal jurisdiction of the Rome Statute for an International Criminal Court. The U.S. is not a party to that Statute.

Under the principal of subsidiarity it is primarily the responsibility of states to prevent and make reparation for human rights violations.

In the decision in *Haitian Centre for Human Rights v. United States*, excerpted in Selected Case Decisions, Appendix J, one can see an actual case decision of the Inter-American Commission on Human Rights, finding that the United States committed a human rights violation under the ADHR. See Document 62.

See Also Terms: 3, 5, 10, 11, 12, 13, 16, 19, 25, 26, 30, 40, 42, 46, 48, 58, 59, 60, 61, 63, 64, 66, 70, 73, 88, 93, 99, 103, 104, 107, 112, 113, 114, 118, 119, 124, 128, 130, 132, 133, 143, 144, 145, 146, 147, 148, 150, 153, 157, 159, 162, 165, 175, 177, 179, 181, 182, 184, 187, 199, 202, 206, 208, 215, 222, 223, 224, 244, 246, 253, 259, 264, 267, 268, 272, 273, 289, 290, 291, 293, 297, 306, 307, 309, 316, 318.

152. HUMAN SECURITY

Definition: The quality or state of being or feeling secure from danger and harm, or from interference with desired activity, or with physical freedom.

Significance: Human security is what everyone in the world in some way desires and needs. It is security that places the individual human being at the center of discussion or debate about security in a local, national or international society. Human beings want to feel safe and to know that they and their family's needs will be met so that they can live a decent, safe, healthy and dignified life. As a result of the need for human security in relation to one's own government the international community has articulated and codified international human rights law and humanitarian law. These bodies of law give individuals rights which are meant to assure their human security and well-being, whether in time of peace or during armed conflict. In order to maximize human security all international human rights law and humanitarian law must be interpreted and applied in domestic law in a manner which is most protective of human dignity and security, and which allows the full development of all human beings.

There has historically been a tendency of states, through their governments, to place national security above individual human security. The theory is that if the whole nation is in danger the security of the individuals in that nation will also be in danger. This leads governments to cause individuals to give up some of their freedom in order for the security of the whole society to be protected. There is a line between the maximum freedom and the proper limitation of individual freedoms for the needs of the greater society. Human rights norms have factored in this balance. It is a balance between the maximum of individual freedom and maximum protection of the nation, such as in the war on terrorism.

But all measures of national security are limited by human rights law. The state cannot do what it wants just because it thinks that will help protect national security. The obvious example is the person who knows where a bomb is planted that is going to go off. How far can the state go in restricting the freedom of, or violating the physical and mental integrity of the person in order to protect the rest of society? The answer is, as regards torture, for example, that the government can never commit torture on the claim that it is necessary to do so to protect that nation. Torture is over the line. It is prohibited by international human rights law. The reason being that historically it has been well documented that where governments allow any torture at all the agents of the state will justify torturing when and where they wish and will seek to justify everything as necessary to protect national security. Torture cannot be legally limited because the state wlll make exceptions to the point where the entire rule is eaten up and rendered useless.

Human security has two necessary forces against the various dangers and risks in life: hard power and soft power. Hard power means things like police and the armed forces, street signs, courts, government offices, spy networks, high technology surveillance. Soft power means things like altruism, charity, morality, compliance with human rights norms, civil society advocacy, and human rights education. The U.S government in the Obama Administration has been telling Americans that America needs recourse to, and development of, more soft power and less hard power. It sees the solutions to major problems as not so much matters for the military and police and weapons. It is of the opinion that one is more powerful if one is more just and righteous and less bellicose than if one merely has all the military hardware to force anyone into doing or not doing what we want them to do or not do. Hard power is increasingly being looked at as too destructive to the innocent and too economically wasteful, and a bullying tactic that assumes that the strongest one is the right or the best one.

Human security requires finding the proper balance between soft power and hard power and human rights law norms give us the criteria. The yardstick for determining where the balance should lie in a rule of law society governed by human rights. Good governance in a democratic society characterized by rule of law and human rights and participatory sustainable development are presented by the international human rights community as the way to maximize human security and minimize the chances of international armed conflict and violent internal conflict.

As a rule of human rights law, human beings cannot be asked to give up their human rights in order to gain human security. It is true that the exercise of most, but not all, of their human rights can be limited for legitimate aims such as national security and public order, but there are legal limits to those permissible limitations and states cannot violate human rights for purposes of protecting human rights or human security. This is the principle of inalienability of human rights articulated in the Declaration of Independence which Americans celebrate every July 4. Fundamental rights are not created, nor given, by the state, and the state cannot demand they be given back or waived by individuals in return for security. But states do this all the time. Human rights are inherent characteristics of the human personality. Human beings can never, never, be placed in a position to decide between security or freedom. They have an inalienable human right to human security with full respect for their individual human freedom, as set forth in the international legal obligations undertaken by the state. These obligations can only be limited as expressly stated in the human rights instruments.

Human security requires the state to fulfill its four international legal obligations to respect, protect, ensure and fulfill all human rights all of the time.

Suspension of the exercise of certain expressly listed human rights can arise during periods of "derogation." Periods of derogation are where there is a public emergency affecting the life of the whole nation, and this is officially decreed. (See ICCPR Article 4, Document 8). A proclamation of a period of derogation, for example, an invasion by foreign armies, allows a state to suspend or derogate certain human rights in a human rights treaty, such as freedom of movement in the ICCPR. But such derogation is strictly supervised by the treaty monitoring body. The state must announce which human rights are being derogated and can only derogated rights not expressly listed in the treaty to be "non derogable rights." If a state properly complies with the restraints on its limitation measures and properly uses periods of derogation and respect for the wording of the so called "derogation clause," it will result in maximum human security. As stated in the preamble of the UDHR, "recognition of the equal and inalienable rights of all members of the human family is the foundation of freedom, justice and peace in the world." Human security requires respect for human rights obligations.

See Also Terms: 1, 3, 11, 12, 20, 21, 24, 32, 33, 34, 35, 42, 45, 48, 59, 70, 72, 75, 83, 88, 92, 93, 97, 99, 100, 113, 119, 120, 122, 123, 129, 134, 136, 141, 142, 144, 145, 146, 147, 148, 153, 154, 160, 162, 167, 169, 177, 178, 179, 180, 181, 182, 184, 192, 193, 195, 196, 203, 204, 205, 207, 208, 223, 224, 226, 230, 231, 242, 243, 244, 250, 252, 263, 264, 267, 268, 272, 283, 289, 295, 296, 309, 316, 323.

153. HUMANITARIAN INTERVENTION

Definition: A doctrine of international law, established in the 18th century, which states that it is legally permissible under international law for one country to use military force in the territory of another country to stop that country from committing widespread and brutal mistreatment of its own citizens in a way that shocks the conscience of all humankind.

Significance: This was the first doctrine of international law that asserted that states were limited in how they could treat their own citizens. It suggests that where the acts of a state against its own people are so widespread and brutal as to shock the conscience of all nations, then the doctrine of sovereignty becomes subjected to the right and obligation of the international community to see all human beings treated humanely everywhere. It would allow one or more states to violate the sovereignty of another state by entering and using violent force to protect the victims from further atrocities.

This was the key legal doctrine relied on by the Clinton Administration in the late 1990's for engaging with NATO in bombing Yugoslavia over the Kosovo human rights crisis. This doctrine became abused by states that used it as an excuse to overthrow a government or change the political situation. Most scholars believe that the U.N. Charter, Article 2.4 made resorting to unilateral humanitarian intervention by a state unlawful, thus forcing states to work through the United Nations to prevent or remedy such human rights violations. See Document 5.

To be considered humanitarian intervention, an entry would be:

1. motivated by widespread and brutal atrocities committed by a state against its own people;
2. not requested by the guilty parties;
3. made only to effectuate protection of the victim population; and
4. not part of a U.N. action.

Every time a country acts in violation of another country's territorial integrity or sovereignty it must have a legal basis for doing so. The United States has used this doctrine several times. The U.N. Charter intended for states not to make such unilateral judgments about when to use force but to use collective measures through the United Nations and other international organizations to stop such atrocities.

The problem with humanitarian intervention is that if a state acts under that doctrine and violates the sovereignty or territorial integrity of another state it is subject to being accused of committing the crime of aggression, which is an international crime against peace. This could involve the ICC because the crime of aggression has been defined for purposes of the ICC jurisdiction. The issue of humanitarian intervention was one of the issues involved in the process of defining aggression so as not to prevent legitimate acts of humanitarian intervention.

In the late 2000s the international community started to talk about the concept of Responsibility to Protect, abbreviated "R2P." It was the idea that there was a responsibility of the international community and states to protect people from the more serious and extensive human rights violations. It was an attempt to prevent political indifference in the face of another human rights horror such as Rwanda. The "responsibility to protect" (R2P) doctrine outlines the conditions in which the international community is obligated to intervene in another country, militarily if necessary, to prevent genocide, ethnic cleansing and other atrocities. National governments are responsible for preventing large-scale losses of life and ethnic cleansing in their own populations. In the event that a national government is unable or unwilling to prevent such atrocities, the international community, acting through the United Nations, has a responsibility to act and protect the suffering population, with or without the consent of the recalcitrant or wrongdoing government. This is a contested and vague doctrine.

See Also Terms: 19, 26, 48, 63, 64, 70, 72, 73, 101, 119, 124, 130, 133, 136, 137, 143, 144, 145, 151, 152, 167, 169, 173, 177, 184, 185, 200, 213, 215, 218, 221, 228, 235, 259, 271, 272, 276, 283, 287, 292, 302, 308, 309, 316, 317, 318, 319.

154. HUMANITARIAN LAW

Definition: Humanitarian law is the body of international law that applies to armed conflict, both international (between two or more states) and noninternational (such as civil wars), and that seeks to limit the damage, destruction, pain, suffering and loss caused to human beings by violence resulting from military force. It sets forth legal norms governing the actions of the parties to the conflict, regarding how they treat the victims of the conflict, combatants and noncombatants, and limiting the methods and means (tactics and weapons) by which they fight.

Significance: Humanitarian law is part of international law and has historically been considered different from human rights law, though the ultimate purpose is to protect human beings from the calamity of armed conflict. Sometimes it is referred to as part of the "Law of War," but this is incorrect. In international humanitarian law one does not refer to "war," which is a legal relationship between two or more states where diplomatic relations are broken off. They are broken off due to a *casus belli*, a reason for starting a war. It is not the existence of armed hostilities, bullets flying or bombs dropping which makes a war. For this reason the international community refers to "armed conflict." Humanitarian law is part of the Law of Armed Conflict. The Law of Armed Conflict is comprised of two parts. The first part is the *jus ad bellum*, which deals with when a state has the legal right in international law to use military force, such as pursuing rebels into a neighboring country or for self-defense. The second part is the *jus in bello*, which concerns how a state fights the armed conflict, its methods and means of conflict, such as with what kinds of weapons, and how it treats victims of the conflict such as prisoners of war. Humanitarian Law is the *jus in bello*.

Humanitarian law consists primarily of the four Geneva Conventions of 1949 and Protocol I of 1977 covering international armed conflicts (and a few specified non international conflicts) and Protocol I, covering non international armed conflicts. See Documents 72, 73. In addition, Humanitarian Law includes the so called "Hague Law" or "Hague Rules" of 1899 and 1907, which is part of what is called the Customary Law of Armed Conflict. See Document 69. The famous Leiber Code used in the U.S. Civil War is part of this body of law. Geneva Convention I covers sick and wounded soldiers in the field; Geneva Convention II covers sick and wounded soldiers at sea; Geneva III covers prisoners of war; and Geneva IV covers civilian victims.

Violations of the Geneva Conventions can either be grave breaches, for the more serious violations, and minor breaches. Grave breaches constitute war crimes and are international criminal offenses giving rise to universal jurisdiction of every state. See entry for Grave Breaches.

The U.S. has ratified and is bound by the four Geneva Conventions but has not signed nor ratified either of the two Protocols, though it does recognize certain norms of Protocol I as reflective of Customary International Law, thus binding the U.S. military. It is up to the armed forces themselves to repress or suppress violations within their ranks. This is one of the things court martials and military commissions do. A major principle of this law is "command responsibility." This principle states that commanding officers can be held criminally responsible for the war crimes of their subordinates under certain circumstances. Another principle is that it is not a defense to a charge of committing a war crime that a soldier was "just following orders." This might lighten a sentence but is no legal excuse.

Another principle is proportionality. In all measures of armed conflict regarding an armed attack a military force will be subject to the principle of proportionality. This means roughly that a state can only use such force as is militarily necessary.

In every armed conflict the U.S. is engaged in there are many military lawyers advising officers on what they can and cannot do, or what is within the Law of Armed Conflict, particularly the Geneva Conventions. Humanitarian Law does not apply to the so called war on terrorism, but does apply to the actual armed conflicts such as the Iraq and Afghanistan conflicts.

There is an increasing convergence between the bodies of law known as human rights law and humanitarian law even though they have different juridical structures. Humanitarian law is about limiting what a state does to persons who are citizens of another state during armed conflict, such as prisoners of war. Human rights law is about norms dealing with what a state does to persons within that same state, or how a state treats its own people.

In the war on terrorism, humanitarian law is extremely important because it limits how American troops can fight armed conflicts against guerilla and insurgent forces in what is called "asymmetrical conflict."

Humanitarian law is primarily monitored by the International Committee of the Red Cross which has its headquarters in Geneva. When an armed conflict is going on and humanitarian law is applicable, this does not extinguish or suspend international human rights norms. Human rights norms apply during armed conflict. Certain norms are subject to derogation in certain circumstances for the duration of the public emergency, if officially declared. (See Derogation.)

The ICRC has developed a summary of humanitarian law principles entitled Basic Rules of International Humanitarian Law. This encapsulates the whole of humanitarian law in six separate rules disseminated by the ICRC.

1. Attacks may be made solely against military objectives. People who do not or can no longer take part in the hostilities are entitled to respect for their lives and for their physical and mental integrity. Such people must in all circumstances be protected and treated with humanity, without any unfavorable distinction whatever.

2. It is forbidden to kill or wound an adversary who surrenders or who can no longer take part in the fighting.

3. Neither the parties to the conflict nor members of their armed forces have an unlimited right to choose methods and means of warfare. It is forbidden to use weapons or methods of warfare that are likely to cause unnecessary losses or excessive suffering.

4. The wounded and sick must be collected and cared for by the party to the conflict which has them in its power. Medical personnel and medical establishments, transports and equipment must be spared.

5. The red cross or red crescent on a white background is the distinctive sign indicating that such persons and objects must be respected.

6. Captured combatants and civilians who find themselves under the authority of the adverse party are entitled to respect for their lives, their dignity, their personal rights and their political, religious and other convictions. They must be protected against all acts of violence or reprisal. They are entitled to exchange news with their families and receive aid. They must enjoy basic judicial guarantees.

These rules are not legally binding but synthesize the binding legal norms of humanitarian law. See Document 71. These should be known by everybody so they can know if their government is respecting international humanitarian law.

The four Geneva Conventions require that every state party disseminate the basic principles, not only to soldiers, but to all members of society, including civilians, during peacetime as well as during armed conflict. The U.S. does not do this except to the military.

See Documents 69-75, all of which are part of the body of humanitarian law. Read each one's accompanying Document Overview and Information Sheet.

See Also Terms: 13, 19, 20, 23, 26, 37, 38, 40, 41, 42, 45, 49, 58, 59, 63, 70, 72, 73, 79, 81, 82, 84, 86, 90, 95, 96, 99, 100, 104, 110, 113, 124, 125, 129, 132, 134, 135, 144, 145, 151 ,152, 164, 166, 170, 171, 177, 178, 181, 182, 184, 185, 191, 192, 197, 201, 202, 203, 210, 211, 215, 216, 221, 222, 223, 224, 251, 252, 253, 257, 258, 259, 272, 275, 283, 291, 293, 306, 314, 315, 316, 317, 318, 319, 320, 322.

155. ILLEGAL ALIEN

Definition: A person who is in a country in which he or she is not a citizen and in which he or she has no legal right or permission to be, and who can be removed by that country.

Significance: Every state has the sovereign power to decide which noncitizens it will let enter and remain within its borders. Even though an illegal alien may have no legal right to enter or remain within a country like the United States, he remains a human being. As human beings illegal aliens still possess inherent human dignity and hold all human rights, even though some of those rights can be limited. The ICCPR, Article 2.1, to which the United States is legally bound, recognizes certain civil and political human rights in "all individuals within its territory and subject to its jurisdiction," which includes illegal aliens. Article 2.1 also states that everyone can exercise all the human rights in the ICCPR "without distinction of any kind, such as race, colour,... birth or other status." See Document 8. This language precludes most discrimination against aliens.

In U.S. law there is a legal fiction that certain aliens who were excludable when they entered the U.S. are considered as not legally present in the U.S. for purposes of U.S. law and the Constitution. The government seeks to exclude them from entering even when they have already entered. This deprives the alien of access to the fullness of U.S. Constitutional protections. This fiction is in itself a human rights violation. It violates Article 26 of the ICCPR concerning equality of legal status before the law, and to some extent Article 16 on recognition as a person before the law. This does not mean that the state cannot remove such persons from the U.S. It can. It just means that while any person is in our territory and subject to our effective control, he or she enjoys all human rights in the ICCPR. The implication of ICCPR Articles 16 and 26 is that such persons although "illegal" under U.S. immigration law are human beings entitled to respect for their inherent human dignity and inherent and inalienable human rights, as are guaranteed under international law binding on the U.S. under the Constitution. The fact that the ICCPR is deemed "non self-executing" does nothing to change that legal reality.

In the U.S. Constitutional scheme the jurisdiction of immigration is delegated solely to the federal government, not the states. See Document 2. In the Constitution the colonies delegated to the federal government plenary power over immigration. It is the Departments of Homeland Security (DHS) and Immigration and Customs Enforcement (ICE) who have charge of this, as immigration is deemed a matter of great national security in light of immigration issues raised by the 9/11 attack.

There have been several times when states have tried to legislate in the area of immigration, particularly regarding illegal aliens who were perceived to be a state problem. The states claim that the reason they do this is because the federal government is failing in its job of effectively sealing the border and getting rid of the illegals. The states are acting primarily to give a wakeup call to the federal government to do something more effective to solve the state's problem. These state efforts are invariably struck down as an intrusion into the federal domain.

In 2010, an issue arose in the U.S. as to a law passed in the State of Arizona giving rise to a response from different places around the world. Arizona passed a law aimed at identifying, arresting and deporting illegal aliens in cooperation with the federal government. It allowed the police to question people about their legal status in the U.S., arrest them if they were illegal and turn them over to ICE for removal. The goal was to discourage illegal aliens from coming to Arizona and for those there to leave. The legality of this law is a matter of U.S. Constitutional law but the issue is government by the ICCPR via the federal clause and Article VI of the Constitution which makes international law the supreme law of the land:

> ... all Treaties made, or which shall be made, under the Authority of the United States, shall be
> the supreme Law of the Land; and the Judges in every State shall be bound thereby, anything in
> the Constitution or Laws of any State to the Contrary notwithstanding.

The Arizona issue is being discussed without any reference to the applicable international human rights law, but only in a Constitutional framework. What is necessary is to use both U.S. Constitution and international human rights law in the debate and resolution.

The Convention on Elimination of All Forms of Racial Discrimination (CERD) also applies to discrimination based on national origin, and it could apply to discrimination against aliens of a particular state, such as Mexico. See Document 25.

In 2010 the administration began pushing for a new comprehensive immigration law. Any such law legally must factor in the international legal considerations such as norms binding on the U.S. in the ICCPR and CERD.

The following documents go into more detail on the treatment of aliens in the United States: The U.S. Second and Third Periodic Reports to the U.N. Human Rights Committee, Document 15, on how the United States says it treats illegal aliens in law and practice; Appendix item General Comments No. 15 on "The Position of Aliens under the [ICCPR] Covenant"; Appendix L item, Report of the Special Rapporteur on Racism; Document 42, U.N. Declaration on the Rights of Individuals Who are not Nationals of the Country in Which they Live; Appendix N item The Rights of Non-Citizens (UNHCHR 2006); Second Periodic Report to CERD 2007, Document 25, where the U.S. uses the term "unauthorized population."

See Also Terms: 11, 12, 13, 16, 18, 20, 21, 24, 28, 29, 33, 34, 35, 48, 55, 59, 70, 75, 76, 78, 79, 81, 82, 84, 86, 90, 92, 93, 100, 102, 113, 120, 124, 127, 134, 136, 139, 140, 144, 145, 146, 147, 152, 156, 160, 167, 169, 177, 179, 180, 184, 185, 188, 195, 196, 198, 205, 210, 211, 216, 219, 222, 237, 240, 242, 243, 252, 253, 254, 255, 256, 258, 259, 260, 261, 263, 272, 282, 283, 287, 292, 294, 297, 304, 309, 316, 323, 324.

156. IMMIGRATION

Definition: The act of moving permanently or indefinitely to a country where one is not a native or citizen. Immigration can either be illegal or legal. An immigrant is a person who has entered a state with the intent to reside there permanently or indefinitely, abandoning residence in the former state of citizenship or residence.

Significance: In discussing this issue in the American context one has to be careful about how one understands and uses the word "state." As used in this book, state refers to a country. In American law the state refers to one of the 50 states of the U.S. This is important because it must be remembered that under the U.S. Constitutional scheme the fifty states have given over (ceded) to the federal government the exclusive power and authority over the field of immigration. (See Document 2, Article 1, sec. 8, Powers of Congress). So in the discussion of this issue "state" refers to the U.S. and every other nation state not the fifty states of the U.S.

Every nation state (country) retains the legal sovereignty to determine who enters its territory and for how long and for what purposes, and who can be considered a citizen by birth or naturalization. In the U.S. it is the United States federal government which holds this sovereignty. The Constitution has given plenary power to Congress to legislate in this area and it is then duty of the Head of State, the President, as chief executive, to carry out and enforce these immigration laws. A nation state has the power to determine the eligibility criteria for a person from another state to enter and immigrate to the state. The eligibility criteria and process whereby one becomes a legal immigrant are subject to certain legal norms in international human rights law and international refugee law, such as the equality and non discrimination clauses and the principle of non refoulement. That latter principle from customary international law states that a state may not return or expel a person to the frontiers of any state in which his life or freedom would be threatened on account of race, religion, nationality, political opinion, or membership in a particular social group. That principle is codified in Article 33 of the 1951 Refugee Convention. See Document 36.

A legal immigrant is a person who comes to settle in a country with the legal permission of its government. An illegal or undocumented immigrant is a person residing in a country without the legal permission of its government. They are people who come to a country where they intend to settle permanently or at least indefinitely, and many of them intend to seek to obtain citizenship, if eligible. All non citizens in the U.S. are called aliens. They are either legal aliens or illegal aliens.

Immigrants are people who intend to live here permanently or indefinitely, whereas alien just means they are here in the U.S. but are not citizens of the U.S.

States wishing to remove illegal aliens, which includes illegal immigrants, from their territory must do so consistent with their international human rights obligations, and while they are present in the U.S. they must be accorded all the human rights within the treaties to which they are states parties, such as the ICCPR. In the ICCPR the U.S legal obligation to recognize illegal aliens comes primarily from Article 2.1 where it states that "Each state party to the present Covenant undertakes to respect and to ensure to all individuals within its territory and subject to its jurisdiction the rights recognized in the present Covenant, without distinction of any kind, such as race, colour, sex, language, religion, political or other opinion, national or social origin, property, birth or other status." It also comes from Article 26, equality before the law. See Document 8.

A state has the legal right to remove illegal aliens, however International human rights law will not permit states to violate the human rights of illegal aliens who possess their human rights while in the U.S. because they are human beings and the U.S. accepted the legal obligation of the ICCPR regarding all individual within its territory and subject to its jurisdiction. International human rights law will not permit a state to create any legal fiction to deny the applicability of this clause to illegal aliens, such as claiming that since they came illegally they are not really present in the United States. Such a claim would violate ICCPR Article 2.1 as well as Articles 5.1, 14, 16 and 26. Illegal aliens can be arrested, detained, subject to certain limitations, and removed from the U.S. But nothing an illegal alien is or does nullifies their inherent human dignity and their human rights which flow from such dignity.

ICCPR Article 13 provides that aliens lawfully in the territory, which would include lawful permanent residents, may be expelled from the country only pursuant to a decision reached in accordance with the law, and to submit reasons against the expulsion.

The legal norms of the Convention on the Elimination of Racial Discrimination (CERD) also apply fully to immigrants both legal and illegal. See Document 23.

In 2006, the U.N. High Commissioner for Human Rights issued a report which details the human rights of persons who are not citizens of the country in which they are living. (See See Appendix N) It is called "The Rights of Non Citizens." All immigrants, legal and illegal, are covered in the scope of this report. Written by an eminent American law professor, this report describes the human rights which every immigrant in the U.S. holds, whether legal or illegal, regardless of their particular status and whether they have been "admitted" or "excluded" or otherwise. The categorization of American law cannot effect a change in the human rights of non citizens or nationals because these rights are inherent, universal, and inalienable.

Human rights are all about human beings and their human dignity and rights, not about states and nationalities and legal status. In reading the human rights treaties such as the ICCPR one sees the substantive human rights starting with "Every human being has..." or "All persons ..." or "No one shall be ..." or "Everyone shall have..." The U.S. has accepted to be bound by these legal obligations expressed in human rights norms applicable to "all individuals within its territory and subject to its jurisdiction." All immigrants and indeed all aliens, including visitors and tourists are included within the legal scope of that treaty.

Any laws passed or programs established regarding immigration in the U.S. must meet international human rights standards, particularly with regards to the ICCPR, CERD, and CAT.

In August 2010, the U.S. issued its national UPR report to the OHCHR. See Document 86. In that report it makes reference to immigration at paragraphs 92-96. In that report it states at para. 96:

> President Obama remains firmly committed to fixing our broken immigration system, because he recognizes that our ability to innovate, our ties to the world, and our economic prosperity depend on our capacity to welcome and assimilate immigrants. The Administration will continue its efforts to work with the U.S. Congress and affected communities toward this end.

See Also Terms: 11, 12, 13, 16, 17, 18, 20, 24, 32, 33, 34, 35, 48, 55, 68, 70, 72, 78, 79, 81, 82, 84, 86, 87, 90, 92, 93, 99, 100, 102, 124, 136, 139, 140, 144, 145, 152, 155, 158, 160, 167, 169, 170, 171, 176, 177, 179, 180, 184, 185, 194, 195, 196, 198, 205, 210, 211, 216, 222, 231, 232, 237, 238, 242, 243, 255, 256, 259, 260, 261, 263, 272, 283, 287, 292, 294, 297, 304, 316, 324.

157. IMMUNITY

Definition: Freedom from bearing any legal responsibility or from being sued for one's violations of human rights or other rights. Immunity usually comes from a principle that a sovereign state and its agents cannot be sued for its acts without its consent. Immunity is usually granted in a statute, which may provide for immunity only in certain situations.

Immunity is also a word used generally in the law to mean not having to suffer legal consequences for one's acts.

Significance: The case decisions in *Kadic v. Karadzic,* and *Samantar vs. Yousuf* found in Appendix J are examples of defendants in a human rights lawsuit trying to establish legal immunity from their actions that violated human rights norms.

The Foreign Sovereign Immunities Act of 1976, found in Document 105, is U.S. legislation that grants judicial immunity to states and their agents for certain acts. This statute is often raised in lawsuits against states for human rights violations. In 2010, the U.S. Supreme Court rendered a very important opinion in *Samantar vs. Yousuf* limiting sovereign immunity to the state only, and not to a former member of the Somali state government who was being sued in U.S. District Court. This takes away individual immunity from some human rights violators who were government members when they committed their violations.

See Also Terms: 3, 13, 23, 42, 48, 70, 71, 73, 89, 93, 94, 103, 110, 111, 118, 144, 145, 154, 159, 166, 181, 182, 184, 185, 210, 211, 221, 222, 223, 223, 234, 253, 254, 259, 272, 283, 287, 292, 293, 302, 316, 317, 318.

158. IMPLEMENTING LEGISLATION

Definition: Laws and regulations enacted by the U.S. Congress for purposes of putting into U.S. law the legal obligations of the U.S. human rights treaties ratified by the United States.

Significance: In most cases, international human rights treaty norms are only binding upon the United States where Congress has passed specific national laws, transforming those norms into federal statutes and regulations.

When the United States ratifies a human rights treaty, the United States becomes bound to comply with the treaty in international law. However, that treaty does not become part of U.S. law unless it is self-executing. Self-executing means that the treaty is meant to create binding national law applicable in U.S. courts upon its ratification. It does not need the Congress to pass laws that make that treaty binding as U.S. law. If, as is most often the case, the treaty is not self-executing (called "non-self-executing"), then it cannot be applied in U.S. courts and creates no actual legal rights for any U.S. citizen. It must be implemented, that is, put into law by the passage of federal laws that reword the treaty language into more specific judicially applicable law.

For example, the U.S. Congress passed the Refugee Act of 1980 as implementing legislation contained in the U.N. Convention on Refugees and its 1967 Protocol. The U.S. ratified that protocol in 1968, and the U.S. Congress took twelve years both to ratify the treaty by its advice and consent under Article II of the Constitution, and to pass the implementing legislation, the Refugee Act of 1980. This Act set up the system of legal asylum-seeking in the United States and set forth the rights of those persons applying for or receiving a grant of asylum who have met the definition of refugee. When the U.S. Congress ratifies most human rights treaties, it usually expressly provides that the treaty is deemed to be a non-self-executing treaty. Thus, it creates no legal rights to a private cause of action until Congress next passes implementing legislation. One reason Congress uses this procedure is that, as a matter of U.S. law where there is a treaty norm and a U.S. federal law, the last in time is considered the legally binding law.

Congress wants the congressional implementing legislation to prevail over any interpretation of the treaty.

In Appendix F there is a chart on how an international human rights norm becomes binding U.S. law.

See Also Terms: 6, 10, 25, 27, 53, 55, 56, 70, 74, 88, 93, 94, 98, 124, 128, 144, 145, 152, 160, 167, 169, 177, 179, 184, 185, 194, 211, 220, 222, 225, 226, 243, 259, 262, 269, 272, 279, 287, 288, 291, 293, 297, 303, 306, 318.

159. IMPUNITY

Definition: The situation where those who have committed human rights violations are legally or factually allowed to avoid any civil or criminal responsibility, accountability, punishment, loss or harm to them for the violations.

Significance: Very often government agents commit human rights violations but are never held responsible for their conduct, whether it was officially ordered or not. Many violators enjoy impunity because their violations are concealed or covered up after the fact. Governments sometimes refuse or fail to take action against the violators because the governments approved or even ordered the acts. Impunity can also be granted by an official act or grant of amnesty, whereby a state officially and formally forgives and forgets such offenses. Sometimes impunity is enjoyed because the violator has a certain legal immunity status, such as head of state or legislative or diplomatic immunity, and thus cannot be prosecuted. Augusto Pinochet used this claim in 1998 to avoid extradition from the United Kingdom to Spain. In every case of impunity, the violations continue to go unanswered and the victim's or their family's loss is compounded and perpetuated.

The international community has long tolerated impunity for human rights violations. Many a general, prime minister, prince and emperor have committed gross and systematic human rights violations, including genocides, and have never been called to account for it. The international community has done so mainly for reasons of political expediency or lack of political will. Impunity is inconsistent with respect for human rights. It is highly disfavored in international human rights law because it makes a sham of the enforcement of the norms that are essential to establishing universal human rights based on inherent human dignity. It is especially hard to accept where such impunity directly contradicts a state's clear and unambiguous international human rights treaty commitments and obligations to the whole international community.

Impunity is contrasted with accountability for violations. The United States is generally in favor of accountability for violations but has historically been directly involved in grants of impunity to violators, and has not acted to arrest and prosecute violators when it had the power and authority to do so, for example, Haiti/Raoul Cedras and Bosnian war criminals. The reasons for this failure were the perceived political value of Cedras and certain Bosnian leaders, the feared loss of life of U.S. service personnel, and political repercussions in the United States.

The establishment of the permanent International Criminal Court in Rome in July 1998 indicated that such normative impunity was no longer to be accepted. It remains to be seen how much international politics and the U.S. position and influence will help or hinder this goal.

See Also Terms: see entry for Culture of Impunity

160. INALIENABLE RIGHTS

Definition: Rights that, at least in theory, cannot be voluntarily or involuntarily transferred, surrendered or waived by the holder or bearer of the right. Human rights are legal rights that can never be taken away or annulled by another person or by the state.

Significance: Human rights are inalienable because they are the natural, intrinsic attributes of the human personality and "inhere" in all human beings because of their possession of inherent human dignity. Human dignity can never be lost, taken, diminished or given away. Thus, rights based on human dignity cannot be taken away either; they cannot be alienated. Inalienable rights are not created or granted by the legislature or any government official of the state.

The terms "inalienable" and "unalienable" are used interchangeably. Unalienable is the adjective used in the Declaration of Independence of July 4, 1776 ("and endowed by their Creator with certain unalienable rights"). Of the two terms, however, inalienable is now more commonly used. See Document 1.

The preambles to most human rights instruments make explicit reference to human rights as being inalienable. The preamble to the ICCPR, an instrument ratified by the United States, states, "Considering that ... recognition of the inherent dignity and of the equal and *inalienable* rights of all members of the human family is the foundation of freedom, justice and peace in the world....Recognizing that these rights derive from the inherent dignity of the human person...." See Document 8.

This is consonant with the Declaration of Independence, the philosophical source of the concept of inalienable human rights. Reference to this concept is often made in debates over issues of capital punishment; that is, does capital punishment constitute an absolute and permanent alienation of the capital defendant's human rights, such as the right to life, the right to marry, the right to vote, freedom of religion and so on.

Although all human rights are inalienable, human rights law recognizes certain limitations and restrictions that can legitimately be placed on the exercise of human rights, such as for national security, public health or public order (see ICCPR, Article 18.3). Certain human rights can be temporarily suspended during public emergency situations under "derogation clauses" in human rights treaties (see ICCPR, Article 4). The state's legal derogation or limitation of human rights does not constitute an act of alienating such rights.

Since 9/11 there has been a debate on how much of their freedom Americans must give up in order to allow the government to fight the war on terrorism. This is presented as if the government cannot effectively fight or win the war on terrorism unless Americans give up some of their freedom, such as freedom from unreasonable search and seizure. As a matter of international human rights law the government cannot take human rights away because it did not create or give them, and it cannot demand that Americans waive them or give them up. They are inalienable and unalienable. They are meant to reflect a fair balance between the needs of state on the one hand, and maximum personal freedom on the other.

See Also Terms: 11, 12, 20, 21, 24, 30, 32, 33, 34, 53, 54, 55, 56, 57, 63, 65, 66, 68, 69, 70, 73, 74, 75, 85, 86, 90, 92, 99, 100, 108, 110, 111, 113, 116, 117, 120, 121, 122, 123, 124, 125, 126, 127, 130, 133, 134, 136, 144, 145, 146, 147, 148, 152, 153, 161, 167, 169, 177, 179, 180, 184, 185, 189, 195, 196, 213, 222, 242, 252, 256, 259, 260, 265, 272, 281, 282, 297, 298, 302, 306, 308, 309, 312, 316, 317, 318, 322.

161. Incommunicado Detention

Definition: An act by which a government holds a person in physical custody and does not permit the person to communicate with his or her family, legal representatives, or other interested persons or organizations, and prevents those on the outside from contacting the detainee, and often conceals their whereabouts and identity.

Significance: When a government takes a person into physical custody on suspicion of committing a crime or of being part of some law-breaking group, it sometimes holds the person in jail, prison or other confinement place and does not permit the person to communicate with anyone outside that place. Very often, the person is held secretly, leaving the person with no means of seeking freedom through legal means.

Incommunicado detention is almost always a violation of human rights norms. It would, for example, violate the right to seek habeas corpus-type legal proceedings (ICCPR, Article 9.3 and 4); the right against cruel and inhuman treatment (ICCPR, Article 7); the right of persons deprived of their liberty to be treated with humanity (ICCPR, Article 10.1); the right to have legal representation and the means and time to prepare a defense (ICCPR, Article 14.3b and d); the right to freedom from government interference with private and family life (ICCPR, Article 17); and the right to freedom of expression (ICCPR, Article 19.2). See Document 8.

Since the beginning of the war on terrorism the U.S. government has been detaining many individuals and trying to keep them as incommunicado as possible. This was initially the case at Guantanamo but eventually the detainees were able to be contacted by lawyers and some contact was established. There have been allegations and reports about so-called secret detention centers or ghost sites where unknown war on terror detainees were kept incommunicado.

Normally the excuse for incommunicado detention is to prevent any outside interference such as a break out or to prevent sensitive information from getting out. Quite often the reason is because the government wants to treat the detainees in a way which may be too robust to the point of being torture, inhuman or degrading treatment and the government does not want anyone, particularly the media, to find out about it. Most situations of incommunicado detentions would be characterized as human rights violations no matter how noble or urgent the cause.

The U.N. Human Rights Council has a Special Rapporteur on Protection of Human Rights while Countering Terrorism who has been reporting on these ghost detention centers. In addition a joint special rapporteurs report was submitted in 2010 entitled: "Joint Study On Global Practices In Relation To Secret Detention In The Context Of Countering Terrorism Of The Special Rapporteur On The Promotion And Protection Of Human Rights And Fundamental Freedoms While Countering Terrorism, Martin Scheinin; The Special Rapporteur On Torture And Other Cruel, Inhuman Or Degrading Treatment Or Punishment, Manfred Nowak; The Working Group On Arbitrary Detention Represented By Its Vice-Chair, Shaheen Sardar Ali; and The Working Group On Enforced Or Involuntary Disappearances Represented By Its Chair, Jeremy Sarkin." This report is about the global phenomenon of secret detention and not just that of the U.S. See Appendix M. In that report the Special Rapporteurs state about incommunicado or secret detention as follows:

> Secret detention is irreconcilable with international human rights law and international humanitarian law. It amounts to a manifold human rights violation that cannot be justified under any circumstances, including during states of emergency.
>
> 1. Secret detention and the right to liberty of the person
>
> 18. Secret detention violates the right to liberty and security of the person and the prohibition of arbitrary arrest or detention. Article 9, paragraph 1, of the International Covenant on Civil and Political Rights affirms that everyone has the right to liberty and security of person, that no one should be subjected to arbitrary arrest or detention nor be deprived of his or her liberty except on such grounds and in accordance with such procedure as are established by law. Furthermore, Article 9, paragraph 4, of the Covenant stipulates that anyone deprived of their liberty by arrest or detention should be entitled to take proceedings before a court, in order that that court may decide, without delay, on the lawfulness of their detention and order their release if the detention is not lawful. The Human Rights Committee, in its general comment No. 8, highlighted that Article 9, paragraphs 1 and 4, and paragraph 3, of the International Covenant on Civil and
>
> Political Rights as far as the right to be informed at the time of the arrest about the reasons therefore, is applicable to all deprivations of liberty, "whether in criminal cases or in other cases such as, for example, mental illness, vagrancy, drug addiction, educational purposes, immigration control, etc."
>
> 19. The practice of secret detention in itself violates the above-mentioned guarantees, or in most cases, automatically or inherently entails such consequences that amount to a violation. As secret detainees are held outside the reach of the law, no procedure established by law is being applied to them as required by Article 9 of the International Covenant on Civil and Political Rights.

162. INDEPENDENT AND IMPARTIAL JUDICIARY

Definition: A judicial (court) system that handles cases and whose judges dispense justice with complete fairness to all parties appearing before the court. The judges must have no biases for or against any party and cannot in any way prejudge the case.

Significance: A court cannot, in making a decision, be influenced in any way by the government. They must base all decisions only on the law and the facts, according to established procedures and rules of evidence. The ICCPR, Article 14, states that all persons shall be equal before the courts of law and that everyone in judicial proceedings has the right to a "fair and public hearing by a competent and impartial tribunal established by law." See Document 8.

Some U.S. law and practice regarding independent and impartial judiciaries is treated in the Second and Third Reports of the United States to the U.N. Human Rights Committee. See Document 15A.

In the war on terrorism, serious issues of independence and impartiality of tribunals arose on connection with the detention of so-called enemy combatants and other terrorists suspects in relation to their access to justice. For the most part they were denied any access to lawyers or justice. They were being detained in Guantanamo mostly without charges and without trial. After a while, the government started to establish a military commission to try the detainees. The first Commission was ruled unconstitutional as not properly constituted and the second military commission was challenged and found wanting in due process.

What the inherent problem in such tribunals is, is that in a military commission there is a military judge or judges, and a military prosecutor and, most often, a military defense attorney a military bailiff and court reporter and translators. In this judicial context the issue of the independence and impartiality of the court can be seriously questioned. This is a court created by the executive branch of the government (Department of Defense) with judges who are members of the executive branch, with lawyers, both prosecution and defense members of the executive branch, and, at best a few outsiders monitoring the process. There is certainly a place for military justice through such commissions but the perception that the case is stacked in favor of the prosecution cannot be denied.

The U.S. Supreme Court has ruled that these detainees have a right to access to civil courts and this commission process began to take a different tack and unwind with the coming of the Obama Administration and sweeping policy changes.

163. INDIGENOUS PEOPLES OR POPULATIONS

Definition: There is as yet no official or authoritative definition of this term in the field of human rights, though attempts are being made in the international community to craft one. However, generally speaking, indigenous peoples or populations are those who originally inhabit a particular land before an immigration of other people occurs and those people become dominant. It is a group of people with a particular language and culture that is trying to preserve its cultural identity, customs and language in relation to the rest of society.

Significance: In the U.S. context there are three main groups of indigenous peoples: American Indians, Alaskan Eskimos, and Native Hawaiians. These peoples historically inhabited the lands of America before the many later migrations from other countries. The word "indigenous" generally means having originated in and living or occurring naturally in a particular region or environment. When used with "people(s)" or "population(s)," it is difficult to define. There is no universally accepted, authoritative definition of this term. The following suggested descriptions, taken from several sources, give some sense of definition: the people native to the area; the people in residence when "civilization" arrived (some define this as dating back to prehistoric times); communities or nations having an important historical continuity with societies that inhabited the same general territory and that predated colonization or invasion by other peoples. Some say the basic elements of such groups are the following:

Pre-existence: The group is descended from those who inhabited an area prior to arrival of another group.

Nondominance: The group is usually subservient to, or marginalized from, the rest of the later-arriving inhabitants of the society or state.

Cultural difference: The group has essential differences in culture from the later arrivals.

Self-identification as an indigenous group: The group believes itself to be the descendants of the original inhabitants and wishes to preserve its distinct identity, culture and control of its land and resources.

In the United States, the government has long recognized the American Indians as a separate nation and has concluded treaties with the tribes, giving them some form of autonomy and limited sovereignty over tribal lands and activities. The U.S. Congress in 1994 recognized that the takeover of the Hawaiian people and annexation of the Hawaiian Islands in the late 1800s was illegal as a matter of international law. The U.S. government has told the Hawaiians that they may seek, as a people, to exercise their international rights by deciding for themselves whether to remain a part of the United States under federal sovereignty (maintaining their current status), to seek some form of autonomy within the U.S. system, or even to declare their independence from the United States and form their own country (state). As a "people" they have a human right under international law to determine their own political status and destiny. Known as the human right to self-determination, this right is found in ICCPR, Article 1, which is binding upon the United States, since it ratified the ICCPR in 1992. (See Documents 8 and 9.) As of early 2000, the Native Hawaiian people were in the process of debating and voting for the form of political identity and status they wished to have. Different groups had different ideas about what their future status and identity should be.

Indigenous peoples in the United States enjoy all the internationally recognized human rights under the ICCPR, which the United States has ratified. These rights include those described in Article 27 on the rights of ethnic, racial and religious minorities because the term "ethnic" has been interpreted as including indigenous minority groups within its meaning. Because indigenous peoples are ethnic minorities, they are included within the scope of the nonbinding U.N. Declaration on the Rights of Persons Belonging to National or Ethnic, Religious or Linguistic Minorities. This Declaration was adopted by the U.N. General Assembly on 18 December 1992 (GA Res. 47/135). See Document 41.

Also in the context of the United Nations, the U.N. Human Rights Council (on which a U.S. representative sits) has undertaken a lot of activity regarding human rights of indigenous peoples (including American Indians, Eskimos, and Native Hawaiians) around the world. They have done many reports and studies and have begun setting standards in relation to human rights for all indigenous peoples. The United Nations General Assembly adopted the Declaration on the Rights of Indigenous Peoples, which had been prepared and adopted by the former U.N. Sub-Commission on 20 April 1994 (Res. 1994/45). (See Document 39) The intent of the international community seems to be to eventually craft a legally binding Convention on Indigenous Rights, based on this declaration.

The general position of the international community is that indigenous peoples should be allowed some form of group autonomy within a state, but not necessarily the right to break off and create their own (country) state.

In general, the most common human rights issues dealt with in the United States in relation to indigenous populations are preservation of culture (language, customs, art); practice of religion and protection of sacred sites and burial grounds; hunting and use of natural resources; jurisdiction over criminal activity and family relations; and control of health care, education, gambling and other revenue-raising industries.

See the Second and Third Reports of the United States to the U.N. Human Rights Committee, Document 15A, for U.S. law and practice regarding indigenous people under Articles 1, 2, and 27 of the ICCPR. See also: the decision in the case of *Cherokee Nation v. United States* in Appendix J, a decision of the Inter-American Commission on Human Rights. This decision gives an example of how some indigenous groups in the United States have sought to remedy past injustices by resorting to the international human rights system.

In its 2010, UPR report to the OHCHR for the UPR process, Document 86, the administration spent five paragraphs concerning the relationship of the U.S. with the indigenous people here, including Native Americans, Eskimos and Native Hawaiians. The report stated:

> The U.S. took the UPR process to "Indian Country." One of our UPR consultations was hosted on tribal land in Arizona. The New Mexico consultation addressed American Indian and Alaska Native issues, and other consultations included tribal representatives. The United States has a unique legal relationship with federally recognized tribes. By virtue of their status as sovereigns that pre-date the federal Union, as well as subsequent treaties, statutes, executive orders, and judicial decisions, Indian tribes are recognized as political entities with inherent powers of self-government. The U.S. government therefore has a government-to-government relationship with 564 federally recognized Indian tribes and promotes tribal self-governance over a broad range of internal and local affairs. The United States also recognizes past wrongs and broken promises in the federal government's relationship with American Indians and Alaska Natives, and recognizes the need for urgent change.
>
> In November of last year, President Obama hosted a historic summit with nearly 400 tribal leaders to develop a policy agenda for Native Americans where he emphasized his commitment to regular and meaningful consultation with tribal officials regarding federal policy decisions that have tribal implications. In March, the President signed into law important health provisions for American Indians and Alaska Natives. In addition, President Obama recognizes the importance of enhancing the role of tribes in Indian education and supports Native language immersion and Native language restoration programs.

The report mentioned the problems still existing among Americans indigenous peoples, particularly high unemployment and domestic violence.

See Also Terms: 11, 12, 20, 24, 33, 34, 35, 39, 55, 60, 67, 68, 70, 83, 86, 87, 92, 97, 99, 100, 101, 102, 120, 124, 130, 144, 145, 146, 147, 152, 160, 167, 169, 176, 177, 179, 180, 184, 185, 195, 205, 21, 216, 237, 242, 243, 259, 264, 272, 274, 278, 283, 287, 292, 297, 309, 316, 323.

164. INDISCRIMINATE ATTACK/FORCE

Definition: A military attack or use of force that uses weapons or other means that are not, or cannot be, targeted to damage only military persons and objects and not civilian persons and objects.

Significance: International law prohibits combatants in an international armed conflict or internal armed conflict, like a civil war, from engaging in any kind of attack in which both civilians and civilian property are attacked just like military targets. International humanitarian law requires that all sides must distinguish at all times between civilian and military targets and may only attack military targets. If there is damage to civilians and civilian objects (called "collateral damage"), such damage cannot be disproportionate to the military advantage to be achieved by the attack.

In an indiscriminate attack or indiscriminate use of force, there is no way to make sure that only military targets are targeted and damaged. Some say that nuclear weapons and other weapons of mass destruction (WMDs) are unlawful because their use always constitutes an indiscriminate attack. The damage caused cannot be limited to combatants and cannot be controlled. Use of weapons of mass destruction will most always result in violation of both international human rights law and humanitarian law also because their damage effect violates the principle of proportionality. The United States opposes this position, saying that nuclear weapons are unique and must be dealt with in the political context of disarmament and not in the legal context under humanitarian law.

The attempt to prohibit land mines is premised on the fact that land mines cannot discriminate between civilians and combatants and, as such, are indiscriminate weapons. Indiscriminate weapons are prohibited in international humanitarian law. There is an international movement to get land mines to be manufactured so that they self-detonate or self-neutralize after a certain time so that they do not continue to present a danger for an extensive period of time. Most persons harmed by landmines are mostly civilians. Twenty-six thousand people a year become victims, which translates to 70 people a day, or around one person every 15 minutes. Three hundred thousand children and counting are severely disabled because of landmines.

In 2010, a Convention on Cluster Munitions entered into force. The U.S. has not signed or ratified it. Cluster bombs drop many small bomblets which spread out widely and render large areas off limits and dangerous. They cannot discriminate between civilians and military persons and objects, and often kill civilians who innocently pick up the long-lasting unexploded bomblets which then explode.

In U.S. law one definition of Weapons of Mass Destruction is found in U.S. Code. Title 50, Chapter 40 as follows:

§ 2302 Definitions

In this chapter:

(1) The term "weapon of mass destruction" means any weapon or device that is intended, or has the capability, to cause death or serious bodily injury to a significant number of people through

(2) the release, dissemination, or impact of—

(A) toxic or poisonous chemicals or their precursors:

(B) a disease organism; or

(C) radiation or radioactivity.

(2) The term "independent states of the former Soviet Union" has the meaning given that term in section 5801 of title 22.

(3) The term "highly enriched uranium" means uranium enriched to 20 percent or more in the isotope U–235.

There is no accepted definition of WMD in international treaty or customary law.

Indiscriminate attacks are prohibited by the humanitarian law standards set forth in Documents 68, 69, 71, 73, and 76. In the ICJ Advisory Opinion on the Legality of the Use of Nuclear Weapons, the International Court of Justice discussed this issue as it relates to human rights and humanitarian law. See Appendix J.

See Also Terms: 3, 8, 20, 26, 33, 34, 38, 42, 48, 63, 64, 70, 72, 73, 104, 129, 132, 135, 137, 144, 145, 151, 152, 154, 166, 177, 178, 181, 182, 184, 185, 191, 192, 197, 200, 201, 215, 222, 223, 224, 257, 259, 272, 2316, 317, 318, 319, 321, 323.

165. Individual Complaint

Definition: A written complaint submitted by a person or group of people which claims that a certain country has violated its international human rights treaty obligation toward them. The complaint is filed in an international human rights forum that handles complaints, such as the U.N. Human Rights Committee, for purposes of revealing, remedying and redressing the violation.

Significance: This term is contrasted with interstate complaints, which are complaints filed by one or more states against another state.

If the United States were to ratify the First Optional Protocol to the ICCPR, it would give American victims of violations the right ("standing") to file individual complaints against the United States in the U.N. Human Rights Committee. They could only do so after exhausting all their domestic remedies in the U.S. legal system. The case decision of *Ng v. Canada* in Appendix J is a decision in an individual complaint case filed under the Optional Protocol against Canada, but it concerns extradition to the United States.

See Also Terms: 5, 11, 12, 26, 33, 46, 48, 70, 76, 88, 90, 93, 107, 113, 145, 146, 148, 151, 167, 177, 179, 184, 208, 215, 222, 229, 246, 254, 259, 264, 272, 293, 297.

166. INDIVIDUAL CRIMINAL RESPONSIBILITY

Definition: A principle of international criminal law established in the Nuremberg trials that states that individual human beings are responsible for their acts that constitute international crimes, such as genocide, war crimes, crimes against humanity and starting an aggressive war without legal justification, regardless of what that person's official position or status was when they committed the acts.

Significance: In human rights law, it is essential to establish an atmosphere of accountability where states are concerned. The culture of human rights is established when those in power recognize that they do not *give* people rights but only *recognize* the rights that are inherent to them as human beings.

At Nuremberg, the defense against the Nazi claims of sovereignty and assertions of the legality of their actions relative to their own culture was that there is a "law above the law." That law is that you cannot violate the basic human dignity of any human being, no matter what the reason. With that understanding, the modern era of human rights was born and has continued to grow to this day. When those who would violate this principle again try to perpetrate their crimes, the international community has now created mechanisms to punish them, with hopes of eventually causing the atrocities to cease.

One of the reasons for this principle was that there was a tendency to demonize and attack whole populations of people from the perceived wrongful acts of a few individuals. To stop the tendency of people hating a whole group of demonized people for the wrong of a few, the international community decided that only those who are guilty should be punished and not a collective nation or peoples. So it was at the Nuremberg Trials of Nazi war criminals that the victorious powers decided that only those Germans who committed internationally unlawful acts should be punished, so that people would not hold the whole German population responsible for the holocaust and other WW II atrocities.

In 1998 the international community created the International Criminal Court, which sought to codify much of existing conventional and customary criminal law, to prosecute individuals who commit those acts. Article 1 states: "The International Criminal Court is hereby established. It shall be a permanent institute and shall have the power to exercise its jurisdiction <u>over persons</u> for the most serious crimes of international concern." See Document 76. The ICC is aimed at establishing individual criminal responsibility for crimes which affect all humankind. National criminal law systems also prosecute and punish under this principle. The case of *United States of America vs. Roy M. Belfast*, aka "Chuckie Taylor" is a good example of a U.S. Federal criminal court imposing individual criminal responsibility over a torturer who committed his acts in another country. Chuckie Taylor was prosecuted here under universal jurisdiction under the U.S. statute against torture. He was sentenced to 97 years in a U.S. prison. Chuckie Taylor violated our law, international human rights law and international criminal law while he was in Liberia when his father was president of that country. It was not just his government that committed wrongdoing. He, as an individual, had engaged in internationally criminal conduct for which he was personally held accountable. This was individual criminal responsibility. Even sitting presidents can be subject to such responsibility and official position is no shield. The sitting President of Sudan, Ali Bashir, was indicted in 2009, by the ICC for international crimes in the Sudan. Individual criminal responsibility is necessary to assure accountability for serious human rights violations.

See Also Terms: 3, 13, 23, 25, 26, 41, 42, 45, 48, 63, 64, 70, 71, 72, 103, 129, 130, 132, 133, 132, 145, 151, 152, 154, 157, 159, 181, 182, 185, 192, 201, 211, 215, 221, 222, 223, 224, 234, 244, 253, 259, 266, 272, 283, 293, 302, 310, 317, 318, 319.

167. INDIVIDUAL RIGHTS

Definition: Human rights held by one person as that person's own rights and not as a member of a group of persons.

Significance: Human rights are most properly defined as legal rights by individual human beings in relation to the state.

There are two types of rights found in the field of human rights: individual human rights and collective, or group, human rights. Individual rights are held by individuals, and group or collective rights are said to be held either by the group for its individual members, or by each member individually, but exercised together as a group. This latter type of right is not accepted by everyone as properly human rights, because human rights are said to come from the inherent human dignity of the person and not from the society or group to which a person belongs.

The ICCPR, for example, contains mostly individual human rights. Article 27, however, which sets forth the rights of ethnic, religious or linguistic minorities, is considered a collective or group right. See Document 8.

The U.S. Declaration of Independence of 1776 sets forth the philosophy of individual rights, those not granted by society or by a state but held by individuals as endowments of the Creator. See Document 1. States only recognize, respect, protect and ensure individual human rights, they do not grant or legislatively create them. They are inherent attributes of the human personality.

See Also Terms: 11, 12, 20, 24, 25, 26, 32, 33, 34, 35, 39, 53, 54, 55, 57, 70, 98, 116, 120, 124, 136, 144, 145, 146, 147, 152, 160, 177, 179, 180, 184, 185, 222, 236, 242, 244, 259, 272, 282, 283, 291, 297, 309, 312, 316, 322.

168. INDIVISIBILITY (PRINCIPLE OF)

Definition: A principle of international human rights law which says that all human rights together form one whole set of rights that cannot be divided into subsets and that states cannot choose to respect certain human rights or types or sets of human rights and exclude or not respect other rights. It is the concept that there is no hierarchy of rights; civil and political rights are equally as important as social, economic and cultural rights.

Significance: Historically there were times when certain states claimed that they could pick and choose which human rights or types of rights they would recognize and respect within their state. This was particularly pronounced during the time when it was common to refer to or characterize human rights according to "generation." There were "first generation" human rights which were the civil and political rights, "second generation" human rights which were the economic, social and cultural rights. Some said there were also "third generation" human rights, the so-called "solidarity rights" such as the right to peace, the right to a clean environment, the right to development, to humanitarian assistance, and to international solidarity, all which were not generally accepted by the international legal community.

Some states such as the former east bloc states would say that they only accept economic, social and cultural rights, whereas the west said it only accepted first generation. This led to discussions, debates and claims of a hierarchy of human rights and the option of states to choose which types of rights they accept. The international community saw this as a problem and when it came to rearticulate and consolidate human rights in the early 1990s, particularly at the 1993 Vienna Conference on Human Rights, the international community, including the United States, affirmed the principle of indivisibility of human rights, at least the so-called first and second generation human rights. Since that time there has been an concerted attempt by the international human rights legal community to get states and IGOs and NGOs to not use the language of "generations" of human rights, because it leads to confusion of human rights. This was reaffirmed in the consensus document issuing from that Conference: the Vienna Declaration and Programme of Action. See Document 51. This Declaration also reaffirmed the principle of indivisibility in order to counter the claim of cultural relativism, that some human rights could be subject to cultural differences or interpretations in different societies and were not "universal."

At a minimum it can be said that there are no such things as first and second generation human rights any more and that civil, political, economic, social and cultural rights form a whole indivisible set of internationally recognized and accepted human rights, all of which must be recognized by all states. One of the problems with this regarding the United States is that it has had a history of rejecting economic, social and cultural rights, particularly economic human rights. The latter was because much of the Government erroneously believed that acceptance of economic human rights meant that everyone could claim the human right to a free lunch, free medical care, and welfare for doing nothing.

The U.S has signed (1977) the U.N. International Covenant on Economic, Social and Cultural Rights but has never ratified this major human rights treaty adopted in1966. See Document 16. Thus, the U.S. is not yet legally bound to respect, protect, ensure and fulfill economic, social and cultural human rights under that general human rights treaty. The U.S. has issued cautious acceptance of economic human rights but still prefers not to ratify this treaty because of the continued belief in the "free lunch" misunderstanding of economic rights.

See Also Terms: 11, 12, 20, 25, 70, 94, 120, 124, 144, 145, 172, 174, 177, 179, 180, 184, 259, 293, 309, 316, 323.

169. INHERENT HUMAN RIGHTS

Definition: Human rights that are part of human nature itself, as an attribute of human personhood. Human rights are inherent rights held by human beings because of their inherent human dignity.

Significance: Human rights are not created or granted by a government. They inhere in every human being because every human being has human dignity, that is, human worth that cannot be taken away. It is nature or, to some, nature's God, which endows human beings with this dignity. Every state in the world recognizes that the rights of human beings are inherent. Governments have the duty to protect human rights. Very often governments, even the United States, fail to act in a way respectful of an individual's human rights.

Because these rights are inherent, they cannot be taken away. By an individual's acts he or she can allow the government to take a certain action that does limit one's human rights, such as when one is jailed for drunk driving. Such a person loses the right to exercise their human right to freedom of movement for a time, while in jail. They do not lose the right itself, only the right to exercise it as they will.

The concept of inherent human rights comes from the U.S. Declaration of Independence which states, "We hold these truths self-evident: That all men are created equal; that they are endowed by their Creator with certain unalienable rights; that among these are life, liberty, and the pursuit of happiness; that, to secure these rights, governments are instituted among men...."

The preambles to the major human rights instruments, such as the UDHR and ICCPR, make reference to human rights as inherent rights, not humanly granted rights. See Documents 6, 8.

See Also Terms: 11, 12, 20, 21, 24, 33, 52, 53, 54, 55, 56, 57, 58, 62, 65, 66, 68, 70, 73, 75, 120, 122, 124, 136, 144, 145, 146, 147, 152, 155, 160, 167, 177, 179, 180, 184, 185, 213, 222, 242, 250, 252, 259, 265, 282, 283, 297, 306, 308, 309, 312, 316, 322, 323.

170. INHUMAN TREATMENT OR PUNISHMENT

Definition: Government treatment or punishment of human beings under its jurisdiction in a way that suggests the victim is less than human or of less human dignity than others. It is the kind of treatment that deliberately causes intense physical and mental suffering but does not rise to the level of torture.

Significance: Human rights are legal limitations on the use of power by government, whether federal, state, county or city, in relation to individual members of society and anyone present within its jurisdiction. It limits how a government treats or punishes human beings. It requires that government treat people in a way that recognizes their human dignity and legal equality. This obligation applies both to people in the custody of government agents, such as criminal suspects, defendants and convicted people, and to those not in penal custody, such as welfare applicants and forcibly confined mental patients. All have the right to be treated with respect for their human dignity.

In international human rights instruments, inhuman treatment is usually prohibited in a human rights norm that also prohibits torture and cruel or degrading treatment or punishment. All of these represent different levels of severity and unacceptability of treatment or punishment of a human being; the common denominator is that they are inconsistent with human dignity.

Inhuman treatment and inhuman punishment are two different things. They deal with two different kinds of situations. The term "inhuman treatment" is used if the inhuman acts are not being done for purposes of punishment of the victim for a prior act, such as for a criminal or other legal violation. The term "inhuman punishment" is used if the inhuman acts were done for purposes of punishing the victim for his prior conduct, as when a sentence is imposed after a criminal conviction.

The international instrument that partly governs the U.S. law regarding inhuman treatment or punishment is the ICCPR. See Document 8. Such treatment or punishment is inconsistent with a victim's inherent human dignity and violates human rights norms under Article 7 of the ICCPR. Article 7 states, "No one shall be subjected to torture or to cruel, inhuman or degrading treatment or punishment. In particular, no one shall be subjected without his free consent to medical or scientific experimentation."

The United States submitted a reservation to its 1992 ratification of the ICCPR to the effect that the terms "torture, cruel, inhuman and degrading treatment or punishment would be interpreted consistent with the 5th, 8th and 14th amendment to the U.S. Constitution, which offers much less protection than Article 7 of the ICCPR, as interpreted by the Human Rights Committee." See Document 9.

Certain acts of police brutality, jail overcrowding, or such acts as governmental medical experiments on prisoners without their consent would be considered inhuman treatment. The infamous Rodney King beating by police would be considered inhuman treatment. Use of electronic shock stun belts on potentially disruptive criminal trial defendants would also fall into this category. Imposing the death penalty and executing a person using certain means can be considered inhuman punishment. But inhuman government conduct goes far beyond the law enforcement and criminal justice system. It covers *any* activity of any government agent. A public university professor could commit acts of inhuman treatment, as could a nurse in a public hospital, a soldier on the battlefield or an IRS agent. The only question is whether the action of the government is consistent with the inherent human dignity of the victim. If it is not, then there can be no possible justification for it under international human rights law. Under international human rights law, everyone, from the baby to the mass murderer, has the human right to be protected from inhuman treatment or punishment.

Under normal U.S. legal analysis, almost all issues of inhuman treatment or punishment would be looked at principally in terms of the 8th Amendment (applicable to the states under the 14th Amendment) to the Constitution, the "cruel and unusual punishment" clause. To a lesser degree they would involve the 5th Amendment. Because of the U.S. reservation to Article 7 of the ICCPR, the United States can only be legally bound to comply with those U.S. constitutional standards as interpreted by the U.S. court—a lower standard of protection. This reservation allows the United States to get away with acts that would not be permissible under the international human rights standards as interpreted by international human rights bodies, such as the U.N. Human Rights Committee. The U.S. government knew it could not meet the international standard and so opted for the reservation to allow it more legal latitude. (See Document 15A, the Second and Third Reports of the United States to the Human Rights Committee, on Article 7.)

The United States has also ratified the Convention against Torture, subject to certain reservations, declarations and understandings. (See Documents 19 and 20.) This convention also prohibits inhuman treatment or punishment, but in greater detail than the ICCPR. The Second U.S. Report to the U.N. Committee against Torture, contains an exposition of the U.S. law and practice from the U.S. government's perspective. See Document 21A.

The case of *In Re Cincinnati Radiation Litigation*, Appendix J, is an example of inhuman treatment in the form of medical experimentation with massive doses of radiation without the victim's consent.

Inhuman treatment or punishment is sometimes confused with *inhumane* treatment. They have slightly different meanings and are used in different legal contexts. (See the following entry.)

See Also Terms: 11, 12, 19, 20, 24, 26, 30, 33, 34, 35, 49, 53, 58, 63, 65, 66, 70, 73, 75, 81, 82, 84, 96, 106, 110, 111, 115, 120, 124, 125, 133, 136, 144, 145, 146, 147, 151, 152, 167, 171, 177, 179, 181, 182, 184, 185, 192, 215, 222, 235, 238, 256, 259, 275, 283, 297, 302, 309, 316, 317, 318, 320.

171. INHUMANE TREATMENT

Definition: Treatment of a human being in a brutal and barbarous manner with no human compassion, particularly during an armed conflict, as might occur with a captured enemy soldier (prisoner of war).

Significance: Even during a time of war and armed conflict it is the norm of all civilized countries, including the United States, that everyone be treated humanely, that is, in a manner respectful of one's human dignity. This respectful treatment should be accorded to both combatants and civilians, but particularly to civilians. Although it may be legally permissible to kill an armed enemy combatant when military necessity requires it, combatants and civilians must treat the other humanely. This is a principle of humanitarian law, which is a sort of human rights law applicable in times of armed conflict. It is no longer historically or legally the case that opposing enemies may do whatever they want to the soldiers or civilians of their adversary.

The law of armed conflict, as expressed in the Geneva Conventions of 1949, states that even in times of noninternational armed conflict no one may be treated inhumanely. The United States has ratified the Geneva Conventions and is thus required to treat humanely all enemy prisoners of war, or even civilians of the enemy state under its power. (See Articles 3 and 27, Documents 72.)

Sometimes the word inhumane is used in other contexts, such as when speaking of prison conditions, treatment of detainees by law enforcement agents, or living conditions of poor people. ICCPR Article 10.1 states that "All persons deprived of their liberty shall be treated with humanity and with respect for their inherent dignity of the human person." This allows anyone in any form of detention or imprisonment to be treated with respect for their human dignity.

This issue arose in the famous photos taken in Abu Ghraib prison in Iraq in the mid 2000s. These photos showed both inhumane and degrading treatment of the Iraqi prisoners. The detention facilities at Guantanamo's Camp Xray were called inhumane by some.

See Also Terms: 11, 12, 20, 24, 48, 49, 53, 58, 65, 66, 70, 73, 75, 81, 82, 84, 96, 104, 110, 111, 117, 120, 124, 129, 132, 133, 136, 144, 145, 146, 147, 151, 152, 154, 170, 177, 178, 179, 181, 182, 184, 185, 192, 215, 222, 223, 235, 238, 248, 259, 272, 283, 297, 302, 30, 316, 317, 318, 320.

172. INTER-DEPENDENCE (PRINCIPLE OF)

Definition: A principle applicable to all human rights that states that whatever type of human rights is involved, each and every individual human right is dependent upon each and every other human right, so that every human rights is potentially at risk even if only one is.

Significance: The principle of inter-dependence of all human rights is somewhat like saying that all human rights are like a house of cards. Taking one away will cause all the others to topple and the structure to fall. This term is usually seen with its fellow principles of "indivisibility," and "inter-relatedness." This principle is used to combat arguments of cultural relativism and attempts at hierarchical separation and differentiation between norms and so called "generations" of norms. An example would be that the right to vote is dependent on the right to freedom of movement and freedom of expression, and the right to have food to sustain oneself so one can vote. An adequate standard of living with adequate food depends on voting which depends on movement and which is exercised by expression of one's choice.

See Also Terms: 11, 12, 20, 25, 70, 94, 120, 124, 144, 145, 172, 174, 177, 179, 180, 184, 259, 293, 309, 316, 323.

173. INTER-GOVERNMENTAL ORGANIZATION (IGO)

Definition: An organization whose members are the governments of different countries. These governments convene to deal with political, legal, economic or other such matters that are important to them and that need the attention and resources of all the member states to deal with them. The head of the government, or the head of state, is the person who represents the government, though usually a deputy sits in the leader's place.

Significance: The United Nations is an intergovernmental organization, as is the Organization of American States (OAS), both of which count the United States as a member. Most international human rights activity of the United States takes place in the political context of international inter-governmental organizations, such as in the U.N. Human Rights Council.

Inter-governmental organizations are either global, meaning open to every country, such as the United Nations, or regional, meaning open only to states in a particular geographical region, such as the OAS in the western hemisphere.

In Appendix D there is a chart of global and regional human rights systems, including IGOs.

See Also Terms: 11, 12, 50, 70, 131, 142, 145, 146, 147, 151, 181, 183, 185, 208, 211, 217, 218, 221, 222, 230, 231, 259, 264, 272, 276, 289, 290, 296, 306, 307, 308.

174. INTER-RELATEDNESS (PRINCIPLE OF)

Definition: The concept of a mutual or reciprocal relation among all human rights. A principle of human rights that says that all human rights are closely related to each other, e.g., the rights to food, expression, movement, association, and the right to vote.

Significance: In the theory of international human rights law there is a logical and conceptual legal relationship between all human rights, and this relationship must be factored into any application or interpretation of human rights. This term is usually seen with its fellow principles of "indivisibility," and "inter-dependence." While this sounds very much like the principle of inter-dependence, it is not quite the same. The ultimate goal of the principle is to require that in the interpretation and application of human rights one is always aware that human rights form a whole, of which all the parts must make sense in relation to each other for the protection of human dignity. The right to freedom of expression is related to religion, which is related to freedom of movement which is related to freedom of assembly. This comes into play regarding the U.S. because the U.S. has not concretely accepted economic, social and cultural rights, particularly economic human rights, because it has signed but not ratified the ICESCR. See Document 16. This makes it awkward to talk about protecting human rights as the U.S. always says it does, although in reality it has not accepted ICESCR rights, which are inter-related and indivisible and inter-dependent with civil and political human rights. It is the intent of the international community that all states ratify and become bound by all human rights treaties.

Not all states have ratified all human rights treaties which they are entitled to ratify and so the U.S. is not unusual in that regard. However the U.S. cannot get beyond the political and legal obstacles to the acceptance of economic, social and cultural rights which would make their respect for civil and political rights all the more credible and beneficial to the whole international community. Economic, social and cultural rights are and will remain inter-related to, indivisible from, and inter-dependent on all civil and political human rights. One can even say that this is referred to in a sense in the Constitution, whose preamble states that the U.S. was created, among other things, "to promote the general welfare, and secure the blessings of liberty to ourselves and our posterity." See Document 2.

See Also Terms: 11, 20, 25, 70, 94, 120, 124, 144, 145, 172, 174, 177, 179, 180, 184, 259, 293, 309, 316, 323.

175. INTERFERENCE

Definition: An act by the state which impedes the full exercise of a person's substantive human right. It is an act which, if not made pursuant to a limitation clause, will result in a breach of a human rights norm and constitute a human right violation.

Significance: In the field of international human rights law there are many substantive human rights norm with which the state has to comply. As a rule states may not interfere with the exercise of a human right by an individual. If the state does so interfere, there will be a violation of the human rights, unless the state has a legitimate reason found in a limitation or restriction clause for doing so.

When one tries to determine whether a state has violated a human rights norm found in a treaty, one first has to ask the question whether the act or omission constituted an interference. As an example, let us say that the state had an arrangement with a political activist to provide a venue, a platform and a sound system for a political demonstration. On the day of the demonstration the state had not set up the platform or sound system and the activist was not able to hold his demonstration and give his speech. In this example, in determining whether the state's omission to act constituted an interference with the activist freedom of expression will first depend on whether there was an interference with the exercise of the right to expression. If the activist could not give his speech, clearly that would constitute an interference. Or, let's say that the states set up the platform and sound system and then cancelled the demonstration permit. This affirmative act of the state, too, would be an interference. In both instances the activist was presented from holding his demonstration.

But this is not the end of the determination of a violation. After determining that there was an interference we then have to ask whether there was a legitimate justification for the failure to provide the platform and sound system, or for canceling the permit. Some human rights are absolute an allow no exceptions or imitations for any reason. Slavery and torture are examples. If there is an interference there is a violation. But most human rights norms are conditional and allow states to take measures that limit or restrict the exercise of rights, and which make a state interference legal under human right law. These measures can be made under limitations clauses in certain situations. These are called "legitimate aims." If a state takes a certain measure which interferes with exercise of a right, and if the measure seeks to achieve an aim set forth in the limitations clause and the measure is proportionate, necessary, and prescribed by law, then such measures can justify an interference.

Now let us say in relation to our demonstration example that the state had been sent a terrorist threat the night before the demonstration threatening to detonate a bomb at the demonstration. Then the cancellation that interfered with the exercise freedom of expression can be said to have been a legitimate restriction of that right for purposes of public safety or order. Look at this process in terms of Article 19 of the ICCPR. That Article says:

Everyone shall have the right to freedom of expression;....
The exercise of the rights provided for in paragraph 2 of this article carries with it special duties and responsibilities. It may therefore be subject to certain restrictions, but these shall only be such as are provided by law and are necessary:
For respect of the rights or reputations of others;
For the protection of national security or of public order (ordre public), or of public health or morals.

The interference in the example would be argued by the state to be legitimate under Article 19.3(b). If the restriction does not meet the exact wording of the limitation clause (19.3) it will be invalid and the interference will constitute a human rights violation.

See Also Terms: 3, 5, 11, 12, 26, 48, 70, 73, 112, 124, 132, 133, 134, 145, 146, 151, 165, 181, 182, 184, 187, 193, 198, 206, 215, 222, 223, 226, 227, 234, 259, 269, 272, 291, 293, 297, 306, 307, 317, 318.

176. INTERNALLY DISPLACED PERSON (IDP)

Definition: Internally displaced persons are those who are forced by circumstances to leave their home areas and move to other places within the state and who are temporarily or permanently prevented from returning home.

Significance: Many people are living in places away from their homes because they are prevented from returning home. The cause can be a civil war, unchecked violence or lawlessness. It can be done by a government policy of forcing inhabitants to leave an area to get rid of their racial, ethnic, religious, national or political group from an area. It can also be caused by such natural disasters as floods, fires, famine, earthquakes or volcanic eruptions.

It is often a human rights violation for a government to forcibly or legally displace people against their will and prevent them from returning home, especially when they must live in temporary dwellings and makeshift camps. It would possibly be a violation of the UDHR ICCPR, and ICESCR articles. See Documents 6, 8, 16.

Internally displaced persons flee their homes but not their country. They are not refugees. Refugees are people who flee into another country to escape past or feared future persecution based on race, religion, nationality or membership in a particular social group.

In 1998, an important instrument was adopted in the U.N. called the Guiding Principles on Internal Displacement. These guiding principles which might be deemed soft law found their legal underpinnings based on existing international human rights law, humanitarian law and refugee law. They have been incorporated into national laws and policies, inter-governmental organizations and U.N. agencies. These Guidelines seek to protect IDPs in internal armed conflict situations by identifying the rights of IDPs and guarantees relevant to those rights.

See Also Terms: 20, 32, 33, 34, 35, 37, 48, 53, 54, 55, 56, 57, 70, 72, 83, 92, 99, 100, 101, 102, 120, 124, 136, 144, 145, 146, 147, 151, 152, 160, 167, 169, 175, 177, 179, 180, 184, 185, 205, 211, 215, 216, 218, 222, 228, 243, 259, 263, 271, 272, 282, 283, 286, 292, 293, 297, 309, 316.

177. INTERNATIONAL BILL OF RIGHTS

Definition: A term used in the field of human rights to refer to the human rights, fundamental freedoms and implementation mechanisms contained in four of the key foundational international instruments of human rights. The International Bill of Rights consists of the following instruments combined:

1. The Universal Declaration of Human Rights of 1948 (Document 6).

2. The United Nations International Covenant on Civil and Political Rights of 1966 (Document 8).

3. The Optional Protocol (First) to the U.N. Covenant on Civil and Political Rights of 1966 (Document 10).

4. United Nations Covenant on Economic, Social and Cultural Rights of 1966 (Document 16).

Some experts and scholars have stated their belief that the Second Protocol to the ICCPR, which abolishes the death penalty in states that ratify it, has become the fifth instrument of the International Bill of Human Rights. This view is not widely accepted, and definitely not accepted by the United States.

Significance: These instruments together set forth all of the human rights and remedies deemed by the international community as the most basic and necessary to protect human dignity. Some of the wording is difficult to understand because it is technical treaty language, but the reader will get a sense of the substance and procedures of basic human rights as they form part of U.S. discourse in the fields of law and politics. The importance of these documents on both the national and international level makes such familiarity essential for anyone wanting to understand U.S. law and public policy.

The term "International Bill of Rights" was modeled after the U.S. Bill of Rights, the first 10 amendments to the Constitution, upon which the United States relies for the basic constitutional rights of those subject to its sovereignty and jurisdiction. See Document 2. Likewise, when the member states of the United Nations enacted these four instruments they felt that, together, the instruments constituted an international set of minimum constitutional rights of all human beings in the world.

The United States has ratified the ICCPR, which is now part of U.S. law. See Document 8, 9. This ratification was, however, subject to certain qualifications expressly stated by the United States, which limit the U.S. legal obligations under this instrument. The U.S. ratification stated that this instrument was "non-self-executing" and therefore Congress would have to pass implementing legislation to transform the norms of the ICCPR into U.S. national law.

The United States has not ratified, or even signed, the first Optional Protocol to the ICCPR, which would give individuals who are victims of U.S. violations in the United States the right to file a complaint in the U.N. Human Rights Committee. Although the United States signed the ICESCR in 1977, it has not ratified it, largely because the U.S. government has not, until recently, accepted that socio-economic rights are human rights, but considered them only as desirable goals of public policy.

Thus, the United States cannot be said to have fully accepted and endorsed all of the International Bill of Rights as part of U.S. law, even though this term is occasionally used in congressional and executive speeches and reports and even in judicial decisions, and is found in human rights literature and discussion in the United States.

At the 1993 Vienna World Conference on Human Rights these human rights were expressly considered by the consensus of all states of the world to be the "birthright of all human beings." See Document 51. The states also agreed that "their protection and promotion is the first responsibility of Governments" (Vienna Declaration and Programme of Action, para. 1). The United States was a prime mover of states to get them to adopt this language. The philosophy of this language comes from the 1776 Declaration of Independence. See Document 1.

See Also Terms: 20, 21, 24, 33, 48, 49, 51, 62, 66, 68, 70, 72, 74, 80, 81, 82, 84, 86, 88, 90, 92, 93, 98, 99, 100, 113, 114, 116, 121, 123, 124, 126, 127, 136, 144, 145, 146, 147, 148, 149, 150, 151, 152, 158, 160 165, 167, 168, 169, 172, 174, 179, 180, 184, 185, 195, 198, 205, 208, 210, 211, 213, 215, 216, 220, 222, 225, 226, 229, 233, 238, 242, 244, 245, 247, 254, 258, 259, 260, 262, 268, 269, 272, 278, 279, 280, 282, 283, 286, 287, 291, 293, 296, 297, 306, 307, 308, 309, 312, 316, 322, 323.

178. INTERNATIONAL COMMITTEE OF THE RED CROSS (ICRC)

Definition: An international organization, not a government, that is primarily responsible for seeing that all states fulfill their legal obligations under humanitarian law, especially under the Geneva Conventions and Protocols, when there is an international or non-international armed conflict. Its main function is to protect humanity from unnecessary human loss and suffering during armed conflicts. It is headquartered in Geneva, Switzerland, and has a white flag with a red cross as its main symbol.

Significance: Most people think about the Red Cross as an organization that helps in times of natural disasters, such as hurricanes or floods. This is only part of the mission of the Red Cross. Its major function, and the one for which it was founded in the late 1860s, is to engage in humanitarian efforts aimed at alleviating human loss and suffering during war times. The main headquarters for the movement is the International Committee of the Red Cross (ICRC) in Geneva, Switzerland.

There are national Red Cross movements in almost all countries, some of them called Red Crescent Society in Islamic countries. The ICRC was the organization responsible for the international community establishing the four Geneva Conventions of 1949, which provide legal protection for victims of armed conflicts. The ICRC is engaged all over the world trying to make governments and fighting rebel groups wage armed conflict according to the Geneva Conventions and other international laws applicable to armed conflict. Two of its best known functions are visiting captured enemy soldiers, called prisoners of war, in POW camps and setting up services to locate and communicate with lost or captured soldiers and civilians and to reunite families. The ICRC visited the three U.S. servicemen who were captured by Yugoslavia in early 1999 and briefly held as POWs during the Kosovo crisis.

A great part of its work is dealing with issues of compliance with humanitarian law and engaging in education and training in the law of armed conflict, of which human rights are an important part.

The ICRC seeks to protect the dignity and well-being of human beings and to alleviate the suffering of people in every country in extreme crisis and conflict; however, it is politically neutral, independent and objective in its work.

With the increase in the number of detainees in the armed conflicts in Iraq and Afghanistan there was an increase in the activity of the ICRC to monitor the U.S. treatment of these detainees and to try to determine the existence and extent of secret detention sites. There are not supposed to be any secret detention sites that the ICRC cannot visit. It has the right to do this because the U.S. ratified the Geneva Conventions, which give the ICRC certain rights to monitor armed conflict-related detention facilities.

The ICRC in 2007 made a report about the U.S. on the detention center at Guantanamo. It reported on its interviews with 14 "high value" war on terror detainees. This "confidential" report was entitled "ICRC Report on the Treatment of Fourteen "High Value Detainees" in CIA Custody." See Appendix M.

The ICRC is supposed to be neutral and objective in its work. It is an independent organization.

See Also Terms: 4, 13, 37, 38, 40, 41, 42, 45, 48, 49, 58, 59, 63, 66, 70, 71, 72, 73, 81, 82, 84, 85, 86, 90, 95, 96, 104, 110, 111, 112, 113, 117, 120, 124, 129, 130, 132, 135, 136, 144, 145, 151, 152, 154, 157, 159, 161, 164, 166, 167, 170, 171, 181, 182, 185, 192, 191, 197, 201, 203, 206, 215, 216, 217, 221, 222, 223, 224, 226, 227, 251, 252, 257, 259, 272, 275, 291, 293, 306, 307, 313, 314, 315, 316, 317, 319, 320, 321.

179. INTERNATIONAL COVENANT ON CIVIL AND POLITICAL RIGHTS (ICCPR)

Definition: A general human rights treaty adopted by the United Nations in 1966 and entered into force in 1977, which established legally binding civil and political human rights norms of individual member states that ratify it.

Significance: Modern human rights instruments started in 1948, with the adoption of the Universal Declaration of Human Rights (UDHR) in the United Nations. This instrument set forth the first list of specific, internationally recognized human rights. But the UDHR was not a legal document that created binding obligations on states. The ICCPR was intended to put into a legal instrument those civil and political rights found in the UDHR, in more expansive form. See Document 6.

The UDHR contained civil, political, economic, social, and cultural rights. Because of the philosophical differences between East and West after World War II, there could be no agreement on one legal instrument containing all those types of rights. Therefore, the states of the United Nations decided to make two separate treaties (called covenants), one setting forth civil and political rights and the other setting forth economic, social and cultural rights (the ICESCR).

The United States signed the ICCPR in 1977, but its ratification was stalled in Congress by bitter opposition, which resulted in it being tabled year after year. Finally in 1992, the Senate ratified the ICCPR with certain reservations, declarations, and understandings. See Document 9. The Senate specifically declared the ICCPR to be "non-self-executing," meaning that it could not be directly applied as U.S. law until it was implemented by congressional legislation.

Some argue that the ICCPR can be applied in U.S. courts in cases other than individual claims of violation, whereas others say it cannot. Even if the ICCPR cannot be directly applied in U.S. courts as the rule of decision, it can serve as an element of proof of customary international law. It can also be used as an aid in the interpretation of constitutional rights because, according to a Supreme Court decision, U.S. law must be interpreted consistently with international law whenever possible. Whether or not it is binding in U.S. law, it can serve as a basis for political examination and scrutiny of U.S. government actions. By its ratification in 1992, the United States is now bound by international law to abide by its terms, looked at in light of the reservations, declarations and understandings submitted with its ratification.

State compliance with the ICCPR is supervised by the Human Rights Committee. This organ can hear individual complaints of violations by victims from states that ratify the First Optional Protocol to the ICCPR (see Ng v. Canada, a decision of the Human Rights Committee, in Appendix J), and complaints by one or more states parties against another state, if the complaining states submitted a declaration accepting the power of the committee to do so under Article 41. The United States declared that it accepts the jurisdiction of the committee under Article 41. However, no state has ever filed a complaint against another state for violation. The United States has not ratified the First Optional Protocol on individual complaints. Approximately 166 countries have ratified this treaty.

Since 9/11 and the so-called war on terrorism began, a major issue has arisen implicitly concerning the territorial scope of the application of the ICCPR. That pertains to the extension of the legal obligations undertaken by the U.S. when it ratified the ICCPR. Most people assume wrongly that the ICCPR only applies to the actions of the U.S. government (Army, CIA, FBI etc.) within the territory of the U.S. This is not legally true. According to the jurisprudence and General Comments of the Human Rights Committee the ICCPR legal norms apply to all U.S. government actions where the U.S. exerts "effective control" over human beings in an area. The U.S. has argued that this would not, for example, include Guantanamo. This is incorrect. The terms of the ICCPR apply to the U.S. activity in Guantanamo. In finding U.S. law reaching Guantanamo for the 9/11 detainees, the U.S. Supreme Court in Rasul and Hamdan, Hamdi and Boumedienne, looked beyond the sovereignty/no sovereignty form to the actual reality, the substance of U.S. absolute and exclusive jurisdiction there. The Supreme Court ruled that the Constitution and the Habeas Corpus statute apply there, even in land belonging ultimately to Cuba. Again, international law legal human rights obligations such in as the ICCPR, will apply extraterritorially anywhere the U.S. exercises effective control, which is the ultimate criteria for sovereignty. The reason this issue arises is because the wording of the ICCPR itself means that states parties must "undertake to ensure to all individuals within its territory and subject to its jurisdiction the rights recognized in the present Covenant." The U.S. does not accept the more expansive reading of this territorial scope of the ICCPR.

A Second Optional Protocol was adopted by the United Nations in 1991. States that ratify this protocol are thereby abolishing the use of the death penalty. The U.S. has not signed or ratified the Second Optional Protocol.

See the Second and Third Report of the United States to the U.N. Human Rights Committee, Document 15A, for an example of how the United States sees itself in light of the standards of the ICCPR. Additionally, see the comments and observations of the Human Rights Committee in Appendix L, and the decision of the Human Rights Committee in the case of Ng v. Canada, a decision applying the ICCPR to the death penalty in the United States, in Appendix J.

See Also Terms: 3, 16, 17, 18, 20, 25, 30, 33, 34, 35, 39, 48, 49, 51, 58, 62, 66, 70, 72, 7, 80, 81, 82, 84, 86, 88, 90, 91, 93, 96, 98, 99, 100, 104, 110, 111, 113, 114, 120, 121, 122, 123, 124, 126, 127, 136, 142, 144, 145, 146, 147, 148, 151, 152, 155, 156, 160, 161, 162, 165, 167, 169, 170, 171, 177, 184, 185, 189, 193, 195, 196, 198, 205, 211, 215, 216, 220, 222, 225, 226, 229, 233, 236, 238, 240, 242, 243, 244, 245, 248, 250, 252, 253, 254, 256, 259, 260, 262, 265, 268, 269, 272, 275, 278, 281, 283, 286, 291, 293, 297, 302, 306, 307, 309, 311, 316, 320.

180. INTERNATIONAL COVENANT ON ECONOMIC, SOCIAL AND CULTURAL RIGHTS (ICESCR)

Definition: A general human rights treaty adopted by the United Nations in 1966 and entered into force in 1976, which established legally binding human rights standards regarding the economic, social and cultural human rights of individual members of states that ratify it.

Significance: This treaty was signed by the United States in October 1977, but has never been ratified by the U.S. Senate. As such, it does not, strictly speaking, create any binding legal obligations on the United States to protect economic, social and cultural human rights. One can argue that because the U.S. has signed the ICESCR it has an "interim" or "soft" legal obligation under Article 18 of the Vienna Convention on Treaties not to do anything which would impede the object and purpose of this treaty.

Some of the substantive rights in this treaty were taken from the UDHR. See Document 16.

The human right to health care is discussed in this treaty in Article 12. That article provides for the "right of everyone to the enjoyment of the highest attainable standard of physical and mental health" and, to that end, that states parties will take steps towards achieving "the full realization of this right" which shall include steps necessary to "the creation of conditions which would assure to all medical service and medical attention in the event of sickness." These rights are progressive and do not imply any rights to demand free health care.

Implementation of this treaty is supervised by the Committee on Economic, Social, and Cultural Rights. This treaty has 160 states parties at the time of this book writing.

See Also Terms: 6, 20, 48, 62, 70, 72, 83, 92, 97, 98, 160, 167, 169, 177, 179, 184, 185, 204, 211, 216, 222, 225, 226, 233, 244, 259, 268, 269, 272, 274, 282, 283, 286, 291, 293, 297, 306, 307, 309, 316, 322, 323.

181. INTERNATIONAL CRIMINAL COURT (ICC)

Definition: A permanent international court set up under the auspices of the United Nations but independent of it, to prosecute the most serious international crimes which are violations of human rights and humanitarian law, where national courts have been unable or unwilling to fully and fairly prosecute such crimes. It is a penal tribunal which functions in complementarity to national courts.

Significance: The International Criminal Court (ICC) was established in the United Nations via a Statute, a multilateral treaty that was adopted by the international community at a diplomatic conference in Rome in 1998. This was called the Rome Statute for an International Criminal Court, sometimes called the ICC Statute or Rome Statute. This Court is a permanent, international, judicial organ (court) to investigate, prosecute and punish individuals who are accused of committing the most serious international crimes. This would include crimes such as genocide, war crimes, crimes against humanity and aggression (starting an aggressive war). The crime of aggression was considered extremely important but the states could not come to agreement on a definition of aggression. So they put it in the Statute with a reference that it would be defined at a later date.

This court does not have primary jurisdiction over these crimes. It is expected that states prosecute these crimes when they happen on their territory or are done by their nationals. But when the subject state is either unable or unwilling to prosecute, then the ICC can start a prosecution. This is referred to as "complementary jurisdiction" or "complementarity." It is meant to combat the so-called "culture of impunity" by assuring that all such crimes are prosecuted by the international community as a whole. It does this because these crimes affect not only the subject state but the whole human community at large.

Such an international penal court was initially contemplated in the late 1940s after the establishment of the United Nations. This idea was largely influenced by the atrocities of the Holocaust and with the model of the Nuremberg and Tokyo war crimes trials. The idea was that if states do not prosecute those persons who commit such horrible international crimes when they have the power and ability to do so, then the international community should have the right to prosecute those persons. This is because the acts committed by those persons are deemed to have caused harm to the order and peace of every state in the whole world. They are crimes which give rise to universal jurisdiction. Thus, every state in the world has a legitimate interest to protect.

The United States was a major supporter of the idea of establishment of such a court. At that time the United States and other member states of the United Nations expected such a court to be established shortly thereafter, and hoped it would deter future holocausts. The expectation of its creation was so strong that such a court was even referred to in Article VI of the Genocide Conventions of 1948. The process of actually drawing up the international instruments to establish this court began at the United Nations in the 1950s but was shelved due to Cold War political problems.

This process began again in 1989 with the end of the Cold War and gained much momentum from the Bosnia conflict and Rwanda genocide of the early 1990s, and from the establishment of the international criminal courts (tribunals) to punish international crimes committed in those conflicts. It culminated in an international diplomatic conference held in Rome in the summer of 1998 where all states were invited to participate in finalizing the Statute. Almost every state attended. The United States was a strong supporter of the ICC Statute and pushed hard for its acceptance at the Rome conference.

The final draft statute was approved by most states; however, because it contained certain provisions the United States did not like, the United States voted against the adoption of the Statute. The vote was 120 states in favor of the adoption of the ICC Statute, seven against, and 20 abstentions. The United States was one of seven "no" votes. This no vote was largely dictated by U.S. military and Congressional pressure.

With the adoption of the Statute, it was then open for signature and ratification by any states that wished to become part of the ICC criminal justice system. The Court has been established in the Hague, Holland. It was established and became operational in 2002, only after 60 states had ratified the Statute. A Preparatory Commission of the member states began in 1999 to actually set up the Court's rules of procedure and evidence, to list elements of crimes, to define the crime of aggression, and other matters. The United States was allowed to be part of this process even though it is not a party to the Statute.

The governance of the ICC resides with the Assembly of States Parties, a body comprising all states which have ratified the Rome Statute. The Assembly has created rules of procedure and elements of crimes and a prosecutor was selected and is in the process of handling several cases.

This ICC is therefore now acting in a relationship of "complementarity" with the national courts, where they cannot or will not do justice as to the most serious international crimes. It will have jurisdiction only over more serious cases, not isolated individual acts. It only has jurisdiction over cases in states parties where the criminal acts occurred ("territorial state"), or where the defendant is a national of a state (national state) which has ratified the Statute, or where the U.N. Security Council refers a "situation" involving such crimes to it under Chapter VII of the U.N. Charter. See Document 5.

The U.S., again, voted against the Rome Statute. After the Statute was adopted the U.S. administration told the Assembly of States parties it was willing to sign on to the ICC Statute if the ICC granted U.S. military and government persons immunity from prosecution. The Assembly did not accept that. On the last day of the Clinton Administration, President Clinton signed the ICC Statute. Immediately after taking office, President George Bush flatly rejected the ICC statute and the whole ICC process and declared that he was going to "unsign" the Statute and it would never be accepted by the U.S. There was no process for "unsigning" a treaty so he simply declared the U.S. had no intention of ratifying it.

The Bush Administration feared that the ICC would obstruct its operations, particularly after 9/11, and began to take steps to obstruct the court. It got Congress to pass the American Servicemen's Protection Act, which allows the U.S. to use force to free any U.S. personnel apprehended by the ICC. It also started trying to get Bilateral Immunity Agreements (BIAs) entered into with other states, wherein the other states promised not to turn over any U.S. personnel to the ICC. These were also referred to as "Article 98" Agreements after an article in the ICC Statute used by the U.S. to justify it. That Article was not meant to allow such BIAs, or any acts by states parties which worked against the effectiveness of the ICC Statute. (See Document 76.)

The ICC Statute has been signed and is still a signed international treaty which the U.S. has not ratified. Because the U.S. has signed the ICC Statute it has a now uncertain obligation under Article 18 of the Vienna Conventions on the law of Treaties. That article reads:

> Obligation not to defeat the object and purpose of a treaty prior to its entry into force
> A State is obliged to refrain from acts which would defeat the object and purpose of a treaty when: (a) it has signed the treaty or has exchanged instruments constituting the treaty subject to ratification, acceptance or approval, until it shall have made its intention clear not to become a party to the treaty.

Whether the U.S. has no intention to become a party to the treaty is not certain. It remains to be seen what the Obama Administration does with this treaty and this institution, the idea for which it had done so much to promote.

In the meanwhile, in 2010, the Assembly of States parties accomplished a major step in reaching a compromise definition of the crime of aggression. The major issue in that definition process is the role of the U.N. Security Council over what cases alleging aggression are filed. The text can be seen at Document 77, Assembly of States Parties, Resolution RC/res A 4.

See Also Terms: 3, 6, 8, 13, 19, 23, 25, 42, 45, 47, 48, 49, 53, 56, 63, 64, 66, 70, 71, 72, 73, 81, 82, 84, 99, 100, 101, 104, 110, 111, 113, 157, 159, 164, 166, 170, 171, 182, 184, 185, 192, 193, 197, 200, 201, 203, 208, 211, 215, 221, 222, 223, 224, 234, 243, 244, 251, 252, 253, 254, 256, 257, 259, 262, 265, 272, 275, 276, 280, 281, 283, 286, 291, 293, 298, 300, 302, 306, 307, 310, 314, 316, 317, 319, 320, 321, 323.

182. INTERNATIONAL CRIMINAL LAW

Definition: A body of principles and rules in international law which involves defining crimes that are considered as harmful to all humankind, and arresting, prosecuting and punishing persons accused of such crimes.

Significance: In the 17th century, the international community began to consider some acts as violating the peace, order and stability of the whole world with its condemnation of piracy at sea as an international crime which any state could prosecute.

International criminal law developed slowly from that time until World War II, wherein the international community experienced the horrors of the Holocaust and decided to do what it could to punish and prevent such things from happening again. Since the Nuremberg Trials held against the Nazi war criminals in the late 1940s (based largely on the 1907 Hague IV Convention and Rules in Document 69), the international community has been continuing to develop a system of international criminal law that makes it an international crime to commit certain types of human rights violations such as torture, genocide, war crimes and crimes against humanity.

In addition to treaty law international crimes, such as in the Geneva Conventions or ICC Statute, there are customary international law crimes as well, for example genocide and torture.

In 1996 the International Law Commission issued the Draft Code of Crimes Against the Peace and Security of Mankind, which serves as codification of international criminal norms, such as genocide. (See Document 68)

This effort includes the development of international criminal standards and sanctions by multilateral treaties such as the Convention on the Prevention and Punishment of the Crime of Genocide and the Geneva Conventions of 1949 and their 1977 Protocols. (See Documents 17, 72, 73, 74.) It also involved the continued development and articulation of customary international law, such as the Draft Code of Crimes against the Peace and Security of Mankind prepared by the U.N. International Law Commission. It culminated in the attempt of the international community to create a permanent international criminal court by the 1998 adoption of the Statute of the International Criminal Court. When put into place, that Court will prosecute the worst international criminal law violations: genocide, war crimes, crimes against humanity, and waging aggressive wars (aggression). This evolution also included the creation of procedures such as the extradition of suspects or fugitives, the investigation and prevention of crimes, state cooperation in the international criminal process, and the establishment of specific enforcement mechanisms such as the U.N. Ad Hoc International Criminal Tribunal for the former Yugoslavia (ICTY) and International Criminal Tribunal for Rwanda, which apply such law.

Basic principles of this body of international law (Nuremberg Principles) include the principle of individual criminal responsibility, which states that every human being shall be individually responsible for any acts committed against international law, regardless of whether or not they did such acts in an official capacity (such as a soldier or government official) on behalf of a state. There is no official immunity for anyone, even a sitting president, for committing them. This principle was demonstrated by the 1999 indictment of Slobodan Milosevic by the ICTY for crimes against humanity committed in the Kosovo atrocities earlier that year.

The act of the 9/11 attack on the World Trade Towers was, among other things, a crime against humanity. The U.S. in its so-called war on terrorism is trying to apprehend and prosecute those who commit or plan to commit acts of terrorism in the U.S. and elsewhere. Among the charges the U.S. will use are violations of various international criminal law norms, for example war crimes, crimes against humanity and torture. International criminal law is a two-edged sword and the U.S. has to itself not engage in internationally criminal acts as it wages its conflict against terrorism in the world.

See Also Terms: 3, 8, 15, 16, 19, 30, 40, 42, 45, 48, 49, 53, 56, 59, 63, 64, 70, 71, 72, 73, 81, 82, 85, 95, 96, 101, 103, 104, 109, 110, 111, 117, 120, 124, 129, 130, 132, 133, 135, 143, 144, 145, 151, 152, 154, 157, 159, 161, 166, 170, 171, 177, 178, 179, 181, 185, 191, 192, 193, 197, 201, 202, 215, 221, 222, 223, 224, 227, 234, 235, 244, 251, 252, 253, 254, 256, 257, 259, 266, 272, 275, 281, 283, 286, 287, 291, 203, 298, 300, 302, 306, 310, 314, 316, 317, 319, 320, 321, 323.

183. INTERNATIONAL FINANCIAL INSTITUTION (IFI)

Definition: U.S. legislation that is aimed at influencing the activity of international financial institutions, such as the World Bank, the International Finance Corporation and the International Development Association, which make loans to needy countries with money given by wealthy countries like the United States.

Significance: Such legislation is an attempt by the U.S. Congress to introduce human rights considerations into the decision-making processes of the IFI, thus using economic benefit (money loans) as an incentive for borrower states to improve their human rights situations.

After the Second World War and the creation of the United Nations, the international community created international institutions to channel money from the richer countries to the poorer countries. These institutions are known as international financial institutions (IFI).

Because many of these poorer countries, mostly known as "developing countries" or "Third World" countries, usually had bad human rights records, the U.S. Congress felt it could create a positive influence on the human rights situations of these countries by trying to get IFIs to condition loans on improvements in a borrower state's human rights situation. Although the United States could not by itself veto a loan to a country because of its human rights record, it could exercise its "voice and vote" through U.S. members and representatives working in the IFIs. It would use this power in an attempt to get a loan denied to any country guilty of committing gross violations of internationally recognized human rights. This is done through legislation, such as that in title 22 U.S. Code, section 262d of 1988. See Appendix G for the text of section 262d.

See Also Terms: 9, 83, 92, 120, 124, 144, 145, 152, 173, 180, 185, 199, 204, 208, 211, 259, 283, 316, 323.

184. INTERNATIONAL HUMAN RIGHTS LAW

Definition: The part of the body of public international law that sets forth international legal norms (rules and principles) for the protection of human rights. These norms are standards of government conduct to protect the inherent human dignity of human beings from the abuse of power by the state and sometimes other actors.

Significance: Since the Second World War and largely as a consequence of the horrors the world saw then, the international community has attempted to set up international legal rules and implementation systems to monitor how states treat human beings and remedy human rights violations. To do this, the international community has created the system of law known as International Human Rights Law.

This system of law is made up of two major components:

1. Human rights norms applicable in times of peace.
2. Human rights norms applicable in time of armed conflicts, which is known as humanitarian law.

There is some overlap between these two fields of human rights law, though some scholars do not accept the claim that humanitarian law is part of the field of international human rights law. This author does. This body of law sets legal norms, or standards of conduct, for governments, limiting their actions as they relate to human beings under their jurisdiction. Human beings are the "bearers" or "holders" of the rights in this body of law, though some say that humanitarian law gives no rights to individuals but merely creates obligations on states. In any case, both fields generally aim at the protection of human beings from the abuse or consequences of the use of power by a state.

It includes international legal norms whose source is from international treaties (conventional law), from international customary law, from general principles of law, international case law, and scholarly writings and, to a lesser degree, from general principles of "soft" law, which is not technically legally binding but often followed by states.

International human rights law is subsidiary to national laws. It is a backup system to be used when national protection of individual rights does not work. It is the goal of human rights law that each state, including the United States, transform (implement) the international human rights norms into United States domestic (national) law, so that these norms can be enforced in local courts, both state and federal. (The chart in Appendix F shows how international human rights norms are transformed into U.S. law).

International human rights law is found in both global and regional contexts, in such international organizations as the United Nations and the Council of Europe and the Organization of American States. The various human rights norms are implemented by a variety of methods, some judicial, some administrative and some political, at both the national and international levels.

According to some writers, there are approximately 38 separate, substantive human rights in this body of law. Human rights norms are primarily classified as civil, political, economic, social or cultural.

The United States has been one of the main countries working for the development of this field of law, but it has been very reluctant and very slow to ratify human rights treaties and to give them effect in U.S. courts. The U.S. position on international human rights is evolving gradually because of political and legal factors, and varies from administration to administration. The United States generally accepts and implements civil and political human rights but has been especially slow to accept as law the economic, social, and cultural rights.

See Also Terms: 1, 2, 3, 11, 12, 20, 21, 25, 26, 30, 32, 33, 39, 48, 52, 53, 54, 55, 56, 57, 59, 60, 62, 63, 70, 73, 80, 88, 90, 93, 94, 98, 114, 120, 122, 123, 124, 130, 133, 134, 136, 142, 144, 145, 146, 147, 148, 149, 150, 151, 152, 155, 156, 158, 160, 167, 175, 177, 179, 180, 181, 182, 185, 186, 187, 193, 198, 205, 208, 210, 211, 215, 217, 222, 225, 226, 229, 236, 242, 243, 244, 247, 253, 257, 258, 259, 264, 267, 268, 269, 270, 272, 276, 279, 282, 283, 286, 287, 291, 290, 297, 306, 307, 308, 309, 293, 311, 312, 316, 322, 323.

185. INTERNATIONAL LAW/LAW OF NATIONS
See entry for **Public International Law**

186. INTERPRETATION
Definition: There are two different definitions, two distinct meanings to this term, as it is found in the field of human rights:

1. General: The search for the meaning of the language of a treaty norm in order to discover its true meaning in the abstract or as applicable to certain situations.

2. Instrument of Interpretation: A legal instrument filed by a state upon treaty ratification, wherein the state party expresses its written understanding of the meaning of a particular article or words of the treaty. This sometimes happens when a state feels the article/word is vague or ambiguous or when it needs to be understood in light of the state's constitution or high court decisions.

Significance: As for the first meaning "Interpretation of a treaty" is a process that normally requires examination of the treaty text. Sometimes the wording of a treaty is such that it is difficult to determine its true meaning, or its meaning as applied to a particular situation. In order to discover its true meaning one has to go through the process of treaty interpretation. There are rules for doing so. Those rules are found in the Vienna Convention on the Law of Treaties. (See Appendix E.)

Under the Vienna Convention, "A treaty shall be interpreted in good faith in accordance with the ordinary meaning to be given to the terms of the treaty in their context and in the light of its object and purpose."

One may also look to subsequent state practice or instruments and to the preparatory works (*travaux préparatoires*) for further help. See Vienna Convention of 1969, Articles 31 and 32.

As an example, if one were seeking to determine if water boarding were an act or torture, or prohibited as cruel, inhuman or degrading treatment or punishment, one would apply the Vienna Convention rules. Law and not politics determines the correct interpretation of a treaty and the international community has set the rules on how interpretation shall be done. Several principles apply to interpretation. One is the principle of effectiveness which states that one always interprets a treaty such that it renders the treaty more effective in accomplishing the object and purpose of the treaty; and the second is the principle of Pro Homine, also called Pro Personae, which means that one always interprets a treaty in a way that is most protective of the human dignity of human beings.

As to the second meaning, this is a little known international legal instrument which affects the way a state complies with its treaty obligation. This instrument is always found in relation to a state ratifying a treaty. Often an instrument of interpretation is also submitted along with the states' reservations and declarations (RDUs), and always at the time of ratification.

It is also sometimes called an "instrument of understanding" or an "interpretive declaration."

See Also Terms: 48, 52, 62, 70, 73, 74, 94, 127, 144, 145, 146, 151, 184, 185, 211, 215, 220, 222, 225, 243, 245, 247, 259, 264, 269, 272, 279, 291, 306, 307, 323, and see entry for Reservations, Declarations, and Understandings, infra.

187. INTERSTATE COMPLAINT

Definition: A complaint, filed in an international judicial or quasi-judicial body, such as the U.N. Human Rights Committee, by a state (or states) party to a treaty against another state party, usually where both complainant state and respondent state have accepted the competence (jurisdiction) of the body handling the complaint.

Significance: An interstate complaint, petition, application or communication can be filed by one or more states against one other state. In such a complaint, a state or states are alleging that another state has breached its obligations under a human rights treaty and that the body should hear the case and resolve it according to the treaty regime.

The United States has ratified the ICCPR and has declared that it accepts the jurisdiction of the Human Rights Committee to hear cases filed against the United States by other states parties. In theory this means that interstate complaints can be filed against the United States if it violates the ICCPR. However, there has never been a single interstate complaint filed in the Human Rights Committee against any state party, which was a reason why the United States accepted this jurisdiction.

The ICCPR, Article 41, has a provision for interstate complaints.

See Also Terms: 3, 5, 11, 26, 48, 70, 72, 74, 107, 133, 144, 145, 151, 157, 165, 179, 185, 208, 211, 215, 218, 222, 231, 246, 253, 254, 259, 264, 272, 283, 286, 287, 292, 293, 297, 306, 307.

188. INTOLERANCE

Definition: The attitude of a person or group of persons who do not accept or tolerate the differences of other persons or groups, such as people of a different race, religion, language, political opinion or ethnic group. It is not accepting people as they are.

Significance: Many human rights violations happen because people do not accept differences in other people. They look at other people as not as good as them, or not good at all. They refuse to accept others as they are, regardless of race, color, religion, language, political opinion or any other difference. Intolerance involves disrespect for the inherent human dignity of all human beings and, as such, is condemned by the international community as a threat to human rights. This kind of intolerance often leads to such evils as hate crimes, racism, religious intolerance, police brutality and nationalism. Intolerance is contrary to the legal equality and nondiscrimination that are guaranteed to every human being under principles of human rights law. This applies to citizen, noncitizen and even to those who are not legally in a country (though that would not prevent their legal removal). This condemnation of intolerance is consistent with the meaning of the Declaration of Independence, even though it was written at a time when slavery existed and women were disenfranchised or expressly included.

The preamble to the UDHR says, "recognition of the inherent dignity and equal and inalienable rights of all members of the human family is *the* foundation of freedom, justice and peace in the world." Article 1 of the UDHR states, "All human beings are born free and equal in dignity and rights and are endowed with reason and conscience and should act towards one another in a spirit of brotherhood." Article 2 states that everyone is entitled to exercise all human rights without any kind of discrimination based on differences such as "race, colour, sex, language, religion, political opinion, national or social origin, property, birth or other status."

Tolerance is a social quality very much desired and proclaimed in the United States, especially because the United States is such a melting pot of peoples from all corners of the globe, representing every race, language, ethnic group and every other conceivable characteristic. However, intolerance still occurs in the United States and must be dealt with under U.S. law and international human rights law. Where intolerance is manifested by government it is especially problematic and serious and must be remedied.

The United Nations has declared that the best remedy for intolerance is human rights education for everyone in the world according to age and status. It had declared the years 1995 through 2004 as the "Decade for Human Rights Education." The international community believes that education is the key weapon against all forms of intolerance. The United States has unfortunately done very little to participate in broad human rights education as a result of the call of the U.N. Decade. Most Americans know little about human rights, except perhaps a few of the rights in the Bill of Rights.

See Also Terms: 7, 11, 12, 14, 22, 28, 55, 56, 70, 72, 77, 78, 86, 87, 101, 139, 140, 144, 145, 149, 152, 155, 156, 235, 237, 260, 261, 264, 265, 272, 277, 283, 316, 323, 324.

189. INVOLUNTARY SERVITUDE

Definition: Forcing a person to work against his will as a punishment or in order to take economic advantage of him, and keeping the person in a constant state of subjugation so as to keep him working.

Significance: Putting another human being in involuntary servitude is a human rights violation. Very often such a violation is accompanied by other wrongful acts against the victim. Article 1 of the UDHR states, "All human beings are born free and equal in dignity and rights." Article 4 states, "No one shall be held in slavery or servitude; slavery and the slave trade shall be prohibited in all their forms." Article 8 of the ICCPR states:

1. No one shall be held in slavery; slavery and the slave-trade in all their forms shall be prohibited.

2. No one shall be held in servitude.

3. (a) No one shall be required to perform forced or compulsory labour.

Involuntary servitude is a type of human rights violation similar to slavery. It violates the freedom of human beings to determine their own life direction and actions, including where and how they work. Human beings have the right to be free from domination and exploitation by either the state or other persons. In slavery a person is considered the property of someone else to use as they wish. In involuntary servitude a person is merely forced against their will to do work for another person with no choice in the matter.

Involuntary servitude is against the law in the United States. The United States also is bound by its obligations under the ICCPR to prohibit such acts. However, acts of involuntary servitude are occasionally discovered in the United States. One example is the sweatshops where garment workers, who are often illegal aliens, are sometimes kept working for little money and in conditions that they cannot escape.

Much of involuntary servitude in the U.S. is part of the phenomenon of human trafficking. Many people are trafficked into the U.S. to work as indentured servants and sex slaves. In the last decade the U.S. has greatly increased its efforts to discover and dismantle trafficking networks and free the people trapped in such servitude. This phenomenon is found worldwide and is being fought through international inter-governmental organizations and NGOs all over the world.

See Also Terms: 11, 12, 20, 24, 26, 33, 24, 25, 48, 63, 70, 72, 73, 84, 120, 122, 124, 133, 136, 144, 145, 146, 147, 151, 152, 167, 169, 170, 177, 179, 181, 182, 184, 185, 195, 215, 222, 227, 259, 272, 281, 283, 297, 309, 316.

J

190. JACKSON-VANIK AMENDMENT

Definition: The Jackson-Vanik Amendment (19 U.S. Code Section 2432) is an amendment to the Trade Act of 1974 that authorizes the granting of U.S. trade benefits (most favored nation status; now called Normal Trading Status [NTS]) to other countries, and which conditions those trade benefits on a country allowing its people to leave (emigrate) from that country.

Significance: The Jackson-Vanik (See Appendix I) amendment was a congressional amendment made primarily to pressure the former Soviet Union into allowing Soviet Jews to leave and go to other countries, such as Israel and the United States. It involved the granting of most favored nation (MFN) trading status to countries with non-free market economies. The granting of such MFN status allows a country to trade with the U.S. on an equal footing with any other country. This economic advantage was designed to entice a state to allow dissidents or certain persecuted ethnic or religious groups to leave a country. As such, it is a linkage legislation, linking improved human rights practice with foreign trade. Though it was originally enacted for the benefit of Soviet Jews, it is a piece of general human rights legislation and can be applied to any country that denies its people the right to leave the country.

The amendments states that the President must determine if a country is denying or obstructing emigration and that he must certify that fact to Congress and refuse to grant MFN (now NTR) status to that country during any period in which such actions are occurring. A waiver is possible under certain circumstances.

This amendment has become somewhat obsolete since the breakup of the Soviet Union and the new Russia now allowing emigration as a matter of right. But it is still on the books and is still affects U.S. and Russian relations. It also still applies to U.S. trade relations with China. In 2000 President Clinton de-linked trade and human rights as regards China, but the continued existence of the amendment gives Congress a yearly reason to discuss China's human rights records with regard to allowing Chinese dissidents to leave the country.

There is Congressional debate going on over whether to repeal this somewhat archaic law.

See Also Terms: 9, 14, 20, 33, 34, 35, 44, 48, 50, 70, 72, 86, 102, 120, 124, 128, 141, 144, 145, 151, 156, 160, 167, 169, 175, 177, 179, 184, 185, 194, 195, 199, 205, 207, 216, 218, 222, 230, 235, 239, 243, 259, 260, 265, 273, 283, 286, 287, 292, 297, 309, 323.

L

191. LAND MINES

See entry for **Indiscriminate Attack/Force**

192. LAW OF ARMED CONFLICT

Definition: The body of rules and principles found in international law that constitute legal norms applying to situations of armed conflict either between two or more states or within a state, such as a civil war. This body of international law limits when states can use force, how they use it and how they treat victims.

Significance: The law of armed conflict is a body of law that has two parts: first, the law that regulates when a state can legally use armed force against another state or states, which is called the *jus ad bellum*; and second, the law regulating how (by what method and means) a state uses such force and how it treats those who are victims of the conflict, such as the wounded or shipwrecked, prisoners of war, or civilians in occupied territory, called the *jus in bello*. The second part, *jus in bello*, is known as international humanitarian law. Properly speaking, only the second part directly involves human rights norms. As stated in the introductory material of this edition, the author considers this body of law to be part of the larger body of law known as human rights law. It is the part of human rights law that applies when an armed conflict is going on. It applies in both international and internal armed conflicts.

This body of law is based on many rules and principles that have been officially accepted by the member states of the international community. This body of law is a sort of minimum common denominator of conduct of nations during the worst of times, times of armed conflict, that beget death and destruction and that seem irrational and hardly subject to any law.

The truth is that there are many international legal limitations on how military forces can do battle. These limitations have the force of law because they have been established in treaty law, such as in the Geneva Conventions, or are norms that have ripened under the doctrine of customary international law, such as the Nuremberg Principles, or the inherent right of self-defense. The bulk of norms pertaining to when a state can use armed force is contained within the U.N. Charter, sometimes referred to as the "U.N. Charter paradigm." The principle source of the norms of humanitarian law, are contained in the Geneva Conventions of 1949 and its two amendments, the 1977 Protocols to the Geneva Conventions, and in customary international legal norms, commonly referred to as The Laws and Customs of War.

The United States has been a key force in the advancement and evolution of the law of armed conflict because it often participates in military actions in various capacities around the world, such as in Kosovo, Bosnia, Somalia, Iraq, Afghanistan and Vietnam. It has been very active in the advancement of this law ever since the Lieber Code of 1863, written by a U.S. law professor to establish a law of war for union soldiers during the U.S. Civil War. That Lieber Code served as the model for the first Geneva Convention and all subsequent humanitarian law, and is still considered as part of The Laws and Customs of War. Sometimes one hears this set of law called the Law of War. The term "war" is not usually used any more, because war is actually the description of a legal relationship between two or more states, not the hostile military action between them. One now uses the term "armed conflict."

The most important function of the law of armed conflict is to cause the warring parties, whether states or revolutionary forces, to understand that regardless of their military power and ability they cannot do whatever they want, and that the whole international community has an interest in seeing that they play by clearly defined rules, with consequences for violations. As a matter of international humanitarian law it is simply not true that "all is fair in love and war." War is hell, but it is usually more hellish because the parties to a conflict do not follow the rules of this body of law. The goal of this law is to minimize human pain, loss and suffering in a world that still has not been able to prohibit armed conflict all together. The violation of many norms of this law can result in individual criminal responsibility of those directly responsible and often their commanders as well.

Unfortunately, the greatest fault or weakness of this body of law is that it is virtually unknown to Americans. It is known mostly by military lawyers who give legal advice to military commanders about what the law of armed conflict allows or prohibits in a given military action. Soldiers get basic training in it so they do not commit war crimes. There is little civilian oversight to this process on behalf of the civilians who will make up about 80 percent of the victims (dead or wounded) of a given conflict.

Several of the key instruments of this body of law are set forth in the Documents section of this work.

It is primarily up to all the states, such as the United States, to enforce the law of armed conflict. However, there have been international tribunals that have prosecuted violators, such as the Nuremberg trials after World War II. In early 2000, two international tribunals were prosecuting alleged violators of this law, one regarding the Bosnia conflict of the early 1990s and the other regarding those responsible for the Rwanda massacre of 1994.

The main body monitoring compliance with the Law of Armed Conflict is the International Committee of the Red Cross, which has its headquarters in Geneva. That nongovernmental organization has legal and military experts in the area of armed conflict and visits the prisoners of war and internees to see that they are being treated according to the Geneva Conventions. They visited the war on terror detainees in Guantanamo and wrote reports on them to the U.S. government.

The main judicial forum enforcing the Law of Armed Conflict criminally is the new International Criminal Court (ICC), established in 2002 to deal with the most serious violations of international law. These include war crimes, crimes against humanity and genocide, and, as of 2017, the Crime of Aggression, which was finally defined in 2010. This Court only has jurisdiction to try cases when the state where the crime happened or the state of the nationality of the perpetrator is a state party to the ICC Statute, and the state is either genuinely unable or unwilling to prosecute the crimes. It operates under the principle of complementarity, meaning it is a backup to state courts and it can only handle cases if the state courts cannot or do not prosecute. It is meant to deter commissions of crimes against the law of armed conflict and certain other crimes, all of which are deemed to harm all humankind.

The law of armed conflict is supposed to be adhered to or prosecuted by states under the principle of subsidiarity. The international-level protection is for when the states fail to do so.

The Basic Rules of Humanitarian Law, found in Document 71, constitute a summary of the provisions of the humanitarian law side of the law of armed conflict.

Regarding the *jus ad bellum*, that body of law regulates when states can use military force in international law. The main norm is the law of the Crime of Aggression. This is also called a Crime Against Peace. These were prosecuted in the Nuremberg trials in 1945. Because starting an aggressive armed conflict begins the whole catastrophic process of war crimes and crimes against humanity and human rights violations it is considered the mother of all international crimes.

In the post 9/11 context, the law of armed conflict is very important and, along with international human rights law, must be respected by the U.S. In military legal theory if belligerent forces follow humanitarian law there will be less death and destruction, better discipline among the troops, and the conflict will last a shorter time. And when a state sticks to the rules and does not descend into barbarity because the other side did so, the good will of the international community will be on that state's side.

One of the major issues of the law of armed conflict in the so-called war on terrorism is determining who is a combatant and who is not. A combatant is a person who is legally authorized by their government or other authority to participate in the operation of hostilities in an armed conflict. Only combatants have the *jus ad bellum*, the right to engage in armed conflict. The extent of the protections afforded persons under humanitarian law depends on their status. One is either a combatant or a noncombatant. Both are protected by humanitarian law. On the combatant side there are normal combatants and so-called unlawful or unprivileged combatants. The Guantanamo detainees faced this issue. They were captured on a battlefield in the so-called war on terror but were called "enemy combatants" under U.S. law, based on a 1951 U.S. case decision. There is no such category as "enemy combatant" under international humanitarian law. Whether one is a combatant or not depends on fulfilling certain criteria specified in this body of law, such as being under responsible command and following the law of armed conflict. Even unprivileged or unlawful combatants have legal rights under humanitarian law, including certain access to justice and judicial guarantees. When there is a question about the status of a person, whether he is a combatant or not, the person detained has a right under the Geneva Conventions to an "Article 5 hearing" for a determination of their status. It is not the case under the law of armed conflict that if a person does not meet the criteria for being a combatant that that person has no legal rights and can be treated however the capturing power wishes. And, as indicated above, international human rights law will apply to the conduct of the capturing armed force with regard to anyone captured who is in a territory under the effective control of that capturing force. So even if the captured unlawful belligerent did not have the right to be treated a certain way under humanitarian law, which is quite unlikely, he would have the right to treatment according to the international legal obligations in any human rights treaty by which the detaining or capturing state was bound.

The case decision in *Kadic v. Karadzic* is an example of a U.S. court dealing with this body of law. See Appendix J.

See Also Terms: 3, 8, 13, 20, 23, 25, 26, 33, 37, 38, 40, 42, 45, 48, 49, 57, 59, 63, 64, 70, 71, 72, 73, 79, 80, 81, 82, 86, 90, 95, 96, 99, 100, 101, 104, 110, 111, 113, 120, 124, 125, 129, 130, 132, 133, 134, 135, 137, 144, 145, 147, 150, 151, 152, 153, 154, 157, 159, 164, 166, 170, 171, 178, 181, 182, 185, 191, 192, 197, 200, 201, 202, 203, 210, 211, 215, 221, 222, 223, 224, 226, 244, 251, 252, 253, 254, 256, 257, 258, 259, 263, 271, 272, 273, 275, 276, 283, 286, 287, 291, 293, 298, 300, 302, 306, 308, 309, 310, 313, 314, 315, 316, 317, 318, 319, 320, 321, 322.

193. LEGALITY (PRINCIPLE OF)

Definition: A principle of international law and of most national laws which states that no one can be punished for any conduct unless that conduct is prohibited by a law that is specific and detailed and is duly promulgated by a responsible authority and accessible to persons, and which existed before the acts were committed, so that one can know how to regulate their conduct. It is a principle used to create legal certainty in a society by letting everyone know what they can and cannot do, what is lawful and what is unlawful.

Significance: The ability to act within a settled framework without fear of arbitrary or unforeseeable state interference is a human need, a human security need. It has been transformed into a fundamental aspect of the national constitutional order and internationally, reflected in the principle of rule of law. It is the protection of legitimate expectations in society. This principle applies to domestic and international law.

It is normally seen in the context of criminal law regarding the basis on which a state is seeking to punish someone. But it is also applicable in international human rights law in terms of evaluating the legality of criminal prosecutions, regarding whether measures taken by the state violated human rights law.

When it is used in the context of human rights law it applies to limitation clauses. When determining whether a state violated human rights by interfering with someone committing an act, the fact-finder will determine whether the law under which the state acted complied with the principle of legality. This means that the measure is only valid if it was prescribed by legitimate authority, such as a parliament or Congress, and the law behind it is promulgated by an authoritative legal source and the law was specific, clear and accessible, and the results of not complying with it were foreseeable. If the measure is not based on legal authority meeting the principle of legality it will be an invalid measure and a human rights violation.

Accessibility is part of the principle of legality. It comprises the part about a measure being taken according to a clear, precise and understandable law, and that one can find (access) what the law is. It cannot be a hidden, secret measure. This is to prevent government from acting purely on whim outside of the law, and not according to existing law, which too often happens. It is a guard on the principle of rule of law. Human rights are, by definition, limitations on the power of government.

It is primarily applied to penal law where it is expressed by the Latin terrn *Nullum Crimen, Nulla Poena Sine Lege*, which means: there is no crime, no punishment, without a law. This is sometimes framed in terms of ex post facto laws but that is not the only application. It is most often seen in human rights law when a complaint has been filed against a state and the forum is determining if the basis of the state's action was legal or not, in every sense of the word. This would also preclude a vague and ambiguous law.

In international human rights law the principle of legality is found in both the UDHR and ICCPR.

In the UDHR, Article 11.2 reads:

No one shall be held guilty of any penal offence on account of any act or omission which did not constitute a penal offence, under national or international law, at the time when it was committed. Nor shall a heavier penalty be imposed than the one that was applicable at the time the penal offence was committed.

Article 15.1 of the ICCPR reads:

Article 15.1: No one shall be held guilty of any criminal offence on account of any act or omission which did not constitute a criminal offence, under national or international law, at the time when it was committed. Nor shall a heavier penalty be imposed than the one that was applicable at the time when the criminal offence was committed. If, subsequent to the commission of the offence, provision is made by law for the imposition of the lighter penalty, the offender shall benefit thereby.

While these human rights norms seem to speak only about whether acts constitute a criminal offense, the principle of legality is implicit in this norm. And any time the government acts in a way which interferes with the exercise of a human rights it is necessary that the measure taken by the government be done pursuant to law, and that the law pass the principle of legality. Thus, members of society can know what the law expects and may act accordingly.

This issue is dealt with domestically within the 5th Amendment right to procedural due process of law and U.S Constitution, Article I, sec. 9.3.

In applying this to the U.S. in the war on terrorism and to the counter-terrorism measures the government is taking, this principle applies to everything the government does. Nothing in the war on terrorism can supersede the principle of legality. The state can only act pursuant to law.

See Also Terms: 1, 3, 11, 12, 20, 26, 33, 48, 52, 62, 63, 64, 70, 90, 94, 124, 134, 144, 145, 146, 151, 152, 175, 177, 179, 181, 182, 184, 185, 194, 198, 202, 215, 222, 223, 226, 244, 252, 253, 259, 272, 283, 291, 292, 293, 297, 309, 316, 317, 318.

194. Legislation

See entries for **Implementing Legislation** and **General Human Rights Legislation**

195. Liberty

Definition: The quality or state of being free; the power to do as one pleases; the positive enjoyment of various social, political or economic rights or privileges; freedom from arbitrary or despotic control; and freedom to be subject to and follow the rule of law.

Significance: Liberty suggests an absence of restrictions on specific freedoms. The U.S. Constitution and Bill of Rights are the legal assurances of individual liberty in historical U.S. law. See Document 2. International human rights law is a secondary, backup legal system for protection of liberty. Human rights are restrictions on the power of government vis-à-vis individuals. They are legal instruments that are used to protect human liberty from the abuse of power by government.

See Also Terms: 11, 12, 20, 24, 25, 29, 33, 34, 25, 48, 51, 59, 63, 70, 72, 73, 75, 81, 82, 85, 86, 90, 92, 120, 122, 123, 124, 128, 129, 130, 132, 133, 134, 136, 141, 142, 144, 145, 152, 160, 167, 169, 175, 177, 179, 180, 184, 185, 189, 190, 196, 203, 210, 211, 213, 232, 236, 238, 239, 240, 243, 249, 250, 251, 252, 253, 254, 255, 256, 259, 263, 264, 266, 272, 275, 277, 281, 283, 292, 308, 309, 316, 322, 323.

196. Liberty and Security of Person

Definition: The human right of individuals to be free from government searches and seizures and similar restrictions on personal freedom, unless there is a valid legal basis for government to do so. It is the right to feel safe, sound and secure from unjustified government activity, such as stopping for identification, detaining, arresting, using wiretaps, monitoring a person's activities or searching one's home, person or belongings.

Significance: Liberty relates primarily to arrest and detention by law enforcement authorities. Every human being has the human right to liberty and security of person. Human rights are really limitations on the power of government in relation to individuals. They are legal measures aimed at keeping government out of certain areas of the lives of human beings. They are things government cannot do to human beings, as being inconsistent with human dignity. They are a means of protecting the mental and physical integrity of human beings.

Article 3 of the UDHR states, "Everyone has the right to life, liberty and security of person." Article 9 of the ICCPR, Document 8, states:

> Everyone has the right to liberty and security of person. No one shall be subjected to arbitrary arrest or detention. No one shall be deprived of his liberty except on such grounds and in accordance with such procedure as are established by law.
> 2. Anyone who is arrested shall be informed, at the time of arrest, of the reasons for his arrest and shall be promptly informed of any charges against him.
> 3. Anyone arrested or detained on a criminal charge shall be brought promptly before a judge or other officer authorized by law to exercise judicial power and shall be entitled to trial within a reasonable time or to release. It shall not be the general rule that persons awaiting trial shall be detained in custody, but release may be subject to guarantees to appear for trial or at any other stage of the judicial proceedings and, should occasion arise, for execution of the judgment.
> 4. Anyone who is deprived of his liberty by arrest or detention shall be entitled to take proceedings before a court, in order that that court may decide without delay on the lawfulness of his detention and order his release if the detention is not lawful.
> 5. Anyone who has been the victim of unlawful arrest or detention shall have an enforceable right to compensation.

The above norms are the international human rights equivalent of the 4th amendment to the U.S. Constitution, the famous prohibition against unreasonable searches and seizures.

In the Second and Third Report of the United States to the U.N. Human Rights Committee under the ICCPR, the United States explains to the Human Rights Committee its perspective on the United States law and practice in this human rights norm. See Document 15A.

This norm has come to be very important to the U.S. in the so-called war on terrorism because of the large number of persons from many different countries that the U.S. has detained at Guantanamo and elsewhere. The capture of those people interfered with their liberty and security of person. The next question is whether those arrests were justified. These issues are still being litigated, but some cases have made clear that some detainees were completely innocent and had no useful intelligence information. If the deprivation of liberty was not justified then a violation of ICPR Article 9 has occurred. The ICCPR applies to most of the war on terror detainees, at least to those at Guantanamo. Article 9 requires that when someone is found to have been unlawfully deprived of their liberty they have an enforceable right to compensation.

The so-called secret detention or "ghost" sites are also a violation of liberty and security of person, as well as other human rights. See Detention, supra.

See Also Terms: 11, 12, 16, 17, 20, 24, 33, 34, 35, 48, 49, 53, 58, 59, 70, 73, 75, 79, 81, 82, 85, 90, 93, 99, 100, 109, 111, 113, 117, 120, 122, 124, 134, 136, 144, 145, 146, 147, 148, 151, 152, 160, 167, 177, 179, 184, 185, 195, 222, 232, 238, 239, 248, 249, 252, 253, 254, 259, 264, 266, 272, 275, 283, 292, 293, 297, 305, 306, 307, 309, 316.

197. LIEBER CODE

Definition: The first formal military manual setting forth the law of armed conflicts applicable during the U.S. Civil War for union soldiers, for purposes of preventing unnecessary suffering, death and destruction, and preserving discipline. Its formal name was The Instructions for the Government of Armies of the United States in the Field.

Significance: In 1863, Francis Lieber, a Columbia law professor, wrote the Lieber Code for the Union forces, which set a code of how soldiers could fight. It was a codification of existing international law on armed conflicts and served as the basis for later laws on armed conflicts. The present Code of Military Justice is an evolved version of the Lieber Code.

The Lieber Code recognized that even war was subject to law and that those who were not involved as combatants should not be victimized by armed conflicts. To the extent to which it sought to protect human beings from the effects of the Civil War, it was a human rights code.

See Also Terms: 3, 25, 33, 37, 40, 41, 42, 48, 70, 71, 72, 73, 104, 110, 124, 129, 132, 132, 135, 137, 144, 145, 152, 154, 157, 159, 164, 167, 170, 171, 178, 181, 182, 185, 192, 200, 201, 202, 211, 222, 223, 235, 251, 257, 259, 272, 283, 286, 287, 291, 292, 297, 302, 314, 317, 318, 319, 321.

198. LIMITATION

Definition: A lawful restriction placed by the state on the way individuals can exercise their human rights. Such limitations are found in limitation clauses in treaties. A limitation can be imposed by the state if it is done pursuant to law and if such a measure is necessary to meet a pressing social need, such as the protection of public health, public safety, public welfare, morals, national security or the rights and freedoms of others. A limitation is also known as a "restriction." Limitations clauses allow the state some room to act in a way protective of, or beneficial to, the state.

Significance: Some human rights are absolute and apply at all times in all circumstances the same way everywhere. Freedom from torture is an example of an absolute right. The government can never find a valid excuse to commit torture. Other rights are not absolute but are considered to be "prima facie." They can be limited by the government in how they are exercised, because human rights are a balance between the interests of the individual in personal freedoms on the one hand, and the interests of the government in preserving and developing the state on the other. International Human Rights law permits states parties to human rights treaties to take certain measures that limit human rights. For example, a speed limit for automobiles on streets is a limitation on how fast a person may exercise the right to freedom of movement. Measures that limit the disclosure of military secrets can be made for the protection of national security.

However, states may not use limitations as loopholes to avoid or get around their obligations to otherwise respect human rights. If a state, for example, puts a limitation against the movement of a certain group calling it a protection of public order, that limitation cannot have the purpose, in reality, of promoting a racial or religious segregation between peoples, animated by a discriminatory attitude. This type of situation is described in Article 5 of the ICCPR. Limitations will be narrowly and strictly construed against the state.

These limitations, again, are found in "limitations clauses" in human rights instruments, such as in Article 12.2 of the ICCPR. See Document 8.

See Also Terms: 11, 26, 48, 52, 62, 80, 127, 145, 146, 151, 165, 167, 175, 177, 179, 184, 186, 210, 211, 222, 225, 257, 259, 264, 272, 287, 291, 293, 297, 306, 307.

199. LINK/LINKAGE

Definition: The law or policy of a government connecting or conditioning the receipt of some government benefit to another state with that state's human rights record or performance.

Significance: The United States seeks in many different ways to influence other states in regard to improving respect for human rights. One way is by telling a country that it can only get a certain benefit, such as financial aid or military assistance, if it changes its government practices or the actions of its citizens in a way that is in compliance with human rights standards.

An example of U.S. legislation establishing linkage between U.S. foreign relations, foreign aid and human rights practices can be found in the International Religious Freedom Act of 1998. See Document 89.

See Also Terms: 9, 48, 61, 70, 94, 128, 138, 144, 145, 152, 177, 184, 185, 190, 194, 211, 215, 218, 222, 244, 259, 272, 273, 286, 292, 297, 306, 316.

200. MASSACRE

Definition: A violent atrocity committed against human beings involving physical injury and killing, usually indiscriminately and brutally.

Significance: An unfortunate part of the history of the world has been the perpetration of massacres by one group of human beings on another. These massacres have most often occurred during times of armed conflict and during the struggle for power in a particular state. They are marked by violent acts upon men, women and children, not differentiating between them. Massacres can happen in the context of an ethnic cleansing or genocide, but they can occur in other circumstances as well.

The My Lai Massacre, part of the history of the United States, happened during the Vietnam War when a group of U.S. soldiers led by Lt. William Calley massacred a village of Vietnamese because of fears of infiltration by the enemy. Calley was held accountable and prosecuted for this crime. Humanitarian law and the law of armed conflict try to create parameters that keep this kind of atrocity from happening. The Rwanda genocide was a massacre of epic proportions wherein over 800,000 persons were killed in about 100 days.

The greatest obstacle to massacres is the existence of robust national and international legal systems which implement international human rights law and enforce humanitarian law and international criminal law. These systems announce to those who would massacre that the eyes of the world are watching them and they will be prosecuted and punished. This has been happening in the International Criminal Tribunal for the former Yugoslavia and International Criminal Tribunal for Rwanda. The International Criminal Court for those states parties involved has jurisdiction to try the most serious international crimes which would arise from massacres. See Document 76.

See Also Terms: 11, 12, 19, 20, 24, 26, 48, 63, 70, 71, 72, 78, 101, 104, 112, 120, 124, 130, 132, 133, 137, 139, 143, 144, 145, 151, 152, 153, 154, 160, 164, 179, 181, 182, 184, 185, 192, 201, 202, 223, 224, 227, 228, 257, 259, 271, 272, 283, 294, 298, 300, 316, 317, 318, 319, 321.

201. METHODS OR MEANS OF COMBAT

Definition: The legal limitations in international humanitarian law concerning the weapons and tactics used by military combatants in armed conflict. The term refers to how and with what arms and other devices an armed conflict may be fought consistent with respect for human rights.

Significance: It is not true that all is fair in war. There is a well-established body of international law regarding how wars and other armed conflicts are to be fought.

It is a basic principle of humanitarian law, which is a branch of human rights law applicable in armed conflicts, that the two sides to an armed conflict (war) cannot use whatever types of weapons they want and attack the enemy any way they want. This is what the Principle of Humanity implies. They can only use weapons and tactics that will accomplish their military goal with the least amount of physical damage and human death and suffering. This principle must be obeyed by all combatants, even guerrilla warriors. "All-out war" is no longer legally permitted because it hurts innocent people and even harms combatants more than necessary to achieve military goals. A field of combat order which states that anything or anyone in a certain area can be attacked and destroyed is unlawful. The Principle of Distinction in humanitarian law requires that combatants always and everywhere distinguish between combatants and civilians.

Weapons and tactics can only be employed where there is a real "military necessity" for using them, where the damage they cause to noncombatants is proportional to the military advantage gained by the attack, and where the methods or means do not cause unnecessary suffering or damage. Prohibition of the use of napalm, chemical or gas weapons is an example of a regulation of the methods and means of combat. Setting a fire in a field near a town that would kill everyone in the town, both enemy soldiers and civilians, would also be prohibited, as would the dropping of cluster bombs in an area full of civilians.

U.S. forces, whether acting alone, as part of NATO, or as a U.N. peacekeeping force, are subject to these limitations on the methods or means of combat. They must obey international law at all times regarding the methods or means of combat they employ. They also have an obligation to ensure respect for such rules by seeing that other states obey these rules also.

The Nuremberg trials after World War II were partly the prosecution and punishment of Nazi war criminals, who violated international law about the methods and means of combat used in that war, such as mass deportations and the use of lethal gas.

Most recently there has been international action to prohibit the use of antipersonnel land mines, which kill about 26,000 people per year, including many children. Land mines are considered a "means" of armed conflict. These weapons are considered indiscriminate because they cannot distinguish between a combatant and noncombatant. It is estimated that around 20 million potentially harmful land mines are still in the ground all around the world, in places where there is no longer armed conflict.

The attempt to ban these land mines focused on amending the 1980 Convention on Prohibitions or Restrictions on the Use of Certain Conventional Weapons Which May be Deemed to be Excessively Injurious or to Have Indiscriminate Effects. This convention has a protocol dealing with land mines. In the late 1990s the nations of the world held a conference to try to ban such mines. There was strong resistance by the United States to a total ban, which was generated by the Pentagon and caused the United States to refuse to go along with such a ban. The convention set forth in the Documents section shows the 1980 convention, its 1980 protocol on land mines, and the 1996 protocol as finally adopted at the conference. Because most countries were unsatisfied with this result, they had a conference in Ottawa, Canada, without the United States, and adopted a different convention containing a total ban on land mines. That convention is not included here.

In 2010 a Convention on Cluster Munitions (Dublin 2008) entered into force. This Convention seeks to generally prevent use of cluster bombs that would present too much danger to civilians. The U.S. has not signed or ratified this treaty as of the time of this book.

Many argue that the use of nuclear weapons and other weapons of mass destruction are an unlawful means of combat. They are said to violate the Principles of Proportionality, Distinction and Unnecessary Suffering. The United States officially opposes such a position. Nuclear weapons and other weapons of mass destruction have been politically forced into the realm of "disarmament" talks and out of the realm of human rights and humanitarian law, where they belong. This is because within the field of human rights and humanitarian law they cannot be legally justified.

As to the legality of use of nuclear weapons as a method or means of combat (by the United States or any other state), the International Court of Justice (ICJ) ruled in 1996 that the use or threat to use such weapons was limited legally only to situations of extreme national self-defense where the very existence of a state was at stake and there was absolutely no other way of protecting the state from extinction. The ICJ held that such use would still be subject to considerations under the rules and principles of international humanitarian law, such as proportionality and indiscriminate attacks. See Appendix J. Thus, the United States could not legally use or threaten to use such weapons as and when it wants, without possibly violating international law in the U.N. Charter (Article 2.4), international human rights law, humanitarian law and international criminal law.

All new weapons developed by the United States must go through a legal analysis to see if they are consistent with international humanitarian law as to whether they are legitimate methods or means of combat.

See Also Terms: 20, 23, 26, 37, 38, 40, 42, 45, 48, 53, 56, 58, 59, 63, 66, 70, 71, 72, 73, 79, 95, 104, 106, 110, 111, 117, 120, 124, 129, 130, 132, 133, 135, 136, 137, 144, 145, 147, 151, 152, 154, 159, 161, 164, 166, 167, 169, 170, 171, 177, 178, 179, 181, 182, 185, 191, 192, 197, 202, 203, 221, 222, 223, 224, 234, 235, 251, 257, 259, 272, 275, 291, 292, 293, 297, 298, 300, 302, 306, 307, 313, 314, 315, 316, 317, 318, 319, 320, 321.

202. MILITARY COMMISSION/TRIBUNAL

Definition: A judicial body established by a state, normally by a field commander or commander in chief for use in time of armed conflict, normally to try combatants from the enemy side for offenses against the international law of armed conflict (LOAC), such as for committing grave breaches of the Geneva Conventions of 1949, which constitute war crimes. They are called either a military commission or military tribunal. Simply stated, a military commission/tribunal is a type of military court designed to prosecute members of enemy forces during a wartime.

Significance: Military Commissions operate outside the scope of conventional <u>criminal</u> and <u>civil</u> proceedings. The judges are military <u>officers</u> and fulfill the role of <u>jurors</u>. Military tribunals are distinct from <u>courts-martial</u>. A military tribunal is more like an inquisitorial body. In the U.S. context military commissions are institutions which have been setup from time to time as alternatives to courts martial throughout the history of the U.S. With the advent of the war on terrorism the military commission came back under the Bush Administration.

Since 9/11 the U.S. has attempted to set up and hold trials of war on terrorism suspects detained under the legal classification of "enemy combatant." This term does not exist in either international human rights law or international humanitarian law but comes from a 1951 U.S. Supreme Court case, which predates almost all modern human rights law. The recent attempts to set up military commissions in 2006 and 2009 have tried to create a system which is completely under the Executive Branch of the government, under the Department of Defense. These commissions have sought, unsuccessfully, to prosecute the so-called enemy combatants based on charges brought by a military authority, prosecuted by a military authority, judged by military officers, and sentenced by military officers against a member of an adversarial force.

In 2001, President Bush asserted his authority as Commander in Chief to try captives taken in the war on terror before "military commissions." Starting in 2002 Guantanamo detainees, through friends and family, tried to bring habeas corpus petitions before the federal district courts rather than wait to be tried before a military tribunal. The first to reach the U.S. Supreme Court was *Rasul vs. Bush* in 2004. In *Rasul* the Supreme Court dismissed the government's argument that the Naval Base at Guantanamo was beyond the reach of U.S. laws and that the Executive Branch lacks the authority to deny captives access to the U.S. justice system, and that the captives did have the right to initiate *habeas corpus* petitions, and that the Executive Branch was obliged to provide the captives with an opportunity to hear and attempt to refute whatever evidence had caused them to have been classified as "enemy combatants." This also resulted in the Department of Defense creating the Combatant Status Review Tribunals (CSRTs).

In July 2006 the Supreme Court ruled in *Hamdan v. Rumsfeld*, another *habeas corpus* action, that the Executive Branch lacks the Constitutional authority to set up military commissions to try captives taken in the "war on terror." See Appendix J. It ruled that this authority rests only with the United States Congress. In October 2006, the Congress passed the 2006 Military Commissions Act.

On June 12, 2008, The Supreme Court ruled in *Boumedienne vs. Bush* that the prisoners had a right to the habeas corpus under the United States Constitution and that the Military

Commissions Act was an unconstitutional suspension of that right. It ruled that even these enemy aliens, detained as "enemy combatants" on the territory of Cuba, were entitled to the writ of habeas corpus protected in Article I, Section 9 of the U.S. Constitution. It also found the Military Commission procedures falling short of due process standards.

Then in 2009, the Congress passed the Military Commissions Act of 2009. This Act amended some of the provisions of the 2006 Act to improve protections for defendants. The courts will continue to hear cases concerning the military commission process but it appears that the Administration in 2010 is seeking to limit the Commission to certain cases and prosecute other detainees in civil courts elsewhere.

At the international law level, military commissions, including any military commission set up by the U.S. in the war on terrorism, are subject to compliance with international humanitarian law norms (such as GC III, Article 5, PI Article 75 and Common Article 3 of the four GCs) and human rights norms, (such as ICCPR, Articles 2.1, 7, 9, 10, 14, 15, 26). These apply wherever the GCs apply and the U.S. exercises effective control.

In its national UPR report to the OHCHR the U.S. mentions its attempts at military commissions. See Document 86. At paragraph 88 it reads:

> The Administration has expressly acknowledged that international law informs the scope of our detention authority. The President has also made clear that we have a national security interest in prosecuting terrorists, either before Article III courts or military commissions, and that we would exhaust all available avenues to prosecute Guantánamo detainees before deciding whether it would be appropriate to continue detention under the laws of war. Working with our Congress, we have revised our military commissions to enhance their procedural protections, including prohibiting introduction of any statements taken as a result of cruel, inhuman, or degrading treatment.

Most important in the above quote is the fact that international law now will be consciously factored into and control the commission's formation and process. Not only does this pertain to humanitarian law but must include international human rights law. While the U.S. claims that human rights law, basically the ICCPR, does not apply outside of the territorial U.S., this view is legally incorrect as a matter of international law. The ICCPR applies to military commissions wherever established and informs the content of Common Article 3 of the four Geneva Conventions regarding "all the judicial guarantees which are recognized as indispensable by civilized peoples."

See Also Terms: 3, 20, 26, 30, 33, 34, 37, 41, 42, 45, 48, 63, 64, 70, 71, 72, 73, 81, 82, 86, 88, 90, 93, 94, 95, 99, 100, 103, 106, 112, 113, 120, 124, 129, 131, 132, 133, 134, 135, 144, 145, 152, 154, 159, 160, 162, 166, 167, 169, 177, 178, 179, 182, 184, 185, 192, 193, 201, 203, 210, 211, 215, 216, 222, 223, 224, 234, 251, 252, 253, 254, 257, 259, 272, 283, 292, 293, 297, 302, 313, 314, 317, 318, 319, 320, 321.

203. MILITARY/BELLIGERENT OCCUPATION (LAW)

Definition: Military occupation occurs when a belligerent state invades the territory of another state with the intention of holding the territory at least temporarily. While hostilities continue, the occupying state is prohibited by international law from annexing the territory or creating another state out of it, but the occupying state may establish some form of military administration over the territory and the population. Under martial law imposed by this regime, residents are required to obey the occupying authorities and may be punished for not doing so. Civilians may also be compelled to perform a variety of nonmilitary tasks for the occupying authorities, such as the repair of roads and buildings, provided such work does not contribute directly to the enemy war effort.

Significance: Although the power of the occupying army is broad, the military authorities are obligated under international law to maintain public order, respect private property, and honor individual liberties. Civilians may not be deported to the occupant's territory to perform forced labor nor impressed into military service on behalf of the occupying army. Although measures may be imposed to protect and maintain the occupying forces, existing laws and administrative rules are not to be changed. Regulations of the Hague Conventions of 1907 and, more importantly, the 1949 Geneva Convention for the Protection of Civilian Persons in Time of War have attempted to codify and expand the protection afforded the local population during periods of military occupation.

From the second half of the 1700's onward, international law has come to distinguish between the military occupation of a country and territorial acquisition by invasion and annexation. Since the end of the Napoleonic wars in the 1800's this distinction became clear and has been recognized among the general principles of international law. These customary laws of belligerent occupation which evolved as part of the law of armed conflict gave some protection to the population under the military occupation of a belligerent power. Then in 1907 the Hague Conventions further clarified and supplemented these customary laws. See Document 69. This was done in the "Laws and Customs of War on Land" (Hague IV) in 1907. It is set forth in the "Section III Military Authority over the territory of the hostile State." The first two articles of that section read:

Article 42. Territory is considered occupied when it is actually placed under the authority of the hostile army. The occupation extends only to the territory where such authority has been established and can be exercised.

Article 43. The authority of the legitimate power having in fact passed into the hands of the occupant, the latter shall take all the measures in his power to restore, and ensure, as far as possible, public order and safety, while respecting, unless absolutely prevented, the laws in force in the country.

In 1949 these laws governing belligerent occupation of an enemy state's territory were further extended by the adoption of the Fourth Geneva Convention (GC IV). Much of GC IV is relevant to protected persons in occupied territories and Section III: Occupied territories is a specific section covering the occupied territory.

See Also Terms: 20, 25, 33, 34, 37, 40, 42, 48, 53, 54, 55, 56, 57, 59, 68, 69, 70, 72, 73, 79, 80, 81, 82, 86, 90, 92, 93, 99, 100, 108, 113, 120, 122, 124, 125, 126, 129, 130, 132, 135, 136, 144, 145, 147, 151, 152, 154, 160, 162, 166, 167, 169, 177, 178, 179, 180, 181, 182, 184, 185, 192, 195, 196, 197, 201, 202, 211, 216, 222, 223, 224, 236, 252, 253, 257, 259, 260, 263, 265, 272, 277, 292, 297, 299, 302, 306, 308, 309, 314, 316, 317, 318, 319.

204. MILLENNIUM DEVELOPMENT GOALS (MDGs)
See entry for Development. See Document 50.

205. MINORITY/MINORITY RIGHTS
Definition: Minority is a term used to describe a group of human beings classified, among other things, by their race, language, religion, ethnicity or nationality within the context of a larger society in which they are nondominant. There is no one commonly or officially accepted definition of a "minority" in international human rights law as yet. One definition in use in the United Nations says that a minority group is a "group numerically inferior to the rest of the population of a state, in a non-dominant position, whose members—being nationals of the state—possess ethnic, religious or linguistic characteristics differing from those of the rest of the population and show, if only implicitly, a sense of solidarity, directed toward preserving their culture, traditions, religion or language."

Significance: Minority rights is a term generally designating those human rights of whatever type—civil, political, economic, social or cultural—which offer specific protections to members of racial, ethnic, national, religious and linguistic minority groups, or to the entire group as such. One of the most important areas of human rights that has developed since World War II is the protection of various types of minorities, known as minority groups. The Holocaust and other atrocities have taught the world that sometimes a society can demonize and dominate another group of people based on differences such as color, religion or ethnicity, which can result in attempts to destroy, remove or marginalize such groups from that society. Much of the work of defining minorities and their human rights has been conducted at the United Nations.

The main work of the United Nations has been done in standard setting and studies. This work includes specific provisions in general human rights instruments, such as ICCPR, Article 27, and even such nontreaty instruments as the *Declaration on the Rights of Persons Belonging to National or Ethnic, Religious or Linguistic Minorities* (1992), Document 41, and the activity of the U.N. Human Rights Council as they deal with minority issues.

The protection of minorities that are discriminated against on the basis of their racial characteristics, including color or nationality, is covered in the Convention on the Elimination of all Forms of Racial Discrimination, which the United States has ratified. See Document 23.

The United States is also involved in the issue of minority rights in Europe through its participation in the Organization for Security and Cooperation in Europe, which has a High Commissioner for Minorities and a treaty on minorities (which the United States has not signed). The Congressional Commission on Security and Cooperation in Europe oversees the U.S. participation in that OSCE process and often looks into minority issues, such as discrimination and persecution against religious and ethnic minorities.

Some minority human rights issues in the United States are dealt with in the Second and Third Report of the United States to the U.N. Human Rights Committee under the ICCPR regarding the ICCPR Articles 2 and 27, Document 15A. Also, see how the Human Rights Committee sees the interpretation and application of the ICCPR regarding minority groups, in General Comment No. 15(27) and General Comment No. 23(27) of the U.N. Human Rights Committee in Appendix E. An interesting look at the international community's view of minority issues is the Report Submitted by Special Rapporteur, Mr. Doudou Diène, to the U.N. Human Rights Council on the subject of Racism, Racial Discrimination, Xenophobia and Related Intolerance in Appendix L.

See Also Terms: 7, 11, 12, 15, 20, 21, 24, 29, 33, 34, 35, 39, 48, 55, 63, 67, 68, 69, 70, 72, 73, 75, 77, 86, 87, 97, 99, 100, 101, 102, 120, 122, 124, 127, 130, 136, 139, 140, 141, 142, 144, 145, 146, 147, 152, 153, 160, 163, 167, 169, 177, 179, 180, 184, 185, 216, 222, 228, 235, 237, 242, 243, 252, 253, 254, 255, 259, 260, 261, 265, 270, 271, 272, 277, 282, 283, 289, 290, 292, 297, 308, 309, 311, 316, 323, 324.

206. MONITOR

Definition: To watch, observe or check the status of a state's compliance or noncompliance with human rights norms, as a way of assuring that the state is fulfilling its human rights legal obligations.

Significance: Usually an international body charged with implementation of the norm will monitor state parties' compliance, but non-governmental organizations (NGOs) also perform monitoring functions, usually followed by reports of their observations. Such monitoring is a way to ensure that states comply with their obligations. Monitoring is to examine the state's actual practice, as opposed to what a state says it is doing. States oftentimes do not do what they say they are doing. When there are claims of human rights violations against a state, the state often denies it. Sometimes it is only because of persons and groups and human rights bodies monitoring a state's practice, usually on the ground, that the state changes or establishes its practice to conform to the human rights norm. Under the ICCPR, this treaty system established the Human Rights Committee to monitor how states comply with treaty obligations. Monitoring is similar to the practice of treaty "supervision." Monitoring can be done on an unofficial basis by anyone and is most often done by human rights NGOs, such as Human Rights Watch.

A government that knows that its conduct is being monitored is much less likely to commit human rights violations.

See Also Terms: 3, 4, 25, 26, 29, 48, 60, 70, 72, 76, 88, 93, 94, 112, 113, 119, 120, 121, 123, 124, 142, 144, 145, 147, 148, 149, 150, 151, 152, 177, 178, 184, 185, 187, 208, 215, 217, 218, 222, 230, 231, 232, 233, 259, 264, 268, 272, 283, 286, 289, 290, 292, 293, 299, 305, 311, 316.

207. MOST FAVORED NATION (MFN) TRADING STATUS

Definition: A term formerly used to describe a very favorable trading status between two states, whereby a state grants another state tariffs as good as those granted to any other state. In the U.S. context, the term refers to the official granting by the U.S. government of the lowest level of tariffs to other countries with whom it is trading.

Significance: To some degree a state may set the terms of international trade between itself and other states, including the amount of tariff imposed on the import of another state's goods. Conceptually, a state voluntarily chooses, within limits, to grant or not to grant to another state trade conditions at least as favorable as all other trading partners are granted. This system originates in the GATT Treaty (General Agreements on Trade and Tariffs) system.

The grant of MFN status brings about the most favorable and profitable commercial relations to the state that is granted it. In recent years the granting of this status by the United States has often been linked to a state's human rights record. This linkage adds some "leverage" to the U.S. attempt to make another state more attentive to that state's poor human rights practices and to improve them so as to obtain improved status. It is an economic incentive to improve its human rights situation.

Since 1974, U.S. law has required that in order to grant MFN status to a totalitarian state, the president must grant a waiver each year to that country on the basis that such a waiver is in the U.S. national interest. If the president makes a decision to grant MFN status, both houses of Congress must vote in order to overturn the waiver, or it enters into effect.

This waiver has been a major issue in the debate over MFN status for China. In this debate Congress has argued with the president about whether such status should be given to China. This political process often makes human rights performance something to be evaluated in relation to economic benefit to the U.S. economy, and sometimes human rights is subordinated to trade gains. The argument is also made that continuing MFN status keeps trade going between the United States and China, which allows a constructive engagement between the two countries. Through that engagement, the United States can attempt to influence China's human rights policy in a positive direction. The main counter argument is that the failure to penalize China for its poor human rights performance is like telling the Chinese that it is all right to commit human rights violations because they will suffer no adverse consequences in the trade area. They will continue to benefit and profit from trade with the United States, and so there is no economic incentive for them to improve on human rights.

This term has come to be replaced by the term "Normal Trading Relations," or NTR, though both terms are still heard. Normal Trading Relations is the official term.

See Also Terms: 9, 48, 70, 92, 128, 184, 185, 190, 199, 211, 259, 272, 286, 287, 292.

208. MULTILATERAL FORUM

Definition: An international forum where more than two, and usually many, states in the world or in a region, are engaged in matters of mutual interest and can discuss them, make decisions and take collective action on them, including in relation to human rights.

Significance: The United States has historically been involved in legal and political affairs in the international arena of states. With the founding of the United Nations in 1945 in San Francisco, the United States became a member of the key multilateral forum on human rights. In addition to being a multilateral forum, the United Nations is also known as an international intergovernmental organization.

Multilateral means "many sided." The purpose of a multilateral forum is to create an official place where matters of mutual interests between states can be discussed in relation to the human rights norms applicable to that system.

The United States is involved in other multilateral forums, such as the Organization of American States, which deals with human rights issues in the Western Hemisphere, and the Organization for Security and Cooperation in Europe, which deals with human rights political issues in Europe, especially in the former communist countries.

See Also Terms: 3, 11, 12, 43, 48, 50, 70, 72, 146, 147, 150, 151, 152, 173, 181, 183, 211, 214, 221, 222, 230, 231, 259, 264, 268, 276, 291, 292, 293, 306, 307, 308, 311.

209. NATIONAL CONSENSUS

Definition: A basis on which the U.S. Supreme Court analyzes a measure in order to determine whether or not it is constitutional, based on the law and practice of the 50 states.

Significance: In analyzing the constitutionality of certain measures taken by the government, such as application of the death penalty to certain types of offenders, the Supreme Court will look at the laws and practices of the 50 States. By doing this it is seeking to determine whether there is a "national consensus," meaning a similar value held by most states and reflected by their law, policy and practice.

An example of this can be seen in the recent *Graham vs. Florida* opinion of 2010. See Appendix J. That case was about whether it violated the 8th amendment to the Constitution to apply a criminal sentence of life in prison without possibility of parole to a minor who committed a non-deadly crime. Florida imposed such a sentence. The Court had to determine whether such a sentence was cruel and unusual punishment and violated the 8th amendment.

In analyzing whether it was cruel and unusual treatment under contemporary American standards, the Supreme Court looked at what the states did and found that most states do not impose such a penalty because they think it is too harsh to impose on minors.

The court found that the practice of most states showed a national consensus of values regarding such a sentence. It can do this regarding similar analyses concerning, for example, the death penalty on minors or the mentally retarded. The Supreme Court is seeking to determine if there is a weight of authorities arguing for a certain position in the states. If it finds a national consensus it may rule accordingly. It is trying to align the federal system with the state system of values unless there is a clear constitutional rule to the contrary. This type of analysis is used more in legal issues which have stronger moral implications such as the death penalty or sexuality.

See Also Terms: 6, 30, 48, 70, 145, 186, 210, 211, 212, 222, 243, 259, 272, 287, 292, 297, 323.

210. NATIONAL SECURITY

Definition: The concept of national security refers to the protection of the very existence of the state from any internal or external threats or dangers and the measures taken to protect it. In the context of international human rights law, it is one of the permissible bases of restriction or limitation of the exercise of certain human rights norms.

Significance: National security is a relatively new concept which was first introduced in the United States after the Second World War. It is about the state, not the government, trying to protect its existence from within and from outside. When Congress passed the National Security Act of 1947 and it was signed by the President on July 26, 1947, national security became an official guiding principle of foreign policy in the United States.

Protection of national security has become extremely important since 9/11 because the U.S. perceives its enemies as wanting to destroy the United States of America as a country and replace it with another system.

In the field of international law every state has sovereignty, which includes the right to self-defense of the state and its territory. International human rights law is a fair balance between the maximum freedom of the individual on the one hand, and the needs of the state to protect and provide for the well-being of its population. In human rights law norms, most norms are conditional, meaning that they can be interfered with by the government for narrowly prescribed reasons for specific enumerated aims. These aims sometimes include aims such as protection of national security. The protection of national security is one of the legitimate aims in certain limitation/restriction clauses in certain international human rights treaties. By such clauses, a state is allowed to limit or restrict the exercise of certain human rights, such as freedom of expression, if it is necessary, proportional, and prescribed by law for protection of national security. See Document 8, ICCPR, Article 19.3(b). But national security cannot be invoked as a justification for state interference with all human rights. For example, national security can never be claimed as a justification for committing torture or slavery or genocide. National security constitutes a legitimate basis for state measures interfering with human rights norms **only** where the treaty expressly says so. See for example ICCPR Article 19.3, compared with ICCPR Article 7. National security reasons can never be used to violate an absolute human right. No state can commit torture for national security reasons.

National security is a mischievous concept which can be manipulated and misused by government. It can be wrongfully used as a cloak by government to cover up political mistakes, human rights violations, international crimes, to avoid accountability, or to block transparency concerning a society's compliance with human rights obligations. It can be used to cover up embarrassing or politically harmful information. National security can never be used for these reasons and there needs to be a strong civilian control of the military and of the intelligence and police arms of government to make sure they do not misuse this defense. National security is not to be used to protect the government or political party in power. It is to protect the life of the whole nation state, and not just a part of it.

Human rights law, again, recognizes the need to balance the freedom of the individual and the right of the state to protect its existence for the good of the whole society. It allows the government to claim national security as a justification for measures which would otherwise be human rights violations; but there must always be accountability to civilian and preferably judicial institutions to preserve checks and balances.

It should be noted that in the limitations clauses of some human rights treaties, national security is spelled out as one of the legitimate aims justifying certain restrictions of freedom of a certain human right. See, for example, ICCPR Article 19, compared to Article 18.3. There is an express limitation clause provision for national security in Article 19, but not in Article 18. One must read the specific treaty texts to know if national security is a legitimate aim for limitation measures under the treaty. The greatest factor in protecting national security is a rule of law system which respects human rights law and humanitarian law in seeking to protect itself from threats from without and within. Claiming that there is some other legal standard because the U.S. is engaged in a war on terrorism would be incorrect, unlawful and unconstitutional.

See Also Terms: 8, 20, 24, 23, 24, 59, 64, 70, 72, 80, 95, 103, 106, 110, 111, 113, 141, 145, 152, 154, 177, 179, 184, 185, 192, 211, 226, 232, 259, 266, 272, 275, 276, 287, 292, 293, 299, 300, 302, 306, 307, 308, 316, 321, 323.

211. National Self-Interest

Definition: That which seems to a state to be in the best interest of that state. A government is acting in the national self-interest when it acts in a certain way regardless of how it affects another state or anyone else because it believes that this is what most benefits that state itself.

Significance: Even though all states belong to an international community that has established certain principles for the peace and harmony and prosperity of all, very often states act in whatever way they believe will most benefit their individual state. Sometimes this involves economic benefit, sometimes political, sometimes military.

Many times, when people wonder why a government seemed to fail to protect human rights within its own boundaries or elsewhere, the answer is that it was acting in its own perceived national self-interest. National self-interest is judged by those in power in the government to be more important than the protection of human rights or fulfillment of international legal obligations. National self-interest can never be a justification for committing human rights violations. Moreover, national self-interest can never be a reason for neglecting international legal obligations, such as those under international human rights law.

National self-interest is one of the reasons some states do not do certain things in the international arena, such as failing to intervene while the Rwanda genocide was going in, or taking steps against global warming. National self-interest very often has an economic component, meaning that the reason a state does or does not do something is based on the economic effect of an action on the national economy, and economic advantage trumps principle. The United States would probably claim that it has not ratified the ICC Statute because it deems it in the national self-interest militarily not to do so.

States tend to enter into international legal obligations when they deem it in their national self-interest to do so. Sometimes the problem in human rights is to convince a state that limiting its sovereignty for human rights reasons is actually and really in the national self-interest.

See Also Terms: 6, 9, 13, 23, 27, 29, 33, 34, 35, 48, 59, 60, 61, 70, 75, 80, 83, 87, 88, 90, 92, 93, 94, 96, 99, 100, 103, 105, 106, 108, 109, 113, 118, 120, 121, 122, 124, 128, 130, 135, 136, 137, 138, 141, 144, 145, 146, 147, 149, 150, 151, 152, 154, 156, 160, 162, 167, 177, 179, 184, 185, 187, 192, 195, 199, 202, 203, 204, 205, 207, 210, 216, 218, 220, 222, 230, 231, 232, 233, 237, 242, 243, 252, 253, 254, 259, 266, 268, 269, 271, 272, 276, 278, 282, 283, 286, 287, 296, 297, 299, 305, 306, 308, 309, 311, 312, 316, 317, 318, 322, 323.

212. NATIONALISM

Definition: The attitude of a people who identify themselves as a nation, that their nation is the highest good, and highest authority and that everything should be done for the benefit of that nation, regardless of the effect on any other nations or peoples. It is not the same as patriotism, which is a love and respect for, and allegiance to one's own state.

Significance: Under human rights law all people are born equal to all other people. There is no state, nation, people or race superior to any other. There is nothing inherently wrong with nationalism when it exists in the sense of patriotism, that is, a pride in one's people and culture. The problem arises for human rights when nationalism elevates the status and needs of one group of people over another, resulting in demonization, domination, discrimination or violence against the "other"—those who do not belong to the nation. This type of nationalism is often the cause of many human rights violations. It is also seen in the people of one nation trying to remove from their territory all those who are not members of that nation, which is also known as "ethnic cleansing," such as happened in the Bosnia situation in the 1990s.

At its extreme, nationalism can lead to the ultimate human rights violation: genocide. Genocide is the destruction of another group of people because of their nationality, ethnicity, race or religion. This is the lesson of the Holocaust.

Events such as 9/11 can cause a surge in patriotism coming close to nationalism. This is especially so when the nation perceives that there is another people that is threatening its freedom or existence. It is necessary to educate the nation to keep a pluralistic and tolerant perspective in the eyes of the people to assure that nationalism does not lead to discrimination or violence against others leading to conflict, whether international or internal.

See Also Terms: 8, 22, 27, 48, 64, 70, 71, 72, 75, 103, 122, 124, 130, 143, 144, 145, 156, 157, 159, 188, 210, 211, 218, 220, 222, 226, 243, 259, 292, 293, 294, 316, 323, 324.

213. NATURAL LAW

Definition: A philosophy that served as the main basis for the existence of human rights in individual human beings. This philosophy holds that there exist certain laws in the way the world was made. These laws dictate how human actions should occur, whether individually or in a society such as a state, and how a state should treat human beings.

Significance: This law exists outside of any laws made by humankind. Some believe that natural law is transcendent because the universe was created by God, who established these natural laws, such as gravity or the prohibition against murder. Some believe that natural laws exist without any reference to any divinity.

Natural law is the philosophical basis of the Declaration of Independence. See Document 1. In it, the Founding Fathers stated, "When in the course of human events, it becomes necessary for one people to dissolve the political bands which have connected them with another, and to assume among the powers of the earth the separate and equal station to which the *laws of nature* and of nature's God entitle them...We hold these truths to be self-evident: That all men are created equal; that they are endowed by their Creator with certain unalienable rights." This statement reflects their belief that fundamental rights and freedoms are not granted by states but that governments are established in states to protect these rights that the "laws of nature" have given them and requires states to respect and protect.

The natural law ideas of inherency, universality and inalienability of human rights expressed in the Declaration of Independence and in the 1789 French Declaration on the Rights and Duties of Man and of Citizen, are commonly considered to have informed the philosophical basis of all modern international human rights law.

See Also Terms: 20, 21, 24, 30, 33, 34, 35, 63, 64, 69, 70, 72, 75, 120, 122, 124, 144, 145, 152, 153, 154, 160, 167, 169, 177, 184, 195, 222, 259, 272, 283, 297, 309, 312, 316, 323.

214. NON-BINDING RESOLUTION

Definition: A formal procedural act of the Congress whereby Congress votes on a resolution to express the sense of Congress, and thereby the sense of the U.S., regarding the subject of the resolution. Resolutions can be joint or by each house of Congress.

Significance: The U.S. Congress is very involved in international human rights matters, particularly in legislation concerning human rights. From time to time it will scrutinize human rights situations either in a certain country or regarding a certain theme. Sometimes Congress will pass a law obligating the U.S. government to act or not act in a certain way in relation to the country involved or the theme, such as religious persecution. Sometimes it is not possible or advisable to pass legislation. However, if the Congress still wants to express itself on the matter, the entire Congress, or either house of Congress, can pass a non-binding resolution expressing the sense of that body on the issue. This can have substantial political influence in the U.S. and internationally, even though it is not legal binding. See Resolutions in Appendix I.

See Also Terms: 48, 70, 72, 119, 120, 124, 141, 144, 145, 147, 173, 177, 204, 211, 222, 243, 259, 287, 291, 292, 309, 316.

215. NON-COMPLIANCE

Definition: The failure of a state to fulfill its obligation to act or not act in a way consistent with an international human rights norm binding on that state.

Significance: Human rights are legal rights and are recognized by states as already existing in individual human beings. They are found in international law in treaties and in customary legal norms.

States agree that they will order their conduct consistent with these human rights legal norms. For example, if a state has ratified the treaty known as the ICCPR, it accepts to be bound by Article 8, which says that: "No one shall be held in slavery; slavery and the slave-trade in all their forms, shall be prohibited." If a state allows slavery to happen within its territory it is then in non-compliance with its international legal obligation found in Article 8 of the ICCPR. See Document 8. Non-compliance with a human rights legal obligation constitutes a breach of that article and measures can be taken against that state to get the state to stop the violation and make reparations for the resulting harm from the violation.

In the case of treaty based norms, such as in the ICCPR, the supervising body, such as the Human Right Committee, created in the treaty deals with the violation. Once a state accepts to be bound by human rights norms they must change their domestic (national) law and policy to be in harmony with their international legal obligations. If they do not, or if they do make such changes but they later tolerate acts in violation of those norms they are said to be in non-compliance with the legal norms. Legal norms are standards of conduct with which a state must comply.

Compliance with domestic (national) laws and constitutions does not necessarily constitute compliance with international legal obligations. A state can act consistently with its own constitution and at the same time be in non-compliance with its international norms. For example, if a state ratified the ICCPR and its constitution allowed torture and torture to be practiced, the result would be that the state acted in compliance with its own constitution but at the same time was in non-compliance with its international legal obligation under the ICCPR.

In examining the U.S. conduct in relation to detainees in the war on the terrorism one must look to the specific international legal norms found, for example, in the Geneva Conventions, the ICCPR and the Convention against Torture, and examine the facts in light of the international legal norms to determine if the U.S. is or is not in compliance with those norms. In doing so one must also consider any reservations, declarations and understandings which the U.S. has made when ratifying those instruments, where allowed.

Looking for example at the case of *Hamdan vs. Rumsfeld* (see Appendix J) the U.S. Supreme Court found that the U.S. government was in non-compliance with its legal obligation under Article 3 of the Third Geneva Convention, which the Court found applicable to the conflict in Afghanistan. In that case a national court, the U.S. Supreme Court, found the U.S. in violation of, or non-compliance with, an international legal norm in the Geneva Conventions, which was binding under the U.S. Constitution, Article VI, and which U.S. federal districts courts could adjudicate under Article III of the Constitution. See Document 2.

In its 2010 national UPR report to the OHCHR, Document 86, the U.S. administration stated concerning compliance as follows:

> The United States is currently at war with Al Qaeda and its associated forces. President Obama has made clear that the United States is fully committed to **complying** with the Constitution and **with all applicable** domestic and **international law, including the laws of war**, in all aspects of this or any armed conflict. (Emphasis added.)

See Also Terms: 3, 5, 10, 11, 12, 19, 25, 26, 48, 52, 60, 61, 62, 70, 71, 73, 80, 88, 93, 103, 112, 113, 119, 120, 132, 133, 132, 144, 145, 146, 147, 148, 150, 151, 152, 154, 157, 159, 166, 177, 181, 182, 184, 185, 187, 190, 192, 206, 222, 223, 224, 225, 226, 227, 233, 234, 244, 253, 259, 264, 268, 272, 289, 290, 291, 293, 297, 306, 307, 308, 311, 316.

216. NON-DISCRIMINATION

Definition: Non-discrimination is a principle of human rights that states that no one can be denied the exercise and enjoyment of human rights on the basis of their possessing specified characteristics, such as race, religion, nationality, language, sex, birth, social or other status.

Significance: This principle means that a state may not condition or limit the enjoyment of human rights based on any of these characteristics. A state may not treat people differently regarding who enjoys human rights and who does not, unless there is a reasonable and objective justification for such distinction and a reasonable alternative measure cannot be found.

A "non-discrimination clause" is a clause found in a human rights document that sets forth the principle and grounds of non-discrimination. The non-discrimination clause is often used to reinforce the specific substantive rights listed in the body of an instrument. An example of a non-discrimination clause would be Article 2.1 of the ICCPR, which reads: "Each State Party to the present Covenant undertakes to respect and to ensure to all individuals within its territory and subject to its jurisdiction the rights recognized in the present Covenant, without distinction of any kind, such as race, colour, sex, language, religion, political or other opinion, national or social origin, property, birth or other status." See Document 8.

It should be noted that the wording of this section covers all persons "within its territory and subject to its jurisdiction," which would include legal and even illegal aliens in the United States (though not giving the latter the right to stay in the United States). Non-discrimination is a principle largely taken historically from the equality referred to in the Declaration of Independence and U.S. Constitution, 14th Amendment, in the equal protection clause.

U.S. civil rights law also seeks to act against certain types of discrimination, but it is not human rights law, as such.

The non-discrimination principle and U.S. obligation under Article 2 of the ICCPR is discussed in the Second and Third Reports of the United States to the U.N. Human Rights Committee, Document 15A. Also, the Human Rights Committee General Comments nos. 15(27), 22(18), and 23(27), set forth in Appendix E, deal with issues of discrimination.

See Also Terms: 7, 11, 12, 14, 15, 20, 22, 24, 28, 29, 33, 34, 35, 48, 53, 54, 55, 56, 57, 70, 72, 73, 75, 77, 78, 86, 87, 99, 100, 102, 120, 122, 124, 126, 127, 136, 139, 140, 144, 145, 146, 147, 151, 154, 155, 156, 160, 177, 179, 180, 184, 185, 188, 205, 216, 237, 255, 259, 260, 261, 264, 265, 270, 272, 277, 283, 289, 290, 292, 293, 306, 307, 309, 316, 322, 324.

217. NON-GOVERNMENTAL ORGANIZATION (NGO)

Definition: A non-governmental organization (NGO) is a not-for-profit association of people working for the promotion and protection of human rights in either a general (all human rights) or a special (specific, focused on certain human rights issues) focus.

Significance: Generally speaking, an NGO, or Non-Governmental Organization, is defined as an organization which is legally established and created by natural or legal persons, and which operates independently from any government. It is an entity which governments refer to as having no governmental status. In the early days of the U.N. it was designated as "any international organization that is not founded by an international treaty."

NGOs may be local, national, regional or international in structure, presence and activity. They can be permanent or short-term ad hoc organizations; they can focus on a theme or a specific country; and they may have open or closed membership and constitutions. Human rights NGOs monitor and compile information and draft reports on human rights violations; they also circulate information on violations and norms procedures. Occasionally they provide legal and financial support to victims, even to the filing of complaints in international and national human rights organs. They also lobby governments and such inter-governmental organizations as the United Nations, provide input in standard-setting processes, influence public opinion, assist in human rights education, and join together in coalitions with other NGOs on certain issues. They monitor the proceedings of human rights bodies, such as the Commission on Human Rights, and are the "watchdogs" of the human rights that fall within their mandate. NGOs play a major role in influencing U.N. policy, and many of them have official consultative status at the United Nations. Examples of major U.S. NGOs are Human Rights Watch, Human Rights First, Amnesty International USA and Freedom House. Many large and small NGOs come from the United States.

NGOs are a part of what is called "civil society," that sector of society outside of government and business that is involved in public and private issues, laws and policy. NGOs today function primarily as the arm of civil society. They are non-state actors in the field of international law and institutions and are indispensible for monitoring and promoting human rights. NGOs provide a counterweight to the power of state. They sometimes form alliances of NGOs on certain issues, for example, the Coalition for an International Criminal Court (CICC) which brought together 2500 NGOs and other non-state actors from 150 countries to push for the creation of the ICC. Without the CICC NGO the ICC would not have happened.

There are different types of NGOs. Among them is an organization known as a GONGO. This stands for Government Operated Non-Governmental Organization. A GONGO is a fake NGO created by a government and used by the government to serve its political purpose, or promote its financial or economic interest. They may, for example, act to counter allegations of human rights violations by the state.

See Also Terms: 4, 36, 48, 70, 76, 119, 124, 131, 145, 148, 150, 151, 152, 173, 177, 178, 215, 221, 259, 272, 286, 316.

218. NON-INTERFERENCE WITH INTERNAL AFFAIRS

Definition: A principle of international law found in Article 2.7 of the U.N. Charter, which states that no state can legally interfere with matters that are solely within and under the legal authority of another state. This principle is also known as "non-interference in domestic affairs" or the "principle of non-intervention."

Significance: The U.N. Charter provides recognition and legal protection of the sovereignty of all states by providing in Article 2.7 that "Nothing contained in this Charter shall authorize the United Nations to intervene in matters which are essentially within the domestic jurisdiction of any state." See Document 5.

Normally, what happens solely within the territory of a state is only the concern of that state. However, under contemporary international human rights law, human rights violations of a state can be the subject of concern and certain responsive actions by another state or states. Very often, states that are charged with human rights violations by another state will respond by telling that state to stop complaining, because the complaint constitutes an interference in the national affairs of the violating state, and that such a complaint violates the principle of non-interference. This defense is invalid and outdated. Human rights violations are now considered the legitimate concern of all states, especially states who are parties to a particular treaty with the alleged offending state. Human rights violations are not "matters which are essentially within the domestic jurisdiction" of any state. Therefore, Article 2.7 does not apply to human rights violations.

Very often China (PRC) raises this defense when the United States criticizes China for its treatment of dissidents, as it did after the Tien An Men Square Massacre. The defense raised by China is not legally correct. Fewer and fewer states raise this principle as a defense for human rights violations. Now that China has ratified the ICCPR, the United States has the right to call China on its violations of that treaty, without it constituting an "interference" in China's domestic affairs.

See Also Terms: 48, 61, 70, 71, 72, 73, 118, 144, 145, 152, 153, 154, 156, 157, 175, 176, 185, 190, 211, 222, 243, 259, 271, 278, 287, 292, 293, 306, 307, 308, 316.

219. NON-REFOULEMENT

Definition: This French term literally means "not to expel or throw back." It is a principle of customary international law usually seen in the field of refugee law. It asserts that a state may not return or expel a person to the frontiers of any state in which his or her life or freedom would be threatened on account of race, religion, nationality, political opinion, or membership in a particular social group.

Significance: This principle is codified in conventional law in Article 33 of the 1951 Refugee Convention (see Document 36). It served as the basis of the case of *Haitian Centre for Human Rights v. United States*, a case filed in the Inter-American Commission on Human Rights. See Appendix J. An excerpt of the decision in that case is included in Appendix H, Selected Case Briefs and Decisions; it spells out and applies this principle very well.

In U.S. immigration law this principle is set forth in the law on withholding of removal, which is found at 8 USC sec. 241b. Non-refoulement, which may give rise to withholding of removal in immigration proceedings, is different from refugee status. This principle of non-refoulement is largely accepted internationally. (See the *Soering* and *Ng* cases in Appendix J for further application of this principle).

See Also Terms: 11, 12, 18, 20, 33, 34, 48, 53, 55, 59, 70, 73, 79, 109, 111, 120, 122, 124, 136, 144, 145, 151, 152, 155, 156, 160, 167, 169, 177, 179, 184, 185, 210, 211, 222, 226, 246, 259, 263, 266, 272, 283, 287, 292, 293, 294, 297, 306, 309, 316.

220. NON-SELF-EXECUTING TREATY

Definition: A human rights treaty that does not become legally applicable in U.S. courts as a rule of decision when it is ratified by the U.S. Senate. A non-self-executing treaty needs Congress to pass implementing legislation (statutes) to make the rights in the treaty part of U.S. law usable in both its state and federal courts. Otherwise stated, treaty clauses are enforceable by U.S. courts only if they are either self-executing, or have been implemented by Congressional legislation.

Significance: The doctrine of self-executing treaties came from the U.S. Supreme Court, which stated that a treaty clause is self-executing and equivalent to an act of the legislature whenever it operates by itself and without the aid of any legislative provision. Otherwise, such a clause is non-self-executing and cannot be enforced by individuals in a private action. It remains legally binding between the United States and other states that have ratified it. The intent of the treaty-signing party is the true test of whether the clause is self-executing or not. Even if a state has declared a treaty to be non-self-executing, all branches of government must still comply with it as a binding legal obligation. Non-self-executing does not mean not legally binding. It only refers to its status as a rule of law that can be raised by individuals to serve as a "law of the case" for decision-making purposes in U.S. courts.

See the following for a fuller understanding: the U.S. ratification of the ICCPR, Document 9, in which the United States declares that treaty non-self-executing, and the Restatement of the Foreign Relations Law, Third, in Appendix I, for a discussion of U.S. law on this issue.

U.S. case law has established several factors to determine if a treaty clause is self-executing and thus can be used directly as legal norm in U.S. courts. These factors include:

The language and purpose of the agreement as a whole; the circumstances surrounding its execution
The nature of the obligations imposed by the agreement
The availability and feasibility of alternative enforcement mechanisms
The implications of permitting a private right of action
The capability of the judiciary to resolve the dispute
A court trying to decide whether or not a treaty is self-executing will analyze the treaty using these criteria and will make its decision based on one or more of these criteria.

See Also Terms: 2, 6, 25, 26, 27, 48, 53, 55, 70, 74, 88, 93, 94, 98, 129, 145, 151, 158, 160, 167, 169, 179, 184, 185, 194, 211, 215, 222, 226, 229, 243, 259, 262, 269, 272, 279, 287, 288, 291, 293, 297, 306, 307.

221. NON-STATE ACTOR

Definition: Non-state actors, in international relations, are actors on the international level which are not states. The admission of non-state actors into international relations theory is inherently a rebuke to the assumptions of realism and other "black box" theories of international relations, which argue that interactions between states are the main relationships of interest in studying international events.

Significance: States are legal-political entities that are recognized as states by the international community of states. Non-state actor is a term referring to any actor in society who or which is not a recognized state, such as an NGO, national liberation movement, political party, transnational corporation, and even a private individual. Some have defined it as any organization lacking formal or legal status as a state or agent of a state, or any constituent subunit such as a province, autonomous region or municipality, or agent of such entity. Although not strictly private, sometimes IGOs are also referred to as nonstate actors because IGOS are not states, but they have international legal personality.

Traditionally, human rights law, as part of public inter-national law, distinguishes between, and concerns, public actors known as "states," not private actors. In its classical theory, human rights law prevented *states* from violating human rights found in either treaties or customary international law norms binding upon them. These norms were not addressed to, nor considered binding upon, anyone that is not a state. This distinction has become blurred as human rights theory has evolved and seeks to expand responsibility for the protection of human rights to all sectors of society, with accountability for all.

It is often seen in the context of the issue of the "third-party effect" or *"Drittwirkung"* theory of human rights legal obligations, that is, whether the state is responsible for the actions of such private personalities (non-state actors) or whether non-state actors can be legally bound by international human rights obligations.

Examples of these issues would be whether a national liberation army, which is not a state, is bound to follow the Geneva Conventions in combat against the government; or whether the state would be responsible for murders committed by a private paramilitary death squad.

The major issue concerning non-state actors is usually determining the nature of the state government's duty to protect individual rights from violation by third parties not linked to the state, by taking affirmative steps to prevent such third party acts.

Individual agents of non-state actors can be prosecuted for violating certain international crimes, such as genocide and crimes against humanity, under international criminal law and the principle of individual criminal responsibility.

See Also Terms: 3, 4, 25, 26, 36, 48, 70, 71, 76, 91, 93, 112, 113, 119, 124, 131, 144, 145, 147, 148, 149, 150, 151, 152, 166, 177, 178, 222, 227, 234, 259, 268, 272, 291, 300, 302, 304, 316, 323.

222. NORM/NORMATIVE

Definition: A norm is the accepted standard or law of conduct that is legally binding on the state as a matter of international or domestic law.

Significance: In the context of international law a norm is a principle of right action binding upon the member states parties to a treaty; it can also be established by customary international law. In both cases, human rights norms serve to guide, control or regulate proper and acceptable behavior for the state or individual human beings in the area of protection of human dignity. In this sense, the word "norm" does not mean "average," but "a required standard" to be met by the state. A synonym for a norm in human rights law would be a rule. In human rights documents, norms are the *basic* human rights; they are the accepted "rules" of conduct toward each person because of his or her inherent human dignity.

Human rights treaties contain human rights norms that are both *substantive*, that is, describing what is allowed or not allowed to the individual, and *procedural*, that is, describing the mechanisms and procedures for implementing such substantive rights. When it has entered into force, a treaty is known as a "normative" instrument.

The United States is bound to comply with human rights norms found in the international instruments it has ratified, such as the Genocide Convention, the ICCPR, or the Geneva Conventions, and also to comply with customary international law norms, unless a later controlling executive or legislative measure is enacted, because it is the latest intent of the sovereign state.

See Also Terms: 1, 2, 3, 5, 11, 12, 15, 16, 17, 18, 20, 21, 24, 25, 26, 30, 31, 32, 33, 34, 35, 42, 45, 46, 48, 49, 52, 53, 54, 55, 56, 57, 60, 61, 62, 63, 64, 65, 66, 68, 69, 70, 73, 74, 75, 80, 81, 82, 83, 84, 86, 88, 90, 92, 93, 94, 95, 96, 98, 99, 100, 104, 106, 109, 110, 111, 113, 114, 115, 116, 118, 120, 121, 123, 124, 126, 127, 128, 129, 130, 132, 133, 135, 136, 138, 139, 142, 145, 146, 147, 151, 153, 154, 157, 158, 159, 160, 161, 162, 166, 167, 168, 170, 171, 172, 173, 174, 175, 177, 179, 180, 182, 184, 185, 189, 192, 193, 194, 197, 198, 201, 203, 05, 214, 215, 216, 219, 220, 223, 224, 229, 242, 244, 247, 252, 253, 256, 258, 259, 264, 268, 269, 272, 274, 279, 280, 282, 285, 287, 291, 292, 293, 294, 297, 303, 306, 307, 308, 309, 312, 314, 316, 317, 318, 320, 321, 322.

223. NUREMBERG CHARTER AND RULES

Definition: The Nuremberg Charter is the popular name given to the document developed for the 1945 Nuremberg trials of major Nazi war criminals. It set forth the legal basis for criminal prosecution of the Nazis. The Nuremberg Charter was also known as the London Charter, the place it was made. There were actually three sets of crimes mentioned in this charter: (1) war crimes, (2) crimes against peace (aggression), and (3) crimes against humanity.

Significance: These rules established the basis for prosecution of certain international crimes starting at the end of World War II and continuing to the present. These international criminal norms were largely derived from treaty and customary law existing at the time the charter was drafted by the victorious allied powers, upon the defeat of Nazi Germany. The major source was the 1907 Hague IV Convention and Regulations and 1929 Geneva Convention. They were officially recognized by the United Nations as declaratory of international law.

Many of these norms can be seen in the Statutes of the International Criminal Tribunal for the former Yugoslavia, those on Rwanda, and the statute of the International Criminal Court. They are now considered binding as a matter of customary international law. They should be read with the Nuremberg Principles to get a fuller understanding of the Nuremberg legal legacy.

These three sets of crime: (1) war crimes, (2) crimes against peace (aggression), and (3) crimes against humanity, later became known as the Nuremberg Rules and they now form the backbone of international criminal law and the jurisdictional base of the ICC established in 2002. See Document 76. They are also found as crimes within the Code of Crimes against the Peace and Security of Mankind. See Document 68.

The decision in the case of *In Re Cincinnati Radiation Litigation*, concerning the so-called Nuremberg Code on Medical Treatment, gives an idea of how such a body of World War II law can still affect our U.S. legal system 50 years later. That code was a byproduct of the Nuremberg Rules, as applied to the medical profession.

See Also Terms: 3, 8, 25, 26, 31, 33, 42, 48, 53, 56, 63, 64, 70, 71, 72, 73, 120, 129, 130, 132, 133, 135, 136, 143, 144, 145, 154, 157, 159, 166, 181, 182, 184, 185, 192, 197, 201, 211, 213, 215, 221, 222, 224, 234, 243, 259, 272, 283, 291, 310, 317, 318, 319, 323.

224. NUREMBERG PRINCIPLES

Definition: A set of principles taken from the Nuremberg trials and applicable under international law to the international criminal acts of all human beings, regardless of their status or official position. First, anyone who commits an international crime will be individually criminally responsible. Second, the national laws of the place where the acts occurred do not prevent international criminal responsibility. Third, heads of state and other government officials who commit international crimes are not immune from prosecution because of their official status. Fourth, even being an accomplice to such crimes is enough to constitute an international crime.

Significance: These are some of the basic principles of international criminal law that serve as a legal basis for prosecuting individuals for the most serious violations of human rights. These principles are meant to ensure the world that no one, regardless of rank, office or power, is above the law concerning international crimes. They are meant to establish international rule of law in the penal domain.

These principles also serve as the basis of the doctrine of command responsibility, that is, those who are commanders or superiors of the perpetrators of violations of international criminal law may themselves suffer criminal responsibility for the acts of those under them, their subordinates, if they fail to stop such violations when they knew or should have known about them and were able to stop them, but did not.

Under these principles no soldier or other government agent can say as a defense to such crimes that they were "just following orders." Such a defense is not valid at all.

Both the Nuremberg Principles (See Document 70) and the Nuremberg Rules still apply as customary international law and they apply to the actions of the United States in waging its war on terrorism.

See Also Terms: 3, 25, 26, 42, 48, 63, 64, 70, 71, 72, 73, 103, 132, 135, 145, 154, 157, 159, 166, 181, 182, 185, 192, 202, 215, 222, 223, 234, 259, 272, 283, 317, 317, 319, 320.

225. OBJECT AND PURPOSE OF TREATY

Definition: The term used to describe the two factors that must be examined regarding a treaty in order to enable one to properly interpret the meaning of the treaty. To interpret a treaty, one must look at the language in good faith according to its ordinary meaning within the context of the treaty's "object and purpose."

Significance: The object of a human rights treaty is to recognize specific human rights norms and procedures; the purpose may be, for example, to protect the human rights of children or refugees or to eliminate torture.

The main place to look to discern the object and purpose of a treaty is the preamble, the beginning of a treaty. Another source is the preparatory works of the treaty.

When one seeks to apply an international treaty to the conduct of the U.S. government, or to any other country for that matter, one must keep in mind what is the object and purpose of the treaty. For example, when one seeks to determine whether a certain interrogation practice, such as water boarding, is or is not torture under the Convention against Torture, one has to look to and factor in the object and purpose of that instrument. One has to read the preamble, read the specific article of the treaty defining torture, cruel or degrading treatment or punishment, and any RDUs applicable, and decide in light of the treaty's object and purpose. It is also possible that even if there are RDUs applicable to a particular substantive norm, that the RDU may itself be inconsistent with the object and purpose of the treaty and thus objectionable or void.

This term "object and purpose" is found in Article 31 of the Vienna Convention (1969) and is a general principle of international law regarding the interpretation of human rights treaties. (See Appendix E, Vienna Convention). The object is that which the treaty is trying to do, such as to create binding legal norms and a supervisory organ regarding a particular group of humans, such children, and the purpose is what the treaty is ultimately trying to accomplish, such as to prevent abuse and exploitation of children.

See Also Terms: 3, 6, 20, 21, 25, 26, 48, 70, 72, 74, 93, 94, 98, 103, 124, 127, 144, 145, 146, 147, 151, 152, 158, 168, 169, 172, 174, 177, 184, 185, 186, 222, 226, 243, 245, 247, 259, 262, 269, 272, 291, 293, 297, 306, 307, 323.

226. OBLIGATIONS (INTERNATIONAL LEGAL)

Definition: Something a person or a state or an international organization is legally bound to do or refrains from doing as a prescribed conduct or course of action. A requirement imposed on a state by international law or previous agreement enforceable under international law.

Significance: A human rights norm creates an "obligation" or a "duty" on the state to respect that right. Violation or breach of the obligation by non-compliance with a legal norm gives rise to recourse to implementation measures. These depend upon the institutional context, such as individual or interstate complaints seeking reparations or other redress, or possible criminal prosecution, or the imposition of economic sanctions.

All states have four separate legal obligations in regards to international human rights law: the obligations to respect human rights; the obligation to protect all human rights; the obligation to ensure all human rights; the obligation to fulfill all human rights. These obligations are explained in the Introduction section on Concepts. There are positive and negative obligations: negative obligations for the state to refrain from doing something, and positive obligations of the state to do something.

The U.S. national UPR report submitted to the OHCHR in August 2010, Document 86, refers to states' obligations:

Article 1 of the Universal Declaration of Human Rights declares that "all human beings are born free and equal in dignity and rights" and that they are "endowed with reason and conscience." This basic truth suggests the kinds of obligations—both positive and negative—that governments have with regard to their citizens.
…These obligations are what enable people to claim "life, liberty, and the pursuit of happiness" as their just entitlements. These same rights are encoded in international human rights law and in our own Constitution.

See Also Terms: 3, 9, 11, 12, 20, 24, 25, 26, 48, 53, 55, 56, 68, 70, 72, 73, 80, 88, 91, 93, 98, 103, 114, 124, 144, 145, 146, 147, 148, 151, 152, 154, 177, 179, 180, 182, 184, 185, 192, 203, 211, 215, 222, 225, 244, 253, 259, 262, 269, 272, 279, 280, 282, 287, 288, 289, 291, 293, 294, 297, 306, 307, 308, 309, 311, 316, 322.

227. ON-SITE INVESTIGATION/FACT FINDING

(Also known as *in loco* or *in situ* investigation)

Definition: A human rights investigation that takes place at or near the site where a human rights violation occurred. Such an investigation is begun by members of an international human rights body, a governmental agency or a non-governmental organization in response to a complaint or other report of a human rights violation. Members travel to the state and location where the incident happened so that they can get the best possible evidence of what occurred, talk to those involved and see the physical evidence. This *in loco* investigation allows them to make the most accurate report to the organization or judicial or quasi-judicial body about the full and accurate facts.

Significance: After the Kosovo crisis in early 1999, both the U.N. International Criminal Tribunal for the former Yugoslavia and the U.S. Federal Bureau of Investigation, working with them, sent investigators to Kosovo to gather firsthand evidence about alleged atrocities against Kosovo Albanians. These were known as on-site investigations or fact-finding missions. Usually these terms are used to signify someone from outside the state coming into the state to do an investigation on behalf of some non-state interest, such as the United Nations or the Organization of American States.

While these investigations are often conducted just to establish a human rights violation by the state, very often they are for forensic purposes to support prosecution of international crimes in actual criminal cases.

See Also Terms: 3, 4, 46, 48, 61, 70, 76, 94, 112, 133, 142, 144, 145, 146, 147, 150, 151, 178, 181, 184, 200, 206, 234, 244, 253, 259, 268, 289, 290.

228. OPPRESSION

Definition: Excessive and unjustified use of government power or authority that unreasonably and severely burdens those persons against whom it is exercised, denying them the full exercise of their human rights.

Significance: When a society's government intentionally acts toward its people in a way that denies their human rights, it is considered an oppressive society. Oppression is the opposite of freedom and liberty. It is a condition that does not allow human beings the full exercise of their rights in a way that makes possible the fullest development of the human personality.

Human rights are legal tools used to oppose and stop the excessive and unjust use of power or authority by government. When a government acts in violation of human rights norms in any respect, it is oppressing its victims. Many claim, for example, that African-Americans are still an oppressed minority in the United States, even though legally they are free and equal.

Oppression can occur any time in any country, including the United States. This term usually carries the sense of ongoing and systematic acts. Oppression of human beings is not permitted under international human rights law binding on the United States.

See Also Terms: 15, 19, 20, 22, 33, 34, 35, 40, 63, 64, 65, 66, 70, 78, 81, 82, 84, 85, 96, 101, 111, 115, 117, 120, 124, 125, 132, 133, 143, 144, 145, 146, 147, 151, 152, 153, 170, 171, 179, 182, 184, 185, 190, 200, 201, 203, 205, 215, 216, 222, 235, 238, 239, 256, 259, 260, 272, 275, 281, 283, 316, 317, 318, 320, 322, 324.

229. OPTIONAL PROTOCOL

See entry for **Protocol**

230. ORGANIZATION FOR SECURITY AND COOPERATION IN EUROPE (OSCE)

Definition: An international political organization made up of the United States, Canada and about 51 states in Europe for the purposes of providing a political forum for discussion of issues involving conflict prevention and crisis management in member states in Europe. It exists to enhance peace, security and stability in Europe. Until 1994, the OSCE was called the Conference on Security and Cooperation in Europe (CSCE). It has a strong human rights component.

Significance: The OSCE is an organization set up after World War II to settle borders, repatriate refugees and avoid an outbreak of military hostilities between East and West, especially during the Cold War. It continued to have great political importance following the breakup of the former USSR.

The OSCE has always had a component that deals with human rights problems, especially in Central and Eastern Europe. It formerly served as a forum for Eastern bloc–Western bloc discussions of issues, including human rights. This organization based its human rights activities on the Helsinki Final Act of 1975. It has had an increasingly important human rights component, developed in the 1980s and 1990s, known as the Helsinki Human Dimension Mechanisms, and it established a High Commissioner for Minorities. This system relies on existing international human rights standards, such as the UDHR and two U.N. international covenants.

The OSCE (CSCE) was the political forum through which the West was able to get the USSR to allow the exodus of Soviet Jewry to the West in the 1980s. It has been deeply involved in issues of national and ethnic minorities in such places as Chechnya, Bosnia and Kosovo.

The United States monitors the activities of the OSCE through its own agency called the Commission on Security and Cooperation in Europe.

The OSCE has set up an Office of Democratic Institutions and Human Rights (ODIHR) in Warsaw, Poland. The U.S. works in conjunction with this body in promoting human rights in the OSCE states, particularly in the former communist countries.

See Also Terms: 3, 14, 20, 33, 34, 44, 48, 50, 68, 70, 71, 72, 86, 90, 93, 99, 100, 102, 112, 119, 120, 121, 122, 123, 124, 136, 141, 144, 145, 151, 152, 160, 167, 169, 177, 184, 185, 195, 205, 208, 210, 211, 214, 218, 222, 230, 235, 237, 240, 242, 243, 252, 259, 260, 265, 272, 283, 284, 285, 286, 287, 292, 309, 323, 324.

231. ORGANIZATION OF AMERICAN STATES (OAS)

Definition: An international political organization made up of almost all the governments of the states in North, Central and South America. The OAS discusses and takes political and legal action on matters of mutual concern to the member states, including human rights issues.

Significance: This intergovernmental organization contains a regional international human rights system known as the Inter-American human rights system. The OAS was established by the OAS Charter. (See Document 61).

The human rights system created by this Organization is primarily based on the American Declaration on Human Rights and the American Convention on Human Rights and its two protocols. See Documents 62, 63, 64, 65. (Do not confuse the American Declaration on Human Rights with the Declaration of Independence of the United States of America of July 4, 1776. When the term "American Declaration" is used in the international human rights context, it almost always refers to the OAS Declaration of 1948). The system is monitored by the Inter-American Commission on Human Rights, which sits in Washington, D.C., and the Inter-American Court of Human Rights, which sits in San Jose, Costa Rica.

The United States is a member of the Organization of American States. Through this organization the United States most closely deals with its neighbor states in the western hemisphere concerning human rights. A handful of cases have been filed in the Inter-American Commission against the United States for alleged violations of the ADHR. The decisions in the cases of *Cherokee Nation v. United States* and *Haitian Centre for Human Rights v. United States*, and documents on the *Ameziane vs. United States* cases are examples of how this system treats cases of human rights violations by the United States. See Appendix J.

This Commission has become involved in the war on terrorism by receiving complaints against the U.S. by certain terrorism detainees, particularly from Guantanamo, such as *Ameziane*, where the alleged violations are taking place within the geographical sphere of the Commission, Cuba. The Commission has the right to handle such cases, if they are admissible, because the U.S. is a member of the OAS. The Commission's decisions are not legally binding and are seldom the subject of much press in the U.S., even though the Commission sits in Washington D.C.

See Also Terms: 11, 12, 20, 25, 26, 30, 31, 46, 48, 68, 70, 72, 74, 80, 124, 136, 144, 145, 150, 151, 152, 155, 156, 160, 165, 167, 169, 173, 184, 185, 187, 195, 205, 206, 208, 211, 222, 242, 259, 264, 272, 282, 283, 291, 292, 293, 296, 297, 306, 307, 308, 309, 316, 323.

232. PATRIOT ACT

Definition: The Patriot Act was a U.S. law enacted by the U.S. Congress on October 26, 2001, at the request of President George Bush in response to the terrorist acts of September 11, 2001. The full name is the USA Patriot Act, which stands for "Uniting and Strengthening America by Providing Appropriate Tools Required to Intercept and Obstruct Terrorism Act of 2001") See Document 88.

Significance: A law passed by the U.S. Congress right after 9/11. The Patriot Act gave controversial new powers to the Department of Justice in terms of domestic and international surveillance of American citizens and others within its jurisdiction. This act was swiftly passed in the U.S.

after the terrorist attack on the World Trade Centre. The items contained in the Act had been before Congress before 9/11 but the 9/11 attack caused a rush to pass it.

According to its sponsors, the Patriot Act was needed to respond to a situation that had not previously existed. This being the presence of terrorists within America's borders, the need to find them, arrest them and prosecute them. It was hoped that with this Act the government could catch the terrorists before they acted and harmed others. Those who opposed the Act, particularly civil liberties and electronic freedom advocates say that the Act has undone previous checks and balances on government surveillance abuses of the past and that it was unnecessarily endangering our right to privacy and chilling or discouraging free speech.

The Patriot Act increases the ability of law enforcement agencies to search telephone, e-mail communications, medical, financial, and other records; and eases restrictions on foreign intelligence gathering within the United States. It also expands the Secretary of the Treasury's authority to regulate financial transactions, particularly those involving foreign individuals and entities. It also creates broader discretion for law enforcement and immigration authorities in detaining and deporting immigrants suspected of terrorism-related acts. The Act also expands the definition of terrorism, to include **domestic** terrorism, resulting in the enlargement of the number of activities to which the USA Patriot Act's expanded law enforcement powers can be applied.

It was actually a laundry list of government actions most of which had been ruled unlawful by courts. It was the government's move to get those powers back that the judicial branch had taken from the executive branch.

There were many human rights issues with the provisions of the Act. These were vigorously opposed. Opponents of the Act criticized its authorization of indefinite detentions of immigrants; searches through which law enforcement officers search a home or business without the owner's or the occupant's permission or knowledge; the expanded use of National Security Letters, which allows the FBI to search telephone, e-mail, and financial records without a court order; and the expanded access of law enforcement agencies to business records, including library and financial records. Many lawsuits were filed against one or more provisions, and Federal courts have ruled that a number of provisions are unconstitutional.

Civil libertarians, librarians, and others have protested changes made by the Act that have the potential to lead to law enforcement abuses, including reduced judicial oversight of wiretaps, expanded law enforcement access to records held by third-party businesses and organizations. It also ambiguously broadened the criminal definition of what it meant to provide material support to terrorists. Some Patriot Act provisions have lapsed and some have been enacted into permanent law.

The main concern was that of government intruding to far into the privacy and security of Americans, and unreasonable searches and seizures. The human right to privacy and the sanctity of home and correspondence were being threatened. The U.S. discussed this issue in its Second and Third periodic reports to the U.N. Human Rights Committee under the ICCPR in 2005. (See Document 15A, on Article 17.) The report states:

USA PATRIOT ACT. In the wake of the tragedy of 11 September, 2001, Congress passed the USA PATRIOT Act primarily to provide federal prosecutors and investigators with the critical tools needed to fight and win the war against terrorism. The USA PATRIOT Act principally did four things. First, it removed the legal barriers that prevented the law enforcement and intelligence communities from sharing information. By bringing down "the wall" separating law enforcement and intelligence officials, the USA PATRIOT Act has yielded extraordinary dividends, such as by enabling the Department of Justice to dismantle terror cells in such places as Oregon, New York, and Virginia. Second, it updated federal anti-terrorism and criminal laws to bring them up to date with the modern technologies actually used by terrorists, so that the United States no longer had to fight a digital-age battle with legal authorities left over from the era of rotary telephones. Third, it provided terrorism investigators with important tools that were previously available in organized crime and drug trafficking investigations. For example, law enforcement had long used multi-point, or "roving," wiretaps to investigate non-terrorism crimes, such as drug offenses. Now, federal agents are allowed to use multi-point wiretaps, with court approval, to investigate sophisticated international terrorists who are trained to evade detection. Fourth, the USA PATRIOT Act increased the federal criminal penalties for those who commit terrorist crimes and made it easier to prosecute those responsible for funneling money and providing material support to terrorists.

The next Administration brought up the Patriot Act in its 2010 national UPR report to the OHCHR. See Document 86. In paragraphs 90 and 91 the Administration wrote:

> Protecting our national interests may involve new arrangements to confronting threats like terrorism, but these structures and practices must always be in line with our Constitution and preserve the rights and freedoms of our people. Although the departments and agencies of the U.S. Government involved in surveillance and the collection of foreign intelligence information comply with a robust regime of laws, rules, regulations, and policies designed to protect national security and privacy, significant concerns in these areas have been raised by civil society, including concerns that relevant laws have been made outdated by technological changes, and that privacy protections need to be applied more broadly and methodically to surveillance.

The 2001 USA Patriot Act expanded intelligence collection authorities under the Foreign Intelligence Surveillance Act (FISA), which regulates electronic surveillance and physical searches conducted to acquire foreign intelligence information. The U.S. Executive Branch acknowledged in 2005 that the U.S. National Security Agency had been intercepting, without a court order, certain international communications where the government had a reasonable basis to conclude that one person was a member of, or affiliated with, Al Qaeda or a member of an organization affiliated with Al Qaeda and where one party was outside the United States. In response, considerable congressional and public attention focused on issues regarding the authorization, review, and oversight of electronic surveillance programs designed to acquire foreign intelligence information or to address international terrorism. Congress held hearing and enacted new legislation, including the Protecting America Act and a series of amendments to FISA.

In the United Nations the Human Rights Council, through its Special Rapporteur on Protecting Human Rights While Countering Terrorism has questioned laws and practices such as this, and called for the U.S. to make its laws and practice comport with international human rights law norms. (See Documents 58, 87 and Scheinen Documents, Appendixes L and M)

See Also Terms: 17, 24, 30, 59, 70, 71, 75, 81, 82, 88, 90, 91, 93, 96, 99, 100, 103, 111, 113, 120, 122, 1223, 124, 134, 136, 144, 145, 151, 152, 156, 157, 159, 160, 167, 169, 175, 177, 179, 184, 185, 193, 195, 196, 198, 210, 211, 243, 250, 252, 253, 254, 255, 256, 257, 266, 272, 275, 283, 287, 299, 300, 302, 305, 306, 307, 309, 311, 323, 324.

233. PERIODIC STATE REPORT

See entry for **Report/Reporting**

234. PERPETRATOR

Definition: A person or state who commits a human rights violation. The term is sometimes used to describe one who causes such a violation to occur through others.

Significance: A perpetrator can be an individual, group or state, but the term usually refers to individuals. Individuals who cause breaches of human rights norms are perpetrators of human rights violations. This term is applicable to, for example, a policeman who tortures a suspect or a soldier who shoots an innocent civilian. Each person who is responsible for directly or indirectly perpetrating human rights violations should be held accountable before the law and corrected and deterred from future violations.

See Also Terms: 3, 10, 17, 26, 42, 48, 53, 59, 63, 64, 70, 71, 72, 81, 82, 100, 109, 110, 111, 113, 119, 120, 125, 132, 133, 144, 145, 151, 157, 159, 166, 181, 182, 184, 185, 202, 215, 221, 222, 232, 238, 248, 252, 257, 259, 266, 272, 283, 292, 293, 317, 318, 319, 320, 321, 322.

235. PERSECUTION

Definition: Harassment, affliction, injury, grief or serious deprivation intentionally caused to a person or group by the state or its agents. Persecution is the sustained or systematic, intentional violation of basic human rights.

Significance: There is no universally accepted definition of this word in the field of human rights. Its meaning depends on the legal context.

Other synonyms for persecution are oppression, torment, infliction, abuse, maltreatment and ill-treatment. Occasions of persecution against certain persons or groups have often been the reason for establishing international human rights standards. Notably, the modern human rights movement is traced particularly to the Second World War, especially the Holocaust, after which states wanted to establish rules that would not allow that type of violent and genocidal persecution to happen again.

The United States uses this term in many different contexts in dealing with human rights. One of those areas is the law of asylum, in cases before the Immigration and Naturalization Service or immigration courts, when someone has applied for status as a refugee and wishes to be granted asylum. Found in Title 8 of the U.S. Code, the law concerning asylum requires that the applicants prove they were subject to past persecution or have a well-founded fear of future persecution on account of their race, religion, nationality, political opinion or membership in a particular social group. The term persecution in this context is defined as the infliction of suffering or harm upon those who differ in a way regarded as offensive. It is defined in the U.N. High Commissioner for Refugees *Handbook on Procedures and Criteria for Determining Refugee Status* as the threat to life or freedom, or other serious violations of human rights on account of race, religion, nationality, membership in a particular social group or political opinion.

In 1998 the U.S. Congress passed, and President Clinton signed, the International Religious Freedom Act, which set U.S. foreign policy on states that engage in religious persecution. See Document 89.

In 1998 the United States was also engaged in the negotiation and drafting of the Rome Statute of the International Criminal Court. That statute was adopted by the international community by a 120 to 7 vote, with 20 abstentions. See Document 76. The United States voted against it. That statute provided for jurisdiction over crimes against humanity for widespread or systematic attacks against civilians by acts of "persecution against any identifiable group or collectivity on political, racial, national, ethnic, cultural, religion or gender," or other basis "universally recognized as impermissible under international law." (See Article 7 of the statute). Persecution is defined in the statute as "intentional and severe deprivation of fundamental rights contrary to international law by reason of the identity of the group or collectivity." This type of persecution is largely defined as a crime against humanity under customary international law, when done in a widespread or systematic fashion.

See Also Terms: 11, 12, 15, 18, 20, 22, 24, 26, 28, 29, 33, 34, 35, 48, 53, 54, 55, 56, 63, 65, 66, 70, 71, 72, 75, 78, 84, 85, 86, 101, 104, 110, 111, 113, 115, 119, 120, 122, 124, 125, 129, 132, 133, 136. 142, 143, 144, 145, 146, 147, 151, 152, 154, 160, 167, 169, 170, 171, 175, 177, 179, 181, 182, 184, 185, 188, 189, 190, 192, 195, 201, 203, 205, 216, 222, 223, 228, 238, 243, 249, 259, 260, 263, 265, 271, 272, 283, 292, 293, 294, 297, 306, 307, 309, 316, 317, 318, 320, 322, 324.

236. PERSONAL STATUS LAWS

Definition: A national law which regulates, defines and gives procedural process to determine a person's personal identity, status in society as a citizen, or marital or other social status.

Significance: In many countries of the world the legal system contains legal provisions for determining or establishing a person's identity or status in a given state. These laws can give rise to human rights violations such as prohibiting persons from becoming or being recognized as they wish to be, or forcing a person to have a status or identity he or she does not wish to have. In many such states the legal system leaves it to religions and their institutions and laws to define and establish personal status. Thus, personal status is based on religious beliefs or doctrines and not the intention or desire of the individual involved. Moreover, persons who do not belong to the religion whose rules are law on personal status, cannot usually find any alternative means for changing their status.

This often happens in the area of womens' rights, as to their marital status and nationality. Very often the personal status laws are not consistent with international human rights norms, such as CEDAW or the ICCPR. See Documents 8, 27.

See Also Terms: 11, 12, 20, 24, 28, 32, 33, 34, 35, 48, 54, 55, 67, 70, 84, 86, 89, 100, 120, 124, 126, 144, 145, 146, 147, 151, 152, 160, 167, 169, 175, 177, 179, 180, 184, 185, 195, 205, 216, 242, 243, 259, 260, 265, 272, 283, 284, 287, 292, 293, 297, 309, 312, 316, 322, 323.

237. PLURALISM

Definition: Pluralism describes a situation in which many groups of people of different races, languages, ethnicity, religious and philosophical or political opinion live together in a society and accept each other's right to be a member of society and live freely and peacefully within it.

Significance: The population of the United States is made up of people from many nations, languages, religions and political views. They have the human right to exist in the society in which they live and to exercise group autonomy so as to preserve their distinct characteristics, while still belonging to a society that calls itself "American." Pluralism is a necessary feature of a society that seeks to respect human rights. Pluralism allows every group of people the freedom to preserve, practice and nurture that which is important to them and their human identity, while still subjecting them to the jurisdiction of U.S. law, in an attempt to create a harmonious and viable society.

In international human rights law, pluralism is an implied prerequisite of a free society of legally equal human beings. It respects the uniqueness of all human beings by allowing them to possess and express their distinguishing characteristics, which are really manifestations of their inherent human dignity. The United States is a pluralist society.

The human rights principles of non-discrimination based on race, religion, or nationality and so on, as stated in ICCPR Article 2.1 and Article 26 on equality before the law and Article 27 on the rights of members of ethnic, religious and linguistic groups, are the foundational basis for a pluralistic human society. See Document 8.

See Also Terms: 11, 12, 15, 20, 22, 24, 28, 33, 34, 35, 44, 48, 55, 67, 68, 69, 70, 72, 75, 78, 86, 87, 101, 120, 122, 123, 124, 127, 139, 140, 141, 142, 144, 145, 146, 147, 151, 152, 156, 160, 163, 167, 169, 177, 179, 180, 184, 185, 205, 211, 212, 216, 222, 230, 231, 242, 243, 259, 260, 261, 265, 270, 272, 277, 283, 292, 308, 309, 316, 323, 324.

238. POLICE BRUTALITY

Definition: The use of excessive physical force causing injury or harm by members of law enforcement in the exercise of their duties.

Significance: Police are persons whom society trains, hires and places in the local public sector and on whom it relies for the protection of everyone by enforcing the existing law. Police are given legal authority by society to use force to do their job. However, they are only given the legal authority to use a type and amount of force, such as nightsticks, firearms or battering rams, that is reasonable.

Sometimes law enforcement agents use more force than they are allowed by law under the circumstances. When a person is affected by this force it can constitute police brutality. Many believe that police intentionally use excessive force either because they believe it is necessary to deal with a particular situation or because they are angry at the person who is the victim of their abuse. This type of conduct was classically depicted in the famous Rodney King beating in Los Angeles in the early 1990s. The image projected was that of police using force that was unnecessary and was inflicted to punish the victim by causing as much pain as possible.

Police brutality is a violation of human rights. It can constitute a violation of ICCPR Article 7 (torture, cruel, inhuman treatment or punishment); Article 10 on humane treatment in custody; and Article 6, if the victim dies. Police brutality is a particularly dangerous evil in society, especially when it reflects racist attitudes or an attitude that the police are above the law and a law unto themselves, not accountable to society. The Second and Third Report of the United States to the U.N. Human Rights Committee discusses U.S. law and practice under Article 7 of the ICCPR. See Document 15A.

Acts of police brutality can also constitute torture or cruel, inhuman or degrading treatment. As such, they would be human rights violations under the Convention against Torture. The United States has ratified and is bound by this treaty. The Second Report of the United States to the U.N. Committee against Torture is a recent self-examination report of the United States before that Committee. See Document 21A.

"Power corrupts and absolute power corrupts absolutely," as Lord Acton said. Sometimes the power given by society corrupts those very persons who are sworn to uphold and enforce the law. Therefore, a rule of law system with effective civilian supervision of law enforcement personnel is absolutely necessary to preserve society from the abuse of power by the police. Police brutality violates the inherent human dignity of its victims and violates the trust society places in law enforcement.

Human rights are limitations on the use of power by the state. Nowhere is there a greater danger of abuse of power than in police forces. Thus, they need to be well-trained and disciplined. There needs to be civilian oversight, a system for public complaints and accountability through the ranks. Unfortunately there are probably few places in the U.S. where the police are specifically instructed in human rights. They tend to be trained in basic U.S. Constitutional law only. Police need to be instructed in basic human rights law.

See Also Terms: 11, 12, 20, 24, 26, 33, 34, 35, 48, 53, 60, 65, 66, 70, 71, 75, 81, 82, 84, 85, 96, 104, 110, 111, 117, 120, 124, 136, 137, 144, 145, 146, 147, 151, 152, 157, 159, 160, 161, 167, 169, 170, 171, 175, 177, 179, 184, 185, 215, 222, 228, 239, 244, 253, 256, 257, 259, 261, 272, 275, 283, 289, 290, 292, 293, 297, 302, 306, 307, 309, 311, 316.

239. POLICE STATE

Definition: A state or locality whose government strictly controls everyone by threat of arrest or use of force by police or some other government force, usually backed by an extensive surveillance and intelligence network to keep track of everyone.

Significance: A police state is the opposite of a society that respects the basic human rights of all individuals. The culture of human rights is a culture that understands it does not *give* human rights to individuals but only *recognizes* that those rights inhere in all human beings. The government of a state that has this mindset will protect the rights of all individuals, both citizens and noncitizens.

Throughout history, the world has been plagued with the existence of police states, whether their governments have been to the right or the left in political philosophy. A police state and human rights cannot exist together; their basic premises are in opposition to each other.

In the aftermath of 9/11, there are those Americans who fear America may be becoming a police state. The government has much more presence and surveillance cameras are seen

POLITICAL CORRECTNESS/POLITICALLY CORRECT

everywhere. The goal of human rights is to provide for human security. That security means not just security from terrorists and those who would overturn our way of life, it also means security from our own institutions, our police, FBI and other administrative institutions. America will not become a police state as long as it respects and protects human rights in a society characterized by transparency and accountability in a rule of law system based on international human rights norms. Respect for human rights is the best preventative against a police state. But if Americans do not know their human rights they can not very well assert them and demand their respect by the state. This requires human rights education for all, at every age and situation-appropriate level. A population that knows human rights will never become a police state.

See Also Terms: 11, 12, 16, 17, 20, 24, 26, 33, 34, 35, 48, 53, 55, 58, 60, 61, 65, 66, 70, 71, 73, 75, 81, 82, 84, 85, 88, 90, 93, 103, 104, 110, 111, 113, 117, 118, 119, 120, 121, 122. 124, 133, 134, 136, 137, 144, 145, 146, 147, 148, 151, 152, 157, 159, 160, 161, 162, 167, 169, 170, 171, 177, 179, 184, 185, 188, 195, 196, 206, 212, 215, 216, 222, 228, 243, 249, 252, 253, 254, 255, 256, 259, 272, 275, 283, 292, 297, 299, 302, 309, 316, 323.

240. POLITICAL ASYLUM

Definition: A legal status, political asylum is state protection granted under national law to persons who can prove that they meet the definition of a refugee and that they have been persecuted by their home state for their political opinions or have a well-founded fear of such persecution.

Significance: This term is sometimes used loosely to refer to any type of legal asylum granted under U.S. law. However, it only refers to one of the five legal bases for being determined a refugee (race, religion, nationality, membership in a particular social group and political opinion). Political asylum is the legal protection offered by a state, such as the United States, to someone persecuted by his own state for political opinions or actions which the government is trying to suppress or persecute.

The Refugee Convention and Protocol include the definition and bases for asylum. See Documents 36, 37. See the decision in the case of *Haitian Centre for Human Rights v. United States* as an example of how the Inter-American Commission on Human Rights dealt with a case involving Haitian boat people interdicted by the United States at sea while seeking to claim political asylum in the United States in Appendix J.

See Also Terms: 11, 12, 18, 20, 29, 33, 34, 35, 48, 51, 53, 55, 70, 73, 79, 99, 100, 120, 122, 124, 141, 144, 145, 151, 152, 155, 156, 160, 167, 169, 177, 179, 184, 185, 195, 211, 219, 222, 226, 230, 235, 241, 243, 259, 260, 263, 272, 283, 292, 293, 297, 306, 307, 309, 316, 323, 324.

241. POLITICAL CORRECTNESS/POLITICALLY CORRECT

Definition: The quality of an act or message of any kind (e.g., newspaper article, television ad, speech) being consistent with a code of conduct or speech considered sensitive and proper by politically liberal standards because it would not offend any group of people.

Significance: For the most part, political correctness is an attempt to force everyone in a given social context to follow certain rules of speech and conduct in order that no one will give offense to anyone else for what they say or do. Such attempts at protecting people's sensitivities and preserving group harmony and peace run up against, and almost always violate, the human right to freedom of expression as found in UDHR, Article 19, and ICCPR, Article 19. See Documents 6, 8.

Educating people about tolerance, diversity, pluralism and broadmindedness by teaching about the human dignity and human rights of everyone is the key to changing the speech and conduct of those who would otherwise hurt or harm another group of people bearing a certain characteristic. Enforcing political correctness by setting limits on conduct or speech is usually in violation of the human rights to freely express and manifest opinions and ideas.

See Also Terms: 28, 70, 87, 211, 337, 270, 323.

242. POLITICAL HUMAN RIGHTS

Definition: A type of human right that involves the action and participation of individuals in the political processes of society, such as voting, running for office and petitioning the government to make changes.

Significance: Political human rights are found in the ICCPR at Article 25 and in the UDHR at Article 21. See Documents 6, 8. These articles guarantee to everyone the right to try to change a society for the common good by voting, running for office and bringing to the public's and government's attention issues that affect all society. Under human rights principles the source of all legal authority is the will of the people as expressed in voting, and this right to be part of the political workings of a society is necessary for proper protection against the abuse of power by the state.

See Also Terms: 11, 12, 20, 29, 33, 34, 65, 48, 60, 70, 120, 121, 122, 124, 144, 145, 146, 147, 152, 167, 169, 177, 179, 184, 185, 211, 222, 243, 259, 272, 278, 283, 287, 291, 292, 297, 306, 307, 309, 311, 316, 322.

243. POLITICAL WILL

Definition: The collective national will held and expressed by the government of a state to accomplish a certain human rights goal or to conduct its own affairs in a way consistent with its human rights obligations.

Significance: States of the world are sovereign and independent. They can decide to do something or not. Their decision to do something as a state is called the political will of a state.

States will only comply with their international obligations to respect and protect human rights if they have the political will to do so. States should have the political will to fulfill all their human rights obligations, not only within their own boundaries but also outside them, by doing what they can to see that other states do so as well. Human rights are the rightful concern of all states of the world because, as the preambles to the UDHR and ICCPR state, respect for human rights is *the* foundation of freedom, justice, and peace in the world.

It often seems that human rights are mere ideas or rhetoric and respect for human rights is just a sound bite that states like to throw out to improve their image. This is because states often lack the political will to act consistently with their legal obligations or even with what they proclaim as the state's policy and practice on human rights. Political will usually reflects the government's perception about what is in a state's best interest, called "national self-interest," not what is right as a matter of law or principle. It is often a matter of a government wanting to do what will keep it in office, or get it re-elected.

The concept of political will as a state's intention to respect and fulfill its human rights obligations is difficult to decipher. States often make statements or sign international treaties to show that they agree to the concepts, but the actual practice of human rights by a state are better indicators of the degree of respect for these obligations. This may or may not align with human rights law or principles.

As an example of the difficulty in measuring political will, following the U.S.-led invasion of Iraq, documents were discovered exposing confidential "kickback" deals between the Saddam Hussein regime and senior officials in the Russian government, as well as former officials and others connected with the governments of France and China, and even the U.N. administrator of the program and others connected to senior U.N. officials. As France, China and Russia each had voted against the U.S. sponsored U.N. Security Council resolution under Chapter VII of the U.N. Charter authorizing the U.S. to take force, the political will of the countries to act in the interests of human rights rather than state interest was called into question. Moreover, the "oil-for-food" scandal called into question the political will of the entire U.N. body.

An example of lack of political will involving the U.S. was the failure of the U.S. to intervene to stop the genocide in Rwanda in 1994, which killed over 800,000 human beings. Largely based on its recent disastrous experience in Somalia, the U.S. did not send in any military forces to stop the slaughter. It was also a failure of the political will of the entire international community.

In the aftermath of 9/11 the President addressed the nation and stated:

> I ask you to uphold the values of America and remember why so many have come here. We're in a fight for our principles, and our first responsibility is to live by them.

The President was stating that Americans needed to have the political will to uphold our principles, including respect for human dignity and human rights even in the aftermath of that tragic terrorism.

See Also Terms: 3, 6, 9, 10, 27, 28, 29, 34, 35, 48, 70, 72, 74, 75, 79, 89, 103, 105, 106, 108, 110, 111, 114, 118, 119, 120, 128, 138, 145, 146, 147, 152, 155, 156, 157, 158, 159, 173, 177, 179, 180, 184, 185, 187, 190, 199, 209, 211, 214, 222, 259, 262, 266, 269, 271, 272, 276, 278, 287, 288, 292, 293, 297, 305, 322, 323.

244. POSITIVE OBLIGATIONS
See entry for **Obligations (International Legal)**

245. PREAMBLE
Definition: The first part of an international human rights document that states the historical, philosophical, political or legal reasons why a treaty is being made and what the treaty is trying to accomplish. It is not a legally binding part of the treaty but is used in helping to understand, interpret and apply the treaty in actual practice

Significance: The preamble sets the tone of a document and, in that way, gives parameters to its interpretation. It states the motives (the philosophy, object and purpose) for the creation of the document. In the field of human rights law, as in many law-related fields, there is a danger of pulling things out of context to serve one's own purpose or to create "loopholes." The preamble of an international human rights document is a safeguard against that kind of action; it helps keep things in context. The preamble is not legally binding, but does present the aspirations of the people, organizations and states who are presenting it to the international community.

Preambles in treaties and declarations have a series of phrases called "consideranda" that constitute the statements of purpose. These phrases begin with words like *considering that, ... whereas, ... convinced that, ... conscious of,... recalling,* and *recognizing that.* For example, in the UDHR there is a preambular phrase that begins, "Whereas recognition of the inherent dignity and of the equal and inalienable rights of all members of the human family is the foundation of freedom, justice and peace in the world ..." See Document 6.

The preamble of treaties and declarations should always be read first when reading the text of the instrument, or even when searching for a particular article. It sets the tone and context for the whole instrument.

See Also Terms: 11, 12, 53, 54, 55, 56, 57, 70, 144, 145, 177, 179, 180, 186, 258, 259, 306, 307, 309, 323.

246. PRECAUTIONARY/INTERIM MEASURES
See entry for **Communication/Complaint Procedures**

247. PREPARATORY WORKS/TRAVAUX PRÉPARATOIRES
Definition: The written record of the diplomatic work (negotiating and drafting a treaty text) that went into the establishment a treaty instrument and that is sometimes used as an aid in the interpretation of the treaty.

Significance: The name of the written records of the creation of a treaty. It contains the legislative history, deliberations, and discussions about the wording, scope, and content of norms from which one can determine the intent of the instrument's drafters. It is also referred to as the Legislative History or the "travaux préparatoires" abbreviated as TPs.

It often happens when a state is seeking to apply a treaty that it has to interpret the treaty in light of the realities of the state. To do this, the state can look at the preparatory works to see if a particular interpretation is correct in light of the legislative history. One can find evidence of the object and purpose of a treaty which may not be evident in the preamble or text. Preparatory works help us understand what, in American law, is called legislative intent.

It is particularly important for courts to look into the preparatory works to find the correct meaning of treaty provisions so that the judicial body can correctly apply the treaty to the facts before it and correctly adjudicate the merits of case as will achieve the treaty's object and purpose. Looking at the preparatory works can give a court help in determining, for example, if water boarding is within the meaning of torture in the CAT. See Document 19.

Preparatory works are written records of what happened before a treaty's creation. One can also look to any general comments from treaty supervising bodies, such as CERD, to seek understanding of the correct interpretation and application of treaty terms, written after a treaty is created and has been applied and created jurisprudence. While preparatory works are useful tools to jurists they also assist scholars of various disciplines to understand treaties and the political and institutional processes surrounding their creation.

See Also Terms: 25, 26, 48, 52, 62, 70, 72, 94, 107, 127, 144, 145, 154, 179, 180, 184, 185, 186, 208, 222, 225, 226, 244, 245, 259, 264, 269, 272, 291, 293, 297, 306, 307.

248. PRETRIAL DETENTION

Definition: The holding of a person accused of a crime in law enforcement custody after they have been arrested and charged and until their criminal trial can take place to determine whether they are innocent or guilty.

Significance: Under international human rights law, freedom is the rule and any limitation on liberty and freedom of movement is the exception and must be legally justified by the state. The first duty of the state is respect for and protection of the human rights of all people within its jurisdiction. Under the U.S. Constitution, freedom from physical restraint is a substantive due process right guaranteed by the 5th and 14th Amendments. See Document 2. The state may not arrest, detain or otherwise exercise physical restraint on anyone unless it has a valid legal basis for doing so. Its right to do so is limited by international human rights.

Article 3 of the UDHR states: "Everyone has the right to life, liberty and security of person." Security of person is like freedom from unreasonable search and seizure under the 4th Amendment to the U.S. Constitution. Article 9 states: "No one shall be subjected to arbitrary arrest, detention or exile." Under Article 11, everyone charged with a criminal offense is presumed innocent. See Document 6.

Article 9 of the ICCPR, binding on the United States, states: "Everyone has the right to liberty and security of person. No one shall be subject to arbitrary arrest or detention." See Document 8. That Article goes on to list the particular human rights held by someone deprived of liberty. These include the right to be promptly brought before a judge and to have proceedings taken before a court (habeas corpus) so that the court may decide without delay on the lawfulness of the detention and order release if the detention is not proven lawful. The burden of proof of lawfulness is on the government. Those in pretrial detention have a right to a speedy trial and the possibility of release on bail. Those subjected to unlawful arrest have a right to monetary compensation for what they have suffered.

Article 10 sets forth the right of all persons deprived of their liberty to be "treated with humanity and with respect for the inherent dignity of the human person."

Pretrial detention should only be used to protect the public or the accused, or to assure that the accused will appear for all their criminal proceedings.

The Second and Third Reports of the United States to the U.N. Human Rights Committee under the ICCPR shows the U.S. position on its law and practice in light of Article 9 of the ICCPR. See Document 15A. See also the U.N. Body of Principles for the Protection of All Persons under Any Form of Detention. See Document 47.

Pretrial detention has become a major issue in the post 9/11 era. Many people who are suspected terrorists from the U.S. or other states have been put into detention. Some have been charged with offenses and are awaiting trial. There, the applicability to pretrial detention rules is clear. But many are not being charged and so are not actually pretrial detainees. They remain a sort of administrative detainee or a prisoner of war, though the exact status of some of them is still unclear. In any case there needs to be access to judicial process to determine status, and the continued lawfulness of the detention. Where pretrial detention does not meet the international standards there must be access to effective domestic remedies to assure compliance.

The U.S. has been much criticized in its detention programs from immigration to Guantanamo to secret detention sites. There are international standards which apply to detention, pretrial or otherwise. These standards are in effect during the so-called war on terrorism. The U.S. has an obligation to follow the international human rights standards in pretrial detention.

See Also Terms: 3, 11, 12, 17, 20, 24, 33, 34, 35, 48, 49, 53, 58, 59, 65, 66, 70, 73, 81, 82, 85, 86, 90, 93, 95, 96, 99, 100, 103, 104, 106, 110, 111, 113, 117, 120, 122, 124, 125, 127, 129, 134, 136, 144, 145, 146, 147, 150, 151, 152, 154, 155, 160, 162, 167, 169, 170, 171, 175, 177, 179, 181, 184, 185, 192, 193, 195, 196, 202, 210, 211, 216, 222, 232, 234, 238, 244, 252, 253, 254, 256, 259, 264, 266, 272, 275, 283, 287, 289, 290, 293, 294, 297, 302, 305, 306, 307, 309, 311, 316, 317, 318, 319, 320 .

249. PRISONER OF CONSCIENCE (POC)

Definition: A person who is under government custody solely because of some belief he or she holds that the government wants to suppress or eradicate. Such detention violates human rights law.

Significance: Prisoner of conscience is a term often used and probably coined by Amnesty International to describe the people for whose release from government custody they were working. It came to stand for any persons in government custody, such as in a prison, jail or other place of detention, who were being held not for what they did but for what they believed.

See Also Terms: 4, 18, 20, 24, 28, 29, 33, 34, 65, 48, 51, 70, 72, 75, 76, 81, 82, 88, 89, 90, 93, 99, 100, 113, 119, 120, 122, 123, 124, 134, 136, 144, 145, 146, 147, 148, 151, 152, 160, 161, 162, 167, 169, 175, 177, 179, 194, 185, 188, 193, 195, 196, 198, 211, 215, 222, 235, 238, 239, 240, 243, 252, 253, 254, 256, 259, 272, 283, 286, 297, 302, 305, 309, 316, 323 .

250. PRISONER OF WAR (POW)

Definition: A member of the armed forces who has fallen into the hands or power of his adversary by capture, surrender, wounds or unconsciousness.

Significance: A prisoner of war is a protected class of persons under the Geneva Convention III of 1949 and Protocol I of 1977 and is thus entitled to legal protection, humane treatment and a host of other rights by virtue of such status. See Documents 72, 73. Most commonly, prisoners of war are called by the abbreviation "POWs." POWs cannot, as a matter of international humanitarian law, be mistreated. The United States has ratified the Geneva Conventions and thus is legally obligated to treat POWs in accordance with the Geneva Convention III. The difficulty in the post 9/11 so-called war on terrorism is determining the status of captured suspects. What to call them? Why does it matter? It matters because the level of international protection of the person under international humanitarian law depends on their status: combatant or non-combatant.

The United States also uses this convention for judging how other states that have captured U.S. soldiers treat them. For example, the U.S. government used the Geneva Convention III to judge the treatment of the U.S. pilots captured by Sadaam Hussein in the Gulf War and soldiers captured in 1999 during the Kosovo crisis. Whenever one hears the U.S. government accusing another country of "violating international law" with regard to captured U.S. POWs, it is usually referring to the Geneva Convention III.

Violation of certain provisions of the Geneva Convention III can constitute grave breaches of that convention and are considered war crimes. As such, they are subject to the jurisdiction of all countries to prosecute such international crimes.

The most important questions that have arisen concern the captured detainees kept in Guantanamo. From the very beginning there were questions raised about the legal status of the detainees. The ICRC found many to be POWs and some to be civilians for whom no justification for such confinement could be raised. See entry for Combatants. Under the Geneva Conventions, when there is some doubt about status, Article 5 of the Third Geneva Convention requires that there be a judicial process to determine status. Then one knows what legal protection to which they are entitled. This was only started late in the process.

One thing for sure is that, whether one is deemed a POW or not, one has a right to protection under international human rights law and humanitarian law. There is no human being who has no human rights because of anything he or she has done. And there is no place on earth where civilians or combatants or unlawful combatants or enemy combatants have no rights.

See Also Terms: 17, 20, 23, 24, 26, 120, 124, 129, 132, 134, 135, 136, 144, 145, 151, 152, 154, 160, 166, 167, 169, 170, 171, 177, 178, 179, 181, 182, 184, 185, 192, 195, 197, 202, 203, 210, 211, 216, 222, 252, 253, 254, 256, 258, 259, 272, 275, 283, 287, 293, 294, 297, 302, 306, 307, 309, 313, 315, 316, 317, 318, 319, 320, 322, 323.

251. PRIVACY (RIGHT TO)

Definition: A human right which protects the ability of an individual to act within a settled framework without fear of arbitrary or unforeseeable interference.

Significance: The right to privacy is a need of every human being. Everyone needs a reasonable space in their life where there is no unwarranted or unreasonable intrusion by either the government or anyone else. It is a place where the state cannot go. It is a place where no other individual can go unless invited or in emergency. It is the protection of a part of one's human security. Privacy is protected as a substantive human right in international human rights law. The UDHR includes protection of privacy. Article 12 of the UDHR reads:

> No one shall be subjected to arbitrary interference with his privacy, family, home or correspondence, nor to attacks upon his honour and reputation. Everyone has the right to the protection of the law against such interference or attacks.

Though that instrument was originally not a binding legal instrument, some of its norms, called the "hard core" norms, are considered legally binding under customary international law. It is arguable whether or not privacy qualifies as a hard core norm. In any case, that privacy norm has political and moral weight whether or not legally binding in the UDHR. See Document 6.

More importantly for the U.S. is the privacy provision in the ICCPR. Article 17 of the ICCPR is a legally binding norm. See Document 8. Article 17 reads:

1. No one shall be subjected to arbitrary or unlawful interference with his privacy, family, home or correspondence, nor to unlawful attacks on his honour and reputation.
2. Everyone has the right to the protection of the law against such interference or attacks.

The U.S. is bound by the legal norms of the ICCPR because the U.S. ratified that Covenant in 1992. See Document 9. The Covenant was, however, non-self-executing and no implementing legislation was passed on this privacy norm. Privacy in the U.S. is dealt with almost entirely within the terms of the U.S. Constitution as a "penumbral right" under the Bill of Rights and its 4th Amendment protection against unreasonable searches and seizures, all as interpreted by the U.S. courts, particularly the Supreme Court.

One can see how the U.S. perceives its record in relation to this privacy right by examining the U.S. Second and Third periodic reports to the U.N. Human Rights Committee regarding the ICCPR. (See Document 15A on Article 17). There the U.S. describes how it complies with the international norm of Article 17 in the U.S. legal and political context. One notices, however that it is almost exclusively about electronic surveillance and government anti-terrorism and anti-criminal activity. One has to go to the First Periodic Report in 1994 to learn about the other aspects of privacy such as contraception, abortion, bedroom privacy and the classical privacy issues. It is as though the right to privacy has been co-opted by the war on terrorism. It is, of course, a major issue for many people as to how far the government can go into our private lives and data to protect Americans from terror. The debate continues, but there are **international** standards and discourse to be factored into the debate.

In the U.S., the privacy issue has largely come to be much involved with the Patriot Act of 2002. That Act greatly expanded the U.S. government's surveillance powers. In the 2005 Second and Third Reports, the U.S. government informs the Human Rights Committee:

> USA PATRIOT Act. In the wake of the tragedy of 11 September, 2001, Congress passed the USA PATRIOT Act primarily to provide federal prosecutors and investigators with the critical tools needed to fight and win the war against terrorism. The USA PATRIOT Act principally did four things. First, it removed the legal barriers that prevented the law enforcement and intelligence communities from sharing information. By bringing down "the wall" separating law enforcement and intelligence officials, the USA PATRIOT Act has yielded extraordinary dividends, such as by enabling the Department of Justice to dismantle terror cells in such places as Oregon, New York, and Virginia. Second, it updated federal anti-terrorism and criminal laws to bring them up to date with the modern technologies actually used by terrorists, so that the United States no longer had to fight a digital-age battle with legal authorities left over from the era of rotary telephones. Third, it provided terrorism investigators with important tools that were previously available in organized crime and drug trafficking investigations. For example, law enforcement had long used multi-point, or "roving," wiretaps to investigate non-terrorism crimes, such as drug offenses. Now, federal agents are allowed to use multi-point wiretaps, with court approval, to investigate sophisticated international terrorists who are trained to evade detection. Fourth, the USA PATRIOT Act increased the federal criminal penalties for those who commit terrorist crimes and made it easier to prosecute those responsible for funneling money and providing material support to terrorists.

With the advent of the Obama administration there came a shift in government attitude and policy. This came out in the 2010, U.S. national UPR report, which mentions privacy. See Document 86, paragraphs 18, 89–90. In that report the U.S. states:

> We also recognize that privacy is linked to free expression, in that individuals need to feel that they can control the boundaries of their self-disclosure and self-expression in order to be able to express themselves freely: surveillance, especially when practiced by a government, can lead to self-censorship. Although protecting the security of all citizens means that no individual can have an absolute right to privacy or expression, any limitations on these rights are determined in a public process, by representatives of the people in the legislature and by the courts.

It also stated in a later section dedicated only to privacy:

> Privacy
>
> Freedom from arbitrary and unlawful interference with privacy is protected under the Fourth Amendment to the Constitution and federal statutes. In addition, state and local laws

and regulations provide robust protections of individuals' right to privacy and rigorous processes to ensure that investigative authorities are undertaken consistent with the Constitution.

Protecting our national interests may involve new arrangements to confronting threats like terrorism, but these structures and practices must always be in line with our Constitution and preserve the rights and freedoms of our people. Although the departments and agencies of the U.S. Government involved in surveillance and the collection of foreign intelligence information comply with a robust regime of laws, rules, regulations, and policies designed to protect national security and privacy, significant concerns in these areas have been raised by civil society, including concerns that relevant laws have been made outdated by technological changes, and that privacy protections need to be applied more broadly and methodically to surveillance.

The 2001 USA Patriot Act expanded intelligence collection authorities under the Foreign Intelligence Surveillance Act (FISA), which regulates electronic surveillance and physical searches conducted to acquire foreign intelligence information. The U.S. Executive Branch acknowledged in 2005 that the U.S. National Security Agency had been intercepting, without a court order, certain international communications where the government had a reasonable basis to conclude that one person was a member of, or affiliated with, Al Qaeda or a member of an organization affiliated with Al Qaeda and where one party was outside the United States. In response, considerable congressional and public attention focused on issues regarding the authorization, review, and oversight of electronic surveillance programs designed to acquire foreign intelligence information or to address international terrorism. Congress held hearings and enacted new legislation, including the Protecting America Act and a series of amendments to FISA.

See Also Terms: 11, 12, 20, 24, 33, 34, 35, 48, 52, 59, 62, 70, 103, 120, 124, 127, 136, 142, 144, 145, 146, 147, 148, 151, 152, 160, 167, 169, 177, 179, 184, 185, 195, 210, 211, 222, 236, 239, 243, 259, 264, 306, 307, 309, 316, 322.

252. PROCEDURAL DUE PROCESS

See entries for **Procedural Rights** and **Due Process of Law**

253. PROCEDURAL OBLIGATIONS

See entry for **Obligations (International Legal)**

254. PROCEDURAL RIGHTS

Definition: Procedural human rights are legal rights that a person holds toward the government regarding the implementation of their rights; these rights set the manner of implementation of a substantive human right, such as by filing a complaint. They are also the rights that set forth how substantive human rights violations are remedied or how a state otherwise fulfills its international human rights obligations.

Significance: Human rights are either substantive or procedural rights. Substantive rights are what the individual has a right to do or to be free from, such as torture. Procedural rights are part of the mechanism by which the substantive rights are implemented.

The essence of a society that respects human rights and observes the rule of law is the access of individuals to the legal system and other procedures whereby they can bring their grievances and have a reasonable expectation of finding a remedy in a fair and equal manner. These procedures are essential to human rights because, without them, governments can use their ratification of international instruments as merely a public relations tool. The state must in some way be accountable to ensure that the norms to which they have become bound are fully realized by everyone. This requires a set of procedures when the rights are believed to have been violated.

The concept of procedural rights is well known to most Americans through the protections in the Constitution for due process of law. The same concept applies internationally as well and includes those monitoring and supervisory bodies, whether regional or global, that help individuals to obtain remedies for human rights violations. The states are protected in this process as well because of the laws of admissibility that are applied in the process.

Procedural rights are listed and demonstrated throughout the various documents in the Documents section of this work.

See Also Terms: 10, 11, 12, 16, 17, 20, 21, 24, 30, 33, 34, 35, 46, 49, 52, 59, 62, 70, 73, 79, 88, 90, 93, 99, 100, 107, 113, 118, 120, 124, 127, 134, 141, 142, 144, 145, 146, 147, 151, 152, 154, 155, 156, 160, 161, 162, 165, 167, 169, 177, 179, 184, 185, 187, 192, 202, 219, 222, 236, 238, 240, 244, 246, 252, 253, 256, 259, 264, 266, 267, 272, 275, 283, 289, 290, 292, 293, 296, 297, 303, 306, 307, 309, 316.

255. PROFILING

Definition: Racial or ethnic profiling refers to the discriminatory practice by law enforcement or other government officials of targeting individuals for suspicion of crime, misconduct or potential threat based on the individual's race, ethnicity, religion or national origin. Profiling is also defined as the act of suspecting or targeting a person on the basis of observed characteristics or behavior, and also refers to the law enforcement practice of detention, interdiction, or other disparate treatment of an individual on the basis of the racial or ethnic status of such individual.

Significance: Profiling, generally, whether for police or intelligence, or anti-terrorism screening is the reliance on a group of characteristics the government believes to be associated with a common crime or act of terrorism. Examples of racial profiling are the use of race to determine which drivers to stop for minor traffic violations (commonly referred to as "driving while black or brown"), or the use of race to determine which pedestrians to search for illegal contraband. Another example of racial profiling is the targeting, ongoing since the September 11th attacks, of Arabs, Muslims and South Asians for detention on minor immigrant violations in the absence of any connection to the attacks on the World Trade Center or the Pentagon.

Law enforcement agents includes persons acting in a policing capacity for public or private purposes. This includes security guards at department stores, airport security agents, police officers, or, more recently, airline pilots who have ordered passengers to disembark from flights, because the passengers' ethnicity aroused the pilots' suspicions. Members of each of these occupations have been accused of racial profiling.

Racial or ethnic profiling violates the human rights to liberty and security of person and equality before the law and non discrimination. See Document 8, ICCPR, Articles 2, 9, and 26.

Profiling can also be defined in a more general way as the act or process of extrapolating information about a person based on known traits or tendencies, outside of the criminal, terrorism context, such as in "consumer profiling." But it is primarily in the area of police, intelligence, immigration and transportation security where the human rights norms applicable to profiling are most challenged.

In its August 2010, national UPR report to the OHCHR (Document 86) the U.S. government refers to profiling in paragraphs 50–52. The Administration stated in that report:

> The United States recognizes that racial or ethnic profiling is not effective law enforcement and is not consistent with our commitment to fairness in our justice system. For many years, concerns about racial profiling arose mainly in the context of motor vehicle or street stops related to enforcement of drug or immigration laws. Since the September 11, 2001 terrorist attacks, the debate has also included an examination of law enforcement conduct in the context of the country's effort to combat terrorism. Citizens and civil society have advocated forcefully that efforts by law enforcement to prevent future terrorist attacks must be consistent with the government's goal to end racial and ethnic profiling."

Defining racial profiling as relying "solely" on the basis of race, ethnicity, national origin or religion can present problems. This definition found in some state racial profiling laws is unacceptable, because it fails to include when police act on the basis of race, ethnicity, national origin or religion in combination with an alleged violation of all law. Under the "solely" definition, an officer who targeted Asian drivers who were speeding would not be racial profiling because the drivers were not stopped "solely" because of their race but also because they were speeding. This would eliminate the vast majority of racial profiling now occurring. Racial profiling does not refer to the act of a law enforcement agent pursuing a suspect in which the specific description of the suspect includes race or ethnicity in combination with other identifying factors.

Many communities have adopted laws to deal with this illegal practice, and some make racial profiling training available to their law enforcement agencies, as all should do.

Racial profiling laws are generally adopted voluntarily. They also vary from place to place. For example, racial profiling laws may require police to report certain information for analysis, such as: The name, address, gender, and the officer's subjective determination of the race of the person stopped, for example Caucasian, African-American, Hispanic; the alleged traffic violation that led to the stop; the make and year of the vehicle; the date, time and location of the stop; whether a search was conducted of the driver or passenger, and if so whether it was with consent or otherwise; the name and badge number of the police officer.

Racial profiling has been the subject of various U.N. resolutions and human rights reports by Special Rapporteurs from the U.N. Human Rights Council. See Document 54–56, 58 and Appendixes L and M on the war on terrorism and other report documents. The U.S. has been particularly criticized in the international community as engaging in acts of racial or ethnic profiling of Arabs, especially in the aftermath of 9/11.

See Also Terms: 11, 12, 17, 20, 22, 24, 33, 34, 35, 48, 55, 59, 70, 72, 78, 86, 90, 93, 95, 99, 100, 101, 111, 113, 117, 120, 124, 136, 142, 144, 145, 146, 147, 151, 155, 160, 167, 169, 177, 179, 184, 185, 188, 195, 205, 210, 211, 216, 222, 232, 243, 252, 253, 254, 257, 259, 260, 261, 265, 272, 277, 283, 289, 290, 292, 293, 299, 300, 306, 307, 309, 311, 316, 324.

256. PROLONGED ARBITRARY DETENTION

Definition: Holding a person in government custody indefinitely or for an unreasonably long period of time without any valid legal basis for doing so, or even without any charges being filed or criminal proceedings pending.

Significance: Under human rights theory, freedom and liberty are the rule or norm, and restrictions on freedom are the exception and must be carefully limited and scrutinized by the legal system.

The government may take a person under its power and into its custody, depriving that person of liberty, only if it has a proper and valid legal basis for doing so. And even if it has the right to take a person into custody, it may only hold that person only so long as permitted by law. Once a person is arrested on criminal charges, under the Constitution that person must be charged and tried within a reasonable time and can only have their liberty limited by jail or prison for so long as the law allows. If the government holds a person too long, such as beyond the time of a jail sentence, or does not file any charges, then it would most likely be considered a prolonged arbitrary detention. The person held would then have the right to seek their release by a habeas corpus action.

Such detention may violate certain provisions of the U.S. Constitution (4th, 5th, 8th, and 14th Amendments) and even a U.S. state constitution, but it is also a violation of human rights norms binding upon the United States under the International Covenant on Civil and Political Rights (ICCPR). See Documents 2, 8. It could constitute a violation of Article 7 on cruel and inhuman treatment or punishment and Article 9 on liberty and security of person.

Article 9 states:

1. Everyone has the right to liberty and security of person. No one shall be subjected to arbitrary arrest or detention. No one shall be deprived of his liberty except on such grounds and in accordance with such procedures as are established by law.

2. Anyone who is arrested shall be informed, at the time of the arrest, of the reasons for his arrest and shall be promptly informed of the charges against him.

3. Anyone arrested or detained on a criminal charge shall be brought promptly before a judge of other officer authorized by law to exercise judicial power and shall be entitled to trial within a reasonable time or to release. It shall not be the general rule that persons awaiting shall be detained in custody, but release may be subject to guarantees to appear for trial; at any other stage of the judicial proceedings . . . .

4. Anyone who is deprived of his liberty by arrest or detention shall be entitled to take proceedings before a court in order that the court may decide without delay on the lawfulness of his detention and order his release if the detention is not lawful.

Prolonged arbitrary detention violates Article 9 and cannot be justified. This general protection under Article 9, paragraph 1 applies to all persons under detention, whether administrative or criminal. It applies to the detainees at Guantanamo detention. The human rights norm prohibiting prolonged arbitrary detention does not cease to apply during wartime and nothing in the so-called war on terror changes this. When a person is detained they should be promptly processed and interrogated for information and released if they have done nothing criminal. If they have done something criminal they should be promptly charged and promptly prosecuted. Those detained specifically for having committed criminal acts should be charged and prosecuted. Many of the Guantanamo spent their whole time of confinement in Camp Xray never to have had any intelligence information to divulge and no basis for any criminal charges. Some were initially detained by mistake. The detainees were not granted rights under the ICCPR because the U.S. mistakenly believed that the ICCPR did not apply in Guantanamo. It did apply. No title of enemy combatant or fact that Guantanamo is under ultimate Cuban sovereignty change this legal truth.

The United States has had experiences with this human rights violation of prolonged arbitrary detention. The Marielito Cubans who came to the U.S. shores in the late 1970s were mostly convicted criminals and had no lawful right to enter the United States. They were taken into U.S. government custody. The government was unable to file any charges against many of them, and those Marielitos continued to sit in jails and prisons in the United States while the government tried to figure out what to do with them. Cuba refused to discuss taking them back and so blocked the most obvious solution, their repatriation. The U.S. government had to decide between letting these criminals go or holding them without charges. Some Marielitos filed federal habeas corpus actions to seek their release. In one well-known case, *Rodriguez-Fernandez v. Wilkinson*, the district court found that the prohibition of prolonged arbitrary detention had become customary international law. The court found from examining international human rights instruments that this was a standard to which most civilized countries subscribed and was followed as a matter of law (*opinio juris*). The district court could thus ascertain and apply such customary norms in U.S. courts. Prolonged arbitrary detention was a violation of an international norm binding on the United States.

In addition to the Marielitos, an issue of prolonged arbitrary detention arose since 9/11 concerning certain Uyghurs from China who had been held in Guantanamo. Their enemy combatant label was removed in 2004 but they remained in GITMO until 2010. The U.S. could not send them back to China because of a chance of torture, so it continued to hold them because it did not want to release them into U.S. society. After legal actions were filed and NGOs pressured the government, an arrangement was made for the release of some of them from custody into the U.S. Some will be sent to other countries. These Uyghurs did nothing wrong but spent many years in detention with no legal rights for a long time. This is what Article 9 is meant to prevent.

Oftentimes, prolonged arbitrary detention occurs because the persons in custody cannot go back to where they came from because their own country will not take them back. Others are deemed too dangerous to society or it would not be politically expedient to do so.

As for how long one must be in custody, it is up to the courts to scrutinize the facts and legal basis and make its determination. It may look at international human rights treaties as evidence of what the international customary norm is.

The Restatement of the Foreign Relations Law, Third, and the Second and Third Reports of the United States to the U.N. Human Rights Committee under the ICCPR, with its exposition by the United States as to their law and practice under these articles of the ICCPR, will more fully explain this concept in the U.S. context. See Appendix I.

The prolonged arbitrary detention norm, binding on the U.S. by its ratification of the ICCPR, will continue in full force and effect throughout the so-called war on terrorism and will follow U.S. forces everywhere they go and exercise effective control over human beings. As one expert on this subject put it:

> In the context of the so-called war on terror, it is important to recall that the ICCPR applies both in times of peace and in times of armed conflict. In its General Comment No. 31 of 29 March 2004, the Human Rights Committee clarified: "The Covenant applies also in situations of armed conflict to which the rules of international humanitarian law are applicable. While, in respect of certain Covenant rights, more specific rules of international humanitarian law may be especially relevant for the purposes of the interpretation of the Covenant rights, both spheres of law are complementary, not mutually exclusive." (A. de Zayas – Human rights and Indefinite Detention)

See Also Terms: 10, 11, 12, 16, 20, 24, 26, 33, 34, 35, 48, 49, 53, 59, 60, 63, 70, 73, 75, 81, 82, 85, 88, 90, 93, 95, 96, 99, 100, 103, 111, 113, 117, 120, 122, 124, 127, 133, 134, 136, 142, 144, 145, 146, 147, 151, 152, 160, 164, 167, 169, 175, 177, 179, 181, 182, 184, 185, 195, 210, 211, 215, 222, 223, 231, 232, 235, 238, 239, 243, 249, 252, 253, 254, 259, 264, 272, 275, 283, 289, 290, 292, 293, 294, 297, 302, 306, 307, 309, 316.

257. PROPORTIONALITY

Definition: A principle running throughout international rights and humanitarian law. It is the principle that a state and its agents (such as armed forces, police, judges, legislators and government bureaucrats) are only permitted to take measures (for example, enactment of a criminal prohibition of certain conduct, or imposition of a criminal penalty, or an act of armed self defense, or setting a tax rate), wherein the measure taken constitutes a reasonable, fair and justly measured response or solution to a particular problem or societal need.

Significance: The principle of proportionality seeks to limit the actions of government to the least possible intrusion and interference with individual freedom. Human Rights are a balance between the interests of state, such as protection from crime and national security, and individual human rights and fundamental freedoms. Freedom is the rule; government limitations are the exception in human rights philosophy. It requires that the particular measure taken by government must be able to meet the needs of society while minimally burdening freedom, broadly defined. For example, sentencing a criminal to death for shoplifting a candy bar would violate the principle of proportionality because the measure to be taken, that is, death, is not proportional to the seriousness of the crime. It is a safeguard against the unlimited use of legislative and administrative powers and considered to be something of a "rule of common sense," by which an administrative authority may only act to exactly the extent that is needed to achieve its objectives. More specifically, the principle of proportionality means that any measure by a public authority that affects a basic human right must be appropriate in order to achieve the objective which is intended.

This principle is particularly applicable in the Law of Armed Conflict or Humanitarian Law. In this body of law the principle of proportionality requires that a military action be a measured action aimed at achieving a necessary military objective with the least amount of civilian (collateral) damage. Dropping a nuclear bomb on a lightly defended enemy city with little military value would probably not be proportional to the military objective/advantage sought and would likely violate this principle. This principle seeks to regulate the use of state power exercised through criminal laws, military force, police action and judicial action to only that which is reasonably necessary to protect society.

Whenever one examines a state measure aimed at achieving a particular goal, one must always ask not only whether the goal is legitimate, such as public safety, but must determine if the measure is proportional to that goal. Very often, states choose measures which are disproportionate and are thus invalid. One should ask whether the measure is proportional. In the so-called war against terrorism this is particularly important, as in urgent times governments often take urgent and disproportionate measures which intrude too deeply into liberty. The more powerful a state is, the more likely it is to take disproportionate measures.

See Also Terms: 11, 12, 20, 24, 26, 30, 38, 40, 48, 59, 63, 64, 70, 72, 73, 96, 103, 104, 110, 124, 129, 132, 137, 145, 151, 152, 154, 164, 177, 179, 181, 182, 184, 185, 192, 201, 222, 226, 244, 259, 272, 283, 291, 292, 293, 306, 307, 317, 318, 321, 323.

258. PROTOCOL

Definition: An international legal instrument that modifies or amends an international human rights treaty, such as by adding other human rights or adding a new way of implementing the treaty rights.

Significance: International legal instruments known as treaties are contracts between two or more states, governed by international law. Over the course of time, states may wish to change the treaty. They may wish to add more human rights to be included under the treaty's protection, or they may wish to modify or delete something in the treaty. They may also wish to add a new way for implementing the treaty norms, such as adding a reporting procedure whereby a state must report to the treaty supervising body how it is complying with its treaty obligations. Or, the protocol may set up a new organ, such as a commission or a court, to handle formal complaints by individuals or states claiming a state violated the treaty. They do this by means of drafting, signing and ratifying an international legal instrument called a protocol. Because a protocol is itself an international legal instrument, it must go through all the formalities of a treaty (*see* Appendix F, How an International Human Rights Norm Becomes U.S. Law).

One of the four documents of the International Bill of Rights is the First Optional Protocol to the ICCPR. See Document 10. This protocol adds to the ICCPR the procedural right of individuals who are victims of violations to file complaints against their state if their state has ratified the optional protocol. ("Optional" just means that a state that ratifies the ICCPR has the option to ratify the protocol or not). The United States has ratified the ICCPR but not the First Optional Protocol.

When examining an international human rights treaty, one must also examine and apply any protocols to that treaty. They are subject to all the principles and rules regarding the interpretation and application of treaties, such as the principals of effectiveness and *Pro Homine*. See Introduction and Appendix E.

See Also Terms: 2, 11, 25, 52, 62, 70, 94, 98, 129, 132, 154, 177, 178, 179, 180, 184, 185, 191, 192, 220, 222, 225, 226, 229, 231, 244, 259, 262, 264, 269, 272, 279, 280, 287, 291, 293, 297, 306, 307, 317.

259. PUBLIC INTERNATIONAL LAW

Definition: A system of rules and customary practices that regulate relations between states, or between states and international organizations, such as the United Nations, based generally on the consent of sovereign and equal states. Also called just International Law, or the Law of Nations, or *Lex Gentium*.

Significance: International human rights law is one part of the body ("corpus") of public international law. It includes the law of treaties, the law of creation of customary international legal norms, and general principles of law recognized by most civilized societies. This body of law is based on the concept of the acceptance and consent to be bound to such law by sovereign and equal independent states.

Most commonly, this system is simply referred to as international law. However, international law has two parts: public and private. Human rights norms are found in the public side of international law. Human rights norms get their legal status by being established under international law, and then they usually are transformed or incorporated into national legal systems.

Human rights norms found in public international law are to be transformed or incorporated and implemented by states into national law so that they can be fully implemented at the national level.

See in Appendix J the decisions in the cases of *Kadic v. Karadzic, Chuckie Taylor, and Kiobel,* as examples of how U.S. courts deal with public international law in light of U.S. domestic (national) law.

See Also Terms: 2, 6, 8, 10, 11, 12, 15, 20, 23, 25, 29, 30, 31, 32, 33, 37, 38, 39, 40, 41, 42, 44, 45, 46, 47, 48, 49, 52, 53, 54, 55, 56, 57, 60, 62, 63, 64, 66, 68, 69, 70, 71, 72, 73, 74, 77, 80, 84, 85, 86, 88, 90, 91, 92, 93, 94, 95, 97, 98, 99, 100, 107, 113, 114, 123, 124, 127, 128, 129, 130, 131, 132, 133, 135, 136, 141, 142, 143, 144, 145, 146, 147, 150, 151, 152, 153, 154, 158, 160, 165, 166, 167, 169, 170, 171, 172, 173, 174, 175, 177, 178, 179, 180, 181, 182, 183, 184, 185, 186, 187, 190, 191, 192, 193, 196, 197, 198, 201, 202, 203, 204, 205, 208, 211, 214, 215, 218, 219, 220, 221, 222, 223, 224, 225, 226, 229, 230, 231, 233, 240, 242, 243, 244, 245, 246, 247, 253, 254, 256, 257, 258.

260. RACIAL DISCRIMINATION

Definition: Article 1 of the Convention on the Elimination of All Forms of Racial Discrimination (CERD) defines racial discrimination as "any distinction, exclusion, restriction or preference based on race, colour, descent or national or ethnic origin which has the purpose or effect of nullifying or impairing the recognition, enjoyment or exercise, on an equal footing, of human rights and fundamental freedoms in the political, economic, social, cultural or any other field of public life." See Document 23.

Significance: Racial discrimination in the United States is most evident in the early days of the nation when slavery was permitted. To this day there are still reported manifestations of racial discrimination present in the United States, though as a matter of U.S. law, racial discrimination is no longer permitted in all public and most private sectors of U.S. society.

Racial discrimination is a denial of the inherent dignity and equality of all human beings. It is not permitted under international human rights law, such as CERD, except in very rare exceptions. For any distinction on the basis of race to be permissible, there must be a verifiable, reasonable and objective justification for such a measure and no feasible non-discriminating alternative. Under such a test, few racially discriminatory measures would be permissible. The United States has ratified CERD, and it is now part of U.S. law.

Examination of the text of CERD does say that race-related affirmative action programs are not necessarily invalid as measures of racial discrimination. Article 1, paragraph 4, states:

Special measures taken for the sole purpose of securing adequate advancement of certain racial or ethnic groups or individuals requiring such protection as may be necessary in order to ensure such groups or individuals equal enjoyment or exercise of human rights and fundamental freedoms shall not be deemed racial discrimination, provided ... that such measures do not, as a consequence, lead to the maintenance of separate rights for different racial groups and that they shall not be continued after the objectives for which they were taken have been achieved.

If an affirmative action measure is aimed objectively and in good faith at remedying *past* racial discrimination, then such a measure is not "discrimination" so long as it is done pursuant to this article. This principle makes clear that the word "discrimination" has a negative element to it. It is not merely a race-based distinction between two persons or two types of people. The word implies that such distinction is made along with an anti-racial attitude (animus) that wants to do evil to another disliked race. Under international human rights law, race-based affirmative action programs are not discrimination and not acts of racial discrimination if done for the right reason and duration. This would counter an assertion that any race-based affirmative action programs are "reverse discrimination." CERD says they may not be discrimination at all, as discrimination is defined in the field of human rights applicable to the United States. See Document 23.

It should be noted that CERD would permit certain distinctions, exclusions, restrictions or preferences between citizens and noncitizens (CERD, Article 1, para 2).

The Second and Third Reports of the United States to the U.N. Human Rights Committee under the ICCPR, Document 15A, shows how the United States sees itself regarding its law and practice under ICCPR, Article 2. See also General Comments 15(27) and 23(27) of the U.N. Human Rights Committee concerning racial discrimination in Appendix E.

The U.N. also deals with issues of racial discrimination in the context of the Human Rights Council, established in 2006. The Human Rights Council deals with various discrimination issues under its "special mechanisms." These mechanisms include special rapporteurs, special representatives of the Secretary General, independent experts or working groups of five experts. They include a Special Rapporteur on Contemporary Forms of Racism, Racial Discrimination, Xenophobia and Related Intolerance, whose mandate is set by the Council. This person prepares studies about issues within the frame of reference of his or her mandate and reports back to the Council, who uses the rapporteur's work as a starting point for discussions and action regarding certain theses and countries. The rapporteur makes reports periodically or when specifically asked by the Council. It also includes a Working Group on People of African Descent.

In 2009, the Special Rapporteur, Mr. Doudou Diéne, made a fact-finding trip to the United States to examine the situation of racial discrimination in America. His report, set forth in Appendix L, shows how someone from the outside sees America from the prism of international human rights law in the area of race relations.

There was a U.N. World Conference Against Racism, Racial Discrimination, Xenophobia and Related Intolerance in 2001 held in Durban, South Africa (Durban I) to address the problem of racial discrimination. This conference was problematic for the U.S. for different political reasons, especially discussion of compensation for slavery and the actions of Israel towards Palestinians, but when the conference became overshadowed by nations and NGOs utilizing it as a platform to criticize and target Israel, the U.S. delegation, among others, withdrew from the conference. In the end, the Conference issued the Durban Declaration and Programme of Action (DDPA) to push elimination of racial intolerance and wrongdoing in the world, however many considered it seriously flawed for being highly critical of Israel. See Document 52.

In 2009 the U.N. held a follow-up conference to assess the progress made since the first Durban conference (Durban II). The Obama Administration attended the preparatory committee for the conference with the intention of attending the conference; however they and other foreign governments were concerned with a number of issues in the draft outcome document prepared by the preparatory committee. In particular, they were concerned that the draft included references reaffirming the importance of the DDPA adopted by the first Durban conference in 2001, a disproportionate focus on the problem of racism by Israel, and references to the problem of the 'defamation of religions.' While the draft final outcome document for Durban II removed the latter two issues, reference to the DDPA remained, which was a cause of concern for many Western nations that felt it had unjustly targeted Israel as racist, and references to "defamation" were merely repackaged as "incitement." Consequently, as the conference drew near the U.S. decided not to attend.

As many of the nations involved in the preparations for Durban II chose to focus on a perceived link between "defamation of religions" and racism, serious steps to address racism in places such as India, Burma, Indonesia, Sudan, Egypt, China, and elsewhere, where entire ethnic communities have been the victims of discrimination, often directed by the government, were largely ignored at the conference. Laws preventing religions from being defamed exist as "blasphemy laws" in many OIC countries. (This issue is discussed further under "Religious Discrimination"). While there are clearly negative societal attitudes about religion that may at times involve racial communities that are identified by this religion, a legitimate discussion about how to address this intersection was not discussed in the Durban II process. The OIC began to move this issue into Durban II and link defamation with racism to provide greater justification for these domestic laws at the international level, which are often in place solely to limit the freedom of speech and religion of those who dissent from the state's interpretation of a particular religious belief, not to encourage social harmony among diverse religious and ethnic communities.

Since the attacks of 9/11, the issue of racial discrimination has arisen in the context of how Arabs and others associated with the Muslim community are treated, as noted above in the debate over Durban II. In its 2010 UPR national report to the OHCHR for the UPR process (See Document 86) the Administration reports about its efforts regarding racial discrimination at paragraphs 35–36 as follows:

> We have worked to ensure fair treatment of members of Muslim, Arab-American, and South Asian communities. The U.S. Government is committed to protecting the rights of members of these groups, and to combating discrimination and intolerance against them. Examples of such measures include the Justice Department's formation of the 9/11 Backlash Taskforce and civil rights work on religious freedom (e.g., bringing a case on behalf of a Muslim school girl to protect her right to wear a hijab); the civil rights outreach efforts of the Department of Homeland Security; and the Equal Employment Opportunity Commission's enforcement efforts to combat backlash-related employment discrimination which resulted in over $5 million for victims from 2001–2006.
>
> At our UPR consultations, including the meeting in Detroit, Michigan, Muslim, Arab-American, and South Asian citizens shared their experiences of intolerance and pressed for additional efforts to challenge misperceptions and discriminatory stereotypes, to prevent acts of vandalism, and to combat hate crimes. The federal government is committed to ongoing efforts to combat discrimination: the Attorney General's review of the 2003 Guidance Regarding the Use of Race by Federal Law Enforcement Agencies (discussed below), as well as efforts to limit country-specific travel bans, are examples.

It can be pointed out, however, that currently, international law does not recognize religious communities such as Muslims as a racial group for purposes of the Racism Convention, even though they do have specific rights as a racial group within the context of their ethnic identity albeit it South Asian, Arab or other. The distinction between religious discrimination and racial discrimination was made in the U.N. as part of the process of establishing the two documents that deal with this issue: ICERD and the 1981 Declaration on the Elimination of All Forms of Intolerance and Discrimination Based on Religion or Belief. In distinguishing the two concepts, many observers have noted the immutable characteristic of race, whereby religion is a matter of belief which can be changed by the individual. Conflating the two terms by not distinguishing between an individual's religious and racial identity could lead to violations of an individual's right to choose or change their religious beliefs. Race is not religion. Though a person is a Muslim he or she is not necessarily of the Arabic race. Though one is of the Arabic race one is not necessarily Muslim. There is a problem with mixing these two concepts of race and religion.

261. RACISM/RACIST

Definition: Racism is the belief that race is the primary factor in determining human characteristics and abilities, and that racial differences produce an inherent superiority of a particular race. Such a belief leads to intolerance, discrimination and persecution based on race. A racist is a person holding such a belief and attitude. Racism is also defined as a set of mistaken assumptions, opinions and actions resulting from the belief that one group is inherently superior to another. It includes not only attitudes but the structures in society which exclude, restrict and discriminate against individuals on account of race.

Significance: Equality is one of the foundational principles of human rights. Under international human rights law every human being is born with human dignity and possesses that dignity all his or her life. As a result of that dignity, every human being is equal with every other human being. Racism, on the other hand, is a belief and attitude that does not accept that all human beings are of equal dignity and worth and possess the same legal rights. It is an attitude inconsistent with the core of human rights. Any idea that any group or type of human being is superior to any other is dangerous and can lead to intolerance, social division, strife and violence all the way to the point of genocide, the act of trying to destroy a racial group in whole or part.

Race is a term that is broadly defined in international human rights law, particularly in the Convention on the Elimination of All Forms of Racial Discrimination, where race is broadly defined as including "race, colour, descent, or national or ethnic origin." See Document 23. Race is not just the color of one's skin.

Modern human rights law was largely the product of the world's reaction to the Holocaust of World War II. It was believed that the actions of the Nazi regime in killing six million Jews and six million others, such as homosexuals, Gypsies, Catholics and Jehovah's Witnesses, was based on a belief that the Aryan race, of which Germans were part, was superior to all other races. It looked at Jews primarily as a race of people, and a race that jeopardized the safety and security of the Aryan race and thus had to be destroyed. It looked at Negroes as genetically defective and inferior to the blond Aryans. The Final Solution ensued. This historical lesson taught the United States that racism is an evil that must be eradicated. If left unchecked it can again lead to evil, in the United States as well as elsewhere. The killing of almost a million Tutsis in Rwanda in 1994 proved that the world was still capable of genocidal racism, as that term is broadly defined.

The international community has called upon all states, including the United States, to teach human rights to everyone as the solution to racism, thereby creating attitudes of racial tolerance. Racial tolerance and an attitude of racial equality is the opposite of racism, and its solution. The ICCPR, Article 2.1 on nondiscrimination, Article 20 on prohibition of incitement of racial discrimination or violence, Article 26 on equality before the law, and Article 27 on ethnic minorities, supplements the protection of CERD. The United States is bound by both CERD and the ICCPR. See Documents 8, 23.

The U.N. is dealing with racism through the Human Rights Council and its special mechanisms, particularly the Special Rapporteur on Contemporary Forms of Racism, Racial Discrimination, Xenophobia, and Related Intolerance. The Durban World Conference against Racism of 2001 covered this topic and issued the Durban Declaration and Programme of Action. See Document 52. A follow-up conference was held in 2009.

167, 169, 163, 177, 179, 181, 182, 184, 185, 188, 205, 212, 216, 222, 223, 228, 230, 231, 235, 237, 243, 244, 255, 259, 260, 263, 264, 270, 272, 277, 283, 289, 290, 297, 306, 307, 308, 309, 311, 316, 323, 324.

262. RATIFICATION

Definition: The formal legal act of a state to decide and express its consent to accept the legal obligations contained in a treaty. Under the U.S. Constitution, after the President or his representative signs a treaty, that signing must be ratified by the representatives of the U.S. citizenry. The ratification of a treaty signed by the President is undertaken by the U.S. Senate under Article II, Section 2 of the Constitution. This is accomplished when the Senate votes by a two-thirds majority to give its "advice and consent" to the treaty.

Significance: Human rights are contained in instruments called treaties, which are international legal instruments. In order for a state to be bound to obey, or to fulfill, its obligations under a treaty, the state must formally express its acceptance of those legal obligations to the international body establishing that treaty. This usually involves the state going through its national legal (constitutional) processes to formally ratify the act of the head of that state in signing the treaty on behalf of the state.

Under the U.S. Constitution, after the President signs a treaty that signature must be ratified by the representatives of the U.S. citizenry, the Senate.

The ratification is set forth in an "Instrument of Ratification," which is transmitted to and deposited with that person or institution stated in the treaty. See Document 8 Articles 48–49, and Document 9, the U.S. ratification of the ICCPR. Ratifications also often contain "reservations, declarations and understandings" that qualify the legal obligations assumed by the ratifying state. The United States only becomes legally bound to obey the treaty after it has ratified and submitted its instrument of ratification. This ratification usually enters into force as to the United States after a certain number of days after deposit of that instrument of ratification. See the ICCPR, Article 49.2.

Sometimes the words "approval" or "acceptance" or "adhesion" or "accession" are used. They all mean the act of accepting to become legally bound by a treaty.

Regarding accession, the U.S. acceded to the Protocol Relating to the Status of Refugees in 1968. Accession has the same legal effect as ratification, but is not preceded by an act of signature. Accession is also done by states who have not participated in the drafting of a treaty. The formal procedure for accession varies according to the national legislative requirements of the State.

See Also Terms: 2, 11, 25, 26, 27, 31, 48, 52, 53, 54, 55, 56, 57, 62, 70, 74, 98, 114, 129, 144, 145, 146, 151, 154, 158, 167, 169, 175, 175, 179, 180, 184, 185, 211, 220, 222, 225, 226, 229, 244, 258, 259, 264, 269, 272, 279, 280, 287, 288, 291, 293, 297, 306, 307, 308, 316.

263. REFUGEE

Definition: Generally speaking, a refugee is a person who flees from his country to another, seeking safety and protection from the things from which he fled (persecution, civil war, poverty). Most often it is used in the United States in the sense of someone who is seeking asylum in the United States. Asylum is legal protection offered by one country to someone who fled there from another country because of persecution. In order to receive asylum in the United States, a person has to meet the criteria of being a refugee. In United States law, a refugee is defined as "any person who is outside any country of such person's nationality, or in the case of a person having no nationality, is outside any country in which such person last habitually resided, and who is unable or unwilling to return to, and is unable or unwilling to avail himself or herself of the protection of that country because of persecution or a well-founded fear of persecution on account of race, religion, nationality, membership in a particular social group or political opinion..." (8 USC sec. 1101(a)(42)).

Significance: It is important not to confuse the terms immigrants, aliens, illegal aliens and refugees. They are not the same.

The term refugee has come to signify for many anyone who left their country to come to the United States to stay here. In U.S. law, refugees are in one of two categories: (1) conventional or statutory refugees who meet the legal criteria for being determined to be "refugees" on one of the five bases in the immigration statute; or (2) someone who left or fled their country primarily to find better economic possibilities here in the United States. These are commonly referred to as "economic refugees." Economic refugees are not entitled to asylum in the United States, because they do not meet the legal definition of refugee.

The decision in the case of *Haitian Centre for Human Rights v. United States* is an example of an international human rights case involving the United States and refugees. See Appendix J.

See Also Terms: 11, 12, 18, 20, 24, 29, 33, 34, 35, 37, 51, 53, 54, 55, 70, 72, 73, 78, 79, 81, 82, 84, 86, 88, 90, 92, 93, 99, 100, 101, 102, 113, 120, 122, 124, 125, 126, 129, 133, 136, 139, 142, 144, 145, 146, 147, 148, 151, 154, 155, 156, 160, 167, 169, 175, 176, 177, 178, 179, 180, 181, 182, 184, 185, 188, 192, 195, 203, 211, 216, 219, 222, 230, 231, 238, 239, 240, 242, 243, 252, 253, 254, 256, 259, 260, 261, 264, 265, 272, 283, 287, 289, 290, 292, 293, 297, 302, 306, 307, 309, 311, 316, 323, 324.

264. REGIONAL HUMAN RIGHTS SYSTEM OR REGIME

Definition: An international organization of states that creates, adopts and puts into effect an international human rights treaty (convention) and a system of organs and procedures for implementing it, to be applied only within a certain geographical territory, such as Europe, the Western Hemisphere, or Africa. Such a system is contrasted with a "global" or "universal" human rights regime or system, such as under the United Nations.

Significance: See Appendix D for a chart of the regional human rights systems.

The United States is a member of one regional human rights system: The Organization of American States. A handful of cases have been filed against the United States in that system before the Inter-American Commission on Human Rights. A sample of three cases of the Commission concerning alleged violations of the ADHR by the United States are found in excerpted form in Appendix J.

See Also Terms: 11, 12, 20, 25, 26, 33, 46, 48, 52, 68, 70, 72, 74, 80, 90, 92, 93, 99, 100, 107, 112, 113, 114, 122, 123, 124, 126, 133, 136, 144, 145, 150, 151, 152, 156, 160, 165, 167, 169, 173, 175, 177, 184, 185, 186, 187, 198, 205, 206, 208, 211, 222, 225, 226, 227, 231, 233, 242, 243, 244, 246, 247, 253, 254, 258, 259, 262, 267, 268, 269, 272, 280, 282, 283, 287, 291, 292, 293, 296, 297, 306, 307, 308, 309, 316, 322, 323.

265. RELIGIOUS DISCRIMINATION

Definition: The 1981 U.N. Declaration on the Elimination of All Forms of Intolerance and Discrimination Based on Religion or Belief, defines the term religious discrimination and intolerance as follows:

> any distinction, exclusion, restriction, or preference based on religion or belief, and having as its purpose or its effect the nullification or impairment of the recognition, enjoyment, or exercise of human rights and fundamental freedoms on an equal basis.

Significance: As such, religious discrimination and intolerance does not refer to legitimate distinctions such as those made by a community in a statement of faith for membership to that community or other statements by an individual as an expression of their religious beliefs, even when these statements are offensive to others. Instead, the right focuses on any acts which have as their intention and effect the impairment of an individual's ability to have and manifest their religious beliefs, particularly as described in the 1981 Declaration. As a declaration, this definition is not a binding source of international law as such, but it is considered by most to reflect the intention of the right to freedom of religion under Article 18 of both the UDHR and ICCPR. Its frequent, unchallenged use lends support to the argument that it should be accorded very strong moral and political weight, and can be regarded as soft law, a partial guide to compliance with UDHR and ICCPR Articles 18, regarding religious discrimination and intolerance.

Note that this definition would also prohibit intolerance and discrimination based on any non religious type of belief system, such as atheism or agnosticism.

Religious intolerance and discrimination can be a violation of several different human rights, such as freedom of religion, freedom of conscience, freedom of opinion, expression, equality before the law, non discrimination, and freedom of association and assembly. See ICCPR Articles 2.1, 18, 19, 26, 27).

Religious discrimination and intolerance in the public sector is generally prohibited under U.S. law. This phenomenon is the source of much conflict, violence and discrimination in the U.S. and around the world. U.S. law not only prohibits it but U.S. foreign policy in respect to foreign aid regard religious freedom as a pillar of U.S. foreign policy under the International Religious Freedom Act of 1998. This Act looks the respect of the human rights norms in the UDHR, ICCPR and the 1981 Declaration on Religious Intolerance. See Documents 6, 8, 38.

The U.N. Declaration on the Elimination of All Forms of Intolerance and of Discrimination on the Basis of Religion or Belief was adopted on Nov. 25, 1981 (1981 Declaration). While the right to religious freedom was recognized by the U.N. in the 1948 Universal Declaration of Human Rights, the 1981 Declaration reinforces the importance of religious freedom as a fundamental human right. Work on the Declaration began in 1962 in response to an alarming increase in anti-Semitism in West Germany that quickly spread throughout Europe and the Western Hemisphere. This prompted the General Assembly to request the Commission to prepare declarations and conventions for two issues—racial discrimination and religious intolerance. The documents on racial discrimination were promptly completed; however, work on the "religious intolerance" documents moved slowly due to U.N. politics and a lack of consensus reflecting the ideological divisions between countries during the Cold War. Interest in drafting the documents on religious intolerance was revived in 1972 due to vigorous support from non-governmental organizations. However, work on the Declaration was again held back by contentious ideas of what a Declaration on "Religious Intolerance" should protect, leading the Commission to change the Declaration to its current title, which many consider less vague and subjective. The current title also covers discrimination on religious grounds. By 1979, the Commission decided to bypass the need for consensus approval in order to get the first three articles of the Declaration approved. The Commission then established a working group in 1980 to finish its work and by March 1981 the draft Declaration was finally approved.

The Declaration is part of a body of international standards that provide the defining parameters for the right to freedom of thought, conscience, religion and belief. One significant contribution of the Declaration is an extensive—though not exhaustive—list of ways in which religion or belief may be manifested, including through teaching, training or appointing religious leaders, observing holidays, using religious symbols, establishing places for worship or assembling, and soliciting or receiving voluntary contributions, among other areas. Religious intolerance and discrimination can be a violation of several different human rights, such as freedom of religion, freedom of conscience, freedom of opinion, expression, equality before the law, non-discrimination, and freedom of association and assembly under the ICCPR (see Articles 2.1, 18, 19, 26, 27).

In 1986, the U.N. Commission on Human Rights appointed a Special Rapporteur to report annually on U.N. member states' implementation of the Declaration.

The phenomenon of religious intolerance has been the source of much conflict, violence and discrimination in the world, as was seen on 9/11, when individuals justified their attacks and massive killing of innocent civilians in the name of religion, or in the case of hate crimes against individuals on the basis of their religion. Religious discrimination and intolerance in the public sector is generally prohibited under U.S. law in the Civil Rights Act of 1964, and the Department of Justice Civil Rights Division has staff specifically focused on Combating Religious Discrimination and Protecting Religious Freedom. In fact, the U.S. considers religious freedom one of the most fundamental human rights. One of the most significant pieces of U.S. legislation related to the protection against religious discrimination outside of the Civil Rights Act, was the Religious Land Use and Institutionalized Persons Act of 2000 (RLUIPA). (See Document 99.) With respect to U.S. foreign policy, the International Religious Freedom Act of 1998 (IRFA), expresses U.S. support for religious freedom as defined in the 1981 Declaration, UDHR, and ICCPR. (See Documents 6, 8, 38)

In recognizing the special place religious freedom holds in U.S. history—many individuals fled to the United States to seek freedom from religious oppression and their own freedom of religious belief—Congress established the promotion and protection of this right as a key priority in U.S. relations with foreign governments. Under IRFA, Congress established an office at the Department of State to monitor and report on violations of religious freedom throughout the world. Congress also established an independent federal agency, the U.S. Commission on International Religious Freedom, mandated to report on how U.S. officials should engage foreign governments that engage in or allow egregious and persistent violations of this right to occur. These two bodies are critical to helping the President and Secretary of State engage with foreign governments to seek improvements in the protection of religious freedom, and assists Congress in effectively conditioning foreign aid to ensure greater protection of this right. The Commission recommends particular countries to be labeled "countries of particular concern" or CPCs and the Secretary of State and President determines which countries qualify for that designation which carries with it certain requirements for conditioning future aid to that country until significant improvements are made to provide for the freedom of religion. See excerpts from 2010 CIRF country reports in Appendix L.

There is currently a movement within the Obama Administration to refer to this freedom in a more limited context as the "freedom of worship." While Administration spokesmen have claimed that they use the two terms interchangeably, this new terminology does not comport with the full extent of freedom of religion as defined in the 1981 Declaration which includes the freedom to *have* or *change* one's religious beliefs and the freedom to *manifest* that belief "either alone or in community with others and in public or private... in teaching, practice, worship and observance." The State Department's International Religious Freedom reports have long failed to understand the full scope of religious freedom in determining whether this right exists in foreign law. Often, the reports state that religious freedom exists when a more limited right, such as "freedom of worship", is used in the foreign constitution in place of the traditional religious freedom clause. The limited reference to freedom of worship does not incorporate protection for the various rights to manifest or change one's religious beliefs. Moreover, experts on international law related to religious freedom have noted that the limited definitions do not offer full protection for the right as defined under the UDHR and ICCPR to which many of those states have acceded. The right to freedom of religion includes manifesting religion by worship, practice, observance and teaching. One has a right to engage in all four, not just worship.

In its national UPR report to the OHCHR in 2010, the U.S. speaks of freedom of thought, conscience and religion. See Document 86. In paragraph 19-20, the U.S. government states:

> The desire for freedom from religious persecution has brought millions to our shores. Today, freedom of religion protects each individual's ability to participate in and share the traditions of his or her chosen faith, to change his or her religion, or to choose not to believe or participate in religious practice. Citizens continue to avail themselves of freedom of religion protections in the Constitution and in state and federal law.

See Also Terms: 9, 11, 12, 14, 18, 20, 22, 24, 28, 29, 33, 34, 35, 48, 51, 53, 54, 55, 56, 57, 59, 60, 62, 63, 69, 70, 72, 73, 74, 75, 77, 78, 86, 87, 99, 100, 120, 122, 124, 127, 129, 132, 133, 160, 167, 169, 175, 177, 179, 180, 181, 182, 184, 185, 188, 190, 192, 195, 203, 205, 211, 212, 216, 222, 228, 230, 231, 235, 237, 243, 244, 253, 255, 259, 263, 264, 270, 272, 277, 282, 283, 289, 290, 292, 293, 296, 297, 306, 307, 308, 309, 311, 316, 323, 324.

266. RENDITION

Definition: In the context of international law, regular rendition is simply the physical transfer of persons from one state's jurisdiction to another state. It involves the apprehending of a person by one state and turning them over to another state outside of the extradition procedure. Extraordinary rendition is where one state transfers an individual to another state completely outside of any legal framework.

Significance: The issue of rendition, particularly extraordinary or extra-judicial rendition, has become an important issue in relation to the war on terrorism. It has been challenged by civil society organizations and international institutions. It has been alleged that the U.S. has renditioned terrorist suspects to other states with poor human rights records for purposes of interrogation and sometimes for mistreatment in order to obtain information or to get rid of the suspect. This happens without relation to any criminal charges. It has also been alleged that the U.S. was part of whole network of extra ordinary renditions of terrorist suspects and so-called black detention sites housing unknown "ghost detainees."

Regular rendition can be legal as long as the U.S. is not sending the person to a state where his human rights are likely to be violated. Anytime a state puts a person outside of a legal framework where one can challenge the legality of the arrest and detention, and prevent the possibility of harm upon rendition, this constitutes extraordinary rendition. It is a human rights violation. Extraordinary rendition is a violation even if the state is acting in pursuant to the war on terrorism. Unfortunately some extraordinary renditions are done just for that reason, to deprive the detainee of any access to any forum which can legally challenge and halt the detention, and to keep the world from knowing what is happening to the detainees, which is usually mistreatment. It also engages the principle of non-refoulement and some humanitarian law norms, depending on the circumstances and can even constitute a crime against humanity if widespread or systematic.

The attitude of states is usually that the persons who are detained are evil and do not follow the rules and laws of war so why should the apprehending state. There is sometimes an attitude that the absolute existence of the state is at stake and that anything the state does to these individuals is justified. In addition, it is often felt that they (detainees) must be kept in the dark as much as possible so as not to inform their fellow terrorists about the methods and means of operation and whereabouts of the rendering state's counter terrorism mechanisms and apparatus. Resorting to secret detention after extraordinary rendition effectively means taking detainees outside the legal framework and rendering the safeguards contained in international instruments, most importantly habeas corpus, meaningless.

Extraordinary rendition has been the subject of the U.N. Human Rights Council through its Special Rapporteur on Protection of Human Rights While Countering Terrorism, whose mandate is just for such types of counter terrorism actions. It has also been the subject of a study by the Council of Europe which confirmed the existence of such networks involving the U.S. and certain European states.

Extraordinary rendition is prohibited under the ICCPR Articles 6, 7, 9, 10, 14, and 16; under certain customary international norms in the UDHR. See Documents 6, 8. It is a violation of several provisions of the Convention against Torture. See Document 19. All of these human rights treaty norms take into consideration the needs of states to protect the society and allow for derogation of certain rights. Other rights are absolute and allow for no derogation, and as such, violating them can never be justified for reasons of any armed conflict. States can protect society and comply with their human rights obligations. Human rights are inherent, inalienable and universal.

In its national 2010 UPR report the U.S. spoke of its perception of this phenomenon following the change of administration. See Document 86. The report states:

> The United States is currently at war with Al Qaeda and its associated forces. President Obama has made clear that the United States is fully committed to complying with the

Constitution and with all applicable domestic and international law, including the laws of war, in all aspects of this or any armed conflict. We start from the premise that there are no law-free zones, and that everyone is entitled to protection under law. In his Nobel Lecture, the President made clear that "[w]here force is necessary, we have a moral and strategic interest in binding ourselves to certain rules of conduct…[E]ven as we confront a vicious adversary that abides by no rules…the United States of America must remain a standard bearer in the conduct of war."

Detention and treatment of detainees

83. On his second full day in office, President Obama acted to implement this vision by issuing three Executive Orders relating to U.S. detention, interrogation, and transfer policies and the Guantánamo Bay detention facility.

84. Executive Order 13491, *Ensuring Lawful Interrogations*, directed that individuals detained in any armed conflict shall in all circumstances be treated humanely and shall not be subjected to violence to life and person, nor to outrages upon personal dignity, whenever such individuals are in the custody or under the effective control of the United States Government or detained within a facility owned, operated, or controlled by the United States. Such individuals shall not be subjected to any interrogation technique or approach that is not authorized by and listed in the Army Field Manual 2-22.3, which explicitly prohibits threats, coercion, physical abuse, and water boarding. Individuals detained in armed conflict must be treated in conformity with all applicable laws, including Common Article 3 of the 1949 Geneva Conventions, which the President and the Supreme Court have recognized as providing "minimum" standards of protection in all non international armed conflicts, including in the conflict with Al Qaeda.

88. Executive Order 13493, *Review of Detention Policy Options*, established a task force to review and facilitate significant policy decisions regarding broader detention questions. This Special Task Force on Detention Policy has reviewed available options for the apprehension, detention, trial, transfer, release, or other disposition of individuals captured or apprehended in connection with armed conflicts and counterterrorism operations….

The Administration has expressly acknowledged that international law informs the scope of our detention authority. The President has also made clear that we have a national security interest in prosecuting terrorists, either before Article III courts or military commissions, and that we would exhaust all available avenues to prosecute Guantánamo detainees before deciding whether it would be appropriate to continue detention under the laws of war. Working with Congress, our military commissions have been revised to enhance their procedural protections, including prohibiting introduction of any statements taken as a result of cruel, inhuman, or degrading treatment.

See Also Terms: 3, 17, 20, 23, 24, 33, 34, 35, 48, 49, 53, 55, 59, 63, 65, 66, 70, 81, 82, 85, 88, 90, 93, 95, 99, 100, 103, 106, 109, 111, 117, 124, 134, 136, 137, 142, 144, 145, 146, 147, 151, 152, 160, 167, 169, 170, 171, 177, 179, 181, 182, 184, 185, 196, 210, 211, 219, 221, 222, 223, 224, 226, 231, 231, 240, 243, 244, 252, 253, 254, 256, 259, 264, 272, 275, 283, 287, 289, 290, 292, 293, 294, 297, 300, 302, 306, 307, 309, 311, 316, 317, 318, 319.

267. REPARATIONS

Definition: Measures taken to make up for the consequences of a wrongful act, such as a human rights violation, and to make things, as much as possible, the way they were before the act.

Significance: If a state is found to have violated someone's human rights, the state can sometimes be made to make reparations for that illegal act. Most often, reparations are made in the form of monetary payments. They can also be a return of property taken, a public apology or a change to an unjust law. The reparation should be proportional to the harm done by the human rights violation.

Sometimes in the U.S. legal system people are wrongfully convicted and imprisoned for something they did not do, as a result of being framed by government personnel. When eventually they are freed, they often sue for damages for the wrongful imprisonment. If they prove their case and are awarded damages, the award is a form of reparation for the violation of their procedural human rights.

By way of example, Article 9.5 of the ICCPR sets forth a provision for reparations for when one is wrongfully arrested or detained: "Anyone who has been the victim of unlawful arrest or detention shall have an enforceable right to compensation." See Document 8.

The United States, in its ratification of the ICCPR, said that under Article 9.5 it only recognized a person's right to file a request for such reparation, not to automatically receive it. See Document 9.

See Also Terms: 3, 10, 11, 12, 33, 46, 53, 54, 55, 56, 57, 60, 70, 71, 73, 88, 90, 93, 94, 108, 113, 118, 120, 133, 145, 146, 151, 157, 159, 165, 167, 169, 175, 177, 179, 181, 184, 185, 215, 222, 226, 231, 234, 243, 244, 253, 259, 272, 273, 283, 292, 293, 294, 295, 300, 303, 306, 307, 316.

268. REPORTS/REPORTING

Definition: The process of preparation and submission of a formal written report by a state party to a treaty or by an inter-governmental organization, non-governmental organization, or other entity or person, concerning human rights in a particular state or states, or concerning a certain human rights theme.

Significance: No country in the world is in full compliance with all of the human rights standards legally binding upon that state under human rights treaties and customary international law. Every country in the world, including the United States, is trying to bring about enjoyment of human rights gradually and concretely, using human rights norms as their guide and standard. There are certain means of implementation that have been established in international human rights systems to promote the full "implementation" of human rights.

The international community has established procedures and mechanisms for seeing that human rights are able to be exercised by people in reality, not just in theory. One of the ways this is done is by the preparation of reports, which contain facts, stories and evidence of specific violations and analyses concerning human rights. There are four types of reports that are most common to the field of international human rights law and procedure relative to the United States.

1. Reports by states parties to a human rights treaty submitted to the organizational body that was established to monitor state compliance with the treaty. This type of report is done to fulfill the state's "reporting" obligation under the treaty.

For example, under the International Covenant on Civil and Political Rights (ICCPR), Article 40, every state that ratifies that treaty accepts the legal obligation to prepare and submit periodic reports to the U.N. Human Rights Committee. These reports are meant to inform the supervising body of the true human rights situation in that state, so that the supervising body can get a clear picture and take the appropriate steps in the treaty to get the state to comply with the human rights standards.

Generally speaking, these reports serve to inform a supervising entity, such as the Human Rights Committee, as to the state's actual practice and experience regarding enjoyment of the rights, what national legislation and case law applies, what steps are being taken to improve the situation, and what problems or obstacles remain. (Needless to say, these state party reports tend to gloss over problems and sometimes actually conceal essential information).

An example of such a human rights report is found in Document 15A, the Second and Third Reports of the United States to the U.N. Human Rights Committee under the ICCPR. This report was submitted to the HRCee in 2005 pursuant to Article 40 of the ICCPR. The HRCee reviewed this report and responded by issuing observations, comments and recommendations, which can be found in Document 15C. Document 21A is also such report, but submitted by the United States to the U.N. Committee against Torture, under the Torture Convention.

These reports are limited in scope to those specific human rights found in the particular treaty under which the report is submitted. These reports are referred to a Periodic State Reports, because the states have to submit them periodically, every few years.

2. Reports prepared by an inter-governmental body for use by that body in dealing with a general or specific human rights issue. The reports can be about a particular state, called a

country-specific report, or about a particular theme, such as religious freedom or prison conditions, called a thematic report. Inter-governmental human rights bodies such as the U.N. Human Rights Council cause such reports to be made regarding the facts about a particular state or a subject matter of human rights. Most often these reports are prepared by persons called "Special Rapporteurs." These are persons chosen by the particular body and given a mandate to prepare the report, and to submit it to that body for its institutional use. These persons then collect information on the theme or state. This may include a fact-finding mission to a state to gather first-hand evidence and testimony. They seek information from as many credible sources as they can find. These reports are, in effect, studies about human rights in a state or about a theme within the scope of jurisdiction of that body.

Some of the Documents in Appendixes L and M are examples of this type of report. Some are based on the fact-finding missions these special rapporteurs made to the United States.

4. Other reports done primarily by NGOs or even by individuals or other civil society actors to reveal the truth about a general or particular human rights situation. These can also be country specific or thematic.

Civil society, especially human rights NGOs, prepare reports to submit to international human rights bodies such as the U.N. Human Rights Council. These reports are meant to give an objective and factual input into the processes of an inter-governmental organization and work against the political influences and other biases that may exist in the process. Often these reports may be all the information a body is able to obtain about a particular human rights issue. These reports are also sometimes prepared for the general public, academia, national legislators and national human rights institutions to inform them about particular human rights issues or country situations. These reports are very often what gives rise to general and country-specific legislation in the U.S. Congress. An example of legislation enacted as a result of many such written reports is the International Religious Freedom Act of 1998, found in Document 89.

Such reports are often aimed at exposing a particular violator state and the mobilization of public attention to motivate action by exposure of the state to the "forum of shame."

5. Reports prepared by governments for their own internal and external purposes. Governments may prepare written reports to be used by legislators and executive bodies. See Documents 82, 83. An example of this can be found in an excerpt in Appendix L, the U.S. Country Reports, prepared by the U.S. State Department. An excerpt of the actual 2009 country report on China is included in Appendix L. Often the accuracy and objectivity of such government reports is challenged by the states critiqued and by NGOs.

See Also Terms: 3, 48, 53, 54, 55, 57, 60, 70, 76, 112, 119, 127, 142, 144, 145, 146, 147, 148, 150, 151, 152, 173, 179, 180, 184, 185, 190, 206, 208, 211, 215, 217, 227, 231, 233, 244, 253, 259, 264, 272, 289, 290, 292, 293, 305, 306, 307, 311.

269. RESERVATIONS, DECLARATIONS, AND UNDERSTANDINGS (RDUs/RUDs)

Definition: A formal written statement by a state made when it is ratifying a treaty, saying that the state does not accept one or more of the legal obligations set forth in certain parts of the treaty being ratified. It is a statement that alters or excludes certain legal effects of the treaty on the state making the reservation.

Significance: Most human rights are spelled out in international treaties that are international legal instruments. These instruments, such as the ICCPR, contain numerous articles that set forth specific human rights, which states are expected to accept by ratifying the treaty. Sometimes a treaty contains a human right that is not acceptable to a state for certain legal, political or philosophical reasons. Because they are sovereign and independent states, they are free to become legally obligated to obey any treaty they choose. States cannot be forced to sign a treaty and to accept all the specific obligations of a treaty, unless the treaty itself states that no reservations can be made to it.

In order to allow as many states as possible to ratify human rights treaties and become states parties to as many treaties as possible, international law permits states, when they ratify a treaty, to submit written statements that expressly exclude or modify a particular obligation. This helps states to avoid refusing to ratify a treaty only because of one or a few objectionable or unacceptable provisions.

All reservations are valid unless they would be inconsistent with the "object and purpose" for which the treaty was created. This means that a reservation that defeats the goals and purposes of a treaty would not be legally valid. For example, the Torture Convention has as its object prohibiting all torture committed against anyone. If a state ratifies the Torture Convention and submits a reservation stating that it does not accept the obligation not to torture noncitizens, that reservation would be invalid as contrary to the object and purpose of the treaty.

Once a state makes a valid reservation, its obligations under the treaty must be read and applied in light of that reservation. All the other obligations in the treaty are accepted as stated. Using the ICCPR as an example, one can see that the United States ratified that treaty in 1992. See Documents 8 and 9.

> Article 6 of the ICCPR reads:
> 1. Every human being has the inherent right to life. This right shall be protected by law. No one shall be arbitrarily deprived of his life....
> 5. Sentence of death shall not be imposed for crimes committed by persons below eighteen years of age and shall not be carried out on pregnant women.

In following the reservation (Document 9) adopted by the U.S. Senate in 1992, the United States stated that it was not accepting to be legally bound by Article 6:

> "Resolved, ... That the Senate advise and consent to the ratification of the International Covenant on Civil and Political Rights, adopted by the United Nations General Assembly on 16 December 1966, and signed on behalf of the United States on 5 October 1977 (Executive E, 95–2), subject to the following Reservations, Understandings, Declarations and Proviso,
> I. The Senate's advice and consent is subject to the following reservations:
> (2) That the United States reserves the right, subject to its constitutional constraints, to impose capital punishment on any person (other than a pregnant woman) duly convicted under existing or future laws permitting the imposition of capital punishment, including such punishment for crimes committed by persons below 18 years of age."

What this reservation means is that the United States retained the legal right under U.S. law to execute persons who commit capital crimes when they are under age 18. This practice was ruled unconstitutional by the Supreme Court in 2005. See *Roper vs. Simmons*, Appendix J.

U.S. reservations to treaties such as the ICCPR have been controversial in the international human rights context. They have brought about a response by the international community, usually questioning the validity of the extent of U.S. reservations and their compatibility with the object and purpose of such treaties as the ICCPR.

The term "reservations" is usually found along with the terms "declarations" and "understandings" that are abbreviated as "RDUs" or "RUDs."

See Also Terms: 2, 6, 11, 25, 48, 53, 54, 55, 57, 70, 71, 72, 74, 94, 98, 103, 127, 145, 146, 147, 151, 158, 179, 180, 184, 185, 186, 211, 220, 222, 225, 226, 243, 258, 259, 262, 264, 272, 287, 297, 306, 307, 316, 323.

270. RESPONSIBILITY TO PROTECT (R2P)

Definition: A doctrine being advocated in the international community which sets forth the conditions in which the community of nations is legally obligated to intervene in the territory of another country to prevent or terminate genocide, ethnic cleansing, war crimes, and crimes against humanity. This would include all means, including militarily, if absolutely necessary.

Significance: There has been a movement of international NGOs and some states to promote the doctrine of Responsibility to Protect (R2P). By this doctrine every state would have a legal obligation to take action in the context of the international community to prevent or intervene in a state wherein genocide, war crimes, crimes against humanity, or ethnic cleansing are taking place or about to take place.

The Responsibility to Protect doctrine is rooted in the principle that states have a fundamental responsibility to protect their own populations from such international crimes such as genocide, war crimes, crimes against humanity, and ethnic cleansing, and that other states, in turn, have a corollary responsibility to assist if a state fails to fulfill its fundamental responsibility to its citizens and its other residents. If it fails to do so, other states may be obligated to take collective action if a state will not meet that fundamental responsibility. R2P enjoins those other states to bring into play a wide spectrum of policies and measures, both as individual nations and as an international community. It is only rarely, and only in extreme situations, that this will include the use of force. R2P is not a doctrine that allows one state to intervene into another state unilaterally to prevent or end such crimes. It is not the same as the doctrine of humanitarian intervention.

The idea of the responsibility of states to act is not entirely new. A concept similar to this doctrine has already been adopted in the context of the African Union. In 2000, its Constitutive Act invoked a concept of "non-indifference" in the face of grave crimes, and Article 4 of that Act authorized decisive African Union action to put a halt to war crimes, genocide, and crimes against humanity. The idea is that when an event such as the Rwanda Genocide occurs, other states have to get into action to stop it; they cannot just sit by and say it is not a matter affecting their national self-interest. Respect for international rule of law is in the national interest of every state in the world.

It must be emphasized that R2P does not mean immediate resort to military force. That must be the last resort. It means that all measures short of force should be employed to prevent or end such atrocities, before force is used. It also implies a collective state action in the use of means to accomplish this; again, not the unilateral action of one state.

The acceptance of this doctrine has a mixed history in the international community. In a World summit in 2005 there was a vote on accepting the non-binding Outcome Document which included paragraphs on R2P. In that vote all 192 U.N. member states voted affirmatively on R2P.

The two main paragraphs of the non-binding Outcome Document relative to R2P stated:

138. Each individual State has the responsibility to protect its populations from genocide, war crimes, ethnic cleansing and crimes against humanity. This responsibility entails the prevention of such crimes, including their incitement, through appropriate and necessary means. We accept that responsibility and will act in accordance with it. The international community should, as appropriate, encourage and help States to exercise this responsibility and support the United Nations in establishing an early warning capability.

139. The international community, through the United Nations, also has the responsibility to use appropriate diplomatic, humanitarian and other peaceful means, in accordance with Chapters VI and VIII of the Charter, to help protect populations from genocide, war crimes, ethnic cleansing and crimes against humanity. In this context, we are prepared to take collective action, in a timely and decisive manner, through the Security Council, in accordance with the Charter, including Chapter VII, on a case-by-case basis and in cooperation with relevant regional organizations as appropriate, should peaceful means be inadequate and national authorities manifestly fail to protect their populations from genocide, war crimes, ethnic cleansing and crimes against humanity. We stress the need for the General Assembly to continue consideration of the responsibility to protect populations from genocide, war crimes, ethnic cleansing and crimes against humanity and its implications, bearing in mind the principles of the Charter and international law. We also intend to commit ourselves, as necessary

and appropriate, to helping States build capacity to protect their populations from genocide, war crimes, ethnic cleansing and crimes against humanity and to assisting those which are under stress before crises and conflicts break out.

Then in 2006, the U.N. Security Council reaffirmed this commitment and the related principle of protecting civilians, in Security Council Resolution 1674. It can be said that the Council has taken R2P at least partly into consideration in its actions regarding the Democratic Republic of the Congo and Sudan.

The next major advancement in recognition of R2P came in January 2009, when U.N. Secretary-General Ban Ki-moon released a report called *Implementing the Responsibility to Protect*. This report argued for the implementation of R2P. It also set forth the international principles which support the doctrine of R2P.

The first Principle emphasizes that States have the primary responsibility to protect their own populations from genocide, war crimes, ethnic cleansing and crimes against humanity, and such mass atrocities. The second Principle states that if the state is unable to protect its population on its own, the international community has a legal responsibility to assist the state by helping it build its capacity. This could involve building early-warning capabilities, strengthening the security sector, mediating conflicts between political parties, or mobilizing standby forces, and a host of other actions. The third Principle focuses on the responsibility of the international community to take timely and decisive action to prevent and halt such international crimes when a State is manifestly failing to protect its own population.

Under international human rights law, theory states have four separate and distinct legal obligations regarding human rights: the Obligation to Respect, meaning the state itself will not commit human rights violations; the Obligation to Protect, meaning the state will protect individual from the actions of other individuals which threaten their human rights; the Obligation to Ensure, meaning that the states will do all that they can to see that other states respect their human right obligations; and the Obligation to Fulfill, meaning the state will take all affirmative steps to make sure that everyone can exercise all human rights. The doctrine of R2P is consistent with those four obligations.

The position of the United States up to the Obama presidency has been that while it "stands ready" to take collective action to prevent genocide and the other three international crimes in another nation, it is not ready to accept the notion that it is legally obligated in any given situation to intervene to prevent such horrible crimes. That position does not completely renounce the R2P doctrine but it falls short of committing to acceptance of a legal obligation. The current U.S. position as of the time of this book seems to be less nuanced. In his Nobel acceptance speech President Obama stated:

> More and more, we all confront difficult questions about how to prevent the slaughter of civilians by their own government, or to stop a civil war whose violence and suffering can engulf an entire region.
> I believe that force can be justified on humanitarian grounds, as it was in the Balkans, or in other places that have been scarred by war. Inaction tears at our conscience and can lead to more costly intervention later. That's why all responsible nations must embrace the role that militaries with a clear mandate can play to keep the peace.

(Barack Obama, Nobel Peace Prize Acceptance Speech)

Some interpret this as accepting the "strong" R2P approach that states must intervene, including militarily and that this does not require prior action of the Security Council. At the U.N. in July 2009 the U.S. agreed with Russia and China and most other nations on implementing the doctrine.

Those who object to the U.S. accepting this doctrine say, for example, that adopting a doctrine that compels the United States to act to prevent atrocities occurring in other countries would be risky. They claim that U.S. sovereignty and independence could be compromised if the United States consented to be legally bound by the R2P doctrine and that the United States needs to preserve its sovereignty by maintaining a full control on the decision to use diplomatic pressure, political coercion, economic sanctions, and particularly use of its military might. They claim that if the United States intervenes in the affairs of another nation, that decision should be based only on U.S. national interest, not on any other criteria, such as those set forth by the R2P doctrine or any other international standard. Those in favor of the doctrine see the U.S. as part of an international family, the community of nations, which should all actively participate in seeing that international norms are respected and international crimes are not allowed to go unpunished. It sees the "never again" as a collective responsibility of all nations, and wants the prevention of unwarranted unilateral state invasions to happen more for political or economic reasons than for international crime prevention and the protection of vulnerable populations.

As of the time of publication the doctrine of R2P is not accepted as a binding international legal norm, though certain non-governmental organizations, states and international intergovernmental organizations are pushing towards that direction.

It must be remembered, though, that in relation to the Genocide Convention, those states that are states parties to that Convention, as is the U.S., do have a treaty legal obligation under Article 1 to take action where genocide is occurring. This is one of the reasons that the U.S. and some other nations are very slow to use the word genocide to describe a large scale atrocity that is occurring. If they recognize it as genocide they are forced by the Genocide Convention to take action to prevent or punish it.

The problem with R2P for many states is that if this doctrine is accepted then all states will be legally required to act to participate in the protection action and will have no choice in the matter, especially if there is no clear or concrete national self interest. Such actions might cost substantial monies, which may not be politically popular domestically.

See Also Terms: 8, 20, 24, 29, 48, 63, 64, 66, 70, 71, 72, 91, 101, 110, 111, 120, 124, 130, 132, 133, 136, 143, 144, 145, 151, 152, 153, 154, 167, 169, 173, 177, 182, 184, 185, 192, 200, 208, 210, 211, 214, 218, 222, 226, 235, 243, 244, 253, 259, 272, 273, 276, 283, 287, 291, 292, 293, 295, 300, 308, 321, 322, 323.

271. REVERSE DISCRIMINATION

Definition: Discrimination in favor of a certain person or group done for purposes of correcting past adverse discrimination against that person or group. It is discrimination against a person or group which was formerly benefited by discrimination against someone else. The law, policy or practice of treating a person more favorably than someone else because of a particular characteristic or status, for purposes of correcting past discrimination. It is substantially the same as affirmative action.

Significance: Human rights principles require a society to consider all human beings as possessing equality and to treat everyone equally. Society cannot discriminate against persons for reasons such as race, color, religion, gender, political opinion or nationality. Equality is the norm. In a society where much discrimination has occurred, sometimes it is decided to take certain action which will correct the problem and result in a society becoming the way it would have been if the discrimination had not occurred.

Reverse discrimination means that a society makes a law, policy or practice which treats someone more favorably than someone else. For example, if there has been discrimination against women in admission to a certain medical school, a reverse discrimination would occur if the school gave a preference to women candidates over equally qualified males, so as to raise the number of women to what it would have been had there been no previous discrimination against women in admissions.

Any distinction between human beings must have a reasonable and objective justification to be permissible under human rights law applicable to the United States.

See Also Terms: 7, 11, 12, 20, 24, 28, 33, 34, 35, 48, 54, 55, 70, 72, 786, 88, 93, 94, 100, 120, 126, 144, 145, 146, 152, 160, 167, 169, 177, 179, 184, 185, 205, 211, 216, 237, 259, 260, 264, 265, 272, 283, 287, 292, 293, 297, 306, 307, 316, 322, 324.

272. RULE-OF-LAW

Definition: A principle of international law that says that every society in the world must have a system of laws applicable to all persons, that the law is the highest authority in the state, and that no one is above the law. All disputes must be decided pursuant to law and not by the arbitrary or discretionary acts of the government.

Significance: Human rights violations are abuses of power by the state and those acting under or in concert with it. Power of state can only be exercised properly where it is done pursuant to an existing law. Law must rule every action and every person. No one may be immune from responsibility and accountability for actions that violate human rights.

A rule-of-law system has an orderly, express, written, accessible and understandable set of laws equally applicable to everyone. All members of society are legally equal. The United States has a rule-of-law system. Even the President is subject to law, as impeachment trials have demonstrated. This situation is reflected in the famous sayings that "no one is above the law" and "we are a nation of laws and not men." It is the Constitution that is the basis for all law in the United States, though the Constitution leaves certain powers to make law to the individual states, which base their law-making authority on their state constitutions. None of those laws may violate human rights because no government, federal or state, has any legal right to violate human rights.

Rule of law also applies to the international community, where the nations of the world continue to establish norms for human rights and humanitarian law, so that everyone is responsible internationally for his or her acts. A rule-of-law society is considered a prerequisite by the international community for the effective protection of human rights.

In the U.S. legal and political system since 9/11, there have been serious issues arising as to respect for rule of law. As the Executive Branch of the government sought more power and latitude to wage the war on terrorism, and Congress and to some degree the courts allowed it, the edges of rule of law became frayed. The war on terrorism caused a severe imbalance in the checks and balance system, with everything being balanced in favor of the Executive Branch. The courts for a while gave substantial deference to the administration. But with the court cases concerning Guantanamo detainees coming before the U.S. Supreme Court, the situation changed. The U.S. Supreme Court did its job. In four consecutive cases regarding the war on terrorism detainees, the Supreme Court ruled against the U.S. administration, finding it acted unlawfully, particularly with regard to access to justice in challenging the legality of their detention. These were squarely rule-of-law legal opinions. The Court has, in effect, said that the President of the United States, arguably then the most powerful man in the world, was not above the law, even though he was trying to protect America from terrorism. This was about rule-of-law and separation of powers in conflict. The Supreme Court was, in essence, ruling that the war on terrorism had to be waged according to the law of the United States, including international human rights and humanitarian law, which was cited in these cases. The Supreme Court in *Boumedienne* stated solemnly:

> The laws and Constitution are designed to survive, and remain in force, in extraordinary times. Liberty and security can be reconciled; and in our system they are reconciled within the framework of law. . . .
> Security subsists, too, in fidelity to freedom's first principles. Chief among these are freedom from arbitrary and unlawful restraint and the personal liberty secured by the adherence to the separation of powers.

See Also Terms: 1, 3, 10, 11, 12, 13, 20, 23, 46, 47, 48, 52, 53, 54, 55, 56, 57, 59, 62, 63, 64, 70, 71, 72, 73, 75, 80, 88, 89, 90, 93, 94, 98, 103, 1110, 111, 113, 114, 129, 130, 132, 133, 134, 135, 138, 142, 144, 145, 146, 147, 151, 152, 154, 157, 158, 159, 160, 162, 166, 167, 169, 175, 177, 178, 179, 180, 181, 182, 184, 185, 192, 193, 194, 202, 211, 222, 229, 243, 258, 259, 262, 264, 269, 279, 291, 292, 293, 294, 297, 306, 307, 308, 309, 316, 323.

273. SANCTIONS

Definition: Actions taken by one state, a group of states, or an organization against a certain state as a punishment for committing wrongful acts violating human rights, or as a deterrent against the commission of such future wrongful acts against the sanctioning party or a third party.

Significance: Sanctions are one of the means of redress in international law. They are adverse actions taken against a state because of that state's wrongdoing. Sanctions are often imposed collectively through international inter-governmental organizations, such as the United Nations. Often it is through a Chapter VII resolution of the Security Council. See Document 5.

The United States sometimes unilaterally imposes sanctions on countries that have violated human rights. The long-running sanctions against Cuba, Burma, South Africa under the Apartheid government, and North Korea are examples. All have as a major part of their goal punishing a state for its human rights practices and trying to force the target state to change. Some of the general and country-specific legislation found in Appendix I serves as the legal basis for the U.S. imposition of sanctions against human rights violator states. Sanctions can also refer to any negative consequences imposed on a person who commits human rights violations.

After the recent post-election democratic uprising in Iran, the U.S. and many other states sought to increase sanctions against that state for suppressing freedom of speech, movement and association and thus suppressing the move towards democracy. The U.S. has also pressed for a toughening of sanctions for Iran's nuclear enrichment program.

There is a point at which certain sanctions could end up hurting the people of the target country to such as degree as to engage international human rights or even international criminal responsibility. States need to monitor and assess the impact of sanctions on all elements of the target society. Sanctions must be proportional and not otherwise violate international legal obligations.

See Also Terms: 3, 9, 10, 25, 26, 48, 59, 61, 70, 71, 72, 73, 92, 93, 94, 119, 120, 132, 133, 138, 144, 145, 151, 152, 157, 159, 165, 173, 177, 182, 184, 185, 190, 199, 202, 207, 208, 211, 215, 218, 222, 224, 234, 243, 259, 264, 267, 272, 276, 286, 287, 292, 293, 294, 303, 306, 307, 316, 318.

274. SECOND GENERATION HUMAN RIGHTS

Definition: A term formerly used to describe a class or category of human rights that comprises all economic, social, and cultural rights.

Significance: Second generation human rights is a term formerly used to described economic, social and cultural human rights. The International Covenant on Economic, Social and Cultural Rights was commonly considered as the source of so-called second generations rights. The term second generation rights is no longer used to describe a type of human right. This is because it caused too many conceptual problems. However, some people still use this term and the older human rights literature still contains it; thus, it is important to know. The reader is advised not to use this term.

See Also Terms: 116, 301. These three terms should not be used. They are defined and referenced for historical reasons only.

275. SECRET DETENTION

See entries for **Detention** and **Arbitrary Arrest/Detention**

276. SECURITY COUNCIL (U.N.)

Definition: A principal organ of the United Nations charged with dealing with threats to peace, breaches of the peace and acts of aggression. According to the U.N. website, the role of the Security Council is as follows:

> The Security Council has primary responsibility, under the Charter, for the maintenance of international peace and security. It is so organized as to be able to function continuously, and a representative of each of its members must be present at all times at United Nations Headquarters...
>
> When a complaint concerning a threat to peace is brought before it, the Council's first action is usually to recommend to the parties to try to reach agreement by peaceful means. In some cases, the Council itself undertakes investigation and mediation. It may appoint special representatives or request the Secretary-General to do so or to use his good offices. It may set forth principles for a peaceful settlement.
>
> When a dispute leads to fighting, the Council's first concern is to bring it to an end as soon as possible. On many occasions, the Council has issued cease-fire directives which have been instrumental in preventing wider hostilities. It also sends United Nations peace-keeping forces to help reduce tensions in troubled areas, keep opposing forces apart and create conditions of calm in which peaceful settlements may be sought. The Council may decide on enforcement measures, economic sanctions (such as trade embargoes) or collective military action.

Significance: The U.N. Security Council is composed of the five permanent members, the United States, Russia, France, England, and China, referred to as the P5 and has 10 elected non permanent members. On matters other than procedural matters, each of the P5 members can veto any proposed resolution of the Council.

Under the U.N. Charter the Security Council can only handle matters within its competence. See Document 5. That is limited to questions of international breaches of the peace, international threats to the peace, and acts of aggression. Historically it has been seen that human rights and humanitarian law issues have been an important component of problems with which the Council dealt. Human rights and humanitarian law norms were often factored into the resolution of problems and played an important role in Security Council resolutions. The main power of the Council lies in the fact that it can issue resolution binding on all states under Chapter VII of the Charter, including the use of military force. However, it only has powers to act within enumerated purposes in the Charter.

> The Purposes of the United Nations are:
> To maintain international peace and security, and to that end: to take effective collective measures for the prevention and removal of threats to the peace, and for the suppression of acts of aggression or other breaches of the peace, and to bring about by peaceful means, and in conformity with the principles of justice and international law, adjustment or settlement of international disputes or situations which might lead to a breach of the peace;
> ....
> 3. To achieve international co-operation in solving international problems of an economic, social, cultural, or humanitarian character, and in promoting and encouraging respect for human rights and for fundamental freedoms for all without distinction as to race, sex, language, or religion; ....

The Security Council must operate with those purposes and goals in mind, as they are binding because the U.N. Charter is a treaty binding on all states that have ratified it. One of the main questions that has arisen regarding the Council and Human Rights is whether the Council and its activities and resolutions, including Chapter VII resolutions, are subject to international human rights law. The latter question has been dealt with in a number of recent cases in international legal bodies such as the European Court of Human Rights and the U.N. Human Rights Committee. Some of these case have to do with U.N. Security Council resolutions involving counter-terrorism measures. In the case of *Sayadi vs. Belgium* the Human rights Committee found the government of Belgium had violated the petitioner's human right under the ICCPR even if it had been following a U.N. Security Council Chapter VII resolution. The issue was whether Charter Article 103 makes the Council resolutions of higher legal authority than human rights treaties. Article 103 reads: "In the event of a conflict between the obligations of the Members of the United Nations under the present Charter and their obligations under any other international agreement, their obligations under the present Charter shall prevail." The Committee found that this did not give the Security Council the authority to make an order that member states violate human rights norms of the ICCPR. It reasoned that the Security Council cannot act in opposition to the purposes of the Charter, which included Article 1.3 on "promoting and encouraging respect for human rights and for fundamental freedoms,..."

This was said in relation to Article 24 of the Charter which reads:

> In discharging these duties the Security Council shall act in accordance with the Purposes and Principles of the United Nations. The specific powers granted to the Security Council for the discharge of these duties are laid down in Chapters VI, VII, VIII, and XII.

The U.N. Security Council is bound to respect international human rights and humanitarian law norms. Any particular resolution that fails to respect the limits to the powers of the Council would be *ultra vires*, beyond the powers, of the Council. The Security Council will not be acting with impunity if its actions result in human rights or humanitarian law violations.

The Council is an extremely geo-politicized body of states all jockeying among and against each other on delicate and dangerous issues, mostly seeking to accomplish national (or ally) self interest, not protection of individual human beings. There is a potential for devastating effects by the actions of the Council on the human rights of people when, as some have argued "the rule of power overrides the rule of law." Many would argue that the Council has long acted outside the realm of human rights law, as though anything it did was somehow of a higher legal order. It is not.

The question that follows is: By which human rights norms should the Security Council be bound? Some have argued that the Security Council and indeed the whole U.N. organization are at least bound by those human rights norms that are set forth in written treaty instruments adopted within the U.N. organization. One should regard those instruments as an elaboration of the human rights provided for in the Charter. This is because, historically and legally, they were in fact adopted in order to fulfill the mandate concerning human rights, which was expressly provided for in the Charter. This would, of course, apply to the ICCPR, ICESCR, CAT, CERD, CEDAW and the Genocide Convention, among others.

The Security Council deals with issues of human rights in a variety of contexts. One is in debate on the extent to which a wide variety of international actors have obligations with regard to international human rights law. This includes nation-states, intergovernmental organizations, non-governmental organizations, transnational companies, and individuals.

The practice of the Security Council suggests that the following principles have influenced it in dealing with human rights situations:

> The Council recognizes that human rights violations can cause or aggravate threats to international peace and security and thus must be addressed, and done so in the context of international human rights law. Second, human rights must be integrated into conflict resolution peacemaking and peacekeeping. Third Democratic legitimacy and stability depends on respect for political human rights and the election process, and the right to self determination, which is itself a human rights. (See ICCPR, Doc. 8, Article 1).

One major issue for human rights and the Security Council is the relation of the Council to the International Criminal Court (ICC). In 1998 the international community adopted the Rome Statute for an International Criminal. See Document 76. The Court was established in 2002. The U.S. wanted the Security Council to have veto power over the cases brought before the Court. This did not happen. However, the Council can refer cases to the ICC and can ask the ICC to defer handling of cases before it.

The ICC is not a U.N. organ. It is an independent judicial body which has an international agreement stating its relation with the U.N. and agreeing on certain cooperation. Because the ICC deals with the most serious international crimes it deals with matters that are likely before the Security Council also. Those international crimes are mostly human rights and humanitarian law violations. Thus, the Security Council must consider that also. The purpose of the ICC is to prosecute and deter such crimes and eliminate the sense of impunity for such crimes, and thus prevent the kinds of situations which come before the Council.

Of great recent importance is that in 2010 the Assembly of States parties of the ICC has finally adopted a compromise definition of the crime of Aggression. This is meant to deter acts of aggression by which so many human rights and humanitarian law violations originate. The main sticking point in taking so long to resolve this definition of aggression crime was the role of the Security Council in determining when an act of aggression had taken place. It is a complicated definition. See the entry for Aggression, supra. The Security Council does have a role under this newly defined crime.

The Security Council has also had a role in relation to human rights and humanitarian law in relation to the counter measures against terrorism. This is very politically delicate because many states and other voices are reminding the Security Council and particularly the P5 members, of the need and obligation to respect international human rights and humanitarian law while countering terrorism. In a Security Council, a President's Statement on that subject has been issued annually for the past few years, the last one in 2010. In document S/PRST/2010/11) in connection with the Council's consideration of the item entitled "The promotion and strengthening of the rule-of-law in the maintenance of international peace and security," the Council President made the following statement on behalf of the Council:

> "The Security Council reaffirms its commitment to the Charter of the United Nations and international law, and to an international order based on the rule of law and international law, which is essential for peaceful coexistence and cooperation among States in addressing common challenges, thus contributing to the maintenance of international peace and security.
>
> "The Security Council recognizes that respect for international humanitarian law is an essential component of the rule of law in conflict situations and reaffirms its conviction that the protection of the civilian population in armed conflict should be an important aspect of any comprehensive strategy to resolve conflict and recalls in this regard resolution 1894 (2009).
>
> "The Security Council reaffirms its strong opposition to impunity for serious violations of international humanitarian law and human rights law. The Security Council further emphasizes the responsibility of States to comply with their relevant obligations to end impunity and to thoroughly investigate and prosecute persons responsible for war crimes, genocide, crimes against humanity or other serious violations of international humanitarian law in order to prevent violations, avoid their recurrence and seek sustainable peace, justice, truth and reconciliation.
>
> "The Security Council expresses its commitment to ensure that all U.N. efforts to restore peace and security themselves respect and promote the rule of law. The Council recognizes that sustainable peace building requires an integrated approach, which strengthens coherence between political, security, development, human rights and rule of law activities."
> See Document 56.

See Also Terms: 3, 8, 19, 25, 26, 31, 37, 48, 56, 59, 63, 64, 65, 66, 69, 70, 71, 72, 73, 86, 89, 92, 101, 110, 111, 119, 124, 129, 130, 132, 133, 136, 143, 144, 145, 146, 151, 153, 154, 175, 177, 181, 182, 184, 185, 192,

200, 201, 203, 208, 210, 211, 214, 215, 218, 221, 222, 223, 224, 235, 239, 243, 245, 253, 257, 259, 260, 265, 271, 272, 273, 278, 283, 292, 293, 295, 300, 302, 306, 307, 308, 309, 2317, 319, 321, 323, 324.

277. SEGREGATION

Definition: The forced separation, isolation, and keeping apart of different groups of people, based on such characteristics as race, religion, color, nationality, or ethnic identity, as to where they live, work, play, receive education, or participate in any other human activity usually open to members of society.

Significance: U.S. history saw practices of racial segregation primarily against African Americans, both resulting from laws (de jure) or from actual discriminatory practices (de facto). This segregation particularly enforced where they were allowed to live, to use public services, and to attend schools. Segregation was formally ended by U.S. Supreme Court cases, principally *Brown vs. Board of Education.*

As a matter of international human rights law, segregation violates the human rights of equality and nondiscrimination, and it can violate the collective rights of a segregated group, such as a racial or ethnic minority. It is a violation of the Universal Declaration of Human Rights. See Document 6. It is also a violation of the ICCPR, which the U.S. has ratified and is legally binding (See ICCPR, Articles 2.1, 12.1, 26, 27). See Document 8. Racial Segregation also violates the Convention on Elimination of Racial Discrimination, which the U.S. has also ratified. See Document 23.

Segregation of people based on such characteristics as race or religion would be a violation of human rights law, unless there were a reasonable and objective justification consistent with the protection of human rights and with no other alternative. A situation meeting those criteria would be quite exceptional. The prime example of segregation was the system that was in effect in South Africa until 1994, known as *apartheid.* The process of taking steps to reverse segregation and reintegrate a society is called desegregation.

Segregation in the U.S. is discussed in Appendix L, The Report of the Special Rapporteur on contemporary forms of racism, racial discrimination, xenophobia and related intolerance, by U.N. Special Rapporteur, Doudou Diène, on his findings from his fact finding Mission to the United States of America in 2008. Also discussed in Appendix L, is the Report of the Special Rapporteur on adequate housing as a component of the right to an adequate standard of living, and on the right to non-discrimination in this context, by Special Rapporteur Raquel Rolnik on her fact finding Mission to the U.S. in 2009. Segregation is also treated in the U.S. periodic reports to the Human Rights Committee and Committee on Elimination of Racial Discrimination, Documents 15A and 25.

Segregation still exists in some parts of the U.S., and the government and civil society are working on issues related to segregation, through the use of human rights law and other means. As the above special rapporteur reports show, the international community gets involved with segregation issues in the U.S. This is because the U.S. is a member of the U.S. and a state party to the ICCPR and CERD, which engages the action of the treaty bodies created by those treaties in regard to all states parties including the U.S.

See Also Terms: 7, 11, 12, 15, 2-0, 24, 33, 34, 35, 48, 53, 55, 63, 70, 72, 73, 78, 84, 86, 87, 97, 99, 100, 101, 119, 120, 122, 124, 127, 132, 133, 136, 142, 143, 144, 145, 146, 147, 151, 160, 167, 169, 170, 171, 177, 179, 184, 185, 188, 195, 205, 215, 222, 228, 231, 235, 237, 243, 244, 259, 260, 261, 264, 265, 270, 272, 283, 289, 290, 291, 292, 293, 306, 309, 3216, 324.

278. SELF-DETERMINATION

Definition: An internationally recognized human right held by a group of persons who identify themselves as a "people" to determine their own political status and pursue their own economic, social, and cultural development.

Significance: The right to self-determination was recognized to allow people to determine their own political course, so they would not have to feel dominated by another person or group;

thus, they would feel free. This right has been emphasized largely because of the colonialism of the 19th and 20th centuries. The right to self-determination does not in itself mean that every group of people who identify with each other as a group can establish their own country. It may mean that they have the right to autonomy for their group, whereby they make the rules in their particular area. It does not include the right of a people to secede from an existing state at will.

This right is recognized by the United States, but its political application and articulation depends on the particular group of people involved and the state in which they are acting. The native Hawaiians have, since the early 1990s, been in the process of exercising their right to self-determination. This process started when the U.S. Congress recognized in 1991 that the overthrow and annexation of Hawaii by the United States was legally invalid. (See Appendix I, item 17, and P). The right to self-determination is found in Article 1 of the ICCPR and ICESCR, which reads: "All peoples have the right of self-determination." See Document 8.

The Second and Third reports of the United States to the U.N. Human Rights Committee under the ICCPR has an exposition by the United States of its law and practice under Article 1 of the ICCPR, on self-determination. See Document 15A. See also in Appendix J the decision in the case of *Cherokee Nation v. United States*, a decision of the Inter-American Commission on Human Rights, which involved land compensation claims of Native Americans as part of their attempt to remedy past violations of their right to self-determination.

See Also Terms: 11, 12, 28, 29, 33, 39, 48, 70, 72, 73, 75, 92, 102, 122, 124, 144, 145, 146, 147, 152, 160, 163, 167, 169, 177, 179, 180, 184, 185, 193, 205, 210, 211, 213, 221, 222, 242, 243, 259, 264, 272, 276, 283, 287, 292, 297, 306, 307, 308, 309, 316, 323.

279. Self-Executing Treaty

Definition: An international human rights treaty that can be directly applied in U.S. law and used in courts as a rule of decision from the moment the treaty is ratified by the U.S. Senate. Conversely, a non-self-executing treaty, even after being ratified, must first be implemented by congressional legislation before it can be used as law in U.S. courts.

Significance: See Non-Self-Executing Treaty.

See Also Terms: 2, 6, 25, 26, 27, 52, 53, 54, 55, 56, 57, 62, 70, 74, 94, 98, 144, 145, 152, 158, 160, 167, 169, 175, 177, 179, 180, 184, 185, 194, 211, 220, 222, 226, 229, 243, 247, 258, 259, 262, 269, 272, 280, 286, 287, 291, 293, 297, 306, 307.

280. Sign/Signatory

Definition: The legal act of signing a treaty by a state or other legal personality by its authorized representative possessing legal authority ("full powers"). By signing, the states or other party expresses its intent to be legally bound to obey the treaty by subsequent ratification, unless by its terms the treaty provides otherwise, in which case signature alone binds it.

Significance: A treaty is negotiated and then voted on for adoption. If it is adopted, it is then deemed "open for signature" by the adopting parties and anyone else expressly allowed. It is usually necessary for a human rights treaty not only to be signed but also to be ratified by a certain number of states before it enters into force.

Usually signing a treaty, such as a human rights treaty, is the first key step for a state to take on legal obligations under the treaty. The term "signatory" is a designation given to a state or other legal personality that has signed an adopted treaty. Being a signatory only means that the state is on the way to becoming legally bound, not that it *is* legally bound. It is the ratification that binds.

Once a state has signed and ratified a treaty, this ratification is subject, in any case, to reservations, declarations, or understandings submitted by the signatory ratifying state. The ICCPR Articles 48–49 outline the signatory procedure. See Document 8. The U.S. ratification of the ICCPR includes reservations, declarations, and understandings to the treaty. See Document 9.

As a matter of international law expressed in the Vienna Convention on the Law of Treaties, (see Appendix E) when a state has signed a treaty it should act in a manner consistent with that treaty during the time from signing to ratification. This effort is a sign of its good faith and intent to become fully bound. So even if the United States has only signed a human rights treaty, there is an "interim" or "soft" obligation to act in good faith in a manner consistent with any international human rights legal norms contained that treaty.

See Also Terms: 2, 6, 11, 25, 31, 48, 52, 53, 54, 55, 56, 57, 62, 70, 98, 129, 130, 145, 154, 167, 169, 179, 180, 182, 184, 185, 211, 220, 222, 229, 243, 258, 259, 262, 264, 272, 279, 287, 292, 293, 297, 306, 307, 308, 323.

281. SLAVERY

Definition: The status of a person belonging to another person as an object of personal property and having to do whatever the owner commands. Slavery is any exercise of property ownership rights in another person.

Significance: Under modern international human rights law, every human being is free and autonomous, born that way and having that status until death. Slavery, the exercising of acts of property ownership in a human being, is a violation of human rights. Slavery is no longer legally permitted in any country. Certain forms of forced work, such as military service or penal sentence labor, are usually excepted.

Throughout history, the enslavement of one group of people by another has been a continuing problem. Slavery is a particularly degrading violation of human rights that denies the enslaved person his or her inherent dignity as an equal member of the human race. Oftentimes, the enslaved person or persons are legally reclassified as less than human beings, or chattel. The United States took that position before slavery was outlawed. One of the earliest movements of the modern human rights era was to eradicate slavery by treaties and mutual agreement of the states of the world. Although slavery still exists in various parts of the world, it has been thoroughly condemned in international law, both statutory and customary.

The international instruments that address slavery include the Slavery Convention of 1927, the protocol amending the Slavery Convention of 1953, the Supplementary Convention on the Abolition of Slavery, the Slave Trade, and Institutions and Practices Similar to Slavery of 1957, the Convention for the Suppression of the Traffic in Persons and of the Exploitation of the Prostitution of Others of 1951, the Convention Concerning Forced or Compulsory Labour of 1932, and the Abolition of Forced Labor Convention of 1959. The majority of the states of the world have ratified these various instruments, although there are some states which still have not.

With its ratification of the ICCPR in 1992, the United States became bound by a general human rights treaty that specifically prohibits slavery and slavery-like practices. Slavery and similar practices are human rights violations under Article 8 of the ICCPR. See Documents 8, 9. This Convention is the main general human rights treaty to which the United States is a state party. That article states:

1. No one shall be held in slavery; slavery and the slave-trade in all their forms shall be prohibited.
2. No one shall be held in servitude.
3. (a) No one shall be required to perform forced or compulsory labour;
(b) Paragraph 3 (a) shall not be held to preclude, in countries where imprisonment with hard labour may be imposed as a punishment for a crime, the performance of hard labour in pursuance of a sentence to such punishment by a competent court;
(c) For the purpose of this paragraph the term "forced or compulsory labour" shall not include:
(i) Any work or service, not referred to in subparagraph (b), normally required of a person who is under detention in consequence of a lawful order of a court, or of a person during conditional release from such detention;

(ii) Any service of a military character and, in countries where conscientious objection is recognized, any national service required by law of conscientious objectors;

(iii) Any service exacted in cases of emergency or calamity threatening the life or well-being of the community;

(iv) Any work or service which forms part of normal civil obligations.

Slavery, specifically the enslavement of African-Americans, could arguably be called the most important human rights issue in the history of the United States, because the devastating Civil War was fought over it. The most prominent legal case in U.S. history regarding the issue of slavery was the Dred Scott case, accepting slavery. Since the formal abolition of slavery in the United States, instances of slavery have still occurred, notably in situations involving illegal aliens and forced labor.

It was Abraham Lincoln who changed the course of slavery in the U.S. In his historic address entitled the "Emancipation Proclamation" he declared slavery ended. See Document 3. Lincoln declared:

> And by virtue of the power, and for the purpose aforesaid, I do order and declare that all persons held as slaves within said designated States, and parts of States, are, and henceforward shall be free; and that the Executive government of the United States, including the military and naval authorities thereof, will recognize and maintain the freedom of said persons...
>
> And I further declare and make known, that such persons of suitable condition, will be received into the armed service of the United States to garrison forts, positions, stations, and other places, and to man vessels of all sorts in said service.

These violations are being dealt with legally in the U.S. as they are exposed and subjected to the law. Worldwide, although the condemnation of slavery is clear in international law, it is largely NGOs who must watch for outbreaks of the practice, such as the slavery exposed in the Sudan in the 1990s, and make sure that the offending states are held accountable. These outbreaks are an unfortunate reminder of the tendency toward "man's inhumanity to man."

Similar to slavery is the status of involuntary servitude. It is the forcing of individuals to engage in work against their will as a punishment or under an agreement to exploit them economically by keeping them continually in debt and hence under control. The victim is, therefore, being involuntarily subject to a master and in reality lacks individual liberty. Forms of slavery do, from time to time, manifest themselves in the United States, particularly in urban settings, but in rural settings as well: sweatshops full of illegal alien garment workers in Los Angeles and New York, bean fields in central California and in Texas, and houses of ill-repute using drugged and bondaged Southeast Asian women. Citizens as well as aliens can fall into such servitude.

Since the mid-1800s slavery has become, and is now, an international criminal offense, punishable under the law in every country. Nowhere in the world is slavery legally permissible. Slavery, under the name "enslavement," is now a crime within the jurisdiction of the International Criminal Court Statute under crimes against humanity. Where there is widespread or systematic enslavement that can constitute a crime against humanity, the perpetrators are subject to international criminal responsibility. See ICC Statute, Article 7.1(c), Document 76.

See Also Terms: 11, 12, 20, 22, 24, 25, 26, 29, 33, 34, 35, 37, 48, 63, 70, 73, 75, 84, 86, 93, 100, 120, 122, 124, 133, 136, 144, 145, 146, 147, 151, 152, 153, 160, 167, 169, 170, 171, 177, 179, 181, 182, 184, 185, 189, 195, 208, 215, 216, 222, 223, 228, 230, 231, 243, 259, 260, 261, 264, 272, 283, 289, 290, 292, 293, 297, 306, 307, 309, 310, 311, 316.

282. SOCIAL HUMAN RIGHTS

Definition: A type of human right that relates to the protection of human beings in their social context. These rights address how people may establish and regulate their social situation, such as by marriage or adoption, having children, or keeping a family from being separated by government action.

Significance: Social human rights form part of what formerly were known as "second generation" human rights (economic, social, and cultural rights). This term "generation" is no longer used. Social human rights are found primarily in the ICESCR, the classic general human rights instrument. However, there are social human rights found in the ICCPR, a first generation human rights instrument, as well.

The U.S. has signed, but not ratified, the ICESCR and so it is not bound by the hard law of that treaty. (See Vienna Convention, Appendix E). However, as a signatory, it has a soft or interim obligation under the Vienna Convention of 1969 not to do anything inconsistent with the object and purpose of that treaty.

See Also Terms: 11, 12, 20, 21, 24, 25, 26, 29, 32, 48, 215, 222, 230, 231, 236, 243, 57, 62, 70, 92, 120, 124, 142, 144, 145, 146, 147, 151, 152, 160, 167, 169, 177, 179, 180, 184, 185, 250, 253, 259, 264, 272, 289, 290, 292, 293, 297, 306, 307, 309, 311, 316, 322.

283. SOCIAL JUSTICE

Definition: The right ordering of a society according to human rights principles in a manner that guarantees equality, justice, and fairness in reality to every person, with respect for the rule of law and for the inherent human dignity and human rights of every individual, and a decent, safe, and healthy standard of living and living environment.

Significance: This term is not clearly defined in American society. It is very often used in the context of claimed injustices happening to the poor or those in prisons. In many contexts in the United States, human rights are dealt with under the title "social justice." This is particularly true in terms of grassroots organizations, and especially religious organizations. However, with the recent increase in the use and acceptance of the term "human rights" the term social justice is being used less often.

Human rights are essentially about social justice. This is so in relation to how human beings are treated by government and how they are treated by fellow members of society. Human rights emphasize the human dignity of all human beings and the particular rights each human has in a society, such as the right to privacy, freedom of expression and fair criminal trials. Broadly speaking, social justice covers all human rights classified as civil, political, economic, social, and cultural rights.

See Also Terms: 1, 3, 4, 7, 10, 11, 12, 13, 18, 24, 28, 29, 32, 33, 24, 35, 36, 42, 44, 45, 46, 48, 49, 51, 53, 54, 55, 56, 57, 61, 62, 63, 64, 70, 71, 72, 73, 75, 76, 83, 88, 90, 91, 92, 93, 94, 99, 100, 106, 113, 118, 119, 120, 121, 122, 123, 124, 127, 128, 129, 130, 138, 141, 142, 144, 145, 146, 147, 148, 149, 150, 152, 153, 154, 158, 160, 162, 165, 166, 167, 169, 177, 178, 179, 180, 181, 182, 183, 184, 185, 187, 190, 192, 193, 195, 196, 197, 202, 203, 204, 205, 207, 213, 222, 223, 224, 227, 230, 231, 237, 242, 243, 246, 250, 252, 253, 254, 257, 259, 264, 267, 268, 270, 271, 272, 273, 285, 289, 290, 291, 294, 297, 303, 305, 306, 307, 308, 309, 312, 316, 318, 322.

284. SOCIALISM

Definition: A form or system of government which calls for the equal sharing of land and equal return of the product of the land and industry to all member of society.

Significance: Socialism is said to have evolved from the industrial revolution that shook Europe in the first half of the 19th century. It is an economic and social theory that has as its goal to maximize the wealth and opportunity of a society, and minimize want and suffering for all people. It does this through public ownership and control of business and manufacturing and social services. It is an alternative to capitalism, a system wherein the means and profit of production are held by the private sector.

Socialism appeared in the U.S. primarily in the labor movement especially with the creation and expansion of labor unions trying to protect workers' rights. Socialist tenets can be found to some degree in the U.S. social security and welfare systems. The idea that everyone should help

221

one another in society was galvanized by the Great Depression. However, socialism has never posed a serious challenge to capitalism in the United States. And the demise of socialistic regimes in Eastern Europe has shown that it lacks viability as a social and economic theory. Socialism, to most Americans, has a bad connotation of being anti-capitalist. But in historical fact, the U.S. has done a tremendous amount of helping those in need, always under the understanding that it was morally right and humanitarian, and that domestic tranquility was served by eliminating the roots of revolution that one had seen develop into communism in East Europe and Asia.

The use of the term socialist has been used in American political discourse in an attempt to scare people into believing that a harmful trend was occurring in some sector of society. This happened in respect to the battle over health care reform in 2009-2010. There was no question that factually America had an unacceptably high number of completely or partially uninsured persons who could not afford health care. This created problems in the health care system for all Americans. Either society had to find a way to get the private and public sector to solve the problem or the adverse consequences of lack of healthcare would continue to infect American society as a whole.

The attempt by the Administration to propose health care reform was branded by many Americans as "socialism" and the provision of healthcare services to the very poor deemed social-ized medicine. The implication of this use of the terms is that every person should get their own healthcare coverage and it was not the government's job provide it. As matter of international human rights law, the state has a positive legal obligation with respect to taking measure to protect the inherent human dignity of all those within the society. There is a sort of right and duty of every state to continue to increase the general welfare of the state's population. Some of the measures that need to be taken (housing, medical care, and education) are factors in the development of the whole society and, in theory, the measures benefit the whole of society.

It is important, therefore, to be careful how one uses the term socialism. It can be mistaken for government measures which benefit the broader society, including those who do not pay for it. But no where in the discourse of socialism does this issue become more pronounced than with regard to economic human rights. The U.S. has signed but not ratified the International Covenant on Economic, Social and Cultural Rights (ICESCR). That human rights treaty calls upon the states parties to take progressive to take steps, especially economic and technical, to the maximum of its available resources, with a view to progressively realizing the economic, social and cultural human rights in that treaty. These rights include the right to an adequate standard of living including food, clothing and housing, and the right to the enjoyment of the highest attainable standard of physical and mental health. (See Document 16, articles 11 and 12). Neither of these rights can be interpreted as being the right of an individual to have these necessities of life for free. Many have looked at this treaty and felt it was too socialist, allowing for a claim to a free lunch from society. It is not that. The specter of socialism seems to have affected the perceptions of many Americans in relation to economic human rights.

Even so, in the U.S. UPR report, the U.S. mentions the many steps the U.S. has taken to help the poor of this world inside and outside the U.S. It seems America wishes to be perceived as a great humanitarian state, but does not wish to recognize certain basic human needs as human rights.

One has to understand, however, that socialism is often confused by some Americans with the government doing something to help someone in need within society. The Constitution of the United States established a government of the people and for the people in order to "form a more perfect Union, establish justice, insure domestic tranquility, provide for the common defense, **promote the general welfare**, and secure the blessings of liberty to ourselves and our posterity." It cannot be said that taking measures to promote the general welfare of all Americans by doing something to help them is a socialist notion.

See Also Terms: 7, 20, 24, 48, 50, 69, 70, 83, 91, 92, 99, 100, 108, 119, 120, 121, 122, 123, 124, 141, 145, 146, 147, 151, 152, 160, 167, 169, 168, 172, 174, 177, 179, 180, 184, 185, 190, 195, 212, 215, 222, 230, 231, 239, 241, 242, 264, 272, 283, 292, 293, 309, 316, 323, 243.

285. SOFT LAW

Definition: A term describing a doctrine of international law that describes the legal status of certain human rights-related declarations, resolutions, guidelines, and basic principles of inter-governmental organizations. Soft laws are nonbinding norms that set forth nonobligatory but highly recommended standards of state conduct. The term is also used to refer to norms in legal instruments that are so vague or imprecise they are not legally enforceable; these norms are mostly hortatory (advisory) or programmatory.

Significance: In human rights literature it is most often in the first sense that this term is used. It is "soft" law because it is not legally binding, as is "hard" law.

An example of soft law is the 1957 U.N. Standard Minimum Rules for the Treatment of Prisoners (see Document 48). The United States is not bound to comply with these standards but should do so because they represent the opinion of all the states regarding the proper minimum human rights standard.

The way to be most sure that a state is complying with its hard law obligations in international human rights law is to see if it is following the soft law, where applicable. Following soft law is the way to following hard law. Such soft law is usually based on the opinions of international experts in their field. Some countries incorporate certain soft law instruments into their national law, such as regarding treatment of prisoners, or the juvenile justice system.

See Also Terms: 48, 49, 70, 72, 74, 94, 127, 141, 142, 144, 145, 146, 147, 152, 211, 214, 222, 226, 259, 272, 286, 291, 292, 293, 306, 307, 316.

286. SOFT POWER

Definition: Power based on intangible or indirect influences such as culture, values, and ideology. It as defined by the person who coined the term as "co-opting people rather than coercing them."

Significance: The human rights movement has been all about working to get states and their governments to respect and protect human rights. It is about trying to persuade a government to stop violating human rights or persuading another state to intervene with another state to request the other state to stop violation of rights. Certainly a state can be forced by threat of armed force to change its policy and stop violating human rights. But just as effective is the use of soft power. That means the use of human rights norms and discourse and use of administrative and quasi-judicial and judicial procedures to effect change. Soft power is a less destructive and less costly means of change. It seeks to persuade by right, and moral and legal reason, rather than by weapons. The essence of soft power for the U.S. lies in its resort to human values, both in our culture and in the way we as a country handle ourselves internationally. It has been said that soft power is both easy and hard for the U.S. The U.S. is often the model of hard power: the cruise missiles, tanks, drones, and special ops forces. And then sometimes it is the model of soft power. Someone said that the U.S. is "the model and anti-model, the focus of imitation and the target of hatred."

With the new Administration in 2009, there has been more discussion and use of the terms soft power and smart power. The idea seems to seek to change the world and the U.S. domestically, by persuasion and reason, and moral stature, rather than force and political power. This idea fits with human rights, which are abstract concepts which are supposed to limit the power and action of government. If the U.S. were to be a model of soft power through the use of human rights norms and discourse, this would change the geo-political landscape. While many will dismiss the idea of using more soft power as naive in this world of terrorists and asymmetrical warfare, this is an idea which has not been tested and found wanting: it is an idea that has never been tried.

Some say that what the U.S. needs to do is to increase investment in "soft power," not expensive new weapons, which consistently get compromised and neutralized by simple opponents with simple weapons and means. Soft power increases political stature and the state which respects human rights is banking soft power. The more soft power a state gains by its observance of its human rights legal obligations, the more it stands morally capable to respond to the next atrocity, without hypocrisy or double standard.

In this post 9/11 world when many states have criticized the U.S. for its war on terrorism response, it needs to resort to soft power more than ever. It could be argued that America's resort to hard power has created more enemies than it has destroyed. The U.S. needs to use soft power to win back allies and even win over enemies. Respecting human rights at home and abroad is the best way to obtain soft power. This would result in a more favorable world public opinion about the U.S. and increase U.S. credibility and moral strength. To successfully wage the war on terrorism, the U.S. needs the cooperation of other states and international institutions. Soft power is a capacity to do things and to affect the behavior of others to make those things happen.

In the field of international human rights law the biggest U.S. weakness in soft power comes from the U.S. failing to sign or ratify and become part of many major human rights treaties. Much soft power comes from the human rights treaties we have signed and ratified, but much more could be gained from signing or ratifying others, such as the Rome Statute, the Convention on the Rights of the Child, ICESCR, CEDAW, Protocols I and II of the Geneva Conventions, the Convention on the Rights of Migrant Workers, the Kyoto Protocol, the Landmine and the Cluster bomb Conventions, and the Convention against Disappearances. See Documents 16, 27, 28, 36, 44, 45, 46, 63, 64, 65, 73, 74, 76, 86, 87.

If one examines the real reasons why the U.S. has not become bound by these treaties it is either to protect U.S. or ally economic or military interest, both hard power factors. We protect our hard power more than we invest in our soft power. The U.S. has been both the best friend and worst friend of human rights since 9/11. It needs to become single standard and to be soft powered. For this to happen in the U.S. the most necessary factor is human rights education for all Americans at all age appropriate levels. Soft power is learned and modeled and demanded by those who know its power. Lack of country wide human rights education is the soft power Achilles heel of America.

See Also Terms: 4, 7, 9, 10, 11, 12, 20, 24, 28, 29, 34, 35, 36, 44, 46, 47, 48, 50, 51, 53, 54, 55, 56, 57, 60, 61, 63, 64, 68, 70, 72, 73, 75, 83, 90, 92, 93, 94, 99, 100, 112, 113, 118, 119, 120, 128, 129, 130, 132, 133, 134, 135, 136, 137, 138, 141, 142, 143, 144, 146, 147, 148, 149, 150, 152, 154, 158, 160, 162, 167, 169, 173, 177, 178, 179, 180, 181, 184, 185, 187, 190, 193, 195, 196, 197, 204, 208, 216, 217, 222, 223, 224, 229, 231, 237, 243, 252, 253, 254, 259, 264, 267, 272, 276, 289, 290, 292, 293, 305, 306, 307, 309, 311, 316, 318, 322, 323.

287. SOVEREIGNTY

Definition: A principle of public international law that says that every state has the sole and exclusive right to make and enforce the law within its territory and to govern that territory and everything and everyone in it and to defend itself.

Significance: The concept of sovereignty of states was developed with the birth of international law itself in the late 1600s. Before that time, states and international law did not exist as we know them today. Sovereignty allows a group of people who identify as a nation to establish a legal political entity called a "state." A founding principle of international law was that states possessed sovereignty, the sole and exclusive legal control over everything within their territory.

Sovereignty does not include the right of the state to violate the human rights of those within its territory and subject to its jurisdiction (citizens or noncitizens). Sovereignty can be voluntarily limited by a state either by becoming a party to a human rights treaty or by the ripening of customary international human rights norms, which imply state consent. Where states take on legal obligations regarding human rights they give up sovereignty in that area of government conduct. For example, when the United States ratified the Convention against Torture, it gave up its sovereign right to treat people within the United States anyway it wanted, such as by torturing them. Even if the United States would not be violating the U.S. Constitution by torturing someone (it would be), it would still be illegal under international human rights law.

Sovereignty does not permit a state to treat its people any way it wants, in violation of their human rights. Nor does it protect a state from the criticism of other states or non-governmental organizations. Sovereignty is not a legal shield to protect a state from international scrutiny for human rights abuses. In 1993 the nations of the world proclaimed in the Vienna Declaration and Programme of Action that human rights are the birthright of all humankind and the concern of all humankind. See Document 51.

In the United States the notion of sovereignty has become a critically important factor in whether the United States ratifies human rights treaties, such as the Convention on the Rights of the Child. It is perceived by opponents that ratification of such a treaty will result in a loss of sovereignty, preventing the country from determining its own values regarding children and families. Sovereignty for many opposed to U.S. ratification of human rights treaties has become synonymous with the protection of the nation's values and institutions and the country's right to do things "our way." There are fears of a foreign or supranational power intruding on sovereign U.S. space and making citizens do things they do not believe in or that are contrary to the "American way of life."

Recent history, such as in the Bosnia conflict of the 1990s or the Kosovo crisis of 1999, reveals that sovereignty is often a shield behind which government agents who commit human rights violations hide and enjoy immunity from responsibility for their acts.

Although sovereignty does not allow a state to commit human rights violations with impunity, it does limit what the international community or any state can do in response to such violations. All such responses must respect international rule of law and be consistent with international law, including human rights law.

See Also Terms: 2, 6, 25, 26, 27, 48, 70, 71, 72, 73, 75, 79, 80, 103, 105, 106, 109, 114, 118, 137, 138, 141, 152, 153, 185, 187, 207, 210, 211, 218, 222, 243, 259, 262, 264, 266, 269, 272, 276, 278, 292, 293, 294, 308, 316, 323.

288. SOVEREIGNTY PROVISO

Definition: A provision inserted by the U.S. Senate into a Senate resolution that ratifies an international human rights treaty, that says that the president is required to notify all present and prospective states parties to the treaty that nothing in the treaty authorizes legislation that would be prohibited by the U.S. Constitution.

Significance: In the ratification of international human rights instruments, the United States seeks to make them compatible with the laws and principles set forth in the U.S. Constitution. Some in the international community, however, criticize the willingness of the United States to fully submit itself to the international human rights systems by the way it uses the reservations, declarations, and understandings in the ratification process.

See Also Terms: 3, 6, 27, 48, 70, 74, 93, 94, 98, 144, 145, 158, 167, 169, 177, 184, 185, 194, 211, 220, 222, 243, 259, 272, 292, 293, 306, 307.

289. SPECIAL MECHANISMS/PROCEDURES (U.N.)

Definition: "Special Procedures" is the general name given to the mechanisms established by the Commission on Human Rights and assumed by the Human Rights Council to address either specific country situations or thematic issues in all parts of the world. The term "Special Mechanisms" is also used.

Significance: The Office of the High Commissioner for Human Rights provides these mechanisms with personnel, policy, research and logistical support for the discharge of their mandates. Currently, there are about 31 thematic and about eight country mandates. The U.N. Human Rights Council selects and offers to certain human rights experts a mandate to make a report or investigate regarding a certain theme or country. Those who agree to act in such capacity are given a mandate by the Council empowering them to act. They are called mandate holders. The Special Procedures mandates usually call on mandate holders to examine, monitor, advise and publicly report on human rights situations in specific countries or territories, known as country mandates, or on major phenomena of human rights violations worldwide, known as thematic mandates. Various activities are undertaken by special procedures, including responding to individual complaints, conducting studies, providing advice on technical cooperation at the country level, and engaging in general promotional activities.

Special procedures involve either an individual (called "Special Rapporteur," "Special Representative of the Secretary-General" or "Independent Expert"), or a working group, usually composed of five members (one from each global region). The mandates of the special procedures are established and defined by the resolution creating them. mandate-holders of the special procedures serve in their personal capacity, and do not receive salaries or any other financial compensation for their work. The independent status of the mandate-holders is crucial in order to be able to fulfill their functions in all impartiality. Most Special Procedures mandate-holders also receive information on specific allegations of human rights violations and send so called "urgent action" appeals or letters of allegation to governments asking for clarification.

Mandate holders also carry out country visits to investigate the human rights situation at the national level. In the past there have been other U.S. visits of Special Rapporteurs to carry on investigations on certain U.S. human rights practices, such as freedom of religion and racial discrimination.

In its Compilation of information on the U.S. for the UPR (See Appendix K) the OHCHR reports that the following special procedures involved the U.S. and a visit to the U.S.: Special Rapporteur on the human rights of migrants (30 April–18 May 2007); Special Rapporteur on the promotion and protection of human rights and fundamental freedoms while countering terrorism (16–25 May 2007); Special Rapporteur on contemporary forms of racism, racial discrimination, xenophobia and related intolerance (19 May–6 June 2008); Special Rapporteur on extrajudicial, summary or arbitrary executions (16–30 June 2008); Working Group on the use of mercenaries as a means of violating human rights and impeding the exercise of the right of peoples to self-determination (20 July–3 August 2009); Special Rapporteur on adequate housing as a component of the right to an adequate standard of living (22 October–8 November 2009); Working Group of experts on people of African descent (25–29 January 2010).

Included as Document 53 is a report of a Special Rapporteur as part of a special procedure. There are others in Appendix L.

See Also Terms: 3, 20, 26, 30, 48, 70, 72, 77, 115, 117, 119, 124, 125, 126, 144, 145, 147, 150, 151, 152, 163, 173, 177, 184, 185, 211, 259, 260, 261, 265, 268, 272, 286, 290, 311.

290. SPECIAL RAPPORTEUR

Definition: An individual who is selected by the U.N. Human Rights Committee and who is given a specific order and mission (mandate) to investigate, gather information, and prepare a study on either a certain human rights subject or theme or the human rights situation in a particular country, and to report back *(rapporteur)* to the body requesting the study.

Significance: In the U.N. Human Rights Council the United Nations has what are known as "special mechanisms" for making sure states respect human rights. Among those special mechanisms are appointment of special rapporteurs, who compile reports on specific countries or specific themes; appointment of Special Representative of the Secretary General, who function likewise; appointment of independent experts in a given field; and working groups of five experts who work on a specific theme issue such as enforced disappearances.

Special rapporteurs are chosen from around the world for their expertise. They prepare and submit periodic reports to the Human Rights Council, which forms the basis of the work of the Council on a particular issue or country. There were 31 thematic and eight country special rapporteurs in 2010. They sometimes visit states and investigate an issue or a country and usually need the permission of the state to carry out their visit.

They also receive "urgent action" letters from people around the world asking their help on a claimed urgent issue within the terms of reference of the rapporteur. They have no power to force a state to do anything. Their powers have been expanded somewhat to confront the state involved, seeking a response that may lead to a resolution of the issue, such as a disappearance or torture. Examples of reports by special rapporteurs concerning their fact-finding trips to the United States include documents in Appendix L. The August 2010 Compilation of Information on the U.S. for the UPR, lists the following past visits of the Special Rapporteurs to the U.S.: Special Rapporteur on the human rights of migrants (30 April–18 May 2007); Special Rapporteur on the promotion and protection of human rights and fundamental freedoms while countering terrorism (16–25 May 2007); Special Rapporteur on contemporary forms of racism, racial discrimination, xenophobia and related intolerance (19 May–6 June 2008); Special Rapporteur on extrajudicial, summary or arbitrary executions (16–30 June 2008); Special Rapporteur on adequate housing as a component of the right to an adequate standard of living (22 October–8 November 2009).

Document 53 is a Special Rapporteur report. Others are included in the Appendix L, including some specifically about the U.S.

See Also Terms: 48, 49, 59, 70, 77, 81, 82, 85, 112, 113, 133, 142, 144, 145, 147, 150, 151, 162, 163, 173, 177, 184, 185, 202, 206, 208, 215, 222, 227, 243, 259, 268, 286, 289, 292, 293, 302, 298, 324.

291. STANDARD SETTING

Definition: The political process of establishing specific human rights legal norms to serve as the standards of conduct (rules) for state government. This happens when governments convene in the context of an international organization, such as the United Nations, or Organization of American States, to negotiate and adopt both legal and non-legal instruments (treaties, declarations) that set forth the standards upon which they agree and which states are asked to follow.

Significance: Standard-setting instruments are those that set forth human rights norms. These norms are the legal standards accepted by the international community, of which the United States is a key member. The purpose of the international human rights movement is to establish a common denominator of basic human rights norms that uphold the inherent human dignity of each individual worldwide. Normally, first a non-binding declaration of principles concerning a particular topic is adopted by resolution, after which a binding legal instrument, a treaty, is established. The standard setting process culminates in a binding legal norm by which states can agree to become bound in the treaty ratification process.

The following documents in the Primary Documents section are known as "standard-setting" instruments in the field of international human rights law:
2, 5, 6, 8, 10, 11, 16, 17, 19, 23, 27, 28, 29, 31, 33, 34, 35, 36, 37, 38, 39, 40, 41, 42, 43, 44, 45, 46, 47, 48, 49, 50, 60, 61, 62, 63, 64, 65, 66, 68, 69, 70, 71, 72, 73, 74, 75, 76, 77.

Some of these documents are declarations and not binding as such, but are part of the process of standard setting. Some are soft law but can still be considered part of the standard setting process as they articulate how states can most precisely carry out their legal obligations.

See Also Terms: 11, 12, 20, 24, 25, 31, 32, 33, 34, 35, 43, 45, 48, 53, 54, 55, 56, 57, 62, 63, 64, 70, 73, 74, 98, 116, 118, 127, 129, 130, 135, 141, 154, 173, 177, 178, 179, 180, 182, 184, 185, 192, 197, 203, 208, 211, 220, 222, 225, 226, 229, 231, 243, 245, 247, 258, 259, 262, 264, 269, 272, 279, 287, 288, 292, 293, 297, 303, 306, 307, 318, 322, 323.

292. STATE

Definition: An international legal-political entity which meets the following criteria: (1) It has a defined, permanent body of people/population; 2) that occupies a more or less defined territory; 3) that has an organized government capable of maintaining effective control of all its territory; 4) that possesses the capacity to carry on international relations, and 5) that is willing and able to fulfill its international legal obligations to respect and protect human rights. It is the legal term to designate what is in the U.S. commonly called a "country."

Significance: The traditional characteristics of a state were those outlined above. It is increasingly being argued by international legal experts that a state must also fulfill its human rights obligations under international law. This is particularly so if the state is a member of the United Nations, whose Charter sets forth general human rights obligations for every member state. See Document 5, Preamble and Articles 1, 2 and 4.

A state must be independent and exercise sovereignty over its territory. It possesses international legal personality and enjoys "sovereign equality," that is, it is legally equal to all other states in the world. Every state is bound by international legal obligations to protect and respect human rights. No state can claim that human rights violations are acceptable as part of their sovereignty. No state can claim that criticism about its human rights violations is a matter solely within its domestic jurisdiction. Such violations are matters subject to scrutiny and international action by the whole international community according to international law.

See Also Terms: 11, 12, 20, 24, 46, 48, 60, 61, 70, 72, 73, 75, 114, 118, 121, 122, 124, 128, 137, 138, 141, 145, 146, 147, 150, 151, 152, 153, 154, 155, 156, 157, 158, 159, 162, 165, 173, 176, 177, 179, 180, 181, 182, 183, 184, 185, 187, 190, 192, 193, 194, 197, 198, 207, 208, 209, 210, 211, 212, 215, 218, 219, 221, 222, 230, 231, 233, 236, 238, 239, 242, 243, 244, 252, 253, 254, 255, 256, 258, 259, 263, 264, 266, 267, 268, 269, 272, 276, 278, 280, 287, 288, 289, 290, 291, 203, 294, 295, 296, 297, 299, 305, 306, 307, 308, 309, 311, 316, 323.

293. STATE PARTY

Definition: A state which has signed, ratified, and thus become legally bound to obey a treaty, is called a "state party" to that treaty. Sometimes also called a "contracting party."

Significance: A state cannot be accused of violating a human rights treaty unless it is first established that it is a state party to that treaty. The state becomes a state party by signing a treaty and then executing an instrument of ratification (or adhesion, accession, succession, or approval). Whatever it is called, this act is an official act on behalf of the people of the state binding that state and its people to comply with the treaty. The United States is a state party to the International Covenant on Civil and Political Rights (ICCPR) and several other human rights treaties. It is legally bound to comply with these instruments because it is a state party to them. The United States is not yet a state party to many other U.N. conventions, but only a signatory.

An example is the Convention on the Rights of the Child (CRC). Strictly speaking, a signatory state is not fully legally bound to comply with a treaty until it ratifies it. It is not a state party. For example, since it has only signed and not ratified the CRC, the United States is not a state party to that treaty (as of the writing of this book). By signing the CRC the U.S. has expressed its intent to eventually ratify. However, under Article 18 of the Vienna Convention on the Law of Treaties the U.S. has an "interim" obligation to refrain from acts which would defeat the object and purpose of [the] treaty. The object and purpose of the CRC is to recognize certain human rights in children and to protect children from harm.

The U.S. has, however, ratified two protocols to the CRC and it is bound to comply with them. Having ratified these two protocols the U.S. is a state party to those protocols.

It is not the case, therefore, that if a state is not a party to a treaty that it has absolutely no obligations with regards to that treaty. A signatory state does have a soft obligation created under Article 18 of the Vienna Convention.

It must be remembered that when one finds that a certain state is a state party to a treaty one still has to see if there are any Reservations, Declarations and Understandings (RDUs) submitted by such state party when it ratified, before one can determine the extent of the state's obligation in respect to any particular substantive or procedural norm in the treaty. Only then can one be able to determine. if the state has committed any violations of the norms.

294. STATE RESPONSIBILITY FOR INJURY TO ALIENS

Definition: A classical international law doctrine that provided that a state had a legal obligation to treat nationals of another state in a manner that conformed to certain minimum standards of civilization. When a foreign national was injured by the state, that state owed a legal obligation to the state of the injured person's nationality to pay compensation or otherwise remedy the injury, and the latter state could collect the compensation from the offending state for such damages.

Significance: This principle served as one of the historic antecedents to modern human rights law. The principle of Public International Law was based on the premise that individuals held no rights under International Law and that only states did. Thus, if a state harmed a citizen of another state, the state of the victim's nationality had the legal right to seek compensation for the damage to their citizen. This created a legal responsibility of a state to another state for its wrongdoing harming nationals of other states.

Under International Human Rights Law, individuals do now hold ('bear") legal rights, and there are measures that can be taken nationally and internationally for harm done by other states. See the decision in the case of *Kadic vs. Karadizc*, Appendix J, where some of these issues are discussed.

295. STATE TERRORISM/STATE-SPONSORED TERRORISM

See entry for **Terrorism/Terrorist**

296. SUBSIDIARITY (PRINCIPLE OF)

Definition: A principle of international law which says that international law norms and rules and their implementation mechanisms and procedures, whether global or regional, are secondary, a backup, a fallback to domestic (national) laws, rules, judicial systems and procedures.

Significance: In international law the national legal system is primary over the international law system. This means that where there is an issue of a human rights violation one must resort first to the subject state's domestic (national) legal remedies provided in national legal institutions, before having recourse to the international level mechanisms.

Human rights treaties include a provision that each state ratifying the treaty must transform and implement the norms of the treaty into domestic (national) law. This is so that a person who believes that his or her human rights have been violated can go to a local court or other legal or administrative forum to seek respect for their human rights provided in the treaty. Human rights must be protected primarily at the state level, not the international level. The international human rights legal system is a back-up, a secondary system, a subsidiary system. One has to go through the primary state system first before going to the international system, if that is available in the treaty.

For Americans there is only one international human rights legal system in which complaints can be filed and that is in the Inter-American Commission on Human Rights, which is headquartered in Washington, D.C. But in order to file a complaint in that OAS quasi-judicial forum, the complainant has to exhaust all remedies at the national level first. This is according to the principal of subsidiarity. Since, in some cases, it is not possible for an individual to get access to national remedies, or those remedies are not effective to protect human rights in reality, international law allows some exceptions to the exhaustion requirement. See the *Ameziane vs. USA* Petition in Appendix J, pages 35-48. The argument for an exception to the rule of exhaustion of domestic remedies is an argument for exemption from the principle of subsidiarity.

With regard to the other international complaint systems found in international human rights treaties, such as the ICCPR, the U.S. has not accepted the jurisdiction (competence) of the international treaty bodies to handle cases against the U.S. for alleged violation of the rights in the treaty. This is obviously because the U.S. does not want its human rights violations exposed or litigated at the international level. In such cases, all recourse against the U.S. for violating the human rights norms in the treaty can only be brought at the national level.

See Also Terms: 2, 7, 10, 11, 12, 25, 27, 47, 48, 53, 54, 55, 56, 57, 70, 72, 73, 88, 90, 93, 107, 118, 134, 144, 145, 146, 147, 150, 151, 152, 158, 160, 162, 165, 167, 169, 175, 177, 179, 182, 184, 185, 194, 211, 220, 222 226, 231, 233, 243, 244, 252, 253, 259, 262, 264, 268, 270, 272, 279, 287, 288, 2921, 292, 293, 297, 306, 307, 311, 316, 317, 318.

297. SUBSTANTIVE RIGHTS

Definition: Specific human rights found in an international human rights treaty or in a norm of customary international human rights law that express what a human being can do or not be forced to do, or how one is to be treated by government. Examples include freely speaking, freely practicing a religion, voting, movement, association, freedom from torture, and nondiscrimination. This is contrasted with *procedural* rights, which are rights by which the substantive rights come to be respected and protected by the state through commissions or courts, by plaintiffs filing complaints or by a state filing periodic reports on human rights progress or obstacles.

Significance: A major goal of the international human rights movement is to set standards world wide that are a common denominator observed by all states to uphold the inherent human dignity of every human being. To achieve that goal, the documents that make up the body of international human rights law contain these kinds of substantive rights, or norms, in order that the states may agree on what they are and then proceed to implement and enforce them in their various domestic settings. Obviously, because of political and economic differences between states and various, often volatile political climates, this process is a sensitive one. However, without the substantive rights to which states must be accountable being "spelled out," there will always be the temptation for governments to interpret what human rights should be. The standards must be established without confusion in order for human rights to be normalized throughout society.

See Also Terms: 11, 12, 20, 24, 33, 34, 35, 48, 53, 54, 55, 56, 57, 60, 62, 68, 70, 73, 75, 92, 94, 99, 100, 113, 120, 124, 129, 136, 145, 146, 147, 150, 151, 152, 154, 160, 167, 168, 169, 172, 174, 175, 177, 179, 180, 184, 185, 196, 198, 222, 229, 231, 242, 243, 250, 252, 258, 259, 264, 269, 272, 279, 282, 286, 289, 290, 291, 293, 306, 307, 309, 311, 312, 316, 322.

298. SUMMARY EXECUTION

Definition: An unlawful and deliberate killing carried out by order of a government or with its agreement. Such an execution would be carried out by the government's agents or others without prior judicial sentence by a court after a criminal trial capable of imposing capital punishment.

Significance: In human rights circles, it is commonly agreed that while all human rights are important, the right to life is of primary importance. This is because the denial of this particular right negates the enjoyment of any of the other ones. The summary execution is a particularly heinous act perpetrated by governments trying to subdue their political enemies, which denies the right to a fair trial and subsequently the right to life of an individual. The word "summary" in this context refers to an execution done "without delay" or the "formality" of a judicial trial before an independent and impartial court. This situation is ripe for abuses of power and errors in judgment. It can become a lynching mentality where due process of law is suspended for the sake of expediency.

Mass summary executions are observed in countries where dictators come to power and attempt to create a new order without the democratic process of trials for persons accused of treason or other capital crimes. This type of occurrence has historically happened in various South American countries. But in the U.S. context, a summary execution would also occur if, for example, a CIA agent in a foreign country killed someone suspected of being a spy without first giving him a proper trial. The key to understanding both examples is that rights in a society become completely arbitrary unless each person is guaranteed due process of law.

Article 6 of the ICCPR, which has been ratified by the United States, states, "No one shall be arbitrarily deprived of his life." Article 9 of the same treaty details the correct procedural rights to be observed when a person has been arrested or detained. See Document 8. Together, these articles outline the acceptable process to avoid the human rights abuse of a summary execution. With regard to the taking of life without fair trial and all judicial safeguards the issue becomes whether the life was deprived "arbitrarily." This does not just mean that there was a good reason or the person did do something wrong. Just because a person has committed or is about to commit even a heinous crime does not in itself justify a summary execution. Human rights law would foresee an arrest, detention, trial and punishment arbitrary. It recognizes the right to self defense or defense of others but there is a line over which a death caused by the state becomes an arbitrary or summary execution. There is no clear line on this. One must look at the totality of circumstances in light of the the norm which is made to protect inherent human dignity, even of the criminal person and the presumption in favor of life.

Summary executions are also known as "extra-judicial" or "extra-legal" executions or killings, or "arbitrary" executions or killings, depending on the context. In most cases they are government acts of murder that are considered criminal. See Document 104, Item 3, for the definition of extra-judicial killing under the Torture Victim Protection Act. This Act allows U.S. federal court jurisdiction and a cause of action for certain acts of summary execution.

In the war on terrorism the U.S. has been accused of committing violations of the right against summary or extra-judicial execution in its various counter terrorism measures. This is particularly true with the U.S. military drone attacks in the Middle East and in Pakistan, searching to destroy Al Quaeda leaders. See the report submitted to the U.N. Human Rights Council by Phillip Alston, Special Rapporteur on Extrajudicial, Summary or Arbitrary Executions, on "targeted killings" of suspected terrorists, Appendix M. Alston claims that in killing the suspected terrorists there is a likelihood of killing nearby innocent parties in what would amount to a summary execution by the U.S. The killing of the targeted person, whether a terrorist or not, would, strictly speaking, be a summary execution. Claiming that it is being done in the context of an on-going armed conflict does not change that.

See Also Terms: 10, 1Q1, 12, 20, 24, 25, 26, 30, 33, 48, 62, 63, 73, 88, 90, 93, 103, 104, 106, 110, 124, 132, 133, 135, 136, 137, 144, 145, 146, 147, 151, 152, 154, 160, 167, 169, 175, 177, 178, 179, 181, 182, 184, 185, 192, 197, 200, 201, 202, 215, 222, 223, 230, 231, 234, 235, 238, 239, 252, 253, 254, 259, 264, 267, 272, 289, 290, 292, 293, 294, 300, 306, 307, 309, 311, 316, 317, 318, 319.

299. SURVEILLANCE

Definition: Generally speaking, surveillance is the systematic observation of aerospace, surface, or subsurface areas, places, persons, or things, by visual, aural, electronic, photographic, or other means. In the human right context it is the systematic observation by the state or its agents of human beings for anti-crime or anti-terrorism purposes, whether they are or are not under suspicion.

Significance: In the criminal and anti-terrorism sense it is an investigation process by which police or FBI or CIA or other government agents gather evidence about crimes, or suspected crime, or terrorist through continuous observation of persons or places. Observation can be visual or electronic.

The U.S. has for a long time engaged in surveillance at various levels, by various means, and for both military and civilian purposes. The issue for human rights is how far surveillance can go before it violates international human rights norms which are part of U.S. law. Since the start of the war on terrorism the U.S. has engaged in increased surveillance both domestically and internationally. In 2002 the Patriot Act went into effect and increased the powers of the executive branch. See Document 88. A controversy ensued in America over how far the government could intrude into American lives in pursuance of the war on terrorism, and how much surveillance was too much or too far. The state has an obligation to keep Americans and their property safe. It does not enjoy an unlimited choice of methods or means as to how it does so. Its choices are limited by law. That law is primarily the U.S. Constitution and the international legal norms that are binding on the U.S. by virtue of Article VI of the Constitution. See Document 2. Since the start of the war on terrorism the debate, both nationally and internationally, has been whether the U.S. government has gone too far in using terrorism to justify surveillance both here and abroad.

International human rights law seeks to protect inherent human dignity. One aspect of that dignity is personal privacy and the expectation that the state will not violate one's privacy nor engage in unreasonable searches into one's life and property. Human rights norms seek to protect human security by articulating a fair balance between maximum individual freedom from government intrusion and the needs of state to protect society. The line is far from clear. What is clear is that it is the law and not personal choice by government, whatever title or rank, which sets the lines, and courts which determine when that line has been unlawfully crossed.

The particular human rights norms applicable to limiting surveillance by state upon our lives or those who seek to do us harm, are found in the UDHR and ICCPR. (See Documents 6, 8). UDHR Article 3 provides that "Everyone has the right to life, liberty and security of person." Security of person deals mostly with arrest and detention but has an element of how one was arrested which brings into play the surveillance issue. Surveillance deals with the security of the human person. It is not defined nor are its limits stated. What is clear is that everyone, friend or foe, legal or illegal has the human right to security of person and improper or erroneous surveillance can lead to a false or arbitrary arrest.

It is primarily with regard to the human right to privacy that surveillance applies. In UDHR Article 12 states that: "No one shall be subjected to arbitrary interference with his privacy, family, home or correspondence, nor to attacks on his honour and reputation. Everyone has the right to protection of the law against such interference or attacks." Again, this human right to privacy is held by everyone, not just citizens, not just those legally in the U.S., and even to those who seek to do us harm. But this human right is also not unlimited.

A binding legal norm to security of person and privacy can be found in ICCPR Article 9. The U.S. has ratified the ICCPR even though Article 9 has not been implemented by domestic U.S. legislation. Article 9 reads: "Everyone has the right to liberty and security of person." This norm also says that the right to security of person is held by everyone. But it is particularly ICCPR Article 17 which sets the norms limiting surveillance. Article 17 reads:

> No one shall be subject to arbitrary or unlawful interference with his privacy, family, home or correspondence, nor to unlawful attacks upon his honour and reputation.

In prohibiting arbitrary or unlawful interference with privacy in the U.S. is referring to the Constitution and laws and the international legal norms binding on the U.S. Surveillance cannot be arbitrary. There must be a legitimate, articulable justification for any surveillance measure and it must be a proportional measure. Unlawful, again, refers to an interference which is not prescribed by law. In a rule-of-law system everyone is subject to the law, including the President. When anyone disobeys the limits of the law the act becomes *ultra vires*, unlawful, and a violation of human rights. Even in the war on terrorism all surveillance must comply with law and no one is exempt from the law, and that law, again, includes international human rights legal norms, such as outlined in Article 12.

In U.S. law many surveillance laws and amendments have been passed and most all were controversial. Of particular issue was the FISA legislation. See Document 95. On July 10, President Bush signed the FISA Amendments Act of 2008. Until Congress enacted the amendments, FISA generally prohibited the government from conducting electronic surveillance without first obtaining an individualized order from the FISA court. The new law gives the court established by FISA an extremely limited role in overseeing the government's surveillance activities.

The Foreign Intelligence Surveillance Act (FISA) was a product born of the Watergate scandal. It establishes how the government can secretly eavesdrop on Americans inside the U.S. for intelligence investigations. Originally it was passed to authorize the government to collect foreign intelligence information involving communications with "agents of foreign powers."

What do the FISA amendments do? 1. They retroactively legalized a massive electronic operation to spy on the personal communications of many Americans inside the United States; 2. They allow the same kind of unaccountable surveillance online and by telephone; 3. they allow physical searches of homes and work places of Americans without a search warrant or any other proof that anyone undergoing surveillance is suspected of any crime at all; 4. The Attorney General of the United States, who is the person who authorizes the surveillance, is legally the only person with the ability to stop the surveillance.

FISA now gives the Executive Branch extensive, almost unaccountable, power over surveillance not only over suspected terrorists but over any American. Of course, this right to privacy is subject to legitimate law enforcement and intelligence and counter-terrorism measures aimed at keeping Americans safe. But all of these are subject to legal limits in a rule of law system. It is up to victims, civil society and the legal and judicial processes to challenge the state to evaluate and define the limits and the consequence of non-compliance with these limits.

In its Second and Third periodic reports to the U.N. Human Rights Committee 2005, Document 15A, one can read at paragraphs 291 to 312, the U.S. position on the right to privacy in U.S. law and practice specifically in relation to ICCPR Article 17.

In its 2010, national UPR report to the OHCHR the U.S. speaks about surveillance and the right to privacy. (See Document 86.) In its report the Administration stated:

> We also recognize that privacy is linked to free expression, in that individuals need to feel that they can control the boundaries of their self-disclosure and self-expression in order to be able to express themselves freely: surveillance, especially when practiced by a government, can lead to self-censorship. Although protecting the security of all citizens means that no individual can have an absolute right to privacy or expression, any limitations on these rights are determined in a public process, by representatives of the people in the legislature and by the courts.

It also stated in a later section dedicated only to privacy:

> Privacy
> Freedom from arbitrary and unlawful interference with privacy is protected under the Fourth Amendment to the Constitution and federal statutes. In addition, state and local laws and regulations provide robust protections of individuals' right to privacy and rigorous processes to ensure that investigative authorities are undertaken consistent with the Constitution.
>
> Protecting our national interests may involve new arrangements to confronting threats like terrorism, but these structures and practices must always be in line with our Constitution and preserve the rights and freedoms of our people. Although the departments and agencies of the U.S. Government involved in surveillance and the collection of foreign intelligence information comply with a robust regime of laws, rules, regulations, and policies designed to protect national security and privacy, significant concerns in these areas have been raised by civil society, including concerns that relevant laws have been made outdated by technological

changes, and that privacy protections need to be applied more broadly and methodically to surveillance.

The 2001 USA PATRIOT Act expanded intelligence collection authorities under the Foreign Intelligence Surveillance Act (FISA), which regulates electronic surveillance and physical searches conducted to acquire foreign intelligence information. The U.S. Executive Branch acknowledged in 2005 that the U.S. National Security Agency had been intercepting without a court order certain international communications where the government had a reasonable basis to conclude that one person was a member of, or affiliated with, Al Qaeda or a member of an organization affiliated with Al Qaeda and where one party was outside the United States. In response, considerable congressional and public attention focused on issues regarding the authorization, review, and oversight of electronic surveillance programs designed to acquire foreign intelligence information or to address international terrorism. Congress held hearings and enacted new legislation, including the Protecting America Act and a series of amendments to FISA.

See Also Terms: 11, 12, 20, 24, 26, 33, 34, 35, 48, 59, 60, 70, 88, 90, 93, 103, 120, 122, 124, 136, 137, 142, 144, 145, 146, 147, 151, 152, 160, 167, 169, 175, 177, 179, 184, 185, 195, 206, 210, 211, 222, 231, 232, 239, 243, 250, 255, 259, 264, 272, 283, 289, 290, 292, 293, 297, 306, 307, 309, 311, 316.

300. TERRORISM/TERRORIST

Definition: **International:** At the international law level applicable to the international community there is no accepted official legal definition of terrorism.

Even though the international community has not developed a legal definition of terrorism, since 1994, it has used a certain political description in some U.N. sponsored conventions that define and criminalize various types of activities most people associate with terrorism, such as aircraft hijacking and hostage taking. The <u>United Nations General Assembly</u> has used the following political description of terrorism:

> "Criminal acts intended or calculated to provoke a state of terror in the general public, a group of persons or particular persons for political purposes are in any circumstance unjustifiable, whatever the considerations of a political, philosophical, ideological, racial, ethnic, religious or any other nature that may be invoked to justify them."

In 2004 the U.N. Security Council in Resolution 1566 condemned terrorism as:

> "criminal acts, including against civilians, committed with the intent to cause death or serious bodily injury, or taking of hostages, with the purpose to provoke a state of terror in the general public or in a group of persons or particular persons, intimidate a population or compel a government or an international organization to do or to abstain from doing any act, which constitute offences within the scope of and as defined in the international conventions and protocols relating to terrorism, are under no circumstances justifiable by considerations of a political, philosophical, ideological, racial, ethnic, religious or other similar nature,"

National Level: For the U.S. the failure to arrive at an internationally accepted definition has not stopped it from developing its own definition of international terrorism in national law to use in prosecuting what it deems terrorist acts in the international context, that is, which happens outside of the U.S.

That law is found in title 18 of the U.S. Code, which sets forth American law at the federal level, in section 2331, the U.S. Federal Criminal Code. The U.S. considers it an act of international terrorism as a violation of U.S. law as follows :

CRIMES AND CRIMINAL PROCEDURE
PART I-CRIMES CHAPTER 113B–TERRORISM
Sec. 2331. Definitions
    As used in this chapter-
(1) the term "international terrorism" means activities that (A) involve violent acts or acts dangerous to human life that are a violation of the criminal laws of the United States or of any State, or that would be a criminal violation if committed within the jurisdiction of the United States or of any State;
(B) appear to be intended-
(i) to intimidate or coerce a civilian population;
(ii) to influence the policy of a government by intimidation or coercion; or
(iii) to affect the conduct of a government by mass destruction, assassination, or kidnapping; and
(C) occur primarily outside the territorial jurisdiction of the United States, or transcend national boundaries in terms of the means by which they are accomplished, the persons they appear intended to intimidate or coerce, or the locale in which their perpetrators operate or seek asylum;
(2) the term "national of the United States" has the meaning given such term in section 101(a)(22) of the Immigration and Nationality Act;
(3) the term "person" means any individual or entity capable of holding a legal or beneficial interest in property;
(4) the term "act of war" means any act occurring in the course of-
(A) declared war;
(B) armed conflict, whether or not war has been declared, between two or more nations; or
(C) armed conflict between military forces of any origin;

The U.S. Code also contains a definition of terrorism which appears as part of the Annual Country reports on Terrorism, which is submitted by the Secretary of State to Congress every year. It sets forth international terrorism in it definition. This is found in U.S. Code Title 22, Ch.38, Para. 2656f(d):

(d) Definitions
As used in this section—
(1) the term "international terrorism" means terrorism involving citizens or the territory of more than 1 country;
(2) the term "terrorism" means premeditated, politically motivated violence perpetrated against noncombatant targets by subnational groups or clandestine agents;
(3) the term "terrorist group" means any group, or which has significant subgroups which practice, international terrorism;
(4) the terms "territory" and "territory of the country" mean the land, waters, and airspace of the country; and
(5) the terms "terrorist sanctuary" and "sanctuary" mean an area in the territory of the country—
(A) that is used by a terrorist or terrorist organization—
(i) to carry out terrorist activities, including training, fundraising, financing, and recruitment; or
(ii) as a transit point; and
(B) the government of which expressly consents to, or with knowledge, allows, tolerates, or disregards such use of its territory and is not subject to a determination under—
(i) section 2405(j)(1)(A) of the Appendix to title 50;
(ii) section 2371 (a) of this title; or
(iii) section 2780 (d) of this title.

The United States has developed several other definitions of terrorism in different sectors. In the Federal Criminal Code, 18 U.S. Code sec. 2331, it defines domestic terrorism as follows:

> (5) the term "domestic terrorism" means activities that-
> (A) involve acts dangerous to human life that are a violation of the criminal laws of the United States or of any State;
> (B) appear to be intended-
> (i) to intimidate or coerce a civilian population;
> (ii) to influence the policy of a government by intimidation or coercion; or
> (iii) to affect the conduct of a government by mass destruction, assassination, or kidnapping; and
> (C) occur primarily within the territorial jurisdiction of the United States.

The Department of Defense Dictionary of Military Terms has used the following definition of terrorism:

> The calculated use of unlawful violence or threat of unlawful violence to inculcate fear; intended to coerce or to intimidate governments or societies in the pursuit of goals that are generally political, religious, or ideological.

A definition which has been used by the U.S. State Department, terrorism is:
> Premeditated, politically motivated violence perpetrated against noncombatant targets by subnational groups or clandestine agents, usually intended to influence an audience.

The definitions created by the U.S. have no legal force outside of the U.S. legal system. They are solely a part of its domestic law and the legal basis on which the U.S. acts. The U.S. cannot define terrorism for the international community.

Significance: Since 9/11 no term has become so charged with consequence as has terrorism. But ironically it has been the hardest of terms to define outside of the U.S. In fact, major ideological battles are going on both to figure out how to stop terrorism and how to stop some of the counter-measures which some feel go beyond what is legally permissible under human rights law, such as water boarding. Meanwhile, the U.N. is going on with the international community trying to stop what it cannot define, running on political language to get anything done at all.

The problem with trying to defining terrorism in the international community is that it con-flicts with the geo-political and political attitudes and sensitivities of different states and groups of people. This very much so in light of the war on terrorism and U.S. counter-terrorism measures. Among other things, the U.S. is concerned about itself having its own counter-terrorism acts being defined as terrorism. This inability to agree on a definition of terrorism has often been described by the saying that the same violent act that can be observed and described by one person as an act of terrorism will be observed and described by another person as an act of freedom fighting for inde-pendence of a people exercising their legal right to self determination. What is the essence of the definition of terrorism is terror: fear. Terrorism is an act which is meant to cause general fear in the civilian population. The key element to the concept of terrorism is that the subject acts are meant to cause general public terror that makes people feel insecure and in danger for their life or physi-cal well-being. They are terrorized primarily either to show the power and stealth of the terrorist and the weakness and vulnerability of the victim, or to get the terrorized population to get their government leadership to change its policy or practice on a given issue, such as the autonomy of minority group, or to replace that leadership. There are other possible reasons as well. What distin-guishes terrorism from other violent scary acts is that it is politically motivated. Terrorism is about achieving political objectives, even if motivated by other feelings and values, such as religion.

The U.S. has been extensively criticized by many states and groups and national and interna-tional organizations for how it is waging the war on terrorism, such as using drones to assassinate suspected terrorists, and enhanced interrogation techniques and extraordinary rendition to ghost detention sites. The U.S. claims that this is necessary to fight terrorism in an asymmetrical warfare against an enemy it claims follows no rules.

The Appendix M items on the war on terrorism and Documents 54–56, 58 show some of the discourse and international community legal perspective on the relationship between the war against terrorism and the obligation of the U.S. and other states to respect international human rights and humanitarian law obligations.

Within the U.S. the discussion, debate and litigation is about the limits of state power in intruding into the lives of citizens and residents and the protection of human security consistent with human rights. Seldom, however, does one hear anything said about international human rights standards. The victory in the war on terrorism will only be won when there is respect for the human rights of both Americans and other residents on the one hand, and the terrorists whom America seeks to stop. National security as well as human security require a commitment to rule of law and human rights in order to be protected.

In its 2010, national UPR report to the OHCHR the U.S. Administration spends much ink defending and justifying its actions in the war on terrorism and the treatment of minorities such as muslims. See Document 86. At the same time it is making clear and explaining the changes the new Administration has made because it sees certain policies and practices and legal interpretations as not consistent with the Constitution or international human rights and humanitarian law. The U.S. UPR report reads:

> The United States is currently at war with Al Qaeda and its associated forces. President Obama has made clear that the United States is fully committed to complying with the Constitution and with all applicable domestic and international law, including the laws of war, in all aspects of this or any armed conflict. We start from the premise that there are no law-free zones, and that everyone is entitled to protection under law. In his Nobel Lecture, the President made clear that "[w]here force is necessary, we have a moral and strategic interest in binding ourselves to certain rules of conduct...[E]ven as we confront a vicious adversary that abides by no rules...the United States of America must remain a standard bearer in the conduct of war." (paragraph 82)
>
> Executive Order 13493, *Review of Detention Policy Options*, established a task force to review and facilitate significant policy decisions regarding broader detention questions. This Special Task Force on Detention Policy has reviewed available options for the apprehension, detention, trial, transfer, release, or other disposition of individuals captured or apprehended in connection with armed conflicts and counterterrorism operations.... **The Administration has expressly acknowledged that international law informs the scope of our detention authority**. The President has also made clear that we have a national security interest in prosecuting terrorists, either before Article III courts or military commissions, and that we would exhaust all available avenues to prosecute Guantánamo detainees before deciding whether it would be appropriate to continue detention under the laws of war. Working with our Congress, we have revised our military commissions to enhance their procedural protections, including prohibiting introduction of any statements taken as a result of cruel, inhuman, or degrading treatment. (para. 88, emphasis added)
>
> Protecting our national interests may involve new arrangements to confronting threats like terrorism, but these structures and practices must always be in line with our Constitution and preserve the rights and freedoms of our people. Although the departments and agencies of the U.S. Government involved in surveillance and the collection of foreign intelligence information comply with a robust regime of laws, rules, regulations, and policies designed to protect national security and privacy, significant concerns in these areas have been raised by civil society, including concerns that relevant laws have been made outdated by technological changes, and that privacy protections need to be applied more broadly and methodically to surveillance. (para. 90)
>
> The 2001 USA PATRIOT Act expanded intelligence collection authorities under the Foreign Intelligence Surveillance Act (FISA), which regulates electronic surveillance and

physical searches conducted to acquire foreign intelligence information. The U.S. Executive Branch acknowledged in 2005 that the U.S. National Security Agency had been intercepting without a court order certain international communications where the government had a reasonable basis to conclude that one person was a member of, or affiliated with, Al Qaeda or a member of an organization affiliated with Al Qaeda and where one party was outside the United States. In response, considerable congressional and public attention focused on issues regarding the authorization, review, and oversight of electronic surveillance programs designed to acquire foreign intelligence information or to address international terrorism. Congress held hearings and enacted new legislation, including the 2007 Protect America Act and a series of amendments to FISA.

See Also Terms: 11, 12, 19, 20, 24, 26, 29, 33, 34, 35, 48, 59, 62, 63, 64, 70, 71, 72, 73, 75, 101, 110, 120, 124, 129, 132, 133, 136, 137, 142, 144, 145, 146, 147, 151, 152, 154, 160, 164, 167, 169, 175, 177, 179, 181, 182, 184, 185, 188, 192, 200, 202, 208, 215, 222, 223, 230, 231, 232, 234, 243, 259, 264, 272, 276, 289, 290, 291, 292, 295, 297, 306, 307, 308, 309, 310, 311, 316, 317, 318, 319, 320, 321.

301. THIRD GENERATION HUMAN RIGHTS

Definition: A term which was formerly used to describe a class of human rights that are historically newer rights, known as "solidarity rights." The term "generation" does not necessarily connote any chronological difference or hierarchy of human rights.

Third generation human rights are said to include the following separate rights: the right to development, the right to peace, the right to a clean environment, the right to humanitarian assistance, the right to a common heritage, the right to communication, and the right to solidarity.

Significance: This term, along with the terms first generation human rights and second generation human rights, is simply a political-legal conceptual categorization and way of classifying these rights that was used in the earlier days of human rights discourse. Third generation rights are also known as "solidarity rights" or "rights of solidarity." This means rights that require the whole world community of states to work together to achieve, such as the claimed "right to peace," and "right to a clean environment."

These latter terms should not be confused with the so-called right to solidarity, which is itself one of the third generation rights. Third generation human rights are complex, ill-defined conceptually and collectively, and subject to a great deal of dispute about whether they are even rights. In theory, they are rights that can only be realized through the concerted and good faith efforts of all actors in the international scene: states, NGOs, individuals, IGOs, and other public and private bodies, that is, the international community as a whole.

See Also Terms: 116, 274. These three terms should not be used. They are defined and referenced for historical reasons and should be avoided because they cause many conceptual difficulties.

302. TORTURE

Definition:

A. International Law:

1. Treaty Law

The official international law definition, as found in the Convention against Torture, Cruel, Inhuman and Degrading Treatment or Punishment, adopted in the United Nations in 1984 and ratified by the United States in 1994, defines torture as a human rights violation as follows:

> For purposes of this Convention "torture" means any act by which severe pain and suffering, whether physical or mental, is intentionally inflicted on a person for such purposes as obtaining from him or a third person information or a confession, punishing him for an act he has committed, or intimidating or coercing him or a third person, or for any reason based on discrimination of any kind, when such pain or suffering is inflicted by or at the instigation of

or with the consent or acquiescence of a public official or other person acting in an official capacity. It does not include pain or suffering arising only from, inherent in, or incident to, lawful sanctions. (See Document 19).

This international treaty definition has to be read in light of the U.S. "understanding" of that definition set forth below. (See also Document 20).

2. Customary International Law:

Torture has entered as a substantive norm into General International Law. It is prohibited as a matter of customary international law. This is the result of the ripening of Article 5 of the UDHR over time coupled with *opinio juris*, evidenced also by Article 7 of the ICCPR and CAT. (See Appendix I, Restatement of Foreign Relations Law, sec. 702) It is this author's opinion that the content of the definition of torture as a customary norm would be the above definition found in Article 1 of CAT.

B. U.S. Law:

There are three main sources of definitions of torture in U.S. law: 1. the Torture Victim Protection Act; 2. the Torture Act, 18 U.S. Code sec. 2340, for torture occurring outside the U.S.; and 3. the War Crimes Act of 1996 for torture committed within or outside the U.S. as a war crime under Common Article 3 of the Geneva Conventions (18 U.S. Code sec. 2441). (See Appendix I).

1. The Torture Victim Protection Act of 1992 gives U.S. federal courts subject matter jurisdiction over civil lawsuits filed for acts of torture committed outside the U.S. The definition of "torture" under that Act is as follows:

> 1. The term "torture" means any act, directed against an individual in the offender's custody or physical control, by which severe pain or suffering (other than pain or suffering arising from or inherent in, or incidental to, lawful sanctions), whether physical or mental, is intentionally inflicted on that individual for such purposes as obtaining from that individual or a third person information or a confession, punishing that individual for an act that individual or a third person has committed or is suspected of having committed, intimidating or coercing that individual or a third person, or for any reason based on discrimination of any kind; and
>
> 2. that mental pain or suffering refers to prolonged mental harm caused by or resulting from: A. the intentional infliction or threatened infliction of severe physical pain or suffering; B. the administration or application, or threatened administration or application, of mind altering substances or other procedures calculated to disrupt profoundly the senses or the personality; C. the threat of imminent death; or D. the threat that another individual will imminently be subjected to death, severe physical pain or suffering, or the administration or application of mind altering substances or other procedures calculated to disrupt profoundly the senses or the personality.

2. The Torture Act is part of the U.S. criminal code at 18 U.S. Code secs. 2340-2340A. It criminalizes acts of torture committed outside the U.S. In this Act, torture is defined as:

> an act committed by a person acting under the color of law specifically intended to inflict severe physical or mental pain or suffering (other than pain or suffering incidental to lawful sanctions) upon another person within his custody or physical control.
>
> § 2340(1). "Severe mental pain or suffering," in turn, is defined as the prolonged mental harm caused by or resulting from:
>
> (A) the intentional infliction or threatened infliction of severe physical pain or suffering;
>
> (B) the administration or application, or threatened administration or application, of mind-altering substances or other procedures calculated to disrupt profoundly the senses or personality;
>
> (C) the threat of imminent death; or

(D) the threat that another person will imminently be subjected to death, severe physical pain or suffering, or the administration or application of mind-altering substances or other procedures calculated to disrupt profoundly the senses or personality....

3. The War Crimes Act of 1996 definition of torture:

A) **Torture:** The act of a person who commits, or conspires or attempts to commit, an act specifically intended to inflict severe physical or mental pain or suffering (other than pain or suffering incidental to lawful sanctions) upon another person within his custody or physical control for the purpose of obtaining information or a confession, punishment, intimidation, coercion, or any reason based on discrimination of any kind.

Significance: Torture is one of the most serious human rights violations. It violates human dignity by attacking the physical and mental integrity of a person. Committing torture is a human rights violation by the state. It is also an international crime recognized both under the Convention against Torture and as a matter of customary international law.

Above, there are at least five definitions of torture relative to the U.S. Two international law definitions are found in the Convention against Torture and in Customary International Law; three definitions are found in the Torture Victim's Protection Act, the Torture Act, which is an attempt at the criminal implementing legislation of CAT, and the War Crimes Act of 1996. In addition, torture is also dealt with under the U.S. Constitution, particularly the eighth amendment prohibition against "cruel and unusual punishment."

The U.S. international legal obligation regarding torture is found primarily in the Convention Against Torture, Cruel, Inhuman or Degrading Treatment or Punishment (CAT), adopted in 1984. Prior to CAT, torture was first articulated in 1948 as a non-binding human rights principle in Article 5 of the UDHR. See Document 6. In 1966 torture was first made the subject of a legally binding treaty in the International Covenant on Civil and Political Rights. ICCPR Article 7 states:

No one shall be subjected to torture or to cruel, inhuman or degrading treatment or punishment. In particular, no one shall be subjected without his free consent to medical or scientific experimentation.

The United States by its ratification of the ICCPR in 1992 is legally bound by Article 7 not to engage in torture or cruel, inhuman, or degrading treatment or punishment. See Document 8. ICCPR Article 7 is an absolute, non-derogable human right. It applies at all times in all circumstances. Under it the U.S. is also obligated to submit periodic reports to the U.N. Human Rights Committee (HRCee), the treaty-based body elected to supervise the implementation of the ICCPR. The Second and Third Reports of the U.S. to the U.N. HRCee, submitted in 2005, included a statement of the U.S. as to their law and practice under the ICCPR in this area. (See Document 15A, Articles 7 and 10).

But the ICCPR did not define torture. An international definition would come with the creation of the CAT. CAT is known as a "slice instrument" because the international community felt torture was so important as to merit its own treaty and so it took a slice out of the ICCPR, Article 7, and treated torture in detail, along with cruel treatment and punishment and inhuman treatment or punishment and degrading treatment or punishment. All of these Article 7 acts were equally deemed human rights violations, but the international community chose to more specifically and fully define torture and establish its full effect as not only a human rights violation but an international crime giving rise to universal jurisdiction. (See Document 68, Articles 18 and 20).

The United States has ratified and is a state party to the CAT. It is thus bound under international law not to commit acts of torture or cruel, inhuman, or degrading treatment or punishment. The U.S. must provide periodic reports to the Committee Against Torture (also abbreviated CAT), which is the body elected to supervise the implementation of the CAT treaty; it is currently doing this. See Document 21A.

Freedom from torture under CAT is an absolute, non derogable right which applies at all times, in all places in the world, regardless of circumstance. Article 1 of CAT reads:

> 1. Each State Party shall take effective legislative, administrative, judicial or other measures to prevent acts of torture in any territory under its jurisdiction.

Torture is a human rights violation for the state which commits torture. It is also an international crime giving rise to individual criminal responsibility. This applies even in the context of an international or non international armed conflict. Both customary and treaty obligations prohibiting torture under the ICCPR and CAT, fully apply in times of armed conflict, even in the war on terrorism. CAT article 2 reads:

> 2. No exceptional circumstances whatsoever, whether a state of war or a threat of war, internal political in stability or any other public emergency, may be invoked as a justification of torture.

Moreover, no one person, regardless of rank or government position, can be immune from criminal liability by claiming they were "just following orders." Article 3 reads:

> 3. An order from a superior officer or a public authority may not be invoked as a justification of torture.

And, under the Nuremberg Principles (See Document 70) no one can claim immunity from prosecution based on their military rank or their position in the government, even a president or king.

CAT defines and gives special attention to criminalization of torture in domestic law. Article 4 obliges the U.S. as a state party to "ensure that all acts of torture are offences under its criminal law." It must make torture illegal, including acts committed by government or private individuals or groups. The U.S. has not completely fulfilled this obligation in the eyes of the international community, as it has not prohibited torture occurring within the U.S. except under the War Crimes Act context.

CAT Article 12 legally obliges the U.S. to take concrete action to investigate where torture is credibly alleged to have occurred, as follows:

> Each State Party shall ensure that its competent authorities proceed to a prompt and impartial investigation, wherever there is reasonable ground to believe that an act of torture has been committed in any territory under its jurisdiction.

Article 12 applies geographically within the U.S. and any territory under its jurisdiction which would include Guantánamo and arguably much of Afghanistan. Partisan politics cannot be asserted as a justification for failure to fulfill this legal obligation.

In Article 16, CAT deals with state party obligations regarding preventing cruel, inhuman or degrading treatment or punishment. These are all serious human rights violations.

The U.S. is a state party to the Charter of the Organization of American States. See Document 61. As a member of the OAS the U.S. is bound, under Article 25 of the 1948 American Declaration of the Rights and Duties of Man, to ensure that every person in custody or detention "also has the right to humane treatment during the time he is in custody." See Document 62. This would include prohibition of torture. See Appendix J, *Ameziane vs. United States*.

The U.S. has signed (1977) but not ratified the OAS American Convention on Human Rights. See Document 63. That Convention states:

Art. 5. Right to Humane Treatment

1. Every person has the right to have his physical, mental, and moral integrity respected.
2. No one shall be subjected to torture or to cruel, inhuman, or degrading punishment or treatment. All persons deprived of their liberty shall be treated with respect for the inherent dignity of the human person.

Although not fully binding on the U.S., under the Vienna Convention on Treaties the U.S. should not act to defeat the object and purpose of that treaty. See Appendix E, Vienna Convention, Art. 18.

Since 9/11 no human right has generated more controversy involving the U.S. than torture. Much of the controversy involved what the U.S. thinks torture is. And many questions and misunderstandings have arisen as to the relation of torture to the other acts listed in Article 7 and in CAT: inhuman, cruel, and degrading treatment or punishment. It is primarily the purposive element of torture (" for purposes such as obtaining …") which distinguishes it from the other named wrongful acts. The definition of torture requires acts that are intentionally done to the victim for certain specified purposes, purposes such as obtaining information or a confession.

When the U.S. addresses the U.N. Committee Against Torture or the Human Rights Committee it states its view of the prohibition against torture as follows:

The United States is unequivocally opposed to the use and practice of torture. No circumstance whatsoever, including war, the threat of war, internal political instability, public emergency, or an order from a superior officer or public authority, may be invoked as a justification for or defense to committing torture. This is a longstanding commitment of the United States, repeatedly reaffirmed at the highest levels of the U.S. Government. (See Documents 15A and 21A).

It sounds as though the U.S. is fully committed to the eradication of all torture everywhere as it is understood under international law, such as CAT and ICCPR. This is not the case legally. The U.S. has a different definition of torture than most of the rest of the world. The U.S. definition covers fewer acts than the international definition.

The U.S. has been involved in an ongoing controversy with the international community regarding its definition of torture, and certain acts it has committed in waging its war on terrorism. This includes actions taken at Guantánamo and Abu Ghraib. It applies particularly to certain "enhanced interrogation techniques" employed by the U.S. in detention and interrogation of detainees. (See Documents 21B, 21C, and 22). The major issue concerns the U.S. ratification of CAT and the definition of torture which the U.S. said it would follow, and on which U.S. law would be based, specifically the U.S. official understanding of the meaning of the term "torture."

In its 1994 ratification of the Torture Convention, the U.S. submitted an accompanying statement of "Understanding" of the U.S. Senate, which qualified the U.S. ratification of that Convention. That understanding reads as follows:

II. The Senate's Advice and Consent is subject to the following understandings, which shall apply to the obligations of the United States under this Convention:
(1)(a) That with reference to Article 1, the United States understands that, in order to constitute torture, an act must be specifically intended to inflict severe physical pain or suffering and that mental pain or suffering refers to prolonged mental harm caused by or resulting from: (1) the intentional infliction or threatened infliction of severe physical pain or suffering; (2) the administration or application, or threatened administration or application, of mind altering substances or other procedures calculated to disrupt profoundly the senses or

the personality; (3) the threat of imminent death; (4) the threat that another person will imminently be subjected to death, severe physical pain or suffering, or the administration or application of mind altering substances or other procedures calculated to disrupt profoundly the senses or the personality.

By this understanding, the U.S. defines torture more narrowly than the plain wording of the international definition in Article 1 of CAT. This means it offers less protection than CAT or customary international law and this has led to controversy between the international community and the U.S. and certain U.S. civil society actors. How the U.S. defines torture determines what it claims is the scope and extent of its international legal obligation under CAT.

As far as the U.S. is concerned, it is only bound by the Torture Convention within the terms of the above understanding, which is a narrower definition than the international definition, as understood in light of international jurisprudence and scholarship on the CAT. The international community has been calling the U.S. to make its understanding of the definition of torture consistent with the dominantly accepted international definition, which is much more broadly protective against government mistreatment. See Document 21B, paragraph 13.

The main, though not only, problem with the U.S. definition of torture per the above understanding is as follows:

1. The U.S. understanding is that the perpetrator must specifically intend to cause severe mental or physical pain or suffering. ("… an act must be specifically intended to inflict severe physical pain or suffering"). The Torture Convention definition does not say this or mean this. The interpretation of torture in CAT only requires that the perpetrator specifically intends to commit the act, the conduct itself, which results in severe mental or physical pain or suffering. It is the act, not the result that is specifically intended. So, even if the perpetrator only intended moderate pain and suffering, but severe pain and suffering was the actual result, it's still torture. Under the U.S. understanding it is only torture if the perpetrator specifically intends the result, i.e., to cause severe pain and suffering. The U.S. has changed the meaning of the CAT words "any act by which severe pain and suffering, whether physical or mental, is intentionally inflicted." The correct definition refers to the intentionality of the act, such as whipping or beating, not to the level of pain intended. It takes a careful reading of the U.S. wording to see this flaw. According to the legislative history the descriptive word "intentionally" was used to exclude negligent acts and to include only acts deliberately committed.

   Under the U.S. understanding, there is a lot of room for painful acts inflicted by the perpetrators who claim they were only intending moderate pain, not severe pain, even though the actual result was severe pain. In the U.S. understanding, only where the government agent intends severe pain is there an act of Torture. Again, this is not the international standard. The U.S. understanding is aimed at making the definition of torture as narrow as possible, allowing the government to commit more painful acts that escape the scope of the international prohibition. If one intentionally commits an act against someone for one of the specified purposes and intends to inflict only moderate pain and suffering, and in fact inflicts severe pain and suffering upon the victim that is an act of torture under international law. Allowing a perpetrator to claim they just intended moderate pain would lead to a misuse of that defense by torturer. Every torturer would claim to have only intended moderate pain and suffering.

2. While assessing the severity of physical pain and suffering is easier than assessing mental pain and suffering, the U.S. understanding of what constitutes "severe mental pain and suffering" is inconsistent with, and more narrow than, the international legal meaning under CAT. The U.S. understanding states that severe mental pain and suffering "refers

to <u>prolonged</u> mental harm caused by or resulting from" one of four types of acts. This concept of "prolonged mental harm" is not in the CAT definition or jurisprudence. Under CAT, the severe mental suffering does not have to be prolonged to constitute torture. And how long is prolonged? Moreover, the legal definition of torture in CAT does not limit severe mental pain or suffering to that which resulting from only those four types of acts, such as the threat of imminent death. The U.S. understanding of torture deviates from the international definition of torture in ways that allow certain acts to be committed, such as waterboarding, claiming they are not torture because they fall within the scope of this very narrow and problematic understanding. Use of the word <u>prolonged</u> substantially limits the kinds of mental suffering that constitutes torture. Any severe mental suffering, however long experienced, suffices for the CAT definition. It is torture. The U.S. definition makes only very extreme and long lasting mental suffering part of its definition. This allows the U.S. to commit more acts resulting in severe mental pain and suffering and to claim it is not torture because of the duration of the effects.

3. The U.S. understanding defines the level of "severe pain and suffering" as different from the international law meaning. According to international law, torture is <u>not</u> an aggravated form of cruel or inhuman treatment or punishment, and does <u>not</u> involve a different level of pain and suffering. The U.S. understanding defines the level of severe pain and suffering required for torture as higher than that for cruel or inhuman treatment or punishment. This is incorrect. Thus, it has set the severe pain and suffering level for torture higher than that set by CAT, leaving many painful acts outside the scope of torture in the U.S. view. This was based largely on faulty legal precedents from Europe that are no longer valid.

Such understandings in the U.S. definition give rise to much ingenuity and guile in the determination of whether a particular act is or is not torture. Why does it matter? Because torture is an international crime and commission of torture subjects the torturer to universal jurisdiction and individual criminal responsibility in every country in the world. It also engages the responsibility of the state to make sometimes costly reparations for the human rights violation.

Governments tend to believe that what they are doing is not torture or that they will somehow be able get away with it. Under Article 26 of the Vienna Convention on the Law of Treaties, "Every treaty in force is binding upon the parties to it and must be performed by them in good faith." And, under Article 31, "A treaty shall be interpreted in good faith in accordance with the ordinary meaning to be given to the terms of the treaty in their context and in the light of its object and purpose."

Another problem with the U.S. definition is that in order for torture to be combatted globally there needs to be a consistent, harmonious legal definition of torture held by all states. States may deny that a certain act is or is not torture, but there needs to be a standard, universally accepted, definition. The international community intended to do so by CAT Article 1. The weaker U.S. definition promotes the appearance of a dual standard, one for the U.S. and one for other countries, and of exceptionalism, which fuels antipathy and, in some cases, leads to terrorism against the U.S.

In commenting about why torture continues to exist in the world today, Manfred Nowak, present U.N. Special Rapporteur on Torture, recently stated:

The alignment of national legislations with the Convention against Torture and Other Cruel, Inhuman or Degrading Treatment or Punishment is crucial for its effective implementation. Therefore, the definition of torture contained in Article 1, paragraph 1, of the Convention, with all its elements (infliction of severe pain or suffering; intention and specific purpose; and involvement of a public official), must be taken into account by States when making torture an offence under domestic criminal law.

Under international law principals, the U.S. definition is arguably actually a reservation disguised as a declaration of understanding, and invalid for at least two reasons: 1. If it is a "declaration of understanding" it cannot change the meaning of the plain language of a treaty; and 2. Whether it's an understanding or reservation, defining torture in a way that leaves out of its scope many acts which are torture under the international law definition is arguably incompatible with the object and purpose of the CAT and is therefore invalid. The preamble of CAT states one of its purposes as "Desiring to make more effective the struggle against torture and other cruel, inhuman or degrading treatment or punishment throughout the world, ..." The U.S. narrow definition is not consistent with an expansive and broad definition aimed at maximum global prevention.

The U.S. definition of torture is intentionally made to allow the U.S. the maximum amount of perceived legal wiggle room to define certain horrible acts not to be torture, whereas under the Convention definition they would certainly be so. In order to understand this mentality of States trying to control the limitations of their power under human rights law, one is advised to read the so-called "Torture Memos" issued to the Administration from 2002 to 2005 regarding torture in the war on terrorism. See U.S. Torture Memo of 2002, Document 91, and in Documents 15A, 15B, 15C, 15D and 21A, 21B, and 21C. In the 2002 Memo, the U.S. Department of Justice gives the legal counsel for the CIA a legal opinion on whether putting a terrorism suspect in a box with insects, where the suspect is deathly afraid of insects, constitutes torture or not.

Torture committed outside the U.S. can be prosecuted in the U.S. under U.S. law, the Torture Act. For a U.S. court decision which deals with this definition of torture issue see *United States vs. Roy M. Belfast*, known as the *Chuckie Taylor* Case. See Appendix J. Chuckie Taylor got a 97 years prison sentence in a U.S. District Court for violating the U.S. Torture Act for torture committed in Liberia. Defendand Taylor raised the issue of the difference between the U.S. and CAT definitions as a criminal defense. Given that the crime of torture creates universal criminal jurisdiction, the U.S. courts have jurisdiction over it wherever committed.

The United States is also bound by Article 7 of the ICCPR not to engage in torture or cruel, inhuman, or degrading treatment or punishment. See Document 8. The Second and Third Report of the United States to the U.N. Human Rights Committee under the ICCPR, Article 7, submitted in 2005, included a statement of the United States as to their law and practice under the ICCPR in this area. (See Document 15A).

The Convention against Torture offers broader and more topic-specific treatment of this area of human rights than the ICCPR, but both are extremely important international human rights instruments with strong supervising bodies—the Committee against Torture and the Human Rights Committee. There is an Optional Protocol to the CAT which sets up a sub-committee of experts who can visit states parties to fact find and monitor compliance. As of 2010, 56 states had ratified this OP. The U.S. has not signed or ratified this Optional Protocol. The objective of this OP, prevention of torture, is stated as follows:

> The objective of the present Protocol is to establish a system of regular visits undertaken by independent international and national bodies to places where people are deprived of their liberty, in order to prevent torture and other cruel, inhuman or degrading treatment or punishment.
>
> The mandate of the Subcommittee on Prevention is stated as follows:
> (a) Visit the places referred to in Article 4 and make recommendations to States Parties concerning the protection of persons deprived of their liberty against torture and other cruel, inhuman or degrading treatment or punishment;
> (b) In regard to the national preventive mechanisms:
> (i) Advise and assist States Parties, when necessary, in their establishment;
> ....
> (c) Cooperate, for the prevention of torture in general, with the relevant United Nations organs and mechanisms as well as with the international, regional and national institutions or organizations working towards the strengthening of the protection of all persons against torture and other cruel, inhuman or degrading treatment or punishment.

As of 2010, 56 states had ratified this OP.

Torture is also a part of the deportation (removal) law and procedure in the U.S. Immigration Law. The Executive Office for Immigration review, the Immigration Court, can defer the removal of an alien where there is reason believe that the person would be subject to torture, as defined in CAT, as viewed by the U.S. The U.S. Customs and Immigration Service, under the Department of Homeland Security, has implemented a procedure for relief from being removed from the United States. Now an individual who believes he or she will be tortured if removed by the United States to a certain country can use this procedure to stop removal to that state. This is implemented by the immigration court system.

In a 2006 Congressional Research Service legal memo, the legal analyst reports:

> **Application of the Convention against Torture to U.S. Regulations Concerning the Removal of Aliens.** The requirements of CAT Article 3 take the form of a two-track system requiring the withholding or deferral of the alien's removal to the proposed receiving state if it is more likely than not that he would be tortured there....
>
> **General Removal Guidelines Concerning the Convention against Torture.** CAT implementing regulations concerning the removal of aliens from the United States are primarily covered under sections 208. 16-208. 18 and 1208. 16-1208. 18 of title 8 of the Code of Federal Regulations (C.F.R.), and prohibit the removal of aliens to countries where they would more likely than not be subjected to torture. Department of Homeland Security has primary day-to-day authority to implement and enforce these regulations, with the Department of Justice, through the Executive Office of Immigration Review (EOIR), having adjudicative authority over detention and removal. For purposes of these regulations, "torture" is understood to have the meaning prescribed in CAT Article 1, subject to the reservations and understandings, declarations, and provisos contained in the Senate's resolution of ratification of the Convention.

Torture is an international crime under the Rome Statute for an International Criminal Court. It is a crime within the jurisdiction of the International Criminal Court, but only the most serious violations, not individual instances. See Document 76. It can be a crime against humanity, if widespread or systematic, according to Article 7.1. Torture for this section is defined as: e) "Torture" means the intentional infliction of severe pain or suffering, whether physical or mental, upon a person in the custody or under the control of the accused; except that torture shall not include pain or suffering arising only from, inherent in, or incidental to, lawful sanctions."

In Article 8.2(ii) torture can be prosecuted as a war crime when it constitutes a grave breach of the Geneva Conventions. That provision is qualified by the words "in particular when committed as part of a plan or policy or as part of a large-scale commission of such crimes." The U.S. has signed but not ratified the Rome ICC Statute and so is not fully bound by these crimes under the International Criminal Court. It is still bound by the norms against torture in the ICCPR, CAT and customary international law.

Torture is often spoken of in terms of "torture or other ill treatment," the ill treatment referring to other cruel or inhuman or degrading treatment or punishment. When looking at a particular act of government treatment or punishment, if one concludes that an act does not meet the criteria of torture one must still see if it meets the criteria of cruel, inhuman or degrading treatment or punishment, all of which are serious human rights violations, though not international crimes. For example, even if an act such as exposing a terrorist to loud rock music were found not to be torture, such an act might nonetheless be a human rights violation for being a cruel, inhuman or degrading treatment or punishment. Even if a government determines that an act is not torture, it is still prohibited from doing it if it constitutes cruel or inhuman or degrading treatment or punishment. It cannot be said that if an act is torture it is illegal, but that if it is not torture it is completely legal. It may not be torture but still be a human rights violation. One must analyze whether the act falls into one of the other categories of human rights violations in CAT Article

16. If it does, it cannot be committed, regardless of the result. In international human rights law the end cannot justify the means. Political debate does not change the status of an act as a human rights violation.

Freedom from torture is considered one of the most basic of human rights, an absolute, non derogable human right, creating *a jus cogens* obligation on all states. It is an *erge omnes* obligation, meaning towards all other states. It is a peremptory norm of international law which no domestic law can trump. This human right cannot be violated or taken away under any circumstances. Again, commission of torture is not only a human rights violation for the state involved. It is an international crime giving rise to individual criminal responsibility for the perpetrator and certain others under international criminal law.

Most Americans would agree that torture is an unacceptable behavior. However, dilemmas can arise. If, for example, a terrorist is apprehended who is believed to know where a time bomb is planted in a public place with the intention of killing many innocent people, would it be all right, or at least the lesser of two evils, to torture him until he told the location of the bomb? International human rights law says no. It condemns the act of torture even in that scenario. A state cannot violate human dignity in order to protect human dignity, and the terrorist does not lose his or her human dignity, which is inalienable and inherent. He or she can be prosecuted and punished for wrongdoing but only in a manner consistent with human rights. This prohibition is absolute not just because it violates human dignity. There is a practical reason. History has taught us that once we allow to government any exception to the rule, the exceptions will eventually swallow up the whole rule and governments will always find a way to argue their acts fell within the exception. In this area, governments are masters of spin, cover up, plausible deniability, obfuscation and circumlocution. The answer to the ticking bomb dilemma outlined above is to find a way, without torture, to find out where the bomb is. It is not about what the bomber deserves and what will make him or her talk; it is about how barbaric the state will become in fighting barbarity and protecting human dignity. Furthermore, it has been proven that most information obtained from torture is not true and is unreliable. The torture victim will say anything to stop the pain. See Army Field Manual reference below.

One common government claim in defense of torture is that the torture yielded the intelligence information that led directly to preventing a terroristic or disastrous act. Right intention or positive results of the acts of torture, such as getting intelligence information, do not create a justification for torture. Even though torture yields information which saves people's lives, it is still torture. Whether an act of torture has been committed does not depend on whether the perpetrator thought it was torture. The norm against torture fully applies all the time and to everyone during the war on terrorism. Reliance on erroneous legal advice or acting under orders, is not a defense to torture. The one who tortures and the one who orders it are both criminally responsible as a perpetrator of torture. Those who exercise positions of command responsibility and fail to prevent torture when able, can also become criminally responsible.

In its above CAT understanding, the U.S. stated that it considered the death penalty permitted under international law and thus not torture, nor would the period prior to execution, the death row syndrome, constitute a violation of CAT. While the death penalty is still permitted under international law, ironically, the infliction of severe pain and suffering while trying to execute a capital defendant could still be considered torture. For this reason some U.S. courts have, while upholding the death penalty, found that the methods of execution amounted to torture or cruel and unusual punishment. One can argue, in light of ICCPR and CAT, that under certain circumstances death row syndrome prior to execution would constitute a violation of those human rights standards by itself. The U.S. understanding attempts to avoid such a reading and application.

Since the change of U.S. Government in 2009, there has been a change in how the U.S. regards torture. One change was President Obama's Executive Order 13491 on Ensuring Lawful

Interrogation. This sought to change conduct regarding detainee interrogation and treatment. It said that detainees would not be subject to any technique or approach not authorized in the Army Field manual 2-22.3. The U.S. also declared that it considered waterboarding to constitute torture, and was thus thereafter prohibited as such. See Document 92.

The Army Field Manual section 2.22.3, dated 2006, explains why the Government thinks torture is not a good policy or practice. Pages 5-21, paragraphs 5-75, reads as follows:

> Use of torture is not only illegal but also it is a poor technique that yields 'unreliable results, may damage subsequent collection efforts, and can induce the source to say what he thinks the HUMINT collector wants to hear. Use of torture can also have many possible negative conse-quences at national and international levels.'

The Army Field Manual prohibits soldiers from committing torture:

> 3-157 : The following acts are and shall remain prohibited at any time and in any place what-soever with respect to noncombatants:
> Violence to life and person, in particular murder of all kinds, mutilation, cruel treatment, and torture.

As of this writing, nothing has patched the hole described above in the U.S. definition of tor-ture for purposes of CAT or ICCPR. (See Waterboarding definition). Issues on the U.S. definition and application of norms against torture are still in controversy.

In its 2010 UPR Report to the United Nations, Document 86, paragraph 86, the new U.S. Government spoke about its new attitude regarding torture:

> Thus, the United States prohibits torture and cruel, inhuman, or degrading treatment or punishment of persons in the custody or control of the U.S. Government, regardless of their nationality or physical location. It takes vigilant action to prevent such conduct and to hold those who commit acts of official cruelty accountable for their wrongful acts. The United States is a party to the Convention against Torture, and U.S. law prohibits torture at both the federal and state levels. On June 26, 2010, on the anniversary of adoption of the Convention against Torture, President Obama issued a statement unequivocally reaffirming U.S. support for its principles, and committing the United States to continue to cooperate in international efforts to eradicate torture.

This UPR did not reflect any change in the U.S. limited definition of torture, and the inter-national community continues to call on the U.S. Government to conform its law and policies to the international standard by which every other country is obliged to act. It remains an ongoing process. Many of the comments and recommendations of the members of the international com-munity at the U.N. UPR session for the U.S. raised torture related issues, particularly the definition defect. See Document 87 and Appendix K, 1 and 2.

As of this writing, the U.S. still finds itself in the awkward position of working globally for the prevention of torture, by condemning acts of torture as legally defined by other states, but which are not illegal within its own jurisdiction. It weakens a state's moral stature and the impact of its reprimands when it criticizes the actions of other states for action, which is not forbidden under its own laws.

Torture can only be effectively eradicated when it is absolutely and unqualifiedly prohibited globally based on one commonly understood definition. Human rights, by definition, represent universal values.

See Also Terms: 10, 11, 12, 18, 19, 20, 24, 25, 26, 29, 33, 34, 35, 45, 48, 53, 58, 59, 60, 63, 65, 66, 70, 71, 72, 73, 84, 88, 93, 95, 96, 103, 104, 106, 111, 120, 124, 127, 129, 132, 133, 135, 136, 137, 142, 144, 145, 146, 147, 148, 151, 152, 153, 154, 157, 159, 160, 166, 167, 169, 170, 171, 175, 177, 178, 179, 181, 182,

184, 185, 192, 197, 201, 202, 203, 215, 221, 222, 223, 224, 228, 230, 231, 233, 234, 235, 238, 243, 248, 253, 259, 264, 272, 275, 283, 289, 290, 292, 293, 294, 293, 297, 303, 306, 307, 309, 310, 311, 316, 317, 318, 319, 320, 323, 324.

303. TORTURE VICTIM PROTECTION ACT OF 1992 (TVPA)

Definition: A federal statute (28 U.S. Code sec. 1350), partially codifying customary international law, enacted by the U.S. Congress in 1992 to provide a judicial forum in the United States for victims of torture. It expressly created a legal basis (cause of action) in U.S. law that would allow aliens or even U.S. citizens who had been tortured in other countries or the survivors of those who had suffered extrajudicial killing to have cases heard in U.S. federal courts against those who tortured them or killed their deceased relative, if the torturer were found and served legal papers in the United States.

Significance: Under this act, torture is defined as follows:

1. The term "torture" means any act, directed against an individual in the offender's custody or physical control, by which severe pain or suffering (other than pain or suffering arising from or inherent in, or incidental to lawful sanctions), whether physical or mental, is intentionally inflicted on that individual for such purposes as obtaining from that individual or a third person information or a confession, punishing that individual for an act that individual or a third person has committed or is suspected of having committed, intimidating or coercing that individual or a third person, or for any reason based on discrimination of any kind; and

2. mental pain or suffering refers to prolonged mental harm caused by or resulting from-

A. the intentional infliction or threatened infliction of severe physical pain or suffering;

B. the administration or application, or threatened administration or application, of mind altering substances or other procedures calculated to disrupt profoundly the senses or the personality;

C. the threat of imminent death; or

D. the threat that another individual will imminently be subjected to death, severe physical pain or suffering, or the administration or application of mind altering substances or other procedures calculated to disrupt profoundly the senses or the personality.

Under this act, extrajudicial killing is defined as follows:

"a deliberate killing not authorized by a previous judgment pronounced by a regularly constituted court affording all judicial guarantees which are recognized as indispensable by civilized peoples. Such term, however, does not include any such killing that, under international law, is lawfully carried out under the authority of a foreign nation."

The decision in the cases of *Kadic v. Karadzic* is an example of the use of this statute in a U.S. court case. There is also an exposition by the United States in its Second U.S. Report to the U.N. Committee against Torture concerning this U.S. legislation. See Document 21A.

See Also Terms: 3, 10, 11, 12, 25, 26, 46, 48, 53, 70, 71, 72, 88, 93, 94, 118, 119, 120, 124, 128, 136, 144, 145, 151, 152, 157, 158, 159, 160, 165, 167, 169, 175, 179, 184, 194, 211, 215, 221, 222, 234, 243, 253, 267, 272, 273, 283, 286, 292, 293.

304. TRAFFICKING (HUMAN)

Definition: "Trafficking in human beings" shall mean the recruitment, transportation, transfer, harbouring or receipt of persons, by means of the threat or use of force or other forms of coercion, of abduction, of fraud, of deception, of the abuse of power or of a position of vulnerability or of the giving or receiving of payments or benefits to achieve the consent of a person having control over another person, for the purpose of exploitation. Exploitation shall include, at a minimum, the exploitation of the prostitution of others or other forms of sexual exploitation, forced labour or services, slavery or practices similar to slavery, servitude or the removal of organs. A simplified version is that trafficking is the transport of persons, by means of coercion, deception, or consent for the purpose of exploitation, such as forced or consensual labor or prostitution.

Significance: Human trafficking is the fastest-growing criminal industry in the world, with the total annual revenue for trafficking in persons estimated to be between $5 billion and $9 billion.

The above definition comes from a protocol to the <u>Convention against Transnational Organised Crime.</u> It is known as the Protocol to Prevent, Suppress and Punish Trafficking in Persons, especially Women and Children (also referred to as the Trafficking Protocol). It is also known as one of the two <u>Palermo protocols,</u> the other one being the <u>Protocol against the Smuggling of Migrants by Land, Sea and Air,</u> adopted by the <u>United Nations</u> in <u>Palermo, Italy</u> in 2000.

The Trafficking Protocol entered into force on 25 December 2003. By October 2009, the Protocol had been signed by 117 countries, and there were 133 parties. The Protocol covers the following:

- facilitating the return and acceptance of children who have been victims of cross-border trafficking, with due regard to their safety;
- prohibiting the trafficking of children (which is defined as being a person under 18 years of age) for purposes of <u>commercial sexual exploitation of children</u>, exploitative labor practices or the removal of body parts;
- suspending parental rights of parents, caregivers or any other persons who have parental rights in respect of a child should they be found to have trafficked a child;
- ensuring that definitions of trafficking reflect the need for special safeguards and care for children, including appropriate legal protection;
- ensuring that trafficked persons are not punished for any offences or activities related to their having been trafficked, such as prostitution and immigration violations;
- ensuring that victims of trafficking are protected from deportation or return where there are reasonable grounds to suspect that such return would represent a significant security risk to the trafficked person or their family;
- considering temporary or permanent residence in countries of transit or destination for trafficking victims in exchange for testimony against alleged traffickers, or on humanitarian and compassionate grounds;
- providing for proportional criminal penalties to be applied to persons found guilty of trafficking in aggravating circumstances, including offences involving trafficking in children or offences committed or involving complicity by state officials; and,
- providing for the confiscation of the instruments and proceeds of trafficking and related offences to be used for the benefit of trafficked persons.

The Convention and the Protocol obligate ratifying states to introduce national trafficking legislation. The U.S. has enacted anti-trafficking legislation. The Victim of Trafficking and Violence Protection Act of 2002 (PL 106-386) sought to address this international problem which also affected the U.S. It created the Office on Trafficking in Persons in the U.S. State Department. Congress passed the Trafficking Victims Protection Reauthorization Act of 2005. The findings prefacing that Act include the following findings:

Congress finds the following:

(1) The United States has demonstrated international leadership in combating human trafficking and slavery through the enactment of the Trafficking Victims Protection Act of 2000 (division A of Public Law 106–386; 22 U.S.C. 7101 et seq.) and the Trafficking Victims Protection Reauthorization Act of 2003 (Public Law 108–193).

(2) The United States Government currently estimates that 600,000 to 800,000 individuals are trafficked across international borders each year and exploited through forced labor and commercial sex exploitation. An estimated 80 percent of such individuals are women and girls.

(3) Since the enactment of the Trafficking Victims Protection Act of 2000, United States efforts to combat trafficking in persons have focused primarily on the international trafficking in persons, including the trafficking of foreign citizens into the United States.

(4) Trafficking in persons also occurs within the borders of a country, including the United States.

(5) No known studies exist that quantify the problem of trafficking in children for the purpose of commercial sexual exploitation in the United States. According to a report issued by researchers at the University of Pennsylvania in 2001, as many as 300,000 children in the United States are at risk for commercial sexual exploitation, including trafficking, at any given time.

(6) Runaway and homeless children in the United States are highly susceptible to being domestically trafficked for commercial sexual exploitation. According to the National Runaway Switchboard, every day in the United States, between 1,300,000 and 2,800,000 runaway and homeless youth live on the streets. One out of every seven children will run away from home before the age of 18.

(7) Following armed conflicts and during humanitarian emergencies, indigenous populations face increased security challenges and vulnerabilities which result in myriad forms of violence, including trafficking for sexual and labor exploitation. Foreign policy and foreign aid professionals increasingly recognize the increased activity of human traffickers in post conflict settings and during humanitarian emergencies.

. . . .

(11) Further measures are needed to ensure that United States Government personnel and contractors are held accountable for involvement with acts of trafficking in persons, ...

In its 2010 national UPR report, (see Document 86, paragraphs 97-99) the administration reports about trafficking and the U.S. action in that field. Among the description was the following list of specific U.S. activities to stop trafficking:

Hallmarks of the U.S. approach to combating human trafficking include a) vigorous prosecution of traffickers, and funding task forces throughout the nation comprised of local, state and federal law enforcement and a non-governmental victim service provider; b) a victim-centered approach that recognizes victims require specialized care and are an integral part of any investigation and/or prosecution; c) comprehensive victim services such as shelter, health care, mental health care, food, safety, legal services, interpretation, victim advocacy, immigration relief, education, job skills, employment placement, family reunification, and reintegration; d) temporary immigration relief and work authorization for victims assisting investigations and prosecutions and longer term immigration relief for certain victims and their family members which may then lead to permanent residence and citizenship; e) a coordinated identification and enforcement approach among labor, border, and criminal enforcement; and f) an expansive view of prevention activities that includes strengthening labor protections and enforcement, addressing demand for commercial sex, and working with civil society to rid corporate supply chains of forced labor

See Also Terms: 11, 12, 19, 20, 24, 26, 29, 32, 33, 48, 53, 57, 65, 66, 70, 71, 84, 85, 88, 93, 117, 119, 120, 122, 124, 125, 128, 133, 136, 142, 144, 145, 146, 147, 151, 152, 155, 156, 160, 167, 169, 170, 170, 175, 177, 179, 181, 182, 184, 185, 189, 195, 221, 222, 228, 230, 231, 243, 244, 253, 259, 264, 272, 281, 283, 289, 290, 291, 292, 293, 297, 306, 307, 309, 311, 316, 322.

305. TRANSPARENCE
Definition: The quality of a state government being open to monitoring, scrutiny, and examination in all its activities, subject usually to national security interest, resulting in the governed feeling that the government is open, public, accessible, accountable, fair, honest, and follows the rule of law.

Significance: In a government characterized by transparence in its operations, its faults, such as human rights violations or financial malfeasance, can be detected, brought to public attention, and corrected. Transparence helps to ensure the accountability of those who make up the government and civil servants, and it lessens the chance of impunity for people who commit human rights violations or other wrongful acts. Transparence is necessary for openness in resolving public issues, to avoid suspicion and mistrust among the people, especially in critical matters affecting the public interest. Transparence usually leads to public confidence, trust, and support for the state system. These terms are not seen as applying only to states. They can also be applied to any social or political system, such as an IGO or NGO.

In the aftermath of 9/11 the whole U.S. policy changed from day to day into a protective security mode. Major restructuring of the government was done, with the creation of the Department of Homeland Security. The U.S. perceived itself at war against an unseen evil. The institutions of government asked the people of the U.S. to trust them as they took steps to protect them and to give up some of their liberty to allow the government the leeway to act as it felt in U.S. interest.

As a result of the post 9/11 changes in America the government became less transparent. The Patriot Act gave the Executive Branch expansive powers of surveillance and scrutiny into the lives of many. There were many areas of U.S. government activity where even Congress could not look. 9/11 was a blow to transparency of government in America. But slowly the forces of civil society moved and pushed for more transparency and accountability. This became an issue of the elections of 2008. Then came the election of the Obama Administration and major changes occurred in the area of transparency. But transparency in a era of terrorism is not easy. The main problem with a lack of transparency is that it allows the government to violate human rights without anyone finding out about it, which is one of the reasons governments like non-transparency. Transparency leads to accountability and accountability leads to fewer human rights violations and abuses of power by the state. Transparency strengthens a nation.

See Also Terms: 1, 11, 12, 28, 48, 70, 72, 75, 88, 93, 119, 120, 124, 144, 145, 146, 147, 151, 152, 162, 177, 184, 185, 193, 211, 227, 233, 243, 252, 253, 254, 259, 268, 272, 275, 292, 293, 297, 306, 307, 311, 316.

306. TREATY (INTERNATIONAL INSTRUMENT)

Definition: The generic word treaty is defined in the U.S. as defined in the Vienna Convention on the Law of Treaties, that is, an international instrument 'governed by international law, whether embodied in a single instrument or in two or more related instruments and whatever their particular designation.' According to <u>U.S. Treaties In Force</u> as of January 1, 2010, the term "treaty" as a matter of U.S. Constitutional law denotes "international agreements made by the President with the advice and consent of the Senate in accordance with Article II, Section 2 of the Constitution of the United States." (See Document 2.)

Other sources have defined a treaty as a formal, official, written act of a state or states set forth in a document, in which a state expresses its intention with regard to certain legal principles or norms and which is governed by international law.

Significance: Human rights norms are found in international legal instruments that are called treaties. These are agreements between the U.S. and other countries or between the U.S. and an international organization which have the force of law, based on public international law. Public international law is based on the free consent of sovereign and equal states. Treaties are formal, written expressions of that consent to be legally bound. These are actually contracts, which states enter into and promise to fulfill. For states to reach agreement on the international norms to which they are willing to philosophically and legally consent to bind themselves, their duly authorized representatives convene at various times and regarding various subjects of international law, to draft the terms of the instruments.

Oftentimes, the impetus for drafting such documents is provided through one of the committees of an international body, such as the former Commission on Human Rights of the United

Nations. At other times, regional bodies, such as the Council of Europe, might mandate the drafting of an agreement, specifically applicable to the member states of their own region. Sometimes treaties are the product of lobbying by civil society organizations and movements which sees a problem of international stature needing international cooperation and effort to resolve. In any case, it is the beginning of a long process of agreeing on basic norms to be included, in drafting the appropriate wording of the text, then when the text is finished, voting to adopt the text, and then signing or sending the instruments to states to be signed. After a state has signed an instrument that is meant to be legally binding, it must then, according to the legislative processes of its own government, ratify the document and implement it into its domestic law and provide legal procedures to allow an enforceable remedy for protecting the rights.

Treaties create legal obligations for every state which ratifies and become bound by it. It is very important to know that human rights treaties do not create any human rights. Human rights are inherent in the individual. Human rights treaties are only legal acknowledgements of the existence, scope and character of those human rights, and a promise to fulfill the obligations to respect those rights and follow the procedures in the treaty for implementing these rights.

Some instruments set forth human rights principles in a *nonbinding* document, such as a declaration, whereas other instruments, treaty instruments, set forth human rights legal norms that are *binding* upon the states parties who ratify. Declarations are not treaties and normally create no legal obligations. These treaty instruments have different title designations, but all have the same legal effect. The designations include treaty, convention, covenant, charter, and agreement.

Instruments can be of global or regional scope, national, subsidiary. There are various types of treaties, or instruments, including the following:

A *bilateral instrument* is one entered into between only two different states, for example, between the United States and Mexico (NAFTA).

A *multilateral instrument* is one entered into between three or more different states, such as the a treaty between the United States, Canada, and Mexico.

A *global instrument* is one involving all states of the world. Examples include the Geneva Conventions and the ICCPR.

An *international legal instrument* is one used in international relations between two or more states or between states and certain international institutions and is governed by or derives its legal force from international law.

A *regional instrument* is one involving only states in a certain region or political organization. Examples include the Inter-American Convention, used in the context of North and South America, and the European Convention on Human Rights, used in the context of the Council of Europe.

A *national instrument* involves only one state, such as an instrument of ratification submitted by a state ratifying a treaty.

A *subsidiary instrument* covers secondary topics or themes. Examples include the Refugee Convention and the Convention on the Elimination of all Forms of Discrimination against Women.

A *nonlegal instrument* is one that is not legally binding, such as a declaration. Nonlegal instruments are not treaties. This type of instrument often precedes a legally binding treaty. For example, before the Convention on the Rights of the Child was drafted, the Declaration on the Rights of the Child was adopted and set forth the same basic nonbinding principle which later became binding norms in the Convention.

Included in Appendix H and I of this work is a discussion of U.S. law and human rights treaties in *Restatement of the Foreign Relations Law, Third,* and a list of the international human rights treaties signed or ratified by the United States. Those wanting to know up to date what human rights or humanitarian law treaties the U.S. has ratified and which are in force, binding the U.S., should consult the latest edition of <u>Treaties in Force</u>, a U.S. government publication at http://www.state.gov/s/l/treaty/tif/index.htm.

See Also Terms: 2, 3, 6, 11, 20, 23, 25, 26, 27, 29, 31, 33, 45, 48, 52, 53, 54, 55, 56, 57, 62, 68, 70, 72, 73, 74, 80, 88, 92, 93, 94, 98, 114, 124, 127, 129, 130, 132, 135, 144, 145, 146, 147, 151, 152, 154, 158, 160, 167, 169, 173, 175, 177, 179, 180, 184, 185, 186, 203, 208, 211, 215, 220, 222, 225, 226, 229, 230, 231, 233, 242, 243, 244, 245, 247, 253, 258, 259, 262, 264, 269, 272, 279, 280, 282, 283, 286, 287, 291, 293, 297, 306, 307, 308, 311, 316, 317, 323.

307. Treaty Monitoring/Supervising Body

Definition: A judicial organ (court or tribunal) or quasi-judicial organ (commission or committee) established by and within a treaty, under an international intergovernmental organization, to supervise and monitor compliance of states parties to the treaty norms.

Significance: Such a body is established to assure state compliance with the treaty norms by looking for areas and incidents of noncompliance and promoting the carrying out of implementation measures by states parties. This is accomplished by such methods as reporting and complaint systems, which the treaty sets forth in its text.

The U.N. Human Rights Committee, which was established under Article 28 of the ICCPR, is an example of a treaty monitoring or supervising body. See Document 8. An example of its work is its consideration of the U.S. Second and Third Reports under the ICCPR. See Documents 15A, B, C, and D. The decision in the case of *Ng v. Canada* is an example of how a treaty-monitoring body, the Human Rights Committee, handles specific complaints of human rights violations filed by victims against a state party. See Appendix J.

The treaty monitoring bodies also issue General Comments on the interpretation and application of the provision of the treaty they supervise. The members of the supervising bodies are normally experts in the field of human rights and in the subject of the treaty, e.g., children.

A sample General Comment is included as Document 12. Others are included in Appendix E.

See Also Terms: 3, 6, 11, 46, 48, 53, 54, 55, 57, 60, 70, 98, 107, 112, 119, 124, 127, 144, 145, 146, 150, 151, 152, 165, 173, 175, 177, 206, 208, 211, 215, 222, 227, 229, 231, 233, 243, 246, 252, 258, 259, 262, 264, 268, 269, 272, 282, 283, 286, 293, 296, 297, 306, 307, 316.

U

308. United Nations (U.N.) Charter

Definition: The international treaty adopted in San Francisco, California, on 26 June 1945 by 51 states, which established the organization known as the United Nations, and stated its purposes, principles, membership, organs, and procedures, including those aimed at dealing with human rights and fundamental freedoms.

Significance: The U.N. Charter is an international legal instrument, a treaty. It is in international agreement among multiple states to create an international inter-governmental organization called the United Nations. The United States signed and ratified this treaty and was one of its major promoters and drafters. The United States believed that in light of the horrors of the Second World War both in Europe and Asia, and the barbarity involved, that there needed to be an international forum for the peaceful discussion and resolution of disputes among states and certain minimum standards of conduct by states, so as to avoid another war.

The Preamble of the U.N. Charters reads:

We the peoples of the United Nations, determined to save succeeding generations from the scourge of war, which twice in our lifetime has brought untold sorrow to mankind, and
To affirm faith in fundamental human rights, in the dignity and worth of the human person, in the equal rights of men and women and of nations large and small, and

To establish conditions under which justice and respect for the obligations arising from treaties and other sources of international law can be maintained . . .

Article 2 of the U.N. Charter states that one of the purposes of the United Nations is "to achieve international cooperation in solving international problems of an economic, social, cultural, or humanitarian character, and in promoting and encouraging respect for human rights and for fundamental freedoms for all without distinction as to race, sex, language, or religion." Note that it says the U.N. will "promote and encourage respect." It does not say the U.N. will itself protect human rights.

The U.N. Charter set up the international intergovernmental organization (IGO) in which most of the international human rights standards and bodies would arise, and most international human rights activity of the United States would take place.

The Charter serves as the legal basis for the U.N. Human Rights Council and all of the special procedures and mechanisms in the U.N. human rights system. At this time the U.S sits as a member of the Human Rights Council and plays an active role as a governmental member of these systems; American experts and NGOs participate in their human rights activity. These activities occur in the United States, at the U.N. headquarters in New York, but principally in Geneva, Switzerland, where the Office of the High Commissioner for Human Rights, and the U.N. Human Rights Council are located.

See Also Terms: 8, 20, 25, 26, 31, 48, 53, 54, 55, 56, 57, 63, 64, 70, 72, 86, 98, 103, 119, 120, 122, 124, 145, 147, 152, 160, 167, 169, 173, 179, 180, 183, 184, 185, 208, 211, 215, 221, 222, 225, 226, 243, 245, 259, 271, 272, 276, 286, 293, 306, 309, 312, 316, 322, 323, 324.

309. UNIVERSAL DECLARATION OF HUMAN RIGHTS (UDHR)

Definition: An international declaration of human rights principles adopted by the United Nation's General Assembly in 1948, that served as the first international human rights instrument wherein specific substantive human rights standards were identified and states called to observe them. This instrument was, however, not intended to create any legally binding obligations.

Significance: This instrument (document) is known simply as "the Universal Declaration" and is abbreviated UDHR. It is the main historical source of all human rights instruments. It serves as the main point of reference for human rights activity at the United Nations, along with the *Vienna Declaration and Programme of Action* of 1993. It is one of the most translated documents in history.

The Preamble of the UDHR reads:
Whereas recognition of the inherent dignity and of the equal and inalienable rights of all members of the human family is the foundation of freedom, justice and peace in the world,
Whereas disregard and contempt for human rights have resulted in barbarous acts which have outraged the conscience of mankind, and the advent of a world in which human beings shall enjoy freedom of speech and belief and freedom from fear and want has been proclaimed as the highest aspiration of the common people,
Whereas it is essential, if man is not to be compelled to have recourse, as a last resort, to rebellion against tyranny and oppression, that human rights should be protected by the rule of law, . . .
Whereas a common understanding of these rights and freedoms is of greatest importance for the full realization of this pledge,
Now therefore, The General Assembly Proclaims this Universal Declaration of Human Rights as a common standard of achievement for all peoples and all nations, to the end that every individual and every organ of society, keeping this Declaration constantly in mind, shall strive by teaching and education to promote respect for these rights and freedoms by progressive measures, national and international, to secure their universal and effective recognition and observance, . . .

Eleanor Roosevelt was the primary American member of the U.N. Commission on Human Rights responsible for the drafting and promotion of the UDHR. The United States was one of the strongest supporters of this document, as the first international articulation of what universal human rights are.

Though the UDHR was initially intended as nonlegally binding human rights principles, it is considered by most scholars to now be legally binding as a matter of customary international law, at least concerning the most important ("hard core") human rights. There is a discussion of the UDHR and its status in U.S. law in *Restatement of the Foreign Relations Law, Third*. See Appendix I.

Given that it is binding as a matter of customary international law as to its hard core rights on every state in the world, every state must comply with those hard core provisions, such as prohibition of torture, slavery and the right to life.

This instrument is referenced in the initial human rights instruments of most regional human rights systems such as the Council of Europe, and OAS. It forms part of the constitution of some countries.

See Also Terms: 11, 12, 16, 17, 18, 20, 21, 24, 25, 29, 32, 33, 34, 35, 36, 48, 53, 54, 55, 56, 57, 65, 66, 70, 71, 72, 73, 74, 75, 81, 84, 86, 88, 90, 91, 92, 93, 99, 100, 110, 111, 113, 120, 121, 122, 123, 124, 126, 136, 142, 144, 145, 147, 148, 149, 150, 151, 152, 160, 167, 169, 175, 177, 179, 180, 184, 185, 189, 195, 196, 205, 211, 213, 214, 216, 222, 242, 243, 245, 250, 252, 254, 259, 260, 264, 265, 272, 281, 282, 283, 286, 291, 292, 297, 302, 308, 312, 316, 322, 323, 324.

310. UNIVERSAL JURISDICTION

Definition: The legal authority (competence) of all national courts in every state in the world to exercise criminal jurisdiction to prosecute persons who have committed certain international crimes such as genocide, war crimes, crimes against humanity and torture, regardless of their nationality or where the crimes were committed. This is a principle of international criminal law.

Significance: Under public international law, as presently found in international human rights law and international criminal law, some international crimes such as genocide, war crimes, and torture, are accepted by the international community as allowing for universal criminal jurisdiction of every state in the world to arrest and prosecute individual perpetrators of such crimes. This is because these crimes are major human rights violations and are considered by the community of states to be committed against the whole human race, not just against the people of one state, and therefore every state has the right to prosecute and punish those who commit them. This principle arose from the experience of the Holocaust and the attempt to prosecute those who committed those atrocities and who fled to other countries to escape from facing justice. Under the principle of universal jurisdiction, which exists both as a matter of treaty law and customary international law concerning such crimes, every state in the world has the legal right to apprehend, prosecute, and enforce punishment against such evildoers so that they will not escape justice.

Universal jurisdiction promotes, encourages, and facilitates the universal goal of accountability and individual criminal responsibility for committing such crimes. This in turn works against the prevailing culture of impunity and helps bring about a culture of human rights and ultimately a culture of peace.

At the beginning of the new millennium, this principle was being applied to the famous case of Augusto Pinochet in England. He was arrested in the United Kingdom on a request from Spain to transfer (extradite) him to Spain for criminal prosecution there for international crimes he had committed in Chile almost 30 years earlier. Universal jurisdiction would have allowed both Spain and the United Kingdom (and even the United States, if it wanted) to prosecute for such crimes.

The International Criminal Court, established under U.N. auspices in 1998, but independent of it, has jurisdiction over international crimes that have universal jurisdiction. See

Document 76. For cases that fall outside of the jurisdiction of the ICC, international criminal acts can still be prosecuted under treaty law (e.g. Geneva Convention grave breaches) by states parties, or under customary international law by any country in the world. This would mean that if an American committed an international crime such as torture, he or she could be prosecuted in any country in the world if found there. Another principle of international criminal law and universal jurisdiction is that if an international criminal is in a country and the government of that country becomes aware of this, it has an obligation to arrest and prosecute the suspect or to send the suspect to a third country for prosecution, if requested to do so. This is called the principle of *Aut Dedere Aut Judicare*. Moreover, there is no international statute of limitations for international crimes. This is how one still sees arrests and prosecutions for war crimes committed in World War II.

The U.S. has implemented into U.S. law certain international crimes, which U.S. courts are now able to prosecute regardless of where the actions occurred. This includes war crimes and torture. In 2010, a U.S. Court of Appeals ruled in the case of *USA vs. Roy M. Belfast*, the *Chuckie Taylor* case, that torture committed anywhere in the world could now be prosecuted in the U.S. via the Torture Act, found in Title 18 of the U.S. Code. (See entry for Torture, supra.) This act was based on the international law obligation undertaken by the U.S. in ratifying the Convention against Torture. This was a treaty-based universality.

See Also Terms: 3, 26, 48, 53, 56, 63, 64, 70, 72, 73, 88, 93, 94, 103, 110, 111, 119, 129, 130, 132, 144, 145, 151, 152, 154, 181, 182, 185, 192, 211, 215, 221, 222, 223, 224, 234, 243, 253, 259, 272, 281, 283, 291, 292, 293, 306, 307, 316, 317, 319, 320, 321, 323.

311. UNIVERSAL PERIODIC REVIEW

Definition: The Universal Periodic Review (UPR) is an institutional process established by a United Nations General Assembly resolution in March 2006, which involves a review of the human rights records of all of the U.N. Member States by the UPR Working Group once every four years.

Significance: According to the website of the U.S. Human Rights Network (ushrnetwork. org), a U.S.-based NGO focused on the U.S. and the UPR process, whose information informs this entry, the Universal Periodic Review is a mechanism of the U.N. Human Rights Council (HRC). It is based on the proposition that all countries of the world should be subject to equal scrutiny and treatment for all. The process provides for all States to report to the Council on what actions they have taken to improve the human rights situations in their countries and to overcome challenges to the realization and enjoyment of all human rights to which a state is bound.

The ultimate goal of the UPR is the improvement of the human rights situation in every country with significant consequences for people around the globe. The UPR is designed to prompt, support, and expand the promotion and protection of human rights on the ground. To achieve this, the UPR involves assessing States' human rights records and addressing human rights violations wherever they occur. The UPR also aims to provide technical assistance to States and enhance their capacity to deal effectively with human rights challenges and to share best practices in the field of human rights among States and other stakeholders.

The reviews are conducted by the UPR Working Group, which consists of the 47 members of the Council; however any U.N. Member State can take part in the discussion/dialogue with the reviewed States. The state under review is called a "SuR." Each State review is assisted by groups of three States known as "troikas," who serve as rapporteurs, that is to say, parties who submit a report back to the plenary body about the SuR. The selection of the troikas for each State review is done through a drawing of lots prior to each Working Group session.

What are the reviews based on? The documents on which the reviews are based are:

1) Information provided by the State under review, which can take the form of a 20-page national report;

(The United States completed and submitted to the U.N. High Commissioner for Human Rights its national UPR report in August 2010. It was made available on the Department of State website and is included in this book as Document 86).

2) Information contained in the reports of independent human rights experts and groups, known as the Special Procedures, human rights treaty bodies, and other U.N. entities (compiled in a 10-page report by the Office of the High Commissioner for Human Rights (OHCHR));

3) Information from other stakeholders including non-governmental organizations (NGOs) and national human rights institutions. The OHCHR prepares a summary of such information which shall not exceed 10 pages. (Each NGO can submit a 5-page stakeholder report. Collective stakeholder reports can be 10 pages.)

How are the reviews conducted?

Reviews take place through an interactive discussion between the State under review and other U.N. Member States. This takes place during a meeting of the UPR Working Group. During this discussion any U.N. Member State can pose questions, comments and/or make recommendations to the States under review. The troikas (see above) may group issues or questions to be shared with the State under review to ensure that the interactive dialogue takes place in a smooth and orderly manner. The duration of the review will be three hours for each country in the Working Group.

What human rights obligations are addressed?

The UPR will assess the extent to which States respect their human rights obligations set out in:

(1) The U.N. Charter;

(2) The Universal Declaration of Human Rights;

(3) Human rights instruments to which the State is party (human rights treaties ratified by the State concerned.)

According to the August 2010, U.S. UPR report, Document 86, the U.S. states that:

"The United States is at present Party to the following multilateral human rights related treaties:

- Slavery Convention and its amending Protocol;
- Supplementary Convention on the Abolition of Slavery, the Slave Trade and Institutions and Practices Similar to Slavery;
- Protocol Relating to the Status of Refugees;
- Inter-American Convention on the Granting of Political Rights to Women;
- Convention on the Political Rights of Women;
- Convention on the Prevention and Punishment of the Crime of Genocide;
- ILO Convention No. 105 concerning the Abolition of Forced Labor;
- International Covenant on Civil and Political Rights;
- Convention against Torture and Other Cruel, Inhuman or Degrading Treatment or Punishment;
- International Convention on the Elimination of All Forums of Racial Discrimination;
- ILO Convention 182 Concerning the Prohibition and Immediate Action for the Elimination of the Worst Forms of Child Labor;
- Optional Protocol to the Convention on the Rights of the Child on the Involvement of Children in Armed Conflict; and
- Optional Protocol to the Convention on the Rights of the Child on the Sale of Children, Child Prostitution, and Child Pornography.

The United States has signed but not ratified the following multilateral human rights treaties:

- International Covenant on Economic, Social and Cultural Rights;
- American Convention on Human Rights;
- Convention on the Elimination of All Forms of Discrimination Against Women;
- Convention on the Rights of the Child; and
- International Convention on the Rights of Persons with Disabilities.

In addition, the United States has entered into many bilateral treaties (including consular treaties and treaties of friendship, commerce and navigation) that contain provisions guaranteeing various rights and protections to nationals of foreign countries on a reciprocal basis. In some cases, these may be invoked directly in United States courts for that purpose.

(4) Voluntary pledges and commitments made by the State (e.g. national human rights policies and/or programs implemented as well as promises/pledges to be elected to U.N. HR Council); and,

(5) Applicable international humanitarian law.

What is the outcome of the review?

Following the State review by the Working Group, a report is prepared by the troika (see above) with the involvement of the State under review and assistance from the OHCHR. This report, referred to as the "outcome report," provides a summary of the UPR and also includes a sharing of best human rights practices around the globe. It therefore consists of the questions, comments and recommendations made by States to the country under review, as well as the responses by the reviewed State.

How is the review adopted?

During the Working Group session, 30 minutes is allocated to adopt each of the outcome reports. for the States reviewed that session. These take place no sooner than 48 hours after the country review. The reviewed State has the opportunity to make Preliminary comments on the recommendations, choosing to either accept or reject them. Both accepted and refused recommendations are included in the report. After the report has been adopted, editorial modifications can be made to the report by States on their own statements, within the following two weeks. The report then has to be adopted at the following plenary session of the Human Rights Council. During the plenary session, the State under review can reply to questions and issues that were not sufficiently addressed during the Working Group and respond to recommendations that were raised by States during the review. Time is also allotted to member and observer States who may wish to express their opinion on the outcome of the review and for NGOs and other stakeholders to make general comments (2 minutes for NGOs).

For more information please go to www.ushrnetwork.org

Can non-governmental organizations (NGOs) participate in the UPR process?

Yes. NGOs can submit information which can be added to the other stakeholders report which is considered during the review. Information they provide can be referred to by any of the States taking part in the interactive discussion during the review at the Working Group meeting. NGOs can meet with all states and advocate their issues, recommendations and questions to the states. NGOs can request states to pose their recommendations and questions to the state under review. NGOs in consultative relationship with the U.N. Economic and Social Council (ECOSOC) can attend the UPR Working Group sessions and can participate in the regular session of the Human Rights Council when the outcome of the State reviews are considered, including making brief general comments before the adoption of outcome documents by the HRC.

The UPR is meant to complement and not duplicate the work of treaty bodies (i.e. treaty specific U.N. mechanisms such as the Committee on the Elimination of All Forms of Racial Discrimination).

The order of review of countries is by random drawing. For NGO based information see _www. ushrnetwork.org._ The technical guide for the UPR can be found at Document K http://www.ohchr. org/EN/HRBodies/UPR/Documents/TechnicalGuideEN.pdf

The UPR review session of the United States took place on November 5, 2010. The author was present. In its 2010, national report the U.S. Administration addresses the UPR Process itself as follows:

The United States and the Universal Periodic Review: approach and methodology
6. The ultimate objective of the UPR process, and of the U.N. Human Rights Council, is to enhance the protections for and enjoyment of human rights. Our participation signifies our commitment to that end, and we hope to contribute to it by sharing how we have made and will continue to make progress toward it. Some may say that by participating we acknowledge commonality with states that systematically abuse human rights. We do not. There is no comparison between American democracy and repressive regimes. Others will say that our participation, and our assessment of certain areas where we seek continued progress, reflects doubt in the ability of the American political system to deliver progress for its citizens. It does not. As Secretary Clinton said in a speech on human rights last year, "democracies demonstrate their greatness not by insisting they are perfect, but by using their institutions and their principles to make themselves...more perfect." Progress is our goal, and our expectation thereof is justified by the proven ability of our system of government to deliver the progress our people demand and deserve.
7. This document gives a partial snapshot of the current human rights situation in the United States, including some of the areas where problems persist in our society. In addressing those areas, we use this report to explore opportunities to make further progress and also to share some of our recent progress. For us, the primary value of this report is not as a diagnosis, but rather as a roadmap for our ongoing work within our democratic system to achieve lasting change. We submit this report with confidence that the legacy of our past efforts to embrace and actualize universal rights foreshadows our continued success.
8. This report is the product of collaboration between the U.S. Government and representatives of civil society from across the United States. Over the last year, senior representatives from more than a dozen federal departments and agencies traveled the country to attend a series of UPR consultations hosted by a wide range of civil society organizations. At these gatherings, individuals presented their concerns and recommendations and often shared stories or reports as they interacted with government representatives. Those conversations shaped the substance and structure of this report. Nearly a thousand people, representing a diversity of communities and viewpoints, and voicing a wide range of concerns, attended these gatherings in New Mexico; Window Rock, Arizona; the San Francisco Bay Area; Detroit, Michigan; Chicago, Illinois; Birmingham, Alabama; and Washington, D.C. Information about the process was also posted on the website of the U.S. Department of State (www.state). Members of the public were encouraged to contribute questions, comments, and recommendations via that site, and many did so. The consultation process followed a familiar tradition of collaboration and discussion between government and civil society that is vital to the strength of our democracy. The U.S. Government is grateful to all those who hosted meetings and shared their views both in those consultations and online. We also welcome constructive comments and recommendations from other governments and non-governmental organizations through the UPR process.

A compilation of information about the U.S. human rights record has been prepared for the Human Rights Council by the OHCHR. See Appendix K, Compilation Prepared by the Office of the High Commissioner for Human Rights in accordance with paragraph 15 (b) of the annex to Human Rights Council resolution 5/1, United States of America. A Summary (of stakeholder reports and recommendations), prepared by the Office of the High Commissioner for Human Rights in accordance with paragraph 15 (c) of the annex to Human Rights Council resolution 5/1, United States of America, was submitted to the HRC and is also included in Appendix K.

The Draft Outcome Report came out on November 10, 2010, and contains the most recommendations of any state having undergone the UPR process. The final UPR Outcome Report on the U.S. came out in January 2011. See Document 87. The U.S. issued a response to the Outcome Report's 228 recommendations. See Appendix K, #4. The HRC voted to adopt the Outcome Report on March 18, 2011. After this U.S. response, the U.S. needs to be followed to see how much the U.S. complies with and implements the recommendations it has accepted as a result of this process. Four years later, the U.S. will go through the process again and an account will be taken of the progress made or not. (Discussion taken partially from www.ushrnetwork.org).

An excellent publication from the Human Rights Project at the Urban Justice Center entitled *A PRACTICAL GUIDE TO THE UNITED NATIONS' UNIVERSAL PERIODIC REVIEW* is included in Appendix K, which has many documents concerning the UPR process and its legal context. To follow the UPR process of the U.S. one can check on the Department of State website: www.state.gov/g/drl/upr/process/index.htm.

Information on the U.S. UPR process from the U.N. Human Rights Council perspective can be found at the website of the U.N. Office of the High Commissioner for Human Rights, which acts administratively on behalf of the Human Rights Council, can be found at: http://www.ohchr.org/EN/ HRBodies/UPR.

See Also Terms: 3, 20, 25, 29, 32, 33, 34, 35, 48, 49, 53, 55, 57, 59, 60, 62, 65, 66, 70, 72, 79, 81, 82, 84, 85, 86, 88, 90, 92, 93, 95, 96, 97, 99, 100, 102, 103, 104, 106, 110, 111, 114, 117, 119, 120, 122, 124, 125, 126, 137, 139, 140, 142, 144, 145, 147, 148, 150, 151, 152, 154, 155, 156, 159, 161, 162, 163, 164, 166, 167, 169, 170, 171, 175, 177, 179, 184, 185, 196, 201, 203, 205, 208, 210, 211, 215, 216, 217, 222, 226, 232, 233, 235, 238, 243, 244, 248, 250, 252, 253, 254, 255, 256, 259, 260, 261, 265, 266, 268, 272, 275, 292, 297, 299, 302, 317, 319, 320, 322, 324.

312. UNIVERSALITY

Definition: A doctrine of international human rights that states that all human rights of all types ("generations") apply all over the world to everybody in just the same way. They are universal values and are not applied differently based on such differences as race, language, religion, customs, cultures, and ideologies. This doctrine is contrasted with the doctrine of cultural relativism, which says just the opposite.

Significance: The Vienna Declaration and Programme of Action of 1993 expressed the consensus of the international community that universality and not cultural relativism was the predominant and correct worldview on human rights. See Document 51. Article 5 reads:

> All human rights are universal, indivisible and interdependent and interrelated. The international community must treat human rights globally in a fair and equal manner, on the same footing, and with the same emphasis. While the significance of national and regional particularities and various historical, cultural and religious backgrounds must be borne in mind, it is the duty of States, regardless of their political, economic and cultural systems, to promote and protect all human rights and fundamental freedoms. (underscoring added)

This last sentence proclaims the principle of universality of human rights. Religion and culture are not irrelevant to implementation and interpretation. They are not determinative. There is a universal standard that applies to everyone.

This philosophical debate, however, does continue to appear in circles where human rights are discussed, especially relative to differences in cultural and religious practices throughout the world. In places where people perceive human rights negatively as a product of the "western" culture they claim that universality is a sort of cultural imperialism. They view human rights as something the West is trying to impose on them unjustly. This is particularly true where their views are based on religious tenets and where they perceive that the human rights norms are inconsistent with those religious tenets. They want human rights applied in their land in a way that respects their religion and culture. Thus, they want culturally relative implementation of human rights. The tension between these two world views is still in play.

Regarding universality, the U.S. Administration referred to that concept in its 2010 UPR report to the OHCHR, Document 86. The Administration stated at para. 4:

> The ideas that informed and inform the American experiment can be found all over the world, and the people who have built it over centuries have come from every continent. The American experiment is a human experiment; the values on which it is based, including a commitment to human rights, are clearly engrained in our own national conscience, but they are also universal.

And at paragraph 80-81 the Administration states:

> The fundamental truth which grounds the principles of government enshrined in our Constitution—that each person is created with equal value from which flows inalienable rights—is not an exclusively American truth; it is a universal one. It is the truth that anchors the Universal Declaration of Human Rights, it is the truth that underpins the legitimate purposes and obligations not just of our government, but of all governments.
>
> 81. We are committed to that universal truth, and so we are committed to principled engagement across borders and with foreign governments and their citizens. This commitment includes, in the words of our Declaration of Independence, according "decent respect to the opinions of mankind," and seeking always to preserve and protect the dignity of all persons, because the values that we cherish apply everywhere and to everyone.

See Also Terms: 11, 12, 20, 24, 29, 33, 34, 35, 48, 70, 72, 73, 75, 86, 120, 124, 144, 145, 152, 167, 169, 177, 211, 213, 216, 222, 259, 260, 261, 265, 272, 283, 297, 308, 309, 316, 323, 324.

313. UNLAWFUL COMBATANT

See entry for **Combatant**

314. UNNECESSARY SUFFERING

Definition: A term found in the law of armed conflict, humanitarian law, which refers to the principle that all sides of an armed conflict must conduct military operations and use weapons that will not cause any suffering that is not necessary to accomplish legitimate military objectives under the principle of military necessity.

Significance: In the view of many human rights scholars, international human rights law includes the body of law known as humanitarian law, which applies in times of international and noninternational armed conflicts. This is contested by many in the humanitarian law camp. It is true that the nature of the legal obligations in the two areas are different, but the goal is largely the same protection of human beings from the harm of armed conflict.

One of the basic principles of humanitarian law is the principle of humanitarianism. That principle requires that armed conflict be waged in a way that is most humane, which respects human dignity, and is least harmful to human beings. One of the subprinciples to foster that goal is the principle of unneccessary suffering. According to this principle, the parties to an armed conflict do not have the right to engage in hostilities in any way they want with any methods or means that is, tactics or weapons. The methods and means of combat can and have been limited by a norm of the international community as to the causing of unnecessary suffering. According to this principle, it is not permissible in armed conflicts to cause human suffering only for purposes of making people suffer, such as through an act done purely for cruelty, spite, or vengeance to make the other side hurt the most. This norm results from the principle of inherent human dignity and inviolability of the human person. Minimizing human loss and suffering is a basic principle of humanitarianism. Two examples of this are the banning of mustard gas and of dum-dum bullets.

History has taught human kind that causing unnecessary suffering aggravates the emotions that enflame armed conflicts and make them descend into more and more barbarity and last longer and cause more death and destruction.

An "all-out war," where every kind of possible harmful human act is allowed to anyone present, is unacceptable in the international community and not legally permitted. The international community has not yet outlawed all recourse to armed conflict but has established "rules of the game" to protect civilization from barbarity, especially to protect innocent people, who are the main victims of armed conflicts. Because now over 80% of most casualties of armed conflict are civilians it is important to see that especially the innocent do not suffer from military violence. All combatants are duty bound to avoid causing unnecessary suffering.

See Also Terms: 11, 12, 20, 25, 26, 41, 42, 45, 48, 63, 70, 73, 95, 104, 166, 171, 178, 182, 185, 192, 200, 201, 202, 203, 213, 215, 222, 223, 234, 251, 256, 257, 259, 272, 283, 292, 306, 307, 316, 317, 318, 319, 320.

315. UNPRIVILEDGED COMBATANT
See entry for **Combatant**

316. VIENNA DECLARATION AND PROGRAMME OF ACTION
Definition: The final outcome document issued by the 1993 Vienna Conference on Human Rights, which reflected a consensus of the international community as to the basic content and application of international humans rights for the whole world. See Document 51. This document has become the key term of reference for United Nations human rights work.

Significance: In 1993 the nations of the world got together in Vienna for a "stocktaking" of where the world was in terms of its understanding and application of international human rights, and to set policy for and direct the work of the international community through both regional and international inter-governmental organizations such as the United Nations. Several very crucial issues were discussed including the debate over universality versus cultural relativism of human rights. The Conference ended with adoption of this very important consensus document from the international community.

There are two parts to the document: the Declaration and the Programme of Action. In the first part the international community declared its consensus view as to what norms and principles of human rights were part of the accepted body of international human rights.

The second part, the Programme of Action, is a blueprint for the work of the international community primarily through the United Nations, including for example, the institution of the U.N. Office of the High Commissioner for Human Rights. The U.N. administrative staff dealing with human rights issues in any part of the U.N. uses this documents as its main source of understanding of the will of the international community and its priorities and values for rationalizing and improving the U.N. human rights machinery.

The U.S. fully participated in the Vienna Conference and the preparation of the VDPA. However, one seldom ever hears of this document in the U.S. though it should be used and cited by those interested or working in human rights, whether in the U.S. or elsewhere.

See Also Terms: 20, 48, 53, 54, 55, 56, 57, 70, 71, 72, 74, 160, 167, 168, 169, 174, 177, 172, 179, 180, 183, 184, 185, 192, 120, 122, 124, 136, 142, 144, 145, 146, 152, 154, 156, 205, 208, 214, 226, 243, 259, 264, 269, 272, 297, 306, 307, 309, 322, 323, 324.

317. WAR CRIMES

Definition: Criminal offenses against the laws of war, now more commonly called the "law of armed conflict," which are set forth within the particular body of international law known as humanitarian law (known in Latin as the *jus in bello*). These are crimes in violation of international law that are committed by individuals, military or civilian, during an armed conflict. These crimes engage individual criminal responsibility and universal jurisdiction.

Significance: War crimes are defined by referring to the body of humanitarian law. They can be based on humanitarian law as found in treaty law, such as the four Geneva Conventions of 1949 (GCs) and the Protocol I of 1977. They can also be based on customary international law, known as the "laws and customs of war," such as is found in Hague Law of 1907, most particularly in the Hague IV Regulations, as later set forth in the Nuremberg Charter; these instruments are considered "declaratory" of customary international law. In addition to war crimes created by grave breaches of the four GCs, some of the acts that would constitute war crimes include murder, torture, physical mutilation, medical experimentation, inhumane treatment of civilians or POWs, taking hostages, rape, plunder of public or private property, unjustified wanton destruction of property not justified by military necessity, and deportation. Historically, these types of crimes or "atrocities" are like those of the German Third Reich in World War II, which largely precipitated the modern human rights movement. At Nuremberg, these actions were condemned as acts that denied the inherent human dignity of each person, and therefore they were acts that should be universally outlawed. The United States, as part of the Allied forces of World War II, played a major role in the Nuremberg trial proceedings.

War crimes are articulated as international crimes in the Draft Code of Crimes for the Peace and Security of Mankind, which is declaratory of customary international law. See Document 68.

According to the Statute of the International Criminal Court, adopted in July 1998, war crimes fall into four categories:

a. War crimes in international armed conflicts (state versus state) under the grave breaches provisions of the Geneva Conventions of 1949 and Protocol I of 1977.
b. War crimes under customary international law in the Laws and Customs of War (predominantly Hague Law).
c. War crimes in noninternational (internal) armed conflicts under Common Article 3 of the Geneva Conventions of 1949.
d. War crimes in noninternational (internal) armed conflicts under customary international law.

See Document 76, Article 8.

A person who commits a war crime as defined in the above referenced international criminal norms is called a war criminal. He or she is subject to arrest and prosecution for violation of these norms and any country in the world can do so under the principle of universal jurisdiction. Every state has the obligation to arrest and prosecute war criminals, and there is no statute of limitations for these international crimes.

The decision in the case of *Kadic v. Karadzic* is a decision of a U.S. court touching upon war crimes in the Bosnia conflict of the early 1990s. See Appendix J.

See Also Terms: 3, 19, 23, 25, 26, 37, 40, 41, 42, 45, 59, 63, 64, 70, 71, 72, 73, 86, 95, 96, 99, 103, 110, 113, 157, 159, 164, 166, 104, 129, 132, 135, 143, 145, 151, 153, 154, 164, 166, 171, 178, 181, 182, 185, 192, 197, 200, 201, 202, 203, 215, 222, 223, 224, 232, 251, 252, 253, 257, 258, 259, 272, 273, 283, 286, 292, 293, 298, 302, 306, 307, 310, 314, 318, 319, 320, 321.

318. WAR CRIMES ACT OF 1996

Definition: A federal statute enacted in 1996, that would give criminal jurisdiction to U.S. federal courts for the prosecution of any person who commits certain war crimes against a U.S. citizen or soldier anywhere in the world, and for the prosecution of war crimes committed by U.S. soldiers anywhere in the world.

Significance: Under international humanitarian law, all violations that constitute war crimes give rise to universal jurisdiction. In other words, all states can arrest and prosecute any war criminal for any war crime, no matter where it was committed and regardless of the nationality of the one who committed it. However, even though war crimes give every state the right to prosecute, the U.S. legal system requires that a congressional statute be passed expressly granting such jurisdiction to U.S. courts when the actions occur outside of the territory of the United States.

While the United States was reviewing its domestic jurisdiction over war crimes in the mid-1990s, it realized that there was no U.S. legislation allowing U.S. courts to prosecute anyone who would, for example, commit a war crime against a U.S. serviceman acting as a peacekeeper in Bosnia. It also realized that with the possibility of a permanent international criminal court, which was then in the process of creation, it needed to keep its right to exercise criminal jurisdiction over its own military nationals who commit war crimes elsewhere. It decided to pass the War Crimes Act to meet these needs. See Document 97.

The War Crimes Act only included war crimes that were grave breaches as specified in the 1949 Geneva Convention and Protocol I. In 1997, however, Congress undertook legislation called the War Crimes Act Extension of 1997, to add other bases of war crimes, such as those under the Hague Conventions of 1907 and Common Article 3 of the Geneva Conventions of 1949 and arguably Protocol II of 1977 to the Geneva Conventions. This 1997 legislation resulted in all legal bases of war crimes being included within the War Crimes Act, now part of U.S. law. This legislation is found in Title 18 of the U.S. Code.

See Also Terms: 3, 25, 26, 41, 42, 45, 70, 71, 72, 88, 93, 95, 110, 128, 129, 132, 135, 154, 158, 164, 166, 171, 192, 193, 194, 200, 201, 202, 211, 222, 224, 234, 243, 251, 252, 253, 257, 259, 272, 284, 286, 291, 292, 310, 313, 314, 315, 317, 319, 320, 321.

319. WAR CRIMINAL

See entry for **War Crimes**

320. WATERBOARDING

Definition: Waterboarding is an interrogation procedure whereby a suspect is laid down on his back, usually with a gunny sack over his head and has water poured over the gunny sack creating the sensation that the suspect is drowning. It is meant to get the victim to confess to a wrongful act or to provide information sought by the perpetrator.

The U.S. Department of Justice, Office of Legal Counsel, stated the definition of waterboarding for the CIA in a top secret 2002 Torture Memo as follows:

In this procedure, the individual is bound securely to an inclined bench, which is approximately four feet by seven feet. The individual's feet are generally elevated. A cloth is placed over the forehead and eyes. Water is then applied to the cloth in a controlled manner. As this is done, the cloth is lowered until it covers both the nose and mouth. Once the cloth is saturated and completely covers the mouth and nose airflow is slightly restricted for 20-40—seconds due to the presence of the cloth. This causes an increase in carbon dioxide level in the individual's blood. This increase in the carbon dioxide level stimulates increased effort to breath. This effort plus the cloth produces the perception of suffocation and incipient panic, i.e., the perception of drowning."

(See Document 91 for full text of Memo.)

Significance: In the war on terrorism this issue is being heatedly disputed in the politically realm, both nationally and internationally. The answer to the question of whether waterboarding is torture is yes. As a matter of law waterboarding is torture. Waterboarding consists of immobilizing the subject on his back with the head inclined downwards; water is then poured over the face into breathing passages, causing the captive to experience the sensations of drowning. In contrast to submerging the head face-forward in water, waterboarding precipitates an almost immediate gag reflex. Harmful physical consequences can manifest themselves even months after the waterboarding, while the psychological harm can last for years.

The Administration of George W. Bush had argued it was not torture under the above circumscribed definition, and said it was right because it produced information that he claimed was helpful in preventing a terror attack in England. The implication was that if it were necessary to save lives it is permissible to commit torture. Also implied is that if an act is not torture it is therefore fully permissible. The former President admitted to ordering waterboarding on terrorist detainees.

Upon the entry of the Obama Administration the Attorney General, Eric Holder, announced officially that he considered waterboarding to be torture. President Obama, through his AG, issued a rescission of all the so-called Torture Memos and ordered the government to cease any interrogation technique not permitted in the Army Field Manual. See Documents 86, 92. Waterboarding is not permitted under the Army Field manual. The Army Field manual section 2.22.3, dated 2006, at paragraph 5-75 on page 5-21, reads as follows:.

"The Department of Defense Detainee Program"; DOD instructions; and military execute orders including FRAGOs. <u>Use of torture is not only illegal but also it is a poor technique that yields unreliable results, may damage subsequent collection efforts, and can induce the source to say what he thinks the HUMINT collector wants to hear.</u> Use of torture can also have many possible negative consequences at national and international levels.

Cruel, Inhuman or Degrading Treatment Prohibited

All prisoners and detainees, regardless of status, will be treated humanely. Cruel, inhuman and degrading treatment is prohibited. The Detainee Treatment Act of 2005 defines "cruel, inhuman or degrading treatment" as the cruel unusual, and inhumane treatment or punishment prohibited by the Fifth, Eighth, and Fourteenth Amendments to the U.S. Constitution. This definition refers to an extensive body of law developed by the courts of the United States to determine when, under various circumstances, treatment of individuals would be inconsistent with American constitutional standards related to concepts of dignity, civilization, humanity, decency and fundamental fairness. All DOD procedures for treatment of prisoners and detainees have been reviewed and are consistent with these standards, as well as our obligations under international law as interpreted by the United States.....

(underlining added)

. . . .

5-75. **If used in conjunction with intelligence interrogations, prohibited actions include, but are not limited to—**

- Forcing the detainee to be naked, perform sexual acts, or pose in a sexual manner.
- Placing hoods or sacks over the head of a detainee; using duct tape over the eyes.
- Applying beatings, electric shock, burns, or other forms of physical pain.
- **"Waterboarding."**
- Using military working dogs.
- Inducing hypothermia or heat injury.
- Conducting mock executions.

(bolding added)

In the Army Field Manual waterboarding is set forth as a prohibited technique under the rubric of acts which violate the prohibition against cruel, inhuman, or degrading treatment. This is a human rights violation as well, though not at the high level of torture. The fact that the Army Field manual seems to call waterboarding cruel, inhuman, or degrading treatment does not change the fact that <u>internationally</u> waterboarding is still legally torture. The important thing is that even under the Army Field Manual waterboarding is a human rights violation and an absolutely prohibited interrogation technique. Whether torture or cruel, etc. treatment, it is an act which cannot be committed by government even to obtain information from a detainee. No exceptions are given. Whether torture or cruel, etc. treatment, this technique is prohibited. The penal ramifications are different for either but both techniques are prohibited by law. The Obama directive makes waterboarding by U.S. government personnel a human rights violation and illegal. See Document 92.

See Also Terms: 11, 12, 19, 20, 23, 25, 26, 33, 34, 35, 45, 53, 59, 63, 65, 66, 70, 71, 72, 82, 82, 88, 90, 93, 95, 96, 103, 106, 119, 120, 124, 129, 132, 144, 145, 147, 151, 152, 154, 157, 159, 159, 160, 166, 167, 169, 170, 171, 177, 178, 179, 181, 182, 184, 185, 192, 202, 210, 211, 215, 222, 223, 234, 243, 251, 259, 272, 292, 294, 300, 302, 306, 309, 311, 317.

321. WEAPONS OF MASS DESTRUCTION

See entry for **Indiscriminate Attack/Force**

322. WOMEN'S HUMAN RIGHTS

Definition: All of the internationally recognized human rights and fundamental freedoms that are found in international treaties and in customary international law that are aimed at prevention of discrimination against, and protection of women.

Significance: Women's human rights is a term that is used to describe a particular area of human rights advocacy. All the norms in the various universal, regional, and topical human rights instruments that deal with women's access to these human rights and fundamental freedoms are the basis for that advocacy.

These instruments include the United Nations Convention on the Political Rights of Women; the Convention on the Elimination of All Forms of Discrimination against Women (CEDAW); the Convention on Consent to Marriage, Minimum Age for Marriage and Registration of Marriages; the Convention on the Nationality of Women; the Declaration on the Elimination of Violence against Women; and the Final Document of the Beijing Conference of 1995, to name a few. See Documents 27, 33, 43. Within this field of advocacy, worldwide, there are at least 400 documents that can be used in whole or in part to defend women's human rights.

The UDHR and ICCPR also address women's rights in their specific calling for equality and equal protection between the sexes (UDHR, Articles 2 and 7; ICCPR, Articles 2.1, 3, and 26). See the Second and Third Reports of the United States to the U.N. Human Rights Committee under the ICCPR regarding Articles 2.1, 3, and 26. See Documents 6, 8, and 15A.

The issues addressed in the field of women's human rights are numerous. They include the right to political participation; the rights of women in rural areas; the right to food; labor rights, including the protection of pregnant women from dangerous work environments; the right to marry and found a family; the rights of the girl child; the right to health care; the right to education; freedom from violence; the rights of women during armed conflict; and the issue of female circumcision. A study on violence against women in U.S. federal and state prisons was done by a U.N. special rapporteur in 1999 for the U.N. Commission on Human Rights. That report is included in the Appendix section of this work.

Advocacy in the area of women's human rights varies, depending on the specific state in which a person lives, because different states have ratified different instruments and may not be bound by all the norms. Usually, however, even if a state has not ratified a particular document, the state may still be bound to protect that basic right because of customary international law.

Even then, this area of advocacy by necessity includes making sure that governments honor the rights to which they are bound, either by treaty or by customary international law. One often finds that women in the Third World may have fewer accepted rights than women, for example, in Western countries. Group rights or cultural relativism are sometimes factors. Therefore, the approach to establishing women's human rights will have variables, depending on regions and sometimes worldview.

In the United States, it is acknowledged that women in general have a well-established equality of rights. This was not always the case, however; women in the 20th century had to struggle for basic rights, such as the right to vote and hold public office and equal pay for equal work. Individual opinions vary as to whether certain areas of rights still need to be established for women. The United States has ratified, for example, the Convention on the Political Rights of Women, but is only signatory to the Convention on the Elimination of All Forms of Discrimination against Women (CEDAW). Many women's human rights advocates believe that the ratification of that particular document is essential to the full establishment of women's human rights.

Also noteworthy are those who criticize the idea of referring to women's human rights as a separate field of advocacy. They believe that if the ultimate goal is full equality for women, this approach merely emphasizes differences instead of the similarities between the two genders; they feel that the emphasis should be on the inherent dignity of all humankind.

See Also Terms: 7, 11, 12, 20, 24, 28, 33, 34, 35, 48, 54, 57, 60, 63, 69, 70, 86, 88, 89, 90, 92, 93, 100, 115, 119, 120, 124, 125, 126, 127, 129, 144, 145, 146, 147, 151, 152, 154, 160, 167, 169, 176, 177, 179, 180, 181, 182, 183, 2184, 185, 192, 216, 222, 230, 231, 236, 242, 243, 259, 264, 270, 272, 283, 283, 286, 289, 290, 291, 297, 306, 307, 308, 309, 311, 316, 317, 323.

323. WORLDVIEW

Definition: A set of beliefs and opinions regarding the important issues of life. One's worldview determines his or her responses to and decisions regarding the various ethical and moral questions encountered in everyday living. A worldview is sometimes referred to as a "philosophy of life."

Significance: The distinguishing characteristic between human beings and animals is the ability to process rational thought. Using that ability well is the key to living a fruitful personal life as well as functioning positively in society at large. A person's worldview is the combination of beliefs regarding life's most serious and basic questions. These questions include: Where do I come from (e.g., is there a creator God and if so, in what form?), or am I part of a random evolutionary process? What is my purpose in life? How do I respond to other people, and do I owe anything to my fellow man? How should society be run? Is there such a thing as absolute right and wrong, or is all truth relative? The history of the world includes the process of people forming their opinions on these various questions and manifesting them in their lifestyles. One's worldview can be expressed in various theistic belief systems, such as Islam, Christianity, Judaism, and Hinduism. A worldview can also be based on various non-theistic bases, such as those embodied in existentialism, nihilism, humanism, and atheism.

Understanding the concept of "worldview" is essential to human rights because of the existence of so many varying beliefs in the individuals that form society. The concept of the inherent dignity of each person supports the belief that each one has the right to form and hold his or her own opinions. The UDHR, Articles 18 and 19, the ICCPR, Articles 18 and 19, and other international human rights instruments are designed to affirm that right in the various states of the world. See Documents 6, 8. If the government of a state is bound to recognize the individual right to personal belief of each of its citizens, then it must create a climate, through respect for that right, that does not coerce the individual to believe what the majority does. In the U.S. context, this principle is particularly important because of the influx of immigrants from all over the world, with their various worldviews. In the U.S. Bill of Rights, the First Amendment establishes the U.S. commitment to the freedom of each individual to hold his or her own worldview. See Document 2

Although various theistic or non-theistic worldviews may have a prescribed set of tenets or beliefs, individuals will vary on their acceptance of all or part of them. This occurs because most often, the formation of one's worldview is a life process that includes the sum total of life experience: home life and the beliefs of one's parents, individual experiences, socioeconomic considerations, and perhaps most importantly, one's exposure to various competing worldviews. What is of the utmost importance in an enlightened society, however, is that one is aware of this process and uses a rational approach to evaluating the various ideas. Again, from the aspect of human rights, it is essential that each individual is *free* in that pursuit. People who ignore this process may not know how they feel about basic issues of, for example, law and justice, and they can often become the victims of government coercion. Not until it is too late do they realize the loss of their essential freedoms.

A difficulty with this principle of freedom is how a society maintains peace between its citizens who may disagree strongly in everything from their beliefs about God to the tenets on which their government and the economy should be based. It would be naive to say that this is not a problem, because the history of the world demonstrates it with its wars, ethnic cleansings, and so on. The international human rights movement is establishing worldwide an accepted set of norms that allow for individual expression, while reaffirming that individuals also have certain duties to the society at large, including the respect of the rights of other individuals. Tolerance of the worldview of another would by nature preclude coercion to accept that worldview as true. The tenet of Voltaire (paraphrased) that needs to be upheld is "I may disagree with what you believe, but I will defend to the death your right to believe it." This has been the historic approach of the United States.

The major worldview applications in the field of human rights have been about the universality versus the cultural relativism of human rights.

See Also Terms: 4, 22, 28, 70, 72, 75, 77, 87, 89, 103, 119, 120, 121, 122, 123, 124, 140, 148, 152, 153, 157, 160, 167, 169, 177, 204, 211, 212, 217, 222, 223, 224, 232, 236, 237, 241, 243, 259, 261, 264, 265, 271, 284, 286, 292, 293, 300, 308, 309, 316, 324.

324. XENOPHOBIA

Definition: An emotional fear of foreigners, of those who come from other countries. Xenophobia is usually caused by a citizen's perception that the foreigners are substantially different than the citizens of the state and that the foreigners are causing a problem, such as crime or using welfare or somehow threatening the welfare, well-being, or values of the state. It is an emotional attitude that can lead the citizen, alone or as part of a group, to take action against the foreigners, sometimes in a discriminatory or violent way that may violate the human rights of the foreigners.

Significance: This word is derived from the Greek word, *xenos*, meaning "foreign" or "strange," and *phobos*, meaning "fear of." Therefore, it is a fear of something strange or different, and can be manifested when there is an influx of people foreign to a culture. With xenophobia, one determines that a particular group of people with distinguishable characteristics is a threat to the well-being of another group of people or even society as a whole. It can happen between different groups of individuals or a government and a group of individuals.

In dealing with xenophobia, one must distinguish between a fear of something or someone because there is discomfort with strange or different customs, language, physical characteristics, and worldviews, and fear because a specific, provable threat exists. This distinction is usually not analyzed, and, as a result, xenophobes blame anyone of a particular group for any problems in society's functions, merely because they are different. It may even be true that some members of a distinguishable group have violated certain societal norms. However, the xenophobe has a tendency to attach the characteristics to the violation, as if the latter were a logical result of the former. Expressions of this attitude would be such remarks as: "Mexicans and African-Americans are responsible for the problems in welfare," "Italian businessmen are connected to the Mafia," and so on. This denies the basic understanding of an individual's identity, based on more than characteristics, such as race, gender, religion, or creed.

In the history of society worldwide, xenophobia has been blamed for many wars, ethnic cleansings, and occurrences of persecution. The history of the United States has included instances of xenophobia, especially as new ethnic groups as have immigrated. Italian-Americans, Irish-Americans, Jewish-Americans, as well as Mexican-Americans and African-Americans, to name a few, have been the subjects of xenophobic reaction at various times in the nation's history. Unfortunately, human nature tends to react in fear to things that are strange or different. The international human rights instruments, such as the ICCPR emphasize norms that reject the results of xenophobia. Each instrument includes a nondiscrimination clause that protects individuals from being judged unfairly on the basis of "race, color, sex, language, religions, political or other opinion, national or social origin, property, birth or other status." (See Document 8, ICCPR, Article 2.1.) Although it is difficult to control one individual's "xenophobic" response to another individual, these norms are designed to ensure that the government does not institutionalize the practice.

In 1985 a *Declaration on the Human Rights of Individuals Who Are Not Nationals of the Country in Which They Live*, was adopted by the U.N. General Assembly to remind states of the human rights of those members of society who are non citizens and subject to be treated as aliens. However, it does occur that even those who are U.S. citizens, such as some naturalized citizens, can be perceived as foreigners, as not "one of us" and be victims of xenophobia.

In 2006 the U.N. Office of the High Commissioner for Human Rights issued a publication based largely on the work of American professor David Weissbrodt, and entitled "The Rights of Non Citizens." It was meant to respond to this problem of xenophobia as to non-citizens. See Appendix N.

See Also Terms: 11, 12, 15, 20, 22, 28, 55, 56, 63, 68, 69, 70, 120, 122, 124, 127, 139, 140, 142, 144, 145, 146, 147, 151, 152, 155, 156, 163, 177, 179, 184, 185, 188, 205, 211, 212, 216, 228, 230, 231, 237, 243, 259, 260, 261, 272, 283, 289, 290, 292, 297, 306, 307, 309, 311, 316.

HUMAN RIGHTS PRIMARY DOCUMENTS

INTRODUCTION TO PRIMARY DOCUMENTS

In order to understand how international human rights relate to U.S. legal and political matters, one has to look at various human rights related documents. This volume contains many international human rights related documents from a variety of sources. In reality, most of the U.S. activity in the area of international human rights occurs in the context of the United Nations. Thus, most of the documents included here are from that body. It must be stated at the outset that the documents were chosen because either they are primary documents that contain the human rights standards held by the United States in various institutional contexts, or they are examples of the types of documents that come from these bodies and relate to the U.S. law and practice in the field of international human rights. Many documents are not from U.N. sources.

Some of these documents presented as primary documents and as appendix documents may appear to the reader to be critical of U.S. practices in the area of human rights. It is not the intent of this volume to expose the United States to criticism or to make it "look bad." These documents are meant to show the reader the actual processes, policies, positions, and perspectives that relate to the United States. The United States is one of the greatest practitioners of human rights in the world. But we Americans need to be made aware that we do sometimes commit human rights violations both at home and elsewhere in the world. We know that some countries accuse us of violating human rights standards. All countries commit human rights violations to some degree. Honesty, candor, and intellectual integrity require that the whole picture be presented. At the very least, readers will benefit from knowing how we are perceived by the international community as to our human rights practices and how we perceive ourself, such as in the Periodic State Reports done by the U.S., and the U.S. Universal Periodic Review report. The author makes no opinion as to whether these documents are accurate or correct as to facts, events, and opinions. These documents are included for the readers' awareness and learning, not as a political statement concerning or against the United States, which the author loves and supports. He only seeks to improve our country and to make it follow the human rights norms it proclaims to the world and its own citizens that it follows, and by which it judges every other country in the world.

It must be kept in mind, again, that some of the following documents may be dated; that is, they may be wholly or partially out of date at the time you are reading them, and no longer useful for some purposes such as political advocacy. The reader should consult the sources in the bibliography to see if the document has been updated, amended, or replaced by others. This is especially true of treaties and periodic states reports by the U.S. There are some treaties contained in the following documents that had not been either signed or ratified by the United States at the time of this writing but are presented so that if they come up for consideration by the US the reader will have access to the text. Or perhaps the reader will want to take steps to push for consideration of instruments which have not yet been ratified.

An example is the Statute of the International Criminal Court, adopted July 1998 by a vote of 120 states for and 7 against. The United States voted against adopting it but later President Clinton signed it. President George W. Bush repudiated it. Although this Statute has entered into force without the U.S. as a party, the United States has been a key promoter of the ICC (despite voting against it), and has continued to be extremely involved in its negotiation and development, even until the time of this writing. This Statute is so important to the future of protection of human rights and prevention of international crimes such as genocide, that it is included here. However, one cannot at this time apply the terms of this Statute to the United States as a matter of law. The United States is now dealing with it in the geopolitical realm.

Again, the United States could have signed or ratified some of the following treaties after this book was completed. Check the appendix entitled "List of Major International Human Rights Treaties signed or ratified by the United States" for the status of treaties up to the date of publication of this work. For the most current information, a call to your congress member or a quick trip to the Internet can probably help discover the present status of a treaty so that one can determine whether a given treaty is binding on the United States.

The documents included are only a few of the many human rights documents in existence. They do not cover all areas of human rights. They are a representative sample, not a collection of all possible documents.

For some of the other documents one should consult the appendix entitled "List of Names of Major International Human Rights Treaties and Declarations (Global and Regional) with Official Reference Citations." Or go to the University of Minnesota Human Rights library site at: http://www1.umn.edu/humanrts/.

With regards to the subject matter of the documents, the author has included some from the field of humanitarian law, which is basically applicable in times of armed conflicts, such as international or civil wars. This is because such norms are important to the United States, because we were so instrumental in the development of this area of law, and because so many of the worst human rights violations occur during armed conflicts. There are also document from international criminal law, which is the criminalization of certain serious human rights violations. These are included because since 9/11 the U.S. has been involved in what it calls the war on terrorism, and many of these norms are involved to date in places like Iraq and Afghanistan. Human rights are the legal limitation of the use of power, including armed force by government, and nowhere is such force used more excessively and harmfully than in armed conflict such as are seen in this era of terrorism.

Some of the enclosed documents are simply too large to include the whole text. Many have been excerpted by the author at his discretion. He has sought to preserve and present the essence of the documents. Readers are encouraged to find and read the full text for an optimum understanding. The enclosed will at best serve to get the reader started and increase understanding and encourage further study of human rights law.

Types of Documents

There are different types of documents. One needs to know what type of document one is working with in order to understand the legal status and importance of the document.

1. **Nonlegal instruments**, including statements of human rights principles and lists of specific human rights, which are known as declarations. These declarations are proposed and discussed by states within international institutions such as the United Nations or the Organization of American States and voted on by them in a proposed resolution. If adopted by the states by a resolution the declaration becomes an official but not legally binding statement of that institution as to what human rights are in a given system. The Universal Declaration of Human Rights (UDHR) is the classic example. Even though they are not legal documents, states should cause their state practice to be consistent with the declarations and should voluntarily seek to make their national domestic legislation harmonize with it. Sometimes declarations can become legally binding under the doctrine of customary international law, where over the course of time states have consistently acted according to them and have done so out of a sense that the instrument states, in whole or in part, what constitutes the international legal norms of state conduct. (See Document 6 for text and status of the UDHR.) These documents can serve as the primary standards for judging state actions in certain human rights bodies, such as the U.N. Human Rights Council (the UDHR), or the Inter-American Commission on Human Rights (American Declaration on the Rights and Duties of Man). Usually a declaration is done as a first step and a model in arriving at a legally binding treaty. The United States participates in the preparation and drafting of these instruments and in the institutional procedures, such as reporting procedures, in which they are applied.

2. **Legal instruments** that contain the written legal standards (norms) of government conduct required under international law are known as treaties, which are legal contracts between two or more states governed by international law. Treaties are sometimes known by the following titles: covenant, convention, charter, statute, or a protocol (which amends a treaty). The ICCPR (Document 8) is one of the main international human rights legal instruments ratified by the United States.

In dealing with a treaty as it may apply to the United States, it is necessary to first determine whether a treaty has entered into force (see entry on Entry into Force) and secondly whether it has been signed or ratified by the United States. If it has not entered into force the United States cannot be said to be legally bound to obey it. If it has entered into force and the United States has signed it but not yet ratified (by the U.S. Senate), then the United States is still not formally legally bound to obey it. However, the United States should act consistent with the treaty because it has signed it as an expression to the other states that it intends to be bound by and conform state conduct to it. (This is set forth in the 1969 Vienna Convention on the Law of Treaties, Appendix E). If the United States has signed and ratified a treaty that has entered into force, it becomes legally obligated (bound) to obey the treaty.

When the United States ratifies a treaty, it usually undertakes certain legal obligations such as conforming its national legislation and practice to the treaty and setting up effective, accessible domestic legal remedies for violations, so that violations can be remedied within the national legal system. Some of these laws and procedures are set forth in the appendix on U.S. legislation. Ratification of a human rights treaty by the United States most often involves the submission of Reservations, Declarations, and Understandings (abbreviated "RDUs" or "RUDs") with its ratification. See, for example, the United States ratification to the ICCPR (Document 9). One has to read these RDUs to know any qualifications or exceptions or modifications to the obligation as to a given human rights norm. For example, if a treaty stated that children under 18 could not serve in military combat and if the United States did not want to be bound by that norm, it could submit a reservation stating it chose not to be bound by that norm. The U.S. legal obligation about child soldiers would then have to be examined in light of that reservation. Likewise, declarations and understandings affect a state's obligation and may subject it to scrutiny by a certain body or under a certain procedure. In short, anyone wanting to judge U.S.conduct or determine procedures to remedy violations under treaty, must refer to and take into consideration these RDUs to get the whole picture. The RDUs submitted by the United States upon ratification of several of the major human rights treaties have been included herein.

If knowledge is power, then reading the main human rights instruments will give the reader the knowledge of his or her own human rights. With regard to the enumerated rights, the reader is advised to look up the specific human rights in the treaty or declaration articles in Documents 6 and 8. Along with Documents 10 and 16, which the U.S. has not ratified, these are the texts of the four instruments known as the "International Bill of Rights." Document 8 shows how those conceptual rights are articulated in the written legal text from which they are drawn. Reading human rights instruments should result in the individual empowerment of the reader and the creation of a "human rights consciousness," allowing the reader to view local, national, and international situations in their human rights dimension. Every reader of this work will at some time in his or her life face the abuse of power by government, whether federal, state, county, or city. Knowledge of one's human rights in the United States should serve to empower the reader for life. One can only know them if one reads the human rights instruments. But for a short list of your human rights see Appendix R.

3. **U.S. Laws:** In the Document section and in the Appendix are some U.S. laws which the author deems relevant to the most important human rights issues in the U.S. An example is the Military Commissions Act of 2006. As with all documents in this book these are only a sampling and they don't cover every area of activity of the U.S. that affects human rights.

4. **Other Documents:** Among the other documents included in this volume are non legally binding standards, guidelines, and principles adopted by international organizations, aimed at helping states conform their domestic practice with human rights norms. The Basic Principles on Treatment of Prisoners is an example. No state is forced to comply with them, but they are encouraged to implement them because they set forth a standard that is consistent with the human rights treaty standard to which most states are bound. The United States has participated, often very extensively and influentially, in the preparation and adoption of these various standards and principles, most of which were actually fashioned on U.S. constitutional law, practice, and experience. Some of them would be considered in the language of international human rights law as "soft law".

Reports to human rights treaty bodies and their observations, comments, and recommendations are also included in this volume. These are connected to human rights treaties. The legal obligations assumed by U.S. ratification of, for example, the ICCPR also include having to prepare and submit periodic reports on how its national (domestic) law and practice are consistent or inconsistent with the treaty norms, measures taken to implement the treaty, and any obstacles it faces in bringing law and practice into conformity with the human rights norm in the treaty. (See Document 8, ICCPR, Article 40). These reports are submitted to the Human Rights Committee, which is the treaty monitoring body set up by Article 28 of the ICCPR. This body is made up of members who sit not as representatives of their country, but as 18 legal experts in human rights from 18 different countries, representative of the different regions of the world.

There is usually an American sitting as a member of the Human Rights Committee. By choosing to ratify the ICCPR, the United States accepted the power of the Human Rights Committee to examine and comment on such reports and oversee U.S. compliance with this treaty. Included in the following documents are the Second and Third periodic reports of the U.S. State Department to the U.N. Human Rights Committee, which is the United States formally telling the international community how and what the United States does in terms of its human rights obligations under the ICCPR. The first (initial) U.S. report can be found at the U.S. Department of State website. Most of it reads like a treatise on U.S. statutes and case law, but each article of the ICCPR, which sets forth a substantive human right (articles 1-27) is analyzed according to U.S. legal and political experience. This work is how we Americans see our own country's law and judge ourselves by the standards of the ICCPR, which we have voluntarily chosen to obey as a matter of law, binding under the supremacy clause of the U.S. Constitution. The reports are not law nor are the conclusions and recommendations of the human rights bodies, though they should be followed, consistent with Constitutional limitation.

The treaty body, here the Human Rights Committee, examines the report and holds a formal meeting with delegates from the United States to discuss the report. Sometimes it submits a list of items it wishes the state to address. The committee sometimes receives information ("shadow reports") from nongovernmental organisations about the correctness or completeness of the report. The treaty body may issue its own written statement about the report, with its observations, comments, conclusions, and recommendations. These are meant to correct and advise the subject state as to how to best comply with the treaty as the experts see it. The United States is not, strictly speaking, legally bound to follow the recommendations."

This process of report examination can become very contentious, especially where the Human Rights Committee confronts the state on some information received from outside the report that calls into question the accuracy or comprehensiveness of the report.

General Comments of the U.N. human rights treaty bodies, also included in this documents section and in the Appendix, are also connected to human rights treaties. Treaty bodies such as the Human Rights Committee are granted power under the treaty to examine the case law and states reports and state practice and to write formal written statements of the scope and application of a particular norm or set of norms, or how the norms apply to certain situations or people. This is the informal jurisprudence of the treaty. These statements are called "General Comments." (See ICCPR, Article 40.)

One General Comment (No. 22) has been included in the Primary Document section as an example only, and other relevant general comments are found in the Appendix. These should be learned and applied by the U.S. in it law, policy and practice. Getting a state party such as the United States to actually comply with their views and comments involves a process of reconciling the differences between the national system and the international. Ultimately the matter is usually dictated by international and national politics, and the whole process is seldom and little known by the U.S. general population, even the legal community. The serious reader is encouraged to compare these General Comments with the U.S. periodic reports to the Human Rights Committee under the respective ICCPR article, to see how the U.S. government and courts see the human rights and their application, as compared to the international community's legal norms.

Another group of documents is reports/studies/decisions/opinions of non–treaty-based human rights bodies such as the U.N. Human Rights Council, or from one of its special mechanisms such as special rapporteurs or working groups. Special Rapporteurs are appointed by such bodies to study either the human rights situation of a particular state, or a particular theme such as violence against women, and to submit a periodic report on their findings. Various working groups receive written complaints called "communications" and take certain actions on particular problems, such as arbitrary detention or disappearances. As they relate to the United States, the documents in this category concern how the United States is judged to be practicing human rights in a given area such as racial discrimi nation. These are topics that the body is studying on a global basis. The special rapporteur reports included herein are reports based on fact-finding trips by the special rapporteur in the United States. During these trips (called "missions" or "visits"), the Special Rapporteur interviews government people, church leaders, minority groups, human rights activists, prisoners, academics, and anyone else who can provide information on the topic of the report; for example, religious intolerance. In these reports the Special Rapporteur sets forth his or her observations, statements of specific instances of alleged violations by the United States, comments by nongovernmental organizations and nongovernmental persons, a review of U.S. laws and court decisions, conclusions, and recommendations. These reports are transmitted to the body that requested them, such as the Human Rights Council. The body may then discuss these reports in its sessions.

Each document begins with a short overview, "Document Introduction" designed to give you basic information on the document, including: the titles, both official and abbreviated; the general subject matter it contains; its official reference citation for research purposes; where applicable, the dates of its adoption, entry into force, and the states parties to it in an international context; where applicable, the dates of U.S. signature, ratification, and entry into force; the type of document it is; its legal status and nature as to the United States and any relevant comments related to it. With this information and the text of the document itself, it is the author's hope that the reader will have all the basic tools needed to study and put to use these documents that are such an important part of international human rights.

U.S. Founding & Historical Documents

Document 1

Full Official Title: In Congress, July 4, 1776. A Declaration by the Representatives of the United States of America, In General Congress Assembled

Short Title/Acronym/Abbreviation: The Declaration of Independence

Subject: A declaration by the 13 original colonies of the United States that they were declaring their independence from Great Britain and going their separate and independent ways as nation states, and why they were doing so.

Official Citation: Not applicable

Date of Document: July 4, 1776

Date of Adoption: July 4, 1776

Date of General Entry into Force (EIF): Not applicable

Number of States Parties to this treaty as of November 1999: Not a treaty

Date of Signature by United States: Not applicable

Date of Ratification/Accession/Adhesion: Not applicable

Date of Entry into Force as to United States (effective date): Not applicable

Type of Document: A declaration and instrument of secession away from a sovereign state by the 13 colonies

Legal Status/Character of the Instrument/Document as to the United States: It served as a legal notice of secession of the 13 colonies away from the sovereignty of the King on England. Though it is not cited today as law, it is sometimes referred to in cases concerning constitutional rights. It should be.

Comments: Very importantly, this Declaration, which Americans celebrate every 4th of July, stated the reasons why the Colonists were seceding from Britain. It was because the King was causing or tolerating human rights violations in the colonies. This instrument served as one of the key philosophical bases of human rights. It is most important today for its statement that all human beings are born equal and with inalienable human rights, and that these rights do not come from the state, but are inherent in human beings. This is so even though at that time, women and people of color were not considered by many as equal, therefore possessing inalienable rights.

This Declaration makes specific reference to the law of nations, which is international law, as the legal basis of their right to secede from Britain. This is the same body of law from which much of modern international human rights law comes.

Web address: http://info.rutgers.edu/Library/Reference/US/declaration

Declaration of Independence

In Congress July 4, 1776,

The Unanimous Declaration of the Thirteen United States of America. When in the course of human events, it becomes necessary for one people to dissolve the political bands which have connected them with another, and to assume among the powers of the earth, the separate and equal station to which the laws of nature and of nature's God entitle them, a decent respect to the opinions of mankind requires that they should declare the causes which impel them to the separation.

We hold these truths to be self-evident: That all men are created equal; that they are endowed by their Creator with certain unalienable rights; that among these are life, liberty, and the pursuit of happiness; that, to secure these rights, governments are instituted among men, deriving their just powers from the consent of the governed; that whenever any form of government becomes destructive of these ends, it is the right of the people to alter or to abolish it, and to institute new government, laying its foundation on such principles, and organizing its powers in such form, as to them shall seem most likely to effect their safety and happiness. Prudence, indeed, will dictate that governments long established should not be changed for light and transient causes; and accordingly all experience hath shown that mankind are more disposed to suffer, while evils are sufferable than to right themselves by abolishing the forms to which they are accustomed. But when a long train of abuses and usurpations, pursuing invariably the same object, evinces a design to reduce them under absolute despotism, it is their right, it is their duty, to throw off such government, and to provide new guards for their future security. Such has been the patient sufferance of these colonies; and such is now the necessity which constrains them to alter their former systems of government. The history of the present King of Great Britain is a history of repeated injuries and usurpations, all having in direct object the establishment of an absolute tyranny over these states. To prove this, let facts be submitted to a candid world.

He has refused his assent to laws, the most wholesome and necessary for the public good.

He has forbidden his governors to pass laws of immediate and pressing importance, unless suspended in their operation till his assent should be obtained; and, when so suspended, he has utterly neglected to attend to them.

He has refused to pass other laws for the accommodation of large districts of people, unless those people would relinquish the right of representation in the legislature, a right inestimable to them, and formidable to tyrants only.

He has called together legislative bodies at places unusual, uncomfortable, and distant from the depository of their public records, for the sole purpose of fatiguing them into compliance with his measures.

He has dissolved representative houses repeatedly, for opposing, with manly firmness, his invasions on the rights of the people.

He has refused for a long time, after such dissolutions, to cause others to be elected; whereby the legislative powers, incapable of annihilation, have returned to the people at large for their exercise; the state remaining, in the mean time, exposed to all the dangers of invasions from without and convulsions within.

He has endeavored to prevent the population of these states; for that purpose obstructing the laws for naturalization of foreigners; refusing to pass others to encourage their migration hither, and raising the conditions of new appropriations of lands.

He has obstructed the administration of justice, by refusing his assent to laws for establishing judiciary powers.

He has made judges dependent on his will alone, for the tenure of their offices, and the amount and payment of their salaries.

He has erected a multitude of new offices, and sent hither swarms of officers to harass our people and eat out their substance.

He has kept among us, in times of peace, standing armies, without the consent of our legislatures.

He has affected to render the military independent of, and superior to, the civil power.

He has combined with others to subject us to a jurisdiction foreign to our Constitutions and unacknowledged by our laws, giving his assent to their acts of pretended legislation:

For quartering large bodies of armed troops among us;

For protecting them, by a mock trial, from punishment for any murders which they should commit on the inhabitants of these states;

For cutting off our trade with all parts of the world;

For imposing taxes on us without our consent;

For depriving us, in many cases, of the benefits of trial by jury;

For transporting us beyond seas, to be tried for pretended offenses;

For abolishing the free system of English laws in a neighboring province, establishing therein an arbitrary government, and enlarging its boundaries, so as to render it at once an example and fit instrument for introducing the same absolute rule into these colonies;

For taking away our charters, abolishing our most valuable laws, and altering fundamentally the forms of our governments;

For suspending our own legislatures, and declaring themselves invested with power to legislate for us in all cases whatsoever.

He has abdicated government here, by declaring us out of his protection and waging war against us.

He has plundered our seas, ravaged our coasts, burned our towns, and destroyed the lives of our people.

He is at this time transporting large armies of foreign mercenaries to complete the works of death, desolation, and tyranny already begun with circumstances of cruelty and perfidy scarcely paralleled in the most barbarous ages, and totally unworthy the head of a civilized nation.

He has constrained our fellow-citizens, taken captive on the high seas, to bear arms against their country, to become the executioners of their friends and brethren, or to fall themselves by their hands.

He has excited domestic insurrection among us, and has endeavored to bring on the inhabitants of our frontiers the merciless Indian savages, whose known rule of warfare is an undistinguished destruction of all ages, sexes, and conditions.

In every stage of these oppressions we have petitioned for redress in the most humble terms; our repeated petitions have been answered only by repeated injury. A prince, whose character is thus marked by every act which may define a tyrant, is unfit to be the ruler of a free people.

Nor have we been wanting in our attentions to our British brethren. We have warned them, from time to time, of attempts by their legislature to extend an unwarrantable jurisdiction over us. We have reminded them of the circumstances of our emigration and settlement here. We have appealed to their native justice and magnanimity; and we have conjured them, by the ties of our common kindred, to disavow these usurpations which would inevitably interrupt our connections and correspondence. They too, have been deaf to the voice of justice and of consanguinity. We must, therefore, acquiesce in the necessity which denounces our separation, and hold them as we hold the rest of mankind, enemies in war, in peace, friends.

We, therefore, the representatives of the United States of America, in General Congress assembled, appealing to the Supreme Judge of the world for the rectitude of our intentions, do, in the name and by the authority of the good people of these colonies solemnly publish and declare, That these United Colonies are, and of right ought to be, FREE AND INDEPENDENT STATES; that they are absolved from all allegiance to the British crown and that all political connection between them and the state of Great Britain is, and ought to be, totally dissolved; and that, as free and independent states, they have full power to levy war, conclude peace, contract alliances, establish commerce, and do all other acts and things which independent states may of right do. And for the support of this declaration, with a firm reliance on the protection of Divine Providence, we mutually pledge to each other our lives, our fortunes, and our sacred honor.

[Signed by] JOHN HANCOCK [President] [and fifty-five others]

DOCUMENT 2

Full Official Title: The Constitution of the United States of America

Short Title/Acronym/Abbreviation: U.S. Constitution and Bill of Rights

Subject: Establishment of the United States as a state, organizing the basic parts of the U.S. government and proclaiming certain basic, fundamental human rights

Official Citation: Not applicable

Date of Document: September 17, 1787

Date of Adoption: September 17, 1787

Date of General Entry into Force (EIF): June 21, 1788, with the ratification by New Hampshire

Number of States Parties to this Treaty as of November 1999: Originally 14, now 50

Date of Signature by United States: Not applicable

Date of United States Ratification/Accession/Adhesion: Ratified by the original 13 colonies, plus Vermont

Date of Entry into Force (effective date): June 21, 1788

Type of Document: An organic treaty between thirteen colonies, who considered themselves each to be independent nation states, to create a federal state. This was a treaty subject to international law, which treaty had to be ratified by nine of the original thirteen colonies to enter into force.

Legal Status/Character of the Instrument/Document as to the United States: Legally binding upon all states of the United States, all of which voluntarily assumed the binding legal obligations of the Constitution when they were admitted to the Union by vote of the other states according to the Constitution.

Comments: The initial charter of the country (state) known as the United States of America was one of the newly liberated and independent colonies forming a federal state and giving up some of their sovereignty over certain things such as war, immigration, postal service, to the federal government, reserving certain power to the states and people. This Constitution was a document which created a government of limited powers so as to prevent the types of human rights abuses they remembered from their days under British rule. They gave up some of their sovereignty for the power they could find in a union. Human rights are limitations on the power of government, much like the Constitution. This particularly applies to the later (1791) Bill of Rights. The Bill of Rights served as a model for some modern human rights norms.

Web address: http://info.rutgers.edu/Library/Reference/US/constitution/

U.S. Constitution (Including the Bill of Rights) (Excerpts)
Preamble

We, the people of the United States, in order to form a more perfect Union, establish justice, insure domestic tranquillity, provide for the common defense, promote the general welfare, and secure the blessings of liberty to ourselves and our posterity, do ordain and establish this Constitution for the United States of America.

Article I

Section 1. Legislative powers; in whom vested

All legislative powers herein granted shall be vested in a Congress of the United States, which shall consist of a Senate and House of Representatives.

Sec. 2. House of Representatives, how and by whom chosen Qualifications of a Representative. Representatives and direct taxes, how apportioned. Enumeration. Vacancies to be filled. Power of choosing officers, and of impeachment.

1. The House of Representatives shall be composed of members chosen every second year by the people of the several States, and the elector in each State shall have the qualifications requisite for electors of the most numerous branch of the State Legislature.

Sec. 3. Senators, how and by whom chosen. How classified. State Executive, when to make temporary appointments, in case, etc. Qualifications of a Senator. President of the Senate, his right to vote. President pro tem., and other officers of the Senate, how chosen. Power to try impeachments. When President is tried, Chief Justice to preside. Sentence.

1. The Senate of the United States shall be composed of two Senators from each State, [chosen by the Legislature thereof,] (Altered by 17th Amendment) for six years; and each Senator shall have one vote.

...

Sec. 8. Powers of Congress

The Congress shall have the power

1. To lay and collect taxes, duties, imposts and excises, to pay the debts and provide for the common defense and general welfare of the United States; but all duties, imposts and excises shall be uniform throughout the United States:

...

3. To regulate commerce with foreign nations, and among the several states, and with the Indian tribes:

4. To establish an uniform rule of naturalization, throughout the United States:

...

10. To define and punish piracies and felonies committed on the high seas, and offences against the law of nations:

11. To declare war, grant letters of marque and reprisal, and make rules concerning captures on land and water:

12. To make rules for the government and regulation of the land and naval forces:

...

15. To provide for calling forth the militia to execute the laws of the union, suppress insurrections and repel invasions:

16. To make all laws which shall be necessary and proper for carrying into execution the foregoing powers, and all other powers vested by this constitution in the government of the United States, or in any department or officer thereof.

...

Sec. 9. Provision as to migration or importation of certain persons. Habeas Corpus, Bills of attainder, etc. Taxes, how apportioned. No export duty. No commercial preference. Money, how drawn from Treasury, etc. No titular nobility. Officers not to receive presents, etc.

...

2. The privilege of the writ of habeas corpus shall not be suspended, unless when in cases of rebellion or invasion the public safety may require it.

3. No bill of attainder or ex post facto law shall be passed.

4. [No capitation, or other direct tax shall be laid unless in proportion to the census or enumeration herein before directed to be taken.] <<Altered by 16th Amendment>>

Sec. 10. States prohibited from the exercise of certain powers.

1. No state shall enter into any treaty, alliance, or confederation; grant letters of marque and reprisal; pass any bill of attainder, ex post facto law, invaded, or in such imminent danger as will not admit of delay.

Article II

Section 1. President: his term of office. Electors of President; number and how appointed. Electors to vote on same day. Qualification of President. On whom his duties devolve in case of his removal, death, etc. President's compensation. His oath of office.

1. The Executive power shall be vested in a President of the United States of America. He shall hold office during the term of four years, and together with the Vice President, chosen for the same term,

Sec. 2. President to be Commander-in-Chief. He may require opinions of cabinet officers, etc., may pardon. Treaty-making power. Nomination of certain officers. When President may fill vacancies.

1. The President shall be Commander-in-Chief of the Army and Navy of the United States, and of the militia of the several States,

2. He shall have power, by and with the advice and consent of the Senate, to make treaties, provided two-thirds of the Senators present concur; and he shall nominate, and by and with the advice and consent of the Senate, shall appoint ambassadors,

Sec. 3. President shall communicate to Congress. He may convene and adjourn Congress, in case of disagreement, etc. Shall receive ambassadors, execute laws, and commission officers.

Article III

Section 1. Judicial powers. Tenure. Compensation.

The judicial power of the United States, shall be vested in one supreme court, and in such inferior courts as the Congress may, from time to time, ordain and establish.

Sec. 2. Judicial power; to what cases it extends. Original jurisdiction of Supreme Court Appellate. Trial by Jury, etc.

Trial, where

1. The judicial power shall extend to all cases, in law and equity, arising under this constitution, the laws of the United States, and treaties made, or which shall be made under their authority; to controversies to which the United States shall be a party; [to controversies between two or more states, between a state and citizens of another state, between citizens of different states, between citizens of the same state, claiming lands under grants of different states, and between a state, or the citizens thereof, and foreign states, citizens or subjects.] <<Altered by 11th Amendment>>.

. . .

Article VI

. . .

2. This constitution, and the laws of the United States which shall be made in pursuance thereof; and all treaties made, or which shall be made, under the authority of the United States shall be the supreme law of the land; and the judges in every state shall be bound thereby, any thing in the constitution or laws of any state to the contrary notwithstanding.

3. The senators and representatives before-mentioned, and the members of the several state legislatures, and all executive and judicial officers, both of the United States and of the several states, shall be bound by oath or affirmation, to support this constitution; but no religious test shall ever be required as a qualification to any office or public trust under the United States.

BILL OF RIGHTS (WITH OTHER PERTINENT AMENDMENTS)

The Ten Original Amendments: The Bill of Rights. Passed by Congress September 25, 1789. Ratified December 15, 1791.

Amendment I

Congress shall make no law respecting an establishment of religion, or prohibiting the free exercise thereof; or abridging the freedom of speech, or of the press; or the right of the people peaceably to assemble, and to petition the Government for a redress of grievances.

Amendment II

A well-regulated militia, being necessary to the security of a free State, the right of the people to keep and bear arms, shall not be infringed.

Amendment III

No soldier shall, in time of peace be quartered in any house, without the consent of the owner, nor in time of war, but in a manner to be prescribed by law.

Amendment IV

The right of the people to be secure in their persons, houses, papers, and effects, against unreasonable searches and seizures, shall not be violated, and no warrants shall issue, but upon probable cause, supported by oath or affirmation, and particularly describing the place to be searched, and the persons or things to be seized.

Amendment V

No person shall be held to answer for a capital, or otherwise infamous crime, unless on a presentment or indictment of a Grand Jury, except in cases arising in the land or naval forces, or in the militia, when in actual service in time of war or public danger; nor shall any person be subject for the same offense to be twice put in jeopardy of life or limb; nor shall be compelled in any criminal case to be a witness against himself, nor be deprived of life, liberty, or property, without due process of law; nor shall private property be taken for public use without just compensation.

Amendment VI

In all criminal prosecutions, the accused shall enjoy the right to a speedy and public trial, by an impartial jury of the State and district wherein the crime shall have been committed, which district shall have been previously ascertained by law, and to be informed of the nature and cause of the accusation; to be confronted with the witnesses against him; to have compulsory process for obtaining witnesses in his favor, and to have the assistance of counsel for his defense.

Amendment VII

In suits at common law, where the value in controversy shall exceed twenty dollars, the right of trial by jury shall be preserved, and no fact tried by a jury shall be otherwise reexamined in any court of the United States, than according to the rules of the common law.

Amendment VIII

Excessive bail shall not be required, nor excessive fines imposed, nor cruel and unusual punishments inflicted.

Amendment IX

The enumeration in the Constitution, of certain rights, shall not be construed to deny or disparage others retained by the people.

Amendment X

The powers not delegated to the United States by the Constitution, nor prohibited by it to the States, are reserved to the States respectively, or to the people.

...

Amendment XIII

Passed by Congress January 31, 1865. Ratified December 6, 1865.

Section 1.

Neither slavery nor involuntary servitude, except as a punishment for crime whereof the party shall have been duly convicted, shall exist within the United States, or any place subject to their jurisdiction.

Sec. 2.

Congress shall have power to enforce this article by appropriate legislation.

Amendment XIV

Passed by Congress June 13, 1866. Ratified July 9, 1868

Section 1.

All persons born or naturalized in the United States, and subject to the jurisdiction thereof, are citizens of the United States and of the State wherein they reside. No State shall make or enforce any law which shall abridge the privileges or immunities of citizens of the United States; nor shall any State deprive any person of life, liberty, or property, without due process of law; nor to deny to any person within its jurisdiction the equal protection of the laws.

...

Sec. 5.

The Congress shall have the power to enforce, by appropriate legislation, the provisions of this article.

...

Amendment XIX

Passed by Congress June 4, 1919. Ratified August 18, 1920.

The right of citizens of the United States to vote shall not be denied or abridged by the United States or by any State on account of sex. Congress shall have power to enforce this article by appropriate legislation.

Passed by Congress March 23, 1971. Ratified June 30, 1971.

...

Amendment XXVI

Section 1.

The right of citizens of the United States, who are 18 years of age or older, to vote shall not be denied or abridged by the United States or any state on account of age.

Section 2.

The Congress shall have power to enforce this article by appropriate legislation.

DOCUMENT 3

Full Official Title: The Emancipation Proclamation

Short Title/Acronym/Abbreviation: Emancipation Proclamation

Subject: Termination of Slavery

Official Citation: United States. President Abraham Lincoln. *Proclamation*, 95. Washington: September 22, 1862.

Date of Document: September 22, 1862

Date of Adoption: Not applicable

Date of General Entry into Force (EIF): January 1, 1863

Number of States Parties as of this printing: Not applicable

Date of Signature by United States: Not applicable

Date of Ratification/Accession/Adhesion: Not applicable

Date of Entry into Force as to United States (effective date): January 1, 1863

Type of Document: Proclamation by a U.S. President (See dictionary entry on "Executive Orders").

Legal Status/Character of the Instrument/Document as to the United States: This type of act by the president is similar to an executive order except that it typically directs public policy outside the government. It may be seen as part of a directive of the President to fulfill his/her constitutional duty to "take Care that the Laws be faithfully executed" (U.S. Constitution Article 2, Section 3, Clause 4), and is most credible when it follows Congressional action since Congress holds the legislative-making authority. It has been used by presidents since George Washington for issues ranging from ceremonial recognition of specific events to granting presidential pardons. (See http://www.presidency.ucsb.edu/proclamations.) This document called for the freedom of any slave held in a state or part of a state that was in rebellion against the United States. It did not affect any slave in other parts of the United States, including rebel areas under control of the Union forces, but was an important step in the abolition of slavery in the United States. It also proclaimed that black men were allowed to enter the U.S. Army and Navy.

THE EMANCIPATION PROCLAMATION

January 1, 1863

Whereas, on the twenty-second day of September, in the year of our Lord one thousand eight hundred and sixty-two, a proclamation was issued by the President of the United States, containing, among other things, the following, to wit:

"That on the first day of January, in the year of our Lord one thousand eight hundred and sixty-three, all persons held as slaves within any State or designated part of a State, the people whereof shall then be in rebellion against the United States, shall be then, thenceforward, and forever free; and the Executive Government of the United States, including the military and naval authority thereof, will recognize and maintain the freedom of such persons, and will do no act or acts to repress such persons, or any of them, in any efforts they may make for their actual freedom.

"That the Executive will, on the first day of January aforesaid, by proclamation, designate the States and parts of States, if any, in which the people thereof, respectively, shall then be in rebellion against the United States; and the fact that any State, or the people thereof, shall on that day be, in good faith, represented in the Congress of the United States by members chosen thereto at elections wherein a majority of the qualified voters of such State shall have participated, shall, in the absence of strong countervailing testimony, be deemed conclusive evidence that such State, and the people thereof, are not then in rebellion against the United States."

Now, therefore I, Abraham Lincoln, President of the United States, by virtue of the power in me vested as Commander-in-Chief, of the Army and Navy of the United States in time of actual armed rebellion against the authority and government of the United States, and as a fit and necessary war measure for suppressing said rebellion, do, on this first day of January, in the year of our Lord one thousand eight hundred and sixty-three, and in accordance with my purpose so to do publicly proclaimed for the full period of one hundred days, from the day first above mentioned, order and designate as the States and parts of States wherein the people thereof respectively, are this day in rebellion against the United States, the following, to wit:

Arkansas, Texas, Louisiana, (except the Parishes of St. Bernard, Plaquemines, Jefferson, St. John, St. Charles, St. James Ascension, Assumption, Terrebonne, Lafourche, St. Mary, St. Martin, and Orleans, including the City of New Orleans) Mississippi, Alabama, Florida, Georgia, South Carolina, North Carolina, and Virginia, (except the forty-eight counties designated as West Virginia, and also the counties of Berkley, Accomac, Northampton, Elizabeth City, York, Princess Ann, and Norfolk, including the cities of Norfolk and Portsmouth[)], and which excepted parts, are for the present, left precisely as if this proclamation were not issued.

And by virtue of the power, and for the purpose aforesaid, I do order and declare that all persons held as slaves within said designated States, and parts of States, are, and henceforward shall be free; and that the Executive government of the United States, including the military and naval authorities thereof, will recognize and maintain the freedom of said persons.

And I hereby enjoin upon the people so declared to be free to abstain from all violence, unless in necessary self-defence; and I recommend to them that, in all cases when allowed, they labor faithfully for reasonable wages.

And I further declare and make known, that such persons of suitable condition, will be received into the armed service of the United States to garrison forts, positions, stations, and other places, and to man vessels of all sorts in said service.

And upon this act, sincerely believed to be an act of justice, warranted by the Constitution, upon military necessity, I invoke the considerate judgment of mankind, and the gracious favor of Almighty God.

In witness whereof, I have hereunto set my hand and caused the seal of the United States to be affixed.

Done at the City of Washington, this first day of January, in the year of our Lord one thousand eight hundred and sixty three, and of the Independence of the United States of America the eighty-seventh.

By the President: ABRAHAM LINCOLN

WILLIAM H. SEWARD, Secretary of State.

Document 4

Full Official Title: Franklin Roosevelt's Annual Address to Congress—The "Four Freedoms"

Short Title/Acronym/Abbreviation: The Four Freedoms Speech

Subject: Human Rights, War

Official Citation: Franklin D. Roosevelt Annual Message to Congress, January 6, 1941; Records of the United States Senate; SEN 77A-H1; Record Group 46; National Archives.

Date of Document: January 6, 1941

Date of Adoption: Not applicable

Date of General Entry into Force (EIF): Not applicable

Number of States Parties as of this printing: Not applicable

Date of Signature by United States: Not applicable

Date of Ratification/Accession/Adhesion: Not applicable

Date of Entry into Force as to United States (effective date): Not applicable

Type of Document: President's annual State of the Union speech to Congress

Legal Status/Character of the Instrument/Document as to the United States: Non-binding political speech, Presidential Address

Comment: President Franklin D. Roosevelt declared four essential freedoms in his Annual Message to Congress of January 6, 1941. This annual presidential "State of the Union" address called Americans out of isolation to contribute to the war effort. Roosevelt affirmed the essential rights to freedom of speech and expression, freedom to worship, freedom from want, and freedom from fear. These four freedoms were later enshrined in the U.N. Charter. Roosevelt refers in this speech to a "new one-way international law" that dictators would try to impose on other nations as an instrument of oppression and offers an alternative order—a moral order. Roosevelt calls Americans to support the struggle for true freedom which protects the "supremacy of human rights everywhere."

THE FOUR FREEDOMS SPEECH

Mr. President, Mr. Speaker, Members of the Seventy-seventh Congress:

I address you, the Members of the Seventy-seventh Congress, at a moment unprecedented in the history of the Union. I use the word "unprecedented," because at no previous time has American security been as seriously threatened from without as it is today.

Since the permanent formation of our Government under the Constitution, in 1789, most of the periods of crisis in our history have related to our domestic affairs. Fortunately, only one of these—the four-year War Between the States—ever threatened our national unity. Today, thank God, one hundred and thirty million Americans, in forty-eight States, have forgotten points of the compass in our national unity.

It is true that prior to 1914 the United States often had been disturbed by events in other Continents. We had even engaged in two wars with European nations and in a number of undeclared wars in the West Indies, in the Mediterranean and in the Pacific for the maintenance of American rights and for the principles of peaceful commerce. But in no case had a serious threat been raised against our national safety or our continued independence.

What I seek to convey is the historic truth that the United States as a nation has at all times maintained clear, definite opposition, to any attempt to lock us in behind an ancient Chinese wall while the procession of civilization went past. Today, thinking of our children and of their children, we oppose enforced isolation for ourselves or for any other part of the Americas.

That determination of ours, extending over all these years, was proved, for example, during the quarter century of wars following the French Revolution.

While the Napoleonic struggles did threaten interests of the United States because of the French foothold in the West Indies and in Louisiana, and while we engaged in the War of 1812 to vindicate our right to peaceful trade, it is nevertheless clear that neither France nor Great Britain, nor any other nation, was aiming at domination of the whole world.

In like fashion from 1815 to 1914—ninety-nine years—no single war in Europe or in Asia constituted a real threat against our future or against the future of any other American nation.

Except in the Maximilian interlude in Mexico, no foreign power sought to establish itself in this Hemisphere; and the strength of the British fleet in the Atlantic has been a friendly strength. It is still a friendly strength.

Even when the World War broke out in 1914, it seemed to contain only small threat of danger to our own American future. But, as time went on, the American people began to visualize what the downfall of democratic nations might mean to our own democracy.

We need not overemphasize imperfections in the Peace of Versailles. We need not harp on failure of the democracies to deal with problems of world reconstruction. We should remember that the Peace of 1919 was far less unjust than the kind of "pacification" which began even before Munich, and which is being carried on under the new order of tyranny that seeks to spread over every continent today. The American people have unalterably set their faces against that tyranny.

Every realist knows that the democratic way of life is at this moment being directly assailed in every part of the world—assailed either by arms, or by secret spreading of poisonous propaganda by those who seek to destroy unity and promote discord in nations that are still at peace.

During sixteen long months this assault has blotted out the whole pattern of democratic life in an appalling number of independent nations, great and small. The assailants are still on the march, threatening other nations, great and small. Therefore, as your President, performing my constitutional duty to "give to the Congress information of the state of the Union," I find it, unhappily, necessary to report that the future and the safety of our country and of our democracy are overwhelmingly involved in events far beyond our borders.

Armed defense of democratic existence is now being gallantly waged in four continents. If that defense fails, all the population and all the resources of Europe, Asia, Africa and Australasia will be dominated by the conquerors. Let us remember that the total of those populations and their resources in those four continents greatly exceeds the sum total of the population and the resources of the whole of the Western Hemisphere—many times over.

In times like these it is immature—and incidentally, untrue—for anybody to brag that an unprepared America, single-handed, and with one hand tied behind its back, can hold off the whole world.

No realistic American can expect from a dictator's peace international generosity, or return of true independence, or world disarmament, or freedom of expression, or freedom of religion—or even good business.

Such a peace would bring no security for us or for our neighbors. "Those, who would give up essential liberty to purchase a little temporary safety, deserve neither liberty nor safety."

As a nation, we may take pride in the fact that we are softhearted; but we cannot afford to be soft-headed.

We must always be wary of those who with sounding brass and a tinkling cymbal preach the "ism" of appeasement.

We must especially beware of that small group of selfish men who would clip the wings of the American eagle in order to feather their own nests.

I have recently pointed out how quickly the tempo of modern warfare could bring into our very midst the physical attack which we must eventually expect if the dictator nations win this war.

There is much loose talk of our immunity from immediate and direct invasion from across the seas. Obviously, as long as the British Navy retains its power, no such danger exists. Even if there were no British Navy, it is not probable that any enemy would be stupid enough to attack us by landing troops in the United States from across thousands of miles of ocean, until it had acquired strategic bases from which to operate.

But we learn much from the lessons of the past years in Europe—particularly the lesson of Norway, whose essential seaports were captured by treachery and surprise built up over a series of years.

The first phase of the invasion of this Hemisphere would not be the landing of regular troops. The necessary strategic points would be occupied by secret agents and their dupes—and great numbers of them are already here, and in Latin America.

As long as the aggressor nations maintain the offensive, they—not we—will choose the time and the place and the method of their attack.

That is why the future of all the American Republics is today in serious danger.

That is why this Annual Message to the Congress is unique in our history.

That is why every member of the Executive Branch of the Government and every member of the Congress faces great responsibility and great accountability.

The need of the moment is that our actions and our policy should be devoted primarily—almost exclusively—to meeting this foreign peril. For all our domestic problems are now a part of the great emergency.

Just as our national policy in internal affairs has been based upon a decent respect for the rights and the dignity of all our fellow men within our gates, so our national policy in foreign affairs has been based on a decent respect for the rights and dignity of all nations, large and small. And the justice of morality must and will win in the end.

Our national policy is this:

First, by an impressive expression of the public will and without regard to partisanship, we are committed to all-inclusive national defense.

Second, by an impressive expression of the public will and without regard to partisanship, we are committed to full support of all those resolute peoples, everywhere, who are resisting aggression and are thereby keeping war away from our Hemisphere. By this support, we express our determination that the democratic cause shall prevail; and we strengthen the defense and the security of our own nation.

Third, by an impressive expression of the public will and without regard to partisanship, we are committed to the proposition that principles of morality and considerations for our own security will never permit us to acquiesce in a peace dictated by aggressors and sponsored by appeasers. We know that enduring peace cannot be bought at the cost of other people's freedom.

In the recent national election there was no substantial difference between the two great parties in respect to that national policy. No issue was fought out on this line before the American electorate. Today it is abundantly evident that American citizens everywhere are demanding and supporting speedy and complete action in recognition of obvious danger.

Therefore, the immediate need is a swift and driving increase in our armament production.

Leaders of industry and labor have responded to our summons. Goals of speed have been set. In some cases these goals are being reached ahead of time; in some cases we are on schedule; in other cases there are slight but not serious delays; and in some cases—and I am sorry to say very important cases—we are all concerned by the slowness of the accomplishment of our plans.

The Army and Navy, however, have made substantial progress during the past year. Actual experience is improving and speeding up our methods of production with every passing day. And today's best is not good enough for tomorrow.

I am not satisfied with the progress thus far made. The men in charge of the program represent the best in training, in ability, and in patriotism. They are not satisfied with the progress thus far made. None of us will be satisfied until the job is done.

No matter whether the original goal was set too high or too low, our objective is quicker and better results.

To give you two illustrations:

We are behind schedule in turning out finished airplanes; we are working day and night to solve the innumerable problems and to catch up.

We are ahead of schedule in building warships but we are working to get even further ahead of that schedule.

To change a whole nation from a basis of peacetime production of implements of peace to a basis of wartime production of implements of war is no small task. And the greatest difficulty comes at the beginning of the program, when new tools, new plant facilities, new assembly lines, and new ship ways must first be constructed before the actual materiel begins to flow steadily and speedily from them.

The Congress, of course, must rightly keep itself informed at all times of the progress of the program. However, there is certain information, as the Congress itself will readily recognize, which, in the interests of our own security and those of the nations that we are supporting, must of needs be kept in confidence.

New circumstances are constantly begetting new needs for our safety. I shall ask this Congress for greatly increased new appropriations and authorizations to carry on what we have begun.

I also ask this Congress for authority and for funds sufficient to manufacture additional munitions and war supplies of many kinds, to be turned over to those nations which are now in actual war with aggressor nations.

Our most useful and immediate role is to act as an arsenal for them as well as for ourselves. They do not need man power, but they do need billions of dollars worth of the weapons of defense.

The time is near when they will not be able to pay for them all in ready cash. We cannot, and we will not, tell them that they must surrender, merely because of present inability to pay for the weapons which we know they must have.

I do not recommend that we make them a loan of dollars with which to pay for these weapons—a loan to be repaid in dollars.

I recommend that we make it possible for those nations to continue to obtain war materials in the United States, fitting their orders into our own program. Nearly all their materiel would, if the time ever came, be useful for our own defense.

Taking counsel of expert military and naval authorities, considering what is best for our own security, we are free to decide how much should be kept here and how much should be sent abroad to our friends who by their determined and heroic resistance are giving us time in which to make ready our own defense.

For what we send abroad, we shall be repaid within a reasonable time following the close of hostilities, in similar materials, or, at our option, in other goods of many kinds, which they can produce and which we need.

Let us say to the democracies: "We Americans are vitally concerned in your defense of freedom. We are putting forth our energies, our resources and our organizing powers to give you the strength to regain and maintain a free world. We shall send you, in ever-increasing numbers, ships, planes, tanks, guns. This is our purpose and our pledge."

In fulfillment of this purpose we will not be intimidated by the threats of dictators that they will regard as a breach of international law or as an act of war our aid to the democracies which dare to resist their aggression. Such aid is not an act of war, even if a dictator should unilaterally proclaim it so to be.

When the dictators, if the dictators, are ready to make war upon us, they will not wait for an act of war on our part. They did not wait for Norway or Belgium or the Netherlands to commit an act of war.

Their only interest is in a new one-way international law, which lacks mutuality in its observance, and, therefore, becomes an instrument of oppression.

The happiness of future generations of Americans may well depend upon how effective and how immediate we can make our aid felt. No one can tell the exact character of the emergency situations that we may be called upon to meet. The Nation's hands must not be tied when the Nation's life is in danger.

We must all prepare to make the sacrifices that the emergency—almost as serious as war itself—demands. Whatever stands in the way of speed and efficiency in defense preparations must give way to the national need.

A free nation has the right to expect full cooperation from all groups. A free nation has the right to look to the leaders of business, of labor, and of agriculture to take the lead in stimulating effort, not among other groups but within their own groups.

The best way of dealing with the few slackers or trouble makers in our midst is, first, to shame them by patriotic example, and, if that fails, to use the sovereignty of Government to save Government.

As men do not live by bread alone, they do not fight by armaments alone. Those who man our defenses, and those behind them who build our defenses, must have the stamina and the courage which come from unshakable belief in the manner of life which they are defending. The mighty action that we are calling for cannot be based on a disregard of all things worth fighting for.

The Nation takes great satisfaction and much strength from the things which have been done to make its people conscious of their individual stake in the preservation of democratic life in America. Those things have toughened the fibre of our people, have renewed their faith and strengthened their devotion to the institutions we make ready to protect.

Certainly this is no time for any of us to stop thinking about the social and economic problems which are the root cause of the social revolution which is today a supreme factor in the world.

For there is nothing mysterious about the foundations of a healthy and strong democracy. The basic things expected by our people of their political and economic systems are simple. They are:

Equality of opportunity for youth and for others.

Jobs for those who can work.

Security for those who need it.

The ending of special privilege for the few.

The preservation of civil liberties for all.

The enjoyment of the fruits of scientific progress in a wider and constantly rising standard of living.

These are the simple, basic things that must never be lost sight of in the turmoil and unbelievable complexity of our modern world. The inner and abiding strength of our economic and political systems is dependent upon the degree to which they fulfill these expectations.

Many subjects connected with our social economy call for immediate improvement.

As examples:

We should bring more citizens under the coverage of old-age pensions and unemployment insurance.

We should widen the opportunities for adequate medical care.

We should plan a better system by which persons deserving or needing gainful employment may obtain it.

I have called for personal sacrifice. I am assured of the willingness of almost all Americans to respond to that call.

A part of the sacrifice means the payment of more money in taxes. In my Budget Message I shall recommend that a greater portion of this great defense program be paid for from taxation than we are paying today. No person should try, or be allowed, to get rich out of this program; and the principle of tax payments in accordance with ability to pay should be constantly before our eyes to guide our legislation.

If the Congress maintains these principles, the voters, putting patriotism ahead of pocketbooks, will give you their applause.

In the future days, which we seek to make secure, we look forward to a world founded upon four essential human freedoms.

The first is freedom of speech and expression—everywhere in the world.

The second is freedom of every person to worship God in his own way—everywhere in the world.

The third is freedom from want—which, translated into world terms, means economic understandings which will secure to every nation a healthy peacetime life for its inhabitants—everywhere in the world.

The fourth is freedom from fear—which, translated into world terms, means a world-wide reduction of armaments to such a point and in such a thorough fashion that no nation will be in a position to commit an act of physical aggression against any neighbor—anywhere in the world.

That is no vision of a distant millennium. It is a definite basis for a kind of world attainable in our own time and generation. That kind of world is the very antithesis of the so-called new order of tyranny which the dictators seek to create with the crash of a bomb.

To that new order we oppose the greater conception—the moral order. A good society is able to face schemes of world domination and foreign revolutions alike without fear.

Since the beginning of our American history, we have been engaged in change—in a perpetual peaceful revolution—a revolution which goes on steadily, quietly adjusting itself to changing conditions—without the concentration camp or the quick-lime in the ditch. The world order which we seek is the cooperation of free countries, working together in a friendly, civilized society.

This nation has placed its destiny in the hands and heads and hearts of its millions of free men and women; and its faith in freedom under the guidance of God. Freedom means the supremacy of human rights everywhere. Our support goes to those who struggle to gain those rights or keep them. Our strength is our unity of purpose.

To that high concept there can be no end save victory.

FOUNDING & HISTORICAL INTERNATIONAL DOCUMENTS

DOCUMENT 5

Full Official Title: Charter of the United Nations

Short Title/Acronym/Abbreviation: The U.N. Charter/UNCH

Subject: Establishment of the international intergovernmental organization known as the United Nations, setting forth its purposes and goals and establishing its organs and procedures, done at San Francisco, California

Official Citation: 59 Stat. 1031, T.S. No. 993, 3 Bevans 1153

Date of Document: June 26, 1945

Date of Adoption: June 26, 1945

Date of General Entry into Force (EIF): October 24, 1945

Number of States Parties to this Treaty as of this printing: 188

Date of Signature by United States: June 26, 1945

Date of Ratification/Accession/Adhesion: October 24, 1945

Date of Entry into Force as to United States (effective date): October 24, 1945

Type of Document: A legal instrument establishing an international institution under international law. (Most often a "charter" is a legal instrument which establishes an organization. It is the organic document of that body.)

Legal Status/Character of the Instrument/Document as to the United States: Binding upon the United States which ratified it, making it a member state of the United Nations and obligating it to fulfill its legal obligations under the Charter.

Comments: The United States was largely instrumental in the drafting and adoption of the U.N. Charter and in the creation of the United Nations.

Web address: http://www1.umn.edu/humanrts/instree/aunchart.htm

CHARTER OF THE UNITED NATIONS (EXCERPTS)

Preamble

We the Peoples of the United Nations,

Determined to save succeeding generations from the scourge of war, which twice in our lifetime has brought untold sorrow to mankind, and to reaffirm faith in **fundamental human rights**, in the dignity and worth of the human person, in the equal rights of men and women and of nations large and small, and to establish conditions under which justice and respect for the obligations arising from treaties and other sources of international law can be maintained, and to promote social progress and better standards of life in larger freedom,

And for these Ends to practice tolerance and live together in peace with one another as good neighbors, and to unite our strength to maintain international peace and security, and to ensure by the acceptance of principles and the institution of methods, that armed force shall not be used, save in the common interest, and to employ international machinery for the promotion of the economic and social advancement of all peoples,

Have Resolved to Combine ours Efforts to Accomplish these Aims

Accordingly, our respective Governments, through representatives assembled in the city of San Francisco, who have exhibited their full powers found to be in good and due form, have agreed to the present Charter of the United Nations and do hereby establish an international organization to be known as the United Nations.

Chapter I—Purposes and Principles

Article 1

The Purposes of the United Nations are:

1. To maintain international peace and security, and to that end: to take effective collective measures for the prevention and removal of threats to the peace, and for the suppression of acts of aggression or other

breaches of the peace, and to bring about by peaceful means, and in conformity with the principles of justice and international law, adjustment or settlement of international disputes or situations which might lead to a breach of the peace;

2. To develop friendly relations among nations based on respect for the principle of equal rights and self-determination of peoples, and to take other appropriate measures to strengthen universal peace;

3. To achieve international cooperation in solving international problems of an economic, social, cultural, or humanitarian character, and **in promoting and encouraging respect for human rights and for fundamental freedoms for all without distinction as to race, sex, language, or religion; and**

4. To be a center for harmonizing the actions of nations in the attainment of these common ends.

Article 2

The Organization and its Members, in pursuit of the Purposes stated in Article 1, shall act in accordance with the following Principles.

1. The Organization is based on the principle of the sovereign equality of all its Members.

2. All Members, in order to ensure to all of them the rights and benefits resulting from membership, shall fulfill in good faith the obligations assumed by them in accordance with the present Charter.

3. All Members shall settle their international disputes by peaceful means in such a manner that international peace and security, and justice, are not endangered.

4. All Members shall refrain in their international relations from the threat or use of force against the territorial integrity or political independence of any state, or in any other manner inconsistent with the Purposes of the United Nations.

5. All Members shall give the United Nations every assistance in any action it takes in accordance with the present Charter, and shall refrain from giving assistance to any state against which the United Nations is taking preventive or enforcement action.

6. The Organization shall ensure that states which are not Members of the United Nations act in accordance with these Principles so far as may be necessary for the maintenance of international peace and security.

7. Nothing contained in the present Charter shall authorize the United Nations to intervene in matters which are essentially within the domestic jurisdiction of any state or shall require the Members to submit such matters to settlement under the present Charter; but this principle shall not prejudice the application of enforcement measures under Chapter VII.

...

Chapter IX—International Economic and Social Co-operation

Article 55

With a view to the creation of conditions of stability and well-being which are necessary for peaceful and friendly relations among nations based on respect for the principle of equal rights and self-determination of peoples, the United Nations shall promote:

a. higher standards of living, full employment, and conditions of economic and social progress and development;

b. solutions of international economic, social, health, and related problems; and international, cultural and educational co-operation; and

c. **universal respect for, and observance of, human rights and fundamental freedoms for all without distinction as to race, sex, language, or religion.**

Article 56

All Members pledge themselves to take joint and separate action in cooperation with the Organization for the achievement of the purposes set forth in Article 55.

...

Chapter X—The Economic and Social Council Functions and Powers

Article 62

1. The Economic and Social Council may make or initiate studies and reports with respect to international economic, social, cultural, educational, health, and related matters and may make recommendations with respect to any such matters to the General Assembly, to the Members of the United Nations, and to the specialized agencies concerned.

2. **It may make recommendations for the purpose of promoting respect for, and observance of, human rights and fundamental freedoms for all.**

3. It may prepare draft conventions for submission to the General Assembly, with respect to matters falling within its competence.

4. It may call, in accordance with the rules prescribed by the United Nations, international conferences on matters falling within its competence.

...

Article 68

The Economic and Social Council shall set up commissions in economic and social fields and for the promotion of human rights, and such other commissions as may be required for the performance of its functions.

...

Article 71

The Economic and Social Council may make suitable arrangements for consultation with non-governmental organizations which are concerned with matters within its competence. Such arrangements may be made with international organizations and, where appropriate, with national organizations after consultation with the Member of the United Nations concerned.

[Emphasis added]

DOCUMENT 6

Full Official Title: Universal Declaration of Human Rights

Short Title/Acronym/Abbreviation: The Universal Declaration/UDHR

Subject: A statement of substantive human rights and human rights principles for the whole world

Official Citation: G.A. res. 217A (III), U.N. Doc A/810 at 71 (1948)

Date of Document: Not applicable

Date of Adoption: December 10, 1948

Date of General Entry into Force (EIF): Not applicable

Number of States Parties to this Treaty as of this printing: Not a treaty

Date of Signature by United States: Not applicable

Date of Ratification/Accession/Adhesion: This is not a treaty. It does not get signed or ratified. It was adopted by a resolution of the U.N. General Assembly.

Date of Entry into Force as to United States (effective date): Not a treaty

Type of Document: A declaration, not a treaty. An aspirational document initially meant to not create legal obligations, but to encourage states of the world to seek to fulfill its principles and rights.

Legal Status/Character of the Instrument/Document as to the United States: Initially adopted as a non-legal document, this document has come to be considered by most scholars as now binding on all states of the world as a matter of customary international law, at least as to its most important (hard core) human rights. Such legal status is also recognized in American Law. (See "Restatement of the Foreign Relations Law, Third," in Appendix I.) Thus, the UDHR does create binding legal norms on the United States, at least as to those hard core rights. (See entry for Hard Core rights.)

Comments: The United States was largely instrumental in the drafting and adoption of the UDHR and many of its provisions were fashioned with the U.S. Constitution and Declaration of Independence in mind. Eleanor Roosevelt was the U.S. member of the U.N. body which helped draft this UDHR.

This instrument is the first and foremost source of human rights and the document upon which all other systems were created. It was the first document to contain a list of specific human rights applicable to the whole world. It provided a list of the specific human rights recognized by the U.N. member states in 1948, which were referred to in the U.N. Charter. Its words call it a "common standard of achievement" for all nations. It is not just of historical interest. It is now considered to set forth legal norms applicable in some situations where a state is not bound by a treaty, for example torture or summary executions. This instrument serves as the basis of most of the U.N. human rights activity in the U.N. Commission of Human Rights and its Sub-Commission and other bodies.

In judging the conduct of the United States, one can use the UDHR, the ICCPR and any other treaties ratified by the United States. As to what the United States does within the territory of the United States, one should *primarily* use the ICCPR. It is fully legally binding and sets forth civil and political human rights in greater scope and detail. One should judge U.S. conduct using all applicable sources of human rights legal norms both from treaty and from customary international law.

Caution: The status and applicability of this instrument as to the United States may have changed since date of publication. The above information may be updated by referring to the following site:

Web address: http://www1.umn.edu/humanrts/instree/b1udhr.htm

UNIVERSAL DECLARATION OF HUMAN RIGHTS (UDHR)

Preamble

Whereas recognition of the inherent dignity and of the equal and inalienable rights of all members of the human family is the foundation of freedom, justice and peace in the world,

Whereas disregard and contempt for human rights have resulted in barbarous acts which have outraged the conscience of mankind, and the advent of a world in which human beings shall enjoy freedom of speech and belief and freedom from fear and want has been proclaimed as the highest aspiration of the common people,

Whereas it is essential, if man is not to be compelled to have recourse, as a last resort, to rebellion against tyranny and oppression, that human rights should be protected by the rule of law,

Whereas it is essential to promote the development of friendly relations between nations,

Whereas the peoples of the United Nations have in the Charter reaffirmed their faith in fundamental human rights, in the dignity and worth of the human person and in the equal rights of men and women and have determined to promote social progress and better standards of life in larger freedoms,

Whereas Member States have pledged themselves to achieve, in co-operation with the United Nations, the promotion of universal respect for and observance of human rights and fundamental freedoms,

Whereas a common understanding of these rights and freedoms is of the greatest importance for the full realization of this pledge,

Now therefore,

The General Assembly Proclaims this Universal Declaration of Human Rights as a common standard of achievement for all peoples and all nations, to the end that every individual and every organ of society, keeping this Declaration constantly in mind, shall strive by teaching and education to promote respect for these rights and freedoms and by progressive measures, national and international, to secure their universal and effective recognition and observance, both among the peoples of Member States themselves and among the peoples of territories under their jurisdiction.

Article 1

All human beings are born free and equal in dignity and rights. They are endowed with reason and conscience and should act towards one another in a spirit of brotherhood.

Article 2

Everyone is entitled to all the rights and freedoms set forth in this Declaration, without distinction of any kind, such as race, colour, sex, language, religion, political or other opinion, national or social origin, property, birth, or other status. Furthermore, no distinction shall be made on the basis of the political, jurisdictional or international status of the country or territory to which a person belongs, whether it be independent, trust, non-self-governing or under any other limitation of sovereignty.

Article 3

Everyone has the right to life, liberty and security of person.

Article 4

No one shall be held in slavery or servitude; slavery and the slave trade shall be prohibited in all their forms.

Article 5

No one shall be subjected to torture or to cruel, inhuman or degrading treatment or punishment.

Article 6

Everyone has the right to recognition everywhere as a person before the law.

Article 7

All are equal before the law and are entitled without any discrimination to equal protection of the law. All are entitled to equal protection against any discrimination in violation of this Declaration and against any incitement to such discrimination.

Article 8

Everyone has the right to an effective remedy by the competent national tribunals for acts violating the fundamental rights granted him by the constitution or by law.

Article 9

No one shall be subjected to arbitrary arrest, detention or exile.

Article 10

Everyone is entitled in full equality to a fair and public hearing by an independent and impartial tribunal, in the determination of his rights and obligations and of any criminal charge against him.

Article 11

1. Everyone charged with a penal offence has the right to be presumed innocent until proved guilty according to law in a public trial at which he has had all the guarantees necessary for his defense.

2. No one shall be held guilty of any penal offence on account of any act or omission which did not constitute a penal offence, under national or international law, at the time when it was committed. Nor shall a heavier penalty be imposed than the one that was applicable at the time the penal offence was committed.

Article 12

No one shall be subjected to arbitrary interference which his privacy, family, home or correspondence, nor to attacks upon his honour and reputation. Everyone has the right to the protection of the law against such interference or attacks.

Article 13

1. Everyone has the right to freedom of movement and residence within the borders of each State.

2. Everyone has the right to leave any country, including his own, and to return to his country.

Article 14

1. Everyone has the right to seek and to enjoy in other countries asylum from persecution.

2. This right may not be invoked in the case of prosecutions genuinely arising from non-political crimes or from acts contrary to the purposes and principles of the United Nations.

Article 15

1. Everyone has the right to a nationality.

2. No one shall be arbitrarily deprived of his nationality nor denied the right to change his nationality.

Article 16

1. Men and women of full age, without any limitation due to race, nationality or religion, have the right to marry and to found a family. They are entitled to equal rights as to marriage, during marriage and at its dissolution.

2. Marriage shall be entered into only with free and full consent of the intending spouses.

3. The family is the natural and fundamental group unit of society and is entitled to protection by society and the State.

Article 17

1. Everyone has the right to own property alone as well as in association with others.

2. No one shall be arbitrarily deprived of his property.

Article 18

Everyone has the right to freedom of thought, conscience and religion; this right includes freedom to change his religion or belief, and freedom, either alone or in community with others and in public or private, to manifest his religion or belief in teaching, practice, worship and observance.

Article 19

Everyone has the right to freedom of opinion and expression; this right includes freedom to hold opinions without interference and to seek, receive and impart information and ideas through any media and regardless of frontiers.

Article 20

1. Everyone has the right to freedom of peaceful assembly and association.

2. No one may be compelled to belong to an association.

Article 21

1. Everyone has the right to take part in the government of his country, directly or through freely chosen representatives.

2. Everyone has the right to equal access to public service in his country.

3. The will of the people shall be the basis of the authority of government; this will shall be expressed in periodic and genuine elections which shall be by universal and equal suffrage and shall be held by secret vote or by equivalent free voting procedures.

Article 22

Everyone, as a member of society, has the right to social security and is entitled to realization, through national effort and international co-operation and in accordance with the organization and resources of each State, of the economic, social and cultural rights indispensable for his dignity and the free development of his personality.

Article 23

1. Everyone has the right to work, to free choice of employment, to just and favorable conditions of work and to protection against unemployment.

2. Everyone without any discrimination, has the right to equal pay for equal work.

3. Everyone who works has the right to just and favorable remuneration ensuring for himself and his family an existence worthy of human dignity, and supplemented if necessary, by other means of social protection.

4. Everyone has the right to form and to join trade unions for the protection of his interests.

Article 24

Everyone has the right to rest and leisure, including reasonable limitation of working hours and periodic holidays with pay.

Article 25

1. Everyone has the right to a standard of living adequate for the health and well-being of himself and of his family, including food, clothing, housing and medical care and necessary social services, and the right to security in the event of unemployment, sickness, disability, widowhood, old age or other lack of livelihood in circumstances beyond his control.

2. Motherhood and childhood are entitled to special care and assistance. All children, whether born in or out of wedlock, shall enjoy the same social protection.

Article 26

1. Everyone has the right to education. Education shall be free, at least in the elementary and fundamental stages. Elementary education shall be compulsory. Technical and professional education shall be made generally available and higher education shall be equally accessible to all on the basis of merit.

2. Education shall be directed to the full development of the human personality and to the strengthening of respect for human rights and fundamental freedoms. It shall promote understanding, tolerance and friendship among all nations, racial or religious groups, and shall further the activities of the United Nations for the maintenance of peace.

3. Parents have a prior right to choose the kind of education that shall be given to their children.

Article 27

1. Everyone has the right freely to participate in the cultural life of the community, to enjoy the arts and to share in scientific advancement and its benefits.

2. Everyone has the right to the protection of the moral and material interests resulting from any scientific, literary or artistic production of which he is the author.

Article 28

Everyone is entitled to a social and international order in which the rights and freedoms set forth in this Declaration can be fully realized.

Article 29

1. Everyone has duties to the community in which alone the free and full development of his personality is possible.

2. In the exercise of his rights and freedoms, everyone shall be subject only to such limitations as are determined by law solely for the purpose of securing due recognition and respect for the rights and freedoms of others and of meeting the just requirements of morality, public order and the general welfare in a democratic society.

3. These rights and freedoms may in no case be exercised contrary to the purposes and principles of the United Nations.

Article 30

Nothing in this Declaration may be interpreted as implying for any State, group or person any right to engage in any activity or to perform any act aimed at the destruction of any of the rights and freedoms set forth herein.

DOCUMENT 7

Full Official Title: Eleanor Roosevelt's Speech in Paris, France on "The Struggle for Human Rights"
Short Title/Acronym/Abbreviation: "The Struggle for Human Rights"
Subject: Human Rights, United Nations
Official Citation: Eleanor Roosevelt Speech at the Sorbonne in Paris, France, September 24, 1948
Date of Document: September 24, 1948
Date of Adoption: Not applicable
Date of General Entry into Force (EIF): Not applicable
Number of States Parties as of this printing: Not applicable
Date of Signature by the United States: Not applicable
Date of Ratification/Accession/Adhesion: Not applicable
Date of Entry into Force as to United States (effective date): Not applicable
Type of Document: Speech
Legal Status/Character of the Instrument/Document as to the United States: Non-binding political address

Comment: Eleanor Roosevelt gave this speech as the U.N. General Assembly met to consider the adoption of the Universal Declaration of Human Rights, a document which she had a significant leadership role in drafting and getting passed through the U.N. Commission on Human Rights. In her speech which was given in the early days of the General Assembly meeting, she chose to focus on human rights because she believed "the issue of human liberty is decisive for the settlement of outstanding political differences and for the future of the United Nations." She worked throughout the General Assembly meeting to secure the passage of the UDHR.

THE STRUGGLE FOR HUMAN RIGHTS

28 September, 1948

I have come this evening to talk with you on one of the greatest issues of our time—that is the preservation of human freedom. I have chosen to discuss it here in France, at the Sorbonne, because here in this soil the roots of human freedom have long ago struck deep and here they have been richly nourished. It was here the Declaration of the Rights of Man was proclaimed, and the great slogans of the French Revolution—liberty, equality, fraternity—fired the imagination of men. I have chosen to discuss this issue in Europe because this has been the scene of the greatest historic battles between freedom and tyranny. I have chosen to discuss it in the early days of the General Assembly because the issue of human liberty is decisive for the settlement of outstanding political differences and for the future of the United Nations.

The decisive importance of this issue was fully recognized by the founders of the United Nations at San Francisco. Concern for the preservation and promotion of human rights and fundamental freedoms stands at the heart of the United Nations. Its Charter is distinguished by its preoccupation with the rights and welfare of individual men and women. The United Nations has made it clear that it intends to uphold human rights and to protect the dignity of the human personality. In the preamble to the Charter the keynote is set when it declares: "We the people of the United Nations determined ... to reaffirm faith in fundamental human rights, in the dignity and worth of the human person, in the equal rights of men and women and of nations large and small, and ... to promote social progress and better standards of life in larger freedom." This reflects the basic premise of the Charter that the peace and security of mankind are dependent on mutual respect for the rights and freedoms of all.

One of the purposes of the United Nations is declared in Article 1 to be: "to achieve international cooperation in solving international problems of an economic, social, cultural, or humanitarian character, and in promoting and encouraging respect for human rights and for fundamental freedoms for all without distinction as to race, sex, language, or religion."

This thought is repeated at several points and notably in Articles 55 and 56 the Members pledge themselves to take joint and separate action in cooperation with the United Nations for the promotion of "universal respect for, and observance of, human rights and fundamental freedoms for all without distinction as to race, sex, language, or religion."

The Human Rights Commission was given as its first and most important task the preparation of an International Bill of Rights. The General Assembly, which opened its third session here in Paris a few days ago, will have before it the first fruit of the Commission's labors in this task, that is the International Declaration of Human Rights.

The Declaration was finally completed after much work during the last session of the Human Rights Commission in New York in the spring of 1948. The Economic and Social Council has sent it without recommendation to the General Assembly, together with other documents transmitted by the Human Rights Commission.

It was decided in our Commission that a Bill of Rights should contain two parts:

1. A Declaration which could be approved through action of the Member States of the United Nations in the General Assembly. This declaration would have great moral force, and would say to the peoples of the world "this is what we hope human rights may mean to all people in the years to come." We have put down here the rights that we consider basic for individual human beings the world over to have. Without them, we feel that the full development of individual personality is impossible.

2. The second part of the bill, which the Human Rights Commission has not yet completed because of the lack of time, is a covenant which would be in the form of a treaty to be presented to the nations of the world. Each nation, as it is prepared to do so, would ratify this covenant and the covenant would then become binding on the nations which adhere to it. Each nation ratifying would then be obligated to change its laws wherever they did not conform to the points contained in the covenant.

This covenant, of course, would have to be a simpler document. It could not state aspirations, which we feel to be permissible in the Declaration. It could only state rights which could be assured by law and it must contain methods of implementation, and no state ratifying the covenant could be allowed to disregard it. The methods of implementation have not yet been agreed upon, nor have they been given adequate consideration by the Commission at any of its meetings. There certainly should be discussion on the entire question of this world Bill of Human Rights and there may be acceptance by this Assembly of the Declaration if they come to agreement on it. The acceptance of the Declaration, I think, should encourage every nation in the coming months to discuss its meaning with its people so that they will be better prepared to accept the covenant with a deeper understanding of the problems involved when that is presented, we hope, a year from now and, we hope, accepted.

The Declaration has come from the Human Rights Commission with unanimous acceptance except for four abstentions—the U.S.S.R., Yugoslavia, Ukraine, and Byelorussia. The reason for this is a fundamental difference in the conception of human rights as they exist in these states and in certain other Member States in the United Nations.

In the discussion before the Assembly, I think it should be made crystal clear what these differences are and tonight I want to spend a little time making them clear to you. It seems to me there is a valid reason for taking the time today to think carefully and clearly on the subject of human rights, because in the acceptance and observance of these rights lies the root, I believe, of our chance of peace in the future, and for the strengthening of the United Nations organization to the point where it can maintain peace in the future.

We must not be confused about what freedom is. Basic human rights are simple and easily understood: freedom of speech and a free press; freedom of religion and worship; freedom of assembly and the right of petition; the right of men to be secure in their homes and free from unreasonable search and seizure and from arbitrary arrest and punishment.

We must not be deluded by the efforts of the forces of reaction to prostitute the great words of our free tradition and thereby to confuse the struggle. Democracy, freedom, human rights have come to have a definite meaning to the people of the world which we must not allow any nation to so change that they are made synonymous with suppression and dictatorship.

There are basic differences that show up even in the use of words between a democratic and a totalitarian country. For instance "democracy" means one thing to the U.S.S.R. and another the the U.S.A. and, I know, in France. I have served since the first meeting of the nuclear commission on the Human Rights Commission, and I think this point stands out clearly.

The U.S.S.R. Representatives assert that they already have achieved many things which we, in what they call the "bourgeois democracies" cannot achieve because their government controls the accomplishment of these things. Our government seems powerless to them because, in the last analysis, it is controlled by the people. They would not put it that way—they would say that the people in the U.S.S.R. control their government by allowing their government to have certain absolute rights. We, on the other hand, feel that certain rights can never be granted to the government, but must be kept in the hands of the people.

For instance, the U.S.S.R. will assert that their press is free because the state makes it free by providing the machinery, the paper, and even the money for salaries for the people who work on the paper. They state that there is no control over what is printed in the various papers that they subsidize in this manner, such, for instance, as a trade-union paper. But what would happen if a paper were to print ideas which were critical of the basic policies and beliefs of the Communist government? I am sure some good reason would be found for abolishing the paper.

It is true that they have been many cases where newspapers in the U.S.S.R. have criticized officials and their actions and have been responsible for the removal of those officials, but in doing so they did not criticize anything which was fundamental to Communist beliefs. They simply criticized methods of doing things, so one must differentiate between things which are permissible, such as criticism of any individual or of the manner of doing things, and the criticism of a belief which would be considered vital to the acceptance of Communism.

What are the differences, for instance, between trade-unions in the totalitarian states and in the democracies? In the totalitarian state a trade-union is an instrument used by the government to enforce duties, not to assert rights. Propaganda material which the government desires the workers to have is furnished by the trade-unions to be circulated to their members.

Our trade-unions, on the other hand, are solely the instrument of the workers themselves. They represent the workers in their relations with the government and with management and they are free to develop their own opinions without government help or interference. The concepts of our trade-unions and those in totalitarian countries are drastically different. There is little mutual understanding.

I think the best example one can give of this basic difference of the use of terms is "the right to work." The Soviet Union insists that this is a basic right which it alone can guarantee because it alone provides full employment by the government. But the right to work in the Soviet Union means the assignment of workers to do whatever task is given to them by the government without an opportunity for the people to participate in the decision that the government should do this. A society in which everyone works is not necessarily a free society and may indeed be a slave society; on the other hand, a society in which there is widespread economic insecurity can turn freedom into a barren and vapid right for millions of people.

We in the United States have come to realize it means freedom to choose one's job, to work or not to work as one desires. We, in the United States, have come to realize, however, that people have a right to demand that their government will not allow them to starve because as individuals they cannot find work of the kind they are accustomed to doing and this is a decision brought about by public opinion which came as a result of the great depression in which many people were out of work, but we would not consider in the United States that we had gained any freedom if we were compelled to follow a dictatorial assignment to work where and when we were told. The right of choice would seem to us an important, fundamental freedom.

I have great sympathy with the Russian people. They love their country and have always defended it valiantly against invaders. They have been through a period of revolution, as a result of which they were for a time cut off from outside contact. They have not lost their resulting suspicion of other countries and the great difficulty is today that their government encourages this suspicion and seems to believe that force alone will bring them respect.

We, in the democracies, believe in a kind of international respect and action which is reciprocal. We do not think others should treat us differently from the way they wish to be treated. It is interference in other countries that especially stirs up antagonism against the Soviet Government. If it wishes to feel secure in developing its economic and political theories within its territory, then it should grant to others that same security. We believe in the freedom of people to make their own mistakes. We do not interfere with them and they should not interfere with others.

The basic problem confronting the world today, as I said in the beginning, is the preservation of human freedom for the individual and consequently for the society of which he is a part. We are fighting this battle again today as it was fought at the time of the French Revolution and as the time of the American Revolution. The issue of human liberty is as decisive now as it was then. I want to give you my conception of what is meant in my country by freedom of the individual.

Long ago in London during a discussion with Mr. Vyshinsky, he told me there was no such things as freedom for the individual in the world. All freedom of the individual was conditioned by the rights of other individuals. That of course, I granted. I said: "We approach the question from a different point of view/ we here in the United Nations are trying to develop ideals which will be broader in outlook, which will consider first the rights of man, which will consider what makes man more free; not governments, but man."

The totalitarian state typically places the will of the people second to decrees promulgated by a few men at the top.

Naturally there must always be consideration of the rights of others; but in a democracy this is not a restriction. Indeed, in our democracies we make our freedoms secure because each of us is expected to respect the rights of others and we are free to make our own laws. Freedom for our peoples is not only a right, but also a tool. Freedom of speech, freedom of the press, freedom of information, freedom of assembly—these are not just abstract ideals to us; they are tools with which we create a way of life, a way of life in which we can enjoy freedom.

Sometimes the processes of democracy are slow, and I have knows some of our leaders to say that a benevolent dictatorship would accomplish the ends desired in a much shorter time than it takes to go through the democratic processes of discussion and the slow formation of public opinion. But there is no way of insuring that a dictatorship will remain benevolent or that power once in the hands of a few will be returned to the people without struggle or revolution. This we have learned by experience and we accept the slow processes of democracy because we know that shortcuts compromise principles on which no compromise is possible.

The final expression of the opinion of the people with us is through free and honest elections, with valid choices on basic issues and candidates. The secret ballot is an essential to free elections but you must have a choice before you. I have heard my husband say many times that a people need never lose their freedom if they kept their right to a secret ballot and if they used that secret ballot to the full. Basic decisions of our society are made through the expressed will of the people. That is why when we see these liberties threatened, instead of falling apart, our nation becomes unified and our democracies come together as a unified group in spite of our varied backgrounds and many racial strains.

In the United States we have a capitalistic economy. That is because public opinion favors that type of economy under the conditions in which we live. But we have imposed certain restraints; for instance, we have antitrust laws. These are the legal evidence of the determination of the American people to maintain an economy of free competition and not to allow monopolies to take away the people's freedom.

Our trade-unions grow stronger because the people come to believe that this is the proper way to guarantee the rights of the workers and that the right to organize and to bargain collectively keeps the balance between the actual producer an the investor of money and the manage in industry who watches over the man who works with this hands and who produces the materials which are out tangible wealth.

In the United States we are old enough not to claim perfection. We recognize that we have some problems of discrimination but we finds steady progress being made in the solution of these problems. Through normal democratic processes we are coming to understand our needs and how we can attain full equality for all our people. Free discussion on the subject is permitted. Our Supreme Court has recently rendered decisions to clarify a number of our laws to guarantee the rights of all.

The U.S.S.R. claims it has reached a point where all races within her borders are officially considered equal and have equal rights and they insist that they have no discrimination where minorities are concerned.

This is a laudable objective but there are other aspects of the development of freedom for the individual which are essential before the mere absence of discrimination is worth much, and these are lacking in the Soviet Union. Unless they are being denied freedoms which they want and which they see other people have, people do not usually complain of discrimination. It is these other freedoms—the basic freedoms of speech, of the press, of religion and conscience, of assembly, of fair trial and freedom from arbitrary arrest and punishment, which a totalitarian government cannot safely give its people and which give meaning to freedom from discrimination.

It is my belief, and I am sure it is also yours, that the struggle for democracy and freedom is a critical struggle, for their preservation is essential to the great objective of the United Nations to maintain international peace and security. Among free men the end cannot justify the means. We know the patterns of totalitarianism—the single political party, the control of schools, press, radio, the arts, the sciences, and the church to support autocratic authority; these are the age-old patterns against which men have struggled for three thousand years. These are the signs of reaction, retreat, and retrogression. The United Nations must hold fast to the heritage of freedom won by the struggle of its people; it must help us to pass it on to generations to come.

The development of the ideal of freedom and its translation into the everyday life of the people in great areas of the earth is the product of the efforts of many peoples. It is the fruit of a long tradition of vigorous thinking and courageous action. No one race and on one people can claim to have done all the work to achieve greater dignity for human beings and great freedom to develop human personality. In each generation and in each country there must be a continuation of the struggle and new steps forward must be taken since this is preeminently a field in which to stand still its to retreat.

The field of human rights is not one in which compromise on fundamental principles are possible. The work of the Commission on Human Rights is illustrative. The Declaration of Human Rights provides: "Everyone has the right to leave any country, including his own." The Soviet Representative said he would agree to this right if a single phrase was added to it—"in accordance with the procedure laid down in the laws of that country." It is obvious that to accept this would be not only to compromise but to nullify the right stated. This case forcefully illustrates the importance of the proposition that we must ever be alert not to compromise fundamental human rights merely for the sake of reaching unanimity and thus lose them.

As I see it, it is not going to be easy to attain unanimity with respect to our different concepts of government and human rights. The struggle is bound to be difficult and one in which we must be firm but patient. If we adhere faithfully to our principles I think it is possible for us to maintain freedom and to do so peacefully and without recourse to force.

The future must see the broadening of human rights throughout the world. People who have glimpsed freedom will never be content until they have secured it for themselves. In a truest sense, human rights are a fundamental object of law and government in a just society. Human rights exist to the degree that they are respected by people in relations with each other and by governments in relations with their citizens.

The world at large is aware of the tragic consequences for human beings ruled by totalitarian systems. If we examine Hitler's rise to power, we see how the chains are forged which keep the individual a slave and we cans e many similarities in the way things are accomplished in other countries. Politically men must be free to discuss and to arrive at as many facts as possible and there must beat least a two-party system in a country because when there is only one political party, too many things can be subordinated to the interests of that one party and it becomes a tyrant and not an instrument of democratic government.

The propaganda we have witnessed in the recent past, like that we perceive in these days, seeks to impugn, to undermine, and to destroy the liberty and independence of peoples. Such propaganda poses to all peoples the issue whether to doubt their heritage of rights and therefore to compromise the principles by which they live, or try to accept the challenge, redouble their vigilance, and stand steadfast in the struggle to maintain and enlarge human freedoms.

People who continue to be denied the respect to which they are entitled as human beings will not acquiesce forever in such denial.

The Charter of the United Nations is a guiding beacon along the way to the achievement of human rights and fundamental freedoms throughout the world. The immediate test is not only to the extent to which human rights and freedoms have already been achieved, but the direction in which the world is moving. Is there a faithful compliance with the objectives of the Charter if some countries continue to curtail human rights and freedoms instead of to promote the universal respect for an observance of human rights and freedoms for all as called for by the Charter?

The place to discuss the issue of human rights is in the forum of the United Nations. The United Nations has been set up as the common meeting ground for nations, where we can consider together our mutual problems and take advantage of our differences in experience. It is inherent in our firm attachment to democracy and freedom that we stand always ready to use the fundamental democratic procedures of honest discussion and negotiation. It is now as always our hope that despite the wide differences in approach we face in the world today, we can with mutual good faith in the principles of the united Nations Charter, arrive at a common basis of understanding.

We are here to join the meetings of this great international Assembly which meets in your beautiful capital of Paris. Freedom for the individual is an inseparable part of the cherished traditions of France. As one of the Delegates from the United States I pray Almighty God that we may win another victory here for the rights and freedoms of all men.

U.N. RELATED DOCUMENTS

DOCUMENT 8

Full Official Title: International Covenant on Civil and Political Rights

Short Title/Acronym/Abbreviation: The Civil and Political Covenant/ICCPR

Object: Establish international legal obligations regarding civil and political human rights in a multilateral treaty

Official Citation: G.A. res. 2200A (XXI), 21 U.N. GAOR Supp. (No. 16) at 52, U.N. Doc. A/6316 (1966), 999 U.N.T.S. 171

Date of Document: Not applicable

Date of Adoption: December 16, 1966

Date of General Entry into Force (EIF): March 23, 1976

Number of States Parties to this Treaty as of this printing: 166

Date of Signature by United States: October 5, 1977

Date of Ratification/Accession/Adhesion: April 2, 1992

Date of Entry into Force as to United States (effective date): September 8, 1992

Type of Document: This is a treaty, a legal instrument.

Legal Status/Character of the Instrument/Document as to the United States: Legally binding upon the U.S. because the United States has ratified it. This ratification is, however, subject to certain reservations, declarations and understandings, which are set forth in Document 6. Moreover, the ICCPR was declared to be "non self-executing" by the U.S. Senate in its ratification. This means that the rights set forth in the ICCPR cannot be asserted in U.S. courts as a direct basis for decision. Some scholars say it can.

Supervising Body: Human Rights Committee

Comment: This is perhaps the most important international human rights treaty the United States has ratified because it deals with civil and political human rights. When ratified, it gave the U.N. Human Rights Committee the authority to monitor U.S. compliance with this treaty. It also submitted a declaration by which it gave the HRC the power to hear written complaints called "communications" filed against it by other states parties to the ICCPR which had also declared such HRC power. No state has ever filed a communication against another state in this system. Significantly, the United States has refused to accept the following Optional Protocol (see Document 10), which would allow victims of U.S. violations to file individual complaints against the United States, after completing all U.S. legal recourse.

This instrument constitutes one of the principal documents of what is known internationally as the "International Bill of Rights." (See entry on International Bill of Rights.)

Caution: The status and applicability of this instrument as to the United States may have changed since the date of this publication. The above information may be updated by referring to the following site:

Web address: http://www1.umn.edu/humanrts/instree/b3ccpr.htm

INTERNATIONAL COVENANT ON CIVIL AND POLITICAL RIGHTS (ICCPR)

Preamble

The States Parties to the present Covenant,

Considering that, in accordance with the principles proclaimed in the Charter of the United Nations, recognition of the inherent dignity and of the equal and inalienable rights of all members of the human family is the foundation of freedom, justice and peace in the world,

Recognizing that these rights derive from the inherent dignity of the human person,

Recognizing that, in accordance with the Universal Declaration of Human Rights, the ideal of free human beings enjoying civil and political freedom and freedom from fear and want can only be achieved if conditions are created whereby everyone may enjoy his civil and political rights, as well as his economic, social and cultural rights,

Considering the obligation of States under the Charter of the United Nations to promote universal respect for, and observance of, human rights and freedoms,

Realizing that the individual, having duties to other individuals and to the community to which he belongs, is under a responsibility to strive for the promotion and observance of the rights recognized in the present Covenant,

Agree upon the following articles:

PART I

Article 1

1. All peoples have the right of self-determination. By virtue of that right they freely determine their political status and freely pursue their economic, social and cultural development.

2. All peoples may, for their own ends, freely dispose of their natural wealth and resources without prejudice to any obligations arising out of international economic co-operation, based upon the principle of mutual benefit, and international law. In no case may a people be deprived of its own means of subsistence.

3. The States Parties to the present Covenant, including those having responsibility for the administration of Non-Self-Governing and Trust Territories, shall promote the realization of the right of self-determination, and shall respect that right, in conformity with the provisions of the Charter of the United Nations.

PART II

Article 2

1. Each State Party to the present Covenant undertakes to respect and to ensure to all individuals within its territory and subject to its jurisdiction the rights recognized in the present Covenant, without distinction of any kind, such as race, colour, sex, language, religion, political or other opinion, national or social origin, property, birth or other status.

2. Where not already provided for by existing legislative or other measures, each State Party to the present Covenant undertakes to take the necessary steps, in accordance with its constitutional processes and with the provisions of the present Covenant, to adopt such legislative or other measures as may be necessary to give effect to the rights recognized in the present Covenant.

3. Each State Party to the present Covenant undertakes:

(a) To ensure that any person whose rights or freedoms as herein recognized are violated shall have an effective remedy, notwithstanding that the violation has been committed by persons acting in an official capacity;

(b) To ensure that any person claiming such a remedy shall have his right thereto determined by competent judicial, administrative or legislative authorities, or by any other competent authority provided for by the legal system of the State, and to develop the possibilities of judicial remedy;

(c) To ensure that the competent authorities shall enforce such remedies when granted.

Article 3

The States Parties to the present Covenant undertake to ensure the equal right of men and women to the enjoyment of all civil and political rights set forth in the present Covenant.

Article 4

1. In time of public emergency which threatens the life of the nation and the existence of which is officially proclaimed, the States Parties to the present Covenant may take measures derogating from their obligations under the present Covenant to the extent strictly required by the exigencies of the situation, provided that such measures are not inconsistent with their other obligations under international law and do not involve discrimination solely on the ground of race, colour, sex, language, religion or social origin.

2. No derogation from Articles 6, 7, 8 (paragraphs 1 and 2), 11, 15, 16 and 18 may be made under this provision.

3. Any State Party to the present Covenant availing itself of the right of derogation shall immediately inform the other States Parties to the present Covenant, through the intermediary of the Secretary General of the United Nations, of the provisions from which it has derogated and of the reasons by which it was actuated. A further communication shall be made, through the same intermediary, on the date on which it terminates such derogation.

Article 5

1. Nothing in the present Covenant may be interpreted as implying for any State, group or person any right to engage in any activity or perform any act aimed at the destruction of any of the rights and freedoms recognized herein or at their limitation to a greater extent than is provided for in the present Covenant.

2. There shall be no restriction upon or derogation from any of the fundamental human rights recognized or existing in any State Party to the present Covenant pursuant to law, conventions, regulations or custom on the pretext that the present Covenant does not recognize such rights or that it recognizes them to a lesser extent.

PART III
Article 6

1. Every human being has the inherent right to life. This right shall be protected by law. No one shall be arbitrarily deprived of his life.

2. In countries which have not abolished the death penalty, sentence of death may be imposed only for the most serious crimes in accordance with the law in force at the time of the commission of the crime and not contrary to the provisions of the present Covenant and to the Convention on the Prevention and Punishment of the Crime of Genocide. This penalty can only be carried out pursuant to a final judgment rendered by a competent court.

3. When deprivation of life constitutes the crime of genocide, it is understood that nothing in this article shall authorize any State Party to the present Covenant to derogate in any way from any obligation assumed under the provisions of the Convention on the Prevention and Punishment of the Crime of Genocide.

4. Anyone sentenced to death shall have the right to seek pardon or commutation of the sentence. Amnesty, pardon or commutation of the sentence of death may be granted in all cases.

5. Sentence of death shall not be imposed for crimes committed by persons below eighteen years of age and shall not be carried out on pregnant women.

6. Nothing in this article shall be invoked to delay or to prevent the abolition of capital punishment by any State Party to the present Covenant.

Article 7

No one shall be subjected to torture or to cruel, inhuman or degrading treatment or punishment. In particular, no one shall be subjected without his free consent to medical or scientific experimentation.

Article 8

1. No one shall be held in slavery; slavery and the slave-trade in all their forms shall be prohibited.

2. No one shall be held in servitude.

3. (a) No one shall be required to perform forced or compulsory labour;

(b) Paragraph 3 (a) shall not be held to preclude, in countries where imprisonment with hard labour may be imposed as a punishment for a crime, the performance of hard labour in pursuance of a sentence to such punishment by a competent court;

(c) For the purpose of this paragraph the term "forced or compulsory labour" shall not include:

(i) Any work or service, not referred to in subparagraph (b), normally required of a person who is under detention in consequence of a lawful order of a court, or of a person during conditional release from such detention;

(ii) Any service of a military character and, in countries where conscientious objection is recognized, any national service required by law of conscientious objectors;

(iii) Any service exacted in cases of emergency or calamity threatening the life or well-being of the community;

(iv) Any work or service which forms part of normal civil obligations.

Article 9

1. Everyone has the right to liberty and security of person. No one shall be subjected to arbitrary arrest or detention. No one shall be deprived of his liberty except on such grounds and in accordance with such procedure as are established by law.

2. Anyone who is arrested shall be informed, at the time of arrest, of the reasons for his arrest and shall be promptly informed of any charges against him.

3. Anyone arrested or detained on a criminal charge shall be brought promptly before a judge or other officer authorized by law to exercise judicial power and shall be entitled to trial within a reasonable time or to release. It shall not be the general rule that persons awaiting trial shall be detained in custody, but release may be subject to guarantees to appear for trial, at any other stage of the judicial proceedings, and, should occasion arise, for execution of the judgement.

4. Anyone who is deprived of his liberty by arrest or detention shall be entitled to take proceedings before a court, in order that that court may decide without delay on the lawfulness of his detention and order his release if the detention is not lawful.

5. Anyone who has been the victim of unlawful arrest or detention shall have an enforceable right to compensation.

Article 10

1. All persons deprived of their liberty shall be treated with humanity and with respect for the inherent dignity of the human person.

2. (a) Accused persons shall, save in exceptional circumstances, be segregated from convicted persons and shall be subject to separate treatment appropriate to their status as unconvicted persons;

(b) Accused juvenile persons shall be separated from adults and brought as speedily as possible for adjudication.

3. The penitentiary system shall comprise treatment of prisoners the essential aim of which shall be their reformation and social rehabilitation. Juvenile offenders shall be segregated from adults and be accorded treatment appropriate to their age and legal status.

Article 11

No one shall be imprisoned merely on the ground of inability to fulfill a contractual obligation.

Article 12

1. Everyone lawfully within the territory of a State shall, within that territory, have the right to liberty of movement and freedom to choose his residence.

2. Everyone shall be free to leave any country, including his own.

3. The above-mentioned rights shall not be subject to any restrictions except those which are provided by law, are necessary to protect national security, public order (ordre public), public health or morals or the rights and freedoms of others, and are consistent with the other rights recognized in the present Covenant.

4. No one shall be arbitrarily deprived of the right to enter his own country.

Article 13

An alien lawfully in the territory of a State Party to the present Covenant may be expelled therefrom only in pursuance of a decision reached in accordance with law and shall, except where compelling reasons of national security otherwise require, be allowed to submit the reasons against his expulsion and to have his case reviewed by, and be represented for the purpose before, the competent authority or a person or persons especially designated by the competent authority.

Article 14

1. All persons shall be equal before the courts and tribunals. In the determination of any criminal charge against him, or of his rights and obligations in a suit at law, everyone shall be entitled to a fair and public hearing by a competent, independent and impartial tribunal established by law. The press and the public may be excluded from all or part of a trial for reasons of morals, public order (ordre public) or national security in a democratic society, or when the interest of the private lives of the parties so requires, or to the extent strictly necessary in the opinion of the court in special circumstances where publicity would prejudice the interests of justice; but any judgement rendered in a criminal case or in a suit at law shall be made public except where the interest of juvenile persons otherwise requires or the proceedings concern matrimonial disputes or the guardianship of children.

2. Everyone charged with a criminal offence shall have the right to be presumed innocent until proved guilty according to law.

3. In the determination of any criminal charge against him, everyone shall be entitled to the following minimum guarantees, in full equality:

(a) To be informed promptly and in detail in a language which he understands of the nature and cause of the charge against him;

(b) To have adequate time and facilities for the preparation of his defence and to communicate with counsel of his own choosing;

(c) To be tried without undue delay;

(d) To be tried in his presence, and to defend himself in person or through legal assistance of his own choosing; to be informed, if he does not have legal assistance, of this right; and to have legal assistance assigned to him, in any case where the interests of justice so require, and without payment by him in any such case if he does not have sufficient means to pay for it;

(e) To examine, or have examined, the witnesses against him and to obtain the attendance and examination of witnesses on his behalf under the same conditions as witnesses against him;

(f) To have the free assistance of an interpreter if he cannot understand or speak the language used in court;

(g) Not to be compelled to testify against himself or to confess guilt.

4. In the case of juvenile persons, the procedure shall be such as will take account of their age and the desirability of promoting their rehabilitation.

5. Everyone convicted of a crime shall have the right to his conviction and sentence being reviewed by a higher tribunal according to law.

6. When a person has by a final decision been convicted of a criminal offence and when subsequently his conviction has been reversed or he has been pardoned on the ground that a new or newly discovered fact shows conclusively that there has been a miscarriage of justice, the person who has suffered punishment as a result of such conviction shall be compensated according to law, unless it is proved that the non-disclosure of the unknown fact in time is wholly or partly attributable to him.

7. No one shall be liable to be tried or punished again for an offence for which he has already been finally convicted or acquitted in accordance with the law and penal procedure of each country.

Article 15

1. No one shall be held guilty of any criminal offence on account of any act or omission which did not constitute a criminal offence, under national or international law, at the time when it was committed. Nor shall a heavier penalty be imposed than the one that was applicable at the time when the criminal offence was committed. If, subsequent to the commission of the offence, provision is made by law for the imposition of the lighter penalty, the offender shall benefit thereby.

2. Nothing in this article shall prejudice the trial and punishment of any person for any act or omission which, at the time when it was committed, was criminal according to the general principles of law recognized by the community of nations.

Article 16

Everyone shall have the right to recognition everywhere as a person before the law.

Article 17

1. No one shall be subjected to arbitrary or unlawful interference with his privacy, family, home or correspondence, nor to unlawful attacks on his honour and reputation.

2. Everyone has the right to the protection of the law against such interference or attacks.

Article 18

1. Everyone shall have the right to freedom of thought, conscience and religion. This right shall include freedom to have or to adopt a religion or belief of his choice, and freedom, either individually or in community with others and in public or private, to manifest his religion or belief in worship, observance, practice and teaching.

2. No one shall be subject to coercion which would impair his freedom to have or to adopt a religion or belief of his choice.

3. Freedom to manifest one's religion or beliefs may be subject only to such limitations as are prescribed by law and are necessary to protect public safety, order, health, or morals or the fundamental rights and freedoms of others.

4. The States Parties to the present Covenant undertake to have respect for the liberty of parents and, when applicable, legal guardians to ensure the religious and moral education of their children in conformity with their own convictions.

Article 19

1. Everyone shall have the right to hold opinions without interference.

2. Everyone shall have the right to freedom of expression; this right shall include freedom to seek, receive and impart information and ideas of all kinds, regardless of frontiers, either orally, in writing or in print, in the form of art, or through any other media of his choice.

3. The exercise of the rights provided for in paragraph 2 of this article carries with it special duties and responsibilities. It may therefore be subject to certain restrictions, but these shall only be such as are provided by law and are necessary:

(a) For respect of the rights or reputations of others;

(b) For the protection of national security or of public order (ordre public), or of public health or morals.

Article 20

1. Any propaganda for war shall be prohibited by law.

2. Any advocacy of national, racial or religious hatred that constitutes incitement to discrimination, hostility or violence shall be prohibited by law.

Article 21

The right of peaceful assembly shall be recognized. No restrictions may be placed on the exercise of this right other than those imposed in conformity with the law and which are necessary in a democratic society in the interests of national security or public safety, public order (ordre public), the protection of public health or morals or the protection of the rights and freedoms of others.

Article 22

1. Everyone shall have the right to freedom of association with others, including the right to form and join trade unions for the protection of his interests.

2. No restrictions may be placed on the exercise of this right other than those which are prescribed by law and which are necessary in a democratic society in the interests of national security or public safety, public order (ordre public), the protection of public health or morals or the protection of the rights and freedoms of others. This article shall not prevent the imposition of lawful restrictions on members of the armed forces and of the police in their exercise of this right.

3. Nothing in this article shall authorize States Parties to the International Labour Organization Convention of 1948 concerning Freedom of Association and Protection of the Right to Organize to take legislative measures which would prejudice, or to apply the law in such a manner as to prejudice, the guarantees provided for in that Convention.

Article 23

1. The family is the natural and fundamental group unit of society and is entitled to protection by society and the State.

2. The right of men and women of marriageable age to marry and to found a family shall be recognized.

3. No marriage shall be entered into without the free and full consent of the intending spouses.

4. States Parties to the present Covenant shall take appropriate steps to ensure equality of rights and responsibilities of spouses as to marriage, during marriage and at its dissolution. In the case of dissolution, provision shall be made for the necessary protection of any children.

Article 24

1. Every child shall have, without any discrimination as to race, colour, sex, language, religion, national or social origin, property or birth, the right to such measures of protection as are required by his status as a minor, on the part of his family, society and the State.

2. Every child shall be registered immediately after birth and shall have a name.

3. Every child has the right to acquire a nationality.

Article 25

Every citizen shall have the right and the opportunity, without any of the distinctions mentioned in Article 2 and without unreasonable restrictions:

(a) To take part in the conduct of public affairs, directly or through freely chosen representatives;

(b) To vote and to be elected at genuine periodic elections which shall bee by universal and equal suffrage and shall be held by secret ballot; guaranteeing the free expression of the will of the electors;

(c) To have access, on general terms of equality, to public service in his country.

Article 26

All persons are equal before the law and are entitled without any discrimination to the equal protection of the law. In this respect, the law shall prohibit any discrimination and guarantee to all persons equal and effective protection against discrimination on any ground such as race, colour, sex, language, religion, political or other opinion, national or social origin, property, birth or other status.

Article 27

In those States in which ethnic, religious or linguistic minorities exist, persons belonging to such minorities shall not be denied the right, in community with the other members of their group, to enjoy their own culture, to profess and practise their own religion, or to use their own language.

PART IV

Article 28

1. There shall be established a Human Rights Committee (hereafter referred to in the present Covenant as the Committee). It shall consist of eighteen members and shall carry out the functions hereinafter provided.

2. The Committee shall be composed of nationals of the States Parties to the present Covenant who shall be persons of high moral character and recognized competence in the field of human rights, consideration being given to the usefulness of the participation of some persons having legal experience.

3. The members of the Committee shall be elected and shall serve in their personal capacity.

Article 29

1. The members of the Committee shall be elected by secret ballot from a list of persons possessing the qualifications prescribed in Article 28 and nominated for the purpose by the States Parties to the present Covenant.

2. Each State Party to the present Covenant may nominate not more than two persons. These persons shall be nationals of the nominating State.

3. A person shall be eligible for renomination.

Article 30

1. The initial election shall be held not later than six months after the date of the entry into force of the present Covenant.

2. At least four months before the date of each election to the Committee, other than an election to fill a vacancy declared in accordance with Article 34, the Secretary General of the United Nations shall address a written invitation to the States Parties to the present Covenant to submit their nominations for membership of the Committee within three months.

3. The Secretary General of the United Nations shall prepare a list in alphabetical order of all the persons thus nominated, with an indication of the States Parties which have nominated them, and shall submit it to the States Parties to the present Covenant no later than one month before the date of each election.

4. Elections of the members of the Committee shall be held at a meeting of the States Parties to the present Covenant convened by the Secretary General of the United Nations at the Headquarters of the United Nations. At that meeting, for which two thirds of the States Parties to the present Covenant shall constitute a quorum, the persons elected to the Committee shall be those nominees who obtain the largest number of votes and an absolute majority of the votes of the representatives of States Parties present and voting.

Article 31

1. The Committee may not include more than one national of the same State.

2. In the election of the Committee, consideration shall be given to equitable geographical distribution of membership and to the representation of the different forms of civilization and of the principal legal systems.

Article 32

1. The members of the Committee shall be elected for a term of four years. They shall be eligible for re-election if renominated. However, the terms of nine of the members elected at the first election shall expire at the end of two years; immediately after the first election, the names of these nine members shall be chosen by lot by the Chairman of the meeting referred to in Article 30, paragraph 4.

2. Elections at the expiry of office shall be held in accordance with the preceding articles of this part of the present Covenant.

Article 33

1. If, in the unanimous opinion of the other members, a member of the Committee has ceased to carry out his functions for any cause other than absence of a temporary character, the Chairman of the Committee shall notify the Secretary General of the United Nations, who shall then declare the seat of that member to be vacant.

2. In the event of the death or the resignation of a member of the Committee, the Chairman shall immediately notify the Secretary General of the United Nations, who shall declare the seat vacant from the date of death or the date on which the resignation takes effect.

Article 34

1. When a vacancy is declared in accordance with Article 33 and if the term of office of the member to be replaced does not expire within six months of the declaration of the vacancy, the Secretary General of the United Nations shall notify each of the States Parties to the present Covenant, which may within two months submit nominations in accordance with Article 29 for the purpose of filling the vacancy.

2. The Secretary General of the United Nations shall prepare a list in alphabetical order of the persons thus nominated and shall submit it to the States Parties to the present Covenant. The election to fill the vacancy shall then take place in accordance with the relevant provisions of this part of the present Covenant.

3. A member of the Committee elected to fill a vacancy declared in accordance with hold office for the remainder of the term of the member who vacated the seat on the Committee under the provisions of that article.

Article 35

The members of the Committee shall, with the approval of the General Assembly of the United Nations, receive emoluments from United Nations resources on such terms and conditions as the General Assembly may decide, having regard to the importance of the Committee's responsibilities.

Article 36

The Secretary General of the United Nations shall provide the necessary staff and facilities for the effective performance of the functions of the Committee under the present Covenant.

Article 37

1. The Secretary General of the United Nations shall convene the initial meeting of the Committee at the Headquarters of the United Nations.

2. After its initial meeting, the Committee shall meet at such times as shall be provided in its rules of procedure.

3. The Committee shall normally meet at the Headquarters of the United Nations or at the United Nations Office at Geneva.

Article 38

Every member of the Committee shall, before taking up his duties, make a solemn declaration in open committee that he will perform his functions impartially and conscientiously.

Article 39

1. The Committee shall elect its officers for a term of two years. They may be re-elected.

2. The Committee shall establish its own rules of procedure, but these rules shall provide, inter alia, that:

(a) Twelve members shall constitute a quorum;

(b) Decisions of the Committee shall be made by a majority vote of the members present.

Article 40

1. The States Parties to the present Covenant undertake to submit reports on the measures they have adopted which give effect to the rights recognized herein and on the progress made in the enjoyment of those rights:

(a) Within one year of the entry into force of the present Covenant for the States Parties concerned;

(b) Thereafter whenever the Committee so requests.

2. All reports shall be submitted to the Secretary General of the United Nations, who shall transmit them to the Committee for consideration. Reports shall indicate the factors and difficulties, if any, affecting the implementation of the present Covenant.

3. The Secretary General of the United Nations may, after consultation with the Committee, transmit to the specialized agencies concerned copies of such parts of the reports as may fall within their field of competence.

4. The Committee shall study the reports submitted by the States Parties to the present Covenant. It shall transmit its reports, and such general comments as it may consider appropriate, to the States Parties. The Committee may also transmit to the Economic and Social Council these comments along with the copies of the reports it has received from States Parties to the present Covenant.

5. The States Parties to the present Covenant may submit to the Committee observations on any comments that may be made in accordance with paragraph 4 of this Article.

Article 41

1. A State Party to the present Covenant may at any time declare under this article that it recognizes the competence of the Committee to receive and consider communications to the effect that a State Party claims that another State Party is not fulfilling its obligations under the present Covenant. Communications under this Article may be received and considered only if submitted by a State Party which has made a declaration recognizing in regard to itself the competence of the Committee. No communication shall be received by the Committee if it concerns a State Party which has not made such a declaration. Communications received under this Article shall be dealt with in accordance with the following procedure:

(a) If a State Party to the present Covenant considers that another State Party is not giving effect to the provisions of the present Covenant, it may, by written communication, bring the matter to the attention of that State Party. Within three months after the receipt of the communication the receiving State shall afford the State which sent the communication an explanation, or any other statement in writing clarifying the matter which should include, to the extent possible and pertinent, reference to domestic procedures and remedies taken, pending, or available in the matter;

(b) If the matter is not adjusted to the satisfaction of both States Parties concerned within six months after the receipt by the receiving State of the initial communication, either State shall have the right to refer the matter to the Committee, by notice given to the Committee and to the other State;

(c) The Committee shall deal with a matter referred to it only after it has ascertained that all available domestic remedies have been invoked and exhausted in the matter, in conformity with the generally recognized principles of international law. This shall not be the rule where the application of the remedies is unreasonably prolonged;

(d) The Committee shall hold closed meetings when examining communications under this Article;

(e) Subject to the provisions of subparagraph (c), the Committee shall make available its good offices to the States Parties concerned with a view to a friendly solution of the matter on the basis of respect for human rights and fundamental freedoms as recognized in the present Covenant;

(f) In any matter referred to it, the Committee may call upon the States Parties concerned, referred to in subparagraph (b), to supply any relevant information;

(g) The States Parties concerned, referred to in subparagraph (b), shall have the right to be represented when the matter is being considered in the Committee and to make submissions orally and/or in writing;

(h) The Committee shall, within twelve months after the date of receipt of notice under subparagraph (b), submit a report:

(i) If a solution within the terms of subparagraph (e) is reached, the Committee shall confine its report to a brief statement of the facts and of the solution reached;

(ii) If a solution within the terms of subparagraph (e) is not reached, the Committee shall confine its report to a brief statement of the facts; the written submissions and record of the oral submissions made by the States Parties concerned shall be attached to the report. In every matter, the report shall be communicated to the States Parties concerned.

2. The provisions of this Article shall come into force when ten States Parties to the present Covenant have made declarations under paragraph I of this Article. Such declarations shall be deposited by the States Parties with the Secretary General of the United Nations, who shall transmit copies thereof to the other States Parties. A declaration may be withdrawn at any time by notification to the Secretary General. Such a withdrawal shall not prejudice the consideration of any matter which is the subject of a communication already transmitted under this Article; no further communication by any State Party shall be received after the notification of withdrawal of the declaration has been received by the Secretary-General, unless the State Party concerned has made a new declaration.

Article 42

1. (a) If a matter referred to the Committee in accordance with Article 41 is not resolved to the satisfaction of the States Parties concerned, the Committee may, with the prior consent of the States Parties concerned, appoint an ad hoc Conciliation Commission (hereinafter referred to as the Commission). The good offices of the Commission shall be made available to the States Parties concerned with a view to an amicable solution of the matter on the basis of respect for the present Covenant;

(b) The Commission shall consist of five persons acceptable to the States Parties concerned. If the States Parties concerned fail to reach agreement within three months on all or part of the composition of the Commission, the members of the Commission concerning whom no agreement has been reached shall be elected by secret ballot by a two-thirds majority vote of the Committee from among its members.

2. The members of the Commission shall serve in their personal capacity. They shall not be nationals of the States Parties concerned, or of a State not Party to the present Covenant, or of a State Party which has not made a declaration under Article 41.

3. The Commission shall elect its own Chairman and adopt its own rules of procedure.

4. The meetings of the Commission shall normally be held at the Headquarters of the United Nations or at the United Nations Office at Geneva. However, they may be held at such other convenient places as

the Commission may determine in consultation with the Secretary General of the United Nations and the States Parties concerned.

5. The secretariat provided in accordance with Article 36 shall also service the commissions appointed under this Article.

6. The information received and collated by the Committee shall be made available to the Commission and the Commission may call upon the States Parties concerned to supply any other relevant information.

7. When the Commission has fully considered the matter, but in any event not later than twelve months after having been seized of the matter, it shall submit to the Chairman of the Committee a report for communication to the States Parties concerned:

(a) If the Commission is unable to complete its consideration of the matter within twelve months, it shall confine its report to a brief statement of the status of its consideration of the matter;

(b) If an amicable solution to the matter on the basis of respect for human rights as recognized in the present Covenant is reached, the Commission shall confine its report to a brief statement of the facts and of the solution reached;

(c) If a solution within the terms of subparagraph (b) is not reached, the Commission's report shall embody its findings on all questions of fact relevant to the issues between the States Parties concerned, and its views on the possibilities of an amicable solution of the matter. This report shall also contain the written submissions and a record of the oral submissions made by the States Parties concerned;

(d) If the Commission's report is submitted under subparagraph (c), the States Parties concerned shall, within three months of the receipt of the report, notify the Chairman of the Committee whether or not they accept the contents of the report of the Commission.

8. The provisions of this article are without prejudice to the responsibilities of the Committee under Article 41.

9. The States Parties concerned shall share equally all the expenses of the members of the Commission in accordance with estimates to be provided by the Secretary General of the United Nations.

10. The Secretary General of the United Nations shall be empowered to pay the expenses of the members of the Commission, if necessary, before reimbursement by the States Parties concerned, in accordance with paragraph 9 of this Article.

Article 43

The members of the Committee, and of the ad hoc conciliation commissions which may be appointed under Article 42, shall be entitled to the facilities, privileges and immunities of experts on mission for the United Nations as laid down in the relevant sections of the Convention on the Privileges and Immunities of the United Nations.

Article 44

The provisions for the implementation of the present Covenant shall apply without prejudice to the procedures prescribed in the field of human rights by or under the constituent instruments and the conventions of the United Nations and of the specialized agencies and shall not prevent the States Parties to the present Covenant from having recourse to other procedures for settling a dispute in accordance with general or special international agreements in force between them.

Article 45

The Committee shall submit to the General Assembly of the United Nations, through the Economic and Social Council, an annual report on its activities.

PART V

Article 46

Nothing in the present Covenant shall be interpreted as impairing the provisions of the Charter of the United Nations and of the constitutions of the specialized agencies which define the respective responsibilities of the various organs of the United Nations and of the specialized agencies in regard to the matters dealt with in the present Covenant.

Article 47

Nothing in the present Covenant shall be interpreted as impairing the inherent right of all peoples to enjoy and utilize fully and freely their natural wealth and resources.

PART VI

Article 48

1. The present Covenant is open for signature by any State Member of the United Nations or member of any of its specialized agencies, by any State Party to the Statute of the International Court of Justice, and

by any other State which has been invited by the General Assembly of the United Nations to become a Party to the present Covenant.

2. The present Covenant is subject to ratification. Instruments of ratification shall be deposited with the Secretary General of the United Nations.

3. The present Covenant shall be open to accession by any State referred to in paragraph 1 of this Article.

4. Accession shall be effected by the deposit of an instrument of accession with the Secretary General of the United Nations.

5. The Secretary General of the United Nations shall inform all States which have signed this Covenant or acceded to it of the deposit of each instrument of ratification or accession.

Article 49

The present Covenant shall enter into force three months after the date of the deposit with the Secretary General of the United Nations of the thirty-fifth instrument of ratification or instrument of accession.

2. For each State ratifying the present Covenant or acceding to it after the deposit of the thirty-fifth instrument of ratification or instrument of accession, the present Covenant shall enter into force three months after the date of the deposit of its own instrument of ratification or instrument of accession.

Article 50

The provisions of the present Covenant shall extend to all parts of federal States without any limitations or exceptions.

Article 51

1. Any State Party to the present Covenant may propose an amendment and file it with the Secretary-General of the United Nations. The Secretary-General of the United Nations shall thereupon communicate any proposed amendments to the States Parties to the present Covenant with a request that they notify him whether they favour a conference of States Parties for the purpose of considering and voting upon the proposals. In the event that at least one third of the States Parties favours such a conference, the Secretary-General shall convene the conference under the auspices of the United Nations. Any amendment adopted by a majority of the States Parties present and voting at the conference shall be submitted to the General Assembly of the United Nations for approval.

2. Amendments shall come into force when they have been approved by the General Assembly of the United Nations and accepted by a two-thirds majority of the States Parties to the present Covenant in accordance with their respective constitutional processes.

3. When amendments come into force, they shall be binding on those States Parties which have accepted them, other States Parties still being bound by the provisions of the present Covenant and any earlier amendment which they have accepted.

Article 52

Irrespective of the notifications made under Article 48, paragraph 5, the Secretary-General of the United Nations shall inform all States referred to in paragraph I of the same article of the following particulars:

(a) Signatures, ratifications and accessions under Article 48;

(b) The date of the entry into force of the present Covenant under Article 49 and the date of the entry into force of any amendments under Article 51.

Article 53

1. The present Covenant, of which the Chinese, English, French, Russian and Spanish texts are equally authentic, shall be deposited in the archives of the United Nations.

2. The Secretary-General of the United Nations shall transmit certified copies of the present Covenant to all States referred to in Article 48.

DOCUMENT 9

Full Official Title: U.S. Ratification of the [ICCPR] Covenant by the U.S. Senate

Short Title/Acronym/Abbreviation: Advice and Consent of the Senate to the ICCPR

Subject: U.S. Senate ratification of the ICCPR

Official Citation: 138 Cong. Rec. 54781-01 (daily ed., april 2, 1992)

Date of Document: April 2, 1992

Date of Adoption: Not applicable

Date of General Entry into Force (EIF): Not applicable

Number of States Parties to this Treaty as of this printing: Not applicable

Date of Signature by United States: Not applicable

Date of Ratification/Accession/Adhesion: This document contains the reservations, declarations, and understandings that accompany the ratification of the ICCPR.

Date of Entry into Force as to United States (effective date): September 8, 1992

Type of Document: Official advice and consent of the U.S. Senate under the U.S. Constitution, ratifying the ICCPR on behalf of the people of the United States. This legislative act ratified the prior signature of the President to the treaty. It also sets forth the reservations, declarations and understandings to the ICCPR submitted with the ratification.

Legal Status/Character of the Instrument/Document as to the United States: A legal document under U.S. and international law. It served to legally bind the United States to comply with the ICCPR after this instrument of ratification was deposited with the United Nations. These legal obligations are subject to the reservations, declarations and understandings submitted by the United States and contained in this instrument. Moreover, this document states that the ICCPR is non self-executing. This means that the ICCPR norms cannot be asserted as the direct legal basis for a court decision. Some scholars disagree with this effect.

Comments: By ratifying the ICCPR the United States voluntarily accepted the legal obligations of the ICCPR as a matter of International Law, and obligated the United States to comply with all its provisions, subject to the RDUs.

Caution: The status and applicability of this instrument as to the United States may have changed since date of publication. The above information may be updated by referring to the following site:

Web address: http://www1.umn.edu/humanrts/usdocs/civilres.html

U.S. RATIFICATION OF THE ICCPR, WITH RESERVATIONS, DECLARATIONS AND UNDERSTANDINGS (RDUs)

Senate of the United States In Executive Session

2 April 1992

Resolved, (two thirds of the Senators present concurring therein), That the Senate advise and consent to the ratification of the International Covenant on Civil and Political Rights, adopted by the United Nations General Assembly on 16 December 1966, and signed on behalf of the United States on 5 October 1977, (Executive E, 95–2), subject to the following Reservations, Understandings, Declarations and Proviso:

I. The Senate's advice and consent is subject to the following reservations:

(1) That Article 20 does not authorize or require legislation or other action by the United States that would restrict the right of free speech and association protected by the Constitution and laws of the United States.

(2) That the United States reserves the right, subject to its constitutional constraints, to impose capital punishment on any person (other than a pregnant woman) duly convicted under existing or future laws permitting the imposition of capital punishment, including such punishment for crimes committed by persons below 18 years of age.

(3) That the United States considers itself bound by Article 7 to the extent that "cruel, inhuman or degrading treatment or punishment" means the cruel and unusual treatment or punishment prohibited by the Fifth, Eighth and/or Fourteenth Amendments to the constitution of the United States.

(4) That because U.S. law generally applies to an offender the penalty in force at the time the offence was committed, the United States does not adhere to the third clause of paragraph 1 of Article 15.

(5) That the policy and practice of the United States are generally in compliance with and supportive of the Covenant's provisions regarding treatment of juveniles in the criminal justice system. Nevertheless, the United States reserves the right, in exceptional circumstances, to treat juveniles as adults, notwithstanding paragraphs 2 (b) and 3 of Article 10 and paragraph 4 of Article 14. The United States further reserves to these provisions with respect to individuals who volunteer for military service prior to age 18.

II. The Senate's advice and consent is subject to the following understandings, which shall apply to the obligations of the United States under this Covenant:

(1) That the Constitution and laws of the United States guarantee all persons equal protection of the law and provide extensive protections against discrimination. The United States understands distinctions

based upon race, colour, sex, language, religion, political or other opinion, national or social origin, property, birth or any other status—as those terms are used in Article 2, paragraph 1 and Article 26—to be permitted when such distinctions are, at minimum, rationally related to a legitimate governmental objective. The United States further understands the prohibition in paragraph 1 of Article 4 upon discrimination, in time of public emergency, based "solely" on the status of race, colour, sex, language, religion or social origin not to bar distinctions that may have a disproportionate effect upon persons of a particular status.

(2) That the United States understands the right to compensation referred to in Articles 9 (5) and 14 (6) to require the provision of effective and enforceable mechanisms by which a victim of an unlawful arrest or detention or a miscarriage of justice may seek and, where justified, obtain compensation from either the responsible individual or the appropriate governmental entity. Entitlement to compensation may be subject to the reasonable requirements of domestic law.

(3) That the United States understands the reference to "exceptional circumstances" in paragraph 2 (a) of Article 10 to permit the imprisonment of an accused person with convicted persons where appropriate in light of an individual's overall dangerousness, and to permit accused persons to waive their right to segregation from convicted persons. The United States further understands that paragraph 3 of Article 10 does not diminish the goals of punishment, deterrence, and incapacitation as additional legitimate purposes for a penitentiary system.

(4) That the United States understands that subparagraphs 3 (b) and (d) of Article 14 do not require the provision of a criminal defendant's counsel of choice when the defendant is provided with court-appointed counsel on grounds of indigence, when the defendant is financially able to retain alternative counsel, or when imprisonment is not imposed. The United States further understands that paragraph 3 (e) does not prohibit a requirement that the defendant make a showing that any witness whose attendance he seeks to compel is necessary for his defence. The United States understands the prohibition upon double jeopardy in paragraph 7 to apply only when the judgment of acquittal has been rendered by a court of the same governmental unit, whether the Federal Government or a constituent unit, as is seeking a new trial for the same cause.

(5) That the United States understand that this Covenant shall be implemented by the Federal Government to the extent that it exercises legislative and judicial jurisdiction over the matters covered therein, and otherwise by the state and local governments; to the extent that state and local governments exercise jurisdiction over such matters, the Federal Government shall take measures appropriate to the Federal system to the end that the competent authorities of the state or local governments may take appropriate measures for the fulfilment of the Covenant.

III. The Senate's advice and consent is subject to the following declarations:

(1) That the United States declares that the provisions of Articles 1 through 27 of the Covenant are not self-executing.

(2) That it is the view of the United States that States Party to the Covenant should wherever possible refrain from imposing any restrictions or limitations on the exercise of the rights recognized and protected by the Covenant, even when such restrictions and limitations are permissible under the terms of the Covenant. For the United States, Article 5, paragraph 2, which provides that fundamental human rights existing in any State Party may not be diminished on the pretext that the Covenant recognizes them to a lesser extent, has particular relevance to Article 19, paragraph 3, which would permit certain restrictions on the freedom of expression. The United States declares that it will continue to adhere to the requirements and constraints of its Constitution in respect to all such restrictions and limitations.

(3) That the United States declares that it accepts the competence of the Human Rights Committee to receive and consider communications under Article 41 in which a State Party claims that another State Party is not fulfilling its obligations under the Covenant.

(4) That the United States declares that the right referred to in Article 47 may be exercised only in accordance with international law.

IV. The Senate's advice and consent is subject to the following proviso, which shall not be included in the instrument of ratification to be deposited by the President:

Nothing in this Covenant requires or authorizes legislation, or other action, by the United States of America prohibited by the Constitution of the United States as interpreted by the United States.

Attest: Walter J. Stewart
Secretary

DOCUMENT 10

Full Official Title: Optional Protocol to the International Covenant on Civil and Political Rights [First]

Short Title/Acronym/Abbreviation: The Optional Protocol/OP/The First Optional Protocol

Subject: The right of individual victims of violations of the ICCPR to file a complaint against a state which ratifies the ICCPR.

Official Citation: G.A. res. 2200A (XXI), 21 U.N. GAOR Supp. (No. 16) at 59, U.N. Doc. A/6316 (1966), 999 U.N.T.S. 302

Date of Document: December 16, 1966

Date of Adoption: December 16, 1966

Date of General Entry into Force (EIF): March 23, 1976

Number of States Parties to this Treaty as of this printing: 113

Date of Signature by United States: The United States has not signed

Date of Ratification/Accession/Adhesion: Not applicable

Date of Entry into Force as to United States (effective date): Not applicable

Type of Document: This is a legal instrument by which a state which ratifies the ICCPR can also choose to accept the authority of the Human Rights Committee to hear written complaints (communications) filed against it by individual victims of violations. It constitutes an amendment to the ICCPR for states which ratify it.

Legal Status/Character of the Instrument/Document as to the United States: It is legally binding on those states which have ratified it. It is not legally binding on the United States because the United States has neither signed nor ratified it. The United States could choose to sign and ratify this protocol at any time.

Supervising Body: U.N. Human Rights Committee

Comments: The United States seems reticent to grant the right to those within its jurisdiction, citizen or otherwise, to bring alleged violations before the HRC, even though the victim must go through all U.S. legal remedies before filing with the HRC. This document is included for purposes of future discussion of whether the United States should ratify it.

Caution: The status and applicability of this instrument as to the United States may have changed since date of publication. The above information may be updated by referring to the following site:

Web address: http://www1.umn.edu/humanrts/instree/b4ccprp1.htm

FIRST OPTIONAL PROTOCOL TO THE ICCPR

Considering that in order further to achieve the purposes of the International Covenant on Civil and Political Rights (herein after referred to as the Covenant) and the implementation of its provisions it would be appropriate to enable the Human Rights Committee set up in Part IV of the Covenant (hereinafter referred to as the Committee) to receive and consider, as provided in the present Protocol, communications from individuals claiming to be victims of violations of any of the rights set forth in the Covenant.

Have agreed as follows:

Article 1

A State Party to the Covenant that becomes a Party to the present Protocol recognizes the competence of the Committee to receive and consider communications from individuals subject to its jurisdiction who claim to be victims of a violation by that State Party of any of the rights set forth in the Covenant. No communication shall be received by the Committee if it concerns a State Party to the Covenant which is not a Party to the present Protocol.

Article 2

Subject to the provisions of Article 1, individuals who claim that any of their rights enumerated in the Covenant have been violated and who have exhausted all available domestic remedies may submit a written communication to the Committee for consideration.

Article 3

The Committee shall consider inadmissible any communication under the present Protocol which is anonymous, or which it considers to be an abuse of the right of submission of such communications or to be incompatible with the provisions of the Covenant.

Article 4

1. Subject to the provisions of Article 3, the Committee shall bring any communications submitted to it under the present Protocol to the attention of the State Party to the present Protocol alleged to be violating any provision of the Covenant.

2. Within six months, the receiving State shall submit to the Committee written explanations or statements clarifying the matter and the remedy, if any, that may have been taken by that State.

Article 5

1. The Committee shall consider communications received under the present Protocol in the light of all written information made available to it by the individual and by the State Party concerned.

2. The Committee shall not consider any communication from an individual unless it has ascertained that:

(a) The same matter is not being examined under another procedure of international investigation or settlement;

(b) The individual has exhausted all available domestic remedies. This shall not be the rule where the application of the remedies is unreasonably prolonged.

3. The Committee shall hold closed meetings when examining communications under the present Protocol.

4. The Committee shall forward its views to the State Party concerned and to the individual.

Article 6

The Committee shall include in its annual report under Article 45 of the Covenant a summary of its activities under the present Protocol.

Article 7

Pending the achievement of the objectives of resolution 1514 (XV) adopted by the General Assembly of the United Nations on 14 December 1960 concerning the Declaration on the Granting of Independence to Colonial Countries and Peoples, the provisions of the present Protocol shall in no way limit the right of petition granted to these peoples by the Charter of the United Nations and other international conventions and instruments under the United Nations and its specialized agencies.

Article 8

1. The present Protocol is open for signature by any State which has signed the Covenant.

2. The present Protocol is subject to ratification by any State which has ratified or acceded to the Covenant. Instruments of ratification shall be deposited with the Secretary General of the United Nations.

3. The present Protocol shall be open to accession by any State which has ratified or acceded to the Covenant.

4. Accession shall be effected by the deposit of an instrument of accession with the Secretary General of the United Nations.

5. The Secretary General of the United Nations shall inform all States which have signed the present Protocol or acceded to it of the deposit of each instrument of ratification or accession.

Article 9

1. Subject to the entry into force of the Covenant, the present Protocol shall enter into force three months after the date of the deposit with the Secretary General of the United Nations of the tenth instrument of ratification or instrument of accession.

2. For each State ratifying the present Protocol or acceding to it after the deposit of the tenth instrument of ratification or instrument of accession, the present Protocol shall enter in to force three months after the date of the deposit of its own instrument of ratification or instrument of accession.

Article 10

The provisions of the present Protocol shall extend to all parts of federal States without any limitations or exceptions.

Article 11

1. Any State Party to the present Protocol may propose an amendment and file it with the Secretary-General of the United Nations. The Secretary-General shall thereupon communicate any proposed amendments to the States Parties to the present Protocol with a request that they notify him whether they favour a conference of States Parties for the purpose of considering and voting upon the proposal. In the event that at least one third of the States Parties favours such a conference, the Secretary-General shall convene the conference under the auspices of the United Nations. Any amendment adopted by a majority of the States Parties present and voting at the conference shall be submitted to the General Assembly of the United Nations for approval.

2. Amendments shall come into force when they have been approved by the General Assembly of the United Nations and accepted by a two-thirds majority of the States Parties to the present Protocol in accordance with their respective constitutional processes.

3. When amendments come into force, they shall be binding on those States Parties which have accepted them, other States Parties still being bound by the provisions of the present Protocol and any earlier amendment which they have accepted.

Article 12

1. Any State Party may denounce the present Protocol at any time by written notification addressed to the Secretary-General of the United Nations. Denunciation shall take effect three months after the date of receipt of the notification by the Secretary-General.

2. Denunciation shall be without prejudice to the continued application of the provisions of the present Protocol to any communication submitted under Article 2 before the effective date of denunciation.

Article 13

Irrespective of the notifications made under Article 8, paragraph 5, of the present Protocol, the Secretary-General of the United Nations shall inform all States referred to in Article 48, paragraph 1, of the Covenant of the following particulars:

(a) Signatures, ratifications and accessions under Article 8;

(b) The date of the entry into force of the present Protocol under Article 9 and the date of the entry into force of any amendments under Article 11;

(c) Denunciations under Article 12.

Article 14

1. The present Protocol, of which the Chinese, English, French, Russian and Spanish texts are equally authentic, shall be deposited in the archives of the United Nations.

2. The Secretary-General of the United Nations shall transmit certified copies of the present Protocol to all States referred to in Article 48 of the Covenant.

DOCUMENT 11

Full Official Title: Optional Protocol to the International Covenant on Civil and Political Rights, aiming at the abolition of the death penalty [Second]

Short Title/Acronym/Abbreviation: The Second Optional Protocol/OP2

Subject: Elimination of the death penalty by ratifying states

Official Citation: G.A. Res. 44/128 of 15 December 1989

Date of Document: December 15, 1989

Date of Adoption: December 15, 1989

Date of General Entry into Force (EIF): July 11, 1991

Number of States Parties to this Treaty as of this printing: 72

Date of Signature by United States: The United States has not signed

Date of Ratification/Accession/Adhesion: Not applicable

Date of Entry into Force as to United States (effective date): Not applicable

Type of Document: This is a legal instrument by which a state which ratifies the ICCPR can also choose to accept the legal obligation to eliminate the death penalty or to refrain from ever reinstituting it. It constitutes an amendment to the ICCPR for those states which ratify it.

Legal Status/Character of the Instrument/Document as to the United States: It is legally binding on those states which have ratified it. It is not legally binding on the United States because the United States has neither signed nor ratified it. The United States could choose to sign and ratify this protocol at any time.

Supervising Body: U.N. Human Rights Committee

Comments: Given the strong position of the United States in favor of the death penalty, it is doubtful that this document will be signed any time in the near future. However, public opinion is subject to change and this document is included for purposes of future discussion of whether the United States should ratify it.

Caution: The status and applicability of this instrument as to the United States may have changed since date of publication. The above information may be updated by referring to the following site:

Web address: http://www1.umn.edu/humanrts/instree/b5ccprp2.htm

SECOND OPTIONAL PROTOCOL TO THE ICCPR

Adopted and proclaimed by General Assembly resolution 44/128 of 15 December 1989

The States Parties to the present Protocol,

Believing that abolition of the death penalty contributes to enhancement of human dignity and progressive development of human rights, Recalling Article 3 of the Universal Declaration of Human Rights, adopted on 10 December 1948, and Article 6 of the International Covenant on Civil and Political Rights, adopted on 16 December 1966,

Noting that Article 6 of the International Covenant on Civil and Political Rights refers to abolition of the death penalty in terms that strongly suggest that abolition is desirable,

Convinced that all measures of abolition of the death penalty should be considered as progress in the enjoyment of the right to life,

Desirous to undertake hereby an international commitment to abolish the death penalty,

Have agreed as follows:

Article 1

1. No one within the jurisdiction of a State Party to the present Protocol shall be executed.

2. Each State Party shall take all necessary measures to abolish the death penalty within its jurisdiction.

Article 2

1. No reservation is admissible to the present Protocol, except for a reservation made at the time of ratification or accession that provides for the application of the death penalty in time of war pursuant to a conviction for a most serious crime of a military nature committed during wartime.

2. The State Party making such a reservation shall at the time of ratification or accession communicate to the Secretary-General of the United Nations the relevant provisions of its national legislation applicable during wartime.

3. The State Party having made such a reservation shall notify the Secretary-General of the United Nations of any beginning or ending of a state of war applicable to its territory.

Article 3

The States Parties to the present Protocol shall include in the reports they submit to the Human Rights Committee, in accordance with Article 40 of the Covenant, information on the measures that they have adopted to give effect to the present Protocol.

Article 4

With respect to the States Parties to the Covenant that have made a declaration under Article 41, the competence of the Human Rights Committee to receive and consider communications when a State Party claims that another State Party is not fulfilling its obligations shall extend to the provisions of the present Protocol, unless the State Party concerned has made a statement to the contrary at the moment of ratification or accession.

Article 5

With respect to the States Parties to the first Optional Protocol to the International Covenant on Civil and Political Rights adopted on 16 December 1966, the competence of the Human Rights Committee to receive and consider communications from individuals subject to its jurisdiction shall extend to the provisions of the present Protocol, unless the State Party concerned has made a statement to the contrary at the moment of ratification or accession.

Article 6

1. The provisions of the present Protocol shall apply as additional provisions to the Covenant.

2. Without prejudice to the possibility of a reservation under Article 2 of the present Protocol, the right guaranteed in Article 1, paragraph 1, of the present Protocol shall not be subject to any derogation under Article 4 of the Covenant.

Article 7

1. The present Protocol is open for signature by any State that has signed the Covenant.

2. The present Protocol is subject to ratification by any State that has ratified the Covenant or acceded to it. Instruments of ratification shall be deposited with the Secretary-General of the United Nations.

3. The present Protocol shall be open to accession by any State that has ratified the Covenant or acceded to it.

4. Accession shall be effected by the deposit of an instrument of accession with the Secretary-General of the United Nations.

5. The Secretary-General of the United Nations shall inform all States that have signed the present Protocol or acceded to it of the deposit of each instrument of ratification or accession.

Article 8

1. The present Protocol shall enter into force three months after the date of the deposit with the Secretary-General of the United Nations of the tenth instrument of ratification or accession.

2. For each State ratifying the present Protocol or acceding to it after the deposit of the tenth instrument of ratification or accession, the present Protocol shall enter into force three months after the date of the deposit of its own instrument of ratification or accession.

Article 9

The provisions of the present Protocol shall extend to all parts of federal States without any limitations or exceptions.

Article 10

The Secretary-General of the United Nations shall inform all States referred to in Article 48, paragraph 1, of the Covenant of the following particulars:

(a) Reservations, communications and notifications under Article 2 of the present Protocol;

(b) Statements made under articles 4 or 5 of the present Protocol;

(c) Signatures, ratifications and accessions under Article 7 of the present Protocol;

(d) The date of the entry into force of the present Protocol under Article 8 thereof.

Article 11

1. The present Protocol, of which the Arabic, Chinese, English, French, Russian and Spanish texts are equally authentic, shall be deposited in the archives of the United Nations.

2. The Secretary-General of the United Nations shall transmit certified copies of the present Protocol to all States referred to in Article 48 of the Covenant.

DOCUMENT 12

Official Title: General Comments [of the U.N. Human Rights Committee] under art. 40, para. 4, of the ICCPR, General Comment no. 22(18), 1993

Short Title/Acronym/Abbreviation: General Comment on Article 18 of the Covenant

Subject: Freedom of Thought, Conscience and Religion under Article 18 of the ICCPR

Official Citation: U.N Doc. CCPR/C/48/CRP.2/Rev.1(1993)

Date of Document: July 30, 1993

Date of Adoption: Not applicable

Date of General Entry into Force (EIF): Not applicable

Number of States Parties to this Treaty as of this printing: Not applicable

Date of Signature by United States: Not applicable

Date of Ratification/Accession/Adhesion: Not applicable

Date of Entry into Force as to United States (effective date): Not applicable

Type of Document: General Comments from a treaty based body, the Human Rights Committee. This is not a legal instrument, as such.

Legal Status/Character of the Instrument/Document as to the United States: Not legally binding but should be followed and applied by the U.S. because of the authority and competence of the HRC.

Supervising Body: U.N. Human Rights Committee

Comments: By ratifying the ICCPR, the United States accepted the authority of the Human Rights Committee to receive and review and comment on reports received from it. It also accepted the power of the HRC to issue "general" comments about the interpretation and application of the different articles of the ICCPR. This document sets forth the opinion of the U.N. Human Rights Committee as to how Article 18 of the ICCPR on freedom of thought, conscience and religion should be interpreted and applied in certain situations. These views are made in response to legal issues which the HRC encounters in its review of the states reports under Article 40. The comments are made in light of the jurisprudence (case decisions called "views") arising from the complaints it handles, especially under the First Optional Protocol.

Having ratified the ICCPR, the U.S. is obligated by Article 2, para. 2 to take legislative and other measures so as "to give effect to the rights recognized in" the ICCPR. Theoretically, American courts should be using this Comment to inform themselves as to how religious freedom issues should be resolved under the first amendment to the U.S. Constitution in a manner consistent with international law. This is so because American law as decided by the U.S. Supreme Court says that our law must, as a matter of constitutionality, be interpreted consistent with any international law binding upon the United States, whenever possible.

Web address: http://www1.umn.edu/humanrts/gencomm/hrcom22.htm

GENERAL COMMENT 22(18) OF THE U.N. HUMAN RIGHTS COMMITTEE ON FREEDOM OF THOUGHT, CONSCIENCE, AND RELIGION

1. The right to freedom of thought, conscience and religion (which includes the freedom to hold beliefs) in Article 18.1 is far-reaching and profound; it encompasses freedom of thought on all matters, personal conviction and the commitment to religion or belief, whether manifested individually or in community with others. The Committee draws the attention of States parties to the fact that the freedom of thought and the freedom of conscience are protected equally with the freedom of religion and belief. The fundamental character of these freedoms is also reflected in the fact that this provision cannot be derogated from, even in time of public emergency, as stated in Article 4.2 of the Covenant.

2. Article 18 protects theistic, non-theistic and atheistic beliefs, as well as the right not to profess any religion or belief. The terms "belief" and "religion" are to be broadly construed. Article 18 is not limited in its application to traditional religions or to religions and beliefs with institutional characteristics or practices analogous to those of traditional religions. The Committee therefore views with concern any tendency to discriminate against any religion or belief for any reason, including the fact that they are newly established, or represent religious minorities that may be the subject of hostility on the part of a predominant religious community.

3. Article 18 distinguishes the freedom of thought, conscience, religion or belief from the freedom to manifest religion or belief. It does not permit any limitations whatsoever on the freedom of thought and conscience or on the freedom to have or adopt a religion or belief of one's choice. These freedoms are protected unconditionally, as is the right of everyone to hold opinions without interference in Article 19.1. In accordance with articles 18.2 and 17, no one can be compelled to reveal his thoughts or adherence to a religion or belief.

4. The freedom to manifest religion or belief may be exercised "either individually or in community with others and in public or private." The freedom to manifest religion or belief in worship, observance, practice and teaching encompasses a broad range of acts. The concept of worship extends to ritual and ceremonial acts giving direct expression to belief, as well as various practices integral to such acts, including the building of places of worship, the use of ritual formulae and objects, the display of symbols, and the observance of holidays and days of rest. The observance and practice of religion or belief may include not only ceremonial acts but also such customs as the observance of dietary regulations, the wearing of distinctive clothing or head coverings, participation in rituals associated with certain stages of life, and the use of a particular language customarily spoken by a group. In addition, the practice and teaching of religion or belief includes acts integral to the conduct by religious groups of their basic affairs, such as the freedom to choose their religious leaders, priests and teachers, the freedom to establish seminaries or religious schools and the freedom to prepare and distribute religious texts or publications.

5. The Committee observes that the freedom to "have or to adopt" a religion or belief necessarily entails the freedom to choose a religion or belief, including the right to replace one's current religion or belief with another or to adopt atheistic views, as well as the right to retain one's religion or belief. Article 18.2 bars coercion that would impair the right to have or adopt a religion or belief, including the use of threat of physical force or penal sanctions to compel believers or non-believers to adhere to their religious beliefs and congregations, to recant their religion or belief or to convert. Policies or practices having the same intention or effect, such as, for example, those restricting access to education, medical care, employment or the rights guaranteed by Article 25 and other provisions of the Covenant, are similarly inconsistent with Article 18.2. The same protection is enjoyed by holders of all beliefs of a non-religious nature.

6. The Committee is of the view that Article 18.4 permits public school instruction in subjects such as the general history of religions and ethics if it is given in a neutral and objective way. The liberty of parents or legal guardians to ensure that their children receive a religious and moral education in conformity with their own convictions, set forth in Article 18.4, is related to the guarantees of the freedom to teach a religion or belief stated in Article 18.1. The Committee notes that public education that includes instruction in a

particular religion or belief is inconsistent with Article 18.4 unless provision is made for non-discriminatory exemptions or alternatives that would accommodate the wishes of parents and guardians.

7. In accordance with Article 20, no manifestation of religion or belief may amount to propaganda for war or advocacy of national, racial or religious hatred that constitutes incitement to discrimination, hostility or violence. As stated by the Committee in its General Comment 11 [19], States parties are under the obligation to enact laws to prohibit such acts.

8. Article 18.3 permits restrictions on the freedom to manifest religion or belief only if limitations are prescribed by law and are necessary to protect public safety, order, health or morals, or the fundamental rights and freedoms of others. The freedom from coercion to have or to adopt a religion or belief and the liberty of parents and guardians to ensure religious and moral education cannot be restricted. In interpreting the scope of permissible limitation clauses, States parties should proceed from the need to protect the rights guaranteed under the Covenant, including the right to equality and non-discrimination on all grounds specified in articles 2, 3 and 26. Limitations imposed must be established by law and must not be applied in a manner that would vitiate the rights guaranteed in Article 18. The Committee observes that paragraph 3 of Article 18 is to be strictly interpreted: restrictions are not allowed on grounds not specified there, even if they would be allowed as restrictions to other rights protected in the Covenant, such as national security. Limitations may be applied only for those purposes for which they were prescribed and must be directly related and proportionate to the specific need on which they are predicated. Restrictions may not be imposed for discriminatory purposes or applied in a discriminatory manner. The Committee observes that the concept of morals derives from many social, philosophical and religious traditions; consequently, limitations on the freedom to manifest a religion or belief for the purpose of protecting morals must be based on principles not deriving exclusively from a single tradition. Persons already subject to certain legitimate constraints, such as prisoners, continue to enjoy their rights to manifest their religion or belief to the fullest extent compatible with the specific nature of the constraint. States parties' reports should provide information on the full scope and effects of limitations under Article 18.3, both as a matter of law and of their application in specific circumstances.

9. The fact that a religion is recognized as a state religion or that it is established as official or traditional or that its followers comprise the majority of the population, shall not result in any impairment of the enjoyment of any of the rights under the Covenant, including articles 18 and 27, nor in any discrimination against adherents to other religions or non-believers. In particular, certain measures discriminating against the latter, such as measures restricting eligibility for government service to members of the predominant religion or giving economic privileges to them or imposing special restrictions on the practice of other faiths, are not in accordance with the prohibition of discrimination based on religion or belief and the guarantee of equal protection under Article 26. The measures contemplated by Article 20, paragraph 2 of the Covenant constitute important safeguards against infringement of the rights of religious minorities and of other religious groups to exercise the rights guaranteed by articles 18 and 27, and against acts of violence or persecution directed towards those groups. The Committee wishes to be informed of measures taken by States parties concerned to protect the practices of all religions or beliefs from infringement and to protect their followers from discrimination. Similarly, information as to respect for the rights of religious minorities under Article 27 is necessary for the Committee to assess the extent to which the right to freedom of thought, conscience, religion and belief has been implemented by States parties. States parties concerned should also include in their reports information relating to practices considered by their laws and jurisprudence to be punishable as blasphemous.

10. If a set of beliefs is treated as official ideology in constitutions, statutes, proclamations of ruling parties, etc., or in actual practice, this shall not result in any impairment of the freedoms under Article 18 or any other rights recognized under the Covenant nor in any discrimination against persons who do not accept the official ideology or who oppose it.

11. Many individuals have claimed the right to refuse to perform military service (conscientious objection) on the basis that such right derives from their freedoms under Article 18. In response to such claims, a growing number of States have in their laws exempted from compulsory military service citizens who genuinely hold religious or other beliefs that forbid the performance of military service and replaced it with alternative national service. The Covenant does not explicitly refer to a right to conscientious objection, but the Committee believes that such a right can be derived from Article 18, inasmuch as the obligation to use lethal force may seriously conflict with the freedom of conscience and the right to manifest one's religion or belief. When this right is recognized by law or practice, there shall be no differentiation among conscientious objectors on the basis of the nature of their particular beliefs; likewise, there shall be no discrimination against conscientious objectors because they have failed to perform military service. The Committee invites States

parties to report on the conditions under which persons can be exempted from military service on the basis of their rights under Article 18 and on the nature and length of alternative national service.

© Copyright 1999

Office of the United Nations High Commissioner for Human Rights Geneva, Switzerland

DOCUMENT 13

Full Official Title: U.N. International Human Rights Instruments—Compilation Of Guidelines On The Form And Content Of Reports To Be Submitted By States Parties To The International Human Rights Treaties

Short Title/Acronym/Abbreviation: U.N. Human Rights Reporting Guidelines

Subject: Guidelines for all states parties to use in preparing form and content of periodic state reports

Official Citation: HRI/GEN/2/Rev.2

Date of Document: May 7, 2004

Date of Adoption: Not applicable

Date of General Entry into Force (EIF): Not applicable

Number of States Parties as of this printing: Not applicable

Date of Signature by the United States: Not applicable

Date of Ratification/Accession/Adhesion: Not applicable

Date of Entry into Force as to United States (effective date): Not applicable

Type of Document: Inter-governmental organization administrative document by the U.N. for states parties to human rights treaties, to set guidelines to standardize periodic states reports to facilitate their review by U.N. human rights bodies, particularly treaty supervising bodies, such as the Human Rights Committee

Legal Status/Character of the Instrument/Document as to the United States: Not legally binding

This document is an administrative document to expedite submission and review of states human rights reports with the U.N. treaty bodies.

Supervising Body: Every treaty based supervising U.N. human rights body

Comments: An administrative tool to standardize the form and content of states reports. It is supposed to be followed in good faith by all states parties.

U.N. HUMAN RIGHTS REPORTING GUIDELINES (EXCERPTS)

Report of the Secretary-General

In its resolutions 52/118 and 53/138, the General Assembly requested the Secretary-General to compile in a single volume the guidelines regarding the form and content of reports to be submitted by States parties that have been issued by the Human Rights Committee, the Committee on Economic, Social and Cultural Rights, the Committee on the Elimination of Discrimination against Women, the Committee on the Elimination of Racial Discrimination, the Committee on the Rights of the Child and the Committee against Torture.

This document was prepared pursuant to that request. It contains, in addition to the guidelines issued separately by the above bodies, the consolidated guidelines relating to the initial part of State party reports containing information of a general character ("core documents").

Chapter I

INITIAL PARTS OF STATE PARTY REPORTS ("CORE DOCUMENTS") UNDER THE VARIOUS INTERNATIONAL HUMAN RIGHTS INSTRUMENTS*

Land and people

1. This section should contain information about the main ethnic and demographic characteristics of the country and its population, as well as such socio-economic and cultural indicators as per capita income, gross national product, rate of inflation, external debt, rate of unemployment, literacy rate and religion. It should also include information on the population by mother tongue, life expectancy, infant mortality, maternal mortality, fertility rate, percentage of population under 15 and over 65 years of age, percentage of population in rural areas and in urban areas and percentage of households headed by women. As far as possible, States should make efforts to provide all data disaggregated by sex.

General political structure

---

* Contained in the annex to document HRI/CORE/1 entitled Preparation of the initial parts of State party reports ("core documents") under the various international human rights instruments.

2. This section should describe briefly the political history and framework, the type of government and the organization of the executive, legislative and judicial organs.

General legal framework within which human rights are protected

3. This section should contain information on:

(a) Which judicial, administrative or other competent authorities have jurisdiction affecting human rights;

(b) What remedies are available to an individual who claims that any of his rights have been violated; and what systems of compensation and rehabilitation exist for victims;

(c) Whether any of the rights referred to in the various human rights instruments are protected either in the constitution or by a separate bill of rights and, if so, what provisions are made in the constitution or bill of rights for derogations and in what circumstances;

(d) How human rights instruments are made part of the national legal system;

With a view to facilitating the implementation of reporting obligations by States parties, and with the agreement of all of the treaty bodies, the guidelines of the various treaty bodies relating to the part of States reports containing general information were consolidated into a single text. By a note verbale dated 26 April 1991, the Secretary-General transmitted the guidelines, calling for the preparation and submission of a "core document", to all States that were parties to one or more international human rights instruments.

(e) Whether the provisions of the various human rights instruments can be invoked before, or directly enforced by, the courts, other tribunals or administrative authorities or whether they must be transformed into internal laws or administrative regulations in order to be enforced by the authorities concerned;

(f) Whether there exist any institutions or national machinery with responsibility for overseeing the implementation of human rights.

Information and publicity

4. This section should indicate whether any special efforts have been made to promote awareness among the public and the relevant authorities of the rights contained in the various human rights instruments. The topics to be addressed should include the manner and extent to which the texts of the various human rights instruments have been disseminated, whether such texts have been translated into the local language or languages, what government agencies have responsibility for preparing reports and whether they normally receive information or other inputs from external sources, and whether the contents of the reports are the subject of public debate.

...

Chapter III

HUMAN RIGHTS COMMITTEE*

A. Introduction

A.1 These guidelines replace all earlier versions issued by the Human Rights Committee, which may now be disregarded (CCPR/C/19/Rev.1 of 26 August 1982, CCPR/C/5/Rev.2 of 28 April 1995 and Annex VIII to the Committee's 1998 report to the General Assembly (A/53/40)); the Committee's general comment 2 (13) of 1981 is also superseded. The present guidelines do not affect the Committee's procedure in relation to any special reports which may be requested.

A.2 These guidelines will be effective for all reports to be presented after 31 December 1999.

A.3 The guidelines should be followed by States parties in the preparation of initial and all subsequent periodic reports.

A.4 Compliance with these guidelines will reduce the need for the Committee to request further information when it proceeds to consider a report; it will also help the Committee to consider the situation regarding human rights in every State party on an equal basis.

B. Framework of the Covenant concerning reports

B.1 Every State party, upon ratifying the Covenant, undertakes, under Article 40, to submit, within a year of the Covenant's entry into force for that State, an initial report on the measures it has adopted which give effect to the rights recognized in the Covenant ("Covenant rights") and progress made in their enjoyment; and thereafter periodic reports whenever the Committee so requests.

---

* Contained in document CCPR/C/66/GUI/Rev.2 entitled Consolidated guidelines for State reports under the International Covenant on Civil and Political Rights. The guidelines were adopted during the sixty-sixth session (July 1999) of the Human Rights Committee and amended during its seventieth session (October 2000).

B.2 For subsequent periodic reports the Committee has adopted a practice of stating, at the end of its concluding observations, a date by which the following periodic report should be submitted.

C. General guidance for contents of all reports

C.1 The articles and the Committee's general comments. The terms of the articles in Parts I, II and III of the Covenant must, together with general comments issued by the Committee on any such article, be taken into account in preparing the report.

C.2 Reservations and declarations. Any reservation to or declaration as to any article of the Covenant by the State party should be explained and its continued maintenance justified.

C.3 Derogations. The date, extent and effect of, and procedures for imposing and for lifting any derogation under Article 4 should be fully explained in relation to every article of the Covenant affected by the derogation.

C.4 Factors and difficulties. Article 40 of the Covenant requires that factors and difficulties, if any, affecting the implementation of the Covenant should be indicated. A report should explain the nature and extent of, and reasons for every such factor and difficulty, if any such exist; and should give details of the steps being taken to overcome these.

C.5 Restrictions or limitations. Certain articles of the Covenant permit some defined restrictions or limitations on rights. Where these exist, their nature and extent should be set out.

C.6 Data and statistics. A report should include sufficient data and statistics to enable the Committee to assess progress in the enjoyment of Covenant rights, relevant to any appropriate article.

C.7 Article 3. The situation regarding the equal enjoyment of Covenant rights by men and women should be specifically addressed.

C.8 Core document. Where the State party has already prepared a core document, this will be available to the Committee: it should be updated as necessary in the report, particularly as regards "General legal framework" and "Information and publicity" (HRI/CORE/1, see chapter 1 of the present document).

D. The initial report

D.1 General

This report is the State party's first opportunity to present to the Committee the extent to which its laws and practices comply with the Covenant which it has ratified. The report should:

- Establish the constitutional and legal framework for the implementation of Covenant rights;
- Explain the legal and practical measures adopted to give effect to Covenant rights;
- Demonstrate the progress made in ensuring enjoyment of Covenant rights by the people within the State party and subject to its jurisdiction.

D.2 Contents of the report

D.2.1 A State party should deal specifically with every article in Parts I, II and III of the Covenant; legal norms should be described, but that is not sufficient: the factual situation and the practical availability, effect and implementation of remedies for violation of Covenant rights should be explained and exemplified.

D.2.2 The report should explain:

How Article 2 of the Covenant is applied, setting out the principal legal measures which the State party has taken to give effect to Covenant rights; and the range of remedies available to persons whose rights may have been violated;

Whether the Covenant is incorporated into domestic law in such a manner as to be directly applicable;

If not, whether its provisions can be invoked before and given effect to by courts, tribunals and administrative authorities;

Whether the Covenant rights are guaranteed in a Constitution or other laws and to what extent; or

Whether Covenant rights must be enacted or reflected in domestic law by legislation so as to be enforceable.

D.2.3 Information should be given about the judicial, administrative and other competent authorities having jurisdiction to secure Covenant rights.

D.2.4 The report should include information about any national or official institution or machinery which exercises responsibility in implementing Covenant rights or in responding to complaints of violations of such rights, and give examples of their activities in this respect.

D.3 Annexes to the report

D.3.1 The report should be accompanied by copies of the relevant principal constitutional, legislative and other texts which guarantee and provide remedies in relation to Covenant rights.

Such texts will not be copied or translated, but will be available to members of the Committee; it is important that the report itself contains sufficient quotations from or summaries of these texts so as to ensure that the report is clear and comprehensible without reference to the annexes.

E. Subsequent periodic reports

E.1 There should be two starting points for such reports:

The concluding observations (particularly "Concerns" and "Recommendations") on the previous report and summary records of the Committee's consideration (insofar as these exist);

An examination by the State party of the progress made towards and the current situation concerning the enjoyment of Covenant rights by persons within its territory or jurisdiction.

E.2 Periodic reports should be structured so as to follow the articles of the Covenant. If there is nothing new to report under any article it should be so stated.

E.3 The State party should refer again to the guidance on initial reports and on annexes, insofar as these may also apply to a periodic report.

E.4 There may be circumstances where the following matters should be addressed, so as to elaborate a periodic report: There may have occurred a fundamental change in the State party's political and legal approach affecting Covenant rights: in such a case a full article-by-article report may be required;

New legal or administrative measures may have been introduced which deserve the annexure of texts and judicial or other decisions.

F. Optional protocols

F.1 If the State party has ratified the Optional Protocol and the Committee has issued Views entailing provision of a remedy or expressing any other concern, relating to a communication received under that Protocol, a report should (unless the matter has been dealt with in a previous report) include information about the steps taken to provide a remedy, or meet such a concern, and to ensure that any circumstance thus criticized does not recur.

F.2 If the State party has abolished the death penalty the situation relating to the Second Optional Protocol should be explained.

G. The Committee's consideration of reports

G.1 General

The Committee intends its consideration of a report to take the form of a constructive discussion with the delegation, the aim of which is to improve the situation pertaining to Covenant rights in the State.

G.2 List of issues

On the basis of all information at its disposal, the Committee will supply in advance a list of issues which will form the basic agenda for consideration of the report. The delegation should come prepared to address the list of issues and to respond to further questions from members, with such updated information as may be necessary; and to do so within the time allocated for consideration of the report.

G.3 The State party's delegation

The Committee wishes to ensure that it is able effectively to perform its functions under Article 40 and that the reporting State party should obtain the maximum benefit from the page 30 reporting requirement. The State party's delegation should, therefore, include persons who, through their knowledge of and competence to explain the human rights situation in that State, are able to respond to the Committee's written and oral questions and comments concerning the whole range of Covenant rights.

G.4 Concluding observations

Shortly after the consideration of the report, the Committee will publish its concluding observations on the report and the ensuing discussion with the delegation. These concluding observations will be included in the Committee's annual report to the General Assembly; the Committee expects the State party to disseminate these conclusions, in all appropriate languages, with a view to public information and discussion.

G.5 Extra information

G.5.1 Following the submission of any report, subsequent revisions or updating may only be submitted:

(a) No later than 10 weeks prior to the date set for the Committee's consideration of the report (the minimum time required by the United Nations translation services); or, (b) After that date, provided that the text has been translated by the State party into the working languages of the Committee (currently English, Spanish and French).

If one or other of these courses is not complied with, the Committee will not be able to take an addendum into account. This, however, does not apply to updated annexes or statistics.

G.5.2 In the course of the consideration of a report, the Committee may request or the delegation may offer further information; the secretariat will keep a note of such matters which should be dealt with in the next report.

G.6.1 The Committee may, in a case where there has been a long-term failure by a State party, despite reminders, to submit an initial or a periodic report, announce its intention to examine the extent of compliance with Covenant rights in that State party at a specified future session. Prior to that session it will transmit to the State party appropriate material in its possession. The State party may send a delegation to the specified session, which may contribute to the Committee's discussion, but in any event the Committee may issue provisional concluding observations and set a date for the submission by the State party of a report of a nature to be specified.

G.6.2 In a case where a State party, having submitted a report which has been scheduled at a session for examination, informs the Committee, at a time when it is impossible to schedule the examination of another State party report, that its delegation will not attend the session, the Committee may examine the report on the basis of the list of issues either at that session or at another to be specified. In the absence of a delegation, it may decide either to reach provisional concluding observations, or to consider the report and other material and follow the course in paragraph G.4 above.

H. Format of the report

The distribution of a report, and thus its availability for consideration by the Committee, will be greatly facilitated if:

(a) The paragraphs are sequentially numbered;

(b) The document is written on A4-sized paper;

(c) Is single-spaced; and

(d) Allows reproduction by photo-offset (is on one side only of each sheet of paper).

Chapter IV
COMMITTEE ON THE ELIMINATION OF RACIAL DISCRIMINATION

1. In accordance with Article 9, paragraph 1, of the International Convention on the Elimination of All Forms of Racial Discrimination, each State party has undertaken to submit to the Secretary-General of the United Nations, for consideration by the Committee on the Elimination of Racial Discrimination, a report on the legislative, judicial, administrative or other measures which it has adopted and which give effect to the provisions of the Convention: (a) within one year after the entry into force of the Convention for the State concerned, and (b) thereafter every two years and whenever the Committee so requests. Article 9, paragraph 1, also provides that the Committee may request further information from the States parties.

2. In order to assist the Committee in fulfilling the tasks entrusted to it pursuant to Article 9 of the Convention and further to facilitate the task of States parties in the preparation of their reports, the Committee has decided that it would be useful to inform States parties of its wishes regarding the form and content of their reports. Compliance with these guidelines will help to ensure that reports are presented in a uniform manner and enable the Committee and States parties to obtain a complete picture of the situation in each State as regards the implementation of the provisions of the Convention. This will also reduce the need for the Committee to request further information under Article 9 and its rules of procedure.

3. It should also be noted, in this connection, that the Committee stated in its general recommendation II of 24 February 1972 that, since all the categories of information requested from States parties refer to obligations undertaken by States parties under the Convention, the Contained in document CERD/C/70/Rev.5, entitled, General guidelines regarding the form and the contents of reports to be submitted by the States parties under Article 9, paragraph 1, of the Convention. The present guidelines, adopted by the Committee on the Elimination of Racial Discrimination at its 475th meeting (twenty-fifth session) on 9 April 1980, reflect the additional guidelines adopted at the 571st (twenty-fifth session) on 17 March 1982 and the revisions adopted at its 984th meeting (forty-second session) on 13 March 1993. The revisions adopted in 1993 consisted of the insertion, under Part II, of a new paragraph concerning information on the ethnic characteristics of the country. It should be noted that the Committee, at its 913th meeting (thirty-ninth session) adopted a number of revisions to its general reporting guidelines, including the incorporation of former Part I, paragraph (a), under Part II and the deletion of former Part I, paragraph (c). The Committee's revision, adopted at its 1354th meeting (fifty-fifth session) on 16 August 1999, consisted of the insertion, under Part II, of a new paragraph concerning information on the situation of women. The Committee further amended former Part II, paragraph 10, related to reporting under Article 5 of the Convention. The Committee's revision, adopted at its 1429th meeting (fifty-seventh session) on 21 August 2000, consisted of adding references

to the general recommendations adopted by the Committee and eliminating the request for information on the status of relations with the racist regimes of southern Africa.

Those changes have been reflected in the present document.

Necessary information in conformity with these guidelines should be provided by all States parties without distinction, whether or not racial discrimination exists in their respective territories.

4. In selecting information for inclusion in their reports, States parties should bear in mind the definition of the term "racial discrimination" as reflected in Article 1, paragraph 1, of the Convention, as well as the provisions of Article 1, paragraphs 2, 3 and 4, which refer to situations not considered as racial discrimination.

5. The report should also reflect in all its parts the actual situation as regards the practical implementation of the provisions of the Convention and the progress achieved.

PART I. GENERAL

6. General information on the land and people, general political structure, general legal framework within which human rights are protected and information and publicity should be prepared in accordance with the consolidated guidelines for the initial part of reports of States parties to be submitted under the various international human rights instruments, as contained in document HRI/CORE/1 (see chapter I of the present document).

PART II. INFORMATION RELATING TO ARTICLES 2 TO 7 OF THE CONVENTION

7. Describe briefly the policy of eliminating racial discrimination in all its forms and the general legal framework within which racial discrimination as defined in Article 1, paragraph 1, of the Convention is prohibited and eliminated in the reporting State, and the recognition, enjoyment or exercise, on an equal footing, of human rights and fundamental freedoms in the political, economic, social, cultural or any other field of public life are promoted and protected.

8. The ethnic characteristics of the country are of particular importance in connection with the International Convention on the Elimination of All Forms of Racial Discrimination. Many States consider that, when conducting a census, they should not draw attention to factors like race lest this reinforce divisions they wish to overcome. If progress in eliminating discrimination based on race, colour, descent, national and ethnic origin is to be monitored, some indication is needed of the number of persons who could be treated less favourably on the basis of these characteristics. States which do not collect information on these characteristics in their censuses are therefore requested to provide information on mother tongues (as requested in paragraph 1 of HRI/CORE/1) as indicative of ethnic differences, together with any information about race, colour, descent, national and ethnic origins derived from social surveys. In the absence of quantitative information, a qualitative description of the ethnic characteristics of the population should be supplied. The remainder of this part should provide specific information in relation to articles 2 to 7, in accordance with the sequence of those articles and their respective provisions.

9. The inclusion of information on the situation of women is important for the Committee to consider whether racial discrimination has an impact upon women different from that upon men, in conformity with general recommendation XXV on gender-related dimensions of racial discrimination (2000). Reporting officers are asked to describe, as far as possible in quantitative and qualitative terms, factors affecting and difficulties experienced in ensuring for women the equal enjoyment, free from racial discrimination, of rights under the Convention. It is also difficult to protect against racial discrimination the rights of persons, both women and men, who belong to any vulnerable groups, such as indigenous peoples, migrants, and those in the lowest socio-economic categories. Members of such groups often experience complex forms of disadvantage which persist over generations and in which racial discrimination is mixed with other causes of social inequality. Reporting officers are asked to bear in mind the circumstances of such persons, and to cite any available social indictors of forms of disadvantage that may be linked with racial discrimination.

10. The Committee requests States parties to incorporate in this part, under the appropriate headings, the texts of the relevant laws, judicial decisions and regulations referred to therein, as well as all other elements which they consider essential for the Committee's consideration of their reports.

11. The information should be arranged as follows:

Article 2

A. Information on the legislative, judicial, administrative or other measures which give effect to the provisions of Article 2, paragraph 1, of the Convention, in particular:

1. Measures taken to give effect to the undertaking to engage in no act or practice of racial discrimination against persons, groups of persons or institutions and to ensure that all public authorities and public institutions, national and local, shall act in conformity with this obligation;

2. Measures taken to give effect to the undertaking not to sponsor, defend or support racial discrimination by any persons or organizations;

3. Measures taken to review governmental, national and local policies, and to amend, rescind or nullify any laws and regulations which have the effect of creating or perpetuating racial discrimination wherever it exists;

4. Measures taken to give effect to the undertaking to prohibit and bring to an end, by all appropriate means, including legislation as required by circumstances, racial discrimination by any persons, group or organization;

5. Measures taken to give effect to the undertaking to encourage, where appropriate, integrationist multiracial organizations and movements and other means of eliminating barriers between races, and to discourage anything which tends to strengthen racial division.

B. Information on the special and concrete measures taken in the social, economic, cultural and other fields to ensure the adequate development and protection of certain racial groups or individuals belonging to them, for the purpose of guaranteeing them the full and equal enjoyment of human rights and fundamental freedoms, in accordance with Article 2, paragraph 2, of the Convention.

Article 3

Information on the legislative, judicial, administrative or other measures which give effect to the provisions of Article 3 of the Convention, in particular, to the condemnation of racial segregation and apartheid and to the undertaking to prevent, prohibit and eradicate all practices of this nature in territories under the jurisdiction of the reporting State.

Article 4

A. Information on the legislative, judicial, administrative or other measures which give effect to the provisions of Article 4 of the Convention, in particular measures taken to give effect to the undertaking to adopt immediate and positive measures designed to eradicate all incitement to, or acts of, racial discrimination, in particular:

1. To declare an offence punishable by law all dissemination of ideas based on racial superiority or hatred, incitement to racial discrimination, as well as all acts of violence or incitement to such acts against any race or group of persons of another colour or ethnic origin, and also the provision of any assistance to racist activities, including the financing thereof;

2. To declare illegal and prohibit organizations, and also organized and all other propaganda activities, which promote and incite racial discrimination, and to recognize participation in such organizations or activities as an offence punishable by law;

3. Not to permit public authorities or public institutions, national or local, to promote or incite racial discrimination.

B. Information on appropriate measures taken to give effect to general recommendations I of 1972, VII of 1985 and XV of 1993, on Article 4 of the Convention, by which the Committee recommended that the States parties whose legislation was deficient in respect of the implementation of Article 4 should consider, in accordance with their national legislative procedures, the question of supplementing their legislation with provisions conforming to the requirements of Article 4 (a) and (b) of the Convention.

C. Information in response to Decision 3 (VII) adopted by the Committee on 4 May 1973 by which the Committee requested the States parties:

1. To indicate what specific penal internal legislation designed to implement the provisions of Article 4 (a) and (b) has been enacted in their respective countries and to transmit to the Secretary-General in one of the official languages the texts concerned, as well as such provisions of general penal law as must be taken into account when applying such specific legislation;

2. Where no such specific legislation has been enacted, to inform the Committee of the manner, and the extent to which the provisions of the existing penal laws, as applied by the courts, effectively implement their obligations under Article 4 (a) and (b), and to transmit to the Secretary-General in one of the official languages the texts of those provisions.

Article 5

Information on the legislative, judicial, administrative or other measures which give effect to the provisions of Article 5 of the Convention, taking into consideration general recommendations XX on Article 5 of the Convention (1996) and XXII regarding refugees and other displaced persons (1996), in particular, measures taken to prohibit racial discrimination in all its forms and to guarantee the right of everyone, without distinction as to race, colour, or national or ethnic origin, to equality before the law notably in the enjoyment of the rights listed.

The Committee will wish to ascertain to what extent all persons within the State's jurisdiction, and particularly members of vulnerable groups, enjoy these rights in practice free from racial discrimination. In many States there will be no quantitative data relevant to the enjoyment of these rights; in such circumstances it may be appropriate to report the opinions of representatives of disadvantaged groups.

A. The right to equal treatment before the tribunals and all other organs administering justice:

This part of the report is the place in which to provide any information on the training and supervision of law enforcement officials and judicial officers in the avoidance of racial discrimination, together with information on measures for the investigation of complaints.

B. The right to security of person and protection by the State against violence or bodily harm, whether inflicted by government officials or by any individual, group or institution:

Information on the incidence of racially motivated criminal offences, their investigation and punishment, should be reported in this section.

C. Political rights:

Information on the means for guaranteeing these rights, and on their enjoyment in practice, should be reported. For example, do members of indigenous peoples and persons of different ethnic or national origin exercise such rights to the same extent as the rest of the population? Are they proportionately represented in the legislature?

D. Other civil rights:

Certain of these rights (e.g. freedom of expression and assembly) have at times to be balanced against the right to protection from racial discrimination. Any problems in this connection should be reported.

E. Economic, social and cultural rights, in particular:

1. The right to work, and

2. The right to form and join trade unions.

Circumstances vary greatly between different regions of the world, but it will help the Committee if at this point the report can (a) briefly describe employment in the State, in what industries, public or private, and whether persons of different ethnic or national origin are concentrated in particular forms of employment, or are unemployed; (b) describe governmental action to prevent racial discrimination in the enjoyment of the right to work; (c) indicate the extent to which these rights are enjoyed in practice.

3. The right to housing.

It will help the Committee if the report can (a) describe the housing markets in the State, public and private, owner-occupied or rented, and whether ethnic groups are concentrated in particular sectors or tend to concentrate in particular localities; (b) describe governmental action to prevent racial discrimination by those who rent or sell houses or apartments; (c) indicate the extent to which the right to housing without discrimination is enjoyed in practice.

4. The right to public health, medical care, social security and social services. Different ethnic groups within the population may have different needs for health and social services. It will help the Committee if the report can (a) describe any such differences; (b) describe governmental action to secure the equal provision of these services.

5. The right to education and training.

It will help the Committee if the report can (a) indicate any variations in the levels of educational and training attainment between members of different ethnic groups; (b) describe governmental action to prevent racial discrimination in the enjoyment of these rights, bearing in mind the Committee's general recommendation XIX.

6. The right to equal participation in cultural activities.

In some countries it may be appropriate to report on access to sporting facilities and on the prevention of ethnic hostility in competitive sports. Since the adoption of the Convention in 1965 many countries have experienced a great increase in the power of the mass media (press, radio, television) to shape popular images of other ethnic groups and to report on events in ways that may promote either peaceful relations or racial hatred. Negative images can hinder equal participation in all fields of public life. Governmental oversight of any such tendencies may be described in this section of a State report.

7. The right of access to places of service.

In many countries complaints are voiced about racial discrimination that denies the right of access to any place or service intended for use by the general public, such as transport, hotels, restaurants, cafés, theatres and parks. Governmental action to prevent such discrimination, and its effectiveness, should be described here.

Article 6

A. Information on the legislative, judicial, administrative or other measures which give effect to the provisions of Article 6 of the Convention, in particular, measures taken to assure to everyone within the jurisdiction of the reporting State effective protection and remedies, through the competent national tribunals and other State institutions, against any acts of racial discrimination which violate his human rights and fundamental freedoms;

B. Measures taken to assure to everyone the right to seek from such tribunals just and adequate reparation or satisfaction for any damage as a result of such discrimination;

C. Information on the practice and decisions of the courts and other judicial and administrative organs relating to cases of racial discrimination as defined under Article 1 of the Convention;

D. Information in connection with general recommendation XXVI on Article 6 of the Convention (2000).

Article 7

Information on the legislative, judicial, administrative or other measures which give effect to the provisions of Article 7 of the Convention, to general recommendation V of 13 April 1977 and to decision 2 (XXV) of 17 March 1982, by which the Committee adopted its additional guidelines for the implementation of Article 7.

In particular, the reports should provide as much information as possible on each of the main subjects mentioned in Article 7 under the following separate headings:

A. Education and teaching;

B. Culture;

C. Information.

Within these broad parameters, the information provided should reflect the measures taken by the States parties:

1. To combat prejudices which lead to racial discrimination;

2. To promote understanding, tolerance and friendship among nations and racial and ethnic groups.

A. Education and teaching

This part should describe legislative and administrative measures, including some general information on the educational system, taken in the field of education and teaching to combat racial prejudices which lead to racial discrimination. It should indicate whether any steps have been taken to include in school curricula and in the training of teachers and other professionals, programmes and subjects to help promote human rights issues which would lead to better understanding, tolerance and friendship among nations and racial or ethnic groups. It should also provide information on whether the purposes and principles of the Charter of the United Nations, the Universal Declaration of Human Rights, the United Nations Declaration on the Elimination of All Forms of Racial Discrimination and the International Convention on the Elimination of All Forms of Racial Discrimination are included in education and teaching.

B. Culture

Information should be provided in this part of the report on the role of institutions or associations working to develop national culture and traditions, to combat racial prejudices and to promote intra-national and intra-cultural understanding, tolerance and friendship among nations and racial or ethnic groups. Information should also be included on the work of solidarity committees or United Nations Associations to combat racism and racial discrimination and the observance by States parties of Human Rights Days or campaigns against racism and apartheid.

C. Information

This part should provide information:

(a) On the role of State media in the dissemination of information to combat racial prejudices which lead to racial discrimination and to inculcate better understanding of the purposes and principles of the above-mentioned instruments;

(b) On the role of the mass information media, i.e. the press, radio and television, in the publicizing of human rights and disseminating information on the purposes and principles of the above-mentioned human rights instruments.

12. If needed, the reports should be accompanied by sufficient copies in one of the working languages (English, French, Russian or Spanish) of all other supplementary documentation which the reporting States may wish to have distributed to all members of the Committee in connection with their reports.

13. On the basis of reports already submitted and those prepared and submitted according to the above guidelines, the Committee is confident that it will be enabled to develop or continue a constructive and fruitful dialogue with each State party for the purpose of the implementation of the Convention and thereby to contribute to mutual understanding and peaceful and friendly relations among nations in accordance with the Charter of the United Nations.

Chapter V

COMMITTEE ON THE ELIMINATION OF DISCRIMINATION AGAINST WOMEN

A. Introduction

A.1. These guidelines replace all earlier reporting guidelines issued by the Committee on the Elimination of Discrimination against Women (CEDAW/C/7/Rev.3), which may now be disregarded. The present guidelines do not affect the Committee's procedure in relation to any exceptional reports which may be requested which are governed by the Rule 48.5 of the Committee's Rules of Procedure and its Decision 21/I on exceptional reports.

A.2. These guidelines will be effective for all reports to be submitted after 31 December 2002.

A.3. The guidelines should be followed by States parties in the preparation of initial and all subsequent periodic reports.

A.4. Compliance with these guidelines will reduce the need for the Committee to request further information when it proceeds to consider a report; it will also help the Committee to consider the situation regarding human rights in every State party on an equal basis.

B. Framework of the Convention concerning reports

B.1. Every State party, upon ratifying or acceding to the Convention, undertakes, under Article 18, to submit, within a year of the Convention's entry into force for that State, an initial report on the legislative, judicial, administrative or other measures it has adopted to give effect to the provisions of the Convention and progress made in this respect; and thereafter periodic reports at least every four years and further whenever the Committee so requests.

C. General guidance for contents of all reports

C.1. The articles and the Committee's general recommendations. The terms of the articles in Parts I, II, III and IV of the Convention must, together with general recommendations adopted by the Committee on any such article, or on a theme addressed by the Convention, be taken into account in preparing the report.

C.2. Reservations and declarations. Any reservation to or declaration as to any article of the Convention by the State party should be explained and its continued maintenance justified. Taking account of the Committee's statement on reservations adopted at its nineteenth session (see A/53/38/Rev.1, part two, chap. I, sect. A), the precise effect of any reservation or declaration in terms of national law and policy should be explained. States parties that have entered general reservations which do not refer to a specific article, or which are directed at articles 2 and/or 3 should report on the effect and the interpretation of those reservations. States parties should provide information on any reservations or declarations they may have lodged with regard to similar obligations in other human rights treaties.

C.3. Factors and difficulties. Article 18.2 of the Convention provides that factors and difficulties affecting the degree of fulfilment of obligations under the Convention may be indicated. A report should explain the nature and extent of, and reasons for every such factor and difficulty, if any such exist; and should give details of the steps being taken to overcome them.

C.4. Data and statistics. A report should include sufficient data and statistics disaggregated by sex relevant to each article and the general recommendations of the Committee to enable it to assess progress in the implementation of the Convention.

C.5. Core document. Where the State party has already prepared a core document, this will be available to the Committee. It should be updated as necessary in the report, particularly as regards "General legal framework" and "Information and publicity" (HRI/CORE/1, annex).

D. The initial report
D.1. General
D.1.1. This report is the State party's first opportunity to present to the Committee the extent to which its laws and practices comply with the Convention which it has ratified. The report should:

(a) Establish the constitutional, legal and administrative framework for the implementation of the Convention;

(b) Explain the legal and practical measures adopted to give effect to the provisions of the Convention;

(c) Demonstrate the progress made in ensuring enjoyment of the provisions of the Convention by the people within the State party and subject to its jurisdiction.

D.2. Contents of the report
D.2.1. A State party should deal specifically with every article in Parts I, II, III and IV of the Convention; legal norms should be described, but that is not sufficient: the factual situation and the practical availability, effect and implementation of remedies for violation of provisions of the Convention should be explained and exemplified.

D.2.2. The report should explain:

(1) Whether the Convention is directly applicable in domestic law on ratification, or has been incorporated into the national Constitution or domestic law so as to be directly applicable;

(2) Whether the provisions of the Convention are guaranteed in a Constitution or other laws and to what extent; or if not, whether its provisions can be invoked before and given effect to by courts, tribunals and administrative authorities;

(3) How Article 2 of the Convention is applied, setting out the principal legal measures which the State party has taken to give effect to Convention rights; and the range of remedies available to persons whose rights may have been violated.

D.2.3. Information should be given about the judicial, administrative and other competent authorities having jurisdiction with respect to the implementation of the provisions of the Convention.

D.2.4. The report should include information about any national or official institution or machinery which exercises responsibility in implementing the provisions of the Convention or in responding to complaints of violations of those provisions, and give examples of their activities in this respect.

D.2.5. The report should outline any restrictions or limitations, even of a temporary nature, imposed by law, practice or tradition, or in any other manner on the enjoyment of each provision of the Convention.

D.2.6. The report should describe the situation of non-governmental organizations and women's associations and their participation in the implementation of the Convention and the preparation of the report.

D.3. Annexes to the report
D.3.1. The report should contain sufficient quotations from or summaries of the relevant principal constitutional, legislative and other texts which guarantee and provide remedies in relation to Convention rights.

D.3.2. The reports should be accompanied by these texts, which will not be translated or copied, but will be made available to the Committee.

E. Subsequent periodic reports
E.1. In general, the subsequent periodic reports of States parties should focus on the period between the consideration of their previous report and the presentation of the current reports.

There should be two starting points for such reports:

(a) The concluding comments (particularly "Concerns" and "Recommendations") on the previous report;

(b) An examination by the State party of the progress made towards and the current implementation of the Convention within its territory or jurisdiction and the enjoyment of its provisions by those within its territory or jurisdiction.

E.2. Periodic reports should be structured so as to follow the articles of the Convention. If there is nothing new to report under any article, it should be so stated. Periodic reports should also highlight any remaining obstacle to the participation of women on an equal basis with men in the political, social, economic and cultural life of the State party.

E.3. The State party should refer again to the guidance on initial reports and on annexes, insofar as these may also apply to periodic reports.

E.4. There may be circumstances where the following matters should be addressed:

(a) A fundamental change may have occurred in the State party's political and legal approach affecting Convention implementation: in such a case a full article-by-article report may be required;

(b) New legal or administrative measures may have been introduced which require the annexure of texts, and judicial or other decisions.

F. Optional Protocol

F.1. If the State party has ratified or acceded to the Optional Protocol and the Committee has issued Views entailing provision of a remedy or expressing any other concern, relating to a communication received under that Protocol, a report should include information about the steps taken to provide a remedy, or meet such a concern, and to ensure that any circumstance giving rise to the communication does not recur.

F.2. If the State party has ratified or acceded to the Optional Protocol and the Committee has conducted an inquiry under Article 8 of the Optional Protocol, a report should include details of any measures taken in response to an inquiry, and to ensure that the violations giving rise to the inquiry do not recur.

G. Measures to implement outcomes of United Nations conferences, summits and reviews

G.1. In the light of paragraph 323 of the Beijing Platform for Action, adopted at the Fourth World Conference on Women, in September 1995, initial and subsequent reports of States parties should contain information on the implementation of the actions to be taken in regard to the 12 critical areas of concern identified in the Platform. Reports should also contain information on the implementation of the Further actions and initiatives to implement the Beijing Declaration and Platform for Action agreed by the twenty-third special session of the General Assembly, "Women 2000: gender equality, development and peace for the twenty-first session" in June 2000.

G.2. Taking into account the gender dimensions of declarations, platforms and programmes of action adopted by relevant United Nations conferences, summits and special sessions of the General Assembly (such as the World Conference against Racism, Racial Discrimination, Xenophobia and Related Intolerance and the Second World Assembly on Ageing), reports should include information on the implementation of specific aspects of these documents which relate to specific articles of the Convention in the light of the subjects with which they deal (for example, migrant women or older women).

H. The Committee's consideration of reports

H.1. General

H.1.1. The Committee intends its consideration of a report to take the form of a constructive discussion with the delegation, the aim of which is to improve the situation pertaining to Convention rights in the State.

H.2. List of issues and questions with respect to periodic reports

H.2.1. On the basis of all information at its disposal, the Committee will supply in advance a list of issues or questions which will form the basic agenda for consideration of periodic reports.

Written answers to the list of issues of questions will be required from the State party several months in advance of the session at which the report will be considered. The delegation should come prepared to address the list of issues and to respond to further questions from members, with such updated information as may be necessary; and to do so within the time allocated for consideration of the report.

H.3. The State party's delegation

H.3.1. The Committee wishes to ensure that it is able effectively to perform its functions under Article 18 and that the reporting State party should obtain the maximum benefit from the reporting requirement. The State party's delegation should therefore include persons who, through their knowledge of and competence to explain the human rights situation in that State, are able to respond to the Committee's written and oral questions and comments concerning the whole range of the Convention's provisions.

H.4. Concluding comments

H.4.1. Shortly after the consideration of the report, the Committee will publish its concluding comments on the report and the constructive dialogue with the delegation. These concluding comments will be included in the Committee's annual report to the General Assembly; the Committee expects the State party to disseminate these conclusions, in all appropriate languages, with a view to public information and discussion.

H.5. Extra information

H.5.1. In the course of its consideration of a report, the Committee may request, or the delegation may offer, further information; the secretariat will keep a note of such matters, which should be dealt with in the subsequent report.

I. Format of the report

I.1. Reports should be submitted in one of the six official languages of the United Nations (Arabic, Chinese, English, French, Spanish or Russian). They should be submitted in hard and electronic form.

I.2. Reports should be as concise as possible. Initial reports should be no more than 100 pages; periodic reports should be no more than 70 pages.

I.3. Paragraphs should be sequentially numbered.

I.4. The document should be on A4-sized paper; and presented in single-spaced format.

I.5. The document should be printed on one side of each sheet of paper so as to allow for reproduction by photo-offset.

Chapter VI
COMMITTEE AGAINST TORTURE
A. Initial reports
PART I. INFORMATION OF A GENERAL NATURE

This part should:

(a) Describe briefly the general legal framework within which torture as defined in Article 1, paragraph 1, of the Convention as well as other cruel, inhuman or degrading treatment or punishment are prohibited and eliminated in the reporting State;

(b) Indicate whether the reporting State is a party to an international instrument or had national legislation which does or may contain provisions of wider application than those provided for under the Convention;

(c) Indicate what judicial, administrative or other competent authorities have jurisdiction over matters dealt with in the Convention and provide information on cases actually dealt with by those authorities during the reporting period;

(d) Describe briefly the actual situation as regards the practical implementation of the Convention in the reporting State and indicate any factors and difficulties affecting the degree of fulfillment of the obligations of the reporting State under the Convention.

PART II. INFORMATION IN RELATION TO EACH OF THE ARTICLES IN PART I OF THE CONVENTION

This part should provide specific information relating to the implementation by the reporting State of articles 2 to 16 of the Convention, in accordance with the sequence of those articles and their respective provisions. It should include in relation to the provisions of each article:

(a) The legislative, judicial, administrative or other measures in force which give effect to those provisions;

(b) Any factors or difficulties affecting the practical implementation of those provisions;

(c) Any information on concrete cases and situations where measures giving effect to those provisions have been enforced including any relevant statistical data contained in CAT/C/4/Rev.2 entitled General guidelines regarding the form and content of initial reports to be submitted by States parties under Article 19, paragraph 1, of the Convention.

The guidelines were adopted by the Committee at its 82nd meeting (sixth session) on 26 April 1991. The report should be accompanied by sufficient copies in one of the working languages (English, French, Russian or Spanish) of the principal legislative and other texts referred to in the report. These will be made available to members of the Committee. It should be noted, however, that they will not be reproduced for general distribution with the report. It is desirable therefore that, when a text is not actually quoted in or annexed to the report itself, the report should contain sufficient information to be understood without reference to it. The text of national legislative provisions relevant to the implementation of the Convention should be quoted in the report.

B. Periodic reports

Periodic reports by States parties should be presented in three parts, as follows:

PART I. INFORMATION ON NEW MEASURES AND NEW DEVELOPMENTS RELATING TO THE IMPLEMENTATION OF THE CONVENTION FOLLOWING THE ORDER OF ARTICLES 1 TO 16, AS APPROPRIATE

(a) This part should describe in detail:

(i) Any new measures taken by the State party to implement the Convention during the period extending from the date of submission of its previous report to the date of submission of the periodic report to be considered by the Committee;

(ii) Any new developments which have occurred during the same period and are relevant to implementation of the Convention;

(b) The State party should provide, in particular, information concerning:

(i) Any change in the legislation and in institutions that affect the implementation of the Convention on any territory under its jurisdiction in particular on places of detention and on training given to law enforcement and medical personnel;

(ii) Any new case law of relevance for the implementation of the Convention; contained in CAT/C/14/Rev.1 entitled General guidelines regarding the form and content of periodic reports to be submitted by States parties under Article 19, paragraph 1, of the Convention, which were adopted by the Committee against Torture at its 85th meeting (sixth session) on 30 April 1991 and revised at its 318th meeting (twentieth session) on 18 May 1998.

(iii) Complaints, inquiries, indictments, proceedings, sentences, reparation and compensation for acts of torture and other cruel, inhuman or degrading treatment or punishment;

(iv) Any difficulty which would prevent the State party from fully discharging the obligations it has assumed under the Convention.

PART II. ADDITIONAL INFORMATION REQUESTED BY THE COMMITTEE

This part should contain any information requested by the Committee and not provided by the State party, during the Committee's consideration of the State party's preceding report. If the information has been provided by the State party, either in a subsequent communication or in an additional report submitted in accordance with rule 67, paragraph 2, of the Committee's rules of procedure, the State party does not need to repeat it.

PART III. COMPLIANCE WITH THE COMMITTEE'S CONCLUSIONS AND RECOMMENDATIONS

This part should provide information on measures taken by the State party to comply with the conclusions and recommendations addressed to it by the Committee at the end of its consideration of the State party's initial and periodic reports.

[Footnotes omitted]

DOCUMENT 14

Full Official Title: International Human Rights Instruments—Core document forming part of the reports of States parties—United States

Short Title/Acronym/Abbreviation: U.S. Core Report for all U.N. periodic human rights reports

Subject: U.S. periodic states human rights reports in the U.N.

Official Citation: U.N. Doc HRI/CORE/USA/2005

Date of Document: January 16, 2006

Date of Adoption: Not applicable

Date of General Entry into Force (EIF): Not applicable

Number of States Parties as of this printing: Not applicable

Date of Signature by the United States: Not applicable

Date of Ratification/Accession/Adhesion: Not applicable

Date of Entry into Force as to United States (effective date): Not applicable

Type of Document: Updated core document forming part of the reports of the U.S. to human rights treaty bodies for periodic reports

Legal Status/Character of the Instrument/Document as to the United States: Not legally binding. This document is incorporated into each periodic report submitted to a U.N. treaty monitoring body such as the Human Rights Committee. It is mostly basic background information about the U.S. to be considered in reviewing the U.S periodic reports.

Supervising Body: Every treaty-based supervising U.N. human rights body

Comments: Rather than repeating this information in every periodic report submitted by the U.S. to a U.N. treaty monitoring body, the U.S. has prepared a one-size-fits-all document with background information on the U.S., to be incorporated therein.

U.S. Core Report for All U.N. Periodic Human Rights Reports (Excerpts)

I. LAND AND PEOPLE

A. Population

1. When the most recent national census was completed in 2000, the population of the United States of America had reached 281.4 million, a 13.2 percent increase from the 1990 census population of 248.7 million. The Census Bureau estimates the current population to be 293,655,404 (July 1, 2004), which represents a growth of 12,233,498 since the April 1, 2000 Census. This growth corresponds to a 4.3 percent increase in the size of the U.S. population. By the year 2010, the United States population is expected to be 308,935,581. Population growth varied significantly by region in the 1990's, with higher rates in the West and South and much lower rates in the Midwest and Northeast.

2. State population growth for the 1990s ranged from a high of 66 percent in Nevada to a low of 0.5 percent in North Dakota. This decade was the only one in the 20th century in which all states gained population.

3. Females outnumber males, comprising 50.9 percent of the population. The median age of all people increased from 32.9 in 1990 to 35.3 in 2000, reflecting a change in age distribution toward the older ages within the age range 18 to 64 with 25.7 percent under the age of 18, 61.9 percent age 18 to 64, and 12.4 percent age 65 and over. Population by selected age groups for the United States and regions: (See below)

4. The United States is home to a wide variety of ethnic and racial groups; indeed, virtually every national, racial, ethnic, cultural and religious group in the world is represented in its population. According to Census 2000, 97.6 percent of all respondents (274,595,678) reported only one race. The largest group reported White alone, accounting for 75 percent of all people living in the United States. The Black or African American alone population represented 12 percent of the total. Just under 1 percent of all respondents indicated only American Indian and Alaska Native. Approximately 4 percent of all respondents indicated only Asian. The smallest race group was the Native Hawaiian and Other Pacific Islander alone population, representing 0.1 percent of the total population. The remainder of the "one race" respondents—5.5 percent of all respondents—indicated only the "Some other race alone" category which consists predominately (97.0 percent) of people of Hispanic origin, and is not a standard Office of Management and Budget race category. 2.4 percent of all respondents reported two or more races.

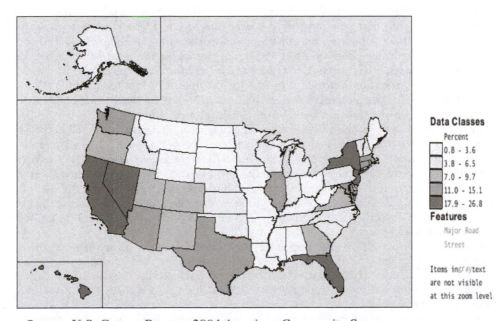

Data Classes

Percent
- 0.8 - 3.6
- 3.8 - 6.5
- 7.0 - 9.7
- 11.0 - 15.1
- 17.9 - 26.8

Features

Major Road
Street

Items in gray text are not visible at this zoom level

Source: U.S. Census Bureau, 2004 American Community Survey.

5. According to the American Community Survey (ACS), in 2004, the foreign-born population was estimated as 34.3 million (or 12.0 percent of the total U.S. household population). The foreign-born population is located throughout the United States. The following map shows the percent of the foreign-born population based on each state's total population. Percent of the people who are foreign born: 2004

6. Within the foreign-born population, 42 percent are naturalized U.S. citizens. About one-in-five entered the United States since 2000. The foreign-born population comes to the United States from all over the world: 54.8 percent were born in the Americas (9.2 percent in the Caribbean, 36.3 percent in Central America, 6.7 percent in South America, and 2.4 percent in Northern America), 30.0 percent were born in Asia, 14.3 percent were born in Europe, 3.3 percent were born in Africa, and 0.6 percent were born in Oceania.

7. The foreign-born population includes naturalized U.S. citizens, legal permanent migrants, temporary migrants (e.g., students), humanitarian migrants (e.g., refugees), and people illegally present in the United States (i.e., unauthorized migrants).

8. Direct estimates of the unauthorized population are not available. Generally, estimates of this population are derived using multiple data sources such as censuses, surveys, and administrative records. Recent efforts have yielded estimates of a residual population that include the unauthorized as well as "quasi-legal" migrants—people who are legally present in the United States, but who have not obtained legal permanent resident (LPR) status.

9. This residual foreign-born population was estimated to be about 3.8 million in 1990 and about 8.7 million in 2000. The residual foreign born were less likely to be male (48 percent) in 1990 than in 2000 (54 percent). Of the residual foreign born, about 27 percent were from Mexico in 1990 and about 47 percent were from Mexico in 2000.

10. Nearly four-fifths (79 percent) of all people in the United States live in urban areas, with "urban" defined as densely populated clusters of 2,500 or more residents.

11. English is the predominant language of the United States. In 2004, of approximately 266 million people aged 5 and over, some 50 million (approximately 19 percent) spoke a language other than English at home. Thirty-one million people spoke Spanish; 7.6 million spoke an Asian or Pacific Island language. Based on data from 2003, French and German were among the next most common. Twenty-two million people in 2004 indicated they did not speak English "very well." The highest percentages of non-English speakers were found in the States of California, New Mexico, and Texas.

B. Vital statistics

12. According to 1999 figures, overall life expectancy in the United States was 76.7 years. Women tend to live longer than men, with a life expectancy of 79.4 years, compared with 73.9 years for men. Whites have a longer life expectancy than minorities. For example, the life expectancy for Whites is 77.3 years, but for African Americans it is only 71.4. From 1998 to 1999, life expectancy has increased for males, but decreased for females. For Black males, it has increased from 67.6 to 67.8 and for White males from 74.5 to 74.6. For Black females, life expectancy has decreased from 74.8 to 74.7 and for White females from 80.0 to 79.9. Overall, the largest gains in life expectancy between 1980 and 1999 were for Black males (4.0 years), White males (3.9 years), Black females (2.2 years), and White females (1.8 years).

13. The total fertility rate for the United States, according to 2000 figures, was 2,130 births per 1,000 women aged 10–49. In other words, women in the United States on average have 2.1 births over the course of their child-bearing years. This is statistically equivalent to the replacement level of 2.1. Over the decade of the 1990s, there has been a convergence between the fertility rate of White women and Black women. In 2000, the total fertility rate of White women was 2,114 births per 1,000 compared with 2,193 births per 1,000 for Black women. In 1990, Black women had a total fertility rate which averaged about 0.5 births per woman higher than that of White women. Overall, one-third (33 percent) of all births in the United States in 2000 were to unmarried women.

14. In 1999, a total of 2,391,399 deaths occurred in the United States, at an age-adjusted rate of 881.9 deaths per 100,000 population. The 1999 rate was the second lowest rate ever. Life expectancy at birth was 76.7 years, the same as the record high achieved in 1998. The infant mortality rate was 7.1 infant deaths per 1,000 live births. This rate continues to trend downward although single year changes have not been statistically different for several years. Gaps between men and women continue to narrow with the age-adjusted death rate for men 1.4 times greater than women and life expectancy for men lagging behind that for women by 5.5 years. Gaps between the Black and White populations persist with age-adjusted death rates 1.3 times

greater, infant mortality rates 2.5 times greater, and maternal mortality 3.7 times greater for the Black population than that for the White population. Life expectancy for the White population exceeds that for the Black population by 5.9 years continuing the trend toward convergence in life expectancy and age-adjusted death rates.

15. Survey data for 2004 indicated that there were 112 million households in the United States, of which 68 percent contained families. However, married couples with children under 18 make up only 23 percent of all households. In recent decades, owing to increases in divorce and single-parenthood, more children are living with only one parent. Among all children under age 18, 28 percent lived with a single parent in 2004, more than double the 12 percent of children who lived with only one parent in 1970. Most children who live with one parent live with their mother. For instance, in 2004 approximately 83 percent of children who lived with one parent lived with their mother. The proportion of children living with one parent varies according to race. Among children under 18, 22 percent of White children lived with one parent, whereas 56 percent of African-American children, 14 percent of Asian children, and 31 percent of Hispanic children lived with one parent. Children in every group were far more likely to live with their mother than their father. Among children living with their mother or father only, 80 percent of White children, 90 percent of African-American children, 86 percent of Asian children, and 83 percent of Hispanic children lived with their mother. In total, approximately 4 percent of children under 18 live with a relative other than their parents or with a non-relative.

Source: 2004 Annual Social and Economic Supplement to the Current Population Survey.

See tables at <http://www.census.gov/population/www/socdemo/hh-fam/cps2004.html>.

16. In 1998, it was estimated that there were 2,256,000 marriages in the United States, at a rate of 8.4 per 1,000 population. Also, there were 1,135,000 divorces, at a rate of 4.2 per 1,000 population. In both cases, the totals were slightly lower than in 1997.

Statistics on women in the workforce

17. The Women's Bureau of the U.S. Department of Labor provides information on a variety of subjects relating to women in the labor force. These include statistics on the number of women in the labor force, their occupational and industrial characteristics, their labor force participation by race and educational attainment, their self-employment, and their earnings; quick facts on women in non-traditional jobs, women in nursing, and older women workers; and fact sheets on hot jobs for the 21st Century, women business owners, and women in high-tech jobs. The statistical data is compiled from Bureau of Labor Statistics reports and is 2004 data unless otherwise noted.

18. *Population*. There are 115,647,000 women compared to 107,710,000 men in the civilian non-institutional population, 16 years or older.

19. *Civilian Labor Force*. This labor force is comprised of 68,421,000 women (59.2% of the civilian population of women age 16 and over) compared with 78,980,000 men (73.3% of the civilian population of men). Women make up 46.4% of the civilian labor force.

20. *Employment, Unemployment.* 64,728,000 women are employed (56% of pop.), and 3,694,000 are unemployed. The unemployment rate for women was 5.4%, and for men, 5.6%.

21. *Full-Time/Part-Time Employment*. 48,073,000 women worked full time (74.3% of all employed women) and 16,654,000 women worked part time (25.7%). 66,444,000 men worked full time (89.2%) and 8,080,000 worked part time (10.8%).

22. *Occupations with the most women employed.* In 2004, the seven occupations in which the largest numbers of women were employed (with the median weekly earnings and estimated annual earnings [weekly earnings x 52 weeks] for women who were full-time wage and salary workers) were as follows:

- *Secretaries and administrative assistants*—3,413,000 women employed; $550 weekly, estimated $28,600 annual earnings.
- *Elementary and middle school teachers*—2,097,000 women employed; $776 weekly, estimated $40,352 annual earnings.
- *Registered Nurses*—2,271,000 women; $895 weekly, estimated $46,540 annual earnings.
- *Nursing, psychiatric and home health aides*—1,614,000 women; $383 weekly, estimated $19,916 annual earnings.
- *Cashiers*—2,261,000 women; $313 weekly, estimated $16,276 annual earnings.
- *First-line supervisors/managers of office and administrative support*—1,001,000 women; $636 weekly, estimated $33,072 annual earnings.

- *First-line supervisors/managers of retail sales workers*—985,000 women; $505 weekly, estimated $26,260 annual earnings.
  - *Retail salespersons*—1,591,000 women; $386 weekly, estimated $20,072 annual earnings.
  - *Bookkeeping, accounting, and auditing clerks*—1,439,000 women; $542 weekly, estimated $28,184 annual earnings.

23. *Occupations with highest earnings for women*. In 2004, the seven occupations in which at least 50,000 women were employed and where women received their highest median weekly earnings were as follows:

- *Pharmacists*—$1,432, with estimated annual earnings of $74,464. There were 110,000 women pharmacists, 47.2 percent of a total 233,000 pharmacists.
- *Chief Executives*—$1,310, with estimated annual earnings of $68,120. There were 392,000 women chief executives, 23.3 percent of a total of 1,680,000 chief executives.
- *Lawyers*—$1,255, with estimated annual earnings of $65,260. There were 280,000 women lawyers, 29.4 percent of a total of 954,000 lawyers.
- *Computer and Information Systems Managers*—$1,228, with estimated annual earnings of $63,856. There were 104,000 women employed as computer and information systems managers, 30.9 percent of a total of 337,000 computer and information systems managers.
- *Computer Software Engineers*—$1,149, with estimated annual earnings of $59,748. There were 204,000 women employed as computer software engineers, 25.1 percent of 813,000 computer software engineers.
- *Computer Programmers*—$1,006, with estimated annual earnings of $52,312. There were 151,000 women employed as computer programmers, 26.8 percent of a total of 564,000 computer programmers.
- *Physicians and Surgeons*—$978, with estimated annual earnings of $50,856. There were 244,000 women physicians and surgeons, 29.4 percent of 830,000 physicians.

24. *Families maintained by women*. There were 76,741,000 primary families and unrelated subfamilies in the United States in March 2004, of which 14,196,000 were families maintained by women, 18.5 percent or slightly less than 1 out of 5 families. Between 2002 and 2004 the number of households headed by women increased by 679,000 (5.0 percent).

25. *Working Mothers*. In 2004, 62.2 percent of mothers with children under six were in the labor force, down from 64.1 percent in 2002. The labor force participation of mothers with children under six has declined since 2000. The total number of women with children under six in the labor force in 2004, 10,131,000, was less than the 10,193,000 mothers in 2002, consistent with the fact that the number of mothers with children under six has been declining since peak levels in 1994. In 2004, 57.3 percent of mothers with children under three were in the labor force (5,401,000 mothers), compared with 60.5 percent (5,600,000 mothers) in 2002.

C. Socio-economic indicators

26. For 2004, the per capita money income in the United States was $23,848 in current dollars. Median money earnings in 2004 for full-time, year-round workers was $40,798 for males compared with $31,223 for females. The gross domestic product (GDP) in billions of current dollars was $11,734 for 2004. The Consumer Price Index, frequently used to measure inflation, increased by 2.3 percent in 2003 and 2.7 percent in 2004.

27. In 2004, 66 percent of the population 16 years and older was in the labor force (totalling 147,401,000), including approximately 25.7 million mothers in the labor force. The overall unemployment rate was 5.5 percent. For men, the figure was 5.6 percent, compared with 5.4 percent for women. Whites' rate of unemployment was 4.8 percent, African-Americans' rate was 10.4 percent, and Hispanics' rate was 7.0 percent. The minimum wage in 2004 was $5.15 an hour.

28. In 2004, 12.7 percent of the population was below the poverty level, the federally established figure below which a person is considered to have insufficient income for his or her basic needs. For a family of four in 2004, this was equal to $19,307. Of all families headed by females, 28.4 percent were below the poverty level. The poverty rate for White, Black and Hispanic families headed by women was respectively, 24.8 percent, 37.6 percent and 38.9 percent. Among related children under 18, 17.3 percent lived in poverty. The rate for related children under six was 19.9 percent.

29. The poverty rate in 2004 varied among racial groups in the United States. While 10.8 percent of Whites (8.6 percent when Hispanics are not included) were below the poverty level, 24.7 percent of Blacks, 21.9 percent of Hispanics and 9.8 percent of Asians fell below the poverty level. Among the poor in 2003, 68.0 percent lived in a household where someone received means-tested assistance (cash or noncash), and 22.6 percent lived in a household where someone received means-tested cash assistance.

30. In 2004, 85.2 percent of the population aged 25 and over had a high school diploma, 53.1 percent had some college or more, and 27.7 percent had a bachelor's degree. Males and females achieved similar levels of education, the primary difference being that 29.4 percent of males versus 26.1 percent of females received a bachelor's degree. Education levels differed more widely, however, on the basis of race. Rates for completing high school and college were 90.0 percent and 30.6 percent for non-Hispanic Whites, versus 80.6 percent and 17.6 percent for the Black population, and 58.4 percent and 12.1 percent for Hispanics. In 2004, 66.7 percent of the most recent graduates of high school had enrolled in colleges and universities.

31. In 2000, approximately four fifths (84%) of all American women ages 25 and over hcve completed high school. Additionally, in 2000 women constitute 56 percent of the students in undergraduate, graduate, and professional degree programs. (Digest Table 174). More specifically, 56.1 percent of undergraduate students are women (Digest Table 189), and 57.9 percent of graduate students are women (Digest Table 190).

32. The United States Department of Education has developed a method for evaluating functional literacy by testing prose, document, and quantitative literacy resulting in five literacy levels. In 1992, the National Adult Literacy Survey (NALS) was conducted with a sample of 26,000 individuals. The NALS found that 21 to 23 percent of the participants scored in the lowest of five levels in each of the three literacy categories. Less than 18–21 percent scored in top 2 levels. The survey found that older adults, who have typically completed the fewest years of schooling, demonstrated lower literacy skills than other age groups. Among participants scoring in the lowest skill level, 62 percent had not completed high school, and 35 percent had eight or fewer years of formal schooling. Additionally, twenty-five percent were born in another country, and 26 percent had some physical or mental condition that prevented them from participating fully in work, school, housework, or other activities. Nearly half, 41 to 44 percent, of these participants lived in poverty. Adults in prison were disproportionately likely to perform in the lowest two levels of literacy skill.

33. Data are from the reports *Adult Literacy and Education in America* (NCES 2001-534) and from *Adult Literacy in America: a first look at the findings of the National Adult Literacy Survey* (NCES 1993-275).

34. Freedom to worship and to follow a chosen religion is constitutionally protected in the United States. As a result, all major world religions are found in the United States and literally hundreds of denominations and sects exist. The population is overwhelmingly Christian, although obtaining accurate statistical data with regard to religion is extremely difficult, as this information is not included in the decennial census of otherwise collected by the government. The available figures are often rough, based on self-reporting studies which leave great room for error. According to the 2001 Yearbook of American and Canadian Churches, practicing church members make up 57% of the general population. Of those church members, the major groups include Protestants (chiefly Baptists, Methodists, Lutherans, Presbyterians, Episcopalians, Pentecostal, and Mormons) (56%), Roman Catholics (40%), and Jews (4%). The latest data available (1990) for Buddhist, Hindu, and Muslim/Islamic groups reported a total membership of 1,155,000 (or 1%). Numbers do not add to 100 percent due to rounding.

D. Land

35. In its totality, the United States of America covers almost 9.4 million square km, including the 48 coterminous states which span the North American continent, Alaska, Hawaii and the various insular areas in the Pacific Ocean and Caribbean Sea.

36. The geography of the continental United States is widely varied, with great mountain ranges, flat open prairies, and numerous rivers. On the Atlantic shore, much of the northern coast is rocky, but the middle and southern Atlantic coast rises gently from the sea. It starts as low, wet ground and sandy flats, but then becomes a rolling coastal lowland somewhat like that of northern and western Europe. The Appalachians, which run roughly parallel to the east coast, are old mountains with many open valleys between them. To the west is the Appalachian plateau underlain by extensive coal deposits, and beyond is the Central Lowland, which resembles the plains of eastern Europe or the Great Plains of Australia. The Central Lowland is drained chiefly by the vast Mississippi-Missouri river system, which extends some 5,970 km and which experienced disastrous flooding during 1993. In the south, the Gulf Coastal Lowlands, including Florida and westward to the Texas Coast, include many lagoons, swamps and sandbars in addition to rolling coastal plain.

. . .

Population and housing profile: 2000

48. The southernmost United States jurisdiction is American Samoa, an unincorporated territory of seven small islands at the eastern end of the Samoan Island chain in the South Pacific Ocean, midway between Honolulu and Sydney, Australia. They include Tutuila Aunu'u, the Manu'a group, Rose Island and Swains Island, covering 199 square km. Volcanic and mountainous, and surrounded by coral reefs, the islands

retain much of their original Polynesian culture. The population of 57,291 is composed of United States nationals approximately 92 percent of whom are Samoan or part Samoan with the remainder being primarily Tongan or other Pacific Island origin.

. . .

II. GENERAL POLITICAL STRUCTURE
A. Republican form of government

52. The United States of America is a federal republic of 50 states, together with a number of commonwealths, territories and possessions. The United States Constitution is the central instrument of government and the supreme law of the land. Adopted in 1789, the Constitution is the world's oldest written constitution still in force, and owes its staying power to its simplicity and flexibility. Originally designed to provide a framework for governing 4 million people in 13 very different former British colonies along the Atlantic coast, its basic provisions were so soundly conceived that, with only 27 amendments, it now serves the needs of some 250 million people in 50 even more diverse states and other constituent units which stretch from the Atlantic to the Pacific Ocean.

53. Although the Constitution has changed in a number of respects since it was first adopted, most of its basic principles remain the same as they were in 1789:

• The will of the people forms the basis of governmental legitimacy, and the people have the right to change their form of national government by legal means defined in the Constitution itself.

• The three main branches of the federal government (the executive, legislative, and judicial) are separate and distinct from one another. The powers given to each are delicately balanced by the powers of the other two. Each branch serves as a check on potential excesses of the others.

• The Constitution stands above all other laws, executive acts and regulations, including treaties.

• All persons are equal before the law and are equally entitled to its protection. All states are equal, and none can receive special treatment from the federal government. Within the limits of the Constitution, each state must give "full faith and credit to the public acts, records, and judicial proceedings of every other state." [It is well settled that the constitutional "full faith and credit" requirement allows states, for public policy reasons, to decline to "recognize and respect" the laws of other states in certain circumstances. *See e.g., Nevada v. Hall* 440 U.S. 410, 422 (1979).] State governments, like the federal government, must be republican in form, with final authority resting with the people.

• Powers not granted to the federal government are reserved to the states or the people.

54. The Constitution and the federal government stand at the peak of a governmental pyramid which includes the 50 states and many hundreds of local jurisdictions. In the United States system, each level of government has a large degree of autonomy. Disputes between different jurisdictions are typically resolved by the courts. However, there are questions involving the national interest which require the cooperation of all levels of government simultaneously, and the Constitution makes provision for this as well. By way of example, the public (government-funded) schools are largely administered by local jurisdictions, adhering to statewide standards even at the university level. Private schools are also generally required to meet the same standards. Nevertheless, the federal government also aids the schools, as literacy and educational attainment are matters of vital national interest. In other areas, such as housing, health and welfare, there is a similar partnership between the various levels of government.

55. Within the states there are generally two or more layers of government. Most states are divided into counties, and areas of population concentration are incorporated in municipalities or other forms of local government (cities, towns, townships, boroughs, parishes or villages). In addition, school districts and special service districts provide systems of public education and various other services (for example, water and sewer services, fire and emergency services, higher education, hospital services, public transportation). The leaders of the federal, state, county, municipal and other local governments are for the most part democratically elected, although some are appointed by other officials who are themselves democratically elected. The leaders of special service districts are likewise either elected or appointed, with election more common in the case of school districts.

56. The federal Constitution establishes a democratic system of governance at the federal level and guarantees a republican system at the state and local levels. Elected at the federal level are the President, the Vice President, and members of the United States Senate and House of Representatives. There is considerable variation in the governmental structures of the states and of lesser governmental units. From state to state there are large differences in the number of officials who are elected per unit of government and in the number

of officials elected per capita. Elected at the state level typically are the governor, a lieutenant governor, an attorney-general, other leaders of state governmental departments, and members of a bicameral legislature (Nebraska has a unicameral legislature). In many states, justices of the state supreme court and judges in various lower courts are also elected. Elected at the county level typically are members of a county governing body, a chief executive, a sheriff, a clerk, an auditor, a coroner, and the like, and minor judicial officials, such as justices of the peace and constables. Officials elected at the municipal level usually include a mayor and members of a governing council, board or commission. All elections, even those for federal office, are conducted by the states or their political subdivisions.

57. Officials at all levels are elected at regularly scheduled elections to terms of fixed duration, usually varying in length between one and six years. Vacancies are filled either through special elections or by appointment or by a combination of the two methods. Elections are conducted by secret ballot.

58. While the Constitution does not establish or regulate political parties, most federal and state elections are in fact dominated by two long-established parties: the Democratic party, the origins of which may be traced to Thomas Jefferson, who was President from 1801 to 1809, and the Republican party, founded in 1854. Each party is a loose alliance of private organizations formed at the state and local levels which unite every four years for the presidential election. While the Democratic party is generally considered more liberal and the Republican party more conservative in terms of ideology, there are no tests for party registration and beliefs vary widely across the country. Some Democrats are more conservative than most Republicans, and some Republicans are more liberal than most Democrats. Where one party dominates the local politics, the only truly competitive electoral race may in fact be an initial, intra-party election of the party's candidate for office. Particularly during a presidential election, each party tends to compete for voters with a "moderate" or centrist ideology, considered to comprise the majority of voters nationwide. Nonetheless, each party has both a liberal and a conservative "wing" or group of members.

59. While the United States may generally be said to have a "two party" system, many Americans consider themselves "independents" or unaffiliated with either the Democratic or Republican party. Currently, two independents hold seats in the United States Congress, one in the House of Representatives and one in the Senate. An independent candidate for President won 18.9 percent of the popular vote in the 1992 election. In the 2004 Election, an independent candidate won 1 percent of the popular vote.

60. Most elections involve a two-step process. The first (or "primary") step involves the selection or designation of a candidate to represent a political party; second, the respective parties' candidates run against each other and any independent candidates in a general election. Local and state party organizations vary widely in the degree to which a voter must demonstrate party allegiance before participating in the party's nominating methods. Commonly, "primary" elections are held among a party's candidates to determine who will be the nominee of that party for office. Other methods include party caucuses and conventions. Primary elections usually require a voter to demonstrate at least a minimal commitment to a particular party. Although a state may not require by law that political parties conduct "closed primaries" limited to registered members of their party, see e.g., *Tashjian v. Republican Party of Conn.*, 479 U.S. 208 (1986), states may nevertheless choose to permit "closed primaries". On the other hand, party caucuses and conventions typically require a greater degree of party affiliation by the voter and may be open only to certain party officials. Once the parties have designated their candidates for office, state-run general elections are held. In almost all elections, voters are permitted to "split" their ballots by, for example, voting for a Democrat for President and a Republican for Senator. The result is that at both the federal and state levels, the individual holding the highest executive office (e.g., President or Governor) may be of a different political party from the majority of elected representatives in the legislative branch.

B. Federal government

61. The federal government consists of three branches: the executive, the legislative and the judicial.

1. The executive branch

62. The executive branch of government is headed by the President, who under the Constitution must be a natural-born United States citizen, at least 35 years old, and a resident of the country for at least 14 years. Candidates for the presidency are chosen by political parties several months before the presidential election, which is held every four years (in years divisible evenly by four) on the first Tuesday after the first Monday in November.

63. The method of electing the President is peculiar to the United States system. Although the names of the candidates appear on the ballots, technically the people of each state do not vote directly for the President

and Vice President. Instead, they select a slate of "presidential electors" equal to the number of Senators and Representatives each state has in Congress. The law of each state determines how its "presidential electors" are chosen. All but two of the states have adopted a "winner-take-all" system, in which the entire slate of "presidential electors" is awarded to the candidate with the highest number of state-wide votes. The other two states have adopted a system in which the citizens of each congressional district choose one presidential elector, and the remaining two electors are chosen in accordance with the highest number of state-wide votes.

64. According to the Constitution the President must "take care that the laws be faithfully executed". To carry out this responsibility, the President presides over the executive branch of government, with broad powers to manage national affairs and the workings of the federal government. The President can issue instructions called executive orders, which are binding upon federal agencies. As commander-in-chief of the armed forces of the United States, the President may also call into federal service the state units of the National Guard. The Congress may by law grant the President or federal agencies broad powers to make rules and regulations under standards set in those laws. In time of war or national emergency, these grants may be broader than in peacetime.

65. The President chooses the heads of all executive departments and agencies, together with hundreds of other high-ranking federal officials. The large majority of federal workers, however, are selected through the Civil Service system, in which appointment and promotion are based on ability and experience rather than political affiliation.

66. Under the Constitution, the President is the federal official primarily responsible for the relations of the United States with foreign nations. In this sense the President is both "head of government" and "head of State". Presidents appoint ambassadors, ministers, and consuls, subject to confirmation by the Senate, and receives foreign ambassadors and other public officials. With the Secretary of State, the President manages all official communication with foreign governments. On occasion, the President may personally participate in summit conferences where heads of government meet for direct consultation.

67. Through the Department of State, the President is responsible for the protection of United States citizens abroad. Presidents decide whether to recognize new nations and new governments, and negotiate treaties with other nations, which are binding on the United States when approved by two thirds of the Senators present and voting. The President may also negotiate executive agreements with foreign powers that are not subject to Senate advice and consent, based on statutory authority as well as inherent constitutional powers.

68. Although the Constitution provides that "all legislative powers" shall be vested in the Congress, the President, as the chief formulator of public policy, also has a major role in the legislative process. The President can veto any bill passed by Congress, and, unless two thirds in each house vote to override the veto, the bill does not become law. Much of the legislation dealt with by Congress is drafted at the initiative of the executive branch. In his annual report (the "State of the Union" address) and in other special messages to Congress, the President may propose legislation he believes is necessary. The President has the power to call the Congress into special session. Furthermore, the President, as head of a political party and as chief executive officer of the United States government, is in a position to influence public opinion and thereby to influence the course of legislation in Congress.

69. The President also appoints federal judges, including Justices of the Supreme Court of the United States, subject to the advice and consent of the Senate. The President has the power to grant a full or conditional pardon to anyone convicted of breaking a federal law, except in a case of impeachment. The pardoning power has come to embrace the authority to shorten prison terms and reduce fines.

70. The day-to-day enforcement and administration of federal laws is in the hands of the various executive departments created by Congress to deal with specific areas of national and international affairs. The heads of the departments, chosen by the President and approved by the Senate, form a council of advisers generally known as the President's Cabinet. The Cabinet is an informal consultative and advisory body, not provided for by the Constitution. Currently, the members of the Cabinet include the secretaries of Agriculture, Commerce, Defense, Education, Energy, Health and Human Services, Housing and Urban Development, Interior, Labor, State, Transportation, Treasury, and Veterans Affairs, as well as the Attorney-General, who heads the Justice Department. Some executive departments include major subordinate agencies, such as the Federal Aviation Administration (the Department of Transportation), the Federal Bureau of Investigation (the Department of Justice), and the Bureau of Indian Affairs and the National Park Service (the Department of the Interior).

71. On November 25, 2002, President George W. Bush signed into law the Homeland Security Act of 2002, Public Law 107–296, 116 Stat. 2135, establishing the Department of Homeland Security (DHS), a new cabinet-level agency. The primary mission of DHS, as described in the Homeland Security Act, is to prevent terrorist attacks within the United States; to reduce the vulnerability of the United States to terrorism; to minimize the damage and assist in the recovery from terrorist attacks that do occur within the United States; to carry out all functions of entities transferred to the Department, including by acting as a focal point regarding natural and manmade crises and emergency planning; to ensure that the function of the agencies and subdivisions within the Department that are not related directly to securing the homeland are not diminished or neglected except by a specific explicit Act of Congress; and to monitor the connection between illegal drug trafficking and terrorism, coordinate efforts to sever such connections, and otherwise contribute to efforts to interdict illegal drug trafficking.

72. The Homeland Security Act consolidated into the new department 22 government agencies and 180,000 employees to accomplish that mission. Overseeing the various DHS components is the Office of the Secretary, which includes several sub-offices such as the Office of the Chief Privacy Officer, the Office of Civil Rights and Civil Liberties, the Office of Counter Narcotics, the Office of the General Counsel, the Office of the Inspector General, the Office of Legislative Affairs, the Office of the Private Sector, the Office of Public Affairs, and the Office of State and Local Government Coordination and Preparedness. The many agencies incorporated into DHS are generally located in one of four major directorates: Border and Transportation Security, Emergency Preparedness and Response, Science and Technology, and Information Analysis and Infrastructure Protection.

73. The Border and Transportation Security Directorate encompasses the government's major border security and transportation operations, including (1) the former U.S. Customs Service (formerly within U.S. Department of the Treasury), now U.S. Customs and Border Protection (CBP); (2) the enforcement components of the former Immigration and Naturalization Service (formerly within U.S. Department in Justice), now U.S. Immigration and Customs Enforcement (ICE); (3) the Federal Protective Service (formerly within U.S. General Services Administration); and (4) the Transportation Security Administration (formerly within the U.S. Department of Transportation).

74. The Emergency Preparedness and Response Directorate oversees domestic disaster preparedness training and coordinates government disaster response. It encompasses (1) the Federal Emergency Management Agency (FEMA) (formerly an independent agency); (2) the Strategic National Stockpile and the National Disaster Medical System (formerly within the U.S. Department of Health and Human Services); (3) the Nuclear Incident Response Team (formerly within the U.S. Department of Energy); and (4) the National Domestic Preparedness Office (formerly within the U.S. Department of Justice (FBI)).

75. The Science and Technology Directorate seeks to utilize all scientific and technological advantages when securing the homeland and includes (1) the Environmental Measurements Laboratory (formerly within U.S. Department of Energy); (2) the National Bio-Weapons Defense Analysis Center (formerly within U.S. Department of Defense); and (3) the Plum Island Animal Disease Center (formerly within U.S. Department of Agriculture).

76. The Information Analysis and Infrastructure Protection Directorate analyzes intelligence and information from other agencies (including the CIA and FBI) involving threats to homeland security and evaluates vulnerabilities in the nation's infrastructure.

77. The Department of Homeland Security also includes the U.S. Secret Service (formerly within U.S. Department of the Treasury), the U.S. Coast Guard (formerly within U.S. Department of Transportation), and U.S. Citizenship and Immigration Services (USCIS) (executing immigration benefits and services functions of former Immigration and Naturalization Service (formerly within U.S. Department of Justice)).

78. In addition to the secretaries of the 14 executive departments, the chiefs of a number of other governmental organizations are also considered part of the Cabinet. Currently, these include the chiefs of the White House staff, the National Security Council, the Office of Management and Budget, the Council of Economic Advisers, the Office of the United States Trade Representative, the Environmental Protection Agency, Drug Control Policy, Domestic Policy Council, the National Economic Council, and the United States Ambassador to the United Nations. The Office of the President includes certain other organizations such as the Office of Science and Technology and the Office of Environmental Policy.

79. In addition to the executive departments, more than 50 other agencies within the executive branch have important responsibilities for keeping the government and the economy working. These are often

called independent agencies, as they are technically not part of the executive departments. Some are regulatory groups, with powers to supervise certain sectors of the economy, such as the Securities and Exchange Commission, the Nuclear Regulatory Commission and the Interstate Commerce Commission. Others provide special services, either to the government or to people, such as the United States Postal Service, the Central Intelligence Agency, and the Federal Election Commission. In most cases, the agencies have been created by Congress to deal with matters that have become too complex for the scope of ordinary legislation. Among the best known independent agencies are the Peace Corps and the National Aeronautics and Space Administration (NASA). All together, the executive branch currently employs approximately 2.8 million civilian personnel.

. . .

2. The legislative branch

81. The legislative branch of the federal government is the Congress, which has two houses: the Senate and the House of Representatives. Powers granted Congress under the Constitution include the powers to levy taxes, borrow money, regulate interstate commerce, and declare war. In addition, each house may discipline its own membership and determine its rules of procedure. Including related entities such as the Library of Congress, the General Accounting Office, the Government Printing Office and the Congressional Budget Office, the legislative branch employs some 38,000 people.

The Senate

82. Each state elects two senators. Senators must be at least 30 years old, residents of the state from which they are elected, and citizens of the United States for at least nine years. Each term of service is for six years, and terms are arranged so that one third of the members are elected every two years.

83. The Senate has certain powers especially reserved to that body, including the authority to confirm presidential appointments of high officials and ambassadors of the federal government, as well as authority to give its advice and consent to the ratification of treaties by a two thirds vote.

84. The Constitution provides that the Vice President of the United States shall be president of the Senate. The Vice President has no vote, except in the case of a tie. The Senate chooses a president *pro tempore* from the majority party to preside when the Vice President is absent.

The House of Representatives

85. The 435 members of the House of Representatives are chosen by direct vote of the electorate in each state, with the number of representatives allotted to each state on the basis of population. Each representative represents a single congressional district. Members must be at least 25 years old, residents of the states from which they are elected, and previously citizens of the United States for at least seven years. They serve for a two-year period.

86. The House of Representatives chooses its own presiding officer, the Speaker of the House. The Speaker is always a member of the political party with the majority in the House.

87. The leaders of the two political parties in each house of Congress are respectively the majority floor leader and the minority floor leader; they are helped by party whips who maintain communication between the leadership and the members of the House. Legislative proposals (termed "bills" prior to enactment as "statutes") introduced by members in the House of Representatives are received by the standing committees which can amend, expedite, delay, or kill the bills. The committee chairmen attain their positions on the basis of seniority. Among the most important House committees are those on Appropriations, the Judiciary, Foreign Affairs, Ways and Means, and Rules.

88. Each house of Congress has the power to introduce legislation on any subject, except that revenue bills must originate in the House of Representatives. Each house can vote against legislation passed by the other house. Often, a conference committee made up of members from both houses must work out a compromise acceptable to both houses before a bill becomes law.

The role of committees

89. One of the major characteristics of the Congress is the dominant role committees play in its proceedings. Committees have assumed their present-day importance by evolution, not design, as the Constitution makes no provision for their establishment. At present, the Senate has 16 standing committees; the House of Representatives has 22. The Houses share a number of joint committees, such as the Joint Committee on Taxation, and each also has a number of special and select committees. Each specializes in specific areas of legislation and governmental activity, such as foreign affairs, defense, banking, agriculture, commerce, appropriations and other fields. Every bill introduced in either house is referred to a committee

for study and recommendation. The committee may approve, revise, reject or ignore any measure referred to it. It is nearly impossible for a bill to reach the House or Senate floor without first winning committee approval. In the House, a petition to discharge a bill from committee requires the signatures of 218 members; in the Senate, a majority of all members is required. In practice, such discharge motions rarely receive the required support.

90. The majority party in each house controls the committee process. Committee chairs are selected by a caucus of members of the majority party in that house or by specially designated groups of members. Minority parties are proportionately represented in the committees according to their strength in each house.

91. Bills are developed by a variety of methods. Some are drawn up by standing committees, some by special committees created to deal with specific legislative issues, and some are suggested by the President or other executive branch officers. Citizens and organizations outside the Congress may suggest legislation to members, and individual members themselves may initiate bills. Each bill must be sponsored by at least one member of the house in which it is introduced. After introduction, bills are sent to designated committees which may schedule a series of public hearings to permit presentation of views by persons who support or oppose the legislation. The hearing process, which can last several weeks or months, opens the legislative process to public participation.

92. When a committee has acted favorably on a bill, the proposed legislation may then be brought to the floor for open debate. In the Senate, the rules permit virtually unlimited debate. In the House, because of the large number of members, the Rules Committee usually sets limits. When debate is ended, members vote to approve the bill, defeat it, table it (set it aside), or return it to committee. A bill passed by one house is sent to the other for action. If the bill is amended by the second house, the bill may return to the first house for another vote, or a conference committee composed of members of both houses may attempt to reconcile the differences.

93. Once passed by both houses, the bill is sent to the President for his action. The President generally has the option of signing the bill, in which case it becomes law, or vetoing it. A bill vetoed by the President must be re-approved by a two thirds vote of each house in order to become law. If the President refuses either to sign or veto a bill, it becomes law without his signature 10 days after it reaches him (not including Sundays). The single exception to this rule is when Congress adjourns after sending a bill to the President and before the 10-day period has expired; the President's refusal to take any action then negates the bill—a process known as the "pocket veto".

Congressional powers of oversight and investigation

94. Among the most important functions of the Congress are oversight and investigation. Oversight functions include reviewing the effectiveness of laws already passed and assessing their implementation by the executive branch, as well as inquiring into the qualifications and performance of members and officials of the other branches. In addition, investigations are conducted to gather information on the need for future legislation. Frequently, committees call on outside (non-governmental) experts to assist in conducting investigative hearings and to make detailed studies of issues.

95. There are important corollaries to the powers of oversight and investigation. One is the power to publicize the proceedings and their results. Most committee hearings are open to the public and are widely reported in the mass media. Congressional hearings thus represent one important tool available to lawmakers to inform the citizenry and arouse public interest in national issues. A second power is to compel testimony from unwilling witnesses and to cite for contempt of Congress witnesses who refuse to testify, and for perjury those who give false testimony.

3. The judicial branch

96. The third branch of the federal government, the judiciary, consists of a system of courts headed by the Supreme Court of the United States and including subordinate courts throughout the country. The federal judicial power extends to cases arising under the Constitution, laws, and treaties of the United States; to cases affecting ambassadors, other public ministers and consuls; to cases of admiralty and maritime jurisdiction; to controversies to which the United States is a party; to controversies between two or more states; between a state and citizens of another state; between citizens of different states; between citizens of the same state claiming lands under grants of different states, and between a state, or the citizens thereof, and foreign states, citizens or subjects. In practice the vast majority of litigation in federal courts is based on federal law or involves disputes between citizens of different states under the courts' "diversity" jurisdiction.

...

The Supreme Court

99. The Supreme Court is the highest court of the United States and the only one specifically created by the Constitution. A decision of the Supreme Court cannot be appealed to any other court. Congress has the power to fix the number of judges sitting on the Court (currently a Chief Justice and eight Associate Justices) and, within limits, to decide what kind of cases it may hear, but it cannot change the powers given to the Supreme Court by the Constitution itself.

100. The Supreme Court may exercise original jurisdiction (i.e. the authority to hear cases directly rather than on appeal) in only two kinds of cases: those affecting ambassadors, other public ministers and consuls; and those in which a state is a party. All other cases reach the Supreme Court on appeal from lower federal courts or from the various state courts. The right of appeal is not automatic in all cases, however, and the Supreme Court exercises considerable discretion in selecting the cases it will consider. A significant amount of the work of the Supreme Court consists of determining whether legislation or executive acts conform to the Constitution. This power of judicial review is not expressly provided for by the Constitution. Rather, it is a doctrine inferred by the Court from its reading of the Constitution, and stated in the landmark case of *Marbury v. Madison*, 5 U.S. 137 (1803). In *Marbury*, the Court held that "a legislative act contrary to the Constitution is not law", and observed that "it is emphatically the province and duty of the judicial department to say what the law is". The doctrine of judicial review also covers the activities of state and local governments for conformity with federal law.

101. Decisions of the Court need not be unanimous; a simple majority prevails, provided at least six Justices participate in the decision. In split decisions, the Court usually issues both a majority and a minority or dissenting opinion, both of which may form the basis for future decisions by the Court. Often Justices will write separate concurring opinions when they agree with a decision, but for reasons other than those given by the majority.

Courts of appeals and district courts

102. The second highest level of the federal judiciary is made up of the courts of appeals. The United States is currently divided into 12 appellate circuits, each served by a court of appeals. The courts of appeals have appellate jurisdiction over decisions of the district courts (trial courts with federal jurisdiction) within their respective geographic areas. They are also empowered to review orders of the independent regulatory agencies, such as the Federal Trade Commission, in cases where the internal review mechanisms of the agencies have been exhausted and there still exists substantial disagreement over legal issues. There is also a thirteenth court of appeals, which hears appeals from certain courts with specialized jurisdiction. Approximately 180 judges sit on the various courts of appeals.

103. Below the courts of appeals are the federal district courts. The 50 states are divided into 89 districts so that litigants may have a trial within easy reach. Additionally, there are district courts in the District of Columbia, the Commonwealth of Puerto Rico, the Commonwealth of the Northern Marianas, and the territories of Guam and the Virgin Islands. Congress fixes the boundaries of the districts according to population, size, and volume of work. Some states (such as Alaska, Hawaii, Idaho and Vermont) constitute a district by themselves, while the larger states (such as New York, California and Texas) have four districts each. In total, there are approximately 650 federal district judges.

Courts with specialized jurisdiction

104. In addition to the federal courts of general jurisdiction, it has been necessary from time to time to set up courts for special purposes. Perhaps the most important of these special courts is the United States Court of Federal Claims, established in 1855 to render judgment on monetary claims against the United States. Other special courts include United States Tax Court, the Court of Veterans Appeals, and the Court of International Trade, which has exclusive jurisdiction over civil actions involving taxes or quotas on imported goods.

Military courts

105. A separate system exists for military justice. Members of the military are subject to the Uniform Code of Military Justice for disciplinary matters. Cases of alleged criminal conduct are investigated and, when substantiated, are resolved in appropriate forums ranging from nonjudicial punishment to one of three types of courts-martial. In a trial by court-martial, an accused is accorded the full range of constitutional rights, including representation by a qualified defense counsel at no charge to the individual. Any court-martial that results in a sentence of confinement for a year or more, discharge from the service or capital punishment is automatically reviewed by the relevant court of criminal appeals for the Military Department concerned.

Those courts, which are composed of senior military (and sometimes civilian) attorneys serving as appellate judges, examine the records of trial for both factual and legal error. Decisions can be appealed to the United States Court of Appeals for the Armed Forces, comprised of five civilian judges. Adverse decisions can be further reviewed by the United States Supreme Court on a discretionary basis.

Relationship between federal and state courts

106. Over the course of the nation's history, a complex set of relationships between state and federal courts has arisen. Ordinarily, federal courts do not hear cases arising under the laws of individual states. However, some cases over which federal courts have jurisdiction may also be heard and decided by state courts. Both court systems thus have exclusive jurisdiction in some areas and concurrent jurisdiction in others. Taking into account that there are 50 separate state court systems, which often include subordinate judicial bodies (e.g., county and city courts), as well as the judicial systems of the insular areas, the District of Columbia and other nonstate entities, there are over 2,000 courts with general jurisdiction and approximately 18,000 judicial districts of either general or limited jurisdiction in the United States. Many states have large numbers of courts with very limited jurisdiction, such as New York (which has 2300 town and village justice courts) and Texas (which has approximately 850 municipal courts and 920 justice of the peace courts).

C. The state governments

107. The governments of the 50 states have structures closely paralleling those of the federal government, each with a constitution and executive, legislative, and judicial branches. The state Governor acts as the head of the executive, but not all states bestow the same amount of power upon their governors; some are quite powerful, others less so. All state legislatures have two houses, except Nebraska's, which is unicameral. The size of state legislatures varies widely; the largest include those in New Hampshire (424 representatives), Pennsylvania (253), and Georgia (236), while the smallest are found in Nebraska (49) and Alaska (60). Most state judicial systems mirror the federal system, with lower trial courts, appellate courts, and a court of last resort. States and insular areas divide relatively evenly among those that elect their judges (22), those that appoint judges (16 including the District of Columbia and four of the insular areas), and those where judges are initially appointed and subsequently run on a retention ballot (18 including Guam).

108. The power of state governments is vast. Essentially, each state is a sovereign entity, free to promulgate and enforce policy and law that pertain exclusively to that state, limited under the Constitution only to the extent that the relevant authority has been delegated to the federal government. The power of a state and its cities and localities to regulate its own general welfare has traditionally been termed the "police power." Besides enforcement of criminal laws, the police power encompasses agriculture and conservation, highway and motor vehicle supervision, public safety and correction, professional licensing, regulation of intrastate business and industry, and broad aspects of education, public health, and welfare. The interpretation of a state's constitution falls exclusively within the domain of that state's own court system. Only where there is direct conflict with federal law or the federal Constitution, or where the federal government has "pre-empted" the field, can state law be overridden or invalidated. The retention of most aspects of governmental authority at the state and local levels generally serves to keep that authority in the hands of the people.

109. Distribution of authority between the states and the federal government has historically been among the most basic dynamics of the federal system. Although the powers of Congress are limited to those expressly enumerated in the Constitution, and those powers not expressly delegated to the federal government are reserved to the states or to the people, the twentieth century has seen increasingly broad judicial interpretation of the national legislative power. Today there is an abundance of federal legislation, touching on many areas which 100 years ago would have been exclusively considered a state concern. One result of this expansion of federal authority, especially in the latter half of this century, has been a substantial increase in legislation and government regulations protecting civil and political rights.

D. Other governmental levels

110. A significant number of United States citizens and/or nationals live in areas outside the 50 states and yet within the political framework and jurisdiction of the United States. They include people living in the District of Columbia, American Samoa, Puerto Rico, the United States Virgin Islands, Guam, the Northern Marianas, and the remaining islands of the Trust Territory of the Pacific. The governmental framework in each is largely determined by the area's historical relationship to the United States and the will of its residents.

111. The *District of Columbia* was established at the founding of the Republic to serve as the home of the nation's capital outside of any state. In 1783 the Continental Congress voted to establish a federal city; the specific site was chosen by President George Washington in 1790. Congress moved to the District from Philadelphia in 1800, and the District remains the seat of the federal government today. Originally, Maryland and Virginia donated land for the District. The land donated by Virginia was given back in 1845 and the District now covers 179.2 km² located on the west central edge of Maryland, along the eastern bank of the Potomac River. Residents of the District, numbering about 550,000, are United States citizens and have been entitled to vote in presidential elections since 1964. Residents elect a non-voting delegate to the United States Congress as well as a mayor and a city council with authority to levy its own taxes. The United States Congress retains final authority in a number of important areas, including the District's laws and budget. Whether the District should be admitted to statehood or whether its residents should be afforded full voting rights in Congress remains an issue of active public debate.

...

III. GENERAL FRAMEWORK FOR THE PROTECTION OF HUMAN RIGHTS
A. Legal framework
118. The essential guarantees of human rights and fundamental freedoms within the United States are set forth in the Constitution and statutes of the United States, as well as the constitutions and statutes of the several states and other constituent units. In practice, the enforcement of these guarantees ultimately depends on the existence of an independent judiciary with the power to invalidate acts by the other branches of government which conflict with those guarantees. Maintenance of a republican form of government with vigorous democratic traditions, popularly elected executives and legislatures, and the deep-rooted legal protection of freedoms of opinion, expression and the press, all contribute to the protection of fundamental rights against governmental limitation and encroachment.

United States Constitution
119. The Constitution has been amended 27 times since it was ratified in 1789. Amending the Constitution requires approval by two thirds of each house of the Congress, or by a national convention, followed by ratification by three quarters of the states. The first 10 amendments, known collectively as the Bill of Rights, were added in 1791. These amendments provide for the basic protection of those individual rights which are fundamental to the democratic system of government. They remain at the heart of the United States legal system today, just as they were written two centuries ago, although the specific rights they guarantee have been extensively elaborated by the judiciary over the course of time. Individuals may assert these rights against the government in judicial proceedings.

120. The First Amendment guarantees freedom of worship, speech and press, the right of peaceful assembly, and the right to petition the government to correct wrongs. The Second Amendment prohibits the federal government from infringing on the right of citizens to keep and bear arms, bearing in mind the necessity for a "well regulated militia". The Third Amendment provides that troops may not be quartered in a private home without the owner's consent. The Fourth Amendment guards against unreasonable searches, arrests and seizures of persons and property.

121. The next four amendments deal with the system of justice. The Fifth Amendment forbids trial for a major crime except after indictment by a grand jury; it prohibits repeated trials for the same offence, forbids punishment without due process of law, and provides that an accused person may not be compelled to testify against him or herself. The Sixth Amendment guarantees a speedy public trial for criminal offences; it requires trial by an unbiased jury, guarantees the right to legal counsel for the accused in criminal proceedings, and provides that witnesses shall be compelled to attend the trial and testify in the presence of the accused. The Seventh Amendment assures trial by jury in civil cases involving anything valued at more than 20 United States dollars. The Eighth Amendment forbids excessive bail or fines and cruel and unusual punishments.

122. The Ninth Amendment declares that the enumeration in the Constitution of certain rights shall not be construed to deny or disparage others retained by the people. The Tenth Amendment sets forth the federal and democratic nature of the United States system of government, providing that powers not delegated by the Constitution to the federal government, nor prohibited by it to the states, are reserved to the states or the people. The Tenth Amendment recognizes that the federal government is a government of limited jurisdiction, empowered to do only what the Constitution authorizes it to do, and that all other powers remain vested in the people, and in their duly constituted state governments.

123. Amendments to the Constitution subsequent to the original Bill of Rights cover a wide range of subjects. One of the most far-reaching is the Fourteenth Amendment, by which a clear and simple definition of citizenship was established and broadened guarantees of due process, equal treatment, and equal protection of the law were confirmed. In essence, this amendment, adopted in 1868, has been interpreted to apply the protections of the Bill of Rights to the states. By other amendments, the judicial power of the national government was limited; the method of electing the president was changed; slavery was forbidden; the right to vote was protected against denial because of race, color, sex or previous condition of servitude; the congressional power to levy taxes was extended to incomes; and the election of United States Senators by popular vote was instituted.

124. The Constitution provides explicitly that it is the "supreme Law of the Land". This clause is taken to mean that when state constitutions or laws passed by state legislatures or laws adopted by the federal government are found to conflict with the Constitution, they have no force or effect. Decisions handed down by the Supreme Court of the United States and subordinate federal courts over the course of two centuries have confirmed and strengthened this doctrine of constitutional supremacy.

State constitutions

125. As indicated above, the protections provided by the federal Constitution and statutes are applicable nationwide, generally providing a minimum standard of guarantees for all persons in the United States. While the laws of individual states cannot detract from the protections afforded to their citizens by federal law, states are, except where prohibited by federal law or it infringes on a protected federal right, free to offer their citizens greater protections of civil and political rights.

126. Historically, states individually or collectively have led the federal government in the advancement and protection of civil and political rights. For example, starting with Vermont in 1777, and through 1862, most Northern states curtailed or abolished slavery. Likewise, women first gained the right to vote in Wyoming Territory in 1869, while federal law did not extend that right until 1920.

127. More recently, in the latter half of the twentieth century, federal law and the federal courts played a more active role in civil rights protections. State courts, however, continue to play an important role in this arena. In many cases, in keeping with the federal system of government, individual state's laws afford their citizens greater protections than the federal Constitution requires. *See Prune Yard Shopping Center v. Robins*, 447 U.S. 74 (1980) (holding that broader state protections for free speech, protecting expression in a public shopping center, did not effect a taking violating the federal Constitution; upholding the California Supreme Court in *Robins v. Prune Yard Shopping Center*, 592 P.2d 341 (Cal. 1979)).

128. State law has provided broader protections than federal law in a number of areas, including free speech, religious liberty, property rights, victims' rights, and the provision of government services. State constitutions vary widely in length, detail, and similarity to the United States Constitution. As a result, a state court decision, while it may expand upon a right protected by the United States Constitution, may rest on grounds very different from those upon which a similar federal case would be decided.

129. One area in which federal law provides broader protection than some state laws is protection of freedom of religion. The federal Constitution permits students who choose freely to do so to attend parochial schools with the use of public funds. *See Zelman v. Harris*, 536 U.S. 639 (2002). Some states, on the other hand, prohibit much more rigidly the use of public funds for religious endeavors. For instance, based on the state constitution's broad prohibition of governmental assistance to an institution not owned by the state, the Supreme Court of Nebraska found unconstitutional a statute under which public school books were loaned to parochial schools; on similar grounds, the Supreme Court of Idaho struck down a statute authorizing publicly provided transportation of students to nonpublic schools. *See Gaffney v. State Department of Education*, 220 N.W.2d 550 (Neb. 1974); *Epeldi v. Engelking*, 488 P.2d 860 (Id. 1971). While the United States Supreme Court has upheld the display of a nativity scene on public property, the California Supreme Court has nonetheless held that the state constitution's ban on preference for religious sects prohibited the display of a lighted cross on public grounds in celebration of Christmas and Easter. *See, Lynch v. Donnelly*, 465 U.S. 668 (1984); *Fox v. City of Los Angeles*, 587 P.2d 663 (Cal. 1978).

130. State courts have also interpreted a state right to equal access to government benefits more broadly than the Supreme Court has interpreted a similar federal right. While the Supreme Court has held that governments may not place an "undue burden" on a woman's ability to obtain an abortion before viability, *see Planned Parenthood v. Casey*, 505 U.S. 833 (1992), the Court has also held that the federal government need not provide financial support and federal health benefits for obtaining an abortion, *see Harris v.*

McRae, 448 U.S. 297 (1980). The Massachusetts Supreme Judicial Court, in contrast, has held that under the Massachusetts Declaration of Rights, once the state has allocated public funds for child-bearing and health in general, the state must show "genuine indifference" in that allocation and consequently fund abortions as well. *See Moe v. Secretary of Administration*, 417 N.E.2d 387 (Mass. 1981).

131. Despite these examples, state courts are not uniform in their willingness to find greater protections within the state constitutions than those guaranteed by the federal government. As is appropriate in a federal system, each state's protections are tailored by that state's democratic process. States are prohibited simply from subverting established federal protections.

Statutes

132. There is no single statute or mechanism by which basic human rights and fundamental freedoms are guaranteed or enforced in the United States legal system. Rather, domestic law provides extensive protection through enforcement of the constitutional provisions cited above and a variety of statutes, which typically provide for judicial and/or administrative remedies.

133. At the federal level, for example, the constitutional protection afforded by the Equal Protection Clause of the Fourteenth Amendment against discrimination by the state governments on the basis of race, color or national origin has been applied to the federal government through the Fifth Amendment. It has also been supplemented by a number of specific federal statutes, including the 1866 and 1871 Civil Rights Acts (protecting property rights, freedom to contract, and providing federal remedies for private individuals subjected to unlawful discrimination by persons acting "under color of law"), the 1964 Civil Rights Act (ensuring equal treatment in places of public accommodation, non-discrimination in federally funded programs, and non-discrimination in employment), the 1965 Voting Rights Act (invalidating discriminatory voter qualifications), and the 1968 Fair Housing Act (providing the right to be free from discrimination in housing). Similarly, in the area of gender discrimination, individuals benefit from the protections of the Equal Protection Clause, the 1963 Equal Pay Act (equal pay for equal work), the Civil Rights Act of 1964 (non-discrimination in hiring and employment practices and policies), the Education Amendments of 1972 (assuring gender equality in education), the Equal Credit Opportunity Act (equal access and non-discrimination in credit and lending), the Fair Housing Act (non-discrimination in housing, real estate and brokerage), the Pregnancy Discrimination Act of 1978, and the Religious Land Use and Institutionalized Persons Act. Protection against age discrimination is provided by the Age Discrimination in Employment Act of 1967 (prohibiting discrimination in employment against workers or applicants 40 years of age or older). The Civil Rights of Institutionalized Persons Act of 1980 provides protection to mentally disabled persons in state facilities. Although disabled persons have long been protected against discrimination in the federal service, an important and much broader set of protections was recently added with the enactment of the Americans with Disabilities Act of 1990, which prohibits discrimination against disabled individuals in employment, public accommodations, state and local government services, and public transportation. The Indian Civil Rights Act of 1968 imposes upon tribes such basic requirements as free speech protection, free exercise of religion, due process and equal protection.

134. Most states and large cities have adopted their own statutory and administrative schemes for protecting and promoting basic rights and freedoms. For the most part, state statutory protections mirror those provided by the United States Constitution and federal law. Typically, state constitutions and statutes protect individuals from discrimination in housing, employment, accommodations, credit and education. For example, Minnesota's statute prohibits discrimination in sales, rentals or lease of housing. Minn. Stat. § 363.03 (1992). Massachusetts makes it unlawful to refuse to hire or to discharge someone from employment on discriminatory grounds, or to discriminate in education. Mass. Ann. Laws ch. 151B, § 4; ch. 151C, § 1 (1993). California requires that all persons be "free and equal" in accommodations, advantages, facilities, privileges and services of business establishments. Cal. Civ. Code § 51 (1993). Texas prohibits discrimination in credit or loans. Texas Revised Civil Statutes Annotated art. 5069-207 (1993).

Derogation/states of emergency

135. Neither the Constitution nor the laws of the United States provide for the declaration of a general state of emergency entailing suspension of the normal operations of the government or permitting derogations from fundamental rights. On the contrary, the basic requirement for a republican form of government, the general functions of the three branches of the federal government, and most of the fundamental civil and political rights enjoyed by individuals, are all enshrined in the Constitution and thus remain in effect at all times, even during crisis situations.

136. The one exception to this rule concerns the privilege of the writ of habeas corpus. Article I, § 9, cl. 2 of the Constitution states that the privilege shall not be suspended, "unless when in cases of rebellion or invasion the public safety may require it". Congress is considered to hold the authority to suspend the privilege. *See Ex Parte Bollman*, 8 U.S. 74, 101 (1807). President Lincoln suspended the privilege during the Civil War but sought congressional authorization for his actions. *See Ex Parte Merryman*, 17 Fed. Cas. 144 (No. 9487) (C.C.D. Md. 1861) (Chief Justice Taney sitting as a Circuit Judge for the 4th Circuit found Lincoln's action invalid). The privilege has been suspended only three other times, each pursuant to an act of Congress.

137. At the national level, there is a general statutory prohibition against the use of the armed forces for domestic law enforcement purposes. However, the President is authorized in limited circumstances to order the use of federal troops to assist state and local authorities in controlling violence and to suppress insurrections and enforce federal law. The President may also declare an emergency with respect to catastrophic domestic situations (for example, in the event of an earthquake, a hurricane, flooding or a drought), thus permitting the federal government to provide disaster relief and emergency assistance to state and local governments and to the individual victims of the crisis. These laws do not, however, permit the executive branch to interfere with the responsibilities of the legislative or judicial branches of the federal government or to arrogate the authority of the states.

138. Other statutes permit the President to declare national emergencies with respect to foreign affairs and international economic transactions (thus providing a basis, for example, for implementation of international sanctions imposed by the United Nations Security Council or other competent international authority). While these laws permit the imposition of civil and criminal penalties for prohibited activities, they remain subject to constitutional limitations and do not circumscribe basic human rights or permit interference in the normal functioning of the government.

139. Under state and local law, the responsible authorities (state Governors, city mayors, county executives) are typically permitted to take a wide range of emergency actions pursuant to the general "police power" in order to respond to emergencies (for example, by imposing curfews in cases of civil unrest, establishing quarantines in response to public health concerns, and restricting water usage in the event of drought). While the "police power" is reserved to the states under the Constitution, actions taken pursuant to it may not limit or infringe upon federally protected rights. Individuals thus retain their constitutional protections and human rights at all times and may challenge the exercise of emergency authority in the courts. As a general rule, the exercise of emergency authority by the government—at any level is given particularly careful judicial scrutiny when it infringes upon individual rights and liberties. *See, e.g., The Amy Warwick* 67 U.S. 635 (1863); *Toyosaburo Korematsu v. United States*, 323 U.S. 214 (1944). It is rare, however, for the United States Supreme Court to invalidate presidential actions taken in emergency situations. *See Youngstown Co. v. Sawyer*, 343 U.S. 579 (1952).

B. Responsible authorities

140. Within the federal government, all three branches share responsibility for the protection and promotion of fundamental rights under the Constitution and the statutes of the United States. The President is responsible for enforcing the law. Within the Department of Justice, the Civil Rights Division bears principal responsibility for the effective enforcement of federal civil rights laws. These include the various civil rights acts mentioned above as well as specific criminal statutes prohibiting wilful deprivation of constitutional rights by officials acting with actual or apparent legal authority or through conspiracy, involuntary servitude, and violent interference with federally protected activities. In addition, most other agencies have civil rights sections charged with enforcing civil rights issues within their scope of authority.

141. The United States Commission on Civil Rights, a statutorily established independent agency within the executive branch, collects and studies information on discrimination or denials of equal protection of the laws because of race, color, religion, sex, age, handicap, national origin or in the administration of justice in such areas as voting rights, enforcement of civil rights laws, and equality of opportunity in education, employment and housing. It also evaluates federal laws and the effectiveness of governmental equal opportunity programs and serves as a clearing house for civil rights information. The Commission makes findings of fact and recommendations for the President and the Congress but has no independent enforcement authority.

142. The United States Equal Employment Opportunity Commission, also an independent agency within the executive branch, works to eliminate discrimination based on race, color, religion, sex, national

origin, disability or age in all aspects of the employment relationship. The Commission conducts investigations of alleged discrimination, makes determinations based on gathered evidence, attempts conciliation when discrimination has occurred, files lawsuits, and conducts voluntary assistance programs for employers, unions and community organizations. The Commission has oversight responsibility for all compliance and enforcement activities relating to equal employment opportunity among federal employees and applicants, including discrimination against individuals with disabilities.

143. At the state and local levels, a variety of schemes and mechanisms exist to protect and promote basic rights. At the state level, enforcement responsibility is typically found in the Attorney-General's Office or in separate civil or human rights offices within the state government or at the county level. Examples include the Massachusetts Commission Against Discrimination, the Illinois Department of Human Rights, the Cook County (Illinois) Human Rights Commission, the California Fair Employment and Housing Department, and the Texas Commission on Human Rights. Many large city governments have also established offices or commissions to address civil rights and discrimination issues. These organizations vary. Some emphasize enforcement of housing and employment anti-discrimination laws. Others facilitate community development and strategies to address human rights issues. Examples include the Boston (Massachusetts) Human Rights Commission, the Chicago (Illinois) Commission on Human Relations, the Los Angeles (California) Human Relations Commission, and the Austin (Texas) Human Rights Commission.

144. Non-governmental organizations also play an important role in ensuring the protection and promotion of human rights within the United States. Professional groups provide legal expertise as well as forums for the development of considered positions on legal developments and matters of human rights concern. Numerous private organizations representing diverse interests and constituencies with particular human rights and civil rights concerns, (including race, religion, sex, private property, children, the disabled, and the indigenous people), are actively involved in the consideration and application of human and civil rights laws relating to their constituencies.

C. Remedies

145. United States law provides extensive remedies and avenues for seeking redress for alleged violations of basic rights and fundamental freedoms. The principal method, if administrative remedies are insufficient to produce the desired result, is through recourse to court. A person claiming to have been denied a constitutionally protected right may assert that right directly in a judicial proceeding in state or federal court. In addition, in instances involving "state action" or actions "under color of state law", the injured party may seek civil damages and injunctive relief against the individual responsible for the denial of rights under the Civil Rights Act of 1871, 42 U.S.C. § 1983. Federal officials may be sued for damages directly under provisions of the Constitution, subject to various doctrines of immunity from liability.

146. Many federal statutes specifically provide for enforcement through administrative procedures or by civil actions filed in court. All states have judicial procedures by which official action may be challenged, though the procedure may go by various names (such as "petition for review").

147. Where Congress has so provided, the federal government may bring civil actions to enjoin acts or patterns of conduct that violate some constitutional rights. This is the case, for example, under the principal civil rights acts discussed above. Thus, the Attorney-General can sue under the Civil Rights of Institutionalized Persons Act to vindicate the rights of persons involuntarily committed to prisons, jails, hospitals, and institutions for the mentally retarded. Similarly, the Voting Rights Act of 1965 authorizes the Attorney-General to bring suit to vindicate the right to vote without discrimination based on race. The federal government may also prosecute criminally the violations of some civil rights, for example, the denial of due process through the abuse of police power and conspiracies to deny civil rights. The government may also bring criminal prosecutions against defendants for use of force or threat of force to violate a person's rights, or for the trafficking of humans.

148. Any person prosecuted under a statute or in conjunction with a governmental scheme (such as jury selection) which he or she believes to be unconstitutional may challenge that statute as part of the defense. This may be done in the context of federal or state prosecutions. Even in civil actions, the defendant may pose a constitutional challenge to the statute that forms the basis of the suit. Any court, from the lowest to the United States Supreme Court, may consider such a claim of unconstitutionality, though normally it must be raised at the earliest opportunity to be considered at all. Detention pursuant to a statute believed to be unconstitutional or as a result of a procedure that allegedly violated a constitutional right may also be challenged by a writ of habeas corpus in state and federal courts. To a limited degree, post-conviction relief is also

available by state and federal writs of habeas corpus or, in the case of federal convictions, by a motion for relief from a sentence. All states have similar remedies as part of their criminal procedure.

D. Human rights instruments

Multilateral treaties

149. The United States is at present Party to the following multilateral human rights instruments:

- Slavery Convention and its amending Protocol; Supplementary Convention on the Abolition of Slavery, the Slave Trade and Institutions and Practices Similar to Slavery;
- Protocol Relating to the Status of Refugees;
- Inter-American Convention on the Granting of Political Rights to Women;
- Convention on the Political Rights of Women;
- Convention on the Prevention and Punishment of the Crime of Genocide;
- ILO Convention No. 105 concerning the Abolition of Forced Labor;
- International Covenant on Civil and Political Rights;
- Convention against Torture and Other Cruel, Inhuman or Degrading Treatment or Punishment;
- International Convention on the Elimination of All Forms of Racial Discrimination;
- ILO Convention 182 Concerning the Prohibition and Immediate Action for the Elimination of the Worst Forms of Child Labor;
- The Optional Protocol to the Convention on the Rights of the Child on Children in Armed Conflict;
- The Optional Protocol to the Convention on the Rights of the Child on Sale of Children, Child Prostitution, and Child Pornography.

150. Moreover, the United States has signed but not yet ratified the following multilateral human rights treaties:

- International Covenant on Economic, Social and Cultural Rights;
- American Convention on Human Rights;
- Convention on the Elimination of All Forms of Discrimination against Women.

151. In addition, the United States has entered into many bilateral treaties (including consular treaties and treaties of friendship, commerce and navigation) which contain provisions guaranteeing various rights and protections to nationals of foreign countries on a reciprocal basis. In some cases, these may be invoked directly in United States courts for that purpose.

Treaties as law

152. Duly ratified treaties are binding on the United States as a matter of international law. Whether a given treaty has the force of domestic law, and if so, to what extent, will depend on the specific provisions of the treaty, including any reservations, understandings, or declarations made by the United States. For example, not all treaty provisions create judicially enforceable individual rights in the courts of the United States. In some cases where a treaty provision does not by its own force grant a judicially enforceable individual right, the federal government may enact implementing legislation that grants such a right as a means of implementing the treaty provision.

153. Historically, the prospect that the constitutional treaty power could be used to override or invalidate state and local law generated considerable domestic political controversy. Although it has been recognized that the treaty power is not limited by the scope of congressional authority over domestic matters (*see Missouri v. Holland*, 252 U.S. 416 (1920)), reliance upon that power to pre-empt State and local law has been considered by some to be an interference with the rights of the constituent States reserved to them under the Constitution. Consequently, the expectation has been that any changes to United States law required by treaty ratification will be accomplished in the ordinary legislative process.

154. Also, treaties as well as statutes must conform to the requirements of the Constitution. *Reid v. Covert*, 354 U.S. 1 (1957). Thus, the United States is unable to accept a treaty obligation which limits constitutionally protected rights, as in the case of Article 20 of the International Covenant on Civil and Political Rights, which infringes upon freedom of speech and association guaranteed under the First Amendment to the Constitution.

155. Consequently, in giving advice and consent to ratification of a treaty concerning the rights of individuals, Congress must give careful consideration to the specific provisions of the treaty and to the question of consistency with existing state and federal law, both constitutional and statutory. When elements or clauses of a treaty conflict with the Constitution, it is necessary for the United States to take reservations to

those elements or clauses, simply because neither the President nor Congress has the power to override the Constitution. In some cases, it has been considered necessary for the United States to state its understanding of a particular provision or undertaking in a treaty, or to make a declaration of how it intends to apply that provision or undertaking.

Implementation

156. When necessary to carry out its treaty obligations, the United States generally enacts implementing legislation rather than relying on a treaty to be "self-executing". Thus, for example, to implement the Genocide Convention, the United States Congress adopted the Genocide Convention Implementation Act of 1987, codified at 18 U.S.C. § 1091-93. When such legislation is required, the United States' practice with respect to certain treaties has been to enact the necessary legislation before depositing its instrument of ratification. It is for this reason, for example, that the United States did not deposit its instrument of ratification for the Convention Against Torture until 1994, even though the Senate gave its advice and consent to ratification of that treaty in 1990, as Congress did not approve the necessary implementing legislation until May 1994.

157. However, the United States does not believe it necessary to adopt implementing legislation when domestic law already makes adequate provision for the requirements of the treaty. Again, the Convention Against Torture provides a case in point. While final ratification awaited enactment of legislation giving United States courts criminal jurisdiction over extraterritorial acts amounting to torture which had not previously been covered by United States law, no new implementing legislation was proposed with respect to torture within the United States because United States law at all levels already prohibited acts of torture within the meaning of the Convention. Similarly, because the basic rights and fundamental freedoms guaranteed by the International Covenant on Civil and Political Rights (other than those to which the United States took a reservation) have long been protected as a matter of federal constitutional and statutory law, it was not considered necessary to adopt special implementing legislation to give effect to the Covenant's provisions in domestic law. That important human rights treaty was accordingly ratified in 1992 shortly after the Senate gave its advice and consent.

IV. INFORMATION AND PUBLICITY

158. Information concerning human rights treaties is readily available to any interested person in the United States. All treaties, including human rights treaties, to which the United States is a Party are published by the federal government, first in the Treaties and International Agreements Series (TIAS) and thereafter in the multi-volume United States Treaties (UST) series. Annually, the Department of State publishes a comprehensive listing of all treaties to which the United States is a Party, known as Treaties in Force (TIF). The constitutional requirement that the Senate give advice and consent to ratification of all treaties ensures that there is a public record of its consideration, typically including a formal transmission of the treaty from the President to the Senate, a record of the Senate Foreign Relations Committee's public hearing and the Committee's report to the full Senate, together with the action of the Senate itself.

159. The texts of all human rights treaties (whether or not the United States has ratified) can also be readily obtained from the government or virtually any public or private library, as they have been published in numerous non-governmental compilations and are also available in major computerized databases. The United Nations Compilation of International Instruments on Human Rights (ST/HR/1) is also widely available.

160. Although there is no national educational curriculum in the United States, instruction in fundamental constitutional, civil and political rights occurs throughout the educational system, from grammar and secondary school through the college and university levels. Most institutions of higher education, public and private, include courses on constitutional law in their departments of political science or government. Constitutional law is a required subject in law school curricula, and most law schools now offer advanced or specialized instruction in the area of civil and political rights, non-discrimination law and related fields. Nearly every law school curriculum includes instruction in international law including basic human rights law. Several textbooks have been published in the field, including documentary supplements which contain the texts of the more significant human rights instruments. The numerous non-governmental human rights advocacy groups in the United States, which operate freely, also contribute to public awareness and understanding of domestic and international rights and norms.

161. With particular respect to the International Covenant on Civil and Political Rights, the original transmittal of the treaty to the Senate was published in 1978 (Message from the President of the United

States Transmitting Four Treaties Pertaining to Human Rights, 95th Cong., 2d Sess., Exec. E, 23 Feb. 1978). The record of Senate consideration has also been published (see Hearing before the Senate Committee on Foreign Relations, 102d Cong., 1st Sess., 21 Nov. 1991, S. Hrg. 102-478; Report of the Senate Foreign Relations Committee, Exec. Rept. 102-23, 24 March 1992; 102 Cong. Rec. S4781-4784 (daily ed. 2 April 1992). The full text of the treaty has also been published in the official journal of the federal government (see 58 Federal Register 45934-45942, No. 167, 31 Aug. 1993). Copies of the Covenant have also been sent to the attorneys-general of each state and constituent unit in the United States, with a request that they be further distributed to relevant officials. The fact of United States ratification and the text of the treaty have also been brought to the attention of state bar associations. Governmental officials have participated in a number of presentations at academic and professional meetings to highlight the significance of United States ratification.

162. Finally, the advice and input of various non-governmental organizations and other human rights professionals was sought and considered during the preparation of this report, and the report will be given wide distribution to the public and through interested groups such as the bar associations and human rights organizations.

(For information on confidentiality protection, nonsampling error, and definitions, see *www.census.gov/prod/cen2000/doc/sf1.pdf*)

Area	1990						2000					
		Under 18		65 and over		Median age		Under 18		65 and over		Median age
	Total	Number	Per-cent	Number	Per-cent		Total	Number	Per-cent	Number	Per-cent	
United States	248,709,873	63,604,432	25.6	31,241,831	12.6	32.9	281,421,906	72,293,812	25.7	34,991,753	12.4	35.3
Region												
Northeast.........	50,809,229	11,913,007	23.4	6,995,156	13.8	34.2	53,594,378	13,047,783	24.3	7,372,282	13.8	36.8
Midwest..........	59,668,632	15,614,783	26.2	7,749,130	13.0	32.9	64,392,776	16,647,666	25.9	8,259,075	12.8	35.6
South..........	85,445,930	22,008,378	25.8	10,724,182	12.6	32.7	100,236,820	25,566,903	25.5	12,438,267	12.4	35.3
West	52,786,082	14,068,264	26.7	5,773,363	10.9	31.8	63,197,932	17,031,460	26.9	6,922,129	11.0	33.8

Source: U.S. Census Bureau, Census 2000 Summary File 1; 1990 Census of Population, General Population Characteristics, United States (1990 CP-1-1).

Population by Race and Hispanic Origin for the United States: 2000

Race and Hispanic or Latino	Number	Percent of total population
RACE		
Total population	281,421,906	100.0
One race	274,595,678	97.6
White	211,460,626	75.1
Black or African American	34,658,190	12.3
American Indian and Alaska Native	2,475,956	0.9
Asian..	10,242,998	3.6
Native Hawaiian and Other Pacific Islander	398,835	0.1
Some other race................................	15,359,073	5.5
Two or more races...............................	6,826,228	2.4
HISPANIC OR LATINO		
Total population	281,421,906	100.0
Hispanic or Latino	35,305,818	12.5
Not Hispanic or Latino............................	246,116,088	87.5

Source: U.S. Census Bureau, Census 2000 Redistricting (Public Law 94-171) Summary File, Tables PL1 and PL2.

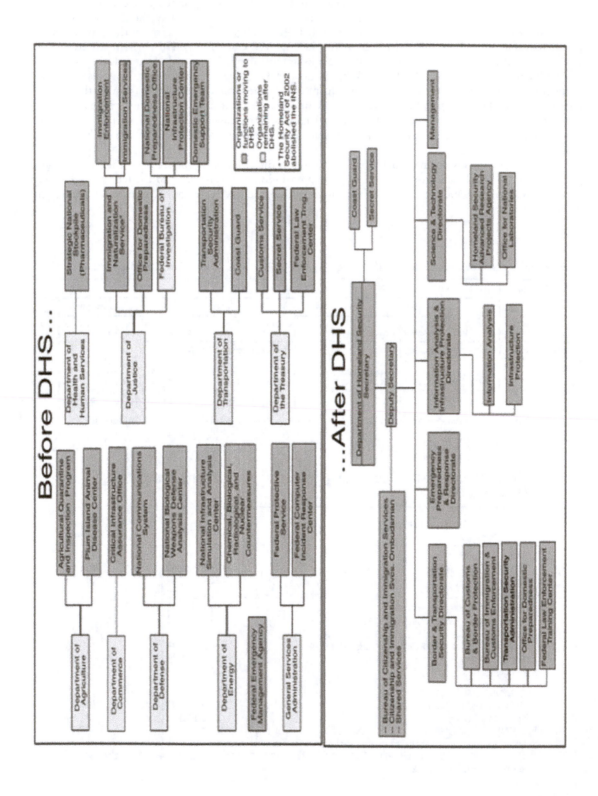

DOCUMENT 15A (SERIES)

Document 15A: (Series 15A to 15D—This is a series of documents related to the U.S. Periodic Report to the U.N. Human Rights Committee; they all form part of a single process)

Full Official Title: Second and Third Periodic Report of the United States of America to the U.N. Committee on Human Rights Concerning the International Covenant on Civil and Political Rights (U.S. Department of State)

Short Title/Acronym/Abbreviation: Second and Third U.S. Periodic Reports to the Human Rights Committee

Type of Document: This is a state periodic report submitted by the U.S. to a U.N. treaty body in compliance with Article 40 of the ICCPR, to which it is a party.

Subject: How the U.S. implements civil and political rights under the ICCPR

Official Citation: United States. Department of State. Second and Third Periodic Report of the United States of America to the U.N. Committee on Human Rights Concerning the International Covenant on Civil and Political Rights. Washington, October 21, 2005.U.N. Doc CCPR/C/USA/3

Date of Document: October 21, 2005

Date of Adoption: Not applicable

Date of General Entry into Force (EIF): Not applicable

Number of States Parties as of this printing: Not applicable

Date of Signature by the United States: Not applicable

Date of Ratification/Accession/Adhesion: Not applicable

Date of Entry into Force as to United States (effective date): Not applicable

Legal Status/Character of the Instrument/Document as to the United States: This is not a legal instrument but a document that is required to be filed by all state parties to fulfill their legal obligations under Article 40 of the ICCPR, which is a legally binding treaty.

Comments: By ratifying the ICCPR, the U.S. agreed under Article 40 to report to the Human Rights Committee on measures they have adopted to give effect to the rights recognized in the Covenant or any progress they have made or obstacles in the enjoyment of those rights. Each state is required to submit an initial report to the Committee within one year of the treaty entering into force, and subsequently whenever the Committee requests information. The Committee may submit to the State a list of issues it wants the state to address. The State may respond in writing. The U.S. responses to the List of Issues is contained in Document 15B. The state will appear before the Committee in Geneva and have a discussion on issues of concern to the Committee or to clarify things. The Committee then reviews all the information and issues its Concluding observations and recommendations. These are contained in Document 15C. It is up to the state to then decide whether and how to implement these recommendations or contest the conclusions. The state may respond to those recommendations in follow up comments. These are contained in Document 15D. This is an administrative and not a judicial process. The results are not legally binding.

This is the United States' second and third report and addresses several of the Committee's specific concerns with the implementation of the Covenant. The report is an important tool to reiterate the U.S. position on its treaty obligations and any differences of opinion it may have with the Committee over how they interpret specific obligations, such as the territorial scope of the application of the Covenant. This is a particularly important report because it is the first one submitted during the so-called war on terrorism and the Committee is obviously very concerned about some of the U.S. counter-terrorism measures, such as detainee treatment, interrogations and racial profiling. The U.S., on the other hand, doesn't want anything that occurs outside of the U.S. territory, such as Guantánamo, to be brought up by the Committee.

This report should be read along with the following three documents to get an idea of the give and take between the international community, represented by the Committee and the U.S. represented by a Department of State delegation. First document to be read is Document 15A, which forms the basis for everything else in this periodic reporting process.

The Second and Third Reports document is very large and could not be reprinted in its entirety. Only selected excerpts corresponding to certain articles of the ICCPR are included. The reader should consult the following website to obtain the full text.

Web Address: http://www.state.gov/g/drl/rls/55504.htm

Second and Third Report of the U.S. to the U.N. Human Rights Committee (Excerpts)

I. INTRODUCTION

1. The Government of the United States of America welcomes this opportunity to provide the Human Rights Committee the U.S. combined second and third periodic report on measures giving effect to U.S. undertakings under the International Covenant on Civil and Political Rights ("the Covenant") in accordance with Article 40 thereof. The organization of this periodic report follows the General Guidelines of the Human Rights Committee regarding the form and content of periodic reports to be submitted by States Parties (CCPR/C/66/GUI/Rev.2).

2. The following information supplements that provided in the U.S. Initial Report of July 1994 (CCPR/C/81/Add.4, published 24 August 1994; and HRI/CORE/1/Add.49, published 17 August 1994). It also supplements the information provided by the U.S. delegation at the meetings of the Human Rights Committee, which discussed the Initial Report on 31 March 1995 (CCPR/C/SR. 1401-1402 and SR. 1405-1406, published 24 April 1995). The information also takes into account the concluding observations of the Committee, CCPR/C/79/Add.50; A/50/40, paras. 266-304, published 3 October 1995, and the 27 July 2004 letter of the Committee to the United States in which the Committee invited the United States to address several of its specific concerns.

3. In this consolidated report, the United States has sought to respond to the Committee's concerns as fully as possible, notwithstanding the continuing difference of view between the Committee and the United States concerning certain matters relating to the import and scope of provisions of the Covenant. In particular, in regard to the latter, the United States respectfully reiterates its firmly held legal view on the territorial scope of application of the Covenant.

See Annex I.

II. IMPLEMENTATION OF SPECIFIC PROVISIONS OF THE COVENANT

Article 1—Self-determination

4. The basic principle of self-determination remains at the core of American political life, as the nation was born in a struggle against the colonial regime of the British during the eighteenth century. The right to self-determination, set forth in Article 1 of the Covenant, is reflected in Article IV, Section 4 of the United States Constitution, which obliges the federal government to guarantee to every state a "Republican Form of Government."

5. *The Insular Areas.* The United States continues to exercise sovereignty over a number of Insular Areas, each of which is unique and constitutes an integral part of the U.S. political family.

. . .

American Indians

9. The United States is home to more than 560 federally recognized tribes with about 50 percent of the American Indian and Alaska Native population residing on or near 280 reservations. These tribal lands represent about four percent of the United States' total land area.

10. In addition, there are approximately 56 million acres held in federal trust for the use and benefit of tribes and individual Indians. Trust land is maintained both on and off Indian reservations, and may not be alienated, encumbered, or otherwise restricted without the approval of the Secretary of the Interior. A significant number of acres of land are owned in fee status whereby the United States holds the fee to the land as a means of acquisition prior to converting the land to trust land.

11. *History of Indian Trust Accounts.* The federal government-Indian trust relationship dates back over a century. As to individual Indians, pursuant to its assimilationist policy in the 19th century, Congress passed the General Allotment Act of 1887, also known as the "Dawes Act." 25 U.S.C. § 331, et seq. (as amended). Under the General Allotment Act, beneficial title of allotted lands vested in the United States as trustee for individual Indians. *See Cobell v. Norton*, 240 F.3d 1081, 1087 (D.C. Cir. 2001). The trust had a term of 25 years, at which point a fee patent would issue to the individual Indian allottee. *See id.* Allotment of tribal lands ceased with the enactment of the Indian Reorganization Act of 1934 ("IRA"). *See id.* (citing 48 Stat. 984 (codified as amended at 25 U.S.C. § 461 et seq.)). Allotted lands remained allotted, but the IRA provided that unallotted surplus Indian lands return to tribal ownership.

. . .

15. *Committee Recommendation*: **That steps be taken to ensure that previously recognized aboriginal Native American rights cannot be extinguished.** The term "recognized aboriginal rights" does not have a

meaning per se in U.S. Indian law and practice. Moreover, under U.S. law recognized tribal property rights are subject to diminishment or elimination under the plenary authority reserved to the U.S. Congress for conducting Indian affairs.

16. *Committee Recommendation*: **That the government ensure that there is a full judicial review in respect of determinations of federal recognition of tribes**. The U.S. regulatory process for recognizing tribal governments is set forth in 25 C.F.R. Part 83; it provides that determinations may be reviewed in federal court. In particular, an administrative decision not to recognize a tribe can be challenged in federal court. Also, Congress retains the authority, subject to some constitutional constraints, to recognize Indian groups as tribes.

17. *Committee Recommendation*: **That the Self-Governance Demonstration Project and similar programs be strengthened to continue to fight the high incidence of poverty, sickness and alcoholism among Native Americans**. The Self-Governance Demonstration Project became a permanent program for the U.S. Department of the Interior in 1994 and for the U.S. Department for Health and Human Services in 2003. *See* 25 U.S.C. § 458aa et seq. As of 2003, more than 200 tribes had participated in the program under 81 agreements with the United States which were funded at a total cost of $304,857,315. The Self-Governance Program continues to be credited with the improved delivery of services to American Indians and Alaska Natives.

18. *Committee Request*: **Describe the constitutional and political processes—including the legislative, administrative or other measures in force—which in practice allow the exercise of the right of self-determination within the U.S.** Under the concept of tribal self-determination, the tribes have the right to operate under their own governmental systems within the American political framework. In Article 1, Section 8, Clause 3 of the United States Constitution, tribes are recognized as political entities with a government-to-government relationship with the United States. The United States enables, assists, and supports the exercise of tribal self-determination. One example of this government support of the exercise of tribal self-determination and self-governance is through Indian Self-Determination Contracts and Grants for the entire range of governmental programs frequently administered by tribal governments, including health, education, human services, public safety and justice, community development, resources management, trust services, and general administration.

19. *Current policy*. As stated by President George W. Bush on 23 September 2004, "my administration is committed to continuing to work with federally recognized tribal governments on a government to government basis and strongly supports and respects tribal sovereignty and self-determination for tribal governments in the United States." George W. Bush, Memorandum for the Heads of Executive Departments and Agencies. President Bush stated that his administration would continue to provide Native Americans "with new economic and educational opportunities." Proclamation No. 7500, 66 Fed. Reg. 57, 641 (Nov. 12, 2001). *See also*, George W. Bush, Letter Celebrating the 35th Anniversary of President Richard Nixon's Special Message to Congress on Indian Affairs, (July 1, 2005); George W. Bush, Proclamation of National American Indian Heritage Month, (Nov. 4, 2004); and, George W. Bush, Government-to-Government Relationship with Tribal Governments, (Sept. 23, 2004).

20. *Committee Request*: **Describe the factors or difficulties which prevent the free disposal by peoples of their natural wealth and resources contrary to the provisions of Article 1 of the Covenant and the extent to which such prevention affects the enjoyment of other rights set forth in the Covenant**. Under the concept of tribal self-determination, the tribes have the right to operate under their own governmental systems within the American political framework. In some circumstances, the United States may require that Native Americans secure the consent of the federal government prior to disposing of their property or natural resources. Native Americans are the owners of land and resources, which may be held in either trust or in fee. In either case, there are processes available for the disposal or alienation of the land or the natural resources if they so choose, with the consent of the federal government.

...

Article 2—Equal protection of rights in the Covenant

26. The enjoyment by all individuals within the United States of the rights enumerated in the Covenant without regard to race, color, sex, language, religion, political or other opinion, national or social origin, property, birth or other status, was elaborated upon in paragraphs 77–100 of the Initial Report.

27. Since submission of its Initial Report, the United States has ratified the International Convention on the Elimination of All Forms of Racial Discrimination; that Convention entered into force for the United

States on 20 November, 1994. The United States Initial Report under that Convention was submitted to the U.N. Committee on the Elimination of Racial Discrimination in September 2000. Committee on the Elimination of Racial Discrimination; Third periodic reports of States Parties due in 1999: United States of America, U.N. Doc. CERD/C/351/Add.1 (2000). The United States was examined by that Committee on that report in August 2001. Concluding Observations of the Committee on the Elimination of Racial Discrimination: United States of America, Comm. on the Elimination of Racial Discrimination, 59th Sess., U.N. Doc. CERD/C/59/Misc.17/Rev.3 (2001).

28. *Classifications*. Under the doctrine of equal protection, it has long been recognized that the government must treat persons who are "similarly situated" on an equal basis, but can treat persons in different situations or classes in different ways with respect to a permissible state purpose. The general rule is that legislative classifications are presumed valid if they bear some reasonable relation to a legitimate governmental purpose. *See FCC v. Beach Communication, Inc.*, 508 U.S. 307 (1993); *McGowan v. Maryland*, 366 U.S. 420, 425-36 (1961). The most obvious example is economic regulation. Both state and federal governments are able to apply different rules to different types of economic activities, and the courts will review such regulation under a very deferential standard. *See, e.g., Williamson v. Lee Optical Co.*, 348 U.S. 483 (1955). Similarly, the way in which a state government chooses to allocate its financial resources among categories of needy people will be reviewed under a very deferential standard. *See Dandridge v. Williams*, 397 U.S. 471 (1970).

29. *Suspect classifications*. On the other hand, certain distinctions or classifications have been recognized as inherently invidious and therefore have been subjected to more exacting scrutiny and judged against more stringent requirements. For example, classifications on the basis of racial distinctions are automatically "suspect" and must be justified as necessary to a compelling govern- mental purpose and as narrowly tailored to achieving a valid compelling government interest. *See, e.g., Adarand Constructors, Inc. v. Pena*, 515 U.S. 200 (1995); *Korematsu v. United States*, 323 U.S. 214 (1944); *Brown v. Board of Education*, 347 U.S. 483 (1954); *McLaughlin v. Florida*, 379 U.S. 184 (1961); *Loving v. Virginia*, 388 U.S. 1 (1967).

30. This rule was recently reiterated by the Supreme Court in *Johnson v. California*, 125 S. Ct. 1141 (2005). Petitioner, a prison inmate, sued the California Department of Corrections (CDC), alleging that the CDC's unwritten policy of segregating new and transferred prisoners by race violated the inmate's constitutional right to equal protection of the laws. The CDC contended that the policy was necessary to prevent violence caused by racial prison gangs and was thus reasonably related to legitimate penological interests.

31. The Supreme Court held that the policy was subject to strict judicial scrutiny since it was based on racial classification, and thus the classification was required to be narrowly tailored to further compelling CDC interests. The court found that compromising the inmate's equal protection rights was not necessarily needed for proper prison administration. The CDC's discretion and expertise in the unique area of managing daily prison operations did not warrant deference to the CDC's use of race as a means of controlling prison violence.

32. The court has also affirmed the application of an intermediate level of scrutiny to classifications by gender. *See United States v. Virginia*, 518 U.S. 515 (1996) (stating military college's male-only policy was unconstitutional because the state failed to provide an "exceedingly persuasive justification" for categorically excluding admission of women).

33. *Corrective or affirmative action*. It remains a matter of continuing interest in the United States whether legislation may classify by race for purposes of compensating for past racial discrimination. The general rule that has evolved is that because race is a "suspect classification," in this context as in all others, it will be subject to "strict scrutiny" by the courts. *See, e.g., Adarand Constructors, Inc. v. Perla*, 515 U.S. 200 (1995); *Richmond v. Croson*, 488 U.S. 469 (1989). However, where an employer or other entity has engaged in racial discrimination in the past, it will generally be permitted (and may sometimes be required) to accord narrowly tailored racial preferences for a limited period of time, to correct the effects of its past conduct. *See Wygant v. Jackson Bd. of Educ.*, 476 U.S. 267 (1986). Government entities, however, may also attempt to address discriminatory acts of others when the effects of such discrimination may be extended by government policies.

34. *Black Farmers*. One of the major issues addressed by the U.S. Department of Agriculture (USDA) is the ongoing implementation of the historic civil rights Consent Decree in the federal district court case of *Pigford v. Veneman*, 355 F. Supp. 2d 148 (D.D.C. 2005); *see also Pigford v. Glickman*, 185 F.R.D. 82 (D.D.C. 1999). *Pigford* is a class action lawsuit brought by African American farmers who alleged that USDA discriminated against them on the basis of their race in its farm credit and non-credit benefit programs.

35. On 14 April, 1999, the U.S. District Court for the District of Columbia approved a Consent Decree resolving the case. *See Pigford v. Glickman*, 185 F.R.D. 82 (D.D.C. 1999). (A consent decree is an order of

a judge based upon an agreement, almost always put in writing, between the parties to a lawsuit instead of continuing the case through trial or hearing. A consent decree is a common practice when the government has sued to make a person or corporation comply with the law or the defendant agrees to the consent decree in return for the government not pursuing criminal penalties.)

36. The *Pigford* Consent Decree set up a claims process under which the individual claims of class members would be adjudicated. Class members could either choose Track A, which is an expedited process with a lesser evidentiary standard and automatic relief for prevailing claimants; or Track B, which entitles the claimant to a one-day hearing before the Consent Decree Arbitrator in which the typical evidentiary standard applies and the claimant can receive any relief that the Arbitrator awards.

. . .

40. *Federal statutes.* The Religious Land Use and Institutionalized Persons Act of 2000 (RLUIPA), 42 U.S.C. § 2000cc, et seq., (2004), prohibits governments from imposing a substantial burden on the exercise of religion or otherwise discriminating against individuals or organizations based on their religion through land use regulation. RLUIPA also prohibits government-run institutions, such as prisons, jails, and hospitals, from imposing a substantial burden on the religious exercise of an institutionalized individual. The Attorney General can bring civil actions for injunctive relief to enforce compliance with RLUIPA.

. . .

42. *Aliens.* Under United States immigration law, an alien is "any person not a citizen or national of the United States." 8 U.S.C. § 1101(a)(3). Aliens who are admitted and legally residing in the United States, even though not U.S. citizens, generally enjoy the constitutional and Covenant rights and protections of citizens, including the right to life; freedom from torture or cruel, inhuman or degrading treatment or punishment; prohibition of slavery; the right to liberty and security of person; the right to humane treatment for persons deprived of their liberty; freedom from imprisonment for breach of contractual obligation; freedom of movement; the right to fair trial; prohibition of ex post facto laws; recognition as a person under the law; freedom from arbitrary interference with privacy, family and home in the United States; freedom of thought, conscience and religion; freedom of opinion and expression; freedom of assembly; and freedom of association.

43. Legal aliens enjoy equal protection rights as well. Distinctions between lawful permanent resident aliens and citizens require justification, but not the compelling state interests required for distinctions based on race. Consistent with Article 25 of the Covenant, aliens are generally precluded from voting or holding federal elective office. A number of federal statutes, some of which are discussed above, prohibit discrimination on account of alienage and national origin.

44. Throughout the Immigration and Nationality Act, Congress distinguishes lawful permanent residents (LPRs) and non-LPRs. The federal courts have held that Congress may draw such distinctions consistently with the Equal Protection Clause of the Fifth Amendment so long as there is a facially legitimate and bona fide reason for treating the two classes disparately. *See, e.g., De Leon-Reynoso v. Ashcroft*, 293 F.3d 633 (3d Cir. 2002); *Jankowski-Burczyk v. INS*, 291 F.3d 172 (2d Cir. 2002); *Lara-Ruiz v. INS*, 241 F.3d 934(7th Cir. 2001).

45. With the creation of the Department of Homeland Security (DHS) in 2003, Congress established an Officer for Civil Rights and Civil Liberties. The Officer is charged with reviewing and assessing information concerning abuses of civil rights, civil liberties, and discrimination on the basis of race, ethnicity and religion, by employees or officials of the Department of Homeland Security. The Officer has a unique internal function of assisting the senior leadership to develop policies and initiatives in ways that protect civil rights and civil liberties. The Officer conducts outreach activities to non-governmental organizations and others to communicate the Office's role and the Department's commitment to the protection of individual liberties. The DHS Office for Civil Rights and Civil Liberties has been actively working to develop relationships with the Arab-American and Muslim-American communities. Reaching out to immigrant communities is an important part of a dialogue to address concerns regarding racial, ethnic, and religious discrimination.

46. *Education.* The Equal Protection Clause of the United States Constitution bars public schools and universities from discrimination on the grounds of race, sex, religion, or national origin. Under Title IV of the Civil Rights Act of 1964, the U.S. Department of Justice may bring suit against a school board that deprives children of equal protection of the laws, or against a public university that denies admission to any person on the rounds of "race, color, religion, sex or national origin." The Department of Justice continues to enforce court-issued consent decrees against local school boards that had engaged in racial segregation in the past in cases that may date back 40 years. The Department of Justice also investigates and brings new cases of education discrimination.

47. The Department of Justice has investigated a number of cases involving discrimination against or harassment of Muslim or Arab children in public schools. For example, the Department brought an action against a school district that barred a Muslim girl from wearing a hijab to school, resulting in a consent decree that will protect the rights of students to wear religious garb. Similarly, the Department obtained a settlement in a case in which another girl was harassed by a teacher and students because she was a Muslim.

. . .

52. The Supreme Court ruled that under the Americans with Disabilities Act of 1990 (ADA), states are required to place individuals with mental disabilities who are in the state's care in community settings rather than in institutions when the state's treatment professionals have determined that community placement is appropriate, the individual does not oppose the transfer from institutional care to a less restrictive setting and the community setting placement can be reasonably accommodated, taking into account the state's resources and the needs of others with mental disabilities. *See Olmstead v. L.C.*, 527 U.S. 581 (1999). In Executive Order 13217, President Bush selected the top officials in several federal agencies, including the Departments of Education, Labor, and Housing and Urban Development, to assist the states and localities in swift implementation of the *Olmstead* decision to help ensure that all Americans have the opportunity to live close to their families and friends, to live more independently, to engage in productive employment, and to participate in community life. Executive Order 13217(June 18, 2001).

53. While the Equal Protection Clause of the Constitution bars governmental discrimination on the basis of race, the Supreme Court has permitted the use of race as a factor when it serves a compelling government interest and is narrowly tailored to achieve that interest. In *Grutter v. Bollinger*, 539 U.S. 306 (2003), the Supreme Court upheld the University of Michigan Law School's "affirmative action" program, which allowed the racial and ethnic background of applicants to be considered as a factor in admission decisions. The Court found that the Law School's use of race in admissions to obtain the educational benefits that flow from a diverse student body is constitutional, i.e., that attaining a diverse student body may qualify as a "compelling" interest and that the Law School's use of race is narrowly tailored to achieve this goal. On the issue of whether attaining a diverse student body was a compelling interest, the Court deferred to the Law School's educational judgment that such student body diversity is essential to its educational mission. The Court found the Law School's program to be narrowly tailored to achieve this goal because its interest in achieving a critical mass of minority students was a flexible goal and not a quota, it did not preempt a holistic review of each applicant's file, and it did not "unduly burden" individuals who are not members of the favored racial and ethnic groups. The Court opined that unlike the University of Michigan's undergraduate admissions program, the Law School awarded no "mechanical, predetermined diversity 'bonuses' based on race or ethnicity." The Court also held that "race-conscious admissions policies must be limited in time" and expressed an expectation that "25 years from now, the use of racial preferences will no longer be necessary to further the interest approved today." At the same time, the Court in *Gratz v. Bollinger*, 539 U.S. 244 (2003), struck down the admissions policies of the same university's undergraduate program on the ground that it operated as a mechanical quota that was not narrowly tailored to achieve its goal of racial diversity.

. . .

58. *Education and aliens.* The courts have held that the constitutional guarantee of equal protection of the laws applies to aliens who have made an entry into the United States, even if such entry was unlawful. In *Plyer v. Doe*, 457 U.S. 202 (1982), the Supreme Court invalidated a Texas law which withheld state funds from local school districts for the education of undocumented alien children, and allowed local school districts to refuse to enroll the children.

The Court first found that the Equal Protection Clause of the Constitution applies to the undocumented alien children. Then, although the Court did not treat the aliens as a suspect class entitled to strict scrutiny of their differing treatment, the Court nonetheless required the state to demonstrate a rational basis for its restrictions. The Court concluded that the state could not meet this test, rejecting the state's arguments that denial of benefits was justified due to the children's lack of legal status and based on the state's desire to preserve resources for the education of the state's lawful residents.

. . .

Article 3—Equal rights of men and women

60. *Constitutional protections.* As discussed in paragraphs 101–109 of the Initial Report, the rights enumerated in the Covenant and provided by U.S. law are guaranteed equally to men and women in the United States through the Equal Protection and Due Process Clauses of the Fourteenth and Fifth Amendments of

the United States Constitution. These provisions prohibit both the federal government and the states from arbitrarily or irrationally discriminating on the basis of gender.

61. *Gender Classifications.* In *Craig v. Boren*, 429 U.S. 190 (1976), the Supreme Court articulated a standard which governed the field of gender distinctions for several years:"[t]o withstand constitutional challenge … classifications by gender must serve important governmental objectives and must be substantially related to achievement of those objectives. *Id.* at 197; *see also, Califano v. Goldfarb*, 430 U.S. 199 (1977); *Taylor v. Louisiana*, 419 U.S. 522 (1975).

62. However, in *United States v. Virginia*, 518 U.S. 515 (1996), the Supreme Court articulated the current standard for equal protection review of gender distinctions. The justification for such distinctions must be "exceedingly persuasive." *Id.* at 533. "The burden of justification is demanding and it rests entirely on the state. The state must show 'at least that the [challenged] classification serves important governmental objectives and that the discriminatory means employed are substantially related to the achievement of those objectives.'" *Id.*, (quoting *Mississippi Univ. for Women v. Hogan*, 458 U.S. 718, 724 (1982)). Furthermore, "[t]he justification must be genuine, not hypothesized or invented post hoc in response to litigation. And it must not rely on overbroad generalizations about the different talents, capacities, or preferences of males and females." *Id.*.

63. In *Nguyen v. INS*, 533 U.S. 53 (2001), the Supreme Court applied the *Virginia* standard to uphold a federal immigration statute that makes gender-based distinctions in the methods of establishing citizenship for a child born out-of-wedlock overseas where one parent is a U.S. citizen and the other is an alien. The statute, 8 U.S.C. § 1409(a), requires that certain steps be taken to document parenthood when the citizen-parent is the child's father but not when the citizen-parent is the child's mother. The Court found that the statute substantially serves the important governmental objectives of ensuring the existence of a biological relationship between the citizen-parent and the child, as the mother-child relationship is verifiable from the child's birth. *Id.* at 62. The Court also reasoned that the statute ensures at least the opportunity for the development of ties between the child and the citizen-parent, and, in turn, the United States, as the very event of birth provides such an opportunity for the mother and child. *Id.* at 64–65. Because fathers and mothers are not similarly situated with regard to proof of parentage, the Court held that the gender-based distinctions in the statute were justified. *Id.* at 63, 73. The Court also noted that the additional requirements imposed upon fathers were "minimal" and that the statute did not impose "inordinate and unnecessary hurdles to the conferral of citizenship on the children of citizen fathers[.]" *Id.* at 70–71.

64. On 23 June, 2000, Executive Order 13160 was issued prohibiting discrimination on the basis of a number of classifications, including sex, in federally-conducted education and training programs. 65 Fed. Reg. 39,775 (2000). This order applies to all federally conducted education and training programs as a supplement to existing laws and regulations that already prohibit many forms of discrimination in both federally conducted and federally assisted educational programs.

65. *Discrimination based on pregnancy.* The Pregnancy Discrimination Act (PDA) of 1978, 42 U.S.C. § 2000e(k)(2004), amended Title VII of the Civil Rights Act of 1964 to provide that discrimination "on the basis of sex" includes discrimination "because of or on the basis of pregnancy, childbirth, or related medical conditions[.]" The PDA requires that pregnancy be treated the same as other physical or medical conditions.

66. The PDA has been held to protect not only female employees, but also the spouses of male employees. In *Newport News Shipbuilding and Dry Dock Co. v. E.E.O.C.*, 462U.S. 669, 684-85 (1983), the Supreme Court held that a provision in an employer's health insurance plan that provided female employees with hospitalization benefits for pregnancy-related conditions, but provided less extensive benefits for spouses of male employees, discriminated against male employees in violation of the Civil Rights Act of 1964, as amended by the PDA. The Court stated that the PDA "makes clear that it is discriminatory to treat pregnancy-related conditions less favorably than other medical conditions." *Id.* at 684.67. In *International Union v. Johnson Controls, Inc.*, 499 U.S. 187, 206 (1991), the Supreme Court held that a battery manufacturer's policy prohibiting women capable of bearing children from working in jobs involving lead exposure violated Title VII of the Civil Rights Act of 1964, as amended by the PDA. The Court recognized that the PDA prohibits discrimination not only on the basis of pregnancy, but also on the basis of a woman's capacity to become pregnant. *Id.*

…

68. The PDA has been found to apply to contraceptive coverage in employer health insurance plans. On 14 December, 2000, the U.S. Equal Employment Opportunity Commission (EEOC) decided that the

exclusion of prescription contraceptives from a health insurance plan that covered other comparable medical treatments was a violation of Title VII of the Civil Rights Act of 1964, as amended by the PDA. However, this was an administrative reasonable cause determination, and not an authoritative construction of the PDA.

69. *Prohibition of Sex Discrimination in Education.* Title IX of the Education Amendments of 1972 (20 U.S.C. § 1681 et seq.) is the principal federal law that prohibits sex discrimination in education programs or activities that receive federal financial assistance. Federal regulations and guidelines require and assist schools in addressing such issues as sexual harassment and nondiscrimination in admissions, financial assistance, course offerings, parental or marital status, and opportunities to participate in interscholastic and inter-collegiate athletics. Each school or educational institution is required to designate an employee to coordinate its Title IX responsibilities, including investigating complaints alleging violations of Title IX.

70. Title IX is primarily enforced by the Department of Education's Office for Civil Rights which investigates complaints, issues policy guidance, and provides technical assistance to schools (such as training, and sponsorship of and participation in civil rights conferences). Students and school employees may also bring private lawsuits against schools for violations of Title IX.

71. Furthermore, every federal agency that provides financial assistance to education programs is required to enforce Title IX. In August 2000, twenty federal agencies issued a final common rule for the enforcement of Title IX. In addition, Executive Order 13160, issued in June 2000, prohibits discrimination based on sex, race, color, national origin, disability, religion, age, sexual orientation, and status as a parent in education and training programs conducted by the federal government.

72. *Prohibition of Discrimination in Education on the Basis of Pregnancy.* The Title IX implementing regulation at 34 C.F.R. 106.40(a) specifically prohibits educational institutions that are recipients of federal financial assistance from applying any rule concerning a student's actual or potential parental, family, or marital status, which treats students differently on the basis of sex. The Title IX implementing regulation at 34 C.F.R. 106.40(b)(1) prohibits a recipient from discriminating against any student, or excluding any student from its education programs or activities, including any class or extracurricular activity, on the basis of such student's pregnancy or pregnancy related condition, unless the student requests voluntarily to participate in a separate portion of the program or activity of the recipient. The Title IX implementing regulation at 34 C.F.R. 106.40(b)(3) provides that if a recipient operates a portion of its education program or activity separately for pregnant students, to which admittance is completely voluntary on the part of the student, a recipient shall ensure that the instructional program in the separate program is comparable to that offered to non-pregnant students.

73. The Title IX implementing regulation at 34 C.F.R. 106.40(b)(2) provides that a recipient may require a pregnant student to obtain the certification of a physician that the student is physically and emotionally able to continue participation in the normal education program or activity so long as such a certification is required of all students for other physical or emotional conditions requiring the attention of a physician. With respect to a recipient that does not have leave of absence policies for students, or in the case of a student who does not otherwise qualify for leave under such a policy, the Title IX implementing regulation at 34 C.F.R. 106.40(b)(5) provides that a recipient shall treat pregnancy and pregnancy-related conditions as a justification for a leave of absence for so long a period of time as is deemed medically necessary by the student's physician, at the conclusion of which the student shall be reinstated to the status which she held when the leave began.

74. A recipient shall treat pregnancy and pregnancy-related conditions in the same manner and under the same policies as any temporary disability with respect to any medical or hospital benefit, service, plan, or policy which such recipient administers, operates, offers, or participates in with respect to students admitted to the recipient's educational program or activity. 34 C.F.R. 106.40(b)(4).

75. *Sexual Harassment.* Sexual harassment has been found to be a form of sex discrimination. Thus, federal statutes prohibiting discrimination on the basis of sex in employment, Title VII of the Civil Rights Act of 1964, 42 U.S.C. § 2000e et seq, and in federally assisted education programs, Title IX of the Education Amendments of 1972, 20 U.S.C. 1681, also prohibit sexual harassment. In a series of decisions, the Supreme Court has established the principles underlying the application of these statutes to sexual harassment. First, it is clear that same-sex harassment is actionable, as long as the harassment is based upon sex. *See Oncale v. Sundowner Offshore Servs., Inc.*, 523 U.S. 75 (1998). With respect to employment, where harassment by a supervisor results in a "tangible employment action" such as demotion, discharge, or undesirable reassignment, the employer is liable for a Title VII violation. Even if there has been no such tangible employment

action by the employer, there may nonetheless be a Title VII violation if workplace harassment is "sufficiently severe or pervasive to alter the conditions of [the victim's] employment and create an abusive working environment." *See, Meritor Sav. Bank, FSB v. Vinson*, 477 U.S. 57, 67 (1986) (citations and internal quotation marks omitted). In such cases, however, an employer may avoid liability if it demonstrates that: 1) it exercised reasonable care to prevent and correct promptly any sexually harassing behavior; and 2) the employee unreasonably failed to take advantage of any preventive opportunities provided by the employer or to avoid harm otherwise. *See, e.g., Faragher v. City of Boca Raton*, 524 U.S. 775, 807 (1998); *Burlington Indus. v. Ellerth*, 524 U.S. 742, 765 (1998).

76. With respect to education, educational institutions that receive federal financial assistance may be liable for damages in sexual harassment suits if school officials have actual notice of the harassment, and respond to that notice with deliberate indifference. *See, e.g., Franklin v. Gwinnett County Pub. Sch.*, 503 U.S. 60 (1992); *Gebser v. Lago Vista Indep. Sch. Dist.*, 524 U.S. 274 (1998); *Davis v. Monroe County Bd. of Educ.*, 526 U.S. 629 (1999).

77. *Compensation for sex discrimination.* Section 706(g) of the Civil Rights Act of 1964 provides that courts may enjoin respondents from engaging in unlawful employment practices, and order such affirmative action as may be appropriate, including reinstatement or hiring of employees with or without back pay, or any other equitable relief the court may require. 42 U.S.C. § 2000e-5(g)(1). Section 102 of the Civil Rights Act of 1991 provides that Title VII claims not involving disparate impact may result in compensatory and punitive damages in addition to the relief authorized by Section 706(g) of the Civil Rights Act. 42 U.S.C. § 1981a(a)(1). Punitive damages are allowed when the plaintiff can demonstrate that the defendant acted with malice or reckless indifference to the plaintiff's federally protected rights, but are not allowed against governmental entities. 42 U.S.C. § 1981a(b)(1). The sum of compensatory and punitive damages for each plaintiff cannot exceed $50,000 for employers with between 14 and 100 employees, $100,000 for employers with 100 to 200 employees, $200,000 for employers with 201 to 500 employees, and $300,000 for employers with more than 500 employees. 42 U.S.C. § 1981a(b)(3). Federally assisted educational institutions may also be liable for damages for sex discrimination. *See Gebser, supra.*

78. *Family Leave.* The federal Family and Medical Leave Act (FMLA), 29 U.S.C. § 2601 et seq., guarantees that employees who work for companies with 50 or more employees can take up to 12 weeks of unpaid leave a year for the birth or adoption of a child, or for a serious health condition of the employee or a family member of the employee, including a child, spouse or parent. The FMLA defines a serious health condition as an illness, injury, impairment, or physical or mental condition that involves in-patient care in a hospital, hospice, or residential medical care facility, or continuing treatment by a health care provider. 29 U.S.C. § 2611(11).

79. The FMLA allows states to provide additional protections, and several states have family leave laws that are more generous than the FMLA. For example, some states have family and medical leave laws that apply to employers with fewer than 50 employees, provide longer time periods for family and medical leave, use a more expansive definition of "family member," or require leave for participation in children's educational activities.

80. Title VII of the Civil Rights Act of 1964, as amended by the Pregnancy Discrimination Act (PDA), also imposes certain obligations on employers with respect to maternity leave. The PDA requires that women affected by pregnancy or childbirth be treated the same as others for all employment-related purposes, including receipt of benefits under fringe benefit programs and leave time. Although an employer need not treat pregnancy more favorably than other conditions, an employer may choose to do so. *See California Federal Savings & Loan Ass'n v. Guerra*, 479 U.S. 272, 285 (1987) (agreeing with lower court that "Congress intended the PDA to be a 'floor beneath which pregnancy disability benefits may not drop—not a ceiling above which they may not rise'") (quoting *California Federal Savings & Loan Ass'n v. Guerra*, 758 F.2d 390, 396 (9th Cir. 1985)).

81. *Violence Against Women.* On 13 September, 1994, the U.S. Congress passed the Violence Against Women Act (VAWA), a comprehensive legislative package aimed at ending violence against women. Violent Crime Control and Law Enforcement Act of 1994, 42 U.S.C. § 13701 (2004).

82. VAWA was designed to improve criminal justice responses to domestic violence, sexual assault, and stalking and to increase the availability of services for victims of these crimes. VAWA requires a coordinated community response to domestic violence, sexual assault, and stalking crimes, encouraging jurisdictions to bring together multiple players to share information and to use their distinct roles to improve community responses. These players often include: victim advocates; police officers, prosecutors, judges, probation and

corrections officials; health care professionals; leaders within faith communities; survivors of violence against women; and others.

83. VAWA and subsequent legislation created new federal crimes involving interstate domestic violence, interstate violation of a protection order, interstate stalking, and firearms, strengthened penalties for repeat sex offenders, and required states and territories to enforce protection orders issued by other states, tribes and territories. VAWA also created legal relief for certain battered immigrants to prevent abusers from discouraging undocumented alien victims from calling the police or seeking safety due to their unlawful status.

84. VAWA also created the National Domestic Violence Hotline and authorized funds to support domestic violence shelters, rape prevention education, domestic violence intervention and prevention programs, and programs to improve law enforcement, prosecution, court, and victim services responses to violence against women.

85. The Violence Against Women Act of 2000 (VAWA 2000), Pub. L. No. 106-386, 114 Stat. 1464, enacted on 28 October, 2000, and codified at 42 U.S.C. § 3796gg, continued and strengthened the federal government's commitment to helping communities change the way they respond to these crimes. VAWA 2000 reauthorized critical grant programs created by VAWA and subsequent legislation and established new programs such as initiatives addressing elder abuse, violence against women with disabilities, and supervised visitation with children in domestic violence cases. VAWA 2000 also strengthened the original law by improving protections for battered immigrants, sexual assault survivors, and victims of dating violence and creating a new federal cyberstalking crime.

86. *The Office on Violence Against Women (OVW).* This office, a component of the U.S. Department of Justice, was created in 1995. OVW implements VAWA and subsequent legislation and provides national leadership against domestic violence, sexual assault, and stalking. Since its inception, OVW has launched a multifaceted approach to responding to these crimes. In 2002, Congress passed the Violence Against Women Office Act (Pub.L. 107-273, Div. A, Title IV, Nov. 2, 2002, 116 Stat. 1789) which statutorily established the office. A description of the comprehensive programs to protect women from violence implemented by OVM, recent initiatives to protect women from what is referred to as "stalking", and other federal and state initiatives on this subject is provided in Annex II.

87. *Women and the economy.* Several U.S. federal agencies sponsor programs to advance the ability of women to participate in the workplace. One such agency is the Women's Bureau at the U.S. Department of Labor. The Women's Bureau promotes 21st century solutions to improve the status of working women and their families. For example, GEM-Nursing (Group E-Mentoring in Nursing) encourages young men and women ages 15 to 21 to choose careers in nursing through a Web site featuring information on nursing occupations and associations, e-mentoring, and regional events. It is modeled after GEM-SET (Girls' E-Mentoring in Science, Engineering, and Technology) which seeks to increase the number of girls age 13 to 18 who pursue careers in science, engineering, and technology through a Web site offering online resources, e-mentoring, and information about regional events. Other Women's Bureau programs address financial security and workplace flexibility. To improve women's financial savvy, the Women's Bureau developed the Wi$e Up project for Generation X women ages 22 to 35. Wi$e Up includes an eight-unit curriculum available online and in classroom settings, e-mentoring, and monthly teleconferences featuring speakers on financial topics. To promote workplace flexibility options, the Women's Bureau developed Flex-Options for Women. This project brings together corporate executives and entrepreneurs who volunteer to mentor business owners interested in creating or enhancing flexible workplace policies and programs.

88. *Institutional mechanisms for the advancement of women.* The Women's Bureau was created by Congress in 1920 to "formulate standards and policies that shall promote the welfare of wage-earning women, improve their working conditions, increase their efficiency, and advance their opportunities for profitable employment." The Director of the Women's Bureau is the principal advisor to the Secretary of Labor on issues affecting women in the labor force. The Women's Bureau's Fiscal year 2003-8 Strategic Plan includes the following goals: to increase women's employment in high-growth, demand-driven occupations; increase opportunities for women to take steps to improve their economic security and retirement savings; and enhance women's quality of life by increasing the number of employer flexible programs and policies.

Article 4—States of emergency

89. Consistent with the information reported in paragraphs 110–127 of the Initial Report, since submission of that report, the United States has not declared a "state of emergency" within the meaning of Article 4 or otherwise imposed emergency rule by the executive branch.

90. However, as reported in that section of the Initial Report, there are statutory grants of emergency powers to the President. Since the submission of the Initial Report, the President has invoked the National Emergencies Act, 50 U.S.C. § 1601 et seq., to declare a national emergency in the following situations: In 2001, the President of the United States issued a number of executive orders after the September 11 terrorist attacks that declared a national emergency as a result of those attacks pursuant to the National Emergencies Act, 50 U.S.C. §§ 1601–1651 (2005).

91. This invocation was misinterpreted by the (OSCE) as action which required derogation under Article 4 of the Covenant. In correspondence with the OSCE, the United States explained that under U.S. law, declarations of national emergency have been used frequently, in both times of war and times of peace, in order to implement special legal authorities and that the Executive Orders made as a result of the September 11 attacks did not require derogation from its commitments under the Covenant.

92. *Judicial review.* There have been no adverse federal judicial rulings concerning the exercise of emergency powers by the federal authorities since the submission of the Initial Report.

93. In *Hamdi v. Rumsfeld*, 124 S. Ct. 2633 (2004), the Supreme Court stated that the United States is entitled to detain enemy combatants, even American citizens, until the end of hostilities, in order to prevent the enemy combatants from returning to the field of battle and again taking up arms. The Court recognized the detention of such individuals is such a fundamental and accepted incident of war that it is part of the "necessary and appropriate" force that Congress authorized the President to use against nations, organizations, or persons associated with the September 11 terrorist attacks. 124 S.Ct. at 2639–42 (plurality op.); *id.*, at 2679 (Thomas J., dissenting). A plurality of the Court addressed the entitlements of a U.S. citizen designated as an enemy combatant and held that the Due Process Clause of the United States Constitution requires "notice of the factual basis for [the citizen-detainee's] classification, and a fair opportunity to rebut the government's factual assertions before a neutral decision maker." *Id.* at 2648. A plurality of the Court observed: "There remains the possibility that the [due process] standards we have articulated could be met by an appropriately authorized and properly constituted military tribunal," and proffered as a benchmark for comparison the regulations titled, Enemy Prisoners of War, Retained Personnel, Civilian Internees and Other Detainees, Army Regulation 190-8, §1–6 (1997). *Id.* at 2651.

94. On 28 February, 2005, a federal district court held that the Non-Detention Act, 18 U.S.C. § 4001(a), forbids the federal government from detaining Jose Padilla as an "enemy combatant" and that the President lacks any inherent constitutional authority to detain Padilla.

See Padilla v. Hanft, 2005 U.S. Dist. LEXIS 2921 (D.S.C. Feb. 2005). In September of 2005, the district court's decision was reversed by the Fourth Circuit. 2005 U.S. App. LEXIS 19465 (4th Cir. 2005). The Fourth Circuit held that the United States Congress in the Authorization for Use of Military Force Joint Resolution, 115 Stat. 224, provided the President all powers "necessary and appropriate to protect American citizens from terrorist acts by those who attacked the U.S. on September 11, 2001." *Id.* at *30. Those powers included the power to detain identified and committed enemies such as Padilla, who associated with al Qaeda and the Taliban regime, took up arms against the United States in its war against these enemies, a power without which the President could well be unable to protect American citizens. *Id.* at *31.

Article 5—Non-derogable nature of fundamental rights

95. There is no change from the information reported in paragraphs 128—130 of the Initial Report.

Article 6—Right to life

96. *Right to life, freedom from arbitrary deprivation.* The United States constitutional recognition of every human's inherent right to life and the doctrine that that right shall be protected by law were explained in paragraphs 131–148 of the Initial Report.

97. In addition, the Born-Alive Infants Protection Act of 2002, which was signed into federal law on 5 August, 2002, makes it clear that "every infant member of the species homo sapiens who is born alive at any stage of development" is considered a "person", "human being", and "individual" under federal law. *See* 1 U.S.C. § 8. This is true regardless of the nature of the birth, and whether the live birth resulted from a failed abortion procedure. *Id.*

98. Congress also enacted the Unborn Victims of Violence Act of 2004 "to protect unborn children from assault and murder." *See* Pub. L. No. 108-212. Federal law now provides that whoever, in the course of committing certain federal crimes, "causes the death ... of a child, who is in utero at the time the conduct take place," is guilty of a separate offense and shall be punished as if that death had occurred to the unborn child's mother. *See* 18 U.S.C. § 1841(a). If the person engaging in such conduct intentionally kills the unborn

child, he will be punished for intentionally killing a human being. *See* 18 U.S.C. § 1841(a)(2)(C). This law does not, however, authorize the prosecution of any woman with respect to her unborn child, *see* 18 U.S.C. § 1841(c)(3), nor does it criminalize "conduct relating to an abortion for which the consent of the pregnant woman, or a person authorized by law to act on her behalf, has been obtained or for which such consent is implied by law." *See* 18 U.S.C. § 1841(c)(1).

99. *Assisted suicide.* In recent years, debate has intensified in the United States over the question of whether terminally ill people should have the legal right to obtain a doctor's help in ending their lives. The campaign to legalize assisted suicide, also called the right-to-die movement, has been under way since the 1970s but became prominent in the 1990s, at least partly because of the actions of Dr. Jack Kevorkian, a retired Michigan pathologist. Kevorkian helped at least 50 people to die since 1990. In 1999, a Michigan jury convicted Kevorkian of second-degree murder and he is currently serving a 10 to 25 year prison sentence.

100. In November 1994, Oregon became the first state to make assisted suicide legal. Its law, passed by a slim margin in a voter referendum, allows doctors to prescribe a lethal dose of drugs to terminally ill patients who meet certain criteria. In June 1997, the Supreme Court upheld two state laws that barred assisted suicide. *See, e.g., Vacco v. Quill*, 521 U.S. 793 (1997); *Washington v. Glucksberg*, 521 U.S. 702 (1997). While finding that states could make assisted suicide illegal, the court also made it clear that states could legalize assisted suicide if they so chose. The debate over assisted suicide continues in the United States. Legislation legalizing the practice has been introduced in a number of states. However, physician-assisted suicide remains illegal in every state except Oregon.

101. The Attorney General has determined that assisting suicide is not a legitimate medical purpose and therefore that the Controlled Substances Act of 1970 ("CSA"), 21 U.S.C. § 801, bars physicians from prescribing federally-controlled substances to assist in a suicide. The validity of the Attorney General's determination is the subject of litigation and is scheduled for decision by the Supreme Court during the October Term 2005. *See Gonzales v. Oregon*, 125 S.Ct. 1299 (2005).

102. The Supreme Court has recognized that a state has "legitimate interests from the outset of the pregnancy in protecting the life of the fetus that may become a child." *See Planned Parenthood v. Casey*, 505 U.S. 833, 846 (1992). Accordingly, it has held that "subsequent to viability, the state, in promoting its interest in the potentiality of human life, may, if it chooses, regulate, and even proscribe, abortion except where it is necessary, in appropriate medical judgment, for the preservation of the life or health of the mother." *Id.* at 879. At the same time, the Supreme Court has held that a state may not place an "undue burden" on a woman's ability to abort a pregnancy prior to viability, and has invalidated some legislative efforts to protect an unborn child's right to life on this ground. *See e.g, Casey*, 505 U.S. 833; *Stenberg v. Carhart*, 530 U.S. 914 (2000) (invalidating a state-law ban on a procedure known as "partial birth abortion," because it failed to allow an exception for the mother's health, and because the vagueness of the statute's definition of the procedure it prohibited had the effect of placing an "undue burden" on a woman's ability to obtain abortion by prohibiting certain common methods of abortion).

103. In 2003, Congress enacted a federal prohibition on partial-birth abortion, finding that "[i]mplicitly approving such a brutal and inhumane procedure by choosing not to prohibit it will further coarsen society to the humanity of not only newborns, but all vulnerable and innocent human life, making it increasingly difficult to protect such life." *See* Pub. L. No. 108-105 at § 2(14)(M). This statute includes a more precise definition of the procedure it prohibits. In addition, the statute contains a congressional finding that "partial-birth abortion is never necessary to preserve the health of a woman, poses serious risks to a woman's health, and lies outside the standard of medical care." *See* Pub. L. No. 108-105 at § 2(13). The validity of this statute is currently the subject of litigation.

104. *Capital Punishment.* The federal government and 38 states impose capital punishment for crimes of murder or felony murder, and generally only when aggravating circumstances were present in the commission of the crime, such as multiple victims, rape of the victim, or murder-for-hire.

105. Criminal defendants in the United States, especially those in potential capital cases, enjoy many procedural guarantees, which are well respected and enforced by the courts. These include: the right to a fair hearing by an independent tribunal; the presumption of innocence; the minimum guarantees for the defense; the right against self-incrimination; the right to access all evidence used against the defendant; the right to challenge and seek exclusion of evidence; the right to review by a higher tribunal, often with a publicly funded lawyer; the right to trial by jury; and the right to challenge the makeup of the jury, among others.

106. In two major decisions described also in paragraphs 108 and 109, the Supreme Court cut back on the categories of defendants against whom the death penalty may be applied. In *Roper v Simmons*, 125 S.

Ct. 1183 (2005), the Court held that the execution of persons who were under the age of eighteen when their capital crimes were committed violates the Eighth and Fourteenth Amendments. In *Atkins v. Virginia*, 536 U.S. 304 (2002), the Court held that the execution of mentally retarded criminal defendants was cruel and unusual punishment, in violation of the Eighth and Fourteenth Amendments. The Supreme Court has repeatedly refused to consider the contention that a long delay between conviction and execution constitutes cruel and unusual punishment under the Eighth Amendment. *See, e.g., Foster v. Florida*, 537 U.S. 990 (2002). Also, the lower federal courts and state courts have consistently rejected such a claim. *See, e.g., Knight v. Florida*, 528 U.S. 990, 120 S.Ct. 459, 461 (1999) (THOMAS, J., concurring in denial of certiorari).

107. *Federal Death Penalty*. The following three federal capital defendants have been executed since the enactment of the current federal death penalty statutes:

• *Timothy McVeigh* was executed by lethal injection at the U.S. Penitentiary at Terre Haute, Indiana, on 11 June, 2001. He had been charged with multiple offenses arising out of the 19 April, 1995, bombing of the Alfred P. Murrah Federal Building in Oklahoma City, Oklahoma, and resulting deaths of 168 victims. After a jury trial in the U.S. District Court for the District of Colorado, McVeigh was convicted of conspiracy to use a weapon of mass destruction, in violation of 18 U.S.C. § 2332a; use of a weapon of mass destruction, in violation of 18 U.S.C. § 2332a; destruction of government property by means of an explosive, in violation of 18 U.S.C. § 844(f); and eight counts of first degree murder, in violation of 18 U.S.C. § 1111 and 18 U.S.C. § 1114.

McVeigh appealed to the court of appeals, which affirmed the convictions and death sentences. *United States v. McVeigh*, 153 F.3d 1186 (10th Cir. 1998). McVeigh then filed a petition for writ of certiorari in the U.S. Supreme Court, which denied the petition. *McVeigh v. United States*, 526 U.S. 1007 (1999). McVeigh later filed a motion to vacate his sentence under 28 U.S.C. § 2255 in the district court, which denied the motion and declined to issue a certificate of appealability. *United States v. McVeigh*, 118 F. Supp. 2d 1137 (D. Colo. 2000). McVeigh applied to the court of appeals for a certificate of appealability, which the court denied. McVeigh's execution followed that decision.

• *Juan Raul Garza* was executed by lethal injection at Terre Haute on 19 June 2001. After a jury trial in the U.S. District Court for the Southern District of Texas, Garza was convicted of numerous offenses, including engaging in a continuing criminal enterprise, in violation of 21 U.S.C. § 848(a) & (c), and committing three murders while engaged in and in furtherance of a continuing criminal enterprise, in violation of 21 U.S.C. § 848(e). He was sentenced to death for each of the murders. The court of appeals affirmed. *United States v. Flores*, 63 F.3d 1342 (5th Cir. 1995). The U.S. Supreme Court denied his petition for a writ of certiorari. 519 U.S. 825 (1996). Garza filed a motion to vacate his sentence under 28 U.S.C. § 2255, and the district court denied the motion and declined to issue a certificate of appealability. Garza then applied to the court of appeals for a certificate of appealability, and the court of appeals denied the application. *United States v. Garza*, 165 F.3d 312 (5th Cir. 1999). The U.S. Supreme Court again denied certiorari. 528 U.S. 1006. Garza's execution followed that denial.

• *Louis Jones* was executed by lethal injection at Terre Haute on 19 March, 2003. A jury in the U.S. District Court for the Northern District of Texas convicted Jones, a retired U.S. Army Ranger, of kidnapping and killing Tracie McBride, a 19-year-old private in the United States Army, in violation of 18 U.S.C. § 1201(a)(2). The jury sentenced Jones to death. Jones was also convicted of assaulting Private Michael Peacock with resulting serious bodily injury, in violation of 18 U.S.C. § 113(f). Jones appealed his conviction and sentence, which the court of appeals affirmed. *United States v. Jones*, 132 F.3d 232 (5th Cir. 1998). The U.S. Supreme Court granted Jones's certiorari petition and affirmed his conviction and sentence. *Jones v. United States*, 527 U.S. 373 (1999). The Supreme Court denied Jones's petition for rehearing. *See Jones v. United States*, 527 U.S. 1058 (1999).

Jones filed a motion to vacate sentence pursuant to 28 U.S.C. § 2255. Following an evidentiary hearing, the district court denied the motion and Jones's application for a certificate of appealability. Jones applied to the court of appeals for a certificate of appealability, which the court denied on 27 March, 2002. *United States v. Jones*, 287 F.3d 325 (5th Cir. 2002). The Supreme Court denied certiorari. 123 S. Ct. 549 (2002). Jones's execution followed thereafter.

108. *Juvenile Death Penalty*. The application of the death penalty to those who commit capital offences at ages 16 and 17 had continued to be the subject of substantial debate in the United States. This debate was recently concluded by the Supreme Court in its ruling in *Roper v Simmons*, 125 S. Ct. 1183 (2005), holding that the Eighth and Fourteenth Amendments forbid imposition of the death penalty on offenders who were under the age of 18 when their crimes were committed.

109. *Mental defect*. The U.S. Supreme Court has restricted the death penalty, finding that it is a dispro-portionate punishment where the defendant is mentally retarded. *See Atkins v. Virginia*, 536 U.S. 304 (2002). In addition, a death penalty eligible defendant is entitled to an individualized determination that the death sentence is appropriate in his case, and the jury must be able to consider and give effect to any mitigating evidence that a defendant proffers as a basis for a sentence less than death. *See Johnson v. Texas*, 509 U.S. 350 (1993). Moreover, where the prosecution identifies the likelihood that a defendant will engage in violent conduct in the future as a basis for returning a death sentence and the only alternative to a death sentence is life without the possibility of parole, the jury must be informed that the defendant is parole ineligible, in other words, where a life prison sentence could not result in parole. *See Simmons v South Carolina*, 512 U.S. 154 (1994).

110. *Capital Punishment and Consular Notification*. Since the initial report, a number of foreign nation-als who were tried and sentenced to death by one of the states of the United States have sought to have their convictions or sentences overturned based upon the arresting authorities' failure to provide timely consular notification to the foreign national as required under the Vienna Convention on Consular Relations (VCCR). Paraguay, Germany, and Mexico each brought suit against the United States in the International Court of Justice (ICJ) under the Optional Protocol to the VCCR, asking the court, inter alia, to order the United States to provide new trials and sentencing hearings to foreign nationals when the competent authorities in the United States had failed to provide consular notification as required under the VCCR. *See Vienna Convention on Consular Relations (Paraguay v. U.S.)*, 1998; *LaGrand (Germany v. U.S.)*, 2001; *Avena and Other Mexican Nationals (Mexico v. U.S.)*.

111. The ICJ in *LaGrand* found that the appropriate remedy for cases in which German nationals are sentenced to severe penalties without having been provided consular notification was for the United States to provide, by means of its own choosing, review and reconsideration of the conviction and sentence taking into account the VCCR violation. In March 2004, the ICJ reiterated in *Avena* that review and reconsid-eration was the appropriate remedy for 51 Mexican nationals who the court found had not been provided consular notification as required.

112. On 28 February, 2005, President Bush determined that "the United States will discharge its interna-tional obligations under the decision of the International Court of Justice in *Avena* ... by having state courts give effect to the decision in accordance with general principles of comity in cases filed by the 51 Mexican nationals addressed in that decision." The U.S. government subsequently filed briefs with the U.S. Supreme Court and the Texas Court of Criminal Appeals in a case involving Ernesto Medellin, one of the individuals named in *Avena*. The government's *amicus* briefs argue that the President's decision is binding on state courts and, consistent with the U.S. government's longstanding interpretation of the VCCR, that the VCCR does not grant a foreign national a judicially enforceable right to challenge his or her conviction or sentence in the United States.

113. The United States' concerns that the ICJ's decisions had interpreted the VCCR in ways not intended or anticipated by the Parties led the United States to withdraw from the Optional Protocol to the VCCR. The Optional Protocol is a purely jurisdictional treaty separate from the VCCR itself. Only about 30 percent of the countries that are Party to the VCCR have chosen to be a Party to the Optional Protocol.

114. The United States remains a Party to the VCCR and is fully committed to meeting its obligations to provide consular notification and access in the cases of detained foreign nationals. As part of its on-going effort to improve compliance with the VCCR, the Department of State's Bureau of Consular Affairs has continued its aggressive program to advance awareness of consular notification and access. Since 1998, the State Department has distributed to federal, state and local law enforcement over 1,000,000 training videos, booklets and pocket cards that provide instructions for arrests and detentions of foreign nationals (the text of the booklet can be found at http://travel.state.gov/law/notify.html). State Department experts have con-ducted over 350 training seminars on consular notification and access throughout the United States and its territories. These included formal training events, presentations and other briefings at law enforcement and criminal justice agencies conferences, training academies and accreditation organizations, and judicial and legislative groups. The State Department has also produced an online training course that provides personnel with up-to-date, interactive training on the topic.

115. *Victims of Crime*. The Office for Victims of Crime (OVC) in the Department of Justice administers programs authorized by the Victims of Crime Act of 1984, in addition to the Crime Victims Fund (the Fund) also authorized by the same statute. The Fund is composed of criminal fines and penalties, special assess-

ments, and bond forfeitures collected from convicted federal offenders, as well as gifts and donations received from the general public. Money deposited in this fund is used to support a wide range of activities on behalf of crime victims, including victim compensation and assistance services, demonstration programs, training and technical assistance, program evaluation and replication, and programs to assist victims of terrorism and mass violence. OVC administers two major formula grant programs: Victim Assistance and Victim Compensation. During the past decade, these two formula grant programs have greatly improved the accessibility and quality of services for federal and state crime victims nationwide.

116. In 2003, Congress passed the Justice for All Act, which sets out the following rights of victims of federal crimes: The right to be reasonably protected from the accused; the right to reasonable, accurate, and timely notice of any public court proceeding, or any parole proceeding, involving the crime or of any release or escape of the accused; the right not to be excluded from any such public court proceeding, unless the court, after receiving clear and convincing evidence, determines that testimony by the victim would be materially altered if the victim heard other testimony at that proceeding; the right to be reasonably heard at any public proceeding in the district court involving release, plea, sentencing, or any parole proceeding; the reasonable right to confer with the attorney for the government in the case; the right to full and timely restitution as provided in law; the right to proceedings free from unreasonable delay; the right to be treated with fairness and with respect for the victim's dignity and privacy.

117. Officers and employees of the Department of Justice and other departments and agencies of the United States engaged in the detection, investigation, or prosecution of crime are required to make their best efforts to see that crime victims are notified of, and accorded, these rights.

118. In order to enforce these rights, the crime victim, the crime victim's lawful representative, or the government prosecutor may assert the rights in a federal court. Failure to afford a right does not provide a defendant grounds for a new trial, however, and the act does not create a cause of action for damages or create, enlarge, or imply any duty or obligation to any victim or other person for the breach of which the United States or any of its officers or employees could be held liable in damages. In addition, the Department of Justice was required, under the act, to create an ombudsman for victims rights and provide for training and possible disciplinary sanctions for employees who fail to afford victims their rights.

119. In terms of immigration, DHS may grant relief in the form of "U" visas to victims of crimes of violence who have aided in the investigation or prosecution of the perpetrators of violent crime. See Trafficking Victims Protection Act of 2000 (TVPA), Pub. L. 106-386, 114 Stat. 1464 (Oct. 28 2000), Division B, the Violence Against Women Act of 2000 (VAWA). The U visa may be available to a person who suffered substantial physical or mental abuse as a result of having been a victim of a serious crime, including rape, torture, prostitution, sexual exploitation, female genital mutilation, being held hostage, peonage (debtors bound in servitude to creditors), involuntary servitude, slave trade; kidnapping, abduction, unlawful criminal restraint, false imprisonment, blackmail, extortion, manslaughter, murder, felonious assault, witness tampering, obstruction of justice, or perjury. See INA § 101(a) (15)(U); See also VTVPA §1513(b)(3). The U visa implementing regulations have not yet been promulgated. DHS is holding possible U visa cases pending publication of the implementing rule and providing interim employment authorization to applicants who establish prima facie eligibility.

120. *Victim Assistance*. Each year, all 50 states, the District of Columbia and various U.S. territories are awarded OVC funds to support community-based organizations that serve crime victims. Approximately 5,600 grants are made to domestic violence shelters, rape crisis centers, child abuse programs, and victim service units in law enforcement agencies, prosecutors' offices, hospitals, and social service agencies. These programs provide services including crisis intervention, counseling, emergency shelter, criminal justice advocacy, and emergency transportation. States and territories are required to give priority to programs serving victims of domestic violence, sexual assault, and child abuse. Additional funds must be set aside for underserved victims, such as survivors of homicide victims and victims of drunk drivers.

121. *Victim Compensation*. All 50 states, the District of Columbia, Puerto Rico and Guam, have established compensation programs for crime victims. These programs reimburse victims for crime-related expenses such as medical costs, mental health counseling, funeral and burial costs, and lost wages or loss of support. Compensation is paid only when other financial resources, such as private insurance and offender restitution, do not cover the loss. Some expenses, such as replacement of property that is stolen or damaged, are not covered by most compensation programs. Although each state compensation program is administered independently, most programs have similar eligibility requirements and offer comparable benefits.

122. *Victims of International Terrorism.* In addition, the Victims of Crime Act (VOCA) (42 U.S.C. § 10603c) authorizes the OVC Director to establish an International Terrorism Victim Expense Reimbursement Program to compensate eligible "direct" victims of acts of international terrorism that occur outside the United States, for expenses associated with that victimization.

123. *Victims of Trafficking.* Victims who are considered to have been subjected to a severe form of trafficking, and who agree to assist law enforcement in the investigation of trafficking, may be eligible for immigration relief, including "continued presence" and the T-visa. These are self-petitioning visas, under the TVPA. If granted, a T-visa provides the alien with temporary permission to reside in the United States and may lead to legal resident status. The victim also receives an authorization permit to work in the United States.

124. The Department of Homeland Security U.S. Citizenship and Immigration Services (USCIS) processes T-visas; the Department of Homeland Security Immigration and Customs Enforcement (ICE) processes continued presence requests. All victims of trafficking are eligible for victim services upon their identification by federal law enforcement. The types of services available depend on: (1) whether a determination has been made that the victim meets the definition of having been subjected to a severe form of trafficking set out in the TVPA; (2) the page 30 victim's immigration status; and (3) the victim's willingness to assist with an investigation and prosecution. To be eligible for services, minor victims need not demonstrate a willingness to assist law enforcement in an investigation nor are they required to have continued presence status. The Trafficking Victims Protection Reauthorization Act (TVPRA) of 2003 mandated new information campaigns to combat sex tourism, added some refinements to the federal criminal law, and created a new civil action provision that allows trafficking victims to sue their traffickers in federal district courts. The TVPRA provides enhanced protection for victims of trafficking and assistance to family members of victims, including elimination of the requirement that a victim of trafficking between the ages of 15 and 18 must cooperate with the investigation and prosecution of his or her trafficker in order to be eligible for a T-visa, and making benefits and services available to victims of trafficking also available for their family members legally entitled to join them in the United States.

125. *Victims of Trafficking Discretionary Grant Program.* OVC also administers the Services for Trafficking Victims Discretionary Grant Program, which was authorized under the Trafficking Victims Protection Act of 2000. Most trafficking victims do not come to the United States with an immigration status that would allow them to receive benefits and services. The TVPA created a mechanism for allowing non-citizens who were trafficking victims access to benefits and services from which they might otherwise be barred. The TVPA allows for the "certification" of adult victims to receive certain federally–funded or administered benefits and services such as cash assistance, medical care, food stamps and housing. Minor (child) victims do not need to be certified to receive such benefits and services, but instead receive eligibility letters to the same effect. Programs funded by OVC focus on providing comprehensive and specialized services to victims of severe forms of trafficking during the "pre-certification" period, in order to address the emergency and immediate needs of these victims before they are eligible for other benefits and services.

Article 7—Freedom from torture, or cruel, inhuman or degrading treatment or punishment

126. *Torture.* As described in paragraphs 149—187 of the Initial Report, U.S. law prohibits torture at both the federal and state levels within the United States. On 27 October, 1990, the United States ratified the U.N. Convention against Torture and Other Cruel, Inhuman or Degrading Treatment or Punishment ("Convention Against Torture"). The United States deposited its instrument of ratification with the U.N. on 21 October, 1994. The Convention Against Torture entered into force for the United States on 20 November, 1994.

127. *Federal Extraterritorial Offense of Torture.* Coincident with the entry into force of the Convention Against Torture, the United States enacted the Torture Convention Implementation Act, codified at 18 U.S.C. § 2340A, which gave effect to obligations assumed by the United States under Article 5 of the Convention Against Torture. As provided in the statute, whoever commits or attempts to commit torture outside the United States (both terms as defined in the statute) is subject to federal criminal prosecution if the alleged offender is a national of the United States or the alleged offender is present in the United States, irrespective of the nationality of the victim.

128. *Report to the Committee Against Torture.* On 19 October, 1999, the United States submitted its initial report to the U.N. Committee Against Torture describing in detail U.S. compliance with the obligations it had assumed under the Convention Against Torture. Comm. Against Torture, Initial reports of States

Parties due in 1995: United States of America, U.N. Doc. CAT/C/28/Add.5 (2000). The Committee Against Torture began discussion of the U.S. report with a U.S. delegation on 10 May, 2000. Comm. Against Torture, 24th Sess., 424st mtg., pt. 1, U.N. Doc. CAT/C/SR.424 (2000). Discussion occurred over three meetings (May 10, 11, 15)—mtgs 424, 427, 431. Later, the Committee Against Torture offered concluding observations. *Report of the Committee against Torture*, U.N. GAOR, 55th Sess., Supp. No. 44, at 175–80, U.N. Doc. A/55/44 (2000). The United States recently submitted its second periodic report to the Committee Against Torture (*available at* http://www.state.gov/g/drl/rls/45738.htm) and awaits the invitation of the Committee Against Torture to discuss that report.

129. *Committee Request.* In its letter of 27 July 2004, the Human Rights Committee requested, inter alia, that the United States should address: problems relating to the legal status and treatment of persons detained in Afghanistan, Guantánamo, Iraq and other places of detention outside the United States of America (art 7, 9, 10, and 14 of the Covenant).

130. The United States recalls its longstanding position that it has reiterated in paragraph 3 of this report and explained in detail in the legal analysis provided in Annex I; namely, that the obligations assumed by the United States under the Covenant apply only within the territory of the United States. In that regard, the United States respectfully submits that this Committee request for information is outside the purview of the Committee. The United States also notes that the legal status and treatment of such persons is governed by the law of war. Nonetheless, as a courtesy, the United States is providing the Committee pertinent material in the form of an updated Annex to the U.S. report on the Convention Against Torture and Other Cruel, Inhuman or Degrading Treatment or Punishment.

131. *Cruel, inhuman or degrading treatment or punishment.* Cruel, inhuman or degrading treatment or punishment. Below are examples of federal law enforcement prosecutions for the mistreatment of people in custody. Not all of these examples involve conduct constituting cruel, inhuman or degrading treatment or punishment as defined under Article 7, as ratified by the United States. Mistreatment is conduct less severe than that falling within the scope of U.S. obligations under Article 7; in particular, mere violations of the Fourth Amendment do not fall within the scope of those obligations. Such examples are included simply to demonstrate the scope of remedies that are available in the United States for governmental misconduct:

• On 14 July, 2004, an Oklahoma police officer was convicted and awaits sentencing for assaulting and fracturing the hip of a 67-year-old man the officer stopped for a traffic violation. The officer was prosecuted under 18 U.S.C. § 242 for intentional use of unreasonable force under the color of law;

• On 19 May, 2004, a Louisiana detention officer was convicted and is awaiting sentencing for repeatedly throwing a handcuffed detainee against a wall resulting in significant lacerations to the victim's face. The officer was prosecuted under 18 U.S.C. § 242 for the willful use of force amounting to the deprivation of the victim's liberty without due process under color of law;

• On 25 March, 2004, the Eleventh Circuit affirmed the conviction and sentence of a former deputy sheriff with the Jacksonville, Florida Sheriff's Department, who was charged and convicted for kidnapping, murdering, and stealing money from motorists, bank customers, and drug dealers whom he falsely arrested in 1998 and 1999. He was sentenced to life in prison for, among other charges, the violation of 18 U.S.C. § 241 for conspiracy to deprive one of the victims of life and the others of liberty and property without due process under color of law;

• On 24 September, 2003, a North Carolina police officer pleaded guilty to a felony civil rights charge for coercing women, whom he stopped or arrested, into having sex with him. He was sentenced to ten years in prison for willful deprivation of liberty without due process under color of law;

• On 2 November, 2000, seven federal correctional officers from the U.S. Penitentiary in Florence, Colorado, were indicted for systematically beating inmates and lying to cover-up their illegal conduct. On 24 June, 2003, the jury convicted the three ringleaders on conspiracy and substantive counts. They were sentenced to 30 and 41 months in prison for, among other charges, the violation of 18 U.S.C. § 241 for conspiring to impose cruel and unusual punishment under color of law. Three additional defendants pled guilty to violating inmates' civil rights prior to trial;

• On 15 August, 2001, a Maryland, K–9 [canine] officer was convicted and thereafter sentenced to 10 years in prison for releasing her dog on two men who had surrendered, resulting in serious injuries to the men;

• On 9 November, 2000, a correctional officer captain from a state of Florida jail pled guilty to having forcible sexual contact with a female inmate and was thereafter sentenced to 15 months in prison. He was prosecuted under 18 U.S.C. § 242 for willful deprivation of the victim's liberty without due process under color of law;

• On 7 February, 2001, six correctional officers with the Arkansas Department of Corrections beat and repeatedly shocked two naked and handcuffed victims with a hand-held stun gun and six-foot long cattle prod. During a separate incident, three of the six defendants shocked and beat another handcuffed inmate. Ultimately, five officers entered guilty pleas while the sixth was convicted at trial. They were sentenced to terms of incarceration ranging from 24 to 78 months under 18 U.S.C. § 242 for imposing cruel and unusual punishment under color of law;

• Between 3 March, 2001 and 21 August, 2001, three other correctional officers with the Arkansas Department of Corrections pled guilty to assaulting an inmate while he was handcuffed behind his back. They were later sentenced to terms of incarceration ranging from 8 to 18 months in prison under 18 U.S.C. § 242 for imposing cruel and unusual punishment under color of law;

• On 29 January, 2002, a North Carolina chief of police was convicted of using excessive force in seven separate incidents, involving six separate arrestees. The defendant was sentenced to 37 months in prison for willfully using unreasonable force under color of law in violations of 18 U.S.C. § 242;

• On 23 March, 2000, a U.S. Bureau of Prisons correctional officer in Oklahoma City was convicted of engaging in various degrees of sexual misconduct with five female inmates. As a result, he was sentenced to 146 months in prison under 18 U.S.C. § 242 for imposing cruel and unusual punishment under color of law;

• On 27 May, 2001, the last of five male orderlies at a state-run care facility for developmentally disabled adults near Memphis, Tennessee was convicted for routinely beating residents. One of these beatings resulted in the death of a developmentally disabled patient who could not cry out for help because he was mute. The five orderlies received sentences ranging from 60 to 180 months in prison under 18 U.S.C. § 242 for willful deprivation of the victim's liberty without due process under color of law;

• On 23 January, 2001, a Florida Department of Corrections officer with the Metro Dade Jail was convicted of assaulting a female inmate resulting in multiple contusions to her face, back, and neck. He was sentenced to 17 months in prison under 18 U.S.C. § 242 for imposing cruel and unusual punishment under color of law.

132. The civil rights laws have also been used to prosecute judges who abuse their power. For example, in 1997, the U.S. Supreme Court upheld the conviction of a Tennessee judge who was convicted by a jury of multiple counts of sexually assaulting both female litigants who had cases pending before him as well as female courthouse employees. *See United States v. Lanier*, 520 U.S. 259 (1997). Lanier received a sentence of 25 years in prison.

133. *Basic rights of prisoners.* Complaints about failure by individual law enforcement officers to comply with procedural rights continue to be made to federal and state authorities. The Criminal Section of the Civil Rights Division of the United States Department of Justice is charged with reviewing such complaints made to the federal government and ensuring the vigorous enforcement of the applicable federal criminal civil rights statutes. There have been fewer allegations of violation of procedural rights than physical abuse allegations.

134. *Civil Pattern or Practice Enforcement.* The Civil Rights Division of the U.S. Department of Justice may institute civil actions for equitable and declaratory relief pursuant to the Pattern or Practice of Police Misconduct provision of the Crime Bill of 1994, 42 U.S.C. § 14141, which prohibits law enforcement agencies from engaging in a pattern or practice of violating people's civil rights. Since October of 1999, the Civil Rights Division has negotiated 16 settlements with law enforcement agencies. These settlements include two consent decrees regarding the Detroit, Michigan Police Department, and consent decrees covering Prince George's County, Maryland and Los Angeles, California police departments. Other recent settlements include those entered into with police departments in the District of Columbia; Cincinnati, Ohio; Buffalo, New York; Villa Rica, Georgia; and Cleveland, Ohio. There are currently 13 ongoing investigations of law enforcement agencies.

135. *Civil Rights of Institutionalized Persons Act (CRIPA).* The Civil Rights of Institutionalized Persons Act (CRIPA), 42 U.S.C. § 1997 et seq., permits the Attorney General to institute civil lawsuits against state institutions regarding the civil rights of their residents, including the conditions of their confinement and use of excessive force. The Civil Rights Division of the Department of Justice has utilized this statute to prosecute allegations of torture and cruel, inhuman, and degrading treatment or punishment. By August

2004, the Civil Rights Division had initiated CRIPA actions regarding approximately 400 facilities, resulting in approximately 120 consent decrees and settlements governing conditions in about 240 facilities, since CRIPA was enacted in 1980. CRIPA enforcement has been a major priority of the Division. Over the last six years, the Division has opened 52 new investigations covering 66 facilities. The Division has also entered into 39 settlement agreements including seven consent decrees. There are currently 59 active investigations covering 69 facilities.

136. *Prisoner Litigation.* The Civil Rights Division investigates conditions in state prisons and local jail facilities pursuant to CRIPA, and investigates conditions in state and local juvenile detention facilities pursuant to either CRIPA or Section 14141, described above. These statutes allow suit for declaratory or equitable relief for a pattern or practice of unconstitutional conditions of confinement. Over the last 6 years, the Civil Rights Division has authorized 16 investigations concerning 17 adult correctional facilities, and 16 investigations of 26 juvenile detention facilities. Since October of 1999, the Civil Rights Division has entered 13 settlement agreements concerning 26 adult correctional facilities and 11 settlement agreements concerning 26 juvenile detention facilities. Since October 1999, pursuant to CRIPA, the Division has issued so-called findings letters—letters detailing patterns or practices of civil rights violations and minimum remedial measures to remedy the violations—covering 13 adult correctional facilities and 17 juvenile detention facilities. Some examples of these investigations follow:

• On 7 June, 2004, the Civil Rights Division filed a lawsuit challenging the conditions of confinement at the Terrell County Jail in Dawson, Georgia. The Division's complaint alleged that the jail routinely violated federally protected rights, including failing to protect inmate safety, and failing to provide required medical and mental health care. For example, after jail officials allegedly left one detainee with known mental health problems unsupervised despite his being on "suicide watch," he hanged himself;

• On 16 July, 2004, the Division reached an out-of-court agreement with the Wicomico County Detention Center in Salisbury, Maryland regarding systematic violations of prisoners' federally protected civil rights. The Division's three-year investigation revealed evidence that the Detention Center failed to provide required medical and mental health care, failed to provide adequate inmate safety, and failed to provide sufficiently sanitary living conditions. Under the terms of the agreement, the Detention Center will address and correct the deficiencies identified by the Division;

• The Division has also issued letters in 2004 reporting its findings regarding conditions at the McPherson and Grimes Correctional Units in Newport, Arkansas, the Garfield County Jail and County Work Center in Enid, Oklahoma, the Patrick County Jail in Virginia, and the Santa Fe Adult Detention Center in New Mexico;

• On 18 December, 2003, the Division filed suit to remedy a pattern or practice of unconstitutional conditions at the Oakley and Columbia Training Schools—juvenile justice facilities—in Mississippi. The Division's investigation found evidence of numerous abusive practices;

• On 27 August, 2004, the Division reached an out-of-court agreement with the state of Arkansas regarding the McPherson and Grimes Correctional Units in Newport, Arkansas. The agreement requires changes in staffing and security, and medical and mental health care for both male and female inmates;

• Over the last six years, the Division entered into agreements to remedy patterns or practices of unconstitutional conditions of confinement at several local jails or state prisons, including the Wyoming State Prison; the Nassau County Correctional Center in New York State; the Shelby County Jail in Tennessee; the Maricopa County jails in Phoenix, Arizona; and the McCracken County Jail in Kentucky.

137. *Sexual abuse in prison.* The Prison Rape Elimination Act of 2003 (PREA) was enacted to address the problem of sexual assault of persons in the custody of U.S. correctional agencies. The Act, signed into law on 4 September, 2003, applies to all public and private institutions that house adult or juvenile offenders and is also relevant to community-based agencies. The purpose of the Act is to:

• Establish a zero-tolerance standard for the incidence of rape in prisons in the United States;
• Make the prevention of rape a top priority in each prison system;
• Develop and implement national standards for the detection, prevention, reduction, and punishment of prison rape;
• Increase the available data and information on the incidence of prison rape, consequently improving the management and administration of correctional facilities;
• Standardize the definitions used for collecting data on the incidence of prison rape;
• Increase the accountability of prison officials who fail to detect, prevent, reduce, and punish prison rape;

- Protect the Eighth Amendment rights of federal, state, and local prisoners;
- Increase the efficiency and effectiveness of federal expenditures through grant programs such as those dealing with health care; mental health care; disease prevention; crime prevention, investigation, and prosecution; prison construction, maintenance, and operation; race relations; poverty; unemployment; and homelessness; and
- Reduce the costs that prison rape imposes on interstate commerce.

138. Illustrative of the problem of sexual abuse in correctional facilities are *United States v. Arizona* and *United States v. Michigan*, both cases filed under CRIPA in 1997 and dismissed in 1999 and 2000 respectively; the Civil Rights Division sought to remedy a pattern or practice of sexual misconduct against female inmates by male staff, including sexual contact and unconstitutional invasions of privacy. The cases were dismissed after the state prisons agreed to make significant changes in conditions of confinement for female inmates.

139. *Segregation of Prisoners.* In *Sandin v. Conner*, 515 U.S. 472 (1995), the Supreme Court defined the due process requirements for prisoners subjected to segregation for disciplinary reasons. The Court held that a 30-day period of disciplinary segregation from general population did not give rise to a liberty interest that would require a full due process hearing prior to the imposition of the punishment. The Court did leave open the possibility that due process protections would be implicated if the confinement was "atypical and significant."

140. *Psychiatric hospitals.* As reported in paragraphs 172–173 of the Initial Report, individuals with mental illness may be admitted to psychiatric hospitals either through involuntary or voluntary commitment procedures for the purpose of receiving mental health services. Institutionalized persons, including mental patients, are entitled to adequate food, clothing, shelter, medical care, reasonable safety, and freedom from undue bodily restraint.

Complaints tend to focus on inadequate conditions of confinement. Since enactment of the Civil Rights of Institutionalized Persons Act, 42 U.S.C. § 1997, et seq, in 1980, some 400 facilities, including psychiatric facilities, prisons, jails, juvenile facilities, nursing homes, and facilities housing persons with developmental disabilities have been investigated by the U.S. Department of Justice and relief sought, as appropriate. Also, the 1999 U.S. Supreme Court decision in *Olmstead v. L.C.*, 527 U.S. 581 (1999), held that unnecessary segregation of people with disabilities in institutions may be a form of discrimination that violates the 1990 Americans with Disabilities Act, when considering all relevant factors including the cost of a less restrictive environment. In addition, the Protection and Advocacy for Individuals with Mental Illness program, enacted in 1986, protects and advocates for the rights of people with mental illnesses and investigates reports of abuse and neglect in facilities that care for or treat individuals with mental illnesses. Patients are also afforded protections under Medicare and Medicaid "Conditions of Participation on Patients' Rights" and the Children's Health Act of 2001 related to use of seclusion and restraint.

141. *Medical or scientific experimentation.* The United States Constitution protects individuals against non-consensual experimentation. Specifically included are the Fourth Amendment's proscription against unreasonable searches and seizures (including seizing a person's body), the Fifth Amendment's proscription against depriving one of life, liberty or property without due process, and the Eighth Amendment's proscription against the infliction of cruel and unusual punishment. In addition, legislation provides similar guarantees (*See* 21 U.S.C. §§ 355(i)(4) & 3360j(g)(3)(D)).

142. Comprehensive control of unapproved drugs is vested by statute in the federal Food and Drug Administration (FDA) within HHS. The general commercialization of such drugs is prohibited, *See* 21 U.S.C. § 355(a), but HHS/FDA permits their use in experimental research under certain conditions (21 U.S.C. §§ 355(i), 357(d); 21 C.F.R. §§ 50, 56, & 312). The involvement of human beings in such research is prohibited unless the subject or the subject's legally authorized representative has provided informed consent, with the limited exceptions described below. The HHS/FDA regulations state in detail the elements of informed consent (21 C.F.R. §§ 50.–20-50.27).

143. U.S. statute and HHS regulations make an exception to requiring consent when the human subject is confronted by a life-threatening situation that requires use of the test article, legally effective consent cannot be obtained from the subject, time precludes consent from the subject's legal representative, and there is no comparable alternative therapy available (21 C.F.R. 50.23(a)-(c)). HHS/FDA regulations also set forth criteria for the President of the United States to apply in making a decision to waive the prior informed-consent

requirement for the administration of an investigational new drug to a member of the U.S. Armed Forces in connection with the member's participation in a particular military operation (21 C.F.R. 50.23(d)). This regulation implements, in part, 10 U.S.C. § 1107(f) which specifies that only the President may waive informed consent in this connection, and that the President may grant such a waiver only if the President determines in writing that obtaining consent is not feasible, is contrary to the best interests of the military members, or is not in the interests of U.S. national security. The statute further provides that in making a determination to waive prior informed consent on the ground that it is not feasible on the grounds that it is contrary to the best interests of the military members involved, the President shall apply the standards and criteria that are set forth in these regulations. Finally, HHS/FDA regulations provide an exception to informed consent for emergency research (21 C.F.R. 50.24). This exception allows an Institutional Review Board (IRB) to approve research if it finds that the human subjects are in a life threatening situation, available treatments are unproven or unsatisfactory, obtaining informed consent is not feasible, participation in the research holds out the prospect of direct benefit to the subjects, the research could not practicably be carried out without the waiver, and other protections are provided.

144. The Fourth, Fifth, and Eighth Amendments to the United States Constitution, by statutes, and by agency rules and regulations promulgated in response to such provisions, prohibit experimentation on prisoners. As a general matter, in the United States, "[e]very human being of adult years or sound mind has a right to determine what shall be done with his own body." See *Schloendorff v. Society of New York Hospitals*, 105 N.E. 92, 93 (1914). Accordingly, prisoners are almost always free to consent to any regular medical or surgical procedure for treatment of their medical conditions. Consent must be "informed": the inmate must be informed of the risks of the treatment; must be made aware of alternatives to the treatment; and must be mentally competent to make the decision. Because of possible "coercive factors, some blatant and some subtle, in the prison milieu," (James J. Gobert and Neil P. Cohen, *Rights of Prisoners*, New York: McGraw Hill, Inc., 1981, pp. 350–51) prison regulations generally do not permit inmates to participate in medical and scientific research.

145. The U.S. Federal Bureau of Prisons prohibits medical experimentation or pharmaceutical testing of *any* type on all inmates in the custody of the U.S. Attorney General who are assigned to the Bureau of Prisons. 28 C.F.R. § 512.11(c).

146. Moreover, the federal government strictly regulates itself when conducting, or funding research in prison settings. HHS, which sponsors over 90 percent of federally conducted or supported human research promulgated in 1976 regulations (45 C.F.R. § 46 (c)) that protect the rights and welfare of prisoners involved in research. An IRB, which approves and oversees all research conducted or supported by HHS, must have at least one prisoner or prisoner representative if prisoners are to be used as subjects in the study. Research involving prisoners must present risks similar to risks accepted by non-prisoner volunteers (*See* 45 C.F.R. § 46). Furthermore, the regulations established by HHS require that the research proposed must fall into one of four categories.

• Study of the possible causes, effects, and processes of incarceration, and of criminal behavior, provided that the study presents no more than a minimal risk and no more than inconvenience to the subject;

• Study of prisons as institutional structures or of prisoners as incarcerated persons, provided that the study presents no more than minimal risk and no more than inconvenience to the subject;

• Research on conditions particularly affecting prisoners as a class;

• Research on practices, both innovative and accepted, which have the intent and reasonable probability of improving the health and well-being of the subject. 45 C.F.R. § 46.306(a)(2).

147. Research conducted under categories 1 and 2 must present "no more than minimal risk and no more than inconvenience to the subjects." For research conducted under category 3, or conducted under category 4 where "studies require the assignment of prisoners in a manner consistent with protocols approved by the IRB to control groups which may not benefit from the research," "the study may proceed only after the Secretary [of HHS] has consulted with appropriate experts, including experts in penology, medicine, and ethics, and published notice, in the Federal Register, of the intent to approve such research."

148. The Secretary of HHS, pursuant to 45 C.F.R. 46.101(i), has waived the applicability of certain provisions of subpart C of 45 C.F.R. part 46 (Additional HHS Protections Pertaining to Biomedical and Behavioral Research Involving Prisoners as Subjects) to specific types of epidemiological research involving

prisoners as subjects. This waiver, effective 20 June, 2003, allows HHS to conduct or support certain important and necessary epidemiological research that would not otherwise be permitted under subpart C.

149. The Secretary of HHS has also waived the applicability of 45 C.F.R. 46.305(a)(1) and 46.306(a) (2) for certain epidemiologic research conducted or supported by HHS in which the sole purposes are the following:

- To describe the prevalence or incidence of a disease by identifying all cases; or
- To study potential risk factor associations for a disease; and
- Where the institution responsible for the conduct of the research certifies to the HHS Office for Human Research Protections, acting on behalf of the Secretary, that the IRB approved the research and fulfilled its duties under 45 C.F.R. § 46.305(a)(2)–(7) and determined and documented that the research presents no more than minimal risk and no more than inconvenience to the prisoner–subjects; and prisoners are not a particular focus of the research.

Article 8—Prohibition of slavery

150. *Slavery and involuntary servitude.* Abolition of the institution of slavery in the United States dates from the early 1800s, when the charter for the Northwest Territories provided that neither slavery (government–sanctioned ownership of a person) nor involuntary servitude (the holding of a person through compulsion for labor or services, without government sanction) would exist in certain lands being brought into the United States. Restrictions on the trafficking of slaves were adopted throughout the early 1800s. Slavery was abolished throughout the United States and its Territories by the Thirteenth Amendment to the United States Constitution, adopted in 1865.

151. Although slavery and involuntary servitude have been outlawed throughout the United States since 1865, tragically, modern analogs of that horrible practice continue around the world. The United States estimates that each year between 600,000 and 800,000 persons are trafficked across international borders, including an estimated 14,500 to 17,500 persons trafficked into the United States.

152. Prior to 2000, the United States prosecuted instances of slavery/human trafficking under statutes designed to protect persons in the United States in the free enjoyment of their constitutional rights, such as 18 U.S.C. § 241, which criminalizes conspiracies to interfere with the exercise of constitutional rights, and statutes such as 18 U.S.C. § 1584, which criminalizes involuntary servitude. Under these statutes, the Justice Department could prosecute only cases in which involuntary servitude was brought about through use or threatened use of physical or legal coercion; it was not sufficient to show that labor was forced through psychological coercion or other means. *United States v. Kozminski*, 487 U.S. 931 (1988).

153. Recognizing the fact that human traffickers often use various forms of non–physical and psychological manipulation, including threats to victims and their families, document confiscation, and other forms of disorientation, Congress enacted the Trafficking Victims Protection Act of 2000 (TVPA). The TVPA enhanced the United States' ability to prosecute slaveholders and to assist victims of human trafficking.

154. The TVPA set forth a three–pronged strategy to combat modern–day slavery: preventing human trafficking by working with authorities in the victims' home countries, providing protection and assistance to victims, and prosecuting offenders. The TVPA created several new criminal offenses: (i) holding persons for labor or services through a scheme or pattern of coercion (section 1589); (ii) trafficking persons into a condition of servitude or forced labor (section 1590); (iii) trafficking persons for commercial sexual activity through force fraud or coercion, or trafficking minors for commercial sexual activity (section 1591), and (iv) confiscation of identity documents in order to maintain an condition of servitude (section 1592). The TVPA raised the statutory maximum for servitude offenses to twenty years imprisonment, and in cases involving kidnapping, rape, or death of a victim, to life imprisonment. The TVPA provided for victim assistance by allowing trafficking victims to apply for federally funded or federally administered health and welfare benefits and by allowing qualified aliens to remain in the United States. The statute increased penalties for pre–existing crimes including forced labor; trafficking with respect to peonage, slavery, involuntary servitude, or forced labor; sex trafficking of children or by force, fraud, or coercion; and unlawful conduct with respect to documents, criminalized attempts to engage in these acts and provided for mandatory restitution and forfeiture.

155. In 2003, the United States renewed the TVPA and added provisions for information campaigns to combat sex tourism, added refinements to the federal criminal law, and created a new civil action provision that allows trafficking victims to sue their traffickers in federal district court.

156. Trafficking cases involve coercion, sometimes following an initial recruitment through false promises, in order to obtain or maintain the victims' labor or services. Many of the defendants in these cases prey

on the vulnerabilities of children or immigrant populations. While the means of isolation and coercion are often similar, victims are placed into various exploitative situations in a number of different industries. Sometimes, the underlying labor is legitimate, such as agricultural labor or domestic service. Other times, the victims are forced into illegal activities, such as prostitution or other commercial sexual activity. All of the victims of these severe forms of trafficking are held through coercive forces that deny them their essential freedom.

157. Since 1992, the Department of Justice has prosecuted 98 involuntary servitude cases involving 284 defendants, with three–fourths of the cases brought in the past five years. The cases have resulted in 194 convictions and guilty pleas and five acquittals. Since the TVPA's enactment in October 2000 through June 2005, the United States initiated prosecutions of 215 human traffickers, a three–fold increase over the prior four years. During that same period, the United States offered 752 adult and children victims of trafficking health and welfare benefits, including assistance with food, housing, transportation, medical services, and social adjustment services; English language training; job counseling and placement; and legal services. For those victims who wished to be reunited with their families abroad, the United States has assisted in achieving a safe reunion. For those victims who wish to remain in the United States, the United States allows victims to extend their stay in the United States or to apply for a special visa that carries the privilege of applying for permanent residency after three years. The United States is currently one of the few countries that grant the possibility of permanent residency to victims of trafficking. From October 2000 through June 2005, the United States granted immigration benefits to 450 trafficking victims. Additionally, in order to stop trafficking at its source, from October 2001 through June 2005, the United States invested over $295 million on international anti–trafficking efforts.

158. The Department of Justice's enforcement efforts in recent years have uncovered trafficking cases involving persons whose labor or services were forcibly obtained or maintained for, among other things: prostitution, nude dancing, domestic service, migrant agricultural labor, "sweatshop" garment factories, and street peddling/begging. The following examples are illustrative of some of the cases brought by the Department of Justice since the passage of the TVPA in October 2000:

• The owner of a sweatshop in the Territory of American Samoa was sentenced to 40 years in prison after being convicted of conspiring to enslave workers, involuntary servitude, and forced labor for holding Vietnamese factory workers to work as sewing machine operators in the Daewoosa Samoa garment factory. The workers were deprived of food, beaten, and physically restrained in order to force them to work. The lead defendant, Kil Soo Lee, was sentenced to 40 years in prison in June 2005; two other defendants entered guilty pleas to conspiracy for their involvement in the scheme and were sentenced to 70 and 51 months incarceration. *United States v. Kil Soo Lee*, 159 F. Supp. 2d 1241 (D. Haw. 2001);

• A defendant was convicted of forcing a young Cameroonian girl to work as a domestic servant after being brought into the United States illegally. The eleven–year old girl was forced to care for the defendant's two children and performed all the household chores without pay. The defendant beat her, forbade her from speaking of the conditions to anyone, forbade her from leaving the house or opening the door to anyone, and interfered with her mail. The defendant, who fled to Cameroon after being convicted, was sentenced to 210 months in prison and has since been returned to the United States to serve her sentence. *United States v. Mubang*;

• Six defendants pleaded guilty to trafficking Mexican women into the United States illegally and forced them into prostitution in Queens and Brooklyn. The male defendants lured the women into the United States and prostitution through personal relationships or marriage. The traffickers controlled their victims in part by holding the victims' children in Mexico. *United States v. Carreto*, et al;

• Eight defendants were charged with maintaining trailers along the Texas border as safe houses for illegal aliens newly arrived from the U.S./Mexico border. Women aliens were kept at the trailers where they were forced to cook and clean and were raped by the defendants. Seven of the eight defendants entered guilty pleas for their involvement in the scheme and were sentenced to terms of incarceration ranging from 4 months to 23 years in prison. Three of the seven defendants were ordered to pay $11,532 in restitution. The final defendant is a fugitive. *United States v.*

• *Soto-Huarto*, et al;

• Two defendants, who operated a tree cutting business, were convicted for holding two Jamaican immigrants in conditions of forced labor and document servitude in New Hampshire. The defendants obtained workers from Jamaica by means of false promises of good work and pay. Once the workers arrived in New Hampshire, their visas and others documents were confiscated and the workers were paid substantially less than promised, were housed in deplorable conditions, were denied medical treatment, and were routinely threatened. The defendants were sentenced to 70 months in prison, three years supervised release and ordered to pay a $12,500 fine and $13,052 restitution. *United States v. Bradley*, 390 F.3d 145 (1st Cir. 2004);

• Two Russian nationals were convicted at trial of recruiting women from Uzbekistan into the United States under false pretenses, then forcing them to work in strip clubs and bars in order to pay back an alleged $300,000 smuggling fee. The victims' passports were taken away, they were required to work seven days a week, and they were told that their families in Uzbekistan would be harmed if they did not comply with the defendants' demands. The defendants were sentenced to 60 months incarceration and ordered to pay almost $1,000,000 in restitution. *United States v.Gasanova*, 332 F.3d 297 (5th Cir 2003).

159. Since 1992, the Department of Justice has prosecuted 78 involuntary servitude cases involving 245 defendants, with three–fourths of the cases brought in the past five years. The cases have resulted in 187 convictions and guilty pleas and four acquittals.

160. *Forced Labor*. As reported in paragraph 202 of the Initial Report, the United States does not engage in practices of forced labor. In addition, the newly enacted criminal statute, 18 U.S.C. §1589, prohibits forced labor by private parties who obtain or maintain labor or services through coercion that does not rise to the level mandated for other offenses by the U.S. Supreme Court in *United States v. Kozminski*, 487 U.S. 931 (1998).

161. *Worst Forms of Child Labor*. On 2 December, 1999, the United States ratified ILO Convention 182 on The Worst Forms of Child Labor. The treaty came into force for the United States on 2 December, 2000. By ratifying the convention, the United States committed itself to take immediate action to prohibit and eliminate the worst forms of child labor.

Article 9—Liberty and security of person

162. The Supreme Court has used the vagueness doctrine to limit statutory authorizations for arrest of suspected gang members. In *City of Chicago v. Morales*, 527 U.S. 41 (1999), the Court struck down a city ordinance that permitted arrest if a police officer observed those he reasonably believed to be street gang members loitering, ordered the persons to disperse, and the persons disobeyed that order. In *Atwater v. City of Lago Vista*, 532 U.S. 318 (2001), however, the Court held that the Fourth Amendment does not forbid a warrantless arrest for a minor criminal offense, even one punishable only by a fine.

163. In *Dickerson v. United States*, 530 U.S. 428 (2000), the Supreme Court held that Miranda requirements regarding the admissibility of statements during custodial interrogations were constitutionally based and could not be overruled by legislation. The Court subsequently divided over related questions. In *United States v. Patane*, 542 U.S. 630 (2004), a plurality concluded that the Constitution does not generally require suppression of the physical fruits of voluntary statements that were not preceded by Miranda warnings. On the other hand, in *Missouri v. Seibert*, 542 U.S. 600 (2004), a plurality refused to allow deliberate evasions of Miranda, requiring suppression of statements that were made after Miranda warnings had been given but had first been obtained without giving the suspect Miranda warnings.

164. *Hamdi v. Rumsfeld*, 124 S. Ct. 2633 (2004), involved the case of a U.S. citizen, Yaser Esam Hamdi, who was captured by the U.S. military during military operations against al Qaeda and the Taliban in Afghanistan and eventually detained within the United States at a naval brig in South Carolina. Hamdi was a U.S. citizen by birth but had lived with his family in Saudi Arabia for virtually his entire life. The Supreme Court stated that the Authorization for Use of Military Force ("AUMF"), passed by Congress in the wake of the 11 September, 2001 terrorist attacks, authorized the President to detain individuals, including U.S. citizens, determined to be enemy combatants for the duration of armed hostilities. A plurality of the Court further stated that the Constitution requires that U.S. citizens so detained receive notice of the factual basis for their classification as enemy combatants, as well as a fair opportunity to rebut the government's factual assertions before a neutral decision–maker. Subsequent to the Supreme Court's decision, the United States released Hamdi and repatriated him to Saudi Arabia pursuant to a settlement agreement under which he renounced U.S. citizenship and agreed to various restrictions to ensure he would not pose a future threat to the United States.

165. *Rumsfeld v. Padilla*, 124 S. Ct. 2711 (2004), involved the case of a U.S. citizen, Jose Padilla, who associated with forces hostile to the United States in Afghanistan and took up arms against United States forces in their conflict with al Qaeda. He then escaped to Pakistan, where he was recruited, trained, funded, and equipped by al Qaeda leaders to engage in hostile acts within the United States. However, upon traveling to the United States, Padilla was apprehended by the United States at Chicago's O'Hare International

Airport. Padilla was determined to be an enemy combatant and transferred to the custody of the Department of Defense based on Presidential findings that he was associated with al Qaeda and had engaged in hostile and war–like acts including preparation for acts of international terrorism, and was detained at a naval brig in South Carolina, after which a petition for a writ of habeas corpus was filed on his behalf. The Supreme Court held that it was incorrect for that petition to have named the Secretary of Defense as respondent, because the Secretary of Defense was not Padilla's immediate custodian. The Supreme Court also held that the petition should have been filed in the district where Padilla was being confined, South Carolina, rather than New York, where it was actually filed. Subsequent to the Supreme Court decision, Padilla refiled the habeas case in the appropriate district court and against the appropriate respondent. On 9 September, 2005, the U.S. Court of Appeals for the Fourth Circuit held that Padilla's detention was authorized by the AUMF. *Padilla v. Hanft*, 2005 U.S. App. LEXIS 19465 (4th Cir. 2005). In so holding, the Fourth Circuit reversed the decision of a lower court that had found Padilla's detention unlawful and had ordered the government to release him unless it elected to bring criminal charges against him or hold him as a material witness. Rejecting the lower court's analysis, the Fourth Circuit stated that Padilla's "military detention as an enemy combatant by the President is unquestionably authorized by the AUMF as a fundamental incident to the President's prosecution of the war against al Qaeda in Afghanistan."

166. In 1996, thirty–four percent of the 56,982 defendants charged with a federal offense were ordered detained by the court pending adjudication of the charges. Defendants charged with violent (49.7%), immigration (47.9%), or drug trafficking (45.7%) offenses were detained by the court for the entire pretrial period at a greater rate than other offenders. Of the 19,254 defendants for who detention was ordered, 42.3 percent were detained because they were considered a flight risk, 10.6 percent because they were considered a danger either to the community or prospective witnesses or jurors, and 47 percent for both reasons.

167. In 2000, an estimated 62 percent of defendants facing felony charges in the nation's 75 most populous counties were released prior to the disposition of their cases. Murder defendants (13%) were the least likely to be released prior to case disposition, followed by defendants whose most serious arrest charge was robbery (44%), motor vehicle theft (46%), burglary (49%), or rape (56%). Less than half of defendants with an active criminal justice status, such as parole (23%) or probation (41%), at the time of arrest were released, compared to 70 percent of these with no active status.

168. *Detention to secure the presence of a witness.* A person may also be held in custody to secure his presence as a material witness at an upcoming trial. The Supreme Court has stated that the "duty to disclose knowledge of crime ... is so vital that one known to be innocent may be detained in the absence of bail, as a material witness." *See Stein v. New York*, 346 U.S. 156, 184 (1953). Federal law accordingly has a material witness statute, 18 U.S.C. § section 3144, that provides: If it appears from an affidavit filed by a party that the testimony of a person is material in a criminal proceeding, and if it is shown that it may become impracticable to secure the presence of the person by subpoena, a judicial officer may order the arrest of the person and treat the person in accordance with the provisions of [the Bail Reform Act]. No material witness may be detained because of inability to comply with any condition of release if the testimony of such witness can adequately be secured by deposition, and if further detention is not necessary to prevent a failure of justice. Release of a material witness may be delayed for a reasonable period of time until the deposition of the witness can be taken pursuant to the Federal Rules of Criminal Procedure.

169. The government has relied on this statute as authority to detain not only trial witnesses, but grand jury witnesses as well. One federal district court held that § 3144 does not apply to grand jury witnesses. *See United States v. Awadallah*, 202 F. Supp. 55, 61–79 (S.D.N.Y. 2002). Another federal court within the same district rejected *Awadallah*, holding that § 3144 provides clear authority to detain individuals to testify before the grand jury. *In re Application of the United States for a Material Witness Warrant*, 213 F.Supp.2d 287, 288–300 (S.D.N.Y. 2002). The issue went to the Court of Appeals for the Second Circuit which held in 2003 that a grand jury proceeding is a "criminal proceeding" for purposes of § 3244, meaning that material witnesses may be detained under § 3244 for the grand jury process. *See United States v. Awadallah*, 349 F.3d 42, 55 (2d Cir. 2003). A detained witness in a grand jury investigation may have a hearing on the propriety of the detention and is entitled to the protections of §3142" insofar as they are applicable in the grand jury setting." *Id.* at 61. A court may order that a deposition be taken to release a detained witness earlier than would be possible by requiring the witness to testify before the grand jury. *Id.* at 60. The decision of the Second Circuit was not appealed.

170. *Detention of aliens.* The Immigration and Nationality Act ("INA") provides for mandatory detention of certain categories of aliens during immigration proceedings, including certain criminal aliens, and

certain aliens who pose a threat to national security. *See* 8 U.S.C. §§ 1226(c), 1226(a), and 1225(b). Aliens that do not fall under the mandatory detention requirements may be released by the Secretary of Homeland Security on conditions, including bond, if they do not pose a flight risk or danger to the public. In general, aliens who have made an entry into the United States may challenge the Secretary's custody determination in a hearing before an immigration judge. *See* 8 U.S.C. § 1226(a).

171. Once an alien has been ordered removed from the United States, detention is mandatory during removal efforts for the next 90 days for most criminal aliens and those who pose a national security risk. If the alien has not been removed at the end of this 90–day period, the alien may be detained for another 90–day period pending removal or may be released on conditions if the alien does not pose a flight risk or danger to the public. If, after 180 days post–order detention, an alien's removal is not significantly likely in the reasonably foreseeable future, the alien must be released, with certain limited exceptions. *See Zadvydas v. Davis*, 533 U.S. 678 (2001); *Clark v. Martinez*, 125 S. Ct. 716 (2005).

172. *Habeas corpus.* The writ of habeas corpus can be used to review a final conviction—in addition to the statutory right to appeal one's conviction—as well as to challenge execution of a sentence or to challenge confinement that does not result from a criminal conviction, such as the commitment into custody for mental incompetency or detention for immigration reasons. *INS v. St. Cyr*, 533 U.S. 289 (2001). Also, the Supreme Court has held that some individuals detained in connection with hostilities or as enemy combatants are entitled to habeas corpus review.

173. In 2003, petitions for writ of habeas corpus were filed in U.S. courts on behalf of some of the detainees at Guantánamo seeking review of their detention. On 28 June, 2004, the United States Supreme Court, the highest judicial body in the United States, issued two decisionspertinent to many enemy combatants. One of the decisions directly pertained to enemy combatants detained at Guantánamo Bay, and the other pertained to a citizen enemy combatant held in the United States. *See Rasul v. Bush*, 124 S.Ct. 2686 (2004); *Hamdi v. Rumsfeld*, 124 S.Ct. 2633 (2004); *see also Rumsfeld v. Padilla*, 124 S.Ct. 2711 (2004) (involving a decision on which U.S. federal court has jurisdiction over habeas action). In *Rasul v. Bush*, the Supreme Court decided only the question of jurisdiction. The Court ruled that the U.S. District Court for the District of Columbia had jurisdiction to consider habeas challenges to the legality of the detention of foreign nationals at Guantánamo. 124 S.Ct. at 2698. The Court held that aliens apprehended abroad and detained at Guantánamo Bay, Cuba, as enemy combatants, "no less than citizens," could invoke the habeas jurisdiction of a district court. *Id.* at 2696. The Supreme Court left it to the lower courts to decide "[w]hether and what further proceedings may become necessary after [the United States government parties] make their response to the merits of petitioners' claims." *Id.* at 2699. In *Hamdi v. Rumsfeld*, a plurality of the Court addressed the entitlements of a U.S. citizen designated as an enemy combatant and held that the Due Process Clause of the United States Constitution requires "notice of the factual basis for [the citizen–detainee's] classification, and a fair opportunity to rebut the government's factual assertions before a neutral decision maker." 124 S.Ct. at 2648. A plurality of the Court observed: "There remains the possibility that the [due process] standards we have articulated could be met by an appropriately authorized and properly constituted military tribunal," and proffered as a benchmark for comparison the regulations titled, Enemy Prisoners of War, Retained Personnel, Civilian Internees and Other Detainees, Army Regulation 190–8, §1–6 (1997). *Id.* at 2651.

Article 10—Treatment of persons deprived of their liberty

174. *Humane treatment and respect.* As discussed in paragraphs 259–299 of the Initial Report, the Fifth, Eighth and Fourteenth Amendments to the United States Constitution, as well as federal and state statutes, regulate the treatment and conditions of detention of persons deprived of their liberty by state action. When the actual practice of detention in the United States does not meet Constitutional standards, individuals are held accountable.

175. The Civil Rights of Institutionalized Persons Act, 42 U.S.C. § 1997(a), authorizes the Attorney General of the United States to sue for equitable relief when there is reasonable cause to believe that a state or locality is subjecting institutionalized persons to conditions that deprive them of their rights under the United States Constitution or federal laws.

176. *Correctional systems: federal government.* Individuals convicted of federal crimes are sentenced by U.S. District Courts to the custody of the United States Attorney General. The Attorney General is appointed by the President and confirmed by the U.S. Senate, and manages the U.S. Department of Justice (DOJ). The Attorney General delegates custody responsibilities to the Federal Bureau of Prisons (BOP).

The Director of the Bureau of Prisons retains full administrative responsibility for offenders designated to the Attorney General's custody.

177. The BOP operates 106 correctional facilities throughout the nation, including 17 Penitentiaries, 60 correctional institutions, 10 independent prison camps, 12 detention centers, and 7 medical referral centers. The Bureau is responsible for the incarceration of inmates who have been sentenced to imprisonment for federal crimes, the detention of some individuals awaiting trial or sentencing in federal court, and the confinement of the District of Columbia's (D.C.) sentenced felon inmate population. The BOP places sentenced inmates in facilities commensurate with their security and program needs through a system of classification which allows the use of professional judgment within specific guidelines. Persons being detained prior to their trial, or while waiting for their immigration hearings, are normally designated to special "detention" facilities or housing units within correctional institutions. These inmates are, to the extent practicable, managed separately from convicted offenders. *See* 18 U.S.C. § 3142(i)(2).

178. The Bureau of Prisons contracts with privately–operated prisons and community corrections centers (CCCs or halfway houses), with local jails for short–term confinement, and with privately–operated juvenile facilities. The BOP uses contracting to help manage the federal inmate population when the contracting arrangement is cost–effective and complements the agency's operations and programs. Offenders in pre–release CCC are still under the custody of the Attorney General and the BOP, although the daily management of these inmates is administered by the staff of the halfway house. Private halfway houses are monitored regularly by BOP staff who provide training to CCC staff and who inspect the facilities to ensure that the CCC is in compliance with federal regulations regarding offender program needs and facility safety requirements.

179. The operation of federal correctional institutions is directly supervised by the Director of the Bureau of Prisons, who reports to the Attorney General. When problems arise or allegations are raised regarding misconduct, the Attorney General may initiate an investigation. The Office of Inspector General within the Department of Justice conducts such investigations at the Attorney General's request. In addition, the BOP investigates allegations of staff misconduct internally through its Office of Internal Affairs. A separate branch of the Department of Justice may become involved if there is reason to believe the prisoners' rights are being violated. The legislative branch, the U.S. Congress, may initiate an investigation of the BOP's operations where problems are brought to their attention. Finally, federal courts may be called upon to resolve problems.

180. In December 2003, the Office of the Inspector General (OIG) of the Department of Justice issued a report examining allegations that some correctional officers at the Federal Bureau of Prisons' (BOP) Metropolitan Detention Center (MDC) in Brooklyn, New York, physically and verbally abused individuals detained after the 11 September, 2001, attacks on the United States. This report was issued as a supplemental report to the OIG's June 2003 report that examined the treatment of 762 detainees held on immigration charges in connection with the federal government's investigation of the 11 September, 2001 attacks.

181. The OIG's December 2003 report concluded that the evidence substantiated allegations of abuse by some MDC correctional officers of some detainees, and the OIG recommended that the BOP discipline certain MDC employees. After reviewing the matter, the Department of Justice's Civil Rights Division declined criminal prosecution of the correctional officers.

182. While the OIG report did not find evidence that the detainees were brutally beaten, the OIG concluded that the evidence showed that some officers slammed detainees against the wall, twisted their arms and hands in painful ways, stepped on their leg restraint chains, and punished them by keeping them restrained for long periods. In addition, the OIG found that some MDC staff verbally abused some detainees. The OIG determined that the way these MDC officers handled some detainees was in many respects unprofessional, inappropriate, and in violation of BOP policy.

183. The OIG's report also discussed other findings concerning the treatment of detainees at the MDC. For example, the OIG found that the MDC videotaped detainees' meetings with their attorneys. On many videotapes, portions of detainees' conversations with their attorneys were audible. This violated a federal regulation (28 C.F.R. § 543.13(e)) and BOP policy.

184. In an appendix to the OIG's December 2003 report, the OIG provided the BOP with recommendations regarding discipline for specific MDC employees. That section of the report was not released publicly because of the potential of disciplinary proceedings against the correctional officers.

185. The BOP initiated an investigation based on the OIG's findings to determine whether discipline was warranted. The BOP completed its review in July 2005. It sustained many of the OIG's findings and has initiated the disciplinary process.

186. *Complaints*. As reported in paragraphs 276–280 of the Initial Report, the Department of Justice receives and acts on complaints sent directly from both federal and state prisoners. Since the passage of the statute in 1980, some 400 institutions have been investigated.

187. *Prosecutions*. Abuses do occur in jails and prisons in the United States. The Department of Justice has prosecuted a variety of cases involving federal and state prison officials, including the following examples:

• Six correctional officers at the Cummins Unit of the Arkansas Department of Corrections beat and shocked two naked and handcuffed victims with a hand–held stun gun and cattle prod on the buttocks and testicles in retaliation for them throwing urine and water on a female officer. During a separate incident, three of the six defendants shocked and beat another handcuffed inmate as punishment for his earlier refusal to submit to handcuffing. Five defendants entered guilty pleas while the sixth defendant was convicted at trial. The defendants were sentenced to terms of incarceration ranging from 12 to 108 months. *United States v. Bell*;

• Four officers at the Lea County Correctional Facility in Hobbs, New Mexico were charged with kicking an inmate multiple times in the head while he was lying on the floor and while one of the four defendants, a lieutenant, failed to prevent the assault.

• The defendants subsequently prepared and submitted false statements to investigators in order to hide the truth about the assault. Three of the defendants were convicted at trial while the fourth defendant entered a guilty plea pre–trial. The defendants were sentenced to terms of incarceration ranging from 24 to 78 months. *U.S. v.Fuller*, et al;

• A correctional officer at the Federal Correctional Institute in Danbury, Connecticut, pled guilty to engaging in sexual acts with five female inmates. The defendant was sentenced to 20 months in prison. *U.S. v. Tortorella*;

• Seven correctional officers at the United States Penitentiary in Florence, Colorado, participated in frequent, unlawful assaults of inmates in retaliation for inmate misconduct. Three of the seven were convicted at trial and sentenced to terms of incarceration ranging from 30 to 41 months while four officers were acquitted. Three additional defendants pled guilty to civil rights violations prior to trial. *See, U.S. v. LaVallee*, et al., 269 F.Supp.2d 1297 (D. Colo. 2003).

188. Since October 1997, the Department of Justice has filed charges in 270 cases of official misconduct against more than 470 law enforcement officers. Approximately one third of those cases filed involved violations of a prisoner or person in jail.

189. *Adult aliens in immigration custody*. The Department of Homeland Security continues to address allegations that arise about the treatment of aliens held in immigration detention. Within the Department of Homeland Security, the Bureau of Immigration and Customs Enforcement (ICE), Office of Detention and Removal Operations (DRO) detains approximately 19,000 aliens in Service Processing Centers, Contract Detention Facilities and local facilities through Inter-governmental Service Agreements (IGSA). ICE regularly meets at both the national and local levels with various non–governmental organizations (NGOs) (such as the American Immigration Lawyers Association, the American Bar Association, Catholic Legal Immigration Network) to address such allegations. A national NGO working group meets in Washington, D.C. at ICE Headquarters. ICE also regularly meets with consular officials to address allegations of mistreatment.

190. Since the Initial U.S. Report, in November 2000, the former Immigration and Naturalization Service (INS) promulgated the National Detention Standards (NDS). These 36 standards were the result of negotiations between the American Bar Association, the Department of Justice, the INS and other organizations involved in pro bono representation and advocacy for immigration detainees. The NDS provides policy and procedures for detention operations. Previously, policies governing detention operations were not consolidated in one location, but were instead sent to field officers via periodic memoranda containing guidance and policy statements. As a result, local differences among INS detention offices were possible.

191. The NDS are comprehensive, encompassing areas from legal access to religious and medical services, marriage requests to recreation. The four legal access standards concern visitation, access to legal materials, telephone access, and group presentations on legal rights. In July 2003, the 37th standard was introduced for Staff–Detainee Communication. Effective March 2003, the Office of Detention and Removal Operations became a division of ICE within the Department of Homeland Security. Effective September 2004, the Detainee Transfer standard was added. The 38 NDS can be accessed via the Internet at http://www.ice.gov/graphics/dro/opsmanual/index.htm.

192. ICE is committed to ensuring that the conditions of confinement for aliens detained pursuant to ICE authority meet or exceed the National Detention Standards. These standards are based on current ICE

detention policies, Bureau of Prisons' Program Statements and the widely accepted American Correctional Association Standards for Adult Local Detention Facilities, but are tailored to serve the unique needs of ICE detainees. All ICE facilities are required to comply with such standards. Additionally, wherever possible, ICE works with private contract facilities and state, local and federal government agencies which are holding aliens under Intergovernmental Service Agreements to ensure that non-ICE facilities comply with ICE's detention standards.

193. On 24 January, 2002, DRO completed and implemented the Detention Management Control Program (DMCP) to operational components at all levels. The DMCP replaced the outdated INS Jail Inspection Program. The purpose of the DMCP is to prescribe policies, standards, and procedures for ICE detention operations and to ensure detention facilities are operated in a safe, secure and humane condition for both detainees and staff. The DMCP consists of a series of events designed to ensure that reviews/inspections of detention facilities are conducted in a uniform manner.

194. All Service Processing Centers, Contract Detention Facilities, and Intergovernmental Service Agreements are reviewed annually using procedures and guidance as outlined in DMCP. During FY 2003, a cumulative total of 8 Special Assessments were conducted as a result of reported significant incidents, reported deficiencies, at-risk detention reviews or significant media event. Some examples follow:

• A special assessment was prompted at a facility in Oklahoma following an escape. Health, welfare and safety issues were identified during the assessment. Corrective actions taken by ICE included the removal of all ICE detainees from the facility and the termination of the agreement;

• Following an escape of a detainee, a special assessment was conducted at a facility used in Washington. The population was ordered reduced due to health, welfare and safety issues. Monthly site visits were instituted until the facility became compliant with the contract and applicable standards. The contractor removed the Warden and Assistant Warden;

• After allegations of assault on a detainee by staff at a parish jail in Louisiana, a special assessment was conducted. The officer was arrested and prosecuted by the Parish District Attorney, other staff were terminated, and disciplinary action initiated. No further action by ICE was required.

195. ICE concluded capacity studies for its Service Processing Centers (SPCs) in 2003. These studies were conducted by an independent agency. They determined the proper population levels at each facility based on operational, design, and emergency capacity parameters. Pursuant to completion of these studies, ICE issued policy directives mandating facility compliance with assessed appropriate population levels. In addition, the DHS Office for Civil Rights and Civil Liberties reviews certain specific allegations of mistreatment or abuse at immigration detention facilities and makes recommendations to ICE to assist in the implementation of the National Detention Standards.

196. *Care and Placement of Unaccompanied Alien Children.* Effective March 2003, functions under U.S. immigration laws regarding the care and placement of unaccompanied alien children

(UACs) were transferred from the Commissioner of the former Immigration and Naturalization Service to the Office of Refugee Resettlement (ORR) within the Administration for Children and Families (ACF) at the Department of Health and Human Services (HHS). See section 462 of the Homeland Security Act of 2002. DHS and HHS ORR also have joint obligations under the settlement agreement that followed the Supreme Court's decision in *Reno v. Flores*, 507 U.S. 292 (1993). The *Flores* agreement directs that when a child is in the custody of the federal government the child will be treated with dignity, respect and special concern for the particular vulnerabilities of children. The agreement favors release to custodians where consistent with public safety, the safety of the juvenile, and the need for the juvenile to appear for immigration proceedings. Juveniles are only released to a responsible adult.

197. Responsibilities of ORR under the law include: making and implementing placement determinations and policies, identifying sufficient qualified placements to house UACs, ensuring that the interests of the child are considered in decisions related to the care and custody of UACs, reuniting UAC with guardians or sponsors, overseeing the infrastructure and personnel of UAC facilities, conducting investigations and inspections of facilities housing UACs, collecting and comparing statistical information on UACs, and compiling lists of qualified entities to provide legal representation for UACs.

198. The UAC Program has accomplished a great deal since its inception within ORR. The program has made great strides in improving overall services within facilities, including enhanced clinical and mental health services. The program has also been faced with a dramatic increase in the number of apprehended juveniles due to increased Department of Homeland Security border initiatives. As a result, the program has added over 300 shelter or foster care beds to accommodate the influx, marking a significant achievement for

this program. This was accomplished without reliance on secure detention facilities. In fact, since March 2003 the program has dramatically reduced its reliance on secure detention by ensuring that only those with a severe criminal background are placed in a secure juvenile facility. Children are never mixed with an adult population, since the current facilities under contract are licensed to serve only juvenile populations. Currently, less than 2 percent of the total UAC population is in a secure environment. Finally, all facilities are required to ensure an appropriate level of care in terms of education, counseling, recreation and mental health services.

199. *Reform and rehabilitation.* While there is no right under the United States Constitution to rehabilitation, *Coakley v. Murphy*, 884 F.2d 1218 (9th Cir. 1989), all prison systems have as one of their goals the improvement of prisoners to facilitate their successful reintegration into society. The mission of the Federal Bureau of Prisons is to protect society by confining offenders in the controlled environments of prisons and community-based facilities that are safe, humane, cost-efficient, and appropriately secure, and that provide work and other self-improvement opportunities to assist offenders in becoming law-abiding citizens. Moreover, the Bureau of Prisons has a responsibility to provide inmates with opportunities to participate in programs that can provide them with the skills they need to lead crime-free lives after release. The BOP provides many self-improvement programs, including work in prison industries and other institution jobs, vocational training, education, substance abuse treatment, religious observance, counseling, and other programs that teach essential life skills. 28 C.F.R. parts 544, 545, 548, and 550.

200. Some minimum-security inmates from federal prison camps perform labor-intensive work off institutional grounds for other federal entities such as the National Park Service, the U.S. Forest Service, and the U.S. armed services. These inmates work at their job site during the day and return to the institution at night.

201. Federal prisoners are also provided the opportunity to participate in self-improvement programs that can provide them with the skills they need to lead crime-free lives after release. These programs include vocational training, substance abuse treatment, religious observance, parenting, anger management, counseling, and other programs that teach essential life skills. In the Bureau of Prisons, currently 34 percent of the inmates have a substance abuse disorder. The Bureau of Prisons also provides other structured activities designed to teach inmates productive ways to use their time.

Article 11—Freedom from imprisonment for breach of contractual obligation

202. As reported in the Initial Report, in the United States, imprisonment is never a sanction for the inability to fulfill a private contractual obligation.

Article 12—Freedom of movement

203. As reported in the Initial Report, in the United States, the right to travel—both domestically and internationally—is constitutionally protected. The U.S. Supreme Court has held that it is "a part of the 'liberty' of which a citizen cannot be deprived without due process of law under the Fifth Amendment". *See Zemel v. Rusk*, 381 U.S. 1 (1965). As a consequence, governmental actions affecting travel are subject to the mechanisms for judicial review of constitutional questions described elsewhere in this report. Moreover, the United States Supreme Court has emphasized that it "will construe narrowly all delegated powers that curtail or dilute citizens' ability to travel". *See Kent v. Dulles*, 357 U.S. 116, 129 (1958).

204. *Alien travel outside the United States.* Non-citizen residents are generally free to travel outside the United States, but may need special permission to return in some circumstances. For example, lawful permanent residents need permits to re-enter the United States for travel abroad of one year or more. These documents should be applied for before leaving the United States, *see* 8 U.S.C. § 1203, INA § 223; 8 C.F.R. § 223.2(b), but departure before a decision is made on the application does not effect the application. Aliens with pending applications for lawful status who travel abroad must apply for advance permission to return to the United States if they wish to re-enter the country. A departure before a decision is made on such an application is deemed an abandonment of the application, with limited exceptions. A refugee travel document allows people who are refugees or asylees to return to the United States after travel abroad. Although it should be applied for before travel, it may be issued even where the applicant is outside the United States. 8 C.F.R. § 223.2(b)(2)(ii). In addition, the INA vests in the President broad authority to regulate departure of citizens and aliens from the United States. See INA § 215, 8 U.S.C. § 1185.

205. *Alien travel within the United States.* Travel within the United States may be restricted for illegal aliens who are charged as removable and placed in immigration proceedings. As a condition of release from detention, restrictions may be placed on travel outside certain geographical areas to limit risk of flight.

Article 13—Expulsion of aliens

206. On 1 March, 2003, the U.S. Immigration and Naturalization Service ("INS") ceased to exist as an independent agency within the Department of Justice, and its functions were transferred to the newly formed Department of Homeland Security, along with more than 20 other agencies. *See* Homeland Security Act of 2002 ("HSA"), Pub. L. No. 107-296, § 441, 116 Stat. 2135, 2178, 2192 (Nov. 25, 2002). The Executive Office for Immigration Review ("EOIR"), which includes the Immigration Courts and the Board of Immigration Appeals, remained within the Department of Justice. Since the Initial Report, numerous aspects of U.S. immigration law and practice have changed substantially. The following discussion seeks to highlight the most notable developments.

207. At present, the United States provides annually for the legal immigration of over 700,000 aliens each year, with special preferences granted for family reunification and particular employment categories. In 2003, 705,827 aliens immigrated legally to the United States. In addition, each year the United States grants admission to refugees fleeing their home country, and accords asylum to many others already present in the United States. Illegal immigration to the United States, however, continues to grow substantially. The total number of aliens illegally in the United States was estimated in 2000 to be over 7 million. This number rose consistently by approximately 350,000 a year from 1990–1999. Using this estimate, the number of illegal aliens residing in the United States today may be as high as 8.5 million. In response, the United States has sought to balance its legal immigration system with a fair and just removal process that works to expel illegal aliens while securing the borders and protecting United States citizens and lawfully admitted aliens.

208. There have considerable changes in U.S. immigration law since the Initial Report. One significant piece of immigration reform legislation enacted since the last U.S. report is the Anti-Terrorism and Effective Death Penalty Act of 1996, Pub. L. No. 104-132, 110 Stat. 279 (1996) (AEDPA). The AEDPA, among other things, established a ground of inadmissibility to the U.S. for members or representatives of foreign terrorist organizations and provided related bars to various immigration benefits and forms of relief from deportation such as withholding of deportation, voluntary departure, and adjustment of status. The Act also established new alien terrorist removal procedures at title V of the INA, although the special procedures have not yet been employed. In addition, the AEDPA allowed for deportation of nonviolent offenders prior to completion of their sentences and broadened the definition of "aggravated felony", to which significant immigration consequences attach.

209. Several months later, Congress enacted the Illegal Immigration Reform and Immigrant Responsibility Act of 1996, Pub. L. No. 104-208, 110 Stat. 3546 (Sept. 30, 1996) (IIRIRA), which comprehensively overhauled the immigration laws of the United States. IIRIRA replaced exclusion and deportation proceedings with "removal proceedings." 997. An alien in removal proceedings post-IIRIRA can be charged as removable in one of two ways, "inadmissible" or "deportable."

210. Prior to IIRIRA the government looked to whether an alien had made an "entry" into the United States to determine whether exclusion or deportation proceedings applied. Entry referred to those aliens, within the United States, who were inspected and admitted, as well as those who evaded inspection and came into the United States illegally. The INA now requires that the government look not to whether an alien had "entered" the United States, but whether the alien had been "admitted" to the United States. Admission is statutorily defined in the INA as a lawful entry following inspection and authorization by an immigration officer. 8 U.S.C. § 1101(a)(13)(A). Aliens who have been admitted to the United States are charged as deportable when placed into removal proceedings. Aliens who are present in the United States but were never inspected and admitted at an official entry point to the United States are charged as inadmissible. The provisions of the INA apply different grounds of removal to deportable (8 U.S.C. § 1227), and inadmissible (8 U.S.C. § 1182) aliens.

211. *Arriving Aliens Who Are Inspected at the Border.* An alien has the burden of satisfying the immigration officer at the border point of entry that the alien is entitled to be admitted to the United States and is not subject to removal. If the officer concludes the alien is not entitled to be admitted to the United States, the officer may temporarily detain the alien for further inquiry. The purpose of the second inquiry is to gather additional information regarding the alien's admissibility. If DHS determines that the alien will not be admitted, the alien is detained for further proceedings. DHS may at any time permit an alien to withdraw his or her application for admission. 8 C.F.R. § 235.4.

212. *Parole*. DHS may, in its discretion, parole (release) into the United States an arriving alien who is not admitted. In general, parole may be granted on a case-by-case basis for urgent humanitarian reasons or significant public benefit. 8 U.S.C. § 1182(d)(5). Parole may also be granted to aliens who have serious medical conditions where detention would not be appropriate. 8 C.F.R. § 212.5(b)(1).

213. *Unaccompanied Juveniles*. Special rules apply to unaccompanied juveniles. The care and placement of unaccompanied juveniles was recently transferred from DHS to the U.S. Department of Health and Human Services, Office of Refugee Resettlement (ORR), by the Homeland Security Act of 2002. ORR endeavors to place unaccompanied juveniles with a relative or in a licensed shelter care facility. 8 C.F.R. §§ 1212.5(a)(3)(i), 1236.3.

214. *Removal*. Aliens physically present in the United States, who were not stopped at or near the border, may be expelled or "removed" pursuant to extensive procedural safeguards provided by the Immigration and Nationality Act (INA), 8 U.S.C. § 1101 et. seq. Aliens who are illegally present in the United States are subject to removal proceedings. Expedited removal is discussed below in the removal hearing subcategory. Aliens who were admitted (inspected and authorized by an immigration officer upon arrival) are charged as deportable when placed into removal proceedings. Grounds for deportation include, but are not limited to: (i) violation of nonimmigrant status; (ii) marriage fraud; (iii) falsification of documents; (iv) alien smuggling; (v) national security grounds; and (vi) conviction of certain crimes.

215. *Inadmissible Aliens*. Aliens who have not been admitted to the United States are charged as inadmissible when placed into removal proceedings. Grounds of inadmissibility include, but are not limited to: (i) health related grounds; (ii) certain criminal violations; (iii) national security and terrorism grounds; (iv) public charge; (v) aliens present without being admitted or paroled; and (vi) falsification of facts or documents to procure an immigration benefit. Regardless of whether an alien is charged as inadmissible or deportable, removal hearings are held before one of the U.S. Immigration Courts, which reside within the Department of Justice's Executive Office of Immigration Review.

Relief and protection from removal

216. *Waivers*. Various waivers are available for some of the grounds of inadmissibility. For example, a waiver of inadmissibility is available under section 212(h) of the INA for certain minor criminal offenses. To qualify, the alien applicant must demonstrate that he or she is the spouse, parent, son, or daughter of a U.S. citizen or lawful permanent resident of the U.S. and that the U.S. citizen or lawful permanent resident family member would suffer extreme hardship if the alien applicant were removed from the United States. 8 U.S.C. § 1182(h).

217. *Cancellation of Removal*. Section 304 of IIRIRA eliminated the former INA § 212(c) waiver of inadmissibility and the former form of relief called "suspension of deportation" and replaced them with a form of relief from removal called "cancellation of removal." *See* 8 U.S.C. § 1229b(a). One form of cancellation of removal is for lawful permanent residents (LPR), the other for non-LPRs. As a general matter, an immigration judge may cancel the removal of an LPR if the alien has been an LPR for at least five years, has resided continuously in the United States for at least seven years after having been admitted in any status, and has not been convicted of an aggravated felony.

218. Cancellation of removal is also available to a non-LPR who is inadmissible or deportable from the United States if the alien has been physically present in the United States for a continuous period of not less than ten years immediately preceding the date of such application, has been a person of good moral character during such period, has not been convicted of a criminal offense or security or terrorist related crime, and establishes that removal would result in "exceptional and extremely unusual hardship" to the alien's spouse, parent, or child, who is a U.S. citizen or LPR. *See* 8 U.S.C. § 1229b(b).

219. *Asylum*. *See* discussion below under sub-heading "United States refugee and asylum policy."

220. *Convention Against Torture*. Regulations implementing Article 3 of the Convention Against Torture permit aliens to raise Article 3 claims during the course of immigration removal proceedings. These regulations fully implement U.S. obligations under Article 3 and set forth a fair and rule-bound process for considering claims for protection. Individuals routinely assert Article 3 claims before immigration judges within the EOIR, whose decisions are subject to review by the Board of Immigration Appeals, and ultimately, to review in U.S. federal courts. In exceptional cases where an arriving alien is believed to be inadmissible on terrorism-related grounds, Congress has authorized alternate removal procedures in limited circumstances that do not require consideration or review by EOIR. *See* 8 U.S.C. § 1225(c). The implementing regulations provide that removal pursuant to section 235(c) of the Act shall not proceed "under circumstances that violate Article 3 of the Convention Against Torture." *See* 8 C.F.R. § 235.8(b)(4).

221. Article 3 protection is a more limited form of protection than that afforded to aliens granted asylum under the INA. This more limited form of protection is similar to withholding of removal, *see* 8 U.S.C. § 1231(b)(3), through which the United States implements its non-refoulement obligations under the Refugee Protocol. An alien granted protection under the Convention Against Torture may be removed to a third country where there are no substantial grounds for believing that the alien will be subjected to torture. Furthermore, the regulations contain special streamlined provisions for terminating Article 3 protection for an alien who is subject to criminal and security-related bars, when substantial grounds for believing the alien would be tortured if removed to a particular country no longer exist. Finally, in a very small number of appropriate cases, pursuant to 8 C.F.R. § 208.18(c), the United States may consider diplomatic assurances from the country of proposed removal that the alien will not be tortured if removed there. In such removal cases, the Secretary of Homeland Security (and in cases arising prior to the enactment of the Homeland Security Act, the Attorney General), in consultation with the Department of State, would carefully assess such assurances to determine whether they are sufficiently reliable so as to allow the individual's removal consistent with Article 3 of the Torture Convention.

222. Aliens who are subject to criminal- or security-related grounds—and are thus ineligible for other immigration benefits or protection—may be eligible for protection under Article 3. The United States provides a more limited form of protection—"deferral of removal"—to aliens otherwise subject to exclusion grounds.

223. *Voluntary Departure.* The Attorney General or Secretary of Homeland Security may permit an alien voluntarily to depart the United States at the alien's own expense in lieu of being subject to removal proceedings or prior to the completion of removal proceedings. Voluntary departure is beneficial inasmuch as it allows the removable alien to avoid an order of removal, which can trigger a lengthy bar to readmission to the United States. The period within which the alien must voluntarily depart may not exceed 120 days. Certain criminal or terrorist aliens are ineligible for this form of relief from removal. *See* 8 U.S.C. § 1229c(a).

224. An alien, unless subject to the criminal or terrorist bars to voluntary departure, may also request voluntary departure at the conclusion of removal proceedings. *See* 8 U.S.C. § 1229c(b). In order to receive post-hearing voluntary departure, an alien must have been physically present in the United States for at least one year prior to service of the NTA, must show good moral character, must not be subject to the criminal or terrorist bars to such relief, must not have been granted voluntary departure prior to the hearing, and must establish by clear and convincing evidence that he or she can leave at their own expense and that he or she intends to do so. The qualifying alien may only receive up to 60 days to effect a grant of voluntary departure following completion of removal proceedings.

225. *Removal hearing.* In general, proceedings before an immigration judge commence when the Department of Homeland Security (DHS) issues a Notice to Appear (NTA), charging the alien as deportable or inadmissible and thus removable from the United States. 8 C.F.R. § 239.1(a). An alien who concedes removability may apply for discretionary relief from removal provided he or she meets the statutory requirements for such relief. An alien who has not applied for discretionary relief or voluntary departure may be ordered removed from the United States by the immigration judge.

226. In cases where an alien was admitted to the United States and deportability is at issue, the burden is on the government to establish that the alien is deportable by clear and convincing evidence. 8 U.S.C. § 1229a(c)(3)(A). When an alien has been charged as inadmissible, the burden is on the alien to prove that he or she is clearly and beyond doubt entitled to be admitted to the United States, or, that by clear and convincing evidence, he or she is lawfully present in the United States pursuant to a prior admission. 8 U.S.C. § 1229a(c)(2)(A) and (B).

227. Upon issuance of the NTA, DHS may either take the alien into custody upon issuance of a warrant, or release the alien on bond or conditional parole. 8 C.F.R. § 236(a). Such actions occur at the discretion of DHS, with some exceptions noted below. In most cases, an immigration judge may review a custody or bond decision made by DHS at the request of an alien or his or her representative. Exceptions include: (i) aliens who have violated national security grounds; and (ii) aliens convicted of certain serious crimes. 8 C.F.R.§§ 1003.19; 1236.1.

228. Review by the federal courts of the lawfulness of detention remains available through a petition for writ of habeas corpus (habeas petition). DHS is obligated by statute to take into custody any alien convicted of certain criminal offenses or terrorist activity, but in most cases may release the alien if such release is deemed necessary to provide protection to a witness or potential witness cooperating in a major investigation, and DHS decides that the alien's release will not pose a danger and the alien is likely to appear for scheduled

proceedings. 8 U.S.C.§ 1226(c) (2). An alien's release on bond or parole may be revoked at any time in the discretion of DHS. 8 U.S.C. § 1226(b).

229. Removal hearings are open to the public, except that the immigration judge may, due to lack of space, or for the purpose of protecting witnesses, parties, the public interest, or abused alien spouses, limit attendance or hold a closed hearing in any specific case. 8 C.F.R. § 1003.27. Proceedings may also be closed to the public upon a showing by DHS that information to be disclosed in court may harm the national security or law enforcement interests of the United States. 8 C.F.R. § 1003.27(d).

230. At the outset of a proceeding, the immigration judge must advise the alien of their right to representation, information on pro-bono counsel, and that the alien will have the opportunity to examine and object to evidence and to cross-examine witnesses. The immigration judge must also read to the alien the facts alleged in the NTA and request that the alien admit or deny each factual allegation under oath. *See* 8 C.F.R. § 1240(b)(1).

231. During removal proceedings, the immigration judge has the authority to determine whether an alien is inadmissible or deportable, to grant discretionary relief from removal (e.g., voluntary departure, asylum, cancellation of removal), and to determine the country to which an alien's removal will be directed. An alien in removal proceedings retains the right to representation, at no expense to the government, by qualified counsel of his choice. 8 U.S.C. § 1229a(b)(2)(B)(4). An alien must also be afforded a competent, impartial interpreter if the alien is not able to communicate effectively in English.

232. The United and Strengthening America by Providing Appropriate Tools Required to Intercept and Obstruct Terrorism Act of 2001 ("USA PATRIOT Act"), Pub. L. No. 107-56, 115 Stat. 272 (Oct. 26, 2001), amended the INA, significantly expanded the terrorism-related grounds of inadmissibility and deportability. The USA PATRIOT Act also set forth provisions authorizing immigration authorities to detain and remove alien terrorists and those who support them and providing for humanitarian immigration relief to non-citizen victims of the attacks on 11 September, 2001.

233. The Intelligence Reform and Terrorism Prevention Act of 2004, Pub. L. No. 108 458, 118 Stat. 3638 (Dec. 7, 2004), established new grounds of inadmissibility and deportability and bars to immigration relief designed to prevent human rights abusers (i.e., those aliens who have engaged in genocide, torture, extrajudicial killings, or severe violations of religious freedom) from entering or remaining in the United States. The statute also broadened the authority of the Office of Special Investigations (OSI) within the Department of Justice's Criminal Division. The OSI detects, investigates and takes legal action to denaturalize aliens who are inadmissible for having participated in Nazi persecution, genocide, torture or extrajudicial killing. In addition, the law created the Human Smuggling and Trafficking Center within the Department of State to achieve greater integration and overall effectiveness in the U.S. government's efforts to combat alien smuggling, trafficking in persons, and criminal support of clandestine terrorist travel.

234. *Hearing in Absentia.* If an alien fails to appear at his or her removal proceeding, he or she will be ordered removed from the United States if the government establishes by "clear and unequivocal evidence that the written notice was so provided and that the alien is removable." 8 U.S.C. § 1229a(b)(5). An in absentia order may be rescinded in two circumstances. The alien may make a motion to reopen within 180 days of the final order if he or she can show that the failure to appear was due to exceptional circumstances, or he or she may file a motion to reopen at any time showing that he or she did not receive proper notice of the hearing. 8 U.S.C.§ 1229a(b)(5)(C).

Additional removal proceedings in particular circumstances

235. *Expedited Removal of Arriving Aliens.* The IIRIRA established a special, expedited removal procedure for certain aliens. Persons found to be inadmissible at a port-of-entry under sections 212(a)(6)(C) (seeking to procure visa or admission to the United States by fraud or willful misrepresentation) or 212(a)(7) (not possessing valid entry documents) of the INA are subject to immediate removal unless the alien satisfies exceptions defined in the INA. 8 U.S.C. § 1225(b)(1). Expedited removal procedures currently are also applied to two categories of aliens who evade inspection and enter the United States illegally: (1) aliens arriving by sea who have not been in the United States for at least two years; and (2) aliens apprehended within 100 miles of a U.S. international land border within 14 days of entry. Implementation of expedited removal with respect to the latter category has commenced in select areas of the United States and was recently expanded to cover the entire southwest border of the United States. Expedited removal is necessary to prevent potential dangerous mass migrations of economic migrants by sea and to enhance the security and safety of the U.S. land border.

236. Before the expedited removal procedure is used, the examining officer creates a statement of the facts regarding an alien's identity, alienage, and inadmissibility. 8 C.F.R. § 235.3(b)(2)(i). The officer also advises the alien of the charges against him or her and affords the alien the opportunity to respond to those charges. *Id.* If an alien claims to be a permanent resident, a refugee, an asylee, or a United States citizen, the alien is referred to an immigration judge for a determination of that claim or for a removal hearing if the claim is verified. 8 C.F.R. § 235.3(b)(5).

237. Aliens placed in expedited removal are generally not entitled to a hearing before an immigration judge unless they are found to have a "credible fear" of persecution or torture in their country of origin (i.e., a "significant possibility" that the alien could establish eligibility for asylum or for protection under the Convention Against Torture). 8 U.S.C. § 1225(b)(1)(B)(v). If the alien expresses a fear of return to his or her country or indicates a desire to apply for asylum, the alien is referred to an asylum officer for a credible fear interview to determine whether the alien has a credible fear of persecution or torture. 8 C.F.R. § 235.3(b)(4). An alien has the right to contact family members, friends, attorneys, or representatives prior to the interview. 8 C.F.R.§ 1235.3(b) (4)(B). The alien may have a representative present at the interview, and the asylum officer must arrange for an interpreter for the interview if necessary. 8 C.F.R. § 1208.30(d)(5). If the asylum officer finds that the alien does not have a credible fear of persecution or torture, the alien may request review of that determination by an immigration judge. 8 C.F.R. § 1235.3(4)(C). If the officer finds that credible fear exists, the alien is referred to an immigration judge for full consideration of any protection claims. 8 C.F.R. § 208.30(f).

238. Aliens denied admission at the border are considered to be at "the threshold of entry" and thus cannot assert a liberty interest under the Constitution to be admitted into the United States. *Shaughnessy v. Mezei*, 345 U.S. 206 (1953); *U.S. ex rel. Knauff v. Shaughnessy*, 338 U.S. 537 (1950).

239. *Aliens Convicted of Serious Crimes.* An alien who has not been lawfully admitted for permanent residence and has been convicted of an aggravated felony may be placed into a different kind of removal proceeding under section 238 of the INA, 8 U.S.C. § 1228. An alien placed into section 238 proceedings must be given written notice of the allegations and legal charges. 8 C.F.R. § 1238.1(i). The alien may inspect the evidence supporting the charges and may rebut the charges within 10 days (13 days by mail) of service of the notice. 8 C.F.R. § 1238.1(ii). During this period, the alien may request in writing the country he or she elects as the country of removal. *Id.* The alien has the right to representation by counsel of his or her choice, at no expense to the government, during this process and retains the right to request withholding of removal under 8 U.S.C. § 1231(b)(3) if he or she fears persecution or torture in the designated country of removal.

240. *Decisions and appeals.* A decision of an immigration judge in a removal hearing may be written or oral. 8 C.F.R. § 1003.37. Appeal from the decision lies with the Board of Immigration Appeals. 8 C.F.R. § 1003.38.

241. *Federal Court Review.* Judicial review of the Board of Immigration Appeals decision is generally available via a petition for review in a U.S. Court of Appeals. 8 U.S.C. § 1252(a). An alien may not seek judicial review unless and until he or she has exhausted his or her administrative remedies. 8 U.S.C. § 1252(d)(1). An alien, in limited circumstances, may also file a petition for habeas corpus in a federal district court to challenge the lawfulness of his or her detention. *Zadvydas*, 533 U.S. 678.

242. *Post-Order Detention.* Section 241(a)(1)(A) of the INA provides that "when an alien is ordered removed, the Attorney General shall remove the alien from the United States within a period of 90 days." 8 U.S.C. § 1231(a)(1)(A). The law requires that, during the 90-day period, certain criminal and terrorist aliens must be detained. 8 U.S.C. § 1231(a)(2)(A). After 90 days, detention of such aliens is no longer mandatory, and is based on an assessment of the flight and safety risk attributed to the alien given his or her history. 8 C.F.R. § 241.4. If after six months there is no significant likelihood of removal in the reasonably foreseeable future, an alien must be released unless special circumstances exist (e.g., alien's release would endanger national security). *Zadvydas*, 533 U.S. 678; 8 C.F.R § 241.14. Before determining whether a special circumstance applies, DHS makes a determination that no conditions of release can be reasonably expected to avoid the action threatened by the alien. *Id.*

243. In *Clark v. Martinez*, 543 U.S.___, 125 S. Ct. 716 (2005), the Supreme Court interpreted INA § 241(a)(6) to mean that the six-month presumptive detention period noted in *Zadvydas* applies equally to all categories of aliens described in INA § 241(a)(6). As a result, the provisions of 8 C.F.R. §§ 241.13 and .14 apply to inadmissible and excludable aliens, including Mariel Cubans, alien crewman, and stowaways.

244. *Country of removal.* Section 241(b) of the INA, 8 U.S.C. § 1231(b), sets forth what is generally a four-step process to determine the country to which an alien will be removed. First, an alien generally will be removed to the country of his choice. If that removal option is not available, the alien generally will be removed to the country of his citizenship. Third, in the event those removal options are not available, the alien generally will be removed to one of the countries with which he has a lesser connection (e.g., country of birth, country from which he traveled to the United States, country of last residence). Finally, if the preceding removal options are "impracticable, inadvisable, or impossible" other countries of removal will be considered. *See generally Jama v. Immigration and Customs Enforcement,* 125 S. Ct. 694 (2005) (holding that INA generally does not require foreign government's "acceptance" of alien in order for DHS to effect removal to that country).

245. *United States refugee and asylum policy.* The refugee and asylum policy of the United States, remains that set forth primarily in the Refugee Act of 1980 and the Immigration and Nationality Act, in accordance with the United States' historical commitment to the protection of refugees and in compliance with the 1967 United Nations Protocol relating to the Status of Refugees, Jan. 31, 1967, 19 U.S.T. 6224, T.I.A.S. No. 6577 (1968), to which the United States acceded in 1968.

246. *Refugee admissions.* The Immigration and Nationality Act (INA) provides for the admission into the United States of refugees outside the United States. To be considered a refugee for the purpose of admission to the United States a person must meet the definition contained in INA § 101(a)(42), 8 U.S.C. § 1101(a)(42). See below.

247. Each year, after appropriate consultation with Congress, the President determines an authorized admission level for refugees. The admission ceiling for refugees in U.S. fiscal year 1994 was 121,000. The annual ceiling represents the maximum number of refugees allowed to enter the United States in the stated year, allocated by world geographical region. INA § 207(a). The President may accommodate an emergency refugee situation by increasing the refugee admissions ceiling for a 12-month period. INA § 207(b); 8 U.S.C. § 1157(b). The numbers of refugees admitted to the United States in subsequent fiscal years are as follows: FY 1995: 99,490; FY 1996: 75,682; FY 1997: 70,085; FY 1998: 76,554; FY 1999: 85,317; FY 2000: 73,144; FY 2001: 69,304; FY 2002: 27,029; FY 2003: 28,422; and FY 2004: 52,868. See Annex III for more details.

248. *Asylum.* Under the INA, persons at a United States port of entry or within the United States may seek refugee protection through a grant of asylum or withholding of removal. Asylum is a discretionary form of relief from removal that may be granted to an individual determined to be a refugee. The United States definition of refugee, derived from the U.N. Refugee Protocol, is "any person who is outside of any country of such person's nationality or, in the case of a person having no nationality, is outside any country in which such person last habitually resided, and who is unable or unwilling to return to, and is unable or unwilling to avail himself or herself of the protection of, that country because of persecution or a well-founded fear of persecution on account of race, religion, nationality, membership in a particular social group, or political opinion." INA 101(a)(42)(A); 8 U.S.C. § 1101(a)(42)(A). U.S. law further provides that a person "who has been forced to abort a pregnancy or to undergo involuntary sterilization, or who has been persecuted for failure or refusal to undergo such a procedure or for other resistance to a coercive population control program, shall be deemed to have been persecuted on account of political opinion, and a person who has a well-founded fear that he or she will be forced to undergo such a procedure or subject to persecution for such failure, refusal or resistance shall be deemed to have a well founded fear of persecution on account of political opinion." INA § 101(a)(42); 8 U.S.C. § 1101(a)(42).

249. The United States refugee definition excludes "any person who ordered, incited, assisted, or otherwise participated in the persecution of any person on account of race, religion, nationality, membership in a particular social group, or political opinion." INA § 101(a)(42)(B). The statutory provision for withholding of removal (*non-refoulement*), derived from Article 33 of the Convention, provides that an individual cannot be removed to a country where his or her life or freedom would be threatened on account of race, religion, nationality, membership in a particular social group, or political opinion. INA § 241(b)(3), 8 U.S.C. § 1231(b)(3). There are bars to a grant of asylum or withholding of removal, even if eligibility is otherwise established, based on persecution of others, criminal activity, or security concerns, described below. There are certain limitations on the right to apply for asylum, also discussed further below. A related form of protection, temporary protected status, discussed in greater detail below, is available to persons already within the United States when the Homeland Security Secretary determines that certain extreme and temporary conditions in their country of nationality (such as ongoing armed conflict or an environmental disaster) generally do not permit the United States to return them to that country in safety.

250. *Asylum Claims: Numbers.* At present, there are some 100,000 asylum claims pending in various stages of adjudication within the affirmative asylum process. This does not include asylum cases filed by individuals in removal proceedings, which are pending before the Executive Office for Immigration Review within the Department of Justice. All but approximately 30,000 of these applications were submitted by individuals who now are covered by special legislation that allows them to apply for lawful permanent resident status. It is expected that the vast majority of the applicants covered by the special legislation will either become lawful permanent residents under those provisions and withdraw their claims for asylum or, having abandoned their asylum claims, will not appear for an asylum interview when scheduled. It is anticipated the Asylum Program will have addressed the backlog of asylum claims by the end of 2006. The number of new asylum receipts has decreased significantly since 2001 and 2002, when the Asylum Division was receiving approximately 60,000 new cases annually. In fiscal year 2004, the Asylum Division received 28,000 applications. The Asylum Division received approximately 23,500 new applications in fiscal year 2005. page 61

251. *Asylum Claims: Process.* Asylum applications may be submitted by persons who are at a United States port of entry or are physically present in the United States. An asylum applicant may include in his or her application his or her spouse and any unmarried children under age 21 who are present in the United States. Asylum may be granted without regard to the applicant's immigration status or country of origin. There are two paths for an alien present in the United States seeking asylum. First, the alien may come forward to United States Citizenship and Immigration Services (USCIS) within the Department of Homeland Security to apply "affirmatively." Second, the alien may seek asylum as a defense to removal proceedings, even if an ineligibility determination was made during the affirmative process. Under the affirmative process, grants of asylum are within the discretion of the Secretary of the Department of Homeland Security, as executed by Asylum Officers within USCIS. Under the defensive process, grants of asylum are within the discretion of the Attorney General, as executed by immigration judges or the Board of Immigration Appeals within the Department of Justice, Executive Office for Immigration Review.

252. *Asylum Application: Prohibitions.* The IIRIRA of 1996 (discussed supra), which applies to all asylum applications filed on or after 1 April, 1997, included certain prohibitions on the ability to apply for asylum. Under these provisions, an asylum-seeker is not permitted to apply for asylum in the United States if 1) he or she can be returned pursuant to a bilateral or multilateral agreement to a third country where he or she would have access to full and fair procedures for determining a claim to asylum, 2) he or she failed to submit an application for asylum within 1 year from the date of last arrival, unless the person can establish exceptional circumstances relating to the delay or changed circumstances that materially affect eligibility for asylum; or 3) he or she was previously denied asylum in the United States, unless there have been changed circumstances that materially affect eligibility for asylum. INA § 208(a)(2), 8 U.S.C. § 1158(a)(2). These limitations on applying for asylum are Not applicable to requests for withholding of removal (non-refoulement). To date, the United States has entered into only one bilateral agreement to return asylum-seekers to a safe third country under the limitation on filing noted above. In December 2002, the United States entered into such an agreement with Canada. The agreement is limited to individuals seeking asylum at land border ports of entry on the U.S.-Canadian border and contains broad exceptions based on principles of family unity. The agreement went into effect on 29 December, 2004, after both countries issued final implementting regulations.

253. *Affirmative asylum.* Affirmative asylum claims are heard and decided by a corps of USCIS Asylum Officers located in eight regional offices. The Asylum Officer conducts an interview with the applicant "in a non-adversarial manner ... to elicit all relevant and useful information bearing on the applicant's eligibility." 8 C.F.R. § 208.9(b). The applicant may have counsel present at the interview and may submit the affidavits of witnesses. In addition, the applicant may supplement the record at the time of the interview. 8 C.F.R. § 208.9.

254. If the Asylum Officer determines that the applicant is not eligible for asylum and the applicant is not in valid immigration status, the applicant is placed in removal proceedings before an immigration judge within the Department of Justice, and the asylum application is referred to the immigration judge to consider de novo. 8 C.F.R. § 208.14. If an ineligible applicant is in valid status, the Asylum Officer denies the asylum application, after the applicant is provided the reasons for the negative determination and an opportunity to rebut the grounds for denial. The applicant retains his or her valid status (e.g., student status). Each Asylum Officer decision is reviewed by a Supervisory Asylum Officer. The basis for an Asylum Officer's decision to deny or refer an application must be communicated to the applicant in writing and must include an assessment of the applicant's credibility. 8 C.F.R § 208.19. There is no appeal of a grant or denial of asylum by an

Asylum Officer. If a denied asylum seeker no longer retains valid status (either it expired or the asylum seeker took actions inconsistent with that status) and is placed in removal proceedings, he or she can apply for asylum de novo with the immigration judge.

255. *Asylum: Country Conditions Information.* Copies of all asylum applications are forwarded to the Office of Country Reports and Asylum Affairs (CRA) within the Department of State's Bureau of Democracy Rights and Labor (DRL). At its option, DRL may comment on the application or may provide detailed country conditions information relevant to the application.8 C.F.R. § 208.11. In addition to any information from the Department of State, DHS/USCIS Asylum officers consider country conditions information from a wide variety of sources. The Resource Information Center within the Asylum Division of DHS/USCIS is responsible for assisting Asylum Officers with country conditions research and disseminating reliable country conditions information and reports to the eight asylum field offices.

256. *Asylum: Mandatory denials.* Asylum claims cannot be granted when: (i) the alien ordered, incited, assisted or otherwise participated in the persecution of any person on account of race, religion, nationality, membership in a particular social group, or political opinion; (ii) the alien, having been convicted by a final judgment of a particularly serious crime (including an aggravated felony), constitutes a danger to the community of the United States; (iii) there are serious reasons for believing that the alien has committed a serious nonpolitical crime outside the United States prior to arrival in the United States; (iv) there are reasonable grounds for regarding the alien as a danger to the security of the United States; (v) the alien is inadmissible under certain statutory provisions relating to terrorist activity; or (vi) the alien was firmly resettled in another country prior to arriving to the United States. INA § 208(b)(2).

257. *Asylum: Discretionary denials.* An application for asylum may also be denied as a matter of discretion, where appropriate. INA § 208(b)(1); 8 C.F.R. §§ 208.13-.14, 1208.13-.14.

258. *Asylum Termination.* Asylum officers also have limited power to terminate asylum. This power may be exercised when: (i) there is a showing of fraud in the asylum application such that the applicant was not eligible for asylum when it was granted; (ii) the individual no longer meets the definition of refugee owing to a fundamental change in circumstances; (iii) the individual may be removed, pursuant to a bilateral or multilateral agreement to a country other than the country of nationality (or if no nationality, the country of last habitual residence) in which the individual's life or freedom would not be threatened on account of one of the protected characteristics in the refugee definition, and the individual is eligible to receive asylum or equivalent temporary protection (currently the United States has not entered into any such agreements); (iv) the individual has voluntarily availed himself or herself of the protection of his or her country by returning there with permanent resident status or the reasonable possibility of obtaining such status with the same rights and obligations pertaining to other permanent residents of that country; (v) the individual has acquired a new nationality and enjoys the protection of the country of his or her new nationality; or (vi) a mandatory bar to a grant of asylum applies. INA § 208(c)(2), 8 C.F.R. § 208.24(a).

259. *Asylum and withholding of removal in removal proceedings.* If an alien has been served with a Notice to Appear, he must appear before an immigration judge, with whom he may file an asylum application. The filing of an asylum application is also considered a request for withholding of removal under INA section 241(b)(3). 8 C.F.R. §§ 208.3(b), 1208.3(b).

260. *Asylum and withholding of removal for aliens subject to expedited removal.* In 1997, Congress created expedited removal, which provides for the prompt removal of certain aliens who are illegally arriving at or present in the United States. INA § 235(b). Aliens subject to expedited removal may be removed without referral to an immigration judge for a removal hearing. INA § 235(b)(1)(A)(i). However, an alien subject to expedited removal who expresses either an intention to apply for asylum or a fear of persecution must first be interviewed by an asylum officer. INA § 235(b) (1) (A)(ii). If the asylum officer finds that the alien has a significant possibility of establishing eligibility for asylum or withholding of removal, the alien will be served with a Notice to Appear and given an opportunity to seek protection in removal proceedings before an immigration judge. INA § 235(b) (1)(B)(ii). If the asylum officer makes a negative finding, the alien will be removed, unless he or she requests that an immigration judge review the finding. An immigration judge review of an asylum officer's negative finding must be completed within seven days of the finding. INA § 235(b)(1)(B) (iii)(III).

261. Withholding of removal under INA § 241(b)(3) differs from a request for asylum in four ways. First, section 241(b)(3) prohibits the government from removing an alien only to a specific country, while asylum protects the alien from removal generally. Second, in order to qualify for withholding of removal, an alien must demonstrate that his or her "life or freedom would be threatened" in the country of removal, whereas asylum only requires the alien to demonstrate a well-founded fear of persecution. Third, protection under

section 241(b)(3) cannot result in permanent residence, while asylees are eligible to apply for permanent residence after one year. Fourth, relief under section 241(b)(3) is a mandatory restriction imposed on the government while asylum is an immigration benefit which the government has discretion to grant or deny. While asylum claims may be adjudicated either by an asylum officer or an immigration judge, withholding of removal claims made under INA § 241(b)(3) are adjudicated by immigration judges only. 8 C.F.R. §§ 208.16(a), 1208.16(a).

262. An alien will be denied withholding of removal under INA § 241(b)(3) and may be removed to a country, notwithstanding any threat to his or her life or freedom that may exist there, if: (i) he or she has engaged in persecution of others; (ii) he or she has been convicted of a particularly serious crime that constitutes a danger to the community of the United States; (iii) there are serious reasons to believe that he or she has committed a serious non-political crime outside of the United States; or (iv) there are reasonable grounds to believe that he or she may represent a danger to the security of the United States. INA § 241(b)(3)(B).

263. Denial of asylum or withholding of removal by an immigration judge could result in a final order of removal. Aliens granted withholding of removal could also become subject to final orders of removal because the government may remove these aliens to certain countries where their lives or freedom would not be threatened. INA § 241(b)(1), (2). Aliens may appeal immigration judge decisions to the Board of Immigration Appeals within 30 days of the immigration judge's decision. 8 C.F.R. § 1240.15. Appeal, through a "petition for review," to a federal court of appeals is permitted within 30 days of the Board's decision. INA § 242(b)(1).

264. *Rights of refugees and asylees.* An applicant for asylum may be granted employment authorization if: (1) he or she has received a recommended approval of his or her asylum application; or (2) 180 days have elapsed following the filing of the asylum application, and the application has not been denied. 8 C.F.R. § 208.7. An asylum applicant may be granted, in the discretion of the Secretary of Homeland Security, advance parole to travel abroad to a third country. 8 C.F.R. § 212.5(f).

265. *Spouses and Children.* The spouse and children of the person granted asylum or admitted as a refugee may accompany or follow such person without having to apply for protection independently. INA §§ 207(c)(2), 208(b)(3).

266. *Permanent residence.* Persons admitted to the United States as refugees are eligible for permanent resident status after one year of continuous physical presence in the United States. The number of refugees adjusting to permanent resident status is not subject to the annual limitation on immigrants into the United States. INA § 209. An asylee may also apply for permanent resident status after being continuously present in the United States for at least one year after being granted asylum.

267. *Temporary Protected Status.* Under INA § 244, 8 U.S.C. § 1254a, the Secretary of Homeland Security has the authority to grant temporary protected status to aliens in the United States, temporarily allowing foreign nationals to live and work in the United States without fear of being sent back to unstable or dangerous conditions. The United States thus may become, at the Secretary's discretion, a temporary safe haven for foreign nationals already in the country if one of three conditions exist: (i) there is an ongoing armed conflict within the state which would pose a serious threat to the personal safety of returned nationals; (ii) there has been an earthquake, flood, drought, epidemic, or other environmental disaster in the state resulting in a substantial but temporary disruption of living conditions in the area affected; the state is temporarily unable to handle adequately the return of its nationals; and the state officially requests temporary protected status; or (iii) there exist extraordinary and temporary conditions in the state that prevent nationals from returning in safety, as long as permitting such aliens to remain temporarily in the United States is not contrary to the national interest of the United States. INA§ 244(b)(1). A designation of temporary protected status may last for 6 to18 months, with the possibility of extension for an additional 6, 12, or 18 months. INA § 244(b)(2), (3)(C).

268. An alien is ineligible for temporary protected status if he has been convicted of at least one felony or two or more misdemeanors, or is subject to a bar to asylum. INA § 244(c)(2)(B). An alien may also be denied temporary protected status if certain grounds of inadmissibility apply and are not waived. INA § 244(c)(2)(A). The Secretary of Homeland Security must withdraw temporary protected status if: (i) the Secretary finds that the alien was not eligible for such status; (ii) the alien was not continuously physically present in the United States, except for brief, casual, and innocent departures or travel with advance permission; or (iii) the alien failed to re-register annually. INA§ 244(c)(3).

...

Article 14—Right to fair trial

271. *Competent, independent and impartial tribunal.* States may set appropriate standards of conduct for their judges. *See Gruenburg v. Kavanagh*, 413 F. Supp. 1132, 1135 (E.D. Mich.1976). The Supreme Court has held, however, that a state canon of judicial conduct that prohibits candidates for judicial elections from announcing their views on disputed political or legal issues violates the First Amendment. *See Republican Party v. White*, 536 U.S. 765 (2002).

272. *Trial by jury.* The right to trial by jury reflects "a profound judgment about the way in which law should be enforced and justice administered". *See Duncan v. Louisiana*, 391 U.S. at 155. In the U.S. system, the jury is the fact-finder. Therefore, a judge may not direct the jury to return a verdict of guilty, no matter how strong the proof of guilt may be. *See Sparf and Hansen v. United States*, 156 U.S. 51, 105-6 (1895). A criminal defendant is entitled to a jury determination beyond a reasonable doubt of every element of the crime with which he is charged, as well as any fact (other than the fact of a prior conviction) that increases the statutory maximum penalty for the offense. *Apprendi v. New Jersey*, 530 U.S. 466, 490 (2000); *In re Winship*, 397 U.S. 358, 364 (1970). *See also, Blakely v. Washington*, 124 S. Ct. 2531, 159 L. Ed. 2d 403 (2004).

273. *Civil cases.* Guarantees of fairness and openness also are ensured in the civil context, with federal and state constitutions providing basic and essential protections. In civil disputes, the fundamental features of the United States judicial system—an independent judiciary and bar, due process and equal protection of the law—are common. Most importantly, the Due Process and Equal Protection Clauses of the Constitution—applicable to the states through the Fourteenth Amendment—mandate that judicial decision-making be fair, impartial, and devoid of discrimination. Neutrality is the core value.

274. Neutrality means the absence of discrimination. As is the case with criminal trials, the Equal Protection Clause bars the use of discriminatory stereotypes in the selection of the jury in civil cases. As the Supreme Court held in *Edmonson v. Leesville Concrete Co., Inc.*, 500 U.S. 614, 628 (1991): "Race discrimination within the courtroom raises serious questions as to the fairness of the proceedings conducted there. Racial bias mars the integrity of the judicial system and prevents the idea of democratic government from becoming a reality." In *J.E.B. v. Alabama*, 511 U.S. 127, 129 (1994), the Court extended this principle to cases involving gender-based exclusion of jurors, holding that "gender, like race, is an unconstitutional proxy for juror competence and impartiality." As the Court explained (*id.* at 146): "When persons are excluded from participation in our democratic processes solely because of race or gender, ... the integrity of our judicial system is jeopardized."

275. Fairness of civil proceedings also is ensured by the requirement that where they might result in serious "hardship" to a party adversary hearings must be provided. For instance, where a dispute between a creditor and debtor runs the risk of resulting in repossession, the Supreme Court has concluded that debtors should be afforded a fair adversarial hearing. *See Fuentes v. Shevin*, 407 U.S. 67 (1972). *See also, Sniadach v. Family Finance Corp.*, 395 U.S. 337 (1969).

276. This is particularly true in civil cases involving governmental action, where the Supreme Court, since the 1970s, has recognized the importance of granting procedural rights to individuals. In determining whether procedures are constitutionally adequate, the Court weighs the strength of the private interest, the adequacy of the existing procedures, the probable value of other safeguards, and the government's interest. *See Mathews v. Eldridge*, 424 U.S. 319, 335 (1976). Depending on these factors, the United States Constitution mandates different types of guarantees in civil proceedings involving the government. Basic requirements include an unbiased tribunal; notice to the private party of the proposed action; and the right to receive written findings from the decision maker. Applying these principles, the Court has thus held that persons have had a right to notice of the detrimental action, and a right to be heard by the decision maker. *See Grannis v. Ordean*, 234 U.S. 385, 394 (1918) ("The fundamental requisite of due process of law is the opportunity to be heard"); *See Goldberg v. Kelly*, 397 U.S. 254 (1970) (welfare entitlements cannot be interrupted without a prior evidentiary hearing). In the context of civil forfeiture proceedings, the Court has held that citizens have a Due Process right to a hearing to oppose the forfeiture of their property. *See United States v. James Daniel Good Real Property*, 510 U.S. 43, 48–62 (1993). And in *Degen v. United States*, 517 U.S. 820 (1996), the Court ruled that this right to a hearing applies even when the citizen is a fugitive who refuses to return in person to this country to face criminal charges. When action is taken by a government agency, statutory law embodied in the Administrative Procedure Act also imposes requirements on the government, such as the impartiality of the decision maker and the party's right to judicial review of adverse action. As Justice Frankfurter once wrote, the "validity and moral authority of a

con- clusion largely depend on the mode by which it was reached ... No better instrument has been devised for arriving at truth than to give a person in jeopardy of serious loss notice of the case against him and an opportunity to meet it. Nor has a better way been found for generating the feeling, so important to popular government, that justice has been done." *Joint Anti-Fascist Refugee Committee v. McGrath*, 341 U.S. 123, 171–72 (1951).

277. Although inequalities in wealth distribution certainly have an impact on individuals' access to the courts and to representation, the equal protection components of state and federal constitutions have helped smooth these differences. In particular, the Supreme Court has held that access to judicial proceedings cannot depend on one's ability to pay where such proceedings are "the only effective means of resolving the dispute at hand". *Boddie v. Connecticut*, 401 U.S. 371, 375-76 (1971) (holding unconstitutional a state law conditioning a judicial decree of divorce upon the claimant's ability to pay court fees and costs). *See also*, M.L.B v. S.L.J., 519 U.S. 201 (1996) (holding unconstitutional a state law conditioning a parent's right to appeal from a trial court's decree terminating her parental rights on her ability to pay record preparation fees).

278. Inequalities remain, though, in part because neither the Constitution nor federal statutes provide a right to appointed counsel in civil cases. Nonetheless, the Supreme Court has made it easier for indigent parties to afford legal representation by invalidating prohibitions against concerted legal action. The Court has thus recognized a right for groups to "unite to assert their legal rights as effectively and economically as practicable". *See United Trans. Union v. State Bar of Michigan*, 401 U.S. 576, 580 (1971). In addition, Congress long ago enacted the "federal *in forma pauperis* statute ... to ensure that indigent litigants have meaningful access to the federal courts." *See Neitzke v. Williams*, 490 U.S. 319, 324 (1989). And in the past 40 years, Congress has enacted an increasing number of fee-shifting statutes—such as the Civil Rights Attorneys Fees Awards Act in 1976 and the Equal Access to Justice Act in 1980—that enable prevailing parties in certain kinds of cases to recoup all or part of their attorney's fees and expenses from the losing parties.

Rights of the accused

279. *Right to prepare defense and to communicate with counsel.* Defendants retained in custody acquire their Sixth Amendment right to counsel when formal adversarial judicial proceedings are initiated against them. *See Brewer v. Williams*, 430 U.S. 387, 398 (1977). A suspect's invocation of the right to counsel is specific to the charged offense and does not also invoke the right to counsel for later interrogation concerning another factually related offense, unless the two offenses would be deemed the same for double jeopardy purposes. *See Texas v.Cobb*, 532 U.S. 162, 173 (2001). In a landmark decision, the Supreme Court held that the admission of out-of-court testimonial statements violates the Sixth Amendment's Confrontation Clause unless those witnesses are unavailable for trial and the defendant has had an opportunity to cross-examine those witnesses. *Crawford v. Washington*, 541 U.S. 36 (2004).

280. The Sixth Amendment also guarantees a defendant the right to counsel. Although there is no right to appointment of counsel for misdemeanor offenses where no sentence of actual imprisonment is imposed, a suspended sentence may not be activated based upon a defendant's violation of the terms of probation where he was not provided with counsel during the prosecution of the offense for which he received a sentence of probation. *Alabama v. Shelton*, 535 U.S. 654 (2002).

281. *Right to legal assistance of own choosing.* The right to counsel in all federal criminal Prosecutions is provided for by the Sixth Amendment. This right has been extended to state courts through operation of the Due Process Clause of the Fourteenth Amendment. In the case of *Gideon v. Wainwright*, 372 U.S. 335 (1963), the U.S. Supreme Court mandated that every indigent person accused of a felony in a state court must be provided with counsel. In *Argersinger v. Hamlin*, 407 U.S. 25 (1972), the Supreme Court extended this rule to provide for the appointment of counsel to indigent persons charged with any offense, including misdemeanors, which could result in incar- ceration. In addition, a defendant may not be sentenced to imprisonment based upon his violation of the terms of probation previously imposed for a misdemeanor offense, if he was not provided with counsel during the prosecution of the misdemeanor offense. *See Alabama v. Shelton*, 535 U.S. 654 (2002).

282. *Protection against self-incrimination.* The Fifth Amendment provides that "No person shall be ... compelled in any criminal case to be a witness against himself." This constitutional protection of the individual's right against self-incrimination in criminal cases is applicable to the states as well as the federal government.

283. The Fifth Amendment thus prohibits the use of involuntary statements. It not only bars the government from calling the defendant as a witness at his trial, but also from taking statements from the accused

against the accused's will. If a defendant confesses, he may seek to exclude the confession from trial by alleging that it was involuntary. The court will conduct a factual inquiry into the circumstances surrounding the confession to determine if the law enforcement officers acted in a way to pressure or coerce the defendant into confessing and, if so, whether the defendant lacked a capacity to resist the pressure. *See Colorado v. Connelly*, 479 U.S. 157 (1986). Physical coercion will render a confession involuntary. *See Brown v. Mississippi*, 297 U.S. 278 (1936).

284. An individual's right against compelled self-incrimination applies regardless of whether charges have been formally filed. To ensure that the individual has knowingly waived Fifth Amendment rights when he gives a statement during questioning by government agents, the investigating officer conducting a custodial interrogation is obligated to inform the suspect that the suspect has a right to remain silent, that anything he says can be used against him, and that the suspect has a right to speak with an attorney before answering questions. *See Miranda v. Arizona*, 384 U.S. 436 (1966). *See Dickerson v. United States*, 530 U.S. 428, 444 (2000) ("Miranda announced a constitutional rule" that cannot be overruled by congressional enactment).

285. *Review of conviction and sentence*. Individuals who allege their convictions or punishments are in violation of federal law or the Constitution may seek review in federal court by way of an application for a writ of habeas corpus. *See, e.g., Ex parte Bollman*, 8 U.S. 74, 95 (1807); *Stone v. Powell*, 428 U.S. 465, 474-75 n.6 (1976); *Preiser v. Rodriguez*, 411 U.S. 475, 500 (1973). State prisoners in custody may seek federal court review on the ground that they are in custody in violation of the Constitution or laws or treaties of the United States. 28 U.S.C. §§ 2241, 2254. The prisoner seeking federal review must first exhaust all state appellate remedies. 28 U.S.C. § 2254 (b),(c). Federal courts have imposed limitations on the types of issues that can be raised in habeas corpus applications as well as procedural requirements for raising those issues, largely out of respect for the states' interest in the finality of their criminal convictions. *See Coleman v. Thompson*, 501 U.S. 722 (1991); *McCleskey v. Zant*, 499 U.S. 467 (1991); *Teague v. Lane*, 489 U.S. 288 (1989). In 1996, Congress enacted the Antiterrorism and Effective Death Penalty Act (AEDPA) that modified the habeas corpus statutes by codifying many of the judicially-created limitations. *See* 110 Stat. 1214 (effective April 24, 1996).

286. *Double jeopardy protections for defendants*. The government's *Petite* policy is set out in the United States Attorney's Manual § 9-2.031 (2000). The policy precludes federal prosecution of a defendant after he has been prosecuted by state or federal authorities for "substantially the same act[s] or transaction[s]," unless three requirements are satisfied. First, the case must involve a "substantial federal interest." Second, the "prior prosecution must have left that interest demonstrably unvindicated." The policy notes that this requirement may be met when the defendant was not convicted in the prior proceeding because of "incompetence, corruption, intimidation, or undue influence," "court or jury nullification in clear disregard of the law," or "the unavailability of significant evidence," or when the sentence imposed in the prior proceeding was "manifestly inadequate in light of the federal interest involved." Prosecutions that fall within the Petite policy must be approved in advance by an Assistant Attorney General. In *Smith v. Massachusetts*, 125 S. Ct. 1129 (2005), the Supreme Court held that a judge's ruling during a trial that charges should be dismissed for lack of evidence constituted a "judgment of acquittal," which could not be revisited by that judge or any other under the Double Jeopardy Clause.

287. *Procedure in the case of juvenile persons*. Historically, confidentiality was one of the special aspects of juvenile proceedings and the proceedings and records were generally closed to the public and press. More recently, states have modified or removed traditional confidentiality provisions, making records and proceedings more open.

288. All states and the federal criminal justice system allow juveniles to be tried as adults in criminal court under certain circumstances. In some states, a prosecutor has discretion over whether to bring a case in criminal or juvenile court. Some state laws also provide for automatic prosecution in criminal court for serious offences, repeat offenders, or routine traffic citations. A juvenile who is subject to the adult criminal justice system is entitled to the constitutional and statutory rights and protections provided for adults.

Article 15—Prohibition of ex post facto laws

289. Paragraphs 508—511 of the Initial Report describe the United States Constitutional prohibition against enacting ex post facto laws. Article I, section 9 of the Constitution, addressing the duties of the U.S. Congress, states that "No ... ex post facto Law shall be passed". Article I section 10 provides that "No state shall ... pass any ... ex post facto Law." That legal situation has not changed.

Article 16—Recognition as a person under the law

290. As reported in paragraphs 513 and 514 of the Initial Report, all human beings within the jurisdiction of the United States are recognized as persons before the law. In addition, the Born-Alive Infants Protection Act of 2002, which was signed into federal law on 5 August, 2002, makes it clear that "every infant member of the species homo sapiens who is born alive at any stage of development" is considered a "person," "human being," and "individual" under federal law. *See* 1 U.S.C. § 8. Congress also enacted the Unborn Victims of Violence Act of 2004 "to protect unborn children from assault and murder." *See* Pub. L. No. 108-212. Federal law now provides that whoever, in the course of committing certain federal crimes, "causes the death of ... a child, who is in utero at the time the conduct take place," is guilty of a separate offense and shall be punished as if that death had occurred to the unborn child's mother. *See* 18 U.S.C. § 1841(a). If the person engaging in such conduct intentionally kills the unborn child, he will punished for intentionally killing a human being.

See 18 U.S.C. § 1841(a)(2)(C). This law does not, however, authorize the prosecution of any woman with respect to her unborn child, *See* 18 U.S.C. § 1841(c)(3), nor does it criminalize "conduct relating to an abortion for which the consent of the pregnant woman, or a person authorized by law to act on her behalf, has been obtained or for which such consent is implied by law," *see* 18 U.S.C. § 1841(c)(1).

Article 17—Freedom from arbitrary interference with privacy, family, home

291. *Right to privacy.* As reported in paragraphs 515—544 of the Initial Report, freedom from arbitrary and unlawful interference with privacy is protected under the Fourth Amendment to the Constitution.

292. *Technology: movements and conversations: electronic surveillance.* The U.S. Congress has also recognized that there could be substantial privacy infringements through the use of electronic devices to track the movements of persons or things and to intercept private communications. Such devices include wiretaps, pen registers and trap and trace devices (which record, respectively, outgoing and incoming dialing, routing, addressing, or signaling information used by communication systems, such as telephones or computer network communications), digital "clone" pagers and surreptitiously installed microphones. Note that the there is a significant difference in constitutional and statutory protections afforded to "content" devices, such as wiretaps, as opposed to "non-content" devices, such as pen registers. (See below for a discussion of pen/trap provisions of Titles II and III of ECPA, Pub. L. No. 99-508, 100 Stat. 1848).

293. In 1968, Congress enacted what is generally referred to as Title III to regulate the use of electronic audio surveillance and interception. 18 U.S.C. §§ 2510-21 (Title III of the Omnibus Crime Control and Safe Streets Act of 1968—Wiretapping and Electronic Surveillance, Pub. L. No. 90-351, 82 Stat. 212). Title III essentially bans the use of certain electronic surveillance techniques by private citizens. It makes punishable as a felony any intentional interception of any wire, oral, or electronic communication that would not be otherwise readily accessible to the public; use of an interception device; or disclosure of the contents of any communication that has been unlawfully intercepted. 18 U.S.C. § 2511.

294. Title III, however, exempts law enforcement from the general prohibition if it meets certain explicit conditions. The primary condition is that the government must obtain an appropriate court order authorizing the interception.

295. Before applying for a court order authorizing the interception of wire or oral communications, law enforcement generally must obtain prior approval from specified senior officials in the Department of Justice, in the case of federal law enforcement, or from senior state or local prosecuting officials, in the case of state or local law enforcement. For the interception of electronic communications, which, generally, are non-voice-based communications, federal agents must get approval from a federal prosecutor to seek a court order; state and local law enforcement must get approval from senior state or local prosecuting officials to seek a court order.

296. Having obtained approval, the agent must then apply for an order from a court. The application must set forth sufficient facts to satisfy the court that probable cause exists to believe that (i) certain identified persons have committed, are committing, or will commit one of the felony offences specified by the statute, which include serious felony offenses in the case of federal interceptions of oral or wire communications or any interceptions by state law enforcement, and include any federal felony in the case of an electronic communications interception by federal agents; (ii) all or some of the persons have used, are using, or will use a targeted communication facility or premises in connection with the commission of the listed offence; and (iii) the targeted communication facility or premise has been used, is being used, or will be used in connection with the crime. The agent's application must also satisfy the judge that other less intrusive investigative procedures have been tried without success, would not be likely to succeed, or would be too dangerous to use.

The application must also include a complete statement of all other applications that have been made for electronic surveillance involving the persons, facilities, or premises.

297. The court's order may authorize the interception for no more than 30 days. The court, however, may grant extensions of the order if the government files an application justifying the extension. 18 U.S.C. §2518(5). In addition, the judge issuing the order and the Department of Justice are required to report to the Administrative Office of U.S. Courts on each court-ordered electronic surveillance and the number of arrests, suppression orders, and convictions that resulted from them. 18 U.S.C. § 2519.

298. There is an exception to the requirement of prior judicial approval where there is an emergency involving immediate danger of death or serious bodily injury or conspiratorial activities that threaten national security or are characteristic of organized crime, and there is insufficient time to obtain a prior court order. 18 U.S.C. § 2518(7). When electronic surveillance is utilized in these emergency instances, the government must obtain a court order within 48 hours.

299. During the period of surveillance the agents are under a continuing duty to minimize-that is, to not record or overhear conversations that are not related to the crimes or persons for which the surveillance order was obtained. The recordings must also be sealed in a manner that will protect them from tampering. The government is expressly limited in the purposes for which, and to whom, it may disclose those communications. Section 223 of the USA PATRIOT Act provided for civil liability for unauthorized disclosures and provided that a person aggrieved by certain willful violation may commence an action for money damages against the United States. It also provides for the initiation of administrative proceedings.

300. Title III predated the use of video surveillance and was passed in the wake of two Supreme Court decisions that addressed non-consensual interception of oral communications. Moreover, in 1968, when Title III was enacted, video cameras were too bulky and too noisy to be effective as surreptitious recording devices, and thus were not considered when the electronic surveillance statute was enacted. For both these reasons, the statute did not address the use of electronic video interception for gathering non-aural evidence, and Congress has not passed subsequent legislation addressing the issue. However, the federal appellate courts that have considered the issue all agree that the government may conduct video surveillance. Because interception of visual, non-verbal conduct is not regulated by statute, the courts analyze it under the requirements of the Constitution. As long as the interception is conducted in a manner consistent with the protections provided by the Fourth Amendment, the courts will permit its use. *See, e.g., United States v. Falls*, 34 F.3d. 674 (8th Cir. 1994); *United States v. Koyomejian*, 970 F.2d 536 (9th Cir. 1992) (*en banc*); *United States v. Mesa-Rincon*, 911 F.2d 1433 (10th Cir. 1990); *United States v. Villegas*, 899 F.2d 1324 (2d Cir.1990); *United States v. Cuevas-Sanchez*, 821 F.2d 248 (5th Cir. 1987); *United States v. Biasucci*, 786 F.2d 504 (2d Cir. 1985), *cert. denied*, 479 U.S. 827 (1986); *United States v. Torres*, 751 F.2d 875 (7th Cir. 1984), *cert.denied*, 470 U.S. 1087 (1985).

301. Congress enacted the Electronic Communications Privacy Act ("ECPA") in 11986 to address, among other matters, (i) access to stored wire and electronic communications and transactional records and (ii) the use of pen registers and trap and trace devices. (*See* Titles II and III of ECPA, Pub. L. No. 99-508, 100 Stat. 1848.) Title II of ECPA generally prohibits unauthorized access to or disclosure of stored wire and electronic communications, absent certain statutory exceptions. Title II of ECPA also provides for legal process that law enforcement may use to obtain such stored communications and transactional records. The pen register and trap and trace provisions of ECPA prohibit the installation or use of a pen register or trap and trace device, except as may be provided for in the statue. Except in narrow, specified emergencies, law enforcement may not install a pen register or a trap and trace device without a prior court order.

302. Under the federal statutes, communications can be acquired if one of the parties to the communication has given prior consent to their acquisition. 18 U.S.C. §§ 2511(2)(c), 2701(c)(2), 3123(b)(3) (2004). Similarly, the Fourth Amendment's protection of one's reasonable expectation of privacy does not require that the government obtain a warrant for a consensual interception, i.e. where one of the parties consents. In a case where an undercover agent wore a recording device concealed on his person, the Supreme Court explained:[The] case involves no "eavesdropping" whatever in any proper sense of that term. The government did not use an electronic device to listen in on conversations it could not otherwise have heard. Instead, the device was used only to obtain the most reliable evidence possible of a conversation in which the government's own agent was a participant and which that agent was fully entitled to disclose. And the device was not planted by means of an unlawful physical invasion of [the suspect's] premises under circumstances which would violate the Fourth Amendment. It was carried in and out by an undercover agent who

was there with [the suspect's] assent, and it neither saw nor heard more than the agent himself. *See Lopez v. United States*, 373 U.S. 427, 439 (1963).

303. Though federal judges need not authorize interception orders where one party to the conversation has consented to the electronic eavesdropping, the U.S. Department of Justice has adopted certain written guidelines for federal prosecutors. These guidelines are set forth in the Attorney General's Memorandum of May 30, 2002, which states:

304. When a communicating party consents to the monitoring of his or her oral communications, the monitoring device may be concealed on his or her person, in personal effects, or in a fixed location. Each department and agency engaging in such consensual monitoring must ensure that the consenting party will be present at all times when the device is operating. In addition, each department and agency must ensure: (1) that no agent or person cooperating with the department or agency trespasses while installing a device in a fixed location, unless that agent or person is acting pursuant to a court order that authorizes the entry and/or trespass, and (2) that as long as the device is installed in the fixed location, the premises remain under the control of the government or of the consenting party. *See United States v. Yonn*, 702 F.2d 1341, 1347 (11th Cir.), *cert. denied*, 464 U.S. 917 (1983) (rejecting the First Circuit's holding in *United States v. Padilla*, 520 F.2d 526 (1st Cir. 1975), and approving use of fixed monitoring devices that are activated only when the consenting party is present). *See United States v. Shabazz*, 883 F. Supp. 422 (D. Minn. 1995). The same rule applies to consensual videotaping.

305. Another area of note regarding technology and privacy is individuals' privacy with respect to information maintained on computer databases. In general, individuals are entitled to privacy by the Privacy Act, 5 U.S.C. § 552(a). The Privacy Act generally bars federal agencies from using or disclosing information collected for one purpose for a different purpose, unless the use or disclosure falls within one of the specifically enumerated exceptions in the Act. The Computer Matching and Privacy Protection Act of 1988 specifically addresses the use by federal agencies of computer data. The Act regulates the computer matching of federal data for federal benefits eligibility or recouping delinquent debts. The government may not take adverse action based on such computer checks without giving individuals an opportunity to respond. Three other federal laws that protect information commonly maintained on computer database are the Fair Credit Reporting Act (15 U.S.C. §§ 1681-81(v)), the Video Privacy Protection Act (18 U.S.C. § 2710), and the Right to Financial Privacy Act (12 U.S.C. §§ 3401-22). The first regulates the distribution and use of credit information by credit agencies. The second prevents the disclosure and sale of customers' video-rental records without the customers' consent. The last sets procedures regarding when federal agencies may review customers' bank records.

306. A number of federal statutes, in addition to those described above, protect information commonly maintained in computer databases. These include the Fair Credit Reporting Act (15 U.S.C. §§ 1681-1681(v)), which regulates the distribution and use of credit information by credit agencies; the Video Privacy Protection Act (18 U.S.C. § 2710), which addresses the disclosure and sale of customer records regarding video rentals; the Right to Financial Privacy Act (12 U.S.C. § 3401-3422), which sets procedures regarding access to customers' bank records by the federal government; the Privacy Protection Act (42 U.S.C. § 2000aa-2000aa-12), which provides special procedures for government searches or seizures of the press and other publishers; title V of the Gramm-Leach-Bliley Act (Pub. L. No. 106-102, 113 Stat. 1338), which addresses the protection and disclosure of nonpublic customer information by financial institutions; and provisions of the Health Insurance Portability and Accountability Act (42 U.S.C. §§ 1320d-1320d-8), which provides for the creation of protections regarding the privacy of individually identifiable health information.

307. With respect to aliens, a number of laws protect the confidentiality of certain information, with limited exceptions, including asylum applications (8 C.F.R. 208.6 and 1208.6), information relating to battered spouses and children seeking immigration relief (8 U.S.C. § 1186A(c)(4)), and alien registration and fingerprint records (8 U.S.C. § 1304(b)).

308. *USA PATRIOT Act.* In the wake of the tragedy of 11 September, 2001, Congress passed the USA PATRIOT Act primarily to provide federal prosecutors and investigators with the critical tools needed to fight and win the war against terrorism. The USA PATRIOT Act principally did four things. First, it removed the legal barriers that prevented the law enforcement and intelligence communities from sharing information. By bringing down "the wall" separating law enforcement and intelligence officials, the USA PATRIOT Act has yielded extraordinary dividends, such as by enabling the Department of Justice to dismantle ter-

ror cells in such places as Oregon, New York, and Virginia. Second, it updated federal anti-terrorism and criminal laws to bring them up to date with the modern technologies actually used by terrorists, so that the United States no longer had to fight a digital-age battle with legal authorities left over from the era of rotary telephones. Third, it provided terrorism investigators with important tools that were previously available in organized crime and drug trafficking investigations. For example, law enforcement had long used multi-point, or "roving," wiretaps to investigate non-terrorism crimes, such as drug offenses. Now, federal agents are allowed to use multi-point wiretaps, with court approval, to investigate sophisticated international terrorists who are trained to evade detection. Fourth, the USA PATRIOT Act increased the federal criminal penalties for those who commit terrorist crimes and made it easier to prosecute those responsible for funneling money and providing material support to terrorists.

309. The USA PATRIOT Act has been the subject of a vigorous public debate, which has focused on a handful of the Act's many provisions. As noted above, the Act authorizes multi-point wiretap surveillance in foreign intelligence investigations. This authority is directed to the problem of terrorists who seek to avoid surveillance by frequently changing telephones, and allows foreign intelligence investigators in certain specified circumstances to obtain from a federal court a wiretap order that permits surveillance of a specified person rather than a specific phone. This authority has been available in criminal investigations for years, but only became available in foreign intelligence investigations upon enactment of the USA PATRIOT Act. It allows surveillance to continue uninterrupted even though the terrorist changes phones. This authority has been an essential tool in conducting sensitive national security-related surveillance. There have been no verified abuses of this authority.

310. Another provision of the USA PATRIOT Act created a nationally uniform process and standard for obtaining delayed-notice search warrants, which have been available for decades and were common long before the USA PATRIOT Act was enacted. Like all criminal search warrants, a delayed-notice search warrant is issued by a federal judge only upon a showing that there is probable cause to believe that the property sought or seized constitutes evidence of a criminal offense. A delayed-notice warrant differs from an ordinary search warrant only in that the judge authorizes the officers executing the warrant to wait for a limited period of time before notifying the subject of the search because immediate notice would have an "adverse result." In passing the USA PATRIOT Act, Congress recognized that delayed-notice search warrants are a vital aspect of the Department of Justice's strategy of detecting and incapacitating terrorists, drug dealers, and other criminals before they can harm U.S. citizens. A delayed-notice search warrant is an invaluable though rarely used tool; delayed-notice has been used in less than 0.2 percent of all federal warrants authorized in the period of time between the enactment of the USA PATRIOT Act and 31 January, 2005. There have been no verified abuses of this authority.

311. A third provision of the USA PATRIOT Act authorizes federal prosecutors to issue subpoenas for records about an individual that are held by third parties. It is important to understand that federal prosecutors, by obtaining grand-jury subpoenas, have long been able to obtain business records, of exactly the sorts that are the subject of this provision, in ordinary criminal investigations without the involvement of a judge. The USA PATRIOT Act simply extended a similar authority to investigators in international terrorism and espionage investigations, and in addition imposed a requirement that those investigators obtain prior judicial approval. Moreover, because the provision at issue explicitly states that an investigation cannot be conducted of a United States person based solely upon activities protected by the First Amendment of the Constitution, investigators are expressly prohibited from investigating United States persons solely because of, for example, their library habits or the websites they visit. As the Attorney General testified before Congress, between the passage of the USA PATRIOT Act and 30 March, 2005, this business records provision was not used a single time to request library or bookstore records. However, we know from experience that terrorists and spies do use libraries to further their hostile intentions, and we cannot afford to make libraries safe havens. There have been no verified abuses of this authority.

312. The USA PATRIOT Act has helped to protect Americans from terrorist attacks while at the same time safeguarding their civil rights and civil liberties, such as by preserving the important role of judicial and congressional oversight. Many key provisions of the USA PATRIOT Act are scheduled to expire at the end of 2005, and Congress is considering reauthorization of those provisions. The House passed a reauthorization bill on 21 July, 2005, by a vote of 257-171, and the Senate passed a similar bill by unanimous consent on July 29, 2005. The next step in the process will be a conference between the two houses to resolve differences in the two bills. These bills have followed extensive debate and oversight by Congress as it considered whether

to renew these critical intelligence and law enforcement tools. For example, the Attorney General has testified in front of the Senate and House Judiciary Committees and Senate Select Committee on Intelligence on the subject, and in total, the Department of Justice has provided 32 witnesses at 18 congressional hearings on the USA PATRIOT Act in 2005. In his congressional testimony, the Attorney General urged that all 16 sun-setting provisions should be reauthorized without any additional sunsets and opposed any weakening of the Act. As the extensive hearings and public debates have confirmed, there have been no verified abuses of the USA PATRIOT Act provisions.

Article 18—Freedom of thought, conscience, and religion

313. There have been a number of notable changes in United States law to the protections of religious freedom outlined in paragraphs 545–579 of the Initial Report.

314. As noted in the Initial Report, in response to the ruling by the United States Supreme Court in *Employment Div., Dep't of Human Services of Oregon v. Smith*, 494 U.S. 872 (1990), that religious believers may not obtain exemptions to religion-neutral laws of general applicability that infringe on their religious practices, Congress enacted the Religious Freedom Restoration Act of 1993 ("RFRA"). 42 U.S.C. § 2000(b)(b)(2004). This law provided that government action that substantially burdened religious exercise was invalid unless it was justified by a compelling government interest and was the least restrictive way to achieve that interest. In *City of Boerne v. Flores*, 521 U.S. 507 (1997), the Supreme Court struck down RFRA as applied to the states on the grounds that it exceeded Congress's power over states. RFRA continues to apply to actions by the federal government.

315. There have been two major developments in response to the invalidation of RFRA. First, many states have adopted their own versions of RFRA to ensure that religious exercise is not burdened by state action. Second, the Congress enacted the Religious Land Use and Institutionalized Persons Act of 2000 (RLUIPA), 114 Stat. 804, which imposes, among other things, a requirement on states that in most circumstances burdens on religion through land use regulation and burdens on the religious exercise of prisoners must, as with RFRA, be justified by a compelling government interest and through the least restrictive means. The Supreme Court upheld a constitutional challenge to the prisoner-rights portion of RLUIPA in *Cutter v. Wilkinson*, 125 S. Ct. 2113 (2005), finding that the law's protection of inmate religious rights did not violate the Establishment Clause. In *Cutter*, the Court emphasized that there is a long tradition in the United States of accommodating religious practice through laws such as RLUIPA, and the fact that a law may provide exceptions to general rules for religious reasons but not other reasons does not render it invalid.

316. As discussed above, there have been important developments in the area of religion in schools. The Supreme Court has re-emphasized that state-sponsored religious speech in public schools is severely restricted, while at the same time religious speech by students at schools is strongly protected. On the issue of funding, which was discussed at great length in the Initial Report, the Supreme Court has moved toward two principles. First, where an educational benefit such as a scholarship is provided directly to a student, and the student is then free to use it toward education at the school of his choice, whether public or private, secular or religious, the non-Establishment principle of the Constitution is not violated. Second, where aid is given directly to a school, it will be upheld if the aid is secular in nature, is distributed in a neutral manner without regard to religion, and there is no risk of substantial diversion of the aid to religious purposes.

. . .

Article 19—Freedom of opinion and expression

327. The First Amendment to the United States Constitution provides that "Congress shall make no law abridging the freedom of speech." Paragraphs 580—588 of the Initial Report describe how freedom of opinion and expression are zealously guarded in the United States, as well as the limitations on freedom of expression.

328. Freedom of speech also encompasses certain rights to seek and receive information. The most important means by which these rights are promoted is by the First Amendment's special concern for freedom of the press, which is protected from prior restraint (that is, censorship in advance of publication) in the absence of proof of direct, immediate, and irreparable and substantial damage to the public interest. *See New York Times, Inc. v. United States*, 403 U.S. 713 (1971). The First Amendment protects the publication of truthful information about matters of public importance, even where the disclosure of the information affects significant privacy interests, as long as the person who discloses it did not violate the law in obtaining the information. *See, e.g., Florida Star v. B.J.F.*, 491 U.S. 524 (1989); *Bartnicki v. Vopper*, 532 U.S. 514 (2001). In addition to publishing information, the press, and the public as a whole, have been held to have a constitutional right

to gather information concerning matters of public significance in certain circumstances. For example, the public generally has a right of access to observe criminal trials, since such access is viewed as instrumental to the effectuation of the rights to speak and publish concerning the events at trial. This right does not entail a general constitutional obligation on the part of the government to disclose information in its own possession. *See, e.g., Houchins v. KQED, Inc.,* 438 U.S. 1 (1978); *Los Angeles Police Dept. v.United Reporting Pub. Corp.,* 428 U.S. 32 (1999). However, the First Amendment is supplemented by a number of laws that promote access to government, such as the Freedom of Information Act, 5 U.S.C. § 552, the Government in the Sunshine Act, 5 U.S.C. § 552b, and the Federal Advisory Committee Act, 5 U.S.C. App. 2.

329. Under U.S. law and practice, government is accorded broad scope to shape the content of official utterances and is not as a general matter compelled to speak on behalf of those with whom it disagrees. The courts have held, in the context of government or government assisted programs, that the government may limit the extent to which such programs provide access to information for the beneficiaries. Thus, in *Rust v. Sullivan,* 500 U.S. 173 (1991), the U.S. Supreme Court upheld government regulations proscribing abortion counseling in programs receiving federal funding, but noted that the recipient of those funds could still provide counseling and related services through separate and independent programs. The Court noted that its holding merely allowed the government to refrain from funding speech activity that it did not support, and did not suggest that the government could condition or restrict speech in areas that have been traditionally open to the public for free expression, such as public parks or universities. Along similar lines, the government, through the National Endowment for the Arts, can consider factors such as "decency and respect" in deciding whether to help fund the work of controversial artists. *See National Endowment of the Arts v. Finley,* 524 U.S. 569 (1998). The government may not, however, impose viewpoint-specific restrictions within the context of a government-created public forum for speech, such as on a student publication funded by a state university. *Rosenberger v. Univ. of Virginia,* 515 U.S. 819 (1995).

Article 20—Prohibition of propaganda relating to war or racial, national, or religious hatred

330. The following U.S. reservation to Article 20 remains in effect: That Article 20 does not authorize or require legislation or other action by the United States that would restrict the right of free speech and association protected by the Constitution and laws of the United States.

331. The reasons for this reservation, as discussed in paragraphs 596—598 of the Initial Report, remain unchanged.

332. *Hate crimes.* As reported in paragraphs 599—606 of the Initial Report, the Civil Rights Division of the U.S. Department of Justice enforces several criminal statutes which prohibit acts of violence or intimidation motivated by racial, ethnic, or religious hatred and directed against participation in certain activities.

333. Following are several examples of recent cases:

• A self-described "Luciferian," pled guilty to setting a total of twenty-nine fires in eight states throughout the United States. The defendant was sentenced to life in prison without parole for his guilty pleas to setting five church fires in Georgia, including a fire at the New Salem United Methodist Church in which a volunteer firefighter was killed while on duty. *See United States v. Ballinger,* 153 F. Supp. 2d 1361 (N.D. Ga. 2001);

...

Post-September 11 efforts to counter crimes against Muslims

336. After the September 11 attacks on the World Trade Center and the Pentagon, the United States saw a rise in bias crimes against Muslims and Arabs, as well as those wrongly perceived to be Muslim and Arab, including Sikhs and South Asians. These bias crimes included attacks on individuals ranging from Internet and telephone threats and assault to murder, as well as attacks on mosques and businesses ranging from graffiti and vandalism to arson.

337. The Department of Justice has put a priority on investigating and prosecuting these cases. The Department has investigated more than 650 such crimes, resulting in more than 150 state and local prosecutions, as well as the prosecution of 27 defendants on federal civil rights charges.

...

Article 21—Freedom of assembly

339. The First Amendment to the United States Constitution proscribes the making of any law abridging "the right of people peaceably to assemble". This right has been interpreted quite broadly, as discussed in paragraphs 607—612 of the Initial Report.

Article 22—Freedom of association

340. *United States Constitution.* Although the freedom of association is not specifically mentioned in the United States Constitution, it has been found to be implicit in the rights of assembly, speech, and expression.

See NAACP v. Claiborne Hardware Co., 458 U.S. 898 (1982); *Healey v. James*, 408 U.S. 169 (1972). Taken together, these provisions of the First, Fifth and Fourteenth Amendments guarantee freedom of assembly in all contexts, including the right of workers to establish and join organizations of their own choosing, without previous authorization by or interference from either the federal government or the state governments. *See, Brotherhood of Railroad Trainmen v. Virginia*, 377 U.S. 1 (1964); *United Mine Workers v. Illinois State Bar Assn.*, 389 U.S. 217 (1967). Freedom of assembly continues to be practiced in the United States, as described in paragraphs 613—654 of the Initial Report.

341. The right to associate for purposes of expressive activity receives heightened protection. This right, termed the right of "expressive association," encompasses both the expression of ideas within a group among its members, and expression by the group to the wider public. The first category is exemplified by *Boy Scouts v. Dale*, 530 U.S. 640 (2000), in which the Supreme Court held that the Boy Scouts could exclude a homosexual man from a position as assistant scoutmaster, despite a state law barring such discrimination, on the grounds that the Boy Scouts is a group dedicated to instilling certain morals and values in boys, and that homosexuality is contrary to those morals and values. An example of the second type of case is *Hurley v. Irish American Gay, Lesbian and Bisexual Group of Boston*, 515 U.S. 557 (1995), in which the Supreme Court held that a private group that sponsored an annual Saint Patrick's Day parade could not be required by a state to allow an Irish-American homosexual group to march in the parade. In each case, the ability to exclude those with views at odds with the views of the group was deemed fundamental to the group's ability to carry out its expressive mission.

342. In a recent decision, the Supreme Court decided that, because of the impossibility of distinguishing between a state university's ideological and educational activities, state universities can use mandatory student fees to fund organizations whose positions are opposed by particular students as long as the funding decisions are made in a viewpoint-neutral manner. *Univ. of Wisconsin v. Southworth*, 529 U.S. 217 (2000).

. . .

Article 23—Protection of the family

347. *Right to Marry*. United States law has long recognized the importance of marriage as a social institution which is favored in law and society. Marriage has been described as an institution which is the foundation of society "without which there would be neither civilization nor progress". *See Maynard v. Hill*, 125 U.S. 190, 211 (1888).

348. As described in paragraphs 658—673 of the Initial Report, marriage has traditionally been defined in the United States as the status of relation of a man and a woman who have been legally united as husband and wife. Marriage is contractual in nature, in that it creates certain rights and responsibilities between the parties involved. However, the contract of marriage is unique in the eyes of the law. As one court stated: While we may speak of marriage as a civil contract, yet that is a narrow view of it. The consensus of opinion in civilized nations is that marriage is something more than a dry contract. It is a contract different from all others. For instance: only a court can dissolve it. It may not be rescinded at will like other contracts. Only one such can exist at a time. It may not exist between near blood kin. It legitimizes children. It touches the laws of inheritance. It affects title to real estate. It provides for the perpetuity of the race. It makes a hearthstone, a home, a family. It marks the line between the moral of the barnyard and the morals of civilized men, between reasoning affection and animal lust. In fine, it rises to the dignity of a status in which society, morals, religion, reason and the state itself have a live and large interest. *See Bishop v. Brittain Inv. Co.*, 129 S.W. 668, 676 (Mo. 1910).

349. *Same Sex Marriage*. In 1996, Congress passed and President Clinton signed the Defense of Marriage Act ("DOMA"). The DOMA provides that, for purposes of federal law, the word "marriage" means the union of one man and one woman and the word "spouse" means a person of the opposite sex. It also provides that no state could be required to adopt another state's law with respect to same-sex marriage. The only courts to rule on the issue upheld the constitutionality of the DOMA. *See, e.g., Smelt v. County of Orange*, 274 F. Supp. 2d 861 (C.D. Cal. 2005); *In re Kandu*, 315 B.R. 123 (W.D. Wash. 2004); *see also, Order Granting Motion to Dismiss*, Case No: 8:04-cv-1680-T-30-TBM (U.S. District Court for the Middle District of Florida, Jan. 19, 2005).

350. In addition, the Federal Marriage Amendment ("FMA") to the Constitution, which was supported by President Bush, was introduced in Congress in 2004. The FMA states that "marriage" consists only of the union of a man and a woman and that the federal and state constitutions shall not be construed to require marriage for any other union. It failed to pass the Senate on a procedural vote on 7 July, 2004, by 48-50 and failed in the House 227-186 on 30 September, 2004.

351. Same sex marriage has also been an issue at the state level. In 2003, the Massachusetts Supreme Judicial Court held that under the equality and liberty guarantees of the Massachusetts constitution, the marriage licensing statute limiting civil marriage to heterosexual couples was unconstitutional because it was not rationally related to a permissible legislative purpose. *Goodridge v. Dep't of Public Health*, 798 N.E.2d 941 (Mass. 2003). State trial courts in California, New York, and Washington have also found a right to same-sex marriage under their state constitutions, but those cases are on appeal. In contrast, an intermediate appeals court in New Jersey found that the state constitution did not confer a right to same-sex marriage, *Lewis v. Harris*, A-2244-03T5 (June 14, 2005), a decision that has been appealed to the state supreme court. Further, the Supreme Court of Oregon, invalidated marriage licenses to homosexual couples that had been granted by one county. *Liv. Oregon*, No. CC 0403-03057, CA A124877, SC S51612, April 14, 2005.

…

Procedures for marriage

354. *Blood tests*. While many states require a blood test as one of the requirements that must be met before obtaining a marriage license, recently, several states have considered abandoning this requirement. In states that do require testing, the statutes generally require that in order to obtain the marriage license, the parties must be free of certain sexually-transmitted or other communicable diseases. Failure to comply with this requirement generally does not invalidate the marriage, although it may subject the parties and the issuing authority to penalties.

…

Article 24—Protection of children

362. *U.N. Optional Protocol to the Convention on the Rights of the Child on Children in Armed Conflict*. On 19 June, 2002, the United States Senate gave its advice and consent to ratification of the U.N. Optional Protocol to the Convention on the Rights of the Child on Children in Armed Conflict. The United States deposited its instrument of ratification on 23 December, 2002. The Protocol came into effect for the United States on 23 January, 2003.

363. *U.N. Optional Protocol on the Sale of Children, Child Prostitution, and Child Pornography*. On 19 June, 2002, the United States Senate gave its advice and consent to ratification of the U.N. Optional Protocol to the Convention on the Rights of the Child on the Sale of Children, Child Prostitution, and Child Pornography. The United States deposited its instrument of ratification on 23 December, 2002. The Protocol came into effect for the United States on 23 January, 2003.

364. *ILO Convention 182 on the Worst Forms of Child Labor*. On 5 November, 1999, the United States Senate gave its advice and consent to ratify ILO Convention 182 on the Worst Forms of Child Labor on the grounds that the United States was in full compliance with its provisions. (*See* Senate Resolution 145, Cong. Rec. S14226-03 (1999) and Senate Treaty Document 106-5). The resolution contains the U.S. understandings of the terms of the Convention. The President ratified Convention 182 on 2 December, 1999, and it came into effect for the United States on 2 December, 2000.

365. *Children born outside of marriage*. A child born abroad and out of wedlock acquires at birth the nationality of a citizen mother who meets a specified residency requirement. 8 U.S.C. § 1409(c) (2005). However, when the father is the citizen-parent, one of three steps must be taken before the child turns 18: legitimization, a declaration of paternity under oath by the father, or a court order of paternity. *See*, 8 U.S.C. § 1409(a)(4)(2005). *Tuan Anh Nguyen v. INS*, 533 U.S. 53 (2001); *Miller v. Albright*, 523 U.S. 420 (1998).

366. *Non-citizen children*. School children in the United States cannot be denied a free public education on the basis of their immigration status. *See Plyler v. Doe*, 457 U.S. 202 (1982).

367. *Education*. The Office for Civil Rights (OCR) in the U.S. Department of Education is responsible for enforcing federal civil rights laws that prohibit discrimination on the basis of race, color, national origin, sex, disability, and age by recipients of federal financial assistance, as well as a law that ensures equal access to public school facilities for the Boy Scouts of America and certain other youth groups. These civil rights laws represent a national commitment to end discrimination in education programs. Because most educational institutions receive some type of federal financial assistance, these laws apply throughout the nation. Coverage of these civil rights laws extends to nearly 15,000 school districts; more than 4,000 colleges and universities; about 5,000 proprietary organizations, such as training schools for truck drivers and cosmetologists; and thousands of libraries, museums, vocational rehabilitation agencies, and correctional facilities.

Consequently, these civil rights laws protect large numbers of students attending, or applying to attend, U.S. educational institutions. In certain situations, the laws also protect persons who are employed or are seeking employment at educational institutions. Overall, these laws protect nearly 53.2 million students attending elementary and secondary schools; and nearly 15.4 million students attending colleges and universities.

...

393. *Registration and identity.* The United States does not have a system of national identification cards or registration for citizens or nationals. However, aliens over the age of 14 who remain in the United States over 30 days must register and be fingerprinted, with limited exceptions. *See* 8 U.S.C. § 1302. Aliens under the age of 14 must be registered by a parent or legal guardian. Aliens 18 years or older must keep in their possession at all times any evidence of registration issued to them. Registered aliens are required to notify DHS in writing of a change of address within 10 days. *See* 8 U.S.C. § 1305(a).

394. In addition, DHS may prescribe special registration and fingerprinting requirements for selected classes of aliens not lawfully admitted to the United States for permanent residence, *see* 8 U.S.C. § 1303(a), and may require, upon 10 days notice, that natives of specified foreign countries notify DHS of their current address and furnish additional specified information. 8 U.S.C. § 1305(b).

395. The National Security Entry-Exit Registration System (NSEERS), described at 8 C.F.R. § 264.1(f), 67 Fed. Reg. 52584 (Aug. 12, 2002), established special registration procedures for nonimmigrant nationals or citizens of specified countries.

...

Article 25—Access to the political system

397. The U.S. political system is open to all adult citizens without distinction as to gender, race, color, ethnicity, wealth or property. The right to vote is the principal mechanism for participating in the U.S. political system. The requirements for suffrage are determined primarily by state law, subject to limitations of the Constitution and other federal laws that guarantee the right to vote. Over the course of the nation's history, various amendments to the Constitution have marked the process toward universal suffrage. In particular, the Supreme Court's interpretations of the Equal Protection Clause of the Fourteenth Amendment have expanded voting rights in a number of areas.

398. The Presidential election in 2000 saw an extremely close contest, with President George W. Bush winning the state of Florida by fewer than 1,000 votes. The contesting of the result raised some allegations of voting irregularities. However, subsequent investigations by the United States Department of Justice revealed no evidence in support of these allegations, nor any violations of federal voting rights violations that affected the outcome of the election.

...

Minorities in government

435. The representation of minorities at all levels of public service continues to increase.

436. *U.S. Congress.* Like women, minorities have made significant gains in Congressional representation as a result of the 2005 elections. Currently, 42 Blacks are members of the House and 1 is a member of the Senate. There are 24 Hispanics in the House, and 2 in the Senate. There are 4 Asian Americans in the House, and 2 in the Senate.

Article 26—Equality before the law

437. As indicated in the discussion of the Initial Report, all persons in the United States are equal before the law. Subject to certain exceptions, such as the reservation of the right to vote to citizens, they are equally entitled to all the rights specified in the Covenant. In addition, as discussed at length under Article 2, all persons in the United States enjoy the equal protection of the laws. Any distinction must at minimum be rationally related to a legitimate governmental objective, and certain distinctions such as race can be justified only by a compelling governmental interest, a standard that is almost never met.

Article 27—The rights of minorities to culture, religion and language

438. *Linguistic freedom.* The First Amendment to the Constitution guarantees all persons in the United States the right to converse or correspond in any language they wish. Virtually every major language is spoken somewhere in the United States, and there are no restrictions on the use of foreign language in the print or electronic media. Under Sections 203 and 4(f)(4) of the Voting Rights Act, 42 U.S.C. §§ 1973b and 1973aa-1a, the states and political subdivisions are required to provide multilingual election services for all elections in those jurisdictions in which members of a single language minority with limited English proficiency constitute more than 5 percent of the voting age population or more than 10,000 citizens of voting age. The language minorities that are covered are limited to persons who are American Indian, Asian American, Alaskan Natives, or of Spanish Heritage. This requirement of the Voting Rights Act is scheduled

to expire in 2007 unless renewed by Congress. In those jurisdictions that are not covered by the language minority provisions of the Voting Rights Act, Section 208 of the Act, 42 U.S.C. 1973aa-6, mandates that any voter who requires assistance to vote by reason of an inability to read or write the English language may be given assistance by a person of the voter's choice, other than the voter's employer or agent of that employer or officer or agent of the voter's union.

439. *No Child Left Behind.* The No Child Left Behind Act of 2001 (NCLB Act) also will go a long way to ensure that all children receive a quality education, through its comprehensive overhaul of the Elementary and Secondary Education Act of 1965 (ESEA). Title I of the ESEA provides financial assistance to school districts with high concentrations of students from low income families to improve the academic achievement of students who are failing, or at risk of failing, to meet state academic standards. The NCLB Act strengthens Title I accountability by requiring states to implement statewide accountability systems for all schools and students. Each state is required to establish academic content and achievement standards and define adequate yearly progress, for the state as a whole and for schools and school districts, toward ensuring that all students meet these standards. Adequate yearly progress must include separate measurable annual objectives for continuous and substantial improvement for all public elementary and secondary students and for the achievement of economically disadvantaged students, students from major racial and ethnic groups, students with disabilities, and students with limited English proficiency. These accountability systems also will include annual testing for students in grades 3-8. The reauthorized ESEA requires, as a condition of a state's receipt of Title I funds, that the results of annual statewide testing be published and broken down, at the school, school district, and state levels, by poverty, race, ethnicity, gender, migrant status, disability status, and limited English proficiency to ensure that no group is left behind.

...

III. COMMITTEE SUGGESTIONS AND RECOMMENDATIONS

447. The Committee recommended that the United States review its reservations, declarations and understandings with a view to withdrawing them, in particular reservations to Article 6, paragraph 5, and Article 7 of the Covenant.

448. Comment: The United States has reviewed its reservations, declarations and understandings to the Covenant, and concluded that they are appropriate. With reference to Article 6(5) and Article (7) of the Covenant, the United States notes that its reservations are founded in United States constitutional principles. In that regard, with respect to Article 6(5), the United States also notes that, since its Initial Report, the Supreme Court has ruled that the execution of offenders who were under 18 years of age at the time of their offense is prohibited by the United States Constitution. *See Roper v. Simmons,* 125 S. Ct. 1183 (2005).

449. The Committee hopes that the government of the United States will consider becoming a Party to the First Optional Protocol to the Covenant.

450. Comment: The United States has considered this issue and has no current intention of becoming a Party to the First Optional Protocol to the Covenant.

451. The Committee recommends that appropriate inter-federal and state institutional mechanisms be established for the review of existing as well as proposed legislation and other measures with a view to achieving full implementation of the Covenant, including its reporting obligations.

452. Comment: The United States has considered this issue, and on December 18, 1998, the President issued Executive Order 13107 regarding the implementation of human rights treaties. This order declares, inter alia, that it "shall be the policy and practice of the government of the United States, ... fully to implement its obligations under the international human rights treaties to which it is a Party and that all executive departments and agencies ... shall maintain a current awareness of United States international human rights obligations that are relevant to their functions and shall perform such functions so as to respect and implement those obligations fully."

453. The order further establishes an Interagency Working Group on Human Rights Treaties "for the purpose of providing guidance, oversight, and coordination with respect to questions concerning the adherence to and implementation of human rights obligations and related matters. The principal functions of this group include, inter alia, (i) coordinating the preparation of reports that are to be submitted by the United States in fulfillment of its international human rights treaty obligations, (ii) coordinating responses to complaints submitted to the United Nations, the Organization of American States, and other international organizations alleging human rights violations by the United States, and (iii) developing effective mechanisms to review legislation proposed by the Administration for conformity with international human rights obligations and

that these obligations are taken into account in reviewing legislation under consideration by the Congress. Consistent with the order, a variety of inter-agency procedures now exist to ensure that the matters addressed by the order are coordinated among all relevant agencies.

454. With respect to complying with its reporting obligations on a timelier basis, since the fall of 2003, the Department of State has more than doubled the resources it has dedicated to the purpose of completing such reports. The United States government is committed to submitting timely treaty reports.

455. The Committee emphasizes the need for the government to increase its efforts to prevent and eliminate persisting discriminatory attitudes and prejudices against persons belonging to minority groups and women including, where appropriate, through the adoption of affirmative action. State legislation which is not yet in full compliance with the non-discrimination Articles of the Covenant should be brought systematically into line with them as soon as possible.

456. Comment: The United States agrees that efforts to prevent and eliminate public and private discrimination consistent with our Constitution are of the utmost importance. The Civil Rights Division of the Department of Justice, the independent Equal Employment Opportunity Commission, the Office of Federal Contract Compliance Programs of the U.S. Department of Labor, and the Office for Civil Rights of the U.S. Department of Education, among others, vigorously enforce anti-discrimination laws, including, among others, the Civil Rights Act of 1964, the Voting Rights Act of 1965, Executive Order 11246, Title IX of the Education Amendments, the Americans with Disabilities Act of 1992, and the Help America Vote Act of 2002.

457. At the same time, the United States government believes that discriminatory attitudes and prejudices are best fought by promoting equal access and individual merit as the guiding forces behind opportunity and advancement in society. The United States Supreme Court has interpreted the United States Constitution's equal protection principle to be incongruent with fostering racial or gender preferences and classifications except in the most compelling circumstances. *See Gutter v. Bollinger*, 539 U.S. 309 (2003); *United States v. Virginia*, 518 U.S. 515, 531 (1996). Under U.S. law, vague and amorphous allusions to societal discrimination at large are not a compelling interest; policies aimed at remedying discrimination in a particular institution or program can be considered a compelling interest. *Croson*, 488 U.S. at 499-506; *Adarand Constructors, Inc. v. Pena*, 515 U.S. 200 (1995). Furthermore, we note that no provision in the Covenant requires the use of "affirmative action" as a governmental policy.

458. The Committee urges the State Party to revise federal and state legislation with a view to restricting the number of offences carrying the death penalty strictly to the most serious crimes, in conformity with Article 6 of the Covenant and with a view eventually to abolishing it. It exhorts the authorities to take appropriate steps to ensure that persons are not sentenced to death for crimes committed before they were 18. The Committee considers that the determination of methods of execution must take into account the prohibition against causing avoidable pain and recommends the State Party to take all necessary steps to ensure respect of Article 7 of the Covenant.

459. Comment: While, consistent with reservation (2) of the United States to the Covenant, the Covenant imposes no constraint on the crimes for which the United States may impose capital punishment, under the United States Constitution the use of the death penalty is restricted to particularly serious offenses. Also, see our response to Comment 1. Regarding Article 7, the United States reminds the Committee that under U.S. reservation (3), the United States is bound by Article 7 only to the extent that "cruel, inhuman or degrading treatment or punishment" means the cruel and unusual treatment or punishment prohibited by the Fifth, Eighth and/or Fourteenth Amendments to the Constitution. The United States government takes the position that methods of execution currently employed in the United States do not constitute cruel and unusual punishment under our Constitution.

460. The Committee urges the State Party to take all necessary measures to prevent any excessive use of force by the police; that rules and regulations governing the use of weapons by the police and security forces be in full conformity with the United Nations Basic Principles on the Use of Force and Firearms by Law Enforcement Officials; that any violations of these rules be systematically investigated in order to bring those found to have committed such acts before the courts; and that those found guilty be punished and the victims be compensated.

461. Comment: The United States refers the Committee to the various sections of this report that demonstrate that the United States, at the state and federal level, prohibits and punishes excessive use of force by government officials.

462. Regulations limiting the sale of firearms to the public should be extended and strengthened.

463. Comment: This recommendation states a policy preference rather than addressing a duty or obligation under the Covenant. As the Committee is aware, the Second Amendment of the United States Constitution states that "[a] well regulated militia being necessary to the security of a free State, the right of the people to keep and bear arms, shall not be infringed." The United States recognizes that this Amendment protects a right of the public to possess firearms. The Second Amendment, however, allows for reasonable restrictions designed to prevent unfit persons from possessing firearms or to restrict possession of firearms particularly suited to criminal misuse, and there are many such restrictions at both the federal and state level.

Pursuant to federal law, a person seeking to purchase firearms from a Federal Firearm Licensee is subject to a background check to determine whether the transfer should be denied because the person falls within a prohibited category. In addition, the United States government, under its Project Safe Neighborhoods initiative and in partnership with state and local law enforcement, vigorously prosecutes prohibited persons found in possession of firearms.

464. The Committee recommends that appropriate measures be adopted as soon as possible to ensure to excludable aliens the same guarantees of due process as are available to other aliens and guidelines be established which would place limits on the length of detention of persons who cannot be deported.

465. Comment: The Department of Homeland Security and the Department of Justice have promulgated extensive regulations governing the continued detention of aliens who are subject to an order of removal, deportation, or exclusion. See generally 8 C.F.R. 241.13, 241.14, 1241.14.

466. The United States Supreme Court has long held that aliens who have been stopped at the border and are seeking admission in the first instance or who have been inspected and denied admission have no constitutional or statutory entitlement to be admitted or released into the United States. See generally Zadvydas v. Davis, 533 U.S. 678, 693–694 (2001); Shaughnessy v. United States ex rel. Mezei, 345 U.S. 206, 212 (1953); U.S. ex rel. Knauff v. Shaughnessy, 338 U.S. 537 (1950); see also United States v. Flores-Montano, 124 S. Ct. 1582, 1585 (2004) ("The government's interest in preventing the entry of unwanted persons ... is at its zenith at the international border."); Landon v. Plasencia, 459 U.S. 21, 32 (1982) ("This Court has long held that an alien seeking initial admission to the United States requests a privilege and has no constitutional rights regarding his application, for the power to admit or exclude aliens is a sovereign prerogative... [H]owever, once an alien gains admission to our country and begins to develop the ties that go with permanent residence, his constitutional status changes accordingly."). In neither Zadvydas v. Davis, 533 U.S. 678 (2001), nor Clark v. Martinez, 125 S. Ct. 716 (2005), did the Supreme Court purport to impose constitutional limits on the government's detention authority, especially with regard to aliens who are dangerous to national security or who pose threats to public safety.

467. The Committee's recommendation was given careful consideration, but it is the view of the United States that current U.S. law fully satisfies the obligations the United States has assumed under the Covenant. United States immigration law draws reasonable distinctions, with respect to the nature and quantum of rights afforded in the detention and removal process, between aliens who were stopped at the border and not lawfully admitted to the United States and those who were lawfully admitted. Governments may make such reasonable distinctions under national law consistent with the Covenant. In addition, the United States has a legitimate interest in taking steps so that aliens who pose a threat to the public safety or national security are removed from the country as soon as practicable and, while awaiting removal, are subject to appropriate custody or detention.

468. The Committee does not share the view expressed by the government that the Covenant lacks extraterritorial reach under all circumstances. Such a view is contrary to the consistent interpretation of the Committee on this subject, that, in special circumstances, persons may fall under the subject-matter jurisdiction of a State Party even when outside that state's territory.

469. Comment: The United States continues to consider that its view is correct that the obligations it has assumed under the Covenant do not have extraterritorial reach. Please note Annex I to this report.

470. The Committee expresses the hope that measures be adopted to bring conditions of detention of persons deprived of liberty in federal or state prisons in full conformity with Article 10 of the Covenant. Legislative, prosecutorial and judicial policy in sentencing must take into account that overcrowding in prisons causes violation of Article 10 of the Covenant.

471. Comment: All prisons in the United States are subject to the strictures of the federal Constitution and federal civil rights laws. Prisons must ensure that "inmates receive adequate food, clothing, shelter, and medical care and must 'take reasonable measures to guarantee the safety of inmates.'" *Farmer v. Brennan*, 511 U.S. 825, 832-33 (1994). The Americans with Disabilities Act and the Rehabilitation Act generally require prison physical spaces and page 106 programs to be accessible to inmates with impairments, subject to appropriate security and safety concerns, and the Individuals with Disabilities in Education Act requires prisons to provide inmates with appropriate special educational services.

472. As noted, the federal Constitution prohibits prison conditions, including overcrowding, when such constitutes "cruel and unusual punishment." *Rhodes v. Chapman*, 452 U.S. 337, 352(1981). However, in making such a determination, "courts cannot assume that state legislatures and prison officials are insensitive to the requirements of the Constitution or to the perplexing sociological problems of how best to achieve the goals of the penal function in the criminal justice system: to punish justly, to deter future crime, and to return imprisoned persons to society with an improved change of being useful, law-abiding citizens." *Id.* Overcrowding, standing alone, does not violate federal law. Nor does the United States agree that overcrowding, standing alone, violates Article 10(1).

473. Existing legislation that allows male officers access to women's quarters should be amended so as to provide at least that they will always be accompanied by women officers.

474. Comment: It is not the practice of the federal Bureau of Prisons or of most state corrections departments to restrict corrections officers to work only with inmates of the same sex. Furthermore, requiring female officers always to be present during male officers' access to women's quarters would be extremely burdensome on prison resources. Appropriate measures are taken, however, to protect female prisoners. Staff are trained to respect offenders' safety, dignity, and privacy, and procedures exist for investigation of complaints and disciplinary action-including criminal prosecution-against staff who violate applicable laws and regulations.

475. Conditions of detention in prisons, in particular in maximum security prisons, should be scrutinized with a view to guaranteeing that persons deprived of their liberty be treated with humanity and with respect for the inherent dignity of the human person, and implementing the United Nations Standard Minimum Rules for the Treatment of Prisoners and the Code of Conduct for Law Enforcement Officials therein.

476. Comment: All prisoners in the United States are guaranteed treatment that does not constitute cruel and unusual punishment prohibited by the United States Constitution. Also, *see* the response to Question 10, supra. It is also worth noting that the United Nations Standard Minimum Rules for the Treatment of Prisoners and the Code of Conduct for Law Enforcement Officials are non-binding recommendations.

477. Appropriate measures should be adopted to provide speedy and effective remedies to compensate persons who have been subjected to unlawful or arbitrary arrests as provided in Article 9, paragraph 5, of the Covenant.

478. Comment: The Constitution of the United States prohibits unreasonable seizures of persons, and the Supreme Court has allowed the victims of such unconstitutional seizures to sue in court for money damages. *See, e.g., Bivens v. Six Unnamed Known Agents of Federal Bureau of Narcotics*, 403 U.S. 388 (1971). In addition, the United States reminds the Committee of the understanding (2) of the United States concerning Article 9(5).

479. The Committee recommends that further measures be taken to amend any federal or state regulation which allow, in some states, non-therapeutic research to be conducted on minors or mentally-ill patients on the basis of surrogate consent.

480. Comment: The U.S. government's position in the protection of human subject regulations is grounded in extensive public review and debate, based on the recommendations of the National Commission for the Protection of Human Subjects of Biomedical and Behavioral Research. Fourteen federal government departments and agencies have adopted regulations that provide protection for human subjects in federally-conducted or -supported research. Under these rules, a legally authorized representative may consent to a subject's participation in research, including non-therapeutic research. This includes mentally ill subjects or subjects with impaired decision-making capacity, including minors. The rules provide rigorous safeguards for research subjects in general and recognize that additional protections may be necessary for vulnerable populations. The U.S. government does not see a need to reexamine that position.

481. The Committee recommends that the current system in a few states in the appointment of judges through elections be reconsidered with a view to its replacement by a system of appointment on merit by an independent body.

482. Comment: The United States does not believe there is any reason to reconsider the state practice of election of judges. Popular election of judges, though not provided for in the federal Constitution, is one means of ensuring democratic accountability of the state and local judicial branch of government. Furthermore, each state is entitled to determine the structure of its government, with only limited, circumscribed restrictions in federal law.

483. The Committee recommends that steps be taken to ensure that previously recognized aboriginal Native American rights cannot be extinguished. The Committee urges the government to ensure that there is a full judicial review in respect of determinations of federal recognition of tribes. The Self-Governance Demonstration Project and similar programs should be strengthened to continue to fight the high incidence of poverty, sickness and alcoholism among Native Americans.

484. Comment: Under United States Constitutional law, the Congress has plenary power over Native American communal rights.

485. Indigenous groups seeking recognition as federally recognized tribes may submit an application for recognition to the Department of the Interior, or else be recognized through Congressional or other Executive Branch actions. Indigenous groups who are unsuccessful in this process may seek review of a recognition decision in a United States federal court.

486. The United States also provides a diverse array of funding and training opportunities, as well as direct services, available to Native Americans and Alaska Natives, some of which promote home ownership and small business development, combat drug and alcohol abuse, promote health and healthy living, and equip and train law enforcement officials.

487. The Committee expresses the hope that, when determining whether currently permitted affirmative action programs for minorities and women should be withdrawn, the obligation to provide Covenant's rights in fact as well as in law be borne in mind.

488. Comment: See response to Question 4, supra.

489. The Committee recommends that measures be taken to ensure greater public awareness of the provisions of the Covenant and that the legal profession as well as judicial and administrative authorities at federal and state levels be made familiar with these provisions in order to ensure their effective application.

490. Comment: There is extensive awareness of the provisions of the Covenant at the state and federal levels. [Footnotes omitted]

[Author's Note: Because of the importance of the following Annex to the issue of the territorial applicability of the ICCPR in the eyes of the U.S. Government the Author is leaving in the notes. It is this Author' opinion that the position of the U.S., that the ICCPR does not apply at all outside of the territorial boundaries of the U.S., was to protect the U.S. from claims of human rights violations in relation to its actions abroad in the war on terrorism, for example Guantánamo, Cuba. On this issue see Appendix E, General Comment #31, paragraphs 10–12.]

Annex I

TERRITORIAL APPLICATION OF THE INTERNATIONAL COVENANT ON CIVIL AND POLITICAL RIGHTS

The Vienna Convention on the Law of Treaties[1] states the basic rules for the interpretation of treaties. In Article 31(1), it states that:

A treaty shall be interpreted in good faith in accordance with the ordinary meaning to be given to the terms of the treaty in their context and in the light of its object and purpose. Resort to this fundamental rule of interpretation leads to the inescapable conclusion that the obligations assumed by a State Party to the International Covenant on Civil and Political Rights (Covenant) apply only within the territory of the State Party.

Article 2(1) of the Covenant states that "[e]ach State Party to the present Covenant undertakes to respect and to ensure to all individuals *within its territory and subject to its jurisdiction* the rights recognized in the present Covenant, without distinction of any kind." Hence, based on the plain and ordinary meaning of its text, this Article establishes that States Parties are required to ensure the rights in the Covenant only to individuals who are both *within* the territory of a State Party *and* subject to that State Party's sovereign authority.

This evident interpretation was expressed in 1995 by Conrad Harper, the Legal Adviser of the U.S. Department of State, in response to a question posed by the U.N. Committee on Human Rights, as follows: Mr. HARPER (United States of America) said:

Mr. Klein had asked whether the United States took the view that the Covenant did not apply to government actions outside the United States. The Covenant was not regarded as having extra territorial application. In general, where the scope of application of a treaty was not specified, it was presumed to apply only within a Party's territory.

Article 2 of the Covenant expressly stated that each State Party undertook to respect and ensure the rights recognized "to all individuals within its territory and subject to its jurisdiction". That dual requirement restricted the scope of the Covenant to persons under United States jurisdiction and within United States territory. During the negotiating history, the words "within its territory" had been debated and were added by vote, with the clear understanding that such wording would limit the obligations to within a Party's territory.[2]

A further rule of interpretation contained in the Vienna Convention on the Law of Treaties states in Article 32 that: Recourse may be had to supplementary means of interpretation, including the preparatory work of the treaty and the circumstances of its conclusion, in order to confirm the meaning resulting from the application of Article 31, or to determine the meaning when the interpretation according to Article 31: leaves the meaning ambiguous or obscure; or leads to a result which is manifestly absurd or unreasonable.

In fact, there is no ambiguity in Article 2(1) of the Covenant and its text is neither manifestly absurd nor unreasonable. Thus there is no need to resort to the travaux preparatoires of the Covenant to ascertain the territorial reach of the Covenant. However, resort to the travaux serves to underscore the intent of the negotiators to limit the territorial reach of obligations of States Parties to the Covenant.

The preparatory work of the Covenant establishes that the reference to "within its territory" was included within Article 2(1) of the Covenant to make clear that states would not be obligated to ensure the rights recognized therein outside their territories. In 1950, the draft text of Article 2 then under consideration by the Commission on Human Rights would have required that states ensure Covenant rights to everyone "within its jurisdiction." The United States, however, proposed the addition of the requirement that the individual also be "within its territory."[3] Eleanor Roosevelt, the U.S. representative and then-Chairman of the Commission emphasized that the United States was "particularly anxious" that it not assume "an obligation to ensure the rights recognized in it to citizens of countries under United States occupation."[4] She explained that: The purpose of the proposed addition [is] to make it clear that the draft Covenant would apply only to persons within the territory and subject to the jurisdiction of the contracting states. The United States [is] afraid that without such an addition the draft Covenant might be construed as obliging the contracting states to enact legislation concerning persons, who although outside its territory were technically within its jurisdiction for certain purposes. An illustration would be the occupied territories of Germany, Austria and Japan: persons within those countries were subject to the jurisdiction of the occupying states in certain respects, but were outside the scope of legislation of those states. Another illustration would be leased territories; some countries leased certain territories from others for limited purposes, and there might be question of conflicting authority between the lessor nation and the lessee nation.[5]

Several delegations spoke against the U.S. amendment, arguing that a nation should guarantee fundamental rights to its *citizens* abroad as well as at home. René Cassin (France), proposed that the U.S. proposal should be revised in the French text replacing "*et*" with "*ou*" so that states would not "lose their jurisdiction over their foreign citizens."[6] Charles Malik (Lebanon) cited three possible cases in which the United States amendment was open to doubt: First, ... [the] amendment conflicted with Article [12], which affirmed the right of a citizen abroad to return to his own country; it might not be possible for him to return if, while abroad, he were not under the jurisdiction of his own government. Secondly, if a national of any state, while abroad were informed of a suit brought against him in his own country, he might be denied the rightful fair hearing because of his residence abroad. Thirdly, there was the question whether a national of a state, while abroad, could be accorded a fair and public hearing in a legal case in the country in which he was resident.[7]

Mrs. Roosevelt in responding to Malik's points, could "see no conflict between the United States' amendment and Article [12]; the terms of Article [12] would naturally apply in all cases."[8] Additionally, she asserted that "any citizen desiring to return to his home country would receive a fair and public hearing in any case brought against him."[9] Finally, she reiterated generally that "it was not possible for any nation to guarantee such rights [e.g., the right to a fair trial in foreign courts] under the terms of the draft Covenant to its nationals resident abroad."[10] Ultimately, the U.S. amendment was adopted at the 1950 session by a vote of 8-2 with 5 abstentions.[11] Subsequently, after similar debates, the United States and others defeated French proposals to delete the phrase "within its territory" at both the 1952 session of the Commission[12] and the 1963 session of the General Assembly.[13]

Notes

1 Although the United States has not ratified the Vienna Convention [on the Law of Treaties], the United States generally recognizes the Convention as an authoritative guide to principles of treaty interpretation. *See, e.g., Fujitsu Ltd. v. Federal Express Corp.*, 247 F.3d 423, 433 (2d Cir.), *cert. denied*, 534 U.S. 891 (2001); *see also* Vienna Convention on the Law of Treaties, S. Exec. Doc.L, 92d Cong., 1st Sess. 1, 19 (1971).

2 *Summary record of the 1405th meeting: United States of America*, U.N. ESCOR Hum. Rts. Comm., 53rd Sess., 1504th mtg. at 7, 20, U.N. Doc. CCPR/C/SR.1405 (1995).

3 *Compilation of the Comments of Governments on the Draft International Covenant on Human Rights and on the Proposed Additional Articles*, U.N. ESCOR Hum. Rts. Comm., 6th Sess. at 14, U.N. Doc. E/CN.4/365 (1950) (U.S. proposal). The U.S. amendment added the words "territory and subject to its" before "jurisdiction" in Article 2(1).

4 *Summary Record of the Hundred and Ninety-Third Meeting*, U.N. ESCOR Hum. Rts. Comm., 6th Sess., 193rd mtg. at 13, 18, U.N. Doc. E/CN.4/SR.193 at 13, 18 (1950) (Mrs. Roosevelt); *Summary Record of the Hundred and Ninety-Fourth Meeting*, U.N. ESCOR Hum. Rts. Comm., 6th Sess., 194rd mtg. at 5, 9, U.N. Doc. E/CN.4/SR.194 (1950).

5 *Summary Record of the Hundred and Thirty-Eighth Meeting*, U.N. ESCOR Hum. Rts. Comm., 6th Sess., 138th mtg at 10, U.N. Doc. E/CN.4/SR.138 (1950) (emphasis added).

6 *Summary Record of the Hundred and Ninety-Third Meeting, supra* note 2, at 21. (Mr. René Cassin). Several states maintained similar positions. *See, Summary Record of the Hundred and Ninety-Fourth Meeting, supra* note 2, at 5 (Mauro Mendez, representative of Philippines); *Id.* (Alexis Kryou, representative of Greece); *Id.* at 7 (Joseph Nisot, representative of Belgium); *Id.* at 8 (Branko Jevremovic, representative of Yugoslavia).

7 *Id.* at 7 (Charles Malik proposed the addition of the words "'in so far as internal laws are applicable' following the U.S. amendment.").

8 *Id.* (Mrs. Roosevelt) ICCPR Article 12(4) provides that "No one shall be arbitrarily deprived of the right to enter his own country."

9 *Summary Record of the Hundred and Ninety-Fourth Meeting, supra* note 2, at 7 (Mrs. Roosevelt).

10 *Id..* Several states maintained that the United States position was the most sound and logical one. *See, Id.* at 6 (Dr. Carlos Valenzuela, representative of Chile); *Id.* at 8 (E.N. Oribe, representative of Uruguay).

11 *Id.* at 11.

12 *Draft International Convention on Human Rights and Measures of Implementation*, U.N. ESCOR Hum. Rts. Comm., 8th Sess., Agenda Item 4, U.N. Doc. E/CN.4/L.161 (1952)(French amendment); *Summary Record of the Three Hundred and Twenty-Ninth Meeting*, U.N. ESCOR Hum. Rts. Comm., 8th Sess., 329th mtg. at 14, U.N. Doc. E/CN.4/SR.329 (1952) (vote rejecting amendment). During the debate France and Yugoslavia again urged deletion of the phrase within its territory because states should be required to guarantee Covenant rights to citizens abroad. *Id.* at 13 (P. Juvigny, representative of France); *Id.* at 13 (Branko Jevremovic, representative of Yugoslavia).

13 U.N. GAOR 3rd Comm., 18th Sess., 1259th mtg. 30, U.N. Doc. A/C.3/SR.1259 (1963) (rejection of French and Chinese proposal to delete "within its territory"). Several states again maintained that the Covenant should guarantee rights to citizens abroad. *See*, U.N. GAOR 3rd Comm., 18th Sess., 1257th mtg. 1 U.N. Doc. A/C.3/SR.1257 (1963) (Mrs. Mantaoulinos, representative of Greece); *Id.* at 10 (Mr. Capotorti, representative of Italy); *Id.* at 21(Mr. Combal, representative of France); U.N. GAOR 3rd Comm., 18th Sess., 1258th mtg. 29,U.N. Doc. A/C.3/ SR.1258 (1963) (Mr. Cha, representative of China); *Id.* at 39 (Antonio Belaunde, representative of Peru).

DOCUMENT 15B (SERIES)

Full Official Title: [Written Response Of The United States To The] List Of Issues To Be Taken Up In Connection With The Consideration Of The Second And Third Periodic Reports Of The United States of America

Short Title/Acronym/Abbreviation: U.S. Responses to Human Rights Committee List of Issues, Second and Third Reports

Type of Document: This is a governmental document consisting of U.S. responses to a list of issue the Human Rights Committee wanted addressed by the U.S. regarding its Second and Third Reports. The List was prepared by the Human Rights Committee and sent to the U.S. State Department. The State Department prepared these responses to the issues the Committee wants the U.S. to address when the U.S.

delegation appears before the Committee in Geneva to review its Second and Third periodic reports. These are not legal documents but administrative documents of a treaty based body. This was a response to a the List document dated April 26, 2006, from the HR Cee.

Subject: Specific Issues the HRCee wanted addressed by the U.S. before its hearing before the Committee, such as the legal framework of the relation of the U.S. to Native Americans; obstacles to withdrawing reservations to ICCPR articles; the definition of terrorism, how the U.S. will implement the Covenant during operations in Iraq and Afghanistan, Guantánamo detainee identities and arrest info, military commissions, Detainee Treatment Act. The U.S responded to these issues.

Official Citation: U.S. Written Responses to Human Rights Committee document CCPR/C/USA/Q/3 (U.N. site has no reference citation, see http://www2.ohchr.org/english/bodies/hrc/hrcs87.htm. and http://www2.ohchr.org/english/bodies/hrc/docs/AdvanceDocs/USA-writtenreplies.pdf)

Date of Document: July 17, 2006

Date of Adoption: Not applicable

Date of General Entry into Force (EIF): Not applicable

Number of States Parties as of this printing: Not applicable

Date of Signature by the United States: Not applicable

Date of Ratification/Accession/Adhesion: Not applicable

Date of Entry into Force as to United States (effective date): Not applicable

Legal Status/Character of the Instrument/Document as to the United States: This is not a legal instrument but an administrative document, government to intergovernmental organization, that is submitted by a state party to the Human Rights Committee to address the issues of concern to the Committee, in fulfillment of the State's legal obligations under Article 40 of the ICCPR, which is a legally binding treaty.

Comments: By ratifying the ICCPR, the U.S. agreed under Article 40 to report to the Human Rights Committee on measures they have adopted to give effect to the rights recognized in the Covenant or any progress they have made or obstacles in the enjoyment of those right. Part of this process after the report is submitted is for the State to appear in person before the Committee to discuss issues arising in the report. Because the Committee suspected that the U.S would probably not want to address issues related to the war on terrorism, it sent this list of items for them to respond to at the hearing. There are also non-war-on-terrorism items listed. The Committee mainly wants to address U.S counter terrorism measures to determine whether they think the U.S. is or is not complying with its obligations under the ICCPR. This document is the U.S. response to that request. The document sets forth the specific items listed by the Committee followed by its response. After the hearing took place, the Committee prepared the outcome (See Document 15C), giving its conclusions and recommendations to the U.S. It is up to the state to then decide whether and how to implement these recommendations or contest the conclusions. This is an administrative and not a judicial process. The results are not legally binding.

This document should be read along with the three other 15-series documents to get an idea of the give and take between the international community, represented by the Human Rights Committee, and the U.S., represented by a Department of State delegation. This process also happens in the other treaty bodies, CERD and CAT.

Website: For the text of the Human Rights Committee List of Issues see the following website: http://daccess-dds-ny.un.org/doc/UNDOC/GEN/G06/426/26/PDF/G0642626.pdf?OpenElement

For the full text of the U.S. written responses to the Human Rights Committee List of issues see the following website: http://www.state.gov/g/drl/rls/70385.htm or http://www2.ohchr.org/english/bodies/hrc/docs/AdvanceDocs/USA-writtenreplies.pdf

LIST OF ISSUES TO BE TAKEN UP IN CONNECTION WITH THE CONSIDERATION OF THE SECOND AND THIRD PERIODIC REPORTS OF THE UNITED STATES OF AMERICA (EXCERPTS)

(Bold wording is Human Rights Committee Issue; unbolded is the U.S. response)

1. Does the State party rely on the doctrine of discovery in its relationship with indigenous peoples, and if so what are the legal consequences of such approach? What is the status and force of law of treaties with Indian tribes? Please indicate how the principle set forth in U.S. law and practice, by which recognized tribal property rights are subject to diminishment or elimination under the plenary authority reserved to the U.S. Congress for conducting Indian affairs, complies with articles 1 and 27 of the Covenant? (Previous concluding observations, s. 290 and 302; Periodic report, s. 15 and 484)

In the July 1994 U.S. Initial Report on its implementation of the Covenant and in the March 1995 discussions before the Human Rights Committee, the United States described at length the complex history of U.S. relations with Native American tribes and the legal regime within the United States that applies to such tribes, including the concept of "tribal self determination" under U.S. law. While it would not be possible to repeat that discussion in the space limitations imposed by the Committee, the United States response to this question is premised on that information. To address the Committee's specific question, the doctrine of discovery in U.S. law was first discussed by the Supreme Court in Johnson v. M'Intosh, 21 U.S. 543 (1823). The Court noted this was not a doctrine that originated in the United States but rather with "European potentates."

The United States, when breaking away from England, inherited the rights England had with respect to lands in what is now the United States. They included the exclusive right of purchase of lands held or occupied by Indian tribes. They did not deny to the tribes the rights to their lands but only limited to whom those lands could be sold or transferred. In fact, the states of the Union could not enter into treaties with tribes to acquire their lands.

The majority of the land that is now the United States was not acquired by conquest or "discovery" by the United States. The Louisiana Purchase from the French (1803), the Gadsden Purchase from Mexico (1853), cession from Mexico of what is now California, Nevada, Utah, New Mexico and Arizona, the Oregon compromise with Britain, and the purchase of Alaska from Russia all comprise the majority of U.S. territory. In each of those cases the Indian tribes retained the rights to their lands, and the United States, in some 67 other transactions with the tribes, by treaty, acquired actual title from the Indians.

During its first hundred years of existence, the United States engaged with Indian tribes through federal legislation and the treaty making process. Treaty making between the federal government and the Indian tribes ended in 1871, but the treaties retain their full force and effect even today as they are considered the equivalent of treaties with foreign governments and have the force of federal law. Unlike treaties with foreign governments, treaties with Indian tribes are subject to special canons of construction that tend to favor Indian interests. Treaties with Indian tribes are interpreted, to the extent that such original intention is relevant, as they would have been understood by the Indians at the time of their signing, not by the American authors of the treaties; and where the treaty is ambiguous as to its interpretation, the Court will interpret it to favor the Indians specifically because it was not written by them or in their language.

Constitutional and legal framework within which the Covenant is implemented (art. 2)

2. Please explain further what are the obstacles to the withdrawal of reservations, in particular to articles 6(5) and 7 of the Covenant. (Periodic report, s. 448; Previous concluding observations, s. 278–279 and 292).

The U.S. reservation to Article 6(5) states:

"(2) That the United States reserves the right, subject to its constitutional constraints, to impose capital punishment on any person (other than a pregnant woman) duly convicted under existing or future laws permitting the imposition of capital punishment, including such punishment for crimes committed by persons below eighteen years of age."

This reservation remains in effect, and the United States has no current intention of withdrawing it. We note, as a courtesy to the Committee, that U.S. judicial decisions, independent of any obligation of the United States under the Covenant, recently have tightened restrictions on the death penalty in the United States. In Roper v. Simmons, 543 U.S. 551 (2005), the U.S. Supreme Court held that imposition of capital punishment on those who were under 18 years of age at the time of the offense violates the U.S. Constitution's Eighth Amendment protection against cruel and unusual punishment. Id. at 578. Although the decision in the Roper case does not change the formal scope of the U.S. treaty reservation to Article 6(5), the effect of the decision is that the United States, as a matter of its own constitutional law, will not execute persons who were below the age of 18 years at the time of the offense. Thus, while the last sentence in the above-referenced reservation preserves the discretion of the United States under the Covenant to impose the death penalty "for crimes committed by persons below eighteen years of age," the fact is that the United States does not do so.

The U.S. reservation to Article 7 states:

(3) That the United States considers itself bound by Article 7 to the extent that "cruel, inhuman or degrading treatment or punishment" means the cruel and unusual treatment or punishment prohibited by the Fifth, Eighth and/or Fourteenth Amendments to the Constitution of the United States.

The United States entered this reservation because of concern over the uncertain meaning of the phrase "cruel, inhuman or degrading treatment or punishment" ("CIDTP"), and this reservation was undertaken to ensure that existing U.S. constitutional standards would satisfy U.S. obligations under Article 7. The reasons underlying the decision by the United States to file its reservation to Article 7 have not changed, as the underlying vagueness of this provision remains. Because of the concern that certain practices that are constitutional in the United States might be considered impermissible under possible interpretations of the vaguely-worded standard in Article 7, the United States does not currently intend to withdraw that reservation.

...

Counter-terrorism measures and respect of Covenant guarantees

3. Please comment on the compatibility with the Covenant of the definition of terrorism under national law and of the Congress' Authorization for Use of Military Force Joint Resolution, which provides the President all powers "necessary and appropriate to protect American citizens from terrorist acts by those who attacked the U.S. on September 11, 2001". (Periodic report, s. 90–94 and s. 164–165; Core document, s. 135–138)

A. Definition of Terrorism. The Covenant does not address the question of how a State Party might define the term "terrorism" under its domestic law. Within the United States, there is no uniform "definition of terrorism under [U.S.] national law." Some federal statutes use the term "terrorism" and define that term in a manner consistent with the specific purpose of those particular statutes. Such statutes arise in many different subject areas including, among other things, with respect to law enforcement, economic sanctions, immigration, and executive branch reporting requirements. This response will focus on one particular type of legal mechanism—established by statute and executive order—under which a person or organization is "designated" as a terrorist and that designation has a serious of financial consequences. This authority is crucial to the counter-terrorism efforts of the United States Government.

Specifically:

(i) Under 8 U.S.C. 1189(1)(a), the U.S. government has the authority to designate as a "foreign terrorist organization" (FTO) any organization that either engages in "terrorist activity" as defined in 8 U.S.C. 1182(a)(3)(B)(iii) or "terrorism" as defined in 22 U.S.C. 2656f, and that meets other relevant legal criteria. Multiple consequences flow from an FTO designation. Certain financial assets may be frozen; aliens having certain associations with the organization are inadmissible to, and may be deported from, the United States; and it becomes criminally prohibited knowingly to provide material support to the organization.

(ii) Under 8 U.S.C. 1182(a)(3)(B)(vi)(II), the U.S. government has the authority to include on the Terrorist Exclusion List any organization that "engages in terrorist activity" as defined in 8 U.S.C. 1182(a)(3)(B)(iii). If an organization is included on the Terrorist Exclusion List, aliens having certain associations with that organization are inadmissible and may be deported from the United States.

(iii) Under Executive Order 13224, the U.S. government has the authority to designate as "Specially Designated Global Terrorists" individuals and entities that commit acts of "terrorism" as defined in the Executive Order, or who have certain associations with already-designated individuals and entities. Designation under Executive Order 13224 results in the imposition of asset-blocking sanctions. Moreover, it is a criminal act willfully or intentionally to have dealings or transactions with an SDGT.

The definitions of "terrorism" and "terrorist activity" referred to above are set forth in Annex A. As is clear upon inspection, these definitions simply establish the ways in which terrorist activity is distinguishable from other forms of violent and dangerous activity, and contain nothing that is on their face incompatible with U.S. obligations under the Covenant. Moreover, the designation authorities of which these definitions form an integral part are themselves subject to appropriate procedural safeguards, and are compatible with U.S. obligations under the Covenant. (We additionally note that these designation authorities form an essential part of the legal framework by which the U.S. government implements its law enforcement, sanctions, and other obligations under international legal instruments such as U.N. Security Council Resolutions 1267 and 1373, and successor resolutions, and the U.N. counterterrorism conventions.) The U.S. government accordingly considers that the above-referenced definitions are compatible with U.S. obligations under the Covenant.

Paragraphs 4–9

In paragraphs 4 through 9, the Committee poses a number of questions about the conduct of U.S. military and other activities outside the territory of the United States. Many of these questions are similar to matters addressed at length by the United States in its public statements as well as in its May, 2006 discussion of its report on its implementation of the Convention Against Torture and Other Cruel, Inhuman or Degrading Treatment or Punishment with the U.N. Committee Against Torture.

In addressing these questions, the United States notes and reaffirms paragraph 130 of its Second and Third Periodic Report:

"130. The United States recalls its longstanding position that it has reiterated in paragraph 3 of this report and explained in detail in the legal analysis provided in Annex I; namely, that the obligations assumed by the United States under the Covenant apply only within the territory of the United States. In that regard, the United States respectfully submits that this Committee request for information is outside the purview of the Committee. The United States also notes that the legal status and treatment of such persons is governed by the law of war. Nonetheless, as a courtesy, the United States is providing the Committee pertinent material in the form of an updated Annex to the U.S. report on the Convention Against Torture and Other Cruel, Inhuman or Degrading Treatment or Punishment."

While it reiterates this position, as a courtesy to the Committee, the United States provides additional written information to the Committee appended to this response as Annex B.

Question 4 also asks

"how the State Party ensures full respect for the rights enshrined in the Covenant in relation to its actions to combat terrorism ... (d) on its own territory, in particular when it holds detainees. How would such practices comply with the Covenant, in particular with articles 7, 9 and 10?"

This question—which appears to ask how all U.S. actions to combat terrorism comply with the Covenant—is of extraordinary breadth. As the answer to particular aspects of this question is contained in U.S. responses to other questions, this reply addresses the broader question of how U.S. counterterrorism measures as a general matter satisfy U.S. obligations under the Covenant.

The struggle against al Qaida and its affiliates poses new kinds of challenges for all members of the international community. The United States is a democracy founded on the rule of law and is absolutely committed to conducting its actions in response to these challenges in a manner consistent with the rule of law, its core values, and its obligations under both its domestic law—most notably the United States Constitution—and under the applicable international law. The U.S. Initial Report on its implementation of the Covenant from 1994 and its Second and Third Periodic Report from October 2005 describe in great detail the operation of the U.S. legal system that enables the United States to implement its obligations under the Covenant. Those mechanisms, including the operation of a well ordered legal system governed under the rule of law and implemented, inter alia, by an independent judiciary, continue to apply in full measure to U.S. measures to combat terrorism. In its Initial Report, the United States explained in detail the manner in which the comprehensive protections to individuals provided under the U.S. Constitution enabled the United States to implement its treaty obligations under the Covenant and indeed in many instances offered greater protections than those required under the Covenant. Terrorist suspects within the United States are subject to the protections under the U.S. Constitution and other laws, and these protections fully implement U.S. obligations under the Covenant.

10. Has the State party adopted a policy to send, or to assist in the sending of suspected terrorists to third countries, either from U.S. or other States' territories, for purposes of detention and interrogation? If so, please indicate the number of affected persons and their place of detention and/or interrogation. What measures have been adopted to ensure that their rights under the Covenant are fully respected? Please provide information on cases where removal/transfer was carried out based on diplomatic assurances received from a foreign government. Please explain in more detail whether there are exceptions, in particular for suspected terrorists, to the right of aliens to challenge their deportation before a court on the basis of the *non-refoulement* rule. Do such remedies have a suspensive effect? What were the results of the investigations conducted by the State party, if any, into the numerous allegations that persons have been sent to third countries where they have undergone torture and ill-treatment? In this regard, please comment on the case of Maher Arar, a Canadian citizen deported in October 2002 to Jordan and then Syria, and who was allegedly tortured, (articles 6, 7, 9, 10) (Periodic report, s. 220–241; CAT/C/48/ Add.3/Rev. 1, Annexes, Part I, s. 45^7)

As an initial matter, the United States would like to emphasize that, unlike the Convention Against Torture and Other Cruel, Inhuman, Degrading Treatment or Punishment ("Convention Against Torture"), the Covenant does not impose a non-refoulement obligation upon States Parties. We are familiar with the Committee's statement in General Comment 20 regarding Article 7 of the Covenant that:

"States parties must not expose individuals to the danger of torture or cruel, inhuman or degrading treatment or punishment upon return to another country by way of their extradition, expulsion or refoulement."

However, the United States disagrees that States Parties have accepted that obligation under the Covenant.

. . .

As has been stated publicly, the United States does not comment on information or reports relating to alleged intelligence operations. That being said, Secretary of State Condoleezza Rice recently explained that the United States and other countries have long used renditions to transport terrorist suspects from the country where they were captured to their home country or to other countries where they can be questioned, held, or brought to justice. The United States considers rendition a vital tool in combating international terrorism, which takes terrorists out of action and saves lives. However, as is true with the case of immigration removals and extraditions, in conducting renditions, the United States acts in accordance with its obligations under the CAT and, even in instances in which the CAT does not apply, does not transport individuals to a country when it believes that the individuals would more likely than not be tortured in that country.

. . .

11. Please indicate how many persons have been or are still being detained on the basis of the Material Witness Statute, for how long, how many of them have been charged with crimes related to terrorism, and how their rights under the Covenant were and continue to be ensured. Please comment also on withholding information regarding such detainees and how far closing of the immigration court hearings to the public is compatible with the Covenant, (articles 9, 10 and 14) (Periodic report, 168–169)

Material witness warrants are used to secure testimony before a grand or petit jury by witnesses who are flight risks. Their use is a long-standing practice authorized by statute and dating back to 1789 and the first Congress. These warrants are used in various cases, predominantly alien-smuggling, but also organized crime investigations and terrorism.

Every instance of detention of a material witness is subject to independent oversight by the Judicial Branch of the U.S. government. The Federal Bureau of Investigation cannot unilaterally arrest and detain an individual as a material witness, but rather must comply with a regimen of procedural requirements. The government must establish probable cause to believe that the witness's testimony is material and that it would be impracticable to secure that witness's appearance by subpoena. Furthermore, every person held as a material witness has the right to be represented by an attorney, and an attorney will be appointed if the material witness cannot afford to pay for a lawyer. Every material witness has the right to challenge, in court, before a judicial officer, his or her confinement as a material witness. If a juvenile is confined as a material witness, statutes governing the treatment, segregation, and processing of detained juveniles (including but not limited to material witnesses) guide the handling of each particular case. Once a material witness gives full and complete testimony, he or she is released, unless there is some other source of authority for continued detention, such as an immigration detainer or criminal charges. At that point, the witness will be afforded the due process rights available in those types of proceedings.

An informal estimate by the Department of Justice in early 2005 revealed that approximately 10,000 material witness warrants had been issued nationwide since September 11, 2001, about 9600 of which were used in alien smuggling cases. About 230 warrants were issued in drug, weapons or other violent crime cases, and approximately 90 were used in terrorism cases. The exact number of those arrested who were subsequently ordered detained by a court is not available, nor is an individual breakdown of the types of cases.

12. Please report in more detail on the compliance with the Covenant of: (a) Section 213 of the Patriot Act, expanding the possibility of delayed notification of home and office searches; (b) Section 215 of the Patriot Act, regarding access to individuals' personal records and belongings; (c) Section 505, relating to the issuance of national security letters; and (d) Section 412, regarding the possibility of indefinite detention of foreigners suspected to be terrorists. Please be more specific about the power granted to the judiciary to oversee the implementation of these provisions, and indicate to what extent affected individuals may challenge their implementation before a court. Please provide updated information on the extent to which the State party has invoked the above-mentioned provisions, and provide examples. (Periodic report, 308–312)

Section 213 of the USA Patriot Act codified existing U.S. common law regarding delayed-notice search warrants, which have been available for decades and were in use long before the USA PATRIOT Act was enacted. In this way, section 213 was not a significant grant of new authority to law enforcement officials; rather, it simply created a nationally uniform process and standard for obtaining such search warrants. The judiciary continues to play an integral role in the use of such warrants. As with all criminal search warrants, a delayed-notice search warrant is issued by a federal judge only upon a showing that there is probable cause to believe that the property sought or seized constitutes evidence of a criminal offense.

The USA PATRIOT Improvement and Reauthorization Act of 2005 added new protection for subjects of the warrant. Section 213 of the initial Act had required that notice be given within a "reasonable" period of time, as determined by the judge. Section 114 of the reauthorization legislation provides a presumption that notice must be given within 30 days after the warrant is executed, with extensions limited to periods of 90 days or less. Congress also imposed a reporting requirement designed to provide information on how often delayed-notice search warrants are used and the periods of delay authorized. In fact, delayed-notice warrants are rare; according to an informal estimate in early 2005, they were used in less than 0.2 percent of all federal warrants authorized since the enactment of the USA PATRIOT Act.

. . .

13. The State Party, including through the National Security Agency (NSA), reportedly has monitored and still monitors phone, email, and fax communications of individuals both within and outside the U.S., without any judicial oversight. Please comment and explain how such practices comply with Article 17 of the Covenant.

Article 17 of the Covenant provides, in relevant part, that "[n]o one shall be subjected to arbitrary or unlawful interference with his privacy, family, home or correspondence, nor to unlawful attacks on his honour and reputation." For reasons described in this response, the Terrorist Surveillance Program is consistent with this article.

Pursuant to the Terrorist Surveillance Program described by the President in December 2005, the National Security Agency targets for interception communications where one party to the communication is outside of the United States and where there are reasonable grounds to believe that either party is a member of al Qaeda or an affiliated terrorist organization. The "reasonable grounds to believe" standard is a "probable cause" standard of proof of the type incorporated into the Fourth Amendment. *See Maryland v. Pringle*, 540 U.S. 366, 371 (2003) ("We have stated . . . that [t]he substance of all the definitions of probable cause is a reasonable ground for belief of guilt."). Thus, this program does not involve an arbitrary intrusion into personal privacy. Due to the speed and agility required to prevent a subsequent terrorist attack within the United States, judgments about whether individual communications meet these criteria are made by experienced intelligence officers rather than courts.

The Terrorist Surveillance Program fully complies with Article 17 of the Covenant. Under the Terrorist Surveillance Program, experienced intelligence officers carefully ensure that each communication involves a member of a terrorist organization—or its affiliates—that has executed or is planning terrorist attacks on the United States. In addition, the President reviews the need for and safeguards underlying this program every forty-five days. These standards and procedures prevent the "arbitrary or unlawful interference with . . . privacy" prohibited by Article 17.

. . .

14. Please provide information on measures taken by the State Party to reduce de facto segregation in public schools, reportedly caused by discrepancies between the racial and ethnic composition of large urban districts and their surrounding suburbs, and the manner in which schools districts are created, funded and regulated. (Periodic report, 46–49)

The Department of Justice is currently involved in monitoring 300 cases of de jure segregation, or segregation caused by intentional discriminatory action, under the authority of Title IV of the Civil Rights Act of 1964 and the Equal Educational Opportunities Act of 1974. Each of these statutes prohibits unlawful intentional segregation proscribed by the Equal Protection Clause of the 14th Amendment. In this regard, the United States prohibits the discrimination covered by Article 26 of the Covenant and the understanding of the United States thereto deposited with its instrument of ratification. As noted in paragraph 49 of the U.S. Report, the Department of Education's Office for Civil Rights (OCR) enforces laws that prohibit discrimination on the basis of race, color, national origin, sex, disability, and age in programs that receive federal financial assistance from the Department of Education. These laws include: Title VI of the Civil Rights Act of 1964 (prohibiting discrimination based on race, color and national origin); Title IX of the Education Amendments of 1972 (prohibiting sex discrimination in education programs); Section 504 of the Rehabilitation Act of 1973 (prohibiting disability discrimination); Age Discrimination Act of 1975 (prohibiting age discrimination); and Title II of the Americans with Disabilities Act of 1990 (prohibiting disability discrimination by public entities, whether or not they receive federal financial assistance). OCR also enforces the Boy Scouts of America Equal Access Act of 2002. Under this law, no public elementary or secondary school, local educational agency, or State educational agency that provides an opportunity for outside groups to meet in school facilities may deny such access to, or discriminate against, the Boy Scouts of America or other patriotic youth groups. Pursuant to Title VI of the Civil Rights Act of 1964, OCR monitors a number of agreements with school districts designed to remedy school segregation.

Although it is unclear what would be meant by the phrase "de facto segregation", the United States assumes that the term may refer to situations where particular schools or other educational facilities have a strong preponderance of one race or other group described in Article 26 of the Covenant. This situation can arise through many different reasons, including a pre-existing preponderance of various groups living in a particular geographic area. Although the government authorities within the United States work to prevent discrimination, they cannot act under law absent an indication of discriminatory intent of state or local authorities. Accordingly, numerical preponderance by certain groups, in itself, is not actionable under the statutes enforced by the federal government and would not be inconsistent with Article 26 of the Covenant.

...

15. What measures has the State party adopted to assess and eliminate reported practices of racial profiling by law enforcement officials, in particular in the administration of the criminal justice system?

In a 2001 address to a Joint Session of Congress, President George W. Bush declared that racial profiling is "wrong and we will end it in America." He directed the Attorney General to review the use by federal law enforcement authorities of race as a factor in conducting stops, searches, and other law enforcement procedures. The Attorney General, in turn, issued guidance to all federal law enforcement agencies to prevent the use of racial profiling in law enforcement. The guidance, developed by the Civil Rights Division (CRD) of the Department of Justice, prohibits the use of racial profiling by federal law enforcement officers. Specifically, the guidance states: "In making routine or spontaneous law enforcement decisions, such as ordinary traffic stops, federal law enforcement officers may not use race or ethnicity to any degree, except that officers may rely on race and ethnicity in a specific suspect description. This prohibition applies even where the use of race or ethnicity might otherwise be lawful."

...

16. Please report on measures implemented during and after the disaster caused by Hurricane Katrina in order to ensure equal treatment of victims, without discrimination based on race, social origin and age, in particular in the context of evacuations. Please comment on the information that measures taken have exacerbated problems in respect of the Afro-American population, with regard to homelessness, loss of property, inadequate access to healthcare, loss of educational opportunities, legal remedies and voting rights.

Right to life (art. 6)

As President Bush has acknowledged, the magnitude of destruction resulting from Hurricane Katrina strained and initially overwhelmed federal, state and local capabilities as never before during a domestic incident within our country. Valuable lessons are learned from all disaster responses, and certainly from one of Hurricane Katrina's magnitude. The United States federal government is aggressively moving forward with implementing lessons learned from Hurricane Katrina, including improving procedures to enhance the protection of, and assistance to economically disadvantaged members of society.

The Committee has requested information about the measures taken to prevent discrimination in the context of evacuation after the disaster caused by Hurricane Katrina. With respect to evacuations specifically, it is important to note that, as set forth in the U.S. constitutional framework and most state laws, state and local governments bear primary responsibility for providing initial lifesaving and life support assistance in the event of a disaster. This includes evacuations such as those that occurred during Hurricane Katrina.

The Federal Emergency Management Agency (FEMA), an agency within the Department of Homeland Security (DHS), works with, and supports, state and local first responders, particularly when needs exceed state and local capabilities. FEMA is chiefly responsible for coordinating post-disaster relief and recovery efforts on behalf of the federal government.

...

17. Has the State party taken steps to review federal and state legislation with a view to assessing whether offences carrying the death penalty are strictly restricted to the most serious crimes? Please also

indicate whether the death penalty has been expanded to new offences over the reporting period. What steps, if any, has the State party adopted to ensure that the application of death penalty is not imposed disproportionately on ethnic minorities as well as on low-income population, and to improve the quality of legal representation provided to indigent defendants? (Periodic report, s. 459; Previous concluding observations, s. 281 and 296)

As an initial matter, the United States took a reservation to the Covenant, permitting it to impose capital punishment within its own constitutional limits. ("The United States reserves the right, subject to its Constitutional restraints, to impose capital punishment on any person (other than a pregnant woman) duly convicted under existing or future laws permitting the imposition of capital punishment.") Accordingly, the scope of the conduct subject to the death penalty in the United States is not a matter relevant to the obligations of the United States under the Covenant.

Nevertheless, U.S. constitutional restraints, federal and state laws, and governmental practices have limited the death penalty to the most serious offenses and has prevented the racially discriminatory imposition of the death penalty. Federal laws providing for the death penalty involve serious crimes which result in death, such as murder committed during a drug-related shooting, civil rights offenses resulting in murder, murder related to sexual exploitation of children, murder related to a carjacking or kidnapping, and murder related to rape. There are also a few very serious non-homicide crimes that may result in a death sentence, *e.g.*, espionage, treason, and possessing very large quantities of drugs or drug receipts as part of a continuing criminal enterprise. Recently, Congress enacted several carefully circumscribed capital offenses intended to combat the threat of terrorist attacks resulting in widespread loss of life. (*See* 18 U.S.C. secs. 1991, 1992, 1993, 2282A, 2283, 2291). These exceptionally grave criminal acts all have catastrophic effects on society.

. . .

18. In the view of the State party, what impact on the rights of women under articles 3, 6, 24 and 26 of the Covenant have (a) government regulations proscribing abortion counseling in programs receiving federal funding; (b) the reported policy of the State party to promote sexual education programs that sanction abstinence as the sole method of pregnancy and disease prevention; and (c) the reported states and federal legislation authorizing health care providers to refuse contraception, sterilization or other reproductive health services on the basis of moral disapproval? (Periodic report, 329)

None of the examples described in this question adversely affect the rights of women set forth in articles 3, 6, 24 and 26 of the Covenant. The United States does not interfere with the equality of men and women under the law (3, 26), the rights of children under the law (24), and does not arbitrarily deny life (6) when it determines to fund some activities and view-points. The U.S. Constitution does not impose an affirmative obligation to finance the exercise of every right it recognizes. As explained below, the United States Government does not restrict or inhibit the rights of its citizens by declining to subsidize the exercise of those rights.

As a matter of domestic constitutional law, the Supreme Court recognized the right of a competent adult woman to terminate her pregnancy under certain circumstances. U.S. law also protects healthcare providers who object to taking part in abortions on religious or moral grounds. For example, no court or public official may require recipients of funds under the Public Health Service Act to perform or make their facilities available for abortions or sterilization procedures if it would be against the entities religious beliefs or moral convictions. 42 U.S.C. s. 300a-7. The same law also forbids discrimination against individual healthcare personnel for refusing to take part in such procedures. These measures protect rights important under the Covenant itself, including Article 18 ("Everyone shall have the right to freedom of thought, conscience, and religion") and Article 26 (requiring freedom from discrimination because of religion).

. . .

Prohibition of torture and cruel, inhuman or degrading treatment or punishment (art. 7)

19. Please comment on the use of electronic control equipment (lasers, stun guns, stun belts etc.) by law enforcement officials. It is reported to the Committee that more than 160 people have died following the use of taser guns by law enforcement personnel since 2001. Please provide information on the results of investigations conducted into these deaths. Please report about current regulations for the use of such electronic equipment by the police and other law enforcement personnel.

Electro-muscular disruption devices (EMDs) have been in use by law enforcement agencies in the United States for many years. Several companies sell EMD-based devices, but Taser International, Inc. now dominates the market. Police agencies have deployed two models from Taser International, Inc., the M26 and X26, in large numbers in recent years. These weapons deliver high-voltage, low amperage electrical pulses to a targeted individual through two wire contacts and induce muscle tetany, thus incapacitating the individual. EMD devices are considered "less-lethal weapons," because they incapacitate without intending to kill the targeted individual. After the deployment of EMD devices, many jurisdictions have seen dramatic drops in injuries and deaths in suspects, officers, and bystanders involved in use-of-force incidents.

...

20. Please report on the compliance with Article 7 of the Covenant of (a) the practice of nontherapeutic research conducted on mentally ill persons or persons with impaired decision-making capacity, including minors, and (b) domestic regulations authorizing the President to waive the prior informed-consent requirement for the administration of an investigational new drug to a member of the U.S. Armed Forces, if the President determines that obtaining consent is not feasible, is contrary to the best interests of the military members, or is not in the interests of U.S. national security. (Periodic report, s. 143 and 480; Previous concluding observations, s. 286 and 300)

The U.S. Government maintains extensive and longstanding programs to protect the rights of welfare on humans involved as subjects in research. The national system oversees all human subjects research conducted or supported by the Federal Government, and all clinical investigations of health care products that require marketing approval from the Food and Drug Administration (FDA) within the U.S. Department of Health and Human Services (HHS). In addition to the Federal Policy for the Protection of Human Research Subjects, informally known as the "Common Rule," which provides basic protections for subjects in all research covered by the regulations, all research conducted or supported by HHS or regulated by HHS/FDA must comply with regulations that provide additional protections for children.

Treatment of persons deprived of liberty (art. 10)

21. What are the conditions of detention and the rights of detainees in federal and state maximum security prisons, in comparison with ordinary prisoners? Please comment on the information that many inmates confined in these prisons do not meet the criteria required to be held in such facilities, and that many of them suffer from mental illness. What measures has the State Party taken to protect inmates in federal or state prisons against rape, abuse or other acts of violence? Please also comment on information of shackling women when giving birth in detention. (Periodic report, s 476; Previous concluding observations, s. 285 and 299)

<u>Maximum Security</u>

The objective of the Bureau of Prisons' Administrative Maximum (ADX) facility, located in Florence, Colorado, is to confine inmates under close controls while providing them opportunities to demonstrate progressively responsible behavior; participate in programs in a safe, secure environment; and establish readiness for transfer to a less secure institution. The BOP ensures, through careful case reviews, that the ADX is used for only those offenders who clearly need the controls available there. As a result, it houses less than one-third of one percent of the BOP's overall inmate population. Since inmates in this facility are considered the most dangerous in the BOP, all general population inmates are restrained at all times when they are in contact with staff. However, the central operating philosophy of this institution is to allow inmates as much unrestrained movement and program access within the institution as possible, consistent with staff and inmate safety.

...

<u>Rape</u>

Let us be clear at the outset: the rape of an inmate is a serious crime in the United States and is vigorously prosecuted. In this regard, the United States has charged 44 defendants with acts of sexual misconduct ranging from inappropriate sexual contact to forcible rape since October 1999. Of these defendants, sixteen were prison officials and the vast majority of the remaining defendants were police officers. (We have also prosecuted other state officials who committed sexual assault under color of law, such as judges and city officials.) Prison rapes within prisons operated by the fifty states are similarly criminal offenses and are prosecuted by the state law enforcement authorities.

<u>Shackling</u>

Regarding the Committee's request for information on shackling women when giving birth in detention, it is not the general policy or practice of the United States Government to shackle female prisoners during childbirth. Although the use of restraints is not prohibited, the Bureau of Prisons does not generally restrain inmates in any manner during labor and delivery. An inmate would be restrained only in the unlikely case that she posed a threat to herself, her baby, or others around her. The determination of whether the shackling of inmates in labor is permissible therefore depends on the facts of each case.

...

22. The Prison Litigation Reform Act of 1995 bars claims based on emotional and psychological mistreatment unless they are accompanied by physical injury. Please explain what the reasons for such restrictions are, and how these restrictions comply with articles 2(3), 7 and 10 of the Covenant.

The Prison Litigation Reform Act of 1995 (PLRA) contains several provisions designed to curtail frivolous lawsuits by prison inmates. One provision is that no federal civil action for damages may be brought by a prisoner for mental or emotional injury suffered while in custody without a prior showing of physical injury. 42 U.S.C. s.1997e(e). This provision is fully compatible with U.S. obligations under the Covenant.

Section 1997e (e) allows a prisoner to bring a federal civil action to redress allegations of torture or cruel, inhuman or degrading treatment or punishment. In this way, it permits redress for activities covered by Article 7 of the Covenant. Although nothing in the Covenant requires the availability of monetary damages as a remedy, a prisoner alleging actual physical injury may seek compensatory, nominal, and punitive damages, and injunctive and declaratory relief.

...

Freedom of association (art. 22)

23. Please explain any restriction imposed on the right to form and join trade unions of, inter alia, agricultural workers, domestic workers, federal, state and local government employees, and immigrant workers, including undocumented workers. Please comment on the information that meatpacking and poultry companies, for example in North Carolina (1996) and Nebraska (2001), have harassed, intimidated, and retaliated against workers—of whom a large proportion are immigrant workers—who have tried to organize, and provide information on measures adopted to combat such practices. In light of the Supreme Court's decision in Hoffman Plastic Compounds, Inc. v. NLRB, please indicate what judicial remedies are made available to undocumented workers in such cases. (Articles 2, 22, 26)

United States law and practice impose no restrictions on the right of individuals to form and join trade unions, including immigrant and undocumented workers, as well as individuals employed as agricultural workers, domestic workers, and federal, state, and local government workers. As indicated in the Second and Third Periodic Reports of the United States, freedom of association is principally protected by the First Amendment of the U.S. Constitution, which has been interpreted by the Supreme Court to include an employee's right to form and join a union without interference from state actors. [See *Thomas v. Collins*, 323 U.S. 516 (1945)]. The First Amendment provides that "Congress shall make no law respecting an establishment of religion, or prohibiting the free exercise thereof; or abridging the freedom of speech, or of the press, or the right of the people peaceably to assemble, and to petition the Government for a redress of grievances."

...

Annex B

Factual Information Related to Human Rights Committee Questions 4 Through 9 Provided on the Basis Described in Paragraph 130 of the U.S. Second and Third Periodic Report

The United States notes and reaffirms paragraph 130 of its Second and Third Periodic Report:

"130. The United States recalls its longstanding position that it has reiterated in paragraph 3 of this report and explained in detail in the legal analysis provided in Annex I; namely, that the obligations assumed by the United States under the Covenant apply only within the territory of the United States. In that regard, the United States respectfully submits that this Committee request for information is outside the purview of the Committee. The United States also notes that the legal status and treatment of such persons is governed by the law of war. Nonetheless, as a courtesy, the United States is providing the Committee pertinent material in the form of an updated Annex to the U.S. report on the Convention Against Torture and Other Cruel, Inhuman or Degrading Treatment or Punishment."

It remains the position of the United States that the questions contained in this Annex fall outside the scope of the Covenant. As a courtesy, the United States directs the Committee to the following information provided to the Committee Against Torture and in other public statements it has made on the issues and questions raised by the Committee.

4. Please indicate in detail how the State Party ensures full respect for the rights enshrined in the Covenant in relation to its actions to combat terrorism (a) in Afghanistan; (b) in Iraq, (c) in any other place outside its territory, and (d) on its own territory, in particular when it holds detainees. In particular, please comment on the allegation that the State party has established secret detention facilities, on U.S.

vessels and aircrafts as well as outside the U.S., and that is has not acknowledged all detentions of individuals captured within the framework of counter-terrorism activities. How would such practices comply with the Covenant, in particular with articles 7, 9 and 10?

While the United States reiterates paragraph 130 of its second and third periodic report that the terms of the Covenant apply exclusively within the territory of the United States and that U.S. military operations in Iraq and Afghanistan are outside the scope of the Covenant, the United States also notes the exceptional breadth of the question (i.e., requesting a description "in detail" about how U.S. operations in two different theaters of combat would implement twenty seven operative articles of the Covenant).

The United States has made available to the Committee extensive detailed information provided to the United Nations Committee Against Torture on the treatment of detainees in its military operations in Iraq, Afghanistan, and Guantánamo Bay, Cuba. In addition to the October 2005 Annex to the U.S. report on its implementation of the Convention Against Torture, the United States has provided electronically to the Committee the United States Government's written responses to the questions of the Committee Against Torture, the opening statement by State Department Assistant Secretary Barry Lowenkron, the opening remarks by State Department Legal Adviser John B. Bellinger, the responses to questions from the Committee Against Torture delivered May 5, 2006, the responses to questions from the Committee Against Torture delivered May 8, 2006 and the U.S. delegation departure statement. Comments of the U.S. delegation during the May 2006 U.S. appearance before the Committee Against Torture include information about the U.S combat against terrorism.

...

U.S. officials from all government agencies are prohibited from engaging in torture, at all times, and in all places. All U.S. officials, wherever they may be, are also prohibited by statute from engaging in cruel, inhuman or degrading treatment or punishment against any person in U.S. custody, as defined by our obligations under the Convention Against Torture. Despite these prohibitions and mechanisms for enforcing them, some individuals have committed abuses against detainees being held in the course of our current armed conflict in Iraq and against Al Qaida and its affiliates. The United States Government deplores those abuses. The United States investigates all allegations of abuse vigorously and when they are substantiated, holds accountable the perpetrators. These processes are all ongoing.

With respect to the request for U.S. "comment on the allegation that the State party has established secret detention facilities, on U.S. vessels and aircraft as well as outside the U.S., and that it is has not acknowledged all detentions of individuals captured within the framework of counter-terrorism activities", as it informed the Committee Against Torture: "The United States, like other countries, does not to comment on allegations of intelligence activities."

...

5. Please provide updated information on the identity, place of origin, place of deprivation of liberty and number of persons held in Guantánamo as well as information on the release of such persons and the date of their release, where applicable. Please provide also information on the status of proceedings of cases where detainees have challenged their detention and their legal status before a U.S. federal court, and on the outcome of such challenges. Please report on the significance of Section 1005 of the Detainee Treatment Act of 2005 in this regard, and on its impact on challenges already made by Guantánamo detainees. What are the guarantees ensuring the independence of Combatant Status Review Tribunals (CSRTs) and Administrative Review Boards (ARBs) from the executive branch and the army, and how are the restrictions on the rights of detainees to have access to all proceedings and evidence justified? Please also report on the number of Guantánamo detainees who have been or are still on hunger strikes, and provide information on the methods used and the reasons justifying force-feeding. (Periodic report, s. 173; CAT/C/48/Add.3/Rev.l, Annexes, Parts, s. 29–43 and 55–62)

For further information, the United States refers the Committee to the information the United States provided at its meeting with the Committee Against Torture in May 2006.

As the United States informed the Committee Against Torture:

"With respect to persons under the control of the United States Department of Defense (DoD), detainees are accounted for fully as required under DoD policies. Detainees under the control of the Department of Defense are issued an internment serial number, or "ISN," as soon as practicable, normally within 14 days of capture.

"Because of operational security considerations, public disclosure of transfers or releases from DoD control are not announced publicly until the movement of detainees from DoD control is completed. The U.S.

government will not transfer an individual to a country where it is more likely than not that the individual will be tortured.

"As of February 20, 2006, the Department of Defense holds approximately 490 detainees at its facilities in Guantánamo Bay, Cuba; approximately 400 detainees at its facilities in Afghanistan; and approximately 14,000 detainees at its facilities in Iraq.

...

6. Please provide more information on the extent to which the 2001 Presidential Military Order, which authorizes the trial of non U.S. citizens suspected of terrorism before military commissions, complies with the Covenant. Please indicate how proceedings before these commissions ensure due process, and guarantee that evidence obtained via torture or ill-treatment shall not be used. Please comment also on how restrictions to the right to appeal sentences are compatible with the Covenant, (articles 2, 6, 7, 14 and 26) (CAT/C/48/Add.3/Rev.l, Annexes, Part I, s. 48–54)

In June of 2006, in the case *Hamdan v. Rumsfeld (548 U.S.(no. 05-184)(2006))*, the U.S. Supreme Court ruled that the military commissions established pursuant to the President's Military Order of November 13, 2001 would violate existing U.S. law. All military commission activity under that order has, consequently, ceased. The U.S. Government is carefully reviewing the Court's opinion in that case in order to determine how to proceed.

...

7. Please report on interrogation techniques authorized or practised in Guantánamo, Afghanistan, Iraq, or other places of detention under U.S. control or by U.S. agents outside the U.S., including non-military services or contract employees. Has the State party authorized, and does it still authorise, the use of techniques such as stress positions, isolation, sensory deprivation, hooding, exposure to cold or heat, sleep and dietary adjustments, 20-hour interrogations, removal of clothing and of all comfort items, forced shaving, removal of religious items, use of dogs to instill fear and mock-drowning? If so, please report on the compliance of such techniques with articles 7, 10 and 18 of the Covenant. (CAT/C/48/Add.3/Rev. 1, Annexes, Part I, s. 78–82)

As the United States informed the Committee Against Torture:

"The Detainee Treatment Act of 2005 prohibits cruel, inhuman, and degrading treatment or punishment, as that term is defined by U.S. obligations under Article 16 of the Convention Against Torture, and applies as a matter of statute to protect any persons "in the custody or under the physical control of the United States Government, regardless of nationality or physical location." The Act also provides for uniform interrogation standards that "[n]o person in the custody or under the effective control of the Department of Defense or under detention in a Department of Defense facility shall be subject to any treatment or technique of interrogation not authorized by and listed in the United States Army Field Manual on Intelligence Interrogation." These standards apply to military, DoD civilians, and contract interrogators.

"A revised version of the United States Army Field Manual on Intelligence Interrogation will be released soon. While it would not be appropriate to report on the contents of this document until it is released, the United States can confirm that it will clarify that certain categories of interrogation techniques are prohibited. For example, the revised manual will confirm that waterboarding, which the manual has never authorized, is not authorized.

"As already noted, the United States does not comment publicly on alleged intelligence activities. But, like any other U.S. government agency, any activities of the CIA would be subject to the extraterritorial criminal torture statute and the Detainee Treatment Act's prohibition on cruel, inhuman, or degrading treatment or punishment."

8. Please comment on measures adopted to ensure full implementation of Section 1003 of the Detainee Treatment Act of 2005, including in relation to persons detained by nonmilitary services and contract employees, as well as on remedies available in cases of non-implementation of this provision. Does the State Party believe that there are any circumstances in which methods prohibited by Article 7 of the Covenant may be lawfully used?

Consistent with the provisions of the Detainee Treatment Act of 2005, the Department of Defense will provide the United States Congress with a report as specified under the Act on its implementation.

As the United States informed the Committee Against Torture:

"The prohibitions on torture and on cruel, inhuman or degrading treatment or punishment contained in Section 1003 of the Detainee Treatment Act of 2005 apply to all U.S. officials from all government at all times and in all places. Accordingly, it is clear that the United States does not believe that there are any circumstances in which the methods prohibited by these statutes may lawfully be used. These prohibitions are codified in United States law. All allegations are thoroughly investigated and violations punished."

9. **Please provide information about the independence and impartiality of the official investigations conducted into allegations of torture and ill-treatment by agents of U.S. military and non-military services, or contract employees, in detention facilities in Guantánamo, Afghanistan and Iraq, and into alleged cases of suspicious death in custody in any of these locations. Please also indicate whether the role of all U.S. agencies, including the Central Intelligence Agency, was fully investigated. What made it possible for such acts to occur? Please provide updated information on the results of the criminal investigations on the allegations of torture and ill-treatment by U.S. military or nonmilitary services, or contract employees in the Abu Ghraib prison, as well as on prosecutions launched and sentences passed. Has compensation been granted to the victims? (Articles 6 and 7) (CAT/C/48/Add.3/Rev.l, Annexes, Part I, s. 83-93 and Part II, s. 110-125)**

As the United States informed the Committee Against Torture:

"The Department of Defense has conducted 12 major reviews of its detention operations. These reviews have focused on all aspects of detention operations from the point of capture to theatre level detention facility operations. The investigations were not overseen or directed by DoD officials. Panels were allowed access to all materials and individuals they requested. They were provided any resources for which they asked, including the assignment of more senior personnel when investigations required it. Finally, senior DoD officials did not direct the conclusions drawn by the panels. "All investigations conducted by the Department have been impartial fact-finding reviews of detention operations. The recommendations generated by these investigations have been taken seriously."

...

Extensive additional information relating to investigations conducted with regard to allegations of abuse arising outside the territory of the United States were provided to the Committee Against Torture and are available to the Human Rights Committee. For example, as the United States informed the Committee Against Torture:

"With respect to the question related to investigations of activities of U.S. intelligence agencies, the United States notes that U.S. intelligence activities are also subject to monitoring and oversight. All of the activities of our Central Intelligence Agency are subject to inspection and investigation by the CIA's independent Inspector General and to oversight by the intelligence committees of the United States Congress. The CIA continues to review and, where appropriate, revise its procedures, including training and legal guidance, to ensure that they comply with U.S. Government policies and all applicable legal obligations, including the Convention Against Torture and the Detainee Treatment Act. To this end, the CIA has put new guidelines and procedures in place during the last several years."

[Endnotes Omitted]

DOCUMENT 15C (SERIES)

Full Official Title: Concluding Observations of the Human Rights Committee,

Consideration of Reports Submitted by States Parties under Article 40 Of The Covenant, United States Of America, Second and Third Periodic Reports

Short Title/Acronym/Abbreviation: Concluding Observations of the Human Rights Committee on the U.S. Second and Third Reports.

Type of Document: This is the outcome document of the periodic state report review process, prepared by the Human Rights Committee. It informs the state under review, the U.S., of the Committee's conclusions as an expert body, based on the U.S. reports and written responses submitted, the oral hearing, and information deduced thereat, and possible shadow reports submitted by NGOs.

Subject: How well the U.S. is complying with its legal obligations under the ICCPR, in the opinion of the Human Rights Committee

Official Citation: CCPR/C/USA/CO/3/Rev.1

Date of Document: December 18, 2006

Date of Adoption: Not applicable

Date of General Entry into Force (EIF): Not applicable

Number of States Parties as of this printing: Not applicable

Date of Signature by the United States: Not applicable

Date of Ratification/Accession/Adhesion: Not applicable

Date of Entry into Force as to United States (effective date): Not applicable

Legal Status/Character of the Instrument/Document as to the United States: This is not a legal instrument but an administrative document that is submitted to a state party to inform the state of the conclusions of the Committee on whether the U.S is fulfilling its legal obligations under the ICCPR, which is a legally binding treaty.

Comments: By ratifying the ICCPR, the U.S. agreed under Article 40 to report to the Human Rights Committee on measures they have adopted to give effect to the rights recognized in the Covenant or any progress they have made or obstacles in the enjoyment of those right. Part of this process after the report is submitted is for the State to appear in person before the Committee to discuss issues arising in the report. After the hearing took place the Committee prepared the Outcome Document, 15C, giving its conclusions and recommendations to the U.S. It is up to the state to then decide whether and how to implement these recommendations or contest the conclusions. This not a judicial process. The recommendations are not legally binding but are part of a treaty obligation and should be implemented in good faith, consistent with the U.S. Constitution.

This report should be read along with the three 15-series documents to get an idea of the give and take, between the international community, represented by the Human Rights Committee and the U.S., represented by a Department of State delegation. This process also happens in the other treaty bodies, CERD and CAT.

The reader should consult Documents 15A, 15B and 15D to get the full effect of this process. For the full text of the U.S. report Document 15A see the following website.

Web Address: http://www.state.gov/g/drl/rls/55504.htm, or
http://daccess-dds-ny.un.org/doc/UNDOC/GEN/G06/459/61/PDF/G0645961.pdf ?OpenElement

CONCLUDING OBSERVATIONS OF THE HUMAN RIGHTS COMMITTEE ON THE U.S. SECOND AND THIRD REPORTS (EXCERPTS)

1. The Committee considered the second and third periodic reports of the United States of America (CCPR/C/USA/3) at its 2379th, 2380th and 2381st meetings (CCPR/C/SR.2379–2381), held on 17 and 18 July 2006, and adopted the following concluding observations at its 2395th meeting (CCPR/C/SR.2395), held on 27 July 2006.

A. Introduction

2. The Committee notes the submission of the State party's second and third periodic combined report, which was seven years overdue, as well as the written answers provided in advance. It appreciates the attendance of a delegation composed of experts belonging to various agencies responsible for the implementation of the Covenant, and welcomes their efforts to answer to the Committee's written and oral questions.

3. The Committee regrets that the State party has not integrated into its report information on the implementation of the Covenant with respect to individuals under its jurisdiction and outside its territory. The Committee notes however that the State party has provided additional material "out of courtesy". The Committee further regrets that the State party, invoking grounds of non-applicability of the Covenant or intelligence operations, refused to address certain serious allegations of violations of the rights protected under the Covenant.

4. The Committee regrets that only limited information was provided on the implementation of the Covenant at the State level.

B. Positive aspects

5. The Committee welcomes the Supreme Court's decision in *Hamdan v. Rumsfeld* (2006) establishing the applicability of common Article 3 of the Geneva Conventions of 12 August 1949, which reflects fundamental rights guaranteed by the Covenant in any armed conflict.

6. The Committee welcomes the Supreme Court's decision in *Roper v. Simmons* (2005), which held that the Eighth and Fourteenth Amendments forbid imposition of the death penalty on offenders who were under the age of 18 when their crimes were committed. In this regard, the Committee reiterates the recommendation made in its previous concluding observations, encouraging the State party to withdraw its reservation to Article 6 (5) of the Covenant.

7. The Committee welcomes the Supreme Court's decision in *Atkins v. Virginia* (2002), which held that executions of mentally retarded criminals are cruel and unusual punishments, and encourages the State party

to ensure that persons suffering from severe forms of mental illness not amounting to mental retardation are equally protected.

8. The Committee welcomes the promulgation of the National Detention Standards in 2000, establishing minimum standards for detention facilities holding Department of Homeland Security detainees, and encourages the State party to adopt all measures necessary for their effective enforcement.

9. The Committee welcomes the Supreme Court's decision in *Lawrence et al. v. Texas* (2003), which declared unconstitutional legislation criminalizing homosexual relations between consenting adults.

C. Principal subjects of concern and recommendations

10. The Committee notes with concern the restrictive interpretation made by the State party of its obligations under the Covenant, as a result in particular of (a) its position that the Covenant does not apply with respect to individuals under its jurisdiction but outside its territory, nor in time of war, despite the contrary opinions and established jurisprudence of the Committee and the International Court of Justice; (b) its failure to take fully into consideration its obligation under the Covenant not only to respect, but also to ensure the rights prescribed by the Covenant; and (c) its restrictive approach to some substantive provisions of the Covenant, which is not in conformity with the interpretation made by the Committee before and after the State party's ratification of the Covenant. (Articles 2 and 40)

The State party should review its approach and interpret the Covenant in good faith, in accordance with the ordinary meaning to be given to its terms in their context, including subsequent practice, and in the light of its object and purpose. The State party should in particular (a) acknowledge the applicability of the Covenant with respect to individuals under its jurisdiction but outside its territory, as well as its applicability in time of war; (b) take positive steps, when necessary, to ensure the full implementation of all rights prescribed by the Covenant; and (c) consider in good faith the interpretation of the Covenant provided by the Committee pursuant to its mandate.

11. The Committee expresses its concern about the potentially overbroad reach of the definitions of terrorism under domestic law, in particular under 8 U.S.C. § 1182 (a) (3) (B) and Executive Order 13224 which seem to extend to conduct, e.g. in the context of political dissent, which, although unlawful, should not be understood as constituting terrorism (Articles 17, 19 and 21).

The State party should ensure that its counter-terrorism measures are in full conformity with the Covenant and in particular that the legislation adopted in this context is limited to crimes that would justify being assimilated to terrorism, and the grave consequences associated with it.

12. The Committee is concerned by credible and uncontested information that the State party has seen fit to engage in the practice of detaining people secretly and in secret places for months and years on end, without keeping the International Committee of the Red Cross informed. In such cases, the rights of the families of the detainees are also being violated. The Committee is also concerned that, even when such persons may have their detention acknowledged, they have been held incommunicado for months or years, a practice that violates the rights protected by articles 7 and 9. In general, the Committee is concerned by the fact that people are detained in places where they cannot benefit from the protection of domestic or international law or where that protection is substantially curtailed, a practice that cannot be justified by the stated need to remove them from the battlefield. (Articles 7 and 9)

The State party should immediately cease its practice of secret detention and close all secret detention facilities. It should also grant the International Committee of the Red Cross prompt access to any person detained in connection with an armed conflict. The State party should also ensure that detainees, regardless of their place of detention, always benefit from the full protection of the law.

13. The Committee is concerned with the fact that the State party has authorized for some time the use of enhanced interrogation techniques, such as prolonged stress positions and isolation, sensory deprivation, hooding, exposure to cold or heat, sleep and dietary adjustments, 20-hour interrogations, removal of clothing and deprivation of all comfort and religious items, forced grooming, and exploitation of detainees' individual phobias. Although the Committee welcomes the assurance that, according to the Detainee Treatment Act of 2005, such interrogation techniques are prohibited by the present Army Field Manual on Intelligence Interrogation, the Committee remains concerned that (a) the State party refuses to acknowledge that such techniques, several of which were allegedly applied, either individually or in combination, over a protracted period of time, violate the prohibition contained by Article 7 of the Covenant; (b) no sentence has been pronounced against an officer, employee, member of the Armed Forces, or other agent of the United States Government for using harsh interrogation techniques that had been approved; (c) these interrogation techniques may still be authorized or used by other agencies, including intelligence agencies and "private contrac-

tors"; and (d) the State party has provided no information to the fact that oversight systems of such agencies have been established to ensure compliance with Article 7.

The State party should ensure that any revision of the Army Field Manual only provides for interrogation techniques in conformity with the international understanding of the scope of the prohibition contained in Article 7 of the Covenant; the State party should also ensure that the current interrogation techniques or any revised techniques are binding on all agencies of the United States Government and any others acting on its behalf; the State party should ensure that there are effective means to follow suit against abuses committed by agencies operating outside the military structure and that appropriate sanctions be imposed on its personnel who used or approved the use of the now prohibited techniques; the State party should ensure that the right to reparation of the victims of such practices is respected; and it should inform the Committee of any revisions of the interrogation techniques approved by the Army Field Manual.

14. The Committee notes with concern shortcomings concerning the independence, impartiality and effectiveness of investigations into allegations of torture and cruel, inhuman or degrading treatment or punishment inflicted by United States military and non-military personnel or contract employees, in detention facilities in Guantánamo Bay, Afghanistan, Iraq, and other overseas locations, and to alleged cases of suspicious death in custody in any of these locations.

The Committee regrets that the State party did not provide sufficient information regarding the prosecutions launched, sentences passed (which appear excessively light for offences of such gravity) and reparation granted to the victims. (Articles 6 and 7)

The State party should conduct prompt and independent investigations into all allegations concerning suspicious deaths, torture or cruel, inhuman or degrading treatment or punishment inflicted by its personnel (including commanders) as well as contract employees, in detention facilities in Guantánamo Bay, Afghanistan, Iraq and other overseas locations. The State party should ensure that those responsible are prosecuted and punished in accordance with the gravity of the crime. The State party should adopt all necessary measures to prevent the recurrence of such behaviors, in particular by providing adequate training and clear guidance to its personnel (including commanders) and contract employees, about their respective obligations and responsibilities, in line with Articles 7 and 10 of the Covenant.

During the course of any legal proceedings, the State party should also refrain from relying on evidence obtained by treatment incompatible with Article 7. The Committee wishes to be informed about the measures taken by the State party to ensure the respect of the right to reparation for the victims.

15. The Committee notes with concern that section 1005 (e) of the Detainee Treatment Act bars detainees in Guantánamo Bay from seeking review in case of allegations of ill-treatment or poor conditions of detention. (Articles 7 and 10)

The State party should amend section 1005 of the Detainee Treatment Act so as to allow detainees in Guantánamo Bay to seek review of their treatment or conditions of detention before a court.

16. The Committee notes with concern the State party's restrictive interpretation of Article 7 of the Covenant according to which it understands (a) that the obligation not to subject anyone to treatment prohibited by Article 7 of the Covenant does not include an obligation not to expose them to such treatment by means of transfer, rendition, extradition, expulsion or refoulement; (b) that in any case, it is not under any other obligation not to deport an individual who may undergo cruel, inhumane or degrading treatment or punishment other than torture, as the State party understands the term; and (c) that it is not under any international obligation to respect a nonrefoulement rule in relation to persons it detains outside its territory. It also notes with concern the "more likely than not" standard it uses in non-refoulement procedures. The Committee is concerned that in practice the State party appears to have adopted a policy to send, or to assist in the sending of, suspected terrorists to third countries, either from the United States of America or other States' territories, for purposes of detention and interrogation, without the appropriate safeguards to prevent treatment prohibited by the Covenant. The Committee is moreover concerned by numerous well-publicized and documented allegations that persons sent to third countries in this way were indeed detained and interrogated while receiving treatment grossly violating the prohibition contained in Article 7, allegations that the State party did not contest. Its concern is deepened by the so far successful invocation of State secrecy in cases where the victims of these practices have sought a remedy before the State party's courts (e.g.: the cases of *Maher Arar v. Ashcroft* (2006) and *Khaled Al-Masri v. Tenet* (2006)). (Article 7)

The State party should review its position, in accordance with the Committee's general comments 20 (1992) on Articles 7 and 31 (2004) on the nature of the general legal obligation imposed on States parties. The State party should take all necessary measures to ensure that individuals, including those it detains outside its own territory, are not returned to another country by way of inter alia, their transfer, rendition, extradition, expulsion or refoulement if there are substantial reasons for believing that they would be in danger of being subjected to torture or cruel, inhuman or degrading treatment or punishment. The State party should conduct thorough and independent investigations into the allegations that persons have been sent to third countries where they have undergone torture or cruel, inhuman or degrading treatment or punishment, modify its legislation and policies to ensure that no such situation will recur, and provide appropriate remedy to the victims.

The State party should exercise the utmost care in the use of diplomatic assurances and adopt clear and transparent procedures with adequate judicial mechanisms for review before individuals are deported, as well as effective mechanisms to monitor scrupulously and vigorously the fate of the affected individuals. The State party should further recognize that the more systematic the practice of torture or cruel, inhuman or degrading treatment or punishment, the less likely it will be that a real risk of such treatment can be avoided by such assurances, however stringent any agreed follow-up procedures may be.

17. The Committee is concerned that the Patriot Act and the 2005 REAL ID Act of 2005 may bar from asylum and withholding of removal any person who has provided "material support" to a "terrorist organization", whether voluntarily or under duress. It regrets having received no response on this matter from the State party. (Article 7)

The State party should ensure that the "material support to terrorist organisations" bar is not applied to those who acted under duress.

18. The Committee is concerned that, following the Supreme Court ruling in *Rasul v. Bush* (2004), proceedings before Combatant Status Review Tribunals (CSRTs) and Administrative Review Boards (ARBs), mandated respectively to determine and review the status of detainees, may not offer adequate safeguards of due process, in particular due to : (a) their lack of independence from the executive branch and the army, (b) restrictions on the rights of detainees to have access to all proceedings and evidence, (c) the inevitable difficulty CSRTs and ARBs face in summoning witnesses, and (d) the possibility given to CSRTs and ARBs, under Section 1005 of the 2005 Detainee Treatment Act, to weigh evidence obtained by coercion for its probative value. The Committee is further concerned that detention in other locations, such as Afghanistan and Iraq, is reviewed by mechanisms providing even fewer guarantees. (Article 9)

The State party should ensure, in accordance with Article 9 (4) of the Covenant, that persons detained in Guantánamo Bay are entitled to proceedings before a court to decide, without delay, on the lawfulness of their detention or order their release. Due process, independence of the reviewing courts from the executive branch and the army, access of detainees to counsel of their choice and to all proceedings and evidence, should be guaranteed in this regard.

19. The Committee, having taken into consideration information provided by the State party, is concerned by reports that, following the September 11 attacks, many non-U.S. citizens, suspected to have committed terrorism-related offences have been detained for long periods pursuant to immigration laws with fewer guarantees than in the context of criminal procedures, or on the basis of the Material Witness Statute only. The Committee is also concerned with the compatibility of the Statute with the Covenant since it may be applied for up-coming trials but also to investigations or proposed investigations. (Article 9)

The State party should review its practice with a view to ensuring that the Material Witness Statute and immigration laws are not used so as to detain persons suspected of terrorism or any other criminal offences with fewer guarantees than in criminal proceedings. The State party should also ensure that those improperly so detained receive appropriate reparation.

20. The Committee notes that the decision of the Supreme Court in *Hamdan v. Rumsfeld*, according to which Guantánamo Bay detainees accused of terrorism offences are to be judged by a regularly constituted court affording all the judicial guarantees required by common Article 3 of the Geneva Conventions of 12 August 1949, remains to be implemented. (Article 14)

The State party should provide the Committee with information on its implementation of the decision.

21. The Committee, while noting some positive amendments introduced in 2006, notes that section 213 of the Patriot Act, expanding the possibility of delayed notification of home and office searches; section 215 regarding access to individuals' personal records and belongings; and section 505, relating to the issuance of national security letters, still raise issues of concern in relation to Article 17 of the Covenant. In particular, the Committee is concerned about the restricted possibilities for the concerned persons to be informed about

such measures and to effectively challenge them. Furthermore, the Committee is concerned that the State Party, including through the National Security Agency (NSA), has monitored and still monitors phone, email, and fax communications of individuals both within and outside the U.S., without any judicial or other independent oversight. (Articles 2(3) and 17)

The State party should review sections 213, 215 and 505 of the Patriot Act to ensure full compatibility with Article 17 of the Covenant. The State party should ensure that any infringement on individual's rights to privacy is strictly necessary and duly authorized by law, and that the rights of individuals to follow suit in this regard are respected.

22. The Committee is concerned with reports that some 50 % of homeless people are African American although they constitute only 12 % of the United States population. (Articles 2 and 26)

The State party should take measures, including adequate and adequately implemented policies, to bring an end to such de facto and historically generated racial discrimination.

23. The Committee notes with concern reports of de facto racial segregation in public schools, reportedly caused by discrepancies between the racial and ethnic composition of large urban districts and their surrounding suburbs, and the manner in which schools districts are created, funded and regulated. The Committee is concerned that the State party, despite measures adopted, has not succeeded in eliminating racial discrimination such as regarding the wide disparities in the quality of education across school districts in metropolitan areas, to the detriment of minority students. It also notes with concern the State party's position that federal government authorities cannot take legal action if there is no indication of discriminatory intent by state or local authorities. (Articles 2 and 26)

The Committee reminds the State party of its obligation under articles 2 and 26 of the Covenant to respect and ensure that all individuals are guaranteed effective protection against practices that have either the purpose or the effect of discrimination on a racial basis. The State party should conduct in-depth investigations into the de facto segregation described above and take remedial steps, in consultation with the affected communities.

24. The Committee, while welcoming the mandate given to the Attorney General to review the use by federal enforcement authorities of race as a factor in conducting stops, searches, and other enforcement procedures, and the prohibition of racial profiling made in guidance to federal law enforcement officials, remains concerned about information that such practices still persist in the State party, in particular at the state level. It also notes with concern information about racial disparities and discrimination in prosecuting and sentencing processes in the criminal justice system. (Articles 2 and 26)

The State party should continue and intensify its efforts to put an end to racial profiling used by federal as well as state law enforcement officials. The Committee wishes to receive more detailed information about the extent to which such practices still persist, as well as statistical data on complaints, prosecutions and sentences in such matters.

25. The Committee notes with concern allegations of widespread incidence of violent crime perpetrated against persons of minority sexual orientation, including by law enforcement officials. It notes with concern the failure to address such crime in the legislation on hate crime adopted at the federal level and in many states. It notes with concern the failure to outlaw employment discrimination on the basis of sexual orientation in many states. (Articles 2 and 26)

The State party should acknowledge its legal obligation under articles 2 and 26 to ensure to everyone the rights recognized by the Covenant, as well as equality before the law and equal protection of the law, without discrimination on the basis of sexual orientation. The State party should ensure that its hate crime legislation, both at the federal and state levels, address sexual orientation-related violence and that federal and state employment legislation outlaw discrimination on the basis of sexual orientation.

26. The Committee, while taking note of the various rules and regulations prohibiting discrimination in the provision of disaster relief and emergency assistance, remains concerned about information that the poor, and in particular African-Americans, were disadvantaged by the rescue and evacuation plans implemented when Hurricane Katrina hit the United States, and continue to be disadvantaged under the reconstruction plans. (Articles 6 and 26)

The State party should review its practices and policies to ensure the full implementation of its obligation to protect life and of the prohibition of discrimination, whether direct or indirect, as well as of the United Nations Guiding Principles on Internal Displacement, in matters related to disaster prevention and preparedness, emergency assistance and relief measures. In the aftermath of Hurricane Katrina, the State party should increase its efforts to ensure that the rights of the poor, and in particular

African-Americans, are fully taken into consideration in the reconstruction plans with regard to access to housing, education and healthcare. The Committee wishes to be informed about the results of the inquiries into the alleged failure to evacuate prisoners at the Parish prison, as well as the allegations that New Orleans residents were not permitted by law enforcement officials to cross the Greater New Orleans Bridge to Gretna, Louisiana.

27. The Committee regrets that it has not received sufficient information on the measures the State party considers adopting in relation to the reportedly nine million undocumented migrants now in the United States. While noting the information provided by the delegation that National Guard troops will not engage in direct law enforcement duties in the apprehension or detention of aliens, the Committee remains concerned about the increased level of militarization on the southwest border with Mexico. (Articles 12 and 26)

The State party should provide the Committee with more detailed information on these issues, in particular on the concrete measures adopted to ensure that only agents who have received adequate training on immigration issues enforce immigration laws, which should be compatible with the rights guaranteed by the Covenant.

28. The Committee regrets that many federal laws which address sex-discrimination are limited in scope and restricted in implementation. The Committee is especially concerned about the reported persistence of employment discrimination against women. (Articles 3 and 26)

The State party should take all steps necessary, including at state level, to ensure the equality of women before the law and equal protection of the law, as well as effective protection against discrimination on the ground of sex, in particular in the area of employment.

29. The Committee regrets that the State party does not indicate that it has taken any steps to review federal and state legislation with a view to assessing whether offences carrying the death penalty are restricted to the most serious crimes, and that, despite the Committee's previous concluding observations, the State party has extended the number of offences for which the death penalty is applicable. While taking note of some efforts towards the improvement of the quality of legal representation provided to indigent defendants facing capital punishment, the Committee remains concerned by studies according to which the death penalty may be imposed disproportionately on ethnic minorities as well as on low-income groups, a problem which does not seem to be fully acknowledged by the State party. (Articles 6 and 14)

The State party should review federal and state legislation with a view to restricting the number of offences carrying the death penalty. The State party should also assess the extent to which death penalty is disproportionately imposed on ethnic minorities and on low-income population groups, as well as the reasons for this, and adopt all appropriate measures to address the problem. In the meantime, the State party should place a moratorium on capital sentences, bearing in mind the desirability of abolishing death penalty.

30. The Committee reiterates its concern about reports of police brutality and excessive use of force by law enforcement officials. The Committee is concerned in particular by the use of so-called less lethal restraint devices, such as electro-muscular disruption devices (EMDs), in situations where lethal or other serious force would not otherwise have been used. It is concerned about information according to which police have used tasers against unruly schoolchildren; mentally disabled or intoxicated individuals involved in disturbed but non-life threatening behaviour; elderly people; pregnant women; unarmed suspects fleeing minor crime scenes and people who argue with officers or simply fail to comply with police commands, without in most cases the responsible officers being found to have violated their departments' policies. (Articles 6 and 7)

The State party should increase significantly its efforts towards the elimination of police brutality and excessive use of force by law enforcement officials. The State party should ensure that EMDs and other restraint devices are only used in situations where greater or lethal force would otherwise have been justified, and in particular that they are never used against vulnerable persons. The State party should bring its policies into line with the United Nations Basic Principles on the Use of Force and Firearms by Law Enforcement Officials.

31. The Committee notes that (a) waivers of consent in research regulated by the U.S Department of Health and Human Services and the Food and Drug Administration may be given in case of individual and national emergencies; (b) some research may be conducted on persons vulnerable to coercion or undue influence such as children, prisoners, pregnant women, mentally disabled persons, or economically disadvantaged persons; (c) non-therapeutic research may be conducted on mentally ill persons or persons with impaired decision-making capacity, including minors; and (d) although no waivers have been given so far, domestic

law authorizes the President to waive the prior informed-consent requirement for the administration of an investigational new drug to a member of the U.S. Armed Forces, if the President determines that obtaining consent is not feasible, is contrary to the best interests of the military members, or is not in the interests of U.S. national security. (Article 7)

The State party should ensure that it meets its obligation under Article 7 of the Covenant not to subject anyone without his/her free consent to medical or scientific experimentation. The Committee recalls in this regard the non-derogable character of this obligation under Article 4 of the Covenant. When there is doubt as to the ability of a person or a category of persons to give such consent, e.g. prisoners, the only experimental treatment compatible with Article 7 would be treatment chosen as the most appropriate to meet the medical needs of the individual.

32. The Committee reiterates its concern that conditions in some maximum security prisons are incompatible with the obligation contained in Article 10 (1) of the Covenant to treat detainees with humanity and respect for the inherent dignity of the human person. It is particularly concerned by the practice in some such institutions to hold detainees in prolonged cellular confinement, and to allow them out-of-cell recreation for only five hours per week, in general conditions of strict regimentation in a depersonalized environment. It is also concerned that such treatment cannot be reconciled with the requirement in Article 10 (3) that the penitentiary system shall comprise treatment the essential aim of which shall be the reformation and social rehabilitation of prisoners. It also expresses concern about the reported high numbers of severely mentally ill persons in these prisons, as well as in regular in U.S. jails.

The State party should scrutinize conditions of detention in prisons, in particular in maximum security prisons, with a view to guaranteeing that persons deprived of their liberty be treated in accordance with the requirements of Article 10 of the Covenant and the United Nations Standard Minimum Rules for the Treatment of Prisoners.

33. The Committee, while welcoming the adoption of the Prison Rape Elimination Act of 2003, regrets that the State party has not implemented its previous recommendation that legislation allowing male officers access to women's quarters should be amended to provide at least that they will always be accompanied by women officers. The Committee also expresses concern about the shackling of detained women during childbirth. (Articles 7 and 10)

The Committee reiterates its recommendation that male officers should not be granted access to women's quarters, or at least be accompanied by women officers.

The Committee also recommends the State party to prohibit the shackling of detained women during childbirth.

34. The Committee notes with concern reports that forty-two states and the Federal Government have laws allowing persons under the age of eighteen at the time the offence was committed, to receive life sentences, without parole, and that about 2,225 youth offenders are currently serving life sentences in United States prisons. The Committee, while noting the State party's reservation to treat juveniles as adults in exceptional circumstances notwithstanding Articles 10 (2) (b) and (3) and 14 (4) of the Covenant, remains concerned by information that treatment of children as adults is not only applied in exceptional circumstances. The Committee is of the view that sentencing children to life sentence without parole is of itself not in compliance with Article 24 (1) of the Covenant. (Articles 7 and 24)

The State party should ensure that no such child offender is sentenced to life imprisonment without parole, and should adopt all appropriate measures to review the situation of persons already serving such sentences.

35. The Committee is concerned that about five million citizens cannot vote due to a felony conviction, and that this practice has significant racial implications. The Committee also notes with concern that the recommendation made in 2001 by the National Commission on Federal Election Reform that all states restore voting rights to citizens who have fully served their sentences has not been endorsed by all states. The Committee is of the view that general deprivation of the right vote for persons who have received a felony conviction, and in particular those who are no longer deprived of liberty, do not meet the requirements of Articles 25 of 26 of the Covenant, nor serves the rehabilitation goals of Article 10 (3).

The State party should adopt appropriate measures to ensure that states restore voting rights to citizens who have fully served their sentences and those who have been released on parole. The Committee also recommends that the State party review regulations relating to deprivation of votes for felony conviction to ensure that they always meet the reasonableness test of Article 25. The State party should

also assess the extent to which such regulations disproportionately impact on the rights of minority groups and provide the Committee with detailed information in this regard.

36. The Committee, having taken note of the responses provided by the delegation, remains concerned that residents of the District of Columbia do not enjoy full representation in Congress, a restriction which does not seem to be compatible with Article 25 of the Covenant. (Articles 2, 25 and 26)

The State party should ensure the right of residents of the District of Columbia to take part in the conduct of public affairs, directly or through freely chosen representatives, in particular with regard to the House of Representatives.

37. The Committee notes with concern that no action has been taken by the State party to address its previous recommendation relating to the extinguishment of aboriginal and indigenous rights. The Committee, while noting that the guarantees provided by the Fifth Amendment apply to the taking of land in situations where treaties concluded between the Federal Government and Indian tribes apply, is concerned that in other situations, in particular where land was assigned by creating a reservation or is held by reason of long possession and use, tribal property rights can be extinguished on the basis of the plenary authority of Congress for conducting Indian affairs without due process and fair compensation. The Committee is also concerned that the concept of permanent trusteeship over the Indian and Alaska native tribes and their land as well as the actual exercise of this trusteeship in managing the so called Individual Indian Money (IIM) accounts may infringe upon the full enjoyment of their rights under the Covenant. Finally, the Committee regrets that it has not received sufficient information on the consequences on the situation of Indigenous Native Hawaiians of Public Law 103-150 apologizing to the Native Hawaiians Peoples for the illegal overthrow of the Kingdom of Hawaii, which resulted in the suppression of the inherent sovereignty of the Hawaiian people. (Articles 1, 26 and 27 in conjunction with Article 2, paragraph 3 of the Covenant).

The State party should review its policy towards indigenous peoples as regards the extinguishment of aboriginal rights on the basis of the plenary power of Congress regarding Indian affairs and grant them the same degree of judicial protection that is available to the non-indigenous population. The State party should take further steps to secure the rights of all indigenous peoples, under Articles 1 and 27 of the Covenant, so as to give them greater influence in decision-making affecting their natural environment and their means of subsistence as well as their own culture.

38. The Committee sets 1st August 2010 as the date for the submission of the fourth periodic report of the United States of America. It requests that the State party's second and third periodic reports and the present concluding observations be published and widely disseminated in the State party, to the general public as well as to the judicial, legislative and administrative authorities, and that the fourth periodic report be circulated for the attention of the nongovernmental organizations operating in the country.

39. In accordance with rule 71, paragraph 5, of the Committee's rules of procedure, the State party should submit within one year information on the follow-up given to the Committee's recommendations in paragraphs 12, 13, 14, 16, 20 and 26 above. The Committee requests the State party to include in its next periodic report information on its remaining recommendations and on the implementation of the Covenant as a whole, as well as about the practical implementation of the Covenant, the difficulties encountered in this regard, and the implementation of the Covenant at state level. The State party is also encouraged to provide more detailed information on the adoption of effective mechanisms to ensure that new and existing legislation, at federal and at state level, is in compliance with the Covenant, and about mechanisms adopted to ensure proper follow-up of the Committee's concluding observations.

DOCUMENT 15D (SERIES)

Full Official Title: Consideration Of Reports Submitted By States Parties Under Article 40 Of The Covenant, United States Of America, Addendum, Comments by the Government of the United States of America on the Concluding Observations of the Human Rights Committee

Short Title/Acronym/Abbreviation: U.S. follow up Comments to the Human Rights Committee on its Concluding Observations, Second and Third Reports.

Type of Document: This is the U.S written communication to the Human Rights Committee regarding the response of the U.S. to the Committee's conclusions and recommendations, Document 15C.

Subject: U.S. response disagreeing with Human Rights Committee's conclusions and recommendations on Second and Third Reports.

Official Citation: CCPR/C/USA/CO/3/Rev.1/Add.1

Date of Document: February 12, 2008

Date of Adoption: Not applicable

Date of General Entry into Force (EIF): Not applicable

Number of States Parties as of this printing: Not applicable

Date of Signature by the United States: Not applicable

Date of Ratification/Accession/Adhesion: Not applicable

Date of Entry into Force as to United States (effective date): Not applicable

Legal Status/Character of the Instrument/Document as to the United States: This is not a legal instrument but an administrative document that is submitted by a state party to a treaty body, the Human Rights Committee, to inform the body of its response to the conclusions of the Committee on its compliance with the ICCPR.

Comments: By ratifying the ICCPR the U.S. agreed under Article 40 to report to the Human Rights Committee on measures they have adopted to give effect to the rights recognized in the Covenant or any progress they have made or obstacles in the enjoyment of those right. Part of this process after the report is submitted is for the State to appear in person before the Committee to discuss issues arising in the report. After the hearing took place the Committee prepared the Outcome Document, 15C, giving its conclusions and recommendations to the U.S. It is up to the state to then decide whether and how to implement these recommendations or contest the conclusions. This is a statement, "comments", by the U.S contesting some of the conclusions and recommendations by the Committee. This is not a judicial process. The recommendations are not legally binding but are part of a treaty obligation and should be implemented in good faith, consistent with the U.S. Constitution.

This report should be read along with the three 15-series documents to get an idea of the give and take, back and forth, between the international community, represented by the Human Rights Committee and the U.S., represented by a Department of State delegation. This process also happens in the other treaty bodies, CERD and CAT.

For the full text of this Document 15D, see the following website:

Web Address: http://daccess-dds-ny.un.org/doc/UNDOC/GEN/G08/404/60/ PDF/G0840460. pdf? OpenElement

U.S. FOLLOW UP COMMENTS TO THE HUMAN RIGHTS COMMITTEE ON ITS CONCLUDING OBSERVATIONS, SECOND AND THIRD REPORTS (EXCERPTS)

United States Responses to Selected Recommendations of the Human Rights Committee October 10, 2007

In its concluding observations of the second and third periodic reports of the United States of America, the Human Rights Committee requested that the United States provide, within one year, information pertaining to selected recommendations.[1] These specific recommendations and the United States' responses to them are provided below.

Scope of Application of the Covenant

As a preliminary matter, the United States notes that most of the Committee's requests for information on follow-up to its recommendations concern matters outside of the territory of the United States. These matters relate to "secret detention" (para. 12), "interrogation techniques" (para. 13), investigations into allegations of abuse (para. 14), "transfer, rendition, extradition, expulsion or refoulement" of detainees "in facilities outside [United States] territory" (para. 16), and the applicability of Common Article 3 of the Geneva Conventions (para. 20).

The United States takes this opportunity to reaffirm its long-standing position that the Covenant does not apply extraterritorially. States Parties are required to ensure the rights in the Covenant only to individuals who are (1) within the territory of a State Party and (2) subject to that State Party's jurisdiction. The United States Government's position on this matter is supported by the plain text of Article 2 of the Covenant and is confirmed in the Covenant's negotiating history (*travaux preparatoires*). Since the time that U.S. delegate Eleanor Roosevelt successfully proposed the language that was adopted as part of Article 2 providing that the Covenant does not apply outside the territory of a State Party, the United States has interpreted the treaty in that manner.[2]

The views of the United States on this matter were described at length in Annex 1 of the U.S. report to the Committee and were discussed at length during the U.S. presentation of its report in July 2006.

Accordingly, the United States respectfully disagrees with the view of the Committee that the Covenant applies extraterritorially. Nevertheless, as a courtesy, the United States provides herein additional information on the topics requested by the Committee, including information on matters outside the scope of the Covenant.

Paragraph 12 Recommendation:

"The State party should immediately cease its practice of secret detention and close all secret detention facilities. It should also grant the International Committee of the Red Cross prompt access to any person detained in connection with an armed conflict. The State party should also ensure that detainees, regardless of their place of detention, always benefit from the full protection of the law."

Response:

The United States is engaged in an armed conflict with al Qaida, the Taliban, and their supporters. As part of this conflict, the United States captures and detains enemy combatants, and is entitled under the law of war to hold them until the end of hostilities. The law of war, and not the Covenant, is the applicable legal framework governing these detentions.

In certain rare cases, the United States moves enemy combatants to secret locations. As the President of the United States stated in a September 6, 2006 speech, "Questioning the detainees in this program has given us information that has saved innocent lives by helping us stop new attacks —here in the United States and across the world." Under the law of war there is no legal obligation for the United States to provide ICRC notice and access to these enemy combatants who are held during the ongoing armed conflict with al Qaida, the Taliban, and their supporters.

All of the detainees who were in this secret interrogation program as of September 6, 2006, were moved to the Department of Defense detention facility at Guantánamo Bay. The ICRC has been notified and has access to these detainees, as they have to all detainees at Guantánamo. Moving forward, as the President of the United States explained, "[a]s more high-ranking terrorists are captured, the need to obtain intelligence from them will remain critical—and having a CIA program for questioning terrorists will continue to be crucial to getting life-saving information."

Paragraph 13 Recommendation:

"The State party should ensure that any revision of the Army Field Manual only provides for interrogation techniques in conformity with the international understanding of the scope of the prohibition contained in Article 7 of the Covenant; the State party should also ensure that the current interrogation techniques or any revised techniques are binding on all agencies of the United States Government and any others acting on its behalf; the State party should ensure that there are effective means to follow suit against abuses committed by agencies operating outside the military structure and that appropriate sanctions be imposed on its personnel who used or approved the use of the now prohibited techniques; the State party should ensure that the right to reparation of now prohibited techniques; the State party should ensure that the right to reparation of now prohibited techniques; the State party should ensure that the right to reparation of the victims of such practices is respected; and it should inform the Committee of any revisions of the interrogation techniques approved by the Army Field Manual."

Response:

As noted elsewhere in this submission, the United States is engaged in an armed conflict with al Qaida, the Taliban, and their supporters. As part of this conflict, the United States captures and detains enemy combatants, and is entitled under the law of war to hold them until the end of hostilities. The law of war, and not the Covenant, is the applicable legal framework governing these detentions. There are, of course, many analogous protections under the law of war, which the United States fully respects.

For instance, international humanitarian law prohibits torture of detainees in international or non-international armed conflict. Consistent with international humanitarian law, there is a statutory prohibition in U.S. criminal law against the torture of anyone in the custody or under the physical control of the United States Government outside the territory of the United States. In addition, cruel, inhuman, and degrading treatment or punishment of anyone in the custody or under the physical control of the United States Government is prohibited both within and outside of the territory of the United States. All detainee interrogations are conducted in a manner consistent with these prohibitions, as well with Common Article 3 of the Geneva Conventions.

In September 2006, following the U.S. presentation of its report to the Committee, the Department of Defense released the updated detainee program Directive 2310.01e ("The Department of Defense Detainee Program") and the Army released its revised Field Manual on interrogation. These documents are attached in Annexes 1 and 2, respectively. They provide guidance to military personnel to ensure compliance with the law, including Common Article 3 of the Geneva Conventions. For instance, the revised Army Field Manual states that "[a]ll captured or detained personnel, regardless of status, shall be treated humanely, and in accordance with the Detainee Treatment Act of 2005 and DOD Directive 2310.1E … and no person in the custody or under the control of DOD, regardless of nationality or physical location, shall be subject to torture or cruel, inhuman, or degrading treatment or punishment, in accordance with and as defined in U.S. law." The Field Manual also provides specific guidance, including a non-exclusive list of actions—such as "waterboarding" and placing a hood or sack over the head of a detainee, among others—that are prohibited when used in conjunction with interrogations. Finally, the Field Manual provides guidance to be used while formulating interrogation plans for approval. For example, the Field Manual states:

"In attempting to determine if a contemplated approach or technique should be considered prohibited … consider these two tests before submitting the plan for approval:

• If the proposed approach technique were used by the enemy against one of your fellow soldiers, would you believe the soldier had been abused?

• Could your conduct in carrying out the proposed technique violate a law or regulation? Keep in mind that even if you personally would not consider your actions to constitute abuse, the law may be more restrictive.

If you answer yes to either of these tests, the contemplated action should not be conducted." We would also note that U.S. law provides several avenues for the domestic prosecution of United States Government officials and contractors who commit torture and other serious crimes overseas. For example, section 2340A of title 18 of the United States Code authorizes the prosecution of any U.S. national who commits torture outside of the United States, while section 2441 does the same for serious violations of Common Article 3. Similarly, under the provisions of the Military Extraterritorial Jurisdiction Act ("MEJA"), persons employed by or accompanying the Armed Forces outside the United States may be prosecuted domestically if they commit a serious criminal offense overseas. MEJA specifically covers all civilian employees and contractors directly employed by the Department of Defense and, as amended in October 2004, also those employed by other United States Government agencies, to the extent that such employment relates to supporting the mission of the Department of Defense overseas.

In addition, U.S. nationals who are not currently covered by MEJA are still subject to domestic prosecution for certain serious crimes committed overseas if the crime was committed within the special maritime and territorial jurisdiction of the United States defined in section 7 of title 18 (e.g., U.S. diplomatic and military missions overseas).

These crimes include murder under section 1111 of title 18, assault under section 113, and sexual abuse under section 2241. Finally, in 2006 the Uniform Code of Military Justice ("UCMJ") was amended so that it now includes within its scope of application, "[i]n time of declared war or a contingency operation, persons serving with or accompanying an armed force in the field." This amendment broadens the coverage of the UCMJ to provide court-martial jurisdiction over these individuals not only during conflicts where the United States has issued a declaration of war, but also during certain other significant military operations.

Notes

1 *See* Human Rights Committee, Concluding Observations of the Human Rights Committee — United States of America. Doc. No. CCPR/C/USA/CO/3/Rev.1 at para. 39 (Dec. 18, 2006).

2 *See e.g.*, Statement by Eleanor Roosevelt, *Summary Record of the Hundred and Thirty-Eighth Meeting*, U.N. ESCOR Hum. Rts. Comm., 6th Sess., 138th mtg at 10, U.N. Doc. E/CN.4/SR.138 (1950). This interpretation was also conveyed to the Human Rights Committee in 1995 by Conrad Harper, the Legal Adviser of the U.S. Department of State. In response to a question posed by the Committee, Mr. Harper stated that "Article 2 of the Covenant expressly stated that each State Party undertook to respect and ensure the rights recognized 'to all individuals within its territory and subject to its jurisdiction.' That dual requirement restricted the scope of the Covenant to persons under United States jurisdiction and within United States territory. During the negotiating history, the words 'within its territory' had been debated and were added by vote, with the clear understanding that such wording would limit the obligations to within a Party's territory. Summary record of the 1405th meeting: United States of America, U.N. ESCOR Hum. Rts. Comm., 53rd Sess., 1504th mtg. at ¶¶ 7, 20, U.N. Doc. CCPR/C/SR 1405 (1995).

[All remaining footnotes omitted]

Paragraph 14 Recommendation:

"The State party should conduct prompt and independent investigations into all allegations concerning suspicious deaths, torture or cruel, inhuman or degrading treatment or punishment inflicted by its personnel (including commanders) as well as contract employees, in detention facilities in Guantánamo Bay, Afghanistan, Iraq and other overseas locations. The State party should ensure that those responsible are prosecuted and punished in accordance with the gravity of the crime. The State party should adopt all necessary measures to prevent the recurrence of such behaviors, in particular by providing adequate training and clear guidance to its personnel (including commanders) and contract employees, about their respective obligations and responsibilities, in line with Articles 7 and 10 of the Covenant. During the course of any legal proceedings, the State party should also refrain from relying on evidence obtained by treatment incompatible with Article 7. The Committee wishes to be informed about the measures taken by the State party to ensure the respect of the right to reparation for the victims."

Response:

As noted elsewhere in this submission, as a matter of application of the Covenant, the United States is engaged in an armed conflict with al Qaida, the Taliban, and their supporters. As part of this conflict, the United States captures and detains enemy combatants, and is entitled under the law of war to hold them until the end of hostilities. The law of war, and not the Covenant, is the applicable legal framework governing these detentions. In addition, because Guantánamo Bay is not within the territory of the United States, U.S. obligations under the Covenant do not apply there. Although the Covenant as such does not apply to U.S. activities outside of its territory, the United States does not permit its personnel to engage in acts of torture or cruel, inhuman or degrading treatment of people in its custody either within or outside U.S. territory and takes vigilant action to prevent such conduct and to hold any such perpetrators accountable for their wrongful acts.

U.S. personnel engaged in detention operations are required to comply with U.S. domestic law, the law of war, and applicable international treaty obligations. Cruel, inhuman and degrading treatment or punishment by all U.S. personnel in all locations is prohibited under United States law. We recognize that there have been violations of the law by U.S. personnel. But those who failed to adhere to these treatment standards have been, and will continue to be, held accountable. As described in the U.S. report and in its answers to the Committee's questions during its July 2006 appearance before the Committee, the United States takes proactive measures not only to punish perpetrators of abuse but to train its personnel to prevent such acts, in particular by providing adequate training and clear guidance to its personnel (including commanders) and contract employees, about their respective obligations and responsibilities.

Education programs and information for military personnel (including contractors) that are involved in the custody, interrogation or treatment of individuals in detention include extensive training on the law of war. This training is provided on an annual basis (or more frequently, as appropriate) for the members of every military service and every person, including contractors, who works with detainees. This training on the law of war includes instruction on the prohibition against torture and the requirement of humane treatment.

The United States submitted a lengthy annex with information about actions taken with regard to Defense Department personnel who were accused of abusing detainees in their custody and provided additional factual information during its July 2006 discussions with the Committee.

In accordance with the National Defense Authorization Act, the Department of Defense is required to report to the U.S. Congress certain statistics regarding detainee abuse cases and their final disposition. During the most recent reporting period (June 2005 through September 30, 2006), the Department reported that there were 92 new cases of alleged detainee abuse that were determined to be founded on the basis of the evidence developed during the initial investigation. Of these 92 cases: 16 were referred for further investigation and 55 were closed. In the remaining cases there were 24 courts martial, 21 non-judicial punishments, 12 reprimands, and three administrative discharges.

The Department of Defense continues to take seriously allegations of abuse and will, according to U.S. law and regulation, hold individuals accountable for violations of the law. As noted above, the Department promulgated, on September 5, 2006, a Department-wide directive that prescribes the minimum care and treatment requirements applicable to all detainees under the Department's control as well as provisions for the reporting of violations of Department standards and policies as well as U.S. law (Annex 1).

Paragraph 16 Recommendation:

"The State party should review its position, in accordance with the Committee's general comments 20 (1992) on Article 7 and 31 (2004) on the nature of the general legal obligation imposed on States parties. The State party should take all necessary measures to ensure that individuals, including those it detains outside its own territory, are not returned to another country by way of inter alia, their transfer, rendition, extradition, expulsion or refoulement if there are substantial reasons for believing that they would be in danger of being subjected to torture or cruel, inhuman or degrading treatment or punishment. The State party should conduct thorough and independent investigations into the allegations that persons have been sent to third countries where they have undergone torture or cruel, inhuman or degrading treatment or punishment, modify its legislation and policies to ensure that no such situation will recur, and provide appropriate remedy to the victims. The State party should exercise the utmost care in the use of diplomatic assurances and adopt clear and transparent procedures with adequate judicial mechanisms for review before individuals are deported, as well as effective mechanisms to monitor scrupulously and vigorously the fate of the affected individuals. The State party should further recognize that the more systematic the practice of torture or cruel, inhuman or degrading treatment or punishment, the less likely it will be that a real risk of such treatment can be avoided by such assurances, however stringent any agreed follow-up procedures may be."

Response:

The United States does not transfer or return persons to countries where it determines that it is more likely than not that the person will be tortured. This policy applies to all components of the U.S. Government and to all individuals in U.S. custody, including those outside U.S. territory. Within the territory of the United States, the United States applies this policy in implementation of its international treaty obligations under Article 3 of the Convention Against Torture and Other Cruel, Inhuman or Degrading Treatment or Punishment (Convention Against Torture or "CAT"). As elaborated below, however, United States policy and legal obligations on this matter are not governed by the International Covenant on Civil and Political Rights.

The scope of obligations of States Parties under Article 7 of the Covenant is a subject on which the United States is in fundamental disagreement with the Committee. Unlike Article 3 of the CAT, Article 7 of the ICCPR contains no reference to the concept of non-refoulement, stating only that: "No one shall be subjected to torture or to cruel, inhuman or degrading treatment or punishment. In particular, no one shall be subjected without his free consent to medical or scientific experimentation."

As noted in our July 2006 written responses to Committee questions, the Covenant does not impose a non-refoulement obligation upon States Parties. The United States Government is familiar with the Committee's statements in General Comments 20 and 31 regarding Article 7 (stating that such an obligation exists). The non-binding opinions offered by the Committee in General Comments 20 and 31 have no firm legal basis in the text of the treaty or the intention of its States Parties at the time they negotiated or became party to the instrument. Moreover, as the United States explained during its July 2006 appearance, the States Parties under Article 40 of the Covenant did not give the Human Rights Committee authority to issue legally binding or authoritative interpretations of the Covenant. Accordingly, the United States does not consider General Comments 20 and 31 to reflect the "legal obligation" under the Covenant that is claimed by the Committee.

Indeed, the adoption of a provision on non-refoulement was one of the important innovations of the later-negotiated CAT, an innovation necessary because of the fact that the Covenant did not contain any non-refoulement prohibition. States Parties to the Covenant that wished to assume a new treaty obligation with respect to non-refoulement for torture were free to become States Parties to the CAT, and a very large number of countries, including the United States, chose to do so. Accordingly, States Parties to the Convention Against Torture have a non-refoulement obligation under Article 3 of that Convention not to "expel, return ("refouler") or extradite a person to another State where there are substantial grounds for believing that he would be in danger of being subjected to torture." It should be noted that not even the later-in-time CAT contains a provision on non-refoulement that would apply with respect to cruel, inhuman or degrading treatment or punishment.

As the United States recently explained to the Committee Against Torture, pursuant to its obligations under the CAT, the United States does not expel, return ('refouler'), or extradite a person from the territory of the United States to another country where it is more likely than not that such person will be tortured. Although the Committee "notes with concern" the "more likely than not" evidentiary standard used by the United States, as described more fully below, this is the obligation assumed by the United States and formally notified to the depositary and all States Parties to the CAT in the form of a formal understanding when the United States became party to that treaty.

The totality of the international legal obligations the United States has assumed with respect to non-refoulement in the human rights and refugee context are contained in Article 33 of the Convention Relating to the Status of Refugees (applicable to the United States by virtue of its being a State Party to the Protocol Relating to the Status of Refugees) and Article 3 of the Convention Against Torture. With respect to the latter instrument, at the time the United States became a State Party to the Convention Against Torture, it filed a formal understanding with respect to the scope of the treaty law obligation it was assuming under that article, stating "[t]hat the United States understands the phrase 'where there are substantial grounds for believing that he would be in danger of being subjected to torture,' as used in Article 3 of the Convention, to mean 'if it is more likely than not that he would be tortured.'" The United States filed the understanding not to articulate a different standard, nor to modify the legal effect of Article 3 as it applies to the United States, but rather simply as a clarification of the definitional scope of Article 3. The United States has not assumed obligations under international human rights and refugee law with respect to non-refoulement other than those described in this paragraph and has specifically assumed no such obligation under the Covenant.

With respect to the scope of the "non-refoulement" obligations in the CAT and the Convention Relating to the Status of Refugees, the United States has read those obligations to apply once a person has entered the territory of the United States. In the context of the Convention Relating to the Status of Refugees, this interpretation has been upheld by the United States Supreme Court. Thus, as to persons who may come into contact with U.S. personnel outside the territory of the United States, the United States is not subject to a legal obligation regarding "refoulement" under either treaty.

Although the United States does not have non-refoulement human rights treaty obligations with respect to persons in U.S. custody outside of its territory, the United States as a matter of policy follows a standard similar to its obligations under Article 3 of the CAT and, accordingly, does not transfer or return persons to countries where it determines that it is more likely than not that the person will be tortured.

The Committee also offered certain recommendations with respect to "the use of diplomatic assurances...." Although the United States, as noted above, does not believe that this subject falls within the scope of the ICCPR, it is pleased as a matter of courtesy to provide to the Committee information on this topic. Where appropriate, the United States may seek assurances that it considers to be credible that transferred persons will not be tortured. It is important to note that diplomatic assurances are a tool that may be used in appropriate cases as a part of a case-specific assessment in order to be satisfied that it is not "more likely than not" that the individual in question will be tortured upon return. Diplomatic assurances are not used as a substitute for such a case specific assessment. In the context of immigration and extradition removals from the United States, the practice of obtaining torture-related diplomatic assurances from foreign governments is infrequent. There also have been cases where the United States has considered the use of diplomatic assurances, but declined to seek them because the United States was not convinced such an assurance would satisfy its "more likely than not" standard, discussed above.

In assessing the credibility of assurances that it receives, the United States Government looks at, among other things, a country's human rights record, its record of compliance with past assurances, the level at which the assurances were given, and any risk factors that are presented by the individual being returned or transferred. If, taking into account all relevant information, including any assurances received, the United States believes that the "more likely than not" standard is not met, it does not approve the return of the person to that country.

A transfer pursuant to a diplomatic assurance is not the end of U.S. interest or attention to the treatment the person may receive following such a transfer. Where we receive credible reports that a country has abused a transferred individual, we investigate those reports by engaging government representatives and other groups and individuals with relevant knowledge. Any determination that a government failed to comply with its assurances would constitute a serious issue in the context of our bilateral relationship with that government and would, of course, have an adverse impact on our ability to do future transfers to that country.

Paragraph 20 Recommendation:

Regarding the U.S. Supreme Court decision in Hamdan v. Rumsfeld, "[t]he State party should provide the Committee with information on its implementation of the decision."

Response:

In *Hamdan v. Rumsfeld*, the Supreme Court of the United States held that Common Article 3 of the Geneva Conventions applies to the conflict with al Qaida. Since meeting with the Committee, the United States has confirmed that all U.S. government practices with respect to detainees are consistent with the Court's decision.

On July 7, 2006, shortly after the Hamdan decision, the Deputy Secretary of Defense, Gordon England, issued a directive instructing the Department of Defense to conduct a review to ensure that all of its operations are consistent with Common Article 3 of the Geneva Conventions (Annex 3). The United States has also confirmed that all agencies of the United States are required to comply with Common Article 3 in the conduct of all detention operations in the conflict against al Qaida.

On October 17, 2006, President Bush signed into law the Military Commissions Act of 2006 (MCA) (Annex 4). The purpose of the Act is to establish procedures—consistent with the Hamdan decision—governing the use of military commissions to try alien unlawful enemy combatants engaged in hostilities against the United States for violations of the law of war and other offenses. The MCA makes numerous changes to the original military commissions in order to address the substantive concerns raised by the United States Supreme Court and the international community, and to ensure that military commissions are consistent with Common Article 3's requirement that individuals be tried by "a regularly constituted court, affording all the judicial guarantees which are recognized as indispensable by civilized peoples."

On January 18, 2007, the Secretary of Defense submitted to Congress a Manual for Military Commissions (Annex 5)—a comprehensive manual for the full and fair prosecution of alien unlawful enemy combatants by military commissions. In accordance with the MCA, the Manual specifies the rules for the military commissions, including the rules of evidence and the elements of crimes. The Manual is intended to further ensure that alien unlawful enemy combatants who are suspected of war crimes and certain other offenses are prosecuted before regularly constituted courts, affording all the judicial guarantees which are recognized as indispensable by civilized peoples.

Paragraph 26 Recommendation:

"The State party should review its practices and policies to ensure the full implementation of its obligation to protect life and of the prohibition of discrimination, whether direct or indirect, as well as of the United Nations Guiding Principles on Internal Displacement, in matters related to disaster prevention and preparedness, emergency assistance and relief measures. In the aftermath of Hurricane Katrina, the State party should increase its efforts to ensure that the rights of the poor, and in particular African-Americans, are fully taken into consideration in the reconstruction plans with regard to access to housing, education and healthcare. The Committee wishes to be informed about the results of the inquiries into the alleged failure to evacuate prisoners at the Parish prison, as well as the allegations that New Orleans residents were not permitted by law enforcement officials to cross the Greater New Orleans Bridge to Gretna, Louisiana."

Response:

The United States Federal Government is aggressively moving forward with implementing lessons learned from Hurricane Katrina, including improving procedures to enhance the protection of, and assistance to, economically disadvantaged members of society. In our July 2006 written responses to Committee questions, the United States provided extensive information on measures taken in the context of the disaster caused by Hurricane Katrina.

Following Hurricane Katrina, which devastated the Gulf Coast region of the United States, there were media reports of alleged ill-treatment perpetrated by law-enforcement personnel. One of the reports included allegations that individuals were not permitted to cross the Greater New Orleans Bridge to Gretna, Louisiana. The Louisiana Attorney General's Office conducted an exhaustive inquiry into that allegation. The investigation currently is under review by the local prosecutor's office. After that office determines whether it will seek any criminal charges in connection with this incident, the Department of Justice's Civil Rights Division will determine whether additional investigation is necessary and whether the facts implicate a violation of any federal statute.

Additionally, in September 2005, the Civil Rights Division requested the FBI to conduct an investigation into allegations that correctional officers did not properly transfer inmates from the Orleans Parish Prison during the aftermath of Hurricane Katrina. After completing its initial investigation, the FBI forwarded the results of that investigation to the Division. The Division reviewed the results of the initial FBI investigation and concluded that there was insufficient evidence to establish a violation of federal criminal law. Thereafter, the FBI informed the Division that it was pursuing additional leads regarding the treatment of prisoners at the Orleans Parish Prison. Based on that additional information, the Division asked the FBI to continue the investigation. That investigation is ongoing.

In providing assistance to individuals affected by Katrina, the Federal Government is committed to helping all victims, and in particular those who are in the greatest need. In that regard, on February 15, 2006, the Attorney General announced a major new civil rights initiative, Operation Home Sweet Home. This fair housing initiative was inspired by victims of Hurricane Katrina who had lost their homes and were seeking new places to live. This is a concentrated initiative to expose and eliminate housing discrimination in the United States. The initiative will focus on improved targeting of discrimination tests, increased testing, and public awareness efforts. One of the key components of Operation Home Sweet Home is concentrated testing for housing discrimination in areas recovering from the effects of Hurricane Katrina and in areas where Katrina victims have been relocated. In addition, the Division is operating a new website devoted to fair housing enforcement: http://www.usdoj.gov/fairhousing. It has an online mechanism for citizens to submit tips and complaints, as well as obtain information about what constitutes housing-based discrimination.

Further, in the aftermath of Katrina, the U.S. Department of Housing and Urban Development has initiated a number of efforts to prevent discrimination in relocation housing. These include grants of $1.2 million to Gulf Coast Fair Housing groups for outreach to evacuees and investigation of discrimination complaints. The U.S. Department of Health and Human Services has also dedicated substantial resources to help redesign and rebuild Louisiana's health-care system to enhance health care in Louisiana.

The Government of the United States is committed to do what it takes to help residents of the Gulf Coast rebuild their lives in the wake of this disaster and has committed $110.6 billion in federal aid alone for relief, recovery and rebuilding efforts. A partial list of the work Federal agencies have accomplished to help not only get the region back on its feet but also to provide for a stronger and better future for the residents of the Gulf Coast can be found at: http://www.dhs.gov/katrina. We assure the Committee that the needs of the poor and most affected communities, including with respect to "access to housing, education and healthcare," are being taken into account in the government's responses to Katrina.
[Footnotes omitted]

DOCUMENT 16

Full Official Title: International Covenant on Economic, Social and Cultural Rights

Short Title/Acronym/Abbreviation: The Economic, Social and Cultural Covenant/ICESCR

Subject: Establish recognition of international legal obligations regarding economic, social and cultural human rights in a multilateral treaty.

Official Citation: G.A. res. 2200A (XXI), 21 U.N GAOR Supp. (No. 16) at 49, U.N. Doc. A/6316 (1966), 993 U.N.T.S. 3

Date of Document: December 16, 1966

Date of Adoption: December 16, 1966

Date of General Entry into Force (EIF): January 3, 1976.

Number of States Parties to this Treaty as of this printing: 160

Date of Signature by United States: October 5, 1977

Date of Ratification/Accession/Adhesion: United States has not ratified this treaty.

Date of Entry into Force as to United States (effective date): Has not entered into force as to United States.

Type of Document: An international legal instrument, a treaty, with the title of "covenant."

Legal Status/Character of the Instrument/Document as to the United States: This instrument was signed by the United States in 1977 but has never been ratified by the U.S. Senate. The Senate has historically been unreceptive to economic, social and cultural rights, especially as to economic rights. There has been a general reluctance in the United States to fully accept these rights as human rights capable of legal implementation. The reluctance stems, in part from questions as to how far the United States, which has a free market economy, would be expected to go in providing jobs, guaranteed income, health services, and other items in these categories that are regularly provided in countries with a more socialistic economy. Thus, it has never ratified this Covenant. However, under certain principles of international law contained in the

Vienna Convention on the Law of Treaties, the United States should act consistently with legal instruments it has signed, as an indication of its good faith intent to act accordingly. Some scholars suggest that the ICESCR could be analyzed and possibly applied, as much as possible, using a free market economy as the standard. In that way, the process of ratification might be expedited.

Caution: The status and applicability of this instrument as to the United States may have changed since date of publication. The above information may be updated by referring to the following site:

Web address: http://www1.umn.edu/humanrts/instree/b2esc.htm

INTERNATIONAL COVENANT ON ECONOMIC, SOCIAL AND CULTURAL RIGHTS (ICESCR)

Preamble

The States Parties to the present Covenant, considering that, in accordance with the principles proclaimed in the Charter of the United Nations, recognition of the inherent dignity and of the equal and inalienable rights of all members of the human family is the foundation of freedom, justice and peace in the world.

Recognizing that these rights derive from the inherent dignity of the human person.

Recognizing that, in accordance with the Universal Declaration of Human Rights, the ideal of free human beings enjoying freedom from fear and want can only be achieved if conditions are created whereby everyone may enjoy his economic, social and cultural rights, as well as his civil and political rights.

Considering the obligation of States under the Charter of the United Nations to promote universal respect for, and observance of, human rights and freedoms,

Realizing that the individual, having duties to other individuals and to the community to which he belongs, is under a responsibility to strive for the promotion and observance of the rights recognized in the present Covenant,

Agree upon the following articles:

PART I

Article 1

1. All peoples have the right of self-determination. By virtue of that right they freely determine their political status and freely pursue their economic, social and cultural development.

2. All peoples may, for their own ends, freely dispose of their natural wealth and resources without prejudice to any obligations arising out of international economic cooperation, based upon the principle of mutual benefit, and international law. In no case may a people be deprived of its own means of subsistence.

3. The States Parties of the present Covenant, including those having responsibility for the administration of Non-Self-Governing and Trust Territories, shall promote the realization of the right of self-determination, and shall respect that right, in conformity with the provisions of the Charter of The United Nations.

PART II

Article 2

1. Each State Party to the present Covenant undertakes to take steps, individually and through international assistance and co-operation, especially economic and technical, to the maximum of its available resources, with a view to achieving progressively the full realization of the rights recognized in the present Covenant by all appropriate means, including particularly the adoption of legislative measures.

2. The States Parties to the present Covenant undertake to guarantee that the rights enunciated in the present Covenant will be exercised without discrimination of any kind as to race, colour, sex, language, religion, political or other opinion, national or social origin, property, birth or other status.

3. Developing countries, with due regard to human rights and their national economy, may determine to what extent they would guarantee the economic rights recognized in the present Covenant to nonnationals.

Article 3

The States Parties to the present Covenant undertake to ensure the equal right of men and women to the enjoyment of all economic, social and cultural rights set forth in the present Covenant.

Article 4

The States Parties to the present Covenant recognize that, in the enjoyment of those rights provided by the State in conformity with the present Covenant, the State may subject such rights only to such limitations as are determined by law only in so far as this may be compatible with the nature of these rights and solely for the purpose of promoting the general welfare in a democratic society.

Article 5

1. Nothing in the present Covenant may be interpreted as implying for any State, group or person any right to engage in any activity or to perform any act aimed at the destruction of any of the rights or freedoms recognized herein, or at their limitation to a greater extent than is provided for in the present Covenant.

2. No restriction upon or derogation from any of the fundamental human rights recognized or existing in any country in virtue of law, conventions, regulations or custom shall be admitted on the pretext that the present Covenant does not recognize such rights or that it recognizes them to a lesser extent.

PART III

Article 6

1. The States Parties to the present Covenant recognize the right to work, which includes the right of everyone to the opportunity to gain his living by work which he freely chooses or accepts, and will take appropriate steps to safeguard this right.

2. The steps to be taken by a State Party to the present Covenant to achieve the full realization of this right shall include technical and vocational guidance and training programmes, policies and techniques to achieve steady economic, social and cultural development and full and productive employment under conditions safeguarding fundamental political and economic freedoms to the individual.

Article 7

The States Parties to the present Covenant recognize the right of everyone to the enjoyment of just and favourable conditions of work which ensure, in particular:

(a) Remuneration which provides all workers, as a minimum, with:

(i) Fair wages and equal remuneration for work of equal value with distinction of any kind, in particular women being guaranteed conditions of work not inferior to those enjoyed by men, with equal pay for equal work;

(ii) A decent living for themselves and their families in accordance with the provisions of the present Covenant;

(b) Safe and healthy working conditions;

(c) Equal opportunity for everyone to be promoted in his employment to an appropriate higher level, subject to no considerations other than those of seniority and competence;

(d) Rest, leisure and reasonable limitation of working hours and periodic holidays with pay, as well as remuneration for public holidays.

Article 8

1. The States Parties to the present Covenant undertake to ensure:

(a) The right of everyone to form trade unions and join the trade union of his choice, subject only to the rules of the organization concerned, for the promotion and protection of his economic and social interests. No restrictions may be placed on the exercise of this right other than those prescribed by law and which are necessary in a democratic society in the interest of national security or public order or for the protection of the rights and freedoms of others:

(b) The right of trade unions to establish national federations or confederations and the right of the latter to form or join international trade-union organizations;

(c) The right of trade unions to function freely subject to no limitations other than those prescribed by law and which are necessary in a democratic society in the interests of national security or public order or for the protection of the rights and freedoms of others:

(d) The right to strike, provided that it is exercised in conformity with the laws of the particular country.

2. This Article shall not prevent the imposition of lawful restrictions on the exercise of these rights by members of the armed forces or of the police or of the administration of the State.

3. Nothing in this Article shall authorize States Parties to the International Labour Organization Convention of 1948 concerning Freedom of Association and Protection of the Right to Organize to take legislative measures which would prejudice, or apply the law in such a manner as would prejudice, the guarantees provided for in that Convention.

Article 9

The States Parties to the present Covenant recognize the right of everyone to social security, including social insurance.

Article 10

The States Parties to the present Covenant recognize that:

1. The widest possible protection and assistance should be accorded to the family, which is the natural and fundamental group unit of society, particularly for its establishment and while it is responsible for the care and education of dependent children. Marriage must be entered into with the free consent of the intending spouses.

2. Special protection should be accorded to mothers during a reasonable period before and after childbirth. During such period working mothers should be accorded paid leave or leave with adequate social security benefits.

3. Special measures of protection and assistance should be taken on behalf of all children and young persons without any discrimination for reasons of parentage or other conditions. Children and young persons should be protected from economic and social exploitation. Their employment in work harmful to their morals or health or dangerous to life or likely to hamper their normal development should be punishable by law. States should also set age limits below which the paid employment of child labour should be prohibited and punishable by law.

Article 11

1. The States Parties to the present Covenant recognize the right of everyone to an adequate standard of living for himself and his family, including adequate food, clothing and housing, and to the continuous improvement of living conditions. The States Parties will take appropriate steps to ensure the realization of this right, recognizing to this effect the essential importance of international co-operation based on free consent.

2. The States Parties to the present Covenant, recognizing the fundamental right of everyone to be free from hunger, shall take, individually and through international cooperation, the measures, including specific programmes, which are needed:

(a) To improve methods of production, conservation and distribution of food by making full use of technical and scientific knowledge, by disseminating knowledge of the principles of nutrition and by developing or reforming agrarian systems in such a way as to achieve the most efficient development and utilization of natural resources;

(b) Taking into account the problems of both food-importing and food-exporting countries, to ensure an equitable distribution of world food supplies in relation to need.

Article 12

1. The States Parties to the present Covenant recognize the right of everyone to the enjoyment of the highest attainable standard of physical and mental health.

2. The steps to be taken by the States Parties to the present Covenant to achieve the full realization of this right shall include those necessary for:

(a) The provision for the reduction of the stillbirth-rate and of infant mortality and for the healthy development of the child;

(b) The improvement of all aspects of environmental and industrial hygiene;

(c) The prevention, treatment and control of epidemic, endemic, occupational and other diseases;

(d) The creation of conditions which would assure to all medical service and medical attention in the event of sickness.

Article 13

1. The States Parties to the present Covenant recognize the right of everyone to education. They agree that education shall be directed to the full development of the human personality and the sense of its dignity, and shall strengthen the respect for human rights and fundamental freedoms. They further agree that education shall enable all persons to participate effectively in a free society, promote understanding, tolerance and friendship among all nations and all racial, ethnic or religious groups, and further the activities of the United Nations for the maintenance of peace.

2. The States Parties to the present Covenant recognize that with a view to achieving the full realization of this right:

(a) Primary education shall be compulsory and available free to all;

(b) Secondary education in its different forms, including technical and vocational secondary education, shall be made generally available and accessible to all by every appropriate means, and in particular by the progressive introduction of free education;

(c) Higher education shall be made equally accessible to all, on the basis of capacity, by every appropriate means, and in particular by the progressive introduction of free education;

(d) Fundamental education shall be encouraged or intensified as far as possible for those persons who have not received or completed the whole period of their primary education;

(e) The development of a system of schools at all levels shall be actively pursued, an adequate fellowship system shall be established, and the material conditions of teaching staff shall be continuously improved.

3. The States Parties to the present Covenant undertake to have respect for the liberty of parents and, when applicable, legal guardians to choose for their children schools, other than those established by the public authorities, which conform to such minimum educational standards as may be laid down or approved by the State and to ensure the religious and moral education of their children in conformity with their own convictions.

4. No part of this article shall be construed so as to interfere with the liberty of individuals and bodies to establish and direct educational institutions, subject always to the observance of the principles set forth in paragraph I of this article and to the requirement that the education given in such institutions shall conform to such minimum standards as may be laid down by the State.

Article 14

Each State Party to the present Covenant which, at the time of becoming a Party, has not been able to secure in its metropolitan territory or other territories under its jurisdiction compulsory primary education, free of charge, undertakes, within two years, to work out and adopt a detailed plan of action for the progressive implementation, within a reasonable number of years, to be fixed in the plan, of the principle of compulsory education free of charge for all.

Article 15

1. The States Parties to the present Covenant recognize the right of everyone:

(a) To take part in cultural life;

(b) To enjoy the benefits of scientific progress and its applications;

(c) To benefit from the protection of the moral and material interests resulting from any scientific, literary or artistic production of which he is the author.

2. The steps to be taken by the States Parties to the present Covenant to achieve the full realization of this right shall include those necessary for the conservation, the development and the diffusion of science and culture.

3. The States Parties to the present Covenant undertake to respect the freedom indispensable for scientific research and creative activity.

4. The States Parties to the present Covenant recognize the benefits to be derived form the encouragement and development of international contacts and cooperation in the scientific and cultural fields.

PART IV

Article 16

1. The States Parties to the present Covenant undertake to submit in conformity with this part of the Covenant reports on the measures which they have adopted and the progress made in achieving the observance of the rights recognized herein.

2. (a) All reports shall be submitted to the Secretary-General of the United Nations, who shall transmit copies to the Economic and Social Council for consideration in accordance with the provisions of the present Covenant;

(b) The Secretary-General of the United Nations shall also transmit to the specialized agencies copies of the reports, or any relevant parts therefrom, from States Parties to the present Covenant which are also members of these specialized agencies in so far as these reports, or parts therefrom, relate to any matters which fall within the responsibilities of the said agencies in accordance with their constitutional instruments.

Article 17

1. The States Parties to the present Covenant shall furnish their reports in stages, in accordance with a programme to be established by the Economic and Social Council within one year of the entry into force of the present Covenant after consultation with the States Parties and the specialized agencies concerned.

2. Reports may indicate factors and difficulties affecting the degree of fulfilment of obligations under the present Covenant.

3. Where relevant information has previously been furnished to the United Nations or to any specialized agency by any State Party to the present Covenant, it will not be necessary to reproduce that information, but a precise reference to the information so furnished will suffice.

Article 18

Pursuant to its responsibilities under the Charter of the United Nations in the field of human rights and fundamental freedoms, the Economic and Social Council may make arrangements with the specialized agencies i respect of their reporting to it on the progress made in achieving the observance of the provisions of the present Covenant falling within the scope of their activities. These reports may include particulars of decisions and recommendations on such implementation adopted by their competent organs.

Article 19

The Economic and Social Council may transmit to the Commission on Human Rights for study and general recommendation or, as appropriate, for information the reports concerning human rights submitted by States in accordance with Articles 16 and 17, and those concerning human rights submitted by the specialized agencies in accordance with Article 18.

Article 20

The States Parties to the present Covenant and the specialized agencies concerned may submit comments to the Economic and Social Council on any general recommendation under Article 19 or reference to such general recommendation in any report of the Commission on Human Rights or any documentation referred to therein.

Article 21

The Economic and Social Council may submit from time to time to the General Assembly reports with recommendations of a general nature and a summary of the information received from the States Parties to the present Covenant and the specialized agencies on the measures taken and the progress made in achieving general observance of the rights recognized in the present Covenant.

Article 22

The Economic and Social Council may bring to the attention of other organs of the United Nations, their subsidiary organs and specialized agencies concerned with furnishing technical assistance any matters arising out of the reports referred to in this part of the present Covenant which may assist such bodies in deciding, each within its field of competence, on the advisability of international measures likely to contribute to the effective progressive implementation of the present Covenant.

Article 23

The States Parties to the present Covenant agree that international action for the achievement of the rights recognized in the present Covenant includes such methods as the conclusion of conventions, the adoption of recommendations, the furnishing of technical assistance and the holding of regional meetings and technical meetings for the purpose of consultation and study organized in conjunction with the Governments concerned.

Article 24

Nothing in the present Covenant shall be interpreted as impairing the provisions of the Charter of the United Nations and of the constitutions of the specialized agencies which define the respective responsibilities of the various organs of the United Nations and of the specialized agencies in regard to the matters dealt with in the present Covenant.

Article 25

Nothing in the present Covenant shall be interpreted as impairing the inherent right of all peoples to enjoy and utilize fully and freely their natural wealth and resources.

PART V

Article 26

1. The present Covenant is open for signature by any State Member of the United Nations or member of any of its specialized agencies, by any State Party to the Statute of the International Court of Justice, and by any other State which has been invited by the General Assembly of the United Nations to become a party to the present Covenant.

2. The present Covenant is subject to ratification. Instruments of ratification shall be deposited with the Secretary-General of the United Nations.

3. The present Covenant shall be open to accession by any State referred to in paragraph 1 of this Article.

4. Accession shall be effected by the deposit of an instrument of accession with the Secretary-General of the United Nations.

5. The Secretary-General of the United Nations shall inform all States which have signed the present Covenant or acceded to it of the deposit of each instrument of ratification or accession.

Article 27

1. The present Covenant shall enter into force three months after the date of the deposit with the Secretary-General of the United Nations of the Thirty-fifth instrument of ratification or instrument of accession.

2. For each State ratifying the present Covenant or acceding to it after the deposit of the thirty-fifth instrument of ratification or instrument of accession, the present Covenant shall enter into force three months after the date of the deposit of its own instrument of ratification or instrument of accession.

Article 28

The provisions of the present Covenant shall extend to all parts of federal States without any limitations or exceptions.

Article 29

1. Any State Party to the present Covenant may propose an amendment and file it with the Secretary-General of the United Nations. The Secretary-General shall thereupon communicate any proposed amendments to the States Parties to the present Covenant with a request that they notify him whether they favour a conference of States Parties for the purpose of considering and voting upon the proposals. In the event that at least one third of the States Parties favours such a conference, the Secretary-General shall convene the conference under the auspices of the United Nations. Any amendment adopted by a majority of the States Parties present and voting at the conference shall be submitted to the General Assembly of the United Nations for approval.

2. Amendments shall come into force when they have been approved by the General Assembly of the United Nations and accepted by a two-thirds majority of the States Parties to the present Covenant in accordance with their respective constitutional processes.

3. When amendments come into force they shall be binding on those States Parties which have accepted them, other States Parties still being bound by the provisions of the present Covenant and any earlier amendment which they have accepted.

Article 30

Irrespective of the notifications made under Article 26, paragraph 5, the Secretary-General of the United Nations shall inform all States referred to in paragraph I of the same Article of the following particulars:

(a) Signatures, ratifications and accessions under Article 26;

(b) The date of the entry into force of the present Covenant under Article 27 and the date of the entry into force of any amendments under Article 29.

Article 31

1. The present Covenant, of which the Chinese, English, French, Russian and Spanish texts are equally authentic, shall be deposited in the archives of the United Nations.

2. The Secretary-General of the United Nations shall transmit certified copies of the present Covenant to all States referred to in Article 26.

DOCUMENT 17

Full Official Title: Convention on the Prevention and Punishment of the Crime of Genocide

Short Title/Acronym/Abbreviation: The Genocide Convention

Subject: A treaty to make the commission of genocide an international crime and to provide a means of universal prosecution

Official Citation: 78 U.N.T.S. 277

Date of Document: Not applicable

Date of Adoption: December 9, 1948

Date of General Entry into Force (EIF): January 12, 1951

Number of States Parties to this Treaty as of this printing: 141

Date of Signature by United States: December 11, 1948

Date of Ratification/Accession/Adhesion: November 24, 1988

Date of Entry into Force as to United States (effective date): February 23, 1989

Type of Document: A treaty, an international legal instrument.

Legal Status/Character of the Instrument/Document as to the United States: It is legally binding upon the United States. Its ratification is subject to the reservations, declarations and understandings submitted by the United States with its ratification. See the following document.

Comments: The United States was largely instrumental in the drafting and adoption of the Genocide Convention but took many years to ratify it. Genocide is also an international crime as a matter of customary international law and thus binding upon all states of the world. It is a crime for which there is universal criminal jurisdiction in every state because it is a crime which is so serious as to be considered damaging to the whole human race. It was created largely in reaction to the Holocaust, so that such an atrocity would "never again" happen.

Caution: The status and applicability of this instrument as to the United States may have changed since date of publication. The above information may be updated by referring to the following site:

Web address: http://www1.umn.edu/humanrts/instree/x1cppcg.htm

CONVENTION ON THE PREVENTION AND PUNISHMENT OF THE CRIME OF GENOCIDE

The Contracting Parties,

Having considered the declaration made by the General Assembly of the United Nations in its resolution 96 (I) dated 11 December 1946 that genocide is a crime under international law, contrary to the spirit and aims of the United Nations and condemned by the civilized world,

Recognizing that at all periods of history genocide has inflicted great losses on humanity, and Being convinced that, in order to liberate mankind from such an odious scourge, international co-operation is required,

Hereby agree as hereinafter provided:

Article 1

The Contracting Parties confirm that genocide, whether committed in time of peace or in time of war, is a crime under international law which they undertake to prevent and to punish.

Article 2

In the present Convention, genocide means any of the following acts committed with intent to destroy, in whole or in part, a national, ethnical, racial or religious group, as such:

(a) Killing members of the group;

(b) Causing serious bodily or mental harm to members of the group;

(c) Deliberately inflicting on the group conditions of life calculated to bring about its physical destruction in whole or in part;

(d) Imposing measures intended to prevent births within the group;

(e) Forcibly transferring children of the group to another group.

Article 3

The following acts shall be punishable:

(a) Genocide;

(b) Conspiracy to commit genocide;

(c) Direct and public incitement to commit genocide;

(d) Attempt to commit genocide;

(e) Complicity in genocide.

Article 4

Persons committing genocide or any of the other acts enumerated in article III shall be punished, whether they are constitutionally responsible rulers, public officials or private individuals.

Article 5

The Contracting Parties undertake to enact, in accordance with their respective

Constitutions, the necessary legislation to give effect to the provisions of the present Convention, and, in particular, to provide effective penalties for persons guilty of genocide or any of the other acts enumerated in article III.

Article 6

Persons charged with genocide or any of the other acts enumerated in article III shall be tried by a competent tribunal of the State in the territory of which the act was committed, or by such international penal tribunal as may have jurisdiction with respect to those Contracting Parties which shall have accepted its jurisdiction.

Article 7

Genocide and the other acts enumerated in article III shall not be considered as political crimes for the purpose of extradition.

The Contracting Parties pledge themselves in such cases to grant extradition in accordance with their laws and treaties in force.

Article 8

Any Contracting Party may call upon the competent organs of the United Nations to take such action under the Charter of the United Nations as they consider appropriate for the prevention and suppression of acts of genocide or any of the other acts enumerated in article III.

Article 9

Disputes between the Contracting Parties relating to the interpretation, application or fulfilment of the present Convention, including those relating to the responsibility of a State for genocide or for any of the other acts enumerated in article III, shall be submitted to the International Court of Justice at the request of any of the parties to the dispute.

Article 10

The present Convention, of which the Chinese, English, French, Russian and Spanish texts are equally authentic, shall bear the date of 9 December 1948.

Article 11

The present Convention shall be open until 31 December 1949 for signature on behalf of any Member of the United Nations and of any non-member State to which an invitation to sign has been addressed by the General Assembly.

The present Convention shall be ratified, and the instruments of ratification shall be deposited with the Secretary-General of the United Nations.

After 1 January 1950, the present Convention may be acceded to on behalf of any Member of the United Nations and of any non-member State which has received an invitation as aforesaid. Instruments of accession shall be deposited with the Secretary-General of the United Nations.

Article 12

Any Contracting Party may at any time, by notification addressed to the Secretary-General of the United Nations, extend the application of the present Convention to all or any of the territories for the conduct of whose foreign relations that Contracting Party is responsible.

Article 13

On the day when the first twenty instruments of ratification or accession have been deposited, the Secretary-General shall draw up a proces-verbal and transmit a copy thereof to each Member of the United Nations and to each of the non-member States contemplated in Article 11.

The present Convention shall come into force on the ninetieth day following the date of deposit of the twentieth instrument of ratification or accession.

Any ratification or accession effected, subsequent to the latter date shall become effective on the ninetieth day following the deposit of the instrument of ratification or accession.

Article 14

The present Convention shall remain in effect for a period of ten years as from the date of its coming into force.

It shall thereafter remain in force for successive periods of five years for such Contracting Parties as have not denounced it at least six months before the expiration of the current period.

Denunciation shall be effected by a written notification addressed to the Secretary-General of the United Nations.

Article 15

If, as a result of denunciations, the number of Parties to the present Convention should become less than sixteen, the Convention shall cease to be in force as from the date on which the last of these denunciations shall become effective.

Article 16

A request for the revision of the present Convention may be made at any time by any Contracting Party by means of a notification in writing addressed to the Secretary-General.

The General Assembly shall decide upon the steps, if any, to be taken in respect of such request.

Article 17

The Secretary-General of the United Nations shall notify all Members of the United Nations and the non-member States contemplated in Article 11 of the following:

(a) Signatures, ratifications and accessions received in accordance with Article 11;

(b) Notifications received in accordance with Article 12;

(c) The date upon which the present Convention comes into force in accordance with Article 13;

(d) Denunciations received in accordance with Article 14;

(e) The abrogation of the Convention in accordance with Article 15;

(f) Notifications received in accordance with Article 16.

Article 18

The original of the present Convention shall be deposited in the archives of the United Nations.

A certified copy of the Convention shall be transmitted to each Member of the United Nations and to each of the non-member States contemplated in article XI.

Article 19

The present Convention shall be registered by the Secretary-General of the United Nations on the date of its coming into force.

DOCUMENT 18

Full Official Title: U.S. reservations, declarations, and understandings, to the International Convention on the Prevention and Punishment of the Crime of Genocide

Short Title/Acronym/Abbreviation: U.S. Reservations to the Genocide Convention

Subject: A statement of the reservations, declarations and understandings which the United States submitted to the United Nations with its ratification of the Genocide Convention

Official Citation: Cong. Rec. S1355–01 (daily ed., Feb. 19, 1986)

Date of Document: February 1986

Date of Adoption: Not applicable

Date of General Entry into Force (EIF): Not applicable

Number of State Parties to this Treaty as of this printing: Not applicable

Date of Signature by United States: Not applicable

Date of Ratification/Accession/Adhesion: Not applicable

Date of Entry into Force as to United States (effective date): Not applicable

Type of Document: This is not a treaty, but is a legal instrument under U.S. and international law which expresses the terms under which the United States ratifies and thus accepts legal obligations under the Genocide Convention.

Legal Status/Character of the Instrument/Document as to the United States: These RDUs are valid as to U.S. ratification so far as they are consistent with the object and purpose of the Genocide Convention.

Comments: The U.S. obligations under the Genocide Convention must be read in light of these RDUs. As an example of the importance of these RDUs, in 1999, the former Yugoslavia sued the United States and other NATO countries in the International Court of Justice (ICJ) for the bombing of Yugoslavia during the Kosovo crisis, alleging the United States was committing genocide against the Serbian people. Yugoslavia alleged that the extensive bombing constituted genocide and therefore the ICJ had jurisdiction over the United States under article IX of the above Genocide Convention. In the initial case for getting the ICJ to order the United States and NATO to stop the bombing, the United States was successful in claiming that the ICJ had no jurisdiction over it, based on the above U.S. reservation (I.(1)) to the Court's jurisdiction.

Caution: The status and applicability of this instrument as to the United States may have changed since date of publication. The above information may be updated by referring to the following site:

Web address: http://www1.umn.edu/humanrts/usdocs/genres.html

U.S. RESERVATIONS, DECLARATIONS, AND UNDERSTANDINGS, TO THE GENOCIDE CONVENTION

I. The Senate's advice and consent is subject to the following reservations:

(1) That with reference to Article IX of the Convention, before any dispute to which the United States is a party may be submitted to the jurisdiction of the International Court of Justice under this article, the specific consent of the United States is required in each case.

(2) That nothing in the Convention requires or authorizes legislation or other action by the United States of America prohibited by the Constitution of the United States as interpreted by the United States.

II. The Senate's advice and consent is subject to the following understandings, which shall apply to the obligations of the United States under this Convention:

(1) That the term "intent to destroy, in whole or in part, a national, ethnical, racial, or religious group as such" appearing in Article II means the specific intent to destroy, in whole or in substantial part, a national ethnical, racial or religious group as such by the facts specified in Article II.

(2) That the term "mental harm" in Article II(b) means permanent impairment of mental faculties through drugs, torture or similar techniques.

(3) That the pledge to grant extradition in accordance with a state's laws and treaties in force found in Article VII extends only to acts which are criminal under the laws of both the requesting and the requested state and nothing in Article VI affects the right of any state to bring to trial before its own tribunals any of its nationals for acts committed outside a state.

(4) That acts in the course of armed conflicts committed without the specific intent required by Article II are not sufficient to constitute genocide as defined by this Convention.

(5) That with regard to the reference to an international penal tribunal in Article VI of the Convention, the United States declares that it reserves the right to effect its participation in any such tribunal only by a treaty entered into specifically for that purpose with the advice and consent of the Senate.

III. The Senate's advice and consent is subject to the following declaration: That the President will not deposit the instrument of ratification until after the implementing legislation referred to in Article V has been enacted.

IV. The Senate's advice and consent is subject to the following proviso, which shall not be included in the instrument of ratification to be deposited by the President: 12/22/2010 Nothing in this Convention requires or authorizes legislation, or other action, by the United States of America prohibited by the Constitution of the United States as interpreted by the United States.

DOCUMENT 19

Full Official Title: Convention against Torture and Other Cruel, Inhuman or Degrading Treatment or Punishment

Short Title/Acronym/Abbreviation: The Torture Convention/CAT

Object: Recognition and creation of an international human rights legal system against torture, cruel, inhuman or degrading treatment or punishment in the world in a multilateral treaty.

Official Citation: G.A. res. 39/46, annex, 39 U.N. GAOR Supp. (No. 51) at 197, U.N. Doc. A/39/51 (1984) 1465 U.N.T.S. 85

Date of Document: Not applicable

Date of Adoption: December 10, 1984

Date of General Entry into Force (EIF): June 26, 1987

Number of States Parties to this Treaty as of this printing: 118

Date of Signature by United States: April 8, 1988

Date of Ratification/Accession/Adhesion: October 21, 1994

Date of Entry into Force as to United States (effective date): November 20, 1994

Type of Document: An international instrument, a treaty.

Legal Status/Character of the Instrument/Document as to the United States: It is legally binding on the United States, subject to the reservations, declarations and understandings submitted with it by the

United States upon ratification. This treaty is "non self-executing," meaning that its norms cannot be asserted by individuals to serve as the basis of court decisions. Some scholars disagree with this conclusion.

Supervising Body: U.N. Committee against Torture

Comments: The United States was largely instrumental in the drafting and adoption of the Torture Convention and many of its provisions were fashioned with the U.S. Constitution in mind. This Convention recognizes torture as an international crime with universal jurisdiction of all states parties. Torture is also an international crime under customary international law. It was largely based on this Convention that Augusto Pinochet's extradition was sought from England to Spain in 1999.

The Torture Convention was largely implemented into U.S. legislation in the 1998–99.

Caution: The status and applicability of this instrument as to the United States may have changed since date of publication. The above information may be updated by referring to the following site:

Web address: http://www1.umn.edu/humanrts/instree/h2catoc.htm

CONVENTION AGAINST TORTURE, CRUEL, INHUMAN, OR DEGRADING TREATMENT OR PUNISHMENT (CAT)

The States Parties to this Convention, Considering that, in accordance with the principles proclaimed in the Charter of the United Nations, recognition of the equal and inalienable rights of all members of the human family is the foundation of freedom, justice and peace in the world,

Recognizing that those rights derive from the inherent dignity of the human person,

Considering the obligation of States under the Charter, in particular Article 55, to promote universal respect for, and observance of, human rights and fundamental freedoms,

Having regard to Article 5 of the Universal Declaration of Human Rights and Article 7 of the International Covenant on Civil and Political Rights, both of which provide that no one shall be subjected to torture or to cruel, inhuman or degrading treatment or punishment,

Having regard also to the Declaration on the Protection of All Persons from Being Subjected to Torture and Other Cruel, Inhuman or Degrading Treatment or Punishment, adopted by the General Assembly on 9 December 1975,

Desiring to make more effective the struggle against torture and other cruel, inhuman or degrading treatment or punishment throughout the world,

Have agreed as follows:

PART I
Article 1

1. For the purposes of this Convention, the term "torture" means any act by which severe pain or suffering, whether physical or mental, is intentionally inflicted on a person for such purposes as obtaining from him or a third person information or a confession, punishing him for an act he or a third person has committed or is suspected of having committed, or intimidating or coercing him or a third person, or for any reason based on discrimination of any kind, when such pain or suffering is inflicted by or at the instigation of or with the consent or acquiescence of a public official or other person acting in an official capacity. It does not include pain or suffering arising only from, inherent in or incidental to lawful sanctions.

2. This Article is without prejudice to any international instrument or national legislation which does or may contain provisions of wider application.

Article 2

1. Each State Party shall take effective legislative, administrative, judicial or other measures to prevent acts of torture in any territory under its jurisdiction.

2. No exceptional circumstances whatsoever, whether a state of war or a threat of war, internal political in stability or any other public emergency, may be invoked as a justification of torture.

3. An order from a superior officer or a public authority may not be invoked as a justification of torture.

Article 3

1. No State Party shall expel, return ("refouler") or extradite a person to another State where there are substantial grounds for believing that he would be in danger of being subjected to torture.

2. For the purpose of determining whether there are such grounds, the competent authorities shall take into account all relevant considerations including, where applicable, the existence in the State concerned of a consistent pattern of gross, flagrant or mass violations of human rights.

Article 4

1. Each State Party shall ensure that all acts of torture are offences under its criminal law. The same shall apply to an attempt to commit torture and to an act by any person which constitutes complicity or participation in torture.

2. Each State Party shall make these offences punishable by appropriate penalties which take into account their grave nature.

Article 5

1. Each State Party shall take such measures as may be necessary to establish its jurisdiction over the offences referred to in Article 4 in the following cases:

(a) When the offences are committed in any territory under its jurisdiction or on board a ship or aircraft registered in that State;

(b) When the alleged offender is a national of that State;

(c) When the victim is a national of that State if that State considers it appropriate.

2. Each State Party shall likewise take such measures as may be necessary to establish its jurisdiction over such offences in cases where the alleged offender is present in any territory under its jurisdiction and it does not extradite him pursuant to Article 8 to any of the States mentioned in paragraph I of this Article.

3. This Convention does not exclude any criminal jurisdiction exercised in accordance with internal law.

Article 6

1. Upon being satisfied, after an examination of information available to it, that the circumstances so warrant, any State Party in whose territory a person alleged to have committed any offence referred to in Article 4 is present shall take him into custody or take other legal measures to ensure his presence. The custody and other legal measures shall be as provided in the law of that State but may be continued only for such time as is necessary to enable any criminal or extradition proceedings to be instituted.

2. Such State shall immediately make a preliminary inquiry into the facts.

3. Any person in custody pursuant to paragraph I of this Article shall be assisted in communicating immediately with the nearest appropriate representative of the State of which he is a national, or, if he is a stateless person, with the representative of the State where he usually resides.

4. When a State, pursuant to this article, has taken a person into custody, it shall immediately notify the States referred to in Article 5, paragraph 1, of the fact that such person is in custody and of the circumstances which warrant his detention.

The State which makes the preliminary inquiry contemplated in paragraph 2 of this article shall promptly report its findings to the said States and shall indicate whether it intends to exercise jurisdiction.

Article 7

1. The State Party in the territory under whose jurisdiction a person alleged to have committed any offence referred to in Article 4 is found shall in the cases contemplated in Article 5, if it does not extradite him, submit the case to its competent authorities for the purpose of prosecution.

2. These authorities shall take their decision in the same manner as in the case of any ordinary offence of a serious nature under the law of that State. In the cases referred to in Article 5, paragraph 2, the standards of evidence required for prosecution and conviction shall in no way be less stringent than those which apply in the cases referred to in Article 5, paragraph 1.

3. Any person regarding whom proceedings are brought in connection with any of the offences referred to in Article 4 shall be guaranteed fair treatment at all stages of the proceedings.

Article 8

1. The offences referred to in Article 4 shall be deemed to be included as extraditable offences in any extradition treaty existing between States Parties. States Parties undertake to include such offences as extraditable offences in every extradition treaty to be concluded between them.

2. If a State Party which makes extradition conditional on the existence of a treaty receives a request for extradition from another State Party with which it has no extradition treaty, it may consider this Convention as the legal basis for extradition in respect of such offences. Extradition shall be subject to the other conditions provided by the law of the requested State.

3. States Parties which do not make extradition conditional on the existence of a treaty shall recognize such offences as extraditable offences between themselves subject to the conditions provided by the law of the requested State.

4. Such offences shall be treated, for the purpose of extradition between States

Parties, as if they had been committed not only in the place in which they occurred but also in the territories of the States required to establish their jurisdiction in accordance with Article 5, paragraph 1.

Article 9

1. States Parties shall afford one another the greatest measure of assistance in connection with criminal proceedings brought in respect of any of the offences referred to in Article 4, including the supply of all evidence at their disposal necessary for the proceedings.

2. States Parties shall carry out their obligations under paragraph I of this Article in conformity with any treaties on mutual judicial assistance that may exist between them.

Article 10

1. Each State Party shall ensure that education and information regarding the prohibition against torture are fully included in the training of law enforcement personnel, civil or military, medical personnel, public officials and other persons who may be involved in the custody, interrogation or treatment of any individual subjected to any form of arrest, detention or imprisonment.

2. Each State Party shall include this prohibition in the rules or instructions issued in regard to the duties and functions of any such person.

Article 11

Each State Party shall keep under systematic review interrogation rules, instructions, methods and practices as well as arrangements for the custody and treatment of persons subjected to any form of arrest, detention or imprisonment in any territory under its jurisdiction, with a view to preventing any cases of torture.

Article 12

Each State Party shall ensure that its competent authorities proceed to a prompt and impartial investigation, wherever there is reasonable ground to believe that an act of torture has been committed in any territory under its jurisdiction.

Article 13

Each State Party shall ensure that any individual who alleges he has been subjected to torture in any territory under its jurisdiction has the right to complain to, and to have his case promptly and impartially examined by, its competent authorities. Steps shall be taken to ensure that the complainant and witnesses are protected against all ill-treatment or intimidation as a consequence of his complaint or any evidence given.

Article 14

1. Each State Party shall ensure in its legal system that the victim of an act of torture obtains redress and has an enforceable right to fair and adequate compensation, including the means for as full rehabilitation as possible. In the event of the death of the victim as a result of an act of torture, his dependants shall be entitled to compensation.

2. Nothing in this article shall affect any right of the victim or other persons to compensation which may exist under national law.

Article 15

Each State Party shall ensure that any statement which is established to have been made as a result of torture shall not be invoked as evidence in any proceedings, except against a person accused of torture as evidence that the statement was made.

Article 16

1. Each State Party shall undertake to prevent in any territory under its jurisdiction other acts of cruel, inhuman or degrading treatment or punishment which do not amount to torture as defined in Article 1, when such acts are committed by or at the instigation of or with the consent or acquiescence of a public official or other person acting in an official capacity. In particular, the obligations contained in

Articles 10, 11, 12 and 13 shall apply with the substitution for references to torture of references to other forms of cruel, inhuman or degrading treatment or punishment.

2. The provisions of this Convention are without prejudice to the provisions of any other international instrument or national law which prohibits cruel, inhuman or degrading treatment or punishment or which relates to extradition or expulsion.

PART II

Article 17

1. There shall be established a Committee against Torture (hereinafter referred to as the Committee) which shall carry out the functions hereinafter provided. The Committee shall consist of ten experts of high

moral standing and recognized competence in the field of human rights, who shall serve in their personal capacity. The experts shall be elected by the States Parties, consideration being given to equitable geographical distribution and to the usefulness of the participation of some persons having legal experience.

2. The members of the Committee shall be elected by secret ballot from a list of persons nominated by States Parties. Each State Party may nominate one person from among its own nationals. States Parties shall bear in mind the usefulness of nominating persons who are also members of the Human Rights Committee established under the International Covenant on Civil and Political Rights and who are willing to serve on the Committee against Torture.

3. Elections of the members of the Committee shall be held at biennial meetings of States Parties convened by the Secretary-General of the United Nations. At those meetings, for which two thirds of the States Parties shall constitute a quorum, the persons elected to the Committee shall be those who obtain the largest number of votes and an absolute majority of the votes of the representatives of States Parties present and voting.

4. The initial election shall be held no later than six months after the date of the entry into force of this Convention. At least four months before the date of each election, the Secretary-General of the United Nations shall address a letter to the States Parties inviting them to submit their nominations within three months. The Secretary-General shall prepare a list in alphabetical order of all persons thus nominated, indicating the States Parties which have nominated them, and shall submit it to the States Parties.

5. The members of the Committee shall be elected for a term of four years. They shall be eligible for re-election if renominated. However, the term of five of the members elected at the first election shall expire at the end of two years; immediately after the first election the names of these five members shall be chosen by lot by the chairman of the meeting referred to in paragraph 3 of this Article.

6. If a member of the Committee dies or resigns or for any other cause can no longer perform his Committee duties, the State Party which nominated him shall appoint another expert from among its nationals to serve for the remainder of his term, subject to the approval of the majority of the States Parties. The approval shall be considered given unless half or more of the States Parties respond negatively within six weeks after having been informed by the Secretary-General of the United Nations of the proposed appointment.

7. States Parties shall be responsible for the expenses of the members of the Committee while they are in performance of Committee duties.

Article 18

1. The Committee shall elect its officers for a term of two years. They may be re-elected.

2. The Committee shall establish its own rules of procedure, but these rules shall provide, inter alia, that:

(a) Six members shall constitute a quorum;

(b) Decisions of the Committee shall be made by a majority vote of the members present.

3. The Secretary-General of the United Nations shall provide the necessary staff and facilities for the effective performance of the functions of the Committee under this Convention.

4. The Secretary-General of the United Nations shall convene the initial meeting of the Committee. After its initial meeting, the Committee shall meet at such times as shall be provided in its rules of procedure.

5. The States Parties shall be responsible for expenses incurred in connection with the holding of meetings of the States Parties and of the Committee, including reimbursement to the United Nations for any expenses, such as the cost of staff and facilities, incurred by the United Nations pursuant to paragraph 3 of this article.

Article 19

1. The States Parties shall submit to the Committee, through the Secretary-General of the United Nations, reports on the measures they have taken to give effect to their undertakings under this Convention, within one year after the entry into force of the Convention for the State Party concerned. Thereafter the States Parties shall submit supplementary reports every four years on any new measures taken and such other reports as the Committee may request.

2. The Secretary-General of the United Nations shall transmit the reports to all States Parties.

3. Each report shall be considered by the Committee which may make such general comments on the report as it may consider appropriate and shall forward these to the State Party concerned. That State Party may respond with any observations it chooses to the Committee.

4. The Committee may, at its discretion, decide to include any comments made by it in accordance with paragraph 3 of this Article, together with the observations thereon received from the State Party concerned,

in its annual report made in accordance with Article 24. If so requested by the State Party concerned, the Committee may also include a copy of the report submitted under paragraph 1 of this Article.

Article 20

1. If the Committee receives reliable information which appears to it to contain well-founded indications that torture is being systematically practised in the territory of a State Party, the Committee shall invite that State Party to co-operate in the examination of the information and to this end to submit observations with regard to the information concerned.

2. Taking into account any observations which may have been submitted by the State Party concerned, as well as any other relevant information available to it, the Committee may, if it decides that this is warranted, designate one or more of its members to make a confidential inquiry and to report to the Committee urgently.

3. If an inquiry is made in accordance with paragraph 2 of this article, the Committee shall seek the co-operation of the State Party concerned. In agreement with that State Party, such an inquiry may include a visit to its territory.

4. After examining the findings of its member or members submitted in accordance with paragraph 2 of this article, the Commission shall transmit these findings to the State Party concerned together with any comments or suggestions which seem appropriate in view of the situation.

5. All the proceedings of the Committee referred to in paragraphs 1 to 4 of this Article shall be confidential, and at all stages of the proceedings the co-operation of the State Party shall be sought. After such proceedings have been completed with regard to an inquiry made in accordance with paragraph 2, the Committee may, after consultations with the State Party concerned, decide to include a summary account of the results of the proceedings in its annual report made in accordance with Article 24.

Article 21

1. A State Party to this Convention may at any time declare under this article that it recognizes the competence of the Committee to receive and consider communications to the effect that a State Party claims that another State Party is not fulfilling its obligations under this Convention. Such communications may be received and considered according to the procedures laid down in this article only if submitted by a State Party which has made a declaration recognizing in regard to itself the competence of the Committee. No communication shall be dealt with by the Committee under this article if it concerns a State Party which has not made such a declaration. Communications received under this article hall be dealt with in accordance with the following procedure;

(a) If a State Party considers that another State Party is not giving effect to the provisions of this Convention, it may, by written communication, bring the matter to the attention of that State Party. Within three months after the receipt of the communication the receiving State shall afford the State which sent the communication an explanation or any other statement in writing clarifying the matter, which should include, to the extent possible and pertinent, reference to domestic procedures and remedies taken, pending or available in the matter;

(b) If the matter is not adjusted to the satisfaction of both States Parties concerned within six months after the receipt by the receiving State of the initial communication, either State shall have the right to refer the matter to the Committee, by notice given to the Committee and to the other State;

(c) The Committee shall deal with a matter referred to it under this article only after it has ascertained that all domestic remedies have been invoked and exhausted in the matter, in conformity with the generally recognized principles of international law. This shall not be the rule where the application of the remedies is unreasonably prolonged or is unlikely to bring effective relief to the person who is the victim of the violation of this Convention;

(d) The Committee shall hold closed meetings when examining communications under this Article;

(e) Subject to the provisions of subparagraph (c), the Committee shall make available its good offices to the States Parties concerned with a view to a friendly solution of the matter on the basis of respect for the obligations provided for in this Convention. For this purpose, the Committee may, when appropriate, set up an ad hoc conciliation commission;

(f) In any matter referred to it under this article, the Committee may call upon the States Parties concerned, referred to in subparagraph (b), to supply any relevant information;

(g) The States Parties concerned, referred to in subparagraph (b), shall have the right to be represented when the matter is being considered by the Committee and to make submissions orally and/or in writing;

(h) The Committee shall, within twelve months after the date of receipt of notice under subparagraph (b), submit a report:

(i) If a solution within the terms of subparagraph (e) is reached, the Committee shall confine its report to a brief statement of the facts and of the solution reached;

(ii) If a solution within the terms of subparagraph (e) is not reached, the Committee shall confine its report to a brief statement of the facts; the written submissions and record of the oral submissions made by the States Parties concerned shall be attached to the report. In every matter, the report shall be communicated to the States Parties concerned.

2. The provisions of this Article shall come into force when five States Parties to this Convention have made declarations under paragraph 1 of this article. Such declarations shall be deposited by the States Parties with the Secretary-General of the United Nations, who shall transmit copies thereof to the other States Parties. A declaration may be withdrawn at any time by notification to the Secretary-General. Such a withdrawal shall not prejudice the consideration of any matter which is the subject of a communication already transmitted under this article; no further communication by any State Party shall be received under this article after the notification of withdrawal of the declaration has been received by the Secretary-General, unless the State Party concerned has made a new declaration.

Article 22

1. A State Party to this Convention may at any time declare under this article that it recognizes the competence of the Committee to receive and consider communications from or on behalf of individuals subject to its jurisdiction who claim to be victims of a violation by a State Party of the provisions of the Convention. No communication shall be received by the Committee if it concerns a State Party which has not made such a declaration.

2. The Committee shall consider inadmissible any communication under this article which is anonymous or which it considers to be an abuse of the right of submission of such communications or to be incompatible with the provisions of this Convention.

3. Subject to the provisions of paragraph 2, the Committee shall bring any communications submitted to it under this article to the attention of the State Party to this Convention which has made a declaration under paragraph 1 and is alleged to be violating any provisions of the Convention. Within six months, the receiving State shall submit to the Committee written explanations or statements clarifying the matter and the remedy, if any, that may have been taken by that State.

4. The Committee shall consider communications received under this article in the light of all information made available to it by or on behalf of the individual and by the State Party concerned.

5. The Committee shall not consider any communications from an individual under this article unless it has ascertained that:

(a) The same matter has not been, and is not being, examined under another procedure of international investigation or settlement;

(b) The individual has exhausted all available domestic remedies; this shall not be the rule where the application of the remedies is unreasonably prolonged or is unlikely to bring effective relief to the person who is the victim of the violation of this Convention.

6. The Committee shall hold closed meetings when examining communications under this Article.

7. The Committee shall forward its views to the State Party concerned and to the individual.

8. The provisions of this Article shall come into force when five States Parties to this Convention have made declarations under paragraph 1 of this article. Such declarations shall be deposited by the States Parties with the Secretary-General of the United Nations, who shall transmit copies thereof to the other States Parties. A declaration may be withdrawn at any time by notification to the Secretary-General. Such a withdrawal shall not prejudice the consideration of any matter which is the subject of a communication already transmitted under this Article; no further communication by or on behalf of an individual shall be received under this Article after the notification of withdrawal of the declaration has been received by the Secretary General, unless the State Party has made a new declaration.

Article 23

The members of the Committee and of the ad hoc conciliation commissions which may be appointed under Article 21, paragraph 1 (e), shall be entitled to the facilities, privileges and immunities of experts on mission for the United Nations as laid down in the relevant sections of the Convention on the Privileges and Immunities of the United Nations.

Article 24

The Committee shall submit an annual report on its activities under this Convention to the States Parties and to the General Assembly of the United Nations.

PART III

Article 25

1. This Convention is open for signature by all States.

2. This Convention is subject to ratification. Instruments of ratification shall be deposited with the Secretary-General of the United Nations.

Article 26

This Convention is open to accession by all States. Accession shall be effected by the deposit of an instrument of accession with the Secretary-General of the United Nations.

Article 27

1. This Convention shall enter into force on the thirtieth day after the date of the deposit with the Secretary-General of the United Nations of the twentieth instrument of ratification or accession.

2. For each State ratifying this Convention or acceding to it after the deposit of the twentieth instrument of ratification or accession, the Convention shall enter into force on the thirtieth day after the date of the deposit of its own instrument of ratification or accession.

Article 28

1. Each State may, at the time of signature or ratification of this Convention or accession thereto, declare that it does not recognize the competence of the Committee provided for in Article 20.

2. Any State Party having made a reservation in accordance with paragraph 1 of this article may, at any time, withdraw this reservation by notification to the Secretary-General of the United Nations.

Article 29

1. Any State Party to this Convention may propose an amendment and file it with the Secretary-General of the United Nations. The Secretary General shall thereupon communicate the proposed amendment to the States Parties with a request that they notify him whether they favour a conference of States Parties for the purpose of considering and voting upon the proposal. In the event that within four months from the date of such communication at least one third of the States Parties favours such a conference, the Secretary General shall convene the conference under the auspices of the United Nations. Any amendment adopted by a majority of the States Parties present and voting at the conference shall be submitted by the Secretary-General to all the States Parties for acceptance.

2. An amendment adopted in accordance with paragraph I of this Article shall enter into force when two-thirds of the States Parties to this Convention have notified the Secretary-General of the United Nations that they have accepted it in accordance with their respective constitutional processes.

3. When amendments enter into force, they shall be binding on those States Parties which have accepted them, other States Parties still being bound by the provisions of this Convention and any earlier amendments which they have accepted.

Article 30

1. Any dispute between two or more States Parties concerning the interpretation or application of this Convention which cannot be settled through negotiation shall, at the request of one of them, be submitted to arbitration. If within six months from the date of the request for arbitration the Parties are unable to agree on the organization of the arbitration, any one of those Parties may refer the dispute to the International Court of Justice by request in conformity with the Statute of the Court.

2. Each State may, at the time of signature or ratification of this Convention or accession thereto, declare that it does not consider itself bound by paragraph 1 of this article. The other States Parties shall not be bound by paragraph 1 of this Article with respect to any State Party having made such a reservation.

3. Any State Party having made a reservation in accordance with paragraph 2 of this Article may at any time withdraw this reservation by notification to the Secretary-General of the United Nations.

Article 31

1. A State Party may denounce this Convention by written notification to the Secretary-General of the United Nations. Denunciation becomes effective one year after the date of receipt of the notification by the Secretary-General.

2. Such a denunciation shall not have the effect of releasing the State Party from its obligations under this Convention in regard to any act or omission which occurs prior to the date at which the denunciation becomes effective, nor shall denunciation prejudice in any way the continued consideration of any matter which is already under consideration by the Committee prior to the date at which the denunciation becomes effective.

3. Following the date at which the denunciation of a State Party becomes effective, the Committee shall not commence consideration of any new matter regarding that State.

Article 32

The Secretary-General of the United Nations shall inform all States Members of the United Nations and all States which have signed this Convention or acceded to it of the following:

(a) Signatures, ratifications and accessions under Articles 25 and 26;

(b) The date of entry into force of this Convention under Article 27 and the date of the entry into force of any amendments under Article 29;

(c) Denunciations under Article 31.

Article 33

1. This Convention, of which the Arabic, Chinese, English, French, Russian and Spanish texts are equally authentic, shall be deposited with the Secretary-General of the United Nations.

2. The Secretary-General of the United Nations shall transmit certified copies of this Convention to all States.

Document 20

Full Official Title: U.S. reservations, declarations, and understandings, Convention Against Torture and Other Cruel, Inhuman or Degrading Treatment or Punishment

Short Title/Acronym/Abbreviation: U.S. Reservations to the Torture Convention

Subject: U.S. reservations, declarations and understandings to the Torture Convention

Official Citation: Cong. Rec. S17486–01 (daily ed., Oct. 27, 1990)

Date of Document: October 1990

Date of Adoption: Not applicable

Date of General Entry into Force (EIF): Not applicable

Number of States Parties to this Treaty as of this printing: Not a treaty

Date of Signature by United States: Not applicable

Date of Ratification/Accession/Adhesion: Not applicable

Date of Entry into Force as to United States (effective date): Not applicable

Type of Document: This is not a treaty, but is a legal instrument under U.S. and international law which expresses the terms under which the United States ratifies and thus accepts legal obligations under the Torture Convention.

Legal Status/Character of the Instrument/Document as to the United States: These RDUs are legally binding as to U.S. ratification so far as they are consistent with the object and purpose of the Torture Convention.

Comments: The U.S. obligations under the Torture Convention must be read in light of these RDUs.

Caution: The status and applicability of this instrument as to the United States may have changed since date of publication. The above information may be updated by referring to the following site:

Web address: http://www1.umn.edu/humanrts/usdocs/tortres.html

U.S. Reservations, Declarations, and Understandings to the Convention Against Torture (CAT)

I. The Senate's advice and consent is subject to the following reservations:

(1) That the United States considers itself bound by the obligation under Article 16 to prevent "cruel, inhuman or degrading treatment or punishment," only insofar as the term "cruel, inhuman or degrading treatment or punishment" means the cruel, unusual and inhumane treatment or punishment prohibited by the Fifth, Eighth, and/or Fourteenth Amendments to the Constitution of the United States.

(2) That pursuant to Article 30(2) the United States declares that it does not consider itself bound by Article 30(1), but reserves the right specifically to agree to follow this or any other procedure for arbitration in a particular case.

II. The Senate's advice and consent is subject to the following understandings, which shall apply to the obligations of the United States under this Convention:

(1)(a) That with reference to Article 1, the United States understands that, in order to constitute torture, an act must be specifically intended to inflict severe physical or mental pain or suffering and that mental pain or suffering refers to prolonged mental harm caused by or resulting from:

(1) the intentional infliction or threatened infliction of severe physical pain or suffering;

(2) the administration or application, or threatened administration or application, of mind altering substances or other procedures calculated to disrupt profoundly he senses or the personality;

(3) the threat of imminent death; or

(4) the threat that another person will imminently be subjected to death, severe physical pain or suffering, or the administration or application of mind altering substances or other procedures calculated to disrupt profoundly the senses or personality.

(b) That the United States understands that the definition of torture in Article 1 is intended to apply only to acts directed against persons in the offender's custody or physical control.

(c) That with reference to Article 1 of the Convention, the United States understands that "sanctions" includes judicially imposed sanctions and other enforcement actions authorized by United States law or by judicial interpretation of such law. Nonetheless, the United States understands that a State Party could not through its domestic sanctions defeat the object and purpose of the Convention to prohibit torture.

(d) That with reference to Article 1 of the Convention, the United States understands that the term "acquiescence" requires that the public official, prior to the activity constituting torture, have awareness of such activity and thereafter breach his legal responsibility to intervene to prevent such activity.

(e) That with reference to Article 1 of the Convention, the United States understands that noncompliance with applicable legal procedural standards does not per se constitute torture.

(2) That the United States understands the phrase, "where there are substantial grounds for believing that he would be in danger of being subjected to torture," as used in Article 3 of the Convention, to mean "if it is more likely than not that he would be tortured."

(3) That it is the understanding of the United States that Article 14 requires a State Party to provide a private right of action for damages only for acts of torture committed in territory under the jurisdiction of that State Party.

(4) That the United States understands that international law does not prohibit the death penalty, and does not consider this Convention to restrict or prohibit the United States from applying the death penalty consistent with the Fifth, Eighth and/or Fourteenth Amendments to the Constitution of the United States, including any constitutional period of confinement prior to the imposition of the death penalty.

(5) That the United States understands that this Convention shall be implemented by the United States Government to the extent that it exercises legislative and judicial jurisdiction over the matters covered by the Convention and otherwise by the state and local governments. Accordingly, in implementing Articles 10–14 and 16, the United States Government shall take measures appropriate to the Federal system to the end that the competent authorities of the constituent units of the United States of America may take appropriate measures for the fulfillment of the Convention.

III. The Senate's advice and consent is subject to the following declarations:

(1) That the United States declares that the provisions of Articles 1 through 16 of the Convention are not self-executing.

(2) That the United States declares, pursuant to Article 21, paragraph 1, of the Convention, that it recognizes the competence of the Committee against Torture to receive and consider communications to the effect that a State Party claims that another State Party is not fulfilling its obligations under the Convention. It is the understanding of the United States that, pursuant to the above mentioned article, such communications shall be accepted and processed only if they come from a State Party which has made a similar declaration.

IV. The Senate's advice and consent is subject to the following proviso, which shall not be included in the instrument of ratification to be deposited by the President: The President of the United States shall not deposit the instrument of ratification until such time as he has notified all present and prospective ratifying parties to this Convention that nothing in this Convention requires or authorizes legislation, or other action, by the United States of America prohibited by the Constitution of the United States as interpreted by the United States.

Document 21A (Series)

Full Official Title: Second Periodic Report of the United States of America to the Committee Against Torture (U.S. Department of State)

Short Title/Acronym/Abbreviation: U.S. Second Report to the U.N. Committee Against Torture

Type of Document: This is a state report submitted by the U.S. to a U.N. treaty body in compliance with Article 19 of the CAT, to which it is a party.

Subject: Torture, cruel, inhuman, degrading treatment or punishment

Official Citation: United States. Department of State. Second Periodic Report of the United States of America to the Committee Against Torture. Washington, May 6, 2005. On-line. OR—U.N. Doc CAT/C/48/Add.3

Date of Document: May 6, 2005

Date of Adoption: Not applicable

Date of General Entry into Force (EIF): Not applicable

Number of States Parties as of this printing: Not applicable

Date of Signature by the United States: Not applicable

Date of Ratification/Accession/Adhesion: Not applicable

Date of Entry into Force as to United States (effective date): Not applicable

Legal Status/Character of the Instrument/Document as to the United States: This is not a legal instrument but a document that is required to be filed by all state parties to fulfill their legal obligations under Article 19 of the CAT.

Comments: By ratifying the CAT, the U.S. agreed, under Article 19, to report to the Committee Against Torture on measures they have adopted to give effect to the rights recognized in the Covenant or any progress they have made in the enjoyment of those rights. Each state is required to submit an initial report to the Committee within one year of the treaty entering into force, and every four years subsequently or whenever the Committee requests information. The Committee has decided that subsequent reports may be prepared using a list of issues prepared by the Committee prior to the state party's submission to allow the state to focus on specific areas of concern. The Committee reviews and issues its observations and comments on the state's report and makes recommendations. The state may then respond to those recommendations in a subsequent report.

This is the United States' second report and addresses several of the Committee's specific concerns with the implementation of the Covenant. The report is an important tool to reiterate the U.S. position on its treaty obligations and any differences of opinion it may have with the Committee over how they interpret specific obligations, such as the definition of torture or the status of "enemy combatants." This document forms the principal document in a series, 21A, 21B, and 21C, which are part of a single periodic report process before the CAT. They are best understood read together, especially in relation to the Convention Against Torture itself, Document 19.

The report is very large and could not be reprinted in its entirety. Only selected excerpts corresponding to certain articles of the CAT are included. The reader should consult the following website to obtain the full text.

Web Address: http://www.state.gov/g/drl/rls/45738.htm

U.S. Second Report to the U.N. Committee Against Torture (Excerpts)

I. INTRODUCTION

1. The Government of the United States of America welcomes the opportunity to report to the Committee Against Torture on measures giving effect to its undertakings under the Convention Against Torture and Other Cruel, Inhuman or Degrading Treatment or Punishment (Torture Convention), pursuant to Article 19 thereof and on other information that may be helpful to the Committee. The organization of this Second Periodic report follows the General guidelines regarding the form and contents of periodic reports to be submitted by states parties.

2. This report was prepared by the U.S. Department of State ("Department of State") with extensive assistance from the U.S. Department of Justice ("Department of Justice"), the U.S. Department of Homeland Security ("Department of Homeland Security"), the U.S. Department of Defense ("Department of Defense") and other relevant departments and agencies of the United States Government. Except where otherwise noted, the report covers the situation for the period after October 1999 and prior to March 1, 2005.

3. The United States submitted its Initial Report to the Committee Against Torture in October 1999 (CAT/C/28/Add.5), hereafter referred to as "Initial Report". It made its oral presentation of that report to the Committee on May 10–15, 2000. Accordingly, the purpose of this Second Periodic Report is to provide an update of relevant information arising since the submission of the Initial Report.

4. Since the Initial Report, with the attacks against the United States of September 11, 2001, global terrorism has fundamentally altered our world. In fighting terrorism, the U.S. remains committed to respecting the rule of law, including the U.S. Constitution, federal statutes, and international treaty obligations, including the Torture Convention.

5. The President of the United States has made clear that the United States stands against and will not tolerate torture under any circumstances. On the United Nations International Day in Support of Victims of Torture, June 26, 2004, the President confirmed the continued importance of these protections and of U.S. obligations under the Torture Convention, stating:

> … [T]he United States reaffirms its commitment to the worldwide elimination of torture.… . To help fulfill this commitment, the United States has joined 135 other nations in ratifying the Convention Against Torture and other Cruel, Inhuman or Degrading Treatment or Punishment. America stands against and will not tolerate torture. We will investigate and prosecute all acts of torture and undertake to prevent other cruel and unusual punishment in all territory under our jurisdiction.…
>
> These times of increasing terror challenge the world. Terror organizations challenge our comfort and our principles. The United States will continue to take seriously the need to question terrorists who have information that can save lives. But we will not compromise the rule of law or the values and principles that make us strong. Torture is wrong no matter where it occurs, and the United States will continue to lead the fight to eliminate it everywhere. *See* Annex 2.

6. The United States is unequivocally opposed to the use and practice of torture. No circumstance whatsoever, including war, the threat of war, internal political instability, public emergency, or an order from a superior officer or public authority, may be invoked as a justification for or defense to committing torture. This is a longstanding commitment of the United States, repeatedly reaffirmed at the highest levels of the U.S. Government.

7. All components of the United States Government are obligated to act in compliance with the law, including all United States constitutional, statutory, and treaty obligations relating to torture and cruel, inhuman or degrading treatment or punishment. The U.S. Government does not permit, tolerate, or condone torture, or other unlawful practices, by its personnel or employees under any circumstances. U.S. laws prohibiting such practices apply both when the employees are operating in the United States and in other parts of the world.

8. The legal and policy framework through which the United States gives effect to its Convention undertakings has not changed fundamentally since the Initial Report. Unless otherwise noted, the scope of the relevant protections afforded by the United States Constitution and comparable state constitutions, as well as the statutory and regulatory provisions governing the criminal justice system, detention conditions, and the relevant immigration laws and policies continue to apply. Furthermore, the U.S. federal court cases that have referenced the Torture Convention in some way since October, 1999, numbering well over 1000, illustrate the real impact of U.S. Convention undertakings on the U.S. legal system.

9. By letter of May 21, 2004, the Committee requested "updated information concerning the situation in places of detention in Iraq, up to the time of the submission of the report." In Annex 1, Part Two the United States provides a discussion and related materials relevant to its detention of individuals under the control of U.S. Armed Forces in Iraq captured during military operations. The United States provides similar information in Annex 1, Part One, with respect to detentions of individuals under the control of U.S. Armed Forces in Afghanistan and Guantánamo Bay, Cuba.

10. The United States is aware of allegations that detainees held in U.S. custody pursuant to the global war on terrorism have been subject to torture or other mistreatment. The President of the United States, as noted above, has clearly stated that torture is prohibited. When allegations of torture or other unlawful treatment arise, they are investigated and, if substantiated, prosecuted. These issues are addressed in detail in this report and its annexes with a view to conveying the seriousness of the commitment of the United States on these issues.

II. INFORMATION ON NEW MEASURES AND NEW DEVELOPMENTS RELATING TO THE IMPLEMENTATION OF THE CONVENTION

Article 1 (Definition)

11. The definition of torture accepted by the United States upon ratification of the Convention and reflected in the understanding issued in its instrument of ratification remains unchanged. The definition of torture is codified in U.S. law in several contexts.

12. As explained in the Initial Report, this definition is codified at Chapter 113B of Title 18 of the United States Code, which provides federal criminal jurisdiction over an extraterritorial act or attempted act of torture if (1) the alleged offender is a national of the United States or (2) if the alleged offender is present in the United States, irrespective of the nationality of the victim or alleged offender. *See* 18 U.S.C. §§ 2340 and 2340A, as amended (the extraterritorial criminal torture statute), which is set forth in Annex 5. On October 26, 2001, the Uniting and Strengthening America by Providing Appropriate Tools Required to Intercept and Obstruct Terrorism Act of 2001 (USA PATRIOT Act), Pub. L. 107-56, Title VIII, § 811(g), amended § 2340A to add an explicit conspiracy provision with strengthened penalties to the substantive offense described in the extraterritorial criminal statute. This prohibition on torture and conspiracy to torture extends, inter alia, to U.S. employees and U.S. contractors of the United States anywhere in the world outside of the United States, provided that the conduct falls within the enumerated elements of the statute. At the time of the enactment of 18 U.S.C.§§ 2340, 2340A, 18 U.S.C. § 2 already punished those who aid, abet, counsel, command, induce, procure or cause the commission of an offense against the United States.

...

Article 2 (Prohibition)

16. As indicated in the Initial Report, in the U.S. legal system, acts of torture are prohibited by law and contrary to U.S. policy, subject to prompt and impartial investigations, and punished by appropriate sanction. As noted above, the core legal framework through which the United States gives effect to its Convention undertakings to prevent acts of torture has not changed fundamentally since the Initial Report. As explained in the Initial Report, it is clear that any act of torture falling within the Torture Convention definition would in fact be criminally prosecutable in every jurisdiction within the United States. Such acts may be prosecuted, for example, as assault, battery or mayhem in cases of physical injury; as homicide, murder or manslaughter, when a killing results; as kidnapping, false imprisonment or abduction where an unlawful detention is concerned; as rape, sodomy, or molestation; or as part of an attempt, or a conspiracy, an act of racketeering, or a criminal violation of an individual's civil rights.

...

20. **Federal criminal prosecutions of complaints about abuse.** Since the Initial Report, complaints about abuse including physical injury by individual law enforcement officers continue to be made and are investigated, and if the facts so warrant, officers are prosecuted by federal and state authorities. As described in the Initial Report, the Criminal Section of the Department of Justice's Civil Rights Division is charged with reviewing such complaints made to the Federal Government and ensuring the vigorous enforcement of the federal statutes that make torture, or any willful use of excessive force, illegal. The Department of Justice is committed to investigating all incidents of willful use of excessive force by law enforcement officers and to prosecuting federal law violations should action by the local and state authorities fail to vindicate the federal interest. Between October 1, 1999 and January 1, 2005, 284 officers were convicted of violating federal civil rights statutes. Most of these law enforcement officers were charged with using excessive force.

...

22. **Criminal prosecutions of complaints of abuse at the state and local level.** Additionally, prosecutions of abuse at the state and local level continue, some examples of which are cited below:

• In July 2004, a District of Columbia police officer was found guilty by a D.C. Superior Court jury of simple assault after shoving the barrel of his gun into the cheek of a man, following a confrontation at a gas station;

...

23. **Federal criminal prosecutions of violations of procedural rights.** Complaints about failures to accord due process or "procedural rights" by individual law enforcement officers continue to be made to federal and state authorities. As described in the Initial Report, the Criminal Section of the Department of Justice's Civil

Rights Division is charged with reviewing such complaints made to the Federal Government and ensuring the vigorous enforcement of the applicable federal criminal civil rights statutes. The Department of Justice is committed to investigating all allegations of willful violations of constitutional rights and to prosecute federal law violations should action by the local and state authorities fail to vindicate the federal interest. For example, as of January 1, 2005, the Civil Rights Division is conducting two separate ongoing investigations in two different states involving allegations that local police officers used threats of force to coerce information or a confession from an arrestee.

24. **Civil Pattern or Practice Enforcement**. As discussed in the Initial Report, the Department of Justice's Civil Rights Division may institute civil actions for equitable and declaratory relief pursuant to the Pattern or Practice of Police Misconduct provision of the Crime Bill of 1994, 42 U.S.C. § 14141 (Section 14141), which prohibits law enforcement page 11 agencies from engaging in a pattern or practice of violating people's civil rights. Since October 1999, the Civil Rights Division has negotiated 16 settlements with law enforcement agencies. These settlements include two consent decrees regarding the Detroit, Michigan Police Department, and consent decrees covering Prince George's County, Maryland and Los Angeles California police departments. Other recent settlements include those entered into with police departments in the District of Columbia; Cincinnati, Ohio; Buffalo, New York; Villa Rica, Georgia; and Cleveland, Ohio. As of January 1, 2005, there are currently 13 ongoing

...

26. **CRIPA**. The Civil Rights of Institutionalized Persons Act (CRIPA), 42 U.S.C. § 1997 et seq., which permits the Attorney General to bring civil lawsuits against state institutions regarding the civil rights of their residents, including the conditions of their confinement and use of excessive force, is another statute pursuant to which the Department of Justice's Civil Rights Division continues to prevent unlawful use of force. By August 2004, the Civil Rights Division had initiated CRIPA actions regarding approximately 400 facilities, resulting in approximately 120 consent decrees and settlements governing conditions in about 240 facilities, since CRIPA was enacted in 1980. CRIPA enforcement has been a major priority of the Division. Since October 1999, the Division has opened 52 new investigations covering 66 facilities. The Division has also entered into 39 settlement agreements including seven consent decrees. As of January 1, 2005, there are currently 59 active investigations covering 69 facilities.

27. **Federal enforcement actions addressing prison conditions**. As stated above, the Civil Rights Division investigates conditions in state prisons and local jail facilities pursuant to CRIPA, and investigates conditions in state and local juvenile detention facilities pursuant to either CRIPA or Section 14141. These statutes allow the Department of Justice to bring legal actions for declaratory or equitable relief for a pattern or practice of unconstitutional conditions of confinement. Some examples of these investigations follow:

• On July 16, 2004, the Civil Rights Division reached an out-of-court agreement with the Wicomico County Detention Center in Salisbury, Maryland regarding systematic violations of prisoners' federally protected civil rights. The Division's three-year investigation revealed evidence that the Detention Center failed to provide required medical and mental health care, failed to provide adequate inmate safety, and failed to provide sufficiently sanitary living conditions. Under the terms of the agreement, the Detention Center will address and correct the deficiencies identified by the Division;

...

Article 3 (Non-refoulement)

30. The United States continues to recognize its obligation not to "expel, return ('refouler') or extradite a person to another state where there are substantial grounds for believing that he would be in danger of being subjected to torture". The United States is aware of allegations that it has transferred individuals to third countries where they have been tortured. The United States does not transfer persons to countries where the United States believes it is "more likely than not" that they will be tortured. This policy applies to all components of the United States government. The United States obtains assurances, as appropriate, from the foreign government to which a detainee is transferred that it will not torture the individual being transferred. If assurances were not considered sufficient when balanced against treatment concerns, the United States would not transfer the person to the control of that government unless the concerns were satisfactorily resolved. The procedures for evaluating torture concerns in the immigration removal and extradition context are described in greater detail below.

31. **Creation of the Department of Homeland Security (DHS)**. Since the United States submitted the Initial Report and subsequent to the terrorist attacks of September 11, 2001, the United States Government

restructured several agencies within the Executive Branch, creating the U.S. Department of Homeland Security (DHS). *See* Homeland Security Act of 2002, Public Law 107-296, 116 Stat. 2310. As part of this restructuring, the Immigration and Naturalization Service (INS) was abolished and its functions were transferred from the U.S. Department of Justice to the new DHS. Pursuant to the Homeland Security Act, all authorities exercised by the Commissioner of the INS, on behalf of the Attorney General, were transferred to the Secretary of Homeland Security. The Executive Office for Immigration Review (EOIR), whose immigration judges preside over removal proceedings and adjudicate Torture Convention claims, remain within the Department of Justice. Immigration removal proceedings, and the adjudication of Torture Convention claims within those proceedings, remain unchanged since the Initial Report, but the functions described in that report as implemented by INS are now performed by DHS.

32. **Observance of Article 3 obligations in the immigration removal context**. As discussed in the Initial Report, regulations implementing Article 3 of the Torture Convention permit aliens to raise Article 3 claims during the course of immigration removal proceedings. These regulations fully implement U.S. obligations under Article 3 and set forth a fair and rule-bound process for considering claims for protection. Individuals routinely assert Article 3 claims before immigration judges within the EOIR, whose decisions are subject to review by the Board of Immigration Appeals, and ultimately, to review in U.S. federal courts. In exceptional cases where an arriving alien is believed to be inadmissible on terrorism-related grounds, Congress has authorized alternate removal procedures in limited circumstances that do not require consideration or review by EOIR. *See* INA § 235(c). The implementing regulations provide that removal pursuant to section 235(c) of the Act shall not proceed "under circumstances that violate ... Article 3 of the Convention Against Torture." *See* 8 C.F.R. 235.8(b)(4).

. . .

Article 4 (Torture as a criminal offense)

44. As discussed in the Initial Report and as restated in paragraph 16 above, within the United States, acts which would constitute torture under the Convention are punishable under state or federal law. This is also true of attempts to commit torture, conspiracies to commit torture and those who aid and abet the commission of an act of torture. Acts of torture committed outside the United States, as defined by the extraterritorial criminal torture statute, codified at 18 U.S.C. § 2340, in which the alleged offender is a national of the United States, or the alleged offender is present in the United States (irrespective of the nationality of the victim or alleged offender), are punishable under 18 U.S.C. § 2340A. The same prohibitions apply to persons who attempt to commit, conspire to commit, or aid and abet the commission of acts of torture within the definition contained in 18 U.S.C. § 2340.

Article 5 (Jurisdiction)

45. Since the submission of the Initial Report, two pieces of legislation, described below, were enacted that provide additional but distinct statutory bases for asserting jurisdiction over acts committed beyond the territory of the United States in addition to those discussed at paragraph 185 of the Initial Report. In addition to the extraterritorial criminal torture statute, which establishes extra-territorial jurisdiction over certain offenses involving torture, the statutes discussed below extend criminal jurisdiction over an array of offenses, which may include torture, when committed within the "Special Maritime and Territorial Jurisdiction of the United States" (SMTJ). *See* 18 U.S.C. § 7. As discussed in the Initial Report, certain provisions of the federal criminal code apply to acts taking place outside United States geographical territory, but which fall within the SMTJ.

46. On November 22, 2000, the President signed into law the "Military Extraterritorial Jurisdiction Act (MEJA)," codified at 18. U.S.C. §§ 3261 et seq. This statute extends criminal jurisdiction over certain categories of individuals for conduct outside the United States that would constitute an offense punishable by imprisonment for more than 1 year if the conduct had been engaged in within the SMTJ. As reflected in House Report No. 106-778(I) which was adopted by the House Judiciary Committee when it considered the statute, the background and purpose of the statute was to amend federal law to extend the application of its criminal jurisdiction to persons, including civilians, both United States citizens and foreign nationals, who commit acts while employed by or otherwise accompanying the U.S. Armed Forces outside the United States. It also extends federal jurisdiction to active duty members of the Armed Forces who commit acts while outside the United States, with one or more other defendants, at least one of whom is not subject to the UCMJ. See 18 USC 3261(d)(2). It also extends federal jurisdiction to former members of the Armed Forces who commit such acts while they were members of the Armed Forces, but who are not

tried for those crimes by military authorities and later cease to be subject to the Uniform Code of Military Justice. Because many federal crimes, such as sexual assault, arson, robbery, larceny, embezzlement, and fraud, did not have extraterritorial effect, there was a "jurisdictional gap" that in many cases allowed such crimes to go unpunished. Although host nations have jurisdiction to prosecute such acts committed within their territory, they frequently declined to exercise jurisdiction when an American was the victim or when the crime involved only property owned by Americans. Accordingly, the statute was designed to close this gap by establishing a new federal crime involving conduct that would constitute an offense punishable by imprisonment for more than 1 year if the conduct had been engaged in within the special maritime and territorial jurisdiction of the U.S. As of January 1, 2005, there have been two prosecutions under MEJA, neither involving torture.

. . .

50. **The extraterritorial criminal torture statute**. As discussed above in paragraph 12, the USA PATRIOT Act amended the extraterritorial criminal torture statute, codified at 18 U.S.C. §§ 2340, 2340A, to also provide extraterritorial jurisdiction over conspiracy to commit such offenses. As of January 1, 2005, the United States has considered applying the statute in several cases, but it has not initiated any prosecutions under this provision to date. In some cases, investigations are pending. As is necessarily true of any successful criminal prosecution, the available evidence must establish the various elements of the offense. Accordingly, in order for the extraterritorial criminal torture statute to apply, the conduct must fall within the definition of torture, it must have been committed subsequent to the effective date of the statute (November 20, 1994), and it must have been committed "outside the United States."

. . .

Article 8 (Extraditable offenses)

54. Consistent with Article 8 of the Convention, any act of torture within the meaning of the Convention continues to be an extraditable offense under relevant United States law and extradition treaties with countries that are also party to the Convention. The crime of torture continues to fall within the scope of extradition treaties concluded by the United States since the time of its Initial Report.

55. Since the Initial Report, the United States has received a small number of requests for extradition involving individuals wanted for serious human rights abuses or war crimes. Since October 1999, the United States extradited Elizaphan Ntakirutimana to the International Criminal Tribunal for Rwanda, which had requested his extradition for genocide, complicity in genocide, and crimes against humanity.

Article 9 (Mutual legal assistance)

56. As discussed in the Initial Report, United States law permits both law enforcement authorities and the courts to request and to provide many forms of "mutual legal assistance" in criminal cases covered by the provisions of the Torture Convention.

Article 10 (Education and Information)

57. As described in the Initial Report, a variety of training programs exist at the federal, state and local level to educate law enforcement personnel, corrections officers and immigration officials in the proper treatment of persons in custody, including information related to the prohibition against torture and other abuses. Training programs for the U.S. Armed Forces, particularly regarding the prohibition of torture and other standards governing detentions by the U.S. Armed Forces in Afghanistan, Guantánamo Bay, and Iraq are described in greater detail in Annex 1.

. . .

Article 11 (Interrogation techniques)

60. As described in the Initial Report, police interrogation of criminal suspects is strictly regulated by court-made rules based on constitutional law. As a result, the methods and practices of interrogation of criminal suspects and their treatment while in custody are routinely subject to judicial review and revision.

61. Concerns have been raised about what detention and interrogation practices were authorized on the basis of the memorandum drafted by the Department of Justice's Office of Legal Counsel in August 2002 interpreting the extraterritorial criminal torture statute (discussed at paragraph 13). On June 22, 2004, upon the release of numerous government documents related to interrogation techniques and U.S. laws regarding torture, then White House Counsel Alberto Gonzales stated the following:

> "The administration has made clear before and I will reemphasize today that the President has not authorized, ordered or directed in any way any activity that would transgress the standards of the torture conventions or the torture statute, or other applicable laws. [L]et me say that the U.S. will treat people in

our custody in accordance with all U.S. obligations including federal statutes, the U.S. Constitution and our treaty obligations. The President has said we do not condone or commit torture. Anyone engaged in conduct that constitutes torture will be held accountable."

62. Interrogation techniques employed by U.S. government personnel and contractors have been reviewed in light of the revised Department of Justice Office of Legal Counsel memorandum of December 30, 2004. *See* Annex 1.

Article 12 (Prompt and impartial investigation)

63. As noted in the Initial Report, as a matter of law, policy and practice, the competent authorities at all levels of Government and in all components of the U.S. government should proceed with a thorough, prompt and impartial investigation whenever they have reason to believe that an act of torture or other abuse has been committed within their jurisdiction. The discussion under Article 2 above demonstrates the commitment of the law enforcement mechanisms in the United States to investigate and rigorously prosecute such abuses in cases within their respective spheres of jurisdiction. Depending on the circumstances, and as noted in the discussion referred to above, this may include prosecutions of misconduct that may arise at the federal, state, county or local law enforcement levels.

Article 13 (Right to complain)

64. As indicated in the Initial Report, individuals who allege that they have been subject to torture or other forms of mistreatment have numerous opportunities to bring complaints and to have their cases promptly and impartially examined by competent authorities.

65. **Legislation on Victims' Rights.** On October 30, 2004, President Bush signed H.R. 5107, known as the Justice for All Act of 2004. [Pub. L. 108-405] Title I of that Act amends the Federal criminal code to grant victims specified rights, including: (1) the right to be protected from the accused, to be heard at any public proceeding involving release, plea, or sentencing, and to be treated with fairness and respect; (2) the right to timely notice of any public proceeding involving the crime or any release or escape of the accused and to proceedings free from unreasonable delay; (3) the right to confer with the Government attorney; and (4) the right to full and timely restitution. It also authorizes grants to help states implement and enforce their own victims' rights laws. Other provisions of the law relate to the expanded and improved use of DNA evidence in the criminal justice system.

. . .

75. **Foreign Assistance to Victims of Torture.** In keeping with its legislative mandate under the Torture Victims Relief Act of 1998 and its subsequent reauthorizations, the U.S. Agency for International Development (USAID) works through the Victims of Torture Fund (VTF) to assist the treatment and rehabilitation of individuals who suffer from the physical and psychological effects of torture. According to the International Rehabilitation Council for Torture Victims (IRCT), rehabilitation aims to empower the torture victim to regain the capacity, confidence, and ability to resume as full a life as possible. In FY 2000, Congress appropriated $7,500,000 to USAID for assistance to survivors of torture. For FY 2001 and 2002, Congress appropriated $10,000,000 in each year. The appropriation levels for FY 2003 and 2004 were $7,950,000 each year.

. . .

Article 14 (Right of redress and/or compensation)

79. As described in the Initial Report, the legal system of the United States provides a variety of mechanisms through which persons subjected to torture or other abuse may seek redress, which are consistent with the obligations assumed by the United States upon ratification of the Convention.

80. **Civil actions in state and federal courts.** Individuals continue to file civil suits in state and federal courts seeking redress against officials for allegedly violating their rights, which may involve seeking monetary damages or equitable or declaratory relief. One of the most common methods by which prisoners seek redress against state and municipal officials is by means of a civil law suit for violations of fundamental rights pursuant to 42 U.S.C. § 1983. Some examples of such civil litigation follow:

• On September 26, 2002, the Court of Appeals of Arizona upheld the decision of a trial court jury that handed down a judgment against a local sheriff in an incident where an inmate in the county jail brutally attacked another inmate. The incident gave rise to a civil rights claim for damages under § 1983. The sheriff was found by the jury to have demonstrated deliberate indifference to inmate safety. The jury awarded, and the appellate court affirmed the award of compensatory and punitive damages;

. . .

81. **Alien Tort Statute**. As discussed in the Initial Report, the Alien Tort Statute (ATS), which was enacted in 1789 and is currently codified at 28 U.S.C. § 1350, provides that "[the] district courts shall have original jurisdiction in any civil action by an alien for a tort only, committed in violation of the law of nations or a treaty of the United States." The United States Supreme Court recently had occasion to consider the ATS in *Sosa v. Alvarez-Machain*, 124 S.Ct. 2739 (2004). While adopting a restrictive interpretation of the range of civil actions that could be brought under this statute consistent with the intent of the legislators who originally enacted it, the Court left open the possibility that federal courts may recognize as a matter of federal common law claims for damages based on alleged violations of the law of nations.

82. **Torture Victims Protection Act (TVPA)**. As described in the Initial Report, the 1992 Torture Victims Protection Act allows both foreign nationals and United States citizens to claim damages against any individual who engages in torture or extrajudicial killing under "actual or apparent authority, or under color of law of any foreign nation." It allows suits for redress for torture or extrajudicial killings perpetrated by officials of foreign governments. In July 2002, following a four week trial of a suit brought under the TVPA, a federal jury in the Southern District of Florida in West Palm Beach returned a verdict of $54.6 million against two Salvadoran generals for their responsibility for the torture of three Salvadorans in the early 1980s. *Romagoza Arce v. Garcia*, No. 99-8364 CIV-Hurley (S.D. Fla. Feb 17, 2000). The U.S. Court of Appeals for the Eleventh Circuit subsequently reversed this decision on the grounds that the claims were time-barred by the statute of limitations. *Romagoza Arce v. Garcia*, No. 02-14427 (11th Cir. 2005).

83. **Treatment and rehabilitation**. As noted in the Initial Report, the United States continues to hold the view that in addition to monetary compensation, States should take steps to make available other forms of remedial benefits to victims of torture, including medical and psychiatric treatment as well as social and legal services. For examples of the U.S. commitment to such programs, see paragraphs 66–78.

...

Article 15 (Coerced statements)

85. United States law continues to provide strict rules regarding the exclusion of coerced statements and the inadmissibility of illegally obtained evidence in criminal trials.

86. Also, some states have taken steps recently to further protect the rights of the accused In 2003, Illinois passed a crime law that requires police to videotape or audiotape questioning of suspects in homicide cases for the entirety of the interview. The reform measure joins Illinois with Alaska and Minnesota as the leading states to require such tapings.

Article 16 (Other cruel, inhuman or degrading treatment or punishment)

87. As the President of the United States explained on the United Nations International Day in Support of Victims of Torture, in addition to its commitment to investigating and prosecuting all acts of torture, the United States will "undertake to prevent other cruel and unusual punishment in all territory under our jurisdiction." *See* Annex 2.

88. In the United States a robust legal and policy framework operates to give effect to U.S. obligations under Article 16 of the Torture Convention. Article 16 requires that States parties act to "prevent in any territory under its jurisdiction other acts of cruel, inhuman or degrading treatment or punishment which do not amount to torture as defined in Article 1, when such acts are committed by or at the instigation of or with the consent or acquiescence of a public official or other person acting in an official capacity." The particular undertakings of Article 16 are those specified in Articles 10–13, "with the substitution for references to torture of references to other forms of cruel, inhuman or degrading treatment or punishment." As we did in the Initial Report, we note the reservation to Article 16 included by the United States in its instrument of ratification: "That the United States considers itself bound by the obligation under Article 16 to prevent 'cruel, inhuman or degrading treatment or punishment,' only insofar as the term 'cruel, inhuman or degrading treatment or punishment' means the cruel, unusual, and inhumane treatment or punishment prohibited by the Fifth, Eighth, and/or Fourteenth Amendments to the Constitution of the United States." As described in the Initial Report, federal and state law provide extensive protections against conduct that may amount to cruel, inhuman or degrading

...

92. **Conditions of Confinement**. U.S. law enforcement authorities continue to work to improve conditions of confinement in detention facilities within the United States. In fact, the discussion in paragraph 27 above provides an illustration of such problems, as well as the mechanisms employed by the Civil Rights Division of the Department of Justice to challenge conditions of confinement in various prisons and other

remedies available under federal and state law. United States law, at both the federal and state level, continues to provide inmates themselves with several methods to challenge conditions of confinement. Indeed, it is common practice in prisons and jails throughout the United States for inmates to challenge conditions of confinement in federal and state courts as evidenced by the numerous district and appellate court decisions handed down every year in federal reporters (collections of federal case decisions), and as further exemplified by the discussion under paragraph 27 above. Additionally, various non-governmental organizations continue to employ advocacy and litigation to draw attention to sub-standard conditions in the nation's prisons. For example, as a result of a class-action lawsuit over conditions for prisoners in a county jail in Washington State filed by the ACLU's National Prison Project in February 2002, a U.S. District Court approved a settlement agreement in January 2004 to improve conditions for inmates in the jail.

. . .

95. **Supermaximum security prisons**. For certain violent inmates, supermaximum security ("supermax") facilities may be necessary, for among other reasons, to protect the safety of the community at large and of other members of the prison population. As discussed in the preceding paragraphs, U.S. law requires that prisons throughout the United States satisfy U.S. constitutional requirements. When they fail to do so, a variety of remedies are available, as described under Article 2 above. For example, in March 2003, the ACLU and others settled a lawsuit brought against Wisconsin's Department of Corrections regarding conditions at its supermax prison in Boscobel, Wisconsin. The settlement agreement included a ban on seriously mentally ill prisoners being housed in the facility; a modest improvement to exercise provision and rehabilitation programs; and a reduction in the use of restraints and electro-shock control devices.

96. **Sexual abuse of prisoners**. Law enforcement authorities in the United States continue to prevent and punish acts of sexual abuse committed against prisoners. Illustrative of the problem of sexual abuse in correctional facilities are the facts animating *United States v. Arizona* and *United States v. Michigan*, both filed in 1997 and dismissed in 1999 and 2000, respectively, subject to a settlement whereby state prisons agreed to make significant changes in conditions of confinement for female inmates. In these cases, brought pursuant to CRIPA, described above, the Department of Justice's Civil Rights Division sought to remedy a pattern or practice of sexual misconduct against female inmates by male staff, including sexual contact and unconstitutional invasions of privacy.

. . .

102. **Restraint devices**. The use of restraint and electro-shock devices continues to form the basis of allegations of abuse by law enforcement officers. Advocacy groups have directed considerable attention to publicizing such allegations and taking legal action to remedy alleged abuses. According to a 2002 Amnesty International report, between 2000 and 2002, at least four inmates died in the United States after being subdued in a restraint chair. In February 2001, the American Civil Liberty Union's National Prison Project and the Connecticut branch of the ACLU filed a lawsuit against the Connecticut Department of Corrections alleging that Connecticut prisoners held in a Virginia state prison, Wallens Ridge State Prison, were being subjected to cruel and unusual punishment in violation of the U.S. Constitution, by being placed in mechanical restraints for prolonged periods for minor offenses.

. . .

107. The stun belt is a defensive device. Only trained, qualified staff members at the supervisory level are authorized to apply and activate a stun belt during an escorted trip. When activated, it produces a medically tested, less than lethal electrical charge of 50,000 volts, which temporarily immobilizes the inmate without causing permanent injury, allowing staff to regain immediate control of the situation. The stun belt has been determined to be essentially harmless to individuals in good health. The BOP medical staff have reviewed the stun belt and concluded the technology is medically safe for use on the great majority of the BOP's inmate population. The exceptions are: 1) pregnant female inmates, 2) inmates with heart disease, 3) inmates with multiple sclerosis, 4) inmates with muscular dystrophy, and 5) inmates who are epileptic. As part of pre-escort screening, inmates identified as having these conditions are prohibited from wearing the belt.

108. When federal pretrial detainees are remanded to the custody of the U.S. Marshals Service, USMS policies and procedures regarding restraints apply. However, the USMS does not operate any facilities that house pretrial detainees. Rather, the USMS contracts with state, local, and private jails throughout the United States to house and care for federal pretrial detainees. Although the daily safekeeping and care of federal pretrial detainees is the responsibility of these jails, the jails must nonetheless undergo regular USMS inspections under the standards promulgated by the U.S. Department of Justice and the American Correctional Association.

109. Stun belts are also used for courtroom security purposes to control potentially violent defendants. The stun belt is placed underneath the clothing of the individual, on the individual's waist, and is activated by remote control.

...

114. **Detention of juveniles**. The Department of Justice continues to make it a priority to investigate and remedy unlawful conditions in juvenile justice facilities across America. Between October 1, 1999 and January 1, 2005, the Civil Rights Division authorized 16 investigations covering 26 juvenile justice facilities, issued eight findings letters—letters detailing patterns or practices of civil rights violations and minimum remedial measures to remedy the violations - regarding conditions in 17 juvenile justice facilities, and entered 11 settlement agreements involving 26 facilities. In fiscal year 2004, the Civil Rights Division authorized five investigations of five facilities; issued three findings letters regarding conditions at six facilities; filed one lawsuit involving two facilities; and entered three consent decrees agreements regarding four facilities.

...

116. Although practice varies within prisons at the state level, in federal prisons, juveniles are not regularly held in prison with the regular prison population. Federal law prohibits juvenile offenders held in custody of federal authorities from being placed in correctional institutions or detention facilities in which they could have regular contact with adult offenders. See 18 U.S.C. § 5039

117. **Care and Placement of Unaccompanied Alien Children**. In March 2003, § 462 of the Homeland Security Act of 2002 transferred functions under U.S. immigration laws regarding the care and placement of unaccompanied alien children (UACs) from the Commissioner of the Immigration and Naturalization Service to the Office of Refugee Resettlement (ORR) within the Administration for Children and Families (ACF) at the Department of Health and Human Services.

...

120. **Abuse of the institutionalized**. Between October 1 1999 and January 1, 2005, pursuant to CRIPA, described above in paragraph 26, the Civil Rights Division authorized 5 investigations covering 8 facilities housing persons with mental illness, 6 investigations covering 6 facilities housing persons with developmental disabilities, and 10 investigations covering 10 nursing homes. During that period, the Civil Rights Division entered into four settlement agreements concerning three facilities housing persons with mental illness, 10 settlement agreements concerning 17 facilities housing persons with developmental disabilities, and 3 settlements concerning 3 nursing homes. During that period, pursuant to CRIPA, the Civil Rights Division issued findings letters regarding conditions in 7 facilities for persons with mental illness, 5 facilities for persons with developmental disabilities, and 11 nursing homes. Some examples of these investigations follow:

• On January 12, 2004, the U.S. Department of Justice's Civil Rights Division and the State of Louisiana filed a complaint and consent decree in *United States v. Louisiana* (M.D. La.) regarding the Hammond and Pinecrest Developmental Centers. The action resolved an investigation into allegations of a pattern or practice of violations at the two facilities. Pinecrest and Hammond are the two largest state-owned and operated residential facilities in Louisiana serving persons with developmental disabilities. Staff at one of the facilities have been arrested for abuse such as kicking a resident, dragging him to his room, placing a blanket over his head, and hitting him. At the other facility, staff had left residents alone for long periods of time and when the residents were eventually found, they were found in appalling and unclean conditions. The Department of Justice's Civil Rights Division and the State of Louisiana entered into a consent decree in which the State agreed to remedy the alleged constitutional deficiencies;

...

121. **Prisoners on chain gangs**. Chain gangs are employed by a minority of states, where their use has sparked controversy. However, the use of chain gangs is not *per se* unconstitutional.

122. The Bureau of Prisons does not employ chain gangs. While only a minority of states and some local jurisdictions employ chain gang work crews, one county in Arizona has attracted particular attention for its approach. Maricopa County, Arizona operates four chain gangs, two for adult males, one for females, and one for juveniles. Common duty for chain gang members is to bury indigent members of the community. In the past, federal authorities have in some instances taken measures to regulate state authorities who have employed chain gangs.

123. Some states have stopped using chain gangs for a variety of reasons, including safety concerns for inmates. Although Alabama was the first state to resurrect the practice in 1995, it ended its chain gangs only

two years later. Inmate safety was a significant factor behind Alabama's decision after a guard shot an inmate who attacked a fellow prisoner while they were chained together and the victim could not escape. Also, in 2002, the Alabama Supreme Court ruled that prison guards could be held liable for injuries suffered by a prisoner while on a chain gang.

. . .

125. **Adult aliens in immigration custody**. The Department of Homeland Security continues to address allegations that arise about the treatment of aliens held in immigration detention. Within the Department of Homeland Security, the Bureau of Immigration and Customs Enforcement (ICE), Office of Detention and Removal Operations (DRO) detains approximately 19,000 aliens in Service Processing Centers, Contract Detention Facilities and local facilities through Inter-governmental Service Agreements (IGSA). ICE regularly meets at both the national and local levels with various non-governmental organizations (NGOs) (such as the American Immigration Lawyers Association, the American Bar Association, Catholic Charities, Las Americas) to address such allegations. A national NGO working group meets in Washington, D.C. at ICE Headquarters. ICE also regularly meets with consular officials to address allegations of mistreatment.

. . .

134. **Immigration detentions connected with September 11 investigations**. In response to the attacks against the United States on September 11, 2001, the United States initiated an investigation to identify any accomplices to the terrorists who committed the September 11 attacks and to prevent a future attack. Department of Justice officials from numerous components, including employees of the Federal Bureau of Investigation (FBI), the former Immigration and Naturalization Service, the United States Marshals Service, the Bureau of Prisons, the Criminal Division, and many United States Attorney's Offices, along with officials at the state level, worked tirelessly to do everything within their legal authority to protect against another terrorist attack. As a result of the Federal Bureau of Investigation's (FBI) investigation, known as "PENTTBOM" (Pentagon Twin Towers Bombing), 762 aliens were detained on immigration charges after the attacks.

. . .

140. **Capital punishment**. The issue of capital punishment remains a matter of active discussion within the United States. As was true when the United States submitted its Initial Report, a majority of the people in a majority of the states, and of the country as a whole, have chosen through their democratically elected representatives to provide the possibility of capital punishment for the most serious of crimes. Capital punishment is permitted by 38 states and by the Federal Government, whereas 12 states and the District of Colombia prohibit its use.

141. As has been explained elsewhere in this report and as discussed in detail in the Initial Report, the reservation to Article 16 contained in the U.S. instrument of ratification limits U.S. obligations under Article 16 of the Convention to the prohibitions against "cruel, unusual and inhumane treatment or punishment prohibited by the Fifth, Eighth, and/or Fourteenth Amendments to the Constitution of the United States." Moreover, the United States understanding, also included in the U.S. instrument of ratification, states that "The United States understands that international law does not prohibit the death penalty, and does not consider this Convention to restrict or prohibit the United States from applying the death penalty consistent with the Fifth, Eighth and/or Fourteenth Amendments to the Constitution of the United States, including any constitutional period of confinement prior to the imposition of the death penalty."

142. Accordingly, as stated in the Initial Report, the United States considers the issue of capital punishment to be outside the scope of its reporting obligations under the Torture Convention. Nevertheless, in an annex to the Initial Report, the United States provided for the information of the Committee a summary of some aspects of the issue. As a matter of courtesy to the Committee, the United States provides updated information on this issue in Annex 7.

III. ADDITIONAL INFORMATION REQUESTED BY THE COMMITTEE

143. By letter of May 21, 2004, the Committee requested "updated information concerning the situation in places of detention in Iraq, up to the time of the submission of the report." This and other relevant information regarding U.S. military operations is provided in Annex 1 for the Committee's review.

IV. OBSERVATIONS ON THE COMMITTEE'S CONCLUSIONS AND RECOMMENDATIONS

144. The United States has carefully considered the Committee's Conclusions and Recommendations. Observations of the United States on those conclusions and recommendations appear below.

The Committee expressed concern over "The failure of the State Party to enact a federal crime of torture in terms consistent with Article 1 of the Convention."

145. As was discussed in considerable detail in the Initial Report, every act of torture within the meaning of the Convention, as ratified by the United States, is illegal under existing federal and/or state law, and any individual who commits such an act is subject to penal sanctions as specified in criminal statutes at either the state or federal level. While the specific legal nomenclature and definitions vary from jurisdiction to jurisdiction, it is clear that any act of torture falling within the Convention would in fact be criminally prosecutable in every jurisdiction within the United States. The United States appreciates many merits in the suggestion advanced by the Committee. However, as the United States substantively has fulfilled the requirements of the Convention in this respect and for the reasons it determined to apply at the time it became party to the Convention, the United States has decided to retain the current statutory regime within the United States on this point.

The Committee expressed concern over "The reservation lodged to Article 16, in violation of the Convention, the effect of which is to limit the application of the Convention."

146. The Committee's use of the phrase "in violation of the Convention" is confusing as a matter of international treaty law. By their nature, reservations alter the scope of treaty obligations assumed by State Parties. Accordingly, reservations that are not prohibited by a treaty or by the applicable international law rules relating to reservations are not violations of that treaty. As the Torture Convention does not prohibit the making of a reservation and as the reservation in question is not incompatible with the object and purpose of the Convention, there is nothing in the U.S. reservation that would be unlawful or otherwise constitute a violation of the Convention.

147. The decision by the United States to condition its ratification upon a reservation to Article 16 (construing its obligations under Article 16 to prevent "cruel, inhuman or degrading treatment or punishment" only insofar as the term means the cruel, unusual and inhumane treatment or punishment prohibited by the Fifth, Eighth and/or Fourteenth Amendments to the U.S. Constitution) was made after careful deliberation. Indeed, the existence of this reservation was a critical element in the decision by the United States to become a State Party to the Convention. The rationale set forth in the Initial Report, in particular the vague and ambiguous nature of the term "degrading treatment," remains equally valid at this time.

The Committee expressed concern over "The number of cases of police ill-treatment of civilians, and ill-treatment in prisons (including instances of inter-prisoner violence). Much of this ill-treatment by police and prison guards seems to be based upon discrimination."

148. Please see discussion under under Article 2 and Article 16 above. In a country of some 280 million people with a prison population of over 2 million people it is perhaps unavoidable, albeit unfortunate, that there are cases of abuse. Continuing U.S. efforts to deal with these problems and punish perpetrators of such acts are set out throughout this report. The United States fully agrees that the rights of detainees should be protected, in particular against unlawful discrimination.

The Committee expressed concern over "Alleged cases of sexual assault upon female detainees and prisoners by law enforcement officers and prison personnel. Female detainees and prisoners are also very often held in humiliating and degrading circumstances."

149. Please see discussion under Article 16 above.

The Committee expressed concern over "The use of electro-shock devices and restraint chairs as methods of constraint, which may violate the provisions of Article 16 of the Convention."

150. Please see discussion under Article 16 above.

The Committee expressed concern over "The excessively harsh regime of the 'supermaximum' prisons."

151. Please see discussion under Article 16 above.

The Committee expressed concern over "The use of 'chain gangs', particularly in public."

152. Please see discussion under Article 16 above.

The Committee expressed concern over "The legal action by prisoners seeking redress, which has been significantly restricted by the requirement of physical injury as a condition for bringing a successful action under the Prison Litigation Reform Act."

153. The Prison Litigation Reform Act of 1996 (PLRA), which was enacted as part of Pub. L. 104-134, contains several provisions designed to curtail frivolous lawsuits by prison inmates. One such provision is the

requirement that no action shall be brought with respect to prison conditions under federal law by a prisoner until such administrative remedies as are available are exhausted. Another is the provision that no federal civil action may be brought by a prisoner for mental or emotional injury suffered while in custody without a prior showing of physical injury. Courts of appeals have held that the physical injury requirement does not prevent a prisoner from obtaining injunctive or declaratory relief. E.g., *Thompson v. Carter*, 284 F.3d 411, 418 (2d Cir. 2002). Moreover, the "physical injury" requirement has been challenged in U.S. courts and its constitutionality has been upheld. Since their enactment in 1996, the statutory amendments provided by the PLRA have achieved their fundamental purpose of restricting frivolous lawsuits by inmates that were disrupting the efficient operation of the federal judicial system.

The Committee expressed concern over "The holding of minors (juveniles) with adults in the regular prison population."

154. Please see discussion under Article 16.

Recommendations *"enact a federal crime of torture in terms consistent with Article 1 of the Convention and withdraw its reservations, interpretations and understandings relating to the Convention."*

155. As described above, the United States respectfully disagrees with the Committee regarding the necessity and advisability of enacting a new federal crime of torture when existing U.S. law already provides that every act of torture within the meaning of the Torture Convention, as ratified by the United States, is prohibited by criminal law under existing federal and/or state law.

156. The United States respectfully reminds the Committee that the United States reached its conclusion that it would be necessary to condition U.S. ratification of the Convention on certain reservations, understandings and declarations as a result of a serious and careful review of U.S. law. The Initial Report sets forth the rationale for each of those reservations, understandings and declarations. While the United States has considered its existing reservations, understandings, and declarations in light of the Committee's recommendation, there have been no developments in the interim that have caused the United States to revise its view of the continuing validity and necessity of the conditions set forth in its instrument of ratification.

"take such steps as are necessary to ensure that those who violate the Convention are investigated, prosecuted and punished, especially those who are motivated by discriminatory purposes or sexual gratification."

157. Much of this report has described actions taken within the United States that are consistent with this recommendation. The United States Government is aware of continuing allegations of specific types of abuse and ill-treatment in particular cases. The United States believes that, overall, the country's law enforcement agencies and correctional institutions set and maintain high standards of conduct for their officers and treatment for persons in their custody. The United States believes that there is a deterrent effect on prospective individual conduct due to the successful federal and state criminal prosecutions of law enforcement officers who are responsible for abuse. It also realizes that such conduct has not been eradicated and that its efforts in this regard must continue.

158. The discussion under Article 2 above provides accounts of examples of the Department of Justice's efforts to prosecute law enforcement officers for misconduct, as exemplified by the 284 convictions of law enforcement officers for violating federal civil rights statutes between October 1, 1999 and January 1, 2005. When sufficient evidence of a violation of an individual's constitutional rights is established, such cases are prosecuted by the Federal Government and substantial sentences are adjudged. Please refer also to the discussion under Article 16 above regarding police brutality and the action taken to remedy such abuses. In addition to federal law enforcement efforts, local and state prosecutions are also brought.

159. Recognizing that female offenders have different social, psychological, educational, family, and health care needs than male offenders, the Bureau of Prisons continues to design and implement special programs for women offenders. However, the BOP treats all inmates, male and female, in a firm, fair, and consistent manner, with a primary focus being the maintenance of the inmates' dignity and humanity. Prospective employees undergo a rigorous pre-employment screening and background check to ensure the highest standards of integrity. Once employed, staff receive initial training and refresher training at least annually throughout their careers regarding the importance of proper treatment of inmates, and appropriate boundaries between staff and inmates.

160. Despite these measures, there have been unfortunate instances where staff have violated these standards of trust. Federal law expressly criminalizes sexual activity between correctional workers and inmates

in federal prisons. Every allegation is investigated thoroughly. In cases where an allegation of inappropriate conduct by a staff member towards an inmate is substantiated, offending staff are referred for prosecution, to eradicate this deplorable behavior. Examples of prosecutions of such conduct are provided in the discussion under Article 16 above.

"Abolish electro-shock stun belts and restraint chairs as methods of restraining those in custody; their use almost invariably leads to breaches of Article 16 of the Convention."

161. The policies regarding the use of restraint chairs adopted by the Department of Justice reflect an awareness that the use of restraint chairs and stun belts, while lawful, should nevertheless be carefully circumscribed. The Bureau of Prisons' use of restraint chairs is intended only for short-term use, such as transporting an inmate on or off of an airplane. In the course of several investigations, the Civil Rights Division of the Department of Justice has investigated the use of the restraint chair in non-federal jails and prisons. The Civil Rights Division has recommended that such devices should only be used to keep an inmate from hurting himself or others, when less restrictive means of controlling the inmate have failed. The use of such devices should be carefully controlled and the inmate should be monitored at least every 15 minutes, vital signs should be checked and opportunities for movement, eating, and toileting should be provided. Restraints should be removed as soon as the inmate is no longer a threat to himself or others.

162. In the course of its investigations of adult correctional facilities, juvenile correctional facilities and law enforcement agencies pursuant to the Civil Rights of Institutionalized Persons Act (CRIPA) and the Pattern or Practice of Police Misconduct provision of the Crime Bill of 1994, described above, the Civil Rights Division has recommended limitations on the use of electro-shock weapons in both law enforcement agencies and corrections facilities, as well as increased training for officers using such weapons. However, the *per se* use of such restraints does not violate constitutional standards. Used appropriately, stun belts, stun guns, certain types of choke holds, and pepper spray can be effective tools for law enforcement under certain conditions where use of force is warranted due to the actions of a suspect whom the police are justifiably attempting to detain or arrest and in the correctional setting. In particular, these devices sometimes can be used as effective alternatives where more serious or deadly force would otherwise be justified. In the corrections setting, medical screening is required to determine if use of stun devices and pepper spray is contraindicated.

"Consider declaring in favor of Article 22 of the Convention."

163. At the time it undertook its domestic procedures to become a State Party to the Convention, the United States Executive and Legislative Branches gave substantial thought to the question of whether to avail the United States of the procedure set forth in Article 22. Since receiving the Committee's recommendation, the United States has further considered whether to make a declaration recognizing the competence of the Committee to consider communications made by or on behalf of individuals claiming to be victims of a violation of the Convention by the United States. While noting that at any time it could decide to reconsider the issue, the United States continues to decline to make such a declaration. As has been discussed at considerable length throughout this report, the United States legal system affords numerous opportunities for individuals to complain of abuse, and to seek remedies for such alleged violations. Accordingly, the United States will continue to direct its resources to addressing and dealing with violations of the Convention pursuant to the operation of its own domestic legal system.

"Ensure that minors (juveniles) are not held in prison with the regular prison population."

164. As stated under Article 16 above, in federal prisons, juveniles are not regularly held in prison with the regular prison population. Federal law prohibits juvenile offenders held in custody of federal authorities from being placed in correctional institutions or detention facilities in which they could have regular contact with adult offenders. *See* 18 U.S.C. § 5039. When a juvenile must be temporarily detained in an adult facility, it is for a minimal period of time and "sight and sound" separation from the adult offenders is ensured within the institution. The Bureau of Prisons has less than 300 juvenile offenders in its custody, and all such offenders are housed in contract facilities. All juvenile offenders in BOP custody are required to receive 50 hours per week of quality programming (e.g., GED, drug treatment, sex offender treatment, violent offender treatment).

165. The United States appreciates this opportunity to update its Initial Report on the operation of the Convention within the United States and looks forward to further work with the Committee Against Torture on these important issues.

V. ANNEXES
Annex 1
PART ONE
INDIVIDUALS UNDER THE CONTROL OF U.S. ARMED FORCES CAPTURED DURING OPERATIONS AGAINST AL-QAIDA, THE TALIBAN AND THEIR AFFILIATES AND SUPPORTERS I. BACKGROUND ON THE WAR AGAINST AL-QAIDA, THE TALIBAN AND THEIR AFFILIATES AND SUPPORTERS

1. The United States and its coalition partners are engaged in a war against al-Qaida, the Taliban, and their affiliates and supporters. There is no question that under the law of armed conflict, the United States has the authority to detain persons who have engaged in unlawful belligerence until the cessation of hostilities. Like other wars, when they start we do not know when they will end. Still, we may detain combatants until the end of the war.

2. At the same time, the commitment of the United States to treat detainees humanely is clear and well documented. A discussion of allegations of mistreatment of detainees appears in Part One, III.B and Part Two, III.B.

3. To understand U.S. actions in continuing to detain members of al-Qaida, the Taliban, and their affiliates and supporters, whether captured committing acts of belligerency themselves or directly supporting hostilities in aid of such enemy forces, the United States submits a brief summary of events in its war against al-Qaida, the Taliban, and their affiliates and supporters.

Summary of unlawful belligerent acts committed by al-Qaida

4. Although the events of September 11, 2001 indisputably brought conflict to U.S. soil al-Qaida had engaged in acts of war against the United States long before that date. The reality is that for almost a decade before September 11, 2001, al-Qaida and its affiliates waged a war against the United States, although it did not show the depth of its goals until the morning of September 11, 2001.

5. In 1996, Usama bin Ladin issued a fatwa declaring war on the United States. In February 1998, he repeated the fatwa stating that it was the duty of all Muslims to kill U.S. citizens—civilian or military—and their allies everywhere. Six months later, on August 7, 1998, al-Qaida attacked two U.S. Embassies in Kenya and Tanzania, killing over 200 people and injuring approximately 5,000.

6. In 1999, an al-Qaida member attempted to carry out a bombing plot at the Los Angeles International Airport during the Millennium Celebrations. U.S. law enforcement foiled this attack, arresting Ahmed Ressam at Port Angeles at the U.S./Canadian border. The United States now knows that in October 2000, al-Qaida directed the attack on a U.S. naval warship, the USS Cole, while docked in the port of Aden, Yemen.13 This attack killed 17 U.S. sailors and injured 39.

7. The horrific events of September 11, 2001 are well known. On that day, the United States suffered massive and brutal attacks carried out by nineteen al-Qaida suicide hijackers who crashed three U.S. commercial jets into the World Trade Center and the Pentagon, and were responsible for the downing of one commercial jet in Shanksville, Pennsylvania. These attacks resulted in approximately 3,000 individuals of 78 different nationalities reported dead or missing.

8. The United Nations Security Council immediately condemned these terrorist acts as a "threat to international peace and security" and recognized the "inherent right of individual or collective self-defense in accordance with the United Nations Charter." U.N. Sec. Council Res. 1368, U.N. Doc. No. S/RES/1368 (Sept. 12, 2001) (at http://daccessdds.un.org/doc/UNDOC/GEN /N01/533/82/PDF/N0153382.pdf?OpenElement (visited October 13, 2005)); see U.N. Sec. Council Res. 1373, U.N. Doc. No. S/RES/1373 (Sept. 28, 2001) (at http://www.un.org/ News/Press/docs/2001/sc7158.doc.htm (visited October 13, 2005)) (deciding that all States shall take certain steps to combat terrorism).

9. On September 12, 2001, less than 24 hours after the terrorist attacks against the United States, NATO declared the attacks to be an attack against all the 19 NATO member countries. The Allies—for the first time in NATO's history—invoked Article 5 of the Washington Treaty, which states that an armed attack against one or more NATO member countries is an attack against all. NATO followed this landmark decision by implementing practical measures aimed at assisting the United States. (At http://www.nato.int/terrorism/index.htm#a (visited October 13, 2005)).

10. On September 11, 2001, the Organization of American States (OAS) General Assembly immediately "condemned in the strongest terms, the terrorist acts visited upon the cities of New York and Washington,

D.C." and expressed "full solidarity" with the government and people of the United States. Immediately thereafter, the foreign ministers of the States Parties to the 1947 Inter-American Treaty of Reciprocal Assistance (the Rio Treaty) declared, "these terrorist attacks against the United States of America are attacks against all American states."

. . .

19. In conclusion, it is clear that al-Qaida and its affiliates and supporters have planned and continue to plan and perpetrate armed attacks against the United States and its coalition partners, and they directly target civilians in blatant violation of the law of war.

II. DETAINEES—CAPTURING, HOLDING, RELEASING AND/OR TRYING
A. Brief overview of the detainee populations held by the U.S. armed forces at Guantánamo Bay and in Afghanistan

20. During the course of the war in Afghanistan, the U.S. Armed Forces and allied forces have captured or procured the surrender of thousands of individuals fighting as part of the al-Qaida and Taliban effort. The law of war has long recognized the right to detain combatants until the cessation of hostilities. Detaining enemy combatants prevents them from returning to the battlefield and engaging in further armed attacks against innocent civilians and U.S. forces. Further, detention serves as a deterrent against future attacks by denying the enemy the fighters needed to conduct war. Interrogations during detention enable the United States to gather important intelligence to prevent future attacks during ongoing hostilities.

21. The first group of enemy combatants captured in the war against al-Qaida, the Taliban, and their affiliates and supporters arrived in Guantánamo Bay, Cuba, in January 2002. The United States has approximately 505 detainees in custody at Guantánamo (at http://www.defenselink.mil/releases/2005/nr20050822-4501.html (visited October 13, 2005)) and slightly more than 400 detainees in Afghanistan. These numbers represent a small percentage of the total number of individuals the United States has detained, at one point or another, in fighting the war against al-Qaida and the Taliban.

22. Since the war began in Afghanistan (and long before the U.S. Supreme Court decisions in the detainee cases of June 2004), the United States has captured, screened and released more than 10,000 individuals. It transferred to Guantánamo fewer than ten percent of those screened. The United States only wishes to hold those enemy combatants who are part of or are supporting Taliban or al-Qaida forces (or associated forces) and who, if released, would present a threat of reengaging in belligerent acts or directly aiding and supporting ongoing hostilities against the United States or its allies. We have made mistakes: of the detainees we have released, we have later recaptured or killed about 5% of them while they were engaged in hostile action against U.S. forces.

23. Detainees in Afghanistan and Guantánamo include many senior al-Qaida and Taliban operatives and leaders, in addition to rank-and-file jihadists who took up arms against the United States. The individuals currently held by the United States were at one time actively committing belligerent terrorist acts as part of al-Qaida, the Taliban or their affiliates and supporters who engaged in hostilities against the United States and its allies. Generally, the enemy combatants held at Guantánamo Bay comprise enemy combatants who are part of al-Qaida, the Taliban, or affiliated forces, or their supporters, whether captured committing acts of belligerency themselves or directly supporting hostilities in aid of such enemy forces.

Examples of enemy combatants held in U.S. custody include:

• Terrorists linked to major al-Qaida attacks on the United States, such as the East Africa U.S. Embassy bombings and the USS Cole attack;

• Terrorists who taught or received training on arms, explosives, surveillance, and interrogation resistance techniques at al-Qaida camps;

• Terrorists continuing to express their desire to kill Americans if released. In particular, some have threatened their guards and the families of the guards;

• Terrorists who have sworn personal allegiance ("bayat") to Usama bin Ladin; and Terrorists linked to several al-Qaida operational plans, including the targeting of U.S. facilities and interests.

24. Representative examples of specific Guantánamo detainees include:

• An al-Qaida explosives trainer who has provided information on the September 2001 assassination of Northern Alliance leader Ahmad Shah Masoud;

. . .

B. Status of detainees at Guantánamo Bay and in Afghanistan

25. On February 7, 2002, shortly after the United States began operations in Afghanistan, President Bush's Press Secretary announced the President's determination that the Geneva Convention "appl[ies] to the Taliban detainees, but not to the al Qaeda international terrorists" because Afghanistan is a party to the Geneva Convention, but al Qaeda—an international terrorist group—is not. Statement by the U.S. Press Secretary, The James S. Brady Briefing Room, in Washington, D.C. (Feb. 7, 2002) (at http://www. state.gov/s/l/38727.htm (visited October 13, 2005)). Although the President determined that the Geneva Convention applies to Taliban detainees, he determined that, under Article 4, such detainees are not entitled to POW status. *Id.* He explained that: Under Article 4 of the Geneva Convention, ... Taliban detainees are not entitled to POW status.... The Taliban have not effectively distinguished themselves from the civilian population of Afghanistan. Moreover, they have not conducted their operations in accordance with the laws and customs of war.... Al Qaeda is an international terrorist group and cannot be considered a state party to the Geneva Convention. Its members, therefore, are not covered by the Geneva Convention, and are not entitled to POW status under the treaty.

26. Statement by the U.S. Press Secretary, The James S. Brady Briefing Room, in Washington, D.C. (Feb. 7, 2002) (at http://www.state.gov/s/l/38727.htm (visited October 13, 2005)); *see also*, White House Memorandum—Humane Treatment of al Qaeda CAT/C/48/Add.3/Rev.1and Taliban Detainees, February 7, 2002, at 2(c) & (d) (released and declassified in full on June 17, 2004). (At http://www.washingtonpost.com/ wp-srv/nation/documents/020702bush.pdf (visited March 1, 2005)).

27. After the President's decision, the United States concluded that those who are part of al-Qaida, the Taliban or their affiliates and supporters, or support such forces are enemy combatants whom we may detain for the duration of hostilities; these unprivileged combatants do not enjoy the privileges of POWs (*i.e.*, privileged combatants) under the Third Geneva Convention.15 International law, including the Geneva Conventions, has long recognized a nation's authority to detain unlawful enemy combatants without benefit of POW status. *See, e.g.*, INGRID DETTER, THE LAW OF WAR 148 (2000) ("Unlawful combatants... though they are a legitimate target for any belligerent action, are not, if captured, entitled to any prisoner of war status."); *see also United States v. Lindh*, 212 F. Supp. 2d. 541, 558 (E.D. Va. 2002) (confirming the Executive branch view that "the Taliban falls far short when measured against the four GPW criteria for determining entitlement to lawful combatant immunity").

28. Because there is no doubt under international law as to the status of al-Qaida, the Taliban, their affiliates and supporters, there is no need or requirement to review individually whether each enemy combatant detained at Guantánamo is entitled to POW status. For example, Article 5 of the Third Geneva Convention requires a tribunal in certain cases to determine whether a belligerent (or combatant) is entitled to POW status under the Convention only when there is doubt under any of the categories enumerated in Article 4. The United States concluded that Article 5 tribunals were unnecessary because there is no doubt as to the status of these individuals.

29. After the decisions of the U.S. Supreme Court in *Rasul v. Bush*, 124 S.Ct. 2686 (2004), and *Hamdi v. Rumsfeld*, 124 S.Ct. 2633 (2004), which are described below in Section G, the U.S. Government established a process on July 7, 2004, to conduct Combatant Status Review Tribunals (CSRTs) at Guantánamo Bay. (At http://www.defenselink.mil/transcripts/2004/tr20040707-0981.html (visited October 13, 2005) (Department of Defense Briefing on Combatant Status Review Tribunal, dated July 7, 2004)). Consistent with the Supreme Court decision in *Rasul*, these tribunals supplement the prior screening procedures and serve as fora for detainees to contest their designation as enemy combatants and thereby the legal basis for their detention. The tribunals were established in response to the Supreme Court decision in *Rasul* and draw upon guidance contained in the U.S. Supreme Court decision in *Hamdi* that would apply to citizen-enemy combatants in the United States.

C. Combatant Status Review Tribunals (CSRTs) for detainees at Guantánamo Bay

30. Between August 2004 and January 2005, various Combatant Status Review Tribunals (CSRTs) have reviewed the status of all individuals detained at Guantánamo, in a fact-based proceeding, to determine whether the individual is still classified as an enemy combatant. As reflected in the Order establishing the CSRTs, an enemy combatant is "an individual who was part of or supporting Taliban or al Qaeda forces, or associated forces that are engaged in hostilities against the United States or its coalition partners. This includes any person who has committed a belligerent act or has directly supported hostilities in aid of enemy armed forces." CSRT Order (at http://www.defenselink.mil/news/Jul2004/d20040707review.pdf (visited October 13, 2005)). Each detainee has the opportunity to contest such designation. The Deputy

Secretary of Defense appointed the Secretary of the Navy, The Honorable Gordon England, to implement and oversee this process. On July 29, 2004, Secretary England issued the implementation directive for the CSRTs, giving specific procedural and substantive guidance. (At http://www.defenselink.mil/news/Jul2004/d20040730comb.pdf (visited October 13, 2005)). On July 12–14, 2004, the United States notified all detainees then at Guantánamo of their opportunity to contest their enemy combatant status under this process, and that a federal court has jurisdiction to entertain a petition for habeas corpus brought on their behalf. The Government has also provided them with information on how to file habeas corpus petitions in the U.S. court system. (At http://www.defenselink.mil/news/Dec2004/d20041209ARB.pdf (visited October 13, 2005)). When the Government has added new detainees, it has also informed them of these legal rights.

31. CSRTs offer many of the procedures contained in U.S. Army Regulation 190-8. The Supreme Court specifically cited these Army procedures as sufficient for U.S. citizen-detainees entitled to due process under the U.S. Constitution. For example:

• Tribunals are composed of three neutral commissioned officers, plus a non-voting officer who serves as a recorder;

• Decisions are by a preponderance of the evidence by a majority of the voting members who are sworn to execute their duties impartially;

• The detainee has the right to (a) call reasonably available witnesses, (b) question witnesses called by the tribunal, (c) testify or otherwise address the tribunal, (d) not be compelled to testify, and (e) attend the open portions of the proceedings;

• An interpreter is provided to the detainee, if necessary; and

• The Tribunal creates a written report of its decision that the Staff Judge Advocate reviews for legal sufficiency. *See* CSRT Implementation Memorandum, July 29, 2004 (at http://www.defenselink.mil/news/Jul2004/d20040730comb.pdf (visited October 13, 2005)).

32. Unlike an Article 5 tribunal, the CSRT guarantees the detainee *additional* rights, such as the right to a personal representative to assist in reviewing information and preparing the detainee's case, presenting information, and questioning witnesses at the CSRT. The rules entitle the detainee to receive an unclassified summary of the evidence in advance of the hearing in the detainee's native language, and to introduce relevant documentary evidence. *See* CSRT Order (1); Implementation Memorandum Encl. (1) F(8), H (5); CSRT Order (10); Implementation Memorandum Encl. (1) F (6). In addition, the rules require the Recorder to search government files for, and provide to the Tribunal, any "evidence to suggest that the detainee should not be designated as an enemy combatant." *See* Implementation Memorandum Encl. (2), (1). The detainee's Personal Representative also has access to the government files and can search for and provide relevant evidence that would support the detainee's position.

33. A higher authority (the CSRT Director) automatically reviews the result of every CSRT. He has the power to return the record to the tribunal for further proceedings if appropriate. *See* CSRT Order h; Implementation Memorandum Encl. (1) I (8). The CSRT Director is a two-star admiral—a senior military officer. CSRTs are transparent proceedings. Members of the media, the International Committee of the Red Cross (ICRC), and non-governmental organizations may observe military commissions and the unclassified portions of the CSRT proceedings. They also have access to the unclassified materials filed in Federal court. Every detainee now held at Guantánamo Bay has had a CSRT hearing. New detainees will have the same rights.

34. As of March 29, 2005, the CSRT Director had taken final action in all 558 cases. Thirty-eight detainees were determined no longer to be enemy combatants; twenty-eight of them have been subsequently released to their home countries, and at the time of this Report's submission, arrangements are underway or being pursued for the release of the others. (At http://www.defenselink.mil/releases/2005/nr20050419-2661.html (visited October 13, 2005)).

D. Assessing detainees for release/transfer

1. Guantánamo Bay

35. The detention of each Guantánamo detainee is reviewed annually by an Administrative Review Board (ARB), established by an order on May 11, 2004 (*Review Procedure Announced for Guantánamo Detainees*, Department of Defense Press Release, May 18, 2004) (at http://www.defenselink.mil/releases/2004/nr20040518-0806.html (visited October 13, 2005)) and supplemented by an implementing directive on September 14, 2004. *See Implementation of Administrative Review Procedures for Enemy Combatants Detained at U.S. Naval Base Guantánamo Bay, Cuba* (at http://www.defenselink.mil/news/ Sep2004/ d20040914 admin review.pdf (visited October 13, 2005)).

...

2. Afghanistan

44. Detainees under DoD control in Afghanistan are subject to a review process that first determines whether an individual is an enemy combatant. The detaining Combatant Commander, or designee, shall review the initial determination that the detainee is an enemy combatant. This review is based on all available and relevant information available on the date of the review and may be subject to further review based upon newly discovered evidence or information. The Commander will review the initial determination that the detainee is an enemy combatant within 90 days from the time that a detainee comes under DoD control. After the initial 90-day status review, the detaining combatant commander, on an annual basis, is required to reassess the status of each detainee. Detainees assessed to be enemy combatants under this process remain under DoD control until they no longer present a threat. The review process is conducted under the authority of the Commander, U.S. Central Command (USCENTCOM). If, as a result of the periodic Enemy Combatant status review (90-day or annual), a detaining combatant commander concludes that a detainee no longer meets the definition of an enemy combatant, the detainee is released.

E. Transfers or releases to third countries

45. After it is determined that a detainee no longer continues to pose a threat to the U.S. security interests or that a detainee no longer meets the criteria of enemy combatant and is eligible for release or transfer, the United States generally seeks to return the detainee to his or her country of nationality. The Department of Defense has transferred detainees to the control of their governments of nationality when those governments are prepared to take the steps necessary to ensure that the detainees will not pose a continuing threat to the United States and only after the United States receives assurances that the government concerned will treat the detainee humanely and in a manner consistent with its international obligations. A detainee may be considered for transfer to a country other than his country of nationality, such as in circumstances where that country requests transfer of the detainee for purposes of criminal prosecution. Of particular concern to the United States is whether the foreign government concerned will treat the detainee humanely, in a manner consistent with its international obligations, and will not persecute the individual because of his race, religion, nationality, membership in a social group, or political opinion. In some cases, however, transfers cannot easily be arranged.

46. U.S. policy is not to transfer a person to a country if it is determined that it is more likely than not that the person will be tortured or, in appropriate cases, that the person has a well-founded fear of persecution and would not be disqualified from persecution protection on criminal- or security-related grounds. If a case were to arise in which the assurances obtained from the receiving government are not sufficient when balanced against treatment concerns, the United States would not transfer a detainee to the control of that government unless the concerns were satisfactorily resolved. Circumstances have arisen in the past where the Department of Defense elected not to transfer detainees to their country of origin because of torture concerns.

47. With respect to the application of these policies to detainees at Guantánamo Bay, the U.S. Government in February of 2005 filed factual declarations with a Federal court for use in domestic litigation. These declarations describe in greater detail the application of the policy described above as it applies to the detainees at Guantánamo Bay, and are attached to this document as Tab 1.

F. Military commissions to try detainees held at Guantánamo Bay

48. In 2001, the President authorized military commissions to try certain individuals for violations of the law of war and other applicable laws. See Detention, Treatment, and Trial of Certain Non-Citizens in the War Against Terrorism, November 13, 2001 (at http://www.whitehouse.gov/news/releases/2001/11/print/20011113-27.html (visited October 13, 2005)).

...

G. Access to U.S. courts

55. In 2003, petitions for writ of habeas corpus were filed in U.S. courts on behalf of some of the detainees at Guantánamo seeking review of their detention. On June 28, 2004, the United States Supreme Court, the highest judicial body in the United States, issued two decisions pertinent to many enemy combatants. One of the decisions directly pertained to enemy combatants detained at Guantánamo Bay, and the other pertained to a citizen enemy combatant held in the United States. *See Rasul v. Bush*, 124 S.Ct. 2686 (2004); *Hamdi v. Rumsfeld*, 124 S.Ct. 2633 (2004); *see also Rumsfeld v. Padilla*, 124 S.Ct. 2711 (2004) (involving a decision on which U.S. Federal court has jurisdiction over habeas action). In *Rasul v. Bush*, the Supreme Court decided only the question of jurisdiction. The Court ruled that the U.S.

District Court for the District of Columbia had jurisdiction to consider habeas challenges to the legality of the detention of foreign nationals at Guantánamo. 124 S.Ct. at 2698. The Court held that aliens apprehended abroad and detained at Guantánamo Bay, Cuba, as enemy combatants, "no less than citizens," could invoke the habeas jurisdiction of a district court. *Id.* at 2696. The Supreme Court left it to the lower courts to decide "[w]hether and what further proceedings may become necessary after [the United States Government parties] make their response to the merits of petitioners' claims." *Id.* at 2699. In *Hamdi v. Rumsfeld*, the Supreme Court held that the United States is entitled to detain enemy combatants, even American citizens, until the end of hostilities, in order to prevent the enemy combatants from returning to the field of battle and again taking up arms. 124 S.Ct. at 2639-40. The Court recognized the detention of such individuals is such a fundamental and accepted incident of war that it is part of the "necessary and appropriate" force that Congress authorized the President to use against nations, organizations, or persons associated with the September 11 terrorist attacks. 124 S.Ct. at 2639-42 (plurality op.); *id.*, at 2679 (Thomas J., dissenting).

III. DETAINEES—TREATMENT

A. Description of conditions of detention at Department of Defense facilities

1. Guantánamo Bay

63. The Department of Defense has released to the public several photographs of the detention facilities in Guantánamo Bay. (At http://www.defenselink.mil/home/features/gtmo (visited October 13, 2005)). These photographs reflect U.S. policy and practices regarding treatment of detainees at Guantánamo Bay, including the U.S. requirement that all detainees receive adequate housing, recreation facilities, and medical facilities.

64. Detainees receive:

- Three meals per day that meet cultural dietary requirements;
- Adequate shelter, including cells with beds, mattresses, and sheets;
- Adequate clothing, including shoes, uniforms, and hygiene items; Opportunity to worship, including prayer beads, rugs, and copies of the Koran;
- The means to send and receive mail;
- Reading materials, including allowing detainees to keep books in their cells; and
- Excellent medical care.

65. All enemy combatants get state-of-the art medical and dental care that is comparable to that received by U.S. Armed Forces deployed overseas. Wounded enemy combatants are treated humanely and nursed back to health, and amputees are fitted with modern prosthetics.

66. Detainees write to and receive mail from their families and friends. Detainees who are illiterate, but trustworthy enough for a classroom setting, are taught to read and write in their native language so they, too, can communicate with their families and friends.

67. Enemy combatants at Guantánamo may worship as desired and in accordance with their beliefs. They have access to the Koran and other prayer accessories. Traditional garb is available for some detainees.

68. Where security permits, detainees are eligible for communal living in a new Medium Security Facility, with fan-cooled dormitories, family-style dinners, and increased outdoor recreation time, where they play board games like chess and checkers, and team sports like soccer.

69. The United States permits the International Committee of the Red Cross to visit privately with every detainee in DoD control at Guantánamo. Communications between the U.S. Government and the ICRC are confidential.

70. In addition, legal counsel representing the detainees in habeas corpus cases have visited detainees at Guantánamo since late August 2004. As of September 2005, counsel in forty cases have personally met with the more than 100 detainees they represent. Some counsel have visited their clients more than once. To date, virtually every request by American counsel of record in the habeas cases to visit detainees at Guantánamo has been granted, after that counsel has received the requisite security clearance, agreed to the terms of the protective order issued by the Federal court and submitted a request at least 20 days in advance of the proposed visit. The proposed visit dates in some cases have been adjusted based on other counsel visits that were already scheduled for the same time period. The Government does not monitor these meetings (or the written correspondence between counsel and detainees), which occur in a confidential manner. The Government also allows foreign and domestic media to visit the facilities.

2. Afghanistan

71. The Department of Defense holds individuals in Afghanistan in a safe, secure, and humane environment. The primary focus of DoD detainee operations in Afghanistan is to secure detainees from harm, recognizing the reality that the U.S. Armed Forces continue to engage in combat in Afghanistan.

. . .

B. Allegations of mistreatment of persons detained by the Department of Defense
1. Introduction

75. The United States is well aware of the concerns about the mistreatment of persons detained by the Department of Defense in Afghanistan and at Guantánamo Bay, Cuba. Indeed, the United States has taken and continues to take all allegations of abuse very seriously. Specifically, in response to specific complaints of abuse in Afghanistan and at Guantánamo Bay, Cuba, the Department of Defense has ordered a number of studies that focused, *inter alia*, on detainee operations and interrogation methods to determine if there was merit to the complaints of mistreatment.

. . .

78. Concerns have also been generated by an August 1, 2002, memorandum prepared by the Office of Legal Counsel (OLC) at the U.S. Department of Justice (DOJ), on the definition of torture and the possible defenses to torture under U.S. law and a DoD Working Group Report on detainee operations, dated April 4, 2003, the latter of which was the basis for the Secretary of Defense's approval of certain counter resistance techniques on April 16, 2003. The 2002 DOJ OLC memorandum was withdrawn on June 22, 2004 and replaced with a December 30, 2004, memorandum interpreting the legal standards applicable under 18 U.S.C. 2340–2340A, also known as the Federal Torture Statute. On March 17, 2005, the Department of Defense determined that the Report of the Working Group on Detainee Interrogations is to be considered as having no standing in policy, practice, or law to guide any activity of the Department of Defense.

. . .

2. Reports of abuses, summary of abuse investigations and actions
to hold persons accountable - Guantánamo Bay

83. As described above in the introductory section, there have been multiple reports resulting from/investigations concerning the treatment of detainees at Guantánamo Bay. For example, the Naval Inspector General reviewed the intelligence and detainee operations at Guantánamo Bay to ensure compliance with DoD orders and policies. The review, conducted in May 2004, concluded that the Secretary of Defense's directions with respect to humane treatment of detainees and interrogation techniques were fully implemented. The Naval Inspector General documented eight minor infractions involving contact with detainees as stated below (two additional incidents occurred after this investigation was completed). In each of those cases, the chain of command took swift and effective action. Administrative actions ranging from admonishment to reduction in grade.

. . .

3. Reports of abuses, summary of abuse investigations and actions to hold
persons accountable—Afghanistan

88. The United States acted swiftly in response to allegations of serious abuses by DoD personnel in Afghanistan. There have been 29 investigations into allegations of abuse of detainees in Afghanistan, of which 21 were substantiated and one was unsubstantiated. Seven investigations are open and continue to be investigated. As of October 1, 2005, penalties have varied and include 11 courts-martial, 10 non-judicial punishments, and 9 reprimands. A number of actions are still pending.

The following are examples of substantiated abuses and a summary of the status:

• The investigations into the death of two detainees (Mr. Mullah Habibullah and Mr. Dilawar) at the Bagram detention facility on December 4 and 10, 2002 identified 28 military members who may have committed offenses punishable under the UCMJ. Investigations determined that the detainees had been beaten by several military members. Commanders are considering the full range of administrative and disciplinary measures, including trial by court-martial. As of this writing, charges have been preferred against nine military members and a final result reached in eight of those cases. Five soldiers were found guilty of various offenses related to the death of these two detainees, two soldiers were acquitted of all charges, and one case is not yet concluded. Sentences ranged from forfeiture in pay and reduction in rank to confinement for a period of years;

• The Naval Criminal Investigation Service (NCIS) opened an investigation in May 2004 involving allegations of an Afghan police officer who claimed he was abused in while under coalition control in Gardez and Bagram. This investigation remains open.

...

IV. TRAINING OF U.S. ARMED FORCES

90. Personnel assigned to detention operations go through an extensive professional and sensitivity training process to ensure they understand the procedures for protecting the rights and dignity of detainees.

• Personnel mobilizing to detention operations receive training prior to deployment on detention facility operations, self-defense, safety, and rules on the use of force. Before beginning work, personnel again receive training on the law of armed conflict, the rules of engagement, the Standard Operating Procedures, military justice, and specific policies applying to detention operations in their area of responsibility. This is true of all service members deploying to serve in detention operations. All U.S. service members receive general training on the law of armed conflict, including the Geneva Conventions, as well as further law of armed conflict training commensurate with their duties;

• During their operational tours, U.S. service members continue to receive briefings and are briefed again before every detainee movement on the rules, procedures, and policies in operating detention facilities;

...

II. DETAINEES—CAPTURING, HOLDING AND/OR RELEASING

A. Brief overview of the detainee population held by MNF-I

94. As of September 2005, MNF-I was detaining approximately 13,000 persons in Iraq. The vast majority of the detainee population is composed of individuals who are held for imperative reasons of security, consistent with U.N. Security Council Resolution 1546. In addition to security internees, the MNF-I holds a small number of enemy prisoners of war (EPWs) and, on behalf of the ITG, a number of persons suspected of violating Iraqi criminal laws. The MNF-I has established several detention facilities in various locations throughout Iraq that are operated by the U.S. Army under the Commander, MNF-I. The U.S. Army operates three theater internment facilities: Abu Ghraib (Baghdad Central Correction Facility), Camp Cropper, and Camp Bucca.

B. Status review of detainees

95. Detainees under DoD control in Iraq undergo the review process described herein in order to confirm their status and ensure that they are being lawfully detained. Upon capture by a detaining unit, a detainee is moved as expeditiously as possible to a theater internment facility. A military magistrate reviews an individual's detention to assess whether to continue to detain or to release him or her. If detention is continued, the Combined Review and Release Board assumes the responsibility for subsequently reviewing whether continued detention is appropriate.

...

C. Decisions on continued detention or release of detainees

97. The Combined Review and Release Board (CRRB) was created to provide detainees a method by which to have their detention status reviewed. The CRRB first met on August 21, 2004. It consists of nine members: three MNF-I officers, and two members each from the Iraqi Ministry of Justice, Ministry of Interior, and Ministry of Human Rights.

III. DETAINEES—TREATMENT

A. Description of conditions of detention in U.S. Department of Defense facilities

98. The primary goal of U.S. detention operations in Iraq has been to operate safe, secure, and humane facilities consistent with the Geneva Conventions. U.S. and other MNF-I forces continue to make physical improvements to various facilities throughout Iraq. Since the incidents of abuse at Abu Ghraib, the United States has made substantial improvements in all areas of detention operations, including facilities and living conditions. Families may visit detainees at visitation centers set up at each detention facility. Detainees are provided with prayer materials and allowed the open and free expression of religion in detention. Detainees also have access to medical facilities, consistent with the Geneva Conventions.

99. As set forth in CPA Memorandum No. 3 (Revised), and consistent with the provisions of the Geneva Conventions, the ICRC is provided with notice of detainees under the control of the U.S. contingent of MNF-I as soon as reasonably possible and is provided access to such detainees unless reasons of imperative military necessity require otherwise.

B. Allegations of mistreatment of persons detained by the Department of Defense

1. Legal framework

100. As noted above, U.N. Security Council Resolution 1546 provides authority for MNF-I security operations in Iraq, including detention operations. The United States contingent to MNF-I conducts its detention operations consistent with the Geneva Conventions, including pursuant to CPA Memorandum No. 3 (Revised), for operations after June 28, 2004. The Geneva Conventions prohibit the torture or inhumane treatment of protected persons. U.S. Armed Forces in Iraq are instructed to act consistently with these provisions with regard to all detainees and to treat all detainees humanely. Detainees under the control of U.S. Armed Forces receive shelter, food, clothing, water, and medical care, and are able to practice their religion.

101. U.S. military interrogators are instructed to conduct interrogations consistent with the Geneva Conventions. Further, military regulations strictly regulate permissible interrogation techniques. DoD policy prohibits the use of force, mental and physical torture, or any form of inhumane treatment during an interrogation.

102. Army Regulation (AR) 190-8 provides policy, procedures, and responsibilities for the administration and treatment of enemy prisoners of war (EPW), retained personnel (RP), civilian internees (CI), and other detainees in the custody of U.S. Armed Forces. (At http://www.usapa.army.mil/pdffiles/r190_8.pdf (visited October 13, 2005)). A.R. 190-8, paragraph 1–5 provides: General Protection Policy a. U.S. policy, relative to the treatment of EPW, CI and RP in the custody of the U.S. Armed Forces, is as follows:

(1) All persons captured, detained, interned, or otherwise held in U.S. Armed Forces custody during the course of conflict will be given humanitarian care and treatment from the moment they fall into the hands of U.S. forces until final release or repatriation.

(2) All persons taken into custody by U.S. forces will be provided with the protections of the 1949 Geneva Convention Relative to the Treatment of Prisoners of War (GPW) until some other legal status is determined by competent authority.

(3) The punishment of EPW, CI, and RP known to have, or suspected of having committed serious offenses will be administered [in accordance with] due process of law and under legally constituted authority per the GPW, [the 1949 Geneva Convention Relative to the Protection of Civilian Persons in Time of War], the Uniform Code of Military Justice and the Manual for Courts Martial.

(4) The inhumane treatment of EPW, CI, and RP is prohibited and is not justified under the stress of combat or with deep provocation. Inhumane treatment is a serious and punishable violation under international law and the Uniform Code of Military Justice (UCMJ).

. . .

105. Interrogation techniques are developed and approved to ensure compliance with legal and policy requirements. Throughout the conflict in Iraq, military, policy, and legal officials have met and continue to meet regularly to review interrogation policy and procedures to ensure their compatibility with applicable domestic and international legal standards. The United States will continue to review and update its interrogation techniques in order to remain in full compliance with applicable law.

. . .

2. Reports of abuses and summary of abuse investigations

107. In response to these allegations of abuse, the U.S. Government has acted swiftly to investigate and take action to address the abuses. The United States is investigating allegations of abuse thoroughly and making structural, personnel, and policy changes necessary to reduce the risk of further such incidents. All credible allegations of inappropriate conduct by U.S. personnel are thoroughly investigated. A rapid response to allegations of abuse, accompanied by accountability, sends an unequivocal signal to all U.S. military personnel and the international community that mistreatment of detainees will not be tolerated under any circumstances. To the extent allegations of misconduct have been levied against private contractors, the U.S. Department of Justice has conducted or initiated investigations. For example, following the reports at Abu Ghraib, the Department of Justice received referrals from Military Investigators regarding contract employees and their potential involvement in the abuses. DOJ subsequently opened an investigation.

108. At the direction of the President, the Secretary of Defense, and the military chain of command, nine different senior-level investigative bodies convened to review military policy from top-to-bottom in

order to understand the facts in these cases and identify any systemic factors that may have been relevant. The assignment of these entities was to identify and investigate the circumstances of all alleged instances of abuse, review command structure and policy, and recommend personnel and policy changes to improve accountability and reduce the possibility of future abuse.

109. The United States has ordered a number of studies and reports subsequent to allegations of mistreatment in Iraq, particularly at Abu Ghraib. Again, as described in Part One of this Report, it is impossible to characterize and summarize fully these reports, but it can be stated that although these investigations identified problems and made recommendations, none found a governmental policy directing, encouraging, or condoning the abuses that occurred. What follows is a brief summary of each of the investigative reports:

- *Miller Report*

Major General Miller's report on detention and interrogation operations in Iraq was completed on September 9, 2003. General Miller's report assessed the conditions and operations of detention facilities in Iraq.

- *Ryder Report*

Major General Ryder's assessment of detention operations in Iraq was completed on November 6, 2003, as described in Part 1, Section III.B.3. General Ryder's report covered specific operations in Iraq and Afghanistan relating to the conduct of detention operations.

- *Taguba Report*

Major General Taguba completed his investigation into detainee operations and the 800th Military Police Brigade on March 12, 2004. This report focused primarily on the allegations of detainee abuse at the Abu Ghraib detention facility arising from disclosures made by U.S. service members.

- *The Army Inspector General Report*

The Army Inspector General conducted a review of alleged detainee abuse committed by U.S. Army personnel in Iraq and Afghanistan, which was released in July 2004, as described in Part 1, Section III.B.3. (At http://www4.army.mil/ocpa/reports/ArmyIGDetaineeAbuse/DAIG%20Detainee%20 Operations%20 Inspection%20Report.pdf (visited October 13, 2005)).

- *Report by Major General Fay, Lieutenant General Jones, and General Kern*

This was completed on August 13, 2004. This report covered Military Intelligence (MI) and DoD contractor interrogation policies in Iraq. This report revealed that 27 military personnel or civilians appeared to have abused Iraqi prisoners due to criminal activity or confusing interrogation rules. Twenty-three military intelligence personnel and four civilian contractors were alleged to be involved in abuse. Eight others, including six military officers and two civilians, were alleged to have learned of the abuse and to have failed to report the abuse to authorities. This report found 44 cases of abuse. In an interview after the report's release, General Kern told reporters, "We found that the pictures you have seen, as revolting as they are, were not the result of any doctrine, training or policy failures, but violations of the law and misconduct." (At http://www. defenselink.mil/transcripts/2004/tr20040825-1224.html (visited October 13, 2005)). The report found that the abuses were carried out by a small group of "morally corrupt" soldiers and civilians and caused by a lack of discipline by leaders and soldiers of the brigade and a "failure or lack of leadership B multiple echelons" within a unit within the U.S. military forces in Iraq. *See* Report at 2. This report was publicly released and can be found online (at http://news.findlaw.com/hdocs/ docs/dod/fay82504rpt.pdf (visited October 13, 2005)).

- *Schlessinger Report*

This Report was completed in August 2004. The Secretary of Defense named a panel of four distinguished former public officials, including two former Secretaries of Defense, to evaluate the areas under review in the ongoing investigations and to determine if there was a need for additional areas of investigation. The Report found that "[n]o approved procedures called for or allowed the kinds of abuse that in fact occurred. There is no evidence of a policy of abuse promulgated by senior officials or military authorities." *See* Report at 5. It stated that "the most egregious instances of detainee abuse were caused by the aberrant behavior of a limited number of soldiers and the predilections of the non-commissioned officers on the night shift of Tier 1 at Abu Ghraib," although noting that "commanding officers and their staffs at various levels failed in their duties and that such failure contributed directly or indirectly to detainee abuse." *See* Report at p. 43. This report was publicly released and can be found online (at http://www.defenselink.mil/news/Aug2004/d20040824final-report.pdf (visited October 13, 2005)).

- *Formica Report*

Brigadier General Formica initiated a report on May 15, 2004 that focuses on allegations of abuse by Special Operations Forces in Iraq. The investigation is complete. The report's contents are classified because of the highly sensitive operations that were examined and that remain ongoing.

- *Church Report*

Vice Admiral Church's comprehensive review of DoD Detention Operations and Interrogation Techniques was completed on March 10, 2005 and is described in Part One, Section III.B.3. of this Annex to the updated CAT report. The Executive Summary of the Report is available at http://www.defenselink.mil/news/Mar2005/d20050310exe.pdf (visited October 13, 2005).

- *Naval Inspector General Report*

The Naval Inspector General (Vice Admiral Route) is conducting a review of documents recently released under the Freedom of Information Act and is expected to release his findings soon as described in Part 1, Section III.B.3.

110. From the nine reports that have been completed, it is clear that serious abuses occurred, but it is also clear that the vast majority of the 150,000 military personnel who that have been stationed in Iraq have conducted themselves honorably. The U.S. Armed Forces is committed to ensuring that those who committed abuses are accountable and that such abuses do not occur again.

111. It is important to remember that the U.S. Armed Forces began the process of assessing detainee operations, investigating allegations of abuse, and implementing changes at Abu Ghraib, well before the media and the international community began to focus on detainee abuse at that facility. Both before and after the public disclosure of these abuses, the United States pursued swift and thorough investigations of problems.

112. In conducting the major reviews, the United States reached out broadly, interviewed more than 1,700 people, and compiled more than 13,000 pages of information to address detainee abuse. Much of this information is publicly available. In an effort to be transparent and keep the public and our government informed, the Department of Defense delivered more than 60 briefings to the U.S. Congress.

113. The Department of Defense has improved its detention operations in Iraq and elsewhere, improvements have been made based upon the lessons learned, and in part because of the broad investigations and focused inquiries into specific allegations. These comprehensive reports, reforms, investigations and prosecutions make clear the commitment of the Department of Defense to do everything possible to ensure that detainee abuse such as occurred at Abu Ghraib never happens again.

114. Finally, the highest levels of the Department of Defense are reviewing and acting on all of the reports and investigations. The Department has established an inter-departmental committee, called the Senior Leadership Oversight Committee, that comprises senior members of the Joint Staff, the Provost Marshal General's Office, the Office of Detainee Affairs, and the Military Departments engaged in detention operations.

115. This group is specifically responsible for ensuring that the recommendations of the panels and investigations are followed through to their conclusion, and for monitoring changes made by combatant commands and the relevant offices in the Department of Defense. To date, the committee has met three times and has reviewed more than 600 recommendations. The Department has already implemented a significant number of recommendations and is examining the remainder of them. The Oversight Council will continue to meet on a periodic basis until the recommendations of the investigations and panels have been addressed fully.

3. Summary of actions to hold persons accountable

116. The Department of Defense takes all allegations of abuse seriously and investigates them. Those people who are found to have committed unlawful acts are held accountable and disciplined as the circumstances warrant. Investigations are thorough and have high priority.

117. Some criminal investigations have been completed and others continue with respect to abuse of detainees in Iraq. Although it would be inappropriate to comment on the specifics of on-going investigations, as of October 1, 2005, more than 190 incidents of abuse have been substantiated. Some are minor, while others are not: penalties have ranged from administrative to criminal sanctions, including 65 courts-martial, 76 non-judicial punishments, 38 reprimands, and 20 administrative actions, separations, or other administrative relief. A number of actions are pending.

118. Some examples of service members convicted at a court-martial for acts related to detainee maltreatment include:

(1) A Staff Sergeant, charged with numerous offenses related to maltreatment of detainees at the Abu Ghraib Detention Facility, pled guilty on October 21, 2004, at a General Court-Martial to conspiracy, maltreatment of detainees, simple battery, and indecent acts. The Military Judge sentenced him to 10 years confinement, total forfeitures of pay and allowances, reduction from Staff Sergeant (a non-commissioned

officer rank) to the lowest enlisted grade (enlisted grade of Private), and discharge from the U.S. Army with a dishonorable discharge. Because of a plea agreement, the Staff Sergeant will ultimately be confined for eight years, if he cooperates with future prosecutions per the plea arrangement.

...

C. Remedies for victims of abuse

120. The United States is committed to adequately compensating the victims of abuse and mistreatment by U.S. military personnel in Iraq. The U.S. Army is responsible for handling all claims in Iraq. Several claims statutes allow the United States to compensate victims of misconduct by U.S. military personnel. The primary mechanism for paying claims for allegations of abuse and mistreatment by U.S. personnel in Iraq is through the Foreign Claims Act (FCA), 10 U.S.C. § 2734. Under the FCA, Foreign Claims Commissions are tasked with investigating, adjudicating, and settling meritorious claims arising out of an individual's detention. There are currently 78 Foreign Claims Commission personnel in Iraq. Claims may be submitted to the claims personnel, who regularly visit detention facilities, or they may be presented to the Iraqi Assistance Center. For persons with U.S. residency, claims may be brought pursuant to the Military Claims Act, 10 U.S.C. § 2733. All allegations of detainee abuse are investigated by the U.S. Army Claims Service (USARCS), and the Department of the Army Office of the General Counsel is the approval authority.

...

IV. TRAINING OF U.S. ARMED FORCES

122. U.S. Armed Forces receive significant training before being deployed and during their deployment. The United States incorporates by reference that section and reiterates that all employees and Armed Forces deployed in detention missions receive extensive training and education on the laws and customs of armed conflict, including humane treatment procedures and the obligations of the United States in conducting detention operations. With respect to Iraq, U.S. Armed Forces serving as interrogators and detention personnel are also trained to conduct themselves in accordance with the principles (including the prohibition on torture) set forth in the Geneva Conventions and to treat detainees humanely regardless of status.

123. Since allegations of abuse became known, corrections specialists are now stationed at detention facilities to provide additional skills and experience to the detention mission. In addition, the Department of Defense is developing procedures and policies to ensure that contractors used by the Department receive training and understand the U.S. Government's commitments and policies before being deployed in detention operations.

V. LESSONS LEARNED AND POLICY REFORMS

124. It is clear that certain individual service members committed serious abuses during U.S. detention operations in Iraq. Apart from proceedings to hold accountable the perpetrators of abuse, the U.S. Armed Forces have been studying the larger question of how to ensure that these types of abuses will not occur in the future. The eleven detainee reports released to date have made more than 400 recommendations for short and long-term changes to improve detainee handling, accountability, investigation, supervision, and coordination. Further investigations remain in progress. The Office of the Secretary of Defense, the Military Departments, the Combatant Commands, and the Joint Staff have each taken concrete steps to implement many of these changes and will continue to do so.

125. The Department of Defense has responded to the abuses committed by taking steps designed to improve senior-level supervision and coordination of detainee matters. The Secretary of Defense has:

• Established a Detainee Affairs office overseen by the Deputy Assistant Secretary of Defense for Detainee Affairs;

• Established a Joint Detainee Coordination Committee on Detainee Affairs;

• Issued a policy for "Handling of Reports from the International Committee of the Red Cross";

• Issued a policy on "Procedures for Investigations into the Death of Detainees in the Custody of the Armed Forces of the U.S."; and

• Initiated a department-wide review of detainee-related policy directives. Other steps that the Department of Defense has taken include:

• Designation of a Major General as Deputy Commanding General for Detainee Operations, MNF-I. He is the Department's primary point of contact with the Iraqi Transitional Government for detainee operations. He is responsible for ensuring that all persons captured, detained, interned, or otherwise held in under MNF-I control are treated humanely and consistent with the Geneva Conventions and all applicable law from the moment they fall into the hands of U.S. forces until their final release from MNF-I control or their repatriation. He ensures that it is made clear that inhumane treatment is prohibited and is a punishable violation under the Uniform Code of Military Justice. All service members have an obligation to report allegations of detainee abuse to the responsible command or law enforcement agency;

• The posting of the Geneva Conventions and Camp rules in a language the detainee can understand;

• Ensuring widespread publication of the findings of reports and investigations by publishing unclassified information on the Department of Defense website http://www.defenselink.mil. The Department has established an entire sub-site on detainee operations.

[Footnotes omitted]

DOCUMENT 21B (SERIES)

Full Official Title: Consideration of Reports Submitted By States Parties Under Article 19 of the Convention; Conclusions and Recommendations of the Committee against Torture-United States Of America

Short Title/Acronym/Abbreviation: CAT Concluding Observations and Recommendations on U.S. Periodic Report

Type of Document: Written response to a state report, from a treaty-based body, the U.N. Committee Against Torture. This is not a legal document as such. It is a response to the U.S. periodic report and other information received, as to how the U.S. is complying with a legal instrument, the Convention Against Torture, and how it could improve.

Subject: U.S. implementation of CAT (torture, cruel, human and degrading treatment or punishment)

Official Citation: U.N. Doc CAT/C/USA/CO/2

Date of Document: 25 July 2006

Date of Adoption: Not applicable

Date of General Entry into Force (EIF): Not applicable

Number of States Parties as of this printing: Not applicable

Date of Signature by the United States: Not applicable

Date of Ratification/Accession/Adhesion: Not applicable

Date of Entry into Force as to United States (effective date): Not applicable

Legal Status/Character of the Instrument/Document as to the United States: Not legally binding. Theoretically, the comments and concluding observations and recommendations of the Committee Against Torture should be seriously considered, followed and applied by the U.S. because of the authority and competence of the Committee. It should help guide the United States as to how to comply better with the CAT.

Supervising Body: Committee Against Torture (U.N.)

Comments: By ratifying the CAT the U.S. agreed, under Article 19, to report to the Committee Against Torture on measures they have adopted to give effect to the rights recognized in the Covenant or any progress they have made in the enjoyment of those rights, and respond to the Committee's observations, comments, and recommendations on the report. These conclusions and observations, etc. are made in light of CAT's general comments made from its experience in reviewing other reports, and the jurisprudence (case decisions) arising from the complaints it handles. They are not supposed to be made for political reasons or to criticize the reporting state, but to help it fulfill its legal obligations under the CAT. This document should be read after reading Document 21A.

The reader should consult the following website to obtain the full text.

Web Address: http://www.unhchr.ch/tbs/doc.nsf/(Symbol)/CAT.C.USA.CO.2.En?Opendocument; or http://daccess-dds-ny.un.org/doc/UNDOC/GEN/G06/432/25/PDF/G0643225.pdf?OpenElement

CAT CONCLUDING OBSERVATIONS AND RECOMMENDATION ON U.S. REPORT

CONSIDERATION OF REPORTS SUBMITTED BY STATES PARTIES UNDER ARTICLE 19 OF THE CONVENTION

Conclusions and recommendations of the Committee against Torture

UNITED STATES OF AMERICA

1. The Committee against Torture considered the second report of the United States of America (CAT/C/48/Add.3/Rev.1) at its 702nd and 705th meetings (CAT/C/SR.702 and 705), held on 5 and 8 May 2006, and adopted, at its 720th and 721st meetings, on 17 and 18 May 2006 (CAT/C/SR.720 and 721), the following conclusions and recommendations.

A. Introduction

2. The second periodic report of the United States of America was due on 19 November 2001, as requested by the Committee at its twenty-fourth session in May 2000 (A/55/44, para. 180 (f)) and was received on 6 May 2005. The Committee notes that the report includes a point-by-point reply to the Committee's previous recommendations.

3. The Committee commends the State party for its exhaustive written responses to the Committee's list of issues, as well as the detailed responses provided both in writing and orally to the questions posed by the members during the examination of the report. The Committee expresses its appreciation for the large and high-level delegation, comprising representatives from relevant departments of the State party, which facilitated a constructive oral exchange during the consideration of the report.

4. The Committee notes that the State party has a federal structure, but recalls that the United States of America is a single State under international law and has the obligation to implement the Convention against Torture and Other Cruel, Inhuman or Degrading Treatment or Punishment ("the Convention") in full at the domestic level.

5. Recalling its statement adopted on 22 November 2001 condemning utterly the terrorist attacks of 11 September 2001, the terrible threat to international peace and security posed by acts of international terrorism and the need to combat by all means, in accordance with the Charter of the United Nations, the threats caused by terrorist acts, the Committee recognizes that these attacks caused profound suffering to many residents of the State party. The Committee acknowledges that the State party is engaged in protecting its security and the security and freedom of its citizens in a complex legal and political context.

B. Positive aspects

6. The Committee welcomes the State party's statement that all United States officials, from all government agencies, including its contractors, are prohibited from engaging in torture at all times and in all places, and that all United States officials from all government agencies, including its contractors, wherever they may be, are prohibited from engaging in cruel, inhuman or degrading treatment or punishment, in accordance with the obligations under the Convention.

7. The Committee notes with satisfaction the State party's statement that the United States does not transfer persons to countries where it believes it is "more likely than not" that they will be tortured, and that this also applies, as a matter of policy, to the transfer of any individual, in the State party's custody, or control, regardless of where they are detained.

8. The Committee welcomes the State party's clarification that the statement of the United States President on signing the Detainee Treatment Act on 30 December 2005 is not to be interpreted as a derogation by the President from the absolute prohibition of torture.

9. The Committee also notes with satisfaction the enactment of:

(a) The Prison Rape Elimination Act of 2003, which addresses sexual assault of persons in the custody of correctional agencies, with the purpose, inter alia, of establishing a "zero-tolerance standard" for rape in detention facilities in the State party; and

(b) That part of the Detainee Treatment Act of 2005 which prohibits cruel, inhuman, or degrading treatment and punishment of any person, regardless of nationality or physical location, in the custody or under the physical control of the State party.

10. The Committee welcomes the adoption of National Detention Standards in 2000, which set minimum standards for detention facilities holding Department of Homeland Security detainees, including asylum-seekers.

11. The Committee also notes with satisfaction the sustained and substantial contributions of the State party to the United Nations Voluntary Fund for the Victims of Torture.

12. The Committee notes the State party's intention to adopt a new Army Field Manual for intelligence interrogation, applicable to all its personnel, which, according to the State party, will ensure that interrogation techniques fully comply with the Convention.

C. Subjects of concern and recommendations

13. Notwithstanding the statement by the State party that "every act of torture within the meaning of the Convention is illegal under existing federal and/or state law", the Committee reiterates the concern expressed in its previous conclusions and recommendations with regard to the absence of a federal crime of torture, consistent with Article 1 of the Convention, given that sections 2340 and 2340 A of the United States Code limit federal criminal jurisdiction over acts of torture to extraterritorial cases. The Committee

also regrets that, despite the occurrence of cases of extraterritorial torture of detainees, no prosecutions have been initiated under the extraterritorial criminal torture statute (arts. 1, 2, 4 and 5).

The Committee reiterates its previous recommendation that the State party should enact a federal crime of torture consistent with Article 1 of the Convention, which should include appropriate penalties, in order to fulfil its obligations under the Convention to prevent and eliminate acts of torture causing severe pain or suffering, whether physical or mental, in all its forms.

The State party should ensure that acts of psychological torture, prohibited by the Convention, are not limited to "prolonged mental harm" as set out in the State party's understandings lodged at the time of ratification of the Convention, but constitute a wider category of acts, which cause severe mental suffering, irrespective of their prolongation or its duration.

The State party should investigate, prosecute and punish perpetrators under the federal extraterritorial criminal torture statute.

14. The Committee regrets the State party's opinion that the Convention is Not applicable in times and in the context of armed conflict, on the basis of the argument that the "law of armed conflict" is the exclusive lex specialis applicable, and that the Convention's application "would result in an overlap of the different treaties which would undermine the objective of eradicating torture" (arts. 1 and 16).

The State party should recognize and ensure that the Convention applies at all times, whether in peace, war or armed conflict, in any territory under its jurisdiction and that the application of the Convention's provisions are without prejudice to the provisions of any other international instrument, pursuant to paragraph 2 of its articles 1 and 16.

15. The Committee notes that a number of the Convention's provisions are expressed as applying to "territory under [the State party's] jurisdiction" (arts. 2, 5, 13, 16). The Committee reiterates its previously expressed view that this includes all areas under the de facto effective control of the State party, by whichever military or civil authorities such control is exercised. The Committee considers that the State party's view that those provisions are geographically limited to its own de jure territory to be regrettable.

The State party should recognize and ensure that the provisions of the Convention expressed as applicable to "territory under the State party's jurisdiction" apply to, and are fully enjoyed, by all persons under the effective control of its authorities, of whichever type, wherever located in the world.

16. The Committee notes with concern that the State party does not always register persons detained in territories under its jurisdiction outside the United States, depriving them of an effective safeguard against acts of torture (art. 2).

The State party should register all persons it detains in any territory under its jurisdiction, as one measure to prevent acts of torture. Registration should contain the identity of the detainee, the date, time and place of the detention, the identity of the authority that detained the person, the ground for the detention, the date and time of admission to the detention facility and the state of health of the detainee upon admission and any changes thereto, the time and place of interrogations, with the names of all interrogators present, as well as the date and time of release or transfer to another detention facility.

17. The Committee is concerned by allegations that the State party has established secret detention facilities, which are not accessible to the International Committee of the Red Cross. Detainees are allegedly deprived of fundamental legal safeguards, including an oversight mechanism in regard to their treatment and review procedures with respect to their detention. The Committee is also concerned by allegations that those detained in such facilities could be held for prolonged periods and face torture or cruel, inhuman or degrading treatment. The Committee considers the "no comment" policy of the State party regarding the existence of such secret detention facilities, as well as on its intelligence activities, to be regrettable (arts. 2 and 16).

The State party should ensure that no one is detained in any secret detention facility under its de facto effective control. Detaining persons in such conditions constitutes, per se, a violation of the Convention. The State party should investigate and disclose the existence of any such facilities and the authority under which they have been established and the manner in which detainees are treated. The State party should publicly condemn any policy of secret detention.

The Committee recalls that intelligence activities, notwithstanding their author, nature or location, are acts of the State party, fully engaging its international responsibility.

18. The Committee is concerned by reports of the involvement of the State party in enforced disappearances. The Committee considers the State party's view that such acts do not constitute a form of torture to be regrettable (arts. 2 and 16).

The State party should adopt all necessary measures to prohibit and prevent enforced disappearance in any territory under its jurisdiction, and prosecute and punish perpetrators, as this practice constitutes, per se, a violation of the Convention.

19. Notwithstanding the State party's statement that "[u]nder U.S. law, there is no derogation from the express statutory prohibition of torture" and that "[n]o circumstances whatsoever... may be invoked as a justification or defense to committing torture", the Committee remains concerned at the absence of clear legal provisions ensuring that the Convention's prohibition against torture is not derogated from under any circumstances, in particular since 11 September 2001 (arts. 2, 11 and 12).

The State party should adopt clear legal provisions to implement the principle of absolute prohibition of torture in its domestic law without any possible derogation. Derogation from this principle is incompatible with paragraph 2 of Article 2 of the Convention, and cannot limit criminal responsibility. The State party should also ensure that perpetrators of acts of torture are prosecuted and punished appropriately.

The State party should also ensure that any interrogation rules, instructions or methods do not derogate from the principle of absolute prohibition of torture and that no doctrine under domestic law impedes the full criminal responsibility of perpetrators of acts of torture.

The State party should promptly, thoroughly, and impartially investigate any responsibility of senior military and civilian officials authorizing, acquiescing or consenting, in any way, to acts of torture committed by their subordinates.

20. The Committee is concerned that the State party considers that the non-refoulement obligation, under Article 3 of the Convention, does not extend to a person detained outside its territory. The Committee is also concerned by the State party's rendition of suspects, without any judicial procedure, to States where they face a real risk of torture (art. 3).

The State party should apply the non-refoulement guarantee to all detainees in its custody, cease the rendition of suspects, in particular by its intelligence agencies, to States where they face a real risk of torture, in order to comply with its obligations under Article 3 of the Convention. The State party should always ensure that suspects have the possibility to challenge decisions of refoulement.

21. The Committee is concerned by the State party's use of "diplomatic assurances", or other kinds of guarantees, assuring that a person will not be tortured if expelled, returned, transferred or extradited to another State. The Committee is also concerned by the secrecy of such procedures including the absence of judicial scrutiny and the lack of monitoring mechanisms put in place to assess if the assurances have been honoured (art. 3).

When determining the applicability of its non-refoulement obligations under Article 3 of the Convention, the State party should only rely on "diplomatic assurances" in regard to States which do not systematically violate the Convention's provisions, and after a thorough examination of the merits of each individual case. The State party should establish and implement clear procedures for obtaining such assurances, with adequate judicial mechanisms for review, and effective post-return monitoring arrangements. The State party should also provide detailed information to the Committee on all cases since 11 September 2001 where assurances have been provided.

22. The Committee, noting that detaining persons indefinitely without charge constitutes per se a violation of the Convention, is concerned that detainees are held for protracted periods at Guantánamo Bay, without sufficient legal safeguards and without judicial assessment of the justification for their detention (arts. 2, 3 and 16).

The State party should cease to detain any person at Guantánamo Bay and close this detention facility, permit access by the detainees to judicial process or release them as soon as possible, ensuring that they are not returned to any State where they could face a real risk of being tortured, in order to comply with its obligations under the Convention.

23. The Committee is concerned that information, education and training provided to the State party's law-enforcement or military personnel are not adequate and do not focus on all provisions of the Convention, in particular on the non-derogable nature of the prohibition of torture and the prevention of cruel, inhuman and degrading treatment or punishment (arts. 10 and 11).

The State party should ensure that education and training of all law-enforcement or military personnel, are conducted on a regular basis, in particular for personnel involved in the interrogation of suspects. This should include training on interrogation rules, instructions and methods, and specific training on how to identify signs of torture and cruel, inhuman or degrading treatment. Such personnel should also be instructed to report such incidents.

The State party should also regularly evaluate the training and education provided to its law-enforcement and military personnel as well as ensure regular and independent monitoring of their conduct.

24. The Committee is concerned that in 2002 the State party authorized the use of certain interrogation techniques that have resulted in the death of some detainees during interrogation. The Committee also regrets that "confusing interrogation rules" and techniques defined in vague and general terms, such as "stress positions", have led to serious abuses of detainees (arts. 11, 1, 2 and 16).

The State party should rescind any interrogation technique, including methods involving sexual humiliation, "waterboarding", "short shackling" and using dogs to induce fear, that constitutes torture or cruel, inhuman or degrading treatment or punishment, in all places of detention under its de facto effective control, in order to comply with its obligations under the Convention.

25. The Committee is concerned at allegations of impunity of some of the State party's law-enforcement personnel in respect of acts of torture or cruel, inhuman or degrading treatment or punishment. The Committee notes the limited investigation and lack of prosecution in respect of the allegations of torture perpetrated in areas 2 and 3 of the Chicago Police Department (art. 12).

The State party should promptly, thoroughly and impartially investigate all allegations of acts of torture or cruel, inhuman or degrading treatment or punishment by law-enforcement personnel and bring perpetrators to justice, in order to fulfil its obligations under Article 12 of the Convention. The State party should also provide the Committee with information on the ongoing investigations and prosecution relating to the above-mentioned case.

26. The Committee is concerned by reliable reports of acts of torture or cruel, inhuman and degrading treatment or punishment committed by certain members of the State party's military or civilian personnel in Afghanistan and Iraq. It is also concerned that the investigation and prosecution of many of these cases, including some resulting in the death of detainees, have led to lenient sentences, including of an administrative nature or less than one year's imprisonment (art. 12).

The State party should take immediate measures to eradicate all forms of torture and ill-treatment of detainees by its military or civilian personnel, in any territory under its jurisdiction, and should promptly and thoroughly investigate such acts, prosecute all those responsible for such acts, and ensure they are appropriately punished, in accordance with the seriousness of the crime.

27. The Committee is concerned that the Detainee Treatment Act of 2005 aims to withdraw the jurisdiction of the State party's federal courts with respect to habeas corpus petitions, or other claims by or on behalf of Guantánamo Bay detainees, except under limited circumstances. The Committee is also concerned that detainees in Afghanistan and Iraq, under the control of the Department of Defense, have their status determined and reviewed by an administrative process of that department (art. 13).

The State party should ensure that independent, prompt and thorough procedures to review the circumstances of detention and the status of detainees are available to all detainees, as required by Article 13 of the Convention.

28. The Committee is concerned at the difficulties certain victims of abuses have faced in obtaining redress and adequate compensation, and that only a limited number of detainees have filed claims for compensation for alleged abuse and maltreatment, in particular under the Foreign Claims Act (art. 14).

The State party should ensure, in accordance with the Convention, that mechanisms to obtain full redress, compensation and rehabilitation are accessible to all victims of acts of torture or abuse, including sexual violence, perpetrated by its officials.

29. The Committee is concerned at section 1997 e (e) of the 1995 Prison Litigation Reform Act which provides "that no federal civil action may be brought by a prisoner for mental or emotional injury suffered while in custody without a prior showing of physical injury" (art. 14).

The State party should not limit the right of victims to bring civil actions and amend the Prison Litigation Reform Act accordingly.

30. The Committee, while taking note of the State party's instruction number 10 of 24 March 2006, which provides that military commissions shall not admit statements established to be made as a result of torture in evidence, is concerned about the implementation of the instruction in the context of such commissions and the limitations on detainees' effective right to complain. The Committee is also concerned about the Combatant Status Review Tribunals and the Administrative Review Boards (arts. 13 and 15).

The State party should ensure that its obligations under articles 13 and 15 are fulfilled in all circumstances, including in the context of military commissions and should consider establishing an independent mechanism to guarantee the rights of all detainees in its custody.

31. The Committee is concerned at the fact that substantiated information indicates that executions in the State party can be accompanied by severe pain and suffering (arts. 16, 1 and 2).

The State party should carefully review its execution methods, in particular lethal injection, in order to prevent severe pain and suffering.

32. The Committee is concerned at reliable reports of sexual assault of sentenced detainees, as well as persons in pretrial or immigration detention, in places of detention in the State party. The Committee is concerned that there are numerous reports of sexual violence perpetrated by detainees on one another, and that persons of differing sexual orientation are particularly vulnerable. The Committee is also concerned by the lack of prompt and independent investigation of such acts and that appropriate measures to combat these abuses have not been implemented by the State party (arts. 16, 12, 13 and 14).

The State party should design and implement appropriate measures to prevent all sexual violence in all its detention centres. The State party should ensure that all allegations of violence in detention centres are investigated promptly and independently, perpetrators are prosecuted and appropriately sentenced and victims can seek redress, including appropriate compensation.

33. The Committee is concerned at the treatment of detained women in the State party, including gender-based humiliation and incidents of shackling of women detainees during childbirth (art. 16).

The State party should adopt all appropriate measures to ensure that women in detention are treated in conformity with international standards.

34. The Committee reiterates the concern expressed in its previous recommendations about the conditions of the detention of children, in particular the fact that they may not be completely segregated from adults during pretrial detention and after sentencing. The Committee is also concerned at the large number of children sentenced to life imprisonment in the State party (art. 16).

The State party should ensure that detained children are kept in facilities separate from those for adults in conformity with international standards. The State party should address the question of sentences of life imprisonment of children, as these could constitute cruel, inhuman or degrading treatment or punishment.

35. The Committee remains concerned about the extensive use by the State party's law-enforcement personnel of electroshock devices, which have caused several deaths. The Committee is concerned that this practice raises serious issues of compatibility with Article 16 of the Convention.

The State party should carefully review the use of electroshock devices, strictly regulate their use, restricting it to substitution for lethal weapons, and eliminate the use of these devices to restrain persons in custody, as this leads to breaches of Article 16 of the Convention.

36. The Committee remains concerned about the extremely harsh regime imposed on detainees in "supermaximum prisons". The Committee is concerned about the prolonged isolation periods detainees are subjected to, the effect such treatment has on their mental health, and that its purpose may be retribution, in which case it would constitute cruel, inhuman or degrading treatment or punishment (art. 16).

The State party should review the regime imposed on detainees in "supermaximum prisons", in particular the practice of prolonged isolation.

37. The Committee is concerned about reports of brutality and use of excessive force by the State party's law-enforcement personnel, and the numerous allegations of their ill-treatment of vulnerable groups, in particular racial minorities, migrants and persons of different sexual orientation which have not been adequately investigated (art. 16 and 12).

The State party should ensure that reports of brutality and ill-treatment of members of vulnerable groups by its law-enforcement personnel are independently, promptly and thoroughly investigated and that perpetrators are prosecuted and appropriately punished.

38. The Committee strongly encourages the State party to invite the Special Rapporteur on torture and other cruel, inhuman or degrading treatment or punishment, in full conformity with the terms of reference for fact-finding missions by special procedures of the United Nations, to visit Guantánamo Bay and any other detention facility under its de facto control.

39. The Committee invites the State party to reconsider its express intention not to become party to the Rome Statute of the International Criminal Court.

40. The Committee reiterates its recommendation that the State party should consider withdrawing its reservations, declarations and understandings lodged at the time of ratification of the Convention.

41. The Committee encourages the State party to consider making the declaration under Article 22, thereby recognizing the competence of the Committee to receive and consider individual communications, as well as ratifying the Optional Protocol to the Convention.

42. The Committee requests the State party to provide detailed statistical data, disaggregated by sex, ethnicity and conduct, on complaints related to torture and ill-treatment allegedly committed by law-enforcement officials, investigations, prosecutions, penalties and disciplinary action relating to such complaints. It requests the State party to provide similar statistical data and information on the enforcement of the Civil Rights of Institutionalized Persons Act by the Department of Justice, in particular in respect to the prevention, investigation and prosecution of acts of torture, or cruel, inhuman or degrading treatment or punishment in detention facilities and the measures taken to implement the Prison Rape Elimination Act and their impact. The Committee requests the State party to provide information on any compensation and rehabilitation provided to victims. The Committee encourages the State party to create a federal database to facilitate the collection of such statistics and information which assist in the assessment of the implementation of the provisions of the Convention and the practical enjoyment of the rights it provides. The Committee also requests the State party to provide information on investigations into the alleged ill-treatment perpetrated by law-enforcement personnel in the aftermath of Hurricane Katrina.

43. The Committee requests the State party to provide, within one year, information on its response to its recommendations in paragraphs 16, 20, 21, 22, 24, 33, 34 and 42 above.

44. The Committee requests the State party to disseminate its report, with its addenda and the written answers to the Committee's list of issues and oral questions and the conclusions and recommendations of the Committee widely, in all appropriate languages, through official websites, the media and non-governmental organizations.

45. The State party is invited to submit its next periodic report, which will be considered as its fifth periodic report, by 19 November 2011, the due date of the fifth periodic report.

. . .

DOCUMENT 21C (SERIES)

Full Official Title: Consideration Of Reports Submitted By States Parties Under Article 19 Of The Convention, Comments by the Government of the United States of America to the conclusions and recommendations of the Committee against Torture (CAT/C/USA/CO/2)

Short Title/Acronym/Abbreviation: U.S. follow up Comments to CAT on its Concluding Observations, Second and Third Reports

Type of Document: This is the U.S written communication to the CAT regarding the response of the U.S. to the Committee's conclusions and recommendations, Document 21B.

Subject: U.S. report on and disagreeing with CATs conclusions and recommendations on Second and Third Reports.

Official Citation: CAT/C/USA/CO/2/Add. 1

Date of Document: November 6, 2007

Date of Adoption: Not applicable

Date of General Entry into Force (EIF): Not applicable

Number of States Parties as of this printing: Not applicable

Date of Signature by the United States: Not applicable

Date of Ratification/Accession/Adhesion: Not applicable

Date of Entry into Force as to United States (effective date): Not applicable

Legal Status/Character of the Instrument/Document as to the United States: This is not a legal instrument but an administrative document that is submitted by a state party to a treaty body, the Human Rights Committee, to inform the body of its response to the conclusions of the Committee on its compliance with the ICCPR.

Comments: By ratifying the CAT, the U.S. agreed under Article 19 to report to the Committee Against Torture on measures they have adopted to give effect to the rights recognized in the Convention or any progress they have made or obstacles in the enjoyment of those right. Part of this process after the report is submitted is for the State to appear in person before the Committee to discuss issues arising in the report. After the hearing took place the Committee prepared the outcome document, 21B, giving its conclusions and recommendations to the U.S. It is up to the state to then decide whether and how to implement these recommendations or contest the conclusions. This is a statement, "comments", by the U.S. contesting some of the conclusions and recommendations by the Committee. This is not a judicial process. The recommendations are not legally binding but are part of a treaty obligation and should be implemented in good faith, consistent with the U.S. Constitution.

This report should be read along with the three 21-series documents to get an idea of the give and take between the international community, represented by the Committee Against Torture, and the U.S., represented by a Department of State delegation. This process also happens in the other treaty bodies, CERD and HRCee.

For the full text of this document 21C, see the following website:
Web Address: http://2001–2009.state.gov/g/drl/rls/100736.htm

U.S. FOLLOW UP COMMENTS TO CAT ON ITS CONCLUDING OBSERVATIONS, SECOND AND THIRD REPORTS

CONSIDERATION OF REPORTS SUBMITTED BY STATES PARTIES UNDER ARTICLE 19 OF THE CONVENTION, Comments by the Government of the United States of America To The Conclusions and Recommendations of the Committee Against Torture (CAT/C/USA/CO/2) [25 July 2007]

1. In its conclusions and recommendations regarding the Second Period report of the United States of America, the Committee Against Torture requested that the United States provide, within one year, information on its response to specific recommendations identified by the Committee.[1] These specific recommendations and the United States responses to them are provided below.

Paragraph 16

"The State party should register all persons it detains in any territory under its jurisdiction, as one measure to prevent acts of torture. Registration should contain the identity of the detainee, the date, time and place of the detention, the identity of the authority that detained the person, the ground for the detention, the date and time of admission to the detention facility and the state of health of the detainee upon admission and any changes thereto, the time and place of interrogations, with the names of all interrogators present, as well as the date and time of release or transfer to another detention facility."

2. As an initial matter it should be noted that the Convention Against Torture and other Cruel, Inhuman or Degrading Treatment or Punishment (hereinafter referred to as "the Convention") has no provision requiring the registration of prisoners.

3. Although there is no unified national policy governing the registry of persons detained in territory subject to the jurisdiction of the United States, relevant individual federal, state, and local authorities, including military authorities, as a matter of good administrative practice generally maintain appropriate records on persons detained by them.[2] Such records would generally include the information mentioned in the Committee's recommendation.

Paragraph 20

"The State party should apply the *non-refoulement* guarantee to all detainees in its custody, cease the rendition of suspects, in particular by its intelligence agencies, to States where they face a real risk of torture, in order to comply with its obligations under Article 3 of the Convention. The State party should always ensure that suspects have the possibility to challenge decisions of *refoulement*."

4. There are two issues that appear to be raised in this conclusion and recommendation. The first issue is the *evidentiary standard* that would trigger application of CAT Article 3. As the United States described to the Committee,[3] pursuant to a formal understanding the United States filed at the time it became a State Party to the Convention, the United States determines whether it is more likely than not that a person would be tortured, rather than whether a person faces a "real risk" of torture.

5. The second issue addresses the *territorial scope* of Article 3. Although the United States and the Committee hold differing views on the applicability of the non-refoulement obligation in Article 3 of the Convention outside the territory of a State Party, as the United States explained to the Committee at length,[4] with respect to persons outside the territory of the United States as a matter of policy, the United States government does not transfer persons to countries where it determines that it is more likely than not that they will be tortured. This policy applies to all components of the government, including the intelligence agencies.[5] Although there is no requirement under the Convention that individuals should have the possibility to challenge refoulement, United States practice in the different areas in which this provision comes into play is designed to ensure that any torture concerns, whenever raised by the individual to be transferred, are taken into account. For example, in the context of immigration removals from the United States, as noted in the United States periodic report,[6] there are procedures for alleging torture concerns and procedures by which those claims can be advanced.

Paragraph 21

"When determining the applicability of its non-refoulement obligations under Article 3 of the Convention, the State party should only rely on "diplomatic assurances" in regard to States which do not systematically violate the Convention's provisions, and after a thorough examination of the merits of each individual case. The State party should establish and implement clear procedures for obtaining such assurances, with adequate judicial mechanisms for review, and effective post-return monitoring arrangements. The State party should also provide detailed information to the Committee on all cases since 11 September 2001 where assurances have been provided."

6. As explained to the Committee,[7] the United States undertakes a thorough, case-by-case analysis of each potential transfer where diplomatic assurances are involved. This analysis takes into account all relevant factors, including all available information about the compliance of the potential receiving state with its international obligations, including those under the Convention, and the merits of each individual case.

7. The United States would like to emphasize to the Committee, as it did on other occasions,[8] that diplomatic assurances are used sparingly but that assurances may be sought in order to be satisfied that it is not "more likely than not" that the individual in question will be tortured upon return. It is important to note that diplomatic assurances are only a factor that may be considered in appropriate cases and are not used as a substitute for a case-specific assessment as to whether it is not more likely than not that a person will be tortured if returned.

8. Procedures for obtaining diplomatic assurances vary according to the context (*e.g.*, extradition, immigration removal, or military custody transfer) and have been made available to the Committee.[9] For example, the United States report provides information regarding regulatory procedures for consideration of diplomatic assurances in the immigration removal context, which provide for the opportunity to allege torture and advance such claims.[10] In addition, attached in Annex 1 is a declaration by Clint Williamson, Ambassador-at-large for War Crimes Issues at the Department of State, dated June 8, 2007, and filed in United States federal court. This declaration explains in detail the process for obtaining and considering diplomatic assurances for detainees to be transferred from Guantánamo. It supersedes the declaration by former Ambassador Pierre Prosper that was provided to the Committee as part of the Second Periodic Report.[11] For the Committee's information, With regard to post-return monitoring arrangements, the United States agrees that follow-up following return is important. Indeed, the United States has requested and obtained information about the situation of individuals who have been transferred to other countries subject to assurances. As explained to the Committee, the United States would pursue any credible report and take appropriate action if it had reason to believe that those assurances would not be, or had not been, honored.

9. The United States does not unilaterally make public the specific assurances provided to it by foreign governments. Reasons for this policy were articulated in the materials provided to the Committee,[12] including the fact that unilaterally making assurances public might make foreign governments reluctant in the future to communicate frankly with the United States concerning important concerns related to torture or mistreatment.

Paragraph 22

"The State party should cease to detain any person at Guantánamo Bay and close this detention facility, permit access by the detainees to judicial process or release them as soon as possible, ensuring that they are not returned to any State where they could face a real risk of being tortured, in order to comply with its obligations under the Convention."

10. Among the actions purported by the Committee to be governed under the Convention—including, for example, (1) closing Guantánamo; (2) permitting judicial access by enemy combatant detainees in that facility; or (3) not returning individuals who face "a real risk" of being tortured—the first two lack an arguable textual basis in the Convention, while the third issue is discussed at length in materials provided to the Committee[13] as well as in the response to the Committee's recommendation in paragraph 20 above.

11. As the United States explained to the Committee,[14] the United States is in an armed conflict with al-Qaida, the Taliban, and their supporters. As part of this conflict, the United States captures and detains enemy combatants, and is entitled under the law of war to hold them until the end of hostilities. The law of war, and not the Convention, provides the applicable legal framework governing these detentions.

12. Without going into further detail about its legal disagreements with the Committee's sweeping legal assertions regarding the scope of the Convention—which are addressed in other responses[15]—the United States has made it clear in many different settings that it does not want to be the world's jailer. Although the

Committee calls for the closure of Guantánamo, it does not appear to take into account the consequences of releasing dangerous terrorist combatants detained there or explain where those who cannot be repatriated due to humane treatment concerns might be sent. The United States will continue to look to the international community for assistance with resettlement of those detainees approved for transfer or release.

13. The United States does permit access by Guantánamo detainees to judicial process. Every detainee in Guantánamo is evaluated by a Combatant Status Review Tribunal (CSRT), which determines whether the detainee was properly classified as an enemy combatant and includes a number of procedural guarantees. A CSRT decision can be directly appealed to a United States domestic civilian court, the Court of Appeals for the District of Columbia Circuit. Providing such an opportunity for judicial review exceeds the requirements of the law of war and is an unprecedented and expanded protection available to all detainees at Guantánamo. These procedural protections are more extensive than those applied by any other nation in any previous armed conflict to determine a combatant's status.

14. After a CSRT determination, each enemy combatant not charged by a Military Commission receives an annual review to determine whether the United States needs to continue detention. An Administrative Review Board (ARB) conducts this review.

16. Since the Committee's consideration of the United States report in May 2006, approximately 120 detainees have departed Guantánamo. This process is ongoing. Updates are available at http://www.defenselink.mil/news/nrdgb.html.

17. These transfers are a demonstration of the United States' desire not to hold detainees any longer than necessary. It also underscores the processes put in place to assess each individual and make a determination about their detention while hostilities are ongoing—an unprecedented step in the history of warfare.

18. At present, approximately 375 detainees remain at Guantánamo, and approximately 405 have been released or transferred. The Department of Defense has determined—through its comprehensive review processes—that approximately 75 additional detainees are eligible for transfer or release. Departure of these detainees is subject to ongoing discussions between the United States and other nations.

Paragraph 24

"The State party should rescind any interrogation technique, including methods involving sexual humiliation, "waterboarding," "short shackling" and using dogs to induce fear, that constitutes torture or cruel, inhuman or degrading treatment or punishment, in all places of detention under its de facto effective control, in order to comply with its obligations under the Convention."

19. As an initial matter, as the United States has informed the Committee,[16] the United States is in an armed conflict with al-Qaida, the Taliban, and their supporters. As part of this conflict, the United States captures and detains enemy combatants, and is entitled under the law of war to hold them until the end of hostilities. The law of war, and not the Convention, is the applicable legal framework governing these detentions. Moreover, as the Committee is aware,[17] the United States disagrees with the Committee's contention that "de facto effective control" is equivalent to territory subject to a State party's jurisdiction for the purposes of the Convention.

20. Leaving aside interpretive issues arising under the Convention, as a matter of United States law, there is a ban on torture of anyone under the custody or physical control of the United States Government. Torture, attempt to commit torture, and conspiracy to commit torture outside of the United States by U.S. nationals or persons present in the United States are crimes under the extraterritorial torture statute.[18] Moreover, pursuant to the Detainee Treatment Act of 2005,[19] cruel, inhuman, or degrading treatment or punishment of anyone under the custody or physical control of the United States Government is prohibited. All detainee interrogations must be conducted in a manner consistent with these prohibitions, Common Article 3 of the Geneva Conventions, as well as any greater applicable law of war protections.

21. In September 2006, the Department of Defense released the updated DoD detainee program directive 2310.01E, and the Army released its revised Field Manual on Interrogation. These documents are attached in Annexes 2 and 3, respectively. They provide guidance to military personnel to ensure compliance with the law, and require that all personnel subject to the directive treat all detainees, regardless of their legal status, consistently with the minimum standards of Common Article 3 until their final release, transfer out of DoD control, or repatriation. Of course, certain categories of detainees, such as enemy prisoners of war, enjoy protections under the law of war in addition to the minimum standards prescribed by Common Article 3.

22. Furthermore, under the Military Commissions Act of 2006,[20] serious violations of Common Article 3, including torture and cruel or inhuman treatment, are criminal offenses. In defining precisely

those violations that are subject to criminal prosecution, greater clarity is provided to officials involved in detention and interrogation operations on what treatment violates United States and international law. A copy of the Military Commissions Act is attached at Annex 4.

Paragraph 33

"The State party should adopt all appropriate measures to ensure that women in detention are treated in conformity with international standards."

23. The United States provided the Committee with information about its efforts to ensure appropriate treatment of women in detention facilities, including action taken against gender-based violence and sexual abuse.[21] As the United States told the Committee,[22] incidents of shackling of female detainees during childbirth are extremely rare and are not a standard procedure. It also provided the information on these issues in response to other questions from members of the Human Rights Committee.[23]

24. In its written reply to the Committee's List of Issues, the United States provided Bureau of Prisons statistics regarding enforcement actions for sexual abuse against prisoners.[24] These figures were for calendar year 2004, the latest year for which statistics were available at the time. Updated figures are provided below.

25. During Calendar Year (CY) 2005, the latest figures available, there were 17 allegations of *inmate-on-inmate non-consensual sexual acts* (also broadly referred to as "rape"). During CY 2005, there were five guilty findings for *non-consensual sexual acts*. Please note that there is not necessarily a correspondence between allegations and findings because cases may span more than one calendar year.

26. During CY 2005, there were 40 allegations of *inmate-on-inmate abusive sexual contacts* (also broadly referred to as "touching offenses"). During CY 2005, there were 30 guilty findings for abusive sexual contacts. Please note that there is not necessarily a correspondence between allegations and findings because cases may span more than one calendar year.

27. During CY 2005, there were 203 allegations of staff sexual misconduct. During CY 2005, 6 allegations were substantiated. Please note that it is possible for a single case to have multiple subjects; and similarly, the same subject could be charged with multiple allegations in the same case. If a single case involved multiple subjects, an allegation is counted for each subject and for each behavior. Any allegations made during previous years which were closed during CY 2005 are not reflected.

28. Allegations of the sexual abuse of inmates by staff are tracked in accordance with the definitions outlined Title 18, United States Code, Chapter 109A.

29. Additionally, other behaviors such as indecent exposure, staff voyeurism, and inappropriate comments of a sexual nature are also tracked and are included with the sexual abuse allegations. All types of allegations are included in the above figures. These figures are for allegations made against staff working in Bureau of Prisons facilities.

Paragraph 34

"The State party should ensure that detained children are kept in facilities separate from those for adults in conformity with international standards. The State party should address the question of sentences of life imprisonment of children, as these could constitute cruel, inhuman or degrading treatment or punishment."

30. As the United States explained to the Committee,[25] juveniles are not regularly held in federal prison with the adult prison population. Federal law prohibits juvenile offenders held in the custody of federal authorities from being housed in correctional institutions or detention facilities in which they could have regular contact with adults. As a general rule, the state prison populations do not include "juveniles" as that term is defined by the applicable state law.

31. The Convention does not prohibit the sentencing of juveniles to life imprisonment without parole. The United States, moreover, does not believe that the sentencing of juveniles to life imprisonment constitutes cruel, inhuman or degrading treatment or punishment as defined in United States obligations under the Convention. In this context, it is significant to recall the specific treaty obligations of the United States under Article 16 in light of the formal reservation the United States took with respect to that provision at the time it became a State Party to the Convention. Specifically, that reservation stated "[t]hat the United States considers itself bound by the obligation under Article 16 to prevent 'cruel, inhuman or degrading treatment or punishment,' only insofar as the term 'cruel, inhuman or degrading treatment or punishment' means the cruel, unusual and inhumane treatment or punishment prohibited by the Fifth, Eighth, and/or Fourteenth Amendments to the Constitution of the United States." United States courts have considered such sentences on numerous occasions and ruled that juvenile

life imprisonment does not violate the United States Constitution. Accordingly, such sentences do not violate U.S. obligations under the Convention with respect to cruel, inhuman or degrading treatment or punishment.

32. A prohibition of juvenile life imprisonment without parole is an important provision in the later-negotiated Convention on the Rights of the Child (CRC). States that wished to assume new treaty obligations with respect to juvenile sentencing were free to become States Parties to the CRC, and a very large number of countries chose to do so. Accordingly, States Parties to the CRC have an obligation under Article 37 of that Convention to ensure that "neither capital punishment nor life imprisonment without possibility of release shall be imposed for offences committed by persons below eighteen years of age." However, the United States has not become a State Party to the CRC[26] and, accordingly, is under no obligation to prohibit the sentencing of juveniles to life imprisonment without the opportunity for parole.

Paragraph 42

"The Committee requests the State party to provide detailed statistical data, disaggregated by sex, ethnicity and conduct, on complaints related to torture and ill-treatment allegedly committed by law-enforcement officials, investigations, prosecutions, penalties and disciplinary action relating to such complaints. It requests the State party to provide similar statistical data and information on the enforcement of the Civil Rights of Institutionalized Persons Act by the Department of Justice, in particular in respect to the prevention, investigation and prosecution of acts of torture, or cruel, inhuman or degrading treatment or punishment in detention facilities and the measures taken to implement the Prison Rape Elimination Act and their impact. The Committee requests the State party to provide information on any compensation and rehabilitation provided to victims."

33. The United States provided substantial statistical information to the Committee[27] and provides the following updated information.

34. In July 2006, the Department of Justice's Bureau of Justice Statistics released a report, Sexual Violence Reported by Correctional Authorities, 2005. This report is attached as Annex 5 and is also available at: http://www.ojp.usdoj.gov/bjs/pub/pdf/svrca05.pdf. This report has detailed statistical information, including:

35. According to this report, in 2005, in substantiated incidents of staff sexual misconduct and harassment, staff were discharged or resigned in approximately 82% of cases, arrested or referred for prosecution in approximately 45% of cases, and disciplined, transferred, or demoted in approximately 17% of cases (these numbers add to more than 100% because more than one action against a staff member could be taken concerning the same incident).

36. This report also states that in 2005, approximately 15% of allegations of staff sexual misconduct in Federal and state prisons were substantiated, while approximately 6% of allegations of staff sexual harassment in Federal and state prisons were substantiated. The report states that in local jails, approximately 37% of allegations of staff sexual misconduct were substantiated, while approximately 10% of allegations of staff sexual misconduct were substantiated.

37. Finally, the report states that in 2005, in Federal and state prisons approximately 67% of the victims of staff misconduct were male, while approximately 62% of the perpetrators were female. In local jails, however, approximately 78% of the victims of staff misconduct were female, while approximately 87% of the perpetrators were male. With respect to race, approximately 69% of the staff members involved in staff sexual misconduct and harassment were White, approximately 24% were Black (non-Hispanic), approximately 4% were Hispanic, and approximately 4% were Other (this category includes American Indians, Alaska Natives, Asians, Native Hawaiians, and Other Pacific Islanders).

"The Committee encourages the State party to create a federal database to facilitate the collection of such statistics and information which assist in the assessment of the implementation of the provisions of the Convention and the practical enjoyment of the rights it provides."

38. As a result of the decentralized federal structure of the United States, the creation of one unified database would not materially contribute to better implementation of the Convention. Instead, Federal and state authorities compile relevant statistics, including those mentioned by the Committee, and use them for a wide variety of purposes, including assessing the effectiveness of enforcement. Enforcement against torture and cruel, inhuman or degrading treatment or punishment is managed through the laws and procedures described at length in the United States periodic report[28] and its responses to the questions posed by the Committee.[29]

"The Committee also requests the State party to provide information on investigations into the alleged ill-treatment perpetrated by law-enforcement personnel in the aftermath of Hurricane Katrina."

39. For the Committee's information, a partial list of the work done by Federal agencies in response to Hurricanes Katrina and Rita, including enhanced law enforcement operations in the Gulf Coast region, is attached at Annex 6 and is available at http://www.dhs.gov/xprepresp/programs/gc_1157649340100.shtm.

40. Since the Committee has not provided the United States with specific information about the allegations of ill-treatment it mentions, the United States is unable to provide a detailed response to any specific allegations the Committee may have in mind.

41. That said, U.S. law prohibits brutality and discriminatory actions by law enforcement officers. The Civil Rights Division of the Department of Justice, with the aid of United States Attorney's Offices and the FBI, actively enforces those laws. In addition, states have laws and/or other mechanisms that protect individuals from mistreatment by law enforcement officers.

42. Following Hurricane Katrina, which devastated the Gulf Coast region of the United States, there have been media reports of alleged ill-treatment perpetrated by law-enforcement personnel. The Federal government and relevant state entities have attempted to determine the validity of the allegations. Given the dual-sovereign system of government in the United States, as well as the manner in which the Federal government keeps statistics of allegations of police misconduct, it is not possible for the United States to accurately determine how many allegations of law enforcement misconduct were reported or investigated in the aftermath of Hurricane Katrina.

43. The Department of Justice's Civil Rights Division has opened files in connection with at least ten complaints of law-enforcement misconduct in the affected areas following the storm. Three of those complaints have been closed without prosecution because the allegations did not constitute prosecutable violations of federal criminal civil rights law. The three closed files included unsubstantiated allegations of an assault in a Mississippi jail; a civilian who was struck by a patrol car during the evacuation; and officers stealing cars from a car dealership following the storm.

44. Two of the nine matters opened by the Civil Rights Division involve incidents that have led to criminal charges being filed by the State of Louisiana. In October 2005, three New Orleans Police Department officers were charged with battery stemming from the assault of an individual in the New Orleans French Quarter a few weeks after Hurricane Katrina. In December 2006, seven New Orleans Police Department officers were indicted for the fatal shooting of two individuals on the Danziger Bridge in the aftermath of the hurricane. Both cases still are pending, and the Department of Justice will continue to monitor these prosecutions.

45. The remaining files that were opened by the Civil Rights Division still are open and the investigations into those allegations are pending. Applicable federal law and policy requires that information concerning pending investigations into those allegations remain confidential. Nevertheless, the Committee can be assured that if an investigation indicates that there was a violation of a federal criminal civil rights statute, appropriate action will be taken.

46. In addition to the cases reviewed by the Civil Rights Division, the Louisiana Attorney General's Office is conducting an exhaustive inquiry into allegations that New Orleans residents were not permitted by law enforcement officials to cross the Greater New Orleans Bridge to Gretna, Louisiana, during the evacuation of the city. The Civil Rights Division intends to review the results of the state's investigation to determine whether the facts implicate a violation of any federal statutes.

47. The U.S. Department of Homeland Security (DHS) also received complaints alleging ill-treatment by law enforcement personnel in the aftermath of Hurricane Katrina. Specifically, DHS's Immigration and Customs Enforcement Office of Professional Responsibility (ICE OPR) received six complaints and its Office of Inspector General (IG) received three complaints. The allegations raised by these complainants are detailed below:

48. Complaints received by ICE OPR:

a) One complaint regarding an alleged civil rights/false arrest violation.

b) Two complaints regarding alleged looting/theft of electronics.

c) One complaint regarding an alleged rape.

d) One complaint regarding an alleged unauthorized procurement of supplies.

e) One complaint regarding alleged rude conduct.

49. Complaints received by the DHS Inspector General:

a) One complaint regarding alleged intimidation/mismanagement.

b) Two complaints regarding alleged false claims.

50. These allegations are being or have been investigated pursuant to standard procedures.

[Footnotes omitted]

DOCUMENT 22

Full Official Title: List of issues prior to the submission of the fifth periodic report of United States of America (CAT/C/USA/5) Specific information on the implementation of articles 1 to 16 of the Convention, including with regard to the previous recommendations of the Committee

Short Title/Acronym/Abbreviation: CAT List of Issues for the U.S. Fifth Periodic Report

Type of Document: This is an inter-governmental organization document from the U.N. Committee Against Torture consisting of list of specific issues CAT wants to have addressed by the U.S. regarding its Fifth Periodic Report to CAT. The List was prepared by the Committee Against Torture and sent to the U.S. State Department. The State Department will prepare its responses to present when the U.S. delegation appears before the Committee in Geneva to review its Fifth Periodic Reports. These are not a legal documents but administrative documents of a U.N. treaty based body.

Subject: Specific Issues for the U.S. to address before Committee, such as psychological torture, Guantánamo detainees, prison rape, police brutality, lethal injections and capital punishment, treatment of HIV-infected detained illegal immigrants, detention of juveniles, extraordinary rendition.

Official Citation: U.N. Doc. CAT/C/USA/Q/5

Date of Document: January 10, 2010

Date of Adoption: Not applicable

Date of General Entry into Force (EIF): Not applicable

Number of States Parties as of this printing: Not applicable

Date of Signature by the United States: Not applicable

Date of Ratification/Accession/Adhesion: Not applicable

Date of Entry into Force as to United States (effective date): Not applicable

Legal Status/Character of the Instrument/Document as to the United States: This is not a legal instrument but an administrative document, intergovernmental organization to the U.S. government. According to the document, "The present list of issues was adopted by the Committee [Against Torture] at its forty-third session, according to the new optional procedure established by the Committee at its thirty-eighth session, which consists in the preparation and adoption of lists of issues to be transmitted to States parties prior to the submission of their respective periodic report. The replies of the State party to this list of issues will constitute its report under Article 19 of the Convention.

Comments: By ratifying the Convention against Torture the U.S. agreed under Article 19 to report to the CAT on measures they have taken to give effect to their undertakings under the Convention. Part of this process after the report is submitted is for the State to appear in person before the Committee to discuss issues arising in the report. This list of specific items is part of a new optional procedure for a state report instead of just the state preparing its own report, such as Document 21A. The document sets forth the specific items listed by the Committee to which it wants the U.S. to respond at its hearing before the Committee. After the hearing takes place the Committee will prepare the outcome document, which will be like Document 21B, giving its conclusions and recommendations to the U.S. It is up to the state to then decide whether and how to implement these recommendations or contest the conclusions. This is an administrative and not a judicial process. The results are not legally binding.

This document is part of a U.S. periodic report review process which, at the time of this book, had not yet been completed. The reader should follow up at the U.S. Department of State Treaty Report website. This document is connected to and should be read along with 21-series documents to get an idea of the give and take between the international community, represented by the CAT, and the U.S., represented by a Department of State delegation. This process also happens in the other treaty bodies, HRCee and CERD.

For the text of the List of Issues, see the following website:

Website: http://www2.ohchr.org/english/bodies/cat/docs/CAT.C.USA.Q.5.pdf

List of Issues Prior to the Submission of the Fifth Periodic Report of the United States of America (CAT/C/USA/5)

Articles 1 and 4

1. Please provide information on steps taken to enact a federal crime of torture consistent with Article 1 of the Convention, which includes appropriate penalties, as recommended by the Committee in its previous concluding observations (para. 13).

2. Please clarify the State party's position with regard to its understanding of acts of psychological torture, prohibited by the Convention. Does the State party recognize a wider category of acts which cause severe mental suffering, irrespective of their prolongation or its duration, as acts of psychological torture prohibited by the Convention?

3. Please provide updated information on any changes in the State party's position that the Convention is Not applicable at all times, whether in peace, war or armed conflict, in any territory under its jurisdiction and is not without prejudice to the provisions of any other international instrument, pursuant to Article 1, paragraph 2, and 16, paragraph 2, of the Convention.

Article 2

4. In light of the Committee's previous concluding observations (para. 16) and the replies provided in the State party's comments under the follow-up procedure (CAT/C/USA/CO/2/Add.1, para. 3), please provide:

(a) Information on steps taken by the State party to ensure that it registers all persons it detains in any territory under its jurisdiction, including in all areas under its de facto effective control. Please elaborate on whether steps have been taken to adopt legislative measures to make registration obligatory for all authorities, including military authorities. Please clarify in which cases the authorities do not maintain appropriate records on persons detained.

(b) Details of cases in which the registration of persons detained does not contain all the elements mentioned in paragraph 16 of the previous concluding observations as to guarantee an effective safeguard against acts of torture.

5. Please provide information on:

(a) Whether the State party has adopted a policy that ensures that no one is detained in any secret detention facility under its de facto effective control and that publicly condemns secret detention, pursuant the Committee's previous concluding observations (para. 17). Please disclose detailed information on the existence of any such facilities, in the past and present, and the authority under which they have been established. In this respect, please respond to allegations made by the Special Rapporteur on torture and other cruel, inhuman or degrading treatment or punishment and the Council of Europe that the State party has used the British Indian Ocean Territory, Diego Garcia, for the secret detention of high-value "terror" suspects.[1]

(b) The legal safeguards provided to the detainees and the manner in which they are treated.

(c) Steps taken to address the reports of detainees held incommunicado and without the protection of domestic or international law (CCPR/C/USA/CO/3/Rev.1, para. 12). In this respect, please provide information on steps taken to ensure that all detained suspects, including in Diego Garcia and at Bagram Airbase in Afghanistan, are afforded, in practice, fundamental safeguards, including the right to a lawyer and an independent medical examination, as well as the right to inform a relative and have access to a court and the right to challenge the grounds for their detention.

6. Please indicate what specific measures have been taken to ensure that the State party is fulfilling its international responsibility under the Convention during its intelligence activities, notwithstanding the author, nature or location of those activities.

7. Please indicate if the State party has adopted legal provisions to implement the principle of absolute prohibition of torture in its domestic law without any possible derogation, as recommended by the Committee in its previous concluding observations (para. 19).

8. Please provide updated information on practical steps taken to close down Guantánamo Bay. In this respect, please provide detailed information on:

(a) States which have agreed to accept Guantánamo detainees and which conditions they have imposed. Please elaborate on steps taken to ensure that they are not returned to any State where they could face a real risk of being tortured and guarantee effective post-return monitoring arrangements.

(b) Steps taken to bring to justice those still detained at Guantánamo Bay for crimes under criminal law in regularly constituted courts, in accordance with internationally recognized fair trial standards. Please indicate before which judicial authority such detainees are tried and the legal safeguards with which they are provided.

(c) Steps taken to ensure that the State party will not indefinitely detain suspects, including those currently held at Guantánamo Bay, without charge. In case of such prolonged detention without trial, please elaborate on the legal safeguards provided to the detainees. Do they have the right to access to a lawyer of their own choice?

(d) Measures taken to ensure that all detainees who were kept in detention at Guantánamo Bay can have an enforceable right to fair and adequate compensation, in addition to rehabilitation, if a victim of torture or ill-treatment.

9. Please describe steps taken to ensure that the Material Witness Statute and immigration laws are not used so as to detain persons suspected of terrorism or any other criminal offences with fewer guarantees than in criminal proceedings.

Article 3

10. In light of the Committee's previous concluding observations (para. 20), please provide updated information on:

(a) Steps taken to ensure that the State party applies the non-refoulement guarantee to all detainees in its custody, including those detained outside its territory. Please provide information on steps taken to establish adequate judicial mechanisms to challenge all refoulement decisions.

(b) Whether the State party has ceased the "rendition" of suspects, in particular by its intelligence agencies, to States where they face a real risk of torture, as recommended by the Committee in its previous concluding observations.

(c) Steps taken to ensure that the State party conducts investigations into all allegations of violation of Article 3 of the Convention. Please elaborate on the outcome of these investigations and the impact thereof on the State party's policy (CCPR/C/USA/CO/3/Rev.1, para. 16).

11. Please provide detailed information on:

(a) The procedures in place for obtaining "diplomatic assurances", as requested by the Committee in its previous concluding observations (para. 21). A reminder to this effect was sent by the Rapporteur for follow-up in his letter of 8 August 2008.

(b) Steps taken to establish a judicial mechanism for reviewing, in last instance, the sufficiency and appropriateness of diplomatic assurances in any applicable case. Please elaborate on the federal court ruling in the case of Sameh Khouzam, noting that "deporting Khouzam based on diplomatic assurances without court review would render the procedures established for seeking protection under the Convention Against Torture 'a farce'". Please provide information on other cases of this kind, if any.

(c) Steps taken to guarantee effective post-return monitoring arrangements.

(d) All cases since 11 September 2001 where diplomatic assurances have been provided. Furthermore, please indicate if the State party has received information on any assurances that have not been honoured and what appropriate actions were taken in such cases by the State party?

12. Please provide updated information on the security agreement reached between the State Party and Iraq on the transfer of detainees held by the State party to Iraqi custody and the safeguards included to ensure that detainees are not in danger of being tortured. Does each detainee have the opportunity to contest a transfer to Iraqi custody?

Articles 5 and 7

13. Please indicate whether the State party has rejected, for any reason, any request for extradition by another State of an individual suspected of having committed an offence of torture and started its own prosecution proceedings as a result since the consideration of the previous report. If so, please provide information on the status and outcome of such proceedings.

14. Please indicate what are the purposes of the agreements the State party is signing with countries not to transfer its citizens to the International Criminal Court to be prosecuted for war crimes or crimes against humanity and how does the State party ensure that this combats impunity? Please provide examples of such cases, if any. With how many States has the State party signed such agreements? Should these agreements

prove not to be effective in combating impunity, please provide information on any other measures taken by the State party to combat impunity in such cases.

15. Please provide information on any judicial cooperation between the State party and Colombia regarding Colombian paramilitary leaders who were extradited to the State party and their responsibility for gross human rights violations, in order to ensure the prosecution of the perpetrators and satisfy the right to justice, truth and compensation of the victims.

Article 10

16. Please include information on steps taken to:

(a) Ensure that education and training of all law enforcement or military personnel is conducted on a regular basis, in particular for personnel involved in the interrogation of suspects. Does this include training on interrogation rules, instructions and methods, as well as specific training on how to identify signs of torture and cruel, inhuman or degrading treatment? Are personnel instructed to report such incidents?

(b) Ensure specific training for all medical personnel dealing with detainees in the detection of signs of torture and ill-treatment and ensure that the Istanbul Protocol of 1999 becomes an integral part of the training provided to physicians and others involved in care of detainees.

(c) Develop and implement a methodology to evaluate the implementation of its training/educational programmes, and their effectiveness and impact on the reduction of cases of torture and ill-treatment. Please provide information on the content and implementation of such methodology, as well as on the results of the measures implemented.

17. Please indicate steps taken to ensure that acts of health personnel are in full conformity with principle No. 2 of the Principles of Medical Ethics relevant to the Role of Health Personnel in the Protection of Prisoners and Detainees against Torture and Other Cruel, Inhuman or Degrading Treatment or Punishment. In this respect, please provide information on the participation and role of health personnel in interrogations of terror suspects, including in secret detention facilities.

Article 11

18. The Committee and the Human Rights Committee have expressed their concern that the State party authorized the use of enhanced interrogation techniques, such as methods involving sexual humiliation, "waterboarding", "short shackling" and using dogs to induce fear (para. 24 and CCPR/C/USA/CO/3/Rev.1, para. 13). In this respect, please describe steps taken to ensure that interrogation rules, instructions or methods do not derogate from the principle of absolute prohibition of torture. Furthermore, please:

(a) Provide updated information on the content of the Army Field Manual on Interrogation and its conformity with the Convention;

(b) Clarify if the standard for interrogation set in the manual is binding on all components of the State party, including intelligence agencies and private contractors who act on their behalf;

(c) Provide information with regard to the Central Intelligence Agency (CIA) interrogation manual;

(d) Indicate whether all interrogation techniques used in practice are in conformity with the Convention;

(e) Describe any steps taken to adopt legislation that explicitly prohibits interrogation techniques amounting to torture, such as those identified by the Committee in its previous concluding observations.

19. Please provide updated information on the composition and functioning of the inter-agency task force established by an executive order to evaluate the interrogation practices allowed by the Army Field Manual. Please also elaborate on the work of the agency, in particular on whether it has recommended any changes.

20. Please indicate if the International Committee of the Red Cross is granted access to all places of detention in any territory under its jurisdiction, including Bagram Airbase in Afghanistan and Diego Garcia, and under which conditions.

21. Please provide updated information on the establishment, composition and functioning of the "High-Value Interrogation Group", responsible for the interrogation of high-value detainees. Please provide detailed information on steps taken to ensure that the unit will only use interrogation techniques that are in conformity with the Convention. Furthermore, information should be provided on the authority responsible for monitoring such unit.

Articles 12 and 13

22. Please indicate if the State party has investigated, prosecuted and punished perpetrators under the federal extraterritorial criminal torture statute, as recommended by the Committee in its previous concluding observations (para. 13). If so, please provide further information on the relevant cases.

23. In light of the Committee's previous concluding observations, please provide information on:

(a) Steps taken to ensure that all forms of torture and ill-treatment of detainees by its military or civilian personnel, in any territory under its de facto and de jure jurisdiction, as well as in any other place under its effective control, is promptly, impartially and thoroughly investigated, and that all those responsible, including senior military and civilian officials authorizing, acquiescing or consenting in any way to such acts committed by their subordinates are prosecuted and appropriately punished, in accordance with the seriousness of the crime (para. 26). Are all suspects in prima facie cases of torture and ill-treatment as a rule suspended or reassigned during the process of investigation?

(b) The mandate of the prosecutor in charge of the preliminary review into whether United States laws were violated by CIA officers and contractors during the interrogation of detainees at places outside the United States, including Guantánamo Bay. Please elaborate on the outcome of this investigation and, if applicable, on the steps taken to hold the responsible persons accountable.

24. Please describe steps taken to ensure prompt and effective investigation into any allegations of torture or ill-treatment by private military and security companies and prosecute alleged perpetrators. In this respect, please indicate if the Department of Justice has strengthened its investigative resource capacity and appointed an independent prosecutor, as recommended by the Working Group on mercenaries.

25. As requested by the Committee in its previous concluding observations, please provide updated information on the investigations and prosecution relating to the allegations of torture perpetrated in areas 2 and 3 of the Chicago Police Department (para. 25). In this respect, please provide detailed information on the charges filed against Jon Burge and, if applicable, on the outcome of this case. Furthermore, please indicate if any other police officers have been brought to justice in this case.

26. Please provide detailed information on the procedures in place to review the circumstances of detention, as well as on steps taken to ensure that the status of detainees is available to all detainees. In this respect, please elaborate on the status and content of the Military Commission Act, as well as its conformity with the Convention.

Article 14

27. Pursuant the Committee's previous concluding observations (para. 28), please provide:

(a) Information on steps taken to ensure that mechanisms to obtain full redress, compensation and rehabilitation are accessible to all victims of acts or torture, including sexual violence, perpetrated by its officials. In this respect, please provide information about any reparation programmes, including psychological treatment and other forms of rehabilitation, provided to victims of torture and ill-treatment, as well as about the allocation of adequate resources to ensure the effective functioning of such programmes.

(b) Statistical data, disaggregated by sex and age, on the number of requests for redress made, the number granted and the amounts ordered and those actually provided in each case. In particular, information should be provided on the number of cases filed by detainees, including under the Foreign Claims Act, since the examination of the last periodic report in 2006.

28. Please indicate if the State party has amended the Prison Litigation Reform Act, including to guarantee the right of victims to bring civil actions, as recommended by the Committee in its previous concluding observations (para. 29).

Article 15

29. In light of the Committee's previous concluding observations, please provide information on steps taken by the State party to ensure that its obligations under articles 13 and 15 are fulfilled in all circumstances, including in the context of the military commissions (para. 30). Please inform the Committee whether the State party has established an independent mechanism to guarantee the rights of all detainees in custody.

Article 16

30. With reference to the Committee's previous concluding observations, please provide information on measures taken to prohibit and prevent enforced disappearances in any territory under its jurisdiction, and prosecute and punish perpetrators (para. 18).

31. Please address the following:

(a) Is the State party considering abolishing the death penalty?

(b) In light of the Committee's previous concluding observations, please provide information on steps taken to address the continuous concern that executions by lethal injection can cause severe pain and suffering (para. 31). In this respect, please elaborate on the events of the failed execution in the state of Ohio on 15 September 2009 and the proceedings following this, as well as on the fact that the revised execution procedure used by the state of California for carrying out executions continues to be lethal injection.

(c) Furthermore, please also provide information on the Nebraska Supreme Court's ruling that the use of the electric chair constitutes cruel and unusual punishment. Please indicate in how many states executions by electric chair are still performed.

32. With reference to the Committee's previous concluding observations (paras. 32 and 42), please provide:

(a) Information on steps taken to design and implement appropriate measures to prevent all sexual violence in all its detention centres. In this respect, please elaborate on the measures taken to implement the Prison Rape Elimination Act and on the standards developed by the National Prison Rape Elimination Commission in 2009 to detect, prevent, reduce, and punish prison rape, as well as on the implementation thereof.

(b) Please provide data on the prevalence of this problem.

(c) Please indicate steps taken to ensure that all allegations of violence in detention centres are investigated promptly and independently, as well as that perpetrators are prosecuted and appropriately sentenced.

(d) Information on steps taken to ensure that victims can seek redress, including appropriate compensation. Information should also be provided on the number of requests for redress made, the number granted and the amounts ordered and those actually provided in each case.

Please provide information on the impact and effectiveness of these measures in reducing cases of sexual violence in detention centres.

33. In light of the Committee's previous concluding observations, please elaborate on the measures adopted by the State party to ensure that women in detention are treated in conformity with international standards, as well as on the implementation of these measures (para. 33). Furthermore, please provide information on the impact and effectiveness of these measures in reducing cases of ill-treatment of detained women.

34. Please provide updated information on steps taken to address the concern about the conditions of detention of children, in particular about the fact that they may not be completely segregated from adults and the use of excessive force in juvenile prisons (para. 34). Please provide information on the impact and effectiveness of these measures in improving detention of children. Furthermore, please provide information on the status and content of the draft legislation Juvenile Justice and Delinquency Prevention Reauthorization Act of 2009, which would reform the juvenile justice system.

35. Please describe steps taken to prohibit the sentencing of juveniles to life imprisonment without the possibility of parole, as recommended by the Committee in its previous concluding observations (para. 34).

36. Please indicate if the State party has reviewed the use of electroshock devices and regulated their use, restricting it to substitution for lethal weapons, as recommended by the Committee in its previous concluding observations (para. 35). Are such devices still used to restrain persons in custody?

37. Please describe steps taken to improve the extremely harsh regime imposed on detainees in "super-maximum security prisons", in particular the practice of prolonged isolation.

38. Please provide information on steps taken to address the reports of inhumane conditions at Guantánamo Bay, in particular experienced by children, including by allowing phone calls with family members and providing detainees with educational opportunities and materials. Information should be provided on the impact and effectiveness of these measures in improving the detention conditions at Guantánamo Bay.

39. Please inform the Committee of steps taken to address the reports of inconsistent and inadequate medical care for immigrant women held by United States Immigration and Customs Enforcement detention system and for HIV-positive immigration detainees.

40. Please describe steps taken to end the practice of corporal punishment in schools, in particular of mentally and/or physically disabled students.

41. Please provide information on steps taken to:

(a) Prevent and punish violence and abuse of women, in particular women belonging to racial, ethnic and national minorities. Do these measures include providing specific training for those working within the criminal justice system and raising awareness about the mechanisms and procedures provided for in national legislation on racism and discrimination?

(b) Address the report of an increase in incidences of domestic violence, rape and sexual assault (National Crime Victimization Survey, December 2008).

(c) Ensure that reports of violence against women are independently, promptly and thoroughly investigated, and that perpetrators are prosecuted and appropriately punished.

Please include statistical data on the number of complaints concerning violence against women and the related investigations, prosecutions, convictions and sanctions, as well as on compensation provided to victims.

42. The Committee expressed its concern about reports of brutality and use of excessive force by law enforcement officials and ill-treatment of vulnerable groups, in particular racial minorities, migrants and persons of different sexual orientation (para. 37). Such concerns have also been voiced by the Committee on the Elimination of Racial Discrimination and the Human Rights Committee (CERD/C/USA/CO/6, para. 25, and CCPR/USA/CO/3/Rev.1, para. 30). Please:

(a) Describe steps taken to address this concern. Do these steps include establishing adequate systems for monitoring police abuses and developing adequate training for law enforcement officials? Furthermore, please indicate steps taken by the State party to ensure that reports of police brutality and excessive use of force are independently, promptly and thoroughly investigated and that perpetrators are prosecuted and appropriately punished. Information should also be provided on the impact and effectiveness of these measures in reducing cases of police brutality and excessive use of force.

(b) Provide information on measures taken by the State party to put an end to racial profiling used by federal and state law enforcement officials. Have the federal Government and state governments adopted comprehensive legislation prohibiting racial profiling? Statistical data should also be provided on the extent to which such practices persist, as well as on complaints, prosecutions and sentences in such matters.

Other issues

43. Please provide updated information on the State party's position on extending an invitation to the special procedure mandate holders who have requested a visit, especially to the request of the Special Rapporteur on the question of torture to visit Guantánamo Bay, as well as the Special Rapporteur on the promotion and protection of human rights and fundamental freedoms while countering terrorism, the Special Rapporteur on the question of torture, the Working Group on Arbitrary Detention and the Working Group on Enforced or Involuntary Disappearances with regard to their joint study into secret detention. Information should also be provided on the State party's position on extending an open standing invitation to special procedure mechanisms.

44. Please provide:

(a) Information on steps taken to become a party to the Optional Protocol to the Convention.

(b) Clarification of whether the State party is considering becoming a party to the Rome Statute of the International Criminal Court.

45. Please indicate what steps have been taken by the State party to accept the competence of the Committee under Article 22 of the Convention.

46. Please indicate any changes in the State party's position on withdrawing its reservations, declarations and understandings lodged at the time of ratification of the Convention.

47. Please provide information on steps taken to establish an independent national human rights institution in accordance with the Paris Principles.

48. Please clarify the State party's position with regard to the interpretation of "territory under the State party's jurisdiction". Does the State party apply the provisions of the Convention which have been named as applicable to "territory under the State party's jurisdiction" to all persons under the effective control of its authorities, of whichever type, wherever located in the world?

49. Please provide updated statistical data, disaggregated by sex, ethnicity and conduct, on:

(a) Complaints related to torture and ill-treatment allegedly committed by law enforcement officials, and investigations, prosecutions, penalties and disciplinary action relating to such complaints;

(b) The enforcement of the Civil Rights of Institutionalized Persons Act by the Department of Justice, in particular with respect to the prevention, investigation and prosecution of acts of torture, or cruel, inhuman or degrading treatment or punishment in detention facilities.

50. Please describe steps taken to establish a federal database to facilitate the collection of statistics and information, as requested by the Committee (para. 42) and the Rapporteur on follow-up in his letter of 8 August 2008.

51. Please provide updated information on investigations into alleged ill-treatment perpetrated by law enforcement personnel in the aftermath of Hurricane Katrina.

52. Please provide updated information on measures taken by the State party to respond to any threats of terrorism and please describe if, and how, these measures have affected human rights safeguards in law and practice and how it has ensure that those measures taken to combat terrorism comply with all its obligations under international law. Please describe the relevant training given to law enforcement officers, the number and types of convictions under such legislation, the legal remedies available to persons subjected to anti-terrorist measures, whether there are complaints of non-observance of international standards and the outcome of these complaints.

General information on the national human rights situation, including new measures and developments relating to the implementation of the Convention

53. Please provide detailed information on the relevant new developments on the legal and institutional framework within which human rights are promoted and protected at the national level that have occurred since the previous periodic report, including any relevant jurisprudential decisions.

54. Please provide detailed relevant information on the new political, administrative and other measures taken to promote and protect human rights at the national level, since the previous periodic report, including on any national human rights plans or programmes, and the resources allocated thereto, their means, objectives and results.

55. Please provide any other information on new measures and developments undertaken to implement the Convention and the Committee's recommendations since the consideration of the previous periodic report in 2006, including the necessary statistical data, as well as on any events that have occurred in the State party and are relevant under the Convention.

. . .

DOCUMENT 23

Full Official Title: International Convention on the Elimination of all Forms of Racial Discrimination

Short Title/Acronym/Abbreviation: The U.N. Race Convention/The Racial Discrimination Convention/ CERD

Subject: Creating international legal human rights against racial discrimination

Official Citation: 660 U.N.T.S. 195

Date of Document: Not applicable

Date of Adoption: December 21, 1965

Date of General Entry into Force (EIF): January 4, 1969

Number of States Parties to this Treaty as of this printing: 153

Date of Signature by United States: September 28, 1966

Date of Ratification/Accession/Adhesion: October 21, 1994

Date of Entry into Force as to United States (effective date): November 20, 1994

Type of Document: A treaty, an international legal instrument.

Legal Status/Character of the Instrument/Document as to the United States: The United States has ratified this Convention and so is legally bound to comply with it. The United States submitted reservations, declarations and understandings (see following document) with its ratification and so this Convention must be read and applied to the United States in light of those RDUs. Moreover, the U.S. Senate declared this treaty to be nonself-executing and so private individuals cannot assert the norms of this treaty as a legal basis for court decisions.

Supervising Body: Committee on the Elimination of Racial Discrimination

Comments: Of particular note in this Convention is the broad definition of the term "racial discrimination" as being "based on race, colour, descent, or national or ethnic origin." Also of note is Article 1, para. 4, which is a reference to race-related affirmative action type measures. This article defines certain kinds of such measures as not constituting racial discrimination at all, subject to certain limitations.

Caution: The status and applicability of this instrument as to the United States may have changed since date of publication. The above information may be updated by referring to the following site:

Web address: http://www1.umn.edu/humanrts/instree/d1cerd.htm

Convention on the Elimination of All Forms of Racial Discrimination (CERD)

The States Parties to this Convention,

Considering that the Charter of the United Nations is based on the principles of the dignity and equality inherent in all human beings, and that all Member States have pledged themselves to take joint and separate action, in co-operation with the Organization, for the achievement of one of the purposes of the United Nations which is to promote and encourage universal respect for and observance of human rights and fundamental freedoms for all, without distinction as to race, sex, language or religion,

Considering that the Universal Declaration of Human Rights proclaims that all human beings are born free and equal in dignity and rights and that everyone is entitled to all the rights and freedoms set out therein, without distinction of any kind, in particular as to race, colour or national origin,

Considering that all human beings are equal before the law and are entitled to equal protection of the law against any discrimination and against any incitement to discrimination,

Considering that the United Nations has condemned colonialism and all practices of segregation and discriminated associated therewith, in whatever form and wherever they exist, and that the Declaration on the Granting of Independence to Colonial Countries and Peoples of 14 December 1960 (General Assembly Resolution 1514 (XV)) has affirmed and solemnly proclaimed the necessity of bringing them to a speedy and unconditional end,

Considering that the United Nations Declaration on the Elimination of All Forms of Racial Discrimination of 20 November 1963 (General Assembly Resolution 1904 (XVIII)) solemnly affirms the necessity of speedily eliminating racial discrimination throughout the world in all its forms and manifestations and of securing understanding of and respect for the dignity of the human person,

Convinced that any doctrine of superiority based on racial differentiation is scientifically false, morally condemnable, socially unjust and dangerous, and that there is no justification for racial discrimination, in theory or in practice, anywhere,

Reaffirming that discrimination between human beings on the grounds of race, colour or ethnic origin is an obstacle to friendly and peaceful relations among nations and is capable of disturbing peace and security among peoples and the harmony of persons living side by side even within one and the same State,

Convinced that the existence of racial barriers is repugnant to the ideals of any human society,

Alarmed by manifestations of racial discrimination still in evidence in some areas of the world and by governmental policies based on racial superiority or hatred, such as policies of apartheid, segregation or separation,

Resolved to adopt all necessary measures for speedily eliminating racial discrimination in all its forms and manifestations, and to prevent and combat racist doctrines and practices in order to promote understanding between races and to build an international community free from all forms of racial segregation and racial discrimination,

Bearing in mind the Convention concerning Discrimination in respect of Employment and

Occupation adopted by the International Labour Organization in 1958, and the Convention against Discrimination in Education adopted by the United Nations Educational, Scientific and Cultural Organization in 1960,

Desiring to implement the principles embodied in the United Nations Declaration on the Elimination of all Forms of Racial Discrimination and to secure the earliest adoption of practical measures to that end,

Have agreed as follows:

PART I

Article 1

1. In this Convention, the term "racial discrimination" shall mean any distinction, exclusion, restriction or preference based on race, colour, descent, or national or ethnic origin which has the purpose or effect of nullifying or impairing the recognition, enjoyment or exercise, on an equal footing, of human rights and fundamental freedoms in the political, economic, social, cultural or any other field of public life.

2. This Convention shall not apply to distinctions, exclusions, restrictions or preferences made by a State Party to this Convention between citizens and non-citizens.

3. Nothing in this Convention may be interpreted as affecting in any way the legal provisions of States Parties concerning nationality, citizenship or naturalization, provided that such provisions do not discriminate against any particular nationality.

4. Special measures taken for the sole purpose of securing adequate advancement of certain racial or ethnic groups or individuals requiring such protection as may be necessary in order to ensure such groups or individuals equal enjoyment or exercise of human rights and fundamental freedoms shall not be deemed racial discrimination, provided, however, that such measures do not, as a consequence, lead to the maintenance of separate rights for different racial groups and that they shall not be continued after the objectives for which they were taken have been achieved.

Article 2

1. States Parties condemn racial discrimination and undertake to pursue by all appropriate means and without delay a policy of eliminating racial discrimination in all its forms and promoting understanding among all races, and, to this end:

(a) Each State Party undertakes to engage in no act or practice of racial discrimination against persons, groups of persons or institutions and to ensure that all public authorities and public institutions, national and local, shall act in conformity with this obligation;

(b) Each State Party undertakes not to sponsor, defend or support racial discrimination by any persons or organizations;

(c) Each State Party shall take effective measures to review governmental, national and local policies, and to amend, rescind or nullify any laws and regulations which have the effect of creating or perpetuating racial discrimination wherever it exists;

(d) Each State Party shall prohibit and bring to an end, by all appropriate means, including legislation as required by circumstances, racial discrimination by any persons, group or organization;

(e) Each State Party undertakes to encourage, where appropriate, integrationalist multiracial organizations and movements and other means of eliminating barriers between races, and to discourage anything which tends to strengthen racial division.

2. States Parties shall, when the circumstances so warrant, take, in the social, economic, cultural and other fields, special and concrete measures to ensure the adequate development and protection of certain racial groups or individuals belonging to them, for the purpose of guaranteeing them the full and equal enjoyment of human rights and fundamental freedoms. These measures shall in no case entail as a consequence the maintenance of unequal or separate rights for different racial groups after the objectives for which they were taken have been achieved.

Article 3

States Parties particularly condemn racial segregation and apartheid and undertake to prevent, prohibit and eradicate all practices of this nature in territories under their jurisdiction.

Article 4

States Parties condemn all propaganda and all organizations which are based on ideas or theories of superiority of one race or group of persons of one colour or ethnic origin, or which attempt to justify or promote racial hatred and discrimination in any form, and undertake to adopt immediate and positive measures designed to eradicate all incitement to, or acts of, such discrimination and, to this end, with due regard to the principles embodied in the Universal Declaration of Human Rights and the rights expressly set forth in Article 5 of this Convention, inter alia:

(a) shall declare an offence punishable by law all dissemination of ideas based on racial superiority or hatred, incitement to racial discrimination, as well as all acts of violence or incitement to such acts against any race or group of persons of another colour or ethnic origin, and also the provision of any assistance to racist activities, including the financing thereof;

(b) shall declare illegal and prohibit organizations, and also organized and all other propaganda activities, which promote and incite racial discrimination, and shall recognize participation in such organizations or activities as an offence punishable by law;

(c) shall not permit public authorities or public institutions, national or local, to promote or incite racial discrimination.

Article 5

In compliance with the fundamental obligations laid down in Article 2 of this Convention, States Parties undertake to prohibit and to eliminate racial discrimination in all its forms and to guarantee the right of everyone, without distinction as to race, colour, or national or ethnic origin, to equality before the law, notably in the enjoyment of the following rights:

(a) The right to equal treatment before the tribunals and all other organs administering justice;

(b) The right to security of person and protection by the State against violence or bodily harm, whether inflicted by government officials or by any individual group or institution;

(c) Political rights, in particular the right to participate in elections—to vote and to stand for election—on the basis of universal and equal suffrage, to take part in the Government as well as in the conduct of public affairs at any level and to have equal access to public service;

(d) Other civil rights, in particular:

(i) The right to freedom of movement and residence within the border of the State:

(ii) The right to leave any country, including one's own, and to return to one's country;

(iii) The right to nationality;

(iv) The right to marriage and choice of spouse;

(v) The right to own property alone as well as in association with others;

(vi) The right to inherit;

(vii) The right to freedom of thought, conscience and religion;

(viii) The right to freedom of opinion and expression;

(ix) The right to freedom of peaceful assembly and association;

(e) Economic, social and cultural rights, in particular:

(i) The rights to work, to free choice of employment, to just and favorable conditions of work, to protection against unemployment, to equal pay for equal work, to just and favorable remuneration;

(ii) The right to form and join trade unions;

(iii) The right to housing;

(iv) The right to public health, medical care, social security and social services;

(v) The right to education and training;

(vi) The right to equal participation in cultural activities;

(f) The right of access to any place or service intended for use by the general public, such as transport, hotels, restaurants, cafes, theaters and parks.

Article 6

States Parties shall assure to everyone within their jurisdiction effective protection and remedies, through the competent national tribunals and other State institutions, against any acts of racial discrimination which violate his human rights and fundamental freedoms contrary to this Convention, as well as the right to seek from such tribunals just and adequate reparation or satisfaction for any damage suffered as a result of such discrimination.

Article 7

States Parties undertake to adopt immediate and effective measures, particularly in the fields of teaching, education, culture and information, with a view to combating prejudices which lead to racial discrimination and to promoting understanding, tolerance and friendship among nations and racial or ethnical groups, as well as to propagating the purposes and principles of the Charter of the United Nations, the Universal Declaration of Human Rights, the United Nations Declaration on the Elimination of All Forms of Racial Discrimination, and this Convention.

PART II

Article 8

1. There shall be established a Committee on the Elimination of Racial Discrimination

(hereinafter referred to as the Committee) consisting of eighteen experts of high moral standing and acknowledged impartiality elected by States Parties from among their nationals, who shall serve in their personal capacity, consideration being given to equitable geographical distribution and to the representation of the different forms of civilization as well as of the principal legal systems.

2. The members of the Committee shall be elected by secret ballot from a list of persons nominated by the States Parties. Each State Party may nominate one person from among its own nationals.

3. The initial election shall be held six months after the date of the entry into force of this Convention. At least three months before the date of each election the Secretary-General of the United Nations shall address a letter to the States Parties inviting them to submit their nominations within two months. The Secretary-General shall prepare a list in alphabetical order of all persons thus nominated, indicating the States Parties which have nominated them, and shall submit it to the States Parties.

4. Elections of the members of the Committee shall be held at a meeting of States Parties convened by the Secretary-General at United Nations Headquarters. At that meeting, for which two thirds of the States

Parties shall constitute a quorum, the persons elected to the Committee shall be nominees who obtain the largest number of votes and an absolute majority of the votes of the representatives of States Parties present and voting.

5. (a) The members of the Committee shall be elected for a term of four years.

However, the terms of nine of the members elected at the first election shall expire at the end of two years; immediately after the first election the names of these nine members shall be chosen by lot by the Chairman of the Committee;

(b) For the filling of casual vacancies, the State Party whose expert has ceased to function as a member of the Committee shall appoint another expert from among its nationals, subject to the approval of the Committee.

6. States Parties shall be responsible for the expenses of the members of the Committee while they are in performance of Committee duties.

Article 9

1. States Parties undertake to submit to the Secretary-General of the United Nations, for consideration by the Committee, a report on the legislative, judicial, administrative or other measures which they have adopted and which give effect to the provisions of this Convention:

(a) within one year after the entry into force of the Convention for the State concerned; and

(b) thereafter every two years and whenever the Committee so requests. The Committee may request further information from the States Parties.

2. The Committee shall report annually, through the Secretary General, to the General Assembly of the United Nations on its activities and may make suggestions and general recommendations based on the examination of the reports and information received from the States Parties. Such suggestions and general recommendations shall be reported to the General Assembly together with comments, if any, from States Parties.

Article 10

1. The Committee shall adopt its own rules of procedure.

2. The Committee shall elect its officers for a term of two years.

3. The Secretariat of the Committee shall be provided by the Secretary General of the United Nations.

4. The meetings of the Committee shall normally be held at United Nations Headquarters.

Article 11

1. If a State Party considers that another State Party is not giving effect to the provisions of this Convention, it may bring the matter to the attention of the Committee. The Committee shall then transmit the communication to the State Party concerned. Within three months, the receiving State shall submit to the Committee written explanations or statements clarifying the matter and the remedy, if any, that may have been taken by that State.

2. If the matter is not adjusted to the satisfaction of both parties, either by bilateral negotiations or by any other procedure open to them, within six months after the receipt by the receiving State of the initial communication, either State shall have the right to refer the matter again to the Committee by notifying the Committee and also the other State.

3. The Committee shall deal with a matter referred to it in accordance with paragraph 2 of this Article after it has ascertained that all available domestic remedies have been invoked and exhausted in the case, in conformity with the generally recognized principles of international law. This shall not be the rule where the application of the remedies is unreasonably prolonged.

4. In any matter referred to it, the Committee may call upon the States Parties concerned to supply any other relevant information.

5. When any matter arising out of this Article is being considered by the Committee, the States Parties concerned shall be entitled to send a representative to take part in the proceedings of the Committee, without voting rights, while the matter is under consideration.

Article 12

1. (a) After the Committee has obtained and collated all the information it deems necessary, the Chairman shall appoint an ad hoc Conciliation Commission (hereinafter referred to as the Commission) comprising five persons who may or may not be members of the Committee. The members of the Commission shall be appointed with the unanimous consent of the parties to the dispute, and its good offices shall be made available to the States concerned with a view to an amicable solution of the matter on the basis of respect for this Convention.

(b) If the States Parties to the dispute fail to reach agreement within three months on all or part of the composition of the Commission, the members of the Commission not agreed upon by the States Parties to the dispute shall be elected by secret ballot by a two-thirds majority vote of the Committee from among its own members.

2. The members of the Commission shall serve in their personal capacity. They shall not be nationals of the States Parties to the dispute or of a State not Party to this Convention.

3. The Commission shall elect its own Chairman and adopt its own rules of procedure.

4. The meetings of the Commission shall normally be held at United Nations Headquarters or at any other convenient place as determined by the Commission.

5. The secretariat provided in accordance with Article 10, paragraph 3, of this Convention shall also service the Commission whenever a dispute among States Parties brings the Commission into being.

6. The States parties to the dispute shall share equally all the expenses of the members of the Commission in accordance with estimates to be provided by the Secretary-General of the United Nations.

7. The Secretary-General shall be empowered to pay the expenses of the members of the Commission, if necessary, before reimbursement by the States Parties to the dispute in accordance with paragraph 6 of this Article.

8. The information obtained and collated by the Committee shall be made available to the Commission, and the Commission may call upon the States concerned to supply any other relevant information.

Article 13

1. When the Commission has fully considered the matter, it shall prepare and submit to the Chairman of the Committee a report embodying its finding on all questions of fact relevant to the issue between the parties and containing such recommendations as it may think proper for the amicable solution of the dispute.

2. The Chairman of the Committee shall communicate the report of the Commission to each of the States Parties to the dispute. These States shall, within three months, inform the Chairman of the Committee whether or not they accept the recommendations contained in the report of the Commission.

3. After the period provided for in paragraph 2 of this Article, the Chairman of the Committee shall communicate the report of the Commission and the declarations of the States Parties concerned to the other States Parties to this Convention.

Article 14

1. A State Party may at any time declare that it recognizes the competence of the Committee to receive and consider communications from individuals or groups of individuals within its jurisdiction claiming to be victims of a violation by that State Party of any of the rights set forth in this Convention. No communication shall be received by the Committee if it concerns a State Party which has not made such a declaration.

2. Any State Party which makes a declaration as provided for in paragraph 1 of this Article may establish or indicate a body within its national legal order which shall be competent to receive and consider petitions from individuals and groups of individuals within its jurisdiction who claim to be victims of a violation of any of the rights set forth in this Convention and who have exhausted other available local remedies.

3. A declaration made in accordance with paragraph 1 of this Article and the name of any body established or indicated in accordance with paragraph 2 of this Article shall be deposited by the State Party concerned with the Secretary-General of the United Nations, who shall transmit copies thereof to the other States Parties. A declaration may be withdrawn at any time by notification to the Secretary-General, but such a withdrawal shall not affect communications pending before the Committee.

4. A register of petitions shall be kept by the body established or indicated in accordance with paragraph 2 of this Article, and certified copies of the register shall be filed annually through appropriate channels with the Secretary-General on the understanding that the contents shall not be publicly disclosed.

5. In the event of failure to obtain satisfaction from the body established or indicated in accordance with paragraph 2 of this Article, the petitioner shall have the right to communicate the matter to the Committee within six months.

6. (a) The Committee shall confidentially bring any communication referred to it to the attention of the State Party alleged to be violating any provision of this Convention, but the identity of the individual or groups of individuals concerned shall not be revealed without his or their express consent. The Committee shall not receive anonymous communications.

(b) Within three months, the receiving State shall submit to the Committee written explanations or statements clarifying the matter and the remedy, if any, that may have been taken by that State.

7. (a) The Committee shall consider communications in the light of all information made available to it by the State Party concerned and by the petitioner. The Committee shall not consider any communication from a petitioner unless it has ascertained that the petitioner has exhausted all available domestic remedies. However, this shall not be the rule where the application of the remedies is unreasonably prolonged;

(b) The Committee shall forward its suggestions and recommendations if any, to the State Party concerned and to the petitioner.

8. The Committee shall include in its annual report a summary of such communications and, where appropriate, a summary of the explanations and statements of the States Parties concerned and of its own suggestions and recommendations.

9. The Committee shall be competent to exercise the functions provided for in this Article only when at least ten States Parties to this Convention are bound by declarations in accordance with paragraph 1 of this Article.

Article 15

1. Pending the achievement of the objectives of the Declaration on the Granting of Independence to Colonial Countries and Peoples, contained in General Assembly Resolution 1514 (XV) of 14 December 1960, the provisions of this Convention shall in no way limit the right of petition granted to these peoples by other international instruments or by the United Nations and its specialized agencies.

2. (a) the Committee established under Article 8, paragraph 1, of this Convention shall receive copies of the petitions from, and submit expressions of opinion and recommendations on these petitions to, the bodies of the United Nations which deal with matters directly related to the principles and objectives of this Convention in their consideration of petitions from the inhabitants of Trust and Non-Self-Governing Territories and all other territories to which General Assembly Resolution 1514 (XV) applies, relating to matters covered by this Convention which are before these bodies;

(b) The Committee shall receive from the competent bodies of the United Nations copies of the reports concerning the legislative, judicial, administrative or other measures directly related to the principles and objectives of this Convention applied by the administering Powers within the Territories mentioned in sub-paragraph (a) of this paragraph, and shall express opinions and make recommendations to these bodies.

3. The Committee shall include in its report to the General Assembly a summary of the petitions and reports it has received from United Nations bodies, and the expressions of opinion and recommendations of the Committee relating to the said petitions and reports.

4. The Committee shall request from the Secretary-General of the United Nations all information relevant to the objectives of this Convention and available to him regarding the Territories mentioned in paragraph 2 (a) of this Article.

Article 16

The provisions of this Convention concerning the settlement of disputes or complaints shall be applied without prejudice to other procedures for settling disputes or complaints in the field of discrimination laid down in the constituent instruments of, or conventions adopted by, the United Nations and its specialized agencies, and shall not prevent the States Parties from having recourse to other procedures for settling a dispute in accordance with general or special international agreements in force between them.

PART III

Article 17

1. This Convention is open for signature by any State Member of the United Nations or member of any of its specialized agencies, by any State Party to the Statute of the International Court of Justice, and by any other State which has been invited by the General Assembly of the United Nations to become a Party to this Convention.

2. This Convention is subject to ratification. Instruments of ratification shall be deposited with the Secretary-General of the United Nations.

Article 18

1. This Convention shall be open to accession by any State referred to in Article 17, paragraph 1, of the Convention.

2. Accession shall be effected by the deposit of an instrument of accession with the Secretary-General of the United Nations.

Article 19

1. This Convention shall enter into force on the thirtieth day after the date of the deposit with the Secretary-General of the United Nations of the twenty-seventh instrument of ratification or instrument of accession.

2. For each State ratifying this Convention or acceding to it after the deposit of the twenty-seventh instrument of ratification or instrument of accession, the Convention shall enter into force on the thirtieth day after the date of the deposit of its own instrument of ratification or instrument of accession.

Article 20

1. The Secretary-General of the United Nations shall receive and circulate to all States which are or may become Parties to this Convention reservations made by States at the time of ratification or accession. Any State which objects to the reservation shall, within a period of ninety days from the date of the said communication, notify the Secretary-General that it does not accept it.

2. A reservation incompatible with the object and purpose of this Convention shall not be permitted, nor shall a reservation the effect of which would inhibit the operation of any of the bodies established by this Convention be allowed. A reservation shall be considered incompatible or inhibitive if at least two-thirds of the States Parties to this Convention object to it.

3. Reservations may be withdrawn at any time by notification to this effect addressed to the Secretary-General. Such notification shall take effect on the date on which it is received.

Article 21

A State Party may denounce this Convention by written notification to the Secretary-General of the United Nations. Denunciation shall take effect one year after the date of receipt of the notification by the Secretary-General.

Article 22

Any dispute between two or more States Parties with respect to the interpretation or application of this Convention, which is not settled by negotiation or by the procedures expressly provided for in this Convention, shall, at the request of any of the parties to the dispute, be referred to the International Court of Justice for decision, unless the disputants agree to another mode of settlement.

Article 23

1. A request for the revision of this Convention may be made at any time by any State Party by means of a notification in writing addressed to the Secretary-General of the United Nations.

2. The General Assembly of the United Nations shall decide upon the steps, if any, to be taken in respect of such a request.

Article 24

The Secretary-General of the United Nations shall inform all States referred to in Article 17, paragraph 1, of this Convention of the following particulars:

(a) signatures, ratifications and accessions under Articles 17 and 18;

(b) the date of entry into force of this Convention under Article 19;

(c) communications and declarations received under Articles 14, 20 and 23;

(d) denunciations under Article 21.

Article 25

1. This Convention, of which the Chinese, English, French, Russian and Spanish texts are equally authentic, shall be deposited in the archives of the United Nations.

2. The Secretary-General of the United Nations shall transmit certified copies of this Convention to all States belonging to any of the categories mentioned in Article 17, paragraph 1, of the Convention.

DOCUMENT 24

Full Official Title: U.S. reservations, declarations, and understandings, Convention on the Elimination of All Forms of Racial Discrimination

Short Title/Acronym/Abbreviation: U.S. Reservations to the Racial Convention

Subject: U.S. reservations, declarations and understandings to the Convention on the Elimination of All Forms of Racial Discrimination

Official Citation: 140 Cong. Rec. S7634–02

Date of Document: June 24, 1994

Date of Adoption: Not applicable

Date of General Entry into Force (EIF): Not applicable

Number of States Parties to this Treaty as of this printing: Not a treaty

Date of Signature by United States: Not applicable

Date of Ratification/Accession/Adhesion: Not applicable

Date of Entry into Force as to United States (effective date): November 20, 1994

Type of Document: This is not a treaty, but is a legal instrument under U.S. and international law which expresses the terms under which the United States ratifies and thus accepts legal obligations under the Racial Discrimination Convention (previous document).

Legal Status/Character of the Instrument/Document as to the United States: These RDUs are legally binding as to U.S. ratification so far as they are consistent with the object and purpose of the Racial Discrimination Convention.

Comments: The U.S. obligations under the Racial Discrimination Convention must be read in light of these RDUs.

Caution: The status and applicability of this instrument as to the United States may have changed since date of publication. The above information may be updated by referring to the following site:

Web address: http://www1.umn.edu/humanrts/usdocs/racialres.html

U.S. RESERVATIONS, DECLARATIONS, AND UNDERSTANDINGS, TO THE RACIAL DISCRIMINATION CONVENTION

I. The Senate's advice and consent is subject to the following reservations:

(1) That the Constitution and laws of the United States contain extensive protections of individual freedom of speech, expression and association. Accordingly, the United States does not accept any obligation under this Convention, in particular under Articles 4 and 7, to restrict those rights, through the adoption of legislation or any other measures, to the extent that they are protected by the Constitution and laws of the United States.

(2) That the Constitution and the laws of the United States establish extensive protections against discrimination, reaching significant areas of non-governmental activity. Individual privacy and freedom from governmental interference in private conduct, however, are also recognized as among the fundamental values which shape our free and democratic society. The United States understands that the identification of the rights protected under the Convention by reference in Article 1 to the fields of public life reflects a similar distinction between spheres of public conduct that are customarily the subject of governmental regulation, and spheres of private conduct that are not. To the extent, however, that the Convention calls for a broader regulation of private conduct, the United States does not accept any obligation under this Convention to enact legislation or take other measures under paragraph (1) of Article 2, subparagraphs (1)(c) and (d) of Article 2, Article 3 and Article 5 with respect to private conduct except as mandated by the Constitution and laws of the United States.

(3) That with reference to Article 22 of the Convention, before any dispute to which the United States is a party may be submitted to the jurisdiction of the International Court of Justice under this article, the specific consent of the United States is required in each case.

II. The Senate's advice and consent is subject to the following understanding, which shall apply to the obligations of the United States under this Convention: That the United States understands that this Convention shall be implemented by the Federal Government to the extent that it exercises jurisdiction over the matters covered therein, and otherwise by the state and local governments. To the extent that state and local governments exercise jurisdiction over such matters, the Federal Government shall, as necessary, take appropriate measures to ensure the fulfillment of this Convention.

III. The Senate's advice and consent is subject to the following declaration: That the United States declares that the provisions of the Convention are not self-executing.

DOCUMENT 25

Full Official Title: Fourth, Fifth and Sixth-Periodic Reports of the United States of America to the Committee on the Elimination of Racial Discrimination

Short Title/Acronym/Abbreviation: U.S. Fourth, Fifth, and Sixth Periodic Reports to CERD

Type of Document: This is a state report submitted by the U.S. to a U.N. treaty body in compliance with Article 9 of the ICERD, to which it is a party.

Subject: Elimination of racial discrimination

Official Citation: CERD/C/USA/6

Date of Document: May 1, 2007 (April 23, 2007)

Date of Adoption: Not applicable

Date of General Entry into Force (EIF): Not applicable

Number of States Parties as of this printing: Not applicable

Date of Signature by the United States: Not applicable

Date of Ratification/Accession/Adhesion: Not applicable

Date of Entry into Force as to United States (effective date): Not applicable

Legal Status/Character of the Instrument/Document as to the United States: This is not a legal instrument but a document that is required to be filed by all state parties to fulfill their legal obligations under Article 9 of the ICERD.

Comments: By ratifying the ICERD the U.S. agreed, under Article 9, to report to the Committee on the Elimination of Racial Discrimination on measures they have adopted to give effect to the rights recognized in the Covenant or any progress they have made in the enjoyment of those rights. Each state is required to submit an initial report to the Committee within one year of the treaty entering into force, and every two years thereafter or whenever the Committee requests information. The Committee then reviews and issues its observations and comments on the report and makes recommendations. The state may then respond to those recommendations in a subsequent report.

This is the United States' fourth, fifth, and sixth reports and addresses several of the Committee's specific concerns with the implementation of the Covenant. The report is an important tool to reiterate the U.S. position on its treaty obligations and any differences of opinion it may have with the Committee over how they interpret specific obligations.

The report is very large and could not be reprinted in its entirety. Only selected excerpts corresponding to certain articles of the ICERD are included. The reader should consult the following website to obtain the full text, and for subsequent reports:

Web Address: http://www2.ohchr.org/english/bodies/cerd/cerds72.htm or http://www.state.gov/g/drl/rls/cerd_report/83404.htm

U.S. FOURTH, FIFTH AND SIXTH PERIODIC REPORTS TO THE COMMITTEE ON THE ELIMINATION OF RACIAL DISCRIMINATION

Introduction

1. The Government of the United States of America welcomes the opportunity to report to the Committee on the Elimination of Racial Discrimination on measures giving effect to its undertakings under the International Convention on the Elimination of All Forms of Racial Discrimination (CERD), pursuant to Article 9 thereof. This document constitutes the fourth, fifth, and sixth periodic reports of the United States. Its organization follows the General Guidelines regarding the form and contents of periodic reports to be submitted by States parties, adopted by the Committee in August 2000 (CERD/C/70/Rev.5) and the guidelines for Initial Parts of State Party Reports ("Core Documents") (HRI/GEN/2/Rev 3) of 8 May 2006.

2. This report was prepared by the U.S. Department of State with extensive assistance from the White House, the Civil Rights Division of the U.S. Department of Justice, the Equal Employment Opportunity Commission, and other relevant departments and agencies of the federal government and of the states. Contributions were also solicited and received from interested members of the numerous non-governmental organizations and other public interest groups active in the area of civil rights, civil liberties, and human rights in the United States.

3. The United States submitted its initial, second, and third periodic reports as a single document to the Committee on the Elimination of Racial Discrimination in September 2000, hereinafter "Initial U.S. Report" or "Initial Report." A copy can be viewed at http://www.state.gov/. The United States made its oral presentation to the Committee on August 3 and 6, 2001. Accordingly, the purpose of this fourth, fifth, and sixth periodic report is to provide an update of relevant information since the submission of the Initial Report.

4. The legal and policy framework through which the United States gives effect to its Convention undertakings has not changed dramatically since the Initial Report. As described in that Report, the United States Constitution; the constitutions of the various states and territories; and federal, state, and territorial law and practice provide strong and effective protections against discrimination on the basis of race, color, ethnicity, and national origin in all fields of public endeavor and with regard to substantial private conduct as well. These protections, as administered through executive action and the judicial system, continue to apply.

PART I. GENERAL

A. Background

5. The information provided in this report supplements that provided in the Initial U.S. Report filed in 2000 (CERD/C/351/Add.1). It also supplements the information provided by the U.S. delegation at the meetings of the Committee, which discussed the Initial U.S. Report on August 3 and 6, 2001 (CERD/C/SR/1474, 1475, 1476). The information provided herein takes into account the concluding observations of the Committee (CERD/A/56/18, paragraphs 380–407), published on August 14, 2001, as well as relevant general Committee recommendations and other Committee actions.

6. In this consolidated report, the United States has sought to respond to the Committee's concerns as fully as possible. In this regard, the United States notes the discussion of U.S. reservations, understandings, and declarations to the Convention contained in paragraphs 145 through 173 of the Initial U.S. Report. The United States maintains its position with regard to these reservations, understandings, and declarations, and with respect to other issues as discussed in this report.

B. Land and People

7. Neither the land area nor the basic federal-state organization of the United States has changed since submission of the Initial U.S. Report in 2000. Nor has there been change in the relationship between the United States and the outlying areas under U.S. jurisdiction—Puerto Rico, the Virgin Islands, American Samoa, Guam, the Northern Mariana Islands, and several very small islands.

1. Update of General Census Data

8. The population of the United States, which was 281.4 million at the time of the 2000 census, was estimated to be 296.4 million in July 1, 2005—an increase of approximately 5.3 percent. By the year 2010, the population is projected to be 308.9 million—an increase of approximately 9.8 percent from 2000; and by 2050, the population is projected to have increased by 49.2 percent from the 2000 figure, to 419.9 million.

9. The U.S. is a multi-racial, multi-ethnic, and multi-cultural society in which racial and ethnic diversity is ever increasing. Virtually every national, racial, ethnic, cultural, and religious group in the world is represented in the U.S. population. As described in the Initial U.S. Report, the racial and ethnic categories used since 1997 in the U.S. census are: White; Black or African American; American Indian and Alaska Native (AIAN); Asian; and Native Hawaiian and Other Pacific Islander (NHPI). Members of these racial categories are also classified separately as belonging to one of two ethnic categories: Hispanic or Latino origin, or non-Hispanic or Latino origin.[1]

10. In the 2000 census, 97.6 percent of all respondents reported only one race. The group reporting White alone accounted for 75 percent of the population, down from about 80 percent in 1990. The Black or African American alone population represented just over 12 percent of the total, approximately the same as in 1990. Just under 1 percent of all respondents indicated American Indian and Alaska Native only, also approximately the same as in 1990. About 4 percent indicated Asian alone, up from about 3 percent in 1990. The smallest racial group was the Native Hawaiian and Other Pacific Islander alone population, representing 0.1 percent of the total. The remainder of the "one race" respondents—5.5 percent of all respondents—indicated only the "some other race alone" category, which consisted predominately of persons of Hispanic origin. This percentage was up from approximately 4 percent in 1990. Two and fourth tenths of a percent of all respondents reported two or more races, and 0.02 percent reported four or more races.

11. Looking at ethnicity, although the U.S. population remains primarily White non-Hispanic, the proportion of the population falling into that category is decreasing. Census projections from March, 2004 show that the White non-Hispanic portion of the population declined from 75.7 percent in 1990 to 69.4 percent in 2000, and is projected to decline further to 65.1 percent by 2010 and to 50.1 percent by

---

[1] For reasons of simplicity, this report generally uses the single terms "African American" and "Hispanic" to refer to the respective categories of persons, rather than the terms "Black or African American" and "Hispanic or Latino" employed by the Census Bureau. On occasion, however, the terms "Black" or "Latino" are used, depending on the context and the source. Also, on occasion the report uses the single term "American Indian" rather than the full Census term "American Indian and Alaska Native."

2050. Although the number of White non-Hispanic persons in the United States is projected to grow by 2.8 percent from 2000 to 2010, the growth rate for this group is projected to be much lower than the growth rates for other racial and ethnic categories. For example, during the 2000 to 2010 period, the Hispanic (of any race) population is projected to grow by 34.1 percent, the African American population to grow by 12.9 percent, the Asian population to grow by 33.3 percent, and the other races category (American Indian and Alaska Native alone, Native Hawaiian and Other Pacific Islander alone, and two or more races) to grow by 30.7 percent. In addition, in 2000 1.2 million people reported Arab ancestry, up from 610,000 in 1980. This represents a 41 percent rate of growth during the 1980s and a 38 percent growth in the 1990s. The table below contains census data on the projected population of the United States by race and Hispanic origin from 2000 to 2050.

12. The distribution of the U.S. population by urban vs. rural residence and region of the country varied considerably by race and ethnicity in 2000. African Americans, Hispanics, and Asian Americans were more likely to live in urban areas (defined as areas with populations of 50,000 or more) than were non-Hispanic Whites. For example, in 2000, although African Americans alone represented only 12.3 percent of the population overall, they constituted 14.6 percent of the persons living in urban areas. Likewise, although Hispanics made up only 12.5 percent of the population overall, they represented 15.5 percent of urban inhabitants. Asian Americans alone represented 5 percent of urban inhabitants, compared to only 3.6 percent of the population overall. By contrast, non-Hispanic Whites composed 62.7 percent of urban dwellers compared to 69.1 percent of the population overall.

13. Of the total population in 2000, 19 percent lived in the Northeast; 23 percent in the Midwest; 36 percent in the South; and 22 percent in the West. However, over half of the African American population (54 percent) lived in the South, including 54.8 percent of those indicating African American alone, and 53.6 percent of the African American alone or in combination population. Other minority groups were concentrated in the West, including 43 percent of American Indians and Alaska Natives alone or in combination; 49 percent of Asians alone or in combination; 73 percent of Native Hawaiian and Other Pacific Islanders alone or in combination; and 43.5 percent of Hispanics.

14. According to the U.S. Census American Community Survey (ACS), in 2004 the foreign-born population was estimated to be 34.3 million (12 percent of the total U.S. household population). This represented an increase of 73 percent from 1990. The foreign-born population was located throughout the United States.

15. Within the foreign-born population, 42 percent were naturalized U.S. citizens. Of the foreign-born population, about one-in-five had entered the United States since 2000. The foreign-born population comes to the United States from throughout the world: 54.8 percent were born in the Americas (9.2 percent in the Caribbean, 36.3 percent in Central America, 6.7 percent in South America, and 2.4 percent in North America); 27 percent in Asia; 14.3 percent in Europe; 3.3 percent in Africa; and 0.6 percent in Oceania.

16. Although direct estimates of the unauthorized population are not available, recent efforts have yielded estimates of a residual population that includes unauthorized as well as "quasi-legal" migrants—persons who are legally present in the United States, but who have not obtained legal permanent resident (LPR) status. This residual foreign-born population was estimated to be about 3.8 million in 1990 and about 8.7 million in 2000. Of the residual foreign born population, about 27 percent were from Mexico in 1990 and about 47 percent were from Mexico in 2000.

17. Although English is the predominant language of the United States, in 2004 approximately 50 million (19 percent) of the 266 million people aged 5 and above spoke a language other than English at home. Thirty-one million people spoke Spanish, and 7.6 million spoke an Asian or Pacific Island language. French and German were the next most common languages spoken. In 2004, twenty-two million people (8.4 percent of the total population) indicated that they did not speak English "very well." The highest percentages of non-English speakers were found in the states of California, New Mexico, and Texas.

2. Socio-Economic Data on American Indian and Alaska Native Populations and Native Hawaiian and Other Pacific Islander Populations

18. In its comments and recommendations of August 14, 2001, the Committee requested additional socio-economic data on, in particular: (a) the indigenous and Arab American population; and (b) the populations of the States of Alaska and Hawaii. That information is included in this and the following subsections.

19. There are 561 federally-recognized American Indian Tribes and Alaska Native tribal governments in the United States. Each tribe generally has its own language, culture, and tribal political and governmental system. Numerous groups are also petitioning through an established federal process to have their tribal status determined. In 2000, 74 percent of all AIAN respondents reported a specific tribal affiliation. The tribal groupings that included 100,000 or more persons were Cherokee, Navajo, Latin American Indian, Choctaw, Sioux, and Chippewa.[2]

20. Of the total United States population, 2.5 million people (0.9 percent) reported AIAN alone, and an additional 1.6 million reported AIAN and at least one other race. The AIAN population grew at a greater rate than the general population from 1990 to 2000, increasing between 26 percent and 110 percent, depending on whether AIAN alone or AIAN in combination with other races was measured. Forty-three percent of this population lived in the west, and 31 percent lived in the south. The AIAN population has a slightly higher ratio of males to females than does the population as a whole: the AIAN alone population had 99.4 males for every 100 females, and the AIAN alone or in combination population had 97.5 males for every 100 females; by contrast, the total population had 96.1 males for every 100 females. The AIAN population also tends to be somewhat younger than the U.S. population: 33.3 percent were under 19, as compared to 25.6 percent for the nation as a whole.

Table 1a. Projected Population of the United States, by Race and Hispanic Origin: 2000 to 2050
(In thousands except as indicated. As of July 1. Resident population.)
(Leading dots indicate sub-parts.)

Population or percent and race or Hispanic origin	2000	2010	2020	2030	2040	2050
POPULATION						
TOTAL	282,125	308,936	335,805	363,584	391,946	419,854
White alone	228,548	244,995	260,629	275,731	289,690	302,626
Black alone	35,818	40,454	45,365	50,442	55,876	61,361
Asian Alone	10,684	14,241	17,988	22,580	27,992	33,430
All other races 1/	7,075	9,246	11,822	14,831	18,388	22,437
Hispanic (of any race)	35,622	47,756	59,756	73,055	87,585	102,560
White alone, not Hispanic	195,729	201,112	205,936	209,176	210,331	210,283
PERCENT OF TOTAL POPULATION						
TOTAL	100.0	100.0	100.0	100.0	100.0	100.0
White alone	81.0	79.3	77.6	75.8	73.9	72.1
Black alone	12.7	13.1	13.5	13.9	14.3	14.6
Asian Alone	3.8	4.6	5.4	6.2	7.1	8.0
All other races 1/	2.5	3.0	3.5	4.1	4.7	5.3
Hispanic (of any race)	12.6	15.5	17.8	20.1	22.3	24.4
White alone, not Hispanic	69.4	65.1	61.3	57.5	53.7	50.1

1/ Includes American Indian and Alaska Native alone, Native Hawaiian and Other Pacific Islander alone, and Two or More Races

Source: U.S. Census Bureau, 2004, "U.S. Interim Projections by Age, Sex, Race, and Hispanic Origin," http://www.census.gov/ipc/www/usinterimproj/.

---

[2] Note that the term "tribe" or "tribal" as used in this report means an Indian or Alaska Native tribe, band, nation, pueblo, village, or community that the Secretary of the Interior acknowledges to exist as an Indian tribe pursuant to the Federally Recognized Indian Tribe List Act of 1994, 25 U.S.C. 479a.

21. In 2000, 874,000 persons (0.3 percent of the population) identified as Native Hawaiian and Other Pacific Islander. Of these, approximately 46 percent said they were NHPI alone, and 54 percent identified as NHPI in combination with other races. The most common combination was NHPI and Asian. The NHPI category includes diverse populations differing in language and culture, with Polynesian, Micronesian, and Melanesian cultural backgrounds. The NHPI category is unique in that it is the only racial category for which the number of respondents reporting two or more races was higher than the number reporting only one race. The NHPI population increased at a rate between 9 and 140 percent from 1990 to 2000, depending on whether NHPI alone or in combination with other races was measured. About three-quarters of this group lived in the west, and over half lived in Hawaii and California (although the 50 percent figure was a reduction from 1990). Native Hawaiian was the largest group, followed by Samoans, and Guamanians or Chamorros. Together these groups constituted 74 percent of the persons reporting NHPI alone, and 71 percent of the NHPI in combination group.

22. The AIAN population tends to have lower school attendance and rates of educational attainment than the U.S. population as a whole, although these rates are improving. The same is also true for the NHPI population, although the NHPI percentages are closer to the national average. For the U.S. population in general, the high school dropout rate (the percentage of 16–19 year olds not enrolled in high school and not high school graduates) was 9.8 percent in 2000, down from 11.2 percent in 1990. By contrast, 16.1 percent of AIAN alone students had dropped out of high school, down from 18.1 percent in 1990. The dropout rate for NHPI alone students was 11 percent for both 2000 and 1990. Likewise, college attendance for both groups was below the national average. Overall, 34 percent of young adults (18 to 24 years old) in the U.S. attended college in 2000, compared to 21 percent for the corresponding AIAN alone population and 30 percent for the corresponding NHPI alone population. These patterns were reflected in overall educational attainment for persons more than 25 years old:

Overall Educational Attainment	AIAN alone	NHPI alone	Overall
High School Graduate or more	70.9%	78.3%	80.4%
Some college or more	41.7%	44.6%	51.8%
BA or more	11.5%	13.8%	24.4%
Advanced degree	3.9%	4.1%	8.9%

(Source: Census 2000: Educational Attainment of the Population 25 Years and Over by Age, Sex, Race, and Hispanic or Latino Origin.)

23. Lower educational attainment, in turn, is reflected in the statistics concerning employment, occupation, and income. The 2004 American Community Survey showed that unemployment was higher for the AIAN alone (14 percent) and NHPI alone (9.9 percent) populations than for the population as a whole (7.2 percent). Those who were working tended to work less in management and more in jobs such as construction and transportation. For example, while 33.6 percent of the overall population worked in management and professional positions, 24.3 percent of the AIAN alone and 23.3 percent of the NHPI alone populations worked in those professions. American Indians and Alaska Natives alone tended to work more heavily in production, transportation and material moving (16.8 percent compared to 14.6 percent overall), construction (12.9 percent compared to 9.4 percent overall), and farming, fishing and forestry (1.3 percent compared to 0.7 percent overall). Likewise, Native Hawaiians and Other Pacific Islanders alone tended to work more heavily in the service professions (20.8 percent compared to 14.9 percent overall) and in transportation and material moving (16.5 percent compared to 14.6 percent overall).

24. In 1999, household income for these two groups was also less than the national average. Compared to a mean household income of $56,644 for the population overall, the mean for the AIAN alone population was $40,135, and that for the NHPI alone group was $53,096. The 2004 American Community Survey showed poverty rates of 24.7 percent for the AIAN population and 18.1 percent for the NHPI group, compared to 13.3 percent overall. For families, the figures were 10.1 percent for all families, contrasted with 20.5 percent for AIAN families and 15.1 percent for NHPI families. Monthly housing costs were among the lowest for AIAN alone inhabitants—$879 compared to the national median of $1,088 for units with a mortgage, and $216 compared to $295 for units without a mortgage. On the other hand, monthly housing costs for NHPI alone members were higher than the national median for units with a mortgage ($1,261) and close to

the median for non-mortgage units. This may be because NHPI persons are concentrated in California and Hawaii, two states with very high homeowner costs and housing values.

3. Socio-Economic Data on the Arab-American Population

25. Census 2000 was the first U.S. census to analyze data and produce reports specifically on U.S. persons of Arab ancestry. In 1997, when the U.S. Census Bureau revised the federal standards for classification of race and ethnicity, it noted a lack of consensus on the definition of an Arab ethnic category, and recommended further research. The reports from the 2000 census are contributing to this ongoing research, and are being analyzed in consultation and collaboration with experts in the Arab community. Persons considered as being of Arab ancestry for purposes of the census reports were those who indicated ancestries originating from Arabic-speaking countries or areas of the world—persons who reported being Arab, Egyptian, Iraqi, Jordanian, Lebanese, Middle Eastern, Moroccan, North African, Palestinian, Syrian, etc. As many as two ancestries were tabulated per respondent and, if either fell into the definition of Arab, the person was considered to be "of Arab ancestry" for purposes of analysis.

26. In 2000, 1.2 million people reported Arab ancestry—up from 860,000 in 1990 and 610,000 in 1980. This represents a 41 percent increase in the 1980s and 38 percent increase in the 1990s. Approximately 850,000 of these 1.2 million persons reported only Arab ancestry (either one Arab ancestry or two ancestries both of which were Arab). In addition, more than a quarter of the Arab population (28 percent) also reported a second, non-Arab ancestry; among those, 14.7 percent reported Irish, 13.6 percent Italian, and 13.5 percent German. Lebanese, Syrian, and Egyptian ancestry accounted for about three-fifths of the Arab ancestries reported: 37 percent indicated Lebanese ancestry, 12 percent Syrian, and 12 percent Egyptian. The next highest was Palestinian, at 6 percent. A substantial portion of the Arab population (20 percent) identified themselves as having general Arab ancestries, such as Arab, Arabic, Middle Eastern, or North African. Those who described their ancestry in general terms as "Arab," "Arabic," or some other generalized term were most likely to be under 18, while those who made specific designations, such as "Syrian" or "Lebanese," were more likely to be older.

27. The population indicating solely Arab ancestry also tended to be more heavily male than the U.S. population overall—57 percent compared to 49 percent population wide. The median age of the male Arab population was 33 years—two years below the median age for the total U.S. population of males, which was 35 years. The female Arab population tended to be most highly concentrated in the 0–9 and 20–35 age ranges.

28. The Arab population was fairly evenly distributed among the four regions of the United States, with about half of that population concentrated in five states: California, Florida, Michigan, New Jersey, and New York. Michigan had the highest proportion of Arabs in its population, and six of the ten largest cities in the United States were among the ten places with the largest Arab populations (New York, Los Angeles, Chicago, Houston, Detroit, and San Diego).

29. The socio-economic data below describe persons of sole Arab ancestry, i.e., those indicating only one Arab ancestry or two ancestries both of which were Arab. Almost half of the residents of sole Arab ancestry (46 percent) were born in the United States or born abroad to U.S. citizen parents, compared to 89 percent for the U.S. as a whole. Of the 54 percent who were foreign born, approximately half had arrived during the 1990s, and over half had become naturalized citizens by 2000—a higher proportion than for the U.S. foreign-born population as a whole.

30. Persons of sole Arab ancestry tended to be more highly educated than the U.S. population as a whole. More than 40 percent of Arab Americans 25 years of age or older had college degrees or higher, as compared to 24 percent for the population as a whole. Likewise, the proportion of Arabs 25 years or older with high school diplomas or higher (84 percent) exceeds that for the population as a whole (80 percent). The population of sole Arab ancestry also tended to live in married households at a greater rate than the population as a whole—60 percent compared to 53 percent. Female family householders with no husband present were less common among Arab households than among U.S. households as a whole—6 percent as compared to 12 percent. Similar relationships are seen when comparing the Arab population as a whole (including those with two ancestries one of which was not Arab) to the total U.S. population. Although 69 percent of Arabs of sole Arab ancestry spoke a language other than English at home, 65 percent of those indicated that they spoke English "very well"—representing 44 percent of overall Arabs aged five and older.

31. Persons of sole Arab ancestry tended to work in management, professional, and related occupations at a higher rate than the population as a whole; approximately 42 percent of Arabs aged 16 and above worked

in those occupations, compared with 34 percent for the U.S. overall. Likewise, a higher proportion of persons of sole Arab ancestry tended to work in sales and office occupations than the population as a whole (30 percent compared to 27 percent), while the proportion of the sole Arab population working in construction, extraction, and maintenance jobs was lower (5.4 percent compared to 9.4 percent), as was the proportion working in production, transportation, and material moving (10.7 percent compared to 14.6 percent). Men of Arab descent were more likely, and women less likely, to be in the labor force than their counterparts in the total population.

32. Median earnings for the sole Arab population were also higher than those for the U.S. population overall (for men, $41,700 compared to a national median of $37,100, and for women $31,800 compared to a national median of $27,200). This was also true for Arab families, which had higher median incomes than U.S. families in general ($52,300 compared to $50,000). Nevertheless, a higher percentage of persons of sole Arab ancestry fell into the poverty range (17 percent compared to 12 percent). Poverty rates were highest among those younger than 18 years.

4. Socio-Economic Data on the Populations of the States of Alaska and Hawaii

33. Alaska is the largest state in the United States in land area, but has one of the smallest populations—only 626,932 persons in 2000. In 2000, its population was more heavily male and slightly younger than the national average. For persons listing one race, Alaska's population was much more heavily American Indian and Alaska Native than the national average—15.6 percent as opposed to 0.09 percent. By contrast, its African American alone population was smaller (3.5 percent as opposed to 12.3 percent), and its White population was also smaller (69.3 percent as opposed to 75.1 percent) than the national average. Its Asian population was slightly above the national average (4 percent as opposed to 3.6 percent). The percentage of the Alaska population listing Hispanic ethnicity was considerably below the national average (4.1 percent as opposed to 12.5 percent). Persons listing two or more races were also elevated in Alaska—5.4 percent as opposed to 2.4 percent nationally. Alaska had a considerably lower percentage of foreign born residents than the nation as a whole (5.9 percent as opposed to 11.1 percent nationally).

34. Alaska's population was somewhat more educated than the national average. Of the population 25 years and over, 88.3 percent of Alaskans were high school graduates or higher, contrasted with 80.4 percent nationally; and 24.7 percent of Alaskans had a college degree or higher, compared to 24.4 percent nationally. In Alaska, 14.3 percent of the population spoke a language other than English at home, as compared to 17.9 percent of the population in general.

35. A higher proportion of Alaska's 16 years and older population was in the workforce than was true nationally (71.3 percent as opposed to 63.9 percent). Likewise, fewer Alaskan families and individuals fell below the poverty level than was true nationally (6.7 percent compared to 9.2 percent for families, and 9.4 percent compared to 12.4 percent for individuals).

36. By contrast, the population of Hawaii in 2000 was 1,211,537, about twice that of Alaska. Also in contrast to Alaska, Hawaii's population was slightly older than the national average; for example, 13.3 percent of Hawaiians were 65 years and older, compared to 12.4 percent nationally. Hawaii was closer to the national average in its male-female ratio—50.2 percent were male (compared to 49.1 percent nationally), and 49.8 percent were female (compared to 50.9 percent nationally). An unusually large proportion of Hawaiians described themselves as being of two or more races (21.4 percent compared to 2.4 percent nationally). Of those indicating only one race, Native Hawaiian and Other Pacific Islanders constituted 9.4 percent of the population, as opposed to 0.1 percent nationally. Asians also constituted an extremely high percentage of the population—41.6 percent as opposed to 3.6 percent nationally. Conversely, the proportion of Whites was considerably lower—24.3 percent, as compared to 75.1 percent nationally. In addition, African Americans and persons of Hispanic origin were less prevalent in Hawaii than in the nation as a whole. African Americans alone constituted only 1.8 percent of the population, compared to 12.3 percent nationally, while persons of Hispanic ethnicity made up only 7.2 percent of the Hawaiian population, compared to 12.5 percent nationally.

37. Like Alaska, the people of Hawaii tended to have higher levels of education than the national average. Eighty four point six percent of Hawaiians age 25 and older were high school graduates or higher, compared to 80.4 percent of the U.S. population overall. Twenty-six point two percent of Hawaiians had college degrees or higher, compared to 24.4 percent nationally. A considerably greater proportion of Hawaiians said that they spoke a language other than English at home—26.6 percent compared to 17.9 percent nationally.

38. The proportion of Hawaiians in the labor force was slightly higher than the national average (64.5 percent compared to 63.9 percent), and Hawaiian individuals and families tended to fall below the poverty level at a lower rate than the total U.S. population (7.6 percent compared to 9.2 percent for families, and 10.7 percent compared to 12.4 percent for individuals).

C. General Political Structure

39. Since the Initial U.S. Report in 2000, there have been no changes in the political structure of the United States, or its basic relationships with United States territories, or with the AIAN or NHPI populations. The Office of Hawaiian Relations within the Department of the Interior was established in the fall of 2005 to "preserve and promote Hawaii's natural and historic resources and the Native Hawaiian culture."

40. The issue of the federal government relationship with Native Hawaiians continues to be under discussion. The Initial U.S. Report noted that, in response to a U.S. Supreme Court case, *Rice v. Cayetano*, 528 U.S. 495 (2000), which cast doubt on the authority of Congress to legislate in a manner that grants Native Hawaiian preferences, the Departments of Interior and Justice were in the process of preparing a report on a reconciliation process between the federal government and Native Hawaiians. The final report, which encompassed the results of meetings and consultations with the Native Hawaiian community, was issued in October 2000. Based on meetings and consultations with the Native Hawaiian community, the report called for the federal government to honor the unique relationships with Native Hawaiians and to respond to their needs for more local control within the framework of Federal law. A version of the Native Hawaiian Government Reorganization Act has been introduced in every Congress since the 106th (in 2000). When the Native Hawaiian Government Reorganization Act of 2005 was introduced in both chambers of the U.S. Congress, it would have formed a governing entity of and for Native Hawaiians, and extended to it federal recognition similar to the recognition extended to American Indian tribes. Specifically, it would have authorized the U.S. Government to enter into negotiations with this governing entity to address specified matters. The bill was thoroughly debated in a number of public forums, including the U.S. Civil Rights Commission, but failed to reach the floor for a vote in the United States Senate in 2005 or 2006. The Administration opposed the bill on the ground that it would "divide people by their race" and would raise serious and difficult constitutional questions regarding the permissibility of "race-based qualifications for participation in government entities and programs." The Administration also questioned the authority of Congress to grant tribal status to Native Hawaiians. The U.S. Civil Rights Commission advised that this bill risked "further subdivid[ing] the American people into discrete subgroups accorded varying degrees of privilege."

D. General Legal Framework

41. The basic Constitutional and legal framework through which U.S. obligations under the Convention are implemented remains the same. The Constitution provides for equal protection of the laws and establishes a carefully balanced governmental structure to administer those protections. Among other factors:

• Under the Fifth and Fourteenth Amendments, all persons are equal before the law and are equally entitled to constitutional protection. All states are equal, and none may receive special treatment from the federal government. Within the limits of the Constitution, each state must give "full faith and credit" to the public acts, records, and judicial proceedings of every other state. State governments, like the federal government, must be republican in form, with final authority resting with the people;

• The Constitution stands above all other laws, executive acts, and regulations, including treaties;

• Powers not granted to the federal government are reserved to the states or the people.

42. In addition to the civil rights protections of the federal Constitution, laws, and courts—state constitutions, laws, and courts play an important role in civil rights protections. In this regard, state constitutions and laws must, at a minimum, meet the basic guarantees of the U.S. Constitution. Moreover, in keeping with the federal system of government, in many cases state laws actually afford their citizens greater protections than the federal Constitution requires. *See, e.g., Locke v. Davey*, 540 U.S. 712, 724 n. 8 (2004) (noting that, "at least in some respects," Washington State's constitution provides greater protections than the Federal Free Exercise Clause).

43. Day-to-day administration and enforcement of federal laws rests in the hands of various executive departments and independent agencies. Since 2000, there have been only a few changes in the division of responsibilities described in that Report. Except for the changes noted in this report, the governmental structure in place to deal with discrimination remains basically as it was described in 2000.

44. <u>Department of Homeland Security</u>. As a result of the events of 11 September 2001 (hereinafter 9/11), Congress created a new Department of Homeland Security (DHS) in 2003. This Department combines a number of other departments, agencies, and portions of departments, such as the Coast Guard, the Transportation Security Administration, the Federal Emergency Management Agency, and the former

Immigration and Naturalization Service. Within DHS, Congress established an Office for Civil Rights and Civil Liberties, led by the DHS Officer for Civil Rights and Civil Liberties who reports directly to the Secretary of Homeland Security. The Office is charged with investigating allegations of abuses of civil rights, civil liberties, and discrimination on the basis of race, ethnicity, and religion by employees or officials of the Department of Homeland Security. In addition, it assists the senior leadership in developing policies and initiatives that are mindful of fundamental rights and liberties and provides leadership to DHS's Equal Employment Opportunity Program. The Office leads the Department's civic engagement efforts and conducts outreach to non-governmental organizations and others, including the Arab American and Muslim American communities.

45. As part of the creation of the Department of Homeland Security, the Immigration and Naturalization Service (INS) ceased to exist as an independent agency within the Department of Justice. The functions of the former INS were transferred to three bureaus of the new DHS: U.S. Citizenship and Immigration Services (CIS), U.S. Immigration and Customs Enforcement (ICE), and U.S. Customs and Border Protection (CBP). The Executive Office for Immigration Review and Board of Immigration Appeals, however, remained within the Department of Justice. See Homeland Security Act of 2002, 116 Stat. 2135, 2178, 2192, Nov. 25, 2002.

46. Department of Defense. Within the Department of Defense, the former Deputy Assistant Secretary for Equal Opportunity has now been changed to a Deputy Under Secretary for Equal Opportunity. This position remains responsible for implementing and monitoring the Department's civilian and military equal opportunity/affirmative action plan goals and objectives. The Department of Defense has numerous policies and programs designed to ensure equal opportunity in the military. The nature and scope of these programs are generally as described in the Initial U.S. report.

47. Other Agencies. Since 2000, several other agencies have also created new bureaus, offices, or training entities to work on issues related to racial and ethnic discrimination or to work specifically with various racial or ethnic groups. For example, the Department of the Interior (DOI) established the Office of Hawaiian Relations in 2005. In 2006, DOI set up a new bureau and office specifically to assist American Indians and Alaska Natives. DOI established: (1) the Bureau of Indian Education to improve academic achievement of Indian students served in the 184 schools on 63 Indian reservations in 23 states; and (2) the Office of Indian Energy and Economic Development, to bring new jobs, businesses, and funds to American Indian and Native Alaska communities. The Department of Housing and Urban Development (HUD) also formed several offices to address problems of discrimination in housing: (1) the Office of Systemic Investigations (OSI) to investigate cases with significant impact on population groups or geographic locations; (2) the Office of Education and Outreach (OEO) to increase public awareness of federal fair housing laws and HUD's role in enforcing them; and (3) the National Fair Housing Training Academy to train housing discrimination investigators at local, state, and federal levels. The Agriculture Department also established the Office of Minority and Socially Disadvantaged Farmers. Finally, the United States Information Agency—which handles outreach to other nations—has been moved into the Department of State.

E. Information and Publicity

48. Information about human rights is readily available in the United States. As a general matter, persons are well informed about their civil and political rights, including the rights of equal protection, due process, and non-discrimination. The scope and meaning of—and issues concerning enforcement of—individual rights are openly and vigorously discussed in the media, freely debated within the various political parties and representative institutions, and litigated before the courts at all levels.

49. The expansion of internet services and the ever-increasing availability of internet access in the years since 2000 have made information concerning human rights and racial and ethnic discrimination even more readily accessible to the U.S. public. Virtually every federal and state agency has a website on which information about the agency structure and programs—including those of agency offices of civil rights—can be found. Many of these websites include relevant information in languages other than English, which increases dissemination both to persons with limited English proficiency within the U.S. as well as to persons outside the U.S. who may be interested in the civil rights protections that the U.S. affords its citizens and residents.

50. Information concerning the work of the U.N. Committee on Elimination of Racial Discrimination is likewise readily available on the internet in the United States, as are all U.S. reports to the Committee. As part of our public outreach, this periodic report will be published and made available to the public through the U.S. Government Printing Office and the depositary library system. Copies of the report and the Convention will also be widely distributed within the executive branch of the U.S. Government, to federal judicial

authorities, to relevant members of Congress and their staffs, and to relevant state officials, state and local bar associations, and non-government human rights organizations. The report and the Convention will also be available on the Department of State website at http://www.state.gov.

51. Specific examples of publicity and outreach programs undertaken since the Initial U.S. Report are described below in the discussion of Article 5.

F. Factors Affecting Implementation

52. As noted in the Initial U.S. Report, the United States has made significant progress in the improvement of race relations over the past half-century. Due in part to the extensive constitutional and legislative framework that provides for effective civil rights protections, overt discrimination is far less pervasive than it was in the early years of the second half of the Twentieth Century. As the United States continues to become an increasingly multi-ethnic, multi-racial, and multi-cultural society, many racial and ethnic minorities have made strides in civic participation, employment, education, and other areas.

53. Nonetheless, significant challenges still exist. Subtle, and in some cases overt, forms of discrimination against minority individuals and groups continue to plague American society, reflecting attitudes that persist from a legacy of segregation, ignorant stereotyping, and disparities in opportunity and achievement. Such problems are compounded by factors such as inadequate understanding by the public of the problem of racial discrimination, lack of awareness of the government-funded programs and activities designed to address it, lack of resources for enforcement, and other factors.

54. In addition, two subjects of concern have been particularly acute in the years since 2000. The first involves the increase in bias crimes and related discriminatory actions against persons perceived to be Muslim, or of Arab, Middle Eastern, or South Asian descent, after the terrorist attacks of 9/11. The second involves the impacts of the changing demographic caused by high rates of immigration into the United States—both legal and illegal. The continuing legacies described above, in addition to these more recent issues, create on-going challenges for the institutions in the United States that are charged with the elimination of discrimination. Thus, despite significant progress, numerous challenges still exist, and the United States recognizes that a great deal of work remains to be done.

PART II. INFORMATION RELATING TO ARTICLES 2 TO 7 OF THE CONVENTION

55. The United States is a vibrant, multi-racial, multi-ethnic, and multi-cultural democracy in which individuals have the right to be protected against discrimination based, *inter alia*, on race, color, and national origin in virtually every aspect of social and economic life. The U.S. Constitution and federal law prohibit discrimination in a broad array of areas, including education, employment, public accommodation, transportation, voting, housing and mortgage credit access, as well as in the military, and in programs receiving federal financial assistance. In addition, nondiscrimination obligations are imposed on federal contractors and subcontractors by Executive Order. The federal government has established a wide-ranging set of enforcement procedures to administer these laws and Executive Orders, with the U.S. Department of Justice exercising a major coordination and leadership role on most critical enforcement issues. State and local governments also have complementary legislation and enforcement mechanisms to further these goals. At both the federal and state levels, enforcement agencies have worked, and continue to work, to improve enforcement of civil rights laws and to promote education, training, and technical assistance.

56. As noted in the Initial U.S. Report, although the definition used in Article 1 (1) of the Convention contains two specific terms ("descent" and "ethnic origin") not typically used in U.S. federal civil rights legislation and practice, no indication exists in the negotiating history of the Convention that those terms encompass characteristics not already subsumed in the terms "race," "color," and "national origin" as those terms are used in existing U.S. law. *See, e.g., Saint Frances College v. Al-Khazraji*, 481 U.S. 604 (1987); *Shaare Tefila Congregation v. Cobb*, 481 U.S. 615 (1987); *Roach v. Dresser Industrial Valve*, 494 F. Supp. 215 (W.D. La. 1980). The United States thus interprets its undertakings and intends to carry out its obligations under the Convention on that basis.

57. The United States collects its census data in a manner that allows analysis and assessment by racial, ethnic, gender, and other characteristics. In addition, in the 2000 census, information was also collected on Americans of Arab ancestry. Census information relevant to this periodic report was presented in Part I and will be referenced, as appropriate, in this section.

Article 2

A. Information on the legislative, judicial, administrative, or other measures that give effect to the provisions of Article 2, paragraph 1, of the Convention.

1. Measures taken to give effect to the undertaking to engage in no act or practice of racial discrimination against persons, groups of persons or institutions and to ensure that all public authorities and public institutions, national and local, shall act in conformity with this obligation

58. As required by Article 2 (1) (a), racial discrimination by the government is prohibited throughout the United States. The Fifth, Thirteenth, Fourteenth, and Fifteenth Amendments to the U.S. Constitution guarantee that no public authority may engage in any act or practice of racial discrimination against persons, groups of persons, or institutions. These prohibitions apply with equal force at the federal, state, and local levels, and all public authorities and institutions must comply. U.S. law extends this prohibition to private organizations, institutions, and employers under many circumstances. Examples of enforcement actions against both public and private institutions are set forth in subsection 2 below and throughout this report.

2. Measures taken to give effect to the undertaking not to sponsor, defend or support racial discrimination by any persons or organizations

59. As required by Article 2 (1) (b), the U.S. Government does not sponsor, defend, or support discrimination. The U.S. Constitution prohibits discrimination on the basis of race at every level of government—federal, state, and local. A number of federal statutes, including the Civil Rights Act of 1964, prohibit discrimination by state or local governments; private entities in the areas of employment, housing, transportation, and public accommodation; and private entities that receive federal financial assistance. The federal government is actively engaged in the enforcement of anti-discrimination statutes against public and private entities in the areas of employment, housing and housing finance, access to public accommodations, and education. In addition, most states and some localities also have laws prohibiting similar types of activity, and in many cases state and federal authorities have entered into work sharing arrangements to ensure effective handling of cases where state and federal jurisdiction overlap. Examples of federal employment, housing, and education cases, as well as state enforcement in these areas, are set forth in this section. Numerous other examples in areas such as public accommodations, police conduct, prisoner rights, voting rights, hate crimes, and others are described in other sections of the report.

Examples of Enforcement Actions: Employment

60. The Equal Employment Opportunity Commission (EEOC) is charged with enforcing federal civil rights laws with regard to discrimination in public and private sector workplaces. The Department of Justice also brings employment cases, and the Department of Labor's Office of Federal Contract Compliance Programs ensures that federal contractors and subcontractors do not discriminate in employment. Since 2000, the EEOC has received and handled approximately 80,000 charges a year, with well over that number in 2003. This is approximately the same annual rate as in the 1990s, with the exception of 1995, when the number was unusually elevated. In 2006, however, the agency received only 75,768 charges. These charges included 113,765 instances of discrimination in private and public sector workplaces. In 2006, 62 percent of all charges alleged race or gender discrimination, or retaliation in violation of Title VII of the Civil Rights Act of 1964. The Commission filed 371 lawsuits, recovered $44.3 million through litigation, plus $229.9 million in settlement, conciliation, and other closures, bringing the total to $274.2 million. The amounts obtained through settlement in fiscal year 2006 included $61.4 million in settlement, conciliation, and other closures of 5,232 race discrimination charges; $21.2 million in settlement, conciliation, and other closures of 1,666 national origin discrimination charges; and $5.7 million in settlement, conciliation, and other closures of 499 religion discrimination charges. Settlements and court decisions also included non-monetary elements to assist in ensuring that offending behavior does not recur.

61. Examples of cases brought since 2000 by the EEOC, the Department of Justice Civil Rights Division, and the Department of Labor Office of Federal Contract Compliance Programs follow. Others are described in other sections of the report. Enforcement cases that go to court often take a number of years from beginning to end. Thus, cases brought since 2000 that have not been settled may still have been proceeding through the courts at the time this report was written.

• In June 2006, the Commission settled a case involving allegations that a homebuilder had disciplined an African American supervisor and discharged him from his position because of his race. Of the employer's 70 employees, this supervisor was the only African American. During his employment, the supervisor complained about racial hostility on the part of some of the subcontractors (e.g., using racial epithets, refusing to communicate directly with him, completing tasks for him more slowly than for White construction superintendents), but the defendant downplayed the concerns and told him to deal with the problems himself. The supervisor was eventually disciplined and discharged for incidents for which similarly-situated Whites were not disciplined. The parties resolved the case through a two-year consent decree under which the employee will receive $46,000 in compensatory damages. The decree enjoins defendant from racial discrimination, racial harassment, and other discrimination prohibited under Title VII. The decree also prohibits defendant from engaging in reprisal or retaliation. *EEOC v. Bob Ward New Homes*, No. JFM-05CV2728 (D. Md. June 27, 2006).

• In June 2005, the Commission, Ford Motor Co., and the United Auto Workers (UAW) union resolved, through a consent order, thirteen charges concerning a written test for skilled trades apprentice positions that had a disparate impact on African American applicants. The order provides that Ford and the UAW will use a validated apprenticeship selection test. The settlement also provides that the company will select 280 class members for apprentice positions, consisting of current and former employees of African descent who took the prior test over an eight-year period but were not placed on an apprenticeship eligibility list. The thirteen charging parties each received $30,000, and the approximately 3,400 additional class members received $2,400 each, for a total recovery of approximately $8.55 million. *EEOC v. Ford Motor Co. and United Automobile Workers of America*, No. 1:04-CV-00854 (S.D. Ohio 2005).

• In another 2005 case, the Commission found evidence that an employment agency coded and referred applicants based on their race and sex, and that some of the agency's client-employers made requests for individuals of a particular race or gender. Under a consent decree, the employment agency paid $285,000 into a Claim Fund to be distributed among qualified claimants identified by the Commission, and three agency clients paid $50,000 in administrative costs. The agreement also included specific requirements to prevent the recurrence of race- and sex-based exclusion of applicants and to open up employment opportunities for African American and female applicants, including appointment of an outside contractor to provide annual training regarding lawful interviewing, screening, and hiring procedures. *EEOC v. EGW Temps., Inc*, No. 00 CIV 833S (W.D.N.Y. 2005).

• An employer with an all-White workforce relied heavily on word-of-mouth recruiting to fill vacancies. The Commission alleged that the company denied employment to African American applicants because of their race. The case arose out of a Commissioner's Charge and included discriminatory practices going as far back as 1991. Despite receiving applications from many African American workers, the company relied on referrals from its current employees, many of whom were Eastern European immigrants who were not likely to refer African Americans. The case was resolved by a consent decree providing $2.5 million in damages for approximately 325 claimants. The company was enjoined from using race or sex in hiring and job assignments, and is required to fill production positions during the three-year term of the decree by alternating hires between interested claimants and other applicants. *EEOC v. Carl Buddig & Co.* (N.D. Ill. 2004).

62. In addition to filing individual claims, the Justice Department Civil Rights Division is also charged with authority to investigate and challenge patterns or practices of employment discrimination. Such suits are complex, time consuming, and resource-intensive. As a result, the Division has historically managed only one case per year. In 2004, however, the Department prevailed in one major pattern or practice trial and filed four additional lawsuits. It filed two in 2005, and had filed three in 2006 as of October.

• One such case involved a suit against the State of Delaware, the State Department of Public Safety, and the Division of State Police for violation of Title VII of the Civil Rights Act in hiring police. The case alleged that use of a multiple-choice reading comprehension and writing test called "Alert" to screen applicants for employment in the Police Department had created a disparate, negative impact on African American applicants. The Court found no intention to discriminate in using the test; nor did it consider the test itself to be offensive. Nonetheless, it found that the cut-off score set by the state was too high and had discriminated against African American applicants. Thus, the Court held the State of Delaware's administration of the test to be unlawful under Title VII. *U.S. v. State of Delaware*, 2004 WL 609331 (D. Del. 2004).

• A second case alleged that the New York Transit Authority had engaged in a "pattern or practice" of discrimination against Muslim, Sikh, and similarly situated employees who wear religious head coverings by not reasonably accommodating their religious observances, practices, and beliefs through selective enforcement of its uniform policies. *United States v. New York Transit Authority*, No. ____ (E.D.N.Y.). This case is still being litigated before the United States District Court for the Eastern District of New York.

• The Department of Justice sued the University of Guam, alleging that it had discriminated against eleven individuals formerly employed in administrative and faculty positions on the basis of their national origin or race and/or in retaliation for complaints made by them. By virtue of a settlement agreement, the individuals—Filipino American, African American, American Indian, and Caucasian—received monetary payments totaling $775,000. The agreement also required the University to issue a new written policy prohibiting employment discrimination and to provide anti-discrimination training to all management level and supervisory employees. *United States v. University of Guam*, No. _____ (D. Guam, 2004).

• The Department of Justice sued the City of Virginia Beach for its use of a written test that disproportionately excluded African Americans and Hispanics in violation of Title VII. *United States v. City of Virginia Beach*, Virginia, No. _____ (E.D.Va.). The case, which was resolved through the entry of a consent decree, focused on the city's use of a mathematics examination as a selection device for choosing new police officer hires. The Justice Department alleged that in addition to disproportionately excluding African Americans and Hispanics, the test was not valid in that it did not test for skills needed to be an entry-level Virginia Beach Police Officer. Title VII prohibits tests that have a disparate impact on the basis of race or national origin and that cannot be shown to be related to the job in question.

• In March 2004, the Community Relations Service of the U.S. Department of Justice became involved in a 1980s education desegregation case in Roanoke, Alabama that involved, among other factors, the hiring of minority teachers and administrators. CRS was asked to mediate an agreement between the Roanoke school system and the African American community to reduce racial conflicts and tension plaguing the school district. The tensions derived from multiple issues, including allegations that the school system: (1) lacked minority teachers and administrators; (2) had a racially disparate disciplinary policy for minority students; and (3) failed to provide appropriate curriculum containing such subjects as African American history. CRS held mediation sessions with school district officials and African American community leaders for several months to discuss the issues in the case and prepare for formal mediation. As a result of CRS's services: (1) a workable relationship and open lines of communication were established; (2) the parties collaborated and implemented the goals of the agreements; and (3) a capacity-building mechanism was put in place for resolving future tensions. More specifically, the school district has worked with minority community leaders to recruit and retain minority teachers and administrators. The school district also agreed to review disciplinary policies in the school system and reviewed the school curriculum to ensure that appropriate subjects such as African American history are taught in the classrooms. CRS has continued to assist the parties.

63. The Department of Labor's Office of Federal Contract Compliance Programs (OFCCP) ensures that employers doing business with the federal government comply with the laws and regulations requiring non-discrimination in employment. The program enforces its mandate by detecting and remedying systemic discrimination and by providing compliance assistance to employers. In fiscal year 2005 (October 1, 2004 to September 30, 2005), OFCCP recovered a record $45,156,462 for 14,761 American workers who had been subjected to unlawful discrimination. Of that recovery, 97 percent was collected in cases of systemic discrimination, defined as those involving a significant number of workers or applicants subjected to discrimination because of an unlawful employment practice or policy. The fiscal year 2005 results represent a 42 percent increase over the recoveries in fiscal year 2000 and a 56 percent increase over fiscal year 2001. Examples of these cases follow:

• In 2003, DOL filed an Administrative Complaint alleging that INA Bearing, a ball bearing manufacturer, engaged in hiring discrimination based on race, and assignment discrimination based on gender, with respect to machine operators. OFCCP found that 613 minority individuals had not been hired due to discriminatory practices. In addition 62 female employees were hired but were improperly channeled into low-paying jobs. In 2005 the company agreed to a $1.1 million settlement. The settlement included $900,000 in back pay, interest, and benefits (including $30,000 in lieu of retroactive seniority); it also included $200,000 in training for new hires and promoted females that was required to be spent over a two year period. INA also agreed to hire 30 minority applicants from the affected class over a 24-month period and to offer promotions to 27 females from the affected class over a 12-month period.

• In fiscal year 2005, an OFCCP compliance review of American Trans Air, Inc. found that the company discriminated against African Americans and Hispanics in hiring. OFCCP's compliance evaluation was closed after the company agreed to a conciliation agreement that provided for significant back pay as well as job offers to 84 victims of discrimination. The total value of the conciliation agreement, including annualized salaries of those offered employment, was $2,867,840.

• Also in fiscal year 2005, OFCCP signed a conciliation agreement with Benchcraft-Blue Mountain Upholstery after a compliance evaluation found that the company's selection practices were racially discriminatory. The company agreed to provide back pay, to offer positions to 178 of the affected class members, and to train managers and others involved with the hiring process. The total value of the conciliation agreement, including annualized salaries for those offered employment, was $6,283,345.

Examples of Enforcement Actions: Fair Housing and Lending

64. Ensuring equal opportunity in housing is one of the strategic goals of the U.S. Department of Housing and Urban Development (HUD). HUD's Office of Fair Housing and Equal Opportunity (FHEO) carries out this strategic goal by administering laws that prohibit discrimination on the bases of race, color, religion, sex, national origin, disability, and familial status. In addition, FHEO educates lenders, housing providers, developers, architects, home-seekers, landlords, and tenants about their rights and obligations under the law. Working with national, state, and local partners—as well as the private and nonprofit sectors—FHEO is involved in a cooperative effort to increase access to the nation's housing stock so that more Americans can obtain housing of their choice. The laws implemented by FHEO include the Fair Housing Act, which is Title VIII of the Civil Rights Act of 1968, as amended in 1988; and other civil rights laws, including Title VI of the Civil Rights Act of 1964, Section 109 of the Housing and Community Development Act of 1974, and Section 3 of the Housing and Urban Development Act of 1968.

65. Since the initial U.S. report, HUD's Office of Policy Development and Research has published several volumes estimating the national level of racial and ethnic housing discrimination against African Americans, Hispanics, and Asian Americans and Pacific Islanders. In addition, statewide estimates were drawn up for Native Americans and Alaska Natives in three states. The methodology involved matched pairs of testers who sought housing in the sales or rental market; one tester was a non-Hispanic White, and the second was of a minority race or ethnicity. The reports showed that discrimination in the sales market had declined significantly in the decade prior to the report's issuance. However, the decline was more modest in the rental market for African Americans, and there was no change at all for Hispanics. The findings also generally indicated that the treatment shown to the non-Hispanic White tester remained more favorable than that shown to the minority tester, further indicting that the problem of housing discrimination persists in many parts of the nation.

66. The HUD Fair Housing Office includes an enforcement arm that receives complaints and investigates cases. In many regions of the U.S., HUD, through FHEO, also funds state or local government fair housing enforcement agencies to receive complaints and to investigate them, as long as the state or local government can show that it enforces a fair housing law that provides rights, remedies, procedures, and opportunities for judicial review that are substantially equivalent to those provided in the Fair Housing Act. By the end of fiscal year 2005, there were 103 such agencies in 37 states and the District of Columbia. In fiscal year 2005, HUD and the 103 state, county, and city Fair Housing Assistance Program agencies that partner with HUD received 9,254 complaints or cases. Of those complaints, 3,472 were based on race and 860 were based on national origin discrimination against Hispanics. Examples of cases investigated and managed by HUD's Fair Housing Office are set forth below:

• An African American couple, Mr. and Mrs. Benton, made a full-price offer on a home in Scott, Arkansas. The seller's agent, however, advised the buyer's agent that the offer was not acceptable, and inquired if the buyers were African American. Instead, the seller, Mr. Arnett, accepted a lower offer, contingent on financing, from the neighbors, who were White. The neighbors did not apply for financing and, several months later, the house was sold to White buyers for nearly $10,000 less than the original offer. On October 26, 2004, HUD issued a charge of discrimination against the sellers, who agreed to settle the case. Under the terms of the settlement, Mr. Arnett will pay the Bentons $15,000 and will attend fair housing training. *Benton, et al. v. Arnett et al.*

• Ms. Puerto and her husband, a Hispanic couple, sought to purchase a home in Pflugerville, Texas. A couple of days before closing, the owner of Capital Funding Group—the couple's brokers and loan processors—informed them that the interest rate was being raised from 9 to 10 percent and that the down payment was being raised from $5,000 to $12,000. Ms. Puerto terminated the transaction and demanded a refund of her $1,030 deposit. Instead, the broker demanded an additional $300. During the investigation, a former employee of Capital Funding Group admitted that the owners of Capital Funding Group had targeted Hispanics and mistreated them because they felt Hispanics would often sign documents that they did not (or were unable to) read. On July 12, 2005, HUD charged Capital Funding Group with discrimination on the basis of national origin in violation of the Fair Housing Act in this case and three others. On August 8, 2005, an election was made to have the case tried in federal court, where it remains in litigation. *Puerto v. Capital Funding Group, et. al.*

• Ms. Jones, a young White female with a bi-racial daughter rented a house in Saraland, Alabama, but was made to feel so uncomfortable by her landlord (once the landlord had seen the daughter) that she and her daughter moved out. She contacted the Mobile Fair Housing Center, which sent two tester families to the housing development—one a family with an African American husband, White wife and bi-racial child, and the other a White family. After the first family was told no houses were available, and the second family was offered three possible homes, HUD then charged the landlord with discrimination on the basis of race in violation of the Fair Housing Act. On April 21, 2005, the parties elected to have the case heard in federal court where it remains in litigation, *Jones v. Stevens.*

67. The Civil Rights Division of the Justice Department is also charged with ensuring non-discriminatory access to housing, public accommodations, and credit. During fiscal year 2006 (October 2005 through September 2006), the Housing Section filed 31 lawsuits, including 19 pattern or practice cases. One of the programs used aggressively by the Civil Rights Division is its Fair Housing Testing Program, in which persons with different characteristics pose as potential tenants seeking to rent apartments in the same facility at approximately the same time. On February 15, 2006, the Attorney General announced a major new civil rights initiative: Operation Home Sweet Home. He made a public commitment that over the next two years the Division would conduct a record-high number of fair housing tests in order to expose housing providers who are discriminating against people trying to rent or buy homes. During fiscal year 2006, the Civil Rights Division increased the number of fair housing tests conducted by 38 percent compared to fiscal year 2005. Examples of recent cases are described here, including a case involving evidence developed by the Fair Housing Testing Program.

• On January 18, 2005, the Division filed the lawsuit *United States v. Dawson Development Co., L.L.C.,* No. 4:05-cv-0095-CLS (N.D. Ala.), alleging that the defendants—the owner and manager of Park Place Apartments in Boaz, Alabama—discriminated against African Americans in the rental of apartments at Park Place. In testing conducted by the Fair Housing Testing Program, the manager told the African American testers that there were no apartments available, but told the White testers who visited the apartments the same day that apartments were available. The manager also failed to call the African American testers when apartments became available, but left messages with the White testers encouraging them to rent apartments at Park Place. The Division entered into a Consent Order with the owner of the complex, enjoining it from further race discrimination, requiring it to adopt uniform non-discriminatory rental and application procedures, and requiring it to pay $32,700-$49,700 for victims of the defendants' discrimination in addition to a $17,000 civil penalty. The Division then won its trial against the property manager, after which the court imposed a $10,000 civil penalty against that defendant.

• On August 29, 2006, the Court approved and entered a Consent Decree in *United States v. Kreisler, Jr., a/k/a/ Bob Peterson,* No. 03-cv-3599 (D. Minn.). The Division's pattern or practice complaint, filed in 2003, alleged that Kreisler violated the Fair Housing Act when he discriminated against African American tenants at two apartment complexes he owned and managed by: evicting African Americans while not evicting similarly situated non-African Americans, requiring African American tenants to vacate their apartments permanently due to "renovation work" while not requiring non-African American tenants to do so, and failing to provide necessary and requested maintenance to African American tenants while providing such maintenance to non-African American tenants. Under the terms of the Consent Decree, the defendants must pay $525,000 to 19 households, hire an independent management company to operate the rental properties, post and publish a nondiscrimination policy, and correct the rental records of several former tenants against whom defendants filed unlawful detainer actions. The defendants will also pay a $50,000 civil penalty.

• On August 7, 2006, the Division filed a complaint in *United States v. Sterling,* No. CV 06-4885-PJW (C.D. Cal.), a pattern or practice case alleging discrimination on the basis of race, national origin, and familial status. The complaint alleges that the defendants refused to rent to non-Korean prospective tenants, misrepresented the availability of apartment units to non-Korean prospective tenants, and provided inferior treatment to non-Korean tenants in the Koreatown section of Los Angeles.

68. Lawsuits brought by the Civil Rights Division have not only defended the rights of Americans to obtain housing, but also to obtain the financing necessary to purchase homes. While a lender may legitimately take into account a broad range of factors in considering whether to make a loan, race has no place in determining creditworthiness. "Redlining" is the term employed to describe a lender's refusal to lend in certain areas based on the race of the area's residents. In 2006, the Division filed and resolved a major redlining case under the Fair Housing Act and the Equal Credit Opportunity Act (ECOA).

• On October 13, 2006, the Justice Department filed a complaint alleging that Centier Bank discriminated on the basis of race and national origin by refusing to provide its lending services to residents of minority neighborhoods in the Gary, Indiana, metropolitan area, in violation of the Fair Housing Act and the Equal Credit Opportunity Act. The Division successfully resolved the suit with a consent decree, under which Centier will open new offices and expand existing operations in the previously excluded areas, invest $3.5 million in a special financing program, and spend at least $875,000 for consumer financial education, outreach to potential customers, and promotion of its products and services in these previously excluded areas. *United States v. Centier Bank*, No. 2:06-CV-344 (N.D. Ind.).

Examples of Enforcement Action: Education

69. The mainstay of the Justice Department Civil Rights Division's work in the area of education is a substantial docket of open desegregation cases under which school districts remain under court orders. Some of the cases are decades old. Although most of these cases have been inactive for years, each represents an as-of-yet unfilled mandate to root out the vestiges of segregation and return control of constitutionally compliant public school systems to local officials.

70. To promote compliance by school districts, the Division initiates case reviews to monitor issues such as student assignment, faculty assignment and hiring, transportation policies, extracurricular activities, the availability of equitable facilities, and the distribution of resources. In 2004, the Civil Rights Division initiated 44 case reviews—the largest number in any given year. In addition, during that year the Division obtained additional relief through a combination of litigation, consent decrees, and out of court settlements in 23 cases. In 2006, the Division initiated 38 case reviews. Since 2000 the Division has initiated more than 228 reviews, which have resulted in the return of local control in more than 126 school districts.

• *United States v. Chicago Board of Education* is a longstanding case, initiated in 1980, involving the failure of the third largest school district in the United States to comply with an earlier court order covering student and faculty assignments and the funding of certain educational programs. In 2004, the court entered a consent decree requiring that many minority students be given the choice to transfer to racially integrated schools. The consent decree also addressed the district's failure to fund adequately certain minority schools and to provide appropriate services to English Language Learners. In 2006, a Second Amended Consent Decree was entered to ensure further opportunities for English Language Learners.

• In a case brought in the 1960s, the Bertie County Board of Education in North Carolina was ordered to develop a school desegregation plan to eliminate a racially-segregated dual system of schools in the county. In 2002, the Department of Justice sought further relief, alleging that Askewville Elementary School in Bertie County was operating as a racially-identifiable White school, based on its school population, faculty, and staff composition. In 2004, the Court granted the Justice Department's motion for further relief. In 2005, the Justice Department reached an agreement with the school district that resulted in the closing of Askewville Elementary, as well as J.P. Law Elementary, a predominantly Black school with dilapidated facilities. *U.S. v. Bertie County Board of Education*.

• In a case in McComb County, Mississippi, the Civil Rights Division has challenged in federal court the school district's classroom assignment practices that segregate students by assigning or clustering a disproportionate number of White students to classrooms in this predominantly minority district as well as its practice of granting certain student awards on the basis of race. The case was heard in 2006 and the Division is awaiting a decision from the court. *U.S. v. McComb County Board of Education*.

• In another case, the Covington County Board of Education in Alabama, with support from the United States Government, filed a motion to terminate an ongoing case from 1963. Holding that Covington County was now in compliance with anti-discrimination laws, the court dismissed the case. *Lee v. Covington County Board of Education*, 2006 WL 269942 (M.D. Ala. 2006). This case was part of a project started by the court in the Middle District of Alabama to move the cases toward closure and a return to local control.

Enforcement of Anti-Discrimination Laws in the Territories

71. Claims of racial and ethnic discrimination are also actively pursued in U.S. territories. Since 2000, the Virgin Islands has experienced a larger volume of cases than the U.S. territories in the Pacific. Two cases in the courts in the Virgin Islands are: (1) *Petersen v. Budget Marine V I, Inc.*, 2004 WL 3237537 (D. V.I. 2004) in which the plaintiff contends he was let go from his employment and replaced by a White male from the continental United States; and (2) *Frorup-Alie v. V. I. Housing Finance Authority*, 2004 WL 1092317 (D. V.I. 2004), involving a claim of discrimination based on race (African American) and national origin (native Virgin Islander). The plaintiff claims that the Housing Finance Authority created a hostile working

environment in which other employees yelled at her and talked about her in Spanish in her presence. A case involving employment discrimination by the University of Guam is described above. Additionally, the Civil Rights Division of the Department of Justice has prosecuted human trafficking cases and brought suits to protect prisoners' rights in the territories.

Enforcement of Anti-Discrimination Laws by the States

72. Most states have state civil rights or human rights commissions or offices that administer and enforce state laws prohibiting discrimination in areas such as employment, education, housing, and access to public accommodations. These offices generally investigate complaints and ensure, where appropriate, that charges are filed and cases are heard. They generally also have advisory and educational functions, informing residents of the state about enforcement of their civil rights. The few states that do not have designated civil rights or human rights offices or commissions administer their civil rights laws through their Attorney General's Offices. Some counties and cities also have commissions to administer their civil rights laws. For example, a complainant in Chicago may have four choices in bringing an employment claim—the federal Equal Employment Opportunity Commission, the Illinois Department of Human Rights, the Cook County Human Rights Commission, or the Chicago City Human Rights Commission. California also has a full system of civil rights agencies. In addition to three state entities—the California Department of Fair Employment and Housing, the California Department of Justice Civil Rights Enforcement Section, and the California Fair Employment and Housing Commission (a quasi-judicial administrative agency that hears cases and is also involved in regulatory, legislative, and outreach activities), complainants can also contact 13 county civil rights commissions and more than 50 city civil rights bodies. For a full discussion of the human rights/civil rights programs in four states (Illinois, New Mexico, Oregon, and South Carolina) with populations of varying racial and ethnic composition, see Annex I to this report.

73. Most state entities have work sharing agreements with the EEOC and the Department of Housing and Urban Development (HUD) to ensure that complainants' rights are protected under both state and federal law, regardless of where they choose to bring their complaints. Under these agreements, the state civil rights entity and the federal entity (EEOC or HUD) each designate the other as its agent for purpose of receiving and drafting charges. Thus, the state may act as the agent of the EEOC or HUD, receiving, filing, and investigating charges that may fall within federal statutes. Charges can also be transferred from one agency to the other in accordance with the terms of the agreement. For employment cases, state agencies generally adhere to the procedures in the EEOC's state and local handbook. In the employment area, many state laws apply to a wider range of businesses than are covered by the federal law, which applies only to employers with 15 or more employees.

74. Although the processes for handling discrimination complaints differ from state to state, a typical state civil rights process involves several steps. The first is intake of inquiries and complaints. Second is investigation of complaints. Prior to or during this phase, many states offer mediation of disputes at no cost or minimal cost to complainants in order to attempt to resolve issues prior to a formal hearing process. If mediation is not successful, some states also offer conciliation. Third, if the complaint is not settled by mediation or conciliation, and if investigation indicates a possible violation of the law, the case may go to a formal hearing before a hearing officer, an administrative law judge, or a commissioner. The hearing officer, administrative law judge, or commissioner in turn renders a determination or decision—a decision that in some cases must be approved by the entire commission. Decisions may normally be appealed to an appellate authority—usually a state appellate court. In many cases, they may also be enforced in state court through writ of mandamus (ordering the defendant to take action) or injunction (prohibiting the defendant from taking certain actions).

75. Most states also provide for removal of cases directly to state court or to federal courts or agencies during the investigation process. As noted above, under work sharing agreements, cases that fall within federal jurisdiction are sometimes transferred to the EEOC or HUD for further action. In addition, most states offer complainants the option of taking cases to state or federal court if the cases meet jurisdictional guidelines—in some cases by filing directly with the court, and in other cases by requesting a right to sue letter from the state civil rights entity that is processing the claim.

76. A large number of complaints are received and investigated by state authorities. For example:

• During 2005, the Illinois Department of Human Rights and Illinois Human Rights Commission received 15,748 inquiries, which led to the filing of 4,055 charges. During that time, the staff also settled 1,238 cases, and 503 complaints were withdrawn. During that year, of the cases docketed, 90 percent were employment cases, 7 percent were housing cases, and 3 percent were public accommodation cases. Race, national origin/ancestry, and color were the bases of discrimination in 32 percent of the employment cases, 47 percent of the housing cases, and 62 percent of the public accommodation cases.

• During 2005, the Civil Rights Division of the Arizona State Attorney General's Office investigated 10,512 new and pending charges and resolved 1,052 cases. Almost 11 percent were resolved through voluntary settlement agreements between parties, generating more than $200,000 for victims of discrimination. The litigation section resolved 16 lawsuits, the conflict resolution program staff and mediators mediated 234 cases (reaching agreement in 73 percent of them), and the compliance section resolved more than 400 employment discrimination cases. In 2004, the staff also made outreach presentations to more than 3,300 farm workers and trained more than 3,500 persons in law enforcement groups, universities, community groups, businesses, and other organizations. An example of a case from Arizona is *Heredia et al. v. Hacienda San Luis*—a group of six cases that involved allegations of housing discrimination and redlining. The defendant was alleged to have taken advantage of the vulnerable status of non-English speaking farm workers. These cases were settled in favor of the complainants.

• In fiscal year 2003–04, the Tennessee Human Rights Commission pursued 840 employment cases, of which 234 (28 percent) were based on race, and 140 housing discrimination cases, of which 47 percent (66) were based on race. In fiscal year 2004–05, the Commission pursued 915 employment cases of which 237 (26 percent) were based on race, and 67 housing cases of which 30 (45 percent) were based on race. The Commission also reached approximately 1.5 million Tennessee residents with outreach activities concerning pursuit of civil rights.

• The New Mexico Human Rights Act of 1969 established two human rights bodies in the state—the Human Rights Division in the New Mexico Department of Labor, which investigates complaints and provides training and public education, and the New Mexico Human Rights Commission, which hears discrimination cases. The Human Rights Division investigates an average of 600–800 cases per year; in fiscal year 2006, the number was 635. In the same year, the Division mediated 194 cases, of which 149 were successfully settled. Of the 1,304 complaints filed in fiscal year 2006, 170 (13 percent) were based on national origin, 109 (8 percent) on race, and 283 (22 percent) on retaliation. Of the 635 cases investigated and resolved, 135 (21 percent) were resolved through settlement, 404 (63.6 percent) led to findings of no probable cause, and 82 (13 percent) were resolved through the administrative hearing process. For cases resolved in favor of claimants, monetary awards totaled $1,051,237.

• The South Carolina Human Affairs Commission (SCHAC), established by the 1972 South Carolina Human Affairs Law, investigates and hears complaints of discrimination in the areas of employment, housing, and public accommodation. In fiscal years 2005–06, there were 1,238 employment complaints filed and 1,218 final actions in such cases. Mediation was used for 162 cases, with a resolution rate of 70 percent. Fair housing complainants filed 88 complaints, and 86 cases were resolved that year; public accommodations complaint activity involved the filing of 66 complaints, with final resolution of 74 cases.

• During 2006, 1,488 complaints were filed with the Nevada Equal Rights Commission (NERC), resulting in 1,035 charges of discrimination. Under Nevada law, NERC's authority extends to discrimination in employment, public accommodations, and housing. In addition to the authority to hold hearings, NERC has the authority to hold informal settlement conferences and conciliations to resolve complaints prior to litigation. In 2006, the NERC held twenty-five conciliations, of which ten were successfully settled and fifteen were unsuccessful. The unsuccessful employment cases were referred to the federal EEOC for possible further action under the work sharing agreement between Nevada and the EEOC. The NERC also offers educational outreach programs, primarily in the area of employment law.

• The Civil Rights Division of the Oregon Bureau of Labor and Industry administers Oregon's civil rights laws. The Civil Rights Division receives approximately 30,000 inquiries per year, of which approximately 2,000 to 2,500 result in the filing of formal discrimination complaints each year. Approximately 98 percent of the complaints relate to employment, one percent to housing, and one percent to discrimination with regard to public accommodations. In turn, approximately 22 percent of the complaints are based on race, color, or national origin discrimination. The Division also has an active education and outreach program, providing information to employers and the public. On the average, 5,000 to 6,000 managers, supervisors, and employers are trained each year.

• Under Kentucky law, the Kentucky Commission on Human Rights, composed of eleven members appointed by the Governor, administers and enforces the civil rights laws of the Commonwealth of Kentucky.

According to the reports of the Commission, in fiscal year 2004–05 there were 343 civil rights complaints filed, of which 160 (47 percent) were based on race, and in fiscal year 2005–06 there were 383 complaints filed, of which 164 (43 percent) were based on race. One recent case example is as follows: In December 2004, the Kentucky Commission on Human Rights filed suit in state court, seeking civil damages against the perpetrators of a cross-burning in Boone County in Northern Kentucky in 2004. The perpetrators pled guilty to three federal counts of violation of civil rights, intimidation, and aiding and abetting. In addition, the civil suit alleged that the cross-burning violated the U.S. Fair Housing Act and Kentucky Civil Rights Act and sought actual and punitive damages for the victims. The Office of the Attorney General joined as an intervening plaintiff. The case was scheduled for trial in March 2007. The family left the neighborhood after the incident and intervened in the civil action in lieu of an administrative hearing before the Commission.

• Vermont has several laws aimed at protecting citizens against harassment, discrimination, and criminal acts based on race, ethnicity, color, and national origin. In 2004–05, 143 employment charges were filed and 171 cases were resolved, with benefits of $647,459 for complainants. That same year, 50 housing charges were filed and 30 were resolved, with benefits of $28,428 for complainants. Thirty-two public accommodation charges were filed in 2004–05, and 28 were resolved, providing benefits of $5,250.

• During fiscal year 2004–05, the Hawaii Civil Rights Commission received over 6,500 inquiries. Of those, 784 intakes were completed and 612 complaints were actually filed. Three hundred and sixty-two of these cases originated with Hawaiian state investigators, and another 250 originated with the EEOC. The 612 cases included 530 employment cases, 30 public accommodations cases, 50 housing cases, and 2 cases involving the state and state-funded services. Race, national origin/ancestry, and color were the basis of approximately 21 percent of the employment cases and 33 percent of the public accommodations cases.

• During fiscal year 2005, the Maryland Human Relations commission received 943 complaints and completed 915 cases, obtaining over $850,000 for victims of discrimination. The mediation unit held 177 mediations and reached agreement or closed 62 percent of those. The staff also provided training and outreach to more than 7,000 Maryland residents and 137 organizations. Examples of cases in Maryland are: *MCHR v. Triangle Oil Company* (employment discrimination based on race by reducing hours and wages and terminating the complainant from his job); *Newkirk v. Chase Real Estate Company et al.* (racial discrimination in rental of a house); and *MCHR v. Elton Smith, Jr.* (harassment of an interracial couple by an African American neighbor).

Enforcement Against Private Entities: Constitutional Limitations and Reservation

77. As noted in the Initial U.S. Report, the definition of "racial discrimination" under Article 1 (1) of the Convention, the obligation imposed in Article 2 (1) (d) to bring to an end all racial discrimination "by any persons, group or organization," and the specific requirements of paragraphs 2 (1) (c) and (d) and articles 3 and 5 may be read as imposing a requirement on States parties to take action to prohibit and punish purely private conduct of a nature generally held to lie beyond the proper scope of governmental regulation under current U.S. law. For this reason, the United States indicated through formal reservation that U.S. undertakings are limited by the reach of constitutional and statutory protections under U.S. law as they may exist at any given time:

"[T]he Constitution and laws of the United States establish extensive protections against discrimination, reaching significant areas of non-governmental activity. Individual privacy and freedom from governmental interference in private conduct, however, are also recognized as among the fundamental values which shape our free and democratic society. The United States understands that the identification of the rights protected under the Convention by reference in Article 1 to fields of "public life" reflects a similar distinction between spheres of public conduct that are customarily the subject of governmental regulation, and spheres of private conduct that are not. To the extent, however, that the Convention calls for a broader regulation of private conduct, the United States does not accept any obligation under this Convention to enact legislation or take other measures under paragraph (1) of Article 2, subparagraphs (1) (c) and (d) of Article 2, Article 3 and Article 5 with respect to private conduct except as mandated by the Constitution and laws of the United States."

That reservation remains in effect, and the specific delineation of current constitutional and statutory protections, as set forth in the Initial U.S. Report, has not changed.

78. Nonetheless, as seen in the enforcement actions described in this report, U.S. law does extend to private conduct in many instances. Basic United States civil rights laws (42 U.S.C. 1981, 1982) have been

used to prohibit private actors from engaging in racial discrimination in activities such as the sale or rental of private property, admission to private schools, and access to public facilities. In addition, enforcement against private parties who engage in discrimination in public accommodations and employment may also be pursued under Titles II and VII of the 1964 Civil Rights Act, which are based on the commerce power of Congress. Executive Order 11246 provides a basis for public enforcement actions against federal contractors and subcontractors who engage in employment discrimination. The Fair Housing Act forms the basis for enforcement against private parties in the area of discrimination in housing. Finally, the spending powers of Congress form the basis for Title VI of the 1964 Civil Rights Act, which prohibits discrimination by both public and private institutions that receive federal funds.

79. States also enforce against private entities. For example, under Kentucky law, in addition to enforcing the Kentucky Civil Rights Act, the Kentucky Commission on Human Rights has a statutory role in addressing unlawful discrimination in proprietary schools and private clubs (KRS 165A.360(1)—proprietary schools), (KRS 141.010(11)(d) and (13)(f)—private clubs). In the context of proprietary schools, the Commission has authority to block the licensure of schools that discriminate or tolerate discrimination on the basis of race, color, or creed. In the context of private clubs, the Commission has authority to block the availability of tax deductions for payments to clubs that discriminate or tolerate discrimination based on race, color, religion, national origin, or sex. On November 18, 2004, the Kentucky Supreme Court ruled that the Commission has the power to investigate private social clubs for discriminatory membership practices. Represented by staff counsel and the Office of the Attorney General, the Commission asserted investigative authority over the Pendennis Club of Louisville, the Louisville Country Club, and the Idle Hour Country Club of Lexington. The private clubs had refused to provide their membership records for a determination regarding their racial and gender makeup. The Kentucky Supreme Court's decision in *Commonwealth v. Pendennis Club, Inc.*, 153 S.W. 3d 784 (Ky. 2004) reversed lower court rulings.

80. A number of cases brought against private entities are set forth in the sections on employment and housing, above. Others are described in other sections of the report.

3. Measures taken to review governmental, national and local policies and to amend, rescind or nullify any laws and regulations that have the effect of creating or perpetuating racial discrimination wherever it exists

81. Article 2 (1) (c) requires States parties to "take effective measures to review governmental, national and local policies ... which have the effect of creating or perpetuating racial discrimination" and to "amend, rescind or nullify any laws and regulations" that have such effects.

82. The United States continues to satisfy these obligations through its ongoing legislative and administrative processes at all levels of government, as well as through court challenges brought by governmental and private litigants. Laws and regulations in the United States are under continuous legislative and administrative revision and judicial review.

Executive Review

83. White House. President Bush has renewed several initiatives that involve review of existing laws and policies with the goal of promoting racial and ethnic equality in the areas, *inter alia*, of education, and economic competitiveness and prosperity. These include the President's Advisory Commission on Educational Excellence for Hispanic Americans (E.O. 13230, October 12, 2001); the President's Board of Advisors on Historically Black Colleges and Universities (E.O. 13256, February, 12, 2002); the Executive Order on Tribal Colleges and Universities (E.O. 13270, July 3, 2002); and the White House Initiative on Asian Americans and Pacific Islanders (E.O. 13339, May 15, 2004). President Bush also continued the Interagency Group on Insular Areas (E.O. 13299, May, 12, 2003). These Executive Orders involve review of existing laws and policies and consideration of recommendations for further action. In most cases, the President has appointed advisory committees for this purpose. The Advisory Committee on Educational Excellence for Hispanic Americans has completed its work and made recommendations, which are discussed in the next section.

84. A number of Executive Branch departments have also undergone legal and policy reviews since 2000.

85. Department of Justice. Shortly after 9/11, the Department of Justice Civil Rights Division reviewed and assessed existing laws and practices and spearheaded a special Initiative to Combat Post 9/11 Discriminatory Backlash. This initiative reflected a commitment by the U.S. government to combat violations of civil rights laws against Arab, Muslim, Sikh, and South-Asian Americans by: (1) ensuring that processes were in place

for individuals to report violations and that cases were handled expeditiously; (2) implementing proactive measures to identify cases involving bias crimes and discrimination being prosecuted at the state level that might merit federal action; (3) conducting outreach to affected communities to provide information on how to file complaints; (4) working with other offices and agencies to ensure accurate referral, effective outreach, and comprehensive provision of services to victims of civil rights violations; and (5) appointing two senior Department of Justice attorneys to focus on post 9/11 backlash issues—a Special Counsel for Post 9/11 National Origin Discrimination and a Special Counsel for Religious Discrimination. More in-depth descriptions of the programs carried out under this initiative appear under the discussion of Article 5, Right to Security of Person and Protection by the State against Violence or Bodily Harm, below.

86. On June 17, 2003, the Department of Justice issued policy guidance to ban federal law enforcement officials from engaging in racial profiling. This guidance has also been adopted by DHS. It is described in more detail in the section on racial profiling under subsection 4 (below).

87. Equal Employment Opportunity Commission. In 2005, the EEOC set up a task force to recommend improvements to its investigation and litigation of systemic discrimination cases. Systemic cases are defined as pattern or practice, policy and/or class action cases where the alleged discrimination has a broad impact on an industry, profession, company, or geographic location. In April 2006, the EEOC accepted the recommendations of this task force and announced its decision to make the fight against systemic discrimination an agency-wide top priority. The new plan places responsibility for addressing systemic discrimination in EEOC district field offices and requires each district to develop a plan to ensure that systemic discrimination is being identified and investigated in a coordinated, strategic, and effective agency-wide manner. Such plans must specify the steps that will be taken to identify and investigate systemic discrimination and describe how the work will be accomplished. District plans should ensure a coordinated, national approach to combating systemic discrimination. For example, districts are to partner with one another, and staff with significant systemic experience should serve as team leaders, team members, or mentors on systemic charges being handled by other offices. EEOC will staff systemic lawsuits based on the needs of the case, rather than based on the office where the case arose. The EEOC plan also requires the Office of Information Technology to prepare an action plan addressing the issue of systemic discrimination in the area of technology.

88. Department of Homeland Security—U.S. Immigration and Customs Enforcement (ICE). Since November 2000, U.S. Immigration and Customs Enforcement (ICE) and its predecessor agency, the former Immigration and Naturalization Service (INS), have implemented National Detention Standards for facilities holding immigration detainees for over 72 hours. These standards were the result of extensive discussions among the former INS, the American Bar Association, and other organizations involved in *pro bono* representation and advocacy for immigration detainees. The National Detention Standards ensure consistent treatment and care for detainees that are in ICE custody anywhere in the country. Previously, each facility had adopted its own standards, generally in accordance with state regulations or recognized accrediting organizations such as the American Corrections Association. The standards provide that, subject to reasonable regulation: (1) detainees will have access to a law library and supplies to prepare documents for legal proceedings; (2) facilities will permit authorized persons to make legal presentations to detainees to inform them of U.S. immigration law and procedures; (3) detainees will have access to telephones and correspondence and other mail; (4) facilities will permit authorized visits to detainees, including from legal counsel, family, and friends; (5) facilities will implement standard operating procedures that address detainee grievances; (6) detainees will be provided a detainee handbook containing necessary information about the rules and regulations governing the facility; (7) facilities will apply appropriate health standards for meal services; (8) facilities will provide medical services to promote detainee health and well-being, including initial medical screening, primary medical care and emergency care; and (9) facilities will accommodate religious observances of detainees, such as providing for meals after sundown for Muslims participating in the fast during Ramadan.

89. Department of Housing and Urban Development (HUD). In January of 2005, HUD established the Office of Systemic Investigations (OSI) for the purpose of identifying, investigating, and resolving complaints alleging systemic discriminatory practices or cases pertaining to housing. The issues raised in these complaints are often novel or complex and raise legal and policy issues of national importance. These cases include mortgage lending, homeowners insurance, zoning and land use, environmental justice, and design and construction. In some instances, the cases identified for systemic processing include those that affect large numbers of persons. The OSI utilizes various methods to identify persons who may not be aware

that they have been victims of discrimination, and the OSI works to prevent future discriminatory acts by addressing systemic practices. In fiscal year 2005, HUD also created a new Division of Education and Outreach (OEO) to increase public awareness of federal fair housing laws and HUD's role in enforcing those laws; HUD also established a National Fair Housing Training Academy to train housing discrimination investigators at local, state, and federal levels.

90. Department of Labor. During the last five years, the Department of Labor Office of Federal Contract Compliance Programs (OFCCP) has refocused its efforts to better detect and remedy systemic discrimination. Systemic discrimination cases are defined as those involving ten or more employees. The shift is designed to: (1) prioritize agency resources to address the worst offenders, those who allow discrimination to be their "standard operating procedure;" (2) achieve maximum leverage of OFCCP resources to protect the greatest number of workers from discrimination; and (3) encourage employers to engage in self-audits by increasing the tangible consequences of not doing so.

Legislative and Judicial Review

91. The U.S. Congress is constantly assessing the state of U.S. legislation and amending existing legislation or enacting new legislation where deemed necessary. New U.S. laws enacted since the Initial Report are set forth in the next section. In addition, legislation and executive branch actions are constantly being assessed by the judiciary for their consistency with the U.S. Constitution and laws. Examples of court cases since 2000 are set forth throughout this report. The same ongoing executive, legislative, and judicial review occurs in the states and territories of the U.S. with regard to their civil rights laws and enforcement activities.

4. Measures taken to give effect to the undertaking to prohibit and bring to an end, by all appropriate means, including legislation as required by the circumstances, racial discrimination by any persons, group or organization

92. Article 2 (1) (d) requires each State party to "prohibit and bring to an end, by all appropriate means, including legislation as required by the circumstances, racial discrimination by any persons, group or organization." As indicated above, government policy at all levels reflects this undertaking, and numerous mechanisms, including programmatic initiatives, litigation, and legislation, exist to achieve this goal. This section describes a number of specific executive initiatives as well as legislation enacted since 2000 to increase and strengthen U.S. laws and programs in the areas of racial, ethnic, and national origin discrimination.

93. Education. Several Administration initiatives are in place to strengthen federal protections in the area of education. First, the President's Advisory Commission on Educational Excellence for Hispanic Americans, E.O. 13230, established within the Department of Education, is designed to improve opportunities for Hispanic Americans to participate in and benefit from federal education programs, with the specific goal of closing the academic achievement gap. A board of advisors issued a report in 2003, finding, *inter alia*, that despite the high hopes of Hispanic parents, only one of three Hispanic students completed high school, and only one of ten completed college. To empower Hispanic parents and children with regard to education, the initiative includes programs to make Hispanic families aware of their rights and the services to which they are entitled under the No Child Left Behind Act of 2001 (20 U.S.C. 6301 et seq.), including free translation services for parents who do not speak English. It also encompasses a national network of public-private partnerships, denominated Partners for Hispanic Family Learning, to help equip communities and families with educational tools and information resources. Partners for Hispanic Family Learning includes over 200 public and private organizations such as the Hispanic Chamber of Commerce; MANA, a National Latina Organization; the Girl Scouts of the USA; the Parent Institute for Quality Education; State Farm Insurance; and others.

94. The President's Board of Advisors on Historically Black Colleges and Universities (HBCUs), E.O. 13256, also administered by the Department of Education, is designed to strengthen and ensure the viability of the historically Black colleges and universities. The HBCUs, which are open to students of all races and ethnicities, form an important component of the overall United States higher education system, offering strong educational programs in smaller, challenging yet nurturing settings. The Board of Advisors issues an annual federal plan for assistance to HBCUs and makes recommendations to the Secretary of Education and the President. These recommendations address how to increase the private sector role in strengthening these institutions, with particular emphasis on enhancing institutional infrastructure, facility planning and development, and use of new technologies.

95. The Executive Order on Tribal Colleges and Universities, E.O. 13270 is also administered within the Department of Education. Offering high quality college education to students in some of the nation's poorest rural areas, tribal colleges and universities seek to teach and maintain native languages and cultural traditions

while providing education and job training that serve to enhance economic development in the communities they serve. The purpose of the Executive Order is to strengthen the institutional capacity, viability, fiscal stability, and physical infrastructure of tribal colleges and universities so they can maintain high standards of educational achievement. The Executive Order also created a Board of Advisors that provides consultation on tribal colleges and relevant Federal and private sector activities, reports progress on these actions, and makes recommendations to the President for implementing the Executive Order to the fullest.

96. In 2002, Congress enacted the No Child Left Behind Act of 2001 (20 U.S.C. 6301 et seq.). This Act reauthorized the Elementary and Secondary Education Act of 1965, and is designed to promote high educational standards and accountability in public elementary and secondary schools, thus providing an important framework for improving the performance of all students. To enable officials to gauge the progress of various groups, the Act requires, as a condition of a state's receipt of federal funds, that the results of annual statewide testing be published and disaggregated at the school, school district, and state levels, by poverty, race, ethnicity, gender, migrant status, disability status, and limited English proficiency (LEP). Each state is required to establish academic content and achievement standards, to define adequate yearly progress for the state as a whole and for schools and school districts, and to work toward ensuring that all students meet these standards by 2013–2014. Adequate yearly progress must include measurable annual objectives for continuous and substantial improvement for all public elementary and secondary students, and for the achievement of economically disadvantaged students, students from major racial and ethnic groups, students with disabilities, and LEP students. If a school or school district fails to make adequate yearly progress, the school or district is subject to a sequence of steps to address the situation, moving from improvement, to corrective action, to restructuring measures designed to improve performance to meet state standards. The Act also focuses on reading in the early grades, and includes programs for LEP students.

97. In 2004, the U.S. Department of Education also began administering the D.C. Choice Incentive Program. The purpose of this $14 million, five-year demonstration program is to give the parents of school children in the District of Columbia the opportunity to exercise greater choice in the education of their children by providing eligible low-income District of Columbia school children scholarships to attend private schools, including private religious schools. This initiative is one of a number of choice programs administered by the Department of Education.

98. Economic Initiatives. The Administration has also initiated a number of programs to support economic development and job competitiveness of American minority populations. In 2004, President Bush established, within the Department of Commerce, the White House Initiative on Asian Americans and Pacific Islanders, E.O. 13339. This Initiative is designed to increase business participation and improve economic and community development for Asian Americans and Pacific Islanders by ensuring equal opportunity to participate in federal programs and public-sector, private-sector partnerships. The Initiative also called for the creation of the President's Advisory Commission on Asian Americans and Pacific Islanders and the Interagency Working Group composed of Secretaries and Administrators from participating federal agencies. As a result of this initiative, a number of federal agencies, such as the Environmental Protection Agency and the National Science Foundation, have made specific efforts to increase the involvement of Asian Americans and Pacific Islanders in their programs.

99. In 2006, Secretary of the Interior Dirk Kempthorne realigned the Native American and Native Alaskan economic development programs within the Department of the Interior to form the Office of Indian Energy and Economic Development. The Office is organized and sharply focused on the goals of bringing new jobs, new businesses, and new money to American Indian and Alaska Native communities. Secretary Kempthorne tasked the Department to develop innovative, collaborative, and increasingly modern approaches to improve economic development opportunities for Native Americans.

100. Under the leadership of Secretary Elaine L. Chao, the first Asian American woman appointed to a President's cabinet, the Labor Department has contributed to the advancement of the Asian Pacific American community and other American racial and ethnic communities through its partnership activities, targeted compliance assistance, human capital development, and enhanced enforcement of labor laws. Examples of the Department's programs and activities include outreach in appropriate languages; direct enforcement activities in low-wage industries; grants for senior citizen work programs and for training of high-risk youth; and establishment of an internship program that has benefited young Asian Pacific Americans among others. Created in 2001, the Department's annual Asian Pacific American Federal Career Advancement Summit is a free one-day training conference to prepare Asian Pacific Americans for career and leadership opportunities

in the federal government. Since 2003, the Labor Department has also sponsored the annual Opportunity Conference to promote economic development in, and access to, government resources by the Asian Pacific, Hispanic, and African American communities.

101. In 2002, former EEOC Chair, Cari M. Dominguez, announced the Administration's Freedom to Compete Initiative. Freedom to Compete is an outreach, education, and coalition-building program designed to help educate America's workforce, deter potential discrimination, and promote compliance and sound employment practices. It complements the agency's enforcement and litigation responsibilities. Since launching the initiative, the EEOC has engaged a cross-section of stakeholders in a dialogue concerning 21st century workplace needs and established alliances with new organization partners, such as trade and professional groups. It has also held a series of panel discussions to educate and inform employers and employees about workplace and marketplace trends and challenges affecting segments of the nation's changing population—specifically highlighting Hispanic, American Indian and Alaska Native, African American, and Asian American and Pacific Islander perspectives. As part of this initiative, the Commission also created the annual Freedom to Compete Awards. These awards are presented to employers, organizations, and other entities that have demonstrated results through best practices in promoting fair and open competition in the workplace. Recipients have included large multi-national employers, small and independent businesses, federal and state agencies, and non-profit organizations. Each recipient has demonstrated a commitment to ensuring that all persons have the freedom to compete and advance in the workplace.

102. Agriculture. The claims process established under the *Pigford v. Johanns* Consent Decree continues to be administered. The Consent Decree was a settlement of the *Pigford v. Johanns* (D.D.C. 1997) class action brought by African American farmers alleging discrimination in farm credit and non-credit benefit programs. As of November 13, 2006, over 22,000 class members had received more than $921 million in damages and debt relief. In addition, USDA has developed several other initiatives to assist minority and socially disadvantaged farmers, including an Office of Minority and Socially Disadvantaged Farmers, a Minority Farm Register to assist in outreach, and new guidelines for improving minority participation in county committee elections.

103. Insular Areas. Recognizing the needs of people inhabiting U.S. insular areas, in May 2003 President Bush re-established the Interagency Group on Insular Areas (IGIA) within the Department of the Interior, E.O. 13299. In consultation with the governors and elected representatives of American Samoa, the U.S. Virgin Islands, and the Commonwealth of the Northern Mariana Islands, the IGIA has provided a forum for important accomplishments in the areas of health care, taxation, immigration, and other matters of concern to the Insular Areas. The group's mission is to address unique problems of the insular areas—such as their remote locations and dependence on air travel—in order to promote economic development, health, education, and other basic needs of the population of those areas. Specific accomplishments of the IGIA include: (1) development of an all-jurisdiction health vital statistics project, in conjunction with the Department of Health and Human Services; and (2) establishment of a governmental forum to discuss issues confronting the Territorial governments, such as a report required by the Energy Policy Act of 2005, support for rural telemedicine projects, and a variety of other issues, such as taxation and immigration.

104. National Origin Discrimination. In 2005 the EEOC issued guidance on national origin discrimination. The guidance is designed to protect against national origin discrimination in American workplaces at a time when issues of discrimination are particularly sensitive in view of America's increasing diversity and the challenges of post 9/11 national origin discrimination. The new guidance explains the prohibition against national origin discrimination and lays out best practices to foster work environments free of national origin bias—including guidance on hiring decisions, harassment, and language issues. It is accompanied by a fact sheet describing some of the national origin issues faced by small employers in today's multi-ethnic American society. In 2006, the Commission received 8,327 charges alleging national origin discrimination, resolved 8,181 charges, and recovered $21.2 million.

105. In view of the increase in bias experienced by Arab, Muslim, Sikh, South Asian Americans, and others in the wake of 9/11, the administration has also placed a high priority on outreach to these communities

---

[3] While the Convention on the Elimination of All Forms of Racial Discrimination does not encompass anti-Muslim or anti-Sikh religious discrimination, it does encompass discrimination based on other factors at issue in these cases, such as ethnicity and national origin. Therefore, the U.S. has included broad descriptions of its initiatives in this area.

and enforcement against discrimination involving such bias.[3] Examples of such activities are set forth in the section on Article 5, below.

106. Health. The Minority Health and Health Disparities Research and Education Act, P. L. 106-525, was enacted in November of 2000 to address the fact that, despite progress in overall health in the nation, continuing disparities exist in the burden of illness and death experienced by some minority groups, compared to the U.S. population as a whole. Although a higher number of non-Hispanic White residents fall in the medically underserved category, higher proportions of racial and ethnic minorities are represented among that group. The law establishes a National Center on Minority Health and Health Disparities in the National Institutes of Health (NIH) within the U.S. Department of Health and Human Services (HHS). The Center is to oversee basic and applied research on health disparities, and to provide grants to Centers of Excellence for Research, Education, and Training to train members of minority health-disparity populations as professionals in biomedical and/or behavior research. The act also requires the Agency for Healthcare Research and Quality (AHRQ) in HHS to conduct research to: (1) identify populations for which there are significant disparities in quality, outcomes, cost, or use of healthcare services; (2) identify causes of and barriers to reducing healthcare disparities, by taking into account such factors as socioeconomic status, attitudes toward health, language spoken, extent of education, area and community of residence, and other factors; and (3) conduct research and run demonstration projects to identify, test, and evaluate strategies for reducing or eliminating health disparities. Finally, the act calls for a national campaign to inform the public and health-care professionals about health disparities, with specific focus on minority and underserved communities.

107. In response to Congressional mandate, HHS/AHRQ published two annual reports, the *National Healthcare Quality Report* (NHQR) and the *National Healthcare Disparities Report* (NHDR). Together, the NHQR and NHDR assess the quality of, and existing disparities in, care provided to the American people. The reports have led to on-line state forums, where states can identify the strengths and weaknesses of their health systems over time, and compare their performance on selected measures with other states, regionally, and nationally. The NHQR and NHDR track performance on a number of measures and operate as tools to improve the quality of future health care. Providing a benchmark of health-care performance helps policy makers at all levels target their resources to improve the status of health care, and to diminish disparities of care in minority and vulnerable populations.

108. The HHS Health Resources and Services Administration's Health Center Program, which has been a major component of its health-care safety net for U.S. indigent populations for more than 40 years, is leading initiatives to increase health-care access in the most needy communities. The underserved health center patients include migrant and seasonal farm workers; homeless individuals; people living in rural areas; large numbers of unemployed persons; and substance abusers, among others. Approximately two-thirds of the patients are minorities.

109. Maternal and Child Health Block Grants deliver health care to pregnant women and to children, including children with special health-care needs. The funds support vital immunizations and newborn screening services, and also pay for transportation and case management to help families access care. These legislated responsibilities are consistent with the current emphasis of HHS on reducing racial differences, building capacity and infrastructure for child health, and ensuring quality care.

110. The Ryan White CARE Act, enacted in 1990, provides for grants for treatment and prevention of AIDS as well as AIDS training and education centers. In 1999, Congress established a Minority AIDS Initiative to increase resources targeted for minority HIV/AIDS prevention and treatment. An Organ Transplant Program also supports national efforts to increase the numbers of organs made available for transplantation and a national network to facilitate the effective allocation of these scarce life-saving and life-enhancing resources to patients. HHS is making directed efforts to increase minority participation in both donation and usage of organs for transplantation.

111. Racial Profiling. The mission of the Justice Department Civil Rights Division includes combating racial profiling. The current Administration was the first to issue racial profiling guidelines for federal law enforcement officers and remains committed to the elimination of unlawful racial profiling by law enforcement agencies. *See Guidance Regarding the Use of Race by Federal Law Enforcement Agencies.* Specifically, racial profiling is the invidious use of race or ethnicity as a criterion in conducting stops, searches, and other law enforcement investigative procedures, based on the erroneous assumption that a particular individual of one race or ethnicity is more likely to engage in misconduct than any particular individual of another race or

ethnicity. Specifically, the Civil Rights Division enforces the Violent Crime Control and Law Enforcement Act of 1994, 42 U.S.C. 14141, the Omnibus Crime Control and Safe Streets Act of 1968, 42 U.S.C. 3789d, and Title VI of the Civil Rights Act, 42 U.S.C. 2000d. The Civil Rights Division receives and investigates allegations of patterns or practice of racial profiling by law enforcement agencies. If a pattern or practice of unconstitutional policing is detected, the Division will typically seek to work with the local agency to revise its policies, procedures, and training protocols to ensure conformity with the Constitution and federal laws.

112. As noted above, in June of 2003 the Department of Justice issued policy guidance to federal law enforcement officials concerning racial profiling. The guidance bars federal law enforcement officials from engaging in racial profiling, even in some instances where such profiling would otherwise be permitted by the Constitution and laws. Federal law enforcement officers may continue to rely on specific descriptions of the physical appearance of criminal suspects, if a specific suspect description exists in that particular case. However, when conducting investigations of specific crimes, federal law enforcement officials are prohibited from relying on generalized racial or ethnic stereotypes. Under the new policy, a federal law enforcement agent may use race or ethnicity only in extremely narrow circumstances—when there is trustworthy information, relevant to the locality or time frame at issue, that links persons of a particular race or ethnicity to an identified criminal incident, scheme, or organization. In the national and border security context, race and ethnicity may be used, but only to the extent permitted by the applicable laws and the Constitution. On June 1, 2004, then-DHS Secretary Tom Ridge formally adopted the DOJ June 2003 guidance and directed all DHS components to develop agency-specific racial profiling training materials, in concert with the DHS Office for Civil Rights and Civil Liberties. That Office is responsible for implementing the DOJ guidance on racial profiling and continues to work with all DHS components to update and strengthen racial profiling training of law enforcement personnel.

113. Under section 1906 of the 2005 Safe, Accountable, Flexible, Efficient Transportation Equity Act: A Legacy for Users, P. L. 109-59, a new grant program was established to strengthen prohibitions on racial profiling by state and local authorities. The grants are administered by the Department of Transportation. A state may qualify for a section 1906 grant in one of two ways: (1) by enacting and enforcing a law that prohibits the use of racial profiling in the enforcement of state laws regulating the use of federal-aid highways, and making available statistical information on the race and ethnicity of drivers and passengers for each motor vehicle stop on such highways (a "Law State"); or (2) by providing satisfactory assurances that the state is undertaking activities to prohibit racial profiling and to maintain and provide public access to data on the race and ethnicity of drivers and passengers (an "Assurances State"). A state may qualify for a grant as an Assurances State for no more than two years.

114. Government Accountability and Training. In 2002, Congress enacted the Notification and Federal Employee Anti-discrimination and Retaliation Act of 2002 (NoFEARAct), P. L. 107-174. This act makes federal agencies directly accountable for violations of anti-discrimination and whistleblower protection laws. Under the Act, agencies must pay out of their own budgets for settlements, awards, or judgments against them in whistleblower and discrimination cases. In addition, they must provide the following outreach and training:

• Notify employees and applicants for employment about their rights concerning discrimination and whistleblower laws;

• Post statistical data relating to Federal sector equal employment complaints on their websites;

• Ensure that their managers have adequate training in the management of diverse workforces, in early and alternative conflict resolution, and in good communications skills;

• Conduct studies on the trends and causes of complaints of discrimination;

• Implement new measures to improve the complaint process and environment;

• Initiate timely and appropriate discipline against employees who engage in misconduct related to discrimination or reprisal;

• Produce annual reports of status and progress for the Congress, the Attorney General, and the EEOC.

115. Other Legislation. Additional examples of recent legislation are discussed in other sections of the report, below. These include: (1) The Help America Vote Act, discussed under Article 5—Political Rights; (2) The Native American Housing Enhancement Act of 2005, discussed under Article 5—The Right to Housing; and (3) The Crime Victims' Rights Act, discussed under Article 6—General Recommendation XXVI.

5. Measures taken to give effect to the undertaking to encourage, where appropriate, integrationist multi-racial organizations and movements and other means of eliminating barriers between races, and to discourage anything that tends to strengthen racial division

116. Article 2 (1) (e) requires each State party to "encourage, where appropriate, integrationist multi-racial organizations and movements and other means of eliminating barriers between races, and to discourage anything which tends to strengthen racial division." Due to its ever-increasing multi-racial, ethnic, and cultural nature and to the open nature of its society, the United States has a plethora of integrationist organizations and movements that promote ethnic and racial tolerance and coexistence. Many such organizations exist in the non-governmental sector. For example, the Association of Multiethnic Americans (AMEA, www.ameasite.org)—a nationwide confederation of local multiethnic/interracial groups—was founded in November of 1988 by representatives of local multiethnic/multiracial organizations from across the United States. Members of local groups come from all walks of life and include people from many racial/ethnic backgrounds and mixtures. AMEA's primary goal is to promote positive awareness of interracial and multiethnic identity for interracial persons and for the society as a whole. Some of its component multi-racial and multi-ethnic organizations deal with specific racial or ethnic groups (for example, Asian Americans), while others seek to bring together people of all races and ethnicities.

117. Other non-governmental organizations focus less specifically on multi-racial issues, and more on addressing racial and ethnic bias and promoting understanding and tolerance. Examples of such organizations are: Teaching Tolerance (seeking to create a national community committed to human rights); the National Coalition Building Institute (NCBI) (leadership training organization working to eliminate prejudice and inter-group conflict in communities); the Anti-Defamation League (ADL) (combating hate crimes and promoting inter-group cooperation and understanding); Educators for Social Responsibility (promoting character education, violence prevention, and inter-group relations); the National Conference for Community and Justice (NCCJ) (developing young leaders from different racial, ethnic, and religious groups to address prejudice and intolerance); and Facing History and Ourselves (teacher training organization that encourages middle and high school students to examine racism and prejudice and promote a more tolerant society). Some organizations, such as the American-Arab Anti-Discrimination Committee (ADC), the National Association for the Advancement of Colored People (NAACP), and the American Jewish Committee promote tolerance with reference to particular groups of the population.

118. Entities that promote tolerance and understanding also exist in federal, state, and local governments. Within the federal government, for example, the Department of Justice Community Relations Service (CRS) provides conflict resolution services, which include mediation, technical assistance, and training throughout the United States to assist communities in avoiding racial and ethnic conflict. CRS deploys highly skilled professional mediators with experience and cultural awareness to enable affected parties to develop and implement their own solutions to racial and ethnic conflict, tension, and concerns. CRS services are confidential, neutral, and free of charge. In contrast to earlier years when CRS's work dealt mainly with issues concerning the African American population, today its work involves the panoply of racial and ethnic groups in the United States, including new immigrants, Native Americans and Alaska Natives, Hispanic Americans, Asians, South Asians, Somalians, Ethiopians, Arab Americans, and others.

119. After the events of 9/11, CRS conducted an aggressive information, outreach, and conflict resolution effort with Arab American, Muslim, and Sikh communities. First, throughout the remainder of 2001, CRS officials sought guidance from leaders of the national Arab American, Muslim, and Sikh communities. CRS focused its work in cities and states where people of Middle Eastern origin are heavily concentrated and places where hate incidents had occurred against the Middle Eastern communities—in particular the states of California, Michigan, Illinois, New Jersey, New York, Texas, Virginia, Florida, Pennsylvania, Ohio, Massachusetts, Maryland, and the District of Columbia.

120. Based on guidance from the relevant communities, CRS's program goals included: (1) conducting hate crimes training for police departments and school administrators in areas with major Muslim and Arab American populations; (2) helping state and local federal officials establish working groups focusing on 9/11 backlash issues; (3) encouraging municipalities, police departments, schools and colleges, and universities with major Muslim and Arab American populations to plan and organize racial dialogues; (4) assisting local Human Rights Commissions and similar organizations to develop work plans that focus on outreach to the Arab and Muslim communities and strategies to bring about better relations between these communities and

the broader community; and (5) convening superintendents of schools and principals to discuss "best practices" and other measures to address backlash affecting Muslim and Arab American students in their school systems.

121. Response to the events of 9/11 also included issuance of a November 19, 2001 "Joint Statement Against Workplace Bias in the Wake of September 11 Attacks." Issued by the EEOC and the Departments of Justice and Labor, this statement reaffirmed the federal government's commitment to upholding laws, regulations, and Executive Orders mandating workplace nondiscrimination. It also noted the government's focus on "preventing and redressing incidents of harassment, discrimination, and violence in the workplace, including such acts directed toward individuals who are, or are perceived to be, Arab, Muslim, Middle Eastern, South Asian, or Sikh." The Joint Statement is available on line at http://www.eeoc.gov/press/11-19-01-js.html. In response to concerns about housing security after 9/11, HUD's Fair Housing Office also issued a statement reviewing federal fair housing laws, setting forth answers to questions regarding housing discrimination, and notifying the public how to file fair housing complaints (http://www.hud.gov/offices/fheo/library/sept11.cfm).

122. In fiscal years 2005 (October 2004 through September 2005) and 2006 (October 2005 through September 2006), CRS's work continued to be connected to post-9/11 and hate incidents. CRS worked with local communities to mitigate post-9/11 tensions and conflicts by deploying mediators and providing cultural training to community leaders and law enforcement bodies. CRS also responded to specific hate crime incidents targeted toward Arab, Muslim, and Sikh residents, businesses, and houses of worship. In addition, CRS developed and made available on its website a multimedia Arab American and Muslim cultural awareness training video entitled "The First Three to Five Seconds." This police roll-call video, which is widely requested by law enforcement departments and organizations across the country, can be seen on the CRS website at www.usdoj.gov/crs.

123. In fiscal years 2005 and 2006, CRS responded, respectively, to approximately 757 and 851 community incidents and conflicts based on race, color, or national origin. CRS mediators continue to work with community, government, and law enforcement leaders to prevent or resolve racial tensions related to a wide range of issues, including administration of justice/police-community relations, anti-hate activities, protests and special events, post-9/11 concerns, immigrant community issues, Native American issues, conflicts in educational institutions, and hate incidents (including vandalism and arson in houses of worship). Services requested include conciliation and mediation, contingency planning, policy training, technical and communication assistance, and partnership building.

124. Organizations promoting tolerance are also active at state and local levels. For example, the California Endowment—the state's largest health foundation—established a 9/11 Special Opportunities Fund, which made more than $2.4 million in grants to tolerance organizations, Human Relations Commissions, non-governmental organizations, and others to promote understanding of Arab Americans and people of the Islamic faith within the state. Another example is found in Oregon, where the legislature has authorized a Commission on Black Affairs, a Commission on Asian Affairs, and a Commission on Hispanic Affairs, each of which works towards economic, social, political, and legal equality for its corresponding group.

125. The Bush Administration's Faith Based and Community Initiative is also designed to ensure that the nation's religious organizations can and are doing their part to provide social services to underserved populations, and to strengthen their involvement in promoting ethnic and racial tolerance and coexistence. This initiative helps religious organizations obtain grant funds for these purposes.

B. Information on the special and concrete measures taken in the social, economic and cultural and other fields to ensure the adequate development and protection of certain racial groups or individuals belonging to them, for the purpose of guaranteeing them the full and equal enjoyment of human rights and fundamental freedoms, in accordance with Article 2, paragraph 2 of the Convention.

126. Article 2 (2) provides that, when circumstances so warrant, States parties shall take "special and concrete measures" for the "adequate development and protection of certain racial groups or persons belonging to them, for the purpose of guaranteeing to them the full and equal enjoying of human rights and fundamental freedoms." Article 1 (4) specifically excludes from the definition of "racial discrimination" "[s]pecial measures taken for the sole purpose of securing adequate advancement of certain racial or ethnic groups or individuals requiring such protection" in order to provide equal enjoyment of human rights and fundamental freedoms. Such measures may not, however, lead to the maintenance of "unequal or separate rights for different racial groups" or "be continued after the objectives for which they were taken have been achieved."

127. The United States acknowledges that Article 2 (2) requires States parties to take special measures "when circumstances so warrant" and, as described below, the United States has in place numerous such measures. The decision concerning when such measures are in fact warranted is left to the judgment and discretion of each State Party. The decision concerning what types of measures should be taken is also left to the judgment and discretion of each State Party, and the United States maintains its position that, consistent with the Convention, special measures taken for the sole purpose of securing adequate advancement of certain racial or ethnic groups or individuals requiring such protection may or may not in themselves be race-based. For example, a "special measure" might address the development or protection of a racial group without the measure itself applying on the basis of race (e.g., a measure might be directed at the neediest members of society without expressly drawing racial distinctions).

128. A substantial number of existing federal ameliorative measures could be considered "special and concrete measures" for the purposes of Article 2 (2). These include the panoply of efforts designed to promote fair employment, statutory programs requiring affirmative action in federal contracting, race-conscious educational admission policies and scholarships, and direct support for historically Black colleges and universities, Hispanic-serving institutions, and Tribal colleges and universities. Some provisions are hortatory, such as statutory encouragement for recipients of federal funds to use minority-owned and women-owned banks. Others are mandatory; for example, the Community Reinvestment Act, 12 U.S.C. 2901, requires federally chartered financial institutions to conduct and record efforts to reach out to under-served communities, including, but not limited to, minority communities.

129. Statutory programs such as those described in the Initial U.S. Report continue to operate. They include, but are not limited to:

• Small Business Act requirement that federal agencies set goals for contracting with "small and disadvantaged businesses";

• Small Business Administration (SBA) section 8 (a) Business Development Program and Small and Disadvantaged Business Certification and Eligibility Program;

• SBA Native American Tribal Business Information Centers;

• SBA HUBZone Contracting Program for small businesses in historically underutilized business zones;

• SBA section 7 (j) Small Business Development Assistance Grant Program, section 7(a) Small Business Loan Guaranty Program, and section 7(m) Microloan Program;

• Department of Agriculture programs designed for "socially disadvantaged" farmers and ranchers;

• Department of Education Gear Up discretionary grant program for high-poverty middle schools, colleges and universities, community organizations, and businesses;

• Department of Education and state and local efforts to help students overcome language barriers that impede equal participation in educational programs;

• Treasury Department Minority Bank Deposit Program, Federal Deposit Insurance Corporation (FDIC) Minority Deposit Institutions Program, and Department of Energy Bank Deposit Financial Assistance Program; and

• Department of Transportation preferences for small businesses owned and controlled by socially and economically disadvantaged individuals in DOT-assisted contracts.

130. In general, the proper goal of affirmative action programs, such as those noted above, is to remedy the effects of past and present discrimination. Affirmative action measures may not create any form of "quotas" or "numerical straightjackets;" nor may they give preference to unqualified individuals, place undue burdens on persons not beneficiaries of the affirmative action programs, or continue to exist or operate after their purposes have been achieved.

131. Any affirmative action plan that incorporates racial classifications must be narrowly tailored to further a compelling government interest, *see, e.g., Adarand Constructors, Inc., v. Pena*, 515 U.S. 200 (1995). The United States Supreme Court recently addressed the use of racial classifications in university admissions. In *Grutter v. Bollinger*, 539 U.S. 306 (2003), and *Gratz v. Bollinger*, 539 U.S. 244 (2003), the Court recognized a compelling interest that permits the limited consideration of race to attain a genuinely diverse student body, including a critical mass of minority students, at universities and graduate schools. Specifically, the Court held that the University of Michigan Law School's interest in "assembling a class that is ... broadly diverse" is compelling because "attaining a diverse student body is at the heart of [a law school's] proper institutional mission." *Grutter*, 539 U.S. at 329. In so doing, the Court deferred to the Law School's educational judgment that student-body diversity was essential to its educational mission. In

Grutter, the Court further found the Law School's program to be narrowly tailored to achieve this mission because it applied a flexible goal rather than a quota, because it involved a holistic individual review of each applicant's file, and because it did not "unduly burden" individuals who were not members of the favored racial and ethnic groups. The Court also held that "race-conscious admissions policies must be limited in time," and expressed an expectation that "25 years from now, the use of racial preferences will no longer be necessary to further the interest approved today." *Id.* At 342-43. At the same time, however, in *Gratz v. Bollinger*, the Court struck down the admissions policies of the University of Michigan's undergraduate program, which automatically awarded points to an applicant's diversity score depending on the applicant's race, because it operated as a mechanical quota that was not "narrowly tailored" to meet the university's objective. *See id.* at 270.

132. To date, the Court has not recognized the goal of achieving broad diversity as compelling outside of the educational settling. Moreover, whether the goal of achieving simple racial diversity is a compelling interest that would permit the use of racial classifications in an education setting has yet to be determined. In its current term, the Supreme Court is expected to decide whether elementary and secondary schools may use race as a deciding factor in making student assignment decisions in order to achieve (or maintain) racially diverse schools. *See Parents Involved in Community Schools v. Seattle School District No. 1*, 05-908; *Meredith v. Jefferson County Board of Education*, 06-915.

133. Debate concerning reverse discrimination (i.e., that racial preference programs are unfair to persons who do not benefit from them) continues. A number of recent lawsuits allege reverse discrimination, and the courts have articulated the standards described above to define which programs do and do not meet constitutional requirements. It continues to be the view of the United States that, consistent with its obligations under the Convention, the United States may adopt and implement appropriately formulated special measures consistent with U.S. constitutional and statutory provisions, and that the Convention gives the State party broad discretion to determine both when circumstances warrant the taking of special measures and how, in such cases, it shall fashion such special measures.

134. Based on the Equal Educational Opportunities Act of 1974 (EEOA) and Title VI of the Civil Rights Act of 1964, courts have also continued to uphold the responsibility of states and local school districts to take affirmative steps to rectify the language deficiency of children with limited English proficiency, as required by the landmark decision of *Lau v. Nichols*, 414 U.S. 563 (1974). For example, in *Flores v. Arizona*, 405 F. Supp. 2d 1112 (D. Ariz. 2005), the federal district court in Arizona, pursuant to the EEOA, found the State of Arizona's funding of its limited English Proficiency (LEP) programs so inadequate that it enjoined the state from requiring LEP students to pass a particular standardized test as a requirement for graduation from high school until funding was restored to an adequate level.

Article 3

135. Article 3 requires States parties to condemn racial segregation and apartheid and to undertake to prevent, prohibit, and eradicate "all practices of this nature" in territories under their jurisdiction. The Initial U.S. Report described the response of the United States Government, state and local governments, and private institutions to governments and institutions that supported or tolerated apartheid. No such policies or practices are permitted in U.S. territories, and it remains the United States position that such practices should be condemned and eradicated wherever they are found.

Article 4

A. Information on the legislative, judicial, administrative or other measures that give effect to the provisions of Article 4 of the Convention, in particular measures taken to give effect to the undertaking to adopt immediate and positive measures designed to eradicate all incitement to, or acts of, racial discrimination, in particular:

1. To declare an offence punishable by law all dissemination of ideas based on racial superiority or hatred, incitement to racial discrimination, as well as all acts of violence or incitement to such acts against any race or group of persons of another colour or ethnic origin, and also the provision of any assistance to racist activities, including the financing thereof;

2. To declare illegal and prohibit organizations, and also organized and all other propaganda activities, which promote and incite racial discrimination, and to recognize participation in such organizations or activities as an offence punishable by law;

3. Not to permit public authorities or public institutions, national or local, to promote or incite racial discrimination.

136. The American people reject all theories of the superiority of one race or group of persons of one color or ethnic origin, as well as theories that attempt to justify or promote racial hatred and discrimination. It is government policy to condemn such theories, and none is espoused at any level of government. The Convention, however, also requires that States parties "undertake to adopt immediate and positive measures designed to eradicate all incitement to, or acts of, such discrimination" as specified in articles 4 (a), (b) and (c). The Committee has stressed the importance with which it views these obligations, as reflected, for example, in General Recommendation VII (1985), General Recommendation XV (1993), and in the Committee's Concluding Observations on the Initial U.S. Report (A/56/18, para. 391).

137. The United States reiterates that, for the reasons described in paragraphs 147 through 156 of the Initial U.S. Report, its ability to give effect to these requirements is circumscribed by the protections provided in the United States Constitution for individual freedom of speech, expression, and association. Accordingly, at the time it became a State party to the Convention, the United States took a formal reservation to Article 4, and to the corresponding provisions of Article 7, to make clear that it could not accept any obligation that would restrict the constitutional rights of freedom of speech, expression, and association, through the adoption of legislation or any other measures, to the extent that doing so would violate the Constitution and laws of the United States. That reservation remains in effect and reflects fundamental human rights protections accorded to persons under the United States Constitution.

138. In the United States, speech intended to cause imminent violence may constitutionally be restricted, but only under certain narrow circumstances. In 1992, the U.S. Supreme Court struck down a municipal ordinance making it a misdemeanor to "place on public or private property a symbol, object, appellation, characterization, or graffiti, including, but not limited to, a burning cross or Nazi swastika, which one knows or has reasonable grounds to know arouses anger, alarm or resentment in others on the basis of race, color, creed, religion or gender" on the grounds that it unconstitutionally restricted freedom of speech on the basis of its content, *R.A.V. v. City of St. Paul*, 505 U.S. 377 (1992). A more recent Supreme Court decision, however, upheld a statute that prohibited cross-burning with the intent of intimidating any person or group of persons, *Virginia v. Black*, 538 U.S. 343 (2003). Although the Virginia Supreme Court had struck down the statute as unconstitutional on the basis that it singled out a type of speech based on content and viewpoint, the U.S. Supreme Court held that the protections of the first amendment are not absolute, and that cross-burning with the intent to intimidate is in the nature of a true threat—a type of speech that may be banned without infringing the First Amendment, whether or not the person uttering the threat actually intends to carry it out, *see Watts v. United States*, 394 U.S. 705 (1969). In the Court's view, because cross-burning is such a particularly virulent form of intimidation, the First Amendment permits Virginia to outlaw cross-burning with the intent to intimidate.

139. Thus, consistent with the limitations of the U.S. Constitution, the United States can, and does, give effect to Article 4 in numerous areas. For example:

140. Hate Crimes. The Civil Rights Division of the U.S. Department of Justice enforces several criminal statutes that prohibit acts of violence or intimidation motivated by racial, ethnic, or religious hatred and directed against participation in certain activities. Those crimes include: 18 U.S.C. 241 (conspiracy against rights); 18 U.S.C. 245 (interference with federally protected activities); 18 U.S.C. 247(c) (damage to religious property); 42 U.S.C. 3631 (criminal interference with right to fair housing); and 42 U.S.C. 1973 (criminal interference with voting rights). In addition, 47 of the 50 U.S. states enforce state laws prohibiting hate crimes, and organizations to combat hate crimes exist in a number of states.

141. Enforcement against hate crimes—including particular efforts devoted to prosecution of post 9/11 hate crimes targeting Arab Americans and Muslim Americans—is a high priority. Statistics concerning the breakdown of racial and ethnic groups involved in hate crimes cases, as well as specific examples of cases, are set forth in the section on Article 5, Security of Person, below.

142. Hate Crimes on the Internet. The U.S. Supreme Court has made it clear that communications on the internet receive the same constitutional protections under the First Amendment that communications in other media enjoy, *Reno v. ACLU*, 521 U.S. 844 (1997). Nonetheless, when speech contains a direct, credible threat against an identifiable individual, organization, or institution, it crosses the line to criminal conduct and loses that constitutional protection. *See, e.g., Planned Parenthood of the Colombia/Willamette, Inc. v. American Coalition of Life Activists*, 290 F. 3d 1058 (9th Cir. 2002), *cert denied*, 539 U.S. 958 (2003); *see also Virginia v. Black*, 538 U.S. 343 (2003).

143. Because of the difficulties in identifying internet hate crimes and tracking down perpetrators, criminal cases have to date been relatively few in number. As one step in addressing the problem, in 2003 the new Office of Juvenile Justice and Delinquency Prevention in the U.S. Department of Justice, in partnership with Partners Against Hate (a collaboration of the Anti-Defamation League, the Leadership Conference on Civil Rights Education Fund, and the Center for the Prevention of Hate Violence) and the Safe and Drug-Free Schools Program of the U.S. Department of Education published a manual entitled "Investigating Hate Crimes on the Internet." This manual, which can be found at www.partnersagainsthate.org/publications/investigating_hc.pdf, is designed to assist law enforcement and related personnel in their efforts to address criminal internet behavior.

144. The Civil Rights Division of the Department of Justice has prosecuted several internet threats cases. In *U.S. v. Razani* (C.D. Cal.), the defendant sent threatening e-mail, including a death threat, to an Arab American woman. The defendant pled guilty to violating 18 U.S.C. 874 (c) and was sentenced to six months home detention and three years probation on April 3, 2006. In *U.S. v. Middleman* (D.C.), the defendant pled guilty to violating 18 U.S.C. 875 for sending threatening e-mail to the president of the Arab American Institute. This defendant was sentenced to ten months in prison on October 14, 2005. In *U.S. v. Oakley* (D.C.), the defendant sent e-mail threatening to bomb the headquarters of the Council on American Islamic Relations. This defendant pled guilty to violating 18 U.S.C. 844 (e), and was sentenced to three years probation. In *U.S. v. Bratisax* (E.D. Mich.), the defendant sent threatening e-mails to the Islamic Center of America. This defendant plead guilty to violating 18 U.S.C. 247 and was sentenced on March 13, 2006 to two years probation.

145. States also actively prosecute such cases. For example, in 1998, a white supremacist and his organization were charged under the Pennsylvania Ethnic Intimidation Law with terroristic threats, harassment, and harassment by communication in connection with material on a website. The complaint was filed against the White supremacist, Ryan Wilson and his organization, Alpha HQ, as well as against Bluelantern, Inc. and Stormfront, Inc., the internet hosts of the website. The site included threats against two specific local and state civil rights enforcement employees, along with a statement that "traitors" like this should beware because they would be "hung from the neck from nearest tree or lamp post." It also depicted a bomb destroying the office of one of these employees who regularly organized anti-hate activities. Upon the filing of the complaint, the defendants agreed to remove the site from the internet. Thus, the matter was resolved without going to court. *Commonwealth of Pennsylvania v. ALPHA HQ.*

B. Information on appropriate measures taken to give effect to general recommendations I of 1972, VII of 1985 and XV of 1993, on Article 4 of the Convention, by which the Committee recommended that the States parties whose legislation was deficient in respect of the implementation of Article 4 should consider, in accordance with their national legislative procedures, the question of supplementing their legislation with provisions conforming to the requirements of Article 4 (a) and (b) of the Convention.

146. As noted above, the United States implementation of Article 4 (a) and (b) is limited by its constitutional guarantees of freedom of speech, expression, and association. However, the U.S. Department of Justice does enforce a number of criminal statutes that prohibit acts of violence or threats of force motivated by racial, ethnic, or religious hatred and directed against participation in certain activities. In addition, as also noted above, 47 of the 50 states also enforce their own hate crimes laws. United States federal and state laws currently provide adequate legal basis for prosecuting racially and ethnically motivated crimes consistent with the Constitution, and the U.S. Congress and state legislatures are seized with the responsibility to consider new legal authorities if warranted.

C. Information in response to Decision 3 (VII) adopted by the Committee on 4 May 1973 by which the Committee requested the States parties:

1. To indicate what specific penal internal legislation designed to implement the provisions of Article 4 (a) and (b) has been enacted in their respective countries and to transmit to the Secretary-General in one of the official languages the texts concerned, as well as such provisions of general penal law as must be taken into account when applying such specific legislation;

2. Where no such specific legislation has been enacted, to inform the Committee of the manner, and the extent to which the provisions of the existing penal laws, as applied by the courts, effectively implement their obligations under Article 4 (a) and (b), and to transmit to the Secretary-General in one of the official languages the texts of those provisions.

147. In the United States, existing penal laws, as applied by the courts, implement U.S. obligations under Article 4 (a) and (b) consistent with the U.S. Constitution. These laws include:

• 18 U.S.C. 241—Conspiracy Against Rights—This law makes it unlawful for two or more persons to agree to injure, threaten, or intimidate a person in any state, territory, or district in the free exercise or enjoyment of any right or privilege secured to him/her by the Constitution or the laws of the United States, or because of his/her having exercised such rights. Unlike most conspiracy statutes, this section does not require that one of the conspirators commit an overt act prior to the conspiracy's becoming a crime. The offense is punishable by a range of imprisonment up to a life term or the death penalty, depending on the circumstances of the crime and the resulting injury, if any.

• 18 U.S.C. 245 (b) (2)—Federally Protected Activities—This law makes it unlawful to willfully injure, intimidate, or interfere with any person, or attempt to do so, by force or threat of force, because of that person's race, color, religion, or national origin and because he or she is or has been (A) enrolling in or attending any public school or public college; (B) participating in or enjoying any benefit, service, privilege, program, facility, or activity provided or administered by any state or subdivision thereof; (C) applying for or enjoying employment by any private employer or any agency of any state or subdivision thereof, or joining or using the services of any labor organization, hiring hall, or employment agency; (D) serving, or attending upon any court of any state in connection with possible service as a juror; (E) traveling in or using any facility of interstate commerce, or using any vehicle, terminal, or facility of any common carrier by motor, rail, water, or air; or (F) enjoying the goods, services, facilities, privileges, advantages, or accommodations of any inn, hotel, motel, or other establishment which provides lodging to transient guests, or of any restaurant, cafeteria, lunchroom, lunch counter, soda fountain, or other facility which serves the public, or of any gasoline station, or of any motion picture house, theater, concert hall, sports arena, stadium, or any other place of exhibition or entertainment which serves the public, or of any other establishment which serves the public and (i) which is located within the premises of any of the aforesaid establishments or within the premises of which is physically located any of the aforesaid establishments, and (ii) which holds itself out as serving patrons of such establishments. The offense is punishable by a range of imprisonment up to a life term, or the death penalty, depending on the circumstances of the crime and the resulting injury, if any.

• 18 U.S.C. 247 (c)—Damage to Religious Property—This law prohibits anyone from intentionally defacing, damaging, or destroying religious real property, or attempting to do so, because of the race, color, or ethnic characteristics of any individual associated with the property, regardless of any connection to interstate or foreign commerce. The offense is punishable by a range of imprisonment up to a life term or the death penalty, depending on the circumstances of the crime and the resulting injury, if any.

• 42 U.S.C. 3631—Fair Housing Act criminal provisions—This law makes it illegal for an individual to use force or threaten to use force to injure, intimidate, or interfere with, or attempt to injure, intimidate, or interfere with, any person's housing rights because of that person's race, color, religion, sex, handicap, familial status, or national origin. Among the housing rights enumerated in the statute are: the sale, purchase, or rental of a dwelling; the occupation of a dwelling; the financing of a dwelling; contracting or negotiating for any of the rights enumerated above; applying for or participating in any service, organization, or facility relating to the sale or rental of dwellings. The statute also makes it illegal to use force or threaten to use force to injure, intimidate, or interfere with any person who is assisting an individual or class of persons in the exercise of housing rights. The offense is punishable by imprisonment up to a life term, depending on the circumstances of the crime and the resulting injury, if any.

• 42 U.S.C. 1973—Voting Act criminal provisions—Among other aspects, this law makes it illegal to deny or abridge the right of any citizen of the United States to vote on the basis of race, color, or membership in a language minority group. The offense is punishable by monetary fines, or imprisonment of not more than five years, or both.

Copies of these laws are being made available to the Secretary General in English.

Article 5

Information on the legislative, judicial, administrative or other measures that give effect to the provisions of Article 5 of the Convention, taking into consideration general recommendations XX on Article 5 of the Convention (1996) and XXII regarding refugees and other displaced persons (1996), in particular, measures taken to prohibit racial discrimination in all its forms and to guarantee the right of everyone, without distinction as to race, colour, or national or ethnic origin, to equality before the law notably in the enjoyment of the rights listed.

148. Article 5 obligates States parties to prohibit and eliminate racial discrimination in all its forms and to guarantee the right of everyone to equality before the law, without distinction as to race, color, or national or ethnic origin. The protections of the U.S. Constitution meet this fundamental requirement, as do laws, policies, and objectives of government at all levels. Article 5 specifically requires States parties to guarantee equality and non-discrimination in the enjoyment of certain enumerated rights. As noted in the Initial U.S. Report, some of these enumerated rights, which may be characterized as economic, social, and cultural rights, are not explicitly recognized as legally enforceable "rights" under U.S. law. However, Article 5 does not affirmatively require States parties to provide or to ensure observance of each of the listed rights themselves, but rather to prohibit discrimination in the enjoyment of those rights to the extent they are provided in domestic law. In this respect, U.S. law fully complies with the requirements of the Convention. The U.S. continues to work to achieve the desired goals with regard to non-discrimination in each of the enumerated areas.

A. The right to equal treatment before the tribunals and all other organs administering justice.

149. The right to equal treatment before courts in the United States is provided through the operation of the Equal Protection Clause of the Fourteenth Amendment to the U.S. Constitution. This provision is binding on all governmental entities at all levels throughout the United States. The constitutional provision has not changed since 2000.

150. In the United States, potential jurors may not be excluded from a jury solely on account of their race in criminal trials, *Batson v. Kentucky*, 476 U.S. 79 (1986), or civil cases, *Edmonson v. Leesville Concrete Co.*, 500 U.S. 614 (1991). Courts have also generally treated ethnicity and national origin as improper criteria in the selection of jurors. Although the Supreme Court has not squarely decided the issue, it has on two occasions treated *Batson* as extending to ethnic origin. *See, e.g., Hernandez v. New York*, 500 U.S. 352 (1991) (assuming without discussion that *Batson* applies to Hispanic jurors); *U.S. v. Martinez-Salazar*, 528 U.S. 304 (2000) (stating that "[u]nder the Equal Protection Clause, a defendant may not exercise a peremptory challenge to remove a potential juror solely on the basis of the juror's gender, ethnic origin, or race"). Lower courts have also applied this principle in specific cases. *See, e.g., Rico v. Leftridge-Byrd*, 340 F. 3d 178 (3rd Cir. 2003) (holding it not objectively unreasonable for a state court to apply *Batson* to peremptory challenges of Italian American jurors); *U.S. v. Bin Laden*, 91 F. Supp. 2d 600 (S.D.N.Y. 2000) (holding that U.S. citizens cannot be excluded from jury selection based on their nationality because "it is well settled that equal protection principles forbid discriminatory exclusions from jury service on the basis of factors such as race and national origin").

151. In addition, with regard to court access, several federal courts have barred discovery concerning the immigration status of plaintiffs in lawsuits alleging employment discrimination under Title VII of the Civil Rights Act, as well as under other federal laws. *See, e.g., Rivera v. NIBCO, Inc.*, 364 F.3d 1057 (9th Cir. 2004), cert. denied, 544 U.S. 905 (2005) (Title VII); *EEOC v. Restaurant Co.*, 448 F. Supp. 2d 1085 (D. Minn. 2006) (Title VII); *Zeng Liu v. Donna Karan Intern, Inc.*, 207 F. Supp. 2d 191 (S.D.N.Y. 2002) (Fair Labor Standards Act); *Topo v. Dhir*, 210 F.R.D. 76 (S.D.N.Y. 2002) (Alien Tort Claims Act).

152. The Sixth Amendment to the U.S. Constitution provides for the right to counsel in Federal criminal prosecutions. Through a series of landmark decisions by the U.S. Supreme Court, the right to counsel has been extended to all criminal prosecutions—state or federal, felony or misdemeanor—that carry a sentence of imprisonment. By law, counsel for indigent defendants is provided without discrimination based on race, color, ethnicity, and other factors. States and localities use a variety of methods for delivering indigent criminal defense services, including public defender programs, assigned counsel programs, and contract attorneys. The federal system also uses similar types of programs. In addition, in many states counsel is available in some civil cases through state bar *pro bono* attorney programs, and legal aid programs. For example, several organizations in Nevada assist those of limited means in obtaining legal services in civil matters. These include Nevada Legal Services, Clark County Legal Services, and "We the People." The 2000 Bureau of Justice Statistics report "Defense Counsel in Criminal Cases" used data from the Administrative Office of the U.S. Courts, the 1999 National Survey of Indigent Defense Systems, the National Survey of State Court Prosecutors, and State Court Processing Statistics to compare indigent felony defendants in federal and state courts. Among other factors, that study found that conviction rates for indigent defendants and those with their own lawyers were about the same in both federal and state courts. Of those found guilty, defendants represented by publicly financed attorneys were incarcerated at a higher rate than those who paid for their own legal representation (88 percent compared to 77 percent in federal courts and 71 percent compared to 54

percent in the most populous counties), but on average, sentence lengths were shorter for those with publicly-financed attorneys than those who hired counsel.

153. <u>Discrimination by Law Enforcement</u>. The U.S. Constitution and federal statutes prohibit racially discriminatory actions by law enforcement agencies. Where such actions do occur, the Justice Department Civil Rights Division institutes civil actions for equitable and declaratory relief under the Pattern or Practice of Police Misconduct provision of the Violent Crime Control and Law Enforcement Act of 1994, 42 U.S.C. 14141, and the Omnibus Crime Control and Safe Streets Act of 1968, 42 U.S.C. 3789d. Those statutes prohibit law enforcement agencies from engaging in a pattern or practice of violation of civil rights.

154. Since January 2001, the Civil Rights Division has reached 14 settlements with law enforcement agencies under these provisions. These settlements cover police departments in Villa Rica, Georgia; Prince George's County, Maryland; Detroit, Michigan; Cincinnati and Cleveland, Ohio; Los Angeles, California; Washington, D.C.; Mount Prospect, Illinois; the State of New Jersey; and others. Many of these cases involve allegations of excessive use of force, and some also involve allegations of discrimination in conducting stops, detention, and other police activities. For example, a provision in the June 2001 Consent Decree with Los Angeles and the Los Angeles, California Police Department specifically prohibits the use of race, color, ethnicity, or national origin in conducting stops or detention or activities following stops or detentions. As of February 2007, the Division was engaged in ongoing investigations of ten law enforcement agencies, plus monitoring and oversight of ten police settlement agreements involving eight agencies (available on the Justice Department website at www.usdoj.gov/crt/split/index.html).

155. Pursuant to 42 U.S.C. 14141, the Civil Rights Division also investigates and provides technical assistance to law enforcement agencies where there are alleged constitutional violations related to use of force. During these investigations, the Division provides on-going technical assistance to advise law enforcement agencies of best practices and how to conform their policies and practices to constitutional standards. Specifically, by utilizing nationally recognized police practices consultants, the Division provides technical assistance in the areas of uses of force, searches and seizures, non-discriminatory policing, misconduct investigations, early warning systems, citizen complaint intake and follow-up, supervisory review of line officer actions, and in several other areas of policy and practice. Additionally, although section 14141 does not require the Division to issue findings letters or provide the technical assistance noted above to law enforcement agencies, the Division adopts both mechanisms, where appropriate, to identify misconduct and to help agencies improve their policing practices. Since January 2001, the Division has issued 3 findings letters and 19 technical assistance letters.

156. As noted above in the section addressing Article 2 (1) (d), the Administration has also taken action to curb discrimination by law enforcement through DOJ's issuance of racial profiling guidelines for federal law enforcement officers. These guidelines, in turn, have been adopted by the Department of Homeland Security.

157. In addition to the above, private litigants may also sue law enforcement agencies based on allegations of racially discriminatory police activities. *See, e.g., Bennett v. City of Eastpointe*, 410 F.3d 810 (6th Cir. 2005) (upholding summary judgment but outlining requirements of private cause of action pursuant to 42 U.S.C. 1983 for discriminatory policing in violation of Fourteenth Amendment); *Farm Labor Org. Comm. v. Ohio State Highway Patrol*, 308 F.3d 523 (6th Cir. 2002) (applying same Fourteenth Amendment calculus to racial profiling claims in a class action); *see also, United States v. Avery*, 137 F.3d 343, 352 (6th Cir. 1997) (holding that "[i]t is axiomatic that the Equal Protection Clause of the Fourteenth Amendment protects citizens from police action that is based on race."); *Bennett v. City of Eastpointe*, 410 F.3d 810, 818 (6th Cir. 2005) (to establish claim of selective law enforcement, plaintiff must demonstrate that the challenged police action "had a discriminatory effect and that it was motivated by a discriminatory purpose"). To show discriminatory purpose, a plaintiff can proffer "evidence that an official chose to prosecute or engage in some other action at least in part because of, not merely in spite of, its adverse effects upon an identifiable group. King, 86 Fed. Appx. at 802 (citing *Wayte v. U.S.*, 470 U.S. 598 at 610 (1985)).

158. In 2000, there were approximately 800,000 full-time, sworn law enforcement officers in the United States. The Department of Justice, the Department of Homeland Security's Federal Law Enforcement Training Center, and state and local agencies and training academies are heavily involved in training for such officers, including diversity training, and training in defusing racially and ethnically tense situations. Law enforcement officers receive periodic training on these issues during their careers. The Community Relations Service established the Law Enforcement Mediation (LEM) Program, which is designed to equip law enforcement officers with basic knowledge of mediation and conflict resolution skills as they apply directly to law enforce-

ment. The program focuses on the officers' need to respond to any given conflict or dispute, especially those relating to race and ethnic based issues, in a minimum of time and with the maximum effectiveness. In many states, the program is certified for police officers' continuing education credit.

159. In specific circumstances, targeted training efforts are initiated. For example, in the aftermath of 9/11 the Department of Justice Community Relations Service was active in establishing dialogue between government officials and the Arab and Muslim communities. Among other activities, CRS immediately released two publications entitled "Twenty Plus Things Law Enforcement Agencies Can Do to Prevent or Respond to Hate Incidents Against Arab Americans, Muslims, and Sikhs" and "Twenty Plus Things Schools Can Do to Prevent or Respond to Hate Incidents Against Arab Americans, Muslims, and Sikhs." These publications were made widely available and posted on the CRS website to provide immediate information and assistance in an effort to calm immediate tensions, fears, and misunderstandings. As noted above, CRS also created a law enforcement roll call video entitled "The First Three to Five Seconds," which seeks to enhance law enforcement and government officials' outreach capabilities to target communities by addressing cultural behaviors and sensitivities, stereotypes, and expectations encountered in interactions and communications with Arab, Muslim, and Sikh communities. The video can be found at http://www.usdoj.gov/crs/training_video/3to5_lan/transcript.html.

160. The Department of Homeland Security (DHS), one of the largest federal law enforcement agencies in the United States, has emphasized training for its employees, and its Office for Civil Rights and Civil Liberties is developing an online "Civil Liberties University" to provide training on a variety of human rights topics, including cultural awareness regarding Arabs and Muslims. In September 2002, the *Law Enforcement Bulletin*, a magazine published by the Federal Bureau of Investigation (FBI) and distributed to local law enforcement officers throughout the United States, also published an article entitled "Interacting with Arabs and Muslims," which provided information regarding Arab and Muslim culture to assist law enforcement officers to be sensitive to unique and important cultural issues. This article can be found at http://www.fbi.gov/publications/leb/2002/sept02/leb.pdf.

161. Many law enforcement agencies have partnered with NGOs to provide training to their officers. For example, the Islamic Networks Group and the Sikh American Legal Defense and Education Fund have trained hundreds of police agencies, sheriff's departments and prosecutors' offices. The American-Arab Anti-Discrimination Committee also offers a Law Enforcement Outreach Program that has been used by numerous federal law enforcement agencies, including the FBI, DHS, and the U.S. Park Police.

162. Representation in the Criminal Justice System. At yearend 2004, 3.2 percent of African American males, 1.2 percent of Hispanic males, and 0.5 percent of White males in the U.S. were incarcerated in state or federal prisons. Distributions were similar among the female population—the rate for African American females was more than 2 times higher than the rate for Hispanic females and 4 times higher than the rate for white females. Overall, the prison population was estimated to be 41 percent African American, 34 percent White, 19 percent Hispanic, and 6 percent other or two or more races.

163. Jail and prison populations have increased between 1995 and 2005, and changes in the composition of jail and prison populations during that time suggest that the rate of growth for African Americans in both of these incarceration settings has been below that for White Non-Hispanics and Hispanics.

From 1995 to 2005, the composition of the jail population changed as follows:

	1995	2005
White Non Hispanic	40.1%	44.3%
Black Non Hispanic	43.5%	38.9%
Hispanic	14.7%	15.0%
Other races	1.7%	1.7%
Two or more races	N.A.	0.1%

(Source: "Prison and Jail Inmates at Midyear 2005," Bureau of Justice Statistics, p. 8)

The change in composition for prisons from 1995 to 2005 was as follows:

	1995	2005
White Non Hispanic	33.5%	34.6%

Black Non Hispanic	45.7%	39.5%
Hispanic	17.6%	20.2%
Other races	3.2%	2.7%
Two or more races	N.A.	3.0%

(Source: "Prisoners in 2005," Bureau of Justice Statistics, p. 8)

164. Thus, for persons in jail, the population of White Non-Hispanic inmates has grown at a greater rate than the overall jail population, while the African American Non-Hispanic population has grown at a lower rate than the population overall. The Hispanic population has basically mirrored the overall growth. For prisons, on the other hand, the White Non-Hispanic population has grown at about the same rate as the overall population; while the Black Non-Hispanic population grew at a slower rate than the population overall.[4] The Hispanic rate of growth, however, was greater than the overall growth rate.

165. The reasons for the disparities in incarceration rates are complex. Numerous scholars have looked at what aspects of crime, social structure, and the criminal justice system might explain such differential rates. Research by Alfred Blumstein of Carnegie Mellon University and Michael Tonry at the University of Minnesota suggests that the disparities are related primarily to differential involvement in crime by the various groups (with some unexplained disparities particularly related to drug use and enforcement), rather than to differential handling of persons in the criminal justice system.[5] Discussion and debate concerning the reasons for the disparities remains active in the judicial and academic communities.

166. <u>Disparities in Sentencing</u>. The Initial U.S. Report discussed the implications on sentencing of the mandatory minimum sentencing guidelines imposed by the Sentencing Reform Act of 1984 for federal courts, including issues related to sentencing for drug-related offenses. Since 2000, the federal mandatory sentencing guidelines have been held unconstitutional by the U.S. Supreme Court, *United States v. Booker*, 543 U.S. 220 (2005) (holding the guidelines incompatible with the requirement of the Sixth Amendment to the U.S. Constitution that a jury find certain facts related to sentencing). The Court instructed lower courts to consider the guidelines, but to tailor sentences in light of other statutory concerns. It also instructed appellate courts to review the sentences imposed by trial courts to determine their reasonableness. As revised sentencing procedures begin to take effect in the federal courts, the United States Sentencing Commission is reviewing the impact of such procedures on federal sentencing, including the implications for persons of different races, education levels, and other factors, *see, e.g,* "*Report on the Impact of United States v. Booker on Federal Sentencing,*" United States Sentencing Commission, March 2006. While the 2006 report found relatively little change in overall sentencing patterns in the short time since the Supreme Court's decision, the Commission cautioned that the statistics are only very preliminary and that it will be important to continue assessing these matters in future years.

167. <u>Capital Punishment</u>. At the time of the Initial U.S. Report, the federal government and 38 states imposed capital punishment for crimes of murder or felony murder, generally only when aggravating circumstances were present, such as multiple victims, rape of the victim, or murder-for-hire. However, since 2000, the law in New York has been declared unconstitutional under the state constitution, and executions in Illinois and New Jersey have been suspended. Kansas's law was also declared unconstitutional, but that decision was overturned by the U.S. Supreme Court, *Kansas v. Marsh*, 126 S. Ct. 2516 (2006). All criminal defendants in the United States, especially those in potential capital cases, enjoy numerous procedural guarantees, which are respected and enforced by the courts. These include, among others: the right to a fair hearing by an independent tribunal; the presumption of innocence; the right against self-incrimination; the right to access all evidence used against the defendant; the right to challenge and seek exclusion of evidence; the right to review by a higher tribunal, often with a publicly funded lawyer; the right to trial by jury; and the right to challenge the makeup of the jury.

168. Two major Supreme Court decisions since 2000 have narrowed the categories of defendants against whom the death penalty may be applied. In *Roper v. Simmons*, 543 U.S. 551 (2005), the Court held that

---

[4] Some, but not all, of this decrease might be attributable to a change in the classification system that allowed inmates to list two or more races.

[5] Blumstein, Alfred, "Racial Disproportionality of U.S. Prison Populations Revisited," University of Colorado Law Review, Vol. 64 (1993); Tonry, Michael, "Racial Disproportion in U.S. Prisons," British Journal of Criminology, Vol. 34, Special Issue (1994).

the execution of persons who were under the age of eighteen when their capital crimes were committed violates the Eighth and Fourteenth Amendments. *Atkins v. Virginia*, 536 U.S. 304 (2002), held that the execution of mentally retarded criminal defendants constituted cruel and unusual punishment in violation of the Eighth and Fourteenth Amendments. The Supreme Court has repeatedly refused to consider the contention that a long delay between conviction and execution constitutes cruel and unusual punishment under the Eighth Amendment, *see, e.g., Foster v. Florida*, 537 U.S. 990 (2002), leaving in place numerous decisions by lower federal courts rejecting such a claim, *see, e.g., Knight v. Florida*, 528 U.S. 990 (1999) (Thomas, J., concurring in denial of certiorari). However, in June of 2006 the Supreme Court decided that death row inmates may, under civil rights laws, challenge the manner in which death by lethal injection is carried out, *Hill v. McDonough*, 126 S. Ct. 2096 (2006). The underlying constitutional question—whether lethal injection violates the Eighth Amendment prohibition on cruel and unusual punishment—was not addressed by the Supreme Court, but will be decided in the first instance by lower courts in specific cases. In June of 2006, the Supreme Court also ruled that new evidence, including DNA evidence concerning a crime committed long ago, raised sufficient doubt about who had committed the crime to merit a new hearing in federal court for a prisoner who had been on death row in Tennessee for 20 years, *House v. Bell*, 126 S. Ct. 2064 (2006). Five states have authorized the death penalty for sexual assault of a child—Louisiana, Florida, Montana, Oklahoma, and South Carolina, with the last two doing so in 2006. The courts have not yet ruled on the constitutionality of these laws.

169. Both the number of prisoners under sentence of death and the number of executions have declined since 2000. In 2000, 37 states and the federal government held 3,601 prisoners under death sentence. By the end of 2005, this number had decreased to 3,254—a reduction of 9.6 percent. Likewise, while there were 85 executions in 2000, the number of executions fell to 53 in 2006. In 2004, the number of inmates who were put on death row (128) was the lowest since 1973. This was the third consecutive year such admissions had declined. Of the inmates in prison under sentence of death, 56 percent were white and 42 percent were African American. Of the inmates whose ethnicity was known, 13 percent were Hispanic.

170. Since 2000, three federal offenders have been executed: Timothy McVeigh in 2001 (for multiple offenses arising out of the 19 April 1995 bombing of the Alfred P. Murrah Federal Building in Oklahoma City, and the resulting deaths of 168 victims); Juan Raul Garza in 2001 (for numerous offenses, including three murders while engaged in and in furtherance of a continuing criminal enterprise); and Louis Jones in 2003 (for kidnapping and killing a 19-year old private in the United States Army). In 2006, 53 executions were carried out by the states, as follows: Texas executed 24 inmates; Ohio executed five; Florida, North Carolina, Oklahoma and Virginia executed four each; and Indiana, Alabama, Mississippi, South Carolina, Tennessee, California, Montana, and Nevada executed one each.

171. Prisons. The Bureau of Prisons (BOP) operates 114 federal correctional facilities throughout the United States, including 21 penitentiaries, 68 correctional institutions, 6 independent prison camps, 12 detention centers, and 6 medical referral centers. Under U.S. regulations, 28 C.F.R., Part 551.90, federal inmates may not be discriminated against on the basis of race, religious, nationality, sex, disability, or political belief. When problems arise or allegations are raised regarding misconduct, several responses may ensue. First, the Attorney General may initiate an investigation, conducted by the DOJ Office of Inspector General (OIG). In addition, the BOP may investigate allegations of staff misconduct internally through its Office of Internal Affairs, and a separate branch of the Department of Justice may become involved if there is reason to believe that prisoners' rights are being violated. The U.S. Congress may also initiate an investigation of BOP operations where problems are brought to their attention, and federal courts may also be called on to resolve problems.

172. For example, in December 2003, the OIG issued a report concerning allegations that some correctional officers at the BOP Metropolitan Detention (MDC) in Brooklyn, New York, had physically and verbally abused individuals detained after the 9/11 attacks. The report concluded that the evidence substantiated allegations of abuse by some MDC officers of some detainees, and the OIG recommended that the BOP discipline certain employees. The report found evidence that some officers had slammed detainees against the wall, twisted their arms and hands in painful ways, stepped on their leg restraint chains, punished them by keeping them restrained for long periods, and verbally abused some detainees. In addition, in some cases, MDC videotaped detainees' meetings with their attorneys, violating federal regulation and BOP policy. As a result of the OIG's findings, the BOP initiated an investigation, which sustained many of the OIG's findings

and resulted in disciplinary action, including removal of two employees, demotion of three employees, and suspensions of various lengths of eight employees.

173. In addition to BOP oversight of federal prisons, the Department of Justice has jurisdiction to investigate institutional conditions and to bring civil lawsuits against state and local governments for a pattern or practice of egregious or flagrant unlawful conditions in state and local prison facilities, pursuant to the Civil Rights of Institutionalized Persons Act (CRIPA), 42 U.S.C. 1997. The Civil Rights Division also investigates conditions in state prisons and local jail facilities pursuant to CRIPA, and investigates conditions in state and local juvenile detention facilities pursuant to either CRIPA and/or Section 14141. These statutes allow the Department to bring legal actions for declaratory or equitable relief for a pattern or practice of unconstitutional conditions of confinement.

174. When the Civil Rights Division uncovers unconstitutional conditions at prisons, jails, or juvenile detention facilities, it works with local and state authorities to remedy these conditions. Specifically, the Department of Justice utilizes subject matter consultants to develop remedial measures tailored to the identified problems and particularities of the facility. The remedies, often memorialized in negotiated settlement agreements, represent constitutional remedies. Once the reforms are agreed to by the facility (assuming agreement is reachable), the Department will often work cooperatively with the jurisdiction to jointly select a monitor to ensure implementation. A hallmark of the Department's approach is transparency. For instance, the Civil Rights Division ensures that the jurisdiction is fully apprised of problems through the use of exit interviews during each on-site visit and, when appropriate, immediate notification to the jurisdictions of life-threatening conditions.

175. Since the Initial U.S. Report, the Civil Rights Division has used CRIPA and other statutes to prosecute allegations of torture, cruel, inhuman, and degrading treatment or punishment, or other abuse. In particular, since January 20, 2001, the Division has opened 69 CRIPA investigations, issued 53 findings letters, filed 22 cases, and obtained 53 settlement agreements. (These figures cover institutions including nursing homes, mental health facilities, facilities for persons with developmental disabilities, jails, prisons, and juvenile justice facilities.) In fiscal year 2006 alone, the Civil Rights Division conducted over 123 investigatory and compliance tours and handled CRIPA matters and cases involving over 175 facilities in 34 states, the District of Columbia, the Commonwealths of Puerto Rico and the Northern Mariana Islands, and the Territories of Guam and the Virgin Islands. In addition, the Civil Rights Division continued its investigations of 77 facilities and monitored the implementation of consent decrees, settlement agreements, memoranda of understanding, and court orders involving 99 facilities.

176. The monitoring of compliance with CRIPA settlement agreements concerning juvenile facilities included: 30 facilities in Georgia, one in New Jersey, 13 in Puerto Rico, one in the Commonwealth of the Northern Mariana Islands, one in Louisiana, one in Arkansas, three in California, two in Mississippi, one in Hawaii, two in Indiana, one in Nevada, one in Michigan, and two in Arizona. The Division's monitoring of compliance with regard to jails included: four in the Northern Mariana Islands, two in Guam, two in Mississippi, two in Georgia, one in Tennessee, one in Kentucky, one in Oklahoma, one in New Mexico, one in New York, eight in Los Angeles, California and one in Maryland. Finally, monitoring with regard to prisons included one in Guam, one in the Virgin Islands, one in the Northern Mariana Islands, and two in Arkansas. As a result of the Division's CRIPA efforts, institutionalized persons who were living in dire, often life-threatening conditions now receive adequate care and services.

177. In undertaking CRIPA investigations, the Department of Justice receives and acts on complaints from numerous sources. During 2006, for example, it received 4,841 CRIPA-related citizen letters and hundreds of CRIPA-related telephone complaints from sources such as: individuals who live at the facilities and their relatives, former staff of facilities, advocates, concerned citizens, media reports, and referrals from within the Division and other federal agencies. In addition, in 2006 the Division responded to approximately 81 CRIPA-related inquiries from Congress and the White House.

178. As noted above, CRIPA also gives the Department of Justice jurisdiction to investigate institutional conditions and to bring civil lawsuits against state and local governments for a pattern or practice of egregious or flagrant unlawful conditions—including allegations of discriminatory inmate segregation or housing policies. In this vein, the Department has recently reviewed the policies and procedures of one state department of correction in which it was alleged that inmates were being segregated based purely on race, and had little or no chance of being housed with inmates of a different race. The Civil Rights Division provided expert technical assistance to the jurisdiction by reviewing the policies and procedures at issue, and is in the process

of working with the jurisdiction to develop a housing assignment policy that is more consistent with the mandates announced in *Johnson v. California*, 543 U.S. 499 (2005) (holding that racial segregation of prison inmates is a form of racial classification that must be judged by the rigorous constitutional standard of "strict scrutiny," i.e., that prison systems must prove that such policies are designed to further a compelling governmental interest and that they are narrowly tailored to meet that interest).

179. New employees working in the field at correctional facilities receive Institution Familiarization (IF) Training, as well as training through the Staff Training Academy (STA), located at the Federal Law Enforcement Training Center. In IF training, emphasis is placed on treating inmates with respect and in a fair, consistent, and appropriate manner. STA provides entry level knowledge and skills to new correctional staff through a three-week course. Attendance at this course is required for all new institution employees within 60 days of employment. Annual refresher training includes discussions regarding ethics and standards of conduct, the importance of diversity management to the Bureau's mission, and other safety and security issues. The Bureau also trains private contractors on matters such as diversity management, respect for inmate rights and privacy, appropriate communication and interaction, and in some cases, the employee code of conduct. The Director has taken an active role in such training. Where correctional facilities are privately operated, such contractors are required to develop and implement comprehensive training programs for their staffs to be provided during employee orientation and then on an annual basis as part of the facility's in-service training plan.

B. The right to security of person and protection by the State against violence or bodily harm, whether inflicted by government officials or by an individual group or institution.

180. Article 5 (b) obligates States parties to provide equal protection against violence and bodily harm, whether inflicted by governmental officials or by individuals, groups, or institutions. The United States Constitution and laws provide such protection through statutes such as the Violent Crime Control and Law Enforcement Act of 1994, the Civil Rights Acts, and Federal "hate crimes" laws. The law in this area has not changed since 2000. In addition, 47 U.S. states also administer state laws prohibiting similar activity.

181. Racially-motivated Crimes. Through its Uniform Crime Reporting Program, the Federal Bureau of Investigation (FBI) collects hate crimes statistics including both federal and state crimes. In 2005, the most recent year for which statistics are available, 2,037 law enforcement agencies reported the occurrence of 7,163 hate crime incidents involving 8,380 offenses. These included 7,160 single-bias incidents (54.7 percent motivated by racial bias and 13.2 percent motivated by ethnicity/national origin bias). Of the offenses involved in these incidents, 68.2 percent resulted from anti-African American bias, and 19.9 percent were due to anti-White bias. Slightly less than 5 percent of racially motivated offenses were driven by anti-Asian or Pacific Islander bias, 2 percent involved bias against American Indians or Alaskan Natives, and 4.9 percent were directed at groups of individuals in which more than one race was represented.

182. Law enforcement agencies classify hate crimes motivated by ethnic or national origin bias into one of two categories—anti-Hispanic or anti-other ethnicity/national origin. In 2005, agencies reported 1,144 offenses involving single-bias incidents motivated by ethnicity or national origin. Of these offenses, 57.7 percent were motivated by anti-Hispanic bias, and 42.3 percent were directed against other ethnicities or national origins.

183. While the highest proportion of hate crime offenses involved intimidation, destruction, damage, or vandalism, a number of more serious offenses, such as murders, rapes, robberies, and arsons were also represented. Of the six reported bias-motivated murders, three resulted from racial bias—one anti-White and two anti-African American. Of the three forcible rapes, one was anti-African American. Of the 127 bias-motivated robberies, 61 involved racial bias, and 29 involved bias against ethnicity or national origin.

184. An examination of racially-motivated crimes by victim type shows that nearly 68 percent of the victims were the object of anti-African American bias. Slightly less than 20 percent were victims of anti-White bias, 4.9 percent were victims of anti-Asian or Pacific Islander bias, and 1.9 percent were victims of anti-American Indian or Alaska Native bias. Ethnically motivated crimes break down as follows: 58.7 percent of the victims were victimized because of anti-Hispanic bias, while 41.2 percent were victimized because of bias against other ethnicities or national origins.

185. In 2005, the states with the highest numbers of hate crimes were California (19.2 percent of total); New Jersey (9 percent); Michigan (8.8 percent); Massachusetts (5.4 percent), and Texas (3.7 percent).

186. Prosecution of hate crimes is a high priority for the Department of Justice. Since 2000, approximately 240 defendants have been charged by federal authorities in connection with crimes such as cross-burnings, arson, vandalism, shootings, and assault for interfering with various federally-protected rights

(e.g., housing, employment, education, and public accommodation) of African American, Hispanic, Asian, Native American, and Jewish victims. Since 1993, virtually all defendants charged in these cases have been convicted.

187. After 9/11, bias crimes against those perceived to be Muslim or Arab rose sharply. In the three months after 9/11, there were more than 300 such crimes. In 2002 through 2004 there was an average of 100 such crimes per year. Since 2004, however, the number of such crimes has steadily decreased, with 83 in 2005 and 46 in 2006. While such crimes have thus decreased significantly since immediately after 9/11, they are still above pre-9/11 levels.

188. Overall, since 2000 the Department of Justice has investigated more than 700 such crimes, resulting in more than 150 state and local prosecutions, as well as the conviction of 32 defendants. Several experienced attorneys in the Civil Rights Division's Criminal Section have been tasked to review all new allegations involving crimes against Arab Americans and those believed to be of Arab ancestry, and to monitor or participate in investigations to ensure uniform decision-making. A few examples of the types of federal prosecutions brought for crimes against Arab Americans and others are provided here. The defendants charged in these bias crimes have received lengthy prison sentences. For example, in *U.S. v. Irving* (C.D. Cal.), the defendant plotted to bomb a mosque in Los Angeles, California, and the offices of the Muslim Public Affairs Council. The defendant pled guilty to violations of 18 U.S.C. 241 and 18 U.S.C. 844; he was sentenced to 20 years in prison on September 22, 2005. In *U.S. v. Burdick* (E.D. Cal.), the defendant shot a Sikh postal carrier with a pellet gun, and pled guilty to violating 18 U.S.C. 111(a)(1). The defendant was sentenced to 70 months in prison on September 17, 2003. Other examples are *U.S. v. Goldstein* (M.D. Fla.) (defendant conspired to destroy mosques and Islamic centers, and was sentenced to 151 months in prison); *U.S. v. Nunez-Flores* (W.D. Tex) (defendant threw a Molotov cocktail at the Islamic Center of El Paso, Texas, and was sentenced to 171 months in prison); and *U.S. v. Cunningham* (W.D. Wash.) (defendant tried to set fire to cars in a mosque parking lot and fired at worshippers, and was sentenced to 78 months in prison).

189. The Community Relations Service (CRS) of the U.S. Department of Justice is available to state and local jurisdictions to help prevent and resolve racial and ethnic conflict and violence, including hate crimes. From years of experience on a wide range of cases, CRS has developed a set of "best practices" to assist localities in preventing hate crimes and restoring harmony in communities. A few specific examples of CRS hate crimes cases follow:

• In Anchorage, Alaska, after White youths videotaped themselves shooting Alaska Natives with paint balls, CRS worked with community groups, citizens, and state and local officials to calm community concerns. CRS trained Anchorage Police Department Academy recruits to increase their sensitivity when interacting with people of color, and provided officers with conflict resolution skills. Participants were also provided strategies to strengthen government-minority community relations and methods to prevent and reduce racial tensions.

• In Modesto, California, an interracial couple reported a firebomb thrown through their bedroom window. At the request of educators, public officials, law enforcement officers, and community leaders, CRS assisted in developing a community response mechanism for responding to hate crimes to address community concerns.

• With regard to church burnings, CRS staff members have worked directly with hundreds of rural, suburban, and urban governments to help eliminate racial distrust and polarization, promote multiracial programs, conduct race relations training for community leaders and law enforcement officers, conduct community dialogues, and provide assistance to bring together law enforcement agencies and members of minority neighborhoods.

190. Immediately following the 9/11 attacks, the Community Relations Service began assessing community racial and ethnic tensions in communities with concentrations of Arab, Muslim, and South Asian populations. CRS contacted local police departments, school districts, colleges and universities, city and state governments, Muslim and Arab American groups, and civil rights organizations. As reports of violence against Arabs, Muslims, and Sikhs in the U.S. intensified, CRS deployed its staff to promote tolerance. Many forums were held for Arab, Muslim, and Sikh community members to provide information, education, and resources, and to identify and discuss the various laws and enforcement agencies that serve their communities and how each could be of assistance. Among CRS's activities was the presentation of the Arab, Muslim, and Sikh Awareness and Protocol Seminar—a series of educational law enforcement protocols for federal, state, and local officials addressing racial and cultural conflict issues between law enforcement and Arab American, Muslim American,

and Sikh American communities. As noted above, CRS also created a law enforcement roll-call video entitled "The First Three to Five Seconds," which has helped police officers reduce tension by differentiating between threats and cultural norms in non-crisis situations involving Arabs, Muslims, and Sikhs.

191. CRS has also responded to reports of vandalism and arson involving mosques and Sikh gurdwaras. For example, on July 14, 2003, CRS responded to televised news reports of a fire at a mosque in Elizabeth, New Jersey. While the police reported that the fire was not arson, it resulted in increased fears among the local Muslim community. CRS provided assistance to the community and the media to address rumors that the fire was a bias incident. CRS helped local Islamic leaders plan a community forum, which allowed community members to express their concerns and receive reassurance from their local community leaders and officials.

192. State Activity Concerning Hate Crimes. As noted above, 47 states have hate crimes laws. In addition, organizations to combat such crimes exist in a number of states—for example, the Oregon Coalition against Hate Crimes, the North Carolina Hate Violence Information Network (HAVIN), the North Florida Hate Crimes Working Group, the Michigan Alliance against Hate Crimes, the Illinois Governor's Commission on Discrimination and Hate Crimes, the Pennsylvania Inter-Agency Task Force on Civil Tension, and the Kentucky Hate Crimes Advisory Group. The Michigan Alliance against Hate Crimes (a partnership between the Michigan Civil Rights Commission and Department, and the U.S. Attorneys for Michigan) brings together a coalition of more than 70 federal, state and local law enforcement agencies, civil and human rights organizations, community and faith-based groups, educators, victims support groups, and anti-violence advocates to ensure complete and effective response to hate crimes and bias incidents.

193. In Maryland, which publishes statistics on state hate crimes, there were 374 hate incident cases in fiscal year 2005, including 32 race-related incidents in the Maryland public school system, and six race-related incidents in colleges and universities. Race and ethnicity accounted for over 70 percent of the hate crimes cases processed during the year. In one Maryland civil case, *MCHR v. Elton Smith, Jr.*, an African American defendant, who harassed an interracial couple in the neighborhood, was ordered to pay damages of more than $3,500 and a civil penalty of $5,000, plus interest.

194. In Illinois, which also publishes statistics, there were 272 hate incidents in 2003, compared to 230 in the preceding year. Approximately 55 percent of the hate incidents were motivated by racial bias.

195. Pennsylvania's Human Relations Commission compiles a Bias Incident Data Base for use in both preventing and responding to civil tension. That data base, which is compiled by bias-motivation, is quite detailed, including information on the nature and location of each incident as well as on the parties involved. For the year 2006, the data base shows 162 bias incidents—66 anti-African American, 29 anti-Hispanic, 3 anti-Asian-Pacific Islander, 6 anti-Arab American, 2 anti-White, and 56 multi-racial. The data base is shared with and used by the member agencies of the Pennsylvania Inter-Agency Task Force on Civil Tension (www.stopbias.org). The Task Force is convened monthly by the Human Relations Commission to review bias-related incidents reported in the previous month. It has both short-term and longer term responsibilities. For example, it develops and assists local communities in implementing strategies for both prevention and response. It also participates in the development and presentation of numerous training initiatives for law enforcement officers, municipal officials and community leaders; enhances public awareness and effective enforcement of Pennsylvania's hate crime statute (the Ethnic Intimidation and Institutional Vandalism Act); establishes the standardized system for identifying and reporting bias-related incidents; and evaluates and recommends legislative changes. For quick response to incidents, a sub-group of the Task Force, called the Inter-Governmental Response Team, provides rapid response to schools and communities that are experiencing severe inter-group tension.

196. The Kentucky Hate Crimes Advisory Group, which includes representatives from the Office of the Attorney General, the U.S. Attorney for the Eastern and Western Districts of Kentucky, federal and state law enforcement officials, and public justice organizations, is charged with researching reported anecdotal incidents of hate violence, as well as reporting and making recommendations to the Kentucky Commission on Human Rights. In addition to local, state, and federal criminal investigations, the Commission is reviewing a recent 2006 cross-burning incident.

197. Vermont's hate crimes statutes enhance penalties for hate-motivated crimes and provide injunctive relief protection for hate crime victims. Conduct that is maliciously motivated by the victim's actual or perceived race, color, religion, national origin, and other factors is penalized based on the severity of the crime. In 2003–04, there were 56 recorded hate crimes in Vermont, of which 35 were race, ethnicity, or

national origin-based. In 2004–05, there were 34 recorded hate crimes, of which 14 were race, ethnicity, or national origin-based. Vermont-certified police officers receive mandatory training on the hate crimes statute, and the Attorney General's Civil Rights Unit and the Vermont Human Rights Commission conduct public education through school and community programs that explore diversity acceptance and awareness. In 2003, the Vermont legislature substantially amended the law regarding harassment and hazing policies for Vermont education institutions. The law prohibits harassment and hazing, and requires schools to have in place policies and procedures to address complaints in a timely manner and provide remediation. Racial harassment is defined as "conduct directed at the characteristics of a student's or a student's family member's actual or perceived race or color, and includes the use of epithets, stereotypes, racial slurs, comments, insults, derogatory remarks, gestures, threats, graffiti, display, circulation of written or visual material, taunts on manner of speech, or negative references to racial customs" (16 V.S.A. 11 (26)(B)(II)(ii)).

198. Measures to address excessive use of force by law enforcement authorities in a discriminatory manner are discussed above under Article 5—Discrimination by Law Enforcement.

C. Political rights—Information on the means for guaranteeing these rights, and on their enjoyment in practice.

199. U.S. law guarantees the right to participate equally in elections, to vote and stand for election on the basis of universal and equal suffrage, to take part in the conduct of public affairs, and to have equal access to public service. Under the Voting Rights Act, the Department of Justice brings suits in federal court to challenge voting practices or procedures that have the purpose or effect of denying equal opportunity to minority voters to elect their candidates of choice. The Department also reviews changes with respect to voting in certain specially covered jurisdictions. In July of 2006, Congress extended the Voting Rights Act for another 25-year period.

200. <u>Voting</u>. To address problems with balloting in the 2000 election, Congress passed the Help America Vote Act of 2000 (HAVA), Pub. L. No. 107-252. That legislation seeks to improve the administration of elections in the United States in three ways: (1) creation of a new federal agency, the Election Assistance Commission, to serve as a clearinghouse for election administration information; (2) provision of funds to states to improve election administration and replace outdated voting systems; and (3) creation of minimum standards for states to follow in several key areas of election administration. The Attorney General enforces the nationwide standards and requirements established by Section III of the Act. These include, for example, standards for voting systems, including alternative language accessibility; availability of provisional voting; standards for provisional voting; requirements for each state to create a single, interactive, computerized statewide voter registration list; and standards for absentee balloting.

201. The Department of Justice has pursued its enforcement responsibilities through litigation and non-litigation guidance. In 2003, after enactment of the Act, the Attorney General sent letters to the chief election officials, governors, and attorney generals in each of the 50 states, the District of Columbia, Guam, America Samoa, the U.S. Virgin Islands, and Puerto Rico describing the requirements and required timelines for compliance under HAVA and offered the Civil Rights Division's assistance in efforts to comply with the requirements of Title III. Each year, the Justice Department has also advised specific states and territories on actions needed to meet the Act's standards. In early 2004, the Justice Department sent informal advisories to six states raising specific concerns about their ability to comply with HAVA in time for the 2004 federal elections. After that round of elections in February and March of 2004, Justice also conducted a state-by-state analysis of compliance and wrote to three states raising compliance concerns noted by monitors. In 2004 and 2005, respectively, the Justice Department filed the first HAVA lawsuits against San Benito County, California and Westchester County, New York. Both suits involved the failure of poll officials to post required voter information. San Benito County also failed to have a system allowing provisional voters to find out whether their ballots were accepted and counted. Consent agreements were reached in both cases. In 2006, the Department filed lawsuits against the States of Alabama, Maine, New Jersey, and New York, and Cochise County, Arizona. As of March 2007, the Justice Department had filed one HAVA lawsuit, against Cibola County, New Mexico.

202. In addition to enforcement of HAVA, the Justice Department continues to enforce other voting legislation, including the Voting Rights Act of 1965, as amended, the Uniformed and Overseas Citizen Absentee Voting Act of 1986 (UOCAVA), and the National Voter Registration Act of 1993. The Civil Rights Division enforces the civil provisions of these laws, while the Public Integrity Section of the Criminal Division enforces the criminal misconduct and anti-fraud prohibitions. In 2006, for example, the Department

announced an agreement to protect the rights of military and overseas citizens to vote in the federal primary elections in Alabama, North Carolina, and South Carolina, and obtained emergency relief in a consent decree with the State of Connecticut to ensure that UOCAVA voters could have their ballots counted for the federal primary election.

203. In 2004, the Justice Department identified election monitoring as a high priority and requested a number of monitors greatly in excess of prior election-year totals. Those monitors received training in election-related civil rights laws including, for the first time, laws relating to protection of the rights of voters with disabilities. For the 2004 elections, the Justice Department sent 802 monitors and observers to 75 elections in 20 states (as compared with 340 monitors and observers deployed to 21 elections in 11 states pre-election in 2000). On election day itself, Justice deployed an additional 1,073 monitors and observers to watch 87 elections in 25 states (as compared with 363 monitors and observers in 20 elections in 10 states on election day in 2000). In selecting the jurisdictions to be monitored, the Department first identified 14 jurisdictions in nine states that were operating under federal court orders or decrees. The Voting Section then identified 58 additional jurisdictions for monitoring, often through outreach to minority advocates. Finally, Justice received written requests from civil rights and election organizations requesting monitoring personnel for 15 additional jurisdictions, most of which were also assigned monitors or observers. Another record was set in 2006 for the mid-term elections, with 470 federal observers and 358 Department personnel sent to monitor polling places in 69 jurisdictions in 22 states on election day. The Department again targeted jurisdictions operating under court orders or consent decrees (15 in 9 states). Another 54 jurisdictions were selected for monitoring relying, in part, on information provided by civil rights groups. In addition to the November 7 general election, the Justice Department in 2006 sent another 496 federal observers and 217 Department personnel to monitor 50 elections in 46 jurisdictions in 17 states.

204. Section 203 of the Voting Rights Act requires that all election materials and information available in English must also be available in the applicable minority language for those who need it in states and political subdivisions with specified language minority populations. This section, which is designed to ensure that citizens not only have the opportunity to vote, but also to cast informed votes, applies to ballots, instructions, and other materials. Since 2002, the Civil Rights Division has filed approximately 60 percent of all cases ever filed under these provisions in the history of the Act, including the first cases ever filed on behalf of Filipino and Vietnamese voters. Enforcement actions have involved cities and counties across the United States, including the states of Arizona, California, Florida, Massachusetts, New Mexico, New York, Pennsylvania, Texas, and Washington. Often accompanying these lawsuits have been cases under Section 208 of the Act to assure that voters who need assistance in voting have the right to receive such assistance, and to choose any person they wish—other than their employer or union official—to provide that assistance. Since 2002, the Civil Rights Division has filed over 75 percent of the cases under Section 208 ever filed in the history of the Act.

205. The Election Assistance Commission's 2005 Report to Congress on election reform progress in 2004 listed some of the changes that have occurred since the enactment of HAVA:

- 17 states have used provisional ballots for the first time;
- 1.5 million voters cast provisional ballots, and over 1 million of those were counted (68 percent);
- At least 25 percent of voters have used new voting equipment, with another 30 percent scheduled to use new equipment by 2006;
- At least nine states have developed and used a statewide voter registration database to help increase access to the polls.

206. Under section 2 of the Voting Rights Act, 42 USC 1973(b), it is unlawful to re-draw voting districts for purposes of federal elections if the re-districting results in political processes that are not as equally open to members of a racial group as they are to other members of the electorate. In *League of United Latin American Citizens v. Perry*, 126 S. Ct. 2594 (2006), the United States Supreme Court found a violation of the Voting Rights Act in one Texas congressional district, district 23, but found no violations of the Constitution or the Voting Rights Act in the remaining 31 of the state's 32 congressional districts. The Court's decision left the Texas redistricting plan largely intact and left it to the state to determine how to remedy the problem identified as to congressional district 23. The majority's decision as to district 23 was founded on a new principle, under Section 2 of the Voting Rights Act, that the creation of an offsetting majority-minority district may not remedy the loss of a majority-minority district in the same part of the state, if the new district is not compact enough to preserve communities of interest.

207. The Civil Rights Division recently has brought lawsuits challenging racially discriminatory election systems in Osceola County, Florida; Euclid, Ohio; and Port Chester, New York. The Division prevailed in the suit against Osceola County, and the other two cases remain in litigation. Other recent Section 2 lawsuits have focused on discrimination at the polls themselves. In 2005, the Justice Department filed and successfully resolved a suit against the City of Boston, Massachusetts, based on the city's discriminatory treatment of Hispanic, Chinese, and Vietnamese voters. Such treatment included denying voters needed assistance, taking voters' ballots and marking them contrary to, or without regard for, the voters' wishes, rude and abusive treatment, and denial of provisional ballots. The Division also recently brought and successfully resolved a lawsuit under Section 2 to protect Hispanic voters from having their right to vote challenged on racial grounds in *United States v. Long County, Georgia*.

208. <u>Disenfranchisement of Convicted Criminals</u>. The Fourteenth Amendment to the U.S. Constitution explicitly recognizes the right of states to bar an individual from voting "for participation in rebellion, or other crime." Accordingly, most states deny voting rights to persons who have been convicted of certain serious crimes. The standards and procedures for criminal disenfranchisement vary from state to state. In most states, this disability is terminated by the end of a term of incarceration or by the granting of pardon or restoration of rights. In all cases, the loss of voting rights does not stem from a person's membership in a racial group or on the basis of race, color, descent, or national or ethnic origin, but is based on the criminal acts perpetrated by the individual for which he or she has been duly convicted by a court of law pursuant to due process of law.

209. Criminal disenfranchisement is a matter of continuing scrutiny in the states of the United States, and changes have occurred in a number of states since 2000. In 2001, New Mexico repealed the state's lifetime voting ban for persons with felony convictions. In 2003, Alabama enacted a law that permits most felons to apply for a certificate of eligibility to register to vote after completing their sentences. In March 2005, the Nebraska legislature repealed the lifetime ban on all felons and replaced it with a two-year-post-sentence ban. In 2006, Iowa (by Executive Order) restored voting rights to persons who have completed felony sentences, and voters in Rhode Island approved a ballot measure restoring voting rights to persons released from prison on probation or parole. Policy changes that lower barriers to voting for ex-felons have also been enacted in Connecticut, Delaware, Kentucky, Maryland, Nevada, Pennsylvania, Virginia, Wyoming, and Washington.

210. In September 2005, the National Commission on Federal Election Reform, chaired by former Presidents Carter and Ford, recommended that all states restore voting rights to citizens who have fully served their sentences. While there is a lively debate within the United States on the question of voting rights for persons convicted of serious crimes pursuant to due process of law, the longstanding practice of states within the United States does not violate U.S. obligations under the Convention.

211. <u>District of Columbia</u>. The U.S. Constitution gives Congress exclusive jurisdiction over the "Seat of Government of the United States," which is the District of Columbia (D.C.). U.S. Const., art. 1 sec. 8. Because the United States was founded as a federation of formerly sovereign states, this provision was designed to avoid placing the nation's capital under the jurisdiction of any one state. Thus, the reason for this provision was governmental structure, not racial. In any case, the earliest Census population figures for the District indicate that in 1800, ten years after its legislative authorization, the District had 8,144 residents, 69.6 percent of whom were White.

212. The right of the District of Columbia to vote in elections for the President and Vice President is granted by the Twenty-third Amendment to the U.S. Constitution. D.C. residents have no representation in the Senate, but are represented in the House of Representatives by a non-voting Delegate, who sits on committees and participates in debate, but cannot vote. The issue of voting rights for the District of Columbia has been under active discussion during the last several years and is currently under consideration by Congress. In light of the requirement in Article 1, section 2 of the Constitution that the members of the House of Representatives be chosen by the people of the "States," the Administration has taken the position that congressional representation for the District would require a constitutional amendment.

213. <u>Public office</u>. Public office is open to U.S. persons without regard to race or ethnicity, and significant numbers of minorities hold positions in public office in the United States.

214. According to the 3rd edition of the American Bar Association Directory of Minority Judges in the United States, published in 2001, of the nearly 60,000 judges and judicial officers in state, federal, and tribal courts in the United States (including Puerto Rico, Guam, the Virgin Islands, and the Northern Mariana Islands), 4,051 (approximately 6.75 percent) were members of racial or ethnic minority groups. This repre-

sents a modest increase from the number of 3,610 (6 percent) in 1997. Of the 4,051 minority judges and judicial officers, 1,798 were African American, 1,523 were Hispanic, 324 were Asian, 56 were Native American (in state or federal courts), and 350 were serving in Native American tribal courts.

215. With respect to federal elected officials, of the 535 members of the 109th Congress, 41 were African American (8 percent), 24 were Hispanic (4 percent), and 7 were Asian (1 percent). These percentages show modest growth from the levels set forth in the Initial U.S. Report. Of the state and territorial governors, as of January of 2007, six were racial minorities—two Black (Massachusetts and U.S. Virgin Islands); two Hispanic (New Mexico and Puerto Rico); and two Asian and Pacific Islander (American Samoa and Guam).

216. In 2002, the Joint Center for Political and Economic Studies in Washington, D.C. released its year 2000 statistical summary of Black Elected Officials (BEOs). This report encompasses federal, state, municipal, and local officials, including those in law enforcement and education. The report shows a six-fold increase in Black elected officials from approximately 1,500 in 1970 to 9,040 in 2000. It also highlights key trends that are shaping the future of Black political leadership. First, Black women accounted for all of the growth in the number of BEOs for two years prior to 2000 and constituted 34.5 percent of the total figure. Second, younger Black Americans, who often have different views and experiences from their older counterparts, are increasingly being elected. Finally, an increasing number of Black mayors are being elected in large cities (over 50,000) where the majority of the population is not African American. According to the National Conference of Black Mayors, there were 542 Black mayors in the U.S. in 2005, including 47 Black mayors of cities with populations greater than 50,000. The Joint Center BEO report indicates that the five states with the largest number of BEOs were Mississippi (897), Alabama (731), Louisiana (701), Illinois (621), and Georgia (582).

217. In 2004, the size of the non-postal federal workforce was 1,270,366. Of this number, 31.4 percent were minority—approximately 17 percent African American (just slightly less than in 2000), 7.3 percent Hispanic (up from 6.6 percent in 2000), 5.0 percent Asian and Pacific Islander (up from 4.5 percent in 2000), and 2.1 percent American Indian and Alaska Native (slightly less than in 2000). At the highest level of the federal workforce, approximately 14 percent of members of the Senior Executive Service were minority. Likewise, of 2,786 political appointees (generally high level officials) 13 percent were minorities and 37 percent were women. As of June 2006, the President's Cabinet, which is composed of the Vice President and the heads of 15 executive departments, included two Hispanics, two African Americans, and two Asian Americans.

D. Other civil rights.

218. Article 5 (d) obligates States parties to ensure equality of enjoyment of a number of human rights and fundamental freedoms, including freedom of movement and residence; the right to leave and return to one's country; the right to a nationality; the right to marriage and choice of spouse; the right to own property alone as well as in association with others; the right to inherit; the right to freedom of thought, conscience, and religion; the right to freedom of expression; and the right to freedom of peaceful assembly and association. These rights are guaranteed to all persons in the United States in accordance with various constitutional and statutory provisions, and interference with them may be criminally prosecutable under a number of statutes. The constitutional and legal guarantees of these rights without regard to race, ethnicity, or national origin have not changed since the filing of the Initial U.S. Report in 2000.

E. Economic, social and cultural rights.

1. The right to work, and
2. The right to form and join trade unions.

219. Article 5 (e) (i) guarantees equality before the law and non-discrimination based on race, color, and national or ethnic origin, with regard to the right to work, to free choice of employment, to just and favorable conditions of work, to protection against unemployment, to equal pay for equal work, and to just and favorable remuneration. United States laws and regulations meet this requirement. Progress has been made, although disparities of results continue to exist in some areas. The sources of such disparities are complex and depend on a number of economic and social factors.

220. As of January 2007, the Bureau of Labor Statistics reported the following rates of participation in the labor force: Whites—66.6 percent; African Americans—64.7 percent, and Hispanics—69.4 percent. Unemployment rates were highest for African Americans at 8.0 percent, and lowest for Asian Americans at 3.2 percent. White Americans were unemployed at the rate of 4.1 percent, and Hispanics at the rate of 5.7 percent. The overall unemployment rate was 4.6 percent. The 1998 unemployment rates as shown in the Initial U.S. Report were 4.5 percent overall and 8.9 percent for African Americans. The Initial U.S. Report did not report 1998 statistics for the other groups.

221. The overall poverty rate in 2005 was 12.6 percent for individuals and 9.9 percent for families. The poverty rate for non-Hispanic Whites was 8.6 percent—higher than the rate of 8.2 percent reported in 1998. By contrast, the poverty rates for African Americans alone (24.9 percent) and Hispanics (21.8 percent) were slightly lower than the 1998 rates described in the Initial U.S. Report (26.1 percent for African Americans and 25.6 percent for Hispanics). The poverty rate for Asians alone was 11.1 percent, down from 14.1 percent in 1989. Using three-year average data (which are often used for smaller groups to improve the variance), the poverty rate for American Indians in 2002–2004 was 19.2 percent for the AIAN alone or in combination population and 24.3 percent for the AIAN alone population, down from 27.6 for the AIAN population in 1989. In making the comparisons to 1989, however, it should be noted that the race groups are not exactly comparable, because in earlier years respondents were instructed to report only one race, whereas after 2003 respondents could report more or more races. Thus, caution is important in viewing these comparisons.

222. According to the 2000 Census, Asian Americans who reported no other race had the highest percentage of workers employed in management, professional, and related occupations (44.6 percent). Non-Hispanic Whites had the second highest percentage of workers in this occupational group (36.6 percent). They were followed by African Americans alone (25.2 percent), American Indian and Alaska Natives alone (23.3 percent), and Native Hawaiian and other Pacific Islanders alone (23.3 percent). About 18.1 percent of Hispanics were employed in management, professional, and related occupations.

223. Twenty-two percent of African Americans alone were employed in service professions, followed by 20.8 percent of Native Hawaiian and Pacific Islanders alone, and 20.6 percent of American Indian and Alaska Natives alone. The figure for Hispanics was 21.8 percent. White non-Hispanic individuals were less represented, with only 12.8 percent of that group employed in service professions, as were Asians with a rate of 14.1 percent.

224. About 18.6 percent of African Americans reported employment in the production, transportation and material moving occupations. This percentage was higher than for people reporting any other race except the "some other race" category. Approximately one fifth (21.2 percent) of Hispanics were employed in production, transportation, and material moving occupations. By contrast, only 13.2 percent of non-Hispanic Whites were in production, transportation, and material moving.

225. Proportionately more Hispanic women than Hispanic men held managerial or professional jobs. Twenty-three percent of Hispanic women were employed in management and professional occupations, compared to 15 percent for Hispanic men. (Note that for the American population as a whole, women are also found in higher proportions in management and professional positions—36 percent for women compared to 31 percent for men.) A similar trend is seen for African Americans. In 2000, 30 percent of African American women and 20 percent of African American men were in management, professional, and related occupations. Conversely, a higher percentage of African American men (28 percent) than women (10 percent) held production, transportation, and material moving jobs.

226. The four regions of the United States did not differ greatly in distribution of occupations. In each region, the highest percentages of workers were in management, professional, and related occupations, followed by sales and office occupations. Construction, extraction, and maintenance occupations and farming, fishing, and forestry occupations had the lowest percentage of workers. The only regional differences involved service occupations and production, transportation, and material moving occupations. The percentage of workers in service occupations in the Northeast and West was higher than the percentage for production, transportation, and material moving occupations, while in the Midwest and the South, the opposite was true. The District of Columbia and Maryland had the highest percentage (51.1 percent and 41.3 percent respectively) of workers in management, professional, and related occupations, reflecting the large federal workforce and support occupations. Nevada and Hawaii—two states with large tourist industries—led all states in the percentage of workers in service occupations.

227. <u>Employment Discrimination</u>. As noted in the section concerning Article 2 (1) (b) above, the United States has strong legal protections safeguarding the right to free choice of employment and just and fair conditions of employment. Where discrimination is reported, federal and state authorities enforce these protections in areas such as training, promotion, tenure and layoff policies, and treatment in the work environment. In 2006, the EEOC received 75,768 charges. In addition, for the fiscal year 2001 to fiscal year 2006 time period, 357,087 charges were received by state and local fair employment practice agencies. This figure, however, covers only complaints that fall within both state and EEOC jurisdiction—i.e., charges of discrimination based on race, color, national origin, religion, gender, age, disability, and retaliation filed

Table 5.
Selected Occupational Groups by Race and Hispanic Origin for the United States: 2000

(Data based on a sample. For information on confidentiality protection, sampling error, nonsampling error, and definitions, see www.census.gov/prod/cen2000/doc/sf3.pdf)

Race and Hispanic or Latino Origin	Occupational groups						
	Employed civilian population 16 years and over	Management, professional, and related occupations	Service	Sales and office	Farming, fishing, and forestry	Construction, extraction, and maintenance	Production, transportation, and material moving
Total.............................	129,721,512	33.6	14.9	26.7	0.7	9.4	14.6
White alone.............................	102,324,962	35.6	13.4	27.0	0.6	9.8	13.6
Black or African American alone..........	13,001,795	25.2	22.0	27.3	0.4	6.5	18.6
American Indian and Alaska Native alone .	914,484	24.3	20.6	24.0	1.3	12.9	16.8
Asian alone.............................	4,786,782	44.6	14.1	24.0	0.3	3.6	13.4
Native Hawaiian and Other Pacific Islander alone...........................	157,119	23.3	20.8	28.8	0.9	9.6	16.5
Some other race	5,886,427	14.2	22.7	21.7	3.5	14.0	24.0
Two or more races	2,649,943	26.7	19.8	27.1	0.9	9.8	15.7
Hispanic or Latino (of any race)..........	13,347,876	18.1	21.8	23.1	2.7	13.1	21.2
White alone, not Hispanic or Latino	95,834,018	36.6	12.8	27.2	0.5	9.6	13.2

U.S. Census Bureau, Census 2000, Sample Edited Detail File.

against employers with at least 15 (or 20 for age discrimination) employees. Various state and local laws cover additional bases and/or smaller employers—charges that are not included in the above total.

228. Of the discrimination complaints filed with the EEOC in 2006, 61 percent were filed under Title VII of the Civil Rights Act, which covers discrimination based on race, color, gender, religion, and national origin; 21 percent were filed under the Americans with Disabilities Act; and 18 percent were filed under the Age Discrimination in Employment Act. Race discrimination accounted for 36 percent of all charges—following a historical trend. National origin discrimination accounted for about 11 percent of all charges. Gender discrimination accounted for 31 percent of Title VII charges.

229. Specific examples of employment discrimination cases brought by the EEOC, the Department of Justice Civil Rights Division, and the Department of Labor's Office of Federal Contract Compliance Programs are described under the discussion of Article 2 (1) (b) above. As noted, in 2006 the EEOC filed 371 lawsuits against alleged offenders and also settled a large number of complaints without going to trial. EEOC's work on these complaints obtained approximately $274.2 million for the victims of employment discrimination. Equally important is the fact that the consent agreements and court decisions resolving these cases require changes in future behavior by the offending employers. The Department of Justice's experience with respect to the resolution of complaints is similar to that of the EEOC. The majority of the cases filed by the Department of Justice are resolved through the entry of consent decrees or through other settlement before a trial on the merits is held. As with the EEOC, the Department of Justice's consent decrees normally require prospective relief in the form of modifications to an employer's employment practices, as well as monetary relief to victims of the discriminatory practice. In 2005, the Department of Labor's enforcement efforts resulted in over $45 million in remedies, offers of employment to thousands of victims of discrimination, and training designed to ensure that American employers practice equal employment opportunity in the future.

230. In April of 2006, the EEOC issued a major new Compliance Manual section updating guidance on Title VII prohibitions on discrimination in employment based on race and color. The Manual will assist employers, employees, and EEOC staff in understanding specifically how Title VII applies to a wide range of contemporary discrimination issues. It contains specific information—including examples—concerning: what constitutes race, color, and national origin discrimination; how to evaluate employment decisions; what constitutes racial disparate treatment, including how to recognize motive and cases of pattern or practice discrimination; how to assess cases of racial disparate impact; how to ensure equal access to jobs in recruiting, hiring and promotion, diversity and affirmative action; how to ensure equal opportunity for job success, including material on racial harassment and racial bias in the workplace; retaliation; remedies; and protective prevention. This new guidance reflects the strong interest of the Equal Employment Opportunity

Commission in proactive prevention and best practices. A copy of the Manual section can be found at www. eeoc.gov under Race/Color Discrimination.

231. In addition to enforcement by the EEOC, Justice, and the states, the Department of Labor enforces laws that prohibit federal contractors and subcontractors from discriminating on the basis of race, color, religion, sex, national origin, or status as a protected veteran or qualified individual with a disability. The Department employs several strategies, including civil rights enforcement, public education, and strategic partnerships. The Labor Department also promotes training of workers with limited English proficiency.

232. As noted above, most states also enforce state fair employment laws through their state civil rights commissions or Attorney General's offices. In most states, the great majority of discrimination complaints involve employment discrimination, many of which are filed in accordance with state–EEOC work sharing agreements. For example, Oregon enforces laws granting job seekers and employees equal access to jobs, career schools, promotions, and a work environment free from discrimination and harassment. Oregon state law also ensures workers protection when they report worksite safety violations, use family leave provisions, or use the workers compensation system. Of an average of 2,100 discrimination complaints filed annually in Oregon, approximately 98 percent allege unfair employment practices. Likewise, in Florida, 91 percent of the case inventory for the Florida Commission on Human Relations and 88 percent of the complaints received in fiscal year 2004–05 involved employment discrimination. Finally, many U.S. counties and cities also have fair employment practice agencies that receive and process charges of discrimination under work sharing agreements with the EEOC.

233. In December of 2005, the Gallup organization released a national poll on discrimination in the contemporary workplace, conducted in conjunction with the 40th anniversary of the EEOC. That poll suggested that while much progress has been made in fulfilling the promise of equal opportunity, more remains to be done. The survey sampled American workers of varying racial and ethnic backgrounds, asking them about their perceptions of discrimination at work and the effect those perceptions had on performance and retention. Results showed that 15 percent of all workers perceived that they had been subjected to some sort of discriminatory or unfair treatment. When broken down into sub-groups, 31 percent of Asians surveyed reported incidents of discrimination—the largest percentage of any ethnic group. This contrasts markedly with the fact that only about 3 percent of claims were brought by Asians—suggesting that a number of Asian persons who perceive discrimination nonetheless do not choose to file complaints. African Americans constituted the second largest group, with 26 percent of African Americans saying they had perceived discrimination. The Gallup survey also indicated that promotion and pay were the most frequently mentioned discriminatory actions, although the overwhelming number of charges filed with the EEOC allege discriminatory discharge.

234. While African American women and men reported that they had experienced almost identical levels of discrimination according to the poll (27 percent and 26 percent respectively), a large discrepancy existed between the perceptions of discrimination of White women (22 percent) versus White men (3 percent). The overall rate of perceived discrimination for persons identified as Hispanic was 18 percent, with Hispanic men more likely to perceive discrimination (20 percent) when compared with Hispanic women (15 percent). Commenting on the contrast between the Gallup findings and the number of discrimination complaints made to the EEOC, former EEOC Chair Cari Dominguez noted: "When you compare our most recent EEOC charge statistics with the Gallup data, we find that a far greater percentage of Hispanics and Asians perceive themselves to be discriminated against than actually file charges. Through the continuation of strong enforcement and targeted outreach and education, the EEOC is striving to ensure that the promise of the Civil Rights Act of 40 years ago will continue to be fulfilled for succeeding generations of American workers."

235. Minority-owned Businesses. According to the Small Business Administration's advocacy office, minority-owned firms represent the fastest-growing segment of the nation's economy. Asians are the largest sector of minority business owners in terms of both number of businesses and employees. However, Hispanics and African Americans are starting businesses at higher rates. For example, a recent report issued by the U.S. Census Bureau indicates that Hispanics in the United States are opening businesses at a rate three times the national average. From 1997 to 2002, the number of Hispanic-owned firms grew by 31.1 percent, compared to a 10.3 percent growth rate for U.S. firms overall.

236. African American-owned businesses in the United States grew even faster, at more than four times the national rate. From 1997 to 2002, African American-owned firms grew by 45 percent, from 823,499 to nearly 1.2 million. Growth was seen in all states except Wyoming, North Dakota, South Dakota, and

Oregon. Some metropolitan areas, such as those surrounding Washington, D.C., experienced levels of growth of well over 80 percent.

237. Private Sector Initiatives. Due to shortages of candidates for skilled technology jobs in the United States, a number of private entities have also initiated diversity outreach efforts. The Congressionally established Commission on the Advancement of Women and Minorities in Science, Engineering, and Technology Development issued a report in September 2000 that found: "If women, underrepresented minorities, and persons with disabilities were represented in the U.S. science, engineering and technology workforce in parity with their percentages in the total workforce population, the shortage [of skilled technology workers] could largely be ameliorated." One example of a private sector initiative in this area is the Professional Technical Diversity Network, a partnership formed by Microsoft, other corporations, and minority professional organizations that focuses on recruitment in technical disciplines. Among other programs, the partnership works with schools and organizations to increase technology training and educational opportunities for women and minorities. As announced in November of 2000, its efforts included:

• More than $90 million in grants, software, and scholarships to colleges and universities serving African American, Hispanic, and Native American populations;

• $6 million in grants to the Minority and Women's Technical Scholarship program;

• Working Connections, a $40 million effort to help disadvantaged persons prepare for information technology jobs at community colleges;

• The Able to Work Consortium, dedicated to increasing employment opportunities for people with disabilities.

238. Protection of U.S. Citizens and Legal Immigrants from Employment Discrimination on the Basis of National Origin. The Department of Justice's Office of Special Counsel for Immigration Related Unfair Employment Practices (OSC) enforces the anti-discrimination provision of the Immigration and Nationality Act, 8 U.S.C. 1324b, which protects U.S. citizens and legal immigrants from employment discrimination based, among other things, on national origin; from unfair documentary practices relating to the employment eligibility verification process ("document abuse"); and from retaliation. Individuals may file charges of discrimination with OSC and the OSC may also commence investigations on its own initiative. The OSC investigates allegations of discrimination and obtains monetary, job, and injunctive relief through settlement or suit for discrimination, document abuse, and retaliation engaged in by employers of four or more employees. Its jurisdiction over national origin discrimination extends to employers with four to fourteen employees (larger employers are handled by the EEOC).

239. A few examples of recent OSC settlements include back pay totaling $22,654 for four refugees, plus $14,000 in civil penalties and injunctive relief to remedy document discrimination; $12,000 in back pay for an asylee who was terminated because a company refused to accept valid documents he presented to re-verify his employment eligibility; and $11,653 in back pay, plus a civil penalty and injunctive relief, for a permanent resident whose valid documents were unfairly rejected during the hiring process. Also, through its worker and employer hotlines, and OSC routinely brings early, cost-effective resolutions to employment disputes that might otherwise result in the filing of charges, the accumulation of back pay awards, and investigation and litigation expenses. In addition, OSC conducts outreach to educate employers and workers about their rights and responsibilities under the anti-discrimination provision. OSC's educational activities include its fully staffed hotlines; a grant program; distribution of free educational materials; presentations at conferences, seminars, and meetings; a website; and a newsletter. In fiscal year 2006, OSC awarded grants totaling nearly $725,000 to eleven non-profit groups throughout the country. The grant program funds public education programs regarding workers' rights and employers' obligations under the anti-discrimination provision, and is open to public service groups, faith-based and community organizations, associations, and others providing information services to employers and/or potential victims of immigration-related employment discrimination.

240. In addition, the interagency Worker Exploitation Task Force described in the Initial U.S. Report has been expanded to become the Trafficking in Persons and Worker Exploitation Task Force (TPWETF). It continues its efforts to prevent trafficking in persons and worker exploitation throughout the United States, and to enforce laws enacted to combat human trafficking. The TPWETF is co-chaired by the Assistant Attorney General for Civil Rights and the Solicitor of the Department of Labor. Other participants include the Federal Bureau of Investigation, the U.S. Citizenship and Immigration Services, the Executive Office for United States Attorneys, the Justice Department Criminal Division, and the Office of Victims of Crime and the Violence against Women Office. The Task Force also works in coordination with the Department of

State, the Department of Homeland Security, the EEOC, and various United States Attorneys Offices across the country.

241. Data released in 2006 show that in 2005 the jobless rate among immigrants fell below that of U.S.-born workers for the first time in at least a decade. Unemployment among immigrants was 4.6 percent in 2005, down from 5.5 percent in 2004, while the jobless rate among native-born Americans was 5.2 percent, down from 5.5 percent. This contrasts with every other year since 1996, when joblessness among immigrants has been as high or higher than that of native-born Americans. The survey data, compiled by the Labor Department's Bureau of Labor Statistics, include immigrants who arrived in the United States both legally and illegally, and do not distinguish between the two.

242. Unions. As noted in the Initial U.S. Report, U.S. law guarantees all persons equal rights to form and join trade unions. The U.S. Department of Labor also enforces portions of the Labor-Management Reporting and Disclosure Act (LMRDA), which guarantees union members certain rights, such as the right to freedom of speech and assembly, the right to have democratically conducted elections, and the right to be free from violence or coercion while exercising any of their rights under the LMRDA. The LMRDA provides for a private right of action regarding freedom of speech and assembly. The right to form and join trade unions is protected by both the U.S. Constitution (First Amendment) and by statute (e.g., the National Labor Relations Act). In addition, some state constitutions and statutes also protect the right to freedom of association.

1. The right to housing

243. Federal and state laws guarantee a right to equal opportunities in housing and prohibit discriminatory practices in the sale and rental of housing as well as in the mortgage lending and insurance markets related to housing. The rights to housing and mortgage financing without discrimination are enjoyed in practice throughout the United States, and where violations of these rights occur, federal and state authorities prosecute the offenders. A description of this enforcement, and examples of some of the cases brought by the Departments of Justice and HUD since 2000, are set forth in the section on Article 2 (1) (b) above.

244. In 2000, approximately 66 percent of occupied housing units were owned by their occupants, while approximately 34 percent of housing units were rented. The home ownership rate for American Indian and Alaska Native alone-occupied housing units was 56 percent, and for Asian Americans alone, 53 percent. By contrast, African American alone, Native Hawaiian and Pacific Islander alone, and Hispanic householders were more likely than all householders to rent rather than own homes. Among these three groups, 46 percent lived in owner-occupied dwellings, while 54 percent lived in renter-occupied housing units.

245. In 2000 the median value for single-family homes in the United States overall was $119,600. The median value for homes owned by Asian Americans alone was $199,300—more than 50 percent higher than the national median. A large number of these households (45 percent) were located in Hawaii or California—states that recorded the highest median home values. Native Hawaiian and Pacific Islander alone homeowners also had median home values considerably higher than the national estimate ($160,500)—also likely due to concentration in areas of high home values. By contrast, homes owned by African Americans alone or American Indians and Alaska Natives alone had median values of about $81,000—one third below the national median. Median home value for the White non-Hispanic population was $123,400—just slightly above the national median; and median home value for the Hispanic population was $105,600—somewhat below the national median.

246. In addition to prosecution of cases concerning housing and mortgage discrimination, the Administration has a number of programs designed to improve housing availability to racial and ethnic minorities. Following up on President Bush's 2002 announcement that the Administration would work with Congress to achieve broader home ownership, especially among minorities, HUD announced a Minority Housing Initiative that includes: (1) preventing housing discrimination through education, outreach, and enforcement of fair housing laws; (2) promptly resolving housing complaints and reducing the backlog of cases; (3) unlocking the potential of faith-based community organizations to expand homeownership opportunities for low income minority persons; (4) directing resources and attention to unfair and discriminatory practices in the Colonias and farmworker communities; and (5) vigorously enforcing against predatory lenders. In addition, each year HUD provides grants to fair housing groups at state and local levels to assist in the fight against illegal housing discrimination. The funds are to be used to investigate allegations of housing discrimination, to educate the public and housing industry concerning housing discrimination laws, and to work to promote fair housing. Since 2000, these grants have normally been in the range of $17 to $20 million per year, and have been provided to approximately 100 state and local fair housing entities each year. Some of the grants are also designated for projects serving rural and immigrant populations in areas without a fair

housing organization or that are otherwise under-served. HUD has also created the Fair Housing Initiatives Program Performance Based Funding Component (PBFC) to help support exceptional private organizations in conducting long-term investigations of the housing or lending market for evidence of systemic discrimination. This program offers three-year grants of up to $275,000 per year, based on appropriations, to private organizations with proven records in addressing such problems.

247. In addition, in fiscal year 2005, HUD's newly-established Office of Systemic Investigations (OSI) conducted a number of investigations of discriminatory practices that have potentially nationwide impact or otherwise affect large numbers of persons. These included: (1) a Title VI compliance review of the Bay St. Louis Housing Authority in Mississippi in response to allegations of racial steering and segregation; (2) an investigation of a major insurance company in New York, in response to a complaint that the company offered different policies with lesser coverage to minority homeowners; and (3) an investigation of a nationwide management company, its owners, and the City of Gainesville, Florida in response to alleged discrimination in the maintenance of a federally-assisted property. Also during 2005, HUD's Office of Education and Outreach (OEO) conducted more than 400 outreach activities throughout the United States, and issued two publications: "Are you a Victim of Housing Discrimination" and "Equal Opportunity for All." These brochures are available in English, Spanish, Chinese, Vietnamese, Korean, and Arabic.

248. In 2003, the Bush Administration also announced $1.27 billion in homeless assistance, to fund 3,700 local housing and service programs around the country. As part of this initiative, former HHS Secretary Tommy G. Thompson, then-Chair of the Interagency Council on Homelessness, awarded nearly $35 million to help meet the goal of ending chronic homelessness within a decade. With the Secretary of HUD and the Secretary of the U.S. Department of Veterans Affairs (DVA) joined as co-sponsors, the initiative included investments of $20 million from HUD, $10 million from HHS, and $5 million from the DVA. This initiative is a collaborative effort among 20 federal agencies and departments, aimed at helping local communities address the special housing and service needs of homeless persons, many of whom have mental illness, substance dependence or abuse, and physical disabilities. While the initiative is not aimed specifically at racial or ethnic minorities, it will assist such persons who fall in the category of the chronically homeless.

249. HUD is also pursuing an initiative to improve access to housing services for persons with limited English proficiency (LEP) (see Executive Order 13166, issued August 11, 2000). This initiative recognizes that the federal government provides an array of services that could be made accessible to persons who are not proficient in the English language. The Executive Order calls on each federal agency to examine the services it provides and to develop and implement systems by which LEP persons can meaningfully access those services. Agencies are also to ensure that private recipients of federal financial assistance provide meaningful access to LEP recipients. Among other actions, HUD has published guidance to Federal Financial Assistance Recipients with regard to the Title VI prohibition against national origin discrimination affecting LEP persons.

250. Recognizing that Native Americans experience some of the worst housing conditions in the nation and that population growth among Native Americans has increased the need for federal housing services, Congress enacted the Native American Housing Enhancement Act of 2005, P.L. 109-136. The purpose of this act is to allow Indian tribes to leverage other federal and private funds to achieve better housing. Among other things, the act amends the law to permit Indian preference under existing housing acts, such as the Housing Act of 1949. It also makes available to Indians Youth Build grants for housing under the Cranston-Gonzales National Affordable Housing Act, 42 U.S.C. 12899f.

251. Most states also handle housing discrimination complaints. For example, in fiscal year 2005, 5 percent of the case inventory and 16 percent of the new complaints filed with the Florida Commission on Human Relations involved housing. In 2004, 5 percent of the charges docketed by the Illinois Department of Human Rights involved housing; and in 2005, 6.1 percent of the requests for service received by the Michigan Department of Civil Rights involved housing discrimination.

252. As noted above, a number of states, counties, and cities participate in HUD's Fair Housing Assistance Program (FHAP), under which HUD funds them to investigate and manage some complaints that involve violations of state and federal laws. In fiscal year 2005, HUD and the Fair Housing Assistance Program agencies, together, received 9,254 complaints—approximately the same number as in fiscal year 2004. Of these, the FHAP agencies investigated 70 percent. Race accounted for approximately 40 percent of the complaints, and national origin discrimination (primarily Hispanic) accounted for approximately 9 percent of the complaints. HUD's Fair Housing Initiatives Program (FHIP) includes an Asian and Pacific Islander Fair Housing Awareness Component, designed to educate Asian and Pacific Islander communities on their rights, and to

carry out fair housing studies. It also includes a Minority Serving Institution Component, which furthers HUD's goal of establishing partnerships with Tribal Colleges and Universities, Historically Black Colleges and Universities, Hispanic-serving institutions, and Native Hawaiian and Alaska Native-serving institutions. This program funds curricula for students to pursue careers in fair housing law.

253. Examples of two cases managed by states under the Fair Housing Assistance Program are set forth below:

• In Lawrence, Kansas, Ms. Morales, who is Hispanic and Irish, found an apartment for rent for herself and her boyfriend, Mr. Jackson. Despite an enthusiastic reception on her initial visit, the reception was cold when Ms. Morales returned with her African American boyfriend. They were eventually informed that their application had been rejected because they were unmarried. Thereafter, they filed complaints of housing discrimination with the Lawrence County Human Relations Commission. During the investigation, the apartment complex claimed that its policy with regard to renting to unmarried couples had changed at about the time that Ms. Morales and Mr. Jackson were looking for housing. However, at about that time, the complex had rented two apartments to unmarried White couples and continued to permit an unmarried White couple to reside there. On May 12, 2005, a jury in Douglas County District Court determined that the defendants had intentionally engaged in racial discrimination. Ms. Morales and Mr. Jackson were awarded $3,390 in actual damages and $76,000 in punitive damages. In addition, the defendant was required to pay $35,000 in attorney's fees to the Lawrence County Human Relations Commission. *Morales v. Villa 26* and *Jackson v. Villa 26*.

• Ms. Nero and her sixteen-year-old granddaughter, who are African American, sought to rent an apartment at the Carriage House Apartments in Dallas, Texas. Over the phone, Ms. Nero was quoted a rent of $625 and a security deposit of $300. When she and her granddaughter visited the property, however, the manager raised the security deposit to $650 and informed her that she would get it back if "she didn't destroy the property." Two days later when a White friend called about a similar apartment at Carriage House, he was quoted a deposit of $300, which remained at $300 even when he visited the property. The Dallas Fair Housing Office investigated the complaint and found cause to believe that discrimination had occurred. On November 3, 2005, the parties settled the complaint through a judicial consent order; Carriage House was required to pay Ms. Nero $5,000, establish a written non-discriminatory policy covering rental rates and security deposits, and require all employees who accept applications, negotiate, or set terms of rental with prospective tenants to attend fair housing training. *Nero v. Carriage House Apartments*.

254. HUD also carries out several programs designed to provide affordable housing for low-income households. For example, the HOME program provides block grants to state and local governments for construction or rehabilitation of rental units or housing for ownership, direct financial assistance to first-time or other qualified homebuyers, and assistance to rehabilitate eligible owner-occupied properties. In fiscal year 2005, 39 percent of the funding for rental units went to African Americans, 18.5 to Hispanics, 2 percent to Asian Americans, and 0.3 percent to American Indians and Alaska Natives. In the homebuyer program, 29.4 percent went to African Americans, 30.7 percent to Hispanics, and 1.2 percent to Asian Americans. Another program is the Housing Choice Voucher Program, designed for low and very low income families to help them lease or purchase safe, decent, and affordable housing. The beneficiaries of this program in fiscal year 2005 were 47.8 percent African American, 18 percent Hispanic, 2.75 percent Asian and less than 1 percent American Indian and Alaska Native, and Native Hawaiian and Pacific Islander.

255. Concern has been expressed about the disparate effects of Hurricane Katrina on housing for minority residents of New Orleans. Recognizing the overlap between race and poverty in the United States, many commentators conclude nonetheless that the post-Katrina issues were the result of poverty (i.e., the inability of many of the poor to evacuate) rather than racial discrimination *per se*. In providing assistance as a result of Katrina, the federal government is committed to helping all victims, and in particular those who are in the greatest need. In that regard, on February 15, 2006, the Attorney General announced a major new civil rights initiative, Operation Home Sweet Home. This fair housing initiative was inspired by victims of Hurricane Katrina, who lost their homes and were seeking new places to live. The initiative is not limited to the areas hit by Hurricane Katrina but is nationwide in scope. The Attorney General made a public commitment that over the next two years the Division would conduct a record high number of fair housing tests in order to expose housing providers who are discriminating against people trying to rent or buy homes. During fiscal year 2006, the Civil Rights Division increased by 38 percent the number of fair housing tests compared to fiscal year 2005. In addition, in the aftermath of Katrina HUD has initiated

a number of efforts to enforce against discrimination in relocation housing. Those included grants of $1.2 million to Gulf Coast Fair Housing groups for outreach to evacuees and investigation of discrimination complaints. HHS has also dedicated substantial resources to help redesign and rebuild Louisiana's health-care system to enhance health care in Louisiana.

1. The right to public health, medical care, social security and social services

256. Social Security. In the United States, social security retirement benefits are available, without regard to race or ethnicity, to all eligible persons who have worked at least 10 years. Age 65 is regarded as full retirement age for those born after 1938, although benefits may begin as early as age 62. Likewise, Medicare, a health insurance program for people age 65 or older (or under age 65 with certain disabilities) is also available without regard to race or ethnicity. In addition, Medicaid provides health insurance to low-income individuals and families of any age, also without regard to race or ethnic origin. Medicaid programs are administered by the states.

257. The new Medicare Modernization Act has significant potential to reduce racial and ethnic disparities among U.S. seniors, as Medicare will now cover preventive medicine, including screenings for heart disease, cancer, depression, and diabetes—conditions that disproportionately affect racial and ethnic minorities. Also, under the new benefits of Medicare, more than 7.8 million minority beneficiaries have access to a prescription drug benefit for the first time in Medicare's history. This program, which began in early 2006, makes available to Medicare recipients a number of plans to cut the costs of prescription drugs, and is designed to assist the elderly—particularly the elderly poor—in meeting health-care expenses. Overall, approximately 90 percent of all Medicare recipients enrolled to receive some type of prescription drug coverage. Minority populations with Medicare mirrored the overall results for coverage.

258. Health care. Notwithstanding the strong overall care provided by the U.S. health-care system, the Initial U.S. Report described a number of disparities in the prevalence of certain diseases and conditions among racial and ethnic groups, many of which continue to exist since 2000. For example, for American Indians and Alaska Natives, the prevalence of diabetes is more than twice that for all adults in the United States, and for African Americans, the age-adjusted death rate for cancer was approximately 25 percent higher than for White Americans in 2001. Disparities are also seen in women's health issues, such as infant mortality and low birth weight. Although infant mortality decreased among all races during the 1980–2000 time period, the Black-White gap in infant mortality widened. During the same period, however, the Black-White gap with regard to low birth weight infants decreased.

259. To understand such disparities better, in 1999 Congress requested the Institute of Medicine (IOM) of the National Academy of Sciences to: (1) assess the extent of racial and ethnic disparities in health-care, assuming that access-related factors, such as insurance status and the ability to pay for care, are the same; (2) identify potential sources of these disparities, including the possibility that overt or subtle biases or prejudice on the part of health-care providers might affect the quality of care for minorities; and (3) suggest intervention strategies. The IOM issued its report in March of 2002. According to the report, the vast majority of studies indicated that minorities are less likely than Whites to receive needed care, including clinically necessary procedures, in certain types of treatment areas. Disparities were found in treatment for cancer, cardiovascular disease, HIV/AIDS, diabetes, and mental illness, and were also seen across a range of procedures, including routine treatments for common health problems.

260. The study looked at possible explanations for such disparities, including subtle differences in the way members of different racial and ethnic groups respond to treatment, variations in help-seeking behavior, racial differences in preferences for treatment, cultural or linguistic barriers, the fragmentation of health-care systems, and possible unintentional bias on the part of well-intentioned health-care workers. Based on the findings, the IOM recommended a comprehensive, multi-level strategy to eliminate disparities. This would include cross-cultural education and training; policy and regulatory changes to address fragmentation of health plans along socioeconomic lines; health-system interventions to promote the use of clinical-practice guidelines; language and cultural interpretation where needed; and the collection of further data to refine the understanding of the problem.

261. HHS Secretary Michael O. Leavitt has reaffirmed his Department's commitment to eliminating racial and ethnic disparities in health care, and the Department has moved forward on a number of IOM's recommendations, including initiatives to:

• Develop a communication strategy aimed at raising awareness of racial and ethnic disparities among consumers, providers, state and local governments, and community-based and other organizations;

• Promote the collection of health data and the strengthening of data infrastructure to enable the identification and monitoring of health status among U.S. racial and ethnic minorities;

• Emphasize the centrality of patient/provider communications;

• Strengthen U.S. capacity to prepare health professionals to serve minority populations and to increase the diversity of the health-related workforce; and

• Integrate cross-cultural education into the training of all current and future health professions.

262. HHS has also made elimination of health disparities affecting racial and ethnic minority populations, including women's health issues, a critical goal of Healthy People 2010, the nation's public-health agenda for the current decade. As part of this effort, in 2001, HHS and the ABC Radio Networks launched an initiative denominated "Closing the Health Gap." This educational campaign is designed to make health an important issue among racial and ethnic minority populations. Originally launched in African American communities, the campaign was expanded in 2003 to include Hispanic Americans, American Indians and Alaska Natives, Asian Americans, and Native Hawaiians and Pacific Islanders. As part of the campaign, all 240 of ABC Radio's Urban Advantage Network affiliates have aired detailed messages to emphasize specific steps listeners can take to adopt healthier lifestyles.

263. In January 2006, HHS hosted the second National Leadership Summit for Eliminating Racial and Ethnic Disparities in Health. The conference included over 2,000 participants and featured more than 96 workshops and special institutes on current and emerging health issues in the areas of: health-care access, utilization, and quality; health care and the public workforce; research, data, and evaluation; health information technology; health disparities across the lifespan; and culture, language, and health literacy. The Summit served as a vehicle for highlighting, promoting, and applying the knowledge experience and expertise of community-based organizations and other partners across the nation toward more strategic and effective actions. The Summit also served as a launching point for the creation of a national action agenda to eliminate racial and ethnic disparities in health. Scheduled for a 2007 launch, this national action agenda is built on three key tenets: (1) national leadership and community solutions; (2) effective communications; and (3) broad-based partnerships. This national action agenda is also responsive to the 2001 IOM recommendation to increase outreach and education to assist racial and ethnic minorities in taking charge of their health and adopting health behaviors.

264. Environmental Justice. Federal agencies continue to address issues concerning the environmental impacts of activities such as the locating of transportation projects and hazardous waste clean-up projects, on certain population groups, including minority and low income populations. As required by U.S. Executive Order 12898, and informed by the National Environmental Justice Advisory Council, the Environmental Protection Agency (EPA) and other federal agencies integrate environmental justice considerations into their day-to-day decision making processes, principally through environmental impact analysis under the National Environmental Policy Act (NEPA). EPA also runs three programs designed to address environmental justice concerns. The first is the Environmental Justice Collaborative Problem-Solving Cooperative Agreements Program, which provides financial assistance to eligible community-based organizations working to address local environmental or public health concerns in their communities. The second is the Environmental Small Grant Program, which provides small grants to eligible community-based organizations for education and training programs concerning local environmental or public health issues. Finally, the Environmental Justice Community Intern Program places students in local community organizations to experience environmental protection at the grassroots level. In addition, the Federal Interagency Working Group on Environmental Justice coordinates government-wide efforts through three task forces: (1) Health disparities; (2) Revitalization Demonstration Projects; and (3) Native American. The Native American group works to protect tribal cultural resources and sacred places.

265. Analyses under the National Environmental Policy Act (NEPA) commonly address "environmental justice" in analyzing the impacts of potential federal projects on the human environment, see 40 CFR 1508.14. A number of recent federal court cases have assessed whether environmental justice was appropriately considered in proposed federal projects. These include: *Coliseum Square Ass'n v. HUD*, No. 03-30875, No. 04-30522, 206 U.S. App. LEXIS 23726 (5th Cir. Sept. 18, 2006) (upholding Department of Housing and Urban Development's consideration of environmental justice issues involving a housing development revitalization project); *Communities against Runway Expansion Inc. v. F.A.A.*, 355 F.3d 678 (D.C. Cir. 2004) (upholding environmental justice analysis of construction of a new airport runway); *Senville v. Peters*, 327 F. Supp. 2d 335 (D. Vt. 2004) (upholding environmental justice analysis prepared by Federal Highway

Administration with regard to the effects of a new highway project on low income and minority persons); and *Washington County v. Department of Navy*, 317 F. Supp. 2d 626 (E.D.N.C. 2004) (preliminarily enjoining construction of aircraft landing field) (inadequate environmental justice analysis alleged).

266. The Initial U.S. Report noted the view expressed by some that the U.S. Navy's use of Vieques Island in Puerto Rico as a bombing range was having negative environmental consequences on Puerto Ricans living on or near the island. In 2001, the Bush Administration pledged to end military activity on the island, and on May 1, 2003 the Navy withdrew from the island and transferred management of the bombing range to the U.S. Department of the Interior. After extensive clean-up, the U.S. Fish and Wildlife Service, an agency of the Department of the Interior, will turn the 6,000 hectare (15,000 acre) site into the largest wildlife refuge in Puerto Rico.

1. The right to education and training

267. *De jure* racial segregation in education has been illegal in the United States since the landmark decision in *Brown v. Board of Education*, 347 U.S. 483 (1954). As a result of that decision, the Civil Rights Act of 1964, and later cases and statutes, schools became increasingly integrated. The Department of Justice Civil Rights Division continues to monitor compliance of school districts, and initiates case reviews where deemed necessary. Since 2000, it has initiated 228 case reviews and resolved 126 cases leading to declarations of unitary status and dismissal. The issues monitored by the Civil Rights Division include student assignments, faculty hiring and assignments, the availability of equitable facilities, and the distribution of resources. Examples of cases brought by the Civil Rights Division since 2000 are described in the section on Article 2 (1) (b) above.

268. In addition to the Department of Justice, the Office for Civil Rights (OCR) within the Department of Education is the primary federal entity responsible for enforcing the federal anti-discrimination laws in the context of education. It enforces a number of laws prohibiting discrimination in institutions that receive federal financial assistance—a category that includes virtually all educational institutions in the nation, from elementary through graduate or professional schools. OCR's primary objectives are to promptly investigate complainants' allegations of discrimination, and to determine accurately whether the civil rights laws and regulations it enforces have been violated. OCR also initiates compliance reviews and other proactive initiatives to focus on specific civil rights compliance problems in education that are particularly acute or national in scope. In addition, OCR pursues compliance by federal fund recipients by promulgating regulations implementing the civil rights laws; developing clear policy guidance interpreting those laws; broadly disseminating this information in many different media, including the Internet; and providing direct technical assistance to educational institutions, parents, students, and others.

269. Signed into law in 2002, the No Child Left Behind Act of 2001 (NCLB) was designed to bring all students up to grade level in reading and math, to close the achievement gaps between students of different races and ethnicities within a decade, and to hold schools accountable for results through annual assessments. Under NCLB, states administer assessments to students in grades three to eight annually, with one additional test administered in high school. The National Center for Education Statistics in the U.S. Department of Education administers the National Assessment of Educational Progress (NAEP) to students in each state in grades four and eight, which are published as the "Nation's Report Card." The NAEP serves as an external indicator for NCLB state results in grades four and eight and as a national indicator for twelfth grade. Data from 2005 show that although achievement gaps between White and minority students continue to exist for all groups except Asians and Pacific Islanders, the gaps are beginning to narrow, even as student populations are becoming more diverse:

• Overall, fourth-grade and eighth-grade math scores rose to all-time highs, and fourth-grade reading scores match the all-time high. (On a scale of 0–500, average fourth-grade math scores rose from 213 in 1990 to 238 in 2005, and average eighth-grade scores rose from 263 in 1990 to 279 in 2005.)

• In fourth-grade math, African American students' scores rose 17 points from 2000 to 2005, reducing the achievement gap with White students by 5 points (from 31 to 26 points); likewise, scores for Hispanic students rose 18 points in the same period, reducing the gap between White and Hispanic students by 6 points (from 27 to 21 points). These were the smallest gaps since 1990. The gaps for White and American Indian students remained constant at 20 points between 2000 and 2005.

• In eighth-grade math, the achievement gap was likewise reduced by 6 points (from 40 points in 2000 to 34 points in 2005) between African American and White students, and also by four points (from 31 in 2000 to 27 points in 2005) between Hispanic and White students. Math scores for American Indian/Alaska

Native students increased at the same rate as White students during the 2003 to 2005 timeframe, causing the gap to remain the same at 25 points.

• For both fourth-grade and eighth-grade math, Asian/Pacific Islander students performed better than White students by 4 points in 2000 and 6 points in 2005.

• In 2005, in fourth- and eighth-grade math, higher percentages of White, African American, Hispanic, and Asian/Pacific Islander students performed at or above "proficient" levels as defined by NAEP than in any previous year.

• In fourth-grade reading, African American students rose 10 points from 2000 to 2005, reducing the gap with White students by 5 points (from 34 to 29 points); scores for Hispanic students rose 13 points during that same time period, reducing the gap with White students by 9 points (from 35 to 26 points). The gap between White and American Indian/Alaska Native students decreased by two points in the 2003 to 2005 timeframe (from 27 to 25 points). Asian/Pacific Islander students performed approximately the same as White students in both 2000 and 2005.

• In eighth-grade reading, the gap between African American and White students increased by two points (26 to 28 points) in the 1998 to 2005 timeframe, while the gap with Hispanic students decreased by two points (from 27 to 25 points). Asian/Pacific Islander students reduced to zero a gap of 6 points that had existed in 1998. American Indian/Alaska Native students also improved by 3 points in the 2003 to 2005 timeframe, reducing the gap with White students by 4 points (from 26 to 22 points).

270. In 2004, President Bush signed Executive Order 13336, recognizing the "unique educational and culturally related academic needs of American Indian and Alaska Native students." The Executive Order pledged to meet No Child Left Behind's high standards "in a manner that is consistent with tribal traditions, languages and cultures." To initiate work under this E.O., the Secretary of Education hosted a national conference on Indian education with more than 600 national, state, and tribal leaders and experts in April of 2005.

271. At higher levels of education, overall educational attainment by all groups is improving; nonetheless, disparities continue to exist. In 2000, Asians alone were more likely than any other population to have completed a bachelor's degree, at 44 percent. The figures for other populations were 27 percent for the White non-Hispanic population, 14 percent for African Americans alone, 14 percent for Native Hawaiians and Pacific Islanders alone, 11.5 percent for American Indians and Alaska Natives alone, and 10.4 percent for Hispanics of any race. These figures were all higher than those reported in the 1990 Census—37 percent for Asians, 22 percent for Whites, 11 percent for African Americans, 9 percent for American Indians, Eskimos, and Aleuts, and 9 percent for Hispanics. At the high school level, in 2000, White non-Hispanic students were most likely to have received a high school diploma (85.5 percent), with Asian alone students close behind at 80.4 percent. The figures for other groups were African Americans alone, 72.3 percent; Native Hawaiian and Pacific Islanders alone, 78.3 percent; American Indian and Alaska Natives alone, 70.9 percent; and Hispanic of any race, 52.4 percent. These figures are uniformly higher than the figures reported in 1990, but they continue to show disparities similar to those in earlier years.

272. Title III of the No Child Left Behind Act of 2001 specifically requires states to develop and implement English language proficiency standards and to carry out annual assessments of English language learner (ELL) students. Based on data available from the states in 2005, there are approximately 5.1 million ELL students nationwide, compared to 2.8 million noted in Initial U.S. Report. All ELL students must, under Title VI of the Civil Rights Act of 1964, receive from their states and local educational agencies instructional services that are appropriate to their level of English proficiency. Title III of the NCLB law provides for grants to states for English language instruction programs that are estimated to be providing supplemental services to approximately 4 million ELL students, or 80 percent of the overall limited English proficiency (LEP) student population. Once students are identified as ELL, they are recommended for placement in a language instruction educational program. States have the flexibility to use the programs they believe would be most effective in permitting their students to achieve the levels of success expected for all students at the appropriate grade level. Programs under Title III of NCLB are administered by the Office of English Acquisition Enhancement and Academic Achievement for Limited English Proficient Students (OELA) of the U.S. Department of Education. OELA also runs a National Clearinghouse for English Language Acquisition and Language Instruction Education Programs (NCELA) that collects, analyzes, and disseminates information about language instruction, educational programs for English language learners, and related programs.

273. The Department of Education's Office of Civil Rights (OCR) works with school districts on issues related to ELL students. For example, in one case, OCR resolved a complaint alleging that a school

district did not meaningfully communicate school-related information to parents of national-origin minority students with limited English proficiency in a language they could understand, as required by Title VI. The district agreed to develop a plan for communicating with LEP parents, establish methods for notifying LEP parents of school-related activities, translate school documents into languages spoken by LEP parents, and recruit and hire interpreters to serve LEP parents.

1. The right to equal participation in cultural activities.

274. Article 5 (e) (vi) requires States parties to undertake to guarantee the right of everyone, without distinction as to race, color, or national or ethnic origin, to equality before the law in participation in cultural activities. In the United States, this right is protected primarily through the First, Fifth, and Fourteenth Amendments of the Constitution. The Fourteenth Amendment prohibits the states from denying any person the equal protection of the laws. The Supreme Court has interpreted the Fifth Amendment to apply the same equal protection obligation on the federal government. *See Bolling v. Sharpe*, 347 U.S. 497, 498–500 (1954). The First Amendment protects the freedoms of speech, press, and peaceable assembly. These three amendments operate together to ensure that every person enjoys an equal right to participate in cultural activities.

275. The rich and diverse cultural heritage of the United States has become even broader and deeper as our nation has become increasingly multi-racial, multi-ethnic, and multi-cultural. The long tradition of cultural expression in the United States continues to be seen in the thousands of ethnic heritage events, ethnic and cultural clubs, and religious, theatrical, artistic, sports, and musical events that celebrate cultural diversity nationwide. In addition, the U.S. Congress and the U.S. Administration, through the Smithsonian Institution, have supported the initiation and building of two major cultural institutions. One celebrates the American Indian, Alaska Native, and Native Hawaiian cultures as well as Native cultures throughout the hemisphere; the other celebrates African American heritage and culture. In 2004, the National Museum of the American Indian, a Smithsonian Museum, opened on the National Mall in Washington, D.C. with a major cultural celebration involving over 25,000 indigenous representatives from throughout the United States, Latin America, and Canada. This Museum, which was authorized by Congress in 1989 and funded with both public and private funds, showcases the living cultures of indigenous populations throughout North and South America. In turn, in 2003 Congress authorized the establishment, also within the Smithsonian, of the National Museum of African American History and Culture. That museum, which will also be located on the National Mall, will be built in the coming years.

1. The right of access to places of service

276. Consistent with Article 5 (f), U.S. law prohibits privately-owned facilities that offer food, lodging, transport, gasoline, and entertainment to the public from discriminating on the basis of race, color, religion, or national origin. State laws also prohibit such discrimination. In addition, public facilities, such as courthouses, jails, hospitals, parks, and other facilities owned and operated by state and local government entities cannot discriminate on the basis of race, color, religion, national origin, or disability.

277. The Department of Justice Civil Rights Division enforces laws guaranteeing the right of access to public accommodations without discrimination. Since 2000, the Division has filed 12 cases and settled 19 cases in this area. A few examples of public accommodations cases brought and/or settled since 2000 are presented below.

• In December 2006, the Justice Department settled a lawsuit alleging that employees of a nightclub in Milwaukee, Wisconsin told African Americans, but not similarly-situated Whites, that the nightclub was full or was being used for a private party, when that was not the case. Pursuant to the consent decree, the nightclub will adopt new entry procedures designed to prevent racial discrimination and will pay for periodic testing to assure that discrimination does not continue. It will also post a prominent sign at the entries advising that it does not discriminate on the basis of race or color, and will train its managers, send periodic reports to the Department, and adopt an objective dress code approved by the Department.

• In 2004, the Department of Justice settled a lawsuit alleging discrimination against African American customers by Cracker Barrel Old Country Store, Inc., a nationwide family restaurant chain. The complaint alleged that Cracker Barrel allowed White servers to refuse to wait on African-American customers, segregated customer seating by race, seated White customers before African American customers who arrived earlier, provided inferior service to African-American customers after they were seated, and treated African Americans who complained about the quality of Cracker Barrel's food or service less favorably than White customers who lodged similar complaints. Investigation had revealed evidence of such conduct in approximately 50 different Cracker Barrel restaurants in the states of Alabama, Georgia, Louisiana, Mississippi, North Carolina, Tennessee, and Virginia. The settlement order requires Cracker Barrel to adopt and implement effective nondiscrimination policies and procedures; implement new and enhanced training programs to ensure compliance; develop and implement an improved system for investigating, tracking, and resolving discrimination complaints; retain an outside contractor to test compliance; and publicize the company's nondiscrimination policies.

• In 2004, the Department of Justice settled a public accommodation discrimination lawsuit against the owners of a campground located in Concan, Texas. The lawsuit, filed in 2002, alleged that Camp Riverview and its owners denied lodging to Hispanic individuals, harassed Hispanic campground guests, and evicted Hispanic guests from the campground. Under the settlement, the campground and its owners will implement policies and procedures to ensure that all visitors, campers, and prospective campers receive equal treatment.

278. A number of states also handle cases concerning discrimination in public accommodations. For example, during fiscal year 2004–05, the Florida Commission on Human Relations closed 95 public accommodations complaints, of which 38 (40 percent) were based on race and 55 (58 percent) involved complaints of discrimination at food establishments. In fiscal year 2005, 9 percent of the complaints received by the Maryland Human Relations Commission involved discrimination at public accommodations. In Illinois, public accommodations cases represented approximately 3 percent of the charges docketed in 2005, and of those cases 62 percent charged discrimination on the basis of race, national origin, or color.

Article 6

A. Information on the legislative, judicial, administrative or other measures that give effect to the provisions of Article 6 of the Convention, in particular, measures taken to assure to everyone within the jurisdiction of the reporting State effective protection and remedies, through the competent national tribunals and other State institutions, against any acts of racial discrimination which violate his/her human rights and fundamental freedoms.

279. Article 6 requires States parties to assure persons within their jurisdictions effective protection and remedies, through tribunals and other institutions, for acts of racial discrimination that violate their human rights and fundamental freedoms contrary to the Convention, including the right to seek "just and adequate reparation or satisfaction for any damage suffered as a result of such discrimination." U.S. law offers those affected by racial or ethnic discrimination a number of remedies, ranging from individual suits in the courts, to reliance on administrative procedures, to civil or criminal prosecution of offenders by appropriate governmental entities.

280. Private Suits. Federal statutes derived from the Civil Rights Act of 1866, including most of the laws dealing with discrimination by governments and their officials, give individuals the right to sue in federal court to correct the alleged discrimination. See, e.g., 42 U.S.C. 1981–1985. Individuals wishing to bring suits under these provisions are sometimes assisted by non-governmental organizations that promote civil rights. Many state laws also permit private suit.

281. Civil Suits. Under statutes such as the Voting Rights Act; the Fair Housing Act; Titles II, IV, VI and VII of the Civil Rights Act; the Equal Credit Opportunity Act; and others, the federal government is authorized to initiate suits to enforce these laws. The Department of Justice Civil Rights Division is normally the federal litigant in such cases. Under some of the laws, such as the Fair Housing Act or the Equal Employment Opportunity Act, agencies such as the Department of Housing and Urban Development (HUD) and the EEOC may also initiate investigations and file complaints relating to cases of discrimination. Examples of such cases are set forth in various sections of this report. In addition, the EEOC and HUD have work sharing agreements with most states that permit states to investigate and sometimes to prosecute such cases. States also investigate and prosecute cases under state law even when the violations fall outside federal jurisdiction. The basic law in this area has not changed since the filing of the Initial U.S. Report.

282. Criminal Prosecution. The Department of Justice, acting through the Federal Bureau of Investigation, the Civil Rights Division, and the United States Attorney's Offices, initiates investigations into potential violations of federal criminal civil rights laws. If violations are found, the Civil Rights Division, usually acting jointly with the United States Attorney's Office for the particular district, prosecutes the cases in federal district court. States also pursue criminal prosecutions in cases involving violation of state criminal laws.

283. Administrative Proceedings. A number of administrative procedures are also available. For example, the EEOC provides administrative procedures, including mediation and conciliation, with regard to allegations of discrimination in the workplace; the Department of Labor's Office of Federal Contract Compliance Programs reviews the employment practices of Federal contractors and subcontractors to ensure that such employers practice equal employment opportunity in all aspects of employment; and the Department of

Education Office for Civil Rights provides similar services with regard to allegations of discrimination in education. Most states also provide administrative procedures, including hearings before administrative tribunals as well as mediation and conciliation. The basic law in this area has not changed since the filing of the Initial U.S. Report.

284. Policy Oversight. In addition to enforcement, a number of federal Departments and offices provide policy oversight. For example, the Office for Civil Rights in the U.S. Department of Education provides guidance to school districts on federal law and policies concerning discrimination, on the requirements necessary to eliminate the vestiges of desegregation in formerly segregated systems, and on provision of effective educational opportunities to English language learner students. The EEOC provides similar legal and policy oversight with regard to discrimination in employment, as does HUD with regard to housing. The policy oversight responsibilities of all these agencies extend to activities in U.S. territories as well as within the 50 states. In addition, the U.S. Commission on Civil Rights conducts studies and makes recommendations concerning civil rights issues. The U.S. Commission receives input from 51 State Advisory Committees, comprising the 50 states and the District of Columbia.

285. Equal Opportunity Officers. Another method of protecting against discrimination and providing remedies to individuals is the requirement that many larger employers designate an "equal opportunity officer" within their organizations. These officers may consider complaints of discrimination, make recommendations to prevent discriminatory practices, and act as internal advocates within organizations for protection of the rights secured by U.S. law and the Convention. While not "enforcement" officers, they have been effective in helping organizations remain conscious of their responsibilities with regard to nondiscrimination.

286. Legislation. In the United States, both state and federal laws are constantly under review and potential revision by federal, state, and territorial governments. New laws are also enacted where deemed necessary. Examples of legislative changes and new laws designed to protect civil rights are set forth throughout this report.

B. Measures taken to assure to everyone the right to seek from such tribunals just and adequate reparation or satisfaction for any damage as a result of such discrimination.

287. The right of equal access to, and treatment before, tribunals administering justice in the United States is provided through the operation of the Equal Protection Clause of the U.S. Constitution. This provision binds all governmental entities at all levels throughout the United States. Measures in place to assure such access are discussed in the section on Article 5, Equality before Tribunals, above.

C. Information on the practice and decisions of courts and other judicial and administrative organs relating to cases of racial discrimination as defined under Article 1 of the Convention.

288. In private suits, civil suits, and administrative proceedings, settlement may include a number of remedies, such as injunctive relief, requiring the defendant to cease or correct the offending discriminatory conduct; monetary relief, requiring the payment of damages; other requirements placed on the offending party, such as the requirement to develop and publicize new policies or the requirement for staff training; and in some cases payment of punitive damages. Criminal cases may lead to payment of criminal fines or to incarceration, or both. The basic law in this area has not changed since the filing of the Initial U.S. Report. Examples of the actual practice and decisions of courts in discrimination cases are provided throughout this report.

D. Information in connection with general recommendation XXVI on Article 6 of the Convention (2000).

289. General recommendation XXVI suggests that to meet the needs of victims of discrimination, courts and other competent authorities should consider awarding financial compensation for damage—material or moral—to victims, when appropriate, rather than limiting remedies solely to punishment of the perpetrator. As noted above, remedies to assist victims are available in the United States in private suits, civil suits, and administrative proceedings. In those cases settlement may include monetary relief, punitive damages, injunctive relief (prohibiting the perpetrator from taking certain actions with regard to the victim), or mandamus (requiring the perpetrator to do something affirmative with regard to the victim). Furthermore, in 2004 Congress enacted the Crime Victims' Rights Act, P.L. 108-405, which provides a number of additional rights to the victims of criminal activity. The Department of Justice Office of Victims of Crime maintains a full program of grants and other activities designed to assist the victims of crime. Among other activities, this office provides funding to the National Victim Assistance Academy and to state victim's assistance academies, which conduct annual training sessions throughout the United States.

Article 7

Information on the legislative, judicial, administrative or other measures that give effect to the provisions of Article 7 of the Convention, to General Recommendation V of 13 April 1977 and to decision 2 (XXV) of 17 March 1982, by which the Committee adopted its additional guidelines for the implementation of Article 7.

290. Article 7 requires States parties to undertake to adopt immediate and effective measures, particularly in the fields of teaching, culture, and information, with a view to combating prejudices that lead to racial discrimination and to promoting understanding, tolerance, and friendship among nations and racial or ethnic groups.

291. Teaching. A number of federal statutes prohibit discrimination in education: for example, Title IV of the Civil Rights Act of 1964, 42 U.S.C. 2000c et seq. (prohibiting discrimination on the basis of race, color, sex, religion, or national origin by public elementary and secondary schools and public institutions of higher learning); Title VI of the Civil Rights Act of 1964, 42 U.S.C. 2000d et seq. (prohibiting discrimination by recipients of federal funds on the basis of race, color, and national origin) and the Equal Educational Opportunities Act of 1974, 20 U.S.C. 1701–1721 (prohibiting specific discriminatory conduct, including segregating students on the basis of race, color, or national origin; discrimination against faculty and staff; and the failure to take appropriate action to remove language barriers).

292. The Departments of Education and Justice play key roles in the implementation of these laws. The Department of Education's Office for Civil Rights (OCR) is charged with ensuring equal access to education and promoting educational excellence throughout the nation through vigorous enforcement of civil rights. One of OCR's responsibilities is to resolve discrimination complaints. Agency-initiated cases, typically called compliance reviews, permit OCR to target resources on compliance problems that appear particularly acute. OCR also provides technical assistance to help institutions voluntarily comply with civil rights. In addition, the Department of Education also provides funding to deal with prejudice and intolerance in some areas; for example, under section 4115 (b) (2) (E) (xiii) of the Safe and Drug Free Schools and Communities Act, the DOE provides funding that local educational agencies may use to address victimization associated with prejudice and intolerance, as part of their overall drug and violence prevention programs. In addition to the Department of Education, the Department of Justice Civil Rights Division prosecutes cases, and the Department of Justice Community Relations Service works with schools and communities to defuse racial and ethnic tensions and violence.

293. Many schools in the United States feature human rights education as an important part of their curricula. A number of NGOs have assisted schools in providing appropriate human rights coursework. For example, Amnesty International USA established a Human Rights Education program which provides resource materials as well as training and networking opportunities. Its teaching guides and lesson plans focus on ways to combat discrimination in school systems and promote a wider understanding of human rights worldwide. A "September 11th Crisis Response Guide" specifically focuses on the events of 9/11 and the immediate aftermath, placing them within a human rights context. The curriculum topics range from racism and discrimination to International Humanitarian Law. Another resource, "Speak Truth to Power: An Educational and Advocacy Package," explores key human rights issues through the eyes of human rights defenders and the actions of local heroes. Amnesty USA's Rights in Sight initiative also helps teachers bring stronger human rights perspectives to their established curricula. Rights in Sight provides free training and professional development, assistance with curriculum design and implementation, printed resources, and access to an online education community.

294. Curricula at many U.S. higher education institutions also include courses on both civil rights and international human rights. Indeed, many U.S. colleges and universities have educational centers devoted to the study of human rights. For example, the Carr Center for Human Rights at the Harvard University's Kennedy School of Government brings human rights scholars from around the world to participate in discussions and to give lectures on human rights to all students. The University of Minnesota, the University of California at Berkeley, and Columbia University, among others, also have programs dedicated exclusively to the study of human rights. Amnesty International Educators Network provides topical human rights syllabi for college courses. In addition, the Education Caucus, a branch of the U.S. Human Rights Network, works to support and complement current human rights education and training models in schools, universities, and other educational settings.

295. Training of federal and state officials, law enforcement officers, and others in civil rights and racial and ethnic tolerance is widespread. As noted above, the No FEAR law, enacted in 2002, requires that all federal managers receive diversity training. Law enforcement officers also receive regular diversity training,

including training on the handling of hate crimes. The amount and scope of such training has been increased substantially since the events of 9/11 as one measure taken in response to the subsequent increase in allegations of bias toward Arab, Muslim, Sikh, and South Asian Americans. For example, in addition to establishing the DHS Civil Liberties Universities, the DHS Office for Civil Rights and Civil Liberties recently released a training video for DHS employees on Arab and Muslim beliefs and culture.

296. Culture. The right to participate in cultural activities without discrimination is guaranteed by the First, Fifth, and Fourteenth Amendments of the U.S. Constitution. A long and rich tradition of cultural expression exists in the United States. For further description of cultural freedom in the United States, see the section on Cultural Activities under Article 5, above.

297. Information. The year 2004 represented the 50th anniversary of the landmark *Brown v. Board of Education* decision. In celebration of this anniversary, Congress established a *Brown v. Board of Education* 50th Anniversary Commission, P.L. 107-41 (September 18, 2001). The distinguished members of that Commission developed plans and programs to celebrate racial and ethnic integration and to remind all Americans of the meaning and critical importance of the constitutional principle of equality. The 50th anniversary was celebrated throughout the year and throughout the nation. Events included writing contests, public lectures, a call for papers, a reunion in Washington, D.C. of the plaintiffs and attorneys involved in the case, a textbook summit, and a national celebration and opening of the Brown Historic Site in Topeka, Kansas. The work of this Commission was complemented by the American Bar Association (ABA), which appointed an ABA Commission on the 50th Anniversary of *Brown v. Board of Education* and developed a number of programs and resources, including a bibliography of books and articles, court cases, films and videos, and lessons for use with students. ABA outreach events were also held throughout the nation.

298. The Department of Justice, Department of Education, Department of Labor, EEOC, and other federal agencies concerned with discrimination have also put out publications and fact sheets designed to ensure that the issue of discrimination is kept in the consciousness of the American public. For example, the EEOC has published fact sheets on National Origin Discrimination and Race/Color Discrimination in a number of languages, including English, Arabic, Chinese, Spanish, Vietnamese, Hindi, Farsi, Urdu, and others. The EEOC also holds an annual nationwide Conference called EXCEL—Examining Conflicts in Employment Law; and the EEOC district, field, local, and area offices hold annual Technical Assistance Program Seminars (TAPS) around the country. The Department of Education's Office for Civil Rights has produced a number of outreach publications including "Achieving Diversity: Race Neutral Alternatives in American Education" (2004); "Case Resolution and Investigation Manual" (2004); and "How to File a Discrimination Complaint with the Office of Civil Rights" (2002). The Department of Justice Civil Rights Division has published Joint Statements with HUD on group homes, land use and the Fair Housing Act, reasonable accommodations under the Fair Housing Act, and a brochure entitled "Protecting the Religious Freedom of All Americans: Federal Protections Against National Origin Laws Against Religious Discrimination." HUD has published a booklet, "Fair Housing: Equal Opportunity for All," a "Fair Housing Act Design Manual," advertising guidance, and post 9/11 guidance for landlords. The Justice Department Civil Rights Division also provides information on its website specifically related to the civil rights of American Indians, and produces a pamphlet entitled "Protecting the Civil Rights of American Indians and Alaska Natives." In addition, the Department of Labor's website contains a variety of compliance assistance materials, including information about the discrimination complaint filing process and compliance guides for small businesses.

299. The Office of Special Counsel for Immigration Related Unfair Employment Practices (OSC) within the Civil Rights Division publishes numerous pamphlets, brochures, posters, and fact sheets, many of which are available in multiple languages, including English, Spanish, Vietnamese, Korean, and Chinese. Some publications focus on the rights of employees to be free from immigration-related employment discrimination, while others attempt to answer common employer questions. Most of OSC's educational materials are easily accessible online and are available to the public without cost. The Division's Voting Section publishes brochures related to voting rights in English, Spanish, Chinese, Japanese, Korean, and Tagalog. A Vietnamese version is available on the Section's website. Additionally, the Civil Rights Division has made efforts to translate materials on its website into Spanish. Publications by other agencies are also referenced throughout this report.

300. One of the most intense federal outreach activities since 2000 has involved the aftermath of the events of 9/11. Immediately after those terrorist attacks, the U.S. government anticipated the potential for a backlash against Arabs and Muslims in the United States. Within days, the President of the United States and heads of U.S. government agencies, including the Attorney General and the Director of the Federal Bureau of Investigation, publicly and strongly denounced violence and discrimination against Arabs and Muslims.

Shortly after 9/11, the Civil Rights Division of the Justice Department spearheaded a special Initiative to Combat Post-9/11 Discriminatory Backlash. Based on consultations with Arab and Muslim leaders in the U.S., this outreach effort included issuance of informational documents in English and Arabic explaining how the federal anti-discrimination laws apply to post-9/11 backlash discrimination and how to file claims. It also involved a national media campaign, resulting in numerous stories in the national media.

301. The EEOC also conducted outreach to Arab and Muslim organizations, appearing at Mosques, as well as business, labor, and civil rights groups. From September 2003 through 2006, the EEOC conducted 156 outreach activities aimed at the Arab/Middle Eastern community, reaching more than 9,400 individuals throughout the United States. It also conducted an additional 169 activities in partnership with religious groups, most of which were Muslim, reaching another 9,300 individuals. For example, the Houston office took steps to foster its relationship with the approximately 90 Mosques in the Houston area. In addition, the EEOC worked with the media to get its message out to the Arab and Muslim communities. For example, the District Director of the EEOC office in Detroit appeared on an Arab American radio show, broadcast throughout the Arab American community, answering questions about the EEOC, the laws enforced by the agency, case processing procedures, and examples of post 9/11 cases.

302. The Department Justice has also acted to ensure that schools are aware of their responsibilities to ensure that students throughout America can attend school in safe and secure environments free from physical threats and discrimination. In 2004, the Assistant Attorney General for the Civil Rights Division sent a letter to the head of the Departments of Education of each of the 50 states, which stated as follows: "As we approach the third anniversary of 11 September 2001, we must all recognize that our differences provide an invaluable opportunity for further education, and must not lead, rather, to a greater separation."

303. The Department of Housing and Urban Development also clarified that landlords may not request additional paperwork or identification from applicants of Arab ancestry that are not required of other applicants, and must use the same standards in providing access to recreational facilities.

304. Finally, a number of steps have been taken to ensure respect for the rights of Arabs and Muslims among law enforcement officials. In many cases, law enforcement agencies have partnered with NGOs to provide effective training that addresses the concerns of the affected communities. Specific training efforts for law enforcement officials are described in the section on Article 5 above.

305. Racial and ethnic prejudice have also been the focus of attention by both print media and other forms of public communication. Newspapers throughout the United States routinely publish articles on racial and ethnic issues. Moreover, the non-print media are also tackling these difficult issues. In 2005, the Oscar for best film of the year was awarded to "Crash," a film addressing racial and ethnic stereotyping and prejudice in Los Angeles.

306. <u>Promoting understanding, tolerance and friendship among nations and racial and ethnic groups.</u> The United States promotes the goals of Article 7 globally through the activities of the Department of State. The Office of the Under Secretary for Public Diplomacy and Public Affairs has undertaken a number of initiatives to further this goal, including the Citizen Dialogue Program, which empowers American Muslims to tell their personal stories to key overseas audiences; an outreach program to American Muslims to promote interfaith dialogue and tolerance; and numerous public affairs and public information campaigns, including digital outreach, websites, web chats, and other information programs. In addition, the Broadcasting Board of Governors, through the Voice of America, the Middle East Broadcasting Networks, Radio Free Europe and Radio Liberty, and Radio Free Asia broadcast news and information programs on rule of law, tolerance, and other topics related to combating racism and promoting tolerance. These outlets give overseas audiences direct access to experts and policy makers in the United States responsible for issues related to racial and ethnic diversity. The United States also sends speakers and publications to overseas missions to foster discussion on issues important to multi-cultural societies.

307. The United States further promotes the goals of Article 7 through professional and educational exchange programs that increase mutual understanding between Americans and people of other countries, under the Fulbright-Hays Act. Working in cooperation with U.S. non-profit partner organizations, the Department of State devotes substantial resources to a full spectrum of such programs. These include the Fulbright Program, which provides educational exchange and professional development opportunities to U.S. and foreign students, scholars, teachers, and professionals from 150 countries around the world through grants and fellowships; Gilman scholarships for American undergraduates representing the diversity of the U.S. to study abroad in all world regions; English teaching abroad, including programs for high school students from underserved sectors; support for study of foreign languages, including Arabic, the Turkic and Indic languages,

and Chinese, by Americans; student leader institutes on U.S. college campuses for young people from the Middle East, South Asia, indigenous populations of Latin America, and other regions; educational advising to promote study by foreign students in the U.S.; the International Visitor Leadership Program, which brings journalists, government officials, clerics, lawyers, teachers, and other civil society leaders to the United States to meet and confer with their U.S. counterparts; professional and cultural exchanges supported through the Office of Citizen Exchanges, which promote diversity and tolerance through exchanges of journalists and religious community leaders; and a number of youth exchange programs, which fund academic-year and short-term exchanges for young people.

Conclusion

308. The United States is aware of the challenges brought about by its historical legacy of racial and ethnic discrimination as well as other more recent challenges, and it continues to work toward the goal of eliminating discrimination based on race, ethnicity, or national origin. As a vibrant, multi-racial, multi-ethnic, and multi-cultural democracy, the United States, at all levels of government and civil society, continually re-examines and re-evaluates its successes and failures in this regard, recognizing that more work is to be done. The United States looks forward to discussing its experiences and this report with the Committee.

Committee Comments and Recommendations

309. This section addresses the concerns and recommendations set forth in the Committee's concluding observations on the Initial U.S. Report, A/56/18, paras. 380–407, 14/08/2001.

This Committee, concerned by the absence of specific legislation implementing the provisions of the Convention in domestic laws, recommends that the State party undertake the necessary measures to ensure the consistent application of the provisions of the Convention at all levels of government (paragraph 390).

310. The United States has taken, and continues to take, necessary measures to ensure the application of the provisions of the Convention at all levels of government, consistent with the U.S. constitutional structure. This commitment is set out in the understanding adopted with respect to the Convention:

"[T]he United States understands that this Convention shall be implemented by the Federal Government to the extent that it exercises jurisdiction over the matters covered therein, and otherwise by the state and local governments. To the extent that state and local governments exercise jurisdiction over such matters, the Federal government shall, as necessary, take appropriate measures to ensure the fulfillment of this Convention."

311. The ways in which the Convention is implemented by the federal government, by the respective state governments, and in U.S. territories are described throughout this report.

The Committee emphasizes its concern about the State party's far-reaching reservations, understandings and declarations entered at the time of ratification of the Convention. The Committee is particularly concerned about the implication of the State party's reservation on the implementation of Article 4 of the Convention. In this regard the Committee recalls its general recommendations VII and XV, according to which the prohibition of dissemination of all ideas based upon racial superiority or hatred is compatible with the right to freedom of opinion and expression, given that a citizen's exercise of this right carries special duties and responsibilities, among which is the obligation not to disseminate racist ideas. The Committee recommends that the State party review its legislation in view of the new requirements of preventing and combating racial discrimination, and adopt regulations extending the protection against acts of racial discrimination, in accordance with Article 4 of the Convention (para 391).

312. The United States supports the goals of the Convention and believes that its reservations, understandings, and declarations are compatible with the objects and purposes thereof.

313. As the United States has previously noted, its Constitution contains extensive protections for individual freedoms of speech, expression, and association, which (absent a reservation, understanding, or declaration) might be construed in tension with articles 4 and 7. The United States believes that its constitutional protections are fully consistent with the goals of the Convention. The purpose of the First Amendment is to preserve an uninhibited marketplace of ideas in which truth will ultimately prevail. *See, e.g., Abrams v. United States,* 250 U.S. 616 (1919) (dissenting opinion of Oliver Wendell Holmes, Jr., in which Justice Brandeis concurred). Through freedom of expression, ideas can be considered and allowed to stand or fall of their own weight. As the late Gerald Gunther, one of the foremost constitutional law scholars in the history of the United States, explained: "The lesson I have drawn from my childhood in Nazi Germany and my happier adult life in this country is the need to walk the sometimes difficult path of denouncing the bigot's hateful ideas with all my power, yet at the same time challenging any community's attempt to suppress hateful ideas by force of law." *See also Virginia v. Black,* 538 U.S. 343, 367 (2003) (quoting Professor Gunther). To

be sure, the Supreme Court has upheld the suppression of particularly hateful and dangerous speech under certain circumstances. *See, e.g., id.* (upholding a ban on cross-burning with intent to intimidate). In general, however, the United States believes that the goal of eliminating racial discrimination is, in fact, better served by application of the principles of freedom of expression and association than by the application of greater restrictions on those freedoms.

314. The Initial U.S. Report and the sections covering Article 4 and Article 5 (security of persons) in this report describe in greater detail the U.S. constitutional limitations on implementation of Article 4, as well as the activities that may constitutionally be restricted. In addition, it should be noted that in cases such as hate crimes, the racial element of the crime may yield more severe punishment. The United States enforces against all such crimes to the fullest extent of the law, and numerous examples of such enforcement actions are described in this report.

The Committee also notes with concern the position of the State party with regard to its obligation under Article 2, paragraph 1 (c) and (d), to bring to an end all racial discrimination by any person, group or organization, that the prohibition and punishment of purely private conduct lie beyond the scope of governmental regulation, even in situations where the personal freedom is exercised in a discriminatory manner. The Committee recommends that the State party review its legislation so as to render liable to criminal sanctions the largest possible sphere of private conduct that is discriminatory on racial or ethnic grounds (para 392).

315. Although the civil rights protections of the Fourteenth Amendment of the U.S. Constitution reach only "state action," private conduct may be regulated on several other constitutional bases. First, the Thirteenth Amendment's prohibition against slavery and involuntary servitude encompasses both governmental and private action and serves as the basis for several civil rights statutes. *See, e.g.,* 42 U.S.C. 1981, 1982. These statutes have been used to prohibit private actors from engaging in racial discrimination in activities such as the sale and/or rental of private property, the assignment of a lease, the grant of membership in a community swimming pool, the refusal of a private school to admit African American students, the making and enforcement of private contracts, and conspiracy to deprive African Americans of the right of interstate travel. In addition, the commerce power of Article 1 of the Constitution underlies Title II and Title VII of the 1964 Civil Rights Act, which prohibit private entities from discriminating in public accommodations and employment. The authority of Congress over commerce also serves as the basis for the Fair Housing Act, which prohibits private parties from discrimination in housing. The spending powers of Article 1 as well as Section 5 of the Fourteenth Amendment serve as the basis for Title VI of the 1964 Civil Rights Act, which prohibits discrimination by public and private institutions that receive federal funds. This report sets forth numerous examples of enforcement action against private persons with regard to activities such as those noted above.

316. In the U.S. view, it is unclear whether the term "public life" in the definition of "racial discrimination" in the Convention is synonymous with the permissible sphere of governmental regulation under U.S. law. Thus, the United States felt it prudent in acceding to the Convention to indicate through a formal reservation that U.S. undertakings in this regard are limited by the reach of constitutional and statutory protections under U.S. law as they may exist at any given time:

"[T]he Constitution and laws of the United States establish extensive protections against discrimination, reaching significant areas of non-governmental activity. Individual privacy and freedom from governmental interference in private conduct, however, are also recognized as among the fundamental values which shape our free and democratic society. The United States understands that the identification of the rights protected under the convention by reference in Article 1 to fields of "public life" reflects a similar distinction between spheres of public conduct that are customarily the subject of governmental regulation, and spheres of private conduct that are not. To the extent, however, that the Convention calls for a broader regulation of private conduct, the United States does not accept any obligation under this Convention to enact legislation or take other measures under paragraph (1) of Article 2, subparagraphs (1) (c) and (d) of Article 2, Article 3 and Article 5 with respect to private conduct except as mandated by the Constitution and laws of the United States."

The Committee draws the attention of the State party to its obligations under the Convention and, in particular, to Article 1, paragraph 1, and general recommendation XIV, to undertake to prohibit and to eliminate racial discrimination in all its forms, including practices and legislation that may not be discriminatory in purpose, but in effect. The Committee recommends that the State party take all appropriate measures to review existing legislation and federal, State and local policies to ensure effective protection against any form of racial discrimination and any unjustifiably disparate impact (para. 393).

317. The United States recognizes and supports the importance of prohibiting and eliminating racial discrimination in all its forms. Under U.S. law, claims that seemingly neutral laws, procedures, or practices are having disparate impacts or effects on persons or groups of a particular race, color, or national origin may be brought under the Voting Rights Act of 1965, as amended, Title VII of the 1964 Civil Rights Act, and the federal regulations implementing Title VI of the 1964 Civil Rights Act.

318. General Recommendation XIV, which is recommendatory in nature, states that "in seeking to determine whether an action has an effect contrary to the Convention, [the Committee] will look to see whether that action has an unjustifiable disparate impact upon a group distinguished by race, colour, descent, or ethnic origin." The term "unjustifiable disparate impact" indicates the view of the Committee that the Convention reaches only those race-neutral practices that both create statistically significant racial disparities and are unnecessary, i.e., unjustifiable. This reading of Article 2 (1) (c) tracks the standards for litigating disparate impact claims under Title VII and the Title VI regulations in U.S. law. It is also consistent with the standards used in litigation of equal protection claims under the Fifth and Fourteenth Amendments of the U.S. Constitution, for which statistical proof of racial disparity, particularly when combined with other circumstantial evidence, is probative of the discriminatory intent necessary to make out a claim. In the view of the United States, Article 1 (1) (c) does not impose obligations contrary to existing U.S. law.

319. Title VII prohibits employers from using facially neutral employment practices that have an unjustified adverse impact on members of a protected class. Examples of practices that may be subject to disparate impact challenges include: written tests, height and weight requirements, educational requirements, and subjective procedures such as interviews. Once a plaintiff establishes disparate impact, the practice may withstand scrutiny only if the employer proves that the practice is "job related for the position and consistent with business necessity." However, even if the employer so proves, the plaintiff may still prevail by showing that the employer has refused to adopt an alternative practice that would satisfy the employer's legitimate interests without having the disparate impact. Many disparate impact cases are prosecuted by the Department of Justice Office for Civil Rights under the "pattern or practice" authority of section 707 of Title VII. The laws enforced by the Department of Labor's Office of Federal Contract Compliance Programs also prohibit federal contractors and subcontractors from utilizing recruiting and selection procedures that have a disparate impact on a protected group. A number of examples of disparate impact cases in the employment arena are set forth in the section on Article 2 (1) (b) above.

320. Title VI prohibits discrimination on the basis of race, color, or national origin by governmental agencies and any private entity receiving federal funds or assistance. More than 28 federal agencies have adopted regulations implementing Title VI that apply the intent standard and the disparate impact standards to their own operations and the operations of any recipients of funds or assistance. DOJ regulations can be found at www.usdoj.gov/crt/cor/coord/vimanual.htm#III.%. The legal standards in Title VI cases are similar to those for Title VII cases. Once disparate impact is proved, the defendant organization may prevail only if it can show a "substantial legitimate justification" for the practice. If such justification can be shown, then the court focuses on whether there are any "equally effective alternative practices" that would result in less racial or ethnic disproportionality.

321. Since 2000, where deemed necessary, legislation and policies have been reviewed to determine if new enforcement priorities are appropriate in areas involving disparate impact. For example, in 2005 the Equal Employment Opportunity Commission (EEOC) set up a special task force to assess whether the agency was doing enough to combat systemic discrimination—patterns or practices of discriminatory activity that have broad impacts on an industry, profession, company, or geographic location. The task force recommended that the EEOC make the fight against systemic discrimination an agency-wide top priority, and the agency has done so. Although systemic discrimination encompasses more than just disparate impact cases, this re-prioritization will have the effect of increasing the focus on disparate impact prosecutions as well as other cases. Similarly, the Department of Justice reexamined the manner in which it selected employers for investigation to determine if those employers had violated Title VII. As a result of this reexamination, the number of the Department's pattern or practice investigations has increased, and the Department has filed an increased number of cases alleging a pattern or practice of discrimination. Since 2001, the Department of Labor's Office of Federal Contract Compliance Programs has also refocused its efforts on detecting and preventing systemic discrimination. Special emphasis has been placed on eliminating disparities in compensation that affect large numbers of workers.

322. One critical form of disparate impact discrimination involves unintentional discrimination against persons with limited English proficiency (LEP). Since 2000, the Department of Justice has also devoted substantial resources to implementation of Executive Order 13166 of August 11, 2000, "Improving Access to

Services for Persons with Limited English Proficiency." This Order required agencies to examine the services they provide, identify any need for those services by persons who are LEP, and develop and implement systems to ensure meaningful access by such persons. Federal agencies as well as recipients of grants or federal assistance are expected to comply. The Federal Interagency Working Group on LEP, coordinated by the Department of Justice, has issued an LEP video in five languages, a "Know your Rights" brochure directed towards LEP individuals in 10 languages, and a second brochure for federal agencies and recipients that outlines the LEP requirements. The Working Group also hosted a two-day meeting in the Washington, D.C. metropolitan area to discuss delivery of government services to the LEP community and how to ensure greater access to such services. The conference presented attendees with an opportunity to share with and learn from leaders in the field of providing language access, and included federal, state, and local officials; funding organizations; and language service providers. The Working Group's website, www.lep.gov, has been steadily growing and is maintained by the Department of Justice. In addition, the Department of Justice has issued several technical assistance documents for its own recipients, including LEP Planning Tools for departments of correction and law enforcement agencies and a Tips and Tools resource document with specific chapters about providing LEP access in courts, law enforcement agencies, 911 call centers, and domestic violence service providers.

323. Examples of successes in this area include the following. First, after a compliance review showed problems, the Office of Justice Programs collaborated with the Philadelphia, Pennsylvania Police Department and with advocacy groups to help the Department implement a new LEP policy in December of 2005. Today when Philadelphia police are confronted with LEP individuals, they have access to professional interpreters, telephonic interpretation, and vital documents translated into seven languages. Second, after receiving guidance from the Department of Justice, the Minnesota Supreme Court approved a proposed amendment to the Minnesota Rules of Civil Procedure making it clear that foreign language interpreters must be provided for all litigants and witnesses, not only in criminal proceedings, but also in civil cases, at court expense. Third, on October 11, 2006, following the Department of Justice's August on-site investigation and negotiations of a complaint of discrimination, the State of Maine Supreme Judicial Court issued an Administrative Order providing for interpreters in both civil and criminal proceedings as well as in a range of other court proceedings including judicially-assisted mediations.

The Committee notes with concern the incidents of police violence and brutality, including cases of deaths as a result of excessive use of force by law enforcement officials, which particularly affect minority groups and foreigners. The Committee recommends that the State party take immediate and effective measures to ensure the appropriate training of the police force with a view to combating prejudices that may lead to racial discrimination and ultimately to a violation of the right to security of persons. The Committee further recommends that firm action be taken to punish racially motivated violence and ensure the access of victims to effective legal remedies and the right to seek just and adequate reparation for any damage suffered as a result of such actions (para. 394).

324. U.S. law prohibits racially discriminatory actions by law enforcement agencies, including police violence and brutality, and the Civil Rights Division of the Department of Justice, with the aid of United States Attorney's Offices and the FBI, actively enforces those laws. A description of enforcement activities is contained in the section of the report concerning Article 5, Discrimination by Law Enforcement.

325. In order to address the incidence of brutality and discriminatory actions noted in the Initial U.S. Report, the United States has stepped up its training of law enforcement officers with a view to combating prejudice that may lead to violence. In the aftermath of 9/11, one of the focus areas for such training has been the increased bias against Arab Americans and Muslim Americans. The Department of Justice Community Relations Service has established dialogues between government officials and Arab and Muslim communities in the U.S., and has created a training video for law enforcement officers. The Department of Homeland Security—one of the largest federal law enforcement agencies in the United States—has emphasized training for DHS employees and is developing an online "Civil Liberties University." The FBI also expanded cultural sensitivity training to all Special Agents in response to broader post-9/11 FBI investigative jurisdiction in these communities.

326. Further examples of law enforcement training are set forth in the section on Article 5, Discrimination by Law Enforcement. State and local authorities also conduct similar types of training.

The Committee notes with concern that the majority of federal, state and local prison and jail inmates in the State party are members of ethnic or national minorities, and that the incarceration rate is particularly high with regard to African-Americans and Hispanics. The Committee recommends that the State party take firm action to guarantee the right of everyone, without distinction as to race, colour, or

national or ethnic origin, to equal treatment before the courts and all other organs administering justice. Noting the socio-economic marginalization of a significant part of the African-American, Hispanic and Arab populations, it is further recommended that the State party ensure that the high incarceration rate is not a result of the economically, socially and educationally disadvantaged position of these groups (para. 395).

327. The Committee's question seems to be based on the assumption that the existence of differing incarceration rates among racial and ethnic groups is due to failure of the United States to guarantee the right of everyone, without distinction as to race, color, or national or ethnic origin, to equal treatment before the courts and all other organs administering justice. This assumption, however, is inaccurate. As noted above, the U.S. does take firm action to guarantee the right of everyone to equal treatment before the courts and other administrative and judicial entities. Neither race nor ethnicity is a criterion in access to courts or other tribunals, the selection of jurors, or the provision of counsel for the indigent. Likewise, immigration status is not a factor in access to courts. Many factors account for differences in the incarceration rates of various populations. As noted above in the section on Article 5, Representation in the Criminal Justice System, some scholarly research indicates that disparities are related primarily to differential involvement in crime by the various groups (with some unexplained disparities particularly related to drug use and enforcement), rather than to differential handling of persons in the criminal justice system. To the extent that varying incarceration rates may relate to socio-economic factors, the United States will continue to work to eliminate the impact of such factors.

The Committee notes with concern that, according to the Special Rapporteur of the United Nations Commission on Human Rights on extrajudicial, summary or arbitrary executions, there is a disturbing correlation between race, both of the victim and the defendant, and the imposition of the death penalty, particularly in states like Alabama, Florida, Georgia, Louisiana, Mississippi and Texas. The Committee urges the State party to ensure, possibly by imposing a moratorium, that no death penalty is imposed as a result of racial bias on the part of prosecutors, judges, juries and lawyers or as a result of the economically, socially and educationally disadvantaged position of the convicted persons (para 396).

328. Capital punishment continues to be an issue of great public debate in the United States. It continues to be supported by a majority of the citizens in a majority of states in the U.S., although a significant number of citizens do not support it. The serious debate concerning capital punishment in the United States is evidence of the complexity of the issue and strongly held opinions on both sides. *See* discussion above, under Article 5, Capital Punishment.

329. To the extent that capital punishment is applied in the United States, the U. S. Government remains confident that it is imposed only in the most egregious cases and only in the context of the heightened procedural safeguards required by our federal and state constitutions and statutes, and that it is not administered in a manner inconsistent with U.S. human rights obligations, including the Convention.

The Committee is concerned about the political disenfranchisement of a large segment of the ethnic minority population who are denied the right to vote by disenfranchising laws and practices based on the commission of more than a certain number of criminal offences, and also sometimes by preventing them from voting even after the completion of their sentences. The Committee recalls that the right of everyone to vote on a non-discriminatory basis is a right contained in Article 5 of the Convention (para 397).

330. This issue is dealt with above in the discussion under Article 5, Voting. As noted in that discussion, the issue is a matter of continuing scrutiny in the states of the United States, and the law in a number of states has changed in recent years. The longstanding practice of states on this matter, however, does not violate U.S. obligations under the Convention.

While noting the numerous laws, institutions and measures designed to eradicate racial discrimination affecting the equal enjoyment of economic, social and cultural rights, the Committee is concerned about persistent disparities in the enjoying of, in particular, the right to adequate housing, equal opportunities for education and employment, and access to public and private health care. The Committee recommends that the State party take all appropriate measures, including special measures according to Article 2, paragraph 2, of the Convention, to ensure the right of everyone, without discrimination as to race, colour, or national or ethnic origin, to the enjoyment of the rights contained in Article 5 of the Convention (para 398).

331. As noted in the discussion of Article 5, above, some of the rights enumerated in Article 5, which may be characterized as economic, social, and cultural rights, are not explicitly recognized as legally enforce-

able "rights" under U.S. law. Nonetheless, the federal and state constitutions and laws fully comply with the requirements of the Convention that the rights and activities covered by Article 5 be enjoyed on a non-discriminatory basis.

332. As discussed in the sections on Article 2 and Article 5, above, the United States has in place a panoply of legislation and measures, including special measures, to ensure non-discriminatory treatment as provided in Article 5. Substantial progress in addressing disparities in housing, education, employment, and access to health care has been made over the years, and evidence of further progress in a number of areas is set forth in this report. For example, the gap between poverty rates for both African Americans and Hispanics as compared to that for non-Hispanic Whites has closed slightly since the 1998 rates described in the Initial U.S. Report. In addition, the unemployment rate for Hispanics dropped between 1999 and 2005, and the 2005 jobless rate among immigrants fell below that of U.S.-born workers for the first time in at least a decade. Minority-owned businesses represent the fastest-growing segment of the nation's economy, including African American-owned business growth at four times the national average and Hispanic-owned business growth at three times the national rate. Some evidence also suggests that gaps in educational attainment may be beginning to close, at least at the elementary and middle school levels. Special measures are in place for education, business development, contracting, and a number of other areas that contribute to the enjoyment of social and economic rights.

333. Despite progress in addressing the legacy of segregation and disparities in opportunity and achievement, much work remains to be done to overcome challenges that still exist. Thus, it will be critical for the United States, at all levels, to continue to work on these issues.

With regard to affirmative action, the Committee notes with concern the position taken by the State party that the provisions of the Convention permit, but do not require States parties to adopt affirmative action measures to ensure the adequate development and protection of certain racial, ethnic or national groups. The Committee emphasizes that the adoption of special measures by States parties when the circumstances so warrant, such as in the case of persistent disparities, is an obligation stemming from Article 2, paragraph 2, of the Convention (para. 399).

334. It appears from the text of its conclusion and recommendation that the Committee may have misinterpreted the United States Government's position. As described in the section concerning Article 2 (2), above, the United States acknowledges that Article 2 (2) requires States parties to take special measures "when circumstances so warrant" and, as described in this report, the United States has in place a number of such measures. The decision concerning when such measures are in fact warranted is left to the judgment and discretion of each State Party. The determination of the precise nature and scope of such measures is also left to the judgment and discretion of each State Party, and the United States maintains its position that, consistent with the Convention, special measures taken for the sole purpose of securing adequate advancement of certain racial or ethnic groups or individuals requiring such protection may or may not in themselves be race-based. For example, a "special measure" might address the development or protection of a racial group without the measure itself applying on the basis of race (e.g., a measure might be directed at the neediest members of society without expressly drawing racial distinctions).

The Committee notes with concern that treaties signed by the Government and Indian tribes, described as "domestic dependent nations' under national law, can be abrogated unilaterally by Congress and that the land they possess or use can be taken without compensation by a decision of the Government. It further expresses concern with regard to information on plans for expanding mining and nuclear waste storage on Western Shoshone ancestral land, placing their land up for auction for private sale, and other actions affecting the rights of indigenous peoples. The Committee recommends that the State party ensure effective participation by indigenous communities in decisions affecting them, including those on their land rights, as required under Article 5 (c) of the Convention, and draws the attention of the State party to general recommendation XXIII on indigenous peoples which stresses the importance of securing the "informed consent" of indigenous communities and calls, <u>inter alia</u>, for recognition and compensation for loss. The State party is also encouraged to use as guidance the ILO Convention No. 169 concerning Indigenous and Tribal Peoples in Independent Countries (para 400).

335. <u>Treaties</u>. During its first hundred years of existence, the United States dealt with Indian tribes concerning land occupancy and property rights through federal treaties and legislation. Although treaty making between the federal government and the Indian tribes ended in 1871, the treaties retain their full force and effect even today because they are the legal equivalent of treaties with foreign governments and have the

force of federal law. Further, unlike treaties with foreign governments, treaties with Indian tribes are subject to special canons of construction that tend to favor Indian interests. Notably, Indian treaties are interpreted, to the extent that such original intention is relevant, as they would have been understood by the Indians at the time of their signing, as opposed to by the federal authors of the treaties; and where the treaty is ambiguous as to its interpretation, the Court will interpret it to favor the Indians specifically because it was not written by them or in their language.

336. <u>Lands</u>. At the time the United States was founded, Indian tribes held their land in "aboriginal title," which consisted of a right of use and occupancy. Since then, Congress and the Executive Branch have acted to recognize tribal property rights through treaties, statutes, and executive orders. Today, federally recognized tribes hold virtually all their land in fee simple or in trust (with the United States as trustee holding legal title and the tribe exercising all rights to occupation or use). In either case, tribal holdings of land are fully protected by law.

337. Once Congress has acted to recognize Indian property rights, such as through treaty or statute, any impairment of such rights may be compensable under the Fifth Amendment of the U.S. Constitution. Although the Supreme Court long ago held that Congress had authority to alter treaty obligations of the United States, *Lone Wolf v. Hitchcock*, 187 U.S. 553, (1903), alterations that affect property rights may give rise to a Fifth Amendment claim for compensation. It should also be noted that, even where the occupancy right based on aboriginal title has been found to be not compensable, compensation has in fact been paid by the United States for many Indian land cessions at the time they were made.

338. In 1946, the Congress adopted the Indian Claims Commission Act, which provided for a quasi-judicial body, the Indian Claims Commission (ICC), to consider unresolved Indian claims that had accrued against the United States, a large portion of which involved historical (pre-1946) claims for compensation for taken lands. The act authorized claims to be brought on behalf of "any Indian tribe, band, or other identifiable group of American Indians" with respect to "claims arriving from the taking by the United States, whether as a result of a treaty of cession or otherwise, of lands owned or occupied by the claimant without the payment for such lands of compensation agreed to by the claimant... ." Under the Act, recovery of compensation did not depend on proof of recognized title; compensation was available even if a tribe's property interest was aboriginal only. The ICC represented the exclusive remedy for tribes in suits against the United States, which ordinarily would have been barred by statutes of limitations and sovereign immunity laws. The ICC also recognized lower burdens of proof on claimants, more favorable rules of evidence, and broad, equitable bases of relief in order to help Indians establish their historic claims. Such favorable, pro-claimant procedures would not ordinarily have been available under regular court rules. Indian tribes had five years to file their claims, and they could seek compensation for general wrongs that might not otherwise have been actionable under law. The wording of the act and its legislative history make clear that only financial compensation was contemplated by Congress; the ICC had no authority to restore land rights that had been extinguished. The fact that the ICC could only decide financial compensation was confirmed by the Commission's decision in *Osage Nation of Indians v. United States*, 1 Indian Claims Commission 54 (December 30, 1948), *reversed on other grounds*, 119 Ct. Cl. 592, *cert. denied*, 342 U.S. 896 (1951). To encourage lawyers to assist Indian claimants, the Indian Claims Commission Act provided that lawyers could receive as attorneys' fees up to ten percent of the awards that they won for their Indian clients. For many Indian claimants, the ICC provided the possibility of compensation and a measure of justice that would have been denied to them under the historically restrictive laws and policies that had limited their ability to seek such compensation.

339. In describing the special and unique measures accorded to Indian tribes in this and other respects, it is important to note that, based on the separate status of Indian tribes recognized in the U.S. Constitution, tribes also have a special political relationship with the federal government and are afforded special rights, benefits, and treatment that are not afforded to other sub-national groups or members of society. This special and more favorable treatment is permissible without violating the equal protection standards of the Constitution because it is based on the political relationship between tribes and the U.S. Government rather than the racial heritage of tribal members. *Morton v. Mancari*, 417 U.S. 535 (1974). When indigenous individuals deal with the federal government in their individual capacities, they are of course entitled to the same constitutional rights as all other citizens. On tribal matters, the tribal representatives deal with the U.S. Government in respect of the government-to-government relationship between the federal government and tribes.

340. Article 5(c) and Recommendation XXIII. Article 5 (c) calls for States parties to guarantee the right of everyone to equality before the law with respect to political rights, in particular the right to participate in local, state and federal elections, to take part in the government as well as the conduct of public affairs, and to have equal access to public service. General Recommendation XXIII also calls for equal rights in respect of participation in public affairs. The United States Constitution and federal law ensure the right of members of tribes to participate equally in elections at all levels and in the conduct of public affairs. Tribal members have equal access to public service, as well as a preference to be hired, if qualified, by the Bureau of Indian Affairs in the Department of the Interior and the Indian Health Service in the Department of Health and Human Services.

341. Tribes (as a group) are also afforded rights not afforded to other members of American society with respect to the conduct of public affairs. For example, the United States provides for numerous consultation mechanisms with tribes that are not afforded other members of society. Many executive orders that regulate actions of the U.S. Government require consultation with tribes on federal actions specifically affecting tribes. For example, Executive Order 13175 requires federal agencies to have a process for meaningful input from tribes in the development of regulations and policies that may affect tribes. Other examples include executive orders requiring consultation on protecting Indian sacred sites and on tribal colleges and universities. In addition, consultation with tribes is also mandated on the same basis as consultation with states on issues of national application.

342. Western Shoshone Claims. The United States maintains its position that the issues raised by certain Western Shoshone descendents are not appropriate for consideration under early-warning measures and urgent procedures, which are not contemplated or described within the text of the Convention. In this context, it should be borne in mind that the United States has not made a declaration under Article 14 of the Convention to accept individual complaints. As it indicated in response to the Committee's inquiry, the United States instead addresses these matters in this periodic report. The following two paragraphs present a very brief overview of the Western Shoshone claim. Annex II to this report provides a more detailed explanation of this matter.

343. In 1951, the Western Shoshone, represented by the Te-Moak Bands, brought a land claim before the Indian Claims Commission seeking compensation for the value of Western Shoshone lands that had been taken by the United States. Finding that the Te-Moak Bands of Western Shoshone were organized under the Indian Reorganization Act of 1934 and recognized by the Secretary of Interior as having authority to maintain a suit, the ICC ruled expressly that the Te-Moak Bands of Western Shoshone Indians, Nevada, had the right to maintain the action for and on behalf of the Western Shoshone, the land-using entity. 11 Ind. Cl. Comm. 387, 388. In 1962, over the objections of the U.S. Government, the ICC found that the Western Shoshone had possessed aboriginal title to the territory involved and that these lands had been taken both by gradual encroachment of settlers and miners on the land, and by the U.S. Government's treatment of portions of the land as federal or public lands. The parties to the litigation stipulated that the lands had been taken in 1872, a valuation trial was held, and the ICC declared the value of the lands and sub-surface rights to be over $26 million at the valuation date (compensation worth approximately $157 million as of March 2007).

344. (a) In 1974, certain Western Shoshone descendents, who had been part of the original litigating group, attempted to raise objections to the litigation strategy pursued in the claims case. These persons preferred not to claim compensation for a portion of the lands in favor of restoration of those lands. However, because they had failed to raise their objections in a timely manner so that the matter could be dealt with in the litigation under applicable law, their attempts to intervene were rejected. Specifically, the ICC and the appellate court found their attempt to intervene in the proceedings was untimely because:

(1) they had waited 23 years from the start of the case before seeking to participate despite admitting in their filings to the court that they had been aware of the ICC proceedings for a very long time;

(2) they had not presented an excuse to the court for the delay; and

(3) they had not demonstrated fraud or collusion between the Te-Moak bands, which were prosecuting the case on behalf of the Western Shoshone, and the U.S. government. *Western Shoshone Legal Defense & Education Ass'n v. United States*, 35 Ind. Cl. Comm. 457 (1975); *affirmed*, 531 F.2d 495 (Ct. Cl., 1976).

(b) In 1979, the award was certified and placed in an interest bearing account, and the Supreme Court subsequently found that payment of the award into the trust account represented a full discharge of the United States, pursuant to the ICC Act, from all claims and demands of the Western Shoshone with regard to the lands at issue. *United States v. Dann*, 470 U.S. 39 (1985). Other courts in which these Western

Shoshone descendents have continued to file claims, even after the 1985 Supreme Court decision, have reaffirmed that the Western Shoshone no longer have a property right in the lands they claim. Thus, the Court of Federal Claims (CFC) ruled on September 19, 2006 that the issue of Western Shoshone treaty title had been resolved by the Supreme Court in 1985, and that the Treaty of Ruby Valley does not provide the ownership claimed by the tribes and bands in litigation. The Department of the Interior is developing a process to distribute the award, now worth more than $157 million, to the Western Shoshone descendents.

(c) Because they have been unsuccessful in pursuing their objections, the dissenting Western Shoshone descendents now seek to bring before the CERD Committee what is essentially an internal dispute among the Western Shoshone, despite ample recourse before U.S. courts, including the U.S. Supreme Court, and despite the fact that their position is at odds with the decisions of the representatives of the Western Shoshone made at the time the case was litigated, and that their position does not now represent the views of all Western Shoshone descendents, most of whom wish to receive the compensation as awarded by the ICC. *See* discussion in Annex II.

345. Paragraph 8 of Decision 1 (68) recommends that the rights of the Western Shoshone be respected and protected without discrimination based on race, color, or national or ethnic origin, and that particular attention be paid to ensuring that the cultural rights and right to health of the Western Shoshone are not infringed. The United States does respect and protect the human rights of the Western Shoshone and members of Indian tribes without discrimination based on race, color or national or ethnic origin. In this regard, special benefits are accorded to Indian tribes—benefits not available to other groups or the general population. As noted above, these benefits are based on the unique political status of tribes rather than on race or ethnicity. With regard to the Committee's reference to the "right to health" and "cultural rights," the United States notes that Article 5 of the CERD Convention does not require States parties to ensure enjoyment of such rights (some of which are not recognized as "rights" under U.S. law), but rather to prohibit discrimination in the enjoyment of those rights to the extent they are provided by domestic law. U.S. law fully complies with this requirement.

346. Moreover, the special laws and executive orders relating to Indian tribes noted above include numerous programs designed to help preserve and protect the cultural and ethnic identities of Indian tribes. For example:

• The Native American Graves Protection and Repatriation Act (NAGPRA)—a process for transferring possession and control of human remains, funerary objects, sacred objects, and objects of cultural patrimony to culturally affiliated Indian tribes and individual Indians and Native Hawaiian organizations;

• The Archaeological Resources Protection Act—a process for protecting material remains of human life or activities that are at least 100 years of age and of archaeological interest;

• The American Indian Religions Freedom Act—requiring federal agencies to evaluate their policies and procedures, in consultation with native traditional religious leaders, in order to determine appropriate changes necessary to protect and preserve native religious cultural rights and practices;

• The Indian Arts and Craft Act—promoting economic welfare through development of arts and crafts, as well as protecting against misrepresentation;

• The National Historic Preservation Act—a process for protecting historic and prehistoric archeological sites;

• The Native Languages Act—a policy to preserve, protect, and promote the rights and freedom of Native Americans to use, practice, and develop Native American languages;

• Executive Order 13007—to accommodate access to sacred sites on federal lands.

In addition, provisions within some federal criminal statutes also limit their application in order to protect and preserve native religious practices, including, for example, the sale, possession, and use of peyote and the possession and transfer of eagle feathers and eagle parts. Such protections are uniquely made for Indians to ensure that the cultural and spiritual significance Indians accord to their lands and activities are taken into consideration in decision-making. Thus, far from discriminating against the Western Shoshone, U.S. law provides benefits and protections not enjoyed by the general population.

347. Paragraph 9 of Decision 1 (68) urges an immediate dialogue with the Western Shoshone descendents in order to find a solution acceptable to them, in particular in light of General Recommendation XXIII. The United States would welcome a dialogue with the Western Shoshone descendents to resolve outstanding issues, and dialogue occurs in many areas. As noted above, the Western Shoshone people are organized in six different tribes, bands, and groups, including five federally-recognized tribes. These include the Te-Moak Tribes of Western Shoshone Indians, the Duckwater Shoshone Tribe, the Yomba Shoshone Tribe, and the Ely

Shoshone Tribe, the Western Shoshone Committee of the Duck Valley Reservation, and the Fallon Band of Western Shoshone. As an example of government pursuit of such dialogue, the Bureau of Land Management (BLM) in the Department of the Interior engages various bands of the Western Shoshone about many land use issues, such as: traditional cultural properties; consistency of land uses with environmental requirements, particularly fire fuels reduction projects; oil, gas and geothermal leasing and land sales; matters involving the Archaeological Resources Protection Act (ARPA); and pine nut harvesting. More specifically:

- Traditional properties. The Te-Moak Tribe identified Mt. Tenabo as a traditional cultural property (TCP). Evaluation of Mt. Tenabo, in consultation with various Western Shoshone Tribes and Bands, resulted in two designations: the Mt. Tenabo/White Cliffs Property of Cultural and Religious Importance and the Horse Canyon Property of Cultural and Religious Importance. Two other properties, Tosawihi Quarries and Rock Creek, have been determined eligible for listing on the National Register of Historic Places. The BLM has also regularly taken elders from the Duck Valley Shoshone-Paiute Tribes to the Tosawihi Quarries area to monitor cultural sites that were burned over by wildfire and subsequently left exposed to looters.

- Land Acquisition. The BLM Elko Field Office is working with the Te-Moak Tribe of Western Shoshone (Elko, South Fork, Battle Mountain, and Wells Bands) to acquire land. The BLM's efforts include helping to identify available federal land, providing mapping services and serving as mediator among the tribes and city and country governments.

- Resource Impacts. The BLM Battle Mountain Field Office and the Te-Moak Tribe established the "Cortez Hills Tribal Working Group." The group consists of BLM and tribal staff and leadership. They will identify specific resources affected by mining in the Crescent Valley/Cortez area and explore alternatives or mitigation measures. The South Fork Band asked the BLM to work with them to identify borders of their traditional pine nut harvesting areas in the Sulphur Springs Range and the Roberts Mountains, with the intention to exclude or limit use within these areas by commercial pine nut harvesters. In a separate action, the BLM's Nevada Groundwater Projects Office received concerns and met with a group called the Western Shoshone Defense Project (representing numerous Western Shoshone tribes and bands) regarding the Proposed Clark, Lincoln, and White Pine Counties Groundwater Development Project.

Many other examples of consultation are set forth in Annex II.

348. Dialogue has not always proven easy, however. For example, the BLM, which manages public lands with the mandate to maintain them in healthy condition, has sought repeatedly to engage the Western Shoshone Dann family regarding grazing livestock in trespass on public lands. In 1973, Carrie Dann stopped paying grazing fees for the use of public land. Since that time, Dann livestock use in trespass has resulted in severe overgrazing of the areas used. The Danns have been offered more opportunities than any other public land trespasser to resolve their issues with the BLM, but they have refused to do so.

349. Paragraph 10 of Decision 1 (68) urges adoption of three specific measures, including freezing any plan to privatize ancestral lands, desisting from all activities planned and/or conducted in relation to natural resources, and stopping grazing fees, trespass, and collection notices, etc. The recommended measures from the Committee on the Elimination of Racial Discrimination are inconsistent with the status of these lands under U.S. law, as repeatedly determined by U.S. courts. As noted above, under U.S. court decisions, including the 1977 ICC decision, the Court of Claims appellate decision and the 1985 Supreme Court decision, the Western Shoshone no longer have title to the lands claimed by the dissenting Western Shoshone. The Department of the Interior is developing a process to distribute the judgment, worth more than $157 million, to the Western Shoshone descendents for the historic encroachment on their lands. That judgment was rendered according to the relevant legal obligations in effect. U.S. law has provided the Western Shoshone the same access (and in some respects greater access) than would have been provided to other citizens to the U.S. judiciary and to Congress to present their requests. In all events, as noted above, none of the actions taken by the United States with respect to the Western Shoshone descendents is based on the racial or ethnic identity of those individuals and, thus, such actions are not matters within the scope of the Convention.

350. ILO Convention Number 169. With regard to the Committee's reference to ILO Convention Number 169, the United States notes that it is not a State party to that Convention and that very few countries have ratified it. The United States believes it is appropriate to address the issues herein as they relate to its obligations under the CERD Convention, without reference to legal provisions that are Not applicable to the United States or the large majority of other countries that have not assumed treaty obligations under that instrument.

Noting the absence of data regarding racial discrimination in federal and State prisons and jails, the Committee invites the State party to provide, in its next report, information and statistics on complaints and subsequent action taken in this field (para 401).

351. The requested data is contained in the section concerning Article 5, Prisons.

Having noted the establishment under Executive Order 13107 of 10 December 1998 of the Interagency Working Group with the task of raising the awareness of United States federal agencies about the rights and obligations provided by the Convention, the International Covenant on Civil and Political Rights and the Convention against Torture and Other Cruel, Inhuman or Degrading Punishment or Treatment, the Committee invites the State party to provide in its next report further information on the powers of the Working Group and the impact of its activities. In this context, the Committee also notes that the present State party report primarily focuses on the implementation of the Convention at the federal level and recommends that the next periodic report contain comprehensive information on its implementation of the State and local levels and in all territories under United States jurisdiction, including Puerto Rico, the Virgin Islands, America Samoa, Guam and the Northern Mariana Islands (para 402).

352. The Interagency Working Group on the Implementation of Human Rights Treaties continues to function under the leadership of the National Security Council in the White House and, among other things, oversees issues of human rights policy, as well as the preparation of United States reports to the United Nations Human Rights Commission and its constituent bodies. Indeed, the present report, like the May and October 2005 reports on U.S. implementation, respectively, of the Convention Against Torture and Other Cruel, Inhuman or Degrading Treatment or Punishment and the International Covenant on Civil and Political Rights, was organized under the auspices of that Interagency Working Group. The working group further acts as a point of contact and policy coordination on a wide range of U.S. bilateral and multilateral human rights initiatives, including U.S. participation in the United Nations General Assembly's Third Committee and the U.N. Human Rights Council.

353. Representative information concerning implementation at the state, local, and territorial levels is presented in the body of the report. Reporting at length on all 50 separate states and the territories would be extremely burdensome and so lengthy as to be unhelpful to the Committee. As an alternative, in addition to the representative information in the body of the report, we have included an Annex reporting at greater length on the programs in four states with varying geographic locations and varying racial and ethnic population compositions. This represents a milestone in U.S. human rights treaty reporting, which we hope will be of use to the Committee.

The Committee further recommends that the next State party report contain socio-economic data, disaggregated by race, ethnic origin and gender, on, in particular: (a) the indigenous and Arab-American population; and (b) the populations of the States of Alaska and Hawaii (para 403).

354. The requested information is set forth in the section on Land and People, above.

It is noted that the State party has not made the optional declaration provided for in Article 14 of the Convention, and the Committee recommends that the possibility of such a declaration be considered (para 404).

355. In submitting the Convention to the United States Senate for ratification, President Carter recognized that if the Senate gave its advice and consent to ratification, the President would then have the right to decide whether to make a declaration, pursuant to Article 14 of the Convention, recognizing the competence of the Committee on the Elimination of Racial Discrimination to consider communications from individuals. If such a declaration were contemplated, he noted that it would be submitted to the Senate for consent to ratification. The United States remains aware of the possibility of making the optional declaration under Article 14, but has not made any decision to do so.

The Committee recommends that the State party ratify the amendments to Article 8, paragraph 6 of the Convention, adopted on 15 January 1992 at the Fourteenth Meeting of States Parties to the Convention (para 405).

356. It is the general policy of the United States that the financial obligations of treaty bodies should be funded by the States parties to the particular treaty at issue. The United States believes that the costs of the CERD Committee should be funded under the Convention itself by the parties thereto, as required by the Convention in its original form, and thus does not support the amendment to Article 8, paragraph 6.

The Committee recommends that the State party's reports continue to be made readily available to the public from the time they are submitted and that the Committee's observations on them be similarly publicized (para 406).

357. The United States agrees with the Committee's intention that the public have access to its deliberations, and the United States will continue to make available to the public both its reports to the Committee and the Committee's responses, as well as all publicly available Committee documents.

The Committee recommends that the State party submit its fourth periodic report jointly with its fifth periodic report, due on 20 November 2003, and that it address all points raised in the present observations (para 407).

358. This report constitutes the fourth, fifth, and sixth periodic reports of the United States. It addresses the points raised in the Committee's observations concerning the Initial U.S. Report.

DOCUMENT 26

Full Official Title: Consideration of Reports Submitted by States Parties Under Article 9 of the Convention: Concluding Observations of the Committee on the Elimination of Racial Discrimination— United States of America

Short Title/Acronym/Abbreviation: CERD Concluding Observations on the Fourth, Fifth and Sixth U.S. Periodic Reports

Subject: Racial discrimination

Official Citation: U.N. Doc CERD/C/USA/CO/6

Date of Document: May 8, 2008

Date of Adoption: Not applicable

Date of General Entry into Force (EIF): Not applicable

Number of States Parties as of this printing: Not applicable

Date of Signature by the United States: Not applicable

Date of Ratification/Accession/Adhesion: Not applicable

Date of Entry into Force as to United States (effective date): Not applicable

Type of Document: Written response to a state report, from a treaty-based body, the U.N. Committee on the Elimination of Racial Discrimination. This is not a legal document as such, but a response as to how the United States is complying with a legal instrument, the ICERD, and how it could improve.

Legal Status/Character of the Instrument/Document as to the United States: Not legally binding. Theoretically, the comments and concluding observations of the ICERD Committee should be seriously considered, followed, and applied by the U.S. because of the authority and competence of the Committee. It should help guide the United States as to how to comply better with the ICERD.

Supervising Body: Committee on the Elimination of Racial Discrimination

Comments: By ratifying the ICERD the U.S. agreed, under Article 9, to report to the Committee on the Elimination of Racial Discrimination on measures they have adopted to give effect to the rights recognized in the Covenant, or any progress they have made in the enjoyment of those rights, and respond to the Committee's observations, comments, and recommendations on the report. These comments, etc. are made in light of the Committee's general comments made from its experience in reviewing other reports, and the jurisprudence (case decisions called "views") arising from the complaints it handles, especially under Article 14 regarding individual complaints. They are not supposed to be made for political reasons or to criticize the reporting state, but to help it fulfill its legal obligations under the ICERD.

The report is very large and could not be reprinted in its entirety. Only selected excerpts corresponding to certain articles of the ICERD are included. The reader should consult the following website to obtain the full text.

Web Address: http://www.state.gov/documents/organization/107361.pdf

CERD CONCLUDING OBSERVATIONS ON THE U.S. REPORT ON ICERD (EXCERPTS)

1. The Committee considered the fourth, fifth and sixth periodic reports of the Unite States of America, submitted in a single document (CERD/C/USA/6), at its 1853rd and 1854th meetings (CERD/C/SR.1853 and 1854), held on 21 and 22 February 2008. At its 1870th meeting (CERD/C/SR.1870), held on 5 March 2008, it adopted the following concluding observations.

A. Introduction

2. The Committee welcomes the reports, and the opportunity to continue an open and constructive dialogue with the State party. The Committee also expresses appreciation for the detailed responses provided to the list of issues, as well as for the efforts made by the high-level delegation to answer the wide range of questions raised during the dialogue.

B. Positive aspects

3. The Committee welcomes the acknowledgement of the multi-racial, multi-ethnic, and multi-cultural nature of the State party.

4. The Committee notes with satisfaction the work carried out by the various executive departments and agencies of the State party which have responsibilities in the field of the elimination of racial discrimination, including the Civil Rights Division of the U.S Department of Justice, the Equal Employment Opportunity Commission (EEOC) and the Department of Housing and Urban Development (HUD).

5. The Committee welcomes the reauthorisation, in 2005, of the Violence Against Women Act of 1994 (VAWA).

6. The Committee also welcomes the reauthorisation, in 2006, of the Voting Rights Act of 1965 (VRA).

7. The Committee commends the launch, in 2007, of the E-RACE Initiative ("Eradicating Racism and Colorism from Employment"), aimed at raising awareness on the issue of racial discrimination in the workplace.

8. The Committee notes with satisfaction the creation, in 2007, of the National Partnership for Action to End Health Disparities for Ethnic and Racial Minority Populations, as well as the various programmes adopted by the U.S. Department of Health and Human Services (HHS) to address the persistent health disparities affecting low-income persons belonging to racial, ethnic and national minorities.

9. The Committee also notes with satisfaction the California Housing Element Law of 1969, which requires each local jurisdiction to adopt a housing element in its general plan to meet the housing needs of all segments of the population, including low-income persons belonging to racial, ethnic and national minorities.

C. Concerns and recommendations

10. The Committee reiterates the concern expressed in paragraph 393 of its previous concluding observations of 2001 (A/56/18, paras. 380–407) that the definition of racial discrimination used in the federal and state legislation and in court practice is not always in line with that contained in Article 1, paragraph 1, of the Convention, which requires States parties to prohibit and eliminate racial discrimination in all its forms, including practices and legislation that may not be discriminatory in purpose, but in effect. In this regard, the Committee notes that indirect, or de facto,– discrimination occurs where an apparently neutral provision, criterion or practice would put persons of a particular racial, ethnic or national origin at a disadvantage compared with other persons, unless that provision, criterion or practice is objectively justified by a legitimate aim and the means of achieving that aim are appropriate and necessary (art.1 (1)).

The Committee recommends that the State party review the definition of racial discrimination used in the federal and state legislation and in court practice, so as to ensure, in light of the definition of racial discrimination provided for in Article 1, paragraph 1, of the Convention,– that it prohibits racial discrimination in all its forms, including practices and legislation that may not be discriminatory in purpose, but in effect.

11. While appreciating that the Constitution and laws of the State party may be used in many instances to prohibit private actors from engaging in acts of racial discrimination, the Committee remains concerned about the wide scope of the reservation entered by the State party at the time of ratification of the Convention with respect to discriminatory acts perpetrated by private individuals, groups or organisations (art. 2).

The Committee recommends that the State party consider withdrawing or narrowing the scope of its reservation to Article 2 of the Convention, and to broaden the protection afforded by the law against discriminatory acts perpetrated by private individuals, groups or organizations.

12. The Committee notes that no independent national human rights institution established in accordance with the Paris Principles (General Assembly resolution 48/134, annex) exists in the State party (art. 2).

The Committee recommends that the State party consider the establishment of an independent national human rights institution in accordance with the Paris Principles.

13. While welcoming the acknowledgement by the delegation that the State party is bound to apply the Convention throughout its territory and to ensure its effective application at all levels, federal, state, and local, regardless of the federal structure of its Government, the Committee notes with concern the lack of appropriate and effective mechanisms to ensure a coordinated approach towards the implementation of the Convention at the federal, state and local levels (art. 2).

The Committee recommends that the State party establish appropriate mechanisms to ensure a coordinated approach towards the implementation of the Convention at the federal, state and local levels.

14. The Committee notes with concern that despite the measures adopted at the federal and state levels to combat racial profiling, including the elaboration by the Civil Rights Division of the U.S. Department of Justice of the Guidance Regarding the Use of Race by Federal Law Enforcement Agencies,– such practice continues to be widespread. In particular, the Committee is deeply concerned about the increase in racial profiling against Arabs, Muslims and South Asians in the wake of the 11 September 2001 attack, as well as about the development of the National Entry and Exit Registration System (NEERS) for nationals of 25 countries, all located in the Middle East, South Asia or North Africa (arts. 2 and 5 (b)).

Bearing in mind its general recommendation No. 31 (2005) on the prevention of racial discrimination in the administration and functioning of the criminal justice system, the Committee recommends that the State party strengthen its efforts to combat racial profiling at the federal and state levels, inter alia, by moving expeditiously towards the adoption of the End Racial Profiling Act, or similar federal legislation. The Committee also draws the attention of the State party to its general recommendation No. 30 (2004) on discrimination against non-citizens, according to which measures taken in the fight against terrorism must not discriminate, in purpose or effect, on the grounds of race, colour, descent, or national or ethnic origin, and urges the State party, in accordance with Article 2, paragraph 1 (c), of the Convention, to put an end to the National Entry and Exit Registration System (NEERS) and to eliminate other forms of racial profiling against Arabs, Muslims and South Asians.

15. The Committee notes with concern that recent case law of the U.S. Supreme Court and the use of voter referenda to prohibit states from adopting race-based affirmative action measures have further limited the permissible use of special measures as a tool to eliminate persistent disparities in the enjoyment of human rights and fundamental freedoms (art. 2 (2)).

The Committee reiterates that the adoption of special measures "when circumstances so warrant" is an obligation arising from Article 2, paragraph 2, of the Convention. The Committee therefore calls once again upon the State party to adopt and strengthen the use of such measures when circumstances warrant their use as a tool to eliminate the persistent disparities in the enjoyment of human rights and fundamental freedoms and ensure the adequate development and protection of members of racial, ethnic and national minorities.

16. The Committee is deeply concerned that racial, ethnic and national minorities,especially Latino and African American persons, are disproportionately concentrated in poor residential areas characterised by sub-standard housing conditions, limited employment opportunities, inadequate access to health care facilities, under-resourced schools and high exposure to crime and violence (art. 3).

The Committee urges the State party to intensify its efforts aimed at reducing the phenomenon of residential segregation based on racial, ethnic and national origin, as well as its negative consequences for the affected individuals and groups. In particular, the Committee recommends that the State party:

(i) Support the development of public housing complexes outside poor, racially segregated areas;

(ii) Eliminate the obstacles that limit affordable housing choice and mobility for beneficiaries of Section 8 Housing Choice Voucher Program; and (iii) Ensure the effective implementation of legislation adopted at the federal and state levels to combat discrimination in housing, including the phenomenon of "steering" and other discriminatory practices carried out by private actors.

17. The Committee remains concerned about the persistence of de facto racial segregation in public schools. In this regard, the Committee notes with particular concern that the recent U.S. Supreme Court decisions in *Parents Involved in Community Schools* v. Seattle School District No. 1 (2007) and *Meredith* v. *Jefferson County Board of Education* (2007) have rolled back the progress made since the U.S. Supreme Court's landmark decision in *Brown* v. *Board of Education* (1954), and limited the ability of public school districts to address de facto segregation by prohibiting the use of race-conscious measures as a tool to promote integration (arts. (2), 3 and 5 (e) (v)).

The Committee recommends that the State party undertake further studies to identify the underlying causes of de facto segregation and racial inequalities in education, with a view to elaborating effective strategies aimed at promoting school desegregation and providing equal educational opportunity in integrated settings for all students. In this regard, the Committee recommends that the State party take all appropriate measures, including the enactment of legislation,– to restore the possibility for school districts to voluntarily promote school integration through the use of carefully tailored special measures adopted in accordance to Article 2, paragraph 2, of the Convention.

18. While appreciating that some forms of hate speech and other activities designed to intimidate, such as the burning of crosses, are not protected under the First Amendment to the U.S. Constitution, the Committee remains concerned about the wide scope of the reservation entered by the State party at the time of ratification of the Convention with respect to the dissemination of ideas based on racial superiority and hatred (art. 4).

The Committee

The Committee draws the attention of the State party to its general recommendations No. 7 (1985) and 15 (1993) concerning the implementation of Article 4 of the Convention, and request the State party to consider withdrawing or narrowing the scope of its reservations to Article 4 of the Convention. In this regard, the Committee wishes to reiterate that the prohibition of all ideas based on racial superiority or hatred is compatible with the right to freedom of opinion and expression, given that the exercise of this right carries special duties and responsibilities, including the obligation not to disseminate racist ideas.

19. While noting the explanations provided by the State party with regard to the situation of the Western Shoshone indigenous peoples, considered by the Committee under its early warning and urgent action procedure, the Committee strongly regrets that the State party has not followed up on the recommendations contained in paragraphs 8 to 10 of its decision 1 (68) of 2006 (CERD/C/USA /DEC/1) (art.5).

The Committee reiterates its Decision 1 (68) in its entirety, and urges the State party to implement all the recommendations contained therein.

20. The Committee reiterates its concern with regard to the persistent racial disparities in the criminal justice system of the State party, including the disproportionate number of persons belonging to racial, ethnic and national minorities in the prison population, allegedly due to the harsher treatment that defendants belonging to these minorities, especially African American persons, receive at various stages of criminal proceedings (art.5 (a)).

Bearing in mind its general recommendation No. 31 (2005) on the prevention of racial discrimination in the administration and functioning of the criminal justice system, according to which stark racial disparities in the administration and functioning of the criminal justice system, including the disproportionate number of persons belonging to racial, ethnic and national minorities in the prison population, may be regarded as factual indicators of racial discrimination, the Committee recommends that the State party take all necessary steps to guarantee the right of everyone to equal treatment before tribunals and all other organs administering justice, including further studies to determine the nature and scope of the problem, and the implementation of national strategies or plans of action aimed at the elimination of structural racial discrimination.

21. The Committee notes with concern that according to information received, young offenders belonging to racial, ethnic and national minorities, including children, constitute a disproportionate number of those sentenced to life imprisonment without parole (art. 5 (a)).

The Committee recalls the concerns expressed by the Human Rights Committee (CCPR/C/USA/ CO/3/Rev.1, para. 34) and the Committee against Torture (CAT/C/USA/CO/2, para. 34) with regard to federal and state legislation allowing the use of life imprisonment without parole against young offenders, including children. In light of the disproportionate imposition of life imprisonment without parole on young offenders, including children, belonging to racial, ethnic and national minorities, the Committee considers that the persistence of such sentencing is incompatible with Article 5 (a) of the Convention. The Committee therefore recommends that the State party discontinue the use of life sentence without parole against persons under the age of eighteen at the time the offence was committed, and review the situation of persons already serving such sentences.

22. While welcoming the recent initiatives undertaken by the State party to improve the quality of criminal defence programmes for indigent persons, the Committee is concerned about the disproportionate impact that persistent systemic inadequacies in these programmes have on indigent defendants belonging to racial, ethnic and national minorities. The Committee also notes with concern the disproportionate impact that the lack of a generally recognized right to counsel in civil proceedings has on indigent persons belonging to racial, ethnic and national minorities (art. 5 (a)).

The Committee recommends that the State party adopt all necessary measures to eliminate the disproportionate impact that persistent systemic inadequacies in criminal defence programmes for indigent persons have on defendants belonging to racial, ethnic and national minorities, inter alia, by increasing its efforts to improve the quality of legal representation provided to indigent defendants and ensuring that public legal aid systems are adequately funded and supervised. The Committee further recommends that the State party allocate sufficient resources to ensure legal representation of indigent persons belonging to racial, ethnic and national minorities in civil proceedings, with particular regard to those proceedings where basic human needs, such as housing, health care, or child custody, are at stake.

23. The Committee remains concerned about the persistent and significant racial disparities with regard to the imposition of the death penalty, particularly those associated with the race of the victim, as evidenced by a number of studies, including a recent study released in October 2007 by the American Bar Association (ABA)[1] (art. 5 (a)).

Taking into account its general recommendation No. 31 (2005) on the prevention of racial discrimination in the administration and functioning of the criminal justice system, the Committee recommends that the State party undertake further studies to identify the underlying factors of the substantial racial disparities in the imposition of the death penalty, with a view to elaborating effective strategies aimed at rooting out discriminatory practices. The Committee wishes to reiterate its previous recommendation contained in paragraph 396 of its previous concluding observations of 2001, that the State party adopt all necessary measures, including a moratorium, to ensure that death penalty is not imposed as a result of racial bias on the part of prosecutors, judges, juries and lawyers.

24. The Committee regrets the position taken by State party that the Convention is Not applicable to the treatment of foreign detainees held as "enemy combatants", on the basis of the argument that the law of armed conflict is the exclusive *lex specialis* applicable, and that in any event the Convention "would be inapplicable to allegations of unequal treatment of foreign detainees" in accordance to Article 1, paragraph 2, of the Convention. The Committee also notes with concern that the State party exposes non-citizens under its jurisdiction to the risk of being subjected to torture or cruel, inhuman or degrading treatment or punishment by means of transfer, rendition, or refoulement to third countries where there are substantial reasons to believe that they will be subjected to such treatment (arts. 5 (a), 5 (b) and 6).

Bearing in mind its general recommendation No. 30 (2004) on noncitizens, the Committee wishes to reiterate that States parties are under an obligation to guarantee equality between citizens and noncitizens in the enjoyment of the rights set forth in Article 5 of the Convention, including the right to equal treatment before the tribunals and all other organs administering justice, to the extent recognised under international law, and that Article 1, paragraph 2, must be construed so as to avoid undermining the basic prohibition of discrimination set out in Article 1, paragraph 1, of the Convention.

The Committee also recalls its Statement on racial discrimination and measures to combat terrorism (A/57/18), according to which States parties to the Convention are under an obligation to ensure that measures taken in the struggle against terrorism do not discriminate in purpose or effect on grounds of race, colour, descent or national or ethnic origin.

The Committee therefore urges the State party to adopt all necessary measures to guarantee the right of foreign detainees held as "enemy combatants" to judicial review of the lawfulness and conditions of detention, as well as their right to remedy for human rights violations. The Committee further requests the State party to ensure that non-citizens detained or arrested in the fight against terrorism are effectively protected by domestic law, in compliance with international human rights, refugee and humanitarian law.

25. While recognising the efforts made by the State party to combat the pervasive phenomenon of police brutality, the Committee remains concerned about allegations of brutality and use of excessive or deadly force by law enforcement officials against persons belonging to racial, ethnic or national minorities, in particular Latino and African American persons and undocumented migrants crossing the U.S.-Mexico border. The Committee also notes with concern that despite the efforts made by the State party to prosecute law enforcement officials for criminal misconduct, impunity of police officers responsible for abuses allegedly remains a widespread problem (arts. 5 (b) and 6).

---

[1] American Bar Association, "State Death Penalty Assessments: Key Findings," 29 October 2007, http://www.abanet.org/moratorium/assessmentproject/keyfindings.doc.

The Committee recommends that the State party increase significantly its efforts to eliminate police brutality and excessive use of force against persons belonging to racial, ethnic or national minorities, as well as undocumented migrants crossing the U.S.-Mexico border, inter alia, by establishing adequate systems for monitoring police abuses and developing further training opportunities for law enforcement officials. The Committee further requests the State party to ensure that reports of police brutality and excessive use of force are independently, promptly and thoroughly investigated and that perpetrators are prosecuted and appropriately punished.

26. While welcoming the various measures adopted by the State party to prevent and punish violence and abuse against women belonging to racial, ethnic and national minorities, the Committee remains deeply concerned about the incidence of rape and sexual violence experienced by women belonging to such groups, particularly with regard to American Indian and Alaska Native women and female migrant workers, especially domestic workers. The Committee also notes with concern that the alleged insufficient will of federal and state authorities to take action with regard to such violence and abuse often deprives victims belonging to racial, ethnic and national minorities, and in particular Native American women, of their right to access to justice and the right to obtain adequate reparation or satisfaction for damages suffered (arts. 5 (b) and 6).

The Committee recommends that the State party increase its efforts to prevent and punish violence and abuse against women belonging to racial, ethnic and national minorities, inter alia, by:

(i) Setting up and adequately funding prevention and early assistance centres, counselling services and temporary shelters;

(ii) Providing specific training for those working within the criminal justice system, including police officers, lawyers, prosecutors and judges, and medical personnel;

(iii) Undertaking information campaigns to raise awareness among women belonging to racial, ethnic and national minorities about the mechanisms and procedures provided for in national legislation on racism and discrimination; and (iv) Ensuring that reports of rape and sexual violence against women belonging to racial, ethnic and national minorities, and in particular Native American women, are independently, promptly and thoroughly investigated, and that perpetrators are prosecuted and appropriately punished. The Committee requests the State party to include information on the results of these measures and on the number of victims, perpetrators, convictions, and the types of sanctions imposed, in its next periodic report.

27. The Committee remains concerned about the disparate impact that existing felon disenfranchisement laws have on a large number of persons belonging to racial, ethnic and national minorities, in particular African American persons, who are disproportionately represented at every stage of the criminal justice system. The Committee notes with particular concern that in some states, individuals remain disenfranchised even after the completion of their sentences (art. 5 (c)).

Taking into account the disproportionate impact that the implementation of disenfranchisement laws has on a large number of persons belonging to racial, ethnic and national minorities, in particular African American persons, the Committee recommends that the State Party adopt all appropriate measures to ensure that the denial of voting rights is used only with regard to persons convicted of the most serious crimes, and that the right to vote is in any case automatically restored after the completion of the criminal sentence.

28. The Committee regrets that despite the various measures adopted by the State party to enhance its legal and institutional mechanisms aimed at combating discrimination, workers belonging to racial, ethnic and national minorities, in particular women and undocumented migrant workers, continue to face discriminatory treatment and abuse in the workplace, and to be disproportionately represented in occupations characterized by long working hours, low wages, and unsafe or dangerous conditions of work. The Committee also notes with concern that recent judicial decisions of the U.S. Supreme Court—including *Hoffman Plastics Compound, Inc.* v. *NLRB* (2007), *Ledbetter* v. *Goodyear Tire and Rubber Co.* (2007) and *Long Island Care at Home, Ltd.* v. *Coke* (2007)—have further eroded the ability of workers belonging to racial, ethnic and national minorities to obtain legal protection and redress in cases of discriminatory treatment at the workplace, unpaid or withheld wages, or work-related injury or illnesses (arts. 5 (e) (i) and 6).

The Committee recommends that the State party take all appropriate measures, including increasing the use of "pattern and practice" investigations, to combat de facto discrimination in the workplace and ensure the equal and effective enjoyment by persons belonging to racial, ethnic and national minorities of their rights under Article 5 (e) of the Convention. The Committee further recommends that the State party take effective measures, including the enactment of legislation, such as the proposed Civil Rights Act of 2008,– to ensure the right of workers belonging to racial, ethnic and national minorities, including undocumented migrant workers, to obtain effective protection and remedies in case of violation of their human rights by their employer.

29. The Committee is concerned about reports relating to activities, such as nuclear testing, toxic and dangerous waste storage, mining or logging, carried out or planned in areas of spiritual and cultural significance to Native Americans, and about the negative impact that such activities allegedly have on the enjoyment by the affected indigenous peoples of their rights under the Convention (arts. 5 (d) (v), 5 (e) (iv) and 5 (e) (vi)).

The Committee recommends that the State party take all appropriate measures, in consultation with indigenous peoples concerned and their representatives chosen in accordance with their own procedure,— to ensure that activities carried out in areas of spiritual and cultural significance to Native Americans do not have a negative impact on the enjoyment of their rights under the Convention.

The Committee further recommends that the State party recognize the right of Native Americans to participate in decisions affecting them, and consult and cooperate in good faith with the indigenous peoples concerned before adopting and implementing any activity in areas of spiritual and cultural significance to Native Americans. While noting the position of the State party with regard to the United Nations Declaration on the Rights of Indigenous Peoples (A/RES/61/295), the Committee finally recommends that the declaration be used as a guide to interpret the State party's obligations under the Convention relating to indigenous peoples.

30. The Committee notes with concern the reports of adverse effects of economic activities connected with the exploitation of natural resources in countries outside the United States by trans national corporations registered in the State party on the right to land, health, living environment and the way of life of indigenous peoples living in these regions (arts. 2 (1) (d) and 5 (e)).

In light of Article 2, paragraph 1 (d), and 5 (e) of the Convention and of its general recommendation No. 23 (1997) on the rights of indigenous peoples, the Committee encourages the State party to take appropriate legislative or administrative measures to prevent acts of transnational corporations registered in the State party which negatively impact on the enjoyment of rights of indigenous peoples in territories outside the United States. In particular, the Committee recommends that the State party explore ways to hold transnational corporations registered in the United States accountable. The Committee requests the State party to include in its next periodic report information on the effects of activities of trans national corporations registered in the United States on indigenous peoples abroad and on any measures taken in this regard.

31. The Committee, while noting the efforts undertaken by the State party and civil society organizations to assist the persons displaced by Hurricane Katrina of 2005, remains concerned about the disparate impact that this natural disaster continues to have on low income African American residents, many of whom continue to be displaced after more than two years after the hurricane (art. 5 (e) (iii)).

The Committee recommends that the State party increase its efforts in order to facilitate the return of persons displaced by Hurricane Katrina to their homes, if feasible, or to guarantee access to adequate and affordable housing, where possible in their place of habitual residence. In particular, the Committee calls upon the State party to ensure that every effort is made to ensure genuine consultation and participation of persons displaced by Hurricane Katrina in the design and implementation of all decisions affecting them.

32. While noting the wide range of measures and policies adopted by the State party to improve access to health insurance and adequate health-care and services, the Committee is concerned that a large number of persons belonging to racial, ethnic and national minorities still remain without health insurance and face numerous obstacles to access to adequate health care and services (art. 5 (e) (iv)).

The Committee recommends that the State party continue its efforts to address the persistent health disparities affecting persons belonging to racial, ethnic and national minorities, in particular by eliminating the obstacles that currently prevent or limit their access to adequate health care, such as lack of health insurance, unequal distribution of health-care resources, persistent racial discrimination in the provision of health care and poor quality of public health-care services. The Committee requests the State party to collect statistical data on health disparities affecting persons belonging to racial, ethnic and national minorities, disaggregated by age, gender, race, ethnic or national origin, and to include it in its next periodic report.

33. The Committee regrets that despite the efforts of the State party, wide racial disparities continue to exist in the field of sexual and reproductive health, particularly with regard to the high maternal and infant mortality rates among women and children belonging to racial, ethnic and national minorities, especially African Americans, the high incidence of unintended pregnancies and greater abortion rates affecting African American women, and the growing disparities in HIV infection rates for minority women (art. 5 (e) (iv)).

The Committee recommends that the State party continue its efforts to address persistent racial disparities in sexual and reproductive health, in particular by:

(i) Improving access to maternal health care, family planning, pre and post—natal care and emergency obstetric services, inter alia, through the reduction of eligibility barriers for Medicaid coverage;

(ii) Facilitating access to adequate contraceptive and family planning methods; and

(iii) Providing adequate sexual education aimed at the prevention of unintended pregnancies and sexually-transmitted infections.

34. While welcoming the measures adopted by the State party to reduce the significant disparities in the field of education, including the adoption of the No Child Left Behind Act of 2001 (NCLB), the Committee remains concerned about the persistent "achievement gap" between students belonging to racial, ethnic or national minorities, including English Language Learner ("ELL") students, and white students. The Committee also notes with concern that alleged racial disparities in suspension, expulsion and arrest rates in schools contribute to exacerbate the high dropout rate and the referral to the justice system of students belonging to racial, ethnic or national minorities (art.5 (e) (v)).

The Committee recommends that the State party adopt all appropriate measures,—including special measures in accordance with Article 2, paragraph 2, of the Convention,—to reduce the persistent "achievement gap" between students belonging to racial, ethnic or national minorities and white students in the field of education, inter alia, by improving the quality of education provided to these students. The Committee also calls upon the State party to encourage school districts to review their "zero tolerance" school discipline policies, with a view to limiting the imposition of suspension or expulsion to the most serious cases of school misconduct, and to provide training opportunities for police officers deployed to patrol school hallways.

35. While welcoming the clarifications offered by the State party with regard to the burden of proof in racial discrimination claims under civil rights statutes, the Committee remains concerned that claims of racial discrimination under the Due Process Clause of the Fifth Amendment to the U.S. Constitution and the Equal Protection Clause of the Fourteenth Amendment must be accompanied by proof of intentional discrimination (arts. 1 (1) and 6).

The Committee recommends that the State party review its federal and state legislation and practice concerning the burden of proof in racial discrimination claims, with a view to allowing, in accordance with Article 1, paragraph 1 of the Convention, a more balanced sharing of the burden of proof between the plaintiff, who must establish a, prima facie, case of discrimination, whether direct or based on a disparate impact, and the defendant, who should provide evidence of an objective and reasonable justification for the differential treatment. The Committee calls in particular on the State Party to consider adoption of the Civil Rights Act of 2008.

36. The Committee regrets that despite the efforts made by the State party to provide training programmes and courses on anti-discrimination legislation adopted at the federal and state levels, no specific training programmes or courses have been provided to, inter alia, government officials, the judiciary, federal and state law enforcement officials, teachers, social workers and other public officials in order to raise their awareness about the Convention and its provisions. Similarly, the Committee notes with regret that information about the Convention and its provisions has not been brought to the attention of the public in general (art.7).

The Committee recommends that the State party organize public awareness and education programmes on the Convention and its provisions, and step up its efforts to make government officials, the judiciary, federal and state law enforcement officials, teachers, social workers and the public in general aware about the responsibilities of the State party under the Convention, as well as the mechanisms and procedures provided for by the Convention in the field of racial discrimination and intolerance.

37. The Committee requests the State party to provide, in its next periodic report, detailed information on the legislation applicable to refugees and asylum-seekers, and on the alleged mandatory and prolonged detention of a large number of non-citizens, includng undocumented migrant workers, victims of trafficking, asylum-seekers and refugees, as well as members of their families (arts. 5 (b), 5 (e) (iv) and 6).

38. The Committee also requests the State party to provide, in its next periodic report, detailed information on the measures adopted to preserve and promote the culture and traditions of American Indian and Alaska Native (AIAN) and Native Hawaiian and Other Pacific Islander (NHPI) peoples. The Committee further requests the State party to provide information on the extent to which curricula and textbooks for primary and secondary schools reflect the multi-ethnic nature of the State party, and provide sufficient information on the history and culture of the different racial, ethnic and national groups living in its territory (art. 7).

39. The Committee is aware of the position of the State party with regard to the Durban Declaration and Programme of Action and its follow-up, but in view of the importance that such a process has for the achievement of the goals of the Convention, it calls upon the State party to consider participating in the preparatory process as well as in the Durban Review Conference itself.

40. The Committee notes that the State party has not made the optional declaration provided for in Article 14 of the Convention and invites it to consider doing so.

41. The Committee recommends that the State party ratify the amendment to Article 8, paragraph 6, of the Convention, adopted on 15 January 1992 at the fourteenth meeting of States parties to the Convention and endorsed by General Assembly resolution 47/111. In this connection, the Committee cites General Assembly resolution 61/148, in which the Assembly strongly urged States parties to accelerate their domestic ratification procedures with regard to the amendment and to notify the Secretary-General expeditiously in writing of their agreement to the amendment.

42. The Committee recommends that the State party's reports be made readily available to the public at the time of their submission, and that the observations of the Committee with respect to these reports be similarly publicised in the official and national languages.

43. The Committee recommends that the State party, in connection with the preparation of the next periodic report, consult widely with organizations of civil society working in the area of human rights protection, in particular in combating racial discrimination.

44. The Committee invites the State party to update its core document in accordance with the harmonised guidelines on reporting under the international human rights treaties, in particular those on the common core document, as adopted by the fifth inter-Committee meeting of the human rights treaty bodies held in June 2006 (HRI/GEN/2/Rev.4).

45. The State party should, within one year, provide information on the way it has followed up on the Committee's recommendations contained in paragraphs 14, 19, 21, 31 and 36, pursuant to paragraph 1 of rule 65 of the rules of procedure.

46. The Committee recommends that the State party submit its seventh, eighth and ninth periodic reports in a single document, due on 20 November 2011, and that the report be comprehensive and address all points raised in the present concluding observations.

DOCUMENT 27

Full Official Title: Convention on the Elimination of All Forms of Discrimination Against Women
Short Title/Acronym/Abbreviation: The Women's Convention/CEDAW
Subject: Establishing recognition of international human rights protecting women from discrimination in a multilateral treaty
Official Citation: G.A. res. 34/180, 34 U.N. GAOR Supp. (No. 46) at 193, U.N. Doc. A/34/46, at 1249 U.N.T.S. 13
Date of Document: Not applicable
Date of Adoption: December 18, 1979
Date of General Entry into Force (EIF): September 3, 1981
Number of States Parties to this Treaty as of this printing: 186
Date of Signature by United States: December 17, 1980
Date of Ratification/Accession/Adhesion: United States has not ratified as of this printing

Date of Entry into Force as to United States (effective date): Has not entered into force as to United States

Type of Document: A treaty, an international legal instrument

Legal Status/Character of the Instrument/Document as to the United States: The United States has signed but not yet ratified CEDAW as of the date of this publication. It is before the U.S. Senate for debate and is facing much opposition. However, under certain principles of international law contained in the Vienna Convention on the Law of Treaties the United States should act consistently with legal instruments it has signed, as an indication of its good faith intent to act accordingly, until ratification.

Supervising Body: Committee on the Elimination of Discrimination against Women

Comments: A very politically controversial treaty. The reluctance of the Senate to ratify has included concerns on the interpretation of certain articles, for example, those relating to affirmative action considerations. Some opponents question whether or not this treaty is necessary, considering the strong gender equality laws that are already enacted in U.S. law.

Caution: The status and applicability of this instrument as to the United States may have changed since date of publication. The above information may be updated by referring to the following site:

Web address: http://www.unhchr.ch/html/menu3/b/21.htm

Convention on the Elimination of All Forms of Discrimination Against Women (CEDAW)

The States Parties to the present Convention,

Noting that the Charter of the United Nations reaffirms faith in fundamental human rights, in the dignity and worth of the human person and in the equal rights of men and women,

Noting that the Universal Declaration of Human Rights affirms the principle of the inadmissibility of discrimination and proclaims that all human beings are born free and equal in dignity and rights and that everyone is entitled to all the rights and freedoms set forth therein, without distinction of any kind, including distinction based on sex,

Noting that the States Parties to the International Covenants on Human Rights have the obligation to ensure the equal rights of men and women to enjoy all economic, social, cultural, civil and political rights,

Considering the international conventions concluded under the auspices of the United Nations and the specialized agencies promoting equality of rights of men and women,

Noting also the resolutions, declarations and recommendations adopted by the United Nations and the specialized agencies promoting equality of rights of men and women,

Concerned, however, that despite these various instruments extensive discrimination against women continues to exist,

Recalling that discrimination against women violates the principles of equality of rights and respect for human dignity, is an obstacle to the participation of women, on equal terms with men, in the political, social, economic and cultural life of their countries, hampers the growth of the prosperity of society and the family and makes more difficult the full development of the potentialities of women in the service of their countries and of humanity,

Concerned that in situations of poverty women have the least access to food, health, education, training and opportunities for employment and other needs,

Convinced that the establishment of the new international economic order based on equity and justice will contribute significantly towards the promotion of equality between men and women,

Emphasizing that the eradication of apartheid, all forms of racism, racial discrimination, colonialism, neo-colonialism, aggression, foreign occupation and domination and interference in the internal affairs of States is essential to the full enjoyment of the rights of men and women,

Affirming that the strengthening of international peace and security, the relaxation of international tension, mutual co-operation among all States irrespective of their social and economic systems, general and complete disarmament, in particular nuclear disarmament under strict and effective international control, the affirmation of the principles of justice, equality and mutual benefit in relations among countries and the realization of the right of peoples under alien and colonial domination and foreign occupation to self-determination and independence, as well as respect for national sovereignty and territorial integrity, will promote social progress and development and as a consequence will contribute to the attainment of full equality between men and women,

Convinced that the full and complete development of a country, the welfare of the world and the cause of peace require the maximum participation of women on equal terms with men in all fields,

Bearing in mind the great contribution of women to the welfare of the family and to the development of society, so far not fully recognized, the social significance of maternity and the role of both parents in the family and in the upbringing of children, and aware that the role of women in procreation should not be a basis for discrimination but that the upbringing of children requires a sharing of responsibility between men and women and society as a whole;

Aware that a change in the traditional role of men as well as the role of women in society and in the family is needed to achieve full equality between men and women,

Determined to implement the principles set forth in the Declaration on the Elimination of Discrimination against Women and for that purpose, to adopt the measures required for the elimination of such discrimination in all its forms and manifestations,

Have agreed on the following:

PART I
Article 1

For the purposes of the present Convention, the term discrimination against women shall mean any distinction, exclusion or restriction made on the basis of sex which has the effect or purpose of impairing or nullifying the recognition, enjoyment or exercise by women, irrespective of their marital status, on a basis of equality of men and women, of human rights and fundamental freedoms in the political, economic, social, cultural, civil or any other field.

Article 2

States Parties condemn discrimination against women in all its forms, agree to pursue by all appropriate means and without delay a policy of eliminating discrimination against women and, to this end, undertake:

(a) to embody the principle of the equality of men and women in their national constitutions or other appropriate legislation if not yet incorporated therein and to ensure, through law and other appropriate means, the practical realization of this principle;

(b) to adopt appropriate legislative and other measures, including sanctions where appropriate, prohibiting all discrimination against women;

(c) to establish legal protection of the rights of women on an equal basis with men and to ensure through competent national tribunals and other public institutions the effective protection of women against any act of discrimination;

(d) to refrain from engaging in any act or practice of discrimination against women and to ensure that public authorities and institutions shall act in conformity with this obligation;

(e) to take all appropriate measures to eliminate discrimination against women by any person, organization or enterprise;

(f) to take all appropriate measures, including legislation, to modify or abolish existing laws, regulations, customs and practices which constitute discrimination against women;

(g) to repeal all national penal provisions which constitute discrimination against women.

Article 3

States Parties shall take in all fields, in particular in the political, social, economic and cultural fields, all appropriate measures, including legislation, to ensure the full development and advancement of women, for the purpose of guaranteeing them the exercise and enjoyment of human rights and fundamental freedoms on a basis of equality with men.

Article 4

1. Adoption by States Parties of temporary special measures aimed at accelerating de facto equality between men and women shall not be considered discrimination as defined in the present Convention, but shall in no way entail as a consequence the maintenance of unequal or separate standards; these measures shall be discontinued when the objectives of equality of opportunity and treatment have been achieved.

2. Adoption by States Parties of special measures, including those measures contained in the present Convention, aimed at protecting maternity shall not be considered discriminatory.

Article 5

States Parties shall take all appropriate measures:

(a) to modify the social and cultural patterns of conduct of men and women, with a view to achieving the elimination of prejudices and customary and all other practices which are based on the idea of the inferiority or the superiority of either of the sexes or on stereotyped roles for men and women;

(b) to ensure that family education includes a proper understanding of maternity as a social function and the recognition of the common responsibility of men and women in the upbringing and development of their children, it being understood that the interest of the children is the primordial consideration in all cases.

Article 6

States Parties shall take all appropriate measures, including legislation, to suppress all forms of traffic in women and exploitation of prostitution of women.

PART II

Article 7

States Parties shall take all appropriate measures to eliminate discrimination against women in the political and public life of the country and, in particular, shall ensure to women, on equal terms with men, the right:

(a) to vote in all elections and public referenda and to be eligible for election to all publicly elected bodies;

(b) to participate in the formulation of government policy and the implementation thereof and to hold public office and perform all public functions at all levels of government;

(c) to participate in non-governmental organizations and associations concerned with the public and political life of the country.

Article 8

States Parties shall take all appropriate measures to ensure to women, on equal terms with men and without any discrimination, the opportunity to represent their Governments at the international level and to participate in the work of international organizations.

Article 9

1. States Parties shall grant women equal rights with men to acquire, change or retain their nationality. They shall ensure in particular that neither marriage to an alien nor change of nationality by the husband during marriage shall automatically change the nationality of the wife, render her stateless or force upon her the nationality of the husband.

2. States Parties shall grant women equal rights with men with respect to the nationality of their children.

PART III

Article 10

States Parties shall take all appropriate measures to eliminate discrimination against women in order to ensure to them equal rights with men in the field of education and in particular to ensure, on a basis of equality of men and women:

(a) the same conditions for career and vocational guidance, for access to studies and for the achievement of diplomas in educational establishments of all categories in rural as well as in urban areas; this equality shall be ensured in pre-school, general, technical, professional and higher technical education, as well as in all types of vocational training;

(b) access to the same curricula, the same examinations, teaching staff with qualifications of the same standard and school premises and equipment of the same quality;

(c) the elimination of any stereotyped concept of the roles of men and women at all levels and in all forms of education by encouraging coeducation and other types of education which will help to achieve this aim and, in particular, by the revision of textbooks and school programs and the adaptation of teaching methods;

(d) the same opportunities to benefit from scholarships and other study grants;

(e) the same opportunities for access to programs of continuing education, including adult and functional literacy programs, particularly those aimed at reducing, at the earliest possible time, any gap in education existing between men and women;

(f) the reduction of female student drop-out rates and the organization of programs for girls and women who have left school prematurely;

(g) the same opportunities to participate actively in sports and physical education;

(h) access to specific educational information to help to ensure the health and well-being of families, including information and advice on family planning.

Article 11

1. States Parties shall take all appropriate measures to eliminate discrimination against women in the field of employment in order to ensure, on a basis of equality of men and women, the same rights, in particular:

(a) the right to work as an inalienable right of all human beings;

(b) the right to the same employment opportunities, including the application of the same criteria for selection in matters of employment;

(c) the right to free choice of profession and employment, the right to promotion, job security and all the benefits and conditions of service and the right to receive vocational training and retraining, including apprenticeships, advanced vocational training and recurrent training;

(d) the right to equal remuneration, including benefits, and to equal treatment in respect of work of equal value, as well as equality of treatment in the evaluation of the quality of work;

(e) the right to social security, particularly in cases of retirement, unemployment, sickness, invalidity and old age and other incapacity to work, as well as the right to paid leave;

(f) the right to protection of health and to safety in working conditions, including safeguarding of the function of reproduction.

2. In order to prevent discrimination against women on the grounds of marriage or maternity and to ensure their effective right to work, States Parties shall take appropriate measures:

(a) to prohibit, subject to the imposition of sanctions, dismissal on the grounds of pregnancy or of maternity leave and discrimination in dismissals on the basis of marital status;

(b) to introduce maternity leave with pay or with comparable social benefits without loss of former employment, seniority or social allowances;

(c) to encourage the provision of the necessary supporting social services to enable parents to combine family obligations with work responsibilities and participation in public life, in particular through promoting the establishment and development of a network of child-care facilities;

(d) To provide special protection to women during pregnancy in types of work proved to be harmful to them.

3. Protective legislation relating to matters covered in this Article shall be reviewed periodically in the light of scientific and technological knowledge and shall be revised, repealed or extended as necessary.

Article 12

1. States Parties shall take all appropriate measures to eliminate discrimination against women in the field of health care in order to ensure, on a basis of equality of men and women, access to health care services, including those related to family planning.

2. Notwithstanding the provisions of paragraph 1 of this Article, States Parties shall ensure to women appropriate services in connection with pregnancy, confinement and the post-natal period, granting free services where necessary, as well as adequate nutrition during pregnancy and lactation.

Article 13

States Parties shall take all appropriate measures to eliminate discrimination against women in other areas of economic and social life in order to ensure, on a basis of equality of men and women, the same rights, in particular:

(a) the right to family benefits;

(b) the right to bank loans, mortgages and other forms of financial credit;

(c) the right to participate in recreational activities, sports and all aspects of cultural life.

Article 14

1. States Parties shall take into account the particular problems faced by rural women and the significant roles which rural women play in the economic survival of their families, including their work in the non-monetized sectors of the economy, and shall take all appropriate measures to ensure the application of the provisions of the present Convention to women in rural areas.

2. States Parties shall take all appropriate measures to eliminate discrimination against women in rural areas in order to ensure, on a basis of equality of men and women, that they participate in and benefit from rural development and, in particular, shall ensure to such women the right:

(a) to participate in the elaboration and implementation of development planning at all levels;

(b) to have access to adequate health care facilities, including information, counseling and services in family planning;

(c) to benefit directly from social security programs;

(d) to obtain all types of training and education, formal and non-formal, including that relating to functional literacy, as well as, inter alia, the benefit of all community and extension services, in order to increase their technical proficiency;

(e) to organize self-help groups and co-operatives in order to obtain equal access to economic opportunities through employment or self-employment;

(f) to participate in all community activities;

(g) to have access to agricultural credit and loans, marketing facilities, appropriate technology and equal treatment in land and agrarian reform as well as in land resettlement schemes;

(h) to enjoy adequate living conditions, particularly in relation to housing, sanitation, electricity and water supply, transport and communications.

PART IV
Article 15

1. States Parties shall accord to women equality with men before the law.

2. States Parties shall accord to women, in civil matters, a legal capacity identical to that of men and the same opportunities to exercise that capacity. In particular, they shall give women equal rights to conclude contracts and to administer property and shall treat them equally in all stages of procedure in courts and tribunals.

3. States Parties agree that all contracts and all other private instruments of any kind with a legal effect which is directed at restricting the legal capacity of women shall be deemed null and void.

4. States Parties shall accord to men and women the same rights with regard to the law relating to the movement of persons and the freedom to choose their residence and domicile.

Article 16

1. States Parties shall take all appropriate measures to eliminate discrimination against women in all matters relating to marriage and family relations and in particular shall ensure, on a basis of equality of men and women:

(a) the same right to enter into marriage;

(b) the same right freely to choose a spouse and to enter into marriage only with their free and full consent;

(c) the same rights and responsibilities during marriage and at its dissolution;

(d) the same rights and responsibilities as parents, irrespective of their marital status, in matters relating to their children; in all cases the interests of the children shall be paramount;

(e) the same rights to decide freely and responsibly on the number and spacing of their children and to have access to the information, education and means to enable them to exercise these rights;

(f) the same rights and responsibilities with regard to guardianship, wardship, trusteeship and adoption of children, or similar institutions where these concepts exist in national legislation; in all cases the interests of the children shall be paramount;

(g) the same personal rights as husband and wife, including the right to choose a family name, a profession and an occupation;

(h) the same rights for both spouses in respect of the ownership, acquisition, management, administration, enjoyment and disposition of property, whether free of charge or for a valuable consideration.

2. The betrothal and the marriage of a child shall have no legal effect, and all necessary action, including legislation, shall be taken to specify a minimum age for marriage and to make the registration of marriages in an official registry compulsory.

Article 17

1. For the purpose of considering the progress made in the implementation of the present Convention, there shall be established a Committee on the Elimination of Discrimination against Women (hereinafter referred to as the Committee) consisting, at the time of entry into force of the Convention, of eighteen and, after ratification of or accession to the Convention by the thirty-fifth State Party, of twenty-three experts of high moral standing and competence in the field covered by the Convention. The experts shall be elected by States Parties from among their nationals and shall serve in their personal capacity, consideration being given to equitable geographical distribution and to the representation of the different forms of civilization as well as the principal legal systems.

2. The members of the Committee shall be elected by secret ballot from a list of persons nominated by States Parties. Each State Party may nominate one person from among its own nationals.

3. The initial election shall be held six months after the date of the entry into force of the present Convention. At least three months before the date of each election the Secretary-General of the United Nations shall address a letter to the States Parties inviting them to submit their nominations within two months. The Secretary-General shall prepare a list in alphabetical order of all persons thus nominated, indicating the States Parties which have nominated them, and shall submit it to the States Parties.

4. Elections of the members of the Committee shall be held at a meeting of States Parties convened by the Secretary-General at United Nations Headquarters. At that meeting, for which two-thirds of the States Parties shall constitute a quorum, the persons elected to the Committee shall be those nominees who obtain the largest number of votes and an absolute majority of the votes of the representatives of States Parties present and voting.

5. The members of the Committee shall be elected for a term of four years. However, the terms of nine of the members elected at the first election shall expire at the end of two years; immediately after the first election the names of these nine members shall be chosen by lot by the Chairman of the Committee.

6. The election of the five additional members of the Committee shall be held in accordance with the provisions of paragraphs 2, 3 and 4 of this Article, following the thirty-fifth ratification or accession. The terms of two of the additional members elected on this occasion shall expire at the end of two years, the names of these two members having been chosen by lot by the Chairman of the Committee.

7. For the filling of casual vacancies, the State Party whose expert has ceased to function as a member of the Committee shall appoint another expert from among its nationals, subject to the approval of the Committee.

8. The members of the Committee shall, with the approval of the General Assembly, receive emoluments from United Nations resources on such terms and conditions as the Assembly may decide, having regard to the importance of the Committee's responsibilities.

9. The Secretary-General of the United Nations shall provide the necessary staff and facilities for the effective performance of the functions of the Committee under the present Convention.

Article 18

1. States Parties undertake to submit to the Secretary-General of the United Nations, for consideration by the Committee, a report on the legislative, judicial, administrative or other measures which they have adopted to give effect to the provisions of the present Convention and on the progress made in this respect:

(a) within one year after the entry into force for the State concerned;

(b) thereafter at least every four years and further whenever the Committee so requests.

2. Reports may indicate factors and difficulties affecting the degree of fulfillment of obligations under the present Convention.

Article 19

1. The Committee shall adopt its own rules of procedure.

2. The Committee shall elect its officers for a term of two years.

Article 20

1. The Committee shall normally meet for a period of not more than two weeks annually in order to consider the reports submitted in accordance with Article 18 of the present Convention.

2. The meetings of the Committee shall normally be held at United Nations Headquarters or at any other convenient place as determined by the Committee.

Article 21

1. The Committee shall, through the Economic and Social Council, report annually to the General Assembly of the United Nations on its activities and may make suggestions and general recommendations based on the examination of reports and information received from the States Parties. Such suggestions and general recommendations shall be included in the report of the Committee together with comments, if any, from States Parties.

2. The Secretary-General of the United Nations shall transmit the reports of the Committee to the Commission on the Status of Women for its information.

Article 22

The specialized agencies shall be entitled to be represented at the consideration of the implementation of such provisions of the present Convention as fall within the scope of their activities. The Committee may invite the specialized agencies to submit reports on the implementation of the Convention in areas falling within the scope of their activities.

PART VI

Article 23

Nothing in the present Convention shall affect any provisions that are more conducive to the achievement of equality between men and women which may be contained:

(a) in the legislation of a State Party; or

(b) in any other international convention, treaty or agreement in force for that State.

Article 24

States Parties undertake to adopt all necessary measures at the national level aimed at achieving the full realization of the rights recognized in the present Convention.

Article 25

1. The present Convention shall be open for signature by all States.

2. The Secretary-General of the United Nations is designated as the depositary of the present Convention.

3. The present Convention is subject to ratification. Instruments of ratification shall be deposited with the Secretary-General of the United Nations.

4. The present Convention shall be open to accession by all States. Accession shall be effected by the deposit of an instrument of accession with the Secretary-General of the United Nations.

Article 26

1. A request for the revision of the present Convention may be made at any time by any State Party by means of a notification in writing addressed to the Secretary-General of the United Nations.

2. The General Assembly of the United Nations shall decide upon the steps, if any, to be taken in respect of such a request.

Article 27

1. The present Convention shall enter into force on the thirtieth day after the date of deposit with the Secretary-General of the United Nations of the twentieth instrument of ratification or accession.

2. For each State ratifying the present Convention or acceding to it after the deposit of the twentieth instrument of ratification or accession, the Convention shall enter into force on the thirtieth day after the date of the deposit of its own instrument of ratification or accession.

Article 28

1. The Secretary-General of the United Nations shall receive and circulate to all States the text of reservations made by States at the time of ratification or accession.

2. A reservation incompatible with the object and purpose of the present Convention shall not be permitted.

3. Reservations may be withdrawn at any time by notification to this effect addressed to the Secretary-General of the United Nations, who shall then inform all States thereof. Such notification shall take effect on the date on which it is received.

Article 29

1. Any dispute between two or more States Parties concerning the interpretation or application of the present Convention which is not settled by negotiation shall, at the request of one of them, be submitted to arbitration. If within six months from the date of the request for arbitration the parties are unable to agree on the organization of the arbitration, any one of those parties may refer the dispute to the International Court of Justice by request in conformity with the Statute of the Court.

2. Each State Party may at the time of signature or ratification of the present Convention or accession thereto declare that it does not consider itself bound by paragraph 1 of this Article. The other States Parties shall not be bound by that paragraph with respect to any State Party which has made such a reservation.

3. Any State Party which has made a reservation in accordance with paragraph 2 of this Article may at any time withdraw that reservation by notification to the Secretary-General of the United Nations.

Article 30

The present Convention, the Arabic, Chinese, English, French, Russian and Spanish texts of which are equally authentic, shall be deposited with the Secretary-General of the United Nations.

IN WITNESS WHEREOF the undersigned, duly authorized, have signed the present Convention.

DOCUMENT 28

Full Official Title: Convention on the Rights of the Child

Short Title/Acronym/Abbreviation: The Children's Convention/CRC

Subject: Establishing recognition of international legal human rights protecting children from abuse and exploitation in a multilateral treaty.

Official Citation: G.A. res. 44/25, annex, 44 U.N. GAOR Supp. (No. 49) at 167, U.N. Doc. A/44/49 (1989).

Date of Document: Not applicable

Date of Adoption: November 30, 1989

Date of General Entry into Force (EIF): September 2, 1990

Number of States Parties to this Treaty as of this printing: 191

Date of Signature by United States: February 16, 1995

Date of Ratification/Accession/Adhesion: The United States has not ratified as of this printing.

Date of Entry into Force as to United States (effective date): Not applicable

Type of Document: A treaty, an international legal instrument

Legal Status/Character of the Instrument/Document as to the United States: The United States has signed this Convention but the U.S. Senate has not ratified it as of the date of this publication. However, under certain principles of international law contained in the Vienna Convention on the Law of Treaties the United States should act consistently with legal instruments it has signed, as an indication of its good faith intent to act accordingly.

Supervising Body: Committee on the Rights of the Child

Comments: A very politically controversial treaty. This is the most widely ratified treaty in the world, with only the United States and two other states not ratifying. Much of the reluctance of the United States to ratify is due to concerns that the treaty will interfere with parents raising their children as they see fit.

Caution: The status and applicability of this instrument as to the United States may have changed since date of publication. The above information may be updated by referring to the following site:

Web address: http://www1.umn.edu/humanrts/instree/k2crc.htm

CONVENTION ON THE RIGHTS OF THE CHILD (CRC)

Preamble

The States Parties to the present Convention,

Considering that, in accordance with the principles proclaimed in the Charter of the United Nations, recognition of the inherent dignity and of the equal and inalienable rights of all members of the human family is the foundation of freedom, justice and peace in the world,

Bearing in mind that the peoples of the United Nations have, in the Charter, reaffirmed their faith in fundamental human rights and in the dignity and worth of the human person, and have determined to promote social progress and better standards of life in larger freedom,

Recognizing that the United Nations has, in the Universal Declaration of Human Rights and in the International Covenants on Human Rights, proclaimed and agreed that everyone is entitled to all the rights and freedoms set forth therein, without distinction of any kind, such as race, colour, sex, language, religion, political or other opinion, national or social origin, property, birth or other status,

Recalling that, in the Universal Declaration of Human Rights, the United Nations has proclaimed that childhood is entitled to special care and assistance,

Convinced that the family, as the fundamental group of society and the natural environment for the growth and well-being of all its members and particularly children, should be afforded the necessary protection and assistance so that it can fully assume its responsibilities within the community,

Recognizing that the child, for the full and harmonious development of his or her personality, should grow up in a family environment, in an atmosphere of happiness, love and understanding,

Considering that the child should be fully prepared to live an individual life in society, and brought up in the spirit of the ideals proclaimed in the Charter of the United Nations, and in particular in the spirit of peace, dignity, tolerance, freedom, equality and solidarity,

Bearing in mind that the need to extend particular care to the child has been stated in the Geneva Declaration of the Rights of the Child of 1924 and in the Declaration of the Rights of the Child adopted by the General Assembly on 20 November 1959 and recognized in the Universal Declaration of Human

Rights, in the International Covenant on Civil and Political Rights (in particular in articles 23 and 24), in the International Covenant on Economic, Social and Cultural Rights (in particular in Article 10) and in the statutes and relevant instruments of specialized agencies and international organizations concerned with the welfare of children,

Bearing in mind that, as indicated in the Declaration of the Rights of the Child, "the child, by reason of his physical and mental immaturity, needs special safeguards and care, including appropriate legal protection, before as well as after birth,"

Recalling the provisions of the Declaration on Social and Legal Principles relating to the Protection and Welfare of Children, with Special Reference to Foster Placement and Adoption Nationally and Internationally; the United Nations Standard Minimum Rules for the Administration of Juvenile Justice (The Beijing Rules); and the Declaration on the Protection of Women and Children in Emergency and Armed Conflict,

Recognizing that, in all countries in the world, there are children living in exceptionally difficult conditions, and that such children need special consideration,

Taking due account of the importance of the traditions and cultural values of each people for the protection and harmonious development of the child,

Recognizing the importance of international co-operation for improving the living conditions of children in every country, in particular in the developing countries,

Have agreed as follows:

PART I

Article 1

For the purposes of the present Convention, a child means every human being below the age of eighteen years unless under the law applicable to the child, majority is attained earlier.

Article 2

1. States Parties shall respect and ensure the rights set forth in the present Convention to each child within their jurisdiction without discrimination of any kind, irrespective of the child's or his or her parent's or legal guardian's race, colour, sex, language, religion, political or other opinion, national, ethnic or social origin, property, disability, birth or other status.

2. States Parties shall take all appropriate measures to ensure that the child is protected against all forms of discrimination or punishment on the basis of the status, activities, expressed opinions, or beliefs of the child's parents, legal guardians, or family members.

Article 3

1. In all actions concerning children, whether undertaken by public or private social welfare institutions, courts of law, administrative authorities or legislative bodies, the best interests of the child shall be a primary consideration.

2. States Parties undertake to ensure the child such protection and care as is necessary for his or her well-being, taking into account the rights and duties of his or her parents, legal guardians, or other individuals legally responsible for him or her, and, to this end, shall take all appropriate legislative and administrative measures.

3. States Parties shall ensure that the institutions, services and facilities responsible for the care or protection of children shall conform with the standards established by competent authorities, particularly in the areas of safety, health, in the number and suitability of their staff, as well as competent supervision.

Article 4

States Parties shall undertake all appropriate legislative, administrative, and other measures for the implementation of the rights recognized in the present Convention. With regard to economic, social and cultural rights, States Parties shall undertake such measures to the maximum extent of their available resources and, where needed, within the framework of international co-operation.

Article 5

States Parties shall respect the responsibilities, rights and duties of parents or, where applicable, the members of the extended family or community as provided for by local custom, legal guardians or other persons legally responsible for the child, to provide, in a manner consistent with the evolving capacities of the child, appropriate direction and guidance in the exercise by the child of the rights recognized in the present Convention.

Article 6

1. States Parties recognize that every child has the inherent right to life.

2. States Parties shall ensure to the maximum extent possible the survival and development of the child.

Article 7

1. The child shall be registered immediately after birth and shall have the right from birth to a name, the right to acquire a nationality and. as far as possible, the right to know and be cared for by his or her parents.

2. States Parties shall ensure the implementation of these rights in accordance with their national law and their obligations under the relevant international instruments in this field, in particular where the child would otherwise be stateless.

Article 8

1. States Parties undertake to respect the right of the child to preserve his or her identity, including nationality, name and family relations as recognized by law without unlawful interference.

2. Where a child is illegally deprived of some or all of the elements of his or her identity, States Parties shall provide appropriate assistance and protection, with a view to speedily re-establishing his or her identity.

Article 9

1. States Parties shall ensure that a child shall not be separated from his or her parents against their will, except when competent authorities subject to judicial review determine, in accordance with applicable law and procedures, that such separation is necessary for the best interests of the child. Such determination may be necessary in a particular case such as one involving abuse or neglect of the child by the parents, or one where the parents are living separately and a decision must be made as to the child's place of residence.

2. In any proceedings pursuant to paragraph 1 of the present article, all interested parties shall be given an opportunity to participate in the proceedings and make their views known.

3. States Parties shall respect the right of the child who is separated from one or both parents to maintain personal relations and direct contact with both parents on a regular basis, except if it is contrary to the child's best interests.

4. Where such separation results from any action initiated by a State Party, such as the detention, imprisonment, exile, deportation or death (including death arising from any cause while the person is in the custody of the State) of one or both parents or of the child, that State Party shall, upon request, provide the parents, the child or, if appropriate, another member of the family with the essential information concerning the whereabouts of the absent member(s) of the family unless the provision of the information would be detrimental to the well-being of the child. States Parties shall further ensure that the submission of such a request shall of itself entail no adverse consequences for the person(s) concerned.

Article 10

1. In accordance with the obligation of States Parties under Article 9, paragraph 1, applications by a child or his or her parents to enter or leave a State Party for the purpose of family reunification shall be dealt with by States Parties in a positive, humane and expeditious manner. States Parties shall further ensure that the submission of such a request shall entail no adverse consequences for the applicants and for the members of their family.

2. A child whose parents reside in different States shall have the right to maintain on a regular basis, save in exceptional circumstances, personal relations and direct contacts with both parents. Towards that end and in accordance with the obligation of States Parties under Article 9, paragraph 2, States Parties shall respect the right of the child and his or her parents to leave any country, including their own, and to enter their own country. The right to leave any country shall be subject only to such restrictions as are prescribed by law and which are necessary to protect the national security, public order (ordre public), public health or morals or the rights and freedoms of others and are consistent with the other rights recognized in the present Convention.

Article 11

1. States Parties shall take measures to combat the illicit transfer and non-return of children abroad.

2. To this end, States Parties shall promote the conclusion of bilateral or multilateral agreements or accession to existing agreements.

Article 12

1. States Parties shall assure to the child who is capable of forming his or her own views the right to express those views freely in all matters affecting the child, the views of the child being given due weight in accordance with the age and maturity of the child.

2. For this purpose, the child shall in particular be provided the opportunity to be heard in any judicial and administrative proceedings affecting the child, either directly, or through a representative or an appropriate body, in a manner consistent with the procedural rules of national law.

Article 13

1. The child shall have the right to freedom of expression; this right shall include freedom to seek, receive and impart information and ideas of all kinds, regardless of frontiers, either orally, in writing or in print, in the form of art, or through any other media of the child's choice.

2. The exercise of this right may be subject to certain restrictions, but these shall only be such as are provided by law and are necessary:

(a) For respect of the rights or reputations of others; or

(b) For the protection of national security or of public order (ordre public), or of public health or morals.

Article 14

1. States Parties shall respect the right of the child to freedom of thought, conscience and religion.

2. States Parties shall respect the rights and duties of the parents and, when applicable, legal guardians, to provide direction to the child in the exercise of his or her right in a manner consistent with the evolving capacities of the child.

3. Freedom to manifest one's religion or beliefs may be subject only to such limitations as are prescribed by law and are necessary to protect public safety, order, health or morals, or the fundamental rights and freedoms of others.

Article 15

1. States Parties recognize the rights of the child to freedom of association and to freedom of peaceful assembly.

2. No restrictions may be placed on the exercise of these rights other than those imposed in conformity with the law and which are necessary in a democratic society in the interests of national security or public safety, public order (ordre public), the protection of public health or morals or the protection of the rights and freedoms of others.

Article 16

1. No child shall be subjected to arbitrary or unlawful interference with his or her privacy, family, home or correspondence, nor to unlawful attacks on his or her honour and reputation.

2. The child has the right to the protection of the law against such interference or attacks.

Article 17

States Parties recognize the important function performed by the mass media and shall ensure that the child has access to information and material from a diversity of national and international sources, especially those aimed at the promotion of his or her social, spiritual and moral well-being and physical and mental health. To this end, States Parties shall:

(a) Encourage the mass media to disseminate information and material of social and cultural benefit to the child and in accordance with the spirit of Article 29;

(b) Encourage international co-operation in the production, exchange and dissemination of such information and material from a diversity of cultural, national and international sources;

(c) Encourage the production and dissemination of children's books;

(d) Encourage the mass media to have particular regard to the linguistic needs of the child who belongs to a minority group or who is indigenous;

(e) Encourage the development of appropriate guidelines for the protection of the child from information and material injurious to his or her well-being, bearing in mind the provisions of articles 13 and 18.

Article 18

1. States Parties shall use their best efforts to ensure recognition of the principle that both parents have common responsibilities for the upbringing and development of the child. Parents or, as the case may be, legal guardians, have the primary responsibility for the upbringing and development of the child. The best interests of the child will be their basic concern.

2. For the purpose of guaranteeing and promoting the rights set forth in the present Convention, States Parties shall render appropriate assistance to parents and legal guardians in the performance of their child-rearing responsibilities and shall ensure the development of institutions, facilities and services for the care of children.

3. States Parties shall take all appropriate measures to ensure that children of working parents have the right to benefit from child-care services and facilities for which they are eligible.

Article 19

1. States Parties shall take all appropriate legislative, administrative, social and educational measures to protect the child from all forms of physical or mental violence, injury or abuse, neglect or negligent treatment, maltreatment or exploitation, including sexual abuse, while in the care of parent(s), legal guardian(s) or any other person who has the care of the child.

2. Such protective measures should, as appropriate, include effective procedures for the establishment of social programmes to provide necessary support for the child and for those who have the care of the child, as well as for other forms of prevention and for identification, reporting, referral, investigation, treatment and follow-up of instances of child maltreatment described heretofore, and, as appropriate, for judicial involvement.

Article 20

1. A child temporarily or permanently deprived of his or her family environment, or in whose own best interests cannot be allowed to remain in that environment, shall be entitled to special protection and assistance provided by the State.

2. States Parties shall in accordance with their national laws ensure alternative care for such a child.

3. Such care could include, inter alia, foster placement, kafalah of Islamic law, adoption or if necessary placement in suitable institutions for the care of children. When considering solutions, due regard shall be paid to the desirability of continuity in a child's upbringing and to the child's ethnic, religious, cultural and linguistic background.

Article 21

States Parties that recognize and/or permit the system of adoption shall ensure that the best interests of the child shall be the paramount consideration and they shall:

(a) Ensure that the adoption of a child is authorized only by competent authorities who determine, in accordance with applicable law and procedures and on the basis of all pertinent and reliable information, that the adoption is permissible in view of the child's status concerning parents, relatives and legal guardians and that, if required, the persons concerned have given their informed consent to the adoption on the basis of such counselling as may be necessary;

(b) Recognize that inter-country adoption may be considered as an alternative means of child's care, if the child cannot be placed in a foster or an adoptive family or cannot in any suitable manner be cared for in the child's country of origin; (c) Ensure that the child concerned by inter-country adoption enjoys safeguards and standards equivalent to those existing in the case of national adoption;

(d) Take all appropriate measures to ensure that, in inter-country adoption, the placement does not result in improper financial gain for those involved in it;

(e) Promote, where appropriate, the objectives of the present article by concluding bilateral or multilateral arrangements or agreements, and endeavour, within this framework, to ensure that the placement of the child in another country is carried out by competent authorities or organs.

Article 22

1. States Parties shall take appropriate measures to ensure that a child who is seeking refugee status or who is considered a refugee in accordance with applicable international or domestic law and procedures shall, whether unaccompanied or accompanied by his or her parents or by any other person, receive appropriate protection and humanitarian assistance in the enjoyment of applicable rights set forth in the present Convention and in other international human rights or humanitarian instruments to which the said States are Parties.

2. For this purpose, States Parties shall provide, as they consider appropriate, co-operation in any efforts by the United Nations and other competent intergovernmental organizations or non-governmental organizations co-operating with the United Nations to protect and assist such a child and to trace the parents or other members of the family of any refugee child in order to obtain information necessary for reunification with his or her family. In cases where no parents or other members of the family can be found, the child shall be accorded the same protection as any other child permanently or temporarily deprived of his or her family environment for any reason, as set forth in the present Convention.

Article 23

1. States Parties recognize that a mentally or physically disabled child should enjoy a full and decent life, in conditions which ensure dignity, promote self-reliance and facilitate the child's active participation in the community.

2. States Parties recognize the right of the disabled child to special care and shall encourage and ensure the extension, subject to available resources, to the eligible child and those responsible for his or her care, of assistance for which application is made and which is appropriate to the child's condition and to the circumstances of the parents or others caring for the child.

3. Recognizing the special needs of a disabled child, assistance extended in accordance with paragraph 2 of the present article shall be provided free of charge, whenever possible, taking into account the financial resources of the parents or others caring for the child, and shall be designed to ensure that the disabled child has effective access to and receives education, training, health care services, rehabilitation services, preparation for employment and recreation opportunities in a manner conducive to the child's achieving the fullest possible social integration and individual development, including his or her cultural and spiritual development.

4. States Parties shall promote, in the spirit of international cooperation, the exchange of appropriate information in the field of preventive health care and of medical, psychological and functional treatment of disabled children, including dissemination of and access to information concerning methods of rehabilitation, education and vocational services, with the aim of enabling States Parties to improve their capabilities and skills and to widen their experience in these areas. In this regard, particular account shall be taken of the needs of developing countries.

Article 24

1. States Parties recognize the right of the child to the enjoyment of the highest attainable standard of health and to facilities for the treatment of illness and rehabilitation of health. States Parties shall strive to ensure that no child is deprived of his or her right of access to such health care services.

2. States Parties shall pursue full implementation of this right and, in particular, shall take appropriate measures:

(a) To diminish infant and child mortality;

(b) To ensure the provision of necessary medical assistance and health care to all children with emphasis on the development of primary health care;

(c) To combat disease and malnutrition, including within the framework of primary health care, through, inter alia, the application of readily available technology and through the provision of adequate nutritious foods and clean drinking water, taking into consideration the dangers and risks of environmental pollution;

(d) To ensure appropriate pre-natal and post-natal health care for mothers;

(e) To ensure that all segments of society, in particular parents and children, are informed, have access to education and are supported in the use of basic knowledge of child health and nutrition, the advantages of breast feeding, hygiene and environmental sanitation and the prevention of accidents;

(f) To develop preventive health care, guidance for parents and family planning education and services.

3. States Parties shall take all effective and appropriate measures with a view to abolishing traditional practices prejudicial to the health of children.

4. States Parties undertake to promote and encourage international co-operation with a view to achieving progressively the full realization of the right recognized in the present article. In this regard, particular account shall be taken of the needs of developing countries.

Article 25

States Parties recognize the right of a child who has been placed by the competent authorities for the purposes of care, protection or treatment of his or her physical or mental health, to a periodic review of the treatment provided to the child and all other circumstances relevant to his or her placement.

Article 26

1. States Parties shall recognize for every child the right to benefit from social security, including social insurance, and shall take the necessary measures to achieve the full realization of this right in accordance with their national law.

2. The benefits should, where appropriate, be granted, taking into account the resources and the circumstances of the child and persons having responsibility for the maintenance of the child, as well as any other consideration relevant to an application for benefits made by or on behalf of the child.

Article 27

1. States Parties recognize the right of every child to a standard of living adequate for the child's physical, mental, spiritual, moral and social development.

2. The parent(s) or others responsible for the child have the primary responsibility to secure, within their abilities and financial capacities, the conditions of living necessary for the child's development.

3. States Parties, in accordance with national conditions and within their means, shall take appropriate measures to assist parents and others responsible for the child to implement this right and shall in case of need provide material assistance and support programmes, particularly with regard to nutrition, clothing and housing.

4. States Parties shall take all appropriate measures to secure the recovery of maintenance for the child from the parents or other persons having financial responsibility for the child, both within the State Party and from abroad. In particular, where the person having financial responsibility for the child lives in a State different from that of the child, States Parties shall promote the accession to international agreements or the conclusion of such agreements, as well as the making of other appropriate arrangements.

Article 28

1. States Parties recognize the right of the child to education, and with a view to achieving this right progressively and on the basis of equal opportunity, they shall, in particular:

(a) Make primary education compulsory and available free to all;

(b) Encourage the development of different forms of secondary education, including general and vocational education, make them available and accessible to every child, and take appropriate measures such as the introduction of free education and offering financial assistance in case of need;

(c) Make higher education accessible to all on the basis of capacity by every appropriate means;

(d) Make educational and vocational information and guidance available and accessible to all children;

(e) Take measures to encourage regular attendance at schools and the reduction of drop-out rates.

2. States Parties shall take all appropriate measures to ensure that school discipline is administered in a manner consistent with the child's human dignity and in conformity with the present Convention.

3. States Parties shall promote and encourage international cooperation in matters relating to education, in particular with a view to contributing to the elimination of ignorance and illiteracy throughout the world and facilitating access to scientific and technical knowledge and modern teaching methods. In this regard, particular account shall be taken of the needs of developing countries.

Article 29

1. States Parties agree that the education of the child shall be directed to:

(a) The development of the child's personality, talents and mental and physical abilities to their fullest potential;

(b) The development of respect for human rights and fundamental freedoms, and for the principles enshrined in the Charter of the United Nations;

(c) The development of respect for the child's parents, his or her own cultural identity, language and values, for the national values of the country in which the child is living, the country from which he or she may originate, and for civilizations different from his or her own;

(d) The preparation of the child for responsible life in a free society, in the spirit of understanding, peace, tolerance, equality of sexes, and friendship among all peoples, ethnic, national and religious groups and persons of indigenous origin;

(e) The development of respect for the natural environment.

2. No part of the present article or Article 28 shall be construed so as to interfere with the liberty of individuals and bodies to establish and direct educational institutions, subject always to the observance of the principles set forth in paragraph 1 of the present article and to the requirements that the education given in such institutions shall conform to such minimum standards as may be laid down by the State.

Article 30

In those States in which ethnic, religious or linguistic minorities or persons of indigenous origin exist, a child belonging to such a minority or who is indigenous shall not be denied the right, in community with other members of his or her group, to enjoy his or her own culture, to profess and practise his or her own religion, or to use his or her own language.

Article 31

1. States Parties recognize the right of the child to rest and leisure, to engage in play and recreational activities appropriate to the age of the child and to participate freely in cultural life and the arts.

2. States Parties shall respect and promote the right of the child to participate fully in cultural and artistic life and shall encourage the provision of appropriate and equal opportunities for cultural, artistic, recreational and leisure activity.

Article 32

1. States Parties recognize the right of the child to be protected from economic exploitation and from performing any work that is likely to be hazardous or to interfere with the child's education, or to be harmful to the child's health or physical, mental, spiritual, moral or social development.

2. States Parties shall take legislative, administrative, social and educational measures to ensure the implementation of the present article. To this end, and having regard to the relevant provisions of other international instruments, States Parties shall in particular:

(a) Provide for a minimum age or minimum ages for admission to employment;

(b) Provide for appropriate regulation of the hours and conditions of employment;

(c) Provide for appropriate penalties or other sanctions to ensure the effective enforcement of the present article.

Article 33

States Parties shall take all appropriate measures, including legislative, administrative, social and educational measures, to protect children from the illicit use of narcotic drugs and psychotropic substances as defined in the relevant international treaties, and to prevent the use of children in the illicit production and trafficking of such substances.

Article 34

States Parties undertake to protect the child from all forms of sexual exploitation and sexual abuse. For these purposes, States Parties shall in particular take all appropriate national, bilateral and multilateral measures to prevent:

(a) The inducement or coercion of a child to engage in any unlawful sexual activity;

(b) The exploitative use of children in prostitution or other unlawful sexual practices;

(c) The exploitative use of children in pornographic performances and materials.

Article 35

States Parties shall take all appropriate national, bilateral and multilateral measures to prevent the abduction of, the sale of or traffic in children for any purpose or in any form.

Article 36

States Parties shall protect the child against all other forms of exploitation prejudicial to any aspects of the child's welfare.

Article 37

States Parties shall ensure that:

(a) No child shall be subjected to torture or other cruel, inhuman or degrading treatment or punishment. Neither capital punishment nor life imprisonment without possibility of release shall be imposed for offences committed by persons below eighteen years of age;

(b) No child shall be deprived of his or her liberty unlawfully or arbitrarily. The arrest, detention or imprisonment of a child shall be in conformity with the law and shall be used only as a measure of last resort and for the shortest appropriate period of time;

(c) Every child deprived of liberty shall be treated with humanity and respect for the inherent dignity of the human person, and in a manner which takes into account the needs of persons of his or her age. In particular, every child deprived of liberty shall be separated from adults unless it is considered in the child's best interest not to do so and shall have the right to maintain contact with his or her family through correspondence and visits, save in exceptional circumstances;

(d) Every child deprived of his or her liberty shall have the right to prompt access to legal and other appropriate assistance, as well as the right to challenge the legality of the deprivation of his or her liberty before a court or other competent, independent and impartial authority, and to a prompt decision on any such action.

Article 38

1. States Parties undertake to respect and to ensure respect for rules of international humanitarian law applicable to them in armed conflicts which are relevant to the child.

2. States Parties shall take all feasible measures to ensure that persons who have not attained the age of fifteen years do not take a direct part in hostilities.

3. States Parties shall refrain from recruiting any person who has not attained the age of fifteen years into their armed forces. In recruiting among those persons who have attained the age of fifteen years but who have not attained the age of eighteen years, States Parties shall endeavour to give priority to those who are oldest.

4. In accordance with their obligations under international humanitarian law to protect the civilian population in armed conflicts, States Parties shall take all feasible measures to ensure protection and care of children who are affected by an armed conflict.

Article 39

States Parties shall take all appropriate measures to promote physical and psychological recovery and social re-integration of a child victim of: any form of neglect, exploitation, or abuse; torture or any other form of cruel, inhuman or degrading treatment or punishment; or armed conflicts. Such recovery and re-integration shall take place in an environment which fosters the health, self-respect and dignity of the child.

Article 40

1. States Parties recognize the right of every child alleged as, accused of, or recognized as having infringed the penal law to be treated in a manner consistent with the promotion of the child's sense of dignity and worth, which reinforces the child's respect for the human rights and fundamental freedoms of others and which takes into account the child's age and the desirability of promoting the child's re-integration and the child's assuming a constructive role in society.

2. To this end, and having regard to the relevant provisions of international instruments, States Parties shall, in particular, ensure that:

(a) No child shall be alleged as, be accused of, or recognized as having infringed the penal law by reason of acts or omissions that were not prohibited by national or international law at the time they were committed;

(b) Every child alleged as or accused of having infringed the penal law has at least the following guarantees:

(i) To be presumed innocent until proven guilty according to law;

(ii) To be informed promptly and directly of the charges against him or her, and, if appropriate, through his or her parents or legal guardians, and to have legal or other appropriate assistance in the preparation and presentation of his or her defence;

(iii) To have the matter determined without delay by a competent, independent and impartial authority or judicial body in a fair hearing according to law, in the presence of legal or other appropriate assistance and, unless it is considered not to be in the best interest of the child, in particular, taking into account his or her age or situation, his or her parents or legal guardians;

(iv) Not to be compelled to give testimony or to confess guilt; to examine or have examined adverse witnesses and to obtain the participation and examination of witnesses on his or her behalf under conditions of equality;

(v) If considered to have infringed the penal law, to have this decision and any measures imposed in consequence thereof reviewed by a higher competent, independent and impartial authority or judicial body according to law;

(vi) To have the free assistance of an interpreter if the child cannot understand or speak the language used;

(vii) To have his or her privacy fully respected at all stages of the proceedings.

3. States Parties shall seek to promote the establishment of laws, procedures, authorities and institutions specifically applicable to children alleged as, accused of, or recognized as having infringed the penal law, and, in particular:

(a) The establishment of a minimum age below which children shall be presumed not to have the capacity to infringe the penal law;

(b) Whenever appropriate and desirable, measures for dealing with such children without resorting to judicial proceedings, providing that human rights and legal safeguards are fully respected.

4. A variety of dispositions, such as care, guidance and supervision orders; counselling; probation; foster care; education and vocational training programmes and other alternatives to institutional care shall be available to ensure that children are dealt with in a manner appropriate to their well-being and proportionate both to their circumstances and the offence.

Article 41

Nothing in the present Convention shall affect any provisions which are more conducive to the realization of the rights of the child and which may be contained in:

(a) The law of a State party; or

(b) International law in force for that State.

PART II

Article 42

States Parties undertake to make the principles and provisions of the Convention widely known, by appropriate and active means, to adults and children alike.

Article 43

1. For the purpose of examining the progress made by States Parties in achieving the realization of the obligations undertaken in the present Convention, there shall be established a Committee on the Rights of the Child, which shall carry out the functions hereinafter provided.

2. The Committee shall consist of ten experts of high moral standing and recognized competence in the field covered by this Convention. The members of the Committee shall be elected by States Parties from among their nationals and shall serve in their personal capacity, consideration being given to equitable geographical distribution, as well as to the principal legal systems.

3. The members of the Committee shall be elected by secret ballot from a list of persons nominated by States Parties. Each State Party may nominate one person from among its own nationals.

4. The initial election to the Committee shall be held no later than six months after the date of the entry into force of the present Convention and thereafter every second year. At least four months before the date of each election, the Secretary-General of the United Nations shall address a letter to States Parties inviting them to submit their nominations within two months. The Secretary-General shall subsequently prepare a list in alphabetical order of all persons thus nominated, indicating States Parties which have nominated them, and shall submit it to the States Parties to the present Convention.

5. The elections shall be held at meetings of States Parties convened by the Secretary-General at United Nations Headquarters. At those meetings, for which two thirds of States Parties shall constitute a quorum, the persons elected to the Committee shall be those who obtain the largest number of votes and an absolute majority of the votes of the representatives of States Parties present and voting.

6. The members of the Committee shall be elected for a term of four years. They shall be eligible for re-election if renominated. The term of five of the members elected at the first election shall expire at the end of two years; immediately after the first election, the names of these five members shall be chosen by lot by the Chairman of the meeting.

7. If a member of the Committee dies or resigns or declares that for any other cause he or she can no longer perform the duties of the Committee, the State Party which nominated the member shall appoint another expert from among its nationals to serve for the remainder of the term, subject to the approval of the Committee.

8. The Committee shall establish its own rules of procedure.

9. The Committee shall elect its officers for a period of two years.

10. The meetings of the Committee shall normally be held at United Nations Headquarters or at any other convenient place as determined by the Committee. The Committee shall normally meet annually. The duration of the meetings of the Committee shall be determined, and reviewed, if necessary, by a meeting of the States Parties to the present Convention, subject to the approval of the General Assembly.

11. The Secretary-General of the United Nations shall provide the necessary staff and facilities for the effective performance of the functions of the Committee under the present Convention.

12. With the approval of the General Assembly, the members of the Committee established under the present Convention shall receive emoluments from United Nations resources on such terms and conditions as the Assembly may decide.

Article 44

1. States Parties undertake to submit to the Committee, through the Secretary-General of the United Nations, reports on the measures they have adopted which give effect to the rights recognized herein and on the progress made on the enjoyment of those rights:

(a) Within two years of the entry into force of the Convention for the State Party concerned;

(b) Thereafter every five years.

2. Reports made under the present article shall indicate factors and difficulties, if any, affecting the degree of fulfilment of the obligations under the present Convention. Reports shall also contain sufficient information to provide the Committee with a comprehensive understanding of the implementation of the Convention in the country concerned.

3. A State Party which has submitted a comprehensive initial report to the Committee need not, in its subsequent reports submitted in accordance with paragraph 1 (b) of the present article, repeat basic information previously provided.

4. The Committee may request from States Parties further information relevant to the implementation of the Convention.

5. The Committee shall submit to the General Assembly, through the Economic and Social Council, every two years, reports on its activities.

6. States Parties shall make their reports widely available to the public in their own countries.

Article 45

In order to foster the effective implementation of the Convention and to encourage international co-operation in the field covered by the Convention:

(a) The specialized agencies, the United Nations Children's Fund, and other United Nations organs shall be entitled to be represented at the consideration of the implementation of such provisions of the present Convention as fall within the scope of their mandate. The Committee may invite the specialized agencies, the United Nations Children's Fund and other competent bodies as it may consider appropriate to provide expert advice on the implementation of the Convention in areas falling within the scope of their respective mandates. The Committee may invite the specialized agencies, the United Nations Children's Fund, and other United Nations organs to submit reports on the implementation of the Convention in areas falling within the scope of their activities;

(b) The Committee shall transmit, as it may consider appropriate, to the specialized agencies, the United Nations Children's Fund and other competent bodies, any reports from States Parties that contain a request, or indicate a need, for technical advice or assistance, along with the Committee's observations and suggestions, if any, on these requests or indications;

(c) The Committee may recommend to the General Assembly to request the Secretary-General to undertake on its behalf studies on specific issues relating to the rights of the child;

(d) The Committee may make suggestions and general recommendations based on information received pursuant to articles 44 and 45 of the present Convention. Such suggestions and general recommendations shall be transmitted to any State Party concerned and reported to the General Assembly, together with comments, if any, from States Parties.

PART III

Article 46

The present Convention shall be open for signature by all States.

Article 47

The present Convention is subject to ratification. Instruments of ratification shall be deposited with the Secretary-General of the United Nations.

Article 48

The present Convention shall remain open for accession by any State. The instruments of accession shall be deposited with the Secretary-General of the United Nations.

Article 49

1. The present Convention shall enter into force on the thirtieth day following the date of deposit with the Secretary-General of the United Nations of the twentieth instrument of ratification or accession.

2. For each State ratifying or acceding to the Convention after the deposit of the twentieth instrument of ratification or accession, the Convention shall enter into force on the thirtieth day after the deposit by such State of its instrument of ratification or accession.

Article 50

1. Any State Party may propose an amendment and file it with the Secretary-General of the United Nations. The Secretary-General shall thereupon communicate the proposed amendment to States Parties, with a request that they indicate whether they favour a conference of States Parties for the purpose of

considering and voting upon the proposals. In the event that, within four months from the date of such communication, at least one third of the States Parties favour such a conference, the Secretary-General shall convene the conference under the auspices of the United Nations. Any amendment adopted by a majority of States Parties present and voting at the conference shall be submitted to the General Assembly for approval.

2. An amendment adopted in accordance with paragraph 1 of the present article shall enter into force when it has been approved by the General Assembly of the United Nations and accepted by a two-thirds majority of States Parties.

3. When an amendment enters into force, it shall be binding on those States Parties which have accepted it, other States Parties still being bound by the provisions of the present Convention and any earlier amendments which they have accepted.

Article 51

1. The Secretary-General of the United Nations shall receive and circulate to all States the text of reservations made by States at the time of ratification or accession.

2. A reservation incompatible with the object and purpose of the present Convention shall not be permitted.

3. Reservations may be withdrawn at any time by notification to that effect addressed to the Secretary-General of the United Nations, who shall then inform all States. Such notification shall take effect on the date on which it is received by the Secretary-General

Article 52

A State Party may denounce the present Convention by written notification to the Secretary-General of the United Nations. Denunciation becomes effective one year after the date of receipt of the notification by the Secretary-General.

Article 53

The Secretary-General of the United Nations is designated as the depositary of the present Convention.

Article 54

The original of the present Convention, of which the Arabic, Chinese, English, French, Russian and Spanish texts are equally authentic, shall be deposited with the Secretary-General of the United Nations.

IN WITNESS THEREOF the undersigned plenipotentiaries, being duly authorized thereto by their respective governments, have signed the present Convention.

© Copyright 1997

Office of the United Nations High Commissioner for Human Rights Geneva, Switzerland

---

DOCUMENT 29

Full Official Title: Optional Protocol to the Convention on the Rights of the Child on the Involvement of Children in Armed Conflict [First]

Short Title/Acronym/Abbreviation: First Optional Protocol to the CRC/OP1CRC

Subject: Armed conflict, children

Official Citation: G.A. res. ... (), U.N. Doc entered into force February 12, 2002. A/RES/54/263

Date of Document: May 25, 2000

Date of Adoption: May 25, 2000

Date of General Entry into Force (EIF): February 12, 2002

Number of States Parties as of this printing: 125 (parties—136)

Date of Signature by the United States: July 5, 2000

Date of Ratification/Accession/Adhesion: December 23, 2002

Date of Entry into Force as to United States (effective date): January 23, 2003

Type of Document: This is a treaty, a legal instrument. It constitutes an amendment to the CRC for states that ratify it; however, the U.S. has not ratified the CRC.

Legal Status/Character of the Instrument/Document as to the United States: Legally binding on the United States because the U.S. has ratified it. This ratification is, however, subject to certain reservations, declarations and understandings, which are set forth in Document 12.

Supervising Body: Committee on the Rights of the Child

Comment: While the U.S. has ratified the First Optional Protocol, it has made clear in its RDUs that they do not assume any obligations under the CRC.

Caution: The status and applicability of this instrument as to the United States may have changed since the date of this publication. The above information may be updated by referring to the following site:

Web Address: http://www2.ohchr.org/english/law/crc-conflict.htm

OPTIONAL PROTOCOL TO THE CONVENTION ON THE RIGHTS OF THE CHILD ON THE INVOLVEMENT OF CHILDREN IN ARMED CONFLICT

The States Parties to the present Protocol,

Encouraged by the overwhelming support for the Convention on the Rights of the Child, demonstrating the widespread commitment that exists to strive for the promotion and protection of the rights of the child,

Reaffirming that the rights of children require special protection, and calling for continuous improvement of the situation of children without distinction, as well as for their development and education in conditions of peace and security,

Disturbed by the harmful and widespread impact of armed conflict on children and the long-term consequences it has for durable peace, security and development,

Condemning the targeting of children in situations of armed conflict and direct attacks on objects protected under international law, including places that generally have a significant presence of children, such as schools and hospitals,

Noting the adoption of the Rome Statute of the International Criminal Court, in particular, the inclusion therein as a war crime, of conscripting or enlisting children under the age of 15 years or using them to participate actively in hostilities in both international and non-international armed conflict,

Considering therefore that to strengthen further the implementation of rights recognized in the Convention on the Rights of the Child there is a need to increase the protection of children from involvement in armed conflict,

Noting that Article 1 of the Convention on the Rights of the Child specifies that, for the purposes of that Convention, a child means every human being below the age of 18 years unless, under the law applicable to the child, majority is attained earlier,

Convinced that an optional protocol to the Convention that raises the age of possible recruitment of persons into armed forces and their participation in hostilities will contribute effectively to the implementation of the principle that the best interests of the child are to be a primary consideration in all actions concerning children,

Noting that the twenty-sixth International Conference of the Red Cross and Red Crescent in December 1995 recommended, inter alia, that parties to conflict take every feasible step to ensure that children below the age of 18 years do not take part in hostilities,

Welcoming the unanimous adoption, in June 1999, of International Labour Organization Convention No. 182 on the Prohibition and Immediate Action for the Elimination of the Worst Forms of Child Labour, which prohibits, inter alia, forced or compulsory recruitment of children for use in armed conflict,

Condemning with the gravest concern the recruitment, training and use within and across national borders of children in hostilities by armed groups distinct from the armed forces of a State, and recognizing the responsibility of those who recruit, train and use children in this regard,

Recalling the obligation of each party to an armed conflict to abide by the provisions of international humanitarian law,

Stressing that the present Protocol is without prejudice to the purposes and principles contained in the Charter of the United Nations, including Article 51, and relevant norms of humanitarian law,

Bearing in mind that conditions of peace and security based on full respect of the purposes and principles contained in the Charter and observance of applicable human rights instruments are indispensable for the full protection of children, in particular during armed conflict and foreign occupation,

Recognizing the special needs of those children who are particularly vulnerable to recruitment or use in hostilities contrary to the present Protocol owing to their economic or social status or gender,

Mindful of the necessity of taking into consideration the economic, social and political root causes of the involvement of children in armed conflict,

Convinced of the need to strengthen international cooperation in the implementation of the present Protocol, as well as the physical and psychosocial rehabilitation and social reintegration of children who are victims of armed conflict,

Encouraging the participation of the community and, in particular, children and child victims in the dissemination of informational and educational programmes concerning the implementation of the Protocol,

Have agreed as follows:

Article 1

States Parties shall take all feasible measures to ensure that members of their armed forces who have not attained the age of 18 years do not take a direct part in hostilities.

Article 2

States Parties shall ensure that persons who have not attained the age of 18 years are not compulsorily recruited into their armed forces.

Article 3

1. States Parties shall raise the minimum age for the voluntary recruitment of persons into their national armed forces from that set out in Article 38, paragraph 3, of the Convention on the Rights of the Child, taking account of the principles contained in that article and recognizing that under the Convention persons under the age of 18 years are entitled to special protection.

2. Each State Party shall deposit a binding declaration upon ratification of or accession to the present Protocol that sets forth the minimum age at which it will permit voluntary recruitment into its national armed forces and a description of the safeguards it has adopted to ensure that such recruitment is not forced or coerced.

3. States Parties that permit voluntary recruitment into their national armed forces under the age of 18 years shall maintain safeguards to ensure, as a minimum, that:

(a) Such recruitment is genuinely voluntary;

(b) Such recruitment is carried out with the informed consent of the person's parents or legal guardians;

(c) Such persons are fully informed of the duties involved in such military service;

(d) Such persons provide reliable proof of age prior to acceptance into national military service.

4. Each State Party may strengthen its declaration at any time by notification to that effect addressed to the Secretary-General of the United Nations, who shall inform all States Parties. Such notification shall take effect on the date on which it is received by the Secretary-General.

5. The requirement to raise the age in paragraph 1 of the present article does not apply to schools operated by or under the control of the armed forces of the States Parties, in keeping with articles 28 and 29 of the Convention on the Rights of the Child.

Article 4

1. Armed groups that are distinct from the armed forces of a State should not, under any circumstances, recruit or use in hostilities persons under the age of 18 years.

2. States Parties shall take all feasible measures to prevent such recruitment and use, including the adoption of legal measures necessary to prohibit and criminalize such practices.

3. The application of the present article shall not affect the legal status of any party to an armed conflict.

Article 5

Nothing in the present Protocol shall be construed as precluding provisions in the law of a State Party or in international instruments and international humanitarian law that are more conducive to the realization of the rights of the child.

Article 6

1. Each State Party shall take all necessary legal, administrative and other measures to ensure the effective implementation and enforcement of the provisions of the present Protocol within its jurisdiction.

2. States Parties undertake to make the principles and provisions of the present Protocol widely known and promoted by appropriate means, to adults and children alike.

3. States Parties shall take all feasible measures to ensure that persons within their jurisdiction recruited or used in hostilities contrary to the present Protocol are demobilized or otherwise released from service. States Parties shall, when necessary, accord to such persons all appropriate assistance for their physical and psychological recovery and their social reintegration.

Article 7

1. States Parties shall cooperate in the implementation of the present Protocol, including in the prevention of any activity contrary thereto and in the rehabilitation and social reintegration of persons who are victims of acts contrary thereto, including through technical cooperation and financial assistance. Such assistance and cooperation will be undertaken in consultation with the States Parties concerned and the relevant international organizations.

2. States Parties in a position to do so shall provide such assistance through existing multilateral, bilateral or other programmes or, inter alia, through a voluntary fund established in accordance with the rules of the General Assembly.

Article 8

1. Each State Party shall, within two years following the entry into force of the present Protocol for that State Party, submit a report to the Committee on the Rights of the Child providing comprehensive information on the measures it has taken to implement the provisions of the Protocol, including the measures taken to implement the provisions on participation and recruitment.

2. Following the submission of the comprehensive report, each State Party shall include in the reports it submits to the Committee on the Rights of the Child, in accordance with Article 44 of the Convention, any further information with respect to the implementation of the Protocol. Other States Parties to the Protocol shall submit a report every five years.

3. The Committee on the Rights of the Child may request from States Parties further information relevant to the implementation of the present Protocol.

Article 9

1. The present Protocol is open for signature by any State that is a party to the Convention or has signed it.

2. The present Protocol is subject to ratification and is open to accession by any State. Instruments of ratification or accession shall be deposited with the Secretary-General of the United Nations.

3. The Secretary-General, in his capacity as depositary of the Convention and the Protocol, shall inform all States Parties to the Convention and all States that have signed the Convention of each instrument of declaration pursuant to Article 3.

Article 10

1. The present Protocol shall enter into force three months after the deposit of the tenth instrument of ratification or accession.

2. For each State ratifying the present Protocol or acceding to it after its entry into force, the Protocol shall enter into force one month after the date of the deposit of its own instrument of ratification or accession.

Article 11

1. Any State Party may denounce the present Protocol at any time by written notification to the Secretary-General of the United Nations, who shall thereafter inform the other States Parties to the Convention and all States that have signed the Convention. The denunciation shall take effect one year after the date of receipt of the notification by the Secretary-General. If, however, on the expiry of that year the denouncing State Party is engaged in armed conflict, the denunciation shall not take effect before the end of the armed conflict.

2. Such a denunciation shall not have the effect of releasing the State Party from its obligations under the present Protocol in regard to any act that occurs prior to the date on which the denunciation becomes effective. Nor shall such a denunciation prejudice in any way the continued consideration of any matter that is already under consideration by the Committee on the Rights of the Child prior to the date on which the denunciation becomes effective.

Article 12

1. Any State Party may propose an amendment and file it with the Secretary-General of the United Nations. The Secretary-General shall thereupon communicate the proposed amendment to States Parties with a request that they indicate whether they favour a conference of States Parties for the purpose of considering and voting upon the proposals. In the event that, within four months from the date of such communication, at least one third of the States Parties favour such a conference, the Secretary-General shall convene the conference under the auspices of the United Nations. Any amendment adopted by a majority of States Parties present and voting at the conference shall be submitted to the General Assembly of the United Nations for approval.

2. An amendment adopted in accordance with paragraph 1 of the present article shall enter into force when it has been approved by the General Assembly and accepted by a two-thirds majority of States Parties.

3. When an amendment enters into force, it shall be binding on those States Parties that have accepted it, other States Parties still being bound by the provisions of the present Protocol and any earlier amendments they have accepted.

Article 13

1. The present Protocol, of which the Arabic, Chinese, English, French, Russian and Spanish texts are equally authentic, shall be deposited in the archives of the United Nations.

2. The Secretary-General of the United Nations shall transmit certified copies of the present Protocol to all States Parties to the Convention and all States that have signed the Convention.

DOCUMENT 30

Full Official Title: Depository Notification of the United States of America with reservations, declarations, and understandings, First Optional Protocol to the Convention on the Rights of the Child on the Involvement of Children in Armed Conflict

Short Title/Acronym/Abbreviation: U.S. Reservations to the First Optional Protocol to the CRC

Subject: Armed conflict, children, U.S. reservations, declarations and understandings

Official Citation: C.N.1361.2002.TREATIES-51

Date of Document: December 23, 2002

Date of Adoption: Not applicable

Date of General Entry into Force (EIF): Not applicable

Number of States Parties as of this printing: Not applicable

Date of Signature by the United States: July 5, 2000

Date of Ratification/Accession/Adhesion: December 23, 2002

Date of Entry into Force as to United States (effective date): January 23, 2003

Type of Document: This is not a treaty but a legal instrument under U.S. and international law that expresses the terms under which the United States ratifies and thus accepts legal obligations under the Protocol to the CRC.

Legal Status/Character of the Instrument/Document as to the United States: These RDUs are legally binding as to U.S. ratification so far as they are consistent with the object and purpose of the First Optional Protocol to the CRC.

Comments: The U.S. obligations under the First Optional Protocol to the CRC must be read in light of these RDUs.

Caution: The status and applicability of this instrument as to the United States may have changed since the date of this publication. The above information may be updated by referring to the following sites:

Web Address: http://treaties.un.org/Pages/ViewDetails.aspx?src=TREATY&mtdsg_no=IV-11-b&chapter=4&lang=en

and

http://treaties.un.org/doc/Treaties/2000/11/20001114%2003-38%20AM/Related%20Documents/CN.1361.2002-Eng.pdf

U.S. RATIFICATION OF CRC OP ON CHILDREN IN ARMED CONFLICT WITH RUDs

Declaration:

"The Government of the United States of America declares, pursuant to Article 3 (2) of the Optional Protocol to the Convention on the Rights of the Child on the Involvement of Children in Armed Conflict that—

(A) the minimum age at which the United States permits voluntary recruitment into the Armed Forces of the United States is 17 years of age;

(B) The United States has established safeguards to ensure that such recruitment is not forced or coerced, including a requirement in section 505 (a) of title 10, United States Code, that no person under 18 years of age may be originally enlisted in the Armed Forces of the United States without the written consent of the person's parent or guardian, if the parent or guardian is entitled to the person's custody and control;

(C) each person recruited into the Armed Forces of the United States receives a comprehensive briefing and must sign an enlistment contract that, taken together, specify the duties involved in military service; and

(D) all persons recruited into the Armed Forces of the United States must provide reliable proof of age before their entry into military service."

Understandings:

(1) NO ASSUMPTION OF OBLIGATIONS UNDER THE CONVENTION ON THE RIGHTS OF THE CHILD—The United States understands that the United States assumes no obligations under the Convention on the Rights of the Child by becoming a party to the Protocol.

(2) IMPLEMENTATION OF OBLIGATION NOT TO PERMIT CHILDREN TO TAKE DIRECT PART IN HOSTILITIES—The United States understands that, with respect to Article 1 of the Protocol—

(A) the term "feasible measures" means those measures that are practical or practically possible, taking into account all the circumstances ruling at the time, including humanitarian and military considerations;

(B) the phrase "direct part in hostilities"-

(i) means immediate and actual action on the battlefield likely to cause harm to the enemy because there is a direct causal relationship between the activity engaged in and the harm done to the enemy; and

(ii) does not mean indirect participation in hostilities, such as gathering and transmitting military information, transporting weapons, munitions, or other supplies, or forward deployment; and

(C) any decision by any military commander, military personnel, or other person responsible for planning, authorizing, or executing military action, including the assignment of military personnel, shall only be judged on the basis of all the relevant circumstances and on the basis of that person's assessment of the information reasonably available to the person at the time the person planned, authorized, or executed the action under review, and shall not be judged on the basis of information that comes to light after the action under review was taken.

(3) MINIMUM AGE FOR VOLUNTARY RECRUITMENT—The United States understands that Article 3 of the Protocol obligates States Parties to the Protocol to raise the minimum age for voluntary recruitment into their national armed forces from the current international standard of 15 years of age.

(4) ARMED GROUPS—The United States understands that the term "armed groups" in Article 4 of the Protocol means nongovernmental armed groups such as rebel groups, dissident armed forces, and other insurgent groups.

(5) NO BASIS FOR JURISDICTION BY ANY INTERNATIONAL TRIBUNAL—The United States understands that nothing in the Protocol establishes a basis for jurisdiction by any international tribunal, including the International Criminal Court."

DOCUMENT 31

Full Official Title: Optional Protocol to the Convention on the Rights of the Child on the Sale of Children, Child Prostitution, and Child Pornography [Second]

Short Title/Acronym/Abbreviation: Second Optional Protocol to the CRC/OP2CRC

Subject: Slavery, prostitution, pornography, children

Official Citation: A/Res/54/263, UNTS vol.2171, p. 220

Date of Document: May 25, 2000

Date of Adoption: May 25, 2000

Date of General Entry into Force (EIF): January 18, 2002

Number of States Parties as of this printing: 117 (parties—139)

Date of Signature by the United States: July 5, 2000

Date of Ratification/Accession/Adhesion: December 23, 2002

Date of Entry into Force as to United States (effective date): January 23, 2003

Type of Document: This is a treaty, a legal instrument. It constitutes an amendment to the CRC for states that ratify it; however, the U.S. has not ratified the CRC.

Legal Status/Character of the Instrument/Document as to the United States: Legally binding on the United States because the U.S. has ratified it. This ratification is, however, subject to certain reservations, declarations and understandings, which are set forth in Document 14.

Supervising Body: Committee on the Rights of the Child

Comment: While the U.S. has ratified the Second Optional Protocol, it has made clear in its RDUs that they do not assume any obligations under the CRC.

Caution: The status and applicability of this instrument as to the United States may have changed since the date of this publication. The above information may be updated by referring to the following site:

Web Address: http://www2.ohchr.org/english/law/crc-sale.htm

OPTIONAL PROTOCOL TO THE CONVENTION ON THE RIGHTS OF THE CHILD ON THE SALE OF CHILDREN, CHILD PROSTITUTION AND CHILD PORNOGRAPHY

The States Parties to the present Protocol,

Considering that, in order further to achieve the purposes of the Convention on the Rights of the Child and the implementation of its provisions, especially articles 1, 11, 21, 32, 33, 34, 35 and 36, it would be appropriate to extend the measures that States Parties should undertake in order to guarantee the protection of the child from the sale of children, child prostitution and child pornography,

Considering also that the Convention on the Rights of the Child recognizes the right of the child to be protected from economic exploitation and from performing any work that is likely to be hazardous or to interfere with the child's education, or to be harmful to the child's health or physical, mental, spiritual, moral or social development,

Gravely concerned at the significant and increasing international traffic in children for the purpose of the sale of children, child prostitution and child pornography,

Deeply concerned at the widespread and continuing practice of sex tourism, to which children are especially vulnerable, as it directly promotes the sale of children, child prostitution and child pornography,

Recognizing that a number of particularly vulnerable groups, including girl children, are at greater risk of sexual exploitation and that girl children are disproportionately represented among the sexually exploited,

Concerned about the growing availability of child pornography on the Internet and other evolving technologies, and recalling the International Conference on Combating Child Pornography on the Internet, held in Vienna in 1999, in particular its conclusion calling for the worldwide criminalization of the production, distribution, exportation, transmission, importation, intentional possession and advertising of child pornography, and stressing the importance of closer cooperation and partnership between Governments and the Internet industry,

Believing that the elimination of the sale of children, child prostitution and child pornography will be facilitated by adopting a holistic approach, addressing the contributing factors, including underdevelopment, poverty, economic disparities, inequitable socio-economic structure, dysfunctioning families, lack of education, urban-rural migration, gender discrimination, irresponsible adult sexual behaviour, harmful traditional practices, armed conflicts and trafficking in children,

Believing also that efforts to raise public awareness are needed to reduce consumer demand for the sale of children, child prostitution and child pornography, and believing further in the importance of strengthening global partnership among all actors and of improving law enforcement at the national level,

Noting the provisions of international legal instruments relevant to the protection of children, including the Hague Convention on Protection of Children and Cooperation in Respect of Intercountry Adoption, the Hague Convention on the Civil Aspects of International Child Abduction, the Hague Convention on Jurisdiction, Applicable Law, Recognition, Enforcement and Cooperation in Respect of Parental Responsibility and Measures for the Protection of Children, and International Labour Organization Convention No. 182 on the Prohibition and Immediate Action for the Elimination of the Worst Forms of Child Labour,

Encouraged by the overwhelming support for the Convention on the Rights of the Child, demonstrating the widespread commitment that exists for the promotion and protection of the rights of the child,

Recognizing the importance of the implementation of the provisions of the Programme of Action for the Prevention of the Sale of Children, Child Prostitution and Child Pornography and the Declaration and Agenda for Action adopted at the World Congress against Commercial Sexual Exploitation of Children, held in Stockholm from 27 to 31 August 1996, and the other relevant decisions and recommendations of pertinent international bodies,

Taking due account of the importance of the traditions and cultural values of each people for the protection and harmonious development of the child, Have agreed as follows:

Article 1

States Parties shall prohibit the sale of children, child prostitution and child pornography as provided for by the present Protocol.

Article 2

For the purposes of the present Protocol:

(a) Sale of children means any act or transaction whereby a child is transferred by any person or group of persons to another for remuneration or any other consideration;

(b) Child prostitution means the use of a child in sexual activities for remuneration or any other form of consideration;

(c) Child pornography means any representation, by whatever means, of a child engaged in real or simulated explicit sexual activities or any representation of the sexual parts of a child for primarily sexual purposes.

Article 3

1. Each State Party shall ensure that, as a minimum, the following acts and activities are fully covered under its criminal or penal law, whether such offences are committed domestically or transnationally or on an individual or organized basis:

(a) In the context of sale of children as defined in Article 2:

(i) Offering, delivering or accepting, by whatever means, a child for the purpose of:

a. Sexual exploitation of the child;

b. Transfer of organs of the child for profit;

c. Engagement of the child in forced labour;

(ii) Improperly inducing consent, as an intermediary, for the adoption of a child in violation of applicable international legal instruments on adoption;

(b) Offering, obtaining, procuring or providing a child for child prostitution, as defined in Article 2;

(c) Producing, distributing, disseminating, importing, exporting, offering, selling or possessing for the above purposes child pornography as defined in Article 2.

2. Subject to the provisions of the national law of a State Party, the same shall apply to an attempt to commit any of the said acts and to complicity or participation in any of the said acts.

3. Each State Party shall make such offences punishable by appropriate penalties that take into account their grave nature.

4. Subject to the provisions of its national law, each State Party shall take measures, where appropriate, to establish the liability of legal persons for offences established in paragraph 1 of the present article. Subject to the legal principles of the State Party, such liability of legal persons may be criminal, civil or administrative.

5. States Parties shall take all appropriate legal and administrative measures to ensure that all persons involved in the adoption of a child act in conformity with applicable international legal instruments.

Article 4

1. Each State Party shall take such measures as may be necessary to establish its jurisdiction over the offences referred to in Article 3, paragraph 1, when the offences are commited in its territory or on board a ship or aircraft registered in that State.

2. Each State Party may take such measures as may be necessary to establish its jurisdiction over the offences referred to in Article 3, paragraph 1, in the following cases:

(a) When the alleged offender is a national of that State or a person who has his habitual residence in its territory;

(b) When the victim is a national of that State.

3. Each State Party shall also take such measures as may be necessary to establish its jurisdiction over the aforementioned offences when the alleged offender is present in its territory and it does not extradite him or her to another State Party on the ground that the offence has been committed by one of its nationals.

4. The present Protocol does not exclude any criminal jurisdiction exercised in accordance with internal law.

Article 5

1. The offences referred to in Article 3, paragraph 1, shall be deemed to be included as extraditable offences in any extradition treaty existing between States Parties and shall be included as extraditable offences in every extradition treaty subsequently concluded between them, in accordance with the conditions set forth in such treaties.

2. If a State Party that makes extradition conditional on the existence of a treaty receives a request for extradition from another State Party with which it has no extradition treaty, it may consider the present

Protocol to be a legal basis for extradition in respect of such offences. Extradition shall be subject to the conditions provided by the law of the requested State.

3. States Parties that do not make extradition conditional on the existence of a treaty shall recognize such offences as extraditable offences between themselves subject to the conditions provided by the law of the requested State.

4. Such offences shall be treated, for the purpose of extradition between States Parties, as if they had been committed not only in the place in which they occurred but also in the territories of the States required to establish their jurisdiction in accordance with Article 4.

5. If an extradition request is made with respect to an offence described in Article 3, paragraph 1, and the requested State Party does not or will not extradite on the basis of the nationality of the offender, that State shall take suitable measures to submit the case to its competent authorities for the purpose of prosecution.

Article 6

1. States Parties shall afford one another the greatest measure of assistance in connection with investigations or criminal or extradition proceedings brought in respect of the offences set forth in Article 3, paragraph 1, including assistance in obtaining evidence at their disposal necessary for the proceedings.

2. States Parties shall carry out their obligations under paragraph 1 of the present article in conformity with any treaties or other arrangements on mutual legal assistance that may exist between them. In the absence of such treaties or arrangements, States Parties shall afford one another assistance in accordance with their domestic law.

Article 7

States Parties shall, subject to the provisions of their national law:

(a) Take measures to provide for the seizure and confiscation, as appropriate, of:

(i) Goods, such as materials, assets and other instrumentalities used to commit or facilitate offences under the present protocol;

(ii) Proceeds derived from such offences;

(b) Execute requests from another State Party for seizure or confiscation of goods or proceeds referred to in subparagraph (a);

(c) Take measures aimed at closing, on a temporary or definitive basis, premises used to commit such offences.

Article 8

1. States Parties shall adopt appropriate measures to protect the rights and interests of child victims of the practices prohibited under the present Protocol at all stages of the criminal justice process, in particular by:

(a) Recognizing the vulnerability of child victims and adapting procedures to recognize their special needs, including their special needs as witnesses;

(b) Informing child victims of their rights, their role and the scope, timing and progress of the proceedings and of the disposition of their cases;

(c) Allowing the views, needs and concerns of child victims to be presented and considered in proceedings where their personal interests are affected, in a manner consistent with the procedural rules of national law;

(d) Providing appropriate support services to child victims throughout the legal process;

(e) Protecting, as appropriate, the privacy and identity of child victims and taking measures in accordance with national law to avoid the inappropriate dissemination of information that could lead to the identification of child victims;

(f) Providing, in appropriate cases, for the safety of child victims, as well as that of their families and witnesses on their behalf, from intimidation and retaliation;

(g) Avoiding unnecessary delay in the disposition of cases and the execution of orders or decrees granting compensation to child victims.

2. States Parties shall ensure that uncertainty as to the actual age of the victim shall not prevent the initiation of criminal investigations, including investigations aimed at establishing the age of the victim.

3. States Parties shall ensure that, in the treatment by the criminal justice system of children who are victims of the offences described in the present Protocol, the best interest of the child shall be a primary consideration.

4. States Parties shall take measures to ensure appropriate training, in particular legal and psychological training, for the persons who work with victims of the offences prohibited under the present Protocol.

5. States Parties shall, in appropriate cases, adopt measures in order to protect the safety and integrity of those persons and/or organizations involved in the prevention and/or protection and rehabilitation of victims of such offences.

6. Nothing in the present article shall be construed to be prejudicial to or inconsistent with the rights of the accused to a fair and impartial trial.

Article 9

1. States Parties shall adopt or strengthen, implement and disseminate laws, administrative measures, social policies and programmes to prevent the offences referred to in the present Protocol. Particular attention shall be given to protect children who are especially vulnerable to such practices.

2. States Parties shall promote awareness in the public at large, including children, through information by all appropriate means, education and training, about the preventive measures and harmful effects of the offences referred to in the present Protocol. In fulfilling their obligations under this article, States Parties shall encourage the participation of the community and, in particular, children and child victims, in such information and education and training programmes, including at the international level.

3. States Parties shall take all feasible measures with the aim of ensuring all appropriate assistance to victims of such offences, including their full social reintegration and their full physical and psychological recovery.

4. States Parties shall ensure that all child victims of the offences described in the present Protocol have access to adequate procedures to seek, without discrimination, compensation for damages from those legally responsible.

5. States Parties shall take appropriate measures aimed at effectively prohibiting the production and dissemination of material advertising the offences described in the present Protocol.

Article 10

1. States Parties shall take all necessary steps to strengthen international cooperation by multilateral, regional and bilateral arrangements for the prevention, detection, investigation, prosecution and punishment of those responsible for acts involving the sale of children, child prostitution, child pornography and child sex tourism. States Parties shall also promote international cooperation and coordination between their authorities, national and international non-governmental organizations and international organizations.

2. States Parties shall promote international cooperation to assist child victims in their physical and psychological recovery, social reintegration and repatriation.

3. States Parties shall promote the strengthening of international cooperation in order to address the root causes, such as poverty and underdevelopment, contributing to the vulnerability of children to the sale of children, child prostitution, child pornography and child sex tourism.

4. States Parties in a position to do so shall provide financial, technical or other assistance through existing multilateral, regional, bilateral or other programmes.

Article 11

Nothing in the present Protocol shall affect any provisions that are more conducive to the realization of the rights of the child and that may be contained in:

(a) The law of a State Party;

(b) International law in force for that State.

Article 12

1. Each State Party shall, within two years following the entry into force of the present Protocol for that State Party, submit a report to the Committee on the Rights of the Child providing comprehensive information on the measures it has taken to implement the provisions of the Protocol.

2. Following the submission of the comprehensive report, each State Party shall include in the reports they submit to the Committee on the Rights of the Child, in accordance with Article 44 of the Convention, any further information with respect to the implementation of the present Protocol. Other States Parties to the Protocol shall submit a report every five years.

3. The Committee on the Rights of the Child may request from States Parties further information relevant to the implementation of the present Protocol.

Article 13

1. The present Protocol is open for signature by any State that is a party to the Convention or has signed it.

2. The present Protocol is subject to ratification and is open to accession by any State that is a party to the Convention or has signed it. Instruments of ratification or accession shall be deposited with the Secretary-General of the United Nations.

Article 14

1. The present Protocol shall enter into force three months after the deposit of the tenth instrument of ratification or accession.

2. For each State ratifying the present Protocol or acceding to it after its entry into force, the Protocol shall enter into force one month after the date of the deposit of its own instrument of ratification or accession.

Article 15

1. Any State Party may denounce the present Protocol at any time by written notification to the Secretary-General of the United Nations, who shall thereafter inform the other States Parties to the Convention and all States that have signed the Convention. The denunciation shall take effect one year after the date of receipt of the notification by the Secretary-General.

2. Such a denunciation shall not have the effect of releasing the State Party from its obligations under the present Protocol in regard to any offence that occurs prior to the date on which the denunciation becomes effective. Nor shall such a denunciation prejudice in any way the continued consideration of any matter that is already under consideration by the Committee on the Rights of the Child prior to the date on which the denunciation becomes effective.

Article 16

1. Any State Party may propose an amendment and file it with the Secretary-General of the United Nations. The Secretary-General shall thereupon communicate the proposed amendment to States Parties with a request that they indicate whether they favour a conference of States Parties for the purpose of considering and voting upon the proposals. In the event that, within four months from the date of such communication, at least one third of the States Parties favour such a conference, the Secretary-General shall convene the conference under the auspices of the United Nations. Any amendment adopted by a majority of States Parties present and voting at the conference shall be submitted to the General Assembly of the United Nations for approval.

2. An amendment adopted in accordance with paragraph 1 of the present article shall enter into force when it has been approved by the General Assembly and accepted by a two-thirds majority of States Parties.

3. When an amendment enters into force, it shall be binding on those States Parties that have accepted it, other States Parties still being bound by the provisions of the present Protocol and any earlier amendments they have accepted.

Article 17

1. The present Protocol, of which the Arabic, Chinese, English, French, Russian and Spanish texts are equally authentic, shall be deposited in the archives of the United Nations.

2. The Secretary-General of the United Nations shall transmit certified copies of the present Protocol to all States Parties to the Convention and all States that have signed the Convention.

Document 32

Full Official Title: Depository Notification of the United States of America with reservations, declarations, and understandings, Second Optional Protocol to the Convention on the Rights of the Child on the Sale of Children, Child Prostitution, and Child Pornography

Short Title/Acronym/Abbreviation: U.S. Ratification, Reservations to the Second Optional Protocol to the CRC

Subject: Armed conflict, children, U.S. reservations, declarations and understandings

Official Citation: C.N.1360.2002.TREATIES-52

Date of Document: December 23, 2002

Date of Adoption: Not applicable

Date of General Entry into Force (EIF): Not applicable

Number of States Parties as of this printing: Not applicable

Date of Signature by the United States: July 5, 2000

Date of Ratification/Accession/Adhesion: December 23, 2002

Date of Entry into Force as to United States (effective date): January 23, 2003

Type of Document: This is a legal instrument under U.S. and international law which expresses the terms by which the United States ratifies, and thus accepts, legal obligations under the Second Optional Protocol. It includes the advice and consent of the U.S. Senate under the U.S. Constitution, ratifying the Second Optional Protocol on behalf of the people of the United States. This legislative act ratified the prior signature of the President to the treaty. The act also sets forth the reservations, declarations and understandings to the Second Optional Protocol, submitted with the ratification.

Legal Status/Character of the Instrument/Document as to the United States: A legal document under U.S. and international law. It served to legally bind the United States to comply with the Second Optional Protocol after this instrument of ratification was deposited with the United Nations. These legal obligations are subject to the reservations, declarations and understandings submitted by the United States and contained in this document. These RDUs are legally binding as to U.S. ratification so far as they are consistent with the object and purpose of the Second Optional Protocol to the CRC.

Comments: The U.S. obligations under the Second Optional Protocol to the CRC must be read in light of these RDUs.

Caution: The status and applicability of this instrument as to the United States may have changed since the date of this publication. The above information may be updated by referring to the following sites:

Web Address: http://treaties.un.org/doc/Treaties/2000/11/20001114%2003-16%20AM/Related%20 Documents/CN.1360.2002-Eng.pdf

and

http://treaties.un.org/Pages/ViewDetails.aspx?src=TREATY&mtdsg_no=IV-11-c&chapter=4&lang=en

U.S. Ratification, Reservations to the Second Optional Protocol to the CRC

Reservation:

"To the extent that the domestic law of the United States does not provide for jurisdiction over an offense described in Article 3 (1) of the Protocol if the offense is committed on board a ship or aircraft registered in the United States, the obligation with respect to jurisdiction over that offense shall not apply to the United States until such time as the United States may notify the Secretary-General of the United Nations that United States domestic law is in full conformity with the requirements of Article 4 (1) of the Protocol.

The Senate's advice and consent is subject to the following understandings:

(1) NO ASSUMPTION OF OBLIGATIONS UNDER THE CONVENTION ON THE RIGHTS OF THE CHILD.—The United States understands that the United States assumes no obligations under the Convention on the Rights of the Child by becoming a party to the Protocol.

(2) THE TERM "CHILD PORNOGRAPHY"—The United States understands that the term "sale of children" as defined in Article 2(a) of the Protocol, is intended to cover any transaction in which remuneration or other consideration is given and received under circumstances in which a person who does not have a lawful right to custody of the child thereby obtains de facto control over the child.

(3) THE TERM "CHILD PORNOGRAPHY"—The United States understands the term "child pornography", as defined in Article 2(c) of the Protocol, to mean the visual representation of a child engaged in real or simulated sexual activities or of the genitalia of a child where the dominant characteristic is depiction for a sexual purpose.

(4) THE TERM "TRANSFER OF ORGANS FOR PROFIT".—The United States understands that—

(A) the term "transfer of organs for profit", as used in Article 3(1)(a)(i) of the Protocol, does not cover any situation in which a child donates an organ pursuant to lawful consent; and

(B) the term "profit", as used in Article 3(1)(a)(i) of the Protocol, does not include the lawful paymeasonable amount associated with the transfer of organs, including any payment for the expense of travel, housing, lost wages, or medical costs.

(5) THE TERMS "APPLICABLE INTERNATIONAL LEGAL INSTRUMENTS" AND "IMPROPERLY INDUCING CONSENT"—

(A) UNDERSTANDING OF "APPLICABLE INTERNATIONAL LEGAL INSTRUMENTS".—The United States understands that the term "applicable international legal instruments" in Articles 3 (1) (a) (ii) and 3 (5) of the Protocol refers to the Convention on Protection of Children and Co-operation in Respect of Intercountry Adoption done at The Hague on May 29, 1993 (in this paragraph referred to as "The Hague Convention").

(B) NO OBLIGATION TO TAKE CERTAIN ACTION—The United States is not a party to The Hague Convention, but expects to become a party. Accordingly, until such time as the United States becomes a party to The Hague Convention, it understands that it is not obligated to criminalize conduct proscribed by Article 3(1)(a)(ii) of the Protocol or to take all appropriate legal and administrative measures required by Article 3(5) of the Protocol.

(C) UNDERSTANDING Of' "IMPROPERLY INDUCING CONSENT"—The United States understands that the term "Improperly inducing consent" in Article 3(1)(a)(ii) of the Protocol means knowingly and willfully inducing consent by offering or giving compensation for the relinquishment of parental rights.

(6) IMPLEMENTATION OF THE PROTOCOL IN THE FEDERAL SYSTEM OF THE UNITED STATES—The United States understands that the Protocol shall be implemented by the Federal Government to the extent that it exercises jurisdiction over the matters covered therein, and otherwise by the State and local governments. To the extent that State and local governments exercise jurisdiction over such matters, the Federal Government shall as necessary, take appropriate measures to ensure the fulfillment of the Protocol.

DOCUMENT 33

Full Official Title: The Convention on the Political Rights of Women
Short Title/Acronym/Abbreviation: Nothing official
Subject: Women, civil and political rights
Official Citation: U.N. General Assembly, *Convention on the Political Rights of Women*, 20 December 1952
Date of Document: December 20, 1952
Date of Adoption: December 20, 1952
Date of General Entry into Force (EIF): July 7, 1954
Number of States Parties as of this printing: 121
Date of Signature by the United States: Not applicable
Date of Ratification/Accession/Adhesion: April 8, 1976
Date of Entry into Force as to United States (effective date): Article VI 2 of the convention says: "For each State ratifying or acceding to the Convention after the deposit of the sixth instrument of ratification or accession the Convention shall enter into force on the ninetieth day after deposit by such State or its instrument of ratification or accession."
Type of Document: This is a treaty, a legal instrument.
Legal Status/Character of the Instrument/Document as to the United States: Legally binding on the United States because the U.S. has ratified it.
Supervising Body:
Comment: Eleanor Roosevelt was very involved in moving this treaty through the U.N. to secure international recognition of some basic but essential rights of women to engage in political life.
Caution: The status and applicability of this instrument as to the United States may have changed since the date of this publication. The above information may be updated by referring to the following site:
Web Address: http://www.un-documents.net/cprw.htm

CONVENTION ON THE POLITICAL RIGHTS OF WOMEN, 193 U.N.T.S. 135

The Contracting Parties,

Desiring to implement the principle of equality of rights for men and women contained in the Charter of the United Nations,

Recognizing that everyone has the right to take part in the government of his country directly or indirectly through freely chosen representatives, and has the right to equal access to public service in his country, and desiring to equalize the status of men and women in the enjoyment and exercise of political rights, in accordance with the provisions of the Charter of the United Nations and of the Universal Declaration of Human Rights,

Having resolved to conclude a Convention for this purpose,

Hereby agree as hereinafter provided:

Article 1

Women shall be entitled to vote in all elections on equal terms with men, without any discrimination.

Article 2

Women shall be eligible for election to all publicly elected bodies, established by national law, on equal terms with men, without any discrimination.

Article 3

Women shall be entitled to hold public office and to exercise all public functions, established by national law, on equal terms with men, without any discrimination.

Article 4

1. This Convention shall be open for signature on behalf of any Member of the United Nations and also on behalf of any other State to which an invitation has been addressed by the General Assembly.

2. This Convention shall be ratified and the instruments of ratification shall be deposited with the Secretary-General of the United Nations.

Article 5

1. This Convention shall be open for accession to all States referred to in paragraph I of article IV.

2. Accession shall be effected by the deposit of an instrument of accession with the Secretary-General of the United Nations.

Article 6

1. This Convention shall come into force on the ninetieth day following the date of deposit of the sixth instrument of ratification or accession.

2. For each State ratifying or acceding to the Convention after the deposit of the sixth instrument of ratification or accession the Convention shall enter into force on the ninetieth day after deposit by such State of its instrument of ratification or accession.

Article 7

In the event that any State submits a reservation to any of the articles of this Convention at the time of signature, ratification or accession, the Secretary-General shall communicate the text of the reservation to all States which are or may become Parties to this Convention. Any State which objects to the reservation may, within a period of ninety days from the date of the said communication (or upon the date of its becoming a Party to the Convention), notify the Secretary-General that it does not accept it. In such case, the Convention shall not enter into force as between such State and the State making the reservation.

Article 8

1. Any State may denounce this Convention by written notification to the Secretary-General of the United Nations. Denunciation shall take effect one year after the date of receipt of the notification by the Secretary General.

2. This Convention shall cease to be in force as from the date when the denunciation which reduces the number of Parties to less than six becomes effective.

Article 9

Any dispute which may arise between any two or more Contracting States concerning the interpretation or application of this Convention, which is not settled by negotiation, shall at the request of any one of the parties to the dispute be referred to the International Court of Justice for decision, unless they agree to another mode of settlement.

Article 10

The Secretary-General of the United Nations shall notify all Members of the United Nations and the non-member States contemplated in paragraph I of article IV of this Convention of the following:

(a) Signatures and instruments of ratification received in accordance with article IV;

(b) Instruments of accession received in accordance with article V;

(c) The date upon which this Convention enters into force in accordance with article VI;

(d) Communications and notifications received in accordance with article VII;

(e) Notifications of denunciation received in accordance with paragraph I of article VIII;

(f) Abrogation in accordance with paragraph 2 of article VIII.

Article 11

1. This Convention, of which the Chinese, English, French, Russian and Spanish texts shall be equally authentic, shall be deposited in the archives of the United Nations.

2. The Secretary-General of the United Nations shall transmit a certified copy to all Members of the United Nations and to the non-member States contemplated in paragraph I of article IV.

DOCUMENT 34

Full Official Title: The Slavery Convention
Short Title/Acronym/Abbreviation: The Slavery Convention
Subject: Prohibtion of slavery
Official Citation: League of Nations Treaty Series, vol. 60, p. 254.
Date of Document: September 25, 1926
Date of Adoption: September 25, 1926
Date of General Entry into Force (EIF): March 9, 1927
Number of States Parties as of this printing: 81
Date of Signature by the United States: Not applicable
Date of Ratification/Accession/Adhesion: March 21, 1929
Date of Entry into Force as to United States (effective date): March 21, 1929
Type of Document: This is a treaty, a legal instrument.
Legal Status/Character of the Instrument/Document as to the United States: Legally binding on the United States because the U.S. has ratified it.
Supervising Body: Any disputes between state parties to the treaty relating to the interpretation or application of the Convention that are not settled by direct negotiation, would be referred for decision to the Permanent Court of International Justice. With the Protocol amending the Slavery Convention, the United Nations and the International Court of Justice carried on the obligations for this treaty from the League of Nations and PCIJ.
Comment: This was the first international treaty intended to abolish slavery and the slave trade.
Caution: The status and applicability of this instrument as to the United States may have changed since the date of this publication. The above information may be updated by referring to the following site. The Convention was amended by a Protocol, which entered into force on December 7, 1953.
Web Address: http://treaties.un.org/doc/Treaties/1926/09/19260925%2003-12%20AM/Ch_XVIII_3p.pdf

THE SLAVERY CONVENTION

Entry into force: 9 March 1927, in accordance with Article 12. The Convention was amended by the Protocol done at the Headquarters of the United Nations, New York, on 7 December 1953; the amended Convention entered into force on 7 July 1955, the date on which the amendments, set forth in the annex to the Protocol of 7 December 1953, entered into force in accordance with article III of the Protocol.

Whereas the signatories of the General Act of the Brussels Conference of 1889–90 declared that they were equally animated by the firm intention of putting an end to the traffic in African slaves,

Whereas the signatories of the Convention of Saint-Germain-en-Laye of 1919, to revise the General Act of Berlin of 1885 and the General Act and Declaration of Brussels of 1890, affirmed their intention of securing the complete suppression of slavery in all its forrns and of the slave trade by land and sea,

Taking into consideration the report of the Temporary Slavery Commission appointed by the Council of the League of Nations on June 12th, 1924,

Desiring to complete and extend the work accomplished under the Brussels Act and to find a means of giving practical effect throughout the world to such intentions as were expressed in regard to slave trade and slavery by the signatories of the Convention of Saint-Germain-en-Laye, and recognising that it is necessary to conclude to that end more detailed arrangements than are contained in that Convention,

Considering, moreover, that it is necessary to prevent forced labour from developing into conditions analogous to slavery,

Have decided to conclude a Convention and have accordingly appointed as their Plenipotentiaries [names omitted] have agreed as follows:

Article 1
For the purpose of the present Convention, the following definitions are agreed upon:
(1) Slavery is the status or condition of a person over whom any or all of the powers attaching to the right of ownership are exercised.

(2) The slave trade includes all acts involved in the capture, acquisition or disposal of a person with intent to reduce him to slavery; all acts involved in the acquisition of a slave with a view to selling or exchanging him; all acts of disposal by sale or exchange of a slave acquired with a view to being sold or exchanged, and, in general, every act of trade or transport in slaves.

Article 2

The High Contracting Parties undertake, each in respect of the territories placed under its sovereignty, jurisdiction, protection, suzerainty or tutelage, so far as they have not already taken the necessary steps:

(a) To prevent and suppress the slave trade;

(b) To bring about, progressively and as soon as possible, the complete abolition of slavery in all its forms.

Article 3

The High Contracting Parties undertake to adopt all appropriate measures with a view to preventing and suppressing the embarkation, disembarkation and transport of slaves in their territorial waters and upon all vessels flying their respective flags. The High Contracting Parties undertake to negotiate as soon as possible a general Convention with regard to the slave trade which will give them rights and impose upon them duties of the same nature as those provided for in the Convention of June 17th, 1925, relative to the International Trade in Arms (Articles 12, 20, 21, 22, 23, 24 and paragraphs 3, 4 and 5 of Section II of Annex II), with the necessary adaptations, it being understood that this general Convention will not place the ships (even of small tonnage) of any High Contracting Parties in a position different from that of the other High Contracting Parties. It is also understood that, before or after the coming into force of this general Convention, the High Contracting Parties are entirely free to conclude between themselves, without, however, derogating from the principles laid down in the preceding paragraph, such special agreements as, by reason of their peculiar situation, might appear to be suitable in order to bring about as soon as possible the complete disappearance of the slave trade.

Article 4

The High Contracting Parties shall give to one another every assistance with the object of securing the abolition of slavery and the slave trade.

Article 5

The High Contracting Parties recognise that recourse to compulsory or forced labour may have grave consequences and undertake, each in respect of the territories placed under its sovereignty, jurisdiction, protection, suzerainty or tutelage, to take all necessary measures to prevent compulsory or forced labour from developing into conditions analogous to slavery.

It is agreed that:

(1) Subject to the transitional provisions laid down in paragraph (2) below, compulsory or forced labour may only be exacted for public purposes.

(2) In territories in which compulsory or forced labour for other than public purposes still survives, the High Contracting Parties shall endeavour progressively and as soon as possible to put an end to the practice. So long as such forced or compulsory labour exists, this labour shall invariably be of an exceptional character, shall always receive adequate remuneration, and shall not involve the removal of the labourers from their usual place of residence.

(3) In all cases, the responsibility for any recourse to compulsory or forced labour shall rest with the competent central authorities of the territory concerned.

Article 6

Those of the High Contracting Parties whose laws do not at present make adequate provision for the punishment of infractions of laws and regulations enacted with a view to giving effect to the purposes of the present Convention undertake to adopt the necessary measures in order that severe penalties may be imposed in respect of such infractions.

Article 7

The High Contracting Parties undertake to communicate to each other and to the Secretary-General of the League of Nations any laws and regulations which they may enact with a view to the application of the provisions of the present Convention.

Article 8

The High Contracting Parties agree that disputes arising between them relating to the interpretation or application of this Convention shall, if they cannot be settled by direct negotiation, be referred for decision to the Permanent Court of International Justice. In case either or both of the States Parties to such a dispute should not be Parties to the Protocol of December 16th, 1920, relating to the Permanent Court of International Justice, the dispute shall be referred, at the choice of the Parties and in accordance with the constitutional procedure of each State, either to the Permanent Court of International Justice or to a court of arbitration constituted in accordance with the Convention of October 18th, 1907, for the Pacific Settlement of International Disputes, or to some other court of arbitration.

Article 9

At the time of signature or of ratification or of accession, any High Contracting Party may declare that its acceptance of the present Convention does not bind some or all of the territories placed under its sovereignty, jurisdiction, protection, suzerainty or tutelage in respect of all or any provisions of the Convention; it may subsequently accede separately on behalf of any one of them or in respect of any provision to which any one of them is not a Party.

Article 10

In the event of a High Contracting Party wishing to denounce the present Convention, the denunciation shall be notified in writing to the Secretary-General of the League of Nations, who will at once communicate a certified true copy of the notification to all the other High Contracting Parties, informing them of the date on which it was received.

The denunciation shall only have effect in regard to the notifying State, and one year after the notification has reached the Secretary-General of the League of Nations.

Denunciation may also be made separately in respect of any territory placed under its sovereignty, jurisdiction, protection, suzerainty or tutelage.

Article 11

The present Convention, which will bear this day's date and of which the French and English texts are both authentic, will remain open for signature by the States Members of the League of Nations until April 1st, 1927.

The Secretary-General of the League of Nations will subsequently bring the present Convention to the notice of States which have not signed it, including States which are not Members of the League of Nations, and invite them to accede thereto.

A State desiring to accede to the Convention shall notify its intention in writing to the Secretary-General of the League of Nations and transmit to him the instrument of accession, which shall be deposited in the archives of the League.

The Secretary-General shall immediately transmit to all the other High Contracting Parties a certified true copy of the notification and of the instrument of accession, informing them of the date on which he received them.

Article 12

The present Convention will be ratified and the instruments of ratification shall be deposited in the office of the Secretary-General of the League of Nations. The Secretary-General will inform all the High Contracting Parties of such deposit.

The Convention will come into operation for each State on the date of the deposit of its ratification or of its accession.

In faith whereof the Plenipotentiaries signed the present Convention.

Done at Geneva the twenty-fifth day of September, one thousand nine hundred and twenty-six, in one copy, which will be deposited in the archives of the League of Nations. A certified copy shall be forwarded to each signatory State.

DOCUMENT 35

Full Official Title: Supplementary Convention on the Abolition of Slavery, the Slave Trade, and Institutions and Practices similar to Slavery

Short Title/Acronym/Abbreviation: The Supplemental Slavery Convention

Subject: Slavery, slave-like practices

Official Citation: U.N.T.S. 266 Vol. P3

Date of Document: September 7, 1956

Date of Adoption: September 7, 1956

Date of General Entry into Force (EIF): April 30, 1957
Number of States Parties as of this printing: 123
Date of Signature by the United States: March 7, 1956
Date of Ratification/Accession/Adhesion: December 6, 1967
Date of Entry into Force as to United States (effective date): December 6, 1967
Type of Document: This is a treaty, a legal instrument.
Legal Status/Character of the Instrument/Document as to the United States: Legally binding on the United States because the U.S. has ratified it
Supervising Body: Any disputes between state parties to the treaty relating to the interpretation or application of the Convention that are not settled by direct negotiation would be referred for decision to the International Court of Justice.
Comment: The treaty is applicable to "all territories for the international relations of which the United States of America is responsible."
Caution: The status and applicability of this instrument as to the United States may have changed since the date of this publication.
Web Address: http://www2.ohchr.org/english/law/slavetrade.htm

SUPPLEMENTARY CONVENTION ON THE ABOLITION OF SLAVERY, THE SLAVE TRADE, AND INSTITUTIONS AND PRACTICES SIMILAR TO SLAVERY

Preamble

The States Parties to the present Convention,

Considering that freedom is the birthright of every human being, Mindful that the peoples of the United Nations reaffirmed in the Charter their faith in the dignity and worth of the human person,

Considering that the Universal Declaration of Human Rights, proclaimed by the General Assembly of the United Nations as a common standard of achievement for all peoples and all nations, states that no one shall be held in slavery or servitude and that slavery and the slave trade shall be prohibited in all their forms,

Recognizing that, since the conclusion of the Slavery Convention signed at Geneva on 25 September 1926, which was designed to secure the abolition of slavery and of the slave trade, further progress has been made towards this end,

Having regard to the Forced Labour Convention of 1930 and to subsequent action by the International Labour Organisation in regard to forced or compulsory labour,

Being aware, however, that slavery, the slave trade and institutions and practices similar to slavery have not yet been eliminated in all parts of the world,

Having decided, therefore, that the Convention of 1926, which remains operative, should now be augmented by the conclusion of a supplementary convention designed to intensify national as well as international efforts towards the abolition of slavery, the slave trade and institutions and practices similar to slavery,

Have agreed as follows:

SECTION I.—INSTITUTIONS AND PRACTICES SIMILAR TO SLAVERY
Article 1

Each of the States Parties to this Convention shall take all practicable and necessary legislative and other measures to bring about progressively and as soon as possible the complete abolition or abandonment of the following institutions and practices, where they still exist and whether or not they are covered by the definition of slavery contained in Article 1 of the Slavery Convention signed at Geneva on 25 September 1926:

(a) Debt bondage, that is to say, the status or condition arising from a pledge by a debtor of his personal services or of those of a person under his control as security for a debt, if the value of those services as reasonably assessed is not applied towards the liquidation of the debt or the length and nature of those services are not respectively limited and defined;

(b) Serfdom, that is to say, the condition or status of a tenant who is by law, custom or agreement bound to live and labour on land belonging to another person and to render some determinate service to such other person, whether for reward or not, and is not free to change his status;

(c) Any institution or practice whereby:

(i) A woman, without the right to refuse, is promised or given in marriage on payment of a consideration in money or in kind to her parents, guardian, family or any other person or group; or

(ii) The husband of a woman, his family, or his clan, has the right to transfer her to another person for value received or otherwise; or

(iii) A woman on the death of her husband is liable to be inherited by another person;

(d) Any institution or practice whereby a child or young person under the age of 18 years, is delivered by either or both of his natural parents or by his guardian to another person, whether for reward or not, with a view to the exploitation of the child or young person or of his labour.

Article 2

With a view to bringing to an end the institutions and practices mentioned in article I (c) of this Convention, the States Parties undertake to prescribe, where appropriate, suitable minimum ages of marriage, to encourage the use of facilities whereby the consent of both parties to a marriage may be freely expressed in the presence of a competent civil or religious authority, and to encourage the registration of marriages.

SECTION II.—THE SLAVE TRADE

Article 3

1. The act of conveying or attempting to convey slaves from one country to another by whatever means of transport, or of being accessory thereto, shall be a criminal offence under the laws of the States Parties to this Convention and persons convicted thereof shall be liable to very severe penalties.

2. (a) The States Parties shall take all effective measures to prevent ships and aircraft authorized to fly their flags from conveying slaves and to punish persons guilty of such acts or of using national flags for that purpose.

(b) The States Parties shall take all effective measures to ensure that their ports, airfields and coasts are not used for the conveyance of slaves.

3. The States Parties to this Convention shall exchange information in order to ensure the practical co-ordination of the measures taken by them in combating the slave trade and shall inform each other of every case of the slave trade, and of every attempt to commit this criminal offence, which comes to their notice.

Article 4

Any slave who takes refuge on board any vessel of a State Party to this Convention shall ipso facto be free.

SECTION III.—SLAVERY AND INSTITUTIONS AND PRACTICES SIMILAR TO SLAVERY

Article 5

In a country where the abolition or abandonment of slavery, or of the institutions or practices mentioned in article I of this Convention, is not yet complete, the act of mutilating, branding or otherwise marking a slave or a person of servile status in order to indicate his status, or as a punishment, or for any other reason, or of being accessory thereto, shall be a criminal offence under the laws of the States Parties to this Convention and persons convicted thereof shall be liable to punishment.

Article 6

1 . The act of enslaving another person or of inducing another person to give himself or a person dependent upon him into slavery, or of attempting these acts, or being accessory thereto, or being a party to a conspiracy to accomplish any such acts, shall be a criminal offence under the laws of the States Parties to this Convention and persons convicted thereof shall be liable to punishment.

2. Subject to the provisions of the introductory paragraph of article I of this Convention, the provisions of paragraph 1 of the present article shall also apply to the act of inducing another person to place himself or a person dependent upon him into the servile status resulting from any of the institutions or practices mentioned in Article 1, to any attempt to perform such acts, to being accessory thereto, and to being a party to a conspiracy to accomplish any such acts.

SECTION IV.—DEFINITIONS

Article 7

For the purposes of the present Convention:

(a) "Slavery" means, as defined in the Slavery Convention of 1926, the status or condition of a person over whom any or all of the powers attaching to the right of ownership are exercised, and "slave" means a person in such condition or status;

(b) "A person of servile status" means a person in the condition or status resulting from any of the institutions or practices mentioned in article I of this Convention;

(c) "Slave trade" means and includes all acts involved in the capture, acquisition or disposal of a person with intent to reduce him to slavery; all acts involved in the acquisition of a slave with a view to selling or exchanging him; all acts of disposal by sale or exchange of a person acquired with a view to being sold or exchanged; and, in general, every act of trade or transport in slaves by whatever means of conveyance.

SECTION V.—CO-OPERATION BETWEEN STATES PARTIES AND COMMUNICATION OF INFORMATION

Article 8

1. The States Parties to this Convention undertake to co-operate with each other and with the United Nations to give effect to the foregoing provisions.

2. The Parties undertake to communicate to the Secretary-General of the United Nations copies of any laws, regulations and administrative measures enacted or put into effect to implement the provisions of this Convention.

3. The Secretary-General shall communicate the information received under paragraph 2 of this article to the other Parties and to the Economic and Social Council as part of the documentation for any discussion which the Council might undertake with a view to making further recommendations for the abolition of slavery, the slave trade or the institutions and practices which are the subject of this Convention.

SECTION VI.—FINAL CLAUSES

Article 9

No reservations may be made to this Convention.

Article 10

Any dispute between States Parties to this Convention relating to its interpretation or application, which is not settled by negotiation, shall be referred to the International Court of Justice at the request of any one of the parties to the dispute, unless the parties concerned agree on another mode of settlement.

Article 11

1. This Convention shall be open until I July 1957 for signature by any State Member of the United Nations or of a specialized agency. It shall be subject to ratification by the signatory States, and the instruments of ratification shall be deposited with the Secretary-General of the United Nations, who shall inform each signatory and acceding State.

2. After I July 1957 this Convention shall be open for accession by any State Member of the United Nations or of a specialized agency, or by any other State to which an invitation to accede has been addressed by the General Assembly of the United Nations. Accession shall be effected by the deposit of a formal instrument with the Secretary-General of the United Nations, who shall inform each signatory and acceding State.

Article 12

1. This Convention shall apply to all non-self-governing trust, colonial and other non-metropolitan territories for the international relations of which any State Party is responsible; the Party concerned shall, subject to the provisions of paragraph 2 of this article, at the time of signature, ratification or accession declare the non-metropolitan territory or territories to which the Convention shall apply ipso facto as a result of such signature, ratification or accession.

2. In any case in which the previous consent of a non-metropolitan territory is required by the constitutional laws or practices of the Party or of the non-metropolitan territory, the Party concerned shall endeavour to secure the needed consent of the non-metropolitan territory within the period of twelve months from the date of signature of the Convention by the metropolitan State, and when such consent has been obtained the Party shall notify the Secretary-General. This Convention shall apply to the territory or territories named in such notification from the date of its receipt by the Secretary General.

3. After the expiry of the twelve-month period mentioned in the preceding paragraph, the States Parties concerned shall inform the Secretary General of the results of the consultations with those non-metropolitan territories for whose international relations they are responsible and whose consent to the application of this Convention may have been withheld.

Article 13

1. This Convention shall enter into force on the date on which two States have become Parties thereto.

2. It shall thereafter enter into force with respect to each State and territory on the date of deposit of the instrument of ratification or accession of that State or notification of application to that territory.

Article 14

1. The application of this Convention shall be divided into successive periods of three years, of which the first shall begin on the date of entry into force of the Convention in accordance with paragraph I of Article 13.

2. Any State Party may denounce this Convention by a notice addressed by that State to the Secretary-General not less than six months before the expiration of the current three-year period. The Secretary-General shall notify all other Parties of each such notice and the date of the receipt thereof.

3. Denunciations shall take effect at the expiration of the current three year period.

4. In cases where, in accordance with the provisions of Article 12, this Convention has become applicable to a non-metropolitan territory of a Party, that Party may at any time thereafter, with the consent of the territory concerned, give notice to the Secretary-General of the United Nations denouncing this Convention separately in respect of that territory. The denunciation shall take effect one year after the date of the receipt of such notice by the Secretary-General, who shall notify all other Parties of such notice and the date of the receipt thereof.

Article 15

This Convention, of which the Chinese, English, French, Russian and Spanish texts are equally authentic, shall be deposited in the archives of the United Nations Secretariat. The Secretary-General shall prepare a certified copy thereof for communication to States Parties to this Convention, as well as to all other States Members of the United Nations and of the specialized agencies.

IN WITNESS WHEREOF the undersigned, being duly authorized thereto by their respective Governments, have signed this Convention on the date appearing opposite their respective signatures.

DONE at the European Office of the United Nations at Geneva, this seventh day of September one thousand nine hundred and fifty-six.

DOCUMENT 36

Full Official Title: Convention Relating to the Status of Refugees

Short Title/Acronym/Abbreviation: Refugee Convention

Subject: Establishing a definition of "refugee" and recognition of international human rights for protection of refugees in a multilateral treaty.

Official Citation/Source: 189 U.N.T.S. 150

Date of Document: Not applicable

Date of Adoption: July 28, 1951

Date of General Entry into Force (EIF): April 22, 1954

Number of States Parties to this Treaty as of this printing: 144

Date of Signature by United States: Not signed by United States

Date of Ratification/Accession/Adhesion: Not ratified by United States

Date of Entry into Force as to United States (effective date): By virtue of the U.S. ratification to the 1967 Protocol on the Status of Refugees (see following document) the United States became indirectly bound by the Refugee Convention.

Type of Document: A treaty, an international legal instrument

Legal Status/Character of the Instrument/Document as to the United States: Indirectly binding on the United States, by its ratification of the Refugee Protocol of 1967.

Supervising Body: In effect, the U.N. High Commissioner for Refugees has the most direct part in seeking the application of this treaty. This is by U.N. institutional evolution. The UNHCR is not a treaty-based body.

Comments: When adopted in 1951, this treaty only applied to refugees from Europe at the time of the end of World War II. The United States never signed nor ratified it. However, the United States acceded to the 1967 Protocol on the Status of Refugees which had the effect of creating a legal obligation of the United States to apply the Refugee Convention, read in light of the changes set forth in the Refugee Protocol. The Refugee Protocol expanded the definition of "refugee" to all parts of the world from after its effective date. The United States implemented these treaties in the 1980 Refugee Act, now part of title 8 of the United States Code. This establishes the legal basis for being eligible for refugee status and receiving asylum in the U.S.

Caution: The status and applicability of this instrument as to the United States may have changed since date of publication. The above information may be updated by referring to the following site:

Web address: http://www1.umn.edu/humanrts/instree/v1crs.htm

CONVENTION RELATING TO THE STATUS OF REFUGEES

Preamble

The High Contracting Parties,

Considering that the Charter of the United Nations and the Universal Declaration of Human Rights approved on 10 December 1948 by the General Assembly have affirmed the principle that human beings shall enjoy fundamental rights and freedoms without discrimination,

Considering that the United Nations has, on various occasions, manifested its profound concern for refugees and endeavoured to assure refugees the widest possible exercise of these fundamental rights and freedoms,

Considering that it is desirable to revise and consolidate previous international agreements relating to the status of refugees and to extend the scope of and the protection accorded by such instruments by means of a new agreement,

Considering that the grant of asylum may place unduly heavy burdens on certain countries, and that a satisfactory solution of a problem of which the United Nations has recognized the international- scope and nature cannot therefore be achieved without international co-operation,

Expressing the wish that all States, recognizing the social and humanitarian nature of the problem of refugees, will do everything within their power to prevent this problem from becoming a cause of tension between States,

Noting that the United Nations High Commissioner for Refugees is charged with the task of supervising international conventions providing for the protection of refugees, and recognizing that the effective co-ordination of measures taken to deal with this problem will depend upon the co-operation of States with the High Commissioner,

Have agreed as follows:

Chapter I—General Provisions

Article 1. Definition of the term "refugee"

A. For the purposes of the present Convention, the term "refugee, shall apply to any person who:

(1) Has been considered a refugee under the Arrangements of 12 May 1926 and 30 June 1928 or under the Conventions of 28 October 1933 and 10 February 1938, the Protocol of 14 September 1939 or the Constitution of the International Refugee Organization;

Decisions of non-eligibility taken by the International Refugee Organization during the period of its activities shall not prevent the status of refugee being accorded to persons who fulfil the conditions of paragraph 2 of this section;

(2) As a result of events occurring before I January 1951 and owing to well-founded fear of being persecuted for reasons of race, religion, nationality, membership of a particular social group or political opinion, is outside the country of his nationality and is unable, or owing to such fear, is unwilling to avail himself of the protection of that country; or who, not having a nationality and being outside the country of his former habitual residence as a result of such events, is unable or, owing to such fear, is unwilling to return to it.

In the case of a person who has more than one nationality, the term "the country of his nationality" shall mean each of the countries of which he is a national, and a person shall not be deemed to be lacking the protection of the country of his nationality if, without any valid reason based on well-founded fear, he has not availed himself of the protection of one of the countries of which he is a national.

B. (1) For the purposes of this Convention, the words "events occurring before I January 1951" in Article 1, section A, shall be understood to mean either (a) "events occurring in Europe before I January 1951"; or (b) "events occurring in Europe or elsewhere before I January 1951"; and each Contracting State shall make a declaration at the time of signature, ratification or accession, specifying which of these meanings it applies for the purpose of its obligations under this Convention.

(2) Any Contracting State which has adopted alternative (a) may at any time extend its obligations by adopting alternative (b) by means of a notification addressed to the Secretary-General of the United Nations.

C. This Convention shall cease to apply to any person falling under the terms of section A if:

(1) He has voluntarily re-availed himself of the protection of the country of his nationality; or

(2) Having lost his nationality, he has voluntarily reacquired it; or

(3) He has acquired a new nationality, and enjoys the protection of the country of his new nationality; or

(4) He has voluntarily re-established himself in the country which he left or outside which he remained owing to fear of persecution; or

(5) He can no longer, because the circumstances in connection with which he has been recognized as a refugee have ceased to exist, continue to refuse to avail himself of the protection of the country of his nationality;

Provided that this paragraph shall not apply to a refugee falling under section A (I) of this article who is able to invoke compelling reasons arising out of previous persecution for refusing to avail himself of the protection of the country of nationality;

(6) Being a person who has no nationality he is, because the circumstances in connection with which he has been recognized as a refugee have ceased to exist, able to return to the country of his former habitual residence;

Provided that this paragraph shall not apply to a refugee falling under section A (I) of this article who is able to invoke compelling reasons arising out of previous persecution for refusing to return to the country of his former habitual residence.

D. This Convention shall not apply to persons who are at present receiving from organs or agencies of the United Nations other than the United Nations High Commissioner for Refugees protection or assistance.

When such protection or assistance has ceased for any reason, without the position of such persons being definitively settled in accordance with the relevant resolutions adopted by the General Assembly of the United Nations, these persons shall ipso facto be entitled to the benefits of this Convention.

E. This Convention shall not apply to a person who is recognized by the competent authorities of the country in which he has taken residence as having the rights and obligations which are attached to the possession of the nationality of that country.

F. The provisions of this Convention shall not apply to any person with respect to whom there are serious reasons for considering that.

(a) He has committed a crime against peace, a war crime, or a crime against humanity, as defined in the international instruments drawn up to make provision in respect of such crimes;

(b) He has committed a serious non-political crime outside the country of refuge prior to his admission to that country as a refugee;

(c) He has been guilty of acts contrary to the purposes and principles of the United Nations.

Article 2. General obligations

Every refugee has duties to the country in which he finds himself, which require in particular that he conform to its laws and regulations as well as to measures taken for the maintenance of public order.

Article 3. Non-discrimination

The Contracting States shall apply the provisions of this Convention to refugees without discrimination as to race, religion or country of origin.

Article 4. Religion

The Contracting States shall accord to refugees within their territories treatment at least as favourable as that accorded to their nationals with respect to freedom to practise their religion and freedom as regards the religious education of their children.

Article 5. Rights granted apart from this Convention

Nothing in this Convention shall be deemed to impair any rights and benefits granted by a Contracting State to refugees apart from this Convention.

Article 6. The term "in the same circumstances"

For the purposes of this Convention, the term "in the same circumstances" implies that any requirements (including requirements as to length and conditions of sojourn or residence) which the particular individual would have to fulfil for the enjoyment of the right in question, if he were not a refugee, must be fulfilled by him, with the exception of requirements which by their nature a refugee is incapable of fulfilling.

Article 7. Exemption from reciprocity

1. Except where this Convention contains more favourable provisions, a Contracting State shall accord to refugees the same treatment as is accorded to aliens generally.

2. After a period of three years' residence, all refugees shall enjoy exemption from legislative reciprocity in the territory of the Contracting States.

3. Each Contracting State shall continue to accord to refugees the rights and benefits to which they were already entitled, in the absence of reciprocity, at the date of entry into force of this Convention for that State.

4. The Contracting States shall consider favourably the possibility of according to refugees, in the absence of reciprocity, rights and benefits beyond those to which they are entitled according to paragraphs 2 and 3, and to extending exemption from reciprocity to refugees who do not fulfil the conditions provided for in paragraphs 2 and 3.

5. The provisions of paragraphs 2 and 3 apply both to the rights and benefits referred to in articles 13, 18, 19, 21 and 22 of this Convention and to rights and benefits for which this Convention does not provide.

Article 8. Exemption from exceptional measures

With regard to exceptional measures which may be taken against the person, property or interests of nationals of a foreign State, the Contracting States shall not apply such measures to a refugee who is formally a national of the said State solely on account of such nationality. Contracting States which, under their legislation, are prevented from applying the general principle expressed in this article, shall, in appropriate cases, grant exemptions in favour of such refugees.

Article 9. Provisional measures

Nothing in this Convention shall prevent a Contracting State, in time of war or other grave and exceptional circumstances, from taking provisionally measures which it considers to be essential to the national security in the case of a particular person, pending a determination by the Contracting State that that person is in fact a refugee and that the continuance of such measures is necessary in his case in the interests of national security.

Article 10. Continuity of residence

1. Where a refugee has been forcibly displaced during the Second World War and removed to the territory of a Contracting State, and is resident there, the period of such enforced sojourn shall be considered to have been lawful residence within that territory.

2. Where a refugee has been forcibly displaced during the Second World War from the territory of a Contracting State and has, prior to the date of entry into force of this Convention, returned there for the purpose of taking up residence, the period of residence before and after such enforced displacement shall be regarded as one uninterrupted period for any purposes for which uninterrupted residence is required.

Article 11. Refugee seamen

In the case of refugees regularly serving as crew members on board a ship flying the flag of a Contracting State, that State shall give sympathetic consideration to their establishment on its territory and the issue of travel documents to them or their temporary admission to its territory particularly with a view to facilitating their establishment in another country.

Chapter II—Juridical Status

Article 12. Personal status

1. The personal status of a refugee shall be governed by the law of the country of his domicile or, if he has no domicile, by the law of the country of his residence.

2. Rights previously acquired by a refugee and dependent on personal status, more particularly rights attaching to marriage, shall be respected by a Contracting State, subject to compliance, if this be necessary, with the formalities required by the law of that State, provided that the right in question is one which would have been recognized by the law of that State had he not become a refugee.

Article 13. Movable and immovable property

The Contracting States shall accord to a refugee treatment as favourable as possible and, in any event, not less favourable than that accorded to aliens generally in the same circumstances, as regards the acquisition of movable and immovable property and other rights pertaining thereto, and to leases and other contracts relating to movable and immovable property.

Article 14. Artistic rights and industrial property

In respect of the protection of industrial property, such as inventions, designs or models, trade marks, trade names, and of rights in literary, artistic and scientific works, a refugee shall be accorded in the country in which he has his habitual residence the same protection as is accorded to nationals of that country. In the territory of any other Contracting States, he shall be accorded the same protection as is accorded in that territory to nationals of the country in which he has his habitual residence.

Article 15. Right of association

As regards non-political and non-profit-making associations and trade unions the Contracting States shall accord to refugees lawfully staying in their territory the most favourable treatment accorded to nationals of a foreign country, in the same circumstances.

Article 16. Access to courts

1. A refugee shall have free access to the courts of law on the territory of all Contracting States.

2. A refugee shall enjoy in the Contracting State in which he has his habitual residence the same treatment as a national in matters pertaining to access to the courts, including legal assistance and exemption from cautio judicatum solvi.

3. A refugee shall be accorded in the matters referred to in paragraph 2 in countries other than that in which he has his habitual residence the treatment granted to a national of the country of his habitual residence.

Chapter III—GAINFUL EMPLOYMENT

Article 17. Wage-earning employment

1. The Contracting States shall accord to refugees lawfully staying in their territory the most favourable treatment accorded to nationals of a foreign country in the same circumstances, as regards the right to engage in wage-earning employment.

2. In any case, restrictive measures imposed on aliens or the employment of aliens for the protection of the national labour market shall not be applied to a refugee who was already exempt from them at the date of entry into force of this Convention for the Contracting State concerned, or who fulfils one of the following conditions:

(a) He has completed three years' residence in the country;

(b) He has a spouse possessing the nationality of the country of residence. A refugee may not invoke the benefit of this provision if he has abandoned his spouse;

(c) He has one or more children possessing the nationality of the country of residence.

3. The Contracting States shall give sympathetic consideration to assimilating the rights of all refugees with regard to wage-earning employment to those of nationals, and in particular of those refugees who have entered their territory pursuant to programmes of labour recruitment or under immigration schemes.

Article 18. Self-employment

The Contracting States shall accord to a refugee lawfully in their territory treatment as favourable as possible and, in any event, not less favourable than that accorded to aliens generally in the same circumstances, as regards the right to engage on his own account in agriculture, industry, handicrafts and commerce and to establish commercial and industrial companies.

Article 19. Liberal professions

1. Each Contracting State shall accord to refugees lawfully staying in their territory who hold diplomas recognized by the competent authorities of that State, and who are desirous of practising a liberal profession, treatment as favourable as possible and, in any event, not less favourable than that accorded to aliens generally in the same circumstances.

2. The Contracting States shall use their best endeavours consistently with their laws and constitutions to secure the settlement of such refugees in the territories, other than the metropolitan territory, for whose international relations they are responsible.

CHAPTER IV—WELFARE

Article 20. Rationing

Where a rationing system exists, which applies to the population at large and regulates the general distribution of products in short supply, refugees shall be accorded the same treatment as nationals.

Article 21. Housing

As regards housing, the Contracting States, in so far as the matter is regulated by laws or regulations or is subject to the control of public authorities, shall accord to refugees lawfully staying in their territory treatment as favourable as possible and, in any event, not less favourable than that accorded to aliens generally in the same circumstances.

Article 22. Public education

1. The Contracting States shall accord to refugees the same treatment as is accorded to nationals with respect to elementary education.

2. The Contracting States shall accord to refugees treatment as favourable as possible, and, in any event, not less favourable than that accorded to aliens generally in the same circumstances, with respect to education other than elementary education and, in particular, as regards access to studies, the recognition of foreign school certificates, diplomas and degrees, the remission of fees and charges and the award of scholarships.

Article 23. Public relief

The Contracting States shall accord to refugees lawfully staying in their territory the same treatment with respect to public relief and assistance as is accorded to their nationals.

Article 24. Labour legislation and social security

1. The Contracting States shall accord to refugees lawfully staying in their territory the same treatment as is accorded to nationals in respect of the following matters;

(a) In so far as such matters are governed by laws or regulations or are subject to the control of administrative authorities: remuneration, including family allowances where these form part of remuneration, hours of work, overtime arrangements, holidays with pay, restrictions on home work, minimum age of employment, apprenticeship and training, women's work and the work of young persons, and the enjoyment of the benefits of collective bargaining;

(b) Social security (legal provisions in respect of employment injury, occupational diseases, maternity, sickness, disability, old age, death, unemployment, family responsibilities and any other contingency which, according to national laws or regulations, is covered by a social security scheme), subject to the following limitations:

(i) There may be appropriate arrangements for the maintenance of acquired rights and rights in course of acquisition;

(ii) National laws or regulations of the country of residence may prescribe special arrangements concerning benefits or portions of benefits which are payable wholly out of public funds, and concerning allowances paid to persons who do not fulfil the contribution conditions prescribed for the award of a normal pension.

2. The right to compensation for the death of a refugee resulting from employment injury or from occupational disease shall not be affected by the fact that the residence of the beneficiary is outside the territory of the Contracting State.

3. The Contracting States shall extend to refugees the benefits of agreements concluded between them, or which may be concluded between them in the future, concerning the maintenance of acquired rights and rights in the process of acquisition in regard to social security, subject only to the conditions which apply to nationals of the States signatory to the agreements in question.

4. The Contracting States will give sympathetic consideration to extending to refugees so far as possible the benefits of similar agreements which may at any time be in force between such Contracting States and non-contracting States.

Chapter V—Administrative Measures

Article 25. Administrative assistance

1. When the exercise of a right by a refugee would normally require the assistance of authorities of a foreign country to whom he cannot have recourse, the Contracting States in whose territory he is residing shall arrange that such assistance be afforded to him by their own authorities or by an international authority.

2. The authority or authorities mentioned in paragraph I shall deliver or cause to be delivered under their supervision to refugees such documents or certifications as would normally be delivered to aliens by or through their national authorities.

3. Documents or certifications so delivered shall stand in the stead of the official instruments delivered to aliens by or through their national authorities, and shall be given credence in the absence of proof to the contrary.

4. Subject to such exceptional treatment as may be granted to indigent persons, fees may be charged for the services mentioned herein, but such fees shall be moderate and commensurate with those charged to nationals for similar services.

5. The provisions of this article shall be without prejudice to articles 27 and 28.

Article 26. Freedom of movement

Each Contracting State shall accord to refugees lawfully in its territory the right to choose their place of residence and to move freely within its territory subject to any regulations applicable to aliens generally in the same circumstances.

Article 27. Identity papers

The Contracting States shall issue identity papers to any refugee in their territory who does not possess a valid travel document.

Article 28. Travel documents

1. The Contracting States shall issue to refugees lawfully staying in their territory travel documents for the purpose of travel outside their territory, unless compelling reasons of national security or public order otherwise require, and the provisions of the Schedule to this Convention shall apply with respect to such documents. The Contracting States may issue such a travel document to any other refugee in their territory; they shall in particular give sympathetic consideration to the issue of such a travel document to refugees in their territory who are unable to obtain a travel document from the country of their lawful residence.

2. Travel documents issued to refugees under previous international agreements by Parties thereto shall be recognized and treated by the Contracting States in the same way as if they had been issued pursuant to this article.

Article 29. Fiscal charges

1. The Contracting States shall not impose upon refugees duties, charges or taxes, of any description whatsoever, other or higher than those which are or may be levied on their nationals in similar situations.

2. Nothing in the above paragraph shall prevent the application to refugees of the laws and regulations concerning charges in respect of the issue to aliens of administrative documents including identity papers.

Article 30. Transfer of assets

1. A Contracting State shall, in conformity with its laws and regulations, permit refugees to transfer assets which they have brought into its territory, to another country where they have been admitted for the purposes of resettlement.

2. A Contracting State shall give sympathetic consideration to the application of refugees for permission to transfer assets wherever they may be and which are necessary for their resettlement in another country to which they have been admitted.

Article 31. Refugees unlawfully in the country of refuge

1. The Contracting States shall not impose penalties, on account of their illegal entry or presence, on refugees who, coming directly from a territory where their life or freedom was threatened in the sense of Article 1, enter or are present in their territory without authorization, provided they present themselves without delay to the authorities and show good cause for their illegal entry or presence.

2. The Contracting States shall not apply to the movements of such refugees restrictions other than those which are necessary and such restrictions shall only be applied until their status in the country is regularized or they obtain admission into another country. The Contracting States shall allow such refugees a reasonable period and all the necessary facilities to obtain admission into another country.

Article 32. Expulsion

1. The Contracting States shall not expel a refugee lawfully in their territory save on grounds of national security or public order.

2. The expulsion of such a refugee shall be only in pursuance of a decision reached in accordance with due process of law. Except where compelling reasons of national security otherwise require, the refugee shall be allowed to submit evidence to clear himself, and to appeal to and be represented for the purpose before competent authority or a person or persons specially designated by the competent authority.

3. The Contracting States shall allow such a refugee a reasonable period within which to seek legal admission into another country. The Contracting States reserve the right to apply during that period such internal measures as they may deem necessary.

Article 33. Prohibition of expulsion or return ("refoulement")

1. No Contracting State shall expel or return ("refouler") a refugee in any manner whatsoever to the frontiers of territories where his life or freedom would be threatened on account of his race, religion, nationality, membership of a particular social group or political opinion.

2. The benefit of the present provision may not, however, be claimed by a refugee whom there are reasonable grounds for regarding as a danger to the security of the country in which he is, or who, having been convicted by a final judgement of a particularly serious crime, constitutes a danger to the community of that country.

Article 34. Naturalization

The Contracting States shall as far as possible facilitate the assimilation and naturalization of refugees. They shall in particular make every effort to expedite naturalization proceedings and to reduce as far as possible the charges and costs of such proceedings.

Chapter VI—Executory and Transitory Provisions
Article 35. Co-operation of the national authorities with the United Nations
1. The Contracting States undertake to co-operate with the Office of the United Nations High Commissioner for Refugees, or any other agency of the United Nations which may succeed it, in the exercise of its functions, and shall in particular facilitate its duty of supervising the application of the provisions of this Convention.

2. In order to enable the Office of the High Commissioner or any other agency of the United Nations which may succeed it, to make reports to the competent organs of the United Nations, the Contracting States undertake to provide them in the appropriate form with information and statistical data requested concerning:

(a) The condition of refugees,

(b) The implementation of this Convention, and

(c) Laws, regulations and decrees which are, or may hereafter be, in force relating to refugees.

Article 36. Information on national legislation
The Contracting States shall communicate to the Secretary-General of the United Nations the laws and regulations which they may adopt to ensure the application of this Convention.

Article 37. Relation to previous conventions
Without prejudice to Article 28, paragraph 2, of this Convention, this Convention replaces, as between Parties to it, the Arrangements of 5 July 1922, 31 May 1924, 12 May 1926, 30 June 1928 and 30 July 1935, the Conventions of 28 October 1933 and 10 February 1938, the Protocol of 14 September 1939 and the Agreement of 15 October 1946.

Chapter VII—Final Clauses
Article 38. Settlement of disputes
Any dispute between Parties to this Convention relating to its interpretation or application, which cannot be settled by other means, shall be referred to the International Court of Justice at the request of any one of the parties to the dispute.

Article 39. Signature, ratification and accession
1. This Convention shall be opened for signature at Geneva on 28 July 1951 and shall thereafter be deposited with the Secretary-General of the United Nations. It shall be open for signature at the European Office of the United Nations from 28 July to 31 August 1951 and shall be re-opened for signature at the Headquarters of the United Nations from 17 September 1951 to 31 December 1952.

2. This Convention shall be open for signature on behalf of all States Members of the United Nations, and also on behalf of any other State invited to attend the Conference of Plenipotentiaries on the Status of Refugees and Stateless Persons or to which an invitation to sign will have been addressed by the General Assembly. It shall be ratified and the instruments of ratification shall be deposited with the Secretary-General of the United Nations.

3. This Convention shall be open from 28 July 1951 for accession by the States referred to in paragraph 2 of this article. Accession shall be effected by the deposit of an instrument of accession with the Secretary-General of the United Nations.

Article 40. Territorial application clause
1. Any State may, at the time of signature, ratification or accession, declare that this Convention shall extend to all or any of the territories for the international relations of which it is responsible. Such a declaration shall take effect when the Convention enters into force for the State concerned.

2. At any time thereafter any such extension shall be made by notification addressed to the Secretary-General of the United Nations and shall take effect as from the ninetieth day after the day of receipt by the Secretary- General of the United Nations of this notification, or as from the date of entry into force of the Convention for the State concerned, whichever is the later.

3. With respect to those territories to which this Convention is not extended at the time of signature, ratification or accession, each State concerned shall consider the possibility of taking the necessary steps in order to extend the application of this Convention to such territories, subject, where necessary for constitutional reasons, to the consent of the Governments of such territories.

Article 41. Federal clause
In the case of a Federal or non-unitary State, the following provisions shall apply:

(a) With respect to those articles of this Convention that come within the legislative jurisdiction of the federal legislative authority, the obligations of the Federal Government shall to this extent be the same as those of parties which are not Federal States;

(b) With respect to those articles of this Convention that come within the legislative jurisdiction of constituent States, provinces or cantons which are not, under the constitutional system of the Federation, bound to take legislative action, the Federal Government shall bring such articles with a favourable recommendation to the notice of the appropriate authorities of States, provinces or cantons at the earliest possible moment;

(c) A Federal State Party to this Convention shall, at the request of any other Contracting State transmitted through the Secretary-General of the United Nations, supply a statement of the law and practice of the Federation and its constituent units in regard to any particular provision of the Convention showing the extent to which effect has been given to that provision by legislative or other action.

Article 42. Reservations

1. At the time of signature, ratification or accession, any State may make reservations to articles of the Convention other than to articles 1, 3, 4, 16 (1), 33, 36–46 inclusive.

2. Any State making a reservation in accordance with paragraph I of this article may at any time withdraw the reservation by a communication to that effect addressed to the Secretary-General of the United Nations.

Article 43. Entry into force

1. This Convention shall come into force on the ninetieth day following the day of deposit of the sixth instrument of ratification or accession.

2. For each State ratifying or acceding to the Convention after the deposit of the sixth instrument of ratification or accession, the Convention shall enter into force on the ninetieth day following the date of deposit by such State of its instrument of ratification or accession.

Article 44. Denunciation

1. Any Contracting State may denounce this Convention at any time by a notification addressed to the Secretary-General of the United Nations.

2. Such denunciation shall take effect for the Contracting State concerned one year from the date upon which it is received by the Secretary-General of the United Nations.

3. Any State which has made a declaration or notification under Article 40 may, at any time thereafter, by a notification to the Secretary-General of the United Nations, declare that the Convention shall cease to extend to such territory one year after the date of receipt of the notification by the Secretary-General.

Article 45. Revision

1. Any Contracting State may request revision of this Convention at any time by a notification addressed to the Secretary-General of the United Nations.

2. The General Assembly of the United Nations shall recommend the steps, if any, to be taken in respect of such request.

Article 46. Notifications by the Secretary-General of the United Nations

The Secretary-General of the United Nations shall inform all Members of the United Nations and non-member States referred to in Article 39:

(a) Of declarations and notifications in accordance with section B of Article 1;

(b) Of signatures, ratifications and accessions in accordance with Article 39;

(c) Of declarations and notifications in accordance with Article 40;

(d) Of reservations and withdrawals in accordance with Article 42;

(e) Of the date on which this Convention will come into force in accordance with Article 43;

(f) Of denunciations and notifications in accordance with Article 44;

(g) Of requests for revision in accordance with Article 45.

IN FAITH WHEREOF the undersigned, duly authorized, have signed this Convention on behalf of their respective Governments.

DONE at Geneva, this twenty-eighth day of July, one thousand nine hundred and fifty-one, in a single copy, of which the English and French texts are equally authentic and which shall remain deposited in the archives of the United Nations, and certified true copies of which shall be delivered to all Members of the United Nations and to the non-member States referred to in Article 39.

© Copyright 1997

Office of the United Nations High Commissioner for Human Rights

Geneva, Switzerland

DOCUMENT 37

Full Official Title: Protocol Relating to the Status of Refugees
Short Title/Acronym/Abbreviation: The Refugee Protocol
Subject: Expanding the scope of application of the 1951 Refugee Convention to cover refugees in all parts of the world
Official Citation: 606 U.N.T.S. 267
Date of Document: Not applicable
Date of Adoption: January 31, 1967
Date of General Entry into Force (EIF): October 4, 1967
Number of States Parties to this Treaty as of this printing: 143
Date of Signature by United States: 1968
Date of Ratification/Accession/Adhesion: November 1, 1968
Date of Entry into Force as to United States (effective date): November 1, 1968
Type of Document: A treaty, an international legal instrument which amends a prior treaty instrument, the 1951Convention on the Status of Refugees, (See Document 36).
Legal Status/Character of the Instrument/Document as to the United States: These RDUs are legally binding as to U.S. ratification so far as they are consistent with the object and purpose of the Torture Convention.
Supervising Body: In effect, the U.N. High Commissioner for Refugees has the most direct part in seeking the application of this treaty. This is by U.N. institutional evolution. The UNHCR is not a treaty-based body.
Comments: This Protocol made the 1951 Convention on the Status of Refugees indirectly binding on the United States. It incorporated that Convention by reference.
Caution: The status and applicability of this instrument as to the United States may have changed since date of publication. The above information may be updated by referring to the following site:
Web address: http://www1.umn.edu/humanrts/instree/v2prsr.htm

PROTOCOL RELATING TO THE STATUS OF REFUGEES

The Protocol was taken note of with approval by the Economic and Social Council in resolution 1186 (XLI) of 18 November 1966 and was taken note of by the General Assembly in resolution 2198 (XXI) of 16 December 1966. In the same resolution the General Assembly requested the Secretary-General to transmit the text of the Protocol to the States mentioned in Article 5 thereof, with a view to enabling them to accede to the Protocol

ENTRY INTO FORCE: 4 October 1967, in accordance with Article 8

The States Parties to the present Protocol,

Considering that the Convention relating to the Status of Refugees done at Geneva on 28 July 1951 (hereinafter referred to as the Convention) covers only those persons who have become refugees as a result of events occurring before I January 1951,

Considering that new refugee situations have arisen since the Convention was adopted and that the refugees concerned may therefore not fall within the scope of the Convention,

Considering that it is desirable that equal status should be enjoyed by all refugees covered by the definition in the Convention irrespective of the dateline I January 1951,

Have agreed as follows:

Article 1. General provision

1. The States Parties to the present Protocol undertake to apply articles 2 to 34 inclusive of the Convention to refugees as hereinafter defined.

2. For the purpose of the present Protocol, the term "refugee" shall, except as regards the application of paragraph 3 of this article, mean any person within the definition of article I of the Convention as if the words "As a result of events occurring before 1 January 1951 and ..." and the words "... as a result of such events," in Article 1 A (2) were omitted.

3. The present Protocol shall be applied by the States Parties hereto without any geographic limitation, save that existing declarations made by States already Parties to the Convention in accordance with article I B (I) (a) of the Convention, shall, unless extended under article I B (2) thereof, apply also under the present Protocol.

Article 2. Co-operation of the national authorities with the United Nations

1. The States Parties to the present Protocol undertake to co-operate with the Office of the United Nations High Commissioner for Refugees, or any other agency of the United Nations which may succeed it, in the exercise of its functions, and shall in particular facilitate its duty of supervising the application of the provisions of the present Protocol.

2. In order to enable the Office of the High Commissioner or any other agency of the United Nations which may succeed it, to make reports to the competent organs of the United Nations, the States Parties to the present Protocol undertake to provide them with the information and statistical data requested, in the appropriate form, concerning:

(a) The condition of refugees;

(b) The implementation of the present Protocol;

(c) Laws, regulations and decrees which are, or may hereafter be, in force relating to refugees.

Article 3. Information on national legislation

The States Parties to the present Protocol shall communicate to the Secretary-General of the United Nations the laws and regulations which they may adopt to ensure the application of the present Protocol.

Article 4. Settlement of disputes

Any dispute between States Parties to the present Protocol which relates to its interpretation or application and which cannot be settled by other means shall be referred to the International Court of Justice at the request of any one of the parties to the dispute.

Article 5. Accession

The present Protocol shall be open for accession on behalf of all States Parties to the Convention and of any other State Member of the United Nations or member of any of the specialized agencies or to which an invitation to accede may have been addressed by the General Assembly of the United Nations. Accession shall be effected by the deposit of an instrument of accession with the Secretary-General of the United Nations.

Article 6. Federal clause

In the case of a Federal or non-unitary State, the following provisions shall apply:

(a) With respect to those articles of the Convention to be applied in accordance with article I, paragraph 1, of the present Protocol that come within the legislative jurisdiction of the federal legislative authority, the obligations of the Federal Government shall to this extent be the same as those of States Parties which are not Federal States;

(b) With respect to those articles of the Convention to be applied in accordance with article I, paragraph 1, of the present Protocol that come within the legislative jurisdiction of constituent States, provinces or cantons which are not, under the constitutional system of the Federation, bound to take legislative action, the Federal Government shall bring such articles with a favourable recommendation to the notice of the appropriate authorities of States, provinces or cantons at the earliest possible moment;

(c) A Federal State Party to the present Protocol shall, at the request of any other State Party hereto transmitted through the Secretary-General of the United Nations, supply a statement of the law and practice of the Federation and its constituent units in regard to any particular provision of the Convention to be applied in accordance with article I, paragraph 1, of the present Protocol, showing the extent to which effect has been given to that provision by legislative or other action.

Article 7. Reservations and declarations

1. At the time of accession, any State may make reservations in respect of article IV of the present Protocol and in respect of the application in accordance with article I of the present Protocol of any provisions of the Convention other than those contained in articles 1, 3, 4, 16(1) and 33 thereof, provided that in the case of a State Party to the Convention reservations made under this article shall not extend to refugees in respect of whom the Convention applies.

2. Reservations made by States Parties to the Convention in accordance with Article 42 thereof shall, unless withdrawn, be applicable in relation to their obligations under the present Protocol.

3. Any State making a reservation in accordance with paragraph I of this article may at any time withdraw such reservation by a communication to that effect addressed to the Secretary-General of the United Nations.

4. Declarations made under Article 40, paragraphs I and 2, of the Convention by a State Party thereto which accedes to the present Protocol shall be deemed to apply in respect of the present Protocol, unless upon accession a notification to the contrary is addressed by the State Party concerned to the Secretary-General of the United Nations. The provisions of Article 40, paragraphs 2 and 3, and of Article 44, paragraph 3, of the Convention shall be deemed to apply muratis mutandis to the present Protocol.

Article 8. Entry into Protocol

1. The present Protocol shall come into force on the day of deposit of the sixth instrument of accession.

2. For each State acceding to the Protocol after the deposit of the sixth instrument of accession, the Protocol shall come into force on the date of deposit by such State of its instrument of accession.

Article 9. Denunciation

1. Any State Party hereto may denounce this Protocol at any time by a notification addressed to the Secretary-General of the United Nations.

2. Such denunciation shall take effect for the State Party concerned one year from the date on which it is received by the Secretary-General of the United Nations.

Article 10. Notifications by the Secretary-General of the United Nations

The Secretary-General of the United Nations shall inform the States referred to in article V above of the date of entry into force, accessions, reservations and withdrawals of reservations to and denunciations of the present Protocol, and of declarations and notifications relating hereto.

Article 11. Deposit in the archives of the Secretariat of the United Nations

A copy of the present Protocol, of which the Chinese, English, French, Russian and Spanish texts are equally authentic, signed by the President of the General Assembly and by the Secretary-General of the United Nations, shall be deposited in the archives of the Secretariat of the United Nations. The Secretary-General will transmit certified copies thereof to all States Members of the United Nations and to the other States referred to in Article 5 above.

DOCUMENT 38

Full Official Title: Declaration on the Elimination of All Forms of Intolerance and of Discrimination Based on Religion or Belief

Short Title/Acronym/Abbreviation: U.N. Declaration on Religious Intolerance

Subject: General Assembly resolution declaring specific human rights against religious intolerance and discrimination

Official Citation: General Assembly resolution 36/55 of 25 November 1981

Date of Document: November 25, 1981

Date of Adoption: November 25, 1981

Date of General Entry into Force (EIF): Not applicable

Number of States Parties to the Treaty as of this printing: Not a treaty

Date of Signature by United States: Not applicable

Date of Ratification/Accession/Adhesion: Not applicable

Date of Entry into Force as to United States (effective date): Not applicable

Type of Document: This is not a treaty, but is a non-legal instrument proclaiming the human rights principles which states should be following.

Legal Status/Character of the Instrument/Document as to the United States: A declaration is not a legal instrument (treaty) and thus creates no binding legal obligation upon member states such as the United States. However, as a matter of political and moral value all states, including the United States, should follow it and use it as a yardstick for understanding the scope of Article 18 of the ICCPR and UDHR on religious freedom. This document will probably serve as the basis of a future legal instrument on religious freedom.

Comments: Religious freedom is one of the most delicate and controversial issues in all U.N. activities and in all of international relations. There has been an attempt for many years to create a specific treaty recognizing legal human rights to religious freedom. This treaty has never succeeded due to strong opposition from certain countries. However, the states were able to come up with this document which attempts to give more substance to the religious freedom norms found in Article 18 of the UDHR and Article 18 of the ICCPR.

This document was finally adopted by the United Nations when it was drafted so as to include atheism and agnosticism and the right not to believe any religious beliefs within its scope. ("... Based on Religion or *Belief*"). This document should be read along with Article 18 of the UDHR and ICCPR.

The United States was very instrumental in getting this document drafted and adopted and continues to push for a full legal treaty on religious freedom.

This document serves as the basis of the study and work of the U.N. Special Rapporteur on Religious Discrimination and Intolerance. A report based on the application of this instrument to the United States is included in these documents, below.(See "Report Submitted by Abdelfatah Amor," to the U.N. Commission on Human Rights, Document 53)

Web address: http://www1.umn.edu/humanrts/instree/d4deidrb.htm

DECLARATION ON THE ELIMINATION OF ALL FORMS OF INTOLERANCE AND OF DISCRIMINATION BASED ON RELIGION OR BELIEF

Proclaimed by General Assembly resolution 36/55 of 25 November 1981

The General Assembly,

Considering that one of the basic principles of the Charter of the United Nations is that of the dignity and equality inherent in all human beings, and that all Member States have pledged themselves to take joint and separate action in co-operation with the Organization to promote and encourage universal respect for and observance of human rights and fundamental freedoms for all, without distinction as to race, sex, language or religion,

Considering that the Universal Declaration of Human Rights and the International Covenants on Human Rights proclaim the principles of nondiscrimination and equality before the law and the right to freedom of thought, conscience, religion and belief,

Considering that the disregard and infringement of human rights and fundamental freedoms, in particular of the right to freedom of thought, conscience, religion or whatever belief, have brought, directly or indirectly, wars and great suffering to mankind, especially where they serve as a means of foreign interference in the internal affairs of other States and amount to kindling hatred between peoples and nations,

Considering that religion or belief, for anyone who professes either, is one of the fundamental elements in his conception of life and that freedom of religion or belief should be fully respected and guaranteed,

Considering that it is essential to promote understanding, tolerance and respect in matters relating to freedom of religion and belief and to ensure that the use of religion or belief for ends inconsistent with the Charter of the United Nations, other relevant instruments of the United Nations and the purposes and principles of the present Declaration is inadmissible,

Convinced that freedom of religion and belief should also contribute to the attainment of the goals of world peace, social justice and friendship among peoples and to the elimination of ideologies or practices of colonialism and racial discrimination,

Noting with satisfaction the adoption of several, and the coming into force of some, conventions, under the aegis of the United Nations and of the specialized agencies, for the elimination of various forms of discrimination,

Concerned by manifestations of intolerance and by the existence of discrimination in matters of religion or belief still in evidence in some areas of the world,

Resolved to adopt all necessary measures for the speedy elimination of such intolerance in all its forms and manifestations and to prevent and combat discrimination on the ground of religion or belief,

Proclaims this Declaration on the Elimination of All Forms of Intolerance and of Discrimination Based on Religion or Belief:

Article 1

1. Everyone shall have the right to freedom of thought, conscience and religion. This right shall include freedom to have a religion or whatever belief of his choice, and freedom, either individually or in community with others and in public or private, to manifest his religion or belief in worship, observance, practice and teaching.

2. No one shall be subject to coercion which would impair his freedom to have a religion or belief of his choice.

3. Freedom to manifest one's religion or belief may be subject only to such limitations as are prescribed by law and are necessary to protect public safety, order, health or morals or the fundamental rights and freedoms of others.

Article 2

1. No one shall be subject to discrimination by any State, institution, group of persons, or person on the grounds of religion or other belief.

2. For the purposes of the present Declaration, the expression "intolerance and discrimination based on religion or belief" means any distinction, exclusion, restriction or preference based on religion or belief and having as its purpose or as its effect nullification or impairment of the recognition, enjoyment or exercise of human rights and fundamental freedoms on an equal basis.

Article 3

Discrimination between human being on the grounds of religion or belief constitutes an affront to human dignity and a disavowal of the principles of the Charter of the United Nations, and shall be condemned as a violation of the human rights and fundamental freedoms proclaimed in the Universal Declaration of Human Rights and enunciated in detail in the International Covenants on Human Rights, and as an obstacle to friendly and peaceful relations between nations.

Article 4

1. All States shall take effective measures to prevent and eliminate discrimination on the grounds of religion or belief in the recognition, exercise and enjoyment of human rights and fundamental freedoms in all fields of civil, economic, political, social and cultural life.

2. All States shall make all efforts to enact or rescind legislation where necessary to prohibit any such discrimination, and to take all appropriate measures to combat intolerance on the grounds of religion or other beliefs in this matter.

Article 5

1. The parents or, as the case may be, the legal guardians of the child have the right to organize the life within the family in accordance with their religion or belief and bearing in mind the moral education in which they believe the child should be brought up.

2. Every child shall enjoy the right to have access to education in the matter of religion or belief in accordance with the wishes of his parents or, as the case may be, legal guardians, and shall not be compelled to receive teaching on religion or belief against the wishes of his parents or legal guardians, the best interests of the child being the guiding principle.

3. The child shall be protected from any form of discrimination on the ground of religion or belief. He shall be brought up in a spirit of understanding, tolerance, friendship among peoples, peace and universal brotherhood, respect for freedom of religion or belief of others, and in full consciousness that his energy and talents should be devoted to the service of his fellow men.

4. In the case of a child who is not under the care either of his parents or of legal guardians, due account shall be taken of their expressed wishes or of any other proof of their wishes in the matter of religion or belief, the best interests of the child being the guiding principle.

5. Practices of a religion or belief in which a child is brought up must not be injurious to his physical or mental health or to his full development, taking into account Article 1, paragraph 3, of the present Declaration.

Article 6

In accordance with article I of the present Declaration, and subject to the provisions of Article 1, paragraph 3, the right to freedom of thought, conscience, religion or belief shall include, inter alia, the following freedoms:

(a) To worship or assemble in connection with a religion or belief, and to establish and maintain places for these purposes;

(b) To establish and maintain appropriate charitable or humanitarian institutions;

(c) To make, acquire and use to an adequate extent the necessary articles and materials related to the rites or customs of a religion or belief;

(d) To write, issue and disseminate relevant publications in these areas;

(e) To teach a religion or belief in places suitable for these purposes;

(f) To solicit and receive voluntary financial and other contributions from individuals and institutions;

(g) To train, appoint, elect or designate by succession appropriate leaders called for by the requirements and standards of any religion or belief;

(h) To observe days of rest and to celebrate holidays and ceremonies in accordance with the precepts of one's religion or belief;

(i) To establish and maintain communications with individuals and communities in matters of religion and belief at the national and international levels.

Article 7

The rights and freedoms set forth in the present Declaration shall be accorded in national legislation in such a manner that everyone shall be able to avail himself of such rights and freedoms in practice.

Article 8

Nothing in the present Declaration shall be construed as restricting or derogating from any right defined in the Universal Declaration of Human Rights and the International Covenants on Human Rights.

© Copyright 1997

Office of the United Nations High Commissioner for Human Rights

Geneva, Switzerland

DOCUMENT 39

Full Official Title: Declaration on the Rights of Indigenous Peoples

Short Title/Acronym/Abbreviation: U.N. Declaration on Indigenous Rights

Subject: Declaration of specific human rights of indigenous peoples, amplifying existing normative protection of persons belonging to such groups of people.

Official Citation: E/CN.4/SUB.2/1994/2/Add.1 (1994)

Date of Document: 1994

Date of Adoption: September 13, 2007 by U.N. General Assembly.

Date of General Entry into Force (EIF): Not applicable

Number of States Parties to this treaty as of this printing: Not a treaty

Date of Signature by United States: Not applicable

Date of United States Ratification/Accession/Adhesion: Not applicable

Date of Entry into Force (effective date)as to United States: Not applicable

Type of Document: Declaration of the Sub Commission on Prevention of Discrimination and Protection of Minorities, submitted to the Commission on Human Rights.

Legal Status/Character of the Instrument/Document as to the United States: Non-legal, non-binding upon the United States or any other state. Adopted by the U.N. General Assembly September 13, 2007. The U.S. was not in favor of it.

Comments: A major topic of international human rights for the 1990s was the subject of indigenous peoples. (For the meaning of "Indigenous Peoples," see Definition and Significance of that term, above). This is a very politically sensitive and divisive issue in many countries that have indigenous people, such as the United States, which has Native Americans, Eskimos, and Native Hawaiians as separate indigenous groups. From a human rights perspective, some members of the international community perceived that indigenous groups were being discriminated against, being forcibly assimilated into the dominant society, marginalized, deprived of their land and resources and means of living, and having all that is sacred to them, such as burial grounds, holy places, and rituals, taken away. The international community came to feel that indigenous peoples were a gift to all humankind, that they had a right to preserve their identity, language, culture, religion, and way of life and even to just continue to exist as distinct peoples with a collective identities. Indigenous peoples were seen as endangered species. Their very existence was threatened in many states.

In order to protect indigenous peoples, the U.N. now defunct Commission on Human Rights, moved by many human rights NGOs and indigenous groups themselves, mandated its Subcommission to prepare certain studies and propose specific human rights standards aimed at protecting the human rights of indigenous peoples. A Draft Declaration resulted. The draft caused a lot of controversy in the Commission, as it was seen by many of the state representatives on the Commission as too favorable to indigenous groups and not adequately considerate of governmental interests.

Many U.S. indigenous peoples, such as Native American tribes, Native Hawaiians, and Eskimos, and many U.S.-based NGOs are active in this U.N. process and have participated in the formulation and lobbying involved in the creation of this draft. The process continues and the reader should consult the following web address for subsequent developments in the U.N. Human Rights Council which replaced the Commission, where alot is going on in the area of indigenous rights through its special mechanisms.

Appendix references: See Appendix I on certain legislation involving Native Americans. See Appendix J, case decisions of *Cherokee Nation vs. United States* and *Hill V. Rincon Band Of Luiseno Indians*.

Web Address: http://www.unhchr.ch/html/menu2/10/c/ind/ind_sub.htm#chrwg

DECLARATION ON THE RIGHTS OF INDIGENOUS PEOPLES

Affirming that indigenous peoples are equal in dignity and rights to all other peoples, while recognizing the right of all peoples to be different, to consider themselves different, and to be respected as such,

Affirming also that all peoples contribute to the diversity and richness of civilizations and cultures, which constitute the common heritage of humankind,

Affirming further that all doctrines, policies and practices based on or advocating superiority of peoples or individuals on the basis of national origin, racial, religious, ethnic or cultural differences are racist, scientifically false, legally invalid, morally condemnable and socially unjust,

Reaffirming also that indigenous peoples, in the exercise of their rights, should be free from discrimination of any kind,

Concerned that indigenous peoples have been deprived of their human rights and fundamental freedoms, resulting, inter alia, in their colonization and dispossession of their lands, territories and resources, thus preventing them from exercising, in particular, their right to development in accordance with their own needs and interests,

Recognizing the urgent need to respect and promote the inherent rights and characteristics of indigenous peoples, especially their rights to their lands, territories and resources, which derive from their political, economic and social structures and from their cultures, spiritual traditions, histories and philosophies,

Welcoming the fact that indigenous peoples are organizing themselves for political, economic, social and cultural enhancement and in order to bring an end to all forms of discrimination and oppression wherever they occur,

Convinced that control by indigenous peoples over developments affecting them and their lands, territories and resources will enable them to maintain and strengthen their institutions, cultures and traditions, and to promote their development in accordance with their aspirations and needs,

Recognizing also that respect for indigenous knowledge, cultures and traditional practices contributes to sustainable and equitable development and proper management of the environment,

Emphasizing the need for demilitarization of the lands and territories of indigenous peoples, which will contribute to peace, economic and social progress and development, understanding and friendly relations among nations and peoples of the world,

Recognizing in particular the right of indigenous families and communities to retain shared responsibility for the upbringing, training, education and well-being of their children,

Recognizing also that indigenous peoples have the right freely to determine their relationships with States in a spirit of coexistence, mutual benefit and full respect,

Considering that treaties, agreements and other arrangements between States and indigenous peoples are properly matters of international concern and responsibility,

Acknowledging that the Charter of the United Nations, the International Covenant on Economic, Social and Cultural Rights and the International Covenant on Civil and Political Rights affirm the fundamental importance of the right of self-determination of all peoples, by virtue of which they freely determine their political status and freely pursue their economic, social and cultural development,

Bearing in mind that nothing in this Declaration may be used to deny any peoples their right of self-determination,

Encouraging States to comply with and effectively implement all international instruments, in particular those related to human rights, as they apply to indigenous peoples, in consultation and cooperation with the peoples concerned,

Emphasizing that the United Nations has an important and continuing role to play in promoting and protecting the rights of indigenous peoples,

Believing that this Declaration is a further important step forward for the recognition, promotion and protection of the rights and freedoms of indigenous peoples and in the development of relevant activities of the United Nations system in this field,

Solemnly proclaims the following United Nations Declaration on the Rights of Indigenous Peoples:

PART I

Article 1

Indigenous peoples have the right to the full and effective enjoyment of all human rights and fundamental freedoms recognized in the Charter of the United Nations, the Universal Declaration of Human Rights and international human rights law.

Article 2

Indigenous individuals and peoples are free and equal to all other individuals and peoples in dignity and rights, and have the right to be free from any kind of adverse discrimination, in particular that based on their indigenous origin or identity.

Article 3

Indigenous peoples have the right of self-determination. By virtue of that right they freely determine their political status and freely pursue their economic, social and cultural development.

Article 4

Indigenous peoples have the right to maintain and strengthen their distinct political, economic, social and cultural characteristics, as well as their legal systems, while retaining their rights to participate fully, if they so choose, in the political, economic, social and cultural life of the State.

Article 5

Every indigenous individual has the right to a nationality.

PART II

Article 6

Indigenous peoples have the collective right to live in freedom, peace and security as distinct peoples and to full guarantees against genocide or any other act of violence, including the removal of indigenous children from their families and communities under any pretext. In addition, they have the individual rights to life, physical and mental integrity, liberty and security of person.

Article 7

Indigenous peoples have the collective and individual right not to be subjected to ethnocide and cultural genocide, including prevention of and redress for:

(a) Any action which has the aim or effect of depriving them of their integrity as distinct peoples, or of their cultural values or ethnic identities;

(b) Any action which has the aim or effect of dispossessing them of their lands, territories or resources;

(c) Any form of population transfer which has the aim or effect of violating or undermining any of their rights;

(d) Any form of assimilation or integration by other cultures or ways of life imposed on them by legislative, administrative or other measures;

(e) Any form of propaganda directed against them.

Article 8

Indigenous peoples have the collective and individual right to maintain and develop their distinct identities and characteristics, including the right to identify themselves as indigenous and to be recognized as such.

Article 9

Indigenous peoples and individuals have the right to belong to an indigenous community or nation, in accordance with the traditions and customs of the community or nation concerned. No disadvantage of any kind may arise from the exercise of such a right.

Article 10

Indigenous peoples shall not be forcibly removed from their lands or territories. No relocation shall take place without the free and informed consent of the indigenous peoples concerned and after agreement on just and fair compensation and, where possible, with the option of return.

Article 11

Indigenous peoples have the right to special protection and security in periods of armed conflict. States shall observe international standards, in particular the Fourth Geneva Convention of 1949, for the protection of civilian populations in circumstances of emergency and armed conflict, and shall not:

(a) Recruit indigenous individuals against their will into the armed forces and, in particular, for use against other indigenous peoples;

(b) Recruit indigenous children into the armed forces under any circumstances;

(c) Force indigenous individuals to abandon their lands, territories or means of subsistence, or relocate them in special centres for military purposes;

(d) Force indigenous individuals to work for military purposes under any discriminatory conditions.

PART III

Article 12

Indigenous peoples have the right to practise and revitalize their cultural traditions and customs. This includes the right to maintain, protect and develop the past, present and future manifestations of their cultures, such as archaeological and historical sites, artifacts, designs, ceremonies, technologies and visual and perform-ing arts and literature, as well as the right to the restitution of cultural, intellectual, religious and spiritual property taken without their free and informed consent or in violation of their laws, traditions and customs.

Article 13

Indigenous peoples have the right to manifest, practise, develop and teach their spiritual and religious traditions, customs and ceremonies; the right to maintain, protect, and have access in privacy to their religious and cultural sites; the right to the use and control of ceremonial objects; and the right to the repatriation of human remains. States shall take effective measures, in conjunction with the indigenous peoples concerned, to ensure that indigenous sacred places, including burial sites, be preserved, respected and protected.

Article 14

Indigenous peoples have the right to revitalize, use, develop and transmit to future generations their histories, languages, oral traditions, philosophies, writing systems and literatures, and to designate and retain their own names for communities, places and persons. States shall take effective measures, whenever any right of indigenous peoples may be threatened, to ensure this right is protected and also to ensure that they can understand and be understood in political, legal and administrative proceedings, where necessary through the provision of interpretation or by other appropriate means.

PART IV

Article 15

Indigenous children have the right to all levels and forms of education of the State. All indigenous peoples also have this right and the right to establish and control their educational systems and institutions providing education in their own languages, in a manner appropriate to their cultural methods of teaching and learning. Indigenous children living outside their communities have the right to be provided access to education in their own culture and language. States shall take effective measures to provide appropriate resources for these purposes.

Article 16

Indigenous peoples have the right to have the dignity and diversity of their cultures, traditions, histories and aspirations appropriately reflected in all forms of education and public information. States shall take effective measures, in consultation with the indigenous peoples concerned, to eliminate prejudice and dis-crimination and to promote tolerance, understanding and good relations among indigenous peoples and all segments of society.

Article 17

Indigenous peoples have the right to establish their own media in their own languages. They also have the right to equal access to all forms of non-indigenous media. States shall take effective measures to ensure that State-owned media duly reflect indigenous cultural diversity.

Article 18

Indigenous peoples have the right to enjoy fully all rights established under international labour law and national labour legislation. Indigenous individuals have the right not to be subjected to any discriminatory conditions of labour, employment or salary.

PART V

Article 19

Indigenous peoples have the right to participate fully, if they so choose, at all levels of decision-making in matters which may affect their rights, lives and destinies through representatives chosen by themselves in accordance with their own procedures, as well as to maintain and develop their own indigenous decision-making institutions.

Article 20

Indigenous peoples have the right to participate fully, if they so choose, through procedures determined by them, in devising legislative or administrative measures that may affect them. States shall obtain the free and informed consent of the peoples concerned before adopting and implementing such measures.

Article 21

Indigenous peoples have the right to maintain and develop their political, economic and social systems, to be secure in the enjoyment of their own means of subsistence and development, and to engage freely in all their traditional and other economic activities. Indigenous peoples who have been deprived of their means of subsistence and development are entitled to just and fair compensation.

Article 22

Indigenous peoples have the right to special measures for the immediate, effective and continuing improvement of their economic and social conditions, including in the areas of employment, vocational training and retraining, housing, sanitation, health and social security. Particular attention shall be paid to the rights and special needs of indigenous elders, women, youth, children and disabled persons.

Article 23

Indigenous peoples have the right to determine and develop priorities and strategies for exercising their right to development. In particular, indigenous peoples have the right to determine and develop all health, housing and other economic and social programmes affecting them and, as far as possible, to administer such programmes through their own institutions.

Article 24

Indigenous peoples have the right to their traditional medicines and health practices, including the right to the protection of vital medicinal plants, animals and minerals. They also have the right to access, without any discrimination, to all medical institutions, health services and medical care.

PART VI

Article 25

Indigenous peoples have the right to maintain and strengthen their distinctive spiritual and material relationship with the lands, territories, waters and coastal seas and other resources which they have traditionally owned or otherwise occupied or used, and to uphold their responsibilities to future generations in this regard.

Article 26

Indigenous peoples have the right to own, develop, control and use the lands and territories, including the total environment of the lands, air, waters, coastal seas, sea-ice, flora and fauna and other resources which they have traditionally owned or otherwise occupied or used. This includes the right to the full recognition of their laws, traditions and customs, land-tenure systems and institutions for the development and management of resources, and the right to effective measures by States to prevent any interference with, alienation of or encroachment upon these rights.

Article 27

Indigenous peoples have the right to the restitution of the lands, territories and resources which they have traditionally owned or otherwise occupied or used, and which have been confiscated, occupied, used or damaged without their free and informed consent. Where this is not possible, they have the right to just and fair compensation. Unless otherwise freely agreed upon by the peoples concerned, compensation shall take the form of lands, territories and resources equal in quality, size and legal status.

Article 28

Indigenous peoples have the right to the conservation, restoration and protection of the total environment and the productive capacity of their lands, territories and resources, as well as to assistance for this purpose from States and through international cooperation. Military activities shall not take place in the lands and territories of indigenous peoples, unless otherwise freely agreed upon by the peoples concerned. States shall take effective measures to ensure that no storage or disposal of hazardous materials shall take place in the lands and territories of indigenous peoples. States shall also take effective measures to ensure, as needed, that programmes for monitoring, maintaining and restoring the health of indigenous peoples, as developed and implemented by the peoples affected by such materials, are duly implemented.

Article 29

Indigenous peoples are entitled to the recognition of the full ownership, control and protection of their cultural and intellectual property. They have the right to special measures to control, develop and protect their sciences, technologies and cultural manifestations, including human and other genetic resources, seeds, medicines, knowledge of the properties of fauna and flora, oral traditions, literatures, designs and visual and performing arts.

Article 30

Indigenous peoples have the right to determine and develop priorities and strategies for the development or use of their lands, territories and other resources, including the right to require that States obtain their free and informed consent prior to the approval of any project affecting their lands, territories and other resources, particularly in connection with the development, utilization or exploitation of mineral, water or other resources. Pursuant to agreement with the indigenous peoples concerned, just and fair compensation shall be provided for any such activities and measures taken to mitigate adverse environmental, economic, social, cultural or spiritual impact.

PART VII

Article 31

Indigenous peoples, as a specific form of exercising their right to self-determination, have the right to autonomy or self-government in matters relating to their internal and local affairs, including culture, religion, education, information, media, health, housing, employment, social welfare, economic activities, land and resources management, environment and entry by non-members, as well as ways and means for financing these autonomous functions.

Article 32

Indigenous peoples have the collective right to determine their own citizenship in accordance with their customs and traditions. Indigenous citizenship does not impair the right of indigenous individuals to obtain citizenship of the States in which they live. Indigenous peoples have the right to determine the structures and to select the membership of their institutions in accordance with their own procedures.

Article 33

Indigenous peoples have the right to promote, develop and maintain their institutional structures and their distinctive juridical customs, traditions, procedures and practices, in accordance with internationally recognized human rights standards.

Article 34

Indigenous peoples have the collective right to determine the responsibilities of individuals to their communities.

Article 35

Indigenous peoples, in particular those divided by international borders, have the right to maintain and develop contacts, relations and cooperation, including activities for spiritual, cultural, political, economic and social purposes, with other peoples across borders. States shall take effective measures to ensure the exercise and implementation of this right.

Article 36

Indigenous peoples have the right to the recognition, observance and enforcement of treaties, agreements and other constructive arrangements concluded with States or their successors, according to their original spirit and intent, and to have States honour and respect such treaties, agreements and other constructive arrangements. Conflicts and disputes which cannot otherwise be settled should be submitted to competent international bodies agreed to by all parties concerned.

PART VIII

Article 37

States shall take effective and appropriate measures, in consultation with the indigenous peoples concerned, to give full effect to the provisions of this Declaration. The rights recognized herein shall be adopted and included in national legislation in such a manner that indigenous peoples can avail themselves of such rights in practice.

Article 38

Indigenous peoples have the right to have access to adequate financial and technical assistance, from States and through international cooperation, to pursue freely their political, economic, social, cultural and spiritual development and for the enjoyment of the rights and freedoms recognized in this Declaration.

Article 39

Indigenous peoples have the right to have access to and prompt decision through mutually acceptable and fair procedures for the resolution of conflicts and disputes with States, as well as to effective remedies for all infringements of their individual and collective rights. Such a decision shall take into consideration the customs, traditions, rules and legal systems of the indigenous peoples concerned.

Article 40

The organs and specialized agencies of the United Nations system and other intergovernmental organizations shall contribute to the full realization of the provisions of this Declaration through the mobilization, inter alia, of financial cooperation and technical assistance. Ways and means of ensuring participation of indigenous peoples on issues affecting them shall be established.

Article 41

The United Nations shall take the necessary steps to ensure the implementation of this Declaration including the creation of a body at the highest level with special competence in this field and with the direct participation of indigenous peoples. All United Nations bodies shall promote respect for and full application of the provisions of this Declaration.

PART IX

Article 42

The rights recognized herein constitute the minimum standards for the survival, dignity and well-being of the indigenous peoples of the world.

Article 43

All the rights and freedoms recognized herein are equally guaranteed to male and female indigenous individuals.

Article 44

Nothing in this Declaration may be construed as diminishing or extinguishing existing or future rights indigenous peoples may have or acquire.

Article 45

Nothing in this Declaration may be interpreted as implying for any State, group or person any right to engage in any activity or to perform any act contrary to the Charter of the United Nations.

DOCUMENT 40

Full Official Title: General Assembly Resolution [adopting the] Declaration on the Right and Responsibility of Individuals, Groups and Organs of Society to Promote and Protect Universally Recognized Human Rights and Fundamental Freedoms

Short Title/Acronym/Abbreviation: Declaration on Human Rights Defenders

Subject: Declaration recognizing specific human rights for human rights defenders and activists, and for everyone to be informed and active concerning human rights

Official Citation: United Nations General Assembly resolution 53/144 of 8 March 1999

Date of Document: March 8, 1999

Date of Adoption: March 8, 1999, but the Declaration was annexed to this resolution.

Date of General Entry into Force (EIF): Not a treaty. Does not enter into force.

Number of States Parties to this Treaty as of this printing: Not a treaty

Date of Signature by United States: Not applicable

Date of Ratification/Accession/Adhesion: Not applicable

Date of Entry into Force as to United States (effective date): Not applicable

Type of Document: Not a treaty. Does not create any binding legal obligations. This is a U.N. General Assembly resolution which adopts the "Declaration on the Right and Responsibility of Individuals, Groups and Organs of Society to Promote and Protect Universally Recognized Human Rights and Fundamental Freedoms, which was prepared and approved by the U.N. Commission on Human Rights and sent to the General Assembly for a vote by all member states. The Declaration itself is attached as an annex to this resolution.

Legal Status/Character of the Instrument/Document as to the United States: This creates no legal obligations on the United States, but because the United States voted for it and was a very strong supporter of this Declaration it should act consistently with it.

Comments: In many countries it is dangerous to be involved in human rights work. This is so because human rights usually involves criticizing what governments do. Human rights defenders often get jailed or killed or at least harassed and threatened for their work because it exposes the abuse of power and mistreatment of human beings by government. This Declaration was drafted to recognize human rights for human rights defenders and activists, and the right for anyone to become informed about human rights and to teach and communicate with others about human rights issues, or about what human rights are. It is meant to protect those who do human rights work.

Caution: The status and applicability of this instrument as to the United States may have changed since date of publication. The above information may be updated by referring to the following site:

Web address: http://www1.umn.edu/humanrts/instree/Res_53_144.html

GENERAL ASSEMBLY RESOLUTION [ADOPTING THE] DECLARATION ON THE RIGHT AND RESPONSIBILITY OF INDIVIDUALS, GROUPS AND ORGANS OF SOCIETY TO PROMOTE AND PROTECT UNIVERSALLY RECOGNIZED HUMAN RIGHTS AND FUNDAMENTAL FREEDOMS

United Nations General Assembly resolution 53/144
8 March 1999

Declaration on the Right and Responsibility of Individuals, Groups and Organs of Society to Promote and Protect Universally Recognized Human Rights and Fundamental Freedoms

The General Assembly

Reaffirming the importance of the observance of the purposes and principles of the Charter of the United Nations for the promotion and protection of all human rights and fundamental freedoms for all persons in all countries of the world,

Taking note of Commission on Human Rights resolution 1998/7 of 3 April 1998, See Official Records of the Economic and Social Council, 1998, Supplement No. 3 (E/1998/23), chap. II, sect. A. in which the Commission approved the text of the draft declaration on the right and responsibility of individuals, groups and organs of society to promote and protect universally recognized human rights and fundamental freedoms,

Taking note also of Economic and Social Council resolution 1998/33 of 30 July 1998, in which the Council recommended the draft declaration to the General Assembly for adoption,

Conscious of the importance of the adoption of the draft declaration in the context of the fiftieth anniversary of the Universal Declaration of Human Rights, Resolution 217 A (III):

1. Adopts the Declaration on the Right and Responsibility of Individuals, Groups and Organs of Society to Promote and Protect Universally Recognized Human Rights and Fundamental Freedoms, annexed to the present resolution;

2. Invites Governments, agencies and organizations of the United Nations system and intergovernmental and non-governmental organizations to intensify their efforts to disseminate the Declaration and to promote universal respect and understanding thereof, and requests the Secretary-General to include the text of the Declaration in the next edition of Human Rights: A Compilation of International Instruments.

ANNEX

85th plenary meeting
9 December 1998

Declaration on the Right and Responsibility of Individuals, Groups and Organs of Society to Promote and Protect Universally Recognized Human Rights and Fundamental Freedoms

Dec. 9, 1998

The General Assembly,

Reaffirming the importance of the observance of the purposes and principles of the Charter of the United Nations for the promotion and protection of all human rights and fundamental freedoms for all persons in all countries of the world,

Reaffirming also the importance of the Universal Declaration of Human Rights and the International Covenants on Human Rights Resolution 2200 A (XXI), annex. as basic elements of international efforts to promote universal respect for and observance of human rights and fundamental freedoms and the importance of other human rights instruments adopted within the United Nations system, as well as those at the regional level,

Stressing that all members of the international community shall fulfil, jointly and separately, their solemn obligation to promote and encourage respect for human rights and fundamental freedoms for all without distinction of any kind, including distinctions based on race, colour, sex, language, religion, political or other opinion, national or social origin, property, birth or other status, and reaffirming the particular importance of achieving international cooperation to fulfil this obligation according to the Charter,

Acknowledging the important role of international cooperation for, and the valuable work of individuals, groups and associations in contributing to, the effective elimination of all violations of human rights and fundamental freedoms of peoples and individuals, including in relation to mass, flagrant or systematic violations such as those resulting from apartheid, all forms of racial discrimination, colonialism, foreign domination or occupation, aggression or threats to national sovereignty, national unity or territorial integrity and from the refusal to recognize the right of peoples to self-determination and the right of every people to exercise full sovereignty over its wealth and natural resources,

Recognizing the relationship between international peace and security and the enjoyment of human rights and fundamental freedoms, and mindful that the absence of international peace and security does not excuse non-compliance,

Reiterating that all human rights and fundamental freedoms are universal, indivisible, interdependent and interrelated and should be promoted and implemented in a fair and equitable manner, without prejudice to the implementation of each of those rights and freedoms,

Stressing that the prime responsibility and duty to promote and protect human rights and fundamental freedoms lie with the State,

Recognizing the right and the responsibility of individuals, groups and associations to promote respect for and foster knowledge of human rights and fundamental freedoms at the national and international levels,

Declares :

Article 1

Everyone has the right, individually and in association with others, to promote and to strive for the protection and realization of human rights and fundamental freedoms at the national and international levels.

Article 2

1. Each State has a prime responsibility and duty to protect, promote and implement all human rights and fundamental freedoms, inter alia by adopting such steps as may be necessary to create all conditions necessary in the social, economic, political and other fields, as well as the legal guarantees required to ensure that all persons under its jurisdiction, individually and in association with others, are able to enjoy all those rights and freedoms in practice.

2. Each State shall adopt such legislative, administrative and other steps as may be necessary to ensure that the rights and freedoms referred to in the present Declaration are effectively guaranteed.

Article 3

Domestic law consistent with the Charter of the United Nations and other international obligations of the State in the field of human rights and fundamental freedoms is the juridical framework within which human rights and fundamental freedoms should be implemented and enjoyed and within which all activities referred to in the present Declaration for the promotion, protection and effective realization of those rights and freedoms should be conducted.

Article 4

Nothing in the present Declaration shall be construed as impairing or contradicting the purposes and principles of the Charter of the United Nations or as restricting or derogating from the provisions of the Universal Declaration of Human Rights, 2. the International Covenants on Human Rights 3. and other international instruments and commitments applicable in this field.

Article 5

For the purpose of promoting and protecting human rights and fundamental freedoms, everyone has the right, individually and in association with others, at the national and international levels:

(a) To meet or assemble peacefully;

(b) To form, join and participate in non-governmental organizations, associations or groups;

(c) To communicate with non-governmental or intergovernmental organizations.

Article 6

Everyone has the right, individually and in association with others:

(a) To know, seek, obtain, receive and hold information about all human rights and fundamental freedoms, including having access to information as to how those rights and freedoms are given effect in domestic legislative, judicial or administrative systems;

(b) As provided for in human rights and other applicable international instruments, freely to publish, impart or disseminate to others views, information and knowledge on all human rights and fundamental freedoms;

(c) To study, discuss, form and hold opinions on the observance, both in law and in practice, of all human rights and fundamental freedoms and, through these and other appropriate means, to draw public attention to those matters.

Article 7

Everyone has the right, individually and in association with others, to develop and discuss new human rights ideas and principles and to advocate their acceptance.

Article 8

1. Everyone has the right, individually and in association with others, to have effective access, on a non-discriminatory basis, to participation in the government of his or her country and in the conduct of public affairs.

2. This includes, inter alia, the right, individually and in association with others, to submit to governmental bodies and agencies and organizations concerned with public affairs criticism and proposals for improving their functioning and to draw attention to any aspect of their work that may hinder or impede the promotion, protection and realization of human rights and fundamental freedoms.

Article 9

1. In the exercise of human rights and fundamental freedoms, including the promotion and protection of human rights as referred to in the present Declaration, everyone has the right, individually and in association with others, to benefit from an effective remedy and to be protected in the event of the violation of those rights.

2. To this end, everyone whose rights or freedoms are allegedly violated has the right, either in person or through legally authorized representation, to complain to and have that complaint promptly reviewed in a public hearing before an independent, impartial and competent judicial or other authority established by law and to obtain from such an authority a decision, in accordance with law, providing redress, including any compensation due, where there has been a violation of that person's rights or freedoms, as well as enforcement of the eventual decision and award, all without undue delay.

3. To the same end, everyone has the right, individually and in association with others, inter alia:

(a) To complain about the policies and actions of individual officials and governmental bodies with regard to violations of human rights and fundamental freedoms, by petition or other appropriate means, to competent domestic judicial, administrative or legislative authorities or any other competent authority provided for by the legal system of the State, which should render their decision on the complaint without undue delay;

(b) To attend public hearings, proceedings and trials so as to form an opinion on their compliance with national law and applicable international obligations and commitments;

(c) To offer and provide professionally qualified legal assistance or other relevant advice and assistance in defending human rights and fundamental freedoms.

4. To the same end, and in accordance with applicable international instruments and procedures, everyone has the right, individually and in association with others, to unhindered access to and communication with international bodies with general or special competence to receive and consider communications on matters of human rights and fundamental freedoms.

5. The State shall conduct a prompt and impartial investigation or ensure that an inquiry takes place whenever there is reasonable ground to believe that a violation of human rights and fundamental freedoms has occurred in any territory under its jurisdiction.

Article 10

No one shall participate, by act or by failure to act where required, in violating human rights and fundamental freedoms and no one shall be subjected to punishment or adverse action of any kind for refusing to do so.

Article 11

Everyone has the right, individually and in association with others, to the lawful exercise of his or her occupation or profession. Everyone who, as a result of his or her profession, can affect the human dignity, human rights and fundamental freedoms of others should respect those rights and freedoms and comply with relevant national and international standards of occupational and professional conduct or ethics.

Article 12

1. Everyone has the right, individually and in association with others, to participate in peaceful activities against violations of human rights and fundamental freedoms.

2. The State shall take all necessary measures to ensure the protection by the competent authorities of everyone, individually and in association with others, against any violence, threats, retaliation, de facto or de jure adverse discrimination, pressure or any other arbitrary action as a consequence of his or her legitimate exercise of the rights referred to in the present Declaration.

3. In this connection, everyone is entitled, individually and in association with others, to be protected effectively under national law in reacting against or opposing, through peaceful means, activities and acts, including those by omission, attributable to States that result in violations of human rights and fundamental freedoms, as well as acts of violence perpetrated by groups or individuals that affect the enjoyment of human rights and fundamental freedoms.

Article 13

Everyone has the right, individually and in association with others, to solicit, receive and utilize resources for the express purpose of promoting and protecting human rights and fundamental freedoms through peaceful means, in accordance with Article 3 of the present Declaration.

Article 14

1. The State has the responsibility to take legislative, judicial, administrative or other appropriate measures to promote the understanding by all persons under its jurisdiction of their civil, political, economic, social and cultural rights.

2. Such measures shall include, inter alia:

(a) The publication and widespread availability of national laws and regulations and of applicable basic international human rights instruments;

(b) Full and equal access to international documents in the field of human rights, including the periodic reports by the State to the bodies established by the international human rights treaties to which it is a party, as well as the summary records of discussions and the official reports of these bodies.

3. The State shall ensure and support, where appropriate, the creation and development of further independent national institutions for the promotion and protection of human rights and fundamental freedoms in all territory under its jurisdiction, whether they be ombudsmen, human rights commissions or any other form of national institution.

Article 15

The State has the responsibility to promote and facilitate the teaching of human rights and fundamental freedoms at all levels of education and to ensure that all those responsible for training lawyers, law enforcement officers, the personnel of the armed forces and public officials include appropriate elements of human rights teaching in their training programme.

Article 16

Individuals, non-governmental organizations and relevant institutions have an important role to play in contributing to making the public more aware of questions relating to all human rights and fundamental freedoms through activities such as education, training and research in these areas to strengthen further, inter alia, understanding, tolerance, peace and friendly relations among nations and among all racial and religious groups, bearing in mind the various backgrounds of the societies and communities in which they carry out their activities.

Article 17

In the exercise of the rights and freedoms referred to in the present Declaration, everyone, acting individually and in association with others, shall be subject only to such limitations as are in accordance with applicable international obligations and are determined by law solely for the purpose of securing due recognition and respect for the rights and freedoms of others and of meeting the just requirements of morality, public order and the general welfare in a democratic society.

Article 18

1. Everyone has duties towards and within the community, in which alone the free and full development of his or her personality is possible.

2. Individuals, groups, institutions and non-governmental organizations have an important role to play and a responsibility in safeguarding democracy, promoting human rights and fundamental freedoms and contributing to the promotion and advancement of democratic societies, institutions and processes.

3. Individuals, groups, institutions and non-governmental organizations also have an important role and a responsibility in contributing, as appropriate, to the promotion of the right of everyone to a social and international order in which the rights and freedoms set forth in the Universal Declaration of Human Rights and other human rights instruments can be fully realized.

Article 19

Nothing in the present Declaration shall be interpreted as implying for any individual, group or organ of society or any State the right to engage in any activity or to perform any act aimed at the destruction of the rights and freedoms referred to in the present Declaration.

Article 20

Nothing in the present Declaration shall be interpreted as permitting States to support and promote activities of individuals, groups of individuals, institutions or non-governmental organizations contrary to the provisions of the Charter of the United Nations.

(Copyright, Office of the United Nations High Commissioner for Human Rights Geneva, Switzerland)

DOCUMENT 41

Full Official Title: Declaration on the Rights of Persons Belonging to National or Ethnic, Religious or Linguistic Minorities

Short Title/Acronym/Abbreviation: U.N. Minority Rights Declaration/ U.N. Declaration on Minorities

Subject: Declaration of specific human rights of racial, ethnic, religious or linguistic minority groups, amplifying ICCPR Article 27 and related articles of other human rights instruments affecting certain minorities.

Official Citation: G.A. res. 47/135, 47 GAOR Supp.(no. 49) at 210, U.N. Doc. A/47/49 (1993)

Date of Document: Not applicable

Date of Adoption: December 18, 1992

Date of General Entry into Force (EIF): Not applicable

Number of States Parties to this treaty as of this printing: Not a treaty

Date of Signature by United States: Not applicable

Date of United States Ratification/Accession/Adhesion: Not applicable

Date of Entry into Force (effective date)as to United States: Not applicable

Type of Document: Non-legal, non-binding declaration

Legal Status/Character of the Instrument/Document as to the United States: Not legally binding upon the United States.

Comments: This instrument adopted by the U.N. General Assembly in 1992 was actually the product of the U.N. Commission on Human Rights and its Subcommission on Prevention of Discrimination and Protection of Minorities. It was done as part of the Commission's mandate to study human rights situations regarding minority groups and to seek formulation of more specific, more detailed, and more effective human rights standards. This was done because of the many places in the world where serious human rights violations were being committed against such minority groups. These situations were seen by the international community as having the potential to cause poverty and marginalization for such groups, and even to result in genocide, ethnic cleansing, war, and regional or global political conflicts. Most of the issues arose in the context of a state trying to force assimilation of the group to that of the majority in a way that would result in the minority group losing its characteristics or sense of identity as a group. This was often caught up and rooted in a ethnic or religious-based nationalism.

Human rights are conceptually understood as the rights of individuals who each hold their own human rights. They are not generally accepted as held collectively by a group of people possessing a certain similar characteristic. However, because of the desire to find human rights protection for such groups, the United Nations began to move in the direction of articulating some collective or group sounding human rights.

Up to the time of this Declaration there were very few human rights that seemed to apply to groups or collectives of people. The prime example and first express legal norm on such rights was Article 27 of the ICCPR. This article states: "In those states in which ethnic, religious or linguistic minorities exist, persons belonging to such minorities shall not be denied the right, in community with other members of their group, to enjoy their own culture, to profess and practice their own religion, or to use their own language."

This Declaration is an attempt to amplify those existing human rights norms that would be used by minority groups to protect their group culture, religion, and language. The scope of the Declaration was expanded to "national or ethnic, religious or linguistic* minorities. A linguistic minority is a group of people who speak a different native language than that spoken by the majority of people in a state. The United States was much a part of this process of formulating and promoting this Declaration. The United States voted for the Declaration at the General Assembly meeting in 1992, had a U.S. representative on the Commission when it was handled by that body, and had an American expert on the Subcommission when its input and draft was prepared.

This declaration does not obligate the United States to do anything or to change any laws regarding minorities. It does, however have substantial moral and political weight as an expression of most of the member states of the international community as to the human rights of these types of minorities. It can be cited as a guideline/standard for discussing social, legal, and political issues involving minorities, such as Native Hawaiians, African Americans, Native Americans, the Amish, Latinos, and Muslims. The term "ethnic" has been interpreted to include groups normally designated as "indigenous peoples." Thus, all indigenous peoples, such as Eskimos, Native Americans, and Native Hawaiians are covered by this Declaration.

Web Address: http://www.unhchr.ch/html/menu3/b/d_minori.htm

DECLARATION ON THE RIGHTS OF PERSONS BELONGING TO NATIONAL OR ETHNIC, RELIGIOUS OR LINGUISTIC MINORITIES

The General Assembly,

Reaffirming that one of the basic aims of the United Nations, as proclaimed in the Charter, is to promote and encourage respect for human rights and for fundamental freedoms for all, without distinction as to race, sex, language or religion,

Reaffirming faith in fundamental human rights, in the dignity and worth of the human person, in the equal rights of men and women and of nations large and small,

Desiring to promote the realization of the principles contained in the Charter, the Universal Declaration of Human Rights, the Convention on the Prevention and Punishment of the Crime of Genocide, the International Convention on the Elimination of All Forms of Racial Discrimination, the International Covenant on Civil and Political Rights, the International Covenant on Economic, Social and Cultural Rights, the Declaration on the Elimination of All Forms of Intolerance and of Discrimination Based on Religion or Belief, and the Convention on the Rights of the Child, as well as other relevant international instruments that have been adopted at the universal or regional level and those concluded between individual States Members of the United Nations,

Inspired by the provisions of Article 27 of the International Covenant on Civil and Political Rights concerning the rights of persons belonging to ethnic, religious or linguistic minorities,

Considering that the promotion and protection of the rights of persons belonging to national or ethnic, religious and linguistic minorities contribute to the political and social stability of States in which they live,

Emphasizing that the constant promotion and realization of the rights of persons belonging to national or ethnic, religious and linguistic minorities, as an integral part of the development of society as a whole and within a democratic framework based on the rule of law, would contribute to the strengthening of friendship and cooperation among peoples and States,

Considering that the United Nations has an important role to play regarding the protection of minorities,

Bearing in mind the work done so far within the United Nations system, in particular by the Commission on Human Rights, the Subcommission on Prevention of Discrimination and Protection of Minorities and the bodies established pursuant to the International Covenants on Human Rights and other relevant international human rights instruments in promoting and protecting the rights of persons belonging to national or ethnic, religious and linguistic minorities,

Taking into account the important work which is done by intergovernmental and non-governmental organizations in protecting minorities and in promoting and protecting the rights of persons belonging to national or ethnic, religious and linguistic minorities,

Recognizing the need to ensure even more effective implementation of international human rights instruments with regard to the rights of persons belonging to national or ethnic, religious and linguistic minorities,

Proclaims this Declaration on the Rights of Persons Belonging to National or Ethnic, Religious and Linguistic Minorities:

Article 1

1. States shall protect the existence and the national or ethnic, cultural, religious and linguistic identity of minorities within their respective territories and shall encourage conditions for the promotion of that identity.

2. States shall adopt appropriate legislative and other measures to achieve those ends.

Article 2

1. Persons belonging to national or ethnic, religious and linguistic minorities (hereinafter referred to as persons belonging to minorities) have the right to enjoy their own culture, to profess and practise their own religion, and to use their own language, in private and in public, freely and without interference or any form of discrimination.

2. Persons belonging to minorities have the right to participate effectively in cultural, religious, social, economic and public life.

3. Persons belonging to minorities have the right to participate effectively in decisions on the national and, where appropriate, regional level concerning the minority to which they belong or the regions in which they live, in a manner not incompatible with national legislation.

4. Persons belonging to minorities have the right to establish and maintain their own associations.

5. Persons belonging to minorities have the right to establish and maintain, without any discrimination, free and peaceful contacts with other members of their group and with persons belonging to other minorities, as well as contacts across frontiers with citizens of other States to whom they are related by national or ethnic, religious or linguistic ties.

Article 3

1. Persons belonging to minorities may exercise their rights, including those set forth in the present Declaration, individually as well as in community with other members of their group, without any discrimination.

2. No disadvantage shall result for any person belonging to a minority as the consequence of the exercise or non-exercise of the rights set forth in the present Declaration.

Article 4

1. States shall take measures where required to ensure that persons belonging to minorities may exercise fully and effectively all their human rights and fundamental freedoms without any discrimination and in full equality before the law.

2. States shall take measures to create favourable conditions to enable persons belonging to minorities to express their characteristics and to develop their culture, language, religion, traditions and customs, except where specific practices are in violation of national law and contrary to international standards.

3. States should take appropriate measures so that, wherever possible, persons belonging to minorities may have adequate opportunities to learn their mother tongue or to have instruction in their mother tongue.

4. States should, where appropriate, take measures in the field of education, in order to encourage knowledge of the history, traditions, language and culture of the minorities existing within their territory. Persons belonging to minorities should have adequate opportunities to gain knowledge of the society as a whole.

5. States should consider appropriate measures so that persons belonging to minorities may participate fully in the economic progress and development in their country.

Article 5

1. National policies and programmes shall be planned and implemented with due regard for the legitimate interests of persons belonging to minorities.

2. Programmes of cooperation and assistance among States should be planned and implemented with due regard for the legitimate interests of persons belonging to minorities.

Article 6

States should cooperate on questions relating to persons belonging to minorities, inter alia, exchanging information and experiences, in order to promote mutual understanding and confidence.

Article 7

States should cooperate in order to promote respect for the rights set forth in the present Declaration.

Article 8

1. Nothing in the present Declaration shall prevent the fulfilment of international obligations of States in relation to persons belonging to minorities. In particular, States shall fulfil in good faith the obligations and commitments they have assumed under international treaties and agreements to which they are parties.

2. The exercise of the rights set forth in the present Declaration shall not prejudice the enjoyment by all persons of universally recognized human rights and fundamental freedoms.

3. Measures taken by States to ensure the effective enjoyment of the rights set forth in the present Declaration shall not prima facie be considered contrary to the principle of equality contained in the Universal Declaration of Human Rights.

4. Nothing in the present Declaration may be construed as permitting any activity contrary to the purposes and principles of the United Nations, including sovereign equality, territorial integrity and political independence of States.

Article 9

The specialized agencies and other organizations of the United Nations system shall contribute to the full realization of the rights and principles set forth in the present Declaration, within their respective fields of competence.

DOCUMENT 42

Full Official Title: Declaration on the Human Rights of Individuals Who Are Not Nationals of the Country in Which They Live

Short Title/Acronym/Abbreviation: Declaration on the Rights of Non Nationals

Type of Document: A declaration, not a treaty. An aspirational document initially meant not to create any legal obligations, but to recognize human rights of non-citizens, and encourage states of the world to seek to fulfill its stated principles and rights within their national legal systems.

Subject: Human rights of non-nationals

Official Citation: G.A. res.40/144, annex, 40 U.N. GAOR Supp., U.N. Doc. A/RES/40/144 (1985)

Date of Document: Not applicable

Date of Adoption: December 13, 1985

Date of General Entry into Force (EIF): Not applicable

Number of States Parties as of this printing: Not applicable

Date of Signature by the United States: Not applicable

Date of Ratification/Accession/Adhesion: Not applicable

Date of Entry into Force as to United States (effective date): Not applicable

Legal Status/Character of the Instrument/Document as to the United States: Not a treaty and therefore not legally binding upon the United States. This is a U.N. General Assembly resolution that adopts the Declaration on the Human Rights of Individuals Who Are Not Nationals of the Country in Which They Live, which was prepared by an open-ended Working Group that met during the 1985 Assembly.

Comments: This instrument, adopted by the U.N. General Assembly in 1985, was written to recognize and ensure the protection of the fundamental human rights provided for in international human rights instruments, with respect to individuals living in a country where they are not nationals, or in which they are "alien." The declaration is meant to ensure that fundamental freedoms are respected no matter where the persons are. Contained within the declaration is a definition of what it means to be an "alien".

Caution: The status and applicability of this instrument as to the United States may have changed since the date of this publication. The above information may be updated by referring to the following site:

Web Address: http://www.unhchr.ch/huridocda/huridoca.nsf/%28symbol%29/a.res.53.144.en

DECLARATION ON THE HUMAN RIGHTS OF INDIVIDUALS WHO ARE NOT NATIONALS OF THE COUNTRY IN WHICH THEY LIVE

The General Assembly,

Considering that the Charter of the United Nations encourages universal respect for and observance of the human rights and fundamental freedoms of all human beings, without distinction as to race, sex, language or religion, Considering that the Universal Declaration of Human Rights proclaims that all human beings are born free and equal in dignity and rights and that everyone is entitled to all the rights and freedoms set forth in that Declaration, without distinction of any kind, such as race, colour, sex, language, religion, political or other opinion, national or social origin, property, birth or other status,

Considering that the Universal Declaration of Human Rights proclaims further that everyone has the right to recognition everywhere as a person before the law, that all are equal before the law and entitled without any discrimination to equal protection of the law, and that all are entitled to equal protection against any discrimination in violation of that Declaration and against any incitement to such discrimination,

Being aware that the States Parties to the International Covenants on Human Rights undertake to guarantee that the rights enunciated in these Covenants will be exercised without discrimination of any kind as to race, colour, sex, language, religion, political or other opinion, national or social origin, property, birth or other status,

Conscious that, with improving communications and the development of peaceful and friendly relations among countries, individuals increasingly live in countries of which they are not nationals, Reaffirming the purposes and principles of the Charter of the United Nations,

Recognizing that the protection of human rights and fundamental freedoms provided for in international instruments should also be ensured for individuals who are not nationals of the country in which they live,

Proclaims this Declaration:

Article 1

For the purposes of this Declaration, the term "alien" shall apply, with due regard to qualifications made in subsequent articles, to any individual who is not a national of the State in which he or she is present.

Article 2

1. Nothing in this Declaration shall be interpreted as legitimizing the illegal entry into and presence in a State of any alien, nor shall any provision be interpreted as restricting the right of any State to promulgate laws and regulations concerning the entry of aliens and the terms and conditions of their stay or to establish differences between nationals and aliens. However, such laws and regulations shall not be incompatible with the international legal obligations of that State, including those in the field of human rights.

2. This Declaration shall not prejudice the enjoyment of the rights accorded by domestic law and of the rights which under international law a State is obliged to accord to aliens, even where this Declaration does not recognize such rights or recognizes them to a lesser extent.

Article 3

Every State shall make public its national legislation or regulations affecting aliens.

Article 4

Aliens shall observe the laws of the State in which they reside or are present and regard with respect the customs and traditions of the people of that State.

Article 5

1. Aliens shall enjoy, in accordance with domestic law and subject to the relevant international obligation of the State in which they are present, in particular the following rights:

(a) The right to life and security of person; no alien shall be subjected to arbitrary arrest or detention; no alien shall be deprived of his or her liberty except on such grounds and in accordance with such procedures as are established by law;

(b) The right to protection against arbitrary or unlawful interference with privacy, family, home or correspondence;

(c) The right to be equal before the courts, tribunals and all other organs and authorities administering justice and, when necessary, to free assistance of an interpreter in criminal proceedings and, when prescribed by law, other proceedings;

(d) The right to choose a spouse, to marry, to found a family;

(e) The right to freedom of thought, opinion, conscience and religion; the right to manifest their religion or beliefs, subject only to such limitations as are prescribed by law and are necessary to protect public safety, order, health or morals or the fundamental rights and freedoms of others;

(f) The right to retain their own language, culture and tradition;

(g) The right to transfer abroad earnings, savings or other personal monetary assets, subject to domestic currency regulations.

2. Subject to such restrictions as are prescribed by law and which are necessary in a democratic society to protect national security, public safety, public order, public health or morals or the rights and freedoms of others, and which are consistent with the other rights recognized in the relevant international instruments and those set forth in this Declaration, aliens shall enjoy the following rights:

(a) The right to leave the country;

(b) The right to freedom of expression;

(c) The right to peaceful assembly;

(d) The right to own property alone as well as in association with others, subject to domestic law.

3. Subject to the provisions referred to in paragraph 2, aliens lawfully in the territory of a State shall enjoy the right to liberty of movement and freedom to choose their residence within the borders of the State.

4. Subject to national legislation and due authorization, the spouse and minor or dependent children of an alien lawfully residing in the territory of a State shall be admitted to accompany, join and stay with the alien.

Article 6

No alien shall be subjected to torture or to cruel, inhuman or degrading treatment or punishment and, in particular, no alien shall be subjected without his or her free consent to medical or scientific experimentation.

Article 7

An alien lawfully in the territory of a State may be expelled therefrom only in pursuance of a decision reached in accordance with law and shall, except where compelling reasons of national security otherwise require, be allowed to submit the reasons why he or she should not be expelled and to have the case reviewed by, and be represented for the purpose before, the competent authority or a person or persons specially designated by the competent authority. Individual or collective expulsion of such aliens on grounds of race, colour, religion, culture, descent or national or ethnic origin is prohibited.

Article 8

1. Aliens lawfully residing in the territory of a State shall also enjoy, in accordance with the national laws, the following rights, subject to their obligations under Article 4:

(a) The right to safe and healthy working conditions, to fair wages and equal remuneration for work of equal value without distinction of any kind, in particular, women being guaranteed conditions of work not inferior to those enjoyed by men, with equal pay for equal work;

(b) The right to join trade unions and other organizations or associations of their choice and to participate in their activities. No restrictions may be placed on the exercise of this right other than those prescribed by law and which are necessary, in a democratic society, in the interests of national security or public order or for the protection of the rights and freedoms of others;

(c) The right to health protection, medical care, social security, social services, education, rest and leisure, provided that they fulfil the requirements under the relevant regulations for participation and that undue strain is not placed on the resources of the State.

2. With a view to protecting the rights of aliens carrying on lawful paid activities in the country in which they are present, such rights may be specified by the Governments concerned in multilateral or bilateral conventions.

Article 9

No alien shall be arbitrarily deprived of his or her lawfully acquired assets.

Article 10

Any alien shall be free at any time to communicate with the consulate or diplomatic mission of the State of which he or she is a national or, in the absence thereof, with the consulate or diplomatic mission of any other State entrusted with the protection of the interests of the State of which he or she is a national in the State where he or she resides.

DOCUMENT 43

Full Official Title: Declaration on the Elimination of Violence against Women

Short Title/Acronym/Abbreviation: Subject: General Assembly resolution recognizing the human rights of women to be free from violence from governmental or private sources

Official Citation: A/RES/48/104, General Assembly, 85th plenary meeting, 20 December 1993

Date of Document: December 20, 1993

Date of Adoption: December 20, 1993

Date of General Entry into Force (EIF): Not a treaty. Does not enter into force.

Number of States Parties to the Treaty as of this printing: Not applicable

Date of Signature by United States: Not applicable

Date of Ratification/Accession/Adhesion: Not applicable

Date of Entry into Force as to United States (effective date): Not applicable

Type of Document: A declaration. This is not a treaty, but is intended to be a non-legal instrument proclaiming the human rights principles which states should be following.

Legal Status/Character of the Instrument/Document as to the United States: A declaration is not a legal instrument (treaty) and thus creates no binding legal obligation upon member states such as the United States. However, as a matter of political and moral value all states, including the United States, should follow it and use it as a yardstick for understanding the scope of rights of those involved in human rights activity, especially those on the side of victims and those attacking government abuses of human rights. This document will probably serve as the basis of a future legal instrument on violence against women.

Comments: This declaration was necessitated by the evidence of widespread violence against women all over the world, particularly in wars and in spousal abuse in the home.

Web address: http://www1.umn.edu/humanrts/instree/e4devw.htm

DECLARATION ON THE ELIMINATION OF VIOLENCE AGAINST WOMEN

85th plenary meeting
20 December 1993
The General Assembly,

Recognizing the urgent need for the universal application to women of the rights and principles with regard to equality, security, liberty, integrity and dignity of all human beings,

Noting that those rights and principles are enshrined in international instruments, including the Universal Declaration of Human Rights, the International Covenant on Civil and Political Rights, the International Covenant on Economic, Social and Cultural Rights, the Convention on the Elimination of All Forms of Discrimination against Women and the Convention against Torture and Other Cruel, Inhuman or Degrading Treatment or Punishment,

Recognizing that effective implementation of the Convention on the Elimination of All Forms of Discrimination against Women would contribute to the elimination of violence against women and that the Declaration on the Elimination of Violence against Women, set forth in the present resolution, will strengthen and complement that process,

Concerned that violence against women is an obstacle to the achievement of equality, development and peace, as recognized in the Nairobi Forward-looking Strategies for the Advancement of Women, in which a set of measures to combat violence against women was recommended, and to the full implementation of the Convention on the Elimination of All Forms of Discrimination against Women,

Affirming that violence against women constitutes a violation of the rights and fundamental freedoms of women and impairs or nullifies their enjoyment of those rights and freedoms, and concerned about the long-standing failure to protect and promote those rights and freedoms in the case of violence against women,

Recognizing that violence against women is a manifestation of historically unequal power relations between men and women, which have led to domination over and discrimination against women by men and to the prevention of the full advancement of women, and that violence against women is one of the crucial social mechanisms by which women are forced into a subordinate position compared with men,

Concerned that some groups of women, such as women belonging to minority groups, indigenous women, refugee women, migrant women, women living in rural or remote communities, destitute women, women in institutions or in detention, female children, women with disabilities, elderly women and women in situations of armed conflict, are especially vulnerable to violence,

Recalling the conclusion in paragraph 23 of the annex to Economic and Social Council resolution 1990/15 of 24 May 1990 that the recognition that violence against women in the family and society was pervasive and cut across lines of income, class and culture had to be matched by urgent and effective steps to eliminate its incidence,

Recalling also Economic and Social Council resolution 1991/18 of 30 May 1991, in which the Council recommended the development of a framework for an international instrument that would address explicitly the issue of violence against women,

Welcoming the role that women's movements are playing in drawing increasing attention to the nature, severity and magnitude of the problem of violence against women, Alarmed that opportunities for women to achieve legal, social, political and economic equality in society are limited, inter alia, by continuing and endemic violence,

Convinced that in the light of the above there is a need for a clear and comprehensive definition of violence against women, a clear statement of the rights to be applied to ensure the elimination of violence against women in all its forms, a commitment by States in respect of their responsibilities, and a commitment by the international community at large to the elimination of violence against women,

Solemnly proclaims the following Declaration on the Elimination of Violence against Women and urges that every effort be made so that it becomes generally known and respected:

Article 1

For the purposes of this Declaration, the term "violence against women" means any act of gender-based violence that results in, or is likely to result in, physical, sexual or psychological harm or suffering to women, including threats of such acts, coercion or arbitrary deprivation of liberty, whether occurring in public or in private life.

Article 2

Violence against women shall be understood to encompass, but not be limited to, the following:

(a) Physical, sexual and psychological violence occurring in the family, including battering, sexual abuse of female children in the household, dowry-related violence, marital rape, female genital mutilation and other traditional practices harmful to women, non-spousal violence and violence related to exploitation;

(b) Physical, sexual and psychological violence occurring within the general community, including rape, sexual abuse, sexual harassment and intimidation at work, in educational institutions and elsewhere, trafficking in women and forced prostitution;

(c) Physical, sexual and psychological violence perpetrated or condoned by the State, wherever it occurs.

Article 3

Women are entitled to the equal enjoyment and protection of all human rights and fundamental freedoms in the political, economic, social, cultural, civil or any other field. These rights include, inter alia:

(a) The right to life;

(b) The right to equality;

(c) The right to liberty and security of person;

(d) The right to equal protection under the law;

(e) The right to be free from all forms of discrimination;

(f) The right to the highest standard attainable of physical and mental health;

(g) The right to just and favourable conditions of work;

(h) The right not to be subjected to torture, or other cruel, inhuman or degrading treatment or punishment.

Article 4

States should condemn violence against women and should not invoke any custom, tradition or religious consideration to avoid their obligations with respect to its elimination. States should pursue by all appropriate means and without delay a policy of eliminating violence against women and, to this end, should:

(a) Consider, where they have not yet done so, ratifying or acceding to the Convention on the Elimination of All Forms of Discrimination against Women or withdrawing reservations to that Convention;

(b) Refrain from engaging in violence against women;

(c) Exercise due diligence to prevent, investigate and, in accordance with national legislation, punish acts of violence against women, whether those acts are perpetrated by the State or by private persons;

(d) Develop penal, civil, labour and administrative sanctions in domestic legislation to punish and redress the wrongs caused to women who are subjected to violence; women who are subjected to violence should be provided with access to the mechanisms of justice and, as provided for by national legislation, to just and effective remedies for the harm that they have suffered; States should also inform women of their rights in seeking redress through such mechanisms;

(e) Consider the possibility of developing national plans of action to promote the protection of women against any form of violence, or to include provisions for that purpose in plans already existing, taking into account, as appropriate, such cooperation as can be provided by non-governmental organizations, particularly those concerned with the issue of violence against women;

(f) Develop, in a comprehensive way, preventive approaches and all those measures of a legal, political, administrative and cultural nature that promote the protection of women against any form of violence, and ensure that the re-victimization of women does not occur because of laws insensitive to gender considerations, enforcement practices or other interventions;

(g) Work to ensure, to the maximum extent feasible in the light of their available resources and, where needed, within the framework of international cooperation, that women subjected to violence and, where appropriate, their children have specialized assistance, such as rehabilitation, assistance in child care and maintenance, treatment, counselling, and health and social services, facilities and programmes, as well as support structures, and should take all other appropriate measures to promote their safety and physical and psychological rehabilitation;

(h) Include in government budgets adequate resources for their activities related to the elimination of violence against women;

(i) Take measures to ensure that law enforcement officers and public officials responsible for implementing policies to prevent, investigate and punish violence against women receive training to sensitize them to the needs of women;

(j) Adopt all appropriate measures, especially in the field of education, to modify the social and cultural patterns of conduct of men and women and to eliminate prejudices, customary practices and all other practices based on the idea of the inferiority or superiority of either of the sexes and on stereotyped roles for men and women;

(k) Promote research, collect data and compile statistics, especially concerning domestic violence, relating to the prevalence of different forms of violence against women and encourage research on the causes, nature, seriousness and consequences of violence against women and on the effectiveness of measures implemented to prevent and redress violence against women; those statistics and findings of the research will be made public;

(l) Adopt measures directed towards the elimination of violence against women who are especially vulnerable to violence;

(m) Include, in submitting reports as required under relevant human rights instruments of the United Nations, information pertaining to violence against women and measures taken to implement the present Declaration;

(n) Encourage the development of appropriate guidelines to assist in the implementation of the principles set forth in the present Declaration;

(o) Recognize the important role of the women's movement and non-governmental organizations world wide in raising awareness and alleviating the problem of violence against women;

(p) Facilitate and enhance the work of the women's movement and non-governmental organizations and cooperate with them at local, national and regional levels;

(q) Encourage inter-governmental regional organizations of which they are members to include the elimination of violence against women in their programmes, as appropriate.

Article 5

The organs and specialized agencies of the United Nations system should, within their respective fields of competence, contribute to the recognition and realization of the rights and the principles set forth in the present Declaration and, to this end, should, inter alia:

(a) Foster international and regional cooperation with a view to defining regional strategies for combating violence, exchanging experiences and financing programmes relating to the elimination of violence against women;

(b) Promote meetings and seminars with the aim of creating and raising awareness among all persons of the issue of the elimination of violence against women;

(c) Foster coordination and exchange within the United Nations system between human rights treaty bodies to address the issue of violence against women effectively;

(d) Include in analyses prepared by organizations and bodies of the United Nations system of social trends and problems, such as the periodic reports on the world social situation, examination of trends in violence against women;

(e) Encourage coordination between organizations and bodies of the United Nations system to incorporate the issue of violence against women into ongoing programmes, especially with reference to groups of women particularly vulnerable to violence;

(f) Promote the formulation of guidelines or manuals relating to violence against women, taking into account the measures referred to in the present Declaration;

(g) Consider the issue of the elimination of violence against women, as appropriate, in fulfilling their mandates with respect to the implementation of human rights instruments;

(h) Cooperate with non-governmental organizations in addressing the issue of violence against women.

Article 6

Nothing in the present Declaration shall affect any provision that is more conducive to the elimination of violence against women that may be contained in the legislation of a State or in any international convention, treaty or other instrument in force in a State.

DOCUMENT 44

Full Official Title: International Convention on the Rights of Persons with Disabilities

Short Title/Acronym/Abbreviation: The Disabilities Convention

Type of Document: This is a treaty, a legal instrument. This convention was adopted by the U.N. General Assembly upon the recommendation of an Ad Hoc Committee established to prepare the draft text. The Ad Hoc Committee established a Working Group that prepared a draft text that was revised in meetings from 2002–2006. The Ad Hoc Committee adopted a draft Convention and an Optional Protocol that was sent to and passed by consensus in the General Assembly on December 13, 2006 during a Plenary Session.

Subject: Human rights of persons with disabilities

Official Citation: General Assembly A/61/611

Date of Document: December 13, 2006

Date of Adoption: December 13, 2006

Date of General Entry into Force (EIF): May 3, 2008

Number of States Parties as of this printing: 90 [89 states have signed the Optional Protocol and 56 states have ratified or become party to the Optional Protocol.]

Date of Signature by the United States: July 30, 2009

Date of Ratification/Accession/Adhesion: Not applicable

Date of Entry into Force as to United States (effective date): Not applicable

Legal Status/Character of the Instrument/Document as to the United States: The United States has signed but not yet ratified this treaty as of the date of this publication. It has not yet been sent to the U.S. Senate by the President, which is necessary before it can be ratified. Under certain principles of international law contained in the Vienna Convention on the law of treaties, the United States should act consistently with legal instruments it has signed, as an indication of its good-faith intent to act accordingly until ratification.

Supervising Body: Committee on the Rights of Persons with Disabilities

Comment: A very politically controversial treaty. The reluctance of the Senate to ratify has involved concerns about the interpretation of certain articles, and the lack of protection that the treaty affords persons with disabilities prior to birth or at the end of life.. Some opponents question whether this treaty is necessary, considering the strong protections for persons with disabilities that are already enacted in U.S. law.

Caution: The status and applicability of this instrument as to the United States may have changed since the date of this publication.

Web Address: http://www.un.org/disabilities/countries.asp?navid=12&pid=166

INTERNATIONAL CONVENTION ON THE RIGHTS OF PERSONS WITH DISABILITIES

Preamble

The States Parties to the present Convention,

(a) *Recalling* the principles proclaimed in the Charter of the United Nations which recognize the inherent dignity and worth and the equal and inalienable rights of all members of the human family as the foundation of freedom, justice and peace in the world,

(b) *Recognizing* that the United Nations, in the Universal Declaration of Human Rights and in the International Covenants on Human Rights, has proclaimed and agreed that everyone is entitled to all the rights and freedoms set forth therein, without distinction of any kind,

(c) *Reaffirming* the universality, indivisibility, interdependence and interrelatedness of all human rights and fundamental freedoms and the need for persons with disabilities to be guaranteed their full enjoyment without discrimination,

(d) *Recalling* the International Covenant on Economic, Social and Cultural Rights, the International Covenant on Civil and Political Rights, the International Convention on the Elimination of All Forms of Racial Discrimination, the Convention on the Elimination of All Forms of Discrimination against Women, the Convention against Torture and Other Cruel, Inhuman or Degrading Treatment or Punishment, the Convention on the Rights of the Child, and the International Convention on the Protection of the Rights of All Migrant Workers and Members of Their Families,

(e) *Recognizing* that disability is an evolving concept and that disability results from the interaction between persons with impairments and attitudinal and environmental barriers that hinders their full and effective participation in society on an equal basis with others,

(f) *Recognizing* the importance of the principles and policy guidelines contained in the World Programme of Action concerning Disabled Persons and in the Standard Rules on the Equalization of Opportunities for Persons with Disabilities in influencing the promotion, formulation and evaluation of the policies, plans, programmes and actions at the national, regional and international levels to further equalize opportunities for persons with disabilities,

(g) *Emphasizing* the importance of mainstreaming disability issues as an integral part of relevant strategies of sustainable development,

(h) *Recognizing also* that discrimination against any person on the basis of disability is a violation of the inherent dignity and worth of the human person,

(i) *Recognizing further* the diversity of persons with disabilities,

(j) *Recognizing* the need to promote and protect the human rights of all persons with disabilities, including those who require more intensive support,

(k) *Concerned* that, despite these various instruments and undertakings, persons with disabilities continue to face barriers in their participation as equal members of society and violations of their human rights in all parts of the world,

(l) *Recognizing* the importance of international cooperation for improving the living conditions of persons with disabilities in every country, particularly in developing countries,

(m) *Recognizing* the valued existing and potential contributions made by persons with disabilities to the overall well-being and diversity of their communities, and that the promotion of the full enjoyment by persons with disabilities of their human rights and fundamental freedoms and of full participation by persons with disabilities will result in their enhanced sense of belonging and in significant advances in the human, social and economic development of society and the eradication of poverty,

(n) *Recognizing* the importance for persons with disabilities of their individual autonomy and independence, including the freedom to make their own choices,

(o) *Considering* that persons with disabilities should have the opportunity to be actively involved in decision-making processes about policies and programmes, including those directly concerning them,

(p) *Concerned* about the difficult conditions faced by persons with disabilities who are subject to multiple or aggravated forms of discrimination on the basis of race, colour, sex, language, religion, political or other opinion, national, ethnic, indigenous or social origin, property, birth, age or other status,

(q) *Recognizing* that women and girls with disabilities are often at greater risk, both within and outside the home, of violence, injury or abuse, neglect or negligent treatment, maltreatment or exploitation,

(r) *Recognizing* that children with disabilities should have full enjoyment of all human rights and fundamental freedoms on an equal basis with other children, and recalling obligations to that end undertaken by States Parties to the Convention on the Rights of the Child,

(s) *Emphasizing* the need to incorporate a gender perspective in all efforts to promote the full enjoyment of human rights and fundamental freedoms by persons with disabilities,

(t) *Highlighting* the fact that the majority of persons with disabilities live in conditions of poverty, and in this regard recognizing the critical need to address the negative impact of poverty on persons with disabilities,

(u) *Bearing in mind* that conditions of peace and security based on full respect for the purposes and principles contained in the Charter of the United Nations and observance of applicable human rights instruments are indispensable for the full protection of persons with disabilities, in particular during armed conflicts and foreign occupation,

(v) *Recognizing* the importance of accessibility to the physical, social, economic and cultural environment, to health and education and to information and communication, in enabling persons with disabilities to fully enjoy all human rights and fundamental freedoms,

(w) *Realizing* that the individual, having duties to other individuals and to the community to which he or she belongs, is under a responsibility to strive for the promotion and observance of the rights recognized in the International Bill of Human Rights,

(x) *Convinced* that the family is the natural and fundamental group unit of society and is entitled to protection by society and the State, and that persons with disabilities and their family members should receive the necessary protection and assistance to enable families to contribute towards the full and equal enjoyment of the rights of persons with disabilities,

(y) *Convinced* that a comprehensive and integral international convention to promote and protect the rights and dignity of persons with disabilities will make a significant contribution to redressing the profound social disadvantage of persons with disabilities and promote their participation in the civil, political, economic, social and cultural spheres with equal opportunities, in both developing and developed countries,

Have agreed as follows:

Article 1

Purpose

The purpose of the present Convention is to promote, protect and ensure the full and equal enjoyment of all human rights and fundamental freedoms by all persons with disabilities, and to promote respect for their inherent dignity.

Persons with disabilities include those who have long-term physical, mental, intellectual or sensory impairments which in interaction with various barriers may hinder their full and effective participation in society on an equal basis with others.

Article 2

Definitions

For the purposes of the present Convention:

"Communication" includes languages, display of text, Braille, tactile communication, large print, accessible multimedia as well as written, audio, plain-language, human-reader and augmentative and alternative modes, means and formats of communication, including accessible information and communication technology; "Language" includes spoken and signed languages and other forms of non spoken languages;

"Discrimination on the basis of disability" means any distinction, exclusion or restriction on the basis of disability which has the purpose or effect of impairing or nullifying the recognition, enjoyment or exercise, on an equal basis with others, of all human rights and fundamental freedoms in the political, economic, social, cultural, civil or any other field. It includes all forms of discrimination, including denial of reasonable accommodation;

"Reasonable accommodation" means necessary and appropriate modification and adjustments not imposing a disproportionate or undue burden, where needed in a particular case, to ensure to persons with disabilities the enjoyment or exercise on an equal basis with others of all human rights and fundamental freedoms;

"Universal design" means the design of products, environments, programmes and services to be usable by all people, to the greatest extent possible, without the need for adaptation or specialized design. "Universal design" shall not exclude assistive devices for particular groups of persons with disabilities where this is needed.

Article 3

General principles

The principles of the present Convention shall be: (*a*) Respect for inherent dignity, individual autonomy including the freedom to make one's own choices, and independence of persons;

(*b*) Non-discrimination;

(*c*) Full and effective participation and inclusion in society;

(*d*) Respect for difference and acceptance of persons with disabilities as part of human diversity and humanity;

(*e*) Equality of opportunity;

(*f*) Accessibility;

(*g*) Equality between men and women;

(*h*) Respect for the evolving capacities of children with disabilities and respect for the right of children with disabilities to preserve their identities.

Article 4

General obligations

1. States Parties undertake to ensure and promote the full realization of all human rights and fundamental freedoms for all persons with disabilities without discrimination of any kind on the basis of disability. To this end, States Parties undertake:(*a*) To adopt all appropriate legislative, administrative and other measures for the implementation of the rights recognized in the present Convention;

(*b*) To take all appropriate measures, including legislation, to modify or abolish existing laws, regulations, customs and practices that constitute discrimination against persons with disabilities;

(*c*) To take into account the protection and promotion of the human rights of persons with disabilities in all policies and programmes;

(*d*) To refrain from engaging in any act or practice that is inconsistent with the present Convention and to ensure that public authorities and institutions act in conformity with the present Convention;

(*e*) To take all appropriate measures to eliminate discrimination on the basis of disability by any person, organization or private enterprise;

(*f*) To undertake or promote research and development of universally designed goods, services, equipment and facilities, as defined in Article 2 of the present Convention, which should require the minimum possible adaptation and the least cost to meet the specific needs of a person with disabilities, to promote their availability and use, and to promote universal design in the development of standards and guidelines;

(*g*) To undertake or promote research and development of, and to promote the availability and use of new technologies, including information and communications technologies, mobility aids, devices and assistive technologies, suitable for persons with disabilities, giving priority to technologies at an affordable cost;

(*h*) To provide accessible information to persons with disabilities about mobility aids, devices and assistive technologies, including new technologies, as well as other forms of assistance, support services and facilities;

(*i*) To promote the training of professionals and staff working with persons with disabilities in the rights recognized in the present Convention so as to better provide the assistance and services guaranteed by those rights.

2. With regard to economic, social and cultural rights, each State Party undertakes to take measures to the maximum of its available resources and, where needed, within the framework of international cooperation, with a view to achieving progressively the full realization of these rights, without prejudice to those obligations contained in the present Convention that are immediately applicable according to international law.

3. In the development and implementation of legislation and policies to implement the present Convention, and in other decision-making processes concerning issues relating to persons with disabilities, States Parties shall closely consult with and actively involve persons with disabilities, including children with disabilities, through their representative organizations.

4. Nothing in the present Convention shall affect any provisions which are more conducive to the realization of the rights of persons with disabilities and which may be contained in the law of a State Party or international law in force for that State. There shall be no restriction upon or derogation from any of the human rights and fundamental freedoms recognized or existing in any State Party to the present Convention pursuant to law, conventions, regulation or custom on the pretext that the present Convention does not recognize such rights or freedoms or that it recognizes them to a lesser extent.

5. The provisions of the present Convention shall extend to all parts of federal States without any limitations or exceptions.

Article 5
Equality and non-discrimination

1. States Parties recognize that all persons are equal before and under the law and are entitled without any discrimination to the equal protection and equal benefit of the law.

2. States Parties shall prohibit all discrimination on the basis of disability and guarantee to persons with disabilities equal and effective legal protection against discrimination on all grounds.

3. In order to promote equality and eliminate discrimination, States Parties shall take all appropriate steps to ensure that reasonable accommodation is provided.

4. Specific measures which are necessary to accelerate or achieve de facto equality of persons with disabilities shall not be considered discrimination under the terms of the present Convention.

Article 6
Women with disabilities

1. States Parties recognize that women and girls with disabilities are subject to multiple discrimination, and in this regard shall take measures to ensure the full and equal enjoyment by them of all human rights and fundamental freedoms.

2. States Parties shall take all appropriate measures to ensure the full development, advancement and empowerment of women, for the purpose of guaranteeing them the exercise and enjoyment of the human rights and fundamental freedoms set out in the present Convention.

Article 7
Children with disabilities

1. States Parties shall take all necessary measures to ensure the full enjoyment by children with disabilities of all human rights and fundamental freedoms on an equal basis with other children.

2. In all actions concerning children with disabilities, the best interests of the child shall be a primary consideration.

3. States Parties shall ensure that children with disabilities have the right to express their views freely on all matters affecting them, their views being given due weight in accordance with their age and maturity, on an equal basis with other children, and to be provided with disability and age-appropriate assistance to realize that right.

Article 8
Awareness-raising

1. States Parties undertake to adopt immediate, effective and appropriate measures:

(a) To raise awareness throughout society, including at the family level, regarding persons with disabilities, and to foster respect for the rights and dignity of persons with disabilities;

(b) To combat stereotypes, prejudices and harmful practices relating to persons with disabilities, including those based on sex and age, in all areas of life;

(c) To promote awareness of the capabilities and contributions of persons with disabilities.

2. Measures to this end include:

(a) Initiating and maintaining effective public awareness campaigns designed:

(i) To nurture receptiveness to the rights of persons with disabilities;

(ii) To promote positive perceptions and greater social awareness towards persons with disabilities;

(iii) To promote recognition of the skills, merits and abilities of persons with disabilities, and of their contributions to the workplace and the labour market;

(b) Fostering at all levels of the education system, including in all children from an early age, an attitude of respect for the rights of persons with disabilities;

(c) Encouraging all organs of the media to portray persons with disabilities in a manner consistent with the purpose of the present Convention;

(d) Promoting awareness-training programmes regarding persons with disabilities and the rights of persons with disabilities.

Article 9
Accessibility

1. To enable persons with disabilities to live independently and participate fully in all aspects of life, States Parties shall take appropriate measures to ensure to persons with disabilities access, on an equal basis with others, to the physical environment, to transportation, to information and communications, including information and communications technologies and systems, and to other facilities and services open or provided to the public, both in urban and in rural areas. These measures, which shall include the identification and elimination of obstacles and barriers to accessibility, shall apply to, inter alia:

(a) Buildings, roads, transportation and other indoor and outdoor facilities, including schools, housing, medical facilities and workplaces;

(b) Information, communications and other services, including electronic services and emergency services.

2. States Parties shall also take appropriate measures:

(a) To develop, promulgate and monitor the implementation of minimum standards and guidelines for the accessibility of facilities and services open or provided to the public;

(b) To ensure that private entities that offer facilities and services which are open or provided to the public take into account all aspects of accessibility for persons with disabilities;

(c) To provide training for stakeholders on accessibility issues facing persons with disabilities;

(d) To provide in buildings and other facilities open to the public signage in Braille and in easy to read and understand forms;

(e) To provide forms of live assistance and intermediaries, including guides, readers and professional sign language interpreters, to facilitate accessibility to buildings and other facilities open to the public;

(f) To promote other appropriate forms of assistance and support to persons with disabilities to ensure their access to information;

(g) To promote access for persons with disabilities to new information and communications technologies and systems, including the Internet;

(h) To promote the design, development, production and distribution of accessible information and communications technologies and systems at an early stage, so that these technologies and systems become accessible at minimum cost.

Article 10
Right to life

States Parties reaffirm that every human being has the inherent right to life and shall take all necessary measures to ensure its effective enjoyment by persons with disabilities on an equal basis with others.

Article 11
Situations of risk and humanitarian emergencies

States Parties shall take, in accordance with their obligations under international law, including international humanitarian law and international human rights law, all necessary measures to ensure the protection and safety of persons with disabilities in situations of risk, including situations of armed conflict, humanitarian emergencies and the occurrence of natural disasters.

Article 12
Equal recognition before the law

1. States Parties reaffirm that persons with disabilities have the right to recognition everywhere as persons before the law.

2. States Parties shall recognize that persons with disabilities enjoy legal capacity on an equal basis with others in all aspects of life.

3. States Parties shall take appropriate measures to provide access by persons with disabilities to the support they may require in exercising their legal capacity.

4. States Parties shall ensure that all measures that relate to the exercise of legal capacity provide for appropriate and effective safeguards to prevent abuse in accordance with international human rights law. Such safeguards shall ensure that measures relating to the exercise of legal capacity respect the rights, will and preferences of the person, are free of conflict of interest and undue influence, are proportional and tailored to the person's circumstances, apply for the shortest time possible and are subject to regular review by a competent, independent and impartial authority or judicial body. The safeguards shall be proportional to the degree to which such measures affect the person's rights and interests.

5. Subject to the provisions of this article, States Parties shall take all appropriate and effective measures to ensure the equal right of persons with disabilities to own or inherit property, to control their own financial affairs and to have equal access to bank loans, mortgages and other forms of financial credit, and shall ensure that persons with disabilities are not arbitrarily deprived of their property.

Article 13
Access to justice

1. States Parties shall ensure effective access to justice for persons with disabilities on an equal basis with others, including through the provision of procedural and age-appropriate accommodations, in order to facilitate their effective role as direct and indirect participants, including as witnesses, in illegal proceedings, including at investigative and other preliminary stages.

2. In order to help to ensure effective access to justice for persons with disabilities, States Parties shall promote appropriate training for those working in the field of administration of justice, including police and prison staff.

Article 14
Liberty and security of person

1. States Parties shall ensure that persons with disabilities, on an equal basis with others:

(*a*) Enjoy the right to liberty and security of person;

(*b*) Are not deprived of their liberty unlawfully or arbitrarily, and that any deprivation of liberty is in conformity with the law, and that the existence of a disability shall in no case justify a deprivation of liberty.

2. States Parties shall ensure that if persons with disabilities are deprived of their liberty through any process, they are, on an equal basis with others, entitled to guarantees in accordance with international human rights law and shall be treated in compliance with the objectives and principles of the present Convention, including by provision of reasonable accommodation.

Article 15
Freedom from torture or cruel, inhuman or degrading treatment or punishment

1. No one shall be subjected to torture or to cruel, inhuman or degrading treatment or punishment. In particular, no one shall be subjected without his or her free consent to medical or scientific experimentation.

2. States Parties shall take all effective legislative, administrative, judicial or other measures to prevent persons with disabilities, on an equal basis with others, from being subjected to torture or cruel, inhuman or degrading treatment or punishment.

Article 16
Freedom from exploitation, violence and abuse

1. States Parties shall take all appropriate legislative, administrative, social, educational and other measures to protect persons with disabilities, both within and outside the home, from all forms of exploitation, violence and abuse, including their gender-based aspects.

2. States Parties shall also take all appropriate measures to prevent all forms of exploitation, violence and abuse by ensuring, inter alia, appropriate forms of gender- and age-sensitive assistance and support for persons with disabilities and their families and caregivers, including through the provision of information and education on how to avoid, recognize and report instances of exploitation, violence and abuse. States Parties shall ensure that protection services are age-, gender- and disability-sensitive.

3. In order to prevent the occurrence of all forms of exploitation, violence and abuse, States Parties shall ensure that all facilities and programmes designed to serve persons with disabilities are effectively monitored by independent authorities.

4. States Parties shall take all appropriate measures to promote the physical, cognitive and psychological recovery, rehabilitation and social reintegration of persons with disabilities who become victims of any form of exploitation, violence or abuse, including through the provision of protection services. Such recovery and reintegration shall take place in an environment that fosters the health, welfare, self-respect, dignity and autonomy of the person and takes into account gender- and age-specific needs.

5. States Parties shall put in place effective legislation and policies, including women- and child-focused legislation and policies, to ensure that instances of exploitation, violence and abuse against persons with disabilities are identified, investigated and, where appropriate, prosecuted.

Article 17
Protecting the integrity of the person

Every person with disabilities has a right to respect for his or her physical and mental integrity on an equal basis with others.

Article 18
Liberty of movement and nationality

1. States Parties shall recognize the rights of persons with disabilities to liberty of movement, to freedom to choose their residence and to a nationality, on an equal basis with others, including by ensuring that persons with disabilities:

(a) Have the right to acquire and change a nationality and are not deprived of their nationality arbitrarily or on the basis of disability;

(b) Are not deprived, on the basis of disability, of their ability to obtain, possess and utilize documentation of their nationality or other documentation of identification, or to utilize relevant processes such as immigration proceedings, that may be needed to facilitate exercise of the right to liberty of movement;

(c) Are free to leave any country, including their own;

(d) Are not deprived, arbitrarily or on the basis of disability, of the right to enter their own country.

2. Children with disabilities shall be registered immediately after birth and shall have the right from birth to a name, the right to acquire a nationality and, as far as possible, the right to know and be cared for by their parents.

Article 19
Living independently and being included in the community

States Parties to the present Convention recognize the equal right of all persons with disabilities to live in the community, with choices equal to others, and shall take effective and appropriate measures to facilitate full enjoyment by persons with disabilities of this right and their full inclusion and participation in the community, including by ensuring that:

(a) Persons with disabilities have the opportunity to choose their place of residence and where and with whom they live on an equal basis with others and are not obliged to live in a particular living arrangement;

(b) Persons with disabilities have access to a range of in-home, residential and other community support services, including personal assistance necessary to support living and inclusion in the community, and to prevent isolation or segregation from the community;

(c) Community services and facilities for the general population are available on an equal basis to persons with disabilities and are responsive to their needs.

Article 20
Personal mobility

States Parties shall take effective measures to ensure personal mobility with the greatest possible independence for persons with disabilities, including by:

(a) Facilitating the personal mobility of persons with disabilities in the manner and at the time of their choice, and at affordable cost;

(b) Facilitating access by persons with disabilities to quality mobility aids, devices, assistive technologies and forms of live assistance and intermediaries, including by making them available at affordable cost;

(c) Providing training in mobility skills to persons with disabilities and to specialist staff working with persons with disabilities;

(d) Encouraging entities that produce mobility aids, devices and assistive technologies to take into account all aspects of mobility for persons with disabilities.

Article 21
Freedom of expression and opinion, and access to information

States Parties shall take all appropriate measures to ensure that persons with disabilities can exercise the right to freedom of expression and opinion, including the freedom to seek, receive and impart information and ideas on an equal basis with others and through all forms of communication of their choice, as defined in Article 2 of the present Convention, including by:

(a) Providing information intended for the general public to persons with disabilities in accessible formats and technologies appropriate to different kinds of disabilities in a timely manner and without additional cost;

(b) Accepting and facilitating the use of sign languages, Braille, augmentative and alternative communication, and all other accessible means, modes and formats of communication of their choice by persons with disabilities in official interactions;

(c) Urging private entities that provide services to the general public, including through the Internet, to provide information and services inaccessible and usable formats for persons with disabilities;

(d) Encouraging the mass media, including providers of information through the Internet, to make their services accessible to persons with disabilities;

(e) Recognizing and promoting the use of sign languages.

Article 22
Respect for privacy

1. No person with disabilities, regardless of place of residence or living arrangements, shall be subjected to arbitrary or unlawful interference with his or her privacy, family, home or correspondence or other types of communication or to unlawful attacks on his or her honour and reputation. Persons with disabilities have the right to the protection of the law against such interference or attacks.

2. States Parties shall protect the privacy of personal, health and rehabilitation information of persons with disabilities on an equal basis with others.

Article 23
Respect for home and the family

1. States Parties shall take effective and appropriate measures to eliminate discrimination against persons with disabilities in all matters relating to marriage, family, parenthood and relationships, on an equal basis with others, so as to ensure that:

(a) The right of all persons with disabilities who are of marriageable age to marry and to found a family on the basis of free and full consent of the intending spouses is recognized;

(b) The rights of persons with disabilities to decide freely and responsibly on the number and spacing of their children and to have access to age-appropriate information, reproductive and family planning education are recognized, and the means necessary to enable them to exercise these rights are provided;

(c) Persons with disabilities, including children, retain their fertility on an equal basis with others.

2. States Parties shall ensure the rights and responsibilities of persons with disabilities, with regard to guardianship, wardship, trusteeship, adoption of children or similar institutions, where these concepts exist in national legislation; in all cases the best interests of the child shall be paramount. States Parties shall render appropriate assistance to persons with disabilities in the performance of their child-rearing responsibilities.

3. States Parties shall ensure that children with disabilities have equal rights with respect to family life. With a view to realizing these rights, and to prevent concealment, abandonment, neglect and segregation of children with disabilities, States Parties shall undertake to provide early and comprehensive information, services and support to children with disabilities and their families.

4. States Parties shall ensure that a child shall not be separated from his or her parents against their will, except when competent authorities subject to judicial review determine, in accordance with applicable law and procedures, that such separation is necessary for the best interests of the child. In no case shall a child be separated from parents on the basis of a disability of either the child or one or both of the parents.

5. States Parties shall, where the immediate family is unable to care for a child with disabilities, undertake every effort to provide alternative care within the wider family, and failing that, within the community in a family setting.

Article 24
Education

1. States Parties recognize the right of persons with disabilities to education. With a view to realizing this right without discrimination and on the basis of equal opportunity, States Parties shall ensure an inclusive education system at all levels and lifelong learning directed to:

(a) The full development of human potential and sense of dignity and self-worth, and the strengthening of respect for human rights, fundamental freedoms and human diversity;

(b) The development by persons with disabilities of their personality, talents and creativity, as well as their mental and physical abilities, to their fullest potential;

(c) Enabling persons with disabilities to participate effectively in a free society.

2. In realizing this right, States Parties shall ensure that:

(a) Persons with disabilities are not excluded from the general education system on the basis of disability, and that children with disabilities are not excluded from free and compulsory primary education, or from secondary education, on the basis of disability;

(b) Persons with disabilities can access an inclusive, quality and free primary education and secondary education on an equal basis with others in the communities in which they live;

(c) Reasonable accommodation of the individual's requirements is provided;

(d) Persons with disabilities receive the support required, within the general education system, to facilitate their effective education;

(e) Effective individualized support measures are provided in environments that maximize academic and social development, consistent with the goal of full inclusion.

3. States Parties shall enable persons with disabilities to learn life and social development skills to facilitate their full and equal participation in education and as members of the community. To this end, States Parties shall take appropriate measures, including:

(a) Facilitating the learning of Braille, alternative script, augmentative and alternative modes, means and formats of communication and orientation and mobility skills, and facilitating peer support and mentoring;

(b) Facilitating the learning of sign language and the promotion of the linguistic identity of the deaf community;

(c) Ensuring that the education of persons, and in particular children, who are blind, deaf or deaf blind, is delivered in the most appropriate languages and modes and means of communication for the individual, and in environments which maximize academic and social development.

4. In order to help ensure the realization of this right, States Parties shall take appropriate measures to employ teachers, including teachers with disabilities, who are qualified in sign language and/or Braille, and to train professionals and staff who work at all levels of education. Such training shall incorporate disability awareness and the use of appropriate augmentative and alternative modes, means and formats of communication, educational techniques and materials to support persons with disabilities.

5. States Parties shall ensure that persons with disabilities are able to access general tertiary education, vocational training, adult education and lifelong learning without discrimination and on an equal basis with others. To this end, States Parties shall ensure that reasonable accommodation is provided to persons with disabilities.

Article 25
Health
States Parties recognize that persons with disabilities have the right to the enjoyment of the highest attainable standard of health without discrimination on the basis of disability. States Parties shall take all appropriate measures to ensure access for persons with disabilities to health services that are gender-sensitive, including health-related rehabilitation. In particular, States Parties shall:

(a) Provide persons with disabilities with the same range, quality and standard of free or affordable health care and programmes as provided to other persons, including in the area of sexual and reproductive health and population-based public health programmes;

(b) Provide those health services needed by persons with disabilities specifically because of their disabilities, including early identification and intervention as appropriate, and services designed to minimize and prevent further disabilities, including among children and older persons;

(c) Provide these health services as close as possible to people's own communities, including in rural areas;

(d) Require health professionals to provide care of the same quality to persons with disabilities as to others, including on the basis of free and informed consent by, inter alia, raising awareness of the human rights, dignity, autonomy and needs of persons with disabilities through training and the promulgation of ethical standards for public and private health care;

(e) Prohibit discrimination against persons with disabilities in the provision of health insurance, and life insurance where such insurance is permitted by national law, which shall be provided in a fair and reasonable manner;

(f) Prevent discriminatory denial of health care or health services or food and fluids on the basis of disability.

Article 26
Habilitation and rehabilitation
1. States Parties shall take effective and appropriate measures, including through peer support, to enable persons with disabilities to attain and maintain maximum independence, full physical, mental, social and vocational ability, and full inclusion and participation in all aspects of life. To that end, States Parties shall organize, strengthen and extend comprehensive habilitation and rehabilitation services and programmes, particularly in the areas of health, employment, education and social services, in such a way that these services and programmes:

(a) Begin at the earliest possible stage, and are based on the multidisciplinary assessment of individual needs and strengths;

(b) Support participation and inclusion in the community and all aspects of society, are voluntary, and are available to persons with disabilities as close as possible to their own communities, including in rural areas.

2. States Parties shall promote the development of initial and continuing training for professionals and staff working in habilitation and rehabilitation services.

3. States Parties shall promote the availability, knowledge and use of assistive devices and technologies, designed for persons with disabilities, as they relate to habilitation and rehabilitation.

Article 27
Work and employment
1. States Parties recognize the right of persons with disabilities to work, on an equal basis with others; this includes the right to the opportunity to gain a living by work freely chosen or accepted in a labour market and work environment that is open, inclusive and accessible to persons with disabilities. States Parties shall safeguard and promote the realization of the right to work, including for those who acquire a disability during the course of employment, by taking appropriate steps, including through legislation, to, inter alia:

(a) Prohibit discrimination on the basis of disability with regard to all matters concerning all forms of employment, including conditions of recruitment, hiring and employment, continuance of employment, career advancement and safe and healthy working conditions;

(b) Protect the rights of persons with disabilities, on an equal basis with others, to just and favourable conditions of work, including equal opportunities and equal remuneration for work of equal value, safe and healthy working conditions, including protection from harassment, and the redress of grievances;

(c) Ensure that persons with disabilities are able to exercise their labour and trade union rights on an equal basis with others;

(d) Enable persons with disabilities to have effective access to general technical and vocational guidance programmes, placement services and vocational and continuing training;

(e) Promote employment opportunities and career advancement for persons with disabilities in the labour market, as well as assistance in finding, obtaining, maintaining and returning to employment;

(f) Promote opportunities for self-employment, entrepreneurship, the development of cooperatives and starting one's own business;

(g) Employ persons with disabilities in the public sector;

(h) Promote the employment of persons with disabilities in the private sector through appropriate policies and measures, which may include affirmative action programmes, incentives and other measures;

(i) Ensure that reasonable accommodation is provided to persons with disabilities in the workplace;

(j) Promote the acquisition by persons with disabilities of work experience in the open labour market;

(k) Promote vocational and professional rehabilitation, job retention and return-to-work programmes for persons with disabilities.

2. States Parties shall ensure that persons with disabilities are not held in slavery or in servitude, and are protected, on an equal basis with others, from forced or compulsory labour.

Article 28
Adequate standard of living and social protection

1. States Parties recognize the right of persons with disabilities to an adequate standard of living for themselves and their families, including adequate food, clothing and housing, and to the continuous improvement of living conditions, and shall take appropriate steps to safeguard and promote the realization of this right without discrimination on the basis of disability.

2. States Parties recognize the right of persons with disabilities to social protection and to the enjoyment of that right without discrimination on the basis of disability, and shall take appropriate steps to safeguard and promote the realization of this right, including measures:

(a) To ensure equal access by persons with disabilities to clean water services, and to ensure access to appropriate and affordable services, devices and other assistance for disability-related needs;

(b) To ensure access by persons with disabilities, in particular women and girls with disabilities and older persons with disabilities, to social protection programmes and poverty reduction programmes;

(c) To ensure access by persons with disabilities and their families living in situations of poverty to assistance from the State with disability related expenses, including adequate training, counselling, financial assistance and respite care;

(d) To ensure access by persons with disabilities to public housing programmes;

(e) To ensure equal access by persons with disabilities to retirement benefits and programmes.

Article 29
Participation in political and public life

States Parties shall guarantee to persons with disabilities political rights and the opportunity to enjoy them on an equal basis with others, and shall undertake:

(a) To ensure that persons with disabilities can effectively and fully participate in political and public life on an equal basis with others, directly or through freely chosen representatives, including the right and opportunity for persons with disabilities to vote and be elected, inter alia, by:

(i) Ensuring that voting procedures, facilities and materials are appropriate, accessible and easy to understand and use;

(ii) Protecting the right of persons with disabilities to vote by secret ballot in elections and public referendums without intimidation, and to stand for elections, to effectively hold office and perform all public functions at all levels of government, facilitating the use of assistive and new technologies where appropriate;

(iii) Guaranteeing the free expression of the will of persons with disabilities as electors and to this end, where necessary, at their request, allowing assistance in voting by a person of their own choice;

(b) To promote actively an environment in which persons with disabilities can effectively and fully participate in the conduct of public affairs, without discrimination and on an equal basis with others, and encourage their participation in public affairs, including:

(i) Participation in non-governmental organizations and associations concerned with the public and political life of the country, and in the activities and administration of political parties;

(ii) Forming and joining organizations of persons with disabilities to represent persons with disabilities at international, national, regional and local levels.

Article 30

Participation in cultural life, recreation, leisure and sport

1. States Parties recognize the right of persons with disabilities to take part on an equal basis with others in cultural life, and shall take all appropriate measures to ensure that persons with disabilities:

(a) Enjoy access to cultural materials in accessible formats;

(b) Enjoy access to television programmes, films, theatre and other cultural activities, in accessible formats;

(c) Enjoy access to places for cultural performances or services, such as theatres, museums, cinemas, libraries and tourism services, and, as far as possible, enjoy access to monuments and sites of national cultural importance.

2. States Parties shall take appropriate measures to enable persons with disabilities to have the opportunity to develop and utilize their creative, artistic and intellectual potential, not only for their own benefit, but also for the enrichment of society.

3. States Parties shall take all appropriate steps, in accordance with international law, to ensure that laws protecting intellectual property rights do not constitute an unreasonable or discriminatory barrier to access by persons with disabilities to cultural materials.

4. Persons with disabilities shall be entitled, on an equal basis with others, to recognition and support of their specific cultural and linguistic identity, including sign languages and deaf culture

5. With a view to enabling persons with disabilities to participate on an equal basis with others in recreational, leisure and sporting activities, States Parties shall take appropriate measures:

(a) To encourage and promote the participation, to the fullest extent possible, of persons with disabilities in mainstream sporting activities at all levels;

(b) To ensure that persons with disabilities have an opportunity to organize, develop and participate in disability-specific sporting and recreational activities and, to this end, encourage the provision, on an equal basis with others, of appropriate instruction, training and resources;

(c) To ensure that persons with disabilities have access to sporting, recreational and tourism venues;

(d) To ensure that children with disabilities have equal access with other children to participation in play, recreation and leisure and sporting activities, including those activities in the school system;

(e) To ensure that persons with disabilities have access to services from those involved in the organization of recreational, tourism, leisure and sporting activities.

Article 31

Statistics and data collection

1. States Parties undertake to collect appropriate information, including statistical and research data, to enable them to formulate and implement policies to give effect to the present Convention. The process of collecting and maintaining this information shall:

(a) Comply with legally established safeguards, including legislation on data protection, to ensure confidentiality and respect for the privacy of persons with disabilities;

(b) Comply with internationally accepted norms to protect human rights and fundamental freedoms and ethical principles in the collection and use of statistics.

2. The information collected in accordance with this article shall be disaggregated, as appropriate, and used to help assess the implementation of States Parties' obligations under the present Convention and to identify and address the barriers faced by persons with disabilities in exercising their rights.

3. States Parties shall assume responsibility for the dissemination of these statistics and ensure their accessibility to persons with disabilities and others.

Article 32

International cooperation

1. States Parties recognize the importance of international cooperation and its promotion, in support of national efforts for the realization of the purpose and objectives of the present Convention, and will undertake appropriate and effective measures in this regard, between and among States and, as appropriate, in partnership with relevant international and regional organizations and civil society, in particular organizations of persons with disabilities. Such measures could include, inter alia:

(a) Ensuring that international cooperation, including international development programmes, is inclusive of and accessible to persons with disabilities;

(b) Facilitating and supporting capacity-building, including through the exchange and sharing of information, experiences, training programmes and best practices;

(c) Facilitating cooperation in research and access to scientific andtechnical knowledge;

(d) Providing, as appropriate, technical and economic assistance, including by facilitating access to and sharing of accessible and assistive technologies, and through the transfer of technologies.

2. The provisions of this article are without prejudice to the obligations of each State Party to fulfil its obligations under the present Convention.

Article 33

National implementation and monitoring

1. States Parties, in accordance with their system of organization, shall designate one or more focal points within government for matters relating to the implementation of the present Convention, and shall give due consideration to the establishment or designation of a coordination mechanism within government to facilitate related action in different sectors and at different levels.

2. States Parties shall, in accordance with their legal and administrative systems, maintain, strengthen, designate or establish within the State Party, a framework, including one or more independent mechanisms, as appropriate, to promote, protect and monitor implementation of the present Convention. When designating or establishing such a mechanism, States Parties shall take into account the principles relating to the status and functioning of national institutions for protection and promotion of human rights.

3. Civil society, in particular persons with disabilities and their representative organizations, shall be involved and participate fully in the monitoring process.

Article 34

Committee on the Rights of Persons with Disabilities

1. There shall be established a Committee on the Rights of Persons with Disabilities (hereafter referred to as "the Committee"), which shall carry out the functions hereinafter provided.

2. The Committee shall consist, at the time of entry into force of the present Convention, of twelve experts. After an additional sixty ratifications or accessions to the Convention, the membership of the Committee shall increase by six members, attaining a maximum number of eighteen members.

3. The members of the Committee shall serve in their personal capacity and shall be of high moral standing and recognized competence and experience in the field covered by the present Convention. When nominating their candidates, States Parties are invited to give due consideration to the provision set out in Article 4, paragraph 3, of the present Convention.

4. The members of the Committee shall be elected by States Parties, consideration being given to equitable geographical distribution, representation of the different forms of civilization and of the principal legal systems, balanced gender representation and participation of experts with disabilities.

5. The members of the Committee shall be elected by secret ballot from a list of persons nominated by the States Parties from among their nationals at meetings of the Conference of States Parties. At those meetings, for which two thirds of States Parties shall constitute a quorum, the persons elected to the Committee shall be those who obtain the largest number of votes and an absolute majority of the votes of the representatives of States Parties present and voting.

6. The initial election shall be held no later than six months after the date of entry into force of the present Convention. At least four months before the date of each election, the Secretary-General of the United Nations shall address a letter to the States Parties inviting them to submit the nominations within two months. The Secretary-General shall subsequently prepare a list in alphabetical order of all persons thus nominated, indicating the State Parties which have nominated them, and shall submit it to the States Parties to the present Convention.

7. The members of the Committee shall be elected for a term of four years. They shall be eligible for re-election once. However, the term of six of the members elected at the first election shall expire at the end of two years; immediately after the first election, the names of these six members shall be chosen by lot by the chairperson of the meeting referred to in paragraph 5 of this article.

8. The election of the six additional members of the Committee shall be held on the occasion of regular elections, in accordance with the relevant provisions of this article.

9. If a member of the Committee dies or resigns or declares that for any other cause she or he can no longer perform her or his duties, the State Party which nominated the member shall appoint another expert

possessing the qualifications and meeting the requirements set out in the relevant provisions of this article, to serve for the remainder of the term.

10. The Committee shall establish its own rules of procedure.

11. The Secretary-General of the United Nations shall provide the necessary staff and facilities for the effective performance of the functions of the Committee under the present Convention, and shall convene its initial meeting.

12. With the approval of the General Assembly of the United Nations, the members of the Committee established under the present Convention shall receive emoluments from United Nations resources on such terms and conditions as the Assembly may decide, having regard to the importance of the Committee's responsibilities.

13. The members of the Committee shall be entitled to the facilities, privileges and immunities of experts on mission for the United Nations as laid down in the relevant sections of the Convention on the Privileges and Immunities of the United Nations.

Article 35
Reports by States Parties

1. Each State Party shall submit to the Committee, through the Secretary-General of the United Nations, a comprehensive report on measures taken to give effect to its obligations under the present Convention and on the progress made in that regard, within two years after the entry into force of the present Convention for the State Party concerned.

2. Thereafter, States Parties shall submit subsequent reports at least every four years and further whenever the Committee so requests.

3. The Committee shall decide any guidelines applicable to the content of the reports.

4. A State Party which has submitted a comprehensive initial report to the Committee need not, in its subsequent reports, repeat information previously provided. When preparing reports to the Committee, States Parties are invited to consider doing so in an open and transparent process and to give due consideration to the provision set out in Article 4, paragraph 3, of the present Convention.

5. Reports may indicate factors and difficulties affecting the degree of fulfillment of obligations under the present Convention.

Article 36
Consideration of reports

1. Each report shall be considered by the Committee, which shall make such suggestions and general recommendations on the report as it may consider appropriate and shall forward these to the State Party concerned. The State Party may respond with any information it chooses to the Committee. The Committee may request further information from States Parties relevant to the implementation of the present Convention.

2. If a State Party is significantly overdue in the submission of a report, the Committee may notify the State Party concerned of the need to examine the implementation of the present Convention in that State Party, on the basis of reliable information available to the Committee, if the relevant report is not submitted within three months following the notification. The Committee shall invite the State Party concerned to participate in such examination. Should the State Party respond by submitting the relevant report, the provisions of paragraph 1 of this article will apply.

3. The Secretary-General of the United Nations shall make available the reports to all States Parties.

4. States Parties shall make their reports widely available to the public in their own countries and facilitate access to the suggestions and general recommendations relating to these reports.

5. The Committee shall transmit, as it may consider appropriate, to the specialized agencies, funds and programmes of the United Nations, and other competent bodies, reports from States Parties in order to address a request or indication of a need for technical advice or assistance contained therein, along with the Committee's observations and recommendations, if any, on these requests or indications.

Article 37
Cooperation between States Parties and the Committee

1. Each State Party shall cooperate with the Committee and assist its members in the fulfillment of their mandate.

2. In its relationship with States Parties, the Committee shall give due consideration to ways and means of enhancing national capacities for the implementation of the present Convention, including through international cooperation.

Article 38
Relationship of the Committee with other bodies

In order to foster the effective implementation of the present Convention and to encourage international cooperation in the field covered by the present Convention:

(a) The specialized agencies and other United Nations organs shall be entitled to be represented at the consideration of the implementation of such provisions of the present Convention as fall within the scope of their mandate.

The Committee may invite the specialized agencies and other competent bodies as it may consider appropriate to provide expert advice on the implementation of the Convention in areas falling within the scope of their respective mandates. The Committee may invite specialized agencies and other United Nations organs to submit reports on the implementation of the Convention in areas falling within the scope of their activities;

(b) The Committee, as it discharges its mandate, shall consult, as appropriate, other relevant bodies instituted by international human rights treaties, with a view to ensuring the consistency of their respective reporting guidelines, suggestions and general recommendations, and avoiding duplication and overlap in the performance of their functions.

Article 39
Report of the Committee

The Committee shall report every two years to the General Assembly and to the Economic and Social Council on its activities, and may make suggestions and general recommendations based on the examination of reports and information received from the States Parties. Such suggestions and general recommendations shall be included in the report of the Committee together with comments, if any, from States Parties.

Article 40
Conference of States Parties

1. The States Parties shall meet regularly in a Conference of States Parties in order to consider any matter with regard to the implementation of the present Convention.

2. No later than six months after the entry into force of the present Convention, the Conference of States Parties shall be convened by the Secretary-General of the United Nations. The subsequent meetings shall be convened by the Secretary-General biennially or upon the decision of the Conference of States Parties.

Article 41
Depositary

The Secretary-General of the United Nations shall be the depositary of the present Convention.

Article 42
Signature

The present Convention shall be open for signature by all States and by regional integration organizations at United Nations Headquarters in New York as of 30 March 2007.

Article 43
Consent to be bound

The present Convention shall be subject to ratification by signatory States and to formal confirmation by signatory regional integration organizations. It shall be open for accession by any State or regional integration organization which has not signed the Convention.

Article 44
Regional integration organizations

1. "Regional integration organization" shall mean an organization constituted by sovereign States of a given region, to which its member States have transferred competence in respect of matters governed by the present Convention. Such organizations shall declare, in their instruments of formal confirmation or accession, the extent of their competence with respect to matters governed by the present Convention. Subsequently, they shall inform the depositary of any substantial modification in the extent of their competence.

2. References to "States Parties" in the present Convention shall apply to such organizations within the limits of their competence.

3. For the purposes of Article 45, paragraph 1, and Article 47, paragraphs 2 and 3, of the present Convention, any instrument deposited by a regional integration organization shall not be counted.

4. Regional integration organizations, in matters within their competence, may exercise their right to vote in the Conference of States Parties, with a number of votes equal to the number of their member States

that are Parties to the present Convention. Such an organization shall not exercise its right to vote if any of its member States exercises its right, and vice versa.

Article 45
Entry into force

1. The present Convention shall enter into force on the thirtieth day after the deposit of the twentieth instrument of ratification or accession.

2. For each State or regional integration organization ratifying, formally confirming or acceding to the present Convention after the deposit of the twentieth such instrument, the Convention shall enter into force on the thirtieth day after the deposit of its own such instrument.

Article 46
Reservations

1. Reservations incompatible with the object and purpose of the present Convention shall not be permitted.

2. Reservations may be withdrawn at any time.

Article 47
Amendments

1. Any State Party may propose an amendment to the present Convention and submit it to the Secretary-General of the United Nations. The Secretary-General shall communicate any proposed amendments to States Parties, with a request to be notified whether they favour a conference of States Parties for the purpose of considering and deciding upon the proposals. In the event that, within four months from the date of such communication, at least one third of the States Parties favour such a conference, the Secretary-General shall convene the conference under the auspices of the United Nations. Any amendment adopted by a majority of two thirds of the States Parties present and voting shall be submitted by the Secretary-General to the General Assembly of the United Nations for approval and thereafter to all States Parties for acceptance.

2. An amendment adopted and approved in accordance with paragraph 1 of this article shall enter into force on the thirtieth day after the number of instruments of acceptance deposited reaches two thirds of the number of States Parties at the date of adoption of the amendment. Thereafter, the amendment shall enter into force for any State Party on the thirtieth day following the deposit of its own instrument of acceptance. An amendment shall be binding only on those States Parties which have accepted it.

3. If so decided by the Conference of States Parties by consensus, an amendment adopted and approved in accordance with paragraph 1 of this article which relates exclusively to articles 34, 38, 39 and 40 shall enter into force for all States Parties on the thirtieth day after the number of instruments of acceptance deposited reaches two thirds of the number of States Parties atthe date of adoption of the amendment.

Article 48
Denunciation

A State Party may denounce the present Convention by written notification to the Secretary-General of the United Nations. The denunciation shall become effective one year after the date of receipt of the notification by the Secretary-General.

Article 49
Accessible format

The text of the present Convention shall be made available in accessible formats.

Article 50
Authentic texts

The Arabic, Chinese, English, French, Russian and Spanish texts of the present Convention shall be equally authentic.

IN WITNESS THEREOF the undersigned plenipotentiaries, being duly authorized thereto by their respective Governments, have signed the present Convention.

DOCUMENT 45

Full Official Title: International Convention for the Protection of all Persons from Enforced Disappearance

Short Title/Acronym/Abbreviation: Convention on Disappearances

Type of Document: This is a treaty, a legal instrument. This convention was adopted by the U.N. General Assembly upon the recommendation of an Inter-sessional Open-ended Working Group established in 2003 by the U.N. Commission on Human Rights to prepare the draft text. The U.N. Human Rights Council adopted the treaty in its first session in June 2006, and sent it to the General Assembly, which passed it in December 2006.

Subject: Enforced disappearances, non-refoulement

Official Citation: General Assembly Doc A/61/488

Date of Document: December 20, 2006

Date of Adoption: December 20, 2006

Date of General Entry into Force (EIF): According to Article 39, the treaty will enter into force after 20 states have ratified it.

Number of States Parties as of this printing: 23

Date of Signature by the United States: Has not signed

Date of Ratification/Accession/Adhesion: Not applicable

Date of Entry into Force as to United States (effective date): Not applicable

Legal Status/Character of the Instrument/Document as to the United States: The United States is not a party to this treaty.

Supervising Body: Committee on Enforced Disappearances

Comment: The United Nations established a Working Group in 1980 that has continued ever since, in order to ensure protection for victims of enforced disappearances. The convention of 2006 defines enforced disappearances as a crime against humanity, and calls for an end to the practice, impunity, and the protection of the individual.

Caution: The status and applicability of this instrument as to the United States may have changed since the date of this publication.

Web Address: http://www2.ohchr.org/english/law/disappearance-convention.htm

International Convention for the Protection of all Persons from Enforced Disappearance (Excerpts)

Preamble

The States Parties to this Convention,

Considering the obligation of States under the Charter of the United Nations to promote universal respect for, and observance of, human rights and fundamental freedoms,

Having regard to the Universal Declaration of Human Rights

Recalling the International Covenant on Economic, Social and Cultural Rights, the International Covenant on Civil and Political Rights and the other relevant international instruments in the fields of human rights, humanitarian law and international criminal law,

Also recalling the Declaration on the Protection of All Persons from Enforced Disappearance adopted by the General Assembly of the United Nations in its resolution 47/133 of 18 December 1992,

Aware of the extreme seriousness of enforced disappearance, which constitutes a crime and, in certain circumstances defined in international law, a crime against humanity,

Determined to prevent enforced disappearances and to combat impunity for the crime of enforced disappearance,

Considering the right of any person not to be subjected to enforced disappearance, the right of victims to justice and to reparation,

Affirming the right of any victim to know the truth about the circumstances of an enforced disappearance and the fate of the disappeared person, and the right to freedom to seek, receive and impart information to this end,

Have agreed on the following articles:

PART I

Article 1

1. No one shall be subjected to enforced disappearance. 2. No exceptional circumstances whatsoever, whether a state of war or a threat of war, internal political instability or any other public emergency, may be invoked as a justification for enforced disappearance.

...

Article 2

For the purposes of this Convention, "enforced disappearance" is considered to be the arrest, detention, abduction or any other form of deprivation of liberty by agents of the State or by persons or groups of persons acting with the authorization, support or acquiescence of the State, followed by a refusal to acknowledge the deprivation of liberty or by concealment of the fate or whereabouts of the disappeared person, which place such a person outside the protection of the law.

Article 3

Each State Party shall take appropriate measures to investigate acts defined in Article 2 committed by persons or groups of persons acting without the authorization, support or acquiescence of the State and to bring those responsible to justice.

Article 4

Each State Party shall take the necessary measures to ensure that enforced disappearance constitutes an offence under its criminal law.

Article 5

The widespread or systematic practice of enforced disappearance constitutes a crime against humanity as defined in applicable international law and shall attract the consequences provided for under such applicable international law.

Article 6

1. Each State Party shall take the necessary measures to hold criminally responsible at least:

(*a*) Any person who commits, orders, solicits or induces the commission of, attempts to commit, is an accomplice to or participates in an enforced disappearance;

(*b*) A superior who:

(i) Knew, or consciously disregarded information which clearly indicated, that subordinates under his or her effective authority and control were committing or about to commit a crime of enforced disappearance;

(ii) Exercised effective responsibility for and control over activities which were concerned with the crime of enforced disappearance; and

(iii) Failed to take all necessary and reasonable measures within his or her power to prevent or repress the commission of an enforced disappearance or to submit the matter to the competent authorities for investigation and prosecution;

(*c*) Subparagraph (*b*) above is without prejudice to the higher standards of responsibility applicable under relevant international law to a military commander or to a person effectively acting as a military commander.

2. No order or instruction from any public authority, civilian, military or other, may be invoked to justify an offence of enforced disappearance.

Article 7

1. Each State Party shall make the offence of enforced disappearance punishable by appropriate penalties which take into account its extreme seriousness.

2. Each State Party may establish:

(*a*) Mitigating circumstances, in particular for persons who, having been implicated in the commission of an enforced disappearance, effectively contribute to bringing the disappeared person forward alive or make it possible to clarify cases of enforced disappearance or to identify the perpetrators of an enforced disappearance;

(*b*) Without prejudice to other criminal procedures, aggravating circumstances, in particular in the event of the death of the disappeared person or the commission of an enforced disappearance in respect of pregnant women, minors, persons with disabilities or other particularly vulnerable persons.

Article 8

Without prejudice to Article 5,

1. A State Party which applies a statute of limitations in respect of enforced disappearance shall take the necessary measures to ensure that the term of limitation for criminal proceedings:

(*a*) Is of long duration and is proportionate to the extreme seriousness of this offence;

(*b*) Commences from the moment when the offence of enforced disappearance ceases, taking into account its continuous nature.

2. Each State Party shall guarantee the right of victims of enforced disappearance to an effective remedy during the term of limitation.

Article 9

1. Each State Party shall take the necessary measures to establish its competence to exercise jurisdiction over the offence of enforced disappearance:

(a) When the offence is committed in any territory under its jurisdiction or on board a ship or aircraft registered in that State;

(b) When the alleged offender is one of its nationals;

(c) When the disappeared person is one of its nationals and the State Party considers it appropriate.

2. Each State Party shall likewise take such measures as may be necessary to establish its competence to exercise jurisdiction over the offence of enforced disappearance when the alleged offender is present in any territory under its jurisdiction, unless it extradites or surrenders him or her to another State in accordance with its international obligations or surrenders him or her to an international criminal tribunal whose jurisdiction it has recognized.

3. This Convention does not exclude any additional criminal jurisdiction exercised in accordance with national law.

Article 10

1. Upon being satisfied, after an examination of the information available to it, that the circumstances so warrant, any State Party in whose territory a person suspected of having committed an offence of enforced disappearance is present shall take him or her into custody or take such other legal measures as are necessary to ensure his or her presence. The custody and other legal measures shall be as provided for in the law of that State Party but may be maintained only for such time as is necessary to ensure the person's presence at criminal, surrender or extradition proceedings.

2. A State Party which has taken the measures referred to in paragraph 1 of this article shall immediately carry out a preliminary inquiry or investigations to establish the facts. It shall notify the States Parties referred to in Article 9, paragraph 1, of the measures it has taken in pursuance of paragraph 1 of this article, including detention and the circumstances warranting detention, and of the findings of its preliminary inquiry or its investigations, indicating whether it intends to exercise its jurisdiction.

3. Any person in custody pursuant to paragraph 1 of this article may communicate immediately with the nearest appropriate representative of the State of which he or she is a national, or, if he or she is a stateless person, with the representative of the State where he or she usually resides.

Article 11

1. The State Party in the territory under whose jurisdiction a person alleged to have committed an offence of enforced disappearance is found shall, if it does not extradite that person or surrender him or her to another State in accordance with its international obligations or surrender him or her to an international criminal tribunal whose jurisdiction it has recognized, submit the case to its competent authorities for the purpose of prosecution.

2. These authorities shall take their decision in the same manner as in the case of any ordinary offence of a serious nature under the law of that State Party. In the cases referred to in Article 9, paragraph 2, the standards of evidence required for prosecution and conviction shall in no way be less stringent than those which apply in the cases referred to in Article 9, paragraph 1.

3. Any person against whom proceedings are brought in connection with an offence of enforced disappearance shall be guaranteed fair treatment at all stages of the proceedings. Any person tried for an offence of enforced disappearance shall benefit from a fair trial before a competent, independent and impartial court or tribunal established by law.

Article 12

1. Each State Party shall ensure that any individual who alleges that a person has been subjected to enforced disappearance has the right to report the facts to the competent authorities, which shall examine the allegation promptly and impartially and, where necessary, undertake without delay a thorough and impartial investigation. Appropriate steps shall be taken, where necessary, to ensure that the complainant, witnesses, relatives of the disappeared person and their defence counsel, as well as persons participating in the investigation, are protected against all ill-treatment or intimidation as a consequence of the complaint or any evidence given.

2. Where there are reasonable grounds for believing that a person has been subjected to enforced disappearance, the authorities referred to in paragraph 1 of this article shall undertake an investigation, even if there has been no formal complaint.

3. Each State Party shall ensure that the authorities referred to in paragraph 1 of this article:

(*a*) Have the necessary powers and resources to conduct the investigation effectively, including access to the documentation and other information relevant to their investigation;

(*b*) Have access, if necessary with the prior authorization of a judicial authority, which shall rule promptly on the matter, to any place of detention or any other place where there are reasonable grounds to believe that the disappeared person may be present.

4. Each State Party shall take the necessary measures to prevent and sanction acts that hinder the conduct of an investigation. It shall ensure in particular that persons suspected of having committed an offence of enforced disappearance are not in a position to influence the progress of an investigation by means of pressure or acts of intimidation or reprisal aimed at the complainant, witnesses, relatives of the disappeared person or their defence counsel, or at persons participating in the investigation.

Article 13

1. For the purposes of extradition between States Parties, the offence of enforced disappearance shall not be regarded as a political offence or as an offence connected with a political offence or as an offence inspired by political motives. Accordingly, a request for extradition based on such an offence may not be refused on these grounds alone.

2. The offence of enforced disappearance shall be deemed to be included as an extraditable offence in any extradition treaty existing between States Parties before the entry into force of this Convention.

3. States Parties undertake to include the offence of enforced disappearance as an extraditable offence in any extradition treaty subsequently to be concluded between them.

4. If a State Party which makes extradition conditional on the existence of a treaty receives a request for extradition from another State Party with which it has no extradition treaty, it may consider this Convention as the necessary legal basis for extradition in respect of the offence of enforced disappearance.

5. States Parties which do not make extradition conditional on the existence of a treaty shall recognize the offence of enforced disappearance as an extraditable offence between themselves.

6. Extradition shall, in all cases, be subject to the conditions provided for by the law of the requested State Party or by applicable extradition treaties, including, in particular, conditions relating to the minimum penalty requirement for extradition and the grounds upon which the requested State Party may refuse extradition or make it subject to certain conditions.

7. Nothing in this Convention shall be interpreted as imposing an obligation to extradite if the requested State Party has substantial grounds for believing that the request has been made for the purpose of prosecuting or punishing a person on account of that person's sex, race, religion, nationality, ethnic origin, political opinions or membership of a particular social group, or that compliance with the request would cause harm to that person for any one of these reasons.

Article 14

1. States Parties shall afford one another the greatest measure of mutual legal assistance in connection with criminal proceedings brought in respect of an offence of enforced disappearance, including the supply of all evidence at their disposal that is necessary for the proceedings.

2. Such mutual legal assistance shall be subject to the conditions provided for by the domestic law of the requested State Party or by applicable treaties on mutual legal assistance, including, in particular, the conditions in relation to the grounds upon which the requested State Party may refuse to grant mutual legal assistance or may make it subject to conditions.

Article 15

States Parties shall cooperate with each other and shall afford one another the greatest measure of mutual assistance with a view to assisting victims of enforced disappearance, and in searching for, locating and releasing disappeared persons and, in the event of death, in exhuming and identifying them and returning their remains.

Article 16

1. No State Party shall expel, return ("refouler"), surrender or extradite a person to another State where there are substantial grounds for believing that he or she would be in danger of being subjected to enforced disappearance.

2. For the purpose of determining whether there are such grounds, the competent authorities shall take into account all relevant considerations, including, where applicable, the existence in the State concerned of a consistent pattern of gross, flagrant or mass violations of human rights or of serious violations of international humanitarian law.

Article 17

1. No one shall be held in secret detention.

2. Without prejudice to other international obligations of the State Party with regard to the deprivation of liberty, each State Party shall, in its legislation:

(a) Establish the conditions under which orders of deprivation of liberty may be given;

(b) Indicate those authorities authorized to order the deprivation of liberty;

(c) Guarantee that any person deprived of liberty shall be held solely in officially recognized and supervised places of deprivation of liberty;

(d) Guarantee that any person deprived of liberty shall be authorized to communicate with and be visited by his or her family, counsel or any other person of his or her choice, subject only to the conditions established by law, or, if he or she is a foreigner, to communicate with his or her consular authorities, in accordance with applicable international law;

(e) Guarantee access by the competent and legally authorized authorities and institutions to the places where persons are deprived of liberty, if necessary with prior authorization from a judicial authority;

(f) Guarantee that any person deprived of liberty or, in the case of a suspected enforced disappearance, since the person deprived of liberty is not able to exercise this right, any persons with a legitimate interest, such as relatives of the person deprived of liberty, their representatives or their counsel, shall, in all circumstances, be entitled to take proceedings before a court, in order that the court may decide without delay on the lawfulness of the deprivation of liberty and order the person's release if such deprivation of liberty is not lawful.

3. Each State Party shall assure the compilation and maintenance of one or more up-to-date official registers and/or records of persons deprived of liberty, which shall be made promptly available, upon request, to any judicial or other competent authority or institution authorized for that purpose by the law of the State Party concerned or any relevant international legal instrument to which the State concerned is a party. The information contained therein shall include, as a minimum:

(a) The identity of the person deprived of liberty;

(b) The date, time and place where the person was deprived of liberty and the identity of the authority that deprived the person of liberty;

(c) The authority that ordered the deprivation of liberty and the grounds for the deprivation of liberty;

(d) The authority responsible for supervising the deprivation of liberty;

(e) The place of deprivation of liberty, the date and time of admission to the place of deprivation of liberty and the authority responsible for the place of deprivation of liberty;

(f) Elements relating to the state of health of the person deprived of liberty;

(g) In the event of death during the deprivation of liberty, the circumstances and cause of death and the destination of the remains;

(h) The date and time of release or transfer to another place of detention, the destination and the authority responsible for the transfer.

Article 18

1. Subject to articles 19 and 20, each State Party shall guarantee to any person with a legitimate interest in this information, such as relatives of the person deprived of liberty, their representatives or their counsel, access to at least the following information:

(a) The authority that ordered the deprivation of liberty;

(b) The date, time and place where the person was deprived of liberty and admitted to the place of deprivation of liberty;

(c) The authority responsible for supervising the deprivation of liberty;

(d) The whereabouts of the person deprived of liberty, including, in the event of a transfer to another place of deprivation of liberty, the destination and the authority responsible for the transfer;

(e) The date, time and place of release;

(f) Elements relating to the state of health of the person deprived of liberty;

(g) In the event of death during the deprivation of liberty, the circumstances and cause of death and the destination of the remains.

2. Appropriate measures shall be taken, where necessary, to protect the persons referred to in paragraph 1 of this article, as well as persons participating in the investigation, from any ill-treatment, intimidation or sanction as a result of the search for information concerning a person deprived of liberty.

Article 19

1. Personal information, including medical and genetic data, which is collected and/or transmitted within the framework of the search for a disappeared person shall not be used or made available for purposes other than the search for the disappeared person. This is without prejudice to the use of such information in criminal proceedings relating to an offence of enforced disappearance or the exercise of the right to obtain reparation.

2. The collection, processing, use and storage of personal information, including medical and genetic data, shall not infringe or have the effect of infringing the human rights, fundamental freedoms or human dignity of an individual.

Article 20

1. Only where a person is under the protection of the law and the deprivation of liberty is subject to judicial control may the right to information referred to in Article 18 be restricted, on an exceptional basis, where strictly necessary and where provided for by law, and if the transmission of the information would adversely affect the privacy or safety of the person, hinder a criminal investigation, or for other equivalent reasons in accordance with the law, and in conformity with applicable international law and with the objectives of this Convention. In no case shall there be restrictions on the right to information referred to in Article 18 that could constitute conduct defined in Article 2 or be in violation of Article 17, paragraph 1.

2. Without prejudice to consideration of the lawfulness of the deprivation of a person's liberty, States Parties shall guarantee to the persons referred to in Article 18, paragraph 1, the right to a prompt and effective judicial remedy as a means of obtaining without delay the information referred to in Article 18, paragraph 1. This right to a remedy may not be suspended or restricted in any circumstances.

Article 21

Each State Party shall take the necessary measures to ensure that persons deprived of liberty are released in a manner permitting reliable verification that they have actually been released. Each State Party shall also take the necessary measures to assure the physical integrity of such persons and their ability to exercise fully their rights at the time of release, without prejudice to any obligations to which such persons may be subject under national law.

Article 22

Without prejudice to Article 6, each State Party shall take the necessary measures to prevent and impose sanctions for the following conduct:

(*a*) Delaying or obstructing the remedies referred to in Article 17, paragraph 2 (*f*), and Article 20, paragraph 2;

(*b*) Failure to record the deprivation of liberty of any person, or the recording of any information which the official responsible for the official register knew or should have known to be inaccurate;

(*c*) Refusal to provide information on the deprivation of liberty of a person, or the provision of inaccurate information, even though the legal requirements for providing such information have been met.

Article 23

1. Each State Party shall ensure that the training of law enforcement personnel, civil or military, medical personnel, public officials and other persons who may be involved in the custody or treatment of any person deprived of liberty includes the necessary education and information regarding the relevant provisions of this Convention, in order to:

(*a*) Prevent the involvement of such officials in enforced disappearances;

(*b*) Emphasize the importance of prevention and investigations in relation to enforced disappearances;

(*c*) Ensure that the urgent need to resolve cases of enforced disappearance is recognized

2. Each State Party shall ensure that orders or instructions prescribing, authorizing or encouraging enforced disappearance are prohibited. Each State Party shall guarantee that a person who refuses to obey such an order will not be punished.

3. Each State Party shall take the necessary measures to ensure that the persons referred to in paragraph 1 of this article who have reason to believe that an enforced disappearance has occurred or is planned report the matter to their superiors and, where necessary, to the appropriate authorities or bodies vested with powers of review or remedy.

Article 24

1. For the purposes of this Convention, "victim" means the disappeared person and any individual who has suffered harm as the direct result of an enforced disappearance.

2. Each victim has the right to know the truth regarding the circumstances of the enforced disappearance, the progress and results of the investigation and the fate of the disappeared person. Each State Party shall take appropriate measures in this regard.

3. Each State Party shall take all appropriate measures to search for, locate and release disappeared persons and, in the event of death, to locate, respect and return their remains.

4. Each State Party shall ensure in its legal system that the victims of enforced disappearance have the right to obtain reparation and prompt, fair and adequate compensation.

5. The right to obtain reparation referred to in paragraph 4 of this article covers material and moral damages and, where appropriate, other forms of reparation such as:

(a) Restitution;

(b) Rehabilitation;

(c) Satisfaction, including restoration of dignity and reputation;

(d) Guarantees of non-repetition.

6. Without prejudice to the obligation to continue the investigation until the fate of the disappeared person has been clarified, each State Party shall take the appropriate steps with regard to the legal situation of disappeared persons whose fate has not been clarified and that of their relatives, in fields such as social welfare, financial matters, family law and property rights.

7. Each State Party shall guarantee the right to form and participate freely in organizations and associations concerned with attempting to establish the circumstances of enforced disappearances and the fate of disappeared persons, and to assist victims of enforced disappearance.

Article 25

1. Each State Party shall take the necessary measures to prevent and punish under its criminal law:

(a) The wrongful removal of children who are subjected to enforced disappearance, children whose father, mother or legal guardian is subjected to enforced disappearance or children born during the captivity of a mother subjected to enforced disappearance;

(b) The falsification, concealment or destruction of documents attesting to the true identity of the children referred to in subparagraph (a) above.

2. Each State Party shall take the necessary measures to search for and identify the children referred to in paragraph 1 (a) of this article and to return them to their families of origin, in accordance with legal procedures and applicable international agreements.

3. States Parties shall assist one another in searching for, identifying and locating the children referred to in paragraph 1 (a) of this article.

4. Given the need to protect the best interests of the children referred to in paragraph 1 (a) of this article and their right to preserve, or to have re-established, their identity, including their nationality, name and family relations as recognized by law, States Parties which recognize a system of adoption or other form of placement of children shall have legal procedures in place to review the adoption or placement procedure, and, where appropriate, to annul any adoption or placement of children that originated in an enforced disappearance.

5. In all cases, and in particular in all matters relating to this article, the best interests of the child shall be a primary consideration, and a child who is capable of forming his or her own views shall have the right to express those views freely, the views of the child being given due weight in accordance with the age and maturity of the child.

PART II

Article 26

1. A Committee on Enforced Disappearances (hereinafter referred to as "the Committee") shall be established to carry out the functions provided for under this Convention. The Committee shall consist of ten experts of high moral character and recognized competence in the field of human rights, who shall serve in their personal capacity and be independent and impartial. The members of the Committee shall be elected by the States Parties according to equitable geographical distribution. Due account shall be taken of the usefulness of the participation in the work of the Committee of persons having relevant legal experience and of balanced gender representation.

2. The members of the Committee shall be elected by secret ballot from a list of persons nominated by States Parties from among their nationals, at biennial meetings of the States Parties convened by the Secretary-General of the United Nations for this purpose. At those meetings, for which two thirds of the States Parties

shall constitute a quorum, the persons elected to the Committee shall be those who obtain the largest number of votes and an absolute majority of the votes of the representatives of States Parties present and voting.

3. The initial election shall be held no later than six months after the date of entry into force of this Convention. Four months before the date of each election, the Secretary-General of the United Nations shall address a letter to the States Parties inviting them to submit nominations within three months. The Secretary-General shall prepare a list in alphabetical order of all persons thus nominated, indicating the State Party which nominated each candidate, and shall submit this list to all States Parties.

4. The members of the Committee shall be elected for a term of four years. They shall be eligible for re-election once. However, the term of five of the members elected at the first election shall expire at the end of two years; immediately after the first election, the names of these five members shall be chosen by lot by the chairman of the meeting referred to in paragraph 2 of this article.

5. If a member of the Committee dies or resigns or for any other reason can no longer perform his or her Committee duties, the State Party which nominated him or her shall, in accordance with the criteria set out in paragraph 1 of this article, appoint another candidate from among its nationals to serve out his or her term, subject to the approval of the majority of the States Parties. Such approval shall be considered to have been obtained unless half or more of the States Parties respond negatively within six weeks of having been informed by the Secretary-General of the United Nations of the proposed appointment.

6. The Committee shall establish its own rules of procedure.

7. The Secretary-General of the United Nations shall provide the Committee with the necessary means, staff and facilities for the effective performance of its functions. The Secretary-General of the United Nations shall convene the initial meeting of the Committee.

8. The members of the Committee shall be entitled to the facilities, privileges and immunities of experts on mission for the United Nations, as laid down in the relevant sections of the Convention on the Privileges and Immunities of the United Nations.

9. Each State Party shall cooperate with the Committee and assist its members in the fulfilment of their mandate, to the extent of the Committee's functions that the State Party has accepted.

Article 27

A Conference of the States Parties will take place at the earliest four years and at the latest six years following the entry into force of this Convention to evaluate the functioning of the Committee and to decide, in accordance with the procedure described in Article 44, paragraph 2, whether it is appropriate to transfer to another body—without excluding any possibility—the monitoring of this Convention, in accordance with the functions defined in articles 28 to 36.

Article 28

1. In the framework of the competencies granted by this Convention, the Committee shall cooperate with all relevant organs, offices and specialized agencies and funds of the United Nations, with the treaty bodies instituted by international instruments, with the special procedures of the United Nations and with the relevant regional intergovernmental organizations or bodies, as well as with all relevant State institutions, agencies or offices working towards the protection of all persons against enforced disappearances.

2. As it discharges its mandate, the Committee shall consult other treaty bodies instituted by relevant international human rights instruments, in particular the Human Rights Committee instituted by the International Covenant on Civil and Political Rights, with a view to ensuring the consistency of their respective observations and recommendations.

Article 29

1. Each State Party shall submit to the Committee, through the Secretary-General of the United Nations, a report on the measures taken to give effect to its obligations under this Convention, within two years after the entry into force of this Convention for the State Party concerned.

2. The Secretary-General of the United Nations shall make this report available to all States Parties.

3. Each report shall be considered by the Committee, which shall issue such comments, observations or recommendations as it may deem appropriate. The comments, observations or recommendations shall be communicated to the State Party concerned, which may respond to them, on its own initiative or at the request of the Committee.

4. The Committee may also request States Parties to provide additional information on the implementation of this Convention.

Article 30

1. A request that a disappeared person should be sought and found may be submitted to the Committee, as a matter of urgency, by relatives of the disappeared person or their legal representatives, their counsel or any person authorized by them, as well as by any other person having a legitimate interest.

2. If the Committee considers that a request for urgent action submitted in pursuance of paragraph 1 of this article:

(*a*) Is not manifestly unfounded;

(*b*) Does not constitute an abuse of the right of submission of such requests;

(*c*) Has already been duly presented to the competent bodies of the State Party concerned, such as those authorized to undertake investigations, where such a possibility exists;

(*d*) Is not incompatible with the provisions of this Convention; and

(*e*) The same matter is not being examined under another procedure of international investigation or settlement of the same nature; it shall request the State Party concerned to provide it with information on the situation of the persons sought, within a time limit set by the Committee.

3. In the light of the information provided by the State Party concerned in accordance with paragraph 2 of this article, the Committee may transmit recommendations to the State Party, including a request that the State Party should take all the necessary measures, including interim measures, to locate and protect the person concerned in accordance with this Convention and to inform the Committee, within a specified period of time, of measures taken, taking into account the urgency of the situation. The Committee shall inform the person submitting the urgent action request of its recommendations and of the information provided to it by the State as it becomes available.

4. The Committee shall continue its efforts to work with the State Party concerned for as long as the fate of the person sought remains unresolved. The person presenting the request shall be kept informed.

Article 31

1. A State Party may at the time of ratification of this Convention or at any time afterwards declare that it recognizes the competence of the Committee to receive and consider communications from or on behalf of individuals subject to its jurisdiction claiming to be victims of a violation by this State Party of provisions of this Convention. The Committee shall not admit any communication concerning a State Party which has not made such a declaration.

2. The Committee shall consider a communication inadmissible where:

(*a*) The communication is anonymous;

(*b*) The communication constitutes an abuse of the right of submission of such communications or is incompatible with the provisions of this Convention;

(*c*) The same matter is being examined under another procedure of international investigation or settlement of the same nature; or where

(*d*) All effective available domestic remedies have not been exhausted. This rule shall not apply where the application of the remedies is unreasonably prolonged.

3. If the Committee considers that the communication meets the requirements set out in paragraph 2 of this article, it shall transmit the communication to the State Party concerned, requesting it to provide observations and comments within a time limit set by the Committee.

4. At any time after the receipt of a communication and before a determination on the merits has been reached, the Committee may transmit to the State Party concerned for its urgent consideration a request that the State Party will take such interim measures as may be necessary to avoid possible irreparable damage to the victims of the alleged violation. Where the Committee exercises its discretion, this does not imply a determination on admissibility or on the merits of the communication.

5. The Committee shall hold closed meetings when examining communications under the present article. It shall inform the author of a communication of the responses provided by the State Party concerned. When the Committee decides to finalize the procedure, it shall communicate its views to the State Party and to the author of the communication.

Article 32

A State Party to this Convention may at any time declare that it recognizes the competence of the Committee to receive and consider communications in which a State Party claims that another State Party is not fulfilling its obligations under this Convention. The Committee shall not receive communications concerning a State Party which has not made such a declaration, nor communications from a State Party which has not made such a declaration.

Article 33

1. If the Committee receives reliable information indicating that a State Party is seriously violating the provisions of this Convention, it may, after consultation with the State Party concerned, request one or more of its members to undertake a visit and report back to it without delay.

2. The Committee shall notify the State Party concerned, in writing, of its intention to organize a visit, indicating the composition of the delegation and the purpose of the visit. The State Party shall answer the Committee within a reasonable time.

3. Upon a substantiated request by the State Party, the Committee may decide to postpone or cancel its visit.

4. If the State Party agrees to the visit, the Committee and the State Party concerned shall work together to define the modalities of the visit and the State Party shall provide the Committee with all the facilities needed for the successful completion of the visit.

5. Following its visit, the Committee shall communicate to the State Party concerned its observations and recommendations.

Article 34

If the Committee receives information which appears to it to contain well-founded indications that enforced disappearance is being practised on a widespread or systematic basis in the territory under the jurisdiction of a State Party, it may, after seeking from the State Party concerned all relevant information on the situation, urgently bring the matter to the attention of the General Assembly of the United Nations, through the Secretary-General of the United Nations.

Article 35

1. The Committee shall have competence solely in respect of enforced disappearances which commenced after the entry into force of this Convention.

2. If a State becomes a party to this Convention after its entry into force, the obligations of that State vis-à-vis the Committee shall relate only to enforced disappearances which commenced after the entry into force of this Convention for the State concerned.

Article 36

1. The Committee shall submit an annual report on its activities under this Convention to the States Parties and to the General Assembly of the United Nations.

2. Before an observation on a State Party is published in the annual report, the State Party concerned shall be informed in advance and shall be given reasonable time to answer. This State Party may request the publication of its comments or observations in the report.

PART III

Article 37

Nothing in this Convention shall affect any provisions which are more conducive to the protection of all persons from enforced disappearance and which may be contained in:

(*a*) The law of a State Party;

(*b*) International law in force for that State.

Article 38

1. This Convention is open for signature by all Member States of the United Nations.

2. This Convention is subject to ratification by all Member States of the United Nations. Instruments of ratification shall be deposited with the Secretary-General of the United Nations.

3. This Convention is open to accession by all Member States of the United Nations. Accession shall be effected by the deposit of an instrument of accession with the Secretary-General.

Article 39

1. This Convention shall enter into force on the thirtieth day after the date of deposit with the Secretary-General of the United Nations of the twentieth instrument of ratification or accession.

2. For each State ratifying or acceding to this Convention after the deposit of the twentieth instrument of ratification or accession, this Convention shall enter into force on the thirtieth day after the date of the deposit of that State's instrument of ratification or accession.

Article 40

The Secretary-General of the United Nations shall notify all States Members of the United Nations and all States which have signed or acceded to this Convention of the following:

(*a*) Signatures, ratifications and accessions under Article 38;

(*b*) The date of entry into force of this Convention under Article 39.

Article 41

The provisions of this Convention shall apply to all parts of federal States without any limitations or exceptions.

Article 42

1. Any dispute between two or more States Parties concerning the interpretation or application of this Convention which cannot be settled through negotiation or by the procedures expressly provided for in this Convention shall, at the request of one of them, be submitted to arbitration. If within six months from the date of the request for arbitration the Parties are unable to agree on the organization of the arbitration, any one of those Parties may refer the dispute to the International Court of Justice by request in conformity with the Statute of the Court.

2. A State may, at the time of signature or ratification of this Convention or accession thereto, declare that it does not consider itself bound by paragraph 1 of this article. The other States Parties shall not be bound by paragraph 1 of this article with respect to any State Party having made such a declaration.

3. Any State Party having made a declaration in accordance with the provisions of paragraph 2 of this article may at any time withdraw this declaration by notification to the Secretary-General of the United Nations.

Article 43

This Convention is without prejudice to the provisions of international humanitarian law, including the obligations of the High Contracting Parties to the four Geneva Conventions of 12 August 1949 and the two Additional Protocols thereto of 8 June 1977, or to the opportunity available to any State Party to authorize the International Committee of the Red Cross to visit places of detention in situations not covered by international humanitarian law.

Article 44

1. Any State Party to this Convention may propose an amendment and file it with the Secretary-General of the United Nations. The Secretary-General shall thereupon communicate the proposed amendment to the States Parties to this Convention with a request that they indicate whether they favour a conference of States Parties for the purpose of considering and voting upon the proposal. In the event that within four months from the date of such communication at least one third of the States Parties favour such a conference, the Secretary-General shall convene the conference under the auspices of the United Nations.

2. Any amendment adopted by a majority of two thirds of the States Parties present and voting at the conference shall be submitted by the Secretary-General of the United Nations to all the States Parties for acceptance.

3. An amendment adopted in accordance with paragraph 1 of this article shall enter into force when two thirds of the States Parties to this Convention have accepted it in accordance with their respective constitutional processes.

4. When amendments enter into force, they shall be binding on those States Parties which have accepted them, other States Parties still being bound by the provisions of this Convention and any earlier amendment which they have accepted.

Article 45

1. This Convention, of which the Arabic, Chinese, English, French, Russian and Spanish texts are equally authentic, shall be deposited with the Secretary-General of the United Nations.

2. The Secretary-General of the United Nations shall transmit certified copies of this Convention to all States referred to in Article 38.

DOCUMENT 46

Full Official Title: International Convention for the Protection of Migrant Workers and Their Families

Short Title/Acronym/Abbreviation: Migrant Worker Convention

Type of Document: This is a treaty, a legal instrument. This convention was adopted by the U.N. General Assembly.

Subject: Human right of migrant workers

Official Citation: United Nations, *Treaty Series*, vol. 2220, p. 3; Doc. A/RES/45/158

Date of Document: December 18, 1990
Date of Adoption: December 18, 1990
Date of General Entry into Force (EIF): July 1, 2003
Number of States Parties as of this printing: 44
Date of Signature by the United States: Has not signed
Date of Ratification/Accession/Adhesion: Not applicable
Date of Entry into Force as to United States (effective date): Not applicable
Legal Status/Character of the Instrument/Document as to the United States: The United States is not a party to this treaty as of the date of this publication.
Supervising Body: Committee on the Protection of the Rights of All Migrant Workers and Members of their Families (Committee on Migrant Workers)
Comment: Given the politically charged relation to the whole immigration and illegal alien issue, the U.S. has chosen not to be part of this treaty up to the time of this book.
Caution: The status and applicability of this instrument as to the United States may have changed since the date of this publication.
Web Address: http://www2.ohchr.org/english/law/cmw.htm

INTERNATIONAL CONVENTION FOR THE PROTECTION OF THE RIGHTS OF ALL MIGRANT WORKERS AND MEMBERS OF THEIR FAMILIES (EXCERPTS)

Adopted by General Assembly resolution 45/158 of 18 December 1990
Preamble

The States Parties to the present Convention,

Taking into account the principles embodied in the basic instruments of the United Nations concerning human rights, in particular the Universal Declaration of Human Rights, the International Covenant on Economic, Social and Cultural Rights, the International Covenant on Civil and Political Rights, the International Convention on the Elimination of All Forms of Racial Discrimination, the Convention on the Elimination of All Forms of Discrimination against Women and the Convention on the Rights of the Child,

Taking into account also the principles and standards set forth in the relevant instruments elaborated within the framework of the International Labour Organisation, especially the Convention concerning Migration for Employment (No. 97), the Convention concerning Migrations in Abusive Conditions and the Promotion of Equality of Opportunity and Treatment of Migrant Workers (No.143), the Recommendation concerning Migration for Employment (No. 86), the Recommendation concerning Migrant Workers (No.151), the Convention concerning Forced or Compulsory Labour (No. 29) and the Convention concerning Abolition of Forced Labour (No. 105), Reaffirming the importance of the principles contained in the Convention against Discrimination in Education of the United Nations Educational, Scientific and Cultural Organization,

Recalling the Convention against Torture and Other Cruel, Inhuman or Degrading Treatment or Punishment, the Declaration of the Fourth United Nations Congress on the Prevention of Crime and the Treatment of Offenders, the Code of Conduct for Law Enforcement Officials, and the Slavery Conventions,

Recalling that one of the objectives of the International Labour Organisation, as stated in its Constitution, is the protection of the interests of workers when employed in countries other than their own, and bearing in mind the expertise and experience of that organization in matters related to migrant workers and members of their families,

Recognizing the importance of the work done in connection with migrant workers and members of their families in various organs of the United Nations, in particular in the Commission on Human Rights and the Commission for Social Development, and in the Food and Agriculture Organization of the United Nations, the United Nations Educational, Scientific and Cultural Organization and the World Health Organization, as well as in other international organizations,

Recognizing also the progress made by certain States on a regional or bilateral basis towards the protection of the rights of migrant workers and members of their families, as well as the importance and usefulness of bilateral and multilateral agreements in this field,

Realizing the importance and extent of the migration phenomenon, which involves millions of people and affects a large number of States in the international community,

Aware of the impact of the flows of migrant workers on States and people concerned, and desiring to establish norms which may contribute to the harmonization of the attitudes of States through the acceptance of basic principles concerning the treatment of migrant workers and members of their families,

Considering the situation of vulnerability in which migrant workers and members of their families frequently-find themselves owing, among other things, to their absence from their State of origin and to the difficulties they may encounter arising from their presence in the State of employment,

Convinced that the rights of migrant workers and members of their families have not been sufficiently recognized everywhere and therefore require appropriate international protection,

Taking into account the fact that migration is often the cause of serious problems for the members of the families of migrant workers as well as for the workers themselves, in particular because of the scattering of the family,

Bearing in mind that the human problems involved in migration are even more serious in the case of irregular migration and convinced therefore that appropriate action should be encouraged in order to prevent and eliminate clandestine movements and trafficking in migrant workers, while at the same time assuring the protection of their fundamental human rights,

Considering that workers who are non-documented or in an irregular situation are frequently employed under less favourable conditions of work than other workers and that certain employers find this an inducement to seek such labour in order to reap the benefits of unfair competition,

Considering also that recourse to the employment of migrant workers who are in an irregular situation will be discouraged if the fundamental human rights of all migrant workers are more widely recognized and, moreover, that granting certain additional rights to migrant workers and members of their families in a regular situation will encourage all migrants and employers to respect and comply with the laws and procedures established by the States concerned,

Convinced, therefore, of the need to bring about the international protection of the rights of all migrant workers and members of their families, reaffirming and establishing basic norms in a comprehensive convention which could be applied universally,

Have agreed as follows:

Part I: Scope and Definitions

Article 1

1. The present Convention is applicable, except as otherwise provided hereafter, to all migrant workers and members of their families without distinction of any kind such as sex, race, colour, language, religion or conviction, political or other opinion, national, ethnic or social origin, nationality, age, economic position, property, marital status, birth or other status.

2. The present Convention shall apply during the entire migration process of migrant workers and members of their families, which comprises preparation for migration, departure, transit and the entire period of stay and remunerated activity in the State of employment as well as return to the State of origin or the State of habitual residence.

Article 2

For the purposes of the present Convention:

1. The term "migrant worker" refers to a person who is to be engaged, is engaged or has been engaged in a remunerated activity in a State of which he or she is not a national.

2. (a) The term "frontier worker" refers to a migrant worker who retains his or her habitual residence in a neighbouring State to which he or she normally returns every day or at least once a week;

(b) The term "seasonal worker" refers to a migrant worker whose work by its character is dependent on seasonal conditions and is performed only during part of the year;

(c) The term "seafarer", which includes a fisherman, refers to a migrant worker employed on board a vessel registered in a State of which he or she is not a national;

(d) The term "worker on an offshore installation" refers to a migrant worker employed on an offshore installation that is under the jurisdiction of a State of which he or she is not a national;

(e) The term "itinerant worker" refers to a migrant worker who, having his or her habitual residence in one State, has to travel to another State or States for short periods, owing to the nature of his or her occupation;

(f) The term "project-tied worker" refers to a migrant worker admitted to a State of employment for a defined period to work solely on a specific project being carried out in that State by his or her employer;

(g) The term "specified-employment worker" refers to a migrant worker:

(i) Who has been sent by his or her employer for a restricted and defined period of time to a State of employment to undertake a specific assignment or duty; or

(ii) Who engages for a restricted and defined period of time in work that requires professional, commercial, technical or other highly specialized skill; or

(iii) Who, upon the request of his or her employer in the State of employment, engages for a restricted and defined period of time in work whose nature is transitory or brief; and who is required to depart from the State of employment either at the expiration of his or her authorized period of stay, or earlier if he or she no longer undertakes that specific assignment or duty or engages in that work;

(h) The term "self-employed worker" refers to a migrant worker who is engaged in a remunerated activity otherwise than under a contract of employment and who earns his or her living through this activity normally working alone or together with members of his or her family, and to any other migrant worker recognized as self-employed by applicable legislation of the State of employment or bilateral or multilateral agreements.

Article 3

The present Convention shall not apply to:

(a) Persons sent or employed by international organizations and agencies or persons sent or employed by a State outside its territory to perform official functions, whose admission and status are regulated by general international law or by specific international agreements or conventions;

(b) Persons sent or employed by a State or on its behalf outside its territory who participate in development programmes and other co-operation programmes, whose admission and status are regulated by agreement with the State of employment and who, in accordance with that agreement, are not considered migrant workers;

(c) Persons taking up residence in a State different from their State of origin as investors;

(d) Refugees and stateless persons, unless such application is provided for in the relevant national legislation of, or international instruments in force for, the State Party concerned;

(e) Students and trainees;

(f) Seafarers and workers on an offshore installation who have not been admitted to take up residence and engage in a remunerated activity in the State of employment.

Article 4

For the purposes of the present Convention the term "members of the family" refers to persons married to migrant workers or having with them a relationship that, according to applicable law, produces effects equivalent to marriage, as well as their dependent children and other dependent persons who are recognized as members of the family by applicable legislation or applicable bilateral or multilateral agreements between the States concerned.

Article 5

For the purposes of the present Convention, migrant workers and members of their families:

(a) Are considered as documented or in a regular situation if they are authorized to enter, to stay and to engage in a remunerated activity in the State of employment pursuant to the law of that State and to international agreements to which that State is a party;

(b) Are considered as non-documented or in an irregular situation if they do not comply with the conditions provided for in subparagraph (a) of the present article.

Article 6

For the purposes of the present Convention:

(a) The term "State of origin" means the State of which the person concerned is a national;

(b) The term "State of employment" means a State where the migrant worker is to be engaged, is engaged or has been engaged in a remunerated activity, as the case may be;

(c) The term "State of transit,' means any State through which the person concerned passes on any journey to the State of employment or from the State of employment to the State of origin or the State of habitual residence.

Part II: Non-discrimination with Respect to Rights

Article 7

States Parties undertake, in accordance with the international instruments concerning human rights, to respect and to ensure to all migrant workers and members of their families within their territory or subject to their jurisdiction the rights provided for in the present Convention without distinction of any kind such as to sex, race, colour, language, religion or conviction, political or other opinion, national, ethnic or social origin, nationality, age, economic position, property, marital status, birth or other status.

Part III: Human Rights of All Migrant Workers and Members of their Families

Article 8

1. Migrant workers and members of their families shall be free to leave any State, including their State of origin. This right shall not be subject to any restrictions except those that are provided by law, are necessary to protect national security, public order (ordre public), public health or morals or the rights and freedoms of others and are consistent with the other rights recognized in the present part of the Convention.

2. Migrant workers and members of their families shall have the right at any time to enter and remain in their State of origin.

Article 9

The right to life of migrant workers and members of their families shall be protected by law.

Article 10

No migrant worker or member of his or her family shall be subjected to torture or to cruel, inhuman or degrading treatment or punishment.

Article 11

1. No migrant worker or member of his or her family shall be held in slavery or servitude.

2. No migrant worker or member of his or her family shall be required to perform forced or compulsory labour.

3. Paragraph 2 of the present article shall not be held to preclude, in States where imprisonment with hard labour may be imposed as a punishment for a crime, the performance of hard labour in pursuance of a sentence to such punishment by a competent court.

4. For the purpose of the present article the term "forced or compulsory labour" shall not include:

(a) Any work or service not referred to in paragraph 3 of the present article normally required of a person who is under detention in consequence of a lawful order of a court or of a person during conditional release from such detention;

(b) Any service exacted in cases of emergency or calamity threatening the life or well-being of the community;

(c) Any work or service that forms part of normal civil obligations so far as it is imposed also on citizens of the State concerned.

Article 12

1. Migrant workers and members of their families shall have the right to freedom of thought, conscience and religion. This right shall include freedom to have or to adopt a religion or belief of their choice and freedom either individually or in community with others and in public or private to manifest their religion or belief in worship, observance, practice and teaching.

2. Migrant workers and members of their families shall not be subject to coercion that would impair their freedom to have or to adopt a religion or belief of their choice.

3. Freedom to manifest one's religion or belief may be subject only to such limitations as are prescribed by law and are necessary to protect public safety, order, health or morals or the fundamental rights and freedoms of others.

4. States Parties to the present Convention undertake to have respect for the liberty of parents, at least one of whom is a migrant worker, and, when applicable, legal guardians to ensure the religious and moral education of their children in conformity with their own convictions.

Article 13

1. Migrant workers and members of their families shall have the right to hold opinions without interference.

2. Migrant workers and members of their families shall have the right to freedom of expression; this right shall include freedom to seek, receive and impart information and ideas of all kinds, regardless of frontiers, either orally, in writing or in print, in the form of art or through any other media of their choice.

3. The exercise of the right provided for in paragraph 2 of the present article carries with it special duties and responsibilities. It may therefore be subject to certain restrictions, but these shall only be such as are provided by law and are necessary:

(a) For respect of the rights or reputation of others;

(b) For the protection of the national security of the States concerned or of public order (ordre public) or of public health or morals;

(c) For the purpose of preventing any propaganda for war;

(d) For the purpose of preventing any advocacy of national, racial or religious hatred that constitutes incitement to discrimination, hostility or violence.

Article 14

No migrant worker or member of his or her family shall be subjected to arbitrary or unlawful interference with his or her privacy, family, correspondence or other communications, or to unlawful attacks on his or her honour and reputation. Each migrant worker and member of his or her family shall have the right to the protection of the law against such interference or attacks.

Article 15

No migrant worker or member of his or her family shall be arbitrarily deprived of property, whether owned individually or in association with others. Where, under the legislation in force in the State of employment, the assets of a migrant worker or a member of his or her family are expropriated in whole or in part, the person concerned shall have the right to fair and adequate compensation.

Article 16

1. Migrant workers and members of their families shall have the right to liberty and security of person.

2. Migrant workers and members of their families shall be entitled to effective protection by the State against violence, physical injury, threats and intimidation, whether by public officials or by private individuals, groups or institutions.

3. Any verification by law enforcement officials of the identity of migrant workers or members of their families shall be carried out in accordance with procedure established by law.

4. Migrant workers and members of their families shall not be subjected individually or collectively to arbitrary arrest or detention; they shall not be deprived of their liberty except on such grounds and in accordance with such procedures as are established by law.

5. Migrant workers and members of their families who are arrested shall be informed at the time of arrest as far as possible in a language they understand of the reasons for their arrest and they shall be promptly informed in a language they understand of any charges against them.

6. Migrant workers and members of their families who are arrested or detained on a criminal charge shall be brought promptly before a judge or other officer authorized by law to exercise judicial power and shall be entitled to trial within a reasonable time or to release. It shall not be the general rule that while awaiting trial they shall be detained in custody, but release may be subject to guarantees to appear for trial, at any other stage of the judicial proceedings and, should the occasion arise, for the execution of the judgement.

7. When a migrant worker or a member of his or her family is arrested or committed to prison or custody pending trial or is detained in any other manner:

(a) The consular or diplomatic authorities of his or her State of origin or of a State representing the interests of that State shall, if he or she so requests, be informed without delay of his or her arrest or detention and of the reasons therefor;

(b) The person concerned shall have the right to communicate with the said authorities. Any communication by the person concerned to the said authorities shall be forwarded without delay, and he or she shall also have the right to receive communications sent by the said authorities without delay;

(c) The person concerned shall be informed without delay of this right and of rights deriving from relevant treaties, if any, applicable between the States concerned, to correspond and to meet with representatives of the said authorities and to make arrangements with them for his or her legal representation.

8. Migrant workers and members of their families who are deprived of their liberty by arrest or detention shall be entitled to take proceedings before a court, in order that that court may decide without delay on the lawfulness of their detention and order their release if the detention is not lawful. When they attend such proceedings, they shall have the assistance, if necessary without cost to them, of an interpreter, if they cannot understand or speak the language used.

9. Migrant workers and members of their families who have been victims of unlawful arrest or detention shall have an enforceable right to compensation.

Article 17

1. Migrant workers and members of their families who are deprived of their liberty shall be treated with humanity and with respect for the inherent dignity of the human person and for their cultural identity.

2. Accused migrant workers and members of their families shall, save in exceptional circumstances, be separated from convicted persons and shall be subject to separate treatment appropriate to their status as unconvicted persons. Accused juvenile persons shall be separated from adults and brought as speedily as possible for adjudication.

3. Any migrant worker or member of his or her family who is detained in a State of transit or in a State of employment for violation of provisions relating to migration shall be held, in so far as practicable, separately from convicted persons or persons detained pending trial.

4. During any period of imprisonment in pursuance of a sentence imposed by a court of law, the essential aim of the treatment of a migrant worker or a member of his or her family shall be his or her reformation and social rehabilitation. Juvenile offenders shall be separated from adults and be accorded treatment appropriate to their age and legal status.

5. During detention or imprisonment, migrant workers and members of their families shall enjoy the same rights as nationals to visits by members of their families.

6. Whenever a migrant worker is deprived of his or her liberty, the competent authorities of the State concerned shall pay attention to the problems that may be posed for members of his or her family, in particular for spouses and minor children.

7. Migrant workers and members of their families who are subjected to any form of detention or imprisonment in accordance with the law in force in the State of employment or in the State of transit shall enjoy the same rights as nationals of those States who are in the same situation.

8. If a migrant worker or a member of his or her family is detained for the purpose of verifying any infraction of provisions related to migration, he or she shall not bear any costs arising therefrom.

Article 18

1. Migrant workers and members of their families shall have the right to equality with nationals of the State concerned before the courts and tribunals. In the determination of any criminal charge against them or of their rights and obligations in a suit of law, they shall be entitled to a fair and public hearing by a competent, independent and impartial tribunal established by law.

2. Migrant workers and members of their families who are charged with a criminal offence shall have the right to be presumed innocent until proven guilty according to law.

3. In the determination of any criminal charge against them, migrant workers and members of their families shall be entitled to the following minimum guarantees:

(a) To be informed promptly and in detail in a language they understand of the nature and cause of the charge against them;

(b) To have adequate time and facilities for the preparation of their defence and to communicate with counsel of their own choosing;

(c) To be tried without undue delay;

(d) To be tried in their presence and to defend themselves in person or through legal assistance of their own choosing; to be informed, if they do not have legal assistance, of this right; and to have legal assistance assigned to them, in any case where the interests of justice so require and without payment by them in any such case if they do not have sufficient means to pay;

(e) To examine or have examined the witnesses against them and to obtain the attendance and examination of witnesses on their behalf under the same conditions as witnesses against them;

(f) To have the free assistance of an interpreter if they cannot understand or speak the language used in court;

(g) Not to be compelled to testify against themselves or to confess guilt.

4. In the case of juvenile persons, the procedure shall be such as will take account of their age and the desirability of promoting their rehabilitation.

5. Migrant workers and members of their families convicted of a crime shall have the right to their conviction and sentence being reviewed by a higher tribunal according to law.

6. When a migrant worker or a member of his or her family has, by a final decision, been convicted of a criminal offence and when subsequently his or her conviction has been reversed or he or she has been pardoned on the ground that a new or newly discovered fact shows conclusively that there has been a miscarriage of justice, the person who has suffered punishment as a result of such conviction shall be compensated according to law, unless it is proved that the non-disclosure of the unknown fact in time is wholly or partly attributable to that person.

7. No migrant worker or member of his or her family shall be liable to be tried or punished again for an offence for which he or she has already been finally convicted or acquitted in accordance with the law and penal procedure of the State concerned.

Article 19

1. No migrant worker or member of his or her family shall be held guilty of any criminal offence on account of any act or omission that did not constitute a criminal offence under national or international law at the time when the criminal offence was committed, nor shall a heavier penalty be imposed than the one that was applicable at the time when it was committed. If, subsequent to the commission of the offence, provision is made by law for the imposition of a lighter penalty, he or she shall benefit thereby.

2. Humanitarian considerations related to the status of a migrant worker, in particular with respect to his or her right of residence or work, should be taken into account in imposing a sentence for a criminal offence committed by a migrant worker or a member of his or her family.

Article 20

1. No migrant worker or member of his or her family shall be imprisoned merely on the ground of failure to fulfill a contractual obligation.

2. No migrant worker or member of his or her family shall be deprived of his or her authorization of residence or work permit or expelled merely on the ground of failure to fulfill an obligation arising out of a work contract unless fulfillment of that obligation constitutes a condition for such authorization or permit.

Article 21

It shall be unlawful for anyone, other than a public official duly authorized by law, to confiscate, destroy or attempt to destroy identity documents, documents authorizing entry to or stay, residence or establishment in the national territory or work permits. No authorized confiscation of such documents shall take place without delivery of a detailed receipt. In no case shall it be permitted to destroy the passport or equivalent document of a migrant worker or a member of his or her family.

Article 22

1. Migrant workers and members of their families shall not be subject to measures of collective expulsion. Each case of expulsion shall be examined and decided individually.

2. Migrant workers and members of their families may be expelled from the territory of a State Party only in pursuance of a decision taken by the competent authority in accordance with law.

3. The decision shall be communicated to them in a language they understand. Upon their request where not otherwise mandatory, the decision shall be communicated to them in writing and, save in exceptional circumstances on account of national security, the reasons for the decision likewise stated. The persons concerned shall be informed of these rights before or at the latest at the time the decision is rendered.

4. Except where a final decision is pronounced by a judicial authority, the person concerned shall have the right to submit the reason he or she should not be expelled and to have his or her case reviewed by the competent authority, unless compelling reasons of national security require otherwise. Pending such review, the person concerned shall have the right to seek a stay of the decision of expulsion.

5. If a decision of expulsion that has already been executed is subsequently annulled, the person concerned shall have the right to seek compensation according to law and the earlier decision shall not be used to prevent him or her from re-entering the State concerned.

6. In case of expulsion, the person concerned shall have a reasonable opportunity before or after departure to settle any claims for wages and other entitlements due to him or her and any pending liabilities.

7. Without prejudice to the execution of a decision of expulsion, a migrant worker or a member of his or her family who is subject to such a decision may seek entry into a State other than his or her State of origin.

8. In case of expulsion of a migrant worker or a member of his or her family the costs of expulsion shall not be borne by him or her. The person concerned may be required to pay his or her own travel costs.

9. Expulsion from the State of employment shall not in itself prejudice any rights of a migrant worker or a member of his or her family acquired in accordance with the law of that State, including the right to receive wages and other entitlements due to him or her.

Article 23

Migrant workers and members of their families shall have the right to have recourse to the protection and assistance of the consular or diplomatic authorities of their State of origin or of a State representing the interests of that State whenever the rights recognized in the present Convention are impaired. In particular, in case of expulsion, the person concerned shall be informed of this right without delay and the authorities of the expelling State shall facilitate the exercise of such right.

Article 24

Every migrant worker and every member of his or her family shall have the right to recognition everywhere as a person before the law.

Article 25

1. Migrant workers shall enjoy treatment not less favourable than that which applies to nationals of the State of employment in respect of remuneration and:

(a) Other conditions of work, that is to say, overtime, hours of work, weekly rest, holidays with pay, safety, health, termination of the employment relationship and any other conditions of work which, according to national law and practice, are covered by these terms;

(b) Other terms of employment, that is to say, minimum age of employment, restriction on work and any other matters which, according to national law and practice, are considered a term of employment.

2. It shall not be lawful to derogate in private contracts of employment from the principle of equality of treatment referred to in paragraph 1 of the present article.

3. States Parties shall take all appropriate measures to ensure that migrant workers are not deprived of any rights derived from this principle by reason of any irregularity in their stay or employment. In particular, employers shall not be relieved of any legal or contractual obligations, nor shall their obligations be limited in any manner by reason of such irregularity.

Article 26

1. States Parties recognize the right of migrant workers and members of their families:

(a) To take part in meetings and activities of trade unions and of any other associations established in accordance with law, with a view to protecting their economic, social, cultural and other interests, subject only to the rules of the organization concerned;

(b) To join freely any trade union and any such association as aforesaid, subject only to the rules of the organization concerned;

(c) To seek the aid and assistance of any trade union and of any such association as aforesaid.

2. No restrictions may be placed on the exercise of these rights other than those that are prescribed by law and which are necessary in a democratic society in the interests of national security, public order (ordre public) or the protection of the rights and freedoms of others.

Article 27

1. With respect to social security, migrant workers and members of their families shall enjoy in the State of employment the same treatment granted to nationals in so far as they fulfill the requirements provided for by the applicable legislation of that State and the applicable bilateral and multilateral treaties. The competent authorities of the State of origin and the State of employment can at any time establish the necessary arrangements to determine the modalities of application of this norm.

2. Where the applicable legislation does not allow migrant workers and members of their families a benefit, the States concerned shall examine the possibility of reimbursing interested persons the amount of contributions made by them with respect to that benefit on the basis of the treatment granted to nationals who are in similar circumstances.

Article 28

Migrant workers and members of their families shall have the right to receive any medical care that is urgently required for the preservation of their life or the avoidance of irreparable harm to their health on the basis of equality of treatment with nationals of the State concerned. Such emergency medical care shall not be refused them by reason of any irregularity with regard to stay or employment.

Article 29

Each child of a migrant worker shall have the right to a name, to registration of birth and to a nationality.

Article 30

Each child of a migrant worker shall have the basic right of access to education on the basis of equality of treatment with nationals of the State concerned. Access to public pre-school educational institutions or schools shall not be refused or limited by reason of the irregular situation with respect to stay or employment of either parent or by reason of the irregularity of the child's stay in the State of employment.

Article 31

1. States Parties shall ensure respect for the cultural identity of migrant workers and members of their families and shall not prevent them from maintaining their cultural links with their State of origin.

2. States Parties may take appropriate measures to assist and encourage efforts in this respect.

Article 32

Upon the termination of their stay in the State of employment, migrant workers and members of their families shall have the right to transfer their earnings and savings and, in accordance with the applicable legislation of the States concerned, their personal effects and belongings.

Article 33

1. Migrant workers and members of their families shall have the right to be informed by the State of origin, the State of employment or the State of transit as the case may be concerning:

(a) Their rights arising out of the present Convention;

(b) The conditions of their admission, their rights and obligations under the law and practice of the State concerned and such other matters as will enable them to comply with administrative or other formalities in that State.

2. States Parties shall take all measures they deem appropriate to disseminate the said information or to ensure that it is provided by employers, trade unions or other appropriate bodies or institutions. As appropriate, they shall co-operate with other States concerned.

3. Such adequate information shall be provided upon request to migrant workers and members of their families, free of charge, and, as far as possible, in a language they are able to understand.

Article 34

Nothing in the present part of the Convention shall have the effect of relieving migrant workers and the members of their families from either the obligation to comply with the laws and regulations of any State of transit and the State of employment or the obligation to respect the cultural identity of the inhabitants of such States.

Article 35

Nothing in the present part of the Convention shall be interpreted as implying the regularization of the situation of migrant workers or members of their families who are non-documented or in an irregular situation or any right to such regularization of their situation, nor shall it prejudice the measures intended to ensure sound and equitable-conditions for international migration as provided in part VI of the present Convention.

Part IV: Other Rights of Migrant Workers and Members of their Families
who are Documented or in a Regular Situation

Article 36

Migrant workers and members of their families who are documented or in a regular situation in the State of employment shall enjoy the rights set forth in the present part of the Convention in addition to those set forth in part III.

Article 37

Before their departure, or at the latest at the time of their admission to the State of employment, migrant workers and members of their families shall have the right to be fully informed by the State of origin or the State of employment, as appropriate, of all conditions applicable to their admission and particularly those concerning their stay and the remunerated activities in which they may engage as well as of the requirements they must satisfy in the State of employment and the authority to which they must address themselves for any modification of those conditions.

Article 38

1. States of employment shall make every effort to authorize migrant workers and members of the families to be temporarily absent without effect upon their authorization to stay or to work, as the case may be. In doing so, States of employment shall take into account the special needs and obligations of migrant workers and members of their families, in particular in their States of origin.

2. Migrant workers and members of their families shall have the right to be fully informed of the terms on which such temporary absences are authorized.

Article 39

1. Migrant workers and members of their families shall have the right to liberty of movement in the territory of the State of employment and freedom to choose their residence there.

2. The rights mentioned in paragraph 1 of the present article shall not be subject to any restrictions except those that are provided by law, are necessary to protect national security, public order (ordre public), public health or morals, or the rights and freedoms of others and are consistent with the other rights recognized in the present Convention.

Article 40

1. Migrant workers and members of their families shall have the right to form associations and trade unions in the State of employment for the promotion and protection of their economic, social, cultural and other interests.

2. No restrictions may be placed on the exercise of this right other than those that are prescribed by law and are necessary in a democratic society in the interests of national security, public order (ordre public) or the protection of the rights and freedoms of others.

Article 41

1. Migrant workers and members of their families shall have the right to participate in public affairs of their State of origin and to vote and to be elected at elections of that State, in accordance with its legislation.

2. The States concerned shall, as appropriate and in accordance with their legislation, facilitate the exercise of these rights.

Article 42

1. States Parties shall consider the establishment of procedures or institutions through which account may be taken, both in States of origin and in States of employment, of special needs, aspirations and obligations of migrant workers and members of their families and shall envisage, as appropriate, the possibility for migrant workers and members of their families to have their freely chosen representatives in those institutions.

2. States of employment shall facilitate, in accordance with their national legislation, the consultation or participation of migrant workers and members of their families in decisions concerning the life and administration of local communities.

3. Migrant workers may enjoy political rights in the State of employment if that State, in the exercise of its sovereignty, grants them such rights.

Article 43

1. Migrant workers shall enjoy equality of treatment with nationals of the State of employment in relation to:

(a) Access to educational institutions and services subject to the admission requirements and other regulations of the institutions and services concerned;

(b) Access to vocational guidance and placement services;

(c) Access to vocational training and retraining facilities and institutions;

(d) Access to housing, including social housing schemes, and protection against exploitation in respect of rents;

(e) Access to social and health services, provided that the requirements for participation in the respective schemes are met;

(f) Access to co-operatives and self-managed enterprises, which shall not imply a change of their migration status and shall be subject to the rules and regulations of the bodies concerned;

(g) Access to and participation in cultural life.

2. States Parties shall promote conditions to ensure effective equality of treatment to enable migrant workers to enjoy the rights mentioned in paragraph 1 of the present article whenever the terms of their stay, as authorized by the State of employment, meet the appropriate requirements.

3. States of employment shall not prevent an employer of migrant workers from establishing housing or social or cultural facilities for them. Subject to Article 70 of the present Convention, a State of employment may make the establishment of such facilities subject to the requirements generally applied in that State concerning their installation.

Article 44

1. States Parties, recognizing that the family is the natural and fundamental group unit of society and is entitled to protection by society and the State, shall take appropriate measures to ensure the protection of the unity of the families of migrant workers.

2. States Parties shall take measures that they deem appropriate and that fall within their competence to facilitate the reunification of migrant workers with their spouses or persons who have with the migrant worker a relationship that, according to applicable law, produces effects equivalent to marriage, as well as with their minor dependent unmarried children.

3. States of employment, on humanitarian grounds, shall favourably consider granting equal treatment, as set forth in paragraph 2 of the present article, to other family members of migrant workers.

Article 45

1. Members of the families of migrant workers shall, in the State of employment, enjoy equality of treatment with nationals of that State in relation to:

(a) Access to educational institutions and services, subject to the admission requirements and other regulations of the institutions and services concerned;

(b) Access to vocational guidance and training institutions and services, provided that requirements for participation are met;

(c) Access to social and health services, provided that requirements for participation in the respective schemes are met;

(d) Access to and participation in cultural life.

2. States of employment shall pursue a policy, where appropriate in collaboration with the States of origin, aimed at facilitating the integration of children of migrant workers in the local school system, particularly in respect of teaching them the local language.

3. States of employment shall endeavour to facilitate for the children of migrant workers the teaching of their mother tongue and culture and, in this regard, States of origin shall collaborate whenever appropriate.

4. States of employment may provide special schemes of education in the mother tongue of children of migrant workers, if necessary in collaboration with the States of origin.

Article 46

Migrant workers and members of their families shall, subject to the applicable legislation of the States concerned, as well as relevant international agreements and the obligations of the States concerned arising out of their participation in customs unions, enjoy exemption from import and export duties and taxes in respect of their personal and household effects as well as the equipment necessary to engage in the remunerated activity for which they were admitted to the State of employment:

(a) Upon departure from the State of origin or State of habitual residence;

(b) Upon initial admission to the State of employment;

(c) Upon final departure from the State of employment;

(d) Upon final return to the State of origin or State of habitual residence.

Article 47

1. Migrant workers shall have the right to transfer their earnings and savings, in particular those funds necessary for the support of their families, from the State of employment to their State of origin or any other State. Such transfers shall be made in conformity with procedures established by applicable legislation of the State concerned and in conformity with applicable international agreements.

2. States concerned shall take appropriate measures to facilitate such transfers.

Article 48

1. Without prejudice to applicable double taxation agreements, migrant workers and members of their families shall, in the matter of earnings in the State of employment:

(a) Not be liable to taxes, duties or charges of any description higher or more onerous than those imposed on nationals in similar circumstances;

(b) Be entitled to deductions or exemptions from taxes of any description and to any tax allowances applicable to nationals in similar circumstances, including tax allowances for dependent members of their families. 2. States Parties shall endeavour to adopt appropriate measures to avoid double taxation of the earnings and savings of migrant workers and members of their families.

Article 49

1. Where separate authorizations to reside and to engage in employment are required by national legislation, the States of employment shall issue to migrant workers authorization of residence for at least the same period of time as their authorization to engage in remunerated activity.

2. Migrant workers who in the State of employment are allowed freely to choose their remunerated activity shall neither be regarded as in an irregular situation nor shall they lose their authorization of residence by the mere fact of the termination of their remunerated activity prior to the expiration of their work permits or similar authorizations.

3. In order to allow migrant workers referred to in paragraph 2 of the present article sufficient time to find alternative remunerated activities, the authorization of residence shall not be withdrawn at least for a period corresponding to that during which they may be entitled to unemployment benefits.

Article 50

1. In the case of death of a migrant worker or dissolution of marriage, the State of employment shall favourably consider granting family members of that migrant worker residing in that State on the basis of family reunion an authorization to stay; the State of employment shall take into account the length of time they have already resided in that State.

2. Members of the family to whom such authorization is not granted shall be allowed before departure a reasonable period of time in order to enable them to settle their affairs in the State of employment.

3. The provisions of paragraphs I and 2 of the present article may not be interpreted as adversely affecting any right to stay and work otherwise granted to such family members by the legislation of the State of employment or by bilateral and multilateral treaties applicable to that State.

Article 51

Migrant workers who in the State of employment are not permitted freely to choose their remunerated activity shall neither be regarded as in an irregular situation nor shall they lose their authorization of residence by the mere fact of the termination of their remunerated activity prior to the expiration of their work permit, except where the authorization of residence is expressly dependent upon the specific remunerated activity for which they were admitted. Such migrant workers shall have the right to seek alternative employment, participation in public work schemes and retraining during the remaining period of their authorization to work, subject to such conditions and limitations as are specified in the authorization to work.

Article 52

1. Migrant workers in the State of employment shall have the right freely to choose their remunerated activity, subject to the following restrictions or conditions.

2. For any migrant worker a State of employment may:

(a) Restrict access to limited categories of employment, functions, services or activities where this is necessary in the interests of this State and provided for by national legislation;

(b) Restrict free choice of remunerated activity in accordance with its legislation concerning recognition of occupational qualifications acquired outside its territory. However, States Parties concerned shall endeavour to provide for recognition of such qualifications.

3. For migrant workers whose permission to work is limited in time, a State of employment may also:

(a) Make the right freely to choose their remunerated activities subject to the condition that the migrant worker has resided lawfully in its territory for the purpose of remunerated activity for a period of time prescribed in its national legislation that should not exceed two years;

(b) Limit access by a migrant worker to remunerated activities in pursuance of a policy of granting priority to its nationals or to persons who are assimilated to them for these purposes by virtue of legislation or bilateral or multilateral agreements. Any such limitation shall cease to apply to a migrant worker who has resided lawfully in its territory for the purpose of remunerated activity for a period of time prescribed in its national legislation that should not exceed five years.

4. States of employment shall prescribe the conditions under which a migrant worker who has been admitted to take up employment may be authorized to engage in work on his or her own account. Account shall be taken of the period during which the worker has already been lawfully in the State of employment.

Article 53

1. Members of a migrant worker's family who have themselves an authorization of residence or admission that is without limit of time or is automatically renewable shall be permitted freely to choose their remunerated activity under the same conditions as are applicable to the said migrant worker in accordance with Article 52 of the present Convention.

2. With respect to members of a migrant worker's family who are not permitted freely to choose their remunerated activity, States Parties shall consider favourably granting them priority in obtaining permission to engage in a remunerated activity over other workers who seek admission to the State of employment, subject to applicable bilateral and multilateral agreements.

Article 54

1. Without prejudice to the terms of their authorization of residence or their permission to work and the rights provided for in articles 25 and 27 of the present Convention, migrant workers shall enjoy equality of treatment with nationals of the State of employment in respect of:

(a) Protection against dismissal;

(b) Unemployment benefits;

(c) Access to public work schemes intended to combat unemployment;

(d) Access to alternative employment in the event of loss of work or termination of other remunerated activity, subject to Article 52 of the present Convention.

2. If a migrant worker claims that the terms of his or her work contract have been violated by his or her employer, he or she shall have the right to address his or her case to the competent authorities of the State of employment, on terms provided for in Article 18, paragraph 1, of the present Convention.

Article 55

Migrant workers who have been granted permission to engage in a remunerated activity, subject to the conditions attached to such permission, shall be entitled to equality of treatment with nationals of the State of employment in the exercise of that remunerated activity.

Article 56

1. Migrant workers and members of their families referred to in the present part of the Convention may not be expelled from a State of employment, except for reasons defined in the national legislation of that State, and subject to the safeguards established in part III.

2. Expulsion shall not be resorted to for the purpose of depriving a migrant worker or a member of his or her family of the rights arising out of the authorization of residence and the work permit.

3. In considering whether to expel a migrant worker or a member of his or her family, account should be taken of humanitarian considerations and of the length of time that the person concerned has already resided in the State of employment.

Part V: Provisions Applicable to Particular Categories of Migrant Workers and Members of their Families

Article 57

The particular categories of migrant workers and members of their families specified in the present part of the Convention who are documented or in a regular situation shall enjoy the rights set forth in part m and, except as modified below, the rights set forth in part IV.

Article 58

1. Frontier workers, as defined in Article 2, paragraph 2 (a), of the present Convention, shall be entitled to the rights provided for in part IV that can be applied to them by reason of their presence and work in the territory of the State of employment, taking into account that they do not have their habitual residence in that State.

2. States of employment shall consider favourably granting frontier workers the right freely to choose their remunerated activity after a specified period of time. The granting of that right shall not affect their status as frontier workers.

Article 59

1. Seasonal workers, as defined in Article 2, paragraph 2 (b), of the present Convention, shall be entitled to the rights provided for in part IV that can be applied to them by reason of their presence and work in the territory of the State of employment and that are compatible with their status in that State as seasonal workers, taking into account the fact that they are present in that State for only part of the year.

2. The State of employment shall, subject to paragraph 1 of the present article, consider granting seasonal workers who have been employed in its territory for a significant period of time the possibility of taking up other remunerated activities and giving them priority over other workers who seek admission to that State, subject to applicable bilateral and multilateral agreements.

Article 60

Itinerant workers, as defined in Article 2, paragraph 2 (A), of the present Convention, shall be entitled to the rights provided for in part IV that can be granted to them by reason of their presence and work in the territory of the State of employment and that are compatible with their status as itinerant workers in that State.

Article 61

1. Project-tied workers, as defined in Article 2, paragraph 2 (of the present Convention), and members of their families shall be entitled to the rights provided for in part IV except the provisions of Article 43, paragraphs I (b) and (c), Article 43, paragraph I (d), as it pertains to social housing schemes, Article 45, paragraph I (b), and articles 52 to 55.

2. If a project-tied worker claims that the terms of his or her work contract have been violated by his or her employer, he or she shall have the right to address his or her case to the competent authorities of the State which has jurisdiction over that employer, on terms provided for in Article 18, paragraph 1, of the present Convention.

3. Subject to bilateral or multilateral agreements in force for them, the States Parties concerned shall endeavour to enable project-tied workers to remain adequately protected by the social security systems of their States of origin or habitual residence during their engagement in the project. States Parties concerned shall take appropriate measures with the aim of avoiding any denial of rights or duplication of payments in this respect.

4. Without prejudice to the provisions of Article 47 of the present Convention and to relevant bilateral or multilateral agreements, States Parties concerned shall permit payment of the earnings of project-tied workers in their State of origin or habitual residence.

Article 62

1. Specified-employment workers as defined in Article 2, paragraph 2 (g), of the present Convention, shall be entitled to the rights provided for in part IV, except the provisions of Article 43, paragraphs I (b) and (c), Article 43, paragraph I (d), as it pertains to social housing schemes, Article 52, and Article 54, paragraph 1 (d).

2. Members of the families of specified-employment workers shall be entitled to the rights relating to family members of migrant workers provided for in part IV of the present Convention, except the provisions of Article 53.

Article 63

1. Self-employed workers, as defined in Article 2, paragraph 2 (h), of the present Convention, shall be entitled to the rights provided for in part IV with the exception of those rights which are exclusively applicable to workers having a contract of employment.

2. Without prejudice to articles 52 and 79 of the present Convention, the termination of the economic activity of the self-employed workers shall not in itself imply the withdrawal of the authorization for them or for the members of their families to stay or to engage in a remunerated activity in the State of employment except where the authorization of residence is expressly dependent upon the specific remunerated activity for which they were admitted.

Part VI: Promotion of sound, equitable, humane and lawful conditions in connection with international migration of workers and members of their families

Article 64

1. Without prejudice to Article 79 of the present Convention, the States Parties concerned shall as appropriate consult and co-operate with a view to promoting sound, equitable and humane conditions in connection with international migration of workers and members of their families.

2. In this respect, due regard shall be paid not only to labour needs and resources, but also to the social, economic, cultural and other needs of migrant workers and members of their families involved, as well as to the consequences of such migration for the communities concerned.

Article 65

1. States Parties shall maintain appropriate services to deal with questions concerning international migration of workers and members of their families. Their functions shall include, inter alia:

(a) The formulation and implementation of policies regarding such migration;

(b) An exchange of information. consultation and co-operation with the competent authorities of other States Parties involved in such migration;

(c) The provision of appropriate information, particularly to employers, workers and their organizations on policies, laws and regulations relating to migration and employment, on agreements concluded with other States concerning migration and on other relevant matters;

(d) The provision of information and appropriate assistance to migrant workers and members of their families regarding requisite authorizations and formalities and arrangements for departure, travel, arrival, stay, remunerated activities, exit and return, as well as on conditions of work and life in the State of employment and on customs, currency, tax and other relevant laws and regulations.

2. States Parties shall facilitate as appropriate the provision of adequate consular and other services that are necessary to meet the social, cultural and other needs of migrant workers and members of their families.

Article 66

1. Subject to paragraph 2 of the present article, the right to undertake operations with a view to the recruitment of workers for employment in another State shall be restricted to:

(a) Public services or bodies of the State in which such operations take place;

(b) Public services or bodies of the State of employment on the basis of agreement between the States concerned;

(c) A body established by virtue of a bilateral or multilateral agreement.

2. Subject to any authorization, approval and supervision by the public authorities of the States Parties concerned as may be established pursuant to the legislation and practice of those States, agencies, prospective employers or persons acting on their behalf may also be permitted to undertake the said operations.

Article 67

1. States Parties concerned shall co-operate as appropriate in the adoption of measures regarding the orderly return of migrant workers and members of their families to the State of origin when they decide to return or their authorization of residence or employment expires or when they are in the State of employment in an irregular situation.

2. Concerning migrant workers and members of their families in a regular situation, States Parties concerned shall co-operate as appropriate, on terms agreed upon by those States, with a view to promoting adequate economic conditions for their resettlement and to facilitating their durable social and cultural reintegration in the State of origin.

Article 68

1. States Parties, including States of transit, shall collaborate with a view to preventing and eliminating illegal or clandestine movements and employment of migrant workers in an irregular situation. The measures to be taken to this end within the jurisdiction of each State concerned shall include:

(a) Appropriate measures against the dissemination of misleading information relating to emigration and immigration;

(b) Measures to detect and eradicate illegal or clandestine movements of migrant workers and members of their families and to impose effective sanctions on persons, groups or entities which organize, operate or assist in organizing or operating such movements;

(c) Measures to impose effective sanctions on persons, groups or entities which use violence, threats or intimidation against migrant workers or members of their families in an irregular situation.

2. States of employment shall take all adequate and effective measures to eliminate employment in their territory of migrant workers in an irregular situation, including, whenever appropriate, sanctions on employers of such workers. The rights of migrant workers vis-à-vis their employer arising from employment shall not be impaired by these measures.

Article 69

1. States Parties shall, when there are migrant workers and members of their families within their territory in an irregular situation, take appropriate measures to ensure that such a situation does not persist.

2. Whenever States Parties concerned consider the possibility of regularizing the situation of such persons in accordance with applicable national legislation and bilateral or multilateral agreements, appropriate account shall be taken of the circumstances of their entry, the duration of their stay in the States of employment and other relevant considerations, in particular those relating to their family situation.

Article 70

States Parties shall take measures not less favourable than those applied to nationals to ensure that working and living conditions of migrant workers and members of their families in a regular situation are in keeping with the standards of fitness, safety, health and principles of human dignity.

Article 71

1. States Parties shall facilitate, whenever necessary, the repatriation to the State of origin of the bodies of deceased migrant workers or members of their families.

2. As regards compensation matters relating to the death of a migrant worker or a member of his or her family, States Parties shall, as appropriate, provide assistance to the persons concerned with a view to the prompt settlement of such matters. Settlement of these matters shall be carried out on the basis of applicable national law in accordance with the provisions of the present Convention and any relevant bilateral or multilateral agreements.

Part VII: Application of the Convention

Article 72

1. (a) For the purpose of reviewing the application of the present Convention, there shall be established a Committee on the Protection of the Rights of All Migrant Workers and Members of Their Families (hereinafter referred to as "the Committee");

(b) The Committee shall consist, at the time of entry into force of the present Convention, of ten and, after the entry into force of the Convention for the forty-first State Party, of fourteen experts of high moral standing, impartiality and recognized competence in the field covered by the Convention.

2. (a) Members of the Committee shall be elected by secret ballot by the States Parties from a list of persons nominated by the States Parties, due consideration being given to equitable geographical distribution, including both States of origin and States of employment, and to the representation of the principal legal systems. Each State Party may nominate one person from among its own nationals;

(b) Members shall be elected and shall serve in their personal capacity.

3. The initial election shall be held no later than six months after the date of the entry into force of the present Convention and subsequent elections every second year. At least four months before the date of each election, the Secretary-General of the United Nations shall address a letter to all States Parties inviting them to submit their nominations within two months. The Secretary-General shall prepare a list in alphabetical order of all persons thus nominated, indicating the States Parties that have nominated them, and shall submit it to the States Parties not later than one month before the date of the corresponding election, together with the curricula vitae of the persons thus nominated.

4. Elections of members of the Committee shall be held at a meeting of States Parties convened by the Secretary-General at United Nations Headquarters. At that meeting, for which two thirds of the States Parties shall constitute a quorum, the persons elected to the Committee shall be those nominees who obtain the largest number of votes and an absolute majority of the votes of the States Parties present and voting.

5. (a) The members of the Committee shall serve for a term of four years. However, the terms of five of the members elected in the first election shall expire at the end of two years; immediately after the first election, the names of these five members shall be chosen by lot by the Chairman of the meeting of States Parties;

(b) The election of the four additional members of the Committee shall be held in accordance with the provisions of paragraphs 2, 3 and 4 of the present article, following the entry into force of the Convention for the forty-first State Party. The term of two of the additional members elected on this occasion shall expire at the end of two years; the names of these members shall be chosen by lot by the Chairman of the meeting of States Parties;

(c) The members of the Committee shall be eligible for re-election if renominated.

6. If a member of the Committee dies or resigns or declares that for any other cause he or she can no longer perform the duties of the Committee, the State Party that nominated the expert shall appoint another expert from among its own nationals for the remaining part of the term. The new appointment is subject to the approval of the Committee.

7. The Secretary-General of the United Nations shall provide the necessary staff and facilities for the effective performance of the functions of the Committee.

8. The members of the Committee shall receive emoluments from United Nations resources on such terms and conditions as the General Assembly may decide.

9. The members of the Committee shall be entitled to the facilities, privileges and immunities of experts on mission for the United Nations as laid down in the relevant sections of the Convention on the Privileges and Immunities of the United Nations.

Article 73

1. States Parties undertake to submit to the Secretary-General of the United Nations for consideration by the Committee a report on the legislative, judicial, administrative and other measures they have taken to give effect to the provisions of the present Convention:

(a) Within one year after the entry into force of the Convention for the State Party concerned;

(b) Thereafter every five years and whenever the Committee so requests.

2. Reports prepared under the present article shall also indicate factors and difficulties, if any, affecting the implementation of the Convention and shall include information on the characteristics of migration flows in which the State Party concerned is involved.

3. The Committee shall decide any further guidelines applicable to the content of the reports.

4. States Parties shall make their reports widely available to the public in their own countries.

Article 74

1. The Committee shall examine the reports submitted by each State Party and shall transmit such comments as it may consider appropriate to the State Party concerned. This State Party may submit to the Committee observations on any comment made by the Committee in accordance with the present article. The Committee may request supplementary information from States Parties when considering these reports.

2. The Secretary-General of the United Nations shall, in due time before the opening of each regular session of the Committee, transmit to the Director-General of the International Labour Office copies of the

reports submitted by States Parties concerned and information relevant to the consideration of these reports, in order to enable the Office to assist the Committee with the expertise the Office may provide regarding those matters dealt with by the present Convention that fall within the sphere of competence of the International Labour Organisation. The Committee shall consider in its deliberations such comments and materials as the Office may provide.

3. The Secretary-General of the United Nations may also, after consultation with the Committee, transmit to other specialized agencies as well as to intergovernmental organizations, copies of such parts of these reports as may fall within their competence.

4. The Committee may invite the specialized agencies and organs of the United Nations, as well as intergovernmental organizations and other concerned bodies to submit, for consideration by the Committee, written information on such matters dealt with in the present Convention as fall within the scope of their activities.

5. The International Labour Office shall be invited by the Committee to appoint representatives to participate, in a consultative capacity, in the meetings of the Committee.

6. The Committee may invite representatives of other specialized agencies and organs of the United Nations, as well as of intergovernmental organizations, to be present and to be heard in its meetings whenever matters falling within their field of competence are considered.

7. The Committee shall present an annual report to the General Assembly of the United Nations on the implementation of the present Convention, containing its own considerations and recommendations, based, in particular, on the examination of the reports and any observations presented by States Parties.

8. The Secretary-General of the United Nations shall transmit the annual reports of the Committee to the States Parties to the present Convention, the Economic and Social Council, the Commission on Human Rights of the United Nations, the Director-General of the International Labour Office and other relevant organizations.

Article 75

1. The Committee shall adopt its own rules of procedure.

2. The Committee shall elect its officers for a term of two years.

3. The Committee shall normally meet annually.

4. The meetings of the Committee shall normally be held at United Nations Headquarters.

Article 76

1. A State Party to the present Convention may at any time declare under this article that it recognizes the competence of the Committee to receive and consider communications to the effect that a State Party claims that another State Party is not fulfilling its obligations under the present Convention. Communications under this article may be received and considered only if submitted by a State Party that has made a declaration recognizing in regard to itself the competence of the Committee. No communication shall be received by the Committee if it concerns a State Party which has not made such a declaration. Communications received under this article shall be dealt with in accordance with the following procedure:

(a) If a State Party to the present Convention considers that another State Party is not fulfilling its obligations under the present Convention, it may, by written communication, bring the matter to the attention of that State Party. The State Party may also inform the Committee of the matter. Within three months after the receipt of the communication the receiving State shall afford the State that sent the communication an explanation, or any other statement in writing clarifying the matter which should include, to the extent possible and pertinent, reference to domestic procedures and remedies taken, pending or available in the matter;

(b) If the matter is not adjusted to the satisfaction of both States Parties concerned within six months after the receipt by the receiving State of the initial communication, either State shall have the right to refer the matter to the Committee, by notice given to the Committee and to the other State;

(c) The Committee shall deal with a matter referred to it only after it has ascertained that all available domestic remedies have been invoked and exhausted in the matter, in conformity with the generally recognized principles of international law. This shall not be the rule where, in the view of the Committee, the application of the remedies is unreasonably prolonged;

(d) Subject to the provisions of subparagraph (c) of the present paragraph, the Committee shall make available its good offices to the States Parties concerned with a view to a friendly solution of the matter on the basis of the respect for the obligations set forth in the present Convention;

(e) The Committee shall hold closed meetings when examining communications under the present article;

(f) In any matter referred to it in accordance with subparagraph (b) of the present paragraph, the Committee may call upon the States Parties concerned, referred to in subparagraph (b), to supply any relevant information;

(g) The States Parties concerned, referred to in subparagraph (b) of the present paragraph, shall have the right to be represented when the matter is being considered by the Committee and to make submissions orally and/or in writing;

(h) The Committee shall, within twelve months after the date of receipt of notice under subparagraph (b) of the present paragraph, submit a report, as follows:

(i) If a solution within the terms of subparagraph (d) of the present paragraph is reached, the Committee shall confine its report to a brief statement of the facts and of the solution reached;

(ii) If a solution within the terms of subparagraph (d) is not reached, the Committee shall, in its report, set forth the relevant facts concerning the issue between the States Parties concerned. The written submissions and record of the oral submissions made by the States Parties concerned shall be attached to the report. The Committee may also communicate only to the States Parties concerned any views that it may consider relevant to the issue between them.

In every matter, the report shall be communicated to the States Parties concerned.

2. The provisions of the present article shall come into force when ten States Parties to the present Convention have made a declaration under paragraph 1 of the present article. Such declarations shall be deposited by the States Parties with the Secretary-General of the United Nations, who shall transmit copies thereof to the other States Parties. A declaration may be withdrawn at any time by notification to the Secretary-General. Such a withdrawal shall not prejudice the consideration of any matter that is the subject of a communication already transmitted under the present article; no further communication by any State Party shall be received under the present article after the notification of withdrawal of the declaration has been received by the Secretary-General, unless the State Party concerned has made a new declaration.

Article 77

1. A State Party to the present Convention may at any time declare under the present article that it recognizes the competence of the Committee to receive and consider communications from or on behalf of individuals subject to its jurisdiction who claim that their individual rights as established by the present Convention have been violated by that State Party. No communication shall be received by the Committee if it concerns a State Party that has not made such a declaration.

2. The Committee shall consider inadmissible any communication under the present article which is anonymous or which it considers to be an abuse of the right of submission of such communications or to be incompatible with the provisions of the present Convention.

3. The Committee shall not consider any communication from an individual under the present article unless it has ascertained that:

(a) The same matter has not been, and is not being, examined under another procedure of international investigation or settlement;

(b) The individual has exhausted all available domestic remedies; this shall not be the rule where, in the view of the Committee, the application of the remedies is unreasonably prolonged or is unlikely to bring effective relief to that individual.

4. Subject to the provisions of paragraph 2 of the present article, the Committee shall bring any communications submitted to it under this article to the attention of the State Party to the present Convention that has made a declaration under paragraph 1 and is alleged to be violating any provisions of the Convention. Within six months, the receiving State shall submit to the Committee written explanations or statements clarifying the matter and the remedy, if any, that may have been taken by that State.

5. The Committee shall consider communications received under the present article in the light of all information made available to it by or on behalf of the individual and by the State Party concerned.

6. The Committee shall hold closed meetings when examining communications under the present article.

7. The Committee shall forward its views to the State Party concerned and to the individual.

8. The provisions of the present article shall come into force when ten States Parties to the present Convention have made declarations under paragraph 1 of the present article. Such declarations shall be

deposited by the States Parties with the Secretary-General of the United Nations, who shall transmit copies thereof to the other States Parties. A declaration may be withdrawn at any time by notification to the Secretary-General. Such a withdrawal shall not prejudice the consideration of any matter that is the subject of a communication already transmitted under the present article; no further communication by or on behalf of an individual shall be received under the present article after the notification of withdrawal of the declaration has been received by the Secretary-General, unless the State Party has made a new declaration.

Article 78

The provisions of Article 76 of the present Convention shall be applied without prejudice to any procedures for settling disputes or complaints in the field covered by the present Convention laid down in the constituent instruments of, or in conventions adopted by, the United Nations and the specialized agencies and shall not prevent the States Parties from having recourse to any procedures for settling a dispute in accordance with international agreements in force between them.

Part VIII: General provisions

Article 79

Nothing in the present Convention shall affect the right of each State Party to establish the criteria governing admission of migrant workers and members of their families. Concerning other matters related to their legal situation and treatment as migrant workers and members of their families, States Parties shall be subject to the limitations set forth in the present Convention.

Article 80

Nothing in the present Convention shall be interpreted as impairing the provisions of the Charter of the United Nations and of the constitutions of the specialized agencies which define the respective responsibilities of the various organs of the United Nations and of the specialized agencies in regard to the matters dealt with in the present Convention.

Article 81

1. Nothing in the present Convention shall affect more favourable rights or freedoms granted to migrant workers and members of their families by virtue of:

(a) The law or practice of a State Party; or

(b) Any bilateral or multilateral treaty in force for the State Party concerned.

2. Nothing in the present Convention may be interpreted as implying for any State, group or person any right to engage in any activity or perform any act that would impair any of the rights and freedoms as set forth in the present Convention.

Article 82

The rights of migrant workers and members of their families provided for in the present Convention may not be renounced. It shall not be permissible to exert any form of pressure upon migrant workers and members of their families with a view to their relinquishing or foregoing any of the said rights. It shall not be possible to derogate by contract from rights recognized in the present Convention. States Parties shall take appropriate measures to ensure that these principles are respected.

Article 83

Each State Party to the present Convention undertakes:

(a) To ensure that any person whose rights or freedoms as herein recognized are violated shall have an effective remedy, notwithstanding that the violation has been committed by persons acting in an official capacity;

(b) To ensure that any persons seeking such a remedy shall have his or her claim reviewed and decided by competent judicial, administrative or legislative authorities, or by any other competent authority provided for by the legal system of the State, and to develop the possibilities of judicial remedy;

(c) To ensure that the competent authorities shall enforce such remedies when granted.

Article 84

Each State Party undertakes to adopt the legislative and other measures that are necessary to implement the provisions of the present Convention.

Part IX: Final provisions

Article 85

The Secretary-General of the United Nations is designated as the depositary of the present Convention.

. . .

Article 88

A State ratifying or acceding to the present Convention may not exclude the application of any Part of it, or, without prejudice to Article 3, exclude any particular category of migrant workers from its application.

Article 89

1. Any State Party may denounce the present Convention, not earlier than five years after the Convention has entered into force for the State concerned, by means of a notification in writing addressed to the Secretary-General of the United Nations.

...

In witness whereof the undersigned plenipotentiaries, being duly authorized thereto by their respective Governments, have signed the present Convention.

DOCUMENT 47

Full Official Title: Body of Principles for the Protection of All Persons under Any Form of Detention or Imprisonment

Short Title/Acronym/Abbreviation: U.N. Body of Principles on Detention

Subject: Principles for how government treats people who are in the physical custody of the state, so as to protect their human rights

Official Citation: General Assembly resolution 43/173 of 9 December 1988

Date of Document: December 9, 1988

Date of Adoption: December 9, 1988

Date of General Entry into Force (EIF): Not applicable

Number of States Parties to this Treaty as of this printing: Not a treaty

Date of Signature by United States: Not applicable

Date of Ratification/Accession/Adhesion: Not applicable

Date of Entry into Force as to United States (effective date): Not applicable

Type of Document: This is not a treaty. It is a statement of principles, i.e., general rules, called a body of principles, adopted by the United Nations and made consistent with human rights standards.

Legal Status/Character of the Instrument/Document as to the United States: It is not legally binding upon the United States. But because these are adopted within the context of the United Nations, of which the United States is a key member, the United States should consider them when examining its systems of detention and should apply them. These principles are sometimes referred to as having the status of "soft law." There is no U.N. body which enforces these principles because they are not legally binding.

Comments: Some U.N. bodies look to these principles in examining specific issues involving detentions. Some special rapporteurs use these international principles as a standard to judge particular cases in countries they study. Some states in the United States have used these principles in their jail and prison systems as non mandatory guidelines. They are referred to in the U.S. reports to the U.N. Committee against Torture and to the Human Rights Committee, below. The United States recognizes them, but not as legally binding.

Web address: http://www1.umn.edu/humanrts/instree/g3bpppdi.htm

BODY OF PRINCIPLES FOR THE PROTECTION OF ALL PERSONS UNDER ANY FORM OF DETENTION OR IMPRISONMENT

Adopted by General Assembly resolution 43/173 of 9 December 1988

Scope of the Body of Principles

These principles apply for the protection of all persons under any form of detention or imprisonment.

Use of Terms

For the purposes of the Body of Principles:

(a) "Arrest" means the act of apprehending a person for the alleged commission of an offence or by the action of an authority;

(b) "Detained person" means any person deprived of personal liberty except as a result of conviction for an offence;

(c) "Imprisoned person" means any person deprived of personal liberty as a result of conviction for an offence;

(d) "Detention" means the condition of detained persons as defined above;

(e) "Imprisonment" means the condition of imprisoned persons as defined above;

(f) The words "a judicial or other authority" means a judicial or other authority under the law whose status and tenure should affordt he strongest possible guarantees of competence, impartiality and independence.

Principle 1

All persons under any form of detention or imprisonment shall be treated in a humane manner and with respect for the inherent dignity of the human person.

Principle 2

Arrest, detention or imprisonment shall only be carried out strictly in accordance with the provisions of the law and by competent officials or persons authorized for that purpose.

Principle 3

There shall be no restriction upon or derogation from any of the human rights of persons under any form of detention or imprisonment recognized or existing in any State pursuant to law, conventions, regulations or custom on the pretext that this Body of Principles does not recognize such rights or that it recognizes them to a lesser extent.

Principle 4

Any form of detention or imprisonment and all measures affecting the human rights of a person under any form of detention or imprisonment shall be ordered by, or be subject to the effective control of, a judicial or other authority.

Principle 5

1. These principles shall be applied to all persons within the territory of any given State, without distinction of any kind, such as race, colour, sex, language, religion or religious belief, political or other opinion, national, ethnic or social origin, property, birth or other status.

2. Measures applied under the law and designed solely to protect the rights and special status of women, especially pregnant women and nursing mothers, children and juveniles, aged, sick or handicapped persons shall not be deemed to be discriminatory. The need for, and the application of, such measures shall always be subject to review by a judicial or other authority.

Principle 6

No person under any form of detention or imprisonment shall be subjected to torture or to cruel, inhuman or degrading treatment or punishment.* No circumstance whatever may be invoked as a justification for torture or other cruel, inhuman or degrading treatment or punishment.

Principle 7

1. States should prohibit by law any act contrary to the rights and duties contained in these principles, make any such act subject to appropriate sanctions and conduct impartial investigations upon complaints.

*The term "cruel, inhuman or degrading treatment or punishment" should be interpreted so as to extend the widest possible protection against abuses, whether physical or mental, including the holding of a detained or imprisoned person in conditions which deprive him, temporarily or permanently of the use of any of his natural senses, such as sight or hearing, or of his awareness of place and the passing of time.

2. Officials who have reason to believe that a violation of this Body of Principles has occurred or is about to occur shall report the matter to their superior authorities and, where necessary, to other appropriate authorities or organs vested with reviewing or remedial powers.

3. Any other person who has ground to believe that a violation of this Body of Principles has occurred or is about to occur shall have the right to report the matter to the superiors of the officials involved as well as to other appropriate authorities or organs vested with reviewing or remedial powers.

Principle 8

Persons in detention shall be subject to treatment appropriate to their unconvicted status. Accordingly, they shall, whenever possible, be kept separate from imprisoned persons.

Principle 9

The authorities which arrest a person, keep him under detention or investigate the case shall exercise only the powers granted to them under the law and the exercise of these powers shall be subject to recourse to a judicial or other authority.

Principle 10

Anyone who is arrested shall be informed at the time of his arrest of the reason for his arrest and shall be promptly informed of any charges against him.

Principle 11

1. A person shall not be kept in detention without being given an effective opportunity to be heard promptly by a judicial or other authority. A detained person shall have the right to defend himself or to be assisted by counsel as prescribed by law.

2. A detained person and his counsel, if any, shall receive prompt and full communication of any order of detention, together with the reasons therefor.

3. A judicial or other authority shall be empowered to review as appropriate the continuance of detention.

Principle 12

1. There shall be duly recorded:

(a) The reasons for the arrest;

(b) The time of the arrest and the taking of the arrested person to a place of custody as well as that of his first appearance before a judicial or other authority;

(c) The identity of the law enforcement officials concerned;

(d) Precise information concerning the place of custody.

2. Such records shall be communicated to the detained person, or his counsel, if any, in the form prescribed by law.

Principle 13

Any person shall, at the moment of arrest and at the commencement of detention or imprisonment, or promptly thereafter, be provided by the authority responsible for his arrest, detention or imprisonment, respectively with information on and an explanation of his rights and how to avail himself of such rights.

Principle 14

A person who does not adequately understand or speak the language used by the authorities responsible for his arrest, detention or imprisonment is entitled to receive promptly in a language which he understands the information referred to in principle 10, principle 11, paragraph 2, principle 12, paragraph 1, and principle 13 and to have the assistance, free of charge, if necessary, of an interpreter in connection with legal proceedings subsequent to his arrest.

Principle 15

Notwithstanding the exceptions contained in principle 16, paragraph 4, and principle 18, paragraph 3, communication of the detained or imprisoned person with the outside world, and in particular his family or counsel, shall not be denied for more than a matter of days.

Principle 16

1. Promptly after arrest and after each transfer from one place of detention or imprisonment to another, a detained or imprisoned person shall be entitled to notify or to require the competent authority to notify members of his family or other appropriate persons of his choice of his arrest, detention or imprisonment or of the transfer and of the place where he is kept in custody.

2. If a detained or imprisoned person is a foreigner, he shall also be promptly informed of his right to communicate by appropriate means with a consular post or the diplomatic mission of the State of which he is a national or which is otherwise entitled to receive such communication in accordance with international law or with the representative of the competent international organization, if he is a refugee or is otherwise under the protection of an inter-governmental organization.

3. If a detained or imprisoned person is a juvenile or is incapable of understanding his entitlement, the competent authority shall on its own initiative undertake the notification referred to in the present principle. Special attention shall be given to notifying parents or guardians.

4. Any notification referred to in the present principle shall be made or permitted to be made without delay. The competent authority may however delay a notification for a reasonable period where exceptional needs of the investigation so require.

Principle 17

1. A detained person shall be entitled to have the assistance of a legal counsel. He shall be informed of his right by the competent authority promptly after arrest and shall be provided with reasonable facilities for exercising it.

2. If a detained person does not have a legal counsel of his own choice, he shall be entitled to have a legal counsel assigned to him by a judicial or other authority in all cases where the interests of justice so require and without payment by him if he does not have sufficient means to pay.

Principle 18

1. A detained or imprisoned person shall be entitled to communicate and consult with his legal counsel.

2. A detained or imprisoned person shall be allowed adequate time and facilities for consultation with his legal counsel.

3. The right of a detained or imprisoned person to be visited by and to consult and communicate, without delay or censorship and in full confidentiality, with his legal counsel may not be suspended or restricted save in exceptional circumstances, to be specified by law or lawful regulations, when it is considered indispensable by a judicial or other authority in order to maintain security and good order.

4. Interviews between a detained or imprisoned person and his legal counsel may be within sight, but not within the hearing, of a law enforcement official.

5. Communications between a detained or imprisoned person and his legal counsel mentioned in the present principle shall be inadmissible as evidence against the detained or imprisoned person unless they are connected with a continuing or contemplated crime.

Principle 19

A detained or imprisoned person shall have the right to be visited by and to correspond with, in particular, members of his family and shall be given adequate opportunity to communicate with the outside world, subject to reasonable conditions and restrictions as specified by law or lawful regulations.

Principle 20

If a detained or imprisoned person so requests, he shall if possible be kept in a place of detention or imprisonment reasonably near his usual place of residence.

Principle 21

1. It shall be prohibited to take undue advantage of the situation of a detained or imprisoned person for the purpose of compelling him to confess, to incriminate himself otherwise or to testify against any other person.

2. No detained person while being interrogated shall be subject to violence, threats or methods of interrogation which impair his capacity of decision or his judgement.

Principle 22

No detained or imprisoned person shall, even with his consent, be subjected to any medical or scientific experimentation which may be detrimental to his health.

Principle 23

1. The duration of any interrogation of a detained or imprisoned person and of the intervals between interrogations as well as the identity of the officials who conducted the interrogations and other persons present shall be recorded and certified in such form as may be prescribed by law.

2. A detained or imprisoned person, or his counsel when provided by law, shall have access to the information described in paragraph 1 of the present principle.

Principle 24

A proper medical examination shall be offered to a detained or imprisoned person as promptly as possible after his admission to the place of detention or imprisonment, and thereafter medical care and treatment shall be provided whenever necessary. This care and treatment shall be provided free of charge.

Principle 25

A detained or imprisoned person or his counsel shall, subject only to reasonable conditions to ensure security and good order in the place of detention or imprisonment, have the right to request or petition a judicial or other authority for a second medical examination or opinion.

Principle 26

The fact that a detained or imprisoned person underwent a medical examination, the name of the physician and the results of such an examination shall be duly recorded. Access to such records shall be ensured. Modalities therefore shall be in accordance with relevant rules of domestic law.

Principle 27

Non-compliance with these principles in obtaining evidence shall be taken into account in determining the admissibility of such evidence against a detained or imprisoned person.

Principle 28

A detained or imprisoned person shall have the right to obtain within the limits of available resources, if from public sources, reasonable quantities of educational, cultural and informational material, subject to reasonable conditions to ensure security and good order in the place of detention or imprisonment.

Principle 29

1. In order to supervise the strict observance of relevant laws and regulations, places of detention shall be visited regularly by qualified and experienced persons appointed by, and responsible to, a competent authority distinct from the authority directly in charge of the administration of the place of detention or imprisonment.

2. A detained or imprisoned person shall have the right to communicate freely and in full confidentiality with the persons who visit the places of detention or imprisonment in accordance with paragraph 1 of the present principle, subject to reasonable conditions to ensure security and good order in such places.

Principle 30

1. The types of conduct of the detained or imprisoned person that constitute disciplinary offences during detention or imprisonment, the description and duration of disciplinary punishment that may be inflicted and the authorities competent to impose such punishment shall be specified by law or lawful regulations and duly published.

2. A detained or imprisoned person shall have the right to be heard before disciplinary action is taken. He shall have the right to bring such action to higher authorities for review.

Principle 31

The appropriate authorities shall endeavour to ensure, according to domestic law, assistance when needed to dependent and, in particular, minor members of the families of detained or imprisoned persons and shall devote a particular measure of care to the appropriate custody of children left without supervision.

Principle 32

1. A detained person or his counsel shall be entitled at any time to take proceedings according to domestic law before a judicial or other authority to challenge the lawfulness of his detention in order to obtain his release without delay, if it is unlawful.

2. The proceedings referred to in paragraph 1 of the present principle shall be simple and expeditious and at no cost for detained persons without adequate means. The detaining authority shall produce without unreasonable delay the detained person before the reviewing authority.

Principle 33

1. A detained or imprisoned person or his counsel shall have the right to make a request or complaint regarding his treatment, in particular in case of torture or other cruel, inhuman or degrading treatment, to the authorities responsible for the administration of the place of detention and to higher authorities and, when necessary, to appropriate authorities vested with reviewing or remedial powers.

2. In those cases where neither the detained or imprisoned person nor his counsel has the possibility to exercise his rights under paragraph 1 of the present principle, a member of the family of the detained or imprisoned person or any other person who has knowledge of the case may exercise such rights.

3. Confidentiality concerning the request or complaint shall be maintained if so requested by the complainant.

4. Every request or complaint shall be promptly dealt with and replied to without undue delay. If the request or complaint is rejected or, in case of inordinate delay, the complainant shall be entitled to bring it before a judicial or other authority. Neither the detained or imprisoned person nor any complainant under paragraph 1 of the present principle shall suffer prejudice for making a request or complaint.

Principle 34

Whenever the death or disappearance of a detained or imprisoned person occurs during his detention or imprisonment, an inquiry into the cause of death or disappearance shall be held by a judicial or other authority, either on its own motion or at the instance of a member of the family of such a person or any person who has knowledge of the case. When circumstances so warrant, such an inquiry shall be held on the same procedural basis whenever the death or disappearance occurs shortly after the termination of the detention or imprisonment. The findings of such inquiry or a report thereon shall be made available upon request, unless doing so would jeopardize an ongoing criminal investigation.

Principle 35

1. Damage incurred because of acts or omissions by a public official contrary to the rights contained in these principles shall be compensated according to the applicable rules or liability provided by domestic law.

2. Information required to be recorded under these principles shall be available in accordance with procedures provided by domestic law for use in claiming compensation under the present principle.

Principle 36

1. A detained person suspected of or charged with a criminal offence shall be presumed innocent and shall be treated as such until proved guilty according to law in a public trial at which he has had all the guarantees necessary for his defence.

2. The arrest or detention of such a person pending investigation and trial shall be carried out only for the purposes of the administration of justice on grounds and under conditions and procedures specified by law. The imposition of restrictions upon such a person which are not strictly required for the purpose of the detention or to prevent hindrance to the process of investigation or the administration of justice, or for the maintenance of security and good order in the place of detention shall be forbidden.

Principle 37

A person detained on a criminal charge shall be brought before a judicial or other authority provided by law promptly after his arrest. Such authority shall decide without delay upon the lawfulness and necessity of detention. No person may be kept under detention pending investigation or trial except upon the written order of such an authority. A detained person shall, when brought before such an authority, have the right to make a statement on the treatment received by him while in custody.

Principle 38

A person detained on a criminal charge shall be entitled to trial within a reasonable time or to release pending trial.

Except in special cases provided for by law, a person detained on a criminal charge shall be entitled, unless a judicial or other authority decides otherwise in the interest of the administration of justice, to release pending trial subject to the conditions that may be imposed in accordance with the law. Such authority shall keep the necessity of detention under review.

General clause

Nothing in this Body of Principles shall be construed as restricting or derogating from any right defined in the International Covenant on Civil and Political Rights.

Copyright 1997. Office of the United Nations High Commissioner for Human Rights, Geneva, Switzerland.

DOCUMENT 48

Full Official Title: Standard Minimum Rules for the Treatment of Prisoners

Short Title/Acronym/Abbreviation: The Standard Minimum Rules

Subject: Specific rules on how states should treat prisoners in a way that respects their internationally recognized human rights

Official Citation: Adopted by the First United Nations Congress on the Prevention of Crime and the Treatment of Offenders, held at Geneva in 1955, and approved by the Economic and Social Council by its resolution 663 C (XXIV) of 31 July 1957 and 2076 (LXII) of 13 May 1977

Date of Document: May 13, 1977

Date of Adoption: May 13, 1977

Date of General Entry into Force (EIF): Not applicable

Number of States Parties to the Treaty as of this printing: Not a treaty

Date of Signature by United States: Not applicable

Date of Ratification/Accession/Adhesion: Not applicable

Date of Entry into Force as to United States (effective date): Not applicable

Type of Document: This is not a treaty. It is a non-legally binding resolution containing a non-legally binding set of rules, called standard minimum rules. These were adopted within the context of the United Nations and made consistent with international human rights standards.

Legal Status/Character of the Instrument/Document as to the United States: It is not legally binding upon the United States. But because these rules are adopted within the context of the United Nations, of which the United States is a key member, the United States should consider them and apply them when examining its systems of treatment of prisoners. These principles are sometimes referred to as having the status of "soft law." There is no U.N. body which enforces these principles because they are not legally binding.

Comments: Some U.N. bodies look to these rules in examining specific issues involving detentions. Some special rapporteurs use these international rules as a standard to judge particular cases in countries they study. Some states in the United States have used these rules in their jail and prison systems as non-mandatory guidelines. They are referred to in the U.S. reports to the U.N. Committee against Torture and to the Human Rights Committee, below. The United States recognizes them but not as legally binding.

Web address: http://www1.umn.edu/humanrts/instree/g1smr.htm

STANDARD MINIMUM RULES FOR THE TREATMENT OF PRISONERS

Adopted by the First United Nations Congress on the Prevention of Crime and the Treatment of Offenders, held at Geneva in 1955, and approved by the Economic and Social Council by its resolution 663 C (XXIV) of 31 July 1957 and 2076 (LXII) of 13 May 1977

Preliminary Observations

1. The following rules are not intended to describe in detail a model system of penal institutions. They seek only, on the basis of the general consensus of contemporary thought and the essential elements of the most adequate systems of today, to set out what is generally accepted as being good principle and practice in the treatment of prisoners and the management of institutions.

2. In view of the great variety of legal, social, economic and geographical conditions of the world, it is evident that not all of the rules are capable of application in all places and at all times. They should, however, serve to stimulate a constant endeavour to overcome practical difficulties in the way of their application, in the knowledge that they represent, as a whole, the minimum conditions which are accepted as suitable by the United Nations.

3. On the other hand, the rules cover a field in which thought is constantly developing. They are not intended to preclude experiment and practices, provided these are in harmony with the principles and seek to further the purposes which derive from the text of the rules as a whole. It will always be justifiable for the central prison administration to authorize departures from the rules in this spirit.

4. (1) Part I of the rules covers the general management of institutions, and is applicable to all categories of prisoners, criminal or civil, untried or convicted, including prisoners subject to "security measures" or corrective measures ordered by the judge.

(2) Part II contains rules applicable only to the special categories dealt within each section. Nevertheless, the rules under section A, applicable to prisoners under sentence, shall be equally applicable to categories of prisoners dealt with in sections B, C and D, provided they do not conflict with the rules governing those categories and are for their benefit.

5. (1) The rules do not seek to regulate the management of institutions set aside for young persons such as Borstal institutions or correctional schools, but in general part I would be equally applicable in such institutions.

(2) The category of young prisoners should include at least all young persons who come within the jurisdiction of juvenile courts. As a rule, such young persons should not be sentenced to imprisonment.

PART I—RULES OF GENERAL APPLICATION

Basic principle.

6. (1) The following rules shall be applied impartially. There shall be no discrimination on grounds of race, colour, sex, language, religion, political or other opinion, national or social origin, property, birth or other status.

(2) On the other hand, it is necessary to respect the religious beliefs and moral precepts of the group to which a prisoner belongs.

Register

7. (1) In every place where persons are imprisoned there shall be kept a bound registration book with numbered pages in which shall be entered in respect of each prisoner received:

(a) Information concerning his identity;

(b) The reasons for his commitment and the authority therefore;

(c) The day and hour of his admission and release.

(2) No person shall be received in an institution without a valid commitment order of which the details shall have been previously entered in the register.

Separation of categories

8. The different categories of prisoners shall be kept in separate institutions or parts of institutions taking account of their sex, age, criminal record, the legal reason for their detention and the necessities of their treatment. Thus,

(a) Men and women shall so far as possible be detained in separate institutions; in an institution which receives both men and women the whole of the premises allocated to women shall be entirely separate;

(b) Untried prisoners shall be kept separate from convicted prisoners;

(c) Persons imprisoned for debt and other civil prisoners shall be kept separate from persons imprisoned by reason of a criminal offence;

(d) Young prisoners shall be kept separate from adults.

Accommodation

9. (1) Where sleeping accommodation is in individual cells or rooms, each prisoner shall occupy by night a cell or room by himself. If for special reasons, such as temporary overcrowding, it becomes necessary for the central prison administration to make an exception to this rule, it is not desirable to have two prisoners in a cell or room.

(2) Where dormitories are used, they shall be occupied by prisoners carefully selected as being suitable to associate with one another in those conditions. There shall be regular supervision by night, in keeping with the nature of the institution.

10. All accommodation provided for the use of prisoners and in particular all sleeping accommodation shall meet all requirements of health, due regard being paid to climatic conditions and particularly to cubic content of air, minimum floor space, lighting, heating and ventilation.

11. In all places where prisoners are required to live or work,

(a) The windows shall be large enough to enable the prisoners to read or work by natural light, and shall be so constructed that they can allow the entrance of fresh air whether or not there is artificial ventilation;

(b) Artificial light shall be provided sufficient for the prisoners to read or work without injury to eyesight.

12. The sanitary installations shall be adequate to enable every prisoner to comply with the needs of nature when necessary and in a clean and decent manner.

13. Adequate bathing and shower installations shall be provided so that every prisoner may be enabled and required to have a bath or shower, at a temperature suitable to the climate, as frequently as necessary for general hygiene according to season and geographical region, but at least once a week in a temperate climate.

14. All pans of an institution regularly used by prisoners shall be properly maintained and kept scrupulously clean at all times.

Personal hygiene

15. Prisoners shall be required to keep their persons clean, and to this end they shall be provided with water and with such toilet articles as are necessary for health and cleanliness.

16. In order that prisoners may maintain a good appearance compatible with their self-respect, facilities shall be provided for the proper care of the hair and beard, and men shall be enabled to shave regularly.

Clothing and bedding

17. (1) Every prisoner who is not allowed to wear his own clothing shall be provided with an outfit of clothing suitable for the climate and adequate to keep him in good health. Such clothing shall in no manner be degrading or humiliating.

(2) All clothing shall be clean and kept in proper condition. Underclothing shall be changed and washed as often as necessary for the maintenance of hygiene.

(3) In exceptional circumstances, whenever a prisoner is removed outside the institution for an authorized purpose, he shall be allowed to wear his own clothing or other inconspicuous clothing.

18. If prisoners are allowed to wear their own clothing, arrangements shall be made on their admission to the institution to ensure that it shall be clean and fit for use.

19. Every prisoner shall, in accordance with local or national standards, be provided with a separate bed, and with separate and sufficient bedding which shall be clean when issued, kept in good order and changed often enough to ensure its cleanliness.

Food

20. (1) Every prisoner shall be provided by the administration at the usual hours with food of nutritional value adequate for health and strength, of wholesome quality and well prepared and served.

(2) Drinking water shall be available to every prisoner whenever he needs it.

Exercise and sport

21. (1) Every prisoner who is not employed in outdoor work shall have at least one hour of suitable exercise in the open air daily if the weather permits.

(2) Young prisoners, and others of suitable age and physique, shall receive physical and recreational training during the period of exercise. To this end space, installations and equipment should be provided.

Medical services

22. (1) At every institution there shall be available the services of at least one qualified medical officer who should have some knowledge of psychiatry. The medical services should be organized in close relationship to the general health administration of the community or nation. They shall include a psychiatric service for the diagnosis and, in proper cases, the treatment of states of mental abnormality.

(2) Sick prisoners who require specialist treatment shall be transferred to specialized institutions or to civil hospitals. Where hospital facilities are provided in an institution, their equipment, furnishings and pharmaceutical supplies shall be proper for the medical care and treatment of sick prisoners, and there shall be a staff of suitable trained officers.

(3) The services of a qualified dental officer shall be available to every prisoner.

23. (1) In women's institutions there shall be special accommodation for all necessary pre-natal and post-natal care and treatment. Arrangements shall be made wherever practicable for children to be born in a hospital outside the institution. If a child is born in prison, this fact shall not be mentioned in the birth certificate.

(2) Where nursing infants are allowed to remain in the institution with their mothers, provision shall be made for a nursery staffed by qualified persons, where the infants shall be placed when they are not in the care of their mothers.

24. The medical officer shall see and examine every prisoner as soon as possible after his admission and thereafter as necessary, with a view particularly to the discovery of physical or mental illness and the taking of all necessary measures; the segregation of prisoners suspected of infectious or contagious conditions; the noting of physical or mental defects which might hamper rehabilitation, and the determination of the physical capacity of every prisoner for work.

25. (1) The medical officer shall have the care of the physical and mental health of the prisoners and should daily see all sick prisoners, all who complain of illness, and any prisoner to whom his attention is specially directed.

(2) The medical officer shall report to the director whenever he considers that a prisoner's physical or mental health has been or will be injuriously affected by continued imprisonment or by any condition of imprisonment.

26. (1) The medical officer shall regularly inspect and advise the director upon:

(a) The quantity, quality, preparation and service of food;

(b) The hygiene and cleanliness of the institution and the prisoners;

(c) The sanitation, heating, lighting and ventilation of the institution;

(d) The suitability and cleanliness of the prisoners' clothing and bedding;

(e) The observance of the rules concerning physical education and sports, in cases where there is no technical personnel in charge of these activities.

(2) The director shall take into consideration the reports and advice that the medical officer submits according to rules 25 (2) and 26 and, in case he concurs with the recommendations made, shall take immediate steps to give effect to those recommendations; if they are not within his competence or if he does not concur with them, he shall immediately submit his own report and the advice of the medical officer to higher authority.

Discipline and punishment

27. Discipline and order shall be maintained with firmness, but with no more restriction than is necessary for safe custody and well-ordered community life.

28. (1) No prisoner shall be employed, in the service of the institution, in any disciplinary capacity.

(2) This rule shall not, however, impede the proper functioning of systems based on self-government, under which specified social, educational or sports activities or responsibilities are entrusted, under supervision, to prisoners who are formed into groups for the purposes of treatment.

29. The following shall always be determined by the law or by the regulation of the competent administrative authority:

(a) Conduct constituting a disciplinary offence;

(b) The types and duration of punishment which may be inflicted;

(c) The authority competent to impose such punishment.

30. (1) No prisoner shall be punished except in accordance with the terms of such law or regulation, and never twice for the same offence.

(2) No prisoner shall be punished unless he has been informed of the offence alleged against him and given a proper opportunity of presenting his defence. The competent authority shall conduct a thorough examination of the case.

(3) Where necessary and practicable the prisoner shall be allowed to make his defence through an interpreter.

31. Corporal punishment, punishment by placing in a dark cell, and all cruel, inhuman or degrading punishments shall be completely prohibited as punishments for disciplinary offences.

32. (1) Punishment by close confinement or reduction of diet shall never be inflicted unless the medical officer has examined the prisoner and certified in writing that he is fit to sustain it.

(2) The same shall apply to any other punishment that may be prejudicial to the physical or mental health of a prisoner. In no case may such punishment be contrary to or depart from the principle stated in rule 31.

(3) The medical officer shall visit daily prisoners undergoing such punishments and shall advise the director if he considers the termination or alteration of the punishment necessary on grounds of physical or mental health.

Instruments of restraint

33. Instruments of restraint, such as handcuffs, chains, irons and strait-jacket, shall never be applied as a punishment. Furthermore, chains or irons shall not be used as restraints. Other instruments of restraint shall not be used except in the following circumstances:

(a) As a precaution against escape during a transfer, provided that they shall be removed when the prisoner appears before a judicial or administrative authority;

(b) On medical grounds by direction of the medical officer;

(c) By order of the director, if other methods of control fail, in order to prevent a prisoner from injuring himself or others, or from damaging property; in such instances the director shall at once consult the medical officer and report to the higher administrative authority.

34. The patterns and manner of use of instruments of restraint shall be decided by the central prison administration. Such instruments must not be applied for any longer time than is strictly necessary.

Information to and complaints by prisoners

35. (1) Every prisoner on admission shall be provided with written information about the regulations governing the treatment of prisoners of his category, the disciplinary requirements of the institution, the authorized methods of seeking information and making complaints, and all such other matters as are necessary to enable him to understand both his rights and his obligations and to adapt himself to the life of the institution.

(2) If a prisoner is illiterate, the aforesaid information shall be conveyed to him orally.

36. (1) Every prisoner shall have the opportunity each week day of making requests or complaints to the director of the institution or the officer authorized to represent him.

(2) It shall be possible to make requests or complaints to the inspector of prisons during his inspection. The prisoner shall have the opportunity to talk to the inspector or to any other inspecting officer without the director or other members of the staff being present.

(3) Every prisoner shall be allowed to make a request or complaint, without censorship as to substance but in proper form, to the central prison administration, the judicial authority or other proper authorities through approved channels.

(4) Unless it is evidently frivolous or groundless, every request or complaint shall be promptly dealt with and replied to without undue delay.

Contact with the outside world

37. Prisoners shall be allowed under necessary supervision to communicate with their family and reputable friends at regular intervals, both by correspondence and by receiving visits.

38. (1) Prisoners who are foreign nationals shall be allowed reasonable facilities to communicate with the diplomatic and consular representatives of the State to which they belong.

(2) Prisoners who are nationals of States without diplomatic or consular representation in the country and refugees or stateless persons shall be allowed similar facilities to communicate with the diplomatic representative of the State which takes charge of their interests or any national or international authority whose task it is to protect such persons.

39. Prisoners shall be kept informed regularly of the more important items of news by the reading of newspapers, periodicals or special institutional publications, by hearing wireless transmissions, by lectures or by any similar means as authorized or controlled by the administration.

Books

40. Every institution shall have a library for the use of all categories of prisoners, adequately stocked with both recreational and instructional books, and prisoners shall be encouraged to make full use of it.

Religion

41. (1) If the institution contains a sufficient number of prisoners of the same religion, a qualified representative of that religion shall be appointed or approved. If the number of prisoners justifies it and conditions permit, the arrangement should be on a full-time basis.

(2) A qualified representative appointed or approved under paragraph(1) shall be allowed to hold regular services and to pay pastoral visits in private to prisoners of his religion at proper times.

(3) Access to a qualified representative of any religion shall not be refused to any prisoner. On the other hand, if any prisoner should object to a visit of any religious representative, his attitude shall be fully respected.

42. So far as practicable, every prisoner shall be allowed to satisfy the needs of his religious life by attending the services provided in the institution and having in his possession the books of religious observance and instruction of his denomination.

Retention of prisoners' property

43. (1) All money, valuables, clothing and other effects belonging to a prisoner which under the regulations of the institution he is not allowed to retain shall on his admission to the institution be placed in safe custody. An inventory thereof shall be signed by the prisoner. Steps shall be taken to keep them in good condition.

(2) On the release of the prisoner all such articles and money shall be returned to him except in so far as he has been authorized to spend money or send any such property out of the institution, or it has been found necessary on hygienic grounds to destroy any article of clothing. The prisoner shall sign a receipt for the articles and money returned to him.

(3) Any money or effects received for a prisoner from outside shall be treated in the same way.

(4) If a prisoner brings in any drugs or medicine, the medical officer shall decide what use shall be made of them.

Notification of death, illness, transfer, etc.

44. (1) Upon the death or serious illness of, or serious injury to a prisoner, or his removal to an institution for the treatment of mental affections, the director shall at once inform the spouse, if the prisoner is married, or the nearest relative and shall in any event inform any other person previously designated by the prisoner.

(2) A prisoner shall be informed at once of the death or serious illness of any near relative. In case of the critical illness of a near relative, the prisoner should be authorized, whenever circumstances allow, to go to his bedside either under escort or alone.

(3) Every prisoner shall have the right to inform at once his family of his imprisonment or his transfer to another institution.

Removal of prisoners

45. (1) When the prisoners are being removed to or from an institution, they shall be exposed to public view as little as possible, and proper safeguards shall be adopted to protect them from insult, curiosity and publicity in any form.

(2) The transport of prisoners in conveyances with inadequate ventilation or light, or in any way which would subject them to unnecessary physical hardship, shall be prohibited.

(3) The transport of prisoners shall be carried out at the expense of the administration and equal conditions shall obtain for all of them.

Institutional personnel

46. (1) The prison administration, shall provide for the careful selection of every grade of the personnel, since it is on their integrity, humanity, professional capacity and personal suitability for the work that the proper administration of the institutions depends.

(2) The prison administration shall constantly seek to awaken and maintain in the minds both of the personnel and of the public the conviction that this work is a social service of great importance, and to this end all appropriate means of informing the public should be used.

(3) To secure the foregoing ends, personnel shall be appointed on a full-time basis as professional prison officers and have civil service status with security of tenure subject only to good conduct, efficiency and physical fitness. Salaries shall be adequate to attract and retain suitable men and women; employment benefits and conditions of service shall be favourable in view of the exacting nature of the work.

47. (1) The personnel shall possess an adequate standard of education and intelligence.

(2) Before entering on duty, the personnel shall be given a course of training in their general and specific duties and be required to pass theoretical and practical tests.

(3) After entering on duty and during their career, the personnel shall maintain and improve their knowledge and professional capacity by attending courses of in-service training to be organized at suitable intervals.

48. All members of the personnel shall at all times so conduct themselves and perform their duties as to influence the prisoners for good by their example and to command their respect.

49. (1) So far as possible, the personnel shall include a sufficient number of specialists such as psychiatrists, psychologists, social workers, teachers and trade instructors.

(2) The services of social workers, teachers and trade instructors shall be secured on a permanent basis, without thereby excluding part-time or voluntary workers.

50. (1) The director of an institution should be adequately qualified for his task by character, administrative ability, suitable training and experience.

(2) He shall devote his entire time to his official duties and shall not be appointed on a part-time basis.

(3) He shall reside on the premises of the institution or in its immediate vicinity.

(4) When two or more institutions are under the authority of one director, he shall visit each of them at frequent intervals. A responsible resident official shall be in charge of each of these institutions.

51. (1) The director, his deputy, and the majority of the other personnel of the institution shall be able to speak the language of the greatest number of prisoners, or a language understood by the greatest number of them.

(2) Whenever necessary, the services of an interpreter shall be used.

52. (1) In institutions which are large enough to require the services of one or more full-time medical officers, at least one of them shall reside on the premises of the institution or in its immediate vicinity.

(2) In other institutions the medical officer shall visit daily and shall reside near enough to be able to attend without delay in cases of urgency.

53. (1) In an institution for both men and women, the part of the institution set aside for women shall be under the authority of a responsible woman officer who shall have the custody of the keys of all that part of the institution.

(2) No male member of the staff shall enter the part of the institution set aside for women unless accompanied by a woman officer.

(3) Women prisoners shall be attended and supervised only by women officers. This does not, however, preclude male members of the staff, particularly doctors and teachers, from carrying out their professional duties in institutions or parts of institutions set aside for women.

54. (1) Officers of the institutions shall not, in their relations with the prisoners, use force except in self-defence or in cases of attempted escape, or active or passive physical resistance to an order based on law or regulations. Officers who have recourse to force must use no more than is strictly necessary and must report the incident immediately to the director of the institution.

(2) Prison officers shall be given special physical training to enable them to restrain aggressive prisoners.

(3) Except in special circumstances, staff performing duties which bring them into direct contact with prisoners should not be armed. Furthermore, staff should in no circumstances be provided with arms unless they have been trained in their use.

Inspection

55. There shall be a regular inspection of penal institutions and services by qualified and experienced inspectors appointed by a competent authority. Their task shall be in particular to ensure that these institu-

tions are administered in accordance with existing laws and regulations and with a view to bringing about the objectives of penal and correctional services.

PART II—RULES APPLICABLE TO SPECIAL CATEGORIES

A. Prisoners under Sentence

Guiding principles

56. The guiding principles hereafter are intended to show the spirit in which penal institutions should be administered and the purposes at which they should aim, in accordance with the declaration made under Preliminary Observation I of the present text.

57. Imprisonment and other measures which result in cutting off an offender from the outside world are afflictive by the very fact of taking from the person the right of self-determination by depriving him of his liberty. Therefore the prison system shall not, except as incidental to justifiable segregation or the maintenance of discipline, aggravate the suffering inherent in such a situation.

58. The purpose and justification of a sentence of imprisonment or a similar measure deprivative of liberty is ultimately to protect society against crime. This end can only be achieved if the period of imprisonment is used to ensure, so far as possible, that upon his return to society the offender is not only willing but able to lead a law-abiding and self-supporting life.

59. To this end, the institution should utilize all the remedial, educational, moral, spiritual and other forces and forms of assistance which are appropriate and available, and should seek to apply them according to the individual treatment needs of the prisoners.

60. (1) The regime of the institution should seek to minimize any differences between prison life and life at liberty which tend to lessen the responsibility of the prisoners or the respect due to their dignity as human beings.

(2) Before the completion of the sentence, it is desirable that the necessary steps be taken to ensure for the prisoner a gradual return to life in society. This aim may be achieved, depending on the case, by a pre-release regime organized in the same institution or in another appropriate institution, or by release on trial under some kind of supervision which must not be entrusted to the police but should be combined with effective social aid.

61. The treatment of prisoners should emphasize not their exclusion from the community, but their continuing part in it. Community agencies should, therefore, be enlisted wherever possible to assist the staff of the institution in the task of social rehabilitation of the prisoners. There should be in connection with every institution social workers charged with the duty of maintaining and improving all desirable relations of a prisoner with his family and with valuable social agencies. Steps should be taken to safeguard, to the maximum extent compatible with the law and the sentence, the rights relating to civil interests, social security rights and other social benefits of prisoners.

62. The medical services of the institution shall seek to detect and shall treat any physical or mental illnesses or defects which may hamper a prisoner's rehabilitation. All necessary medical, surgical and psychiatric services shall be provided to that end.

63. (1) The fulfilment of these principles requires individualization of treatment and for this purpose a flexible system of classifying prisoners in groups; it is therefore desirable that such groups should be distributed in separate institutions suitable for the treatment of each group.

(2) These institutions need not provide the same degree of security for every group. It is desirable to provide varying degrees of security according to the needs of different groups. Open institutions, by the very fact that they provide no physical security against escape but rely on the self-discipline of the inmates, provide the conditions most favourable to rehabilitation for carefully selected prisoners.

(3) It is desirable that the number of prisoners in closed institutions should not be so large that the individualization of treatment is hindered. In some countries it is considered that the population of such institutions should not exceed five hundred. In open institutions the population should be as small as possible.

(4) On the other hand, it is undesirable to maintain prisons which are so small that proper facilities cannot be provided.

64. The duty of society does not end with a prisoner's release. There should, therefore, be governmental or private agencies capable of lending the released prisoner efficient after-care directed towards the lessening of prejudice against him and towards his social rehabilitation.

Treatment

65. The treatment of persons sentenced to imprisonment or a similar measure shall have as its purpose, so far as the length of the sentence permits, to establish in them the will to lead law-abiding and self-supporting

lives after their release and to fit them to do so. The treatment shall be such as will encourage their self-respect and develop their sense of responsibility.

66. (1) To these ends, all appropriate means shall be used, including religious care in the countries where this is possible, education, vocational guidance and training, social casework, employment counselling, physical development and strengthening of moral character, in accordance with the individual needs of each prisoner, taking account of his social and criminal history, his physical and mental capacities and aptitudes, his personal temperament, the length of his sentence and his prospects after release.

(2) For every prisoner with a sentence of suitable length, the director shall receive, as soon as possible after his admission, full reports on all the matters referred to in the foregoing paragraph. Such reports shall always include a report by a medical officer, wherever possible qualified in psychiatry, on the physical and mental condition of the prisoner.

(3) The reports and other relevant documents shall be placed in an individual file. This file shall be kept up to date and classified in such a way that it can be consulted by the responsible personnel whenever the need arises.

Classification and individualization

67. The purposes of classification shall be:

(a) To separate from others those prisoners who, by reason of their criminal records or bad characters, are likely to exercise a bad influence;

(b) To divide the prisoners into classes in order to facilitate their treatment with a view to their social rehabilitation.

68. So far as possible separate institutions or separate sections of an institution shall be used for the treatment of the different classes of prisoners.

69. As soon as possible after admission and after a study of the personality of each prisoner with a sentence of suitable length, a programme of treatment shall be prepared for him in the light of the knowledge obtained about his individual needs, his capacities and dispositions.

Privileges

70. Systems of privileges appropriate for the different classes of prisoners and the different methods of treatment shall be established at every institution, in order to encourage good conduct, develop a sense of responsibility and secure the interest and co-operation of the prisoners in their treatment.

Work

71. (1) Prison labour must not be of an afflictive nature.

(2) All prisoners under sentence shall be required to work, subject to their physical and mental fitness as determined by the medical officer.

(3) Sufficient work of a useful nature shall be provided to keep prisoners actively employed for a normal working day.

(4) So far as possible the work provided shall be such as will maintain or increase the prisoners, ability to earn an honest living after release.

(5) Vocational training in useful trades shall be provided for prisoners able to profit thereby and especially for young prisoners.

(6) Within the limits compatible with proper vocational selection and with the requirements of institutional administration and discipline, the prisoners shall be able to choose the type of work they wish to perform.

72. (1) The organization and methods of work in the institutions shall resemble as closely as possible those of similar work outside institutions, so as to prepare prisoners for the conditions of normal occupational life.

(2) The interests of the prisoners and of their vocational training, however, must not be subordinated to the purpose of making a financial profit from an industry in the institution.

73. (1) Preferably institutional industries and farms should be operated directly by the administration and not by private contractors.

(2) Where prisoners are employed in work not controlled by the administration, they shall always be under the supervision of the institution's personnel. Unless the work is for other departments of the government the full normal wages for such work shall be paid to the administration by the persons to whom the labour is supplied, account being taken of the output of the prisoners.

74. (1) The precautions laid down to protect the safety and health of free workmen shall be equally observed in institutions.

(2) Provision shall be made to indemnify prisoners against industrial injury, including occupational disease, on terms not less favourable than those extended by law to free workmen.

75. (1) The maximum daily and weekly working hours of the prisoners shall be fixed by law or by administrative regulation, taking into account local rules or custom in regard to the employment of free workmen.

(2) The hours so fixed shall leave one rest day a week and sufficient time for education and other activities required as part of the treatment and rehabilitation of the prisoners.

76. (1) There shall be a system of equitable remuneration of the work of prisoners.

(2) Under the system prisoners shall be allowed to spend at least a part of their earnings on approved articles for their own use and to send a part of their earnings to their family.

(3) The system should also provide that a part of the earnings should be set aside by the administration so as to constitute a savings fund to be handed over to the prisoner on his release.

Education and recreation

77. (1) Provision shall be made for the further education of all prisoners capable of profiting thereby, including religious instruction in the countries where this is possible. The education of illiterates and young prisoners shall be compulsory and special attention shall be paid to it by the administration.

(2) So far as practicable, the education of prisoners shall be integrated with the educational system of the country so that after their release they may continue their education without difficulty.

78. Recreational and cultural activities shall be provided in all institutions for the benefit of the mental and physical health of prisoners.

Social relations and after-care

79. Special attention shall be paid to the maintenance and improvement of such relations between a prisoner and his family as are desirable in the best interests of both.

80. From the beginning of a prisoner's sentence consideration shall be given to his future after release and he shall be encouraged and assisted to maintain or establish such relations with persons or agencies outside the institution as may promote the best interests of his family and his own social rehabilitation.

81. (1) Services and agencies, governmental or otherwise, which assist released prisoners to re-establish themselves in society shall ensure, so far as is possible and necessary, that released prisoners be provided with appropriate documents and identification papers, have suitable homes and work to go to, are suitably and adequately clothed having regard to the climate and season, and have sufficient means to reach their destination and maintain themselves in the period immediately following their release.

(2) The approved representatives of such agencies shall have all necessary access to the institution and to prisoners and shall be taken into consultation as to the future of a prisoner from the beginning of his sentence.

(3) It is desirable that the activities of such agencies shall be centralized or co-ordinated as far as possible in order to secure the best use of their efforts.

B. Insane and Mentally Abnormal Prisoners

82. (1) Persons who are found to be insane shall not be detained in prisons and arrangements shall be made to remove them to mental institutions as soon as possible.

(2) Prisoners who suffer from other mental diseases or abnormalities shall be observed and treated in specialized institutions under medical management.

(3) During their stay in a prison, such prisoners shall be placed under the special supervision of a medical officer.

(4) The medical or psychiatric service of the penal institutions shall provide for the psychiatric treatment of all other prisoners who are in need of such treatment.

83. It is desirable that steps should be taken, by arrangement with the appropriate agencies, to ensure if necessary the continuation of psychiatric treatment after release and the provision of social-psychiatric after-care.

C. Prisoners under Arrest or Awaiting Trial

84. (1) Persons arrested or imprisoned by reason of a criminal charge against them, who are detained either in police custody or in prison custody (jail) but have not yet been tried and sentenced, will be referred to as "untried prisoners," hereinafter in these rules.

(2) Unconvicted prisoners are presumed to be innocent and shall be treated as such.

(3) Without prejudice to legal rules for the protection of individual liberty or prescribing the procedure to be observed in respect of untried prisoners, these prisoners shall benefit by a special regime which is described in the following rules in its essential requirements only.

85. (1) Untried prisoners shall be kept separate from convicted prisoners.

(2) Young untried prisoners shall be kept separate from adults and shall in principle be detained in separate institutions.

86. Untried prisoners shall sleep singly in separate rooms, with the reservation of different local custom in respect of the climate.

87. Within the limits compatible with the good order of the institution, untried prisoners may, if they so desire, have their food procured at their own expense from the outside, either through the administration or through their family or friends. Otherwise, the administration shall provide their food.

88. (1) An untried prisoner shall be allowed to wear his own clothing if it is clean and suitable.

(2) If he wears prison dress, it shall be different from that supplied to convicted prisoners.

89. An untried prisoner shall always be offered opportunity to work, but shall not be required to work. If he chooses to work, he shall be paid for it.

90. An untried prisoner shall be allowed to procure at his own expense or at the expense of a third party such books, newspapers, writing materials and other means of occupation as are compatible with the interests of the administration of justice and the security and good order of the institution.

91. An untried prisoner shall be allowed to be visited and treated by his own doctor or dentist if there is reasonable ground for his application and he is able to pay any expenses incurred.

92. An untried prisoner shall be allowed to inform immediately his family of his detention and shall be given all reasonable facilities for communicating with his family and friends, and for receiving visits from them, subject only to restrictions and supervision as are necessary in the interests of the administration of justice and of the security and good order of the institution.

93. For the purposes of his defence, an untried prisoner shall be allowed to apply for free legal aid where such aid is available, and to receive visits from his legal adviser with a view to his defence and to prepare and hand to him confidential instructions. For these purposes, he shall if he so desires be supplied with writing material. Interviews between the prisoner and his legal adviser may be within sight but not within the hearing of a police or institution official.

D. Civil Prisoners

94. In countries where the law permits imprisonment for debt, or by order of a court under any other non-criminal process, persons so imprisoned shall not be subjected to any greater restriction or severity than is necessary to ensure safe custody and good order. Their treatment shall be not less favourable than that of untried prisoners, with the reservation, however, that they may possibly be required to work.

E. Persons Arrested or Detained Without Charge

95. Without prejudice to the provisions of Article 9 of the International Covenant on Civil and Political Rights, persons arrested or imprisoned without charge shall be accorded the same protection as that accorded under part I and part II, section C. Relevant provisions of part II, section A, shall likewise be applicable where their application may be conducive to the benefit of this special group of persons in custody, provided that no measures shall be taken implying that re-education or rehabilitation is in any way appropriate to persons not convicted of any criminal offence.

DOCUMENT 49

Full Official Title: Safeguards Guaranteeing Protection of the Rights of Those Facing the Death Penalty; Death Penalty, Administration of Justice

Short Title/Acronym/Abbreviation: Nothing official

Subject: Establishing specific international safeguards to be applied to the situation of all persons facing judicially imposed execution (death penalty) so that their human rights are respected until death.

Official Citation: Economic and Social Council resolution 1984/50 of 25 May 1984

Date of Document: May 25, 1984

Date of Adoption: May 25, 1984

Date of General Entry into Force (EIF): Not applicable

Number of States Parties to this Treaty as of this printing: Not a treaty

Date of Signature by United States: Not applicable

Date of Ratification/Accession/Adhesion: Not applicable

Date of Entry into Force as to United States (effective date): Not applicable

Type of Document: A set of measures which a state may take when imposing the death penalty, so that it can do so in a way that is most protective of the human rights of the condemned person.

Supervising Body: None

Legal Status/Character of the Instrument/Document as to the United States: It is not legally binding upon the United States, but because these are adopted within the context of the United Nations, of which the United States is a key member, the United States should consider them when examining its systems of imposing the death penalty. These safeguards are sometimes referred to as having the status of "soft law." There is no U.N. body which enforces these principles because they are not legally binding.

Comments: Some U.N. bodies look to these principles in examining specific issues involving the death penalty or summary executions. Some special rapporteurs use these international safeguards as a standard to judge particular cases in countries they study. They are also referred to in the U.S. reports to the U.N. Committee against Torture and to the Human Rights Committee, Document 21. The United States recognizes them, but not as legally binding.

Caution: The status and applicability of this instrument as to the United States may have changed since date of publication. The above information may be updated by referring to the following site:

Web address: http://www1.umn.edu/humanrts/instree/i8sgpr.htm

SAFEGUARDS GUARANTEEING PROTECTION OF THE RIGHTS OF THOSE FACING THE DEATH PENALTY; DEATH PENALTY, ADMINISTRATION OF JUSTICE

Adopted by Economic and Social Council resolution 1984/50 of 25 May 1984

1. In countries which have not abolished the death penalty, capital punishment may be imposed only for the most serious crimes, it being understood that their scope should not go beyond intentional crimes with lethal or other extremely grave consequences.

2. Capital punishment may be imposed only for a crime for which the death penalty is prescribed by law at the time of its commission, it being understood that if, subsequent to the commission of the crime, provision is made by law for the imposition of a lighter penalty, the offender shall benefit thereby.

3. Persons below 18 years of age at the time of the commission of the crime shall not be sentenced to death, nor shall the death sentence be carried out on pregnant women, or on new mothers, or on persons who have become insane.

4. Capital punishment may be imposed only when the guilt of the person charged is based upon clear and convincing evidence leaving no room for an alternative explanation of the facts.

5. Capital punishment may only be carried out pursuant to a final judgement rendered by a competent court after legal process which gives all possible safeguards to ensure a fair trial, at least equal to those contained in Article 14 of the International Covenant on Civil and Political Rights, including the right of anyone suspected of or charged with a crime for which capital punishment may be imposed to adequate legal assistance at all stages of the proceedings.

6. Anyone sentenced to death shall have the right to appeal to a court of higher jurisdiction, and steps should be taken to ensure that such appeals shall become mandatory.

7. Anyone sentenced to death shall have the right to seek pardon, or commutation of sentence; pardon or commutation of sentence may be granted in all cases of capital punishment.

8. Capital punishment shall not be carried out pending any appeal or other recourse procedure or other proceeding relating to pardon or commutation of the sentence.

9. Where capital punishment occurs, it shall be carried out so as to inflict the minimum possible suffering.

Copyright 1997 Office of the United Nations High Commissioner for Human Rights, Geneva, Switzerland

---

DOCUMENT 50

Full Official Title: United Nations Millennium Declaration

Short Title/Acronym/Abbreviation: The Millenium Declaration or MDG Declaration

Type of Document: A declaration of principles and 8 goals (Millenium Development Goals (MDGs)) for a program of global development

Subject: A global plan for incremental development of every state in the world by 2015.
Official Citation: General Assembly resolution 55/2 of 8 September 2000
Date of Document: September 8, 2000
Date of Adoption: September 8, 2000
Date of General Entry into Force (EIF): Not applicable
Number of States Parties as of this printing: Not applicable
Date of Signature by United States: Not applicable
Date of Ratification/Accession/Adhesion: Not applicable
Date of Entry into Force as to United States (effective date): Not applicable
Legal Status/Character of the Instrument/Document as to the United States: Non-binding declaration; not a legal document. MDGs are voluntary but states are strongly urged to strive to the goals, most of which are tied to human rights.

Almost nothing has been said publicly in the U.S. about these MDGs. The Obama government participated in the U.N. MDG Summit in September 2010 where the 192 nations of the U.N. promised to intensify their efforts to meet the MDGs by 2015.

Web Address: www.umn.edu/humanrts/instree/millennium.html

United Nations Millennium Declaration

General Assembly resolution 55/2 of 8 September 2000

The General Assembly

Adopts the following Declaration:

United Nations Millenium Declaration

I. Values and principles

1. We, heads of State and Government, have gathered at United Nations Headquarters in New York from 6 to 8 September 2000, at the dawn of a new millennium, to reaffirm our faith in the Organization and its Charter as indispensable foundations of a more peaceful, prosperous and just world.

2. We recognize that, in addition to our separate responsibilities to our individual societies, we have a collective responsibility to uphold the principles of human dignity, equality and equity at the global level. As leaders we have a duty therefore to all the world's people, especially the most vulnerable and, in particular, the children of the world, to whom the future belongs.

3. We reaffirm our commitment to the purposes and principles of the Charter of the United Nations, which have proved timeless and universal. Indeed, their relevance and capacity to inspire have increased, as nations and peoples have become increasingly interconnected and interdependent.

4. We are determined to establish a just and lasting peace all over the world in accordance with the purposes and principles of the Charter. We rededicate ourselves to support all efforts to uphold the sovereign equality of all States, respect for their territorial integrity and political independence, resolution of disputes by peaceful means and in conformity with the principles of justice and international law, the right to self-determination of peoples which remain under colonial domination and foreign occupation, non-interference in the internal affairs of States, respect for human rights and fundamental freedoms, respect for the equal rights of all without distinction as to race, sex, language or religion and international cooperation in solving international problems of an economic, social, cultural or humanitarian character.

5. We believe that the central challenge we face today is to ensure that globalization becomes a positive force for all the world's people. For while globalization offers great opportunities, at present its benefits are very unevenly shared, while its costs are unevenly distributed. We recognize that developing countries and countries with economies in transition face special difficulties in responding to this central challenge. Thus, only through broad and sustained efforts to create a shared future, based upon our common humanity in all its diversity, can globalization be made fully inclusive and equitable. These efforts must include policies and measures, at the global level, which correspond to the needs of developing countries and economies in transition and are formulated and implemented with their effective participation.

6. We consider certain fundamental values to be essential to international relations in the twenty-first century. These include:

• Freedom. Men and women have the right to live their lives and raise their children in dignity, free from hunger and from the fear of violence, oppression or injustice. Democratic and participatory governance based on the will of the people best assures these rights.

• Equality. No individual and no nation must be denied the opportunity to benefit from development. The equal rights and opportunities of women and men must be assured.

• Solidarity. Global challenges must be managed in a way that distributes the costs and burdens fairly in accordance with basic principles of equity and social justice. Those who suffer or who benefit least deserve help from those who benefit most.

• Tolerance. Human beings must respect one other, in all their diversity of belief, culture and language. Differences within and between societies should be neither feared nor repressed, but cherished as a precious asset of humanity. A culture of peace and dialogue among all civilizations should be actively promoted.

• Respect for nature. Prudence must be shown in the management of all living species and natural resources, in accordance with the precepts of sustainable development. Only in this way can the immeasurable riches provided to us by nature be preserved and passed on to our descendants. The current unsustainable patterns of production and consumption must be changed in the interest of our future welfare and that of our descendants.

• Shared responsibility. Responsibility for managing worldwide economic and social development, as well as threats to international peace and security, must be shared among the nations of the world and should be exercised multilaterally. As the most universal and most representative organization in the world, the United Nations must play the central role.

7. In order to translate these shared values into actions, we have identified key objectives to which we assign special significance.

II. Peace, security and disarmament

8. We will spare no effort to free our peoples from the scourge of war, whether within or between States, which has claimed more than 5 million lives in the past decade. We will also seek to eliminate the dangers posed by weapons of mass destruction.

9. We resolve therefore:

• To strengthen respect for the rule of law in international as in national affairs and, in particular, to ensure compliance by Member States with the decisions of the International Court of Justice, in compliance with the Charter of the United Nations, in cases to which they are parties.

• To make the United Nations more effective in maintaining peace and security by giving it the resources and tools it needs for conflict prevention, peaceful resolution of disputes, peacekeeping, post-conflict peace-building and reconstruction. In this context, we take note of the report of the Panel on United Nations Peace Operations and request the General Assembly to consider its recommendations expeditiously.

• To strengthen cooperation between the United Nations and regional organizations, in accordance with the provisions of Chapter VIII of the Charter.

• To ensure the implementation, by States Parties, of treaties in areas such as arms control and disarmament and of international humanitarian law and human rights law, and call upon all States to consider signing and ratifying the Rome Statute of the International Criminal Court.

• To take concerted action against international terrorism, and to accede as soon as possible to all the relevant international conventions.

• To redouble our efforts to implement our commitment to counter the world drug problem.

• To intensify our efforts to fight transnational crime in all its dimensions, including trafficking as well as smuggling in human beings and money laundering.

• To minimize the adverse effects of United Nations economic sanctions on innocent populations, to subject such sanctions regimes to regular reviews and to eliminate the adverse effects of sanctions on third parties.

• To strive for the elimination of weapons of mass destruction, particularly nuclear weapons, and to keep all options open for achieving this aim, including the possibility of convening an international conference to identify ways of eliminating nuclear dangers.

• To take concerted action to end illicit traffic in small arms and light weapons, especially by making arms transfers more transparent and supporting regional disarmament measures, taking account of all the recommendations of the forthcoming United Nations Conference on Illicit Trade in Small Arms and Light Weapons.

• To call on all States to consider acceding to the Convention on the Prohibition of the Use, Stockpiling, Production and Transfer of Anti-personnel Mines and on Their Destruction, as well as the amended mines protocol to the Convention on conventional weapons.

10. We urge Member States to observe the Olympic Truce, individually and collectively, now and in the future, and to support the International Olympic Committee in its efforts to promote peace and human understanding through sport and the Olympic Ideal.

III. Development and poverty eradication

11. We will spare no effort to free our fellow men, women and children from the abject and dehumanizing conditions of extreme poverty, to which more than a billion of them are currently subjected. We are committed to making the right to development a reality for everyone and to freeing the entire human race from want.

12. We resolve therefore to create an environment—at the national and global levels alike—which is conducive to development and to the elimination of poverty.

13. Success in meeting these objectives depends, inter alia , on good governance within each country. It also depends on good governance at the international level and on transparency in the financial, monetary and trading systems. We are committed to an open, equitable, rule-based, predictable and non-discriminatory multilateral trading and financial system.

14. We are concerned about the obstacles developing countries face in mobilizing the resources needed to finance their sustained development. We will therefore make every effort to ensure the success of the High-level International and Intergovernmental Event on Financing for Development, to be held in 2001.

15. We also undertake to address the special needs of the least developed countries. In this context, we welcome the Third United Nations Conference on the Least Developed Countries to be held in May 2001 and will endeavour to ensure its success. We call on the industrialized countries:

• To adopt, preferably by the time of that Conference, a policy of duty-and quota-free access for essentially all exports from the least developed countries;

• To implement the enhanced programme of debt relief for the heavily indebted poor countries without further delay and to agree to cancel all official bilateral debts of those countries in return for their making demonstrable commitments to poverty reduction; and

• To grant more generous development assistance, especially to countries that are genuinely making an effort to apply their resources to poverty reduction.

16. We are also determined to deal comprehensively and effectively with the debt problems of low-and middle-income developing countries, through various national and international measures designed to make their debt sustainable in the long term.

17. We also resolve to address the special needs of small island developing States, by implementing the Barbados Programme of Action and the outcome of the twenty-second special session of the General Assembly rapidly and in full. We urge the international community to ensure that, in the development of a vulnerability index, the special needs of small island developing States are taken into account.

18. We recognize the special needs and problems of the landlocked developing countries, and urge both bilateral and multilateral donors to increase financial and technical assistance to this group of countries to meet their special development needs and to help them overcome the impediments of geography by improving their transit transport systems.

19. We resolve further:

• To halve, by the year 2015, the proportion of the world's people whose income is less than one dollar a day and the proportion of people who suffer from hunger and, by the same date, to halve the proportion of people who are unable to reach or to afford safe drinking water.

• To ensure that, by the same date, children everywhere, boys and girls alike, will be able to complete a full course of primary schooling and that girls and boys will have equal access to all levels of education.

• By the same date, to have reduced maternal mortality by three quarters, and under-five child mortality by two thirds, of their current rates.

• To have, by then, halted, and begun to reverse, the spread of HIV/AIDS, the scourge of malaria and other major diseases that afflict humanity.

• To provide special assistance to children orphaned by HIV/AIDS.

• By 2020, to have achieved a significant improvement in the lives of at least 100 million slum dwellers as proposed in the "Cities Without Slums" initiative.

20. We also resolve:

• To promote gender equality and the empowerment of women as effective ways to combat poverty, hunger and disease and to stimulate development that is truly sustainable.

- To develop and implement strategies that give young people everywhere a real chance to find decent and productive work.
- To encourage the pharmaceutical industry to make essential drugs more widely available and affordable by all who need them in developing countries.
- To develop strong partnerships with the private sector and with civil society organizations in pursuit of development and poverty eradication.
- To ensure that the benefits of new technologies, especially information and communication technologies, in conformity with recommendations contained in the ECOSOC 2000 Ministerial Declaration, are available to all.

IV. Protecting our common environment

21. We must spare no effort to free all of humanity, and above all our children and grandchildren, from the threat of living on a planet irredeemably spoilt by human activities, and whose resources would no longer be sufficient for their needs.

22. We reaffirm our support for the principles of sustainable development, including those set out in Agenda 21, agreed upon at the United Nations Conference on Environment and Development.

23. We resolve therefore to adopt in all our environmental actions a new ethic of conservation and stewardship and, as first steps, we resolve:

- To make every effort to ensure the entry into force of the Kyoto Protocol, preferably by the tenth anniversary of the United Nations Conference on Environment and Development in 2002, and to embark on the required reduction in emissions of greenhouse gases.
- To intensify our collective efforts for the management, conservation and sustainable development of all types of forests.
- To press for the full implementation of the Convention on Biological Diversity and the Convention to Combat Desertification in those Countries Experiencing Serious Drought and/or Desertification, particularly in Africa.
- To stop the unsustainable exploitation of water resources by developing water management strategies at the regional, national and local levels, which promote both equitable access and adequate supplies.
- To intensify cooperation to reduce the number and effects of natural and man-made disasters.
- To ensure free access to information on the human genome sequence.

V. Human rights, democracy and good governance

24. We will spare no effort to promote democracy and strengthen the rule of law, as well as respect for all internationally recognized human rights and fundamental freedoms, including the right to development.

25. We resolve therefore:

- To respect fully and uphold the Universal Declaration of Human Rights.
- To strive for the full protection and promotion in all our countries of civil, political, economic, social and cultural rights for all.
- To strengthen the capacity of all our countries to implement the principles and practices of democracy and respect for human rights, including minority rights.
- To combat all forms of violence against women and to implement the Convention on the Elimination of All Forms of Discrimination against Women.
- To take measures to ensure respect for and protection of the human rights of migrants, migrant workers and their families, to eliminate the increasing acts of racism and xenophobia in many societies and to promote greater harmony and tolerance in all societies.
- To work collectively for more inclusive political processes, allowing genuine participation by all citizens in all our countries.
- To ensure the freedom of the media to perform their essential role and the right of the public to have access to information.

VI. Protecting the vulnerable

26. We will spare no effort to ensure that children and all civilian populations that suffer disproportionately the consequences of natural disasters, genocide, armed conflicts and other humanitarian emergencies are given every assistance and protection so that they can resume normal life as soon as possible.

We resolve therefore:

- To expand and strengthen the protection of civilians in complex emergencies, in conformity with international humanitarian law.
- To strengthen international cooperation, including burden sharing in, and the coordination of humanitarian assistance to, countries hosting refugees and to help all refugees and displaced persons to return voluntarily to their s, in safety and dignity and to be smoothly reintegrated into their societies.

• To encourage the ratification and full implementation of the Convention on the Rights of the Child and its optional protocols on the involvement of children in armed conflict and on the sale of children, child prostitution and child pornography.

VII. Meeting the special needs of Africa

27. We will support the consolidation of democracy in Africa and assist Africans in their struggle for lasting peace, poverty eradication and sustainable development, thereby bringing Africa into the mainstream of the world economy.

28. We resolve therefore:

• To give full support to the political and institutional structures of emerging democracies in Africa.

• To encourage and sustain regional and subregional mechanisms for preventing conflict and promoting political stability, and to ensure a reliable flow of resources for peacekeeping operations on the continent.

• To take special measures to address the challenges of poverty eradication and sustainable development in Africa, including debt cancellation, improved market access, enhanced Official Development Assistance and increased flows of Foreign Direct Investment, as well as transfers of technology.

• To help Africa build up its capacity to tackle the spread of the HIV/AIDS pandemic and other infectious diseases.

VIII. Strengthening the United Nations

29. We will spare no effort to make the United Nations a more effective instrument for pursuing all of these priorities: the fight for development for all the peoples of the world, the fight against poverty, ignorance and disease; the fight against injustice; the fight against violence, terror and crime; and the fight against the degradation and destruction of our common.

30. We resolve therefore:

• To reaffirm the central position of the General Assembly as the chief deliberative, policy-making and representative organ of the United Nations, and to enable it to play that role effectively.

• To intensify our efforts to achieve a comprehensive reform of the Security Council in all its aspects.

• To strengthen further the Economic and Social Council, building on its recent achievements, to help it fulfil the role ascribed to it in the Charter.

• To strengthen the International Court of Justice, in order to ensure justice and the rule of law in international affairs.

• To encourage regular consultations and coordination among the principal organs of the United Nations in pursuit of their functions.

• To ensure that the Organization is provided on a timely and predictable basis with the resources it needs to carry out its mandates.

• To urge the Secretariat to make the best use of those resources, in accordance with clear rules and procedures agreed by the General Assembly, in the interests of all Member States, by adopting the best management practices and technologies available and by concentrating on those tasks that reflect the agreed priorities of Member States.

• To promote adherence to the Convention on the Safety of United Nations and Associated Personnel.

• To ensure greater policy coherence and better cooperation between the United Nations, its agencies, the Bretton Woods Institutions and the World Trade Organization, as well as other multilateral bodies, with a view to achieving a fully coordinated approach to the problems of peace and development.

• To strengthen further cooperation between the United Nations and national parliaments through their world organization, the Inter-Parliamentary Union, in various fields, including peace and security, economic and social development, international law and human rights and democracy and gender issues.

• To give greater opportunities to the private sector, non-governmental organizations and civil society, in general, to contribute to the realization of the Organization's goals and programmes.

31. We request the General Assembly to review on a regular basis the progress made in implementing the provisions of this Declaration, and ask the Secretary-General to issue periodic reports for consideration by the General Assembly and as a basis for further action.

32. We solemnly reaffirm, on this historic occasion, that the United Nations is the indispensable common house of the entire human family, through which we will seek to realize our universal aspirations for peace, cooperation and development. We therefore pledge our unstinting support for these common objectives and our determination to achieve them.

DOCUMENT 51

Full Official Title: Vienna Declaration and Programme of Action

Short Title/Acronym/Abbreviation: Vienna Declaration/1993 Vienna Declaration

Subject: An evaluation, declaration of goals and principles, and program of action for the advancement of human rights in the world, in the context of the United Nations.

Official Citation: A/Conf 157/23 of 25 June 1993

Date of Document: June 25, 1993

Date of Adoption: Not applicable

Date of General Entry into Force (EIF): Not applicable

Number of States Parties to this Treaty as of this printing: Not a treaty

Date of Signature by United States: Not applicable

Date of Ratification/Accession/Adhesion: Not applicable

Date of Entry into Force as to United States (effective date): Not applicable

Type of Document: A declaration of the member states of the United Nations gathered in Vienna for a human rights conference to proclaim the state of international human rights in the U.N. context and how that body wants the United Nations to deal with human rights thereafter in its various bodies and mechanisms. Not meant to be a legal instrument.

Legal Status/Character of the Instrument/Document as to the United States: Not legally binding on the United States. However, the fact that this document was adopted by consensus indicates that most all of the states of the world subscribe to its statements on human rights and thus it should be followed on the basis of its political and moral weight. It was voted on for adoption by the states at the Conference.

Comments: The United States was very instrumental in the drafting and adoption of this document, which reaffirms that human rights are the universal "birthright" of all human beings. The U.S. delegation was particularly strong in its pushing for the acceptance of the principle of "universality" of human rights, as opposed to cultural relativism. This document now serves as the basis of the direction of the United Nations in all its human rights activities, especially in the Office of the High Commissioner for Human Rights. It states the strongest and broadest opinion of all the countries of the world as to what human rights are and how they should be protected and respected. It ends with a very strong call for human rights education for everyone, at all levels of society. Everyone should read this document. Every serious work of human rights scholarship should take the substance of this Declaration into account.

Web address: http://www.unhchr.ch/huridocda/huridoca.nsf/(Symbol)/A.CONF.157.23.En? OpenDocument

VIENNA DECLARATION AND PROGRAMME OF ACTION

Note by the secretariat:

Attached is the text of the Vienna Declaration and Programme of Action, as adopted by the World Conference on Human Rights on 25 June 1993.

The World Conference on Human Rights,

Considering that the promotion and protection of human rights is a matter of priority for the international community, and that the Conference affords a unique opportunity to carry out a comprehensive analysis of the international human rights system and of the machinery for the protection of human rights, in order to enhance and thus promote a fuller observance of those rights, in a just and balanced manner,

Recognizing and affirming that all human rights derive from the dignity and worth inherent in the human person, and that the human person is the central subject of human rights and fundamental freedoms, and consequently should be the principal beneficiary and should participate actively in the realization of these rights and freedoms,

Reaffirming their commitment to the purposes and principles contained in the Charter of the United Nations and the Universal Declaration of Human Rights,

Reaffirming the commitment contained in Article 56 of the Charter of the United Nations to take joint and separate action, placing proper emphasis on developing effective international cooperation for the realization of the purposes set out in Article 55, including universal respect for, and observance of, human rights and fundamental freedoms for all,

Emphasizing the responsibilities of all States, in conformity with the Charter of the United Nations, to develop and encourage respect for human rights and fundamental freedoms for all, without distinction as to race, sex, language or religion,

DOCUMENT 51

Recalling the Preamble to the Charter of the United Nations, in particular the determination to reaffirm faith in fundamental human rights, in the dignity and worth of the human person, and in the equal rights of men and women and of nations large and small,

Recalling also the determination expressed in the Preamble of the Charter of the United Nations to save succeeding generations from the scourge of war, to establish conditions under which justice and respect for obligations arising from treaties and other sources of international law can be maintained, to promote social progress and better standards of life in larger freedom, to practice tolerance and good neighbourliness, and to employ international machinery for the promotion of the economic and social advancement of all peoples,

Emphasizing that the Universal Declaration of Human Rights, which constitutes a common standard of achievement for all peoples and all nations, is the source of inspiration and has been the basis for the United Nations in making advances in standard setting as contained in the existing international human rights instruments, in particular the International Covenant on Civil and Political Rights and the International Covenant on Economic, Social and Cultural Rights.

Considering the major changes taking place on the international scene and the aspirations of all the peoples for an international order based on the principles enshrined in the Charter of the United Nations, including promoting and encouraging respect for human rights and fundamental freedoms for all and respect for the principle of equal rights and self -determination of peoples, peace, democracy, justice, equality, rule of law, pluralism, development, better standards of living and solidarity,

Deeply concerned by various forms of discrimination and violence, to which women continue to be exposed all over the world,

Recognizing that the activities of the United Nations in the field of human rights should be rationalized and enhanced in order to strengthen the United Nations machinery in this field and to further the objectives of universal respect for observance of international human rights standards,

Having taken into account the Declarations adopted by the three regional meetings at Tunis, San José and Bangkok and the contributions made by Governments, and bearing in mind the suggestions made by intergovernmental and non-governmental organizations, as well as the studies prepared by independent experts during the preparatory process leading to the World Conference on Human Rights,

Welcoming the International Year of the World's Indigenous People 1993 as a reaffirmation of the commitment of the international community to ensure their enjoyment of all human rights and fundamental freedoms and to respect the value and diversity of their cultures and identities,

Recognizing also that the international community should devise ways and means to remove the current obstacles and meet challenges to the full realization of all human rights and to prevent the continuation of human rights violations resulting thereof throughout the world,

Invoking the spirit of our age and the realities of our time which call upon the peoples of the world and all States Members of the United Nations to rededicate themselves to the global task of promoting and protecting all human rights and fundamental freedoms so as to secure full and universal enjoyment of these rights,

Determined to take new steps forward in the commitment of the international community with a view to achieving substantial progress in human rights endeavours by an increased and sustained effort of international cooperation and solidarity,

Solemnly adopts the Vienna Declaration and Programme of Action

1. The World Conference on Human Rights reaffirms the solemn commitment of all States to fulfil their obligations to promote universal respect for, and observance and protection of, all human rights and fundamental freedoms for all in accordance with the Charter of the United Nations, other instruments relating to human rights, and international law. The universal nature of these rights and freedoms is beyond question.

In this framework, enhancement of international cooperation in the field of human rights is essential for the full achievement of the purposes of the United Nations.

Human rights and fundamental freedoms are the birthright of all human beings; their protection and promotion is the first responsibility of Governments.

2. All peoples have the right of self-determination. By virtue of that right they freely determine their political status, and freely pursue their economic, social and cultural development.

Taking into account the particular situation of peoples under colonial or other forms of alien domination or foreign occupation, the World Conference on Human Rights recognizes the right of peoples to take any legitimate action, in accordance with the Charter of the United Nations, to realize their inalienable right of self-determination. The World Conference on Human Rights considers the denial of the right of self-determination as a violation of human rights and underlines the importance of the effective realization of this right.

In accordance with the Declaration on Principles of International Law concerning Friendly Relations and Cooperation Among States in accordance with the Charter of the United Nations, this shall not be construed as authorizing or encouraging any action which would dismember or impair, totally or in part, the territorial integrity or political unity of sovereign and independent States conducting themselves in compliance with the principle of equal rights and self-determination of peoples and thus possessed of a Government representing the whole people belonging to the territory without distinction of any kind.

3. Effective international measures to guarantee and monitor the implementation of human rights standards should be taken in respect of people under foreign occupation, and effective legal protection against the violation of their human rights should be provided, in accordance with human rights norms and international law, particularly the Geneva Convention relative to the Protection of Civilian Persons in Time of War, of 14 August 1949, and other applicable norms of humanitarian law.

4. The promotion and protection of all human rights and fundamental freedoms must be considered as a priority objective of the United Nations in accordance with its purposes and principles, in particular the purpose of international cooperation. In the framework of these purposes and principles, the promotion and protection of all human rights is a legitimate concern of the international community. The organs and specialized agencies related to human rights should therefore further enhance the coordination of their activities based on the consistent and objective application of international human rights instruments.

5. All human rights are universal, indivisible and interdependent and interrelated. The international community must treat human rights globally in a fair and equal manner, on the same footing, and with the same emphasis. While the significance of national and regional particularities and various historical, cultural and religious backgrounds must be borne in mind, it is the duty of States, regardless of their political, economic and cultural systems, to promote and protect all human rights and fundamental freedoms.

6. The efforts of the United Nations system towards the universal respect for, and observance of, human rights and fundamental freedoms for all, contribute to the stability and well-being necessary for peaceful and friendly relations among nations, and to improved conditions for peace and security as well as social and economic development, in conformity with the Charter of the United Nations.

7. The processes of promoting and protecting human rights should be conducted in conformity with the purposes and principles of the Charter of the United Nations, and international law.

8. Democracy, development and respect for human rights and fundamental freedoms are interdependent and mutually reinforcing. Democracy is based on the freely expressed will of the people to determine their own political, economic, social and cultural systems and their full participation in all aspects of their lives. In the context of the above, the promotion and protection of human rights and fundamental freedoms at the national and international levels should be universal and conducted without conditions attached. The international community should support the strengthening and promoting of democracy, development and respect for human rights and fundamental freedoms in the entire world.

9. The World Conference on Human Rights reaffirms that least developed countries committed to the process of democratization and economic reforms, many of which are in Africa, should be supported by the international community in order to succeed in their transition to democracy and economic development.

10. The World Conference on Human Rights reaffirms the right to development, as established in the Declaration on the Right to Development, as a universal and inalienable right and an integral part of fundamental human rights.

As stated in the Declaration on the Right to Development, the human person is the central subject of development.

While development facilitates the enjoyment of all human rights, the lack of development may not be invoked to justify the abridgement of internationally recognized human rights.

States should cooperate with each other in ensuring development and eliminating obstacles to development. The international community should promote an effective international cooperation for the realization of the right to development and the elimination of obstacles to development.

Lasting progress towards the implementation of the right to development requires effective development policies at the national level, as well as equitable economic relations and a favourable economic environment at the international level.

11. The right to development should be fulfilled so as to meet equitably the developmental and environmental needs of present and future generations. The World Conference on Human Rights recognizes that illicit dumping of toxic and dangerous substances and waste potentially constitutes a serious threat to the human rights to life and health of everyone.

Consequently, the World Conference on Human Rights calls on all States to adopt and vigorously implement existing conventions relating to the dumping of toxic and dangerous products and waste and to cooperate in the prevention of illicit dumping.

Everyone has the right to enjoy the benefits of scientific progress and its applications. The World Conference on Human Rights notes that certain advances, notably in the biomedical and life sciences as well as in information technology, may have potentially adverse consequences for the integrity, dignity and human rights of the individual, and calls for international cooperation to ensure that human rights and dignity are fully respected in this area of universal concern.

12. The World Conference on Human Rights calls upon the international community to make all efforts to help alleviate the external debt burden of developing countries, in order to supplement the efforts of the Governments of such countries to attain the full realization of the economic, social and cultural rights of their people.

13. There is a need for States and international organizations, in cooperation with non-governmental organizations, to create favourable conditions at the national, regional and international levels to ensure the full and effective enjoyment of human rights. States should eliminate all violations of human rights and their causes, as well as obstacles to the enjoyment of these rights.

14. The existence of widespread extreme poverty inhibits the full and effective enjoyment of human rights; its immediate alleviation and eventual elimination must remain a high priority for the international community.

15. Respect for human rights and for fundamental freedoms without distinction of any kind is a fundamental rule of international human rights law. The speedy and comprehensive elimination of all forms of racism and racial discrimination, xenophobia and related intolerance is a priority task for the international community. Governments should take effective measures to prevent and combat them. Groups, institutions, intergovernmental and non-governmental organizations and individuals are urged to intensify their efforts in cooperating and coordinating their activities against these evils.

16. The World Conference on Human Rights welcomes the progress made in dismantling apartheid and calls upon the international community and the United Nations system to assist in this process.

The World Conference on Human Rights also deplores the continuing acts of violence aimed at undermining the quest for a peaceful dismantling of apartheid.

17. The acts, methods and practices of terrorism in all its forms and manifestations as well as linkage in some countries to drug trafficking are activities aimed at the destruction of human rights, fundamental freedoms and democracy, threatening territorial integrity, security of States and destabilizing legitimately constituted Governments. The international community should take the necessary steps to enhance cooperation to prevent and combat terrorism.

18. The human rights of women and of the girl-child are an inalienable, integral and indivisible part of universal human rights. The full and equal participation of women in political, civil, economic, social and cultural life, at the national, regional and international levels, and the eradication of all forms of discrimination on grounds of sex are priority objectives of the international community.

Gender-based violence and all forms of sexual harassment and exploitation, including those resulting from cultural prejudice and international trafficking, are incompatible with the dignity and worth of the human person, and must be eliminated. This can be achieved by legal measures and through national action and international cooperation in such fields as economic and social development, education, safe maternity and health care, and social support.

The human rights of women should form an integral part of the United Nations human rights activities, including the promotion of all human rights instruments relating to women.

The World Conference on Human Rights urges Governments, institutions, intergovernmental and non-governmental organizations to intensify their efforts for the protection and promotion of human rights of women and the girl-child.

19. Considering the importance of the promotion and protection of the rights of persons belonging to minorities and the contribution of such promotion and protection to the political and social stability of the States in which such persons live,

The World Conference on Human Rights reaffirms the obligation of States to ensure that persons belonging to minorities may exercise fully and effectively all human rights and fundamental freedoms without any discrimination and in full equality before the law in accordance with the Declaration on the Rights of Persons Belonging to National or Ethnic, Religious and Linguistic Minorities.

The persons belonging to minorities have the right to enjoy their own culture, to profess and practise their own religion and to use their own language in private and in public, freely and without interference or any form of discrimination.

20. The World Conference on Human Rights recognizes the inherent dignity and the unique contribution of indigenous people to the development and plurality of society and strongly reaffirms the commitment of the international community to their economic, social and cultural well-being and their enjoyment of the fruits of sustainable development. States should ensure the full and free participation of indigenous people in all aspects of society, in particular in matters of concern to them. Considering the importance of the promotion and protection of the rights of indigenous people, and the contribution of such promotion and protection to the political and social stability of the States in which such people live, States should, in accordance with international law, take concerted positive steps to ensure respect for all human rights and fundamental freedoms of indigenous people, on the basis of equality and non-discrimination, and recognize the value and diversity of their distinct identities, cultures and social organization.

21. The World Conference on Human Rights, welcoming the early ratification of the Convention on the Rights of the Child by a large number of States and noting the recognition of the human rights of children in the World Declaration on the Survival, Protection and Development of Children and Plan of Action adopted by the World Summit for Children, urges universal ratification of the Convention by 1995 and its effective implementation by States parties through the adoption of all the necessary legislative, administrative and other measures and the allocation to the maximum extent of the available resources. In all actions concerning children, non-discrimination and the best interest of the child should be primary considerations and the views of the child given due weight. National and international mechanisms and programmes should be strengthened for the defence and protection of children, in particular, the girl-child, abandoned children, street children, economically and sexually exploited children, including through child pornography, child prostitution or sale of organs, children victims of diseases including acquired immunodeficiency syndrome, refugee and displaced children, children in detention, children in armed conflict, as well as children victims of famine and drought and other emergencies. International cooperation and solidarity should be promoted to support the implementation of the Convention and the rights of the child should be a priority in the United Nations system-wide action on human rights.

The World Conference on Human Rights also stresses that the child for the full and harmonious development of his or her personality should grow up in a family environment which accordingly merits broader protection.

22. Special attention needs to be paid to ensuring non-discrimination, and the equal enjoyment of all human rights and fundamental freedoms by disabled persons, including their active participation in all aspects of society.

23. The World Conference on Human Rights reaffirms that everyone, without distinction of any kind, is entitled to the right to seek and to enjoy in other countries asylum from persecution, as well as the right to return to one's own country. In this respect it stresses the importance of the Universal Declaration of Human Rights, the 1951 Convention relating to the Status of Refugees, its 1967 Protocol and regional instruments. It expresses its appreciation to States that continue to admit and host large numbers of refugees in their territories, and to the Office of the United Nations High Commissioner for Refugees for its dedication to its task. It also expresses its appreciation to the United Nations Relief and Works Agency for Palestine Refugees in the Near East.

The World Conference on Human Rights recognizes that gross violations of human rights, including in armed conflicts, are among the multiple and complex factors leading to displacement of people.

The World Conference on Human Rights recognizes that, in view of the complexities of the global refugee crisis and in accordance with the Charter of the United Nations, relevant international instruments and international solidarity and in the spirit of burden-sharing, a comprehensive approach by the international community is needed in coordination and cooperation with the countries concerned and relevant organizations, bearing in mind the mandate of the United Nations High Commissioner for Refugees. This should include the development of strategies to address the root causes and effects of movements of refugees and other displaced persons, the strengthening of emergency preparedness and response mechanisms, the provision of effective protection and assistance, bearing in mind the special needs of women and children, as well as the achievement of durable solutions, primarily through the preferred solution of dignified and safe voluntary repatriation, including solutions such as those adopted by the international refugee conferences. The World Conference on Human Rights underlines the responsibilities of States, particularly as they relate to the countries of origin.

In the light of the comprehensive approach, the World Conference on Human Rights emphasizes the importance of giving special attention including through intergovernmental and humanitarian organizations and finding lasting solutions to questions related to internally displaced persons including their voluntary and safe return and rehabilitation.

In accordance with the Charter of the United Nations and the principles of humanitarian law, the World Conference on Human Rights further emphasizes the importance of and the need for humanitarian assistance to victims of all natural and man-made disasters.

24. Great importance must be given to the promotion and protection of the human rights of persons belonging to groups which have been rendered vulnerable, including migrant workers, the elimination of all forms of discrimination against them, and the strengthening and more effective implementation of existing human rights instruments. States have an obligation to create and maintain adequate measures at the national level, in particular in the fields of education, health and social support, for the promotion and protection of the rights of persons in vulnerable sectors of their populations and to ensure the participation of those among them who are interested in finding a solution to their own problems.

25. The World Conference on Human Rights affirms that extreme poverty and social exclusion constitute a violation of human dignity and that urgent steps are necessary to achieve better knowledge of extreme poverty and its causes, including those related to the problem of development, in order to promote the human rights of the poorest, and to put an end to extreme poverty and social exclusion and to promote the enjoyment of the fruits of social progress. It is essential for States to foster participation by the poorest people in the decision-making process by the community in which they live, the promotion of human rights and efforts to combat extreme poverty.

26. The World Conference on Human Rights welcomes the progress made in the codification of human rights instruments, which is a dynamic and evolving process, and urges the universal ratification of human rights treaties. All States are encouraged to accede to these international instruments; all States are encouraged to avoid, as far as possible, the resort to reservations.

27. Every State should provide an effective framework of remedies to redress human rights grievances or violations. The administration of justice, including law enforcement and prosecutorial agencies and, especially, an independent judiciary and legal profession in full conformity with applicable standards contained in international human rights instruments, are essential to the full and non-discriminatory realization of human rights and indispensable to the processes of democracy and sustainable development. In this context, institutions concerned with the administration of justice should be properly funded, and an increased level of both technical and financial assistance should be provided by the international community. It is incumbent upon the United Nations to make use of special programmes of advisory services on a priority basis for the achievement of a strong and independent administration of justice.

28. The World Conference on Human Rights expresses its dismay at massive violations of human rights especially in the form of genocide, "ethnic cleansing" and systematic rape of women in war situations, creating mass exodus of refugees and displaced persons. While strongly condemning such abhorrent practices it reiterates the call that perpetrators of such crimes be punished and such practices immediately stopped.

29. The World Conference on Human Rights expresses grave concern about continuing human rights violations in all parts of the world in disregard of standards as contained in international human rights instruments and international humanitarian law and about the lack of sufficient and effective remedies for the victims.

The World Conference on Human Rights is deeply concerned about violations of human rights during armed conflicts, affecting the civilian population, especially women, children, the elderly and the disabled. The Conference therefore calls upon States and all parties to armed conflicts strictly to observe international humanitarian law, as set forth in the Geneva Conventions of 1949 and other rules and principles of international law, as well as minimum standards for protection of human rights, as laid down in international conventions.

The World Conference on Human Rights reaffirms the right of the victims to be assisted by humanitarian organizations, as set forth in the Geneva Conventions of 1949 and other relevant instruments of international humanitarian law, and calls for the safe and timely access for such assistance.

30. The World Conference on Human Rights also expresses its dismay and condemnation that gross and systematic violations and situations that constitute serious obstacles to the full enjoyment of all human rights continue to occur in different parts of the world. Such violations and obstacles include, as well as torture and cruel, inhuman and degrading treatment or punishment, summary and arbitrary executions, disappearances, arbitrary detentions, all forms of racism, racial discrimination and apartheid, foreign occupation and alien domination, xenophobia, poverty, hunger and other denials of economic, social and cultural rights, religious intolerance, terrorism, discrimination against women and lack of the rule of law.

31. The World Conference on Human Rights calls upon States to refrain from any unilateral measure not in accordance with international law and the Charter of the United Nations that creates obstacles to trade relations among States and impedes the full realization of the human rights set forth in the Universal Declaration of Human Rights and international human rights instruments, in particular the rights of everyone to a standard of living adequate for their health and well-being, including food and medical care, housing and the necessary social services. The World Conference on Human Rights affirms that food should not be used as a tool for political pressure.

32. The World Conference on Human Rights reaffirms the importance of ensuring the universality, objectivity and non-selectivity of the consideration of human rights issues.

33. The World Conference on Human Rights reaffirms that States are duty-bound, as stipulated in the Universal Declaration of Human Rights and the International Covenant on Economic, Social and Cultural Rights and in other international human rights instruments, to ensure that education is aimed at strengthening the respect of human rights and fundamental freedoms. The World Conference on Human Rights emphasizes the importance of incorporating the subject of human rights education programmes and calls upon States to do so. Education should promote understanding, tolerance, peace and friendly relations between the nations and all racial or religious groups and encourage the development of United Nations activities in pursuance of these objectives. Therefore, education on human rights and the dissemination of proper information, both theoretical and practical, play an important role in the promotion and respect of human rights with regard to all individuals without distinction of any kind such as race, sex, language or religion, and this should be integrated in the education policies at the national as well as international levels. The World Conference on Human Rights notes that resource constraints and institutional inadequacies may impede the immediate realization of these objectives.

34. Increased efforts should be made to assist countries which so request to create the conditions whereby each individual can enjoy universal human rights and fundamental freedoms. Governments, the United Nations system as well as other multilateral organizations are urged to increase considerably the resources allocated to programmes aiming at the establishment and strengthening of national legislation, national institutions and related infrastructures which uphold the rule of law and democracy, electoral assistance, human rights awareness through training, teaching and education, popular participation and civil society.

The programmes of advisory services and technical cooperation under the Centre for Human Rights should be strengthened as well as made more efficient and transparent and thus become a major contribution to improving respect for human rights. States are called upon to increase their contributions to these programmes, both through promoting a larger allocation from the United Nations regular budget, and through voluntary contributions.

35. The full and effective implementation of United Nations activities to promote and protect human rights must reflect the high importance accorded to human rights by the Charter of the United Nations and the demands of the United Nations human rights activities, as mandated by Member States. To this end, United Nations human rights activities should be provided with increased resources.

36. The World Conference on Human Rights reaffirms the important and constructive role played by national institutions for the promotion and protection of human rights, in particular in their advisory capacity to the competent authorities, their role in remedying human rights violations, in the dissemination of human rights information, and education in human rights.

The World Conference on Human Rights encourages the establishment and strengthening of national institutions, having regard to the "Principles relating to the status of national institutions" and recognizing that it is the right of each State to choose the framework which is best suited to its particular needs at the national level.

37. Regional arrangements play a fundamental role in promoting and protecting human rights. They should reinforce universal human rights standards, as contained in international human rights instruments, and their protection. The World Conference on Human Rights endorses efforts under way to strengthen these arrangements and to increase their effectiveness, while at the same time stressing the importance of cooperation with the United Nations human rights activities.

The World Conference on Human Rights reiterates the need to consider the possibility of establishing regional and subregional arrangements for the promotion and protection of human rights where they do not already exist.

38. The World Conference on Human Rights recognizes the important role of non-governmental organizations in the promotion of all human rights and in humanitarian activities at national, regional and international levels. The World Conference on Human Rights appreciates their contribution to increasing public awareness of human rights issues, to the conduct of education, training and research in this field, and to the promotion and protection of all human rights and fundamental freedoms. While recognizing that the primary responsibility for standard-setting lies with States, the conference also appreciates the contribution of non-governmental organizations to this process. In this respect, the World Conference on Human Rights emphasizes the importance of continued dialogue and cooperation between Governments and non-governmental organizations. Non-governmental organizations and their members genuinely involved in the field of human rights should enjoy the rights and freedoms recognized in the Universal Declaration of Human Rights, and the protection of the national law. These rights and freedoms may not be exercised contrary to the purposes and principles of the United Nations. Non-governmental organizations should be free to carry out their human rights activities, without interference, within the framework of national law and the Universal Declaration of Human Rights.

39. Underlining the importance of objective, responsible and impartial information about human rights and humanitarian issues, the World Conference on Human Rights encourages the increased involvement of the media, for whom freedom and protection should be guaranteed within the framework of national law.

A. Increased coordination on human rights within the United Nations system

1. The World Conference on Human Rights recommends increased coordination in support of human rights and fundamental freedoms within the United Nations system. To this end, the World Conference on Human Rights urges all United Nations organs, bodies and the specialized agencies whose activities deal with human rights to cooperate in order to strengthen, rationalize and streamline their activities, taking into account the need to avoid unnecessary duplication. The World Conference on Human Rights also recommends to the Secretary-General that high-level officials of relevant United Nations bodies and specialized agencies at their annual meeting, besides coordinating their activities, also assess the impact of their strategies and policies on the enjoyment of all human rights.

2. Furthermore, the World Conference on Human Rights calls on regional organizations and prominent international and regional finance and development institutions to assess also the impact of their policies and programmes on the enjoyment of human rights.

3. The World Conference on Human Rights recognizes that relevant specialized agencies and bodies and institutions of the United Nations system as well as other relevant intergovernmental organizations whose activities deal with human rights play a vital role in the formulation, promotion and implementation of human rights standards, within their respective mandates, and should take into account the outcome of the World Conference on Human Rights within their fields of competence.

4. The World Conference on Human Rights strongly recommends that a concerted effort be made to encourage and facilitate the ratification of and accession or succession to international human rights treaties and protocols adopted within the framework of the United Nations system with the aim of universal acceptance. The Secretary-General, in consultation with treaty bodies, should consider opening a dialogue with States not having acceded to these human rights treaties, in order to identify obstacles and to seek ways of overcoming them.

5. The World Conference on Human Rights encourages States to consider limiting the extent of any reservations they lodge to international human rights instruments, formulate any reservations as precisely and narrowly as possible, ensure that none is incompatible with the object and purpose of the relevant treaty and regularly review any reservations with a view to withdrawing them.

6. The World Conference on Human Rights, recognizing the need to maintain consistency with the high quality of existing international standards and to avoid proliferation of human rights instruments, reaffirms the guidelines relating to the elaboration of new international instruments contained in General Assembly resolution 41/120 of 4 December 1986 and calls on the United Nations human rights bodies, when considering the elaboration of new international standards, to keep those guidelines in mind, to consult with human rights treaty bodies on the necessity for drafting new standards and to request the Secretariat to carry out technical reviews of proposed new instruments.

7. The World Conference on Human Rights recommends that human rights officers be assigned if and when necessary to regional offices of the United Nations Organization with the purpose of disseminating information and offering training and other technical assistance in the field of human rights upon the request of concerned Member States. Human rights training for international civil servants who are assigned to work relating to human rights should be organized.

8. The World Conference on Human Rights welcomes the convening of emergency sessions of the Commission on Human Rights as a positive initiative and that other ways of responding to acute violations of human rights be considered by the relevant organs of the United Nations system.

Resources

9. The World Conference on Human Rights, concerned by the growing disparity between the activities of the Centre for Human Rights and the human, financial and other resources available to carry them out, and bearing in mind the resources needed for other important United Nations programmes, requests the Secretary-General and the General Assembly to take immediate steps to increase substantially the resources for the human rights programme from within the existing and future regular budgets of the United Nations, and to take urgent steps to seek increased extrabudgetary resources.

10. Within this framework, an increased proportion of the regular budget should be allocated directly to the Centre for Human Rights to cover its costs and all other costs borne by the Centre for Human Rights, including those related to the United Nations human rights bodies. Voluntary funding of the Centre's technical cooperation activities should reinforce this enhanced budget; the World Conference on Human Rights calls for generous contributions to the existing trust funds.

11. The World Conference on Human Rights requests the Secretary-General and the General Assembly to provide sufficient human, financial and other resources to the Centre for Human Rights to enable it effectively, efficiently and expeditiously to carry out its activities.

12. The World Conference on Human Rights, noting the need to ensure that human and financial resources are available to carry out the human rights activities, as mandated by intergovernmental bodies, urges the Secretary-General, in accordance with Article 101 of the Charter of the United Nations, and Member States to adopt a coherent approach aimed at securing that resources commensurate to the increased mandates are allocated to the Secretariat. The World Conference on Human Rights invites the Secretary-General to consider whether adjustments to procedures in the programme budget cycle would be necessary or helpful to ensure the timely and effective implementation of human rights activities as mandated by Member States.

Centre for Human Rights

13. The World Conference on Human Rights stresses the importance of strengthening the United Nations Centre for Human Rights.

14. The Centre for Human Rights should play an important role in coordinating system-wide attention for human rights. The focal role of the Centre can best be realized if it is enabled to cooperate fully with other United Nations bodies and organs. The coordinating role of the Centre for Human Rights also implies that the office of the Centre for Human Rights in New York is strengthened.

15. The Centre for Human Rights should be assured adequate means for the system of thematic and country rapporteurs, experts, working groups and treaty bodies. Follow-up on recommendations should become a priority matter for consideration by the Commission on Human Rights.

16. The Centre for Human Rights should assume a larger role in the promotion of human rights. This role could be given shape through cooperation with Member States and by an enhanced programme of advisory services and technical assistance. The existing voluntary funds will have to be expanded substantially for these purposes and should be managed in a more efficient and coordinated way. All activities should follow strict and transparent project management rules and regular programme and project evaluations should be held periodically. To this end, the results of such evaluation exercises and other relevant

information should be made available regularly. The Centre should, in particular, organize at least once a year information meetings open to all Member States and organizations directly involved in these projects and programmes.

Adaptation and strengthening of the United Nations machinery for human rights, including the question of the establishment of a United Nations High Commissioner for Human Rights

17. The World Conference on Human Rights recognizes the necessity for a continuing adaptation of the United Nations human rights machinery to the current and future needs in the promotion and protection of human rights, as reflected in the present Declaration and within the framework of a balanced and sustainable development for all people. In particular, the United Nations human rights organs should improve their coordination, efficiency and effectiveness.

18. The World Conference on Human Rights recommends to the General Assembly that when examining the report of the Conference at its forty-eighth session, it begin, as a matter of priority, consideration of the question of the establishment of a High Commissioner for Human Rights for the promotion and protection of all human rights.

B. Equality, dignity and tolerance

1. Racism, racial discrimination, xenophobia and other forms of intolerance

19. The World Conference on Human Rights considers the elimination of racism and racial discrimination, in particular in their institutionalized forms such as apartheid or resulting from doctrines of racial superiority or exclusivity or contemporary forms and manifestations of racism, as a primary objective for the international community and a worldwide promotion programme in the field of human rights. United Nations organs and agencies should strengthen their efforts to implement such a programme of action related to the third decade to combat racism and racial discrimination as well as subsequent mandates to the same end. The World Conference on Human Rights strongly appeals to the international community to contribute generously to the Trust Fund for the Programme for the Decade for Action to Combat Racism and Racial Discrimination.

20. The World Conference on Human Rights urges all Governments to take immediate measures and to develop strong policies to prevent and combat all forms and manifestations of racism, xenophobia or related intolerance, where necessary by enactment of appropriate legislation, including penal measures, and by the establishment of national institutions to combat such phenomena.

21. The World Conference on Human Rights welcomes the decision of the Commission on Human Rights to appoint a Special Rapporteur on contemporary forms of racism, racial discrimination, xenophobia and related intolerance. The World Conference on Human Rights also appeals to all States parties to the International Convention on the Elimination of All Forms of Racial Discrimination to consider making the declaration under Article 14 of the Convention.

22. The World Conference on Human Rights calls upon all Governments to take all appropriate measures in compliance with their international obligations and with due regard to their respective legal systems to counter intolerance and related violence based on religion or belief, including practices of discrimination against women and including the desecration of religious sites, recognizing that every individual has the right to freedom of thought, conscience, expression and religion. The Conference also invites all States to put into practice the provisions of the Declaration on the Elimination of All Forms of Intolerance and of Discrimination Based on Religion or Belief.

23. The World Conference on Human Rights stresses that all persons who perpetrate or authorize criminal acts associated with ethnic cleansing are individually responsible and accountable for such human rights violations, and that the international community should exert every effort to bring those legally responsible for such violations to justice.

24. The World Conference on Human Rights calls on all States to take immediate measures, individually and collectively, to combat the practice of ethnic cleansing to bring it quickly to an end. Victims of the abhorrent practice of ethnic cleansing are entitled to appropriate and effective remedies.

2. Persons belonging to national or ethnic, religious and linguistic minorities

25. The World Conference on Human Rights calls on the Commission on Human Rights to examine ways and means to promote and protect effectively the rights of persons belonging to minorities as set out in the Declaration on the Rights of Persons belonging to National or Ethnic, Religious and Linguistic Minorities. In this context, the World Conference on Human Rights calls upon the Centre for Human Rights to provide, at the request of Governments concerned and as part of its programme of advisory services and

technical assistance, qualified expertise on minority issues and human rights, as well as on the prevention and resolution of disputes, to assist in existing or potential situations involving minorities.

26. The World Conference on Human Rights urges States and the international community to promote and protect the rights of persons belonging to national or ethnic, religious and linguistic minorities in accordance with the Declaration on the Rights of Persons belonging to National or Ethnic, Religious and Linguistic Minorities.

27. Measures to be taken, where appropriate, should include facilitation of their full participation in all aspects of the political, economic, social, religious and cultural life of society and in the economic progress and development in their country.

Indigenous people

28. The World Conference on Human Rights calls on the Working Group on Indigenous Populations of the Sub-Commission on Prevention of Discrimination and Protection of Minorities to complete the drafting of a declaration on the rights of indigenous people at its eleventh session.

29. The World Conference on Human Rights recommends that the Commission on Human Rights consider the renewal and updating of the mandate of the Working Group on Indigenous Populations upon completion of the drafting of a declaration on the rights of indigenous people.

30. The World Conference on Human Rights also recommends that advisory services and technical assistance programmes within the United Nations system respond positively to requests by States for assistance which would be of direct benefit to indigenous people. The World Conference on Human Rights further recommends that adequate human and financial resources be made available to the Centre for Human Rights within the overall framework of strengthening the Centre's activities as envisaged by this document.

31. The World Conference on Human Rights urges States to ensure the full and free participation of indigenous people in all aspects of society, in particular in matters of concern to them.

32. The World Conference on Human Rights recommends that the General Assembly proclaim an international decade of the world's indigenous people, to begin from January 1994, including action-orientated programmes, to be decided upon in partnership with indigenous people. An appropriate voluntary trust fund should be set up for this purpose. In the framework of such a decade, the establishment of a permanent forum for indigenous people in the United Nations system should be considered.

Migrant workers

33. The World Conference on Human Rights urges all States to guarantee the protection of the human rights of all migrant workers and their families.

34. The World Conference on Human Rights considers that the creation of conditions to foster greater harmony and tolerance between migrant workers and the rest of the society of the State in which they reside is of particular importance.

35. The World Conference on Human Rights invites States to consider the possibility of signing and ratifying, at the earliest possible time, the International Convention on the Rights of All Migrant Workers and Members of Their Families.

3. The equal status and human rights of women

36. The World Conference on Human Rights urges the full and equal enjoyment by women of all human rights and that this be a priority for Governments and for the United Nations. The World Conference on Human Rights also underlines the importance of the integration and full participation of women as both agents and beneficiaries in the development process, and reiterates the objectives established on global action for women towards sustainable and equitable development set forth in the Rio Declaration on Environment and Development and chapter 24 of Agenda 21, adopted by the United Nations Conference on Environment and Development (Rio de Janeiro, Brazil, 3–14 June 1992).

37. The equal status of women and the human rights of women should be integrated into the mainstream of United Nations system-wide activity. These issues should be regularly and systematically addressed throughout relevant United Nations bodies and mechanisms. In particular, steps should be taken to increase cooperation and promote further integration of objectives and goals between the Commission on the Status of Women, the Commission on Human Rights, the Committee for the Elimination of Discrimination against Women, the United Nations Development Fund for Women, the United Nations Development Programme and other United Nations agencies. In this context, cooperation and coordination should be strengthened between the Centre for Human Rights and the Division for the Advancement of Women.

38. In particular, the World Conference on Human Rights stresses the importance of working towards the elimination of violence against women in public and private life, the elimination of all forms of sexual harassment, exploitation and trafficking in women, the elimination of gender bias in the administration of justice and the eradication of any conflicts which may arise between the rights of women and the harmful effects of certain traditional or customary practices, cultural prejudices and religious extremism. The World Conference on Human Rights calls upon the General Assembly to adopt the draft declaration on violence against women and urges States to combat violence against women in accordance with its provisions. Violations of the human rights of women in situations of armed conflict are violations of the fundamental principles of international human rights and humanitarian law. All violations of this kind, including in particular murder, systematic rape, sexual slavery, and forced pregnancy, require a particularly effective response.

39. The World Conference on Human Rights urges the eradication of all forms of discrimination against women, both hidden and overt. The United Nations should encourage the goal of universal ratification by all States of the Convention on the Elimination of All Forms of Discrimination against Women by the year 2000. Ways and means of addressing the particularly large number of reservations to the Convention should be encouraged. Inter alia, the Committee on the Elimination of Discrimination against Women should continue its review of reservations to the Convention. States are urged to withdraw reservations that are contrary to the object and purpose of the Convention or which are otherwise incompatible with international treaty law.

40. Treaty monitoring bodies should disseminate necessary information to enable women to make more effective use of existing implementation procedures in their pursuits of full and equal enjoyment of human rights and non-discrimination. New procedures should also be adopted to strengthen implementation of the commitment to women's equality and the human rights of women. The Commission on the Status of Women and the Committee on the Elimination of Discrimination against Women should quickly examine the possibility of introducing the right of petition through the preparation of an optional protocol to the Convention on the Elimination of All Forms of Discrimination against Women. The World Conference on Human Rights welcomes the decision of the Commission on Human Rights to consider the appointment of a special rapporteur on violence against women at its fiftieth session.

41. The World Conference on Human Rights recognizes the importance of the enjoyment by women of the highest standard of physical and mental health throughout their life span. In the context of the World Conference on Women and the Convention on the Elimination of All Forms of Discrimination against Women, as well as the Proclamation of Tehran of 1968, the World Conference on Human Rights reaffirms, on the basis of equality between women and men, a woman's right to accessible and adequate health care and the widest range of family planning services, as well as equal access to education at all levels.

42. Treaty monitoring bodies should include the status of women and the human rights of women in their deliberations and findings, making use of gender-specific data. States should be encouraged to supply information on the situation of women de jure and de facto in their reports to treaty monitoring bodies. The World Conference on Human Rights notes with satisfaction that the Commission on Human Rights adopted at its forty-ninth session resolution 1993/46 of 8 March 1993 stating that rapporteurs and working groups in the field of human rights should also be encouraged to do so. Steps should also be taken by the Division for the Advancement of Women in cooperation with other United Nations bodies, specifically the Centre for Human Rights, to ensure that the human rights activities of the United Nations regularly address violations of women's human rights, including gender-specific abuses. Training for United Nations human rights and humanitarian relief personnel to assist them to recognize and deal with human rights abuses particular to women and to carry out their work without gender bias should be encouraged.

43. The World Conference on Human Rights urges Governments and regional and international organizations to facilitate the access of women to decision-making posts and their greater participation in the decision-making process. It encourages further steps within the United Nations Secretariat to appoint and promote women staff members in accordance with the Charter of the United Nations, and encourages other principal and subsidiary organs of the United Nations to guarantee the participation of women under conditions of equality.

44. The World Conference on Human Rights welcomes the World Conference on Women to be held in Beijing in 1995 and urges that human rights of women should play an important role in its deliberations,

in accordance with the priority themes of the World Conference on Women of equality, development and peace.

4. The rights of the child

45. The World Conference on Human Rights reiterates the principle of "First Call for Children" and, in this respect, underlines the importance of major national and international efforts, especially those of the United Nations Children's Fund, for promoting respect for the rights of the child to survival, protection, development and participation.

46. Measures should be taken to achieve universal ratification of the Convention on the Rights of the Child by 1995 and the universal signing of the World Declaration on the Survival, Protection and Development of Children and Plan of Action adopted by the World Summit for Children, as well as their effective implementation. The World Conference on Human Rights urges States to withdraw reservations to the Convention on the Rights of the Child contrary to the object and purpose of the Convention or otherwise contrary to international treaty law.

47. The World Conference on Human Rights urges all nations to undertake measures to the maximum extent of their available resources, with the support of international cooperation, to achieve the goals in the World Summit Plan of Action. The Conference calls on States to integrate the Convention on the Rights of the Child into their national action plans. By means of these national action plans and through international efforts, particular priority should be placed on reducing infant and maternal mortality rates, reducing malnutrition and illiteracy rates and providing access to safe drinking water and to basic education. Whenever so called for, national plans of action should be devised to combat devastating emergencies resulting from natural disasters and armed conflicts and the equally grave problem of children in extreme poverty.

48. The World Conference on Human Rights urges all States, with the support of international cooperation, to address the acute problem of children under especially difficult circumstances. Exploitation and abuse of children should be actively combated, including by addressing their root causes. Effective measures are required against female infanticide, harmful child labour, sale of children and organs, child prostitution, child pornography, as well as other forms of sexual abuse.

49. The World Conference on Human Rights supports all measures by the United Nations and its specialized agencies to ensure the effective protection and promotion of human rights of the girl child. The World Conference on Human Rights urges States to repeal existing laws and regulations and remove customs and practices which discriminate against and cause harm to the girl child.

50. The World Conference on Human Rights strongly supports the proposal that the Secretary-General initiate a study into means of improving the protection of children in armed conflicts. Humanitarian norms should be implemented and measures taken in order to protect and facilitate assistance to children in war zones. Measures should include protection for children against indiscriminate use of all weapons of war, especially anti-personnel mines. The need for aftercare and rehabilitation of children traumatized by war must be addressed urgently. The Conference calls on the Committee on the Rights of the Child to study the question of raising the minimum age of recruitment into armed forces.

51. The World Conference on Human Rights recommends that matters relating to human rights and the situation of children be regularly reviewed and monitored by all relevant organs and mechanisms of the United Nations system and by the supervisory bodies of the specialized agencies in accordance with their mandates.

52. The World Conference on Human Rights recognizes the important role played by non-governmental organizations in the effective implementation of all human rights instruments and, in particular, the Convention on the Rights of the Child.

53. The World Conference on Human Rights recommends that the Committee on the Rights of the Child, with the assistance of the Centre for Human Rights, be enabled expeditiously and effectively to meet its mandate, especially in view of the unprecedented extent of ratification and subsequent submission of country reports.

5. Freedom from torture

54. The World Conference on Human Rights welcomes the ratification by many Member States of the Convention against Torture and Other Cruel, Inhuman or Degrading Treatment or Punishment and encourages its speedy ratification by all other Member States.

55. The World Conference on Human Rights emphasizes that one of the most atrocious violations against human dignity is the act of torture, the result of which destroys the dignity and impairs the capability of victims to continue their lives and their activities.

56. The World Conference on Human Rights reaffirms that under human rights law and international humanitarian law, freedom from torture is a right which must be protected under all circumstances, including in times of internal or international disturbance or armed conflicts.

57. The World Conference on Human Rights therefore urges all States to put an immediate end to the practice of torture and eradicate this evil forever through full implementation of the Universal Declaration of Human Rights as well as the relevant conventions and, where necessary, strengthening of existing mechanisms. The World Conference on Human Rights calls on all States to cooperate fully with the Special Rapporteur on the question of torture in the fulfilment of his mandate.

58. Special attention should be given to ensure universal respect for, and effective implementation of, the Principles of Medical Ethics relevant to the Role of Health Personnel, particularly Physicians, in the Protection of Prisoners and Detainees against Torture and other Cruel, Inhuman or Degrading Treatment or Punishment adopted by the General Assembly of the United Nations.

59. The World Conference on Human Rights stresses the importance of further concrete action within the framework of the United Nations with the view to providing assistance to victims of torture and ensure more effective remedies for their physical, psychological and social rehabilitation. Providing the necessary resources for this purpose should be given high priority, inter alia, by additional contributions to the United Nations Voluntary Fund for the Victims of Torture.

60. States should abrogate legislation leading to impunity for those responsible for grave violations of human rights such as torture and prosecute such violations, thereby providing a firm basis for the rule of law.

61. The World Conference on Human Rights reaffirms that efforts to eradicate torture should, first and foremost, be concentrated on prevention and, therefore, calls for the early adoption of an optional protocol to the Convention against Torture and Other Cruel, Inhuman and Degrading Treatment or Punishment, which is intended to establish a preventive system of regular visits to places of detention.

Enforced disappearances

62. The World Conference on Human Rights, welcoming the adoption by the General Assembly of the Declaration on the Protection of All Persons from Enforced Disappearance, calls upon all States to take effective legislative, administrative, judicial or other measures to prevent, terminate and punish acts of enforced disappearances. The World Conference on Human Rights reaffirms that it is the duty of all States, under any circumstances, to make investigations whenever there is reason to believe that an enforced disappearance has taken place on a territory under their jurisdiction and, if allegations are confirmed, to prosecute its perpetrators.

6. The rights of the disabled person

63. The World Conference on Human Rights reaffirms that all human rights and fundamental freedoms are universal and thus unreservedly include persons with disabilities. Every person is born equal and has the same rights to life and welfare, education and work, living independently and active participation in all aspects of society. Any direct discrimination or other negative discriminatory treatment of a disabled person is therefore a violation of his or her rights. The World Conference on Human Rights calls on Governments, where necessary, to adopt or adjust legislation to assure access to these and other rights for disabled persons.

64. The place of disabled persons is everywhere. Persons with disabilities should be guaranteed equal opportunity through the elimination of all socially determined barriers, be they physical, financial, social or psychological, which exclude or restrict full participation in society.

65. Recalling the World Programme of Action concerning Disabled Persons, adopted by the General Assembly at its thirty-seventh session, the World Conference on Human Rights calls upon the General Assembly and the Economic and Social Council to adopt the draft standard rules on the equalization of opportunities for persons with disabilities, at their meetings in 1993.

C. Cooperation, development and strengthening of human rights

66. The World Conference on Human Rights recommends that priority be given to national and international action to promote democracy, development and human rights.

67. Special emphasis should be given to measures to assist in the strengthening and building of institutions relating to human rights, strengthening of a pluralistic civil society and the protection of groups which

have been rendered vulnerable. In this context, assistance provided upon the request of Governments for the conduct of free and fair elections, including assistance in the human rights aspects of elections and public information about elections, is of particular importance. Equally important is the assistance to be given to the strengthening of the rule of law, the promotion of freedom of expression and the administration of justice, and to the real and effective participation of the people in the decision-making processes.

68. The World Conference on Human Rights stresses the need for the implementation of strengthened advisory services and technical assistance activities by the Centre for Human Rights. The Centre should make available to States upon request assistance on specific human rights issues, including the preparation of reports under human rights treaties as well as for the implementation of coherent and comprehensive plans of action for the promotion and protection of human rights. Strengthening the institutions of human rights and democracy, the legal protection of human rights, training of officials and others, broad-based education and public information aimed at promoting respect for human rights should all be available as components of these programmes.

69. The World Conference on Human Rights strongly recommends that a comprehensive programme be established within the United Nations in order to help States in the task of building and strengthening adequate national structures which have a direct impact on the overall observance of human rights and the maintenance of the rule of law. Such a programme, to be coordinated by the Centre for Human Rights, should be able to provide, upon the request of the interested Government, technical and financial assistance to national projects in reforming penal and correctional establishments, education and training of lawyers, judges and security forces in human rights, and any other sphere of activity relevant to the good functioning of the rule of law. That programme should make available to States assistance for the implementation of plans of action for the promotion and protection of human rights.

70. The World Conference on Human Rights requests the Secretary-General of the United Nations to submit proposals to the United Nations General Assembly, containing alternatives for the establishment, structure, operational modalities and funding of the proposed programme.

71. The World Conference on Human Rights recommends that each State consider the desirability of drawing up a national action plan identifying steps whereby that State would improve the promotion and protection of human rights.

72. The World Conference on Human Rights on Human Rights reaffirms that the universal and inalienable right to development, as established in the Declaration on the Right to Development, must be implemented and realized. In this context, the World Conference on Human Rights welcomes the appointment by the Commission on Human Rights of a thematic working group on the right to development and urges that the Working Group, in consultation and cooperation with other organs and agencies of the United Nations system, promptly formulate, for early consideration by the United Nations General Assembly, comprehensive and effective measures to eliminate obstacles to the implementation and realization of the Declaration on the Right to Development and recommending ways and means towards the realization of the right to development by all States.

73. The World Conference on Human Rights recommends that non-governmental and other grass-roots organizations active in development and/or human rights should be enabled to play a major role on the national and international levels in the debate, activities and implementation relating to the right to development and, in cooperation with Governments, in all relevant aspects of development cooperation.

74. The World Conference on Human Rights appeals to Governments, competent agencies and institutions to increase considerably the resources devoted to building well-functioning legal systems able to protect human rights, and to national institutions working in this area. Actors in the field of development cooperation should bear in mind the mutually reinforcing interrelationship between development, democracy and human rights. Cooperation should be based on dialogue and transparency. The World Conference on Human Rights also calls for the establishment of comprehensive programmes, including resource banks of information and personnel with expertise relating to the strengthening of the rule of law and of democratic institutions.

75. The World Conference on Human Rights encourages the Commission on Human Rights, in cooperation with the Committee on Economic, Social and Cultural Rights, to continue the examination of optional protocols to the International Covenant on Economic, Social and Cultural Rights.

76. The World Conference on Human Rights recommends that more resources be made available for the strengthening or the establishment of regional arrangements for the promotion and protection of human

rights under the programmes of advisory services and technical assistance of the Centre for Human Rights. States are encouraged to request assistance for such purposes as regional and subregional workshops, seminars and information exchanges designed to strengthen regional arrangements for the promotion and protection of human rights in accord with universal human rights standards as contained in international human rights instruments.

77. The World Conference on Human Rights supports all measures by the United Nations and its relevant specialized agencies to ensure the effective promotion and protection of trade union rights, as stipulated in the International Covenant on Economic, Social and Cultural Rights and other relevant international instruments. It calls on all States to abide fully by their obligations in this regard contained in international instruments.

D. Human rights education

78. The World Conference on Human Rights considers human rights education, training and public information essential for the promotion and achievement of stable and harmonious relations among communities and for fostering mutual understanding, tolerance and peace.

79. States should strive to eradicate illiteracy and should direct education towards the full development of the human personality and to the strengthening of respect for human rights and fundamental freedoms. The World Conference on Human Rights calls on all States and institutions to include human rights, humanitarian law, democracy and rule of law as subjects in the curricula of all learning institutions in formal and non-formal settings.

80. Human rights education should include peace, democracy, development and social justice, as set forth in international and regional human rights instruments, in order to achieve common understanding and awareness with a view to strengthening universal commitment to human rights.

81. Taking into account the World Plan of Action on Education for Human Rights and Democracy, adopted in March 1993 by the International Congress on Education for Human Rights and Democracy of the United Nations Educational, Scientific and Cultural Organization, and other human rights instruments, the World Conference on Human Rights recommends that States develop specific programmes and strategies for ensuring the widest human rights education and the dissemination of public information, taking particular account of the human rights needs of women.

82. Governments, with the assistance of intergovernmental organizations, national institutions and non-governmental organizations, should promote an increased awareness of human rights and mutual tolerance. The World Conference on Human Rights underlines the importance of strengthening the World Public Information Campaign for Human Rights carried out by the United Nations. They should initiate and support education in human rights and undertake effective dissemination of public information in this field. The advisory services and technical assistance programmes of the United Nations system should be able to respond immediately to requests from States for educational and training activities in the field of human rights as well as for special education concerning standards as contained in international human rights instruments and in humanitarian law and their application to special groups such as military forces, law enforcement personnel, police and the health profession. The proclamation of a United Nations decade for human rights education in order to promote, encourage and focus these educational activities should be considered.

E. Implementation and monitoring methods

83. The World Conference on Human Rights urges Governments to incorporate standards as contained in international human rights instruments in domestic legislation and to strengthen national structures, institutions and organs of society which play a role in promoting and safeguarding human rights.

84. The World Conference on Human Rights recommends the strengthening of United Nations activities and programmes to meet requests for assistance by States which want to establish or strengthen their own national institutions for the promotion and protection of human rights.

85. The World Conference on Human Rights also encourages the strengthening of cooperation between national institutions for the promotion and protection of human rights, particularly through exchanges of information and experience, as well as cooperation with regional organizations and the United Nations.

86. The World Conference on Human Rights strongly recommends in this regard that representatives of national institutions for the promotion and protection of human rights convene periodic meetings under the auspices of the Centre for Human Rights to examine ways and means of improving their mechanisms and sharing experiences.

87. The World Conference on Human Rights recommends to the human rights treaty bodies, to the meetings of chairpersons of the treaty bodies and to the meetings of States parties that they continue to take

steps aimed at coordinating the multiple reporting requirements and guidelines for preparing State reports under the respective human rights conventions and study the suggestion that the submission of one overall report on treaty obligations undertaken by each State would make these procedures more effective and increase their impact.

88. The World Conference on Human Rights recommends that the States parties to international human rights instruments, the General Assembly and the Economic and Social Council should consider studying the existing human rights treaty bodies and the various thematic mechanisms and procedures with a view to promoting greater efficiency and effectiveness through better coordination of the various bodies, mechanisms and procedures, taking into account the need to avoid unnecessary duplication and overlapping of their mandates and tasks.

89. The World Conference on Human Rights recommends continued work on the improvement of the functioning, including the monitoring tasks, of the treaty bodies, taking into account multiple proposals made in this respect, in particular those made by the treaty bodies themselves and by the meetings of the chairpersons of the treaty bodies. The comprehensive national approach taken by the Committee on the Rights of the Child should also be encouraged.

90. The World Conference on Human Rights recommends that States parties to human rights treaties consider accepting all the available optional communication procedures.

91. The World Conference on Human Rights views with concern the issue of impunity of perpetrators of human rights violations, and supports the efforts of the Commission on Human Rights and the Sub-Commission on Prevention of Discrimination and Protection of Minorities to examine all aspects of the issue.

92. The World Conference on Human Rights recommends that the Commission on Human Rights examine the possibility for better implementation of existing human rights instruments at the international and regional levels and encourages the International Law Commission to continue its work on an international criminal court.

93. The World Conference on Human Rights appeals to States which have not yet done so to accede to the Geneva Conventions of 12 August 1949 and the Protocols thereto, and to take all appropriate national measures, including legislative ones, for their full implementation.

94. The World Conference on Human Rights recommends the speedy completion and adoption of the draft declaration on the right and responsibility of individuals, groups and organs of society to promote and protect universally recognized human rights and fundamental freedoms.

95. The World Conference on Human Rights underlines the importance of preserving and strengthening the system of special procedures, rapporteurs, representatives, experts and working groups of the Commission on Human Rights and the Sub-Commission on the Prevention of Discrimination and Protection of Minorities, in order to enable them to carry out their mandates in all countries throughout the world, providing them with the necessary human and financial resources. The procedures and mechanisms should be enabled to harmonize and rationalize their work through periodic meetings. All States are asked to cooperate fully with these procedures and mechanisms.

96. The World Conference on Human Rights recommends that the United Nations assume a more active role in the promotion and protection of human rights in ensuring full respect for international humanitarian law in all situations of armed conflict, in accordance with the purposes and principles of the Charter of the United Nations.

97. The World Conference on Human Rights, recognizing the important role of human rights components in specific arrangements concerning some peace-keeping operations by the United Nations, recommends that the Secretary-General take into account the reporting, experience and capabilities of the Centre for Human Rights and human rights mechanisms, in conformity with the Charter of the United Nations.

98. To strengthen the enjoyment of economic, social and cultural rights, additional approaches should be examined, such as a system of indicators to measure progress in the realization of the rights set forth in the International Covenant on Economic, Social and Cultural Rights. There must be a concerted effort to ensure recognition of economic, social and cultural rights at the national, regional and international levels.

F. Follow-up to the World Conference on Human Rights

99. The World Conference on Human Rights on Human Rights recommends that the General Assembly, the Commission on Human Rights and other organs and agencies of the United Nations system related to human rights consider ways and means for the full implementation, without delay, of the recommendations contained in the present Declaration, including the possibility of proclaiming a United Nations decade

for human rights. The World Conference on Human Rights further recommends that the Commission on Human Rights annually review the progress towards this end.

100. The World Conference on Human Rights requests the Secretary-General of the United Nations to invite on the occasion of the fiftieth anniversary of the Universal Declaration of Human Rights all States, all organs and agencies of the United Nations system related to human rights, to report to him on the progress made in the implementation of the present Declaration and to submit a report to the General Assembly at its fifty-third session, through the Commission on Human Rights and the Economic and Social Council. Likewise, regional and, as appropriate, national human rights institutions, as well as non-governmental organizations, may present their views to the Secretary-General on the progress made in the implementation of the present Declaration. Special attention should be paid to assessing the progress towards the goal of universal ratification of international human rights treaties and protocols adopted within the framework of the United Nations system.

© Copyright 1999

Office of the United Nations High Commissioner for Human Rights Geneva, Switzerland

---

DOCUMENT 52

Full Official Title: World Conference against Racism, Racial Discrimination, Xenophobia and Related Intolerance Declaration

Short Title/Acronym/Abbreviation: The Durban 1 Declaration. (There were two conferences and two Declarations: Durban I and Durban II)

Type of Document: An outcome document called a Declaration, for a World Conference against Racism, (WCAR) held in Durban, South Africa in 2001.

Subject: Elimination of Racism, Racial Discrimination, Xenophobia and Related Intolerance Declaration

Official Citation:

Date of Document: September 8, 2001

Date of Adoption: September 8, 2001

Date of General Entry into Force (EIF): Not applicable

Number of States Parties as of this printing: Not applicable

Date of Signature by United States: Not applicable

Date of Ratification/Accession/Adhesion: Not applicable

Date of Entry into Force as to United States (effective date): Not applicable

Legal Status/Character of the Instrument/Document as to the United States: non binding declaration of principles regarding Racism, Racial Discrimination, Xenophobia and Related Intolerance.

The U.S. attended the start of this Conference but pulled out along with Israel over some "hurtful language" and did not vote on this Declaration, which was very controversial.

Web Address: www.umn.edu/humanrts/instree/wcardeclaration.html

WORLD CONFERENCE AGAINST RACISM, RACIAL DISCRIMINATION, XENOPHOBIA AND RELATED INTOLERANCE (EXCERPTS)
Declaration

Having met in Durban, South Africa, from 31 August to 8 September 2001,

Expressing deep appreciation to the Government of South Africa for hosting this World Conference,

Drawing inspiration from the heroic struggle of the people of South Africa against the institutionalized system of apartheid, as well as for equality and justice under democracy, development, the rule of law and respect for human rights,

Recalling in this context the important contribution to that struggle of the international community and, in particular, the pivotal role of the people and Governments of Africa, and noting the important role that different actors of civil society, including non-governmental organizations, played in that struggle and in ongoing efforts to combat racism, racial discrimination, xenophobia and related intolerance,

Recalling that the Vienna Declaration and Programme of Action, adopted by the World Conference on Human Rights in June 1993, calls for the speedy and comprehensive elimination of all forms of racism, racial discrimination, xenophobia and related intolerance,

Recalling Commission on Human Rights resolution 1997/74 of 18 April 1997, General Assembly resolution 52/111 of 12 December 1997 and subsequent resolutions of those bodies concerning the convening of the World Conference against Racism, Racial Discrimination, Xenophobia and Related Intolerance and

Recalling also the two World Conferences to Combat Racism and Racial Discrimination, held in Geneva in 1978 and 1983, respectively,

Noting with grave concern that despite the efforts of the international community, the principal objectives of the Three Decades to Combat Racism and Racial Discrimination have not been attained and that countless human beings continue to the present day to be victims of racism, racial discrimination, xenophobia and related intolerance,

Affirming that racism, racial discrimination, xenophobia and related intolerance, where they amount to racism and racial discrimination, constitute serious violations of and obstacles to the full enjoyment of all human rights and deny the self-evident truth that all human beings are born free and equal in dignity and rights, are an obstacle to friendly and peaceful relations among peoples and nations, and are among the root causes of many internal and international conflicts, including armed conflicts, and the consequent forced displacement of populations,

Recognizing that national and international actions are required to combat racism, racial discrimination, xenophobia and related intolerance, in order to ensure the full enjoyment of all human rights, economic, social, cultural, civil and political, which are universal, indivisible, interdependent and interrelated, and to improve the living conditions of men, women and children of all nations,

Reaffirming the importance of the enhancement of international cooperation for the promotion and protection of human rights and for the achievement of the objectives of the fight against racism, racial discrimination, xenophobia and related intolerance,

Strongly rejecting any doctrine of racial superiority, along with theories which attempt to determine the existence of so-called distinct human races,

Dedicating ourselves to combating the scourge of racism, racial discrimination, xenophobia and related intolerance fully and effectively as a matter of priority, while drawing lessons from manifestations and past experiences of racism in all parts of the world with a view to avoiding their recurrence,

Joining together in a spirit of renewed political will and commitment to universal equality, justice and dignity, we salute the memory of all victims of racism, racial discrimination, xenophobia and related intolerance all over the world and solemnly adopt the Durban Declaration and Programme of Action.

General issues

1. We declare that for the purpose of the present Declaration and Programme of Action, the victims of racism, racial discrimination, xenophobia and related intolerance are individuals or groups of individuals who are or have been negatively affected by, subjected to, or targets of these scourges;

2. We recognize that racism, racial discrimination, xenophobia and related intolerance occur on the grounds of race, colour, descent or national or ethnic origin and that victims can suffer multiple or aggravated forms of discrimination based on other related grounds such as sex, language, religion, political or other opinion, social origin, property, birth or other status;

3. We recognize and affirm that, at the outset of the third millennium, a global fight against racism, racial discrimination, xenophobia and related intolerance and all their abhorrent and evolving forms and manifestations is a matter of priority for the international community, and that this Conference offers a unique and historic opportunity for assessing and identifying all dimensions of those devastating evils of humanity with a view to their total elimination through, inter alia, the initiation of innovative and holistic approaches and the strengthening and enhancement of practical and effective measures at the national, regional and international levels;

...

2. We recognize that racism, racial discrimination, xenophobia and related intolerance occur on the grounds of race, colour, descent or national or ethnic origin and that victims can suffer multiple or aggravated forms of discrimination based on other related grounds such as sex, language, religion, political or other opinion, social origin, property, birth or other status;

3. We recognize and affirm that, at the outset of the third millennium, a global fight against racism, racial discrimination, xenophobia and related intolerance and all their abhorrent and evolving forms and manifestations is a matter of priority for the international community, and that this Conference offers a unique and historic opportunity for assessing and identifying all dimensions of those devastating evils of humanity with a view to their total elimination through, inter alia, the initiation of innovative and holistic approaches

and the strengthening and enhancement of practical and effective measures at the national, regional and international levels;

. . .

11. We note that the process of globalization constitutes a powerful and dynamic force which should be harnessed for the benefit, development and prosperity of all countries, without exclusion. We recognize that developing countries face special difficulties in responding to this central challenge. While globalization offers great opportunities, at present its benefits are very unevenly shared, while its costs are unevenly distributed. We thus express our determination to prevent and mitigate the negative effects of globalization. These effects could aggravate, inter alia, poverty, underdevelopment, marginalization, social exclusion, cultural homogenization and economic disparities which may occur along racial lines, within and between States, and have an adverse impact. We further express our determination to maximize the benefits of globalization through, inter alia, the strengthening and enhancement of international cooperation to increase equality of opportunities for trade, economic growth and sustainable development, global communications through the use of new technologies and increased intercultural exchange through the preservation and promotion of cultural diversity, which can contribute to the eradication of racism, racial discrimination, xenophobia and related intolerance. Only through broad and sustained efforts to create a shared future based upon our common humanity, and all its diversity, can globalization be made fully inclusive and equitable;

. . .

Sources, causes, forms and contemporary manifestations of racism, racial discrimination, xenophobia and related intolerance
13. We acknowledge that slavery and the slave trade, including the transatlantic slave trade, were appalling tragedies in the history of humanity not only because of their abhorrent barbarism but also in terms of their magnitude, organized nature and especially their negation of the essence of the victims, and further acknowledge that slavery and the slave trade are a crime against humanity and should always have been so, especially the transatlantic slave trade and are among the major sources and manifestations of racism, racial discrimination, xenophobia and related intolerance, and that Africans and people of African descent, Asians and people of Asian descent and indigenous peoples were victims of these acts and continue to be victims of their consequences;

. . .

16. We recognize that xenophobia against non-nationals, particularly migrants, refugees and asylum-seekers, constitutes one of the main sources of contemporary racism and that human rights violations against members of such groups occur widely in the context of discriminatory, xenophobic and racist practices;

. . .

18. We emphasize that poverty, underdevelopment, marginalization, social exclusion and economic disparities are closely associated with racism, racial discrimination, xenophobia and related intolerance, and contribute to the persistence of racist attitudes and practices which in turn generate more poverty;

. . .

20. We recognize that racism, racial discrimination, xenophobia and related intolerance are among the root causes of armed conflict and very often one of its consequences and recall that non-discrimination is a fundamental principle of international humanitarian law. We underscore the need for all parties to armed conflicts to abide scrupulously by this principle and for States and the international community to remain especially vigilant during periods of armed conflict and continue to combat all forms of racial discrimination;

. . .

25. We express our profound repudiation of the racism, racial discrimination, xenophobia and related intolerance that persist in some States in the functioning of the penal systems and in the application of the law, as well as in the actions and attitudes of institutions and individuals responsible for law enforcement, especially where this has contributed to certain groups being over-represented among persons under detention or imprisoned;

. . .

33. We consider it essential for all countries in the region of the Americas and all other areas of the African Diaspora to recognize the existence of their population of African descent and the cultural, economic, political and scientific contributions made by that population, and recognize the persistence of racism, racial discrimination, xenophobia and related intolerance that specifically affect them, and recognize that, in many countries, their long-standing inequality in terms of access to, inter alia, education, health care and housing has been a profound cause of the socio-economic disparities that affect them;

...

38. We call upon all States to review and, where necessary, revise any immigration policies which are inconsistent with international human rights instruments, with a view to eliminating all discriminatory policies and practices against migrants, including Asians and people of Asian descent;

...

41. We reiterate our conviction that the full realization by indigenous peoples of their human rights and fundamental freedoms is indispensable for eliminating racism, racial discrimination, xenophobia and related intolerance. We firmly reiterate our determination to promote their full and equal enjoyment of civil, political, economic, social and cultural rights, as well as the benefits of sustainable development, while fully respecting their distinctive characteristics and their own initiatives;

...

43. We also recognize the special relationship that indigenous peoples have with the land as the basis for their spiritual, physical and cultural existence and encourage States, wherever possible, to ensure that indigenous peoples are able to retain ownership of their lands and of those natural resources to which they are entitled under domestic law;

...

47. We reaffirm the sovereign right of each State to formulate and apply its own legal framework and policies for migration, and further affirm that these policies should be consistent with applicable human rights instruments, norms and standards, and designed to ensure that they are free of racism, racial discrimination, xenophobia and related intolerance;

48. We note with concern and strongly condemn the manifestations and acts of racism, racial discrimination, xenophobia and related intolerance against migrants and the stereotypes often applied to them; reaffirm the responsibility of States to protect the human rights of migrants under their jurisdiction and reaffirm the responsibility of States to safeguard and protect migrants against illegal or violent acts, in particular acts of racial discrimination and crimes perpetrated with racist or xenophobic motivation by individuals or groups and stress the need for their fair, just and equitable treatment in society and in the workplace;

...

57. We are conscious of the fact that the history of humanity is replete with major atrocities as a result of gross violations of human rights and believe that lessons can be learned through remembering history to avert future tragedies;

58. We recall that the Holocaust must never be forgotten;

59. We recognize with deep concern religious intolerance against certain religious communities, as well as the emergence of hostile acts and violence against such communities because of their religious beliefs and their racial or ethnic origin in various parts of the world which in particular limit their right to freely practise their belief;

...

61. We recognize with deep concern the increase in anti-Semitism and Islamophobia in various parts of the world, as well as the emergence of racial and violent movements based on racism and discriminatory ideas against Jewish, Muslim and Arab communities;

62. We are conscious that humanity's history is replete with terrible wrongs inflicted through lack of respect for the equality of human beings and note with alarm the increase of such practices in various parts of the world, and we urge people, particularly in conflict situations, to desist from racist incitement, derogatory language and negative stereotyping;

63. We are concerned about the plight of the Palestinian people under foreign occupation. We recognize the inalienable right of the Palestinian people to self-determination and to the establishment of an independent State and we recognize the right to security for all States in the region, including Israel, and call upon all States to support the peace process and bring it to an early conclusion;

...

69. We are convinced that racism, racial discrimination, xenophobia and related intolerance reveal themselves in a differentiated manner for women and girls, and can be among the factors leading to a deterioration in their living conditions, poverty, violence, multiple forms of discrimination, and the limitation or denial of their human rights. We recognize the need to integrate a gender perspective into relevant policies, strategies and programmes of action against racism, racial discrimination, xenophobia and related intolerance in order to address multiple forms of discrimination;

...

Measures of prevention, education and protection aimed at the eradication of racism, racial discrimination, xenophobia and related intolerance at the national, regional and international levels

76. We recognize that inequitable political, economic, cultural and social conditions can breed and foster racism, racial discrimination, xenophobia and related intolerance, which in turn exacerbate the inequity. We believe that genuine equality of opportunity for all, in all spheres, including that for development, is fundamental for the eradication of racism, racial discrimination, xenophobia and related intolerance;

...

78. We affirm the solemn commitment of all States to promote universal respect for, and observance and protection of, all human rights, economic, social, cultural, civil and political, including the right to development, as a fundamental factor in the prevention and elimination of racism, racial discrimination, xenophobia and related intolerance;

...

80. We firmly believe that education, development and the faithful implementation of all international human rights norms and obligations, including enactment of laws and political, social and economic policies, are crucial to combat racism, racial discrimination, xenophobia and related intolerance;

81. We recognize that democracy, transparent, responsible, accountable and participatory governance responsive to the needs and aspirations of the people, and respect for human rights, fundamental freedoms and the rule of law are essential for the effective prevention and elimination of racism, racial discrimination, xenophobia and related intolerance. We reaffirm that any form of impunity for crimes motivated by racist and xenophobic attitudes plays a role in weakening the rule of law and democracy and tends to encourage the recurrence of such acts;

...

86. We recall that the dissemination of all ideas based upon racial superiority or hatred shall be declared an offence punishable by law with due regard to the principles embodied in the Universal Declaration of Human Rights and the rights expressly set forth in Article 5 of the International Convention on the Elimination of All Forms of Racial Discrimination;

87. We note that Article 4, paragraph b, of the International Convention on the Elimination of All Forms of Racial Discrimination places an obligation upon States to be vigilant and to proceed against organizations that disseminate ideas based on racial superiority or hatred, acts of violence or incitement to such acts. These organizations shall be condemned and discouraged;

...

90. We recognize the positive contribution that the exercise of the right to freedom of expression, particularly by the media and new technologies, including the Internet, and full respect for the freedom to seek, receive and impart information can make to the fight against racism, racial discrimination, xenophobia and related intolerance; we reiterate the need to respect the editorial independence and autonomy of the media in this regard;

91. We express deep concern about the use of new information technologies, such as the Internet, for purposes contrary to respect for human values, equality, non-discrimination, respect for others and tolerance, including to propagate racism, racial hatred, xenophobia, racial discrimination and related intolerance, and that, in particular, children and youth having access to this material could be negatively influenced by it;

92. We also recognize the need to promote the use of new information and communication technologies, including the Internet, to contribute to the fight against racism, racial discrimination, xenophobia and related intolerance; new technologies can assist the promotion of tolerance and respect for human dignity, and the principles of equality and non-discrimination;

93. We affirm that all States should recognize the importance of community media that give a voice to victims of racism, racial discrimination, xenophobia and related intolerance;

94. We reaffirm that the stigmatization of people of different origins by acts or omissions of public authorities, institutions, the media, political parties or national or local organizations is not only an act of racial discrimination but can also incite the recurrence of such acts, thereby resulting in the creation of a vicious circle which reinforces racist attitudes and prejudices, and which must be condemned;

...

Provision of effective remedies, recourse, redress, and compensatory and other measures at the national, regional and international levels

98. We emphasize the importance and necessity of teaching about the facts and truth of the history of humankind from antiquity to the recent past, as well as of teaching about the facts and truth of the history, causes, nature and consequences of racism, racial discrimination, xenophobia and related intolerance, with a view to achieving a comprehensive and objective cognizance of the tragedies of the past;

...

104. We also strongly reaffirm as a pressing requirement of justice that victims of human rights violations resulting from racism, racial discrimination, xenophobia and related intolerance, especially in the light of their vulnerable situation socially, culturally and economically, should be assured of having access to justice, including legal assistance where appropriate, and effective and appropriate protection and remedies, including the right to seek just and adequate reparation or satisfaction for any damage suffered as a result of such discrimination, as enshrined in numerous international and regional human rights instruments, in particular the Universal Declaration of Human Rights and the International Convention on the Elimination of All Forms of Racial Discrimination;

105. Guided by the principles set out in the Millennium Declaration and the recognition that we have a collective responsibility to uphold the principles of human dignity, equality and equity and to ensure that globalization becomes a positive force for all the world's people, the international community commits itself to working for the beneficial integration of the developing countries into the global economy, resisting their marginalization, determined to achieve accelerated economic growth and sustainable development and to eradicate poverty, inequality and deprivation;

...

Strategies to achieve full and effective equality, including international cooperation and enhancement of the United Nations and other international mechanisms in combating racism, racial discrimination, xenophobia and related intolerance

107. We underscore the need to design, promote and implement at the national, regional and international levels strategies, programmes and policies, and adequate legislation, which may include special and positive measures, for furthering equal social development and the realization of the civil and political, economic, social and cultural rights of all victims of racism, racial discrimination, xenophobia and related intolerance, including through more effective access to the political, judicial and administrative institutions, as well as the need to promote effective access to justice, as well as to guarantee that the benefits of development, science and technology contribute effectively to the improvement of the quality of life for all, without discrimination;

108. We recognize the necessity for special measures or positive actions for the victims of racism, racial discrimination, xenophobia and related intolerance in order to promote their full integration into society. Those measures for effective action, including social measures, should aim at correcting the conditions that impair the enjoyment of rights and the introduction of special measures to encourage equal participation of all racial and cultural, linguistic and religious groups in all sectors of society and to bring all onto an equal footing. Those measures should include measures to achieve appropriate representation in educational institutions, housing, political parties, parliaments and employment, especially in the judiciary, police, army and other civil services, which in some cases might involve electoral reforms, land reforms and campaigns for equal participation;

...

112. We recognize the importance of independent national human rights institutions conforming to the Principles relating to the status of national institutions for the promotion and protection of human rights, annexed to General Assembly resolution 48/134 of 20 December 1993, and other relevant specialized institutions created by law for the promotion and protection of human rights, including ombudsman institutions, in the struggle against racism, racial discrimination, xenophobia and related intolerance, as well as for the promotion of democratic values and the rule of law. We encourage States, as appropriate, to establish such institutions and call upon the authorities and society in general in those countries where they are performing their tasks of promotion, protection and prevention to cooperate to the maximum extent possible with these institutions, while respecting their independence;

...

116. We recognize the fundamental role of civil society in the fight against racism, racial discrimination, xenophobia and related intolerance, in particular in assisting States to develop regulations and strategies, in taking measures and action against such forms of discrimination and through follow-up implementation;

. . .

122. We affirm that our global drive for the total elimination of racism, racial discrimination, xenophobia and related intolerance is undertaken, and that the recommendations contained in the Programme of Action are made, in a spirit of solidarity and international cooperation and are inspired by the purposes and principles of the Charter of the United Nations and other relevant international instruments. These recommendations are made with due consideration for the past, the present and the future, and with a constructive and forward-looking approach. We recognize that the formulation and implementation of these strategies, policies, programmes and actions, which should be carried out efficiently and promptly, are the responsibility of all States, with the full involvement of civil society at the national, regional and international levels.

Programme of Action

Recognizing the urgent need to translate the objectives of the Declaration into a practical and workable Programme of Action, the World Conference against Racism, Racial Discrimination, Xenophobia and Related Intolerance:

I. Sources, causes, forms and contemporary manifestations of racism, racial discrimination, xenophobia and related intolerance

1. Urges States in their national efforts, and in cooperation with other States, regional and international organizations and financial institutions, to promote the use of public and private investment in consultation with the affected communities in order to eradicate poverty, particularly in those areas in which victims of racism, racial discrimination, xenophobia and related intolerance predominantly live;

2. Urges States to take all necessary and appropriate measures to end enslavement and contemporary forms of slavery-like practices, to initiate constructive dialogue among States and implement measures with a view to correcting the problems and the damage resulting therefrom;

II. Victims of racism, racial discrimination, xenophobia and related intolerance
Victims: General

3. Urges States to work nationally and in cooperation with other States and relevant regional and international organizations and programmes to strengthen national mechanisms to promote and protect the human rights of victims of racism, racial discrimination, xenophobia and related intolerance who are infected, or presumably infected, with pandemic diseases such as HIV/AIDS and to take concrete measures, including preventive action, appropriate access to medication and treatment, programmes of education, training and mass media dissemination, to eliminate violence, stigmatization, discrimination, unemployment and other negative consequences arising from these pandemics;

Africans and people of African descent

4. Urges States to facilitate the participation of people of African descent in all political, economic, social and cultural aspects of society and in the advancement and economic development of their countries, and to promote a greater knowledge of and respect for their heritage and culture;

. . .

Indigenous peoples

15. Urges States:

(a) To adopt or continue to apply, in concert with them, constitutional, administrative, legislative, judicial and all necessary measures to promote, protect and ensure the enjoyment by indigenous peoples of their rights, as well as to guarantee them the exercise of their human rights and fundamental freedoms on the basis of equality, non-discrimination and full and free participation in all areas of society, in particular in matters affecting or concerning their interests;

(b) To promote better knowledge of and respect for indigenous cultures and heritage; and welcomes measures already taken by States in these respects;

. . .

Migrants

24. Requests all States to combat manifestations of a generalized rejection of migrants and actively to discourage all racist demonstrations and acts that generate xenophobic behaviour and negative sentiments towards, or rejection of, migrants;

25. Invites international and national non-governmental organizations to include Monitoring and protection of the human rights of migrants in their programmes and activities and to sensitize Governments and increase public awareness in all States about the need to prevent racist acts and manifestations of discrimination, xenophobia and related intolerance against migrants;

...

Refugees

34. Urges States to comply with their obligations under international human rights, refugee and humanitarian law relating to refugees, asylum-seekers and displaced persons, and urges the international community to provide them with protection and assistance in an equitable manner and with due regard to their needs in different parts of the world, in keeping with principles of international solidarity, burden-sharing and international cooperation, to share responsibilities;

...

Other victims

38. Recognizes that victims of trafficking are particularly exposed to racism, racial discrimination, xenophobia and related intolerance. States shall ensure that all measures taken against trafficking in persons, in particular those that affect the victims of such trafficking, are consistent with internationally recognized principles of non-discrimination, including the prohibition of racial discrimination and the availability of appropriate legal redress;

...

III. Measures of prevention, education and protection aimed at the eradication of racism, racial discrimination, xenophobia and related intolerance at the national, regional and international levels

58. Urges States to adopt and implement, at both the national and international levels, effective measures and policies, in addition to existing anti-discrimination national legislation and relevant international instruments and mechanisms, which encourage all citizens and institutions to take a stand against racism, racial discrimination, xenophobia and related intolerance, and to recognize, respect and maximize the benefits of diversity within and among all nations in working together to build a harmonious and productive future by putting into practice and promoting values and principles such as justice, equality and non-discrimination, democracy, fairness and friendship, tolerance and respect within and between communities and nations, in particular through public information and education programmes to raise awareness and understanding of the benefits of cultural diversity, including programmes where the public authorities work in partnership with international and non-governmental organizations and other sectors of civil society;

...

A. National level

1. Legislative, judicial, regulatory, administrative and other measures to prevent and protect against racism, racial discrimination, xenophobia and related intolerance

66. Urges States to establish and implement without delay national policies and action plans to combat racism, racial discrimination, xenophobia and related intolerance, including their gender-based manifestations;

67. Urges States to design or reinforce, promote and implement effective legislative and administrative policies, as well as other preventive measures, against the serious situation experienced by certain groups of workers, including migrant workers, who are victims of racism, racial discrimination, xenophobia and related intolerance. Special attention should be given to protecting people engaged in domestic work and trafficked persons from discrimination and violence, as well as to combating prejudice against them;

68. Urges States to adopt and implement, or strengthen, national legislation and administrative measures that expressly and specifically counter racism and prohibit racial discrimination, xenophobia and related intolerance, whether direct or indirect, in all spheres of public life, in accordance with their obligations under the International Convention on the Elimination of All Forms of Racial Discrimination, ensuring that their reservations are not contrary to the object and purpose of the Convention;

...

Ratification of and effective implementation of relevant international and regional legal instruments on human rights and non-discrimination

75. Urges States that have not yet done so to consider ratifying or acceding to the international human rights instruments which combat racism, racial discrimination, xenophobia and related intolerance, in particular to accede to the International Convention on the Elimination of All Forms of Racial Discrimination

as a matter of urgency, with a view to universal ratification by the year 2005, and to consider making the declaration envisaged under Article 14, to comply with their reporting obligations, and to publish and act upon the concluding observations of the Committee on the Elimination of Racial Discrimination. It also urges States to withdraw reservations contrary to the object and purpose of that Convention and to consider withdrawing other reservations;

...

Prosecution of perpetrators of racist acts

84. Urges States to adopt effective measures to combat criminal acts motivated by racism, racial discrimination, xenophobia and related intolerance, to take measures so that such motivations are considered an aggravating factor for the purposes of sentencing, to prevent these crimes from going unpunished and to ensure the rule of law;

85. Urges States to undertake investigations to examine possible links between criminal prosecution, police violence and penal sanctions, on the one hand, and racism, racial discrimination, xenophobia and related intolerance, on the other, so as to have evidence for taking the necessary steps for the eradication of any such links and discriminatory practices;

86. Calls upon States to promote measures to deter the emergence of and to counter neo-fascist, violent nationalist ideologies which promote racial hatred and racial discrimination, as well as racist and xenophobic sentiments, including measures to combat the negative influence of such ideologies especially on young people through formal and non-formal education, the media and sport;

87. Urges States parties to adopt legislation implementing the obligations they have assumed to prosecute and punish persons who have committed or ordered to be committed grave breaches of the Geneva Conventions of 12 August 1949 and Additional Protocol I thereto and of other serious violations of the laws and customs of war, in particular in relation to the principle of non-discrimination;

...

2. Policies and practices
Data collection and disaggregation, research and study

92. Urges States to collect, compile, analyse, disseminate and publish reliable statistical data at the national and local levels and undertake all other related measures which are necessary to assess regularly the situation of individuals and groups of individuals who are victims of racism, racial discrimination, xenophobia and related intolerance;

(a) Such statistical data should be disaggregated in accordance with national legislation. Any such information shall, as appropriate, be collected with the explicit consent of the victims, based on their self-identification and in accordance with provisions on human rights and fundamental freedoms, such as data protection regulations and privacy guarantees. This information must not be misused;

...

Action-oriented policies and action plans, including affirmative action to ensure nondiscrimination, in particular as regards access to social services, employment, housing, education, health care, etc.

99. Recognizes that combating racism, racial discrimination, xenophobia and related intolerance is a primary responsibility of States. It therefore encourages States to develop or elaborate national action plans to promote diversity, equality, equity, social justice, equality of opportunity and the participation of all. Through, among other things, affirmative or positive actions and strategies, these plans should aim at creating conditions for all to participate effectively in decision-making and realize civil, cultural, economic, political and social rights in all spheres of life on the basis of non-discrimination. The World Conference encourages States, in developing and elaborating such action plans, to establish, or reinforce, dialogue with non-governmental organizations in order to involve them more closely in designing, implementing and evaluating policies and programmes;

...

Employment

103. Urges States to promote and support where appropriate the organization and operation of enterprises owned by persons who are victims of racism, racial discrimination, xenophobia and related intolerance by promoting equal access to credit and to training programmes;

...

Health, environment

109. Urges States, individually and through international cooperation, to enhance measures to fulfil the right of everyone to the enjoyment of the highest attainable standard of physical and mental health, with a

view to eliminating disparities in health status, as indicated in standard health indexes, which might result from racism, racial discrimination, xenophobia and related intolerance;

...

Equal participation in political, economic, social and cultural decision-making

112. Urges States and encourages the private sector and international financial and development institutions, such as the World Bank and regional development banks, to promote participation of individuals and groups of individuals who are victims of racism, racial discrimination, xenophobia and related intolerance in economic, cultural and social decision-making at all stages, particularly in the development and implementation of poverty alleviation strategies, development projects, and trade and market assistance programmes;

...

Role of politicians and political parties

115. Underlines the key role that politicians and political parties can play in combating racism, racial discrimination, xenophobia and related intolerance and encourages political parties to take concrete steps to promote equality, solidarity and non-discrimination in society, inter alia by developing voluntary codes of conduct which include internal disciplinary measures for violations thereof, so their members refrain from public statements and actions that encourage or incite racism, racial discrimination, xenophobia and related intolerance;

...

3. Education and awareness-raising measures

117. Urges States, where appropriate working with other relevant bodies, to commit financial resources to anti-racism education and to media campaigns promoting the values of acceptance, tolerance, diversity and respect for the cultures of all indigenous peoples living within their national borders. In particular, States should promote an accurate understanding of the histories and cultures of indigenous peoples;

...

Access to education without discrimination

121. Urges States to commit themselves to ensuring access to education, including access to free primary education for all children, both girls and boys, and access for adults to lifelong learning and education, based on respect for human rights, diversity and tolerance, without discrimination of any kind;

...

Human rights education

125. Requests States to include the struggle against racism, racial discrimination, xenophobia and related intolerance among the activities undertaken within the framework of the United Nations Decade for Human Rights Education (1995–2004) and to take into account the recommendations of the mid-term evaluation report of the Decade;

126. Encourages all States, in cooperation with the United Nations, the United Nations Educational, Scientific and Cultural Organization and other relevant international organizations, to initiate and develop cultural and educational programmes aimed at countering racism, racial discrimination, xenophobia and related intolerance, in order to ensure respect for the dignity and worth of all human beings and enhance mutual understanding among all cultures and civilizations. It further urges States to support and implement public information campaigns and specific training programmes in the field of human rights, where appropriate formulated in local languages, to combat racism, racial discrimination, xenophobia and related intolerance and promote respect for the values of diversity, pluralism, tolerance, mutual respect, cultural sensitivity, integration and inclusiveness. Such programmes and campaigns should be addressed to all sectors of society, in particular children and young people;

Human rights education for children and youth

129. Urges States to introduce and, as applicable, to reinforce anti-discrimination and anti-racism components in human rights programmes in school curricula, to develop and improve relevant educational material, including history and other textbooks, and to ensure that all teachers are effectively trained and adequately motivated to shape attitudes and behavioural patterns, based on the principles of non-discrimination, mutual respect and tolerance;

130. Calls upon States to undertake and facilitate activities aimed at educating young people in human rights and democratic citizenship and instilling values of solidarity, respect and appreciation of diversity, including respect for different groups. A special effort to inform and sensitize young people to respect demo-

cratic values and human rights should be undertaken or developed to fight against ideologies based on the fallacious theory of racial superiority;

. . .

Human rights education for public officials and professionals

133. Urges States to develop and strengthen anti-racist and gender-sensitive human rights training for public officials, including personnel in the administration of justice, particularly in law enforcement, correctional and security services, as well as among health-care, schools and migration authorities;

134. Urges States to pay specific attention to the negative impact of racism, racial discrimination, xenophobia and related intolerance on the administration of justice and fair trial, and to conduct nationwide campaigns, amongst other measures, to raise awareness among State organs and public officials concerning their obligations under the International Convention on the Elimination of All Forms of Racial Discrimination and other relevant instruments;

135. Requests States, wherever appropriate through cooperation with international organizations, national institutions, non-governmental organizations and the private sector, to organize and facilitate training activities, including courses or seminars, on international norms prohibiting racial discrimination and their applicability in domestic law, as well as on their international human rights obligations, for prosecutors, members of the judiciary and other public officials;

136. Calls upon States to ensure that education and training, especially teacher training, promote respect for human rights and the fight against racism, racial discrimination, xenophobia and related intolerance and that educational institutions implement policies and programmes agreed by the relevant authorities on equal opportunities, anti-racism, gender equality, and cultural, religious and other diversity, with the participation of teachers, parents and students, and follow up their implementation. It further urges all educators, including teachers at all levels of education, religious communities and the print and electronic media, to play an effective role in human rights education, including as a means to combat racism, racial discrimination, xenophobia and related intolerance;

. . .

4. Information, communication and the media, including new technologies

140. Welcomes the positive contribution made by the new information and communications technologies, including the Internet, in combating racism through rapid and wide-reaching communication;

141. Draws attention to the potential to increase the use of the new information and communications technologies, including the Internet, to create educational and awareness-raising networks against racism, racial discrimination, xenophobia and related intolerance, both in and out of school, as well as the ability of the Internet to promote universal respect for human rights and also respect for the value of cultural diversity;

. . .

B. International level

148. Urges all actors on the international scene to build an international order based on inclusion, justice, equality and equity, human dignity, mutual understanding and promotion of and respect for cultural diversity and universal human rights, and to reject all doctrines of exclusion based on racism, racial discrimination, xenophobia and related intolerance;

149. Believes that all conflicts and disputes should be resolved through peaceful means and political dialogue. The Conference calls on all parties involved in such conflicts to exercise restraint and to respect human rights and international humanitarian law;

150. Calls upon States, in opposing all forms of racism, to recognize the need to counter anti-Semitism, anti-Arabism and Islamophobia world-wide, and urges all States to take effective measures to prevent the emergence of movements based on racism and discriminatory ideas concerning these communities;

151. As for the situation in the Middle East, calls for the end of violence and the swift resumption of negotiations, respect for international human rights and humanitarian law, respect for the principle of self-determination and the end of all suffering, thus allowing Israel and the Palestinians to resume the peace process, and to develop and prosper in security and freedom;

. . .

IV. Provision of effective remedies, recourse, redress, and other measures at the national, regional and international levels

158. Recognizes that these historical injustices have undeniably contributed to the poverty, underdevelopment, marginalization, social exclusion, economic disparities, instability and insecurity that affect many

people in different parts of the world, in particular in developing countries. The Conference recognizes the need to develop programmes for the social and economic development of these societies and the Diaspora, within the framework of a new partnership based on the spirit of solidarity and mutual respect, in the following areas:

...

Legal assistance

160. Urges States to take all necessary measures to address, as a matter of urgency, the pressing requirement for justice for the victims of racism, racial discrimination, xenophobia and related intolerance and to ensure that victims have full access to information, support, effective protection and national, administrative and judicial remedies, including the right to seek just and adequate reparation or satisfaction for damage, as well as legal assistance, where required;

161. Urges States to facilitate for victims of racial discrimination, including victims of torture and ill-treatment, access to all appropriate legal procedures and free legal assistance in a manner adapted to their specific needs and vulnerability, including through legal representation;

...

National legislation and programmes

163. For the purposes of effectively combating racism and racial discrimination, xenophobia and related intolerance in the civil, political, economic, social and cultural fields, the Conference recommends to all States that their national legislative framework should expressly and specifically prohibit racial discrimination and provide effective judicial and other remedies or redress, including through the designation of national, independent, specialized bodies;

164. Urges States, with regard to the procedural remedies provided for in their domestic law, to bear in mind the following considerations:

(a) Access to such remedies should be widely available, on a non-discriminatory and equal basis;

(b) Existing procedural remedies should be made known in the context of the relevant action, and victims of racial discrimination should be helped to avail themselves of them in accordance with the particular case;

(c) Inquiries into complaints of racial discrimination and the adjudication of such complaints must be carried out as rapidly as possible;

Remedies, reparations, compensation

165. Urges States to reinforce protection against racism, racial discrimination, xenophobia and related intolerance by ensuring that all persons have access to effective and adequate remedies and enjoy the right to seek from competent national tribunals and other national institutions just and adequate reparation and satisfaction for any damage as a result of such discrimination. It further underlines the importance of access to the law and to the courts for complainants of racism and racial discrimination and draws attention to the need for judicial and other remedies to be made widely known, easily accessible, expeditious and not unduly complicated;

166. Urges States to adopt the necessary measures, as provided by national law, to ensure the right of victims to seek just and adequate reparation and satisfaction to redress acts of racism, racial discrimination, xenophobia and related intolerance, and to design effective measures to prevent the repetition of such acts;

...

V. Strategies to achieve full and effective equality, including international cooperation and enhancement of the United Nations and other international mechanisms in combating racism, racial discrimination, xenophobia and related intolerance and follow-up

168. Urges States that have not yet done so to consider acceding to the Geneva Conventions of 12 August 1949 and their two Additional Protocols of 1977, as well as to other treaties of international humanitarian law, and to enact, with the highest priority, appropriate legislation, taking the measures required to give full effect to their obligations under international humanitarian law, in particular in relation to the rules prohibiting discrimination;

...

171. Urges States to recognize the challenges that people of different socially constructed races, colours, descent, national or ethnic origins, religions and languages experience in seeking to live together and to

develop harmonious multiracial and multicultural societies; also urges States to recognize that the positive examples of relatively successful multiracial and multicultural societies, such as some of those in the Caribbean region, need to be examined and analysed, and that techniques, mechanisms, policies and programmes for reconciling conflicts based on factors related to race, colour, descent, language, religion, or national or ethnic origin and for developing harmonious multiracial and multicultural societies need to be systematically considered and developed, and therefore requests the United Nations and its relevant specialized agencies to consider establishing an international centre for multiracial and multicultural studies and policy development to undertake this critical work for the benefit of the international community;

172. Urges States to protect the national or ethnic, cultural, religious and linguistic identity of minorities within their respective territories and to develop appropriate legislative and other measures to encourage conditions for the promotion of that identity, in order to protect them from any form of racism, racial discrimination, xenophobia and related intolerance. In this context, forms of multiple discrimination should be fully taken into account;

...

176. Urges States to adopt and implement social development policies based on reliable statistical data and centred on the attainment, by the year 2015, of the commitments to meet the basic needs of all set forth in paragraph 36 of the Programme of Action of the World Summit for Social Development, held at Copenhagen in 1995, with a view to closing significantly the existing gaps in living conditions faced by victims of racism, racial discrimination, xenophobia and related intolerance, especially regarding the illiteracy rate, universal primary education, infant mortality, under-five child mortality, health, reproductive health care for all and access to safe drinking water. Promotion of gender equality will also be taken into account in the adoption and implementation of these policies;

International legal framework

177. Urges States to continue cooperating with the Committee on the Elimination of Racial Discrimination and other human rights treaty monitoring bodies in order to promote, including by means of a constructive and transparent dialogue, the effective implementation of the instruments concerned and proper consideration of the recommendations adopted by these bodies with regard to complaints of racism, racial discrimination, xenophobia and related intolerance;

...

General international instruments

179. Endorses efforts of the international community, in particular steps taken under the auspices of the United Nations Educational, Scientific and Cultural Organization, to promote respect for and preserve cultural diversity within and between communities and nations with a view to creating a harmonious multicultural world, including elaboration of a possible international instrument in this respect in a manner consistent with international human rights instruments;

...

Regional/international cooperation

183. Urges States, in consultation with civil society, to support or otherwise establish, as appropriate, regional, comprehensive dialogues on the causes and consequences of migration that focus not only on law enforcement and border control, but also on the promotion and protection of the human rights of migrants and on the relationship between migration and development;

185. Expresses its deep concern over the severity of the humanitarian suffering of affected civilian populations and the burden carried by many receiving countries, particularly developing countries and countries in transition, and requests the relevant international institutions to ensure that urgent adequate financial and humanitarian assistance is maintained for the host countries to enable them to help the victims and to address, on an equitable basis, difficulties of populations expelled from their homes, and calls for sufficient safeguards to enable refugees to exercise freely their right of return to their countries of origin voluntarily, in safety and dignity;

...

Office of the High Commissioner for Human Rights

193. Encourages the United Nations High Commissioner for Human Rights to continue and expand the appointment and designation of goodwill ambassadors in all countries of the world in order, inter alia, to promote respect for human rights and a culture of tolerance and to increase the level of awareness about the scourge of racism, racial discrimination, xenophobia and related intolerance; 194. Calls upon the Office of

the High Commissioner for Human Rights to continue its efforts further to increase awareness of the work of the Committee on the Elimination of Racial Discrimination and the other United Nations human rights treaty bodies;

. . .

195. Invites the Office of the High Commissioner for Human Rights, in consultation with the United Nations Educational, Scientific and Cultural Organization, and non-governmental organizations active in the field of the promotion and protection of human rights, to undertake regular consultations with them and to encourage research activities aimed at collecting, maintaining and adapting the technical, scientific, educational and information materials produced by all cultures around the world to fight racism;

196. Requests the Office of the High Commissioner for Human Rights to pay special attention to violations of the human rights of victims of racism, racial discrimination, xenophobia and related intolerance, in particular migrants, including migrant workers, to promote international cooperation in combating xenophobia and, to this end, to develop programmes which can be implemented in countries on the basis of appropriate cooperation agreements;

197. Invites States to assist the Office of the High Commissioner for Human Rights in developing and funding, upon the request of States, specific technical cooperation projects aimed at combating racism, racial discrimination, xenophobia and related intolerance;

198. (a) Invites the Commission on Human Rights to include in the mandates of the special rapporteurs and working groups of the Commission, in particular the Special Rapporteur on contemporary forms of racism, racial discrimination, xenophobia and related intolerance, recommendations that they consider the relevant provisions of the Declaration and the Programme of Action while exercising their mandates, in particular reporting to the General Assembly and the Commission on Human Rights, and also to consider any other appropriate means to follow up on the outcome on the Conference;

(b) Calls upon States to cooperate with the relevant special procedures of the Commission on Human Rights and other mechanisms of the United Nations in matters pertaining to racism, racial discrimination, xenophobia and related intolerance, in particular with the special rapporteurs, independent experts and special representatives;

199. Recommends that the Commission on Human Rights prepare complementary international standards to strengthen and update international instruments against racism, racial discrimination, xenophobia and related intolerance in all their aspects;

Decades

200. Urges States and the international community to support the activities of the Third Decade to Combat Racism and Racial Discrimination;

201. Recommends that the General Assembly consider declaring a United Nations year or decade against trafficking in persons, especially in women, youth and children, in order to protect their dignity and human rights;

. . .

207. Urges States, in the light of the relationship between racism, racial discrimination, xenophobia and related intolerance and poverty, marginality and social exclusion of peoples and individuals at both the national and international levels, to enhance their policies and measures to reduce income and wealth inequalities and to take appropriate steps, individually and through international cooperation, to promote and protect economic, social and cultural rights on a non-discriminatory basis;

208. Urges States and international financial and development institutions to mitigate any negative effects of globalization by examining, inter alia, how their policies and practices affect national populations in general and indigenous peoples in particular; by ensuring that their policies and practices contribute to the eradication of racism through the participation of national populations and, in particular, indigenous peoples in development projects; by further democratizing international financial institutions; and by consulting with indigenous peoples on any matter that may affect their physical, spiritual or cultural integrity;

. . .

Civil society

210. Calls upon States to strengthen cooperation, develop partnerships and consult regularly with non-governmental organizations and all other sectors of the civil society to harness their experience and expertise, thereby contributing to the development of legislation, policies and other governmental initiatives, as well

as involving them more closely in the elaboration and implementation of policies and programmes designed to combat racism, racial discrimination, xenophobia and related intolerance;

211. Urges leaders of religious communities to continue to confront racism, racial discrimination, xenophobia and related intolerance through, inter alia, promotion and sponsoring of dialogue and partnerships to bring about reconciliation, healing and harmony within and among societies, invites religious communities to participate in promoting economic and social revitalization and encourages religious leaders to foster greater cooperation and contact between diverse racial groups;

...

Non-governmental organizations

213. Urges States to provide an open and conducive environment to enable non-governmental organizations to function freely and openly within their societies and thereby make an effective contribution to the elimination of racism, racial discrimination, xenophobia and related intolerance throughout the world, and to promote a wider role for grass-roots organizations;

...

The private sector

215. Urges States to take measures, including, where appropriate, legislative measures, to ensure that transnational corporations and other foreign enterprises operating within their national territories conform to precepts and practices of non-racism and non-discrimination, and further encourages the business sector, including transnational corporations and foreign enterprises, to collaborate with trade unions and other relevant sectors of civil society to develop voluntary codes of conduct for all businesses, designed to prevent, address and eradicate racism, racial discrimination, xenophobia and related intolerance;

Youth

216. Urges States to encourage the full and active participation of, as well as involve more closely, youth in the elaboration, planning and implementation of activities to fight racism, racial discrimination, xenophobia and related intolerance, and calls upon States, in partnership with non-governmental organizations and other sectors of society, to facilitate both national and international youth dialogue on racism, racial discrimination, xenophobia and related intolerance, through the World Youth Forum of the United Nations system and through the use of new technologies, exchanges and other means;

DOCUMENT 53

Full Official Title: Civil and Political Rights, Including: Freedom of Expression. Report submitted by Mr. Abdelfattah Amor, Special Rapporteur, in accordance with Commission on Human Rights resolution 1998/18

Short Title/Acronym/Abbreviation: Nothing official

Subject: The official report to the U.N. Commission on Human Rights of the findings of the Special Rapporteur mandated to view the situation in the United States related to freedom of religious expression. Results of a Special Procedure.

Official Citation: E/CN.4/1998/58/Add.1, 9 December 1998

Date of Document: December 9, 1998

Date of Adoption: Not applicable

Date of General Entry into Force (EIF): Not a treaty

Number of States Parties to this treaty as of this printing: Not a treaty

Date of Signature by United States: Not applicable

Date of Ratification/Accession/Adhesion: Not applicable

Date of Entry into Force as to United States (effective date): Not applicable

Type of Document: U.N. Commission on Human Rights, Special Rapporteur's Report. Not a legal instrument.

Legal Status/Character of the Instrument/Document as to the United States: Not a legal document. It is a report of a non-treaty-based body, the U.N. Commission on Human Rights, through its thematic special rapporteur mechanism. The Commission no longer exists but special rapporteurs functions continue under the U.N. Human Rights Council since 2006.

Comments: This sample special rapporteur report was made by Mr. Amor in response to his mandate given by the U.N. Commission on Human Rights. He is doing this report as part of his fuller study on the theme of religious intolerance and discrimination in the world. This thematic study is based on the U.N. Declaration on Elimination of All Forms of Intolerance and Discrimination Based on Religion or Belief of 1981. This report is supposed to be objective and non political.

Web address: http://www.unhchr.ch/Huridocda/Huridoca.nsf/TestFrame/3129ccf9f586f 71680256739003494e4?Opendocument

CIVIL AND POLITICAL RIGHTS, INCLUDING: FREEDOM OF EXPRESSION (EXCERPTS)

Report submitted by Mr. Abdelfattah Amor, Special Rapporteur, in accordance with Commission on Human Rights resolution 1998/18

E/CN.4/1999/58/Add.1

9 December 1998

Commission on Human Rights

Fifty-fifth session

Item 11 (c) of the provisional agenda

Addendum

Visit to the United States of America

Contents

Paragraphs

Introduction

1. From 22 January to 6 February 1998, the Special Rapporteur on the question of religious intolerance visited the United States of America in the exercise of his mandate. During his mission, he went to Washington, Chicago, New York, Atlanta (29 January), Salt Lake City, Los Angeles and Arizona.

2. The Special Rapporteur had talks with representatives of the State Department and the Departments of Justice, the Interior and Education, the Immigration and Naturalization Service and the Equal Employment Opportunity Council. ... In addition, he spoke with Justices of the Supreme Court Sandra Day O'Connor and Stephen Breyer.

3. The organization of official meetings presented problems inasmuch as the State Department confined its assistance to meetings held at the federal level, declaring that it was not competent to help with the Special Rapporteur's visits to the states; this highly regrettable lack of cooperation meant that few meetings with official state representatives were arranged....

4. The Special Rapporteur also had consultations with a great number of non-governmental organizations in the field of human rights and with representatives of most religions and beliefs: Native Americans, Christians, Muslims, Jews, Buddhists, Hindus, Jehovah's Witnesses, Seventh-Day Adventists, Mormons, Baha'is, Scientologists, atheists, etc. An essential part was played ... by the assistance of non-governmental organizations and private individuals, including in particular: ... Tandem Project in Minneapolis; ... DePaul University in Chicago; ... Emory University in Atlanta; ... Brigham Young University in Utah; ... NGO Committee on Freedom of Religion or Belief in New York; ... United States Institute for Peace in Washington; ... NGO International Indian Treaty Council; ... Muslim Public Affairs Council and the Interreligious Council of

Southern California in Los Angeles;...International League for Human Rights;...International Religious Liberty Association; and the American Jewish Committee....

5. The Special Rapporteur is unfortunately obliged to draw attention here to the fact that...he came up against a series of obstacles the aim of which was to get his mission put off; he was also the object of various attempts to interfere and take control of his programme. ...What is unacceptable is that these hindrances were the work of international officials of the United Nations, acting, it seems, either on their own initiative or in defence of State interests or certain lobbies. ... the United States Government was not in any way responsible for the obstacles and hindrances. ...

...

I. Legal Situation in the Field of Religion or Belief

7. The principal legal texts concerning freedom of religion or belief are, on the one hand, article VI of the Constitution—"...no religious test shall ever be required as a qualification to any office or public trust under the United States"—and, on the other hand, the First Amendment to the Constitution—"Congress shall make no law respecting an establishment of religion, or prohibiting the free exercise thereof. ..." The two clauses of the First Amendment—free exercise of religion and "non-establishment" of religion—apply equally to the actions of state and local governments since the Supreme Court has ruled that the Fourteenth Amendment's dictum that no state may deprive any person of liberty without due process of law makes the First Amendment applicable to the states. At the federal level, there is no single law on freedom of religion or belief...which provide legal protection essentially by the availability of remedies. ...

8. The Supreme Court has not tried to define religion itself or to answer the delicate question of what constitutes a religious belief to be legally protected; it has, however, considered that some beliefs may be "so bizarre, so clearly non-religious in motivation, as not to be entitled to protection under the free exercise clause" (Thomas v. Review Board, Indiana Employment Security Div., 450 U.S. 707, 715 (1981)). In identifying such "non-religious beliefs," the Court has focused on the credibility and sincerity of an individual's beliefs rather than on the orthodoxy or popularity of a particular faith. ...An individual's right to believe in non-traditional religions or to be an atheist or agnostic is protected. It should be added that the Internal Revenue Code does not define the term "religious." Internal Revenue Service determination concerning the tax-exempt status...looks at whether the asserted religious beliefs of the organization are truly and sincerely held, and whether the practices and rituals...are legal or contrary to clearly defined public policy.

...

A. Constitutional and Jurisprudential Guarantees

1. Free exercise of religion

10. There follows a brief account of the way the Supreme Court's jurisprudence...

11. ...In Reynolds v. United States, 98 U.S. 145 (1879), the Supreme Court rejected Mr. Reynolds' claim that polygamy was an exercise of his religion and said that the free exercise clause protected his right to believe, but not his right to act on those beliefs. Other cases...Wisconsin v. Yoder, 406 U.S. 205 (1972) (exempting Amish children from obligatory school attendance) and Sherbert v. Verner, 374 U.S. 398 (1963) (unemployment compensation may not be denied to a person who refused to make her/himself available for work on Saturday because it was her/his Sabbath), it is suggested that a law which substantially burdens the exercise of religion will be subjected to strict judicial scrutiny...

12. In other cases, the Court has upheld certain neutral laws of general applicability without applying strict scrutiny:...Employment Division v. Smith, 494 U.S. 972 (1990) (state drug laws may be applied to bar the sacramental ingestion of controlled substances such as peyote), the Supreme Court decided that neutral laws of general applicability do not typically offend the free exercise clause merely because in application they incidentally prohibit the exercise of someone's religion....

13. The Religious Freedom Restoration Act of 1993 was enacted by the Congress in order to subject all laws to the strict scrutiny that the Smith case for the most part abandoned. The Act provides that the Government shall not substantially burden a person's exercise of religion...unless the Government demonstrates that the burden furthers a compelling governmental interest and is the least restrictive means of furthering that interest.

14. In Boerne v. Flores, 117 S Ct 2157 (1997), the Supreme Court declared the Religious Freedom Restoration Act unconstitutional because Congress cannot adopt a standard of protection different from that provided by the Constitution unless there is some proportionality between the injury to be prevented and the means adopted to that end....

15. During the Special Rapporteur's mission, many representatives of non-governmental organizations... stress the need for legislation along the lines of the Religious Freedom Restoration Act in order to remedy the decision in the Smith case, regarded as a mistaken interpretation by the Supreme Court...the Smith case means that freedom of religion and belief is and may be affected for the following reasons:

(a) In the past, formally neutral, generally applicable laws were used to persecute minorities...

...

(c) A secular bureaucracy may be indifferent towards the needs of religious communities, or indeed ignorant of them;

(d) Legislators may not be aware of the existence and importance of minority groups in the field of religion or belief...

...

2. "Non-establishment" of Religion

18. The Supreme Court has interpreted the "non-establishment" clause...It recognizes the right of an individual or group to be free from laws and governmental decisions which aid one religion, aid all religions, or prefer one religion over another (Walz v. Tax Commission...) The clause serves to prevent both religious control over Government and political control over religion.

19. In Lemon v. Kutzman, ...three-part test for determining whether a law or decision violates the "non-establishment" clause: the statute or decision must have a secular non-religious purpose, the principal or primary effect must be one that neither advances nor inhibits religion, and the statute or decision must not foster an excessive government entanglement with religion.

20. The interpretation of the "non-establishment" clause is often the subject of debate and has undergone a certain evolution, in particular with respect to the following issues:

(a) Direct public aid to parochial schools....

(b) The recognition and practice of religion in State schools, notably school prayer. ...Supreme Court ruled that Government-sponsored prayer in State schools violates the "non-establishment" clause.... President Clinton has declared that the First Amendment did not convert schools into "religion-free zones"...

(c) Governmental financial assistance that may accrue to the benefit of religious schools. ...Thus the "student benefit" test eventually yielded to the "Lemon test" (see paragraph 19)....

21. In view of the sensitivity of the question of freedom of religion and belief, ...several NGO representatives expressed the wish that the Supreme Court would develop a coherent and comprehensive framework for interpreting and applying the two constitutional clauses. Justices O'Connor and Breyer of the Supreme Court told the Special Rapporteur that the American legal system proceeded case by case, without necessarily spelling out major principles, and that the jurisprudence in the above-mentioned areas was vague and confused. They added that in a pluralist society containing both believers and non-believers, the principle of the separation of religion and the State was a wise one; similarly, the aim should be to be as generous as possible in relation to the practice of religion as long as it did no one else any harm. With regard to the Supreme Court's jurisprudence, described as "chaotic," many non-governmental representatives stressed the need to remedy a kind of insensitivity towards religious minorities. ... and towards the principles of freedom of religion or belief as understood in international human rights law (Declaration on the Elimination of All Forms of Intolerance and of Discrimination Based on Religion or Belief, International Covenant on Civil and Political Rights and jurisprudence of the Human Rights Committee)....

B. Federal Legislation

22. While there is no federal law dealing with freedom of religion or belief stricto sensu, there is a non-homogeneous body of legislation dealing directly or indirectly with certain expressions of these freedoms....

23. Federal statutes make it a crime for:

(a) A person acting under colour of law to deprive another person of any right protected by the Constitution or laws (United States Code (USC), Title 18, sect. 242);

...

(c) And for any person, under colour of law, by force or threat of force, to injure, intimidate or interfere with another person because of that person's race, colour, national origin or religion, because that person is attending a State school, applying for employment, or engaged in other such protected activities (ibid., sect. 245);

24. The Civil Rights Act of 1871 provides a remedy for individuals denied their First Amendment rights or discriminated against on the basis of religion (USC, Title 42, sect. 1983). The Civil Rights Act of 1964 prohibits discrimination on the basis of, inter alia, religion. Title VII bars discrimination in employment

practices while an exception is made for religious institutions to allow them to employ persons of a particular religious background if their work is related to the employer's religious activities....

25. Over and above the question of the Religious Freedom Restoration Act discussed earlier, and faced with federal legislation which is fragmentary, non-governmental representatives called for the adoption of a general law on the freedom of religion or conviction, which might be based in particular on international human rights law. Such a law would provide a greater guarantee of protection for minorities in the field of religion or belief, because it would in particular act as a check on the "might is right" principle....

26. The State Department representatives considered that the First Amendment to the Constitution was a sufficient guarantee and preferable to general legislation, which could only be the result of a compromise in the Congress, where, moreover, minorities were by definition in a weak position. They explained that the First Amendment constituted the general and principal legal framework .... the United States' political system of separation of powers meant there could be no doubt about the matter. Apart from the protective legal framework offered by the Constitution, any violation in the field of religion or belief was punishable under the criminal law. It was therefore considered that any revision of the First Amendment would be pointless. ...According to the Under-Secretary of State, while the system of separation of religion and the State under the Constitution was not perfect, it was preferable to have a fight between freedoms rather than a fight over freedom.

C. Other Matters

27. Many persons deplored the failure of the United States to ratify the Convention on the Rights of the Child, which includes provisions on freedom of religion or belief. We may note that 191 States have ratified this Convention, but that they do not include Somalia and the United States of America. This situation has been interpreted as a manifestation of isolationism and rejection of other people....

28. In general, it appears that international human rights law, including treaties ratified by the United States, is seen as belonging solely to foreign affairs and not to domestic affairs and that domestic law de facto takes precedence over international law...

II. Tolerance and Non-Discrimination Based on Religion or Belief
A. Religions and Beliefs: The Present Picture

29. The Special Rapporteur was unable to obtain official statistics for religions and beliefs because, as the State Department representatives explained, the authorities do not compile such statistics...He therefore had to turn to various non-official sources, such as the World Almanac....

30. The study entitled "The Religious Landscape of the United States," which is to be found in the March 1997 issue of U.S. Society and Values, the electronic review of the United States Information Agency, contains an analysis of the Pluralism Project which yields the following figures:

(a) 163 million Americans (63 per cent) identify themselves as affiliated with a specific religious denomination;

(b) Roman Catholicism is the single largest religious denomination with some 60 million adherents;

(c) American Protestant Churches have a total of some 94 million members of some 220 individual denominations....

(d) There are more than 300,000 local congregations in the United States;

(e) There are more than 530,000 members of the clergy;

(f) Some 3.8 million people identify themselves as Jews, with an additional 2 million defining themselves as primarily culturally or ethnically Jewish;

(g) There are an estimated 3.5–3.8 million Muslims; Islam is the fastest growing religion in the United States;

(h) In terms of personal religious identification, the most rapidly growing group in the United States is atheists/agnostics (currently about 8 million).

31. It is noteworthy that these sources of information make no mention of the traditional beliefs of Native Americans as distinct from the affiliation of part of this group with the Christian religion....

32. It is evident from these figures that the United States of America, which is characterized by an extraordinary religious diversity, offers a mosaic of the world's religions and beliefs. While we find a predominantly European and Judaeo-Christian heritage, ... can nevertheless lead to the view that all denominations are minorities....

33. Before going on to consider these "minority" communities, the Special Rapporteur considers that the situation of the majority Catholic and Protestant religions (each being treated here as a monolithic entity, ... may be practised with less intensity because of their majority position....

B. Situation of Minority Communities in the Field of Religion or Belief
1. Situation of Muslims

34. Within the Muslim community...two main trends: on the one hand, the Afro-Americans who between the end of the nineteenth century and the middle of the twentieth century gradually established the Black Muslim community, rejecting a past of slavery associated with forced conversion to Christianity and reconstructing an identity around Islam, which they think of as their original religion; secondly, the "oriental" Muslim community originally established by Lebanese and Syrian immigrants at the end of the nineteenth century and enriched by newcomers from Pakistan, Bangladesh, India and the Middle East from the 1960s onwards....

35. Most of the Muslim representatives stressed that their community's situation in the religious sphere was satisfactory compared with that of Muslim minorities in other countries, and even with the position of Muslims living in countries where Islam was the majority religion. They emphasized in particular the freedom that prevailed in general with regard to religious activities, including the practice of worship and religious traditions, the management of religious institutions' affairs and the construction of buildings for religious communities. According to the information received, Muslims have 1,250 mosques and Islamic centres. ... There are also about 100 weekday schools, 1,000 weekend schools and about 1,200 community organizations. Inter-denominational dialogue is also encouraged and developed....

36. However, despite a general and comparative situation that is positive, the situation of Muslims within the national religious mosaic is problematic. The Muslim representatives said that they felt that there was both latently and openly a form of islamophobia and racial and religious intolerance in American society. It emerges very clearly that an essential factor in that situation is the particularly harmful role played by the media...the media treatment of the episode when United States diplomats were taken hostage during the Iranian revolution, the explosion at the World Trade Center in New York, the Gulf War, and even the Oklahoma City bombing, which was immediately attributed to Muslims, etc. ...known as the "Nation of Islam."...

37. Such behaviour by the media is very disturbing: these powerful means of communication have a decisive effect on the formation of American public opinion... The result is that most Americans are not only kept in a state of basic ignorance about Islam and Muslims, but are also insidiously and involuntarily conditioned by the...direct or indirect, intentional or unintentional—of intolerance and discrimination, both racial and religious:

(a) Acts of vandalism against mosques and Muslims' private property, verbal and physical attacks, discrimination in the field of employment. ... The 1996/97 report on hate crimes and discrimination against Arab Americans prepared by the American-Arab Anti-Discrimination Committee (ADC) includes 22 instances of hate crime, 55 cases of discrimination in the workplace and 22 cases of discrimination by local or federal government agencies....

(b) A security system used by American airline companies uses a "terrorist profile" that is seen to be discriminatory and humiliating to Arabs and Muslims....

(c) The Anti-Terrorism and Effective Death Penalty Act of 1996 allows the deportation of non-citizens on the grounds of suspicion of links to organizations abroad which the United States designates as "terrorist," and the Illegal Immigration Reform and Immigrant Responsibility Act provides for punishments for minor violations of visa status and makes it more difficult to secure political asylum. ... It is believed that Arabs and Muslims, often associated with terrorists, would be most likely to be affected by this legislation.

38. These manifestations are not, of course, due to any anti-Muslim policy on the part of the United States authorities and are not the general rule for Muslims. They are in fact manifestations which are marginal...

39. The Special Rapporteur would like to refer here to the particular role played by the Afro-American organization "Nation of Islam." During the mission, this organization was described by both Muslim and Jewish representatives as an extremist group in the American Muslim community and as a source of intolerance purveying messages of hatred for whites, Catholics, Jews, Arabs, women, homosexuals, etc. ...

40. The Special Rapporteur wishes in conclusion to refer to the positive action taken on behalf of the Muslim community by some authorities and non-State entities. At the official level, several initiatives directly or indirectly in favour of Muslims deserve to be reported. President Clinton's greetings on the occasion of Ramadan and Mrs. Clinton's invitation of Muslims to the White House for an Iftar dinner (celebrating the end of Ramadan) are gestures of recognition for and communion with the Muslim community... Finally, in society, the Special Rapporteur was very conscious of the role of the interdenominational dialogue and its impact....

2. Situation of Jews

41. The Jewish community is characterized by its diversity. It includes, on the one hand, people who identify with it on a religious or cultural or ethnic basis and, on the other, the three main branches of Judaism in the United States—orthodox, conservative and "reform". ... This is a religion and a community which have made an essential contribution to the different spheres of American life.

42. Representatives of the Jewish community have stated that they have benefited from a privileged—indeed unique—situation in the United States, due in particular to a degree of religious liberty which is without equal in the world. They attributed this situation to the constitutional protections ("non-establishment" and free-exercise clauses) ...

43. Exceptions, however, exist. It was noted that in the Attorney-General's January 1998 report on hate crimes statistics in the United States, of 8,734 crimes classified as "hate crimes" reported to the Federal Bureau of Investigation, 1,400 were "religion-motivated." ...

44. They also drew attention to the Smith case and said that since the 1990 ruling, the Government in most cases is no longer required to demonstrate a compelling reason for restricting religious exercise. This has led to efforts to adopt the Religious Freedom Restoration Act, which the Supreme Court declared unconstitutional and which is being revised....

45. In addition to this situation, considered very satisfactory by the Jewish community, Jewish representatives stressed very strongly the primary role of the constitutional provisions ... They also noted that the Jewish community had played a pioneering role in American society in initiating interreligious dialogue such as the Catholic/Jewish Educational Enrichment Programme which sends rabbis into 30 Catholic high schools to teach about Judaism, anti-Semitism and the Holocaust, and which sends a Catholic professor to teach about Catholicism and the Catholic community in Jewish day schools.

3. Other communities in the field of religion or belief

46. ... "Marginal" religions such as the Jehovah's Witnesses, the Mormons, the Seventh Day Adventists and the Assemblies of God, are also accepted in the society, no doubt because some minorities which in the past suffered from intolerance and discrimination have with time become figures in the landscape of religion and belief which the public have got used to and familiar with. As far as Scientology, on the one hand, and atheism, on the other, are concerned, the situation also appears to be satisfactory ...

   ...

48. The difficulties most often mentioned concern discrimination at the workplace (such as dismissals, non-respect for religious practices—especially in the case of Seventh-Day Adventists—and problems connected with so-called "religious" (particularly in the case of Buddhists, Hindus, Jehovah's Witnesses, Hare Krishna, Mormons outside Utah, etc.), and even isolated attacks on religious buildings.

49. As far as permits for places of worship are concerned, one of the main factors emphasized by the representatives of these communities is the Supreme Court's decision in the Smith case, which affects above all communities in a minority position. .... the Smith case having established that for neutral laws of general applicability, the authorities are no longer obliged to demonstrate a compelling interest unless the law is specifically targeted at a religious practice. This situation was confirmed by the justices of the Supreme Court consulted by the Special Rapporteur. According to Douglas Laycock, a professor at the University of Texas Law School, who based his view on a 1993 survey which concluded, first, that 43 per cent of Americans said they had a very negative or negative opinion of "fundamentalists." ...

50. Concerning Scientology, its representatives declared that their organization had been recognized as a religion in the United States since 1993 and that it had 42 churches with 3 million members. As regards the information collected by the Special Rapporteur during his visit on the existence of forced labour camps—the "Rehabilitation programme"—and Scientology's harassment of its former members and its critics, even including killings, the representatives of the organization firmly rejected those accusations.

51. As far as atheism is concerned, it is a movement which, for the time being, is developing and organizing among the population on a modest scale, generally because of its non-acceptance by the society, in which religion remains a very strong point of reference in social, cultural and identity terms.

C. Situation of Native Americans

52. The situation of the Native Americans was discussed in depth with officials.

53. The Native Americans are without any doubt the community facing the most problematical situation, one inherited from a past of denial of their religious identity, in particular through a policy of assimilation.

54. It was explained to the Special Rapporteur that it must be clearly understood that the continuation and preservation of traditional Native American religion is ensured only through the performance of ceremonies and rites by tribal members.

55. Concerning the situation of Native Americans in the religious domain, regulations restricting traditional ceremonies, including dances, lasted until 1934 when the Indian Reorganization Act was adopted. In 1978 Congress adopted the American Indian Religious Freedom Act (AIRFA) which stipulates, in particular, that: "It shall be the policy of the United States to protect and preserve for American Indians their inherent right of freedom to believe, express and exercise the traditional."

56. With respect to the jurisprudence of the Supreme Court, in Lying v. Northwest Indian Cemetery Protective Association (1988) the Court declared that AIRFA was only a "policy statement." Although the Court recognized that the Government did not have a "compelling interest" in constructing a road on sacred land, as there existed alternatives.

...

58. Concerning the Executive Order in particular, it was stated that while it was very positive for tribes, the Order had no "action clause," leaving tribes without the needed legal "teeth," and that a stronger commitment to effective tribal consultation and higher standards for the protection of sacred sites were needed.

59. Concerning the Native American Graves Protection and Repatriation Act ... Concerns were also expressed on the following issues:

(a) On 24 October 1997, the Advisory Council on Historic Preservation approved regulations that place tribes in a secondary role, in regard to section 106 of the National Historic Preservation Act (16 USC 470), when a tribal sacred site is located off tribal lands;

(b) On 7 January 1997, a bill (HR 193) was introduced to prohibit sites of traditional significance from being listed in the National Register of Historic Places. This bill would have a significant impact on Native American historic and sacred sites.

(c) In April 1994, President Clinton issued an Executive Memorandum on Native American Access to Eagle Feathers, directing the Department of the Interior to take the necessary actions to ensure priority distribution of eagles, a protected species, to Native Americans.

(d) There is a pressing need for federal protection of the religious rights of Native Americans incarcerated in federal, state and local penal and other institutions.

60. In general, the charge is often made that legislation derived from a western legal system is incapable of comprehending Native American values and traditions. Native Americans are being asked to "prove their religion," and in particular the religious significance of sites.

61. Apart from these problems of a legal nature, the representatives of the Native Americans and nongovernmental organizations reported very many cases of what they called intolerance and discrimination in the field of religion, which, in fact, resulted from these legal problems.

62. They involve first of all damage to sites due to the execution or attempted execution of economic projects (for example, mining projects affecting the sacred sites in the Little Rocky Mountains of the Gros Ventre and Assiniboine tribes on the Native American reserve of Fort. In general, these complaints reflect both a real lack of understanding and consideration and an indifference and even hostility on the part of the various officials and other parties.

63. The Special Rapporteur wishes to draw attention here to two situations which have already been the subject of a communication addressed to the United States authorities, in June 1997. First of all, there is the case of Mount Graham, where telescopes are being constructed by the University of Arizona on the sacred site of the Apache nation. The other case concerns the complex and sensitive situation resulting from the Relocation Act (25 USC) following a land dispute between two Native American tribes, the Navajos and the Hopis.

64. A second series of complaints relates to ceremonial instruments and objects (eagles' feathers, tobacco, cactus, peyote, etc.). Persons having them in their possession sometimes run into serious difficulties, including confiscation, especially at frontiers, arrest and prosecution.

65. A fourth category of complaint concerns Native American prisoners (some 7,000) in the United States prison system, both state and federal. Sweat lodges (for cleansing and purification ceremonies), long hair worn in a traditional fashion, headbands, medicine bags, possession of sage, cedar and tobacco and other practices have been banned as "security risks" by one prison or another.

66. Finally, a fifth category of complaints concerns children asked in certain schools to cut their hair.

67. During official consultations, State department representatives said that there were many problems relating to Native Americans. However, while recognizing the existence of very serious abuses in the past, they emphasized that recent years had been marked by progress towards greater protection and autonomy for indigenous peoples.

68. Officials from the Departments of Justice and the Interior described past United States policy as destructive towards Native Americans and biased in favour of the country's economic interests. According to them, President Clinton's policy, on the contrary, took account of Native Americans' interests. They stressed nonetheless the difficulties caused by the conflict between economic values involving vast financial interests and the importance of the concept of private property, on the one hand, and Native Americans' traditional values, on the other.

69. The Office of the Legal Counsel of the Department of Justice stated that while the legislation adopted for the benefit of Native Americans was in general positive, there were problems at the level of courts and public services, which, in many cases, did not abide by it.

III. Conclusions and Recommendations

70. The Special Rapporteur has endeavoured to give an account of the legal situation in the United States of America in the field of religion or belief and at the same time to analyse the situation with regard to tolerance and non-discrimination based on religion or belief. His study has dealt with the present picture with regard to religion and belief, and in particular with the "minority" communities in the field of religion and belief. He has made a special effort to analyse both the religious and the non-religious spheres and the relationship between religions, between beliefs and between society and the State.

71. Concerning the legal situation in the field of religion or belief, the existence of a well-developed Constitution and legislation has to be recognized. The two constitutional clauses relating to "non-establishment" and free exercise constitute fundamental guarantees for the protection of religion and belief, particularly within the context of the mosaic of religions and beliefs that is typical of the United States. It is evident, however, that the interpretation of these two clauses by the Supreme Court creates problems, because they are sometimes seen by some people as prejudicing the freedom of religion and belief, more particularly of religious minorities. Firstly, concerning the clause on free exercise, many religious and non-governmental representatives contest the "new" jurisprudence that emerged from the Smith case, establishing that neutral laws of general applicability do not typically offend the free exercise clause merely because in application they incidentally prohibit someone's exercise of religion, and therefore the Government no longer has to demonstrate a compelling interest unless a law is specifically targeted at a religious practice or infringes upon an additional constitutional right. The religious communities feel that they are thus vulnerable in the face of legislation and political and administrative institutions governed by a conception of the separation of religion and the State which requires that everyone must comply with the same rules and regulations, and which hence regards any request from religions that their specific nature should be respected in their rights and freedoms as a request for privileges. Secondly, concerning the clause on "non-establishment" of religion, the Supreme Court's interpretation, particularly with regard to public aid for religion, recognition of religion in State schools and financial aid given by the Government to religious schools, unfortunately appears from a general viewpoint to be vague and confused, as was stated, incidentally, by members of the Supreme Court. According to John Witte, professor at Emory University in Atlanta, the development of a coherent and comprehensive framework for interpreting and applying the two constitutional religion clauses would be most useful. That unified approach could come in a variety of forms—through grand synthetic cases or through comprehensive statutes, restatements, codes, or even constitutional amendments ("The Essential Rights and Liberties of Religion in the American Constitutional Experiment," Notre Dame Law Review, vol. 71, No. 3, 1996). The Special Rapporteur wholly endorses the approach of taking into account the traditions of other peoples as reflected in the main United Nations human rights instruments, namely, the International Covenant on Civil and Political Rights (Article 18 and General Comment No. 22 of the Human Rights Committee; see paragraph 78 below) and the Declaration on the Elimination of All Forms of Intolerance and Discrimination Based on Religion or Belief. For example, the prioritizing of liberty of conscience, free exercise and equality principles might well serve as a prototype for the integration of the values enshrined in the free exercise and "non-establishment" clauses. This second approach would be a way of correcting the attitude of the United States of America that human rights are to be treated as belonging to international affairs and not as a domestic matter. We may point out here that this attitude was also noted by Mr. Bacre Waly Ndiaye, Special Rapporteur on extrajudicial, summary or arbitrary executions, in his report on his mission to the United States of America (E/CN.4/1998/68/Add.3).

72. There certainly is federal legislation providing protection in the sphere of religion and belief, but it is fragmentary, only dealing with certain aspects of the freedom of religion and belief and certain infringements of that freedom. As regards, in particular, Title VII of the 1964 Civil Rights Act, concerning religious practice at the workplace and the employer's obligation to make "reasonable accommodation," it seems that it has limited effect and that there is a problem of generally restrictive interpretations by the courts in the matter of religion. The Special Rapporteur considers that this legislation needs to be strengthened and hopes that the Religious Freedom in the Workplace Bill and the guidelines for the protection of freedom of religion in federal institutions announced by the Clinton Administration will contribute to that end. In general, the Special Rapporteur considers that in the absence of a consistent and detailed framework within which the two constitutional clauses on "non-establishment" and free exercise of religion could be interpreted and applied, a general law on freedom of religion and belief based on the relevant international human rights instruments and conforming with those two clauses would provide appropriate and necessary legal protection for the freedom of religion and belief in general, but above all for communities in the field of religion or belief. Such a law could also be able to incorporate the advantages of the two constitutional clauses while encouraging State-religion relations based on an appropriate dynamic equilibrium and avoiding extreme situations of "anti-religious clericalism" and "religious clericalism."

73. Finally, ratification of the Convention on the Rights of the Child by the United States is strongly encouraged: it would be a logical consequence of the human rights policy proclaimed by that country at the international level. It will be remembered, however, that as happened in the case of Mr. Bacre Waly Ndiaye's mission, the federal authorities which are supposed to represent the states of the Union at the international level did not take it upon themselves to organize meetings between the Special Rapporteur and the state authorities. Furthermore, most of the official and non-official representatives that the Special Rapporteur met in the states did not seem to know the international human rights instruments. Similarly, statements by certain public figures irritated by United Nations special rapporteurs' visits to the United States are surprising to say the least, in that they would seem to imply that the world's leading Power fears United Nations "domination," on the one hand, and on the other, wishes to set itself up as entitled to give other countries lessons while rejecting criticisms of its domestic situation, which is seen in a positive light without any limitations or reservations. It would therefore be desirable that these individual positions should remain incidental phenomena not affecting the move towards a more open policy both at home and abroad which is evident in the United States and that the country's commitment in the field of human rights should take on a practical aspect -rather than remaining simply a matter of form—both internationally and nationally.

74. As far as tolerance and non-discrimination based on religion or belief are concerned, the Special Rapporteur notes that the United States, a vast mosaic of religions and beliefs (as can be seen in some Washington avenues consisting of an extraordinary succession of places of worship of all denominations), not only extends a welcome to different faiths, but itself begets them, as a country which is free and open to all religions and beliefs. The representation of the United States through the symbol of the mosaic is in fact relevant, because although there is a dominant European and Judaeo-Christian element, the great variety of denominations in the majority Christian religion and of minorities in the field of religion and belief leads one to see all denominations as minorities. At the end of his study, the Special Rapporteur considers that the actual situation in the United States in the field of tolerance and non-discrimination is in general satisfactory. There are nevertheless some evident exceptions that must be pointed out, particularly as regards the situation of Native Americans.

The Jewish Community

75. The Jews are satisfied with their lot as a whole and do not hesitate to describe their situation as privileged, and indeed unique, in particular because of a degree of religious liberty which the representatives of the Jewish community consider to be without equal elsewhere in the world. Faced with problematical situations, which are described as exceptions, involving hate crimes, the Supreme Court's decision in the Smith case and religion at the workplace, the community is displaying real vigour both through the dialogue between religions and through a militancy in making claims and seeking to promote greater awareness in the field of religion.

The Muslim Community

76. The situation of Muslims is distinctly less favourable, although taken all in all it is not negative. The Muslim community can certainly flourish freely in the religious sphere, but it has to be recognized that there is an islamophobia reflecting both racial and religious intolerance. This is not the fault of the authorities, but of very harmful activity by the media in general and the popular press in particular, which consists in putting

out a distorted and indeed hate-filled message treating Muslims as extremists and terrorists. American public opinion—and hence society—is thus informed and formed—by negative representations of the Muslims. The Special Rapporteur raises the question of the responsibility of the media for manifestations—direct or indirect, intentional or not—of racial and religious intolerance and discrimination in society, on the part of citizens, but also of officials acting on their own initiative and of private corporations, manifestations which may be marginal, but nevertheless do really affect Muslims. It is up to the public authorities to help combat the iniquitous representation of Muslims. Here the Special Rapporteur would like to acknowledge the initiatives taken by President Clinton and his Government directly or indirectly for the benefit of Muslims and aimed at the development of strategies for preventing intolerance and discrimination based on religion. Efforts to combat the ignorance and intolerance purveyed by the media, above all through preventive measures in the field of education, should be given priority. The interdenominational dialogue practised in certain States, particularly California, as was evident at the time of the Gulf war, can also serve as an example to the international community. The activities of the Interreligious Council of Southern California deserve to be better known and should be taken as a model.

Other communities in the field of religion or belief

77. The situation of Asian religions (Buddhism, Hinduism, etc.) and "marginal" religions (Jehovah's Witnesses, Mormons outside Utah, Seventh-Day Adventists, Assembly of God, etc.) is generally satisfactory. There are of course exceptions, such as cases of discrimination at the workplace, and obstacles relating to places of worship and attacks on them. These obstacles and acts of discrimination are sometimes the consequences of the Smith case and a form of secularism, as explained in the section on the constitutional clauses. They can also be interpreted in a general way as manifestations of a conflict between intense religion and un-intense religion. In accordance with this interpretation, it appears finally that in general the position of minority communities in the sphere of religion or belief corresponds to that of the majority Christian communities, with the proviso that any difficulties encountered by the latter are less acute precisely because of their majority status.

78. On the subject of atheism, the Special Rapporteur notes that in its general comment No. 22 of 20 July 1993 on Article 18 of the International Covenant on Civil and Political Rights, the Human Rights Committee pointed out that "the freedom to 'have or to adopt' a religion or belief necessarily entails the freedom to choose a religion or belief, including the right to replace one's current religion or belief with another or to adopt atheistic views" (HRI/GEN/1/Rev.3, p. 37, para. 5).

Native Americans

79. A situation which raises a problem is that of the Native Americans: they have in the past been exposed to a policy of assimilation which many of them describe, with surprising insistence, as genocide and which continues to have effects even today. In recent years a policy in favour of these indigenous peoples has been set in motion, particularly under the presidency of Mr. Clinton, but it needs to be strengthened in the religious sphere.

80. As far as legislation is concerned, while noting advances in recent years in the instruments emerging from the legislature and the executive which are designed to protect Native Americans' religion in general (American Indian Religious Freedom Act) and in particular (Native American Graves Protection and Repatriation Act, Executive Order on Indian Sacred Sites, Executive Memorandum on Native American Access to Eagle Feathers), the Special Rapporteur identified weaknesses and gaps which diminish the effectiveness and hinder the application of these legal safeguards. Concerning the American Indian Religious Freedom Act, the Supreme Court has declared that this law was only a policy statement. As for the Executive Order on Indian Sacred Sites, unfortunately, it does not contain an "action clause," leaving the tribes without the needed legal "teeth." Higher standards or the protection of sacred sites are needed and effective tribal consultation should be ensured. These recommendations are all the more necessary in light of the October 1997 Advisory Council on Historic Preservation regulations and the January 1997 bill (see paragraph 59 (a) and (b) above). Concerning the Native American Graves Protection and Repatriation Act of 1990, it is apparent that its coverage was too limited; it is of the utmost importance that concrete solutions be found to solve the repatriation conflict between the scientific community and tribal governments. It is also essential to secure genuine de jure and de facto protection of Native American prisoners' religious rites.

81. In general, the Special Rapporteur recommends that steps should be taken to make sure that there is no conflict or incompatibility between the different federal, state and local laws, so as to arrive at a uniformity—or at least a convergence—in the legal protection of indigenous peoples' religion throughout the ter-

ritory of the United States, while guaranteeing effective application of these texts, by everyone, for everyone and everywhere, all other things being equal (we may cite as an example the 1994 Executive Memorandum on Native American Access to Eagle Feathers -see paragraph 59 (c) above). It is also recommended that in the legal sphere Native Americans' system of values and traditions should be fully recognized, particularly as regards the concept of collective property rights, inalienability of sacred sites and secrecy with regard to their location. Because of the decision in the Smith case, which affects Indians inasmuch as it seems that in their case there is a lack of understanding of their values and religion, since they are asked to "prove" their religion, and in particular the religious significance of their sacred sites, the Special Rapporteur reiterates his recommendations regarding, firstly, the adoption of a unified approach to the interpretation and application of the two constitutional clauses on "non-establishment" and free exercise of religion and, secondly, the adoption of a general law on freedom of religion and conviction, on the understanding that the special status of Native Americans should be taken into account and backed up by the principle of compensatory inequality in order to arrive at greater equality.

82. Because of economic and religious conflicts affecting in particular sacred sites, the Special Rapporteur wishes to point out that the freedom of belief, in this case that of the Native Americans, is a fundamental matter and requires still greater protection. The freedom to manifest one's belief is also recognized, but can be subject to limitations insofar as they are strictly necessary and provided for in Article 1, paragraph 3, of the Declaration on the Elimination of All Forms of Intolerance and Discrimination Based on Religion or Belief and in Article 18 of the International Covenant on Civil and Political Rights. The expression of the belief has to be reconciled with other rights and legitimate concerns, including those of an economic nature, but after the rights and claims of the parties have been duly taken into account, on an equal footing (in accordance with each party's system of values). As far as Native Americans' access to sacred sites is concerned, this is a fundamental right in the sphere of religion, the exercise of which must be guaranteed in accordance with the above-mentioned provisions of international law on the matter.

83. These recommendations apply of course to the two particular situations of Mount Graham and Black Mesa. In the first case, according to information received since the visit, the Italian Parliament has adopted new legislation forbidding Italian participation in the project to set up a telescope, which would be a profanation of the Mount Graham site. As regards the permit delivered to the University of Arizona by the federal water and forest service for the establishment of telescopes on Mount Graham, which is a sacred site of the Apaches, the Special Rapporteur considers it necessary to make sure officially that the conditions stated above with regard to international law have been respected. On the subject of Black Mesa, the Special Rapporteur also calls for the observance of international law on freedom of religion and its manifestations.

84. Concerning the religious rights of Native American prisoners, apart from the recommendation made in the section on legal issues, the Special Rapporteur recommends that the positive and practical action taken in many federal prisons (fully compatible with security requirements, e.g., ending the practice of cutting their hair) should become general throughout the United States prison system and that steps should be taken to ensure, particularly through training, and perhaps through penalties for prison officers and governors, that these rights are not treated as privileges that can be granted or refused at the whim of an authority or official.

85. In general, it is essential to make society and the whole of the administrative and political apparatus aware of the indigenous peoples' religions and spiritual beliefs in order to prevent any attitude—often involuntary because due to ignorance—of discrimination and intolerance in the field of religion (cutting young Native Americans' hair in schools, etc.). The participation of Native Americans in the executive is particularly important and helps to promote greater awareness and reduce the marginalization of these people; it is therefore to be welcomed. It is also desirable that Native Americans, who in general suffer from an accumulation of unfavourable conditions—economic, social, cultural and religious—should benefit in practice from a policy of support to compensate for these inequalities. The Special Rapporteur fully understands that, as the authorities stated, the Native American question is to be viewed in the context of a long-term process, and he welcomes the advances made in recent years. Some official representatives, however, said that more could be done; the Special Rapporteur shares that view and would encourage the authorities to act accordingly.

86. Finally, the Special Rapporteur wishes to emphasize that education can play a primary role in making people aware of the values of tolerance and non-discrimination in the field of religion and belief and of the richness of every denomination and belief. In schools, in particular, it can inculcate values based on human rights and thus encourage a culture of tolerance. The federal authorities have launched such a preventive strategy through

the programme "Preventing Youth Crime: A Manual for Schools and Communities." The Special Rapporteur would encourage the federal Government to extend and develop a national policy coordinated at the federal and state levels in the field of education in order to reach all educational institutions, teachers, pupils and students. It is also strongly recommended that non-governmental organizations should make a contribution.

87. The Special Rapporteur also recommends a campaign for greater sensitivity in the media so that they do not put out a biased and harmful message with regard to religion and beliefs. There have to be limits on the fundamental freedom of the press when it generates actual intolerance, the antithesis of freedom. There is something wrong if certain media hide behind the fundamental principle of freedom in order to pervert it. The Special Rapporteur reiterates his recommendations regarding action to be taken under the advisory services programme (E/CN.4/1995/91, p. 147) and particularly the organization of training workshops for representatives of the media. He also calls for the establishment of machinery for consultation between the media and the religious communities. Finally, he invites media proprietors to show a more acute sense of responsibility in all fields.

88. Last but not least, the Special Rapporteur wishes to emphasize the value of the interdenominational dialogue which he found to be taking place in certain places he visited, and particularly in California.

ANNEX

Membership of religious groups in the United States / Sources: Yearbook of American & Canadian Churches 1997: Prepared and Edited for the Communication

Commission of the National Council of Churches of Christ, Kenneth B. Bedell (ed.), National Council of Churches of Christ, Abingdon Press, 1997; The World Almanac, 1997./

1. These membership figures generally are based on reports made by officials of each group, and not on any religious census. Figures from other sources may vary. Many groups keep careful records; others only estimate. Not all groups report annually. Christian Church membership figures reported in this table are inclusive and refer to all "members," not simply full communicants or confirmed members. Definitions of "member," however, vary from one denomination to another. Only data reported within the past 10 years are included.

2. The number of houses of worship appears in parentheses. An asterisk (*) indicates that the group declines to make membership figures public. Groups reporting fewer than 5,000 members are not included. If membership numbers are not given, only those Churches with 50 or more houses of worship are listed.

Religious group Members
Adventist Churches:
Advent Christian Church (317) 27,100
Church of God General Conference
(Oregon, IL; Morrow, GA) (88) 5,040
Seventh-Day Adventist Church (4,297) 790,731
American Rescue Workers (15) 8,000
Apostolic Christian Churches of America (80) 11,450
Baha'i Faith 130,000 / Based on reliable estimates; figures from other sources may vary.
Baptist Churches
(The list of religious groups continues.)

DOCUMENT 54

Full Official Title: The United Nations Global Counter-Terrorism Strategy
Short Title/Acronym/Abbreviation: Nothing official
Type of Document: A U.N. General Assembly resolution.
Subject: Counter terrorism strategy measures consistent with human rights
Official Citation: A/RES/60/288
Date of Document: September 20, 2006
Date of Adoption: September 20, 2006
Date of General Entry into Force (EIF): Not applicable
Number of States Parties as of this printing: Not applicable
Date of Signature by United States: Not applicable

Date of Ratification/Accession/Adhesion: Not applicable

Date of Entry into Force as to United States (effective date): Not applicable

Legal Status/Character of the Instrument/Document as to the United States: Not a legal document. Not legally binding on the U.S. An attempt by the U.N. General Assembly to come up with a common, joint strategy against terrorism while at the same time reminding states about acting consistent with international law.

Caution: (If this is a legal instrument) The status and applicability of this instrument as to the United States may have changed since the date of this publication. The above information may be updated by referring to the following site:

Web Address: http://www1.umn.edu/humanrts/instree/

THE UNITED NATIONS GLOBAL COUNTER-TERRORISM STRATEGY
Resolution adopted by the General Assembly
[*on the report of the Third Committee (A/64/439/Add.2 (Part II))*]
64/168. Protection of human rights and fundamental freedoms while countering terrorism

The General Assembly,

Reaffirming the purposes and principles of the Charter of the United Nations,

Reaffirming also the Universal Declaration of Human Rights,[1]

Recalling the Vienna Declaration and Programme of Action,[2]

Reaffirming the fundamental importance, including in response to terrorism and the fear of terrorism, of respecting all human rights and fundamental freedoms and the rule of law,

Reaffirming also that States are under the obligation to protect all human rights and fundamental freedoms of all persons,

Reiterating the important contribution of measures taken at all levels against terrorism, consistent with international law, in particular international human rights, refugee and humanitarian law, to the functioning of democratic institutions and the maintenance of peace and security and thereby to the full enjoyment of human rights, as well as the need to continue this fight, including through international cooperation and the strengthening of the role of the United Nations in this respect,

Deeply deploring the occurrence of violations of human rights and fundamental freedoms in the context of the fight against terrorism, as well as violations of international refugee and humanitarian law, *Noting with concern* measures that can undermine human rights and the rule of law, such as the detention of persons suspected of acts of terrorism in the absence of a legal basis for detention and due process guarantees, the deprivation of liberty that amounts to placing a detained person outside the protection of the law, the trial of suspects without fundamental judicial guarantees, the illegal deprivation of liberty and transfer of individuals suspected of terrorist activities, and the return of suspects to countries without individual assessment of the risk of there being substantial grounds for believing that they would be in danger of subjection to torture, and limitations to effective scrutiny of counter-terrorism measures,

Stressing that all measures used in the fight against terrorism, including the profiling of individuals and the use of diplomatic assurances, memorandums of understanding and other transfer agreements or arrangements, must be in compliance with the obligations of States under international law, including international human rights, refugee and humanitarian law,

Recalling Article 30 of the Universal Declaration of Human Rights, and reaffirming that acts, methods and practices of terrorism in all its forms and manifestations are activities aimed at the destruction of human rights, fundamental freedoms and democracy, threatening the territorial integrity and security of States and destabilizing legitimately constituted Governments, and that the international community should take the necessary steps to enhance cooperation to prevent and combat terrorism,[3]

Reaffirming its unequivocal condemnation of all acts, methods and practices of terrorism in all its forms and manifestations, wherever and by whomsoever committed, regardless of their motivation, as criminal and unjustifiable, and renewing its commitment to strengthen international cooperation to prevent and combat terrorism,

---

[1] Resolution 217 A (III).

[2] A/CONF.157/24 (Part I), chap. III.

[3] See sect. I, para. 17, of the Vienna Declaration and Programme of Action adopted by the World Conference on Human Rights on 25 June 1993 (A/CONF.157/24 (Part I), chap. III).

Recognizing that respect for all human rights, respect for democracy and respect for the rule of law are interrelated and mutually reinforcing,

Reaffirming that terrorism cannot and should not be associated with any religion, nationality, civilization or ethnic group,

Emphasizing the importance of properly interpreting and implementing the obligations of States with respect to torture and other cruel, inhuman or degrading treatment or punishment, and of abiding strictly by the definition of torture contained in Article 1 of the Convention against Torture and Other Cruel, Inhuman or Degrading Treatment or Punishment,[4] in the fight against terrorism,

Recalling its resolutions 57/219 of 18 December 2002, 58/187 of 22 December 2003, 59/191 of 20 December 2004, 60/158 of 16 December 2005, 61/171 of 19 December 2006, 62/159 of 18 December 2007 and 63/185 of 18 December 2008, Commission on Human Rights resolutions 2003/68 of 25 April 2003,[5] 2004/87 of 21 April 2004,[6] and 2005/80 of 21 April 2005,[7] and other relevant resolutions and decisions of the General Assembly, the Commission on Human Rights and the Human Rights Council, including Council decision 2/112 of 27 November 2006[8] and Council resolutions 7/7 of 27 March 2008[9] and 10/15 of 26 March 2009,[10]

Recognizing the importance of the United Nations Global Counter-Terrorism Strategy, adopted on 8 September 2006,[11] reaffirming that the promotion and protection of human rights for all and the rule of law are essential to the fight against terrorism, recognizing that effective counter-terrorism measures and the protection of human rights are not conflicting goals but complementary and mutually reinforcing, and stressing the need to promote and protect the rights of victims of terrorism,

Recalling Human Rights Council resolution 6/28 of 14 December 2007,[12] by which the Council decided to extend the mandate of the Special Rapporteur on the promotion and protection of human rights and fundamental freedoms while countering terrorism,

1. *Reaffirms* that States must ensure that any measure taken to combat terrorism complies with their obligations under international law, in particular international human rights, refugee and humanitarian law;

2. *Deeply deplores* the suffering caused by terrorism to the victims and their families, expresses its profound solidarity with them, and stresses the importance of providing them with assistance;

3. *Expresses serious concern* at the occurrence of violations of human rights and fundamental freedoms, as well as international refugee and humanitarian law, committed in the context of countering terrorism;

4. *Reaffirms* that counter-terrorism measures should be implemented in accordance with international law, including international human rights, refugee and humanitarian law, thereby taking into full consideration the human rights of all, including persons belonging to national or ethnic, religious and linguistic minorities, and in this regard must not be discriminatory on grounds such as race, colour, sex, language, religion or social origin;

5. *Also reaffirms* the obligation of States, in accordance with Article 4 of the International Covenant on Civil and Political Rights,[13] to respect certain rights as non-derogable in any circumstances, recalls, in regard to all other Covenant rights, that any measures derogating from the provisions of the Covenant must be in accordance with that article in all cases, and underlines the exceptional and temporary nature of any such derogations,[14] and in this regard calls upon States to raise awareness about the importance of these obligations among national authorities involved in combating terrorism;

6. *Urges* States, while countering terrorism:

(*a*) To fully comply with their obligations under international law, in particular international human rights, refugee and humanitarian law, with regard to the absolute prohibition of torture and other cruel, inhuman or degrading treatment or punishment;

---

[4] United Nations, *Treaty Series*, vol. 1465, No. 24841.

[5] See *Official Records of the Economic and Social Council, 2003, Supplement No. 3* (E/2003/23), chap. II, sect. A.

[6] Ibid., *2004, Supplement No. 3* (E/2004/23), chap. II, sect. A.

[7] Ibid., *2005, Supplement No. 3* and corrigenda (E/2005/23 and Corr.1 and 2), chap. II, sect. A.

[8] See *Official Records of the General Assembly, Sixty-second Session, Supplement No. 53* (A/62/53), chap. I, sect. B.

[9] Ibid., *Sixty-third Session, Supplement No. 53* (A/63/53), chap. II.

[10] Ibid., *Sixty-fourth Session, Supplement No. 53* (A/64/53), chap. II, sect. A.

[11] Resolution 60/288.

[12] See *Official Records of the General Assembly, Sixty-third Session, Supplement No. 53* (A/63/53), chap. I, sect. A.

[13] See resolution 2200 A (XXI), annex.

[14] See, for example, General Comment No. 29 on states of emergency adopted by the Human Rights Committee on 24 July 2001.

(*b*) To take all necessary steps to ensure that persons deprived of liberty, regardless of the place of arrest or detention, benefit from the guarantees to which they are entitled under international law, including the review of the detention and other fundamental judicial guarantees;

(*c*) To ensure that no form of deprivation of liberty places a detained person outside the protection of the law, and to respect the safeguards concerning the liberty, security and dignity of the person, in accordance with international law, including international human rights and humanitarian law;

(*d*) To treat all prisoners in all places of detention in accordance with international law, including international human rights and humanitarian law;

(*e*) To respect the right of persons to equality before the law, courts and tribunals and to a fair trial as provided for in international law, including international human rights law, such as the International Covenant on Civil and Political Rights, and international humanitarian and refugee law;

(*f*) To protect all human rights, including economic, social and cultural rights, bearing in mind that certain counter-terrorism measures may have an impact on the enjoyment of these rights;

(*g*) To ensure that guidelines and practices in all border control operations and other pre-entry mechanisms are clear and fully respect their obligations under international law, particularly international refugee and human rights law, towards persons seeking international protection;

(*h*) To fully respect non-refoulement obligations under international refugee and human rights law and, at the same time, to review, with full respect for these obligations and other legal safeguards, the validity of a refugee status decision in an individual case if credible and relevant evidence comes to light that indicates that the person in question has committed any criminal acts, including terrorist acts, falling under the exclusion clauses under international refugee law;

(*i*) To refrain from returning persons, including in cases related to terrorism, to their countries of origin or to a third State whenever such transfer would be contrary to their obligations under international law, in particular international human rights, humanitarian and refugee law, including in cases where there are substantial grounds for believing that they would be in danger of subjection to torture, or where their life or freedom would be threatened in violation of international refugee law on account of their race, religion, nationality, membership of a particular social group or political opinion, bearing in mind obligations that States may have to prosecute individuals not returned;

(*j*) Insofar as such an act runs contrary to their obligations under international law, not to expose individuals to cruel, inhuman or degrading treatment or punishment by way of return to another country;

(*k*) To ensure that their laws criminalizing acts of terrorism are accessible, formulated with precision, non-discriminatory, non-retroactive and in accordance with international law, including human rights law;

(*l*) Not to resort to profiling based on stereotypes founded on grounds of discrimination prohibited by international law, including on racial, ethnic and/or religious grounds;

(*m*) To ensure that the interrogation methods used against terrorism suspects are consistent with their international obligations and are reviewed to prevent the risk of violations of their obligations under international law, including international human rights, refugee and humanitarian law;

(*n*) To ensure that any person whose human rights or fundamental freedoms have been violated has access to an effective remedy and that victims receive adequate, effective and prompt reparations, where appropriate, including by bringing to justice those responsible for such violations;

(*o*) To ensure due process guarantees, consistent with all relevant provisions of the Universal Declaration of Human Rights,[1] and their obligations under the International Covenant on Civil and Political Rights, the Geneva Conventions of 1949[15] and the Additional Protocols thereto, of 1977,[16] and the 1951 Convention relating to the Status of Refugees [17] and the 1967 Protocol thereto [18] in their respective fields of applicability;

(*p*) To shape and implement all counter-terrorism measures in accordance with the principles of gender equality and non-discrimination;

7. *Encourages* States, while countering terrorism, to take into account relevant United Nations resolutions and decisions on human rights, and encourages them to give due consideration to the recommendations

---

[15] United Nations, *Treaty Series*, vol. 75, Nos. 970–973.
[16] Ibid., vol. 1125, Nos. 17512 and 17513.
[17] Ibid., vol. 189, No. 2545.
[18] Ibid., vol. 606, No. 8791.

of the special procedures and mechanisms of the Human Rights Council and to the relevant comments and views of United Nations human rights treaty bodies;

8. *Acknowledges* the adoption of the International Convention for the Protection of All Persons from Enforced Disappearance in its resolution 61/177 of 20 December 2006, and recognizes that the entry into force of the Convention and its implementation will be an important step in support of the rule of law in countering terrorism;

9. *Recognizes* the need to continue ensuring that fair and clear procedures under the United Nations terrorism-related sanctions regime are strengthened in order to enhance their efficiency and transparency, and welcomes and encourages the ongoing efforts of the Security Council in support of these objectives, including by continuing to review all the names of individuals and entities in the regime, while emphasizing the importance of these sanctions in countering terrorism;

10. *Urges* States, while ensuring full compliance with their international obligations, to ensure the rule of law and to include adequate human rights guarantees in their national procedures for the listing of individuals and entities with a view to combating terrorism;

11. *Requests* the Office of the United Nations High Commissioner for Human Rights and the Special Rapporteur of the Human Rights Council on the promotion and protection of human rights and fundamental freedoms while countering terrorism to continue to contribute to the work of the Counter-Terrorism Implementation Task Force, including by raising awareness about the need to respect human rights and the rule of law while countering terrorism;

12. *Takes note* of the report of the Secretary-General on protecting human rights and fundamental freedoms while countering terrorism[19] and the previous work of the Special Rapporteur on the promotion and protection of human rights and fundamental freedoms while countering terrorism undertaken in accordance with his mandate, based on Commission on Human Rights resolution 2005/80 of 21 April 2005,[7] and Human Rights Council resolutions 5/1 and 5/2 of 18 June 2007[20] and 6/28 of 14 December 2007;[12]

13. *Welcomes* the ongoing dialogue established in the context of the fight against terrorism between the Security Council and its Counter-Terrorism Committee and the relevant bodies for the promotion and protection of human rights, and encourages the Security Council and its Counter-Terrorism Committee to strengthen the links, cooperation and dialogue with relevant human rights bodies, in particular with the Office of the United Nations High Commissioner for Human Rights, the Special Rapporteur on the promotion and protection of human rights and fundamental freedoms while countering terrorism, other relevant special procedures and mechanisms of the Human Rights Council, and relevant treaty bodies, giving due regard to the promotion and protection of human rights and the rule of law in the ongoing work pursuant to relevant Security Council resolutions relating to terrorism;

14. *Calls upon* States and other relevant actors, as appropriate, to continue to implement the United Nations Global Counter-Terrorism Strategy,[11] which, inter alia, reaffirms respect for human rights for all and the rule of law as the fundamental basis of the fight against terrorism;

15. *Requests* the Counter-Terrorism Implementation Task Force to continue its efforts to ensure that the United Nations can better coordinate and enhance its support to Member States in their efforts to comply with their obligations under international law, including international human rights, refugee and humanitarian law, while countering terrorism;

16. *Encourages* relevant United Nations bodies and entities and international, regional and subregional organizations, in particular those participating in the Counter-Terrorism Implementation Task Force, which provide technical assistance, upon request, consistent with their mandates and as appropriate, related to the prevention and suppression of terrorism to step up their efforts to ensure, as an element of technical assistance, respect for international human rights, refugee and humanitarian law, as well as the rule of law;

17. *Urges* relevant United Nations bodies and entities and international, regional and subregional organizations, including the United Nations Office on Drugs and Crime, within its mandate related to the prevention and suppression of terrorism, to step up their efforts to provide, upon request, technical assistance for

---

[19] A/64/186.

[20] See *Official Records of the General Assembly, Sixty-second Session, Supplement No. 53* (A/62/53), chap. IV, sect. A.

building the capacity of Member States in the development and implementation of programmes of assistance and support for victims of terrorism in accordance with relevant national legislation;

18. *Calls upon* international, regional and subregional organizations to strengthen information-sharing, coordination and cooperation in promoting the protection of human rights, fundamental freedoms and the rule of law while countering terrorism;

19. *Requests* the Special Rapporteur on the promotion and protection of human rights and fundamental freedoms while countering terrorism to make recommendations in the context of his mandate, with regard to preventing, combating and redressing violations of human rights and fundamental freedoms in the context of countering terrorism;

20. *Requests* all Governments to cooperate fully with the Special Rapporteur on the promotion and protection of human rights and fundamental freedoms while countering terrorism in the performance of the tasks and duties mandated, including by reacting promptly to the urgent appeals of the Special Rapporteur and providing the information requested, and to give serious consideration to responding favourably to his requests to visit their countries, as well as to cooperate with other relevant procedures and mechanisms of the Human Rights Council regarding the promotion and protection of human rights and fundamental freedoms while countering terrorism;

21. *Welcomes* the work of the United Nations High Commissioner for Human Rights to implement the mandate given to her in 2005, in resolution 60/158, and requests the High Commissioner to continue her efforts in this regard;

22. *Requests* the Secretary-General to submit a report on the implementation of the present resolution to the Human Rights Council and to the General Assembly at its sixty-fifth session;

23. *Decides* to consider at its sixty-fifth session the report of the Special Rapporteur on the promotion and protection of human rights and fundamental freedoms while countering terrorism.

65th plenary meeting
18 December 2009

DOCUMENT 55

Full Official Title: Protection of Human Rights and Fundamental Freedoms While Countering Terrorism

Short Title/Acronym/Abbreviation: Nothing official

Type of Document: Resolution **64/168** adopted by the General Assembly

Subject: Protecting human rights while countering terrorism.

Official Citation: A/RES/64/168

Date of Document: January 22, 2010

Date of Adoption: January 22, 2010

Date of General Entry into Force (EIF): Not applicable

Number of States Parties as of this printing: Not applicable

Date of Signature by United States: Not applicable

Date of Ratification/Accession/Adhesion: Not applicable

Date of Entry into Force as to United States (effective date): Not applicable

Legal Status/Character of the Instrument/Document as to the United States: A non binding resolution expressing the consensus of the U.N General Assembly about protecting human rights while combating terrorism.

Web Address: www.un.org/search/view_doc.asp?symbol=A/Res?64

PROTECTION OF HUMAN RIGHTS AND FUNDAMENTAL FREEDOMS WHILE COUNTERING TERRORISM

Resolution adopted by the General Assembly

[*on the report of the Third Committee (A/64/439/Add.2 (Part II))*]

64/168. Protection of human rights and fundamental freedoms while countering terrorism

The General Assembly,

Reaffirming the purposes and principles of the Charter of the United Nations,

Reaffirming also the Universal Declaration of Human Rights,[1]

Recalling the Vienna Declaration and Programme of Action,[2]

Reaffirming the fundamental importance, including in response to terrorism and the fear of terrorism, of respecting all human rights and fundamental freedoms and the rule of law,

Reaffirming also that States are under the obligation to protect all human rights and fundamental freedoms of all persons,

Reiterating the important contribution of measures taken at all levels against terrorism, consistent with international law, in particular international human rights, refugee and humanitarian law, to the functioning of democratic institutions and the maintenance of peace and security and thereby to the full enjoyment of human rights, as well as the need to continue this fight, including through international cooperation and the strengthening of the role of the United Nations in this respect,

Deeply deploring the occurrence of violations of human rights and fundamental freedoms in the context of the fight against terrorism, as well as violations of international refugee and humanitarian law,

Noting with concern measures that can undermine human rights and the rule of law, such as the detention of persons suspected of acts of terrorism in the absence of a legal basis for detention and due process guarantees, the deprivation of liberty that amounts to placing a detained person outside the protection of the law, the trial of suspects without fundamental judicial guarantees, the illegal deprivation of liberty and transfer of individuals suspected of terrorist activities, and the return of suspects to countries without individual assessment of the risk of there being substantial grounds for believing that they would be in danger of subjection to torture, and limitations to effective scrutiny of counter-terrorism measures,

Stressing that all measures used in the fight against terrorism, including the profiling of individuals and the use of diplomatic assurances, memorandums of understanding and other transfer agreements or arrangements, must be in compliance with the obligations of States under international law, including international human rights, refugee and humanitarian law,

Recalling Article 30 of the Universal Declaration of Human Rights, and reaffirming that acts, methods and practices of terrorism in all its forms and manifestations are activities aimed at the destruction of human rights, fundamental freedoms and democracy, threatening the territorial integrity and security of States and destabilizing legitimately constituted Governments, and that the international community should take the necessary steps to enhance cooperation to prevent and combat terrorism,[3]

Reaffirming its unequivocal condemnation of all acts, methods and practices of terrorism in all its forms and manifestations, wherever and by whomsoever committed, regardless of their motivation, as criminal and unjustifiable, and renewing its commitment to strengthen international cooperation to prevent and combat terrorism,

Recognizing that respect for all human rights, respect for democracy and respect for the rule of law are interrelated and mutually reinforcing,

Reaffirming that terrorism cannot and should not be associated with any religion, nationality, civilization or ethnic group,

Emphasizing the importance of properly interpreting and implementing the obligations of States with respect to torture and other cruel, inhuman or degrading treatment or punishment, and of abiding strictly by the definition of torture contained in Article 1 of the Convention against Torture and Other Cruel, Inhuman or Degrading Treatment or Punishment,[4] in the fight against terrorism,

Recalling its resolutions 57/219 of 18 December 2002, 58/187 of 22 December 2003, 59/191 of 20 December 2004, 60/158 of 16 December 2005, 61/171 of 19 December 2006, 62/159 of 18 December 2007 and 63/185 of 18 December 2008, Commission on Human Rights resolutions 2003/68 of 25 April 2003,[5] 2004/87 of 21 April 2004[6] and 2005/80 of 21 April 2005,[7] and other relevant resolutions and decisions of the General Assembly, the Commission on Human Rights and the Human Rights Council, including Council

---

[1] Resolution 217 A (III).

[2] A/CONF.157/24 (Part I), chap. III.

[3] See sect. I, para. 17, of the Vienna Declaration and Programme of Action adopted by the World Conference on Human Rights on 25 June 1993 (A/CONF.157/24 (Part I), chap. III).

[4] United Nations, *Treaty Series*, vol. 1465, No. 24841.

[5] See *Official Records of the Economic and Social Council, 2003, Supplement No. 3* (E/2003/23), chap. II, sect. A.

[6] Ibid., *2004, Supplement No. 3* (E/2004/23), chap. II, sect. A.

[7] Ibid., *2005, Supplement No. 3* and corrigenda (E/2005/23 and Corr.1 and 2), chap. II, sect. A.

decision 2/112 of 27 November 2006[8] and Council resolutions 7/7 of 27 March 2008[9] and 10/15 of 26 March 2009,[10]

Recognizing the importance of the United Nations Global Counter-Terrorism Strategy, adopted on 8 September 2006, [11] reaffirming that the promotion and protection of human rights for all and the rule of law are essential to the fight against terrorism, recognizing that effective counter-terrorism measures and the protection of human rights are not conflicting goals but complementary and mutually reinforcing, and stressing the need to promote and protect the rights of victims of terrorism,

Recalling Human Rights Council resolution 6/28 of 14 December 2007,[12] by which the Council decided to extend the mandate of the Special Rapporteur on the promotion and protection of human rights and fundamental freedoms while countering terrorism,

1. *Reaffirms* that States must ensure that any measure taken to combat terrorism complies with their obligations under international law, in particular international human rights, refugee and humanitarian law;

2. *Deeply deplores* the suffering caused by terrorism to the victims and their families, expresses its profound solidarity with them, and stresses the importance of providing them with assistance;

3. *Expresses serious concern* at the occurrence of violations of human rights and fundamental freedoms, as well as international refugee and humanitarian law, committed in the context of countering terrorism;

4. *Reaffirms* that counter-terrorism measures should be implemented in accordance with international law, including international human rights, refugee and humanitarian law, thereby taking into full consideration the human rights of all, including persons belonging to national or ethnic, religious and linguistic minorities, and in this regard must not be discriminatory on grounds such as race, colour, sex, language, religion or social origin;

5. *Also reaffirms* the obligation of States, in accordance with Article 4 of the International Covenant on Civil and Political Rights,[13] to respect certain rights as non-derogable in any circumstances, recalls, in regard to all other Covenant rights, that any measures derogating from the provisions of the Covenant must be in accordance with that article in all cases, and underlines the exceptional and temporary nature of any such derogations,[14] and in this regard calls upon States to raise awareness about the importance of these obligations among national authorities involved in combating terrorism;

6. *Urges* States, while countering terrorism:

(*a*) To fully comply with their obligations under international law, in particular international human rights, refugee and humanitarian law, with regard to the absolute prohibition of torture and other cruel, inhuman or degrading treatment or punishment;

(*b*) To take all necessary steps to ensure that persons deprived of liberty, regardless of the place of arrest or detention, benefit from the guarantees to which they are entitled under international law, including the review of the detention and other fundamental judicial guarantees;

(*c*) To ensure that no form of deprivation of liberty places a detained person outside the protection of the law, and to respect the safeguards concerning the liberty, security and dignity of the person, in accordance with international law, including international human rights and humanitarian law;

(*d*) To treat all prisoners in all places of detention in accordance with international law, including international human rights and humanitarian law;

(*e*) To respect the right of persons to equality before the law, courts and tribunals and to a fair trial as provided for in international law, including international human rights law, such as the International Covenant on Civil and Political Rights, and international humanitarian and refugee law;

(*f*) To protect all human rights, including economic, social and cultural rights, bearing in mind that certain counter-terrorism measures may have an impact on the enjoyment of these rights;

(*g*) To ensure that guidelines and practices in all border control operations and other pre-entry mechanisms are clear and fully respect their obligations under international law, particularly international refugee and human rights law, towards persons seeking international protection;

---

[8] See *Official Records of the General Assembly, Sixty-second Session, Supplement No. 53* (A/62/53), chap. I, sect. B.

[9] Ibid., *Sixty-third Session, Supplement No. 53* (A/63/53), chap. II.

[10] Ibid., *Sixty-fourth Session, Supplement No. 53* (A/64/53), chap. II, sect. A.

[11] Resolution 60/288.

[12] See *Official Records of the General Assembly, Sixty-third Session, Supplement No. 53* (A/63/53), chap. I, sect. A.

[13] See resolution 2200 A (XXI), annex.

[14] See, for example, General Comment No. 29 on states of emergency adopted by the Human Rights Committee on 24 July 2001.

(*h*) To fully respect non-refoulement obligations under international refugee and human rights law and, at the same time, to review, with full respect for these obligations and other legal safeguards, the validity of a refugee status decision in an individual case if credible and relevant evidence comes to light that indicates that the person in question has committed any criminal acts, including terrorist acts, falling under the exclusion clauses under international refugee law;

(*i*) To refrain from returning persons, including in cases related to terrorism, to their countries of origin or to a third State whenever such transfer would be contrary to their obligations under international law, in particular international human rights, humanitarian and refugee law, including in cases where there are substantial grounds for believing that they would be in danger of subjection to torture, or where their life or freedom would be threatened in violation of international refugee law on account of their race, religion, nationality, membership of a particular social group or political opinion, bearing in mind obligations that States may have to prosecute individuals not returned;

(*j*) Insofar as such an act runs contrary to their obligations under international law, not to expose individuals to cruel, inhuman or degrading treatment or punishment by way of return to another country;

(*k*) To ensure that their laws criminalizing acts of terrorism are accessible, formulated with precision, non-discriminatory, non-retroactive and in accordance with international law, including human rights law;

(*l*) Not to resort to profiling based on stereotypes founded on grounds of discrimination prohibited by international law, including on racial, ethnic and/or religious grounds;

(*m*) To ensure that the interrogation methods used against terrorism suspects are consistent with their international obligations and are reviewed to prevent the risk of violations of their obligations under international law, including international human rights, refugee and humanitarian law;

(*n*) To ensure that any person whose human rights or fundamental freedoms have been violated has access to an effective remedy and that victims receive adequate, effective and prompt reparations, where appropriate, including by bringing to justice those responsible for such violations;

(*o*) To ensure due process guarantees, consistent with all relevant provisions of the Universal Declaration of Human Rights,[1] and their obligations under the International Covenant on Civil and Political Rights, the Geneva Conventions of 1949[15] and the Additional Protocols thereto, of 1977,[16] and the 1951 Convention relating to the Status of Refugees [17] and the 1967 Protocol thereto [18] in their respective fields of applicability;

(*p*) To shape and implement all counter-terrorism measures in accordance with the principles of gender equality and non-discrimination;

7. *Encourages* States, while countering terrorism, to take into account relevant United Nations resolutions and decisions on human rights, and encourages them to give due consideration to the recommendations of the special procedures and mechanisms of the Human Rights Council and to the relevant comments and views of United Nations human rights treaty bodies;

8. *Acknowledges* the adoption of the International Convention for the Protection of All Persons from Enforced Disappearance in its resolution 61/177 of 20 December 2006, and recognizes that the entry into force of the Convention and its implementation will be an important step in support of the rule of law in countering terrorism;

9. *Recognizes* the need to continue ensuring that fair and clear procedures under the United Nations terrorism-related sanctions regime are strengthened in order to enhance their efficiency and transparency, and welcomes and encourages the ongoing efforts of the Security Council in support of these objectives, including by continuing to review all the names of individuals and entities in the regime, while emphasizing the importance of these sanctions in countering terrorism;

10. *Urges* States, while ensuring full compliance with their international obligations, to ensure the rule of law and to include adequate human rights guarantees in their national procedures for the listing of individuals and entities with a view to combating terrorism;

11. *Requests* the Office of the United Nations High Commissioner for Human Rights and the Special Rapporteur of the Human Rights Council on the promotion and protection of human rights and fundamental freedoms while countering terrorism to continue to contribute to the work of the Counter-Terrorism

---

[15] United Nations, *Treaty Series*, vol. 75, Nos. 970–973.
[16] Ibid., vol. 1125, Nos. 17512 and 17513.
[17] Ibid., vol. 189, No. 2545.
[18] Ibid., vol. 606, No. 8791.

Implementation Task Force, including by raising awareness about the need to respect human rights and the rule of law while countering terrorism;

12. *Takes note* of the report of the Secretary-General on protecting human rights and fundamental freedoms while countering terrorism[19] and the previous work of the Special Rapporteur on the promotion and protection of human rights and fundamental freedoms while countering terrorism undertaken in accordance with his mandate, based on Commission on Human Rights resolution 2005/80 of 21 April 2005,[7] and Human Rights Council resolutions 5/1 and 5/2 of 18 June 2007[20] and 6/28 of 14 December 2007;[12]

13. *Welcomes* the ongoing dialogue established in the context of the fight against terrorism between the Security Council and its Counter-Terrorism Committee and the relevant bodies for the promotion and protection of human rights, and encourages the Security Council and its Counter-Terrorism Committee to strengthen the links, cooperation and dialogue with relevant human rights bodies, in particular with the Office of the United Nations High Commissioner for Human Rights, the Special Rapporteur on the promotion and protection of human rights and fundamental freedoms while countering terrorism, other relevant special procedures and mechanisms of the Human Rights Council, and relevant treaty bodies, giving due regard to the promotion and protection of human rights and the rule of law in the ongoing work pursuant to relevant Security Council resolutions relating to terrorism;

14. *Calls upon* States and other relevant actors, as appropriate, to continue to implement the United Nations Global Counter-Terrorism Strategy,[11] which, inter alia, reaffirms respect for human rights for all and the rule of law as the fundamental basis of the fight against terrorism;

15. *Requests* the Counter-Terrorism Implementation Task Force to continue its efforts to ensure that the United Nations can better coordinate and enhance its support to Member States in their efforts to comply with their obligations under international law, including international human rights, refugee and humanitarian law, while countering terrorism;

16. *Encourages* relevant United Nations bodies and entities and international, regional and subregional organizations, in particular those participating in the Counter-Terrorism Implementation Task Force, which provide technical assistance, upon request, consistent with their mandates and as appropriate, related to the prevention and suppression of terrorism to step up their efforts to ensure, as an element of technical assistance, respect for international human rights, refugee and humanitarian law, as well as the rule of law;

17. *Urges* relevant United Nations bodies and entities and international, regional and subregional organizations, including the United Nations Office on Drugs and Crime, within its mandate related to the prevention and suppression of terrorism, to step up their efforts to provide, upon request, technical assistance for building the capacity of Member States in the development and implementation of programmes of assistance and support for victims of terrorism in accordance with relevant national legislation;

18. *Calls upon* international, regional and subregional organizations to strengthen information-sharing, coordination and cooperation in promoting the protection of human rights, fundamental freedoms and the rule of law while countering terrorism;

19. *Requests* the Special Rapporteur on the promotion and protection of human rights and fundamental freedoms while countering terrorism to make recommendations in the context of his mandate, with regard to preventing, combating and redressing violations of human rights and fundamental freedoms in the context of countering terrorism;

20. *Requests* all Governments to cooperate fully with the Special Rapporteur on the promotion and protection of human rights and fundamental freedoms while countering terrorism in the performance of the tasks and duties mandated, including by reacting promptly to the urgent appeals of the Special Rapporteur and providing the information requested, and to give serious consideration to responding favourably to his requests to visit their countries, as well as to cooperate with other relevant procedures and mechanisms of the Human Rights Council regarding the promotion and protection of human rights and fundamental freedoms while countering terrorism;

21. *Welcomes* the work of the United Nations High Commissioner for Human Rights to implement the mandate given to her in 2005, in resolution 60/158, and requests the High Commissioner to continue her efforts in this regard;

---

[19] A/64/186.

[20] See *Official Records of the General Assembly, Sixty-second Session, Supplement No. 53* (A/62/53), chap. IV, sect. A. at its sixty-fifth session;

22. *Requests* the Secretary-General to submit a report on the implementation of the present resolution to the Human Rights Council and to the General Assembly

23. *Decides* to consider at its sixty-fifth session the report of the Special Rapporteur on the promotion and protection of human rights and fundamental freedoms while countering terrorism.

65th plenary meeting
18 December 2009

DOCUMENT 56

Full Official Title: United Nations Security Council President's Statement
Short Title/Acronym/Abbreviation: Nothing official
Type of Document: A President's Statement, U.N. Security Council
Subject: Protecting human rights while countering terrorism, U.N. Security Council
Official Citation: S/PRST/2010/11
Date of Document: June 29, 2010
Date of Adoption: Not applicable
Date of General Entry into Force (EIF): Not applicable
Number of States Parties as of this printing: Not applicable
Date of Signature by United States: Not applicable
Date of Ratification/Accession/Adhesion: Not applicable
Date of Entry into Force as to United States (effective date): Not applicable
Legal Status/Character of the Instrument/Document as to the United States: Not applicable
Comment: At the 6347th meeting of the Security Council, held on 26 June 2010, in connection with the Council's consideration of the item entitled "The promotion and strengthening of the rule of law in the maintenance of international peace and security," the President of the Security Council made the foregoing statement on behalf of the Security Council to remind all states to comply with international law while combatting terrorism.
Web Address: www.securitycouncilreport.org/atf/cf/%7B65BFCF9B-6D27-4E9C-8CD3-CF6E4FF96FF9%7D/IJ%20SPRST%202010%2011.pdf

UNITED NATIONS SECURITY COUNCIL PRESIDENT'S STATEMENT

At the 6347th meeting of the Security Council, held on 26 June 2010, in connection with the Council's consideration of the item entitled "The promotion and strengthening of the rule of law in the maintenance of international peace and security", the President of the Security Council made the following statement on behalf of the Council:

"The Security Council reaffirms its commitment to the Charter of the United Nations and international law, and to an international order based on the rule of law and international law, which is essential for peaceful coexistence and cooperation among States in addressing common challenges, thus contributing to the maintenance of international peace and security.

"The Security Council is committed to and actively supports the peaceful settlement of disputes and reiterates its call upon Member States to settle their disputes by peaceful means as set forth in Chapter VI of the Charter of the United Nations. The Council emphasizes the key role of the International Court of Justice, the principal judicial organ of the United Nations, in adjudicating disputes among States and the value of its work and calls upon States that have not yet done so to consider accepting the jurisdiction of the Court in accordance with its Statute.

"The Security Council calls upon States to resort also to other dispute settlement mechanisms, including international and regional courts and tribunals which offer States the possibility of settling their disputes peacefully, contributing thus to the prevention or settlement of conflict.

"The Security Council emphasizes the importance of the activities of the United Nations Secretary-General in promoting mediation and in the pacific settlement of disputes between States, recalls in this regard the Secretary-General's Report on enhancing mediation and its support activities of 8 April 2009 (S/2009/189), and encourages the Secretary-General to increasingly and effectively use all the modalities and diplomatic tools at his disposal under the Charter for this purpose.

"The Security Council recognizes that respect for international humanitarian law is an essential component of the rule of law in conflict situations and reaffirms its conviction that the protection of the civilian population in armed conflict should be an important aspect of any comprehensive strategy to resolve conflict and recalls in this regard resolution 1894 (2009).

"The Security Council further reiterates its call for all parties to armed conflict to respect international law applicable to the rights and protection of women and children, as well as displaced persons and humanitarian workers and other civilians who may have specific vulnerabilities, such as persons with disabilities and older persons.

"The Security Council reaffirms its strong opposition to impunity for serious violations of international humanitarian law and human rights law. The Security Council further emphasizes the responsibility of States to comply with their relevant obligations to end impunity and to thoroughly investigate and prosecute persons responsible for war crimes, genocide, crimes against humanity or other serious violations of international humanitarian law in order to prevent violations, avoid their recurrence and seek sustainable peace, justice, truth and reconciliation.

"The Security Council notes that the fight against impunity for the most serious crimes of international concern has been strengthened through the work of the International Criminal Court, ad hoc and mixed tribunals, as well as specialized chambers in national tribunals and takes note of the stocktaking of international criminal justice undertaken by the first Review Conference of the Rome Statute held in Kampala, Uganda from 31 May to 11 June 2010. The Council intends to continue forcefully to fight impunity and uphold accountability with appropriate means and draws attention to the full range of justice and reconciliation mechanisms to be considered, including national, international and mixed criminal courts and tribunals, truth and reconciliation commissions as well as national reparation programs for victims, institutional reforms and traditional dispute resolution mechanisms.

"The Security Council expresses its commitment to ensure that all U.N. efforts to restore peace and security themselves respect and promote the rule of law. The Council recognizes that sustainable peacebuilding requires an integrated approach, which strengthens coherence between political, security, development, human rights and rule of law activities. In this regard, the Council reiterates the urgency of improving U.N. peacebuilding efforts and achieving a coordinated United Nations approach in the field among all parts of the U.N. system, including in ensuring capacity building support to assist national authorities to uphold the rule of law especially after the end of U.N. peacekeeping and other relevant missions.

"The Security Council considers sanctions an important tool in the maintenance and restoration of international peace and security. The Council reiterates the need to ensure that sanctions are carefully targeted in support of clear objectives and designed carefully so as to minimize possible adverse consequences and are implemented by Member States. The Council remains committed to ensure that fair and clear procedures exist for placing individuals and entities on sanctions lists and for removing them, as well as for granting humanitarian exemptions. In this context, the Council recalls the adoption of resolutions 1822 (2008) and 1904 (2009) including the appointment of an Ombudsperson and other procedural improvements in the Al Qaida and Taliban sanctions regime.

"The Security Council welcomes the establishment of the Rule of Law Coordination and Resource Group, chaired by the Deputy Secretary-General and supported by the Rule of Law Unit, and urges greater efforts by the Group to ensure a coordinated and coherent response by the U.N. system to issues on the Council's agenda related to the rule of law.

"The Security Council requests the Secretary-General to provide a follow-up report within 12 months to take stock of the progress made in respect to the implementation of the recommendations contained in the 2004 Report of the Secretary-General (S/2004/616), and to consider in this context further steps in regard with the promotion of the rule of law in conflict and post-conflict situations."

DOCUMENT 57

Full Official Title: Resolution adopted by the General Assembly 60/251. Human Rights Council
Short Title/Acronym/Abbreviation: General Assembly Resolution 60/251
Type of Document: A resolution adopted by the U.N. General Assembly
Subject: Establishment of the U.N. Human Rights Council
Official Citation: A/RES/60/251
Date of Document: 3 April 2006
Date of Adoption: 3 April 2006
Date of General Entry into Force (EIF): Not applicable
Number of States Parties as of this printing: Not applicable
Date of Signature by United States: Not applicable

Date of Ratification/Accession/Adhesion: Not applicable

Date of Entry into Force as to United States (effective date): Not applicable

Legal Status/Character of the Instrument/Document as to the United States: Non-binding resolution creating an organ of an international inter-governmental organization, the U.N. The U.S. fully participates in the work of the Human Rights Council, which was established by this resolution, and is a member of the Council at the time of the writing of this book. The Council is the organ in charge of the Universal Periodic Review process as well as the "special procedures."

Web Address: www.umn.edu/humanrts/hrc60-251.html

RESOLUTION ADOPTED BY THE GENERAL ASSEMBLY 60/251. HUMAN RIGHTS COUNCIL

Resolution adopted by the General Assembly

[*without reference to a Main Committee (A/60/L.48)*]

60/251. Human Rights Council

The General Assembly,

Reaffirming the purposes and principles contained in the Charter of the United Nations, including developing friendly relations among nations based on respect for the principle of equal rights and self-determination of peoples, and achieving international cooperation in solving international problems of an economic, social, cultural or humanitarian character and in promoting and encouraging respect for human rights and fundamental freedoms for all,

Reaffirming also the Universal Declaration of Human Rights[1] and the Vienna Declaration and Programme of Action,[2] and recalling the International Covenant on Civil and Political Rights,[3] the International Covenant on Economic, Social and Cultural Rights[3] and other human rights instruments,

Reaffirming further that all human rights are universal, indivisible, interrelated, interdependent and mutually reinforcing, and that all human rights must be treated in a fair and equal manner, on the same footing and with the same emphasis,

Reaffirming that, while the significance of national and regional particularities and various historical, cultural and religious backgrounds must be borne in mind, all States, regardless of their political, economic and cultural systems, have the duty to promote and protect all human rights and fundamental freedoms,

Emphasizing the responsibilities of all States, in conformity with the Charter, to respect human rights and fundamental freedoms for all, without distinction of any kind as to race, colour, sex, language or religion, political or other opinion, national or social origin, property, birth or other status,

Acknowledging that peace and security, development and human rights are the pillars of the United Nations system and the foundations for collective security and well-being, and recognizing that development, peace and security and human rights are interlinked and mutually reinforcing,

Affirming the need for all States to continue international efforts to enhance dialogue and broaden understanding among civilizations, cultures and religions, and emphasizing that States, regional organizations, non-governmental organizations, religious bodies and the media have an important role to play in promoting tolerance, respect for and freedom of religion and belief,

Recognizing the work undertaken by the Commission on Human Rights and the need to preserve and build on its achievements and to redress its shortcomings,

Recognizing also the importance of ensuring universality, objectivity and non-selectivity in the consideration of human rights issues, and the elimination of double standards and politicization,

Recognizing further that the promotion and protection of human rights should be based on the principles of cooperation and genuine dialogue and aimed at strengthening the capacity of Member States to comply with their human rights obligations for the benefit of all human beings,

Acknowledging that non-governmental organizations play an important role at the national, regional and international levels, in the promotion and protection of human rights,

---

[1] Resolution 217 A (III).

[2] A/CONF.157/24 (Part I), chap. III.

[3] See resolution 2200 A (XXI), annex.

Resolution adopted by the General Assembly 60/251. Human Rights Council

Reaffirming the commitment to strengthen the United Nations human rights machinery, with the aim of ensuring effective enjoyment by all of all human rights, civil, political, economic, social and cultural rights, including the right to development, and to that end, the resolve to create a Human Rights Council,

1. *Decides* to establish the Human Rights Council, based in Geneva, in replacement of the Commission on Human Rights, as a subsidiary organ of the General Assembly; the Assembly shall review the status of the Council within five years;

2. *Decides* that the Council shall be responsible for promoting universal respect for the protection of all human rights and fundamental freedoms for all, without distinction of any kind and in a fair and equal manner;

3. *Decides also* that the Council should address situations of violations of human rights, including gross and systematic violations, and make recommendations thereon. It should also promote the effective coordination and the mainstreaming of human rights within the United Nations system;

4. *Decides further* that the work of the Council shall be guided by the principles of universality, impartiality, objectivity and non-selectivity, constructive international dialogue and cooperation, with a view to enhancing the promotion and protection of all human rights, civil, political, economic, social and cultural rights, including the right to development;

5. *Decides* that the Council shall, inter alia:

(*a*) Promote human rights education and learning as well as advisory services, technical assistance and capacity-building, to be provided in consultation with and with the consent of Member States concerned;

(*b*) Serve as a forum for dialogue on thematic issues on all human rights;

(*c*) Make recommendations to the General Assembly for the further development of international law in the field of human rights;

(*d*) Promote the full implementation of human rights obligations undertaken by States and follow-up to the goals and commitments related to the promotion and protection of human rights emanating from United Nations conferences and summits;

(*e*) Undertake a universal periodic review, based on objective and reliable information, of the fulfillment by each State of its human rights obligations and commitments in a manner which ensures universality of coverage and equal treatment with respect to all States; the review shall be a cooperative mechanism, based on an interactive dialogue, with the full involvement of the country concerned and with consideration given to its capacity-building needs; such a mechanism shall complement and not duplicate the work of treaty bodies; the Council shall develop the modalities and necessary time allocation for the universal periodic review mechanism within one year after the holding of its first session;

(*f*) Contribute, through dialogue and cooperation, towards the prevention of human rights violations and respond promptly to human rights emergencies;

(*g*) Assume the role and responsibilities of the Commission on Human Rights relating to the work of the Office of the United Nations High Commissioner for Human Rights, as decided by the General Assembly in its resolution 48/141 of 20 December 1993;

(*h*) Work in close cooperation in the field of human rights with Governments, regional organizations, national human rights institutions and civil society;

(*i*) Make recommendations with regard to the promotion and protection of human rights;

(*j*) Submit an annual report to the General Assembly;

6. *Decides also* that the Council shall assume, review and, where necessary, improve and rationalize all mandates, mechanisms, functions and responsibilities of the Commission on Human Rights in order to maintain a system of special procedures, expert advice and a complaint procedure; the Council shall complete this review within one year after the holding of its first session;

7. *Decides further* that the Council shall consist of forty-seven Member States, which shall be elected directly and individually by secret ballot by the majority of the members of the General Assembly; the membership shall be based on equitable geographical distribution, and seats shall be distributed as follows among regional groups: Group of African States, thirteen; Group of Asian States, thirteen; Group of Eastern European States, six; Group of Latin American and Caribbean States, eight; and Group of Western European and other States, seven; the members of the Council shall serve for a period of three years and shall not be eligible for immediate re-election after two consecutive terms;

8. *Decides* that the membership in the Council shall be open to all States Members of the United Nations; when electing members of the Council, Member States shall take into account the contribution of candidates to the promotion and protection of human rights and their voluntary pledges and commitments made thereto; the General Assembly, by a two-thirds majority of the members present and voting, may suspend the rights of membership in the Council of a member of the Council that commits gross and systematic violations of human rights;

9. *Decides also* that members elected to the Council shall uphold the highest standards in the promotion and protection of human rights, shall fully cooperate with the Council and be reviewed under the universal periodic review mechanism during their term of membership;

10. *Decides further* that the Council shall meet regularly throughout the year and schedule no fewer than three sessions per year, including a main session, for a total duration of no less than ten weeks, and shall be able to hold special sessions, when needed, at the request of a member of the Council with the support of one third of the membership of the Council;

11. *Decides* that the Council shall apply the rules of procedure established for committees of the General Assembly, as applicable, unless subsequently otherwise decided by the Assembly or the Council, and also decides that the participation of and consultation with observers, including States that are not members of the Council, the specialized agencies, other intergovernmental organizations and national human rights institutions, as well as non-governmental organizations, shall be based on arrangements, including Economic and Social Council resolution 1996/31 of 25 July 1996 and practices observed by the Commission on Human Rights, while ensuring the most effective contribution of these entities;

12. *Decides also* that the methods of work of the Council shall be transparent, fair and impartial and shall enable genuine dialogue, be results oriented, allow for subsequent follow-up discussions to recommendations and their implementation and also allow for substantive interaction with special procedures and mechanisms;

13. *Recommends* that the Economic and Social Council request the Commission on Human Rights to conclude its work at its sixty-second session, and that it abolish the Commission on 16 June 2006;

14. *Decides* to elect the new members of the Council; the terms of membership shall be staggered, and such decision shall be taken for the first election by the drawing of lots, taking into consideration equitable geographical distribution;

15. *Decides also* that elections of the first members of the Council shall take place on 9 May 2006, and that the first meeting of the Council shall be convened on 19 June 2006;

16. *Decides further* that the Council shall review its work and functioning five years after its establishment and report to the General Assembly.

72nd plenary meeting
15 March 2006

DOCUMENT 58

Full Official Title: Report Of The United Nations High Commissioner For Human Rights On The Protection Of Human Rights And Fundamental Freedoms While Countering Terrorism

Short Title/Acronym/Abbreviation: Nothing official

Type of Document: Administrative report of one office of the U.N., the Office of the High Commissioner for Human Rights, to the U.N. Human Rights Council, on a subject requested by the Council.

Subject: Protection of human rights while countering terrorism

Official Citation: A/HRC/13/36

Date of Document: January 22, 2010

Date of Adoption: Not applicable

Date of General Entry into Force (EIF): Not applicable

Number of States Parties as of this printing: Not applicable

Date of Signature by United States: Not applicable

Date of Ratification/Accession/Adhesion: Not applicable

Date of Entry into Force as to United States (effective date): Not applicable

Legal Status/Character of the Instrument/Document as to the United States: Non-binding administrative report to help the Council in its business with human rights. The present report was submitted in accordance with Human Rights Council resolution 10/15 of 26 March 2009, on the protection and promotion of human rights while countering terrorism, in which the Council requested the United Nations High Commissioner for Human Rights "to present [her report], bearing in mind the content of the present resolution, to the Council at its thirteenth session under agenda item 3, in conformity with its annual program of work."

Web Address: www2.ohchr.org/english/bodies/hrcouncil/docs/13session/A-HRC-13-36.pdf

REPORT OF THE UNITED NATIONS HIGH COMMISSIONER FOR HUMAN RIGHTS ON THE PROTECTION OF HUMAN RIGHTS AND FUNDAMENTAL FREEDOMS WHILE COUNTERING TERRORISM*

Human Rights Council
Thirteenth session
Agenda item 3
Promotion and protection of all human rights, civil, political, economic, social and cultural rights, including the right to development

Summary

The present report is submitted in accordance with Human Rights Council resolution 10/15 of 26 March 2009 on the protection and promotion of human rights while countering terrorism, in which the Council requested the United Nations High Commissioner for Human Rights "to present [her report], bearing in mind the content of the present resolution, to the Council at its thirteenth session under agenda item 3, in conformity with its annual programme of work".

In that resolution, the Human Rights Council called upon States to ensure access to an effective remedy in cases where human rights have been violated as a result of counterterrorism measures, and provide adequate, prompt and effective reparations for victims. The Council recalled the absolute prohibition of torture and the right to be equal before courts and tribunals, and urged States to guarantee due process. It also reaffirmed resolution 7/7, in which the Council, among other things, urged States to respect their nonrefoulement obligations as well as the safeguards concerning the liberty, security and dignity of the person.[1]

The present report highlights the need to protect and promote all human rights and to maintain effective counter-terrorism measures. These are mutually reinforcing objectives that must be pursued together as part of the duty of States to protect human rights. It outlines the High Commissioner's activities regarding counter-terrorism measures and her role in the implementation of the United Nations Global Counter-Terrorism Strategy and its Plan of Action. It concludes with the identification of challenges related to complying with human rights obligations, in particular the issues of accountability, ending impunity and effective remedies in the context of countering terrorism.

I. Introduction

1. The present report is submitted in accordance with Council resolution 10/15. In its resolution 7/7, the Human Rights Council requested the United Nations High Commissioner for Human Rights to continue her efforts to implement the mandate given to her by the Commission on Human Rights in its resolution 2005/80 and the General Assembly in its resolution 60/158, and report to the Council. These two resolutions request the High Commissioner for Human Rights, making use of existing mechanisms, to continue:

(a) To examine the question of the protection of human rights and fundamental freedoms while countering terrorism, taking into account reliable information from all sources;

(b) To make general recommendations concerning the obligation of States to promote and protect human rights and fundamental freedoms while taking actions to counter terrorism;

(c) To provide assistance and advice to States, upon their request, on the protection of human rights and fundamental freedoms while countering terrorism, as well as to relevant United Nations bodies.

---

* The present report is submitted late so as to include as much up-to-date information as possible.

[1] In resolutions 7/7 and 10/15 the Human Rights Council reaffirmed the non-derogability of certain rights in all circumstances, as well as the exceptional and temporary nature of derogations.

2. In its resolution 10/15, the Human Rights Council called upon States to ensure access to an effective remedy where human rights are violated as a result of counterterrorism measures, and provide adequate, prompt and effective reparations for victims. The present report addresses developments in respect of the protection of human rights while countering terrorism over the past year. In the same resolution, the Human Rights Council requested the High Commissioner for Human Rights "to present [her report], bearing in mind the content of the present resolution, to the Council at its thirteenth session under its agenda item 3, in conformity with its annual programme of work".

II. Recent developments
A. Implementation of the United Nations Global Counter-Terrorism Strategy and the Counter-Terrorism Implementation Task Force

3. Through the United Nations Global Counter-Terrorism Strategy and Plan of Action, adopted by the General Assembly in its resolution 60/288, Member States reaffirmed that acts, methods and practices of terrorism in all its forms and manifestations are activities aimed at the destruction of human rights, fundamental freedoms and democracy. They committed to adopting measures to ensure respect for human rights for all and to use the rule of law as the fundamental basis of the fight against terrorism. Member States also resolved to ensure that measures taken to counter terrorism comply with their obligations under international human rights law.

4. In the Plan of Action, it was reaffirmed that the Office of the United Nations High Commissioner for Human Rights (OHCHR) should play a lead role in examining the protection of human rights while countering terrorism. OHCHR continued to lead the Working Group on Protecting Human Rights While Countering Terrorism of the Counter-Terrorism Implementation Task Force established by the Secretary-General in 2005, in an effort to ensure a coordinated and coherent approach across the United Nations system to counter-terrorism. In 2008, the Monitoring Team of the Security Council Committee established pursuant to resolution 1267 (1999) (Counter-Terrorism Committee) joined the Working Group and the Office for the Coordination of Humanitarian Affairs and the Office of the United Nations High Commissioner for Refugees as observers. The aim of the Working Group is to support efforts by Member States to ensure the promotion and protection of human rights in the context of counter-terrorism through, among other things, the development and implementation of legislation and policies that are compliant with human rights.

5. To assist Member States in strengthening the protection of human rights in 10 specific areas, my Office, in consultation with Member States, started to develop a series of basic technical reference guides on countering terrorism with the endeavour of providing full respect for human rights. Following consultations with Member States, the first four guides being developed are on (a) proscription of organizations, (b) stopping and searching of persons, (c) designing security infrastructure, and (d) the principle of legality in national counter-terrorism legislation.

6. On 14 and 15 October 2009, my Office participated in the Counter-Terrorism Implementation Task Force retreat in Vienna. This yearly meeting was focused on taking stock of the work that the Task Force and its working groups accomplished in the past year. It also set forth the plans for the future. Key issues discussed included, among others, the institutionalization of the Task Force in accordance with General Assembly resolution 62/272 and the communications strategy of the Task Force.

7. On 12 and 13 October 2009, my Office participated in the first International Workshop for National Counter-Terrorism Focal Points. The workshop was organized by the Counter-Terrorism Implementation Task Force and the United Nations Office on Drugs and Crime and was co-sponsored by the Governments of Austria, Norway, Switzerland and Turkey, as well as by Costa Rica, Japan and Slovakia. It gathered practitioners and policymakers from national Governments to share experiences and to develop strategies for better cooperation in the collective fight against terrorism. Participants represented more than 110 Member States. During the workshop, it was affirmed that the United Nations Global Counter-Terrorism Strategy is the policy framework within which concrete implementation actions need to be strengthened at the national, regional and international levels, and that the Strategy needs to be implemented in a comprehensive manner. Participants noted the importance of the prevention of terrorism. Action in the area of prevention includes promoting economic development, enhancing dialogue among civilizations, supporting victims, and protecting human rights. Participants also discussed steps towards enhancing coordination among governments, United Nations entities and other partners, including the Counter-Terrorism Implementation Task Force.

B. The work of the Security Council

8. On 29 October 2009, I addressed the Counter-Terrorism Committee. Guided by Security Council resolutions 1373 (2001) and 1624 (2005), the Committee has been working to enhance the ability of States

Members of the United Nations to prevent terrorist acts both within their borders and across regions. The Committee is assisted in its efforts by the Counter-Terrorism Committee Executive Directorate, which carries out the policy decisions of the Committee, conducts expert assessments of each Member State and facilitates counter-terrorism technical assistance to countries. This was the third time that a High Commissioner for Human Rights addressed this important body.

9. During this briefing, I reiterated that upholding human rights while countering terrorism is an inescapable imperative, because human rights law offers a framework that can both meet public security concerns and protect human dignity and the rule of law. Some measures taken to counter terrorism, such as resorting to the use of excessive force and indiscriminate repression by the police, security and army personnel, can strengthen terrorists' support bases, undermining the goals that States set out to achieve. Upholding human rights creates trust between the State and those under its jurisdiction, and such trust can serve as the foundation of an effective response to terrorism. I highlighted that meaningful protection also includes tackling the underlying causes of terrorism, such as the obstacles to the enjoyment of economic, social and cultural rights.

10. I sought to underscore that the time had come for the Security Council's counterterrorism bodies to consider a broader approach in their vital work in this area, such as that of the General Assembly in the United Nations Global Counter-Terrorism Strategy and Plan of Action, which stressed not only the need for counter-terrorism measures, but also the impact of such measures on human rights. I noted that because the Counter-Terrorism Committee and the United Nations human rights machinery review counter-terrorism laws and measures in parallel, better cooperation between them could provide additional legitimacy and coherence to the United Nations system as a whole.

11. I shared with the Counter-Terrorism Committee my views that it could play a key role in placing the rule of law and human rights at the core of the fight against terrorism. I mentioned six areas in particular:

(a) The question of legality, including vague definitions of acts of terrorism that have led to the prosecution of individuals for the legitimate, non-violent exercise of their rights to freedom of expression, association and assembly, and which represent a violation of the principle of legality;

(b) The need to respect and protect non-derogable rights. I noted in this respect that national, ethnic, racial or religious profiling raises concerns with regard to the nonderogable principles of equality and non-discrimination. I also raised the question of torture and ill-treatment. These discriminatory and stigmatizing measures affect the rights of communities and may lead to further marginalization and possibly radicalization within those communities;

(c) The expansion of surveillance powers and capacities of law enforcement agencies and the need to adequately protect the right to privacy, which may severely undermine international cooperation; as well as the use of torture and ill-treatment for intelligence gathering, which taints evidence and makes it inadmissible at trial;

(d) Accountability for human rights violations, which is especially crucial to effective counter-terrorism strategies. True security can only be achieved where all members of society cooperate with State authorities and are confident that the measures adopted by these authorities to counter-terrorism are effective, proportionate, and respectful of their human rights and dignity;

(e) The issue of targeted sanctions. I noted that while I welcomed the recent improvements in procedures related to the United Nations targeted sanctions regime, further improvements were necessary to ensure a transparent listing process based on clear criteria, and with a uniformly applied standard of evidence. Accessible and independent mechanisms for review are also necessary;

(f) Issues regarding the proper integration of a human rights approach to the technical work of the Counter-Terrorism Committee. I suggested that consideration should be given to include a human rights expert on all Committee visits to Member States and to devote additional resources to this area of the Committee's work.

I also reaffirmed the OHCHR commitment to supporting the Committee and its Executive Directorate on all issues related to States' compliance with human rights.

12. From 8 to 10 November 2009, the Counter-Terrorism Committee Executive Directorate and the Government of Bangladesh held a regional workshop in Dhaka on effective counter-terrorism practices for senior police officers and prosecutors from Afghanistan, Bangladesh, Bhutan, India, Maldives, Nepal, Pakistan and Sri Lanka; a representative of the South Asian Association for Regional Cooperation (SAARC) also attended. OHCHR participated in this workshop offering views on how human rights can be upheld at the operational level in the context of international legal cooperation.

13. On 17 December 2009 the Security Council adopted resolution 1904 (2009) to meet the challenges faced by Member States in implementing the sanctions regime against Al-Qaida and the Taliban. The resolution was aimed at improving the procedures to ensure that they are fair and the procedures are clear. In it, the Security Council decided, among other things, to create an office of the ombudsperson, which would assist in analysing available information concerning the delisting requests of those seeking removal from the Council's sanctions list.

C. The work of the General Assembly

14. In December 2009, the General Assembly adopted resolution 64/168 on the protection of human rights and fundamental freedoms while countering terrorism. In the resolution, the General Assembly, among other things:

(a) Expresses serious concern at the occurrence of violations of human rights and fundamental freedoms;

(b) Urges States countering terrorism to comply with their obligations in a number of areas, such as the prohibition of torture and other cruel, inhuman or degrading treatment or punishment, the guarantee for liberty and security, the treatment of prisoners, non-refoulement, the legality in the criminalization of acts of terrorism, non-discrimination, the right to an effective remedy, due process and the right to a fair trial;

(c) Highlights the need to protect economic, social and cultural rights;

(d) Notes the need to continue ensuring that fair and clear procedures under the United Nations terrorism-related sanctions regime are strengthened to enhance their efficiency and transparency;

(e) Urges States to ensure the rule of law and to include adequate human rights guarantees in their national listing procedures;

(f) Requests OHCHR to continue to contribute to the work of the Counter-Terrorism Implementation Task Force, including by raising awareness on the need to protect human rights and the rule of law while countering terrorism;

(g) Encourages the Security Council and its Counter-Terrorism Committee to strengthen dialogue with relevant human rights bodies, in particular with OHCHR, the Special Rapporteur on the promotion and protection of human rights and fundamental freedoms while countering terrorism, other relevant special procedures and mechanisms of the Human Rights Council and relevant treaty bodies.

D. Other relevant activities

15. The annual report of the Special Representative of the Secretary-General for Children and Armed Conflict (A/HRC/12/49) presented to the Human Rights Council at its twelfth session addresses terrorism and counter-terrorism and their impact on children. The Special Rapporteur noted that anti-terrorism measures often target children; in some cases, children are arrested or detained for reasons of alleged association with terrorist groups, and legal and practical safeguards are disregarded. The Special Representative also focused on "collateral damage", in which children are often the victims, resulting from precision aerial bombardment and other types of military operation.

16. The United Nations human rights treaty bodies have continued to take up issues related to terrorism in their examination of State party reports and individual complaints. In their concluding observations, different committees have urged States parties to recognize and ensure that the human rights treaties apply at all times, in any territory under their jurisdiction. The Secretary-General has recently reported on key developments in this field to the General Assembly (see A/64/186); I would like to focus on the most recent developments.

17. On 18 and 19 November 2009, my Office participated in a workshop in Jakarta hosted by the Center on Global Counterterrorism Cooperation and Nahdatul Ulama with support from the Governments of Germany and Sweden. The aim of the workshop was to raise awareness of the United Nations Global Counter-Terrorism Strategy among civil society in South-East Asia and to explore the possibilities for greater civil society participation in efforts to implement the global framework in a manner that reflects the needs and priorities across the region.

18. On 30 November 2009, OHCHR participated in an Arria Formula meeting on strengthening a United Nations integrated approach to human rights and counter-terrorism through the role of the Security Council. The meeting was convened by the Government of Mexico, which invited speakers who were members of the Eminent Jurist Panel of the International Commission of Jurists. Participants included members of the Security Council, representatives of the 1267 Committee, the Counter-Terrorism Committee Executive Directorate and the Chair of the Counter-Terrorism Implementation Task Force.

III. Issues of concern: accountability and reparations

19. A major challenge facing States today is accountability for serious violations of human rights that have taken place in the context of counter-terrorism measures and the rights of victims to remedy and reparations. In recent years, serious violations have taken place affecting fundamental rights, including wilful killings, summary executions, disappearances, torture and arbitrary detention. These practices have rarely been investigated thoroughly, perpetrators have often not been punished, and reparations to victims have not been forthcoming.

20. In Article 2, paragraph 3, of the International Covenant on Civil and Political Rights, it is spelled out that in addition to effective protection of Covenant rights, States parties must ensure that individuals have accessible and effective[2] remedies to vindicate those rights,[3] which was restated by the Human Rights Committee in its general comment No. 31 (2004). The Committee stated that it attaches importance to States parties establishing appropriate judicial and administrative mechanisms for addressing claims of rights violations under domestic law. The Committee noted that the enjoyment of the rights recognized under the Covenant can be effectively assured by the judiciary in many different ways, including direct applicability of the Covenant, application of comparable constitutional or other provisions of law, or the interpretive effect of the Covenant in the application of national law. Administrative mechanisms are particularly required to give effect to the general obligation to investigate allegations of violations promptly, thoroughly and effectively through independent and impartial bodies. National human rights institutions, endowed with appropriate powers, can contribute to this end.

21. The Human Rights Committee also stated in general comment No. 31 that Article 2, paragraph 3, requires that States parties make reparation to individuals whose Covenant rights have been violated. Without reparation to individuals whose Covenant rights have been violated, the obligation to provide an effective remedy, which is central to the efficacy of Article 2, paragraph 3, is not discharged. In addition to the explicit reparation required by articles 9, paragraph 5, and 14, paragraph 6, the Committee considered that the Covenant generally entails appropriate compensation. The Committee noted that, where appropriate, reparation can involve restitution, rehabilitation and measures of satisfaction, such as public apologies, public memorials, guarantees of non-repetition and changes in relevant laws and practices, as well as bringing to justice the perpetrators of human rights violations.

A. Accountability

22. Where serious violations of human rights occur, States have the duty to ensure that such violations are properly investigated and, wherever possible, investigation should lead to a judicial or other appropriate response.[4] The failure to conduct an independent investigation of serious human rights violations not only reinforces the violations that have already been committed but can lead to the serious deterioration of larger country-wide human rights situations. On the other hand, a timely and efficient inquiry can have a preventive effect and improve the overall national human rights situation. Failure to investigate also violates the human rights of the victims.[5] Also, a failure by a State party to investigate allegations of violations could give rise to a separate breach of the Covenant. Cessation of an ongoing violation is an essential element of the right to an effective remedy.[6]

23. States are under the obligation to investigate all human rights violations. Under extreme circumstances, where a state of emergency is declared, derogations from some rights and freedoms are permissible

---

[2] See Committee against Torture, communication No. 291/2006, *Ali v. Tunisia*, 21 November 2008.

See also European Court of Human Rights, application No. 52391/99, *Ramsahai and others v. the Netherlands*, 15 May 2007, para. 324. See also CCPR/CO/79/LVA, CCPR/C/LBY/CO/4, CCPR/C/79/Add.121 (Human Rights Committee, 2000), CAT/C/GUY/CO/1 (Committee against Torture, 2006).

[3] Human Rights Committee, communication No. 1332/2004, *Juan García Sánchez and Benvenida González Clares v. Spain*, 31 October 2006.

[4] See Committee against Torture, communication No. 257/2004, *Keremedchiev v. Bulgaria*, 11 November 2008, para. 11. See also Inter-American Court of Human Rights, *Montero Aranguren et al. v. Venezuela*, 5 July 2006, where the Court stated that "the State has the obligation to combat impunity by all available legal means, since it promotes the chronicle repetition of violations to human rights and the defenselessnes of the victims and their next of kin", para. 137.

[5] See Committee against Torture, communication No. 188/2001, *Abdelli v. Tunisia*. See also the independent study on best practices, including recommendations, to assist States in strengthening their domestic capacity to combat all aspects of impunity, by Diane Orentlicher (E/CN.4/2004/88), and "The state of human rights in Europe and the progress of the Assembly's monitoring procedure", Council of Europe, Strasbourg, June 2008.

[6] See Human Rights Committee general comment No. 31, para. 15, 29 March 2004. See also Article 25 of the American Convention on *Human Rights and Velásquez Rodríguez v. Uruguay*, 26 June 1987, para. 91. See also Human Rights Committee, communication No. 1332/2004, *Juan García Sánchez and Benvenida González Clares v. Spain*, 31 October 2006.

under Article 4 of the International Covenant on Civil and Political Rights, but they should not exceed the exigencies of the situation.[7] Article 4 (2) of the Covenant lists various rights which are non-derogable at all times, such as: the right to life; the prohibition of torture and other inhuman or degrading treatment; the prohibition of retroactive criminal laws; freedom of thought, conscience and religion;[8] and the prohibition of the death penalty (Article 6 of the Second Optional Protocol to the International Covenant on Civil and Political Rights).

24. Under Article 2 (1) of the International Covenant on Civil and Political Rights, State parties are obliged to respect and ensure the Covenant rights to all persons who may be within their territory and to all persons subject to their jurisdiction. General comment No. 15 of the Human Rights Committee indicates that this obligation is not limited to a State's citizens, but must be guaranteed to all individuals, regardless of nationality or statelessness, such as asylum-seekers, refugees, migrant workers and others who may find themselves subject to the jurisdictional regulations of the territory in which they are found.

25. Procedurally, States commit themselves to establishing suitable institutions (i.e. primarily judicial institutions, such as criminal, civil, constitutional and special human rights courts, or also national human rights institutions and torture rehabilitation bodies) to enable victims of torture to obtain redress.[9] National mechanisms are required to give prompt, thorough, and effective attention to the obligations to investigate allegations of violations[10] through independent[11] and impartial bodies. National human rights institutions, endowed with appropriate powers, can contribute to this end by referring all those responsible for committing gross human rights violations to the criminal justice system for investigation.

26. The Special Rapporteur on torture and other cruel, inhuman or degrading treatment or punishment indicated that in the light of the consistent international jurisprudence suggesting that the prohibition of amnesties leading to impunity for serious human rights has become a rule of customary international law, he expresses his opposition to the passing, application and non-revocation of amnesty laws which prevent torturers from being brought to justice and hence contribute to a culture of impunity. He called on States to refrain from granting or acquiescing in impunity at the national level, inter alia, by the granting of amnesties, such impunity itself constituting a violation of international law.[12] Article 4 of the Convention against Torture and Other Cruel, Inhuman or Degrading Treatment or Punishment states that each State party must ensure that all acts of torture are offences under its criminal law; this also applies to an attempt to commit torture and to an act by any person which constitutes complicity or participation in torture. It also states that each State party must make these offences punishable by appropriate penalties which take into account their grave nature. The Convention against Torture contains obligations aimed at punishing perpetrators, preventing torture and assisting victims of torture.[13]

---

[7] Article 4 of the International Covenant on Civil and Political Rights cannot be invoked to derogate from the rules of the Geneva Conventions of 1949. Derogation measures must be consistent with State obligations under international humanitarian law. The minimum provided for in Article 3 of the four Geneva Conventions of 1949 must be respected. In particular, the minimum provided in Article 3 for persons taking no active part in hostilities entails, among other things: the prohibition, at any time and in any place, of violence to life and person, in particular murder of all kinds, mutilation, cruel treatment and torture, the taking of hostages, and outrage upon personal dignity. See also general comment No. 29, paras. 9 and 14 of the Human Rights Committee.

[8] Articles 6, 7, 15 and 18 of the International Covenant on Civil and Political Rights. See also Manfred Nowak, *U.N. Covenant on Civil and Political Rights: CCPR Commentary*, second revised edition (Kehl am Rhein, Engle, 2005), p. 94.

[9] See A/HRC/4/33, para. 63; Committee on the Elimination of Racial Discrimination, communication No. 10/1997, *Habassi v. Denmark*, 6 April 1999, paras. 9.3–10; Committee against Torture: conclusions and recommendations on Colombia, 4 February 2004, para. 9 (a); see also conclusions and recommendations on Yemen, 5 February 2004, para. 6 (e); conclusions and recommendations on Morocco, 5 February 2004, para. 7 (c).

[10] See note 7 supra at paras. 15 and 18 of Human Rights Committee general comment No. 31. See also *Helen Mack Chang et al.* Case, Order of the Court of 6 June 2003, Inter-Am. Ct. H.R. (Ser. E) (6 June 2003). *Myrna Mack Chang v. Guatemala*, para. 210. The case can be found at www1.umn.edu/humanrts/iachr/E/chang6-6-03.html.

[11] See Committee against Torture, communication No. 257/2004, *Keremedchiev v. Bulgaria*, 28September 2004; communication No. 1327/2004, *Grioua v. Algeria*, 10 July 2007, para. 7.10. See also European Court of Human Rights, *Barbu Anghelescu v. Romania*, 12 October 2004, on the requirement of independence, which entails not only the absence of all hierarchical or institutional links, but also practical independence. The court found that an inquiry carried out by military prosecutors did not satisfy this criterion.

[12] See A/56/156. See also A/HRC/10/44/Add.2.

[13] See *Official Records of the General Assembly, Fifty-eighth Session, Supplement No. 40* (A/58/40), vol. I, chap. IV, paras. 4, 7 and 12. See conclusions and recommendations of the Committee against Torture: Belgium (CAT/C/CR/30/6). The Committee recommended that Belgium include "a provision in the Penal Code expressly prohibiting the invocation of a state of necessity to justify the violation of the right not to be subjected to torture" (para. 7 (b)). See also CAT/C/XXVII/Concl.5.

27. With regards to the right to life, in general comment No. 6 (1982) the Human Rights Committee specifies that not only do States have a negative obligation not to arbitrarily interfere with the individual right to life, but also, States have a positive obligation to adopt all measures that are appropriate to protect and preserve the right to life and to prevent and punish deprivations of life by criminal acts as well as arbitrary killings by their own security forces.[14] The police have the duty to prepare and plan counter-terrorism operations so as to avoid any loss of life. Public investigations of any death in which State agents may be implicated are necessary.[15]

28. Covert actions raise particular challenges for accountability. Since they are secretive types of action, where information is classified, it is difficult for the legislator and the judiciary to be aware of them. It should be recalled that all measures taken by law enforcement agencies must be lawful under national and international law, and compatible with States' human rights obligations. This means that all activities undertaken by intelligence agencies, including intelligence-gathering, covert surveillance activities, searches and data collection must be regulated by law, monitored by independent agencies, and subject to judicial review. The lack of transparency that prevails in a number of the investigations and trials related to terrorism is a cause for concern. Through the adoption or revival of State secrecy or immunity doctrines or the adoption of other measures to shield intelligence, military or diplomatic sources and information, in the name of national security interests, States have limited the access to the necessary information for an effective investigation and prosecution of cases relating to acts of terrorism. States are required to ensure that confined powers, review of accountability and oversight mechanisms are established against the misuse of exceptional powers granted to intelligence, military agencies or special police to counter terrorism. Such controls might encompass the process or authorizing special powers and the remedies for people claiming abuse of these powers. Controls can occur either before or after the use of powers.

29. The Convention against Torture requires States parties to prevent, within their territory, any acts of torture, or cruel, inhuman or degrading treatment.[16] By virtue of the extraterritorial application of the prohibition of such acts, and the obligations under customary international law and Articles 55 and 56 of the Charter of the United Nations, States must also ensure that their officials do not undertake such practices overseas and that they are not complicit in such conduct by other persons. It is thus essential that those responsible for conducting or colluding in interrogation techniques amounting to torture or cruel, inhuman or degrading treatment are held accountable.[17]

30. The practice of holding terrorist suspects in secret detention has led to the denial of several rights of detainees, not only with respect to their rights associated with liberty, but also for example their right to a fair trial. In such circumstances, where confessions are extracted by torture and evidence gathered illegally through secret agents, the possibility of bringing to justice people who are responsible for committing the above-mentioned violations is unlikely. In its general comment No. 21 on Article 10 of the International Covenant on Civil and Political Rights, the Human Rights Committee imposes on States an obligation to individuals who are vulnerable, such as juveniles, due to their status of persons deprived of liberty to be treated with humanity and with respect for the inherent dignity of the human person.

---

[14] See Human Rights Committee communication No. 1469/2006, *Yasoda Sharma v. Nepal*, 26 April 2006; communication No. 1327/2004, *Grioua v. Algeria*, 10 July 2007, para. 7.10; communication No. 213/1986, *H.C.M.A. v. The Netherlands*, 30 March 1989, para. 11.6; communication No. 612/1995, *Vicente et al. v. Colombia*, 29 July 1997, para. 8.8; communication No. 1196/2003, *Boucherf v. Algeria*, 30 March 2006, para. 11; and communication No. 1297/2004, *Medjnoune v. Algeria*, 14 July 2006, para. 10. See also footnote 11 supra in relation to Human Rights Committee general comment No. 31 on the kinds of effective remedy necessary in cases of violations of the right to life. Inter-American Court of Human Rights, *Myrna Mack Chang v. Guatemala, Bulacio v. Argentina*, 18 September 2003—obligation to adopt all appropriate measures to protect and preserve the right to life under the duty to ensure the full and free exercise of the rights by all persons under their jurisdiction. This obligation extends to all State institutions, the police and the armed forces—States must adopt all necessary measures to prevent, try and punish deprivation of life as a consequence of criminal acts carried out by its own security agents, as well as in general. See also Nils Melzer, *Targeted Killing in International Law* (Oxford Press, 2009), p. 94.

[15] Note 7 supra at para. 18 of general comment No. 31. See also the Basic Principles and Guidelines on the Right to a Remedy and Reparation for Victims of Gross Violations of International Human Rights Law and Serious Violations of International Humanitarian Law (General Assembly resolution 60/147, annex). See also A/HRC/4/33, para. 62: in the leading case on Article 14, *Guridi v. Spain*, the Committee against Torture, without explicit reference to the Guidelines, followed the terminology developed therein in its decision. In that case the perpetrators were subsequently pardoned after they had paid compensation. Despite the payment of compensation, the Committee found a violation of Article 14 of the Basic Principles. It held that reparation should cover all the damages suffered by the victim, which included, among other things, restitution, compensation and rehabilitation of the victim, as well as measures to guarantee the non-repetition of the violations, always bearing in mind the circumstances of each case.

[16] See CAT/C/USA/CO/2, para. 13, 2006; CAT/C/TGO/CO/1, para. 15, 2006; CAT/C/AUS/CO/3, para. 8, 2008.

[17] See A/HRC/10/44/Add.2, para. 64.

31. Accountability and the right to effective remedies are connected to the right to a fair trial as guaranteed by Article 14 of the Covenant, clarified by general comment No. 32 of the Human Rights Committee. Protecting the right of terrorist suspects to a fair trial is critical not only for ensuring that anti-terrorism measures respect the rule of law, but also for ensuring that perpetrators of human rights violations are held accountable. Indeed, violations carried out in the execution of "extraordinary renditions" and collecting evidence by illegal means are very unlikely to be adequately brought to light, and perpetrators brought to justice, if suspects of terrorism are tried in special courts with special procedures or sealed evidence which do not fully guarantee the right to a fair trial. Therefore, the guarantees of a fair trial are essential to ensure accountability and to combat impunity, as well as to provide effective remedies.[18]

32. Article 10 of the International Covenant on Civil and Political Rights has a clear relationship with the protection from torture, inhuman and degrading treatment and punishment. Human Rights Committee general comment No. 21 clarifies that Article 10 imposes on States parties a positive obligation towards persons who are particularly vulnerable because of their status as persons deprived of liberty, and complements for them the ban on torture or other cruel, inhuman or degrading treatment or punishment contained in Article 7 of the Covenant. The Committee also recalls that the principle set forth in Article 10, paragraph 1, constitutes the basis for the more specific obligations of States parties in respect of criminal justice, which are set forth in Article 10, paragraphs 2 and 3.

33. In the endeavour to protect intelligence sources, some States have amended the regulations governing legal or administrative procedures to allow the non-disclosure of materials to suspects.[19] Secrecy and immunity doctrines should not be applied where serious human rights violations are being investigated, such as the absolute prohibition of torture and cases of killings or disappearances. Independent, impartial, transparent and credible investigations are required by law to ensure accountability. Individual responsibility cannot be avoided through amnesties or immunities, and other limitations to the recognition of legal responsibility.

34. States must refrain from granting or acquiescing in impunity at the national level through amnesties.[20] Amnesties for gross and serious violations of human rights and humanitarian law may also violate customary international law,[21] and the continued passing, application and non-revocation of amnesty laws[22] contributes to a culture of impunity.

35. Since September 2001, there has been a trend towards outsourcing the collection of intelligence to private contractors. While the involvement of private actors can be necessary as a technical matter in order to have access to information (for instance for electronic surveillance), there are reasons to be wary of using contractors to interrogate persons who are deprived of their liberty. The responsibility to protect the right to life, physical integrity or liberty of individuals should remain within the exclusive domain of the State. The combination of a lack of proper training, the introduction of a profit motive into situations which are prone to human rights violations, and the often questionable prospect that such contractors will be subject to judicial and parliamentary accountability mechanisms are all elements that should be considered by Member States to ensure that those actors are accountable.

36. A particular concern is that of rendition and extraordinary rendition that arises from increased intelligence cooperation. Extraordinary rendition is almost certain to constitute or facilitate a violation of a

---

[18] Human Rights Committee, communication No. 1416/2005, *Alzery v. Sweden*.

[19] International Commission of Jurists, *Accessing Damage, Urging Action: Report of the Eminent Jurists Panel on Terrorism, Counterterrorism and Human Rights* (2009), p. 78.

[20] See footnote 16 supra in relation to Human Rights Committee general comment No. 31, para. 18. See also principle 36 (a) of the set of principles for the protection and promotion of human rights through action to combat impunity; Human Rights Committee communication No. 45/1979, *Suarez de Guerrero v. Colombia*, 30 March 1982, para. 15; see also Human Rights Committee concluding observations on Venezuela, 26 April 2001 (CCPR/CO/71/VEN), para. 8.

[21] International tribunals have had few opportunities to address the question of whether States' obligations under customary international law may be violated by an amnesty. A 1998 decision by a Trial Chamber of the International Criminal Tribunal for the former Yugoslavia suggested, however, that an amnesty for torture (and, by implication, for other conduct whose prohibition in international law has the status of a peremptory norm) would be "international unlawful" (see *Prosecutor v. Anto Furundzija*, case No. IT-95-17/1-T, Judgement of 10 December 1998, para. 155). See also *Prosecutor v. Morris Kalon* and *Prosecutor v. Brima Bazzy Kamara*, para. 82. See also Inter-American Court of Human Rights, *Barrio Altos v. Peru*, where it found that "Amnesty Laws No. 26479 and No. 26492 are incompatible with the American Convention on Human Rights and, consequently, lack legal effect", 14 March 2001, para. 51/4.

[22] See general comment No. 31 at para. 18. See also Inter-American Court of Human Rights, *Servellón Garcia et al. v. Honduras*, where the Court noted that there is an obligation on States not to resort to legal concepts such as amnesties or other measures to eliminate responsibility, 21 September 2006. See also *Myrna Mack Chang v. Guatemala*, in which the Court noted that the State must "remove all de facto and legal mechanisms and obstacles that maintain impunity", para. 277.

variety of human rights, especially the rights that protect individuals against arbitrary arrest, forcible transfer, enforced disappearance or the subjection of torture and other cruel, inhuman or degrading treatment.[23] States must fulfil their obligations under the different treaties and standards, and ensure that their territory is not used to transfer persons to places where they are likely to be subjected to torture.[24]

37. In the absence of procedural safeguards that protect legal rights such as due process, persons who are subject to such transfers have no means of challenging their transfer. Hence, States should take all practical steps to determine whether foreign movements through their territories involve practices that can lead to irreparable harm. States have an obligation to investigate the role of their agents (both military and intelligence) who may have been involved in facilitating these renditions,[25] to sanction those responsible, and to provide reparation for victims.[26] States also have a responsibility to put in place procedures to address these issues, whether in reference to their own agents or to foreign agents, and to regulate the use of their airspace. States are further required to ensure accountability for past practices.[27]

38. There should be controls against the misuse of exceptional powers by institutions that are not subject to sufficient democratic and civilian control, in particular intelligence or military agencies or special police. States need to ensure confined powers, the review of accountability and oversight mechanisms. Such controls might encompass the process of authorizing special powers and the remedies for people claiming abuse of these powers. Controls can occur either before or after the use of powers.

39. Intelligence-gathering activities must be regulated by law, monitored as much as possible by independent agencies, and subject to judicial review. Under international human rights law, any act that impacts human rights must be lawful; it must be prescribed and regulated by law. This means that any search, seizure, surveillance activity, apprehension or data collection about a person must be clearly authorized by law. States amending regulations governing legal or administrative procedures to prevent the non-disclosure of materials to suspects must ensure they do so in conformity with their human rights obligations, in particular, with due process.[28]

40. Counter-terrorism measures that have an impact on the enjoyment of economic and social rights should also respect the principles of proportionality, effectiveness and legitimacy.[29] Access to justice and the existence of remedies, including adequate reparation for the victims, are key to upholding the accountability of States and to reducing impunity for violations of economic, social and cultural rights. In the context of countering terrorism, evictions and house demolitions are sometimes used as forms of targeted punishment for residents who are suspected of supporting terrorist groups. Where this constitutes a form of collective punishment it is considered a gross violation of human rights. It is often suffered by vulnerable communities, such as women, ethnic, religious and other minorities and indigenous peoples, who are suspected of supporting terrorist groups.

B. Remedies and reparation

41. In addition to States' duties to bring perpetrators of gross human rights violations before the criminal justice system, States' obligations have been described as requiring them to respect the right to truth, to

---

[23] See footnote 20 supra, p. 81.

[24] In the Burgos Case (1981), the Human Rights Committee established that "jurisdiction" was not a reference to where the violation took place, "but rather to the relationship between the individual and the State in relation to a violation of any of the rights set forth in the Covenant, wherever they occurred".

[25] Conclusions and recommendations on Colombia, 4 February 2004 (CAT/C/CR/31/1), para. 9 (d) (iii); conclusions and recommendations on Ecuador, 15 November 1993 (A/49/44), paras. 97–105, at 105. Case *Incal v. Turkey* of 9 June 1998, Reports 1998–IV, paras. 65–73. Committee on the Elimination of Racial Discrimination, Case *L.K. v. the Netherlands*, 16 March 1993 (CERD/C/42/D/1991), paras. 6.4 and 6.6.

[26] In Article 23 of the United Nations Basic Principles and Guidelines on the Right to a Remedy and Reparation for Victims of Gross Violations of International Human Rights Law and Serious Violations of International Humanitarian Law; the jurisprudence and practice have been classified in the United Nations Principles on Reparation as encompassing, among others, measures such as ensuring civilian control over military and security forces, strengthening the independence of the judiciary, protection of legal, medical, media and related personnel and human rights defenders, and human rights training.

[27] See Statement by the United Nations High Commissioner for Human Rights on the International Day in Support of Victims of Torture, 26 June 2009.

[28] See footnote 20 supra, p. 78.

[29] See A/HRC/12/22. For more details, see the summary of discussions of the expert seminar on the impact of terrorism and counterterrorism measures on the enjoyment of economic, social and cultural rights, held in Geneva from 5–7 November 2008, available at www.un.org/terrorism/pdfs/wg_protecting_human_rights.pdf.

justice and to reparation.[30] The right to truth puts an obligation on the State to investigate human rights violations and to present the facts to the public. The right to reparation comprises not only the right to compensation[31] and restitution, but also the right to rehabilitation,[32] satisfaction and guarantees of nonrepetition,[33] as described by the United Nations set of principles for the protection and promotion of human rights through action to combat impunity. These are complementary rights. The right to reparation as established by international law include: restitution *in integrum*, payment of compensation, satisfaction and guarantees of non-repetitions, among others.[34] When restitution, *in integrum*, is not possible, other forms of reparation must afford relief. The different obligations of the State regarding remedies and reparation are unconditional.

42. Article 2, paragraph 3, of the International Covenant on Civil and Political Rights ensures an accessory right to effective remedy against violations of human rights. This obligation was established in order to ensure victims had a means of vindicating their rights. The right to an effective remedy requires that a domestic process to deal with the complaint is available and that it provide the appropriate relief.[35]

The procedural aspect of upholding accountability and reducing impunity for States' human rights violations[36] is access to justice, including proper judicial review, and the existence of remedies, including adequate reparation for the victims. An independent judicial review by States of counterterrorism measures undertaken, including those affecting human rights, serves to ascertain their proportionality, effectiveness and legitimacy.[37]

43. The Human Rights Committee has stressed that the acquisition, development and use of information on terrorist groups and their activities must be in conformity with the International Covenant on Civil and Political Rights.[38] While implementing the United Nations targeted sanctions, such as asset freezing and travel bans against individuals suspected of involvement in terrorist activities, it is necessary to ensure that those victims of wrong listing or listing which violated their rights should be also compensated within the same established set of rules.[39]

44. According to the Declaration of Basic Principles of Justice for Victims of Crime and Abuse of Power,[40] victims include "persons who, individually or collectively, have suffered harm, including physical or mental injury, emotional suffering, economic loss or substantial impairment of their fundamental rights, through acts or omissions that are in violation of criminal laws operative within Member States, including those laws proscribing criminal abuse of power". In the Declaration, it is noted that an individual may be considered a victim "regardless of whether the perpetrator is identified, apprehended, prosecuted or convicted and regardless of the familial relationship between the perpetrator and the victim".

45. In light of frequent shortcomings with respect to victims in domestic jurisdictions, guidelines should be adopted by States to provide victims of counter-terrorism measures that may violate human rights with urgent assistance for their material and psychiatric needs, as well as long-term assistance, including medical and psychological follow-up. Such guidelines should also grant effective access to justice and ensure that evidentiary privileges are not an obstacle to transparency in the conduct of investigations and access to legal remedies.

---

[30] See Article 27.2 of the American Convention on Human Rights; Article 6 of the European Convention on Human Rights; Article 7 of the African Charter on Human and Peoples' Rights. See also Article 2 (3) of the International Covenant on Civil and Political Rights.

[31] See note 7 supra at para. 16. See also *Velásquez Rodríguez v. Uruguay*, Interpretation of Compensatory Damages Judgement, Judgement of August 17, 1990, para. 27.

[31] See note 7 supra, para. 16 of general comment No. 31. See also A/54/426, para. 50.

[33] Code of Conduct for Law Enforcement Officials (General Assembly resolution 34/169 of 17 December 1979), and the Standard Minimum Rules for the Treatment of Prisoners, adopted by the First United Nations Congress on the Prevention of Crime and the Treatment of Offenders, and approved by the Economic and Social Council in its resolutions 663 C (XXIV) of 31 July 1957 and 2076 (LXII) of 13 May 1977.

[34] Inter-American Court of Human Rights, Loayza Tamayo Case, Judgement of 27 November 1998, Series C, No. 42, para. 85.

[35] Jonathan Cooper, *Countering Terrorism, Protecting Human Rights: A Manual* (Warsaw, OSCE Office for Democratic Institutions and Human Rights, 2007), pp. 62–63.

[36] See general comment No. 31, para. 15. See also Committee on the Elimination of Discrimination against Women, general recommendation No. 19, Violence against women, 9 January 1992, para. 24 (t), in which it was held that effective protection included effective legal measures, including penal sanctions, civil remedies and compensatory remedies, preventive measures and protective measures.

[37] Committee against Torture, conclusions and recommendations on Egypt, 23 December 2002 (CAT/C/CR/29/4) para. 6 (c); conclusions and recommendations on Cambodia, 27 May 2003 (CAT/C/CR/30/2) para. 7 (d).

[38] See CCPR/CO/77/EST, para. 8, CCPR/CO/75/NZL, para. 11, CCPR/CO/76/EGY, para. 16, CCPR/CO/75/MDA, para. 8, CCPR/CO/75/YEM, para. 18, CCPR/CO/73/UK, para. 6, CCPR/CO/83/UZB, para. 18, and CCPR/C/NOR/CO/5, para. 9.

[39] Communication No. 1472/2006, *Sayadi and Vinck v. Belgium*, 22 October 2008.

[40] Adopted by the General Assembly in resolution 40/34 of 29 November 1985.

46. Human rights principles and guidelines that would comprehensively address victims of counter-terrorism deserve serious consideration, by drawing on national and international best practice and based on the Basic Principles and Guidelines on the Right to a Remedy and Reparation for Victims of Gross Violations of International Human Rights Law and Serious Violations of International Humanitarian Law (Basic Principles and Guidelines),[41] and the set of principles for the protection and promotion of human rights through action to combat impunity.[42]

47. The Basic Principles and Guidelines provide for different categories of reparation. Since torture constitutes a particularly serious violation of human rights, criminal prosecution and appropriate punishment is perceived by the victim as the most effective means of satisfaction and justice. Criminal investigations serve the purpose of establishing truth and pave the way for other forms of reparation. Guarantees of non-repetition, such as amending relevant laws, fighting impunity and taking effective preventive or deterrent measures, constitute a form of reparation if torture is practised in a widespread or systematic manner. Monetary compensation for the immaterial damage (pain and suffering) or material damage (rehabilitation costs, etc.) may provide satisfaction as an additional form of reparation.

48. In its general comment No. 15, the Human Rights Committee indicates that under Article 2 (1) of the International Covenant on Civil and Political Rights, the obligation is not limited to a State's citizens, but must be guaranteed to all individuals, regardless of nationality or statelessness, such as asylum-seekers, refugees, migrant workers and others who may find themselves subject to the jurisdictional regulations of the territory in which they are found. Such remedies should be appropriately adapted to take account of the special vulnerability of certain categories of person, including in particular children. As was confirmed by general comment No. 31, this principle also applies to those within the power or effective control of the forces of a State acting outside its territory, regardless of the circumstances in which such power or effective control was obtained. States must ensure that individuals have accessible and effective remedies to vindicate the aforementioned rights, which should be appropriately adapted to the special vulnerability of certain categories of persons, particularly children.

IV. Conclusions and recommendations

49. States are urged to ensure that measures taken to combat crimes of terrorism comply with their obligations under international human rights law, in particular the right to an effective remedy for victims of human rights violations.

50. States are urged to respect all rights, in particular non-derogable rights. It is extremely important that the Member States reconfirm their commitment to the absolute prohibition of torture and cruel, inhuman and degrading treatment, which are not to be permitted under any circumstances.

51. States are urged to cooperate with the special procedures of the Human Rights Council in enforcing accountability mechanisms and measures and means of providing remedies to victims.

52. States are urged to issue a standing invitation to all special procedures of the Human Rights Council, and in particular to the Special Rapporteur on the promotion and protection of human rights and fundamental freedoms while countering terrorism, the Special Rapporteur on torture and other cruel, inhuman or degrading treatment or punishment, the Special Rapporteur on extrajudicial, summary or arbitrary executions and the Working Groups on Arbitrary Detention and on Enforced or Involuntary Disappearances.

---

[41] General Assembly resolution 60/147, annex.
[42] E/CN.4/Sub.2/1997/20/Rev.1, annex II, and E/CN.4/2005/102/Add.1.

INTERNATIONAL LABOUR ORGANIZATION DOCUMENTS

DOCUMENT 59

Full Official Title: International Labor Organization Convention on the Abolition of Forced Labor

Short Title/Acronym/Abbreviation: The (ILO) Forced Labor Convention

Type of Document: This is a treaty, a legal instrument. This convention was adopted by the International Labor Organization in 1957.

Subject: Forced labor

Official Citation: ILO No. 105

Date of Document: June 25, 1957

Date of Adoption: June 25, 1957

Date of General Entry into Force (EIF): January 15, 1959

Number of States Parties as of this printing: 169 (Malaysia and Singapore denounced their ratification)

Date of Signature by the United States: Non applicable

Date of Ratification/Accession/Adhesion: September 25, 1991

Date of Entry into Force as to United States (effective date): September 25, 1991

Supervising Body: International labor Organization

Legal Status/Character of the Instrument/Document as to the United States: The United States is a party to this treaty. As a state party to this treaty it is legally bound to comply with this instrument.

Caution: The status and applicability of this instrument as to the United States may have changed since the date of this publication.

Web Address: http://www.ilo.org/ilolex/cgi-lex/convde.pl?C105

THE (ILO) FORCED LABOR CONVENTION

The General Conference of the International Labour Organisation,

Having been convened at Geneva by the Governing Body of the International Labour Office, and having met in its Fortieth Session on 5 June 1957, and

Having considered the question of forced labour, which is the fourth item on the agenda of the session, and

Having noted the provisions of the Forced Labour Convention, 1930, and

Having noted that the Slavery Convention, 1926, provides that all necessary measures shall be taken to prevent compulsory or forced labour from developing into conditions analogous to slavery and that the Supplementary Convention on the Abolition of Slavery, the Slave Trade and Institutions and Practices Similar to Slavery, 1956, provides for the complete abolition of debt bondage and serfdom, and

Having noted that the Protection of Wages Convention, 1949, provides that wages shall be paid regularly and prohibits methods of payment which deprive the worker of a genuine possibility of terminating his employment, and

Having decided upon the adoption of further proposals with regard to the abolition of certain forms of forced or compulsory labour constituting a violation of the rights of man referred to in the Charter of the United Nations and enunciated by the Universal Declaration of Human Rights, and

Having determined that these proposals shall take the form of an international Convention, adopts this twenty-fifth day of June of the year one thousand nine hundred and fifty-seven the following Convention, which may be cited as the Abolition of Forced Labour Convention, 1957:

Article 1

Each Member of the International Labour Organisation which ratifies this Convention undertakes to suppress and not to make use of any form of forced or compulsory labour—

(a) as a means of political coercion or education or as a punishment for holding or expressing political views or views ideologically opposed to the established political, social or economic system;

(b) as a method of mobilising and using labour for purposes of economic development;

(c) as a means of labour discipline;

(d) as a punishment for having participated in strikes;

(e) as a means of racial, social, national or religious discrimination.

Article 2

Each Member of the International Labour Organisation which ratifies this Convention undertakes to take effective measures to secure the immediate and complete abolition of forced or compulsory labour as specified in Article 1 of this Convention.

Article 3

The formal ratifications of this Convention shall be communicated to the Director-General of the International Labour Office for registration.

Article 4

1. This Convention shall be binding only upon those Members of the International Labour Organisation whose ratifications have been registered with the Director-General.

2. It shall come into force twelve months after the date on which the ratifications of two Members have been registered with the Director-General.

3. Thereafter, this Convention shall come into force for any Member twelve months after the date on which its ratification has been registered.

Article 5

1. A Member which has ratified this Convention may denounce it after the expiration of ten years from the date on which the Convention first comes into force, by an act communicated to the Director-General of the International Labour Office for registration. Such denunciation shall not take effect until one year after the date on which it is registered.

2. Each Member which has ratified this Convention and which does not, within the year following the expiration of the period of ten years mentioned in the preceding paragraph, exercise the right of denunciation provided for in this Article, will be bound for another period of ten years and, thereafter, may denounce this Convention at the expiration of each period of ten years under the terms provided for in this Article.

Article 6

1. The Director-General of the International Labour Office shall notify all Members of the International Labour Organisation of the registration of all ratifications and denunciations communicated to him by the Members of the Organisation.

2. When notifying the Members of the Organisation of the registration of the second ratification communicated to him, the Director-General shall draw the attention of the Members of the Organisation to the date upon which the Convention will come into force.

Article 7

The Director-General of the International Labour Office shall communicate to the Secretary-General of the United Nations for registration in accordance with Article 102 of the Charter of the United Nations full particulars of all ratifications and acts of denunciation registered by him in accordance with the provisions of the preceding Articles.

Article 8

At such times as it may consider necessary the Governing Body of the International Labour Office shall present to the General Conference a report on the working of this Convention and shall examine the desirability of placing on the agenda of the Conference the question of its revision in whole or in part.

Article 9

1. Should the Conference adopt a new Convention revising this Convention in whole or in part, then, unless the new Convention otherwise provides:

a) the ratification by a Member of the new revising Convention shall ipso jure involve the immediate denunciation of this Convention, notwithstanding the provisions of Article 5 above, if and when the new revising Convention shall have come into force;

b) as from the date when the new revising Convention comes into force this Convention shall cease to be open to ratification by the Members.

2. This Convention shall in any case remain in force in its actual form and content for those Members which have ratified it but have not ratified the revising Convention.

Article 10

The English and French versions of the text of this Convention are equally authoritative.

DOCUMENT 60

Full Official Title: Convention Concerning the Prohibition and Immediate Action for the Elimination of the Worst Forms of Child Labour

Short Title/Acronym/Abbreviation: Nothing official

Subject: The attempt to prohibit and eliminate the most destructive forms of child labor worldwide in a multilateral treaty.

Official Citation: International Labour Organization, C182 Worst Forms of Child Labour Convention, 1999

Date of Document: Not applicable

Date of Adoption: June 17, 1999

Date of General Entry into Force (EIF): Had not entered into force as of this printing

Number of States Parties to this treaty as of this printing: 172

Date of Signature by United States: November 5, 1999

Date of Ratification/Accession/Adhesion: December 2, 1999

Date of Entry into Force as to United States (effective date): Had not entered into force as of this printing.

Type of Document: An international instrument; a treaty

Legal Status/Character of the Instrument/Document as to the United States: Not legally binding

Comments: The United States is one of the first States to ratify this Convention. It will not be binding on the United States until the treaty enters into force. It will be interpreted in light of the RDU's submitted with the ratification.

Caution: The status and applicability of this instrument as to the United States may have changed since date of publication. The above information may be updated by referring to any of the following sites:

Web address: http://www.ilo.org/public/english/standards/relm/ilc/ilc87/com-chic.htm

CONVENTION CONCERNING THE PROHIBITION AND IMMEDIATE ACTION FOR THE ELIMINATION OF THE WORST FORMS OF CHILD LABOUR (EXCERPTS)

(Note: This convention has not yet come into force):

Convention: C182

Place: Geneva

Session of the Conference: 87

Date of adoption: June 17, 1999

The General Conference of the International Labour Organization,

Having been convened at Geneva by the Governing Body of the International Labour Office, and having met in its 87th Session on 1 June 1999, and

Considering the need to adopt new instruments for the prohibition and elimination of the worst forms of child labour, as the main priority for national and international action, including international cooperation and assistance, to complement the Convention and the Recommendation concerning Minimum Age for Admission to Employment, 1973, which remain fundamental instruments on child labour, and

Considering that the effective elimination of the worst forms of child labour requires immediate and comprehensive action, taking into account the importance of free basic education and the need to remove the children concerned from all such work and to provide for their rehabilitation and social integration while addressing the needs of their families, and

Recalling the resolution concerning the elimination of child labour adopted by the International Labour Conference at its 83rd Session in 1996, and

Recognizing that child labour is to a great extent caused by poverty and that the long-term solution lies in sustained economic growth leading to social progress, in particular poverty alleviation and universal education, and

Recalling the Convention on the Rights of the Child adopted by the United Nations General Assembly on 20 November 1989, and

Recalling the ILO Declaration on Fundamental Principles and Rights at Work and its Follow-up, adopted by the International Labour Conference at its 86th Session in 1998, and

Recalling that some of the worst forms of child labour are covered by other international instruments, in particular the Forced Labour Convention, 1930, and the United Nations Supplementary Convention on the Abolition of Slavery, the Slave Trade, and Institutions and Practices Similar to Slavery, 1956, and

Having decided upon the adoption of certain proposals with regard to child labour, which is the fourth item on the agenda of the session, and

Having determined that these proposals shall take the form of an international Convention;

Adopts this seventeenth day of June of the year one thousand nine hundred and ninety-nine the following Convention, which may be cited as the Worst Forms of Child Labour Convention, 1999.

Article 1

Each Member which ratifies this Convention shall take immediate and effective measures to secure the prohibition and elimination of the worst forms of child labour as a matter of urgency.

Article 2

For the purposes of this Convention, the term *child* shall apply to all persons under the age of 18.

Article 3

For the purposes of this Convention, the term *the worst forms of child labour* comprises:

(a) all forms of slavery or practices similar to slavery, such as the sale and trafficking of children, debt bondage and serfdom and forced or compulsory labour, including forced or compulsory recruitment of children for use in armed conflict;

(b) the use, procuring or offering of a child for prostitution, for the production of pornography or for pornographic performances;

(c) the use, procuring or offering of a child for illicit activities, in particular for the production and trafficking of drugs as defined in the relevant international treaties;

(d) work which, by its nature or the circumstances in which it is carried out, is likely to harm the health, safety or morals of children.

Article 4

1. The types of work referred to under Article 3(d) shall be determined by national laws or regulations or by the competent authority, after consultation with the organizations of employers and workers concerned, taking into consideration relevant international standards, in particular Paragraphs 3 and 4 of the Worst Forms of Child Labour Recommendation, 1999. . . .

. . .

Article 7

1. Each Member shall take all necessary measures to ensure the effective implementation and enforcement. . . .

2. Each Member shall, taking into account the importance of education in eliminating child labour, take effective and time-bound measures to:

(a) prevent the engagement of children in the worst forms of child labour;

(b) provide the necessary and appropriate direct assistance for the removal of children from the worst forms of child labour and for their rehabilitation and social integration;

(c) ensure access to free basic education, and, wherever possible and appropriate, vocational training, for all children removed from the worst forms of child labour;

(d) identify and reach out to children at special risk; and

(e) take account of the special situation of girls. . . .

. . .

Article 10

1. This Convention shall be binding only upon those Members of the International Labour Organization whose ratifications have been registered with the Director-General of the International Labour Office.

2. It shall come into force 12 months after the date on which the ratifications of two Members have been registered with the Director-General.

3. Thereafter, this Convention shall come into force for any Member 12 months after the date on which its ratification has been registered.

Article 11

1. A Member which has ratified this Convention may denounce it after the expiration of ten years from the date on which the Convention first comes into force, by an act communicated to the Director-General of the International Labour Office for registration. Such denunciation shall not take effect until one year after the date on which it is registered....

U.S. RATIFICATION OF THE ILO CONVENTION No. 182

[Congressional Record: November 5, 1999 (Senate)]

[Page S14226]

From the Congressional Record Online

Convention (No. 182) for Elimination of the Worst Forms of Child Labor

The resolution of ratification is as follows:

Resolved (two-thirds of the Senators present concurring therein), That the Senate advise and consent to the ratification of Convention (No. 182) Concerning the Prohibition and Immediate Action for the Elimination of the Worst Forms of Child Labor, adopted by the International Labor Conference at its 87th Session in Geneva on June 17, 1999 (Treaty Doc. 106–5), subject to the understandings of subsection (a), the declaration of subsection (b), and the proviso of subsection (c).

(a) Understandings. The Senate's advice and consent is subject to the following understandings, which shall be included in the instrument of ratification:

Children working on farms. The United States understands that Article 3(d) of Convention 182 does not encompass situations in which children are employed by a parent or by a person standing in the place of a parent on a farm owned or operated by such parent or person, nor does it change, or is it intended to lead to a change in the agricultural employment provisions or any other provision of the Fair Labor Standards Act in the United States.

Basic education. The United States understands that the term "basic education" in Article 7 of Convention 182 means primary education plus one year: eight or nine years of schooling, based on curriculum and not age.

(b) Declaration. The Senate's advice and consent is subject to the following declaration, which shall be binding on the President.

Treaty interpretation. The Senate affirms the applicability to all treaties of the constitutionally based principles of treaty interpretation set forth in Condition

(1) of the resolution of ratification of the INF Treaty, approved by the Senate on May 27, 1988, and Condition (8) of the resolution of ratification of the Document Agreed Among the States Parties to the Treaty on Conventional Armed Forces in Europe, approved by the Senate on May 14, 1997.

(c) Proviso. The resolution of ratification is subject to the following proviso, which shall not be included in the instrument of ratification to be signed by the President.

Supremacy of the constitution. Nothing in the Treaty requires or authorizes legislation or other action by the United States of America that is prohibited by the Constitution of the United States as interpreted by the United States.

ORGANIZATION OF AMERICAN STATES DOCUMENTS

DOCUMENT 61

Full Official Title: Charter of the Organization of American States

Short Title/Acronym/Abbreviation: The OAS Charter

Type of Document: This is a treaty, a legal instrument which establishes an international inter-governmental organization.

Subject: Creating an IGO for states in the North, Central and South American Regions

Official Citation: OAS, Treaty Series, Nos. 1-C and 61

U.N. Registration: 01/16/52 No. 1609 Vol. 119

Date of Document: April 30, 1948

Date of Adoption: April 30, 1948

Date of General Entry into Force (EIF): December 13, 1951

Number of States Parties as of this printing: 35

Date of Signature by the United States: April 30, 1948

Date of Ratification/Accession/Adhesion: May 15, 1951

Date of Entry into Force as to United States (effective date): June 15, 1951

Legal Status/Character of the Instrument/Document as to the Unite States: a binding legal instrument binding on the U.S making it a member of the OAS and obligating it to act consistently with that treaty.

Supervising Body: OAS General Assembly

Caution: The status and applicability of this instrument as to the United States may have changed since the date of this publication. The above information may be updated by referring to the following site:

Web Address: http://treaties.un.org/doc/Treaties/1958/08/19580811%2001-34%20AM/Ch_XVI_2p.pdf

CHARTER OF THE ORGANIZATION OF AMERICAN STATES (A-41)

As amended by the Protocol of Amendment to the Charter of the Organization of American States "Protocol of Buenos Aires", signed on February 27, 1967, at the Third Special Inter-American Conference, by the Protocol of Amendment to the Charter of the Organization of American States "Protocol of Cartagena de Indias", approved on December 5, 1985, at the Fourteenth Special Session of the General Assembly, by the Protocol of Amendment to the Charter of the Organization of American States "Protocol of Washington", approved on December 14, 1992, at the Sixteenth Special Session of the General Assembly, and by the Protocol of Amendment to the Charter of the Organization of American States "Protocol of Managua", adopted on June 10, 1993, at the Nineteenth Special Session of the General Assembly.

CHARTER OF THE ORGANIZATION OF AMERICAN STATES* IN THE NAME OF THEIR PEOPLES, THE STATES REPRESENTED AT THE NINTH INTERNATIONAL CONFERENCE OF AMERICAN STATES,

Convinced that the historic mission of America is to offer to man a land of liberty and a favorable environment for the development of his personality and the realization of his just aspirations;

Conscious that that mission has already inspired numerous agreements, whose essential value lies in the desire of the American peoples to live together in peace and, through their mutual understanding and respect for the sovereignty of each one, to provide for the betterment of all, in independence, in equality and under law;

Convinced that representative democracy is an indispensable condition for the stability, peace and development of the region;

---

*Signed in Bogotá in 1948 and amended by the Protocol of Buenos Aires in 1967, by the Protocol of Cartagena de Indias in 1985, by the Protocol of Washington in 1992, and by the Protocol of Managua in 1993.

Confident that the true significance of American solidarity and good neighborliness can only mean the consolidation on this continent, within the framework of democratic institutions, of a system of individual liberty and social justice based on respect for the essential rights of man;

Persuaded that their welfare and their contribution to the progress and the civilization of the world will increasingly require intensive continental cooperation;

Resolved to persevere in the noble undertaking that humanity has conferred upon the United Nations, whose principles and purposes they solemnly reaffirm;

Convinced that juridical organization is a necessary condition for security and peace founded on moral order and on justice;

and

In accordance with Resolution IX of the Inter-American Conference on Problems of War and Peace, held in Mexico City,

HAVE AGREED

upon the following

CHARTER OF THE ORGANIZATION OF AMERICAN STATES

Part One

Chapter I

NATURE AND PURPOSES

Article 1

The American States establish by this Charter the international organization that they have developed to achieve an order of peace and justice, to promote their solidarity, to strengthen their collaboration, and to defend their sovereignty, their territorial integrity, and their independence. Within the United Nations, the Organization of American States is a regional agency.

The Organization of American States has no powers other than those expressly conferred upon it by this Charter, none of whose provisions authorizes it to intervene in matters that are within the internal jurisdiction of the Member States.

Article 2

The Organization of American States, in order to put into practice the principles on which it is founded and to fulfill its regional obligations under the Charter of the United Nations, proclaims the following essential purposes:

a) To strengthen the peace and security of the continent;

b) To promote and consolidate representative democracy, with due respect for the principle of nonintervention;

c) To prevent possible causes of difficulties and to ensure the pacific settlement of disputes that may arise among the Member States;

d) To provide for common action on the part of those States in the event of aggression;

e) To seek the solution of political, juridical, and economic problems that may arise among them;

f) To promote, by cooperative action, their economic, social, and cultural development;

g) To eradicate extreme poverty, which constitutes an obstacle to the full democratic development of the peoples of the hemisphere; and

h) To achieve an effective limitation of conventional weapons that will make it possible to devote the largest amount of resources to the economic and social development of the Member States.

Chapter II

PRINCIPLES

Article 3

The American States reaffirm the following principles:

a) International law is the standard of conduct of States in their reciprocal relations;

b) International order consists essentially of respect for the personality, sovereignty, and independence of States, and the faithful fulfillment of obligations derived from treaties and other sources of international law;

c) Good faith shall govern the relations between States;

d) The solidarity of the American States and the high aims which are sought through it require the political organization of those States on the basis of the effective exercise of representative democracy;

e) Every State has the right to choose, without external interference, its political, economic, and social system and to organize itself in the way best suited to it, and has the duty to abstain from intervening in the affairs of another State. Subject to the foregoing, the American States shall cooperate fully among themselves, independently of the nature of their political, economic, and social systems;

f) The elimination of extreme poverty is an essential part of the promotion and consolidation of representative democracy and is the common and shared responsibility of the American States;

g) The American States condemn war of aggression: victory does not give rights;

h) An act of aggression against one American State is an act of aggression against all the other American States;

i) Controversies of an international character arising between two or more American States shall be settled by peaceful procedures;

j) Social justice and social security are bases of lasting peace;

k) Economic cooperation is essential to the common welfare and prosperity of the peoples of the continent;

l) The American States proclaim the fundamental rights of the individual without distinction as to race, nationality, creed, or sex;

m) The spiritual unity of the continent is based on respect for the cultural values of the American countries and requires their close cooperation for the high purposes of civilization;

n) The education of peoples should be directed toward justice, freedom, and peace.

Chapter III
MEMBERS
Article 4

All American States that ratify the present Charter are Members of the Organization.

Article 5

Any new political entity that arises from the union of several Member States and that, as such, ratifies the present Charter, shall become a Member of the Organization. The entry of the new political entity into the Organization shall result in the loss of membership of each one of the States which constitute it.

Article 6

Any other independent American State that desires to become a Member of the Organization should so indicate by means of a note addressed to the Secretary General, in which it declares that it is willing to sign and ratify the Charter of the Organization and to accept all the obligations inherent in membership, especially those relating to collective security expressly set forth in Articles 28 and 29 of the Charter.

Article 7

The General Assembly, upon the recommendation of the Permanent Council of the Organization, shall determine whether it is appropriate that the Secretary General be authorized to permit the applicant State to sign the Charter and to accept the deposit of the corresponding instrument of ratification. Both the recommendation of the Permanent Council and the decision of the General Assembly shall require the affirmative vote of two thirds of the Member States.

Article 8

Membership in the Organization shall be confined to independent States of the Hemisphere that were Members of the United Nations as of December 10, 1985, and the nonautonomous territories mentioned in document OEA/Ser. P, AG/doc.1939/85, of November 5, 1985, when they become independent.

Article 9

A Member of the Organization whose democratically constituted government has been overthrown by force may be suspended from the exercise of the right to participate in the sessions of the General Assembly, the Meeting of Consultation, the Councils of the Organization and the Specialized Conferences as well as in the commissions, working groups and any other bodies established.

a) The power to suspend shall be exercised only when such diplomatic initiatives undertaken by the Organization for the purpose of promoting the restoration of representative democracy in the affected Member State have been unsuccessful;

b) The decision to suspend shall be adopted at a special session of the General Assembly by an affirmative vote of two-thirds of the Member States;

c) The suspension shall take effect immediately following its approval by the General Assembly;

d) The suspension notwithstanding, the Organization shall endeavor to undertake additional diplomatic initiatives to contribute to the re-establishment of representative democracy in the affected Member State;

e) The Member which has been subject to suspension shall continue to fulfill its obligations to the Organization;

f) The General Assembly may lift the suspension by a decision adopted with the approval of two-thirds of the Member States;

g) The powers referred to in this article shall be exercised in accordance with this Charter.

Chapter IV

FUNDAMENTAL RIGHTS AND DUTIES OF STATES

Article 10

States are juridically equal, enjoy equal rights and equal capacity to exercise these rights, and have equal duties. The rights of each State depend not upon its power to ensure the exercise thereof, but upon the mere fact of its existence as a person under international law.

Article 11

Every American State has the duty to respect the rights enjoyed by every other State in accordance with international law.

Article 12

The fundamental rights of States may not be impaired in any manner whatsoever.

Article 13

The political existence of the State is independent of recognition by other States. Even before being recognized, the State has the right to defend its integrity and independence, to provide for its preservation and prosperity, and consequently to organize itself as it sees fit, to legislate concerning its interests, to administer its services, and to determine the jurisdiction and competence of its courts. The exercise of these rights is limited only by the exercise of the rights of other States in accordance with international law.

Article 14

Recognition implies that the State granting it accepts the personality of the new State, with all the rights and duties that international law prescribes for the two States.

Article 15

The right of each State to protect itself and to live its own life does not authorize it to commit unjust acts against another State.

Article 16

The jurisdiction of States within the limits of their national territory is exercised equally over all the inhabitants, whether nationals or aliens.

Article 17

Each State has the right to develop its cultural, political, and economic life freely and naturally. In this free development, the State shall respect the rights of the individual and the principles of universal morality.

Article 18

Respect for and the faithful observance of treaties constitute standards for the development of peaceful relations among States. International treaties and agreements should be public.

Article 19

No State or group of States has the right to intervene, directly or indirectly, for any reason whatever, in the internal or external affairs of any other State. The foregoing principle prohibits not only armed force but also any other form of interference or attempted threat against the personality of the State or against its political, economic, and cultural elements.

Article 20

No State may use or encourage the use of coercive measures of an economic or political character in order to force the sovereign will of another State and obtain from it advantages of any kind.

Article 21

The territory of a State is inviolable; it may not be the object, even temporarily, of military occupation or of other measures of force taken by another State, directly or indirectly, on any grounds whatever. No territorial acquisitions or special advantages obtained either by force or by other means of coercion shall be recognized.

Article 22

The American States bind themselves in their international relations not to have recourse to the use of force, except in the case of self-defense in accordance with existing treaties or in fulfillment thereof.

Article 23

Measures adopted for the maintenance of peace and security in accordance with existing treaties do not constitute a violation of the principles set forth in Articles 19 and 21.

Chapter V
PACIFIC SETTLEMENT OF DISPUTES
Article 24

International disputes between Member States shall be submitted to the peaceful procedures set forth in this Charter.

This provision shall not be interpreted as an impairment of the rights and obligations of the Member States under Articles 34 and 35 of the Charter of the United Nations.

Article 25

The following are peaceful procedures: direct negotiation, good offices, mediation, investigation and conciliation, judicial settlement, arbitration, and those which the parties to the dispute may especially agree upon at any time.

Article 26

In the event that a dispute arises between two or more American States which, in the opinion of one of them, cannot be settled through the usual diplomatic channels, the parties shall agree on some other peaceful procedure that will enable them to reach a solution.

Article 27

A special treaty will establish adequate means for the settlement of disputes and will determine pertinent procedures for each peaceful means such that no dispute between American States may remain without definitive settlement within a reasonable period of time.

Chapter VI
COLLECTIVE SECURITY
Article 28

Every act of aggression by a State against the territorial integrity or the inviolability of the territory or against the sovereignty or political independence of an American State shall be considered an act of aggression against the other American States.

Article 29

If the inviolability or the integrity of the territory or the sovereignty or political independence of any American State should be affected by an armed attack or by an act of aggression that is not an armed attack, or by an extracontinental conflict, or by a conflict between two or more American States, or by any other fact or situation that might endanger the peace of America, the American States, in furtherance of the principles of continental solidarity or collective self-defense, shall apply the measures and procedures established in the special treaties on the subject.

Chapter VII
INTEGRAL DEVELOPMENT
Article 30

The Member States, inspired by the principles of inter-American solidarity and cooperation, pledge themselves to a united effort to ensure international social justice in their relations and integral development for their peoples, as conditions essential to peace and security. Integral development encompasses the economic, social, educational, cultural, scientific, and technological fields through which the goals that each country sets for accomplishing it should be achieved.

Article 31

Inter-American cooperation for integral development is the common and joint responsibility of the Member States, within the framework of the democratic principles and the institutions of the inter-American system. It should include the economic, social, educational, cultural, scientific, and technological fields, support the achievement of national objectives of the Member States, and respect the priorities established by each country in its development plans, without political ties or conditions.

Article 32

Inter-American cooperation for integral development should be continuous and preferably channeled through multilateral organizations, without prejudice to bilateral cooperation between Member States.

The Member States shall contribute to inter-American cooperation for integral development in accordance with their resources and capabilities and in conformity with their laws.

Article 33

Development is a primary responsibility of each country and should constitute an integral and continuous process for the establishment of a more just economic and social order that will make possible and contribute to the fulfillment of the individual.

Article 34

The Member States agree that equality of opportunity, the elimination of extreme poverty, equitable distribution of wealth and income and the full participation of their peoples in decisions relating to their own development are, among others, basic objectives of integral development. To achieve them, they likewise agree to devote their utmost efforts to accomplishing the following basic goals:

a) Substantial and self-sustained increase of per capita national product;

b) Equitable distribution of national income;

c) Adequate and equitable systems of taxation;

d) Modernization of rural life and reforms leading to equitable and efficient land-tenure systems, increased agricultural productivity, expanded use of land, diversification of production and improved processing and marketing systems for agricultural products; and the strengthening and expansion of the means to attain these ends;

e) Accelerated and diversified industrialization, especially of capital and intermediate goods;

f) Stability of domestic price levels, compatible with sustained economic development and the attainment of social justice;

g) Fair wages, employment opportunities, and acceptable working conditions for all;

h) Rapid eradication of illiteracy and expansion of educational opportunities for all;

i) Protection of man's potential through the extension and application of modern medical science;

j) Proper nutrition, especially through the acceleration of national efforts to increase the production and availability of food;

k) Adequate housing for all sectors of the population;

l) Urban conditions that offer the opportunity for a healthful, productive, and full life;

m) Promotion of private initiative and investment in harmony with action in the public sector; and

n) Expansion and diversification of exports.

Article 35

The Member States should refrain from practicing policies and adopting actions or measures that have serious adverse effects on the development of other Member States.

Article 36

Transnational enterprises and foreign private investment shall be subject to the legislation of the host countries and to the jurisdiction of their competent courts and to the international treaties and agreements to which said countries are parties, and should conform to the development policies of the recipient countries.

Article 37

The Member States agree to join together in seeking a solution to urgent or critical problems that may arise whenever the economic development or stability of any Member State is seriously affected by conditions that cannot be remedied through the efforts of that State.

Article 38

The Member States shall extend among themselves the benefits of science and technology by encouraging the exchange and utilization of scientific and technical knowledge in accordance with existing treaties and national laws.

Article 39

The Member States, recognizing the close interdependence between foreign trade and economic and social development, should make individual and united efforts to bring about the following:

a) Favorable conditions of access to world markets for the products of the developing countries of the region, particularly through the reduction or elimination, by importing countries, of tariff and nontariff barriers that affect the exports of the Member States of the Organization, except when such barriers are applied in order to diversify the economic structure, to speed up the development of the less-developed Member States, and intensify their process of economic integration, or when they are related to national security or to the needs of economic balance;

b) Continuity in their economic and social development by means of:

i. Improved conditions for trade in basic commodities through international agreements, where appropriate; orderly marketing procedures that avoid the disruption of markets, and other measures designed to promote the expansion of markets and to obtain dependable incomes for producers, adequate and dependable supplies for consumers, and stable prices that are both remunerative to producers and fair to consumers;

ii. Improved international financial cooperation and the adoption of other means for lessening the adverse impact of sharp fluctuations in export earnings experienced by the countries exporting basic commodities;

iii. Diversification of exports and expansion of export opportunities for manufactured and semimanu-factured products from the developing countries; and

iv. Conditions conducive to increasing the real export earnings of the Member States, particularly the developing countries of the region, and to increasing their participation in international trade.

Article 40

The Member States reaffirm the principle that when the more developed countries grant concessions in international trade agreements that lower or eliminate tariffs or other barriers to foreign trade so that they benefit the less-developed countries, they should not expect reciprocal concessions from those countries that are incompatible with their economic development, financial, and trade needs.

Article 41

The Member States, in order to accelerate their economic development, regional integration, and the expansion and improvement of the conditions of their commerce, shall promote improvement and coordination of transportation and communication in the developing countries and among the Member States.

Article 42

The Member States recognize that integration of the developing countries of the Hemisphere is one of the objectives of the inter-American system and, therefore, shall orient their efforts and take the necessary measures to accelerate the integration process, with a view to establishing a Latin American common market in the shortest possible time.

Article 43

In order to strengthen and accelerate integration in all its aspects, the Member States agree to give adequate priority to the preparation and carrying out of multinational projects and to their financing, as well as to encourage economic and financial institutions of the inter-American system to continue giving their broadest support to regional integration institutions and programs.

Article 44

The Member States agree that technical and financial cooperation that seeks to promote regional economic integration should be based on the principle of harmonious, balanced, and efficient development, with particular attention to the relatively less-developed countries, so that it may be a decisive factor that will enable them to promote, with their own efforts, the improved development of their infrastructure programs, new lines of production, and export diversification.

Article 45

The Member States, convinced that man can only achieve the full realization of his aspirations within a just social order, along with economic development and true peace, agree to dedicate every effort to the application of the following principles and mechanisms:

a) All human beings, without distinction as to race, sex, nationality, creed, or social condition, have a right to material well-being and to their spiritual development, under circumstances of liberty, dignity, equality of opportunity, and economic security;

b) Work is a right and a social duty, it gives dignity to the one who performs it, and it should be performed under conditions, including a system of fair wages, that ensure life, health, and a decent standard of living for the worker and his family, both during his working years and in his old age, or when any circumstance deprives him of the possibility of working;

c) Employers and workers, both rural and urban, have the right to associate themselves freely for the defense and promotion of their interests, including the right to collective bargaining and the workers' right to strike, and recognition of the juridical personality of associations and the protection of their freedom and independence, all in accordance with applicable laws;

d) Fair and efficient systems and procedures for consultation and collaboration among the sectors of production, with due regard for safeguarding the interests of the entire society;

e) The operation of systems of public administration, banking and credit, enterprise, and distribution and sales, in such a way, in harmony with the private sector, as to meet the requirements and interests of the community;

f) The incorporation and increasing participation of the marginal sectors of the population, in both rural and urban areas, in the economic, social, civic, cultural, and political life of the nation, in order to achieve the full integration of the national community, acceleration of the process of social mobility, and the consolidation of the democratic system. The encouragement of all efforts of popular promotion and cooperation that have as their purpose the development and progress of the community;

g) Recognition of the importance of the contribution of organizations such as labor unions, cooperatives, and cultural, professional, business, neighborhood, and community associations to the life of the society and to the development process;

h) Development of an efficient social security policy; and

i) Adequate provision for all persons to have due legal aid in order to secure their rights.

Article 46

The Member States recognize that, in order to facilitate the process of Latin American regional integration, it is necessary to harmonize the social legislation of the developing countries, especially in the labor and social security fields, so that the rights of the workers shall be equally protected, and they agree to make the greatest efforts possible to achieve this goal.

Article 47

The Member States will give primary importance within their development plans to the encouragement of education, science, technology, and culture, oriented toward the overall improvement of the individual, and as a foundation for democracy, social justice, and progress.

Article 48

The Member States will cooperate with one another to meet their educational needs, to promote scientific research, and to encourage technological progress for their integral development. They will consider themselves individually and jointly bound to preserve and enrich the cultural heritage of the American peoples.

Article 49

The Member States will exert the greatest efforts, in accordance with their constitutional processes, to ensure the effective exercise of the right to education, on the following bases:

a) Elementary education, compulsory for children of school age, shall also be offered to all others who can benefit from it. When provided by the State it shall be without charge;

b) Middle-level education shall be extended progressively to as much of the population as possible, with a view to social improvement. It shall be diversified in such a way that it meets the development needs of each country without prejudice to providing a general education; and

c) Higher education shall be available to all, provided that, in order to maintain its high level, the corresponding regulatory or academic standards are met.

Article 50

The Member States will give special attention to the eradication of illiteracy, will strengthen adult and vocational education systems, and will ensure that the benefits of culture will be available to the entire population. They will promote the use of all information media to fulfill these aims.

Article 51

The Member States will develop science and technology through educational, research, and technological development activities and information and dissemination programs. They will stimulate activities in the field of technology for the purpose of adapting it to the needs of their integral development. They will organize their cooperation in these fields efficiently and will substantially increase exchange of knowledge, in accordance with national objectives and laws and with treaties in force.

Article 52

The Member States, with due respect for the individuality of each of them, agree to promote cultural exchange as an effective means of consolidating inter-American understanding; and they recognize that regional integration programs should be strengthened by close ties in the fields of education, science, and culture.

Part Two

Chapter VIII

THE ORGANS

Article 53

The Organization of American States accomplishes its purposes by means of:

a) The General Assembly;

b) The Meeting of Consultation of Ministers of Foreign Affairs;

c) The Councils;

d) The Inter-American Juridical Committee;

e) The Inter-American Commission on Human Rights;

f) The General Secretariat;

g) The Specialized Conferences; and

h) The Specialized Organizations. There may be established, in addition to those provided for in the Charter and in accordance with the provisions thereof, such subsidiary organs, agencies, and other entities as are considered necessary.

Chapter IX
THE GENERAL ASSEMBLY
Article 54

The General Assembly is the supreme organ of the Organization of American States. It has as its principal powers, in addition to such others as are assigned to it by the Charter, the following:

a) To decide the general action and policy of the Organization, determine the structure and functions of its organs, and consider any matter relating to friendly relations among the American States;

b) To establish measures for coordinating the activities of the organs, agencies, and entities of the Organization among themselves, and such activities with those of the other institutions of the inter-American system;

c) To strengthen and coordinate cooperation with the United Nations and its specialized agencies;

d) To promote collaboration, especially in the economic, social, and cultural fields, with other international organizations whose purposes are similar to those of the Organization of American States;

e) To approve the program-budget of the Organization and determine the quotas of the Member States;

f) To consider the reports of the Meeting of Consultation of Ministers of Foreign Affairs and the observations and recommendations presented by the Permanent Council with regard to the reports that should be presented by the other organs and entities, in accordance with the provisions of Article 91.f, as well as the reports of any organ which may be required by the General Assembly itself;

g) To adopt general standards to govern the operations of the General Secretariat; and

h) To adopt its own rules of procedure and, by a two-thirds vote, its agenda. The General Assembly shall exercise its powers in accordance with the provisions of the Charter and of other inter-American treaties.

Article 55

The General Assembly shall establish the bases for fixing the quota that each Government is to contribute to the maintenance of the Organization, taking into account the ability to pay of the respective countries and their determination to contribute in an equitable manner. Decisions on budgetary matters require the approval of two thirds of the Member States.

Article 56

All Member States have the right to be represented in the General Assembly. Each State has the right to one vote.

Article 57

The General Assembly shall convene annually during the period determined by the rules of procedure and at a place selected in accordance with the principle of rotation. At each regular session the date and place of the next regular session shall be determined, in accordance with the rules of procedure. If for any reason the General Assembly cannot be held at the place chosen, it shall meet at the General Secretariat, unless one of the Member States should make a timely offer of a site in its territory, in which case the Permanent Council of the Organization may agree that the General Assembly will meet in that place.

Article 58

In special circumstances and with the approval of two thirds of the Member States, the Permanent Council shall convoke a special session of the General Assembly.

Article 59

Decisions of the General Assembly shall be adopted by the affirmative vote of an absolute majority of the Member States, except in those cases that require a two-thirds vote as provided in the Charter or as may be provided by the General Assembly in its rules of procedure.

Article 60

There shall be a Preparatory Committee of the General Assembly, composed of representatives of all the Member States, which shall:

a) Prepare the draft agenda of each session of the General Assembly;

b) Review the proposed program-budget and the draft resolution on quotas, and present to the General Assembly a report thereon containing the recommendations it considers appropriate; and

c) Carry out such other functions as the General Assembly may assign to it. The draft agenda and the report shall, in due course, be transmitted to the Governments of the Member States.

Chapter X

THE MEETING OF CONSULTATION OF MINISTERS OF FOREIGN AFFAIRS

Article 61

The Meeting of Consultation of Ministers of Foreign Affairs shall be held in order to consider problems of an urgent nature and of common interest to the American States, and to serve as the Organ of Consultation.

Article 62

Any Member State may request that a Meeting of Consultation be called. The request shall be addressed to the Permanent Council of the Organization, which shall decide by an absolute majority whether a meeting should be held.

Article 63

The agenda and regulations of the Meeting of Consultation shall be prepared by the Permanent Council of the Organization and submitted to the Member States for consideration.

Article 64

If, for exceptional reasons, a Minister of Foreign Affairs is unable to attend the meeting, he shall be represented by a special delegate.

Article 65

In case of an armed attack on the territory of an American State or within the region of security delimited by the treaty in force, the Chairman of the Permanent Council shall without delay call a meeting of the Council to decide on the convocation of the Meeting of Consultation, without prejudice to the provisions of the Inter-American Treaty of Reciprocal Assistance with regard to the States Parties to that instrument.

Article 66

An Advisory Defense Committee shall be established to advise the Organ of Consultation on problems of military cooperation that may arise in connection with the application of existing special treaties on collective security.

Article 67

The Advisory Defense Committee shall be composed of the highest military authorities of the American States participating in the Meeting of Consultation. Under exceptional circumstances the Governments may appoint substitutes. Each State shall be entitled to one vote.

Article 68

The Advisory Defense Committee shall be convoked under the same conditions as the Organ of Consultation, when the latter deals with matters relating to defense against aggression.

Article 69

The Committee shall also meet when the General Assembly or the Meeting of Consultation or the Governments, by a two-thirds majority of the Member States, assign to it technical studies or reports on specific subjects.

Chapter XI

THE COUNCILS OF THE ORGANIZATION

Common Provisions

Article 70

The Permanent Council of the Organization and the Inter-American Council for Integral Development are directly responsible to the General Assembly, and each has the authority granted to it in the Charter and other inter-American instruments, as well as the functions assigned to it by the General Assembly and the Meeting of Consultation of Ministers of Foreign Affairs.

Article 71

All Member States have the right to be represented on each of the Councils. Each State has the right to one vote.

Article 72

The Councils may, within the limits of the Charter and other inter-American instruments, make recommendations on matters within their authority.

Article 73

The Councils, on matters within their respective competence, may present to the General Assembly studies and proposals, drafts of international instruments, and proposals on the holding of specialized conferences, on the creation, modification, or elimination of specialized organizations and other inter-American agencies, as well as on the coordination of their activities. The Councils may also present studies, proposals, and drafts of international instruments to the Specialized Conferences.

Article 74

Each Council may, in urgent cases, convoke Specialized Conferences on matters within its competence, after consulting with the Member States and without having to resort to the procedure provided for in Article 122.

Article 75

The Councils, to the extent of their ability, and with the cooperation of the General Secretariat, shall render to the Governments such specialized services as the latter may request.

Article 76

Each Council has the authority to require the other Council, as well as the subsidiary organs and agencies responsible to them, to provide it with information and advisory services on matters within their respective spheres of competence. The Councils may also request the same services from the other agencies of the inter-American system.

Article 77

With the prior approval of the General Assembly, the Councils may establish the subsidiary organs and the agencies that they consider advisable for the better performance of their duties. When the General Assembly is not in session, the aforesaid organs or agencies may be established provisionally by the corresponding Council. In constituting the membership of these bodies, the Councils, insofar as possible, shall follow the criteria of rotation and equitable geographic representation.

Article 78

The Councils may hold meetings in any Member State, when they find it advisable and with the prior consent of the Government concerned.

Article 79

Each Council shall prepare its own statutes and submit them to the General Assembly for approval. It shall approve its own rules of procedure and those of its subsidiary organs, agencies, and committees.

Chapter XII
THE PERMANENT COUNCIL OF THE ORGANIZATION

Article 80

The Permanent Council of the Organization is composed of one representative of each Member State, especially appointed by the respective Government, with the rank of ambassador. Each Government may accredit an acting representative, as well as such alternates and advisers as it considers necessary.

Article 81

The office of Chairman of the Permanent Council shall be held by each of the representatives, in turn, following the alphabetic order in Spanish of the names of their respective countries. The office of Vice Chairman shall be filled in the same way, following reverse alphabetic order. The Chairman and the Vice Chairman shall hold office for a term of not more than six months, which shall be determined by the statutes.

Article 82

Within the limits of the Charter and of inter-American treaties and agreements, the Permanent Council takes cognizance of any matter referred to it by the General Assembly or the Meeting of Consultation of Ministers of Foreign Affairs.

Article 83

The Permanent Council shall serve provisionally as the Organ of Consultation in conformity with the provisions of the special treaty on the subject.

Article 84

The Permanent Council shall keep vigilance over the maintenance of friendly relations among the Member States, and for that purpose shall effectively assist them in the peaceful settlement of their disputes, in accordance with the following provisions.

Article 85

In accordance with the provisions of this Charter, any party to a dispute in which none of the peaceful procedures provided for in the Charter is under way may resort to the Permanent Council to obtain its good offices. The Council, following the provisions of the preceding article, shall assist the parties and recommend the procedures it considers suitable for peaceful settlement of the dispute.

Article 86

In the exercise of its functions and with the consent of the parties to the dispute, the Permanent Council may establish ad hoc committees. The ad hoc committees shall have the membership and the mandate that the Permanent Council agrees upon in each individual case, with the consent of the parties to the dispute.

Article 87

The Permanent Council may also, by such means as it deems advisable, investigate the facts in the dispute, and may do so in the territory of any of the parties, with the consent of the Government concerned.

Article 88

If the procedure for peaceful settlement of disputes recommended by the Permanent Council or suggested by the pertinent ad hoc committee under the terms of its mandate is not accepted by one of the parties, or one of the parties declares that the procedure has not settled the dispute, the Permanent Council shall so inform the General Assembly, without prejudice to its taking steps to secure agreement between the parties or to restore relations between them.

Article 89

The Permanent Council, in the exercise of these functions, shall take its decisions by an affirmative vote of two thirds of its Members, excluding the parties to the dispute, except for such decisions as the rules of procedure provide shall be adopted by a simple majority.

Article 90

In performing their functions with respect to the peaceful settlement of disputes, the Permanent Council and the respective ad hoc committee shall observe the provisions of the Charter and the principles and standards of international law, as well as take into account the existence of treaties in force between the parties.

Article 91

The Permanent Council shall also:

a) Carry out those decisions of the General Assembly or of the Meeting of Consultation of Ministers of Foreign Affairs the implementation of which has not been assigned to any other body;

b) Watch over the observance of the standards governing the operation of the General Secretariat and, when the General Assembly is not in session, adopt provisions of a regulatory nature that enable the General Secretariat to carry out its administrative functions;

c) Act as the Preparatory Committee of the General Assembly, in accordance with the terms of Article 60 of the Charter, unless the General Assembly should decide otherwise;

d) Prepare, at the request of the Member States and with the cooperation of the appropriate organs of the Organization, draft agreements to promote and facilitate cooperation between the Organization of American States and the United Nations or between the Organization and other American agencies of recognized international standing. These draft agreements shall be submitted to the General Assembly for approval;

e) Submit recommendations to the General Assembly with regard to the functioning of the Organization and the coordination of its subsidiary organs, agencies, and committees;

f) Consider the reports of the Inter-American Council for Integral Development, of the Inter-American Juridical Committee, of the Inter-American Commission on Human Rights, of the General Secretariat, of specialized agencies and conferences, and of other bodies and agencies, and present to the General Assembly any observations and recommendations it deems necessary; and

g) Perform the other functions assigned to it in the Charter.

Article 92

The Permanent Council and the General Secretariat shall have the same seat.

Chapter XIII

THE INTER-AMERICAN COUNCIL FOR INTEGRAL DEVELOPMENT

Article 93

The Inter-American Council for Integral Development is composed of one principal representative, of ministerial or equivalent rank, for each Member State, especially appointed by the respective Government. In keeping with the provisions of the Charter, the Inter-American Council for Integral Development may establish the subsidiary bodies and the agencies that it considers advisable for the better performance of its duties.

Article 94

The purpose of the Inter-American Council for Integral Development is to promote cooperation among the American States for the purpose of achieving integral development and, in particular, helping to eliminate extreme poverty, in accordance with the standards of the Charter, especially those set forth in Chapter VII with respect to the economic, social, educational, cultural, scientific, and technological fields.

Article 95

In order to achieve its various goals, especially in the specific area of technical cooperation, the Inter-American Council for Integral Development shall:

a) Formulate and recommend to the General Assembly a strategic plan which sets forth policies, programs, and courses of action in matters of cooperation for integral development, within the framework of the general policy and priorities defined by the General Assembly;

b) Formulate guidelines for the preparation of the program-budget for technical cooperation and for the other activities of the Council;

c) Promote, coordinate, and assign responsibility for the execution of development programs and projects to the subsidiary bodies and relevant organizations, on the basis of the priorities identified by the Member States, in areas such as:

1) Economic and social development, including trade, tourism, integration and the environment;

2) Improvement and extension of education to cover all levels, promotion of scientific and technological research, through technical cooperation, and support for cultural activities; and

3) Strengthening of the civic conscience of the American peoples, as one of the bases for the effective exercise of democracy and for the observance of the rights and duties of man. These ends shall be furthered by sectoral participation mechanisms and other subsidiary bodies and organizations established by the Charter and by other General Assembly provisions.

d) Establish cooperative relations with the corresponding bodies of the United Nations and with other national and international agencies, especially with regard to coordination of inter-American technical cooperation programs.

e) Periodically evaluate cooperation activities for integral development, in terms of their performance in the implementation of policies, programs, and projects, in terms of their impact, effectiveness, efficiency, and use of resources, and in terms of the quality, inter alia, of the technical cooperation services provided; and report to the General Assembly.

Article 96

The Inter-American Council for Integral Development shall hold at least one meeting each year at the ministerial or equivalent level. It shall also have the right to convene meetings at the same level for the specialized or sectorial topics it considers relevant, within its province or sphere of competence. It shall also meet when convoked by the General Assembly or the Meeting of Consultation of Foreign Ministers, or on its own initiative, or for the cases envisaged in Article 37 of the Charter.

Article 97

The Inter-American Council for Integral Development shall have the nonpermanent specialized committees which it decides to establish and which are required for the proper performance of its functions. Those committees shall operate and shall be composed as stipulated in the Statutes of the Council.

Article 98

The execution and, if appropriate, the coordination, of approved projects shall be entrusted to the Executive Secretariat for Integral Development, which shall report on the results of that execution to the Council.

Chapter XIV
THE INTER-AMERICAN JURIDICAL COMMITTEE

Article 99

The purpose of the Inter-American Juridical Committee is to serve the Organization as an advisory body on juridical matters; to promote the progressive development and the codification of international law; and to study juridical problems related to the integration of the developing countries of the Hemisphere and, insofar as may appear desirable, the possibility of attaining uniformity in their legislation.

Article 100

The Inter-American Juridical Committee shall undertake the studies and preparatory work assigned to it by the General Assembly, the Meeting of Consultation of Ministers of Foreign Affairs, or the Councils of the Organization. It may also, on its own initiative, undertake such studies and preparatory work as it considers advisable, and suggest the holding of specialized juridical conferences.

Article 101

The Inter-American Juridical Committee shall be composed of eleven jurists, nationals of Member States, elected by the General Assembly for a period of four years from panels of three candidates presented by Member States. In the election, a system shall be used that takes into account partial replacement of membership and, insofar as possible, equitable geographic representation. No two Members of the Committee may be nationals of the same State. Vacancies that occur for reasons other than normal expiration of the terms of office of the Members of the Committee shall be filled by the Permanent Council of the Organization in accordance with the criteria set forth in the preceding paragraph.

Article 102

The Inter-American Juridical Committee represents all of the Member States of the Organization, and has the broadest possible technical autonomy.

Article 103

The Inter-American Juridical Committee shall establish cooperative relations with universities, institutes, and other teaching centers, as well as with national and international committees and entities devoted to study, research, teaching, or dissemination of information on juridical matters of international interest.

Article 104

The Inter-American Juridical Committee shall draft its statutes, which shall be submitted to the General Assembly for approval. The Committee shall adopt its own rules of procedure.

Article 105

The seat of the Inter-American Juridical Committee shall be the city of Rio de Janeiro, but in special cases the Committee may meet at any other place that may be designated, after consultation with the Member State concerned.

Chapter XV

THE INTER-AMERICAN COMMISSION ON HUMAN RIGHTS

Article 106

There shall be an Inter-American Commission on Human Rights, whose principal function shall be to promote the observance and protection of human rights and to serve as a consultative organ of the Organization in these matters. An inter-American convention on human rights shall determine the structure, competence, and procedure of this Commission, as well as those of other organs responsible for these matters.

Chapter XVI

THE GENERAL SECRETARIAT

Article 107

The General Secretariat is the central and permanent organ of the Organization of American States. It shall perform the functions assigned to it in the Charter, in other inter-American treaties and agreements, and by the General Assembly, and shall carry out the duties entrusted to it by the General Assembly, the Meeting of Consultation of Ministers of Foreign Affairs, or the Councils.

Article 108

The Secretary General of the Organization shall be elected by the General Assembly for a five-year term and may not be reelected more than once or succeeded by a person of the same nationality. In the event that the office of Secretary General becomes vacant, the Assistant Secretary General shall assume his duties until the General Assembly shall elect a new Secretary General for a full term.

Article 109

The Secretary General shall direct the General Secretariat, be the legal representative thereof, and, notwithstanding the provisions of Article 91.b, be responsible to the General Assembly for the proper fulfillment of the obligations and functions of the General Secretariat.

Article 110

The Secretary General, or his representative, may participate with voice but without vote in all meetings of the Organization. The Secretary General may bring to the attention of the General Assembly or the Permanent Council any matter which in his opinion might threaten the peace and security of the Hemisphere or the development of the Member States. The authority to which the preceding paragraph refers shall be exercised in accordance with the present Charter.

Article 111

The General Secretariat shall promote economic, social, juridical, educational, scientific, and cultural relations among all the Member States of the Organization, with special emphasis on cooperation for the elimination of extreme poverty, in keeping with the actions and policies decided upon by the General Assembly and with the pertinent decisions of the Councils.

Article 112

The General Secretariat shall also perform the following functions:

a) Transmit ex officio to the Member States notice of the convocation of the General Assembly, the Meeting of Consultation of Ministers of Foreign Affairs, the Inter-American Council for Integral Development, and the Specialized Conferences;

b) Advise the other organs, when appropriate, in the preparation of agenda and rules of procedure;

c) Prepare the proposed program-budget of the Organization on the basis of programs adopted by the Councils, agencies, and entities whose expenses should be included in the program-budget and, after consultation with the Councils or their permanent committees, submit it to the Preparatory Committee of the General Assembly and then to the Assembly itself;

d) Provide, on a permanent basis, adequate secretariat services for the General Assembly and the other organs, and carry out their directives and assignments. To the extent of its ability, provide services for the other meetings of the Organization;

e) Serve as custodian of the documents and archives of the inter-American Conferences, the General Assembly, the Meetings of Consultation of Ministers of Foreign Affairs, the Councils, and the Specialized Conferences;

f) Serve as depository of inter-American treaties and agreements, as well as of the instruments of ratification thereof;

g) Submit to the General Assembly at each regular session an annual report on the activities of the Organization and its financial condition; and

h) Establish relations of cooperation, in accordance with decisions reached by the General Assembly or the Councils, with the Specialized Organizations as well as other national and international organizations.

Article 113

The Secretary General shall:

a) Establish such offices of the General Secretariat as are necessary to accomplish its purposes; and

b) Determine the number of officers and employees of the General Secretariat, appoint them, regulate their powers and duties, and fix their remuneration. The Secretary General shall exercise this authority in accordance with such general standards and budgetary provisions as may be established by the General Assembly.

Article 114

The Assistant Secretary General shall be elected by the General Assembly for a five-year term and may not be reelected more than once or succeeded by a person of the same nationality. In the event that the office of Assistant Secretary General becomes vacant, the Permanent Council shall elect a substitute to hold that office until the General Assembly shall elect a new Assistant Secretary General for a full term.

Article 115

The Assistant Secretary General shall be the Secretary of the Permanent Council. He shall serve as advisory officer to the Secretary General and shall act as his delegate in all matters that the Secretary General may entrust to him. During the temporary absence or disability of the Secretary General, the Assistant Secretary General shall perform his functions. The Secretary General and the Assistant Secretary General shall be of different nationalities.

Article 116

The General Assembly, by a two-thirds vote of the Member States, may remove the Secretary General or the Assistant Secretary General, or both, whenever the proper functioning of the Organization so demands.

Article 117

The Secretary General shall appoint, with the approval of the Inter-American Council for Integral Development, an Executive Secretary for Integral Development.

Article 118

In the performance of their duties, the Secretary General and the personnel of the Secretariat shall not seek or receive instructions from any Government or from any authority outside the Organization, and shall refrain from any action that may be incompatible with their position as international officers responsible only to the Organization.

Article 119

The Member States pledge themselves to respect the exclusively international character of the responsibilities of the Secretary General and the personnel of the General Secretariat, and not to seek to influence them in the discharge of their duties.

Article 120

In selecting the personnel of the General Secretariat, first consideration shall be given to efficiency, competence, and integrity; but at the same time, in the recruitment of personnel of all ranks, importance shall be given to the necessity of obtaining as wide a geographic representation as possible.

Article 121

The seat of the General Secretariat is the city of Washington, D.C.

Chapter XVII

THE SPECIALIZED CONFERENCES

Article 122

The Specialized Conferences are intergovernmental meetings to deal with special technical matters or to develop specific aspects of inter-American cooperation. They shall be held when either the General Assembly or the Meeting of Consultation of Ministers of Foreign Affairs so decides, on its own initiative or at the request of one of the Councils or Specialized Organizations.

Article 123

The agenda and rules of procedure of the Specialized Conferences shall be prepared by the Councils or Specialized Organizations concerned and shall be submitted to the Governments of the Member States for consideration.

Chapter XVIII

THE SPECIALIZED ORGANIZATIONS

Article 124

For the purposes of the present Charter, Inter-American Specialized Organizations are the intergovernmental organizations established by multilateral agreements and having specific functions with respect to technical matters of common interest to the American States.

Article 125

The General Secretariat shall maintain a register of the organizations that fulfill the conditions set forth in the foregoing Article, as determined by the General Assembly after a report from the Council concerned.

Article 126

The Specialized Organizations shall enjoy the fullest technical autonomy, but they shall take into account the recommendations of the General Assembly and of the Councils, in accordance with the provisions of the Charter.

Article 127

The Specialized Organizations shall transmit to the General Assembly annual reports on the progress of their work and on their annual budgets and expenses.

Article 128

Relations that should exist between the Specialized Organizations and the Organization shall be defined by means of agreements concluded between each organization and the Secretary General, with the authorization of the General Assembly.

Article 129

The Specialized Organizations shall establish cooperative relations with world agencies of the same character in order to coordinate their activities. In concluding agreements with international agencies of a worldwide character, the Inter-American Specialized Organizations shall preserve their identity and their status as integral parts of the Organization of American States, even when they perform regional functions of international agencies.

Article 130

In determining the location of the Specialized Organizations consideration shall be given to the interest of all of the Member States and to the desirability of selecting the seats of these organizations on the basis of a geographic representation as equitable as possible.

Part Three

Chapter XIX

THE UNITED NATIONS

Article 131

None of the provisions of this Charter shall be construed as impairing the rights and obligations of the Member States under the Charter of the United Nations.

Chapter XX

MISCELLANEOUS PROVISIONS

Article 132

Attendance at meetings of the permanent organs of the Organization of American States or at the conferences and meetings provided for in the Charter, or held under the auspices of the Organization, shall be in accordance with the multilateral character of the aforesaid organs, conferences, and meetings and shall not depend on the bilateral relations between the Government of any Member State and the Government of the host country.

Article 133

The Organization of American States shall enjoy in the territory of each Member such legal capacity, privileges, and immunities as are necessary for the exercise of its functions and the accomplishment of its purposes.

Article 134

The representatives of the Member States on the organs of the Organization, the personnel of their delegations, as well as the Secretary General and the Assistant Secretary General shall enjoy the privileges and immunities corresponding to their positions and necessary for the independent performance of their duties.

Article 135

The juridical status of the Specialized Organizations and the privileges and immunities that should be granted to them and to their personnel, as well as to the officials of the General Secretariat, shall be determined in a multilateral agreement. The foregoing shall not preclude, when it is considered necessary, the concluding of bilateral agreements.

Article 136

Correspondence of the Organization of American States, including printed matter and parcels, bearing the frank thereof, shall be carried free of charge in the mails of the Member States.

Article 137

The Organization of American States does not allow any restriction based on race, creed, or sex, with respect to eligibility to participate in the activities of the Organization and to hold positions therein.

Article 138

Within the provisions of this Charter, the competent organs shall endeavor to obtain greater collaboration from countries not Members of the Organization in the area of cooperation for development.

Chapter XXI

RATIFICATION AND ENTRY INTO FORCE

Article 139

The present Charter shall remain open for signature by the American States and shall be ratified in accordance with their respective constitutional procedures. The original instrument, the Spanish, English, Portuguese, and French texts of which are equally authentic, shall be deposited with the General Secretariat, which shall transmit certified copies thereof to the Governments for purposes of ratification. The instruments of ratification shall be deposited with the General Secretariat, which shall notify the signatory States of such deposit.

Article 140

The present Charter shall enter into force among the ratifying States when two thirds of the signatory States have deposited their ratifications. It shall enter into force with respect to the remaining States in the order in which they deposit their ratifications.

Article 141

The present Charter shall be registered with the Secretariat of the United Nations through the General Secretariat.

Article 142

Amendments to the present Charter may be adopted only at a General Assembly convened for that purpose. Amendments shall enter into force in accordance with the terms and the procedure set forth in Article 140.

Article 143

The present Charter shall remain in force indefinitely, but may be denounced by any Member State upon written notification to the General Secretariat, which shall communicate to all the others each notice of denunciation received. After two years from the date on which the General Secretariat receives a notice of denunciation, the present Charter shall cease to be in force with respect to the denouncing State, which shall cease to belong to the Organization after it has fulfilled the obligations arising from the present Charter.

Chapter XXII

TRANSITORY PROVISIONS

Article 144

The Inter-American Committee on the Alliance for Progress shall act as the permanent executive committee of the Inter-American Economic and Social Council as long as the Alliance is in operation.

Article 145

Until the Inter-American Convention on Human Rights, referred to in Chapter XV, enters into force, the present Inter-American Commission on Human Rights shall keep vigilance over the observance of human rights.

Article 146

The Permanent Council shall not make any recommendation nor shall the General Assembly take any decision with respect to a request for admission on the part of a political entity whose territory became subject, in whole or in part, prior to December 18, 1964, the date set by the First Special Inter-American Conference, to litigation or claim between an extracontinental country and one or more Member States of the Organization, until the dispute has been ended by some peaceful procedure. This article shall remain in effect until December 10, 1990.

DOCUMENT 62

Full Official Title: American Declaration of the Rights and Duties of Man

Short Title/Acronym/Abbreviation: The American Declaration/ADHR

Subject: Establishment of basic human rights norms in the western hemisphere.

Official Citation: O.A.S. Res.XXX, adopted by the Ninth International Conference of American States (1948), OEA/Ser.L.V/II.82 doc.6, rev1 at 17 (1992).

Date of Document: Not applicable

Date of Adoption: May 2, 1948

Date of General Entry into Force (EIF): Not applicable

Number of States Parties to this Treaty as of this printing: Not a treaty

Date of Signature by United States: Not applicable

Date of Ratification/Accession/Adhesion: Not applicable

Date of Entry into Force as to United States (effective date): Not applicable

Type of Document: Not a legal instrument, a declaration of an international inter-governmental organization as to what human rights are in the Americas.

Legal Status/Character of the Instrument/Document as to the United States: Not legally a treaty. However, it is made applicable to the United States as a basis of human rights standards as to complaints, which can be filed in the Inter-American Commission on Human Rights.

Comments: Several cases have been filed against the United States in the Inter-American Commission alleging violations of the ADHR. See Appendix on Cases: Cherokee Nation and Haitian Refugee Centre cases.

Caution: The status and applicability of this instrument as to the United States may have changed since date of publication. The above information may be updated by referring to the following site:

Web address: http://www.cidh.oas.org/Basic%20Documents/enbas2.htm

AMERICAN DECLARATION OF THE RIGHTS AND DUTIES OF MAN (ADHR)

Whereas:

The American peoples have acknowledged the dignity of the individual, and their national constitutions recognize that juridical and political institutions, which regulate life in human society, have as their principal aim the protection of the essential rights of man and the creation of circumstances that will permit him to achieve spiritual and material progress and attain happiness;

The American States have on repeated occasions recognized that the essential rights of man are not derived from the fact that he is a national of a certain state, but are based upon attributes of his human personality;

The international protection of the rights of man should be the principal guide of an evolving American law;

The affirmation of essential human rights by the American States together with the guarantees given by the internal regimes of the states establish the initial system of protection considered by the American States as being suited to the present social and juridical conditions, not without a recognition on their part that they should increasingly strengthen that system in the international field as conditions become more favorable,

Ninth International Conference of American States,

Agrees to adopt the following American Declaration of the Rights and Duties of Man.

Preamble

All men are born free and equal, in dignity and in rights, and, being endowed by nature with reason and conscience, they should conduct themselves as brothers one to another.

The fulfillment of duty by each individual is a prerequisite to the rights of all. Rights and duties are interrelated in every social and political activity of man. While rights exalt individual liberty, duties express the dignity of that liberty.

Duties of a juridical nature presuppose others of a moral nature which support them in principle and constitute their basis.

Inasmuch as spiritual development is the supreme end of human existence and the highest expression thereof, it is the duty of man to serve that end with all his strength and resources.

Since culture is the highest social and historical expression of that spiritual development, it is the duty of man to preserve, practice and foster culture by every means within his power.

And, since moral conduct constitutes the noblest flowering of culture, it is the duty of every man always to hold it in high respect.

Chapter One—Rights

Article 1. Right to life, liberty and personal security

Every human being has the right to life, liberty and the security of his person.

Article 2. Right to equality before law

All persons are equal before the law and have the rights and duties established in this declaration, without distinction as to race, sex, language, creed or any other factor.

Article 3. Right to religious freedom and worship

Every person has the right freely to profess a religious faith, and to manifest and practice it both in public and in private.

Article 4. Right to freedom of investigation, opinion, expression and dissemination

Every person has the right to freedom of investigation, of opinion, and of the expression and dissemination of ideas, by any medium whatsoever.

Article 5. Right to protection of honor, personal reputation, and private and family life

Every person has the right to the protection of the law against abusive attacks upon his honor, his reputation, and his private and family life.

Article 6. Right to a family and to protection thereof

Every person has the right to establish a family, the basic element of society, and to receive protection therefore.

Article 7. Right to protection for mothers and children

All women, during pregnancy and the nursing period, and all children have the right to special protection, care and aid.

Article 8. Right to residence and movement

Every person has the right to fix his residence within the territory of the state of which he is a national, to move about freely within such territory, and not to leave it except by his own will.

Article 9. Right to inviolability of the home

Every person has the right to the inviolability of his home.

Article 10. Right to the inviolability and transmission of correspondence

Every person has the right to the inviolability and transmission of his correspondence.

Article 11. Right to the preservation of health and to well-being.

Every person has the right to the preservation of his health through sanitary and social measures relating to food, clothing, housing and medical care, to the extent permitted by public and community resources.

Article 12. Right to education.

Every person has the right to an education, which should be based on the principles of liberty, morality and human solidarity.

Likewise every person has the right to an education that will prepare him to attain a decent life, to raise his standard of living, and to be a useful member of society. The right to an education includes the right to equality of opportunity in every case, in accordance with natural talents, merit and the desire to utilize the resources that the state or the community is in a position to provide.

Every person has the right to receive, free, at least a primary education.

Article 13. Right to the benefits of culture

Every person has the right to take part in the cultural life of the community, to enjoy the arts and to participate in the benefits that result from intellectual progress, especially scientific discoveries.

He likewise has the right to the protection of his moral and material interests as regards his inventions or any literary, scientific or artistic works of which he is the author.

Article 14. Right to work and to fair remuneration

Every person has the right to work, under proper conditions, and to follow his vocation freely, in so far as existing conditions of employment permit.

Every person who works has the right to receive such remuneration as will, in proportion to his capacity and skill, assure him a standard of living suitable for himself and for his family.

Article 15. Right to leisure time and to the use thereof

Every person has the right to leisure time, to wholesome recreation, and to the opportunity for advantageous use of his free time to his spiritual, cultural and physical benefit.

Article 16. Right to social security

Every person has the right to social security which will protect him from the consequences of unemployment, old age, and any disabilities arising from causes beyond his control that make it physically or mentally impossible for him to earn a living.

Article 17. Right to recognition of juridical personality and civil rights

Every person has the right to be recognized everywhere as a person having rights and obligations, and to enjoy the basic civil rights.

Article 18. Right to a fair trial

Every person may resort to the courts to ensure respect for his legal rights. There should likewise be available to him a simple, brief procedure whereby the courts will protect him from acts of authority that, to his prejudice, violate any fundamental constitutional rights.

Article 19. Right to nationality

Every person has the right to the nationality to which he is entitled by law and to change it, if he so wishes, for the nationality of any other country that is willing to grant it to him.

Article 20. Right to vote and to participate in government

Every person having legal capacity is entitled to participate in the government of his country, directly or through his representatives, and to take part in popular elections, which shall be by secret ballot, and shall be honest, periodic and free.

Article 21. Right of assembly

Every person has the right to assemble peaceably with others in a formal public meeting or an informal gathering, in connection with matters of common interest of any nature.

Article 22. Right of association

Every person has the right to associate with others to promote, exercise and protect his legitimate interests of a political, economic, religious, social, cultural, professional, labor union or other nature.

Article 23. Right to property

Every person has a right to own such private property as meets the essential needs of decent living and helps to maintain the dignity of the individual and of the home.

Article 24. Right of petition

Every person has the right to submit respectful petitions to any competent authority, for reasons of either general or private interest, and the right to obtain a prompt decision thereon.

Article 25. Right of protection from arbitrary arrest

No person may be deprived of his liberty except in the cases and according to the procedures established by pre-existing law.

No person may be deprived of liberty for nonfulfillment of obligations of a purely civil character.

Every individual who has been deprived of his liberty has the right to have the legality of his detention ascertained without delay by a court, and the right to be tried without undue delay or, otherwise, to be released. He also has the right to humane treatment during the time he is in custody.

Article 26. Right to due process of law

Every accused person is presumed to be innocent until proved guilty.

Every person accused of an offense has the right to be given an impartial and public hearing, and to be tried by courts previously established in accordance with pre-existing laws, and not to receive cruel, infamous or unusual punishment.

Article 27. Right of asylum

Every person has the right, in case of pursuit not resulting from ordinary crimes, to seek and receive asylum in foreign territory, in accordance with the laws of each country and with international agreements.

Article 28. Scope of the rights of man

The rights of man are limited by the rights of others, by the security of all, and by the just demands of the general welfare and the advancement of democracy.

Chapter Two—Duties

Article 29. Duties to society

It is the duty of the individual so to conduct himself in relation to others that each and every one may fully form and develop his personality.

Article 30. Duties toward children and parents

It is the duty of every person to aid, support, educate and protect his minor children, and it is the duty of children to honor their parents always and to aid, support and protect them when they need it.

Article 31. Duty to receive instruction

It is the duty of every person to acquire at least an elementary education.

Article 32. Duty to vote

It is the duty of every person to vote in the popular elections of the country of which he is a national, when he is legally capable of doing so.

Article 33. Duty to obey the law

It is the duty of every person to obey the law and other legitimate commands of the authorities of his country and those of the country in which he may be.

Article 34. Duty to serve the community and the nation

It is the duty of every able-bodied person to render whatever civil and military service his country may require for its defense and preservation, and, in case of public disaster, to render such services as may be in his power.

It is likewise his duty to hold any public office to which he may be elected by popular vote in the state of which he is a national.

Article 35. Duties with respect to social security and welfare

It is the duty of every person to cooperate with the State and the community with respect to social security and welfare, in accordance with his ability and with existing circumstances.

Article 36. Duty to pay taxes

It is the duty of every person to pay the taxes established by law for the support of public services.

Article 37. Duty to work

It is the duty of every person to work, as far as his capacity and possibilities permit, in order to obtain the means of livelihood or to benefit his community.

Article 38. Duty to refrain from political activities in a foreign country

It is the duty of every person to refrain from taking part in political activities that, according to law, are reserved exclusively to the citizens of the state in which he is an alien.

DOCUMENT 63

Full Official Title: American Convention on Human Rights

Short Title/Acronym/Abbreviation: Pact of San Jose/The American Convention/ACHR

Subject: Establishment of basic human rights norms in the Western Hemisphere in a regional multilateral treaty.

Official Citation: O.A.S. Treaty Series No. 36, at 1, O.A.S. off. Rec. OEA/Ser.L/V/II. 23 doc.rev.2

Date of Document: Not applicable

Date of Adoption: November 22, 1969

Date of General Entry into Force (EIF): July 18, 1978

Number of States Parties to this Treaty as of this printing: 25
Date of Signature by United States: June 1, 1977
Date of Ratification/Accession/Adhesion: The United States has not ratified this treaty
Date of Entry into Force as to United States (effective date): Not applicable
Type of Document: An international legal instrument. A treaty. A regional human rights instrument.
Legal Status/Character of the Instrument/Document as to the United States: Not legally binding as to the United States because the United States has not ratified it. However, in legal principles found in the Vienna Convention on the Law of Treaties, the United States should act consistently with this treaty because it has signed it and should do so as to show its good faith intent to follow the treaty norms.
Comments: This treaty is the main human rights legal instrument of the Organization of American States human rights system known as the Inter-American Human Rights System. This treaty is perhaps the most broadly written and pro human rights treaty, of all general human rights instruments. Because of some specific provisions in this treaty, the U.S. Senate has not wanted to give its advice and consent to this treaty. However, the United States is bound to comply with human rights standards of the American Declaration of Human Rights, which is monitored by the Inter-American Commission on Human Rights.
Caution: The status and applicability of this instrument as to the United States may have changed since date of publication. The above information may be updated by referring to the following site:
Web address: http://www.cidh.oas.org/Basic%20Documents/enbas3.htm

AMERICAN CONVENTION ON HUMAN RIGHTS (EXCERPTS)
Signed at the Inter-American Specialized Conference on Human Rights, San José, Costa Rica, Adopted November 22, 1969, entered into force July 18, 1978; O.A.S. Treaty Series No 36, at 1, O.A.S. Off. Rec. OEA/Ser. L./V/II. 23 doc.rev.2

Preamble
The American states signatory to the present Convention,

Reaffirming their intention to consolidate in this hemisphere, within the framework of democratic institutions, a system of personal liberty and social justice based on respect for the essential rights of man;

Recognizing that the essential rights of man are not derived from one's being a national of a certain state, but are based upon attributes of the human personality, and that they therefore justify international protection in the form of a convention reinforcing or complementing the protection provided by the domestic law of the American states;

Considering that these principles have been set forth in the Charter of the Organization of American States, in the American Declaration of the Rights and Duties of Man, and in the Universal Declaration of Human Rights, and that they have been reaffirmed and refined in other international instruments, worldwide as well as regional in scope;

Reiterating that, in accordance with the Universal Declaration of Human Rights, the ideal of free men enjoying freedom from fear and want can be achieved only if conditions are created whereby everyone may enjoy his economic, social, and cultural rights, as well as his civil and political rights; and

Considering that the Third Special Inter-American Conference (Buenos Aires, 1967) approved the incorporation into the Charter of the Organization itself of broader standards with respect to economic, social, and educational rights and resolved that an inter-American convention on human rights should determine the structure, competence, and procedure of the organs responsible for these matters,

Have agreed upon the following:

Part I—State Obligations and Rights Protected
Chapter I—General Obligations
Article 1. Obligation to Respect Rights
1. The States Parties to this Convention undertake to respect the rights and freedoms recognized herein and to ensure to all persons subject to their jurisdiction the free and full exercise of those rights and freedoms, without any discrimination for reasons of race, color, sex, language, religion, political or other opinion, national or social origin, economic status, birth, or any other social condition.

2. For the purposes of this Convention, "person" means every human being.

Article 2. Domestic Legal Effects
Where the exercise of any of the rights or freedoms referred to in Article 1 is not already ensured by legislative or other provisions, the States Parties undertake to adopt, in accordance with their constitutional

processes and the provisions of this Convention, such legislative or other measures as may be necessary to give effect to those rights or freedoms.

Chapter II—Civil and Political Rights

Article 3. Right to Juridical Personality

Every person has the right to recognition as a person before the law.

Article 4. Right to Life

1. Every person has the right to have his life respected. This right shall be protected by law and, in general, from the moment of conception. No one shall be arbitrarily deprived of his life.

2. In countries that have not abolished the death penalty, it may be imposed only for the most serious crimes and pursuant to a final judgment rendered by a competent court and in accordance with a law establishing such punishment, enacted prior to the commission of the crime. The application of such punishment shall not be extended to crimes to which it does not presently apply.

3. The death penalty shall not be reestablished in states that have abolished it.

4. In no case shall capital punishment be inflicted for political offenses or related common crimes.

5. Capital punishment shall not be imposed upon persons who, at the time the crime was committed, were under 18 years of age or over 70 years of age; nor shall it be applied to pregnant women.

6. Every person condemned to death shall have the right to apply for amnesty, pardon, or commutation of sentence, which may be granted in all cases. Capital punishment shall not be imposed while such a petition is pending decision by the competent authority.

Article 5. Right to Humane Treatment

1. Every person has the right to have his physical, mental, and moral integrity respected.

2. No one shall be subjected to torture or to cruel, inhuman, or degrading punishment or treatment. All persons deprived of their liberty shall be treated with respect for the inherent dignity of the human person.

3. Punishment shall not be extended to any person other than the criminal.

4. Accused persons shall, save in exceptional circumstances, be segregated from convicted persons, and shall be subject to separate treatment appropriate to their status as unconvicted persons.

5. Minors while subject to criminal proceedings shall be separated from adults and brought before specialized tribunals, as speedily as possible, so that they may be treated in accordance with their status as minors.

6. Punishments consisting of deprivation of liberty shall have as an essential aim the reform and social readaptation of the prisoners.

Article 6. Freedom from Slavery

1. No one shall be subject to slavery or to involuntary servitude, which are prohibited in all their forms, as are the slave trade and traffic in women.

2. No one shall be required to perform forced or compulsory labor. This provision shall not be interpreted to mean that, in those countries in which the penalty established for certain crimes is deprivation of liberty at forced labor, the carrying out of such a sentence imposed by a competent court is prohibited. Forced labor shall not adversely affect the dignity or the physical or intellectual capacity of the prisoner.

3. For the purposes of this article, the following do not constitute forced or compulsory labor:

a. work or service normally required of a person imprisoned in execution of a sentence or formal decision passed by the competent judicial authority. Such work or service shall be carried out under the supervision and control of public authorities, and any persons performing such work or service shall not be placed at the disposal of any private party, company, or juridical person;

b. military service and, in countries in which conscientious objectors are recognized, national service that the law may provide for in lieu of military service;

c. service exacted in time of danger or calamity that threatens the existence or the well-being of the community; or

d. work or service that forms part of normal civic obligations.

Article 7. Right to Personal Liberty

1. Every person has the right to personal liberty and security.

2. No one shall be deprived of his physical liberty except for the reasons and under the conditions established beforehand by the constitution of the State Party concerned or by a law established pursuant thereto.

3. No one shall be subject to arbitrary arrest or imprisonment.

4. Anyone who is detained shall be informed of the reasons for his detention and shall be promptly notified of the charge or charges against him.

5. Any person detained shall be brought promptly before a judge or other officer authorized by law to exercise judicial power and shall be entitled to trial within a reasonable time or to be released without prejudice to the continuation of the proceedings. His release may be subject to guarantees to assure his appearance for trial.

6. Anyone who is deprived of his liberty shall be entitled to recourse to a competent court, in order that the court may decide without delay on the lawfulness of his arrest or detention and order his release if the arrest or detention is unlawful. In States Parties whose laws provide that anyone who believes himself to be threatened with deprivation of his liberty is entitled to recourse to a competent court in order that it may decide on the lawfulness of such threat, this remedy may not be restricted or abolished. The interested party or another person in his behalf is entitled to seek these remedies.

7. No one shall be detained for debt. This principle shall not limit the orders of a competent judicial authority issued for nonfulfillment of duties of support.

Article 8. Right to a Fair Trial

1. Every person has the right to a hearing, with due guarantees and within a reasonable time, by a competent, independent, and impartial tribunal, previously established by law, in the substantiation of any accusation of a criminal nature made against him or for the determination of his rights and obligations of a civil, labor, fiscal, or any other nature.

2. Every person accused of a criminal offense has the right to be presumed innocent so long as his guilt has not been proven according to law. During the proceedings, every person is entitled, with full equality, to the following minimum guarantees:

a. the right of the accused to be assisted without charge by a translator or interpreter, if he does not understand or does not speak the language of the tribunal or court;

b. prior notification in detail to the accused of the charges against him;

c. adequate time and means for the preparation of his defense;

d. the right of the accused to defend himself personally or to be assisted by legal counsel of his own choosing, and to communicate freely and privately with his counsel;

e. the inalienable right to be assisted by counsel provided by the state, paid or not as the domestic law provides, if the accused does not defend himself personally or engage his own counsel within the time period established by law;

f. the right of the defense to examine witnesses present in the court and to obtain the appearance, as witnesses, of experts or other persons who may throw light on the facts;

g. the right not to be compelled to be a witness against himself or to plead guilty; and

h. the right to appeal the judgment to a higher court.

3. A confession of guilt by the accused shall be valid only if it is made without coercion of any kind.

4. An accused person acquitted by a nonappealable judgment shall not be subjected to a new trial for the same cause.

5. Criminal proceedings shall be public, except insofar as may be necessary to protect the interests of justice.

Article 9. Freedom from Ex Post Facto Laws

No one shall be convicted of any act or omission that did not constitute a criminal offense, under the applicable law, at the time it was committed. A heavier penalty shall not be imposed than the one that was applicable at the time the criminal offense was committed. If subsequent to the commission of the offense the law provides for the imposition of a lighter punishment, the guilty person shall benefit therefrom.

Article 10. Right to Compensation

Every person has the right to be compensated in accordance with the law in the event he has been sentenced by a final judgment through a miscarriage of justice.

Article 11. Right to Privacy

1. Everyone has the right to have his honor respected and his dignity recognized.

2. No one may be the object of arbitrary or abusive interference with his private life, his family, his home, or his correspondence, or of unlawful attacks on his honor or reputation.

3. Everyone has the right to the protection of the law against such interference or attacks.

Article 12. Freedom of Conscience and Religion

1. Everyone has the right to freedom of conscience and of religion. This right includes freedom to maintain or to change one's religion or beliefs, and freedom to profess or disseminate one's religion or beliefs, either individually or together with others, in public or in private.

2. No one shall be subject to restrictions that might impair his freedom to maintain or to change his religion or beliefs.

3. Freedom to manifest one's religion and beliefs may be subject only to the limitations prescribed by law that are necessary to protect public safety, order, health, or morals, or the rights or freedoms of others.

4. Parents or guardians, as the case may be, have the right to provide for the religious and moral education of their children or wards that is in accord with their own convictions.

Article 13. Freedom of Thought and Expression

1. Everyone has the right to freedom of thought and expression. This right includes freedom to seek, receive, and impart information and ideas of all kinds, regardless of frontiers, either orally, in writing, in print, in the form of art, or through any other medium of one's choice.

2. The exercise of the right provided for in the foregoing paragraph shall not be subject to prior censorship but shall be subject to subsequent imposition of liability, which shall be expressly established by law to the extent necessary to ensure:

a. respect for the rights or reputations of others; or

b. the protection of national security, public order, or public health or morals.

3. The right of expression may not be restricted by indirect methods or means, such as the abuse of government or private controls over newsprint, radio broadcasting frequencies, or equipment used in the dissemination of information, or by any other means tending to impede the communication and circulation of ideas and opinions.

4. Notwithstanding the provisions of paragraph 2 above, public entertainments may be subject by law to prior censorship for the sole purpose of regulating access to them for the moral protection of childhood and adolescence.

5. Any propaganda for war and any advocacy of national, racial, or religious hatred that constitute incitements to lawless violence or to any other similar illegal action against any person or group of persons on any grounds including those of race, color, religion, language, or national origin shall be considered as offenses punishable by law.

Article 14. Right of Reply

1. Anyone injured by inaccurate or offensive statements or ideas disseminated to the public in general by a legally regulated medium of communication has the right to reply or to make a correction using the same communications outlet, under such conditions as the law may establish.

2. The correction or reply shall not in any case remit other legal liabilities that may have been incurred.

3. For the effective protection of honor and reputation, every publisher, and every newspaper, motion picture, radio, and television company, shall have a person responsible who is not protected by immunities or special privileges.

Article 15. Right of Assembly

The right of peaceful assembly, without arms, is recognized. No restrictions may be placed on the exercise of this right other than those imposed in conformity with the law and necessary in a democratic society in the interest of national security, public safety or public order, or to protect public health or morals or the rights or freedom of others.

Article 16. Freedom of Association

1. Everyone has the right to associate freely for ideological, religious, political, economic, labor, social, cultural, sports, or other purposes.

2. The exercise of this right shall be subject only to such restrictions established by law as may be necessary in a democratic society, in the interest of national security, public safety or public order, or to protect public health or morals or the rights and freedoms of others.

3. The provisions of this article do not bar the imposition of legal restrictions, including even deprivation of the exercise of the right of association, on members of the armed forces and the police.

Article 17. Rights of the Family

1. The family is the natural and fundamental group unit of society and is entitled to protection by society and the state.

2. The right of men and women of marriageable age to marry and to raise a family shall be recognized, if they meet the conditions required by domestic laws, insofar as such conditions do not affect the principle of nondiscrimination established in this Convention.

3. No marriage shall be entered into without the free and full consent of the intending spouses.

4. The States Parties shall take appropriate steps to ensure the equality of rights and the adequate balancing of responsibilities of the spouses as to marriage, during marriage, and in the event of its dissolution. In case of dissolution, provision shall be made for the necessary protection of any children solely on the basis of their own best interests.

5. The law shall recognize equal rights for children born out of wedlock and those born in wedlock.

Article 18. Right to a Name

Every person has the right to a given name and to the surnames of his parents or that of one of them. The law shall regulate the manner in which this right shall be ensured for all, by the use of assumed names if necessary.

Article 19. Rights of the Child

Every minor child has the right to the measures of protection required by his condition as a minor on the part of his family, society, and the state.

Article 20. Right to Nationality

1. Every person has the right to a nationality.

2. Every person has the right to the nationality of the state in whose territory he was born if he does not have the right to any other nationality.

3. No one shall be arbitrarily deprived of his nationality or of the right to change it.

Article 21. Right to Property

1. Everyone has the right to the use and enjoyment of his property. The law may subordinate such use and enjoyment to the interest of society.

2. No one shall be deprived of his property except upon payment of just compensation, for reasons of public utility or social interest, and in the cases and according to the forms established by law.

3. Usury and any other form of exploitation of man by man shall be prohibited by law.

Article 22. Freedom of Movement and Residence

1. Every person lawfully in the territory of a State Party has the right to move about in it, and to reside in it subject to the provisions of the law.

2. Every person has the right to leave any country freely, including his own.

3. The exercise of the foregoing rights may be restricted only pursuant to a law to the extent necessary in a democratic society to prevent crime or to protect national security, public safety, public order, public morals, public health, or the rights or freedoms of others.

4. The exercise of the rights recognized in paragraph 1 may also be restricted by law in designated zones for reasons of public interest.

5. No one can be expelled from the territory of the state of which he is a national or be deprived of the right to enter it.

6. An alien lawfully in the territory of a State Party to this Convention may be expelled from it only pursuant to a decision reached in accordance with law.

7. Every person has the right to seek and be granted asylum in a foreign territory, in accordance with the legislation of the state and international conventions, in the event he is being pursued for political offenses or related common crimes.

8. In no case may an alien be deported or returned to a country, regardless of whether or not it is his country of origin, if in that country his right to life or personal freedom is in danger of being violated because of his race, nationality, religion, social status, or political opinions.

9. The collective expulsion of aliens is prohibited.

Article 23. Right to Participate in Government

1. Every citizen shall enjoy the following rights and opportunities:

a. to take part in the conduct of public affairs, directly or through freely chosen representatives;

b. to vote and to be elected in genuine periodic elections, which shall be by universal and equal suffrage and by secret ballot that guarantees the free expression of the will of the voters; and

c. to have access, under general conditions of equality, to the public service of his country.

2. The law may regulate the exercise of the rights and opportunities referred to in the preceding paragraph only on the basis of age, nationality, residence, language, education, civil and mental capacity, or sentencing by a competent court in criminal proceedings.

Article 24. Right to Equal Protection

All persons are equal before the law. Consequently, they are entitled, without discrimination, to equal protection of the law.

Article 25. Right to Judicial Protection

1. Everyone has the right to simple and prompt recourse, or any other effective recourse, to a competent court or tribunal for protection against acts that violate his fundamental rights recognized by the constitution or laws of the state concerned or by this Convention, even though such violation may have been committed by persons acting in the course of their official duties.

2. The States Parties undertake:

a. to ensure that any person claiming such remedy shall have his rights determined by the competent authority provided for by the legal system of the state;

b. to develop the possibilities of judicial remedy; and

c. to ensure that the competent authorities shall enforce such remedies when granted.

Chapter III—Economic, Social, and Cultural Rights

Article 26. Progressive Development

The States Parties undertake to adopt measures, both internally and through international cooperation, especially those of an economic and technical nature, with a view to achieving progressively, by legislation or other appropriate means, the full realization of the rights implicit in the economic, social, educational, scientific, and cultural standards set forth in the Charter of the Organization of American States as amended by the Protocol of Buenos Aires.

Chapter IV—Suspension of Guarantees, Interpretation, and Application

Article 27. Suspension of Guarantees

1. In time of war, public danger, or other emergency that threatens the independence or security of a State Party, it may take measures derogating from its obligations under the present Convention to the extent and for the period of time strictly required by the exigencies of the situation, provided that such measures are not inconsistent with its other obligations under international law and do not involve discrimination on the ground of race, color, sex, language, religion, or social origin.

2. The foregoing provision does not authorize any suspension of the following articles: Article 3 (Right to Juridical Personality), Article 4 (Right to Life), Article 5 (Right to Humane Treatment), Article 6 (Freedom from Slavery), Article 9 (Freedom from Ex Post Facto Laws), Article 12 (Freedom of Conscience and Religion), Article 17 (Rights of the Family), Article 18 (Right to a Name), Article 19 (Rights of the Child), Article 20 (Right to Nationality), and Article 23 (Right to Participate in Government), or of the judicial guarantees essential for the protection of such rights.

3. Any State Party availing itself of the right of suspension shall immediately inform the other States Parties, through the Secretary General of the Organization of American States, of the provisions the application of which it has suspended, the reasons that gave rise to the suspension, and the date set for the termination of such suspension.

Article 28. Federal Clause

1. Where a State Party is constituted as a federal state, the national government of such State Party shall implement all the provisions of the Convention over whose subject matter it exercises legislative and judicial jurisdiction.

2. With respect to the provisions over whose subject matter the constituent units of the federal state have jurisdiction, the national government shall immediately take suitable measures, in accordance with its constitution and its laws, to the end that the competent authorities of the constituent units may adopt appropriate provisions for the fulfillment of this Convention.

3. Whenever two or more States Parties agree to form a federation or other type of association, they shall take care that the resulting federal or other compact contains the provisions necessary for continuing and rendering effective the standards of this Convention in the new state that is organized.

Article 29. Restrictions Regarding Interpretation

No provision of this Convention shall be interpreted as:

a. permitting any State Party, group, or person to suppress the enjoyment or exercise of the rights and freedoms recognized in this Convention or to restrict them to a greater extent than is provided for herein;

b. restricting the enjoyment or exercise of any right or freedom recognized by virtue of the laws of any State Party or by virtue of another convention to which one of the said states is a party;

c. precluding other rights or guarantees that are inherent in the human personality or derived from representative democracy as a form of government; or

d. excluding or limiting the effect that the American Declaration of the Rights and Duties of Man and other international acts of the same nature may have.

Article 30. Scope of Restrictions

The restrictions that, pursuant to this Convention, may be placed on the enjoyment or exercise of the rights or freedoms recognized herein may not be applied except in accordance with laws enacted for reasons of general interest and in accordance with the purpose for which such restrictions have been established.

Article 31. Recognition of Other Rights

Other rights and freedoms recognized in accordance with the procedures established in Articles 76 and 77 may be included in the system of protection of this Convention.

Chapter V—Personal Responsibilities

Article 32. Relationship between Duties and Rights

1. Every person has responsibilities to his family, his community, and mankind.

2. The rights of each person are limited by the rights of others, by the security of all, and by the just demands of the general welfare, in a democratic society.

Part II—Means of Protection

Chapter VI—Competent Organs

Article 33

The following organs shall have competence with respect to matters relating to the fulfillment of the commitments made by the States Parties to this Convention:

a. the Inter-American Commission on Human Rights, referred to as "The Commission;" and

b. the Inter-American Court of Human Rights, referred to as "The Court."

Chapter VII—Inter-American Commission on Human Rights

Section 1. Organization

Article 34

The Inter-American Commission on Human Rights shall be composed of seven members, who shall be persons of high moral character and recognized competence in the field of human rights.

Article 35

The Commission shall represent all the member countries of the Organization of American States.

Article 36

1. The members of the Commission shall be elected in a personal capacity by the General Assembly of the Organization from a list of candidates proposed by the governments of the member states.

...

Section 2. Functions

Article 41

The main function of the Commission shall be to promote respect for and defense of human rights. In the exercise of its mandate, it shall have the following functions and powers:

a. to develop an awareness of human rights among the peoples of America;

b. to make recommendations to the governments of the member states, when it considers such action advisable, for the adoption of progressive measures in favor of human rights within the framework of their domestic law and constitutional provisions as well as appropriate measures to further the observance of those rights;

c. to prepare such studies or reports as it considers advisable in the performance of its duties;

d. to request the governments of the member states to supply it with information on the measures adopted by them in matters of human rights;

e. to respond, through the General Secretariat of the Organization of American States, to inquiries made by the member states on matters related to human rights and, within the limits of its possibilities, to provide those states with the advisory services they request;

f. to take action on petitions and other communications pursuant to its authority under the provisions of Articles 44 through 51 of this Convention; and

g. to submit an annual report to the General Assembly of the Organization of American States.

Article 42

The States Parties shall transmit to the Commission a copy of each of the reports and studies that they submit annually to the Executive Committees of the Inter-American Economic and Social Council and the Inter-American Council for Education, Science, and Culture, in their respective fields, so that the Commission may watch over the promotion of the rights implicit in the economic, social, educational, scientific, and cultural standards set forth in the Charter of the Organization of American States as amended by the Protocol of Buenos Aires.

Article 43

The States Parties undertake to provide the Commission with such information as it may request of them as to the manner in which their domestic law ensures the effective application of any provisions of this Convention.

Section 3. Competence

Article 44

Any person or group of persons, or any non-governmental entity legally recognized in one or more member states of the Organization, may lodge petitions with the Commission containing denunciations or complaints of violation of this Convention by a State Party.

Article 45

1. Any State Party may, when it deposits its instrument of ratification of or adherence to this Convention, or at any later time, declare that it recognizes the competence of the Commission to receive and examine communications in which a State Party alleges that another State Party has committed a violation of a human right set forth in this Convention.

2. Communications presented by virtue of this article may be admitted and examined only if they are presented by a State Party that has made a declaration recognizing the aforementioned competence of the Commission. The Commission shall not admit any communication against a State Party that has not made such a declaration.

3. A declaration concerning recognition of competence may be made to be valid for an indefinite time, for a specified period, or for a specific case.

4. Declarations shall be deposited with the General Secretariat of the Organization of American States, which shall transmit copies thereof to the member states of that Organization.

Article 46

1. Admission by the Commission of a petition or communication lodged in accordance with Articles 44 or 45 shall be subject to the following requirements:

a. that the remedies under domestic law have been pursued and exhausted in accordance with generally recognized principles of international law;

b. that the petition or communication is lodged within a period of six months from the date on which the party alleging violation of his rights was notified of the final judgment;

c. that the subject of the petition or communication is not pending in another international proceeding for settlement; and

d. that, in the case of Article 44, the petition contains the name, nationality, profession, domicile, and signature of the person or persons or of the legal representative of the entity lodging the petition.

2. The provisions of paragraphs 1.a and 1.b of this article shall not be applicable when:

a. the domestic legislation of the state concerned does not afford due process of law for the protection of the right or rights that have allegedly been violated;

b. the party alleging violation of his rights has been denied access to the remedies under domestic law or has been prevented from exhausting them; or

c. there has been unwarranted delay in rendering a final judgment under the aforementioned remedies.

Article 47

The Commission shall consider inadmissible any petition or communication submitted under Articles 44 or 45 if:

a. any of the requirements indicated in Article 46 has not been met;

b. the petition or communication does not state facts that tend to establish a violation of the rights guaranteed by this Convention;

c. the statements of the petitioner or of the state indicate that the petition or communication is manifestly groundless or obviously out of order; or

d. the petition or communication is substantially the same as one previously studied by the Commission or by another international organization.

Section 4. Procedure

Article 48

1. When the Commission receives a petition or communication alleging violation of any of the rights protected by this Convention, it shall proceed as follows:

a. If it considers the petition or communication admissible, it shall request information from the government of the state indicated as being responsible for the alleged violations and shall furnish that government a transcript of the pertinent portions of the petition or communication. This information shall be submitted within a reasonable period to be determined by the Commission in accordance with the circumstances of each case.

b. After the information has been received, or after the period established has elapsed and the information has not been received, the Commission shall ascertain whether the grounds for the petition or communication still exist. If they do not, the Commission shall order the record to be closed.

c. The Commission may also declare the petition or communication inadmissible or out of order on the basis of information or evidence subsequently received.

d. If the record has not been closed, the Commission shall, with the knowledge of the parties, examine the matter set forth in the petition or communication in order to verify the facts. If necessary and advisable, the Commission shall carry out an investigation, for the effective conduct of which it shall request, and the states concerned shall furnish to it, all necessary facilities.

e. The Commission may request the states concerned to furnish any pertinent information and, if so requested, shall hear oral statements or receive written statements from the parties concerned.

f. The Commission shall place itself at the disposal of the parties concerned with a view to reaching a friendly settlement of the matter on the basis of respect for the human rights recognized in this Convention.

2. However, in serious and urgent cases, only the presentation of a petition or communication that fulfills all the formal requirements of admissibility shall be necessary in order for the Commission to conduct an investigation with the prior consent of the state in whose territory a violation has allegedly been committed.

Article 49

If a friendly settlement has been reached in accordance with paragraph 1.f of Article 48, the Commission shall draw up a report, which shall be transmitted to the petitioner and to the States Parties to this Convention, and shall then be communicated to the Secretary General of the Organization of American States for publication. This report shall contain a brief statement of the facts and of the solution reached. If any party in the case so requests, the fullest possible information shall be provided to it.

Article 50

1. If a settlement is not reached, the Commission shall, within the time limit established by its Statute, draw up a report setting forth the facts and stating its conclusions. If the report, in whole or in part, does not represent the unanimous agreement of the members of the Commission, any member may attach to it a separate opinion. The written and oral statements made by the parties in accordance with paragraph 1.e of Article 48 shall also be attached to the report.

2. The report shall be transmitted to the states concerned, which shall not be at liberty to publish it.

3. In transmitting the report, the Commission may make such proposals and recommendations as it sees fit.

Article 51

1. If, within a period of three months from the date of the transmittal of the report of the Commission to the states concerned, the matter has not either been settled or submitted by the Commission or by the state concerned to the Court and its jurisdiction accepted, the Commission may, by the vote of an absolute majority of its members, set forth its opinion and conclusions concerning the question submitted for its consideration.

2. Where appropriate, the Commission shall make pertinent recommendations and shall prescribe a period within which the state is to take the measures that are incumbent upon it to remedy the situation examined.

3. When the prescribed period has expired, the Commission shall decide by the vote of an absolute majority of its members whether the state has taken adequate measures and whether to publish its report.

Chapter VIII—Inter-American Court of Human Rights

Section 1. Organization

Article 52

1. The Court shall consist of seven judges, nationals of the member states of the Organization, elected in an individual capacity from among jurists of the highest moral authority and of recognized competence

in the field of human rights, who possess the qualifications required for the exercise of the highest judicial functions in conformity with the law of the state of which they are nationals or of the state that proposes them as candidates.

2. No two judges may be nationals of the same state.

...

Section 2. Jurisdiction and Functions
Article 61
1. Only the States Parties and the Commission shall have the right to submit a case to the Court.

2. In order for the Court to hear a case, it is necessary that the procedures set forth in Articles 48 and 50 shall have been completed.

Article 62
1. A State Party may, upon depositing its instrument of ratification or adherence to this Convention, or at any subsequent time, declare that it recognizes as binding, ipso facto, and not requiring special agreement, the jurisdiction of the Court on all matters relating to the interpretation or application of this Convention.

2. Such declaration may be made unconditionally, on the condition of reciprocity, for a specified period, or for specific cases. It shall be presented to the Secretary General of the Organization, who shall transmit copies thereof to the other member states of the Organization and to the Secretary of the Court.

3. The jurisdiction of the Court shall comprise all cases concerning the interpretation and application of the provisions of this Convention that are submitted to it, provided that the States Parties to the case recognize or have recognized such jurisdiction, whether by special declaration pursuant to the preceding paragraphs, or by a special agreement.

Article 63
1. If the Court finds that there has been a violation of a right or freedom protected by this Convention, the Court shall rule that the injured party be ensured the enjoyment of his right or freedom that was violated. It shall also rule, if appropriate, that the consequences of the measure or situation that constituted the breach of such right or freedom be remedied and that fair compensation be paid to the injured party.

2. In cases of extreme gravity and urgency, and when necessary to avoid irreparable damage to persons, the Court shall adopt such provisional measures as it deems pertinent in matters it has under consideration. With respect to a case not yet submitted to the Court, it may act at the request of the Commission.

Article 64
1. The member states of the Organization may consult the Court regarding the interpretation of this Convention or of other treaties concerning the protection of human rights in the American states. Within their spheres of competence, the organs listed in Chapter X of the Charter of the Organization of American States, as amended by the Protocol of Buenos Aires, may in like manner consult the Court.

2. The Court, at the request of a member state of the Organization, may provide that state with opinions regarding the compatibility of any of its domestic laws with the aforesaid international instruments.

...

Section 3. Procedure
Article 66
1. Reasons shall be given for the judgment of the Court.

2. If the judgment does not represent in whole or in part the unanimous opinion of the judges, any judge shall be entitled to have his dissenting or separate opinion attached to the judgment.

Article 67
The judgment of the Court shall be final and not subject to appeal. In case of disagreement as to the meaning or scope of the judgment, the Court shall interpret it at the request of any of the parties, provided the request is made within ninety days from the date of notification of the judgment.

Article 68
1. The States Parties to the Convention undertake to comply with the judgment of the Court in any case to which they are parties.

2. That part of a judgment that stipulates compensatory damages may be executed in the country concerned in accordance with domestic procedure governing the execution of judgments against the state.

Article 69
The parties to the case shall be notified of the judgment of the Court and it shall be transmitted to the States Parties to the Convention.

...

Part III—General and Transitory Provisions
Chapter X—Ratification, Reservations, Amendments, Protocols, and Denunciation
Article 74

1. This Convention shall be open for signature and ratification by or adherence of any member state of the Organization of American States.

2. Ratification of or adherence to this Convention shall be made by the deposit of an instrument of ratification or adherence with the General Secretariat of the Organization of American States. As soon as eleven states have deposited their instruments of ratification or adherence, the Convention shall enter into force. With respect to any state that ratifies or adheres thereafter, the Convention shall enter into force on the date of the deposit of its instrument of ratification or adherence.

3. The Secretary General shall inform all member states of the Organization of the entry into force of the Convention.

Article 75

This Convention shall be subject to reservations only in conformity with the provisions of the Vienna Convention on the Law of Treaties signed on May 23, 1969.

...

Article 78

1. The States Parties may denounce this Convention at the expiration of a five-year period from the date of its entry into force and by means of notice given one year in advance. Notice of the denunciation shall be addressed to the Secretary General of the Organization, who shall inform the other States Parties.

2. Such a denunciation shall not have the effect of releasing the State Party concerned from the obligations contained in this Convention with respect to any act that may constitute a violation of those obligations and that has been taken by that state prior to the effective date of denunciation.

Chapter XI—Transitory Provisions
Section 1. Inter-American Commission on Human Rights
Article 79

Upon the entry into force of this Convention, the Secretary General shall, in writing, request each member state of the Organization to present, within ninety days, its candidates for membership on the Inter-American Commission on Human Rights. The Secretary General shall prepare a list in alphabetical order of the candidates presented, and transmit it to the member states of the Organization at least thirty days prior to the next session of the General Assembly.

...

American Convention on Human Rights
"Pact of San José, Costa Rica"
(Signed at San José, Costa Rica, 22 November 1969, at the
Inter-American Specialized Conference on Human Rights)
ENTRY INTO FORCE: 18 July 1978, in accordance with Article 74.2 of the Convention.
DEPOSITORY: OAS General Secretariat (Original instrument and ratifications).
TEXT: OAS, Treaty Series, N° 36.

DOCUMENT 64

Full Official Title: Additional Protocol to the American Convention on Human Rights in the Area of Economic, Social and Cultural Rights

Short Title/Acronym/Abbreviation: Protocol of San Salvador

Subject: Amending the ACHR to establish basic norms in the area of economic, social, and cultural rights in the Western Hemisphere.

Official Citation: OAS Treaty Series No. 69, OEA/Ser.A/42 (SEPF)

Date of Document: November 17, 1988

Date of Adoption: November 17, 1988

Date of General Entry into Force (EIF): November 16, 1999

Number of States Parties to this Treaty as of this printing: 15

Date of Signature by United States: United States has not signed.

Date of Ratification/Accession/Adhesion: Not applicable

Date of Entry into Force as to United States (effective date): Not applicable

Type of Document: Treaty Protocol

Legal Status/Character of the Instrument/Document as to the United States: Not binding on the United States because the United States has not ratified either the ACHR or this protocol.

Comments: None

Caution: The status and applicability of this instrument as to the United States may have changed since date of publication. The above information may be updated by referring to the following site:

Web address: http://www.cidh.oas.org/Basic%20Documents/enbas5.htm

FIRST PROTOCOL TO THE ACHR

Preamble

The States Parties to the American Convention on Human Rights "Pact San José, Costa Rica,"

Reaffirming their intention to consolidate in this hemisphere, within the framework of democratic institutions, a system of personal liberty and social justice based on respect for the essential rights of man;

Recognizing that the essential rights of man are not derived from one's being a national of a certain State, but are based upon attributes of the human person, for which reason they merit international protection in the form of a convention reinforcing or complementing the protection provided by the domestic law of the American States;

Considering the close relationship that exists between economic, social and cultural rights, and civil and political rights, in that the different categories of rights constitute an indivisible whole based on the recognition of the dignity of the human person, for which reason both require permanent protection and promotion if they are to be fully realized, and the violation of some rights in favor of the realization of others can never be justified;

Recognizing the benefits that stem from the promotion and development of cooperation among States and international relations;

Recalling that, in accordance with the Universal Declaration of Human Rights and the American Convention on Human Rights, the ideal of free human beings enjoying freedom from fear and want can only be achieved if conditions are created whereby everyone may enjoy his economic, social and cultural rights as well as his civil and political rights;

Bearing in mind that, although fundamental economic, social and cultural rights have been recognized in earlier international instruments of both world and regional scope, it is essential that those rights be reaffirmed, developed, perfected and protected in order to consolidate in America, on the basis of full respect for the rights of the individual, the democratic representative form of government as well as the right of its peoples to development, self-determination, and the free disposal of their wealth and natural resources; and

Considering that the American Convention on Human Rights provides that draft additional protocols to that Convention may be submitted for consideration to the States Parties, meeting together on the occasion of the General Assembly of the Organization of American States, for the purpose of gradually incorporating other rights and freedoms into the protective system thereof,

Have agreed upon the following Additional Protocol to the American Convention on Human Rights "Protocol of San Salvador:"

Article 1. Obligation to Adopt Measures

The States Parties to this Additional Protocol to the American Convention on Human Rights undertake to adopt the necessary measures, both domestically and through international cooperation, especially economic and technical, to the extent allowed by their available resources, and taking into account their degree of development, for the purpose of achieving progressively and pursuant to their internal legislations, the full observance of the rights recognized in this Protocol.

Article 2. Obligation to Enact Domestic Legislation

If the exercise of the rights set forth in this Protocol is not already guaranteed by legislative or other provisions, the States Parties undertake to adopt, in accordance with their constitutional processes and the provisions of this Protocol, such legislative or other measures as may be necessary for making those rights a reality.

Article 3. Obligation of nondiscrimination

The State Parties to this Protocol undertake to guarantee the exercise of the rights set forth herein without discrimination of any kind for reasons related to race, color, sex, language, religion, political or other opinions, national or social origin, economic status, birth or any other social condition.

Article 4. Inadmissibility of Restrictions

A right which is recognized or in effect in a State by virtue of its internal legislation or international conventions may not be restricted or curtailed on the pretext that this Protocol does not recognize the right or recognizes it to a lesser degree.

Article 5. Scope of Restrictions and Limitations

The State Parties may establish restrictions and limitations on the enjoyment and exercise of the rights established herein by means of laws promulgated for the purpose of preserving the general welfare in a democratic society only to the extent that they are not incompatible with the purpose and reason underlying those rights.

Article 6. Right to Work

1. Everyone has the right to work, which includes the opportunity to secure the means for living a dignified and decent existence by performing a freely elected or accepted lawful activity.

2. The State Parties undertake to adopt measures that will make the right to work fully effective, especially with regard to the achievement of full employment, vocational guidance, and the development of technical and vocational training projects, in particular those directed to the disabled. The States Parties also undertake to implement and strengthen programs that help to ensure suitable family care, so that women may enjoy a real opportunity to exercise the right to work.

Article 7. Just, Equitable, and Satisfactory Conditions of Work

The States Parties to this Protocol recognize that the right to work to which the foregoing article refers presupposes that everyone shall enjoy that right under just, equitable, and satisfactory conditions, which the States Parties undertake to guarantee in their internal legislation, particularly with respect to:

a. Remuneration which guarantees, as a minimum, to all workers dignified and decent living conditions for them and their families and fair and equal wages for equal work, without distinction;

b. The right of every worker to follow his vocation and to devote himself to the activity that best fulfills his expectations and to change employment in accordance with the pertinent national regulations;

c. The right of every worker to promotion or upward mobility in his employment, for which purpose account shall be taken of his qualifications, competence, integrity and seniority;

d. Stability of employment, subject to the nature of each industry and occupation and the causes for just separation. In cases of unjustified dismissal, the worker shall have the right to indemnity or to reinstatement on the job or any other benefits provided by domestic legislation;

e. Safety and hygiene at work;

f. The prohibition of night work or unhealthy or dangerous working conditions and, in general, of all work which jeopardizes health, safety, or morals, for persons under 18 years of age. As regards minors under the age of 16, the work day shall be subordinated to the provisions regarding compulsory education and in no case shall work constitute an impediment to school attendance or a limitation on benefiting from education received;

g. A reasonable limitation of working hours, both daily and weekly. The days shall be shorter in the case of dangerous or unhealthy work or of night work;

h. Rest, leisure and paid vacations as well as remuneration for national holidays.

Article 8. Trade Union Rights

1. The States Parties shall ensure:

a. The right of workers to organize trade unions and to join the union of their choice for the purpose of protecting and promoting their interests. As an extension of that right, the States Parties shall permit trade unions to establish national federations or confederations, or to affiliate with those that already exist, as well as to form international trade union organizations and to affiliate with that of their choice. The States Parties shall also permit trade unions, federations and confederations to function freely;

b. The right to strike.

2. The exercise of the rights set forth above may be subject only to restrictions established by law, provided that such restrictions are characteristic of a democratic society and necessary for safeguarding public order or for protecting public health or morals or the rights and freedoms of others. Members of the armed

forces and the police and of other essential public services shall be subject to limitations and restrictions established by law.

3. No one may be compelled to belong to a trade union.

Article 9. Right to Social Security

1. Everyone shall have the right to social security protecting him from the consequences of old age and of disability which prevents him, physically or mentally, from securing the means for a dignified and decent existence. In the event of the death of a beneficiary, social security benefits shall be applied to his dependents.

2. In the case of persons who are employed, the right to social security shall cover at least medical care and an allowance or retirement benefit in the case of work accidents or occupational disease and, in the case of women, paid maternity leave before and after childbirth.

Article 10. Right to Health

1. Everyone shall have the right to health, understood to mean the enjoyment of the highest level of physical, mental and social well-being.

2. In order to ensure the exercise of the right to health, the States Parties agree to recognize health as a public good and, particularly, to adopt the following measures to ensure that right:

a. Primary health care, that is, essential health care made available to all individuals and families in the community;

b. Extension of the benefits of health services to all individuals subject to the State's jurisdiction;

c. Universal immunization against the principal infectious diseases;

d. Prevention and treatment of endemic, occupational and other diseases;

e. Education of the population on the prevention and treatment of health problems, and

f. Satisfaction of the health needs of the highest risk groups and of those whose poverty makes them the most vulnerable

Article 11. Right to a Healthy Environment

1. Everyone shall have the right to live in a healthy environment and to have access to basic public services.

2. The States Parties shall promote the protection, preservation, and improvement of the environment.

Article 12. Right to Food

1. Everyone has the right to adequate nutrition which guarantees the possibility of enjoying the highest level of physical, emotional and intellectual development.

2. In order to promote the exercise of this right and eradicate malnutrition, the States Parties undertake to improve methods of production, supply and distribution of food, and to this end, agree to promote greater international cooperation in support of the relevant national policies.

Article 13. Right to Education

1. Everyone has the right to education.

2. The States Parties to this Protocol agree that education should be directed towards the full development of the human personality and human dignity and should strengthen respect for human rights, ideological pluralism, fundamental freedoms, justice and peace. They further agree that education ought to enable everyone to participate effectively in a democratic and pluralistic society and achieve a decent existence and should foster understanding, tolerance and friendship among all nations and all racial, ethnic or religious groups and promote activities for the maintenance of peace.

3. The States Parties to this Protocol recognize that in order to achieve the full exercise of the right to education:

a. Primary education should be compulsory and accessible to all without cost;

b. Secondary education in its different forms, including technical and vocational secondary education, should be made generally available and accessible to all by every appropriate means, and in particular, by the progressive introduction of free education;

c. Higher education should be made equally accessible to all, on the basis of individual capacity, by every appropriate means, and in particular, by the progressive introduction of free education;

d. Basic education should be encouraged or intensified as far as possible for those persons who have not received or completed the whole cycle of primary instruction;

e. Programs of special education should be established for the handicapped, so as to provide special instruction and training to persons with physical disabilities or mental deficiencies.

4. In conformity with the domestic legislation of the States Parties, parents should have the right to select the type of education to be given to their children, provided that it conforms to the principles set forth above.

Document 64

5. Nothing in this Protocol shall be interpreted as a restriction of the freedom of individuals and entities to establish and direct educational institutions in accordance with the domestic legislation of the States Parties.

Article 14. Right to the Benefits of Culture

1. The States Parties to this Protocol recognize the right of everyone:

a. To take part in the cultural and artistic life of the community;

b. To enjoy the benefits of scientific and technological progress;

c. To benefit from the protection of moral and material interests deriving from any scientific, literary or artistic production of which he is the author.

2. The steps to be taken by the States Parties to this Protocol to ensure the full exercise of this right shall include those necessary for the conservation, development and dissemination of science, culture and Article

3. The States Parties to this Protocol undertake to respect the freedom indispensable for scientific research and creative activity.

4. The States Parties to this Protocol recognize the benefits to be derived from the encouragement and development of international cooperation and relations in the fields of science, arts and culture, and accordingly agree to foster greater international cooperation in these fields.

Article 15. Right to the Formation and the Protection of Families

1. The family is the natural and fundamental element of society and ought to be protected by the State, which should see to the improvement of its spiritual and material conditions.

2. Everyone has the right to form a family, which shall be exercised in accordance with the provisions of the pertinent domestic legislation.

3. The States Parties hereby undertake to accord adequate protection to the family unit and in particular:

a. To provide special care and assistance to mothers during a reasonable period before and after childbirth;

b. To guarantee adequate nutrition for children at the nursing stage and during school attendance years;

c. To adopt special measures for the protection of adolescents in order to ensure the full development of their physical, intellectual and moral capacities;

d. To undertake special programs of family training so as to help create a stable and positive environment in which children will receive and develop the values of understanding, solidarity, respect and responsibility.

Article 16. Rights of Children

Every child, whatever his parentage, has the right to the protection that his status as a minor requires from his family, society and the State. Every child has the right to grow under the protection and responsibility of his parents; save in exceptional, judicially-recognized circumstances, a child of young age ought not to be separated from his mother. Every child has the right to free and compulsory education, at least in the elementary phase, and to continue his training at higher levels of the educational system.

Article 17. Protection of the Elderly

Everyone has the right to special protection in old age. With this in view the States Parties agree to take progressively the necessary steps to make this right a reality and, particularly, to:

a. Provide suitable facilities, as well as food and specialized medical care, for elderly individuals who lack them and are unable to provide them for themselves;

b. Undertake work programs specifically designed to give the elderly the opportunity to engage in a productive activity suited to their abilities and consistent with their vocations or desires;

c. Foster the establishment of social organizations aimed at improving the quality of life for the elderly.

Article 18. Protection of the Handicapped

Everyone affected by a diminution of his physical or mental capacities is entitled to receive special attention designed to help him achieve the greatest possible development of his personality. The States Parties agree to adopt such measures as may be necessary for this purpose and, especially, to:

a. Undertake programs specifically aimed at providing the handicapped with the resources and environment needed for attaining this goal, including work programs consistent with their possibilities and freely accepted by them or their legal representatives, as the case may be;

b. Provide special training to the families of the handicapped in order to help them solve the problems of coexistence and convert them into active agents in the physical, mental and emotional development of the latter;

c. Include the consideration of solutions to specific requirements arising from needs of this group as a priority component of their urban development plans;

d. Encourage the establishment of social groups in which the handicapped can be helped to enjoy a fuller life.

Article 19. Means of Protection

1. Pursuant to the provisions of this article and the corresponding rules to be formulated for this purpose by the General Assembly of the Organization of American States, the States Parties to this Protocol undertake to submit periodic reports on the progressive measures they have taken to ensure due respect for the rights set forth in this Protocol.

2. All reports shall be submitted to the Secretary General of the OAS, who shall transmit them to the Inter-American Economic and Social Council and the Inter-American Council for Education, Science and Culture so that they may examine them in accordance with the provisions of this article. The Secretary General shall send a copy of such reports to the Inter-American Commission on Human Rights.

3. The Secretary General of the Organization of American States shall also transmit to the specialized organizations of the inter-American system of which the States Parties to the present Protocol are members, copies or pertinent portions of the reports submitted, insofar as they relate to matters within the purview of those organizations, as established by their constituent instruments.

4. The specialized organizations of the inter-American system may submit reports to the Inter-American Economic and Social Council and the Inter-American Council for Education, Science and Culture relative to compliance with the provisions of the present Protocol in their fields of activity.

5. The annual reports submitted to the General Assembly by the Inter-American Economic and Social Council and the Inter-American Council for Education, Science and Culture shall contain a summary of the information received from the States Parties to the present Protocol and the specialized organizations concerning the progressive measures adopted in order to ensure respect for the rights acknowledged in the Protocol itself and the general recommendations they consider to be appropriate in this respect.

6. Any instance in which the rights established in paragraph a) of Article 8 and in Article 13 are violated by action directly attributable to a State Party to this Protocol may give rise, through participation of the Inter-American Commission on Human Rights and, when applicable, of the Inter-American Court of Human Rights, to application of the system of individual petitions governed by Article 44 through 51 and 61 through 69 of the American Convention on Human Rights.

7. Without prejudice to the provisions of the preceding paragraph, the Inter-American Commission on Human Rights may formulate such observations and recommendations as it deems pertinent concerning the status of the economic, social and cultural rights established in the present Protocol in all or some of the States Parties, which it may include in its Annual Report to the General Assembly or in a special report, whichever it considers more appropriate.

8. The Councils and the Inter-American Commission on Human Rights, in discharging the functions conferred upon them in this article, shall take into account the progressive nature of the observance of the rights subject to protection by this Protocol.

Article 20. Reservations

The States Parties may, at the time of approval, signature, ratification or accession, make reservations to one or more specific provisions of this Protocol, provided that such reservations are not incompatible with the object and purpose of the Protocol.

DOCUMENT 65

Full Official Title: Protocol to the American Convention on Human Rights to abolish the death penalty

Short Title/Acronym/Abbreviation: Protocol II to the American Convention

Subject: Abolishing the death penalty in the Western Hemisphere.

Official Citation: OAS, Treaty Series, No. 73

Date of Document: June 8, 1990

Date of Adoption: June 8, 1990

Date of General Entry into Force (EIF): August 28, 1991

Number of States Parties to this Treaty: 11

Date of Signature by United States: United States has not signed

Date of Ratification/Accession/Adhesion: Not applicable

Date of Entry into Force as to United States (effective date): Not applicable

Type of Document: a legal instrument. A protocol amending the ACHR

Legal Status/Character of the Instrument/Document as to the United States: Not legally binding; United States has not signed

Comments: In the event public opinion concerning the death penalty changes, the United States may choose to sign and rafity this protocol.

Caution: The status and applicability of this instrument as to the United States may have changed since date of publication. The above information may be updated by referring to the following site:

Web address: http://www.cidh.oas.org/Basic%20Documents/enbas6.htm

Protocol to the American Convention on Human Rights to Abolish the Death Penalty

Preamble

The States parties to this protocol,

Considering:

That Article 4 of the American Convention on Human Rights recognizes the right to life and restricts the application of the death penalty;

That everyone has the inalienable right to respect for his life, a right that cannot be suspended for any reason;

That the tendency among the American States is to be in favor of abolition of the death penalty;

That application of the death penalty has irrevocable consequences, forecloses the correction of judicial error, and precludes any possibility of changing or rehabilitating those convicted;

That the abolition of the death penalty helps to ensure more effective protection of the right to life;

That an international agreement must be arrived at that will entail a progressive development of the American Convention on Human Rights, and

That States Parties to the American Convention on Human Rights have expressed their intention to adopt an international agreement with a view to consolidating the practice of not applying the death penalty in the Americas,

Have agreed to sign the following protocol to the American Convention on Human Rights to Abolish the Death Penalty:

Article 1

The States Parties to this Protocol shall not apply the death penalty in their territory to any person subject to their jurisdiction.

Article 2

1. No reservations may be made to this Protocol. However, at the time of ratification or accession, the States Parties to this instrument may declare that they reserve the right to apply the death penalty in wartime in accordance with international law, for extremely serious crimes of a military nature.

2. The State Party making this reservation shall, upon ratification or accession, inform the Secretary General of the Organization of American States of the pertinent provisions of its national legislation applicable in wartime, as referred to in the preceding paragraph.

3. Said State Party shall notify the Secretary General of the Organization of American States of the beginning or end of any state of war in effect in its territory.

Article 3

1. This Protocol shall be open for signature and ratification or accession by any State Party to the American Convention on Human Rights.

2. Ratification of this Protocol or accession thereto shall be made through the deposit of an instrument of ratification or accession with the General Secretariat of the Organization of American States.

Article 4

This Protocol shall enter into force among the States that ratify or accede to it when they deposit their respective instruments of ratification or accession with the General Secretariat of the Organization of American States.

(Approved at Asunción, Paraguay, on June 8, 1990, at the

twentieth regular session of the General Assembly)

Entry into force: August 28, 1991

Depository: OAS General Secretariat (Original instrument and ratifications).

Text: OAS, Treaty Series, No. 73

DOCUMENT 66

Full Official Title: The Convention on the Nationality of Married Women
Short Title/Acronym/Abbreviation: The Married Women's Nationality Convention
Type of Document: This is a multilateral treaty, a legal instrument.
Subject: Women, civil and political rights, and nationality
Official Citation: UNTS, vol. 309, p. 65.
Date of Document: February 20, 1957
Date of Adoption: February 20, 1957
Date of General Entry into Force (EIF): August 11, 1958
Number of Signatory States/ratifications as of this printing: 74
Date of Signature by the United States: Not applicable
Date of Ratification/Accession/Adhesion: Not applicable
Date of Entry into Force as to United States (effective date): Not applicable
Legal Status/Character of the Instrument/Document as to the United States: The U.S. is not bound by this treaty.
Supervising Body: Not applicable
Comment: Not applicable
Caution: The status and applicability of this instrument as to the United States may have changed since the date of this publication. The above information may be updated by referring to the following site:
Web Address: http://treaties.un.org/doc/Treaties/1958/08/19580811%2001-34%20AM/Ch_XVI_2p.pdf

THE CONVENTION ON THE NATIONALITY OF MARRIED WOMEN

The Contracting States,

Recognizing that, conflicts in law in practice with reference to nationality arise as a result of provisions concerning the loss or acquisition of nationality by women as a result of marriage, of its dissolution or of the change of nationality by the husband during marriage,

Recognizing that, in Article 15 of the Universal Declaration of Human Rights, the General Assembly of the United Nations has proclaimed that "everyone has the right to a nationality" and that "no one shall be arbitrarily deprived of his nationality nor denied the right to change his nationality",

Desiring to co-operate with the United Nations in promoting universal respect for, and observance of, human rights and fundamental freedoms for all without distinction as to sex,

Hereby agree as hereinafter provided:

Article 1

Each Contracting State agrees that neither the celebration nor the dissolution of a marriage between one of its nationals and an alien, nor the change of nationality by the husband during marriage, shall automatically affect the nationality of the wife.

Article 2

Each Contracting State agrees that neither the voluntary acquisition of the nationality of another State nor the renunciation of its nationality by one of its nationals shall prevent the retention of its nationality by the wife of such national.

Article 3

1. Each Contracting State agrees that the alien wife of one of its nationals may, at her request, acquire the nationality of her husband through specially privileged naturalization procedures; the grant of such nationality may be subject to such limitations as may be imposed in the interests of national security or public policy.

2. Each Contracting State agrees that the present Convention shall not be construed as affecting any legislation or judicial practice by which the alien wife of one of its nationals may, at her request, acquire her husband's nationality as a matter of right.

Article 4

1. The present Convention shall be open for signature and ratification on behalf of any State Member of the United Nations and also on behalf of any other State which is or hereafter becomes a member of any specialized agency of the United Nations, or which is or hereafter becomes a Party to the Statute of the International Court of Justice, or any other State to which an invitation has been addressed by the General Assembly of the United Nations.

2. The present Convention shall be ratified and the instruments of ratification shall be deposited with the Secretary-General of the United Nations.

Article 5

1. The present Convention shall be open for accession to all States referred to in paragraph I of Article 4.

2. Accession shall be effected by the deposit of an instrument of accession with the Secretary-General of the United Nations.

Article 6

1. The present Convention shall come into force on the ninetieth day following the date of deposit of the sixth instrument of ratification or accession.

2. For each State ratifying or acceding to the Convention after the deposit of the sixth instrument of ratification or accession, the Convention shall enter into force on the ninetieth day after deposit by such State of its instrument of ratification or accession.

Article 7

1. The present Convention shall apply to all non-self-governing, trust, colonial and other non-metropolitan territories for the international relations of which any Contracting State is responsible; the Contracting State concerned shall, subject to the provisions of paragraph 2 of the present article, at the time of signature, ratification or accession declare the non-metropolitan territory or territories to which the Convention shall apply ipso facto as a result of such signature, ratification or accession.

2. In any case in which, for the purpose of nationality, a non-metropolitan territory is not treated as one with the metropolitan territory, or in any case in which the previous consent of a non-metropolitan territory is required by the constitutional laws or practices of the Contracting State or of the non-metropolitan territory for the application of the Convention to that territory, that Contracting State shall endeavour to secure the needed consent of the non-metropolitan territory within the period of twelve months from the date of signature of the Convention by that Contracting State, and when such consent has been obtained the Contracting State shall notify the Secretary-General of the United Nations. The present Convention shall apply to the territory or territories named in such notification from the date of its receipt by the Secretary-General.

3. After the expiry of the twelve-month period mentioned in paragraph 2 of the present article, the Contracting States concerned shall inform the Secretary-General of the results of the consultations with those non-metropolitan territories for whose international relations they are responsible and whose consent to the application of the present Convention may have been withheld.

Article 8

1. At the time of signature, ratification or accession, any State may make reservations to any article of the present Convention other than articles 1 and 2.

2. If any State makes a reservation in accordance with paragraph 1 of the present article, the Convention, with the exception of those provisions to which the reservation relates, shall have effect as between the reserving State and the other Parties. The Secretary-General of the United Nations shall communicate the text of the reservation to all States which are or may become Parties to the Convention. Any State Party to the Convention or which thereafter becomes a Party may notify the Secretary-General that it does not agree to consider itself bound by the Convention with respect to the State making the reservation. This notification must be made, in the case of a State already a Party, within ninety days from the date of the communication by the Secretary-General; and, in the case of a State subsequently becoming a Party, within ninety days from the date when the instrument of ratification or accession is deposited. In the event that such a notification is made, the Convention shall not be deemed to be in effect as between the State making the notification and the State making the reservation.

3. Any State making a reservation in accordance with paragraph 1 of the present article may at any time withdraw the reservation, in whole or in part, after it has been accepted, by a notification to this effect addressed to the Secretary-General of the United Nations. Such notification shall take effect on the date on which it is received.

Article 9

1. Any Contracting State may denounce the present Convention by written notification to the Secretary-General of the United Nations. Denunciation shall take effect one year after the date of receipt of the notification by the Secretary-General.

2. The present Convention shall cease to be in force as from the date when the denunciation which reduces the number of Parties to less than six becomes effective.

Article 10

Any dispute which may arise between any two or more Contracting States concerning the interpretation or application of the present Convention which is not settled by negotiation, shall, at the request of any one of the parties to the dispute, be referred to the International Court of Justice for decision, unless the parties agree to another mode of settlement.

Article 11

The Secretary-General of the United Nations shall notify all States Members of the United Nations and the non-member States contemplated in paragraph 1 of Article 4 of the present Convention of the following:

(a) Signatures and instruments of ratification received in accordance with Article 4;

(b) Instruments of accession received in accordance with Article 5;

(c) The date upon which the present Convention enters into force in accordance with Article 6;

(d) Communications and notifications received in accordance with Article 8;

(e) Notifications of denunciation received in accordance with paragraph 1 of Article 9;

(f) Abrogation in accordance with paragraph 2 of Article 9.

Article 12

1. The present Convention, of which the Chinese, English, French, Russian and Spanish texts shall be equally authentic, shall be deposited in the archives of the United Nations.

2. The Secretary-General of the United Nations shall transmit a certified copy of the Convention to all States Members of the United Nations and to the non-member States contemplated in paragraph 1 of Article 4.

ORGANIZATION FOR SECURITY & COOPERATION IN EUROPE DOCUMENT

DOCUMENT 67

Full Official Title: Final Act of Helsinki 1975

Short Title/Acronym/Abbreviation: The Helsinki Final Act

Subject: Incorporating human rights principles and consideration into the processes of the Conference on Security and Co-operation in Europe, now Organization on Security and Co-operation in Europe

Official Citation: Not applicable

Date of Document: August 1, 1975

Date of Adoption: August 1, 1975

Date of General Entry into Force (EIF): Not applicable

Number of States Parties to this treaty as of this printing: Not a treaty

Date of Signature by United States: Not applicable

Date of Ratification/Accession/Adhesion: Not applicable

Date of Entry into Force as to United States (effective date): Not applicable

Type of Document: A political instrument, not meant to be a treaty, but sounding much like one.

Legal Status/Character of the Instrument/Document as to the United States: Not a treaty, not legally binding. Some scholars argue that it has become legally binding, as a matter of customary international law. The instrument guiding U.S. activity in the context of the Conference on Security and Cooperation in Europe, which became the Organization for Security and Cooperation in Europe (O.S.C.E.) That body now has an Office for Democratic Institutions and Human Rights ODIHR in Warsaw, Poland.

Comments: The Helsinki Final Act has established a basis for dialogue and critique of Eastern European countries' human rights practices after World War II. It later became the basis for obtaining the emigration of many Russian Jews to Israel and the U.S.

The Helsinki Final Act served as the initial document which was to be become known as the Helsinki Human Dimension, which dealt with human rights. It is part of a larger group of documents including: *Concluding Document of the Vienna Meeting on the Follow-up to the Conference, 1989; Document of the Copenhagen Meeting of the Conference on the Human Dimension of the CSCE; Charter of Paris for a New Europe, 1990; Budapest Summit Declaration, Towards a Genuine Partnership in a New Era, 1994.*

Caution: The status and applicability of this instrument as to the United States may have changed since date of publication. The above information may be updated by referring to the following site:

Web address: http://www.osce.org/indexe-da.htm

FINAL ACT OF HELSINKI 1975 (EXCERPTS)

The Conference on Security and Co-operation in Europe, which opened at Helsinki on 3 July 1973 and continued at Geneva from 18 September 1973 to 21 July 1975, was concluded at Helsinki on 1 August 1975 by the High Representatives of Austria, Belgium, Bulgaria, Canada, Cyprus, Czechoslovakia, Denmark, Finland, France, the German Democratic Republic, the Federal Republic of Germany, Greece, the Holy See, Hungary, Iceland, Ireland, Italy, Liechtenstein, Luxembourg, Malta, Monaco, the Netherlands, Norway, Poland, Portugal, Romania, San Marino, Spain, Sweden, Switzerland, Turkey, the Union of Soviet Socialist Republics, the United Kingdom, the United States of America and Yugoslavia.

During the opening and closing stages of the Conference the participants were addressed by the Secretary-General of the United Nations as their guest of honour. The Director-General of UNESCO and the Executive Secretary of the United Nations Economic Commission for Europe addressed the Conference during its second stage.

During the meetings of the second stage of the Conference, contributions were received, and statements heard, from the following non-participating Mediterranean States on various agenda items: the Democratic and Popular Republic of Algeria, the Arab Republic of Egypt, Israel, the Kingdom of Morocco, the Syrian Arab Republic, Tunisia.

Motivated by the political will, in the interest of peoples, to improve and intensify their relations and to contribute in Europe to peace, security, justice and cooperation as well as to rapprochement among themselves and with the other States of the world,

Determined, in consequence, to give full effect to the results of the Conference and to assure, among their States and throughout Europe, the benefits deriving from those results and thus to broaden, deepen and make continuing and lasting the process of détente,

The High Representatives of the participating States have solemnly adopted the following:

Questions relating to Security in Europe

The States participating in the Conference on Security and Co-operation in Europe,

Reaffirming their objective of promoting better relations among themselves and ensuring conditions in which their people can live in true and lasting peace free from any threat to or attempt against their security;

Convinced of the need to exert efforts to make détente both a continuing and an increasingly viable and comprehensive process, universal in scope, and that the implementation of the results of the Conference on Security and Cooperation in Europe will be a major contribution to this process;

Considering that solidarity among peoples, as well as the common purpose of the participating States in achieving the aims as set forth by the Conference on Security and Cooperation in Europe, should lead to the development of better and closer relations among them in all fields and thus to overcoming the confrontation stemming from the character of their past relations, and to better mutual understanding;

Mindful of their common history and recognizing that the existence of elements common to their traditions and values can assist them in developing their relations, and desiring to search, fully taking into account the individuality and diversity of their positions and views, for possibilities of joining their efforts with a view to overcoming distrust and increasing confidence, solving the problems that separate them and cooperating in the interest of mankind;

Recognizing the indivisibility of security in Europe as well as their common interest in the development of cooperation throughout Europe and among selves and expressing their intention to pursue efforts accordingly;

Recognizing the close link between peace and security in Europe and in the world as a whole and conscious of the need for each of them to make its contribution to the strengthening of world peace and security and to the promotion of fundamental rights, economic and social progress and well-being for all peoples;

Have adopted the following:

1. (a) Declaration on Principles Guiding Relations between Participating States

The participating States,

Reaffirming their commitment to peace, security and justice and the continuing development of friendly relations and co-operation;

Recognizing that this commitment, which reflects the interest and aspirations of peoples, constitutes for each participating State a present and future responsibility, heightened by experience of the past;

Reaffirming, in conformity with their membership in the United Nations and in accordance with the purposes and principles of the United Nations, their full and active support for the United Nations and for the enhancement of its role and effectiveness in strengthening international peace, security and justice, and in promoting the solution of international problems, as well as the development of friendly relations and cooperation among States;

Expressing their common adherence to the principles which are set forth below and are in conformity with the Charter of the United Nations, as well as their common will to act, in the application of these principles, in conformity with the purposes and principles of the Charter of the United Nations;

Declare their determination to respect and put into practice, each of them in its relations with all other participating States, irrespective of their political, economic or social systems as well as of their size, geographical location or level of economic development, the following principles, which all are of primary significance, guiding their mutual relations:

I. Sovereign equality, respect for the rights inherent in sovereignty

The participating States will respect each other's sovereign equality and individuality as well as all the rights inherent in and encompassed by its sovereignty, including in particular the right of every State to juridical equality, to territorial integrity and to freedom and political independence. They will also respect each other's right freely to choose and develop its political, social, economic and cultural systems as well as its right to determine its laws and regulations.

Within the framework of international law, all the participating States have equal rights and duties. They will respect each other's right to define and conduct as it wishes its relations with other States in accordance with international law and in the spirit of the present Declaration. They consider that their frontiers can be changed, in accordance with international law, by peaceful means and by agreement. They also have the right to belong or not to belong to international organizations, to be or not to be a party to bilateral or multilateral treaties including the right to be or not to be a party to treaties of alliance; they also have the right to neutrality.

. . .

VII. Respect for human rights and fundamental freedoms, including the freedom of thought, conscience, religion or belief

The participating States will respect human rights and fundamental freedoms, including the freedom of thought, conscience, religion or belief, for all without distinction as to race, sex, language or religion.

They will promote and encourage the effective exercise of civil, political, economic, social, cultural and other rights and freedoms all of which derive from the inherent dignity of the human person and are essential for his free and full development.

Within this framework the participating States will recognize and respect the freedom of the individual to profess and practice, alone or in community with others, religion or belief acting in accordance with the dictates of his own conscience.

The participating States on whose territory national minorities exist will respect the right of persons belonging to such minorities to equality before the law, will afford them the full opportunity for the actual enjoyment of human rights and fundamental freedoms and will, in this manner, protect their legitimate interests in this sphere.

The participating States recognize the universal significance of human rights and fundamental freedoms, respect for which is an essential factor for the peace, justice and well-being necessary to ensure the development of friendly relations and co-operation among themselves as among all States.

They will constantly respect these rights and freedoms in their mutual relations and will endeavour jointly and separately, including in co-operation with the United Nations, to promote universal and effective respect for them.

They confirm the right of the individual to know and act upon his rights and duties in this field.

In the field of human rights and fundamental freedoms, the participating States will act in conformity with the purposes and principles of the Charter of the United Nations and with the Universal Declaration of Human Rights. They will also fulfil their obligations as set forth in the international declarations and agreements in this field, including inter alia the International Covenants on Human Rights, by which they may be bound.

VIII. Equal rights and self-determination of peoples

The participating States will respect the equal rights of peoples and their right to self-determination, acting at all times in conformity with the purposes and principles of the Charter of the United Nations and with the relevant norms of international law, including those relating to territorial integrity of States.

By virtue of the principle of equal rights and self-determination of peoples, all peoples always have the right, in full freedom, to determine, when and as they wish, their internal and external political status, without external interference, and to pursue as they wish their political, economic, social and cultural development.

The participating States reaffirm the universal significance of respect for and effective exercise of equal rights and self-determination of peoples for the development of friendly relations among themselves as among all States; they also recall the importance of the elimination of any form of violation of this principle.

IX. Co-operation among States

The participating States will develop their co-operation with one another and with all States in all fields in accordance with the purposes and principles of the Charter of the United Nations. In developing their co-operation the participating States will place special emphasis on the fields as set forth within the framework of the Conference on Security and Co-operation in Europe, with each of them making its contribution in conditions of full equality.

They will endeavour, in developing their co-operation as equals, to promote mutual understanding and confidence, friendly and good-neighbourly relations among themselves, international peace, security and justice. They will equally endeavour, in developing their co-operation, to improve the well-being of peoples and contribute to the fulfilment of their aspirations through, inter alia, the benefits resulting from increased mutual knowledge and from progress and achievement in the economic, scientific, technological, social, cultural and humanitarian fields. They will take steps to promote conditions favourable to making these benefits available to all; they will take into account the interest of all in the narrowing of differences in the levels of economic development, and in particular the interest of developing countries throughout the world.

They confirm that governments, institutions, organizations and persons have a relevant and positive role to play in contributing toward the achievement of these aims of their cooperation.

They will strive, in increasing their cooperation as set forth above, to develop closer relations among themselves on an improved and more enduring basis for the benefit of peoples.

X. Fulfilment in good faith of obligations under international law

The participating States will fulfil in good faith their obligations under international law, both those obligations arising from the generally recognized principles and rules of international law and those obligations arising from treaties or other agreements, in conformity with international law, to which they are parties.

In exercising their sovereign rights, including the right to determine their laws and regulations, they will conform with their legal obligations under international law; they will furthermore pay due regard to and implement the provisions in the Final Act of the Conference on Security and Co-operation in Europe.

The participating States confirm that in the event of a conflict between the obligations of the members of the United Nations under the Charter of the United Nations and their obligations under any treaty or other international agreement, their obligations under the Charter will prevail, in accordance with Article 103 of the Charter of the United Nations.

All the principles set forth above are of primary significance and, accordingly, they will be equally and unreservedly applied, each of them being interpreted taking into account the others.

The participating States express their determination fully to respect and apply these principles, as set forth in the present Declaration, in all aspects, to their mutual relations and cooperation in order to ensure to each participating State the benefits resulting from the respect and application of these principles by all.

The participating States, paying due regard to the principles above and, in particular, to the first sentence of the tenth principle, "Fulfilment in good faith of obligations under international law," note that the present Declaration does not affect their rights and obligations, nor the corresponding treaties and other agreements and arrangements.

The participating States express the conviction that respect for these principles will encourage the development of normal and friendly relations and the progress of co-operation among them in all fields. They also express the conviction that respect for these principles will encourage the development of political contacts among them which in time would contribute to better mutual understanding of their positions and views.

The participating States declare their intention to conduct their relations with all other States in the spirit of the principles contained in the present Declaration.

(b) Matters related to giving effect to certain of the above Principles

(i) The participating States,

Reaffirming that they will respect and give effect to refraining from the threat or use of force and convinced of the necessity to make it an effective norm of international life, Declare that they are resolved to respect and carry out, in their relations with one another, inter alia, the following provisions which are in conformity with the Declaration on Principles Guiding Relations between Participating States:

• To give effect and expression, by all the ways and forms which they consider appropriate, to the duty to refrain from the threat or use of force in their relations with one another.

• To refrain from any use of armed forces inconsistent with the purposes and principles of the Charter of the United Nations and the provisions of the Declaration on Principles Guiding Relations between Participating States, against another participating State, in particular from invasion of or attack on its territory.

• To refrain from any manifestation of force for the purpose of inducing another participating State to renounce the full exercise of its sovereign rights.

• To refrain from any act of economic coercion designed to subordinate to their own interest the exercise by another participating State of the rights inherent in its sovereignty and thus to secure advantages of any kind.

• To take effective measures which by their scope and by their nature constitute steps towards the ultimate achievement of general and complete disarmament under strict and effective international control.

• To promote, by all means which each of them considers appropriate, a climate of confidence and respect among peoples consonant with their duty to refrain from propaganda for wars of aggression or for any threat or use of force inconsistent with the purposes of the United Nations and with the Declaration on Principles Guiding Relations between Participating States, against another participating State.

• To make every effort to settle exclusively by peaceful means any dispute between them, the continuance of which is likely to endanger the maintenance of international peace and security in Europe, and to seek, first of all, a solution through the peaceful means set forth in Article 33 of the United Nations Charter.

To refrain from any action which could hinder the peaceful settlement of disputes between the participating States.

(ii) The participating States,

Reaffirming their determination to settle their disputes as set forth in the Principle of Peaceful Settlement of Disputes;

Have adopted the following:

Co-operation in Humanitarian and Other Fields

The participating States,

Desiring to contribute to the strengthening of peace and understanding among peoples and to the spiritual enrichment of the human personality without distinction as to race, sex, language or religion,

Conscious that increased cultural and educational exchanges, broader dissemination of information, contacts between people, and the solution of humanitarian problems will contribute to the attainment of these aims,

Determined therefore to cooperate among themselves, irrespective of their political, economic and social systems, in order to create better conditions in the above fields, to develop and strengthen existing forms of co-operation and to work out new ways and means appropriate to these aims,

Convinced that this co-operation should take place in full respect for the principles guiding relations among participating States as set forth in the relevant document,

Have adopted the following:

1. Human Contacts

The participating States,

Considering the development of contacts to be an important element in the strengthening of friendly relations and trust among peoples,

Affirming, in relation to their present effort to improve conditions in this area, the importance they attach to humanitarian considerations,

Desiring in this spirit to develop, with the continuance of détente, further efforts to achieve continuing progress in this field

And conscious that the questions relevant hereto must be settled by the States concerned under mutually acceptable conditions,

Make it their aim to facilitate freer movement and contacts, individually and collectively, whether privately or officially, among persons, institutions and organizations of the participating States, and to contribute to the solution of the humanitarian problems that arise in that connexion,

Declare their readiness to these ends to take measures which they consider appropriate and to conclude agreements or arrangements among themselves, as may be needed, and

Express their intention now to proceed to the implementation of the following:

(a) Contacts and Regular Meetings on the Basis of Family Ties

In order to promote further development of contacts on the basis of family ties the participating States will favourably consider applications for travel with the purpose of allowing persons to enter or leave their territory temporarily, and on a regular basis if desired, in order to visit members of their families.

Applications for temporary visits to meet members of their families will be dealt with without distinction as to the country of origin or destination: existing requirements for travel documents and visas will be applied in this spirit. The preparation and issue of such documents and visas will be effected within reasonable time limits, cases of urgent necessity—such as serious illness or death—will be given priority treatment. They will take such steps as may be necessary to ensure that the fees for official travel documents and visas are acceptable.

They confirm that the presentation of an application concerning contacts on the basis of family ties will not modify the rights and obligations of the applicant or of members of his family.

(b) Reunification of Families

The participating States will deal in a positive and humanitarian spirit with the applications of persons who wish to be reunited with members of their family, with special attention being given to requests of an urgent character—such as requests submitted by persons who are ill or old.

The receiving participating State will take appropriate care with regard to employment for persons from other participating States who take up permanent residence in that State in connexion with family reunification with its citizens and see that they are afforded opportunities equal to those enjoyed by its own citizens for education, medical assistance and social security.

. . .

(h) Expansion of Contacts

By way of further developing contacts among governmental institutions and non-governmental organizations and associations, including women's organizations, the participating States will facilitate the convening of meetings as well as travel by delegations, groups and individuals.

Follow-up to the Conference

The participating States,

Having considered and evaluated the progress made at the Conference on Security and Co-operation in Europe,

Considering further that, within the broader context of the world, the Conference is an important part of the process of improving security and developing co-operation in Europe and that its results will contribute significantly to this process,

Intending to implement the provisions of the Final Act of the Conference in order to give full effect to its results and thus to further the process of improving security and developing co-operation in Europe,

Convinced that, in order to achieve the aims sought by the Conference, they should make further unilateral, bilateral and multilateral efforts and continue, in the appropriate forms set forth below, the multilateral process initiated by the Conference,

1. Declare their resolve, in the period following the Conference, to pay due regard to and implement the provisions of the Final Act of the Conference:

(a) unilaterally, in all cases which lend themselves to such action;

(b) bilaterally, by negotiations with other participating States;

(c) multilaterally, by meetings of experts of the participating States, and also within the framework of existing international organizations, such as the United Nations Economic Commission for Europe and UNESCO, with regard to educational, scientific and cultural co-operation;

2. Declare furthermore their resolve to continue the multilateral process initiated by the Conference:

(a) by proceeding to a thorough exchange of views both on the implementation of the provisions of the Final Act and of the tasks defined by the Conference, as well as, in the context of the questions dealt with by the latter, on the deepening of their mutual relations, the improvement of security and the development of co-operation in Europe, and the development of the process of détente in the future;

(b) by organizing to these ends meetings among their representatives, beginning with a meeting at the level of representatives appointed by the Ministers of Foreign Affairs. This meeting will define the appropriate modalities for the holding of other meetings which could include further similar meetings and the possibility of a new Conference;

3. The first of the meetings indicated above will be held at Belgrade in 1977. A preparatory meeting to organize this meeting will be held at Belgrade on 15 June 1977. The preparatory meeting will decide on the date, duration, agenda and other modalities of the meeting of representatives appointed by the Ministers of Foreign Affairs;

4. The rules of procedure, the working methods and the scale of distribution for the expenses of the Conference will, mutatis mutandis, be applied to the meetings envisaged in paragraphs 1 (c), 2 and 3 above. All the above- mentioned meetings will be held in the participating States in rotation. The services of a technical secretariat will be provided by the host country.

The original of this Final Act, drawn up in English, French, German, Italian, Russian and Spanish, will be transmitted to the Government of the Republic of Finland, which will retain it in its archives. Each of the participating States will receive from the Government of the Republic of Finland a true copy of this Final Act.

The text of this Final Act will be published in each participating State, which will disseminate it and make it known as widely as possible.

The Government of the Republic of Finland is requested to transmit to the Secretary-General of the United Nations the text of this Final Act, which is not eligible for registration under Article 102 of the Charter of the United Nations, with a view to its circulation to all the members of the Organization as an official document of the United Nations.

The Government of the Republic of Finland is also requested to transmit the text of this Final Act to the Director-General of UNESCO and to the Executive Secretary of the United Nations Economic Commission for Europe.

Wherefore, the undersigned High Representatives of the participating States, mindful of the high political significance which they attach to the results of the Conference, and declaring their determination to act in accordance with the provisions contained in the above texts, have subscribed their signatures below:

Done at Helsinki,
on 1st August 1975